The Reader's Adviser

The Reader's Adviser
A Layman's Guide to Literature
13th EDITION

Barbara A. Chernow and George A. Vallasi, Series Editors

Volume 1
The Best in American and British Fiction, Poetry, Essays, Literary Biography, Bibliography, and Reference
Edited by Fred Kaplan

Books about Books • Bibliography • Reference Books: Literature • Broad Studies and General Anthologies: Literature • British Poetry: Early to Romantic • British Poetry: Middle Period • Modern British and Irish Poetry • American Poetry: Early Period • Modern American Poetry • British Fiction: Early Period • British Fiction: Middle Period • Modern British Fiction • American Fiction: Early Period • Modern American Fiction • Commonwealth Literature • Essays and Criticism • Literary Biography and Autobiography

Volume 2
The Best in American and British Drama and World Literature in English Translation
Edited by Maurice Charney

The Drama • British Drama: Early to Eighteenth Century • Shakespeare • Modern British and Irish Drama • American Drama • World Literature • Greek Literature • Latin Literature • French Literature • Italian Literature • Spanish Literature • Portuguese Literature • German and Netherlandic Literature • Scandinavian Literature • Russian Literature • East European Literatures • Yiddish Literature • Hebrew Literature • Spanish American Literature • African Literature • Middle Eastern Literature • The Literature of the Indian Subcontinent • Chinese Literature • Japanese Literature • Southeast Asian and Korean Literature

Volume 3
The Best in General Reference Literature, the Social Sciences, History, and the Arts
Edited by Paula T. Kaufman

Reference Books: General • Dictionaries • General Biography and Autobiography • The Social Sciences • Education • Ancient History • United States History • Western Hemisphere: Canada and Latin America • British History • World History • Music and Dance • Art and Architecture • The Mass Media • Folklore and Humor • Travel and Exploration

Volume 4
The Best in the Literature of Philosophy and World Religions
Edited by William L. Reese

General Philosophy • Greek and Roman Philosophy • Medieval Philosophy • Renaissance Philosophy • Modern Philosophy, 1600–1900 • Twentieth-Century Philosophy • Ancient Religions and Philosophies • Eastern Religion and Philosophy • Islamic Religion and Philosophy • Judaism • Early Christianity • Late Christianity • The Bible and Related Literature • Minority Religions and Contemporary Religious Movements

Volume 5
The Best in the Literature of Science, Technology, and Medicine
Edited by Paul T. Durbin

General Science • History of Science, Technology, and Medicine • Philosophy of Science and Pseudoscience • Mathematics • Statistics and Probability • Information and Computer Science • Astronomy and Space Science • Earth Sciences • Physics • Chemistry • Biology • Ecology and Environmental Science • Genetics • Medicine and Health • Illness and Disease • Clinical Psychology and Psychiatry • Engineering and Technology • Energy • Science, Technology, and Society • Ethics of Science, Technology, and Medicine

THE
Reader's Adviser

A Layman's Guide to Literature
13th EDITION

Volume 4

The Best in the Literature
of Philosophy and World Religions

Edited by William L. Reese

Barbara A. Chernow and George A. Vallasi, Series Editors

R. R. BOWKER COMPANY
New York & London, 1988

Published by R. R. Bowker Company,
a division of Reed Publishing (USA) Inc.
Copyright © 1988 by Reed Publishing USA

All rights reserved
Printed and bound in the United States of America

International Standard Book Numbers
0-8352-2145-8 (Volume 1)
0-8352-2146-6 (Volume 2)
0-8352-2147-4 (Volume 3)
0-8352-2148-2 (Volume 4)
0-8352-2149-0 (Volume 5)
0-8352-2315-9 (Volume 6)
International Standard Serial Number 0094-5943
Library of Congress Catalog Card Number 57-13277

The paper used in this publication meets the minimum
requirements of American National Standard for
Information Sciences—Permanence of Papers for
Printed Library Materials, ANSI Z39.48-1984.

Contents

Preface

Over its thirteen editions, and since its first publication in 1921, chapters of *The Reader's Adviser* have been expanded and reorganized and new topics have been introduced, thus better to serve the needs of a growing and more diversified population. The first edition, entitled *The Bookman's Manual*, was based on Bessie Graham's course on book salesmanship given at the William Penn Evening High School in Philadelphia. Graham organized the book so that the chapters corresponded to the general classifications familiar to booksellers and, by providing publishers and prices in her text, she simplified book ordering for the bookseller. Since 1921, however, the book industry has experienced significant changes—comparatively few independent book dealers exist, information on titles is available from a wide variety of printed and computerized sources, and publishers are taking fewer risks by printing just enough copies of a title to meet immediate demands. At the same time that these changes were occurring, *The Reader's Adviser* was finding a broader audience; although still used by booksellers, the librarians, general readers, and high school and college students found that the topical organization of the volume with its annotated bibliographies also met their needs. For the nonspecialist who is interested in reading about a particular subject, *The Reader's Adviser* is a perfect starting point. The six-volume set provides annotated bibliographies arranged by subject, with brief biographies of authors, creative artists, and scientists worthy of special mention; in addition, it informs the reader of a book's availability, price, and purchasing source. Since the set is kept up to date by regular revisions, the volumes also serve as a reflection of the current state of the best available literature in print in the United States.

As a result of the growth of new fields of interest to the reading public and the continuing increase in the number of titles published, *The Reader's Adviser* has expanded with each succeeding edition. For this thirteenth edition, it has grown from three to six volumes. The first three volumes appeared simultaneously in 1986; the final three in 1988. The organization of the first two volumes is similar to that in the twelfth edition: Volume 1 covers mainly American and British fiction and poetry and Volume 2 covers drama, Shakespeare, and world literature in English translation. Volume 3, which covers the best in general reference literature, the social sciences, history, and the arts, has experienced the most significant changes—most chapters have been expanded, virtually new chapters have been created for the arts, and several chapters have been moved to form the nuclei of Volumes 4 and 5. Volume 4 covers the Bible, world religions, and philosophy; Volume 5 is devoted to science, technology, and medicine. Except for Volume 6, containing indexes to the entire set and a Publishers' Directory, each of the volumes has been edited by a specialist in the field, the whole project having been coordinated by the series editors.

Although the thirteenth edition of *The Reader's Adviser* retains the essential format and basic structure of the earlier editions, the editors and publisher have made a number of improvements designed to enhance the appearance and usefulness of the volumes. First, the design has been modified to increase readability and provide a more open look. The typeface is easier to read, biographies are printed in a larger face, and the titles in the "books about" sections following the biographies are in alphabetical order according to the authors' surnames. Finally, the authors and anonymous sagas that form the main headings in *The Reader's Adviser* are listed in alphabetical order within the chapters rather than the chronological order of previous editions. In the front matter of each volume, a Chronology of these individuals provides the reader with an overview of the development of a particular genre. For each chapter, the editors chose an eminent scholar or librarian with particular expertise in the subject area, so that the selection of bibliographies and main listings would reflect the best-informed judgment of a specialist in the field.

The greatest challenge was that of selection—which titles and authors to include. Since *The Reader's Adviser* is not a research tool for students and scholars, but rather a reference work designed for the nonspecialist, the editors' goal was to include those books generally available to an intelligent reader through the facilities of the library system of a moderately sized municipality. Books must be currently available in English from a publisher or distributor in the United States. Out-of-print titles are included for those major works which, because of their importance in the field, could not be excluded from the list. If a book is not presently available in English or cannot be purchased in the United States, it is considered out of print (o.p.) by the editors. In some disciplines, such as modern American poetry, publishers allow titles to go out of print quickly and the available literature was found to be surprisingly thin. The reader will also note that Volume 2 (the comparative literature volume) reveals how little of the world's non-English literature has been translated into English.

In selecting authors for main entries, contributing editors weighed a number of criteria—historical importance, current popularity as determined by the number of in-print titles, and space limitations. Particularly in American and British fiction, U.S. and world history, and the social sciences chapters, the necessity of adding new authors sometimes required eliminating authors who were previously the subjects of main entries in earlier editions of *The Reader's Adviser*. Most major authors are represented; other authors were selected as examples of particular movements or styles. The latter category is subjective; although these choices are valid, someone else's choices might have been equally valid. The constraints of space impose their own compromises.

The organization of each volume and of each chapter is designed to move the reader from the general to the specific, from reference books, books of history and criticism, and anthologies to specific authors, scientists, and creative artists. Each chapter opens with a brief introduction that provides a framework for the literature of a particular period or discipline, followed by general reading lists and then, with few exceptions, the main entries. In chapters covering more than one area of study, such as the social sciences, or more than one country, such as Southeast Asia, this pattern repeats itself for each major division. Each author selected as a main entry receives a brief biography followed by bibliographies of books by and about him or her. Wherever possible, the date of first publication follows the title of a work mentioned in the short biography or will instead appear, when available, as the first date in the "Books by..." entries below. In addition to *Books in Print, The New Columbia Encyclopedia* (1975) has served as the authority in verifying dates. The bibliographies of books by an author are mainly composed of collections of works and in-print titles of individual works in the particular genre covered by the chapter. Other titles may be mentioned in the biography, but only those works relevant to the genre under discussion appear in the bibliographies.

The bibliographic entries are so designed that the reader will be able both to locate a book in a library and to know where it is available for purchase and at what price. The editors have included the following information available or applicable for each title: author; title (translated titles or original titles are given in parentheses following the title); editor; series title; translator; authors of prefaces, introductions, and forewords; edition; number of volumes; reprint data; publisher (if more than one, publishers are listed alphabetically); date of publication; and price. The reader should be cautioned that the accuracy and completeness of information depends in large part on the information publishers supply to the *Books in Print* database and the information listed in individual publishers' catalogs.

If a date is listed directly after a title, this indicates the date of the publication of the first edition, regardless of whether that edition is still in print. For reprints, the date of the particular edition from which it was reprinted is given. If a title consists of more than one volume, and is listed with only one price, this is the price of the entire set. As book pricing changes so rapidly, some prices listed in *The Reader's Adviser* may have already changed. Although the editors considered the possibility of deleting prices from *The Reader's Adviser*, it was decided to retain them as an indication to the reader of the general price category into which an individual title falls and to assist the librarian in acquisition. Finally, the reader should be aware that not all in-print editions of a work are necessarily listed, but rather those selected by the editors because of their quality or special features.

To guide the reader through the volumes, *The Reader's Adviser* includes cross-references in three forms. The "see" reference leads the reader to the appropriate volume and chapter for information on a specific author or topic. "See also" refers the reader to additional information in another chapter or volume. Within any introductory narrative portions, the name of an author who appears as a main listing in another chapter or volume is printed in large and small capital letters. In each case, if the chapter cross-referenced is in a different volume from that being consulted, the volume number is also provided.

As with any work of this nature, grouping the material into chapters creates a structure that, while helpful, suggests distinctions greater than actually exist. An understanding of a period requires some knowledge of an earlier one; philosophy and religion are closely interrelated; and Christians, Jews, and Muslims share some common sacred writings. The reader is therefore advised to use the indexes and look for material across the chapter divisions.

Each volume of *The Reader's Adviser* has three indexes—one for names, one for book titles, and one for general subjects. The Name Index includes all authors, editors, compilers, composers, directors, actors, artists, philosophers, and scientists cited in *The Reader's Adviser*. If a name appears as a main listing in the text, the name as well as the first page number of the main listing appear in boldface type. The Title Index includes book titles with two exceptions: collected works or generic titles by authors who receive main listings (e.g., *Selected Prose of T. S. Eliot*) and "books about" titles that follow the main listings and include the name of the main-entry author (e.g., *Booker T. Washington* by Louis R. Harlan). (This does not hold true in the case of Chapter 3, "Shakespeare," in Volume 2, where all works by and about him are included.) Therefore, to ensure locating all titles by and about a main-entry author, the user should look up that author in the Name Index to locate the primary listing.

In preparing the thirteenth edition of *The Reader's Adviser*, the series editors are indebted to a great many people for assistance and advice. We are especially grateful to the many people at R. R. Bowker who have worked with us; in particular, to Olga S. Weber, who provided encouragement, support, and a critical eye in reading manuscripts; to Kathy Kleibacker, for her constant faith in the project; and to Marion Sader, Julia Raymunt, Iris Topel, Nancy Bucenec, and Glorieux Dougherty for their attention to detail and concern for quality in editing and production. We were fortunate in our choice of volume editors. Fred Kaplan, general editor of Volume 1, The Best in American and British Fiction, Poetry, Essays, Literary Biography, Bibliography, and Reference, is Professor of English at Queens College and at the Graduate Center, City University of New York; he is a distinguished Dickens and Carlyle scholar, the editor of *Dickens Studies Annual*, a member of the board of the Carlyle Papers, and is currently writing a biography of Dickens. The general editor of Volume 2, The Best in American and British Drama and World Literature in English Translation, is Maurice Charney, Distinguished Professor at Rutgers University in the department of English. His published works include *How to Read Shakespeare* and a biography of Joe Orton. Paula T. Kaufman, who served as general editor of Volume 3,

The Best in General Reference Literature, the Social Sciences, History, and the Arts, is director of the academic information services group, Columbia University Libraries. Volume 4, The Best in the Literature of Philosophy and World Religions, was developed under the general editorship of William L. Reese. He is Professor of Philosophy at the State University of New York, Albany. His publications include the *Dictionary of Philosophy and Religion*. Paul T. Durbin is general editor of Volume 5, The Best in the Literature of Science, Technology, and Medicine. He is Professor of Philosophy at the University of Delaware and editor of *A Guide to the Culture of Science, Technology, and Medicine*. All made invaluable suggestions for organizing their volumes, recommended contributing editors, and reviewed each chapter for substantive content. A special thanks to David B. Biesel, who first brought the project to us, and to Sanford Kadet, who provided invaluable assistance in coordinating many of the editorial aspects of Volumes 4 and 5. The editors also wish to thank Kathy Martin and Mae Liu, who keyboarded many of the chapters, assisted with verification of bibliographic data, and maintained the project records. For special assistance and advice in the preparation of Volume 4, we also wish to thank Norman J. Girardot, Jeffrey C. Rush, Joseph Frese, S.J., and Claude Conyers.

In the 65 years since *The Reader's Adviser* first appeared, it has grown from a tool for booksellers to a standard reference work. In addition to bibliographic information, the introductions and biographies are enjoyable reading for someone just browsing through the volumes. *The Reader's Adviser* has a distinguished history; it is hoped that these latest volumes will continue in that tradition.

Barbara A. Chernow
George A. Vallasi

Contributing Editors

Gregory D. Alles, ANCIENT RELIGIONS AND PHILOSOPHIES
Assistant Professor, Department of Philosophy and Religious Studies, Western Maryland College, and co-editor of Joachim Wach's *Introduction to the History of Religions* and *Essays in the History of Religions,* as well as author of several journal articles.

John P. Anton, GREEK AND ROMAN PHILOSOPHY
Professor of Philosophy and Director of the Interdisciplinary Center for Greek Studies at the University of South Florida, and author of *Aristotle's Theory of Contrariety, Philosophical Essays, Naturalism and Historical Understanding;* honorary member of Phi Beta Kappa, nominated for "Outstanding Educator" by Emory University in 1970, corresponding member of the Academy of Athens, and President of the Society for Ancient Greek Philosophy (1981–83).

Richard E. Cohen, JUDAISM
Graduate student at Brown University and author of "The Yerushalmi and Its Critics" (*New Perspectives on Ancient Judaism,* Vol. 1, Part 1, by Ernest S. Frerichs, and others) and "The Relationship between Topic, Rhetoric and Logic: Analysis of a Syllogistic Passage in the Palestinian Talmud" (*New Perspectives on Ancient Judaism,* Vol. III, edited by Ernest S. Frerichs and Jacob Neusner).

Robert S. Ellwood, MINORITY RELIGIONS AND CONTEMPORARY RELIGIOUS MOVEMENTS
Professor of Religion, University of Southern California, and author of *Religious and Spiritual Groups in Modern America; One Way: The Jesus Movement and Its Meaning; Alternative Altars: Unconventional and Eastern Spirituality in America.*

Karlfried Froehlich, EARLY CHRISTIANITY
Warfield Professor of Church History at Princeton Theological Seminary; translator and editor of *Biblical Interpretation in the Early Church;* co-author (with H. C. Kee and F. W. Young) of *Understanding the New Testament,* 2nd and 3rd eds.; contributor to numerous historical journals and publications; member of advisory board, *Classics of Western Spirituality,* and of the National Lutheran–Roman Catholic Dialogue in the United States.

Gary H. Gilbert, EARLY CHRISTIANITY
Doctoral candidate in the Department of Religion at Columbia University; his field of speciality is biblical studies.

Norman J. Girardot, EASTERN RELIGION AND PHILOSOPHY
Chair and Professor, Religion Studies Department, Lehigh University; author of *Myth and Meaning in Early Taoism*, co-editor of *Imagination and Meaning: The Scholarly and Literary Worlds of Mircea Eliade*, co-editor of "Myth and Symbol in Chinese Tradition" (Symposium issue of *The Journal of Chinese Religions*); Phi Beta Kappa, Woodrow Wilson Fellow, National Endowment for the Humanities Fellow.

W. Fred Graham, LATE CHRISTIANITY
Professor of Religious Studies, Michigan State University; author of *The Constructive Revolutionary: Calvin's Socio-Economic Impact* and *Picking up the Pieces;* book reviewer and contributor to over 60 publications on such topics as church history, religion and running, church and state, and science and religion; President, Michigan State University Chapter of the National Honors Society Phi Kappa Phi (1986–87); recipient of the American Philosophical Society Grant for study in Scotland and Northern Ireland (1987); he is president-elect of the Sixteenth Century Studies Society.

Leo Hamalian, ISLAMIC RELIGION AND PHILOSOPHY
Professor of English, The City College, City University of New York, and author of *William Saroyan: The Man and the Writer, D. H. Lawrence in Italy, Ladies on the Loose;* editor of *Ararat;* co-editor of *New Writings from the Middle East;* editorial board of *The Literary Review, Columbia,* and *Levant.*

John L. Longeway, MEDIEVAL PHILOSOPHY
Associate Professor, Department of Philosophy, University of Wisconsin at Parkside; author of *William Heytesbury: On Maxima and Minima* and "Nicholas of Cusa and Man's Knowledge of God" (*Philosophy Research Archives*).

Jacob Neusner, JUDAISM
University Professor and Ungerleider Distinguished Scholar of Judaic Studies, Brown University, and author or editor of numerous publications among which are *The Rabbinic Traditions about the Pharisees before 70* (3 volumes); *Eliezer ben Hyrcanus* (2 volumes); *Between Time and the Eternity: The Essentials of Judaism; Judaism: The Evidence of the Mishnah; Invitation to the Talmud; Ancient Judaism: Debates and Disputes; Contemporary Judaic Fellowship in Theory and Practice;* and *Take Judaism for Example: Studies Toward the Comparison of Religion.* Honorary degrees and awards include the University Medal for Excellence (Columbia University, 1974), Doctor of Humane Letters (L.H.D.) (University of Chicago, 1978), Doctor of Philosophy, *Honoris Causa* (Ph.D., h.c.) (University of Cologne, 1979), Von Humboldt Prize (Von Humboldt Foundation, Bonn, 1981), Distinguished Humanitarian Award (Melton Center for Jewish Studies, Ohio State University, 1983), Doctor of Hebrew Letters, *Honoris Causa* (Jewish Theological Seminary, 1987); member of several editorial boards including *Journal of the American Academy of Religion* and *Hebrew Annual Review.*

Richard H. Popkin, MODERN PHILOSOPHY, 1600–1900
Adjunct Professor of Philosophy and History, University of California, Los Angeles, and Professor Emeritus, Washington University; author of *The History of*

Scepticism from Erasmus to Spinoza and *The High Road to Pyrrhonism;* co-editor of *Introduction to Philosophy;* Fulbright Research Fellow (Paris, Utrecht); Guggenheim Fellow; ACLS Fellow; William Andrews Clark Professor (UCLA); Nicholas Murray Butler Medalist (Columbia); President, Journal of the History of Philosophy, Inc.; co-director, International Archive of the History of Ideas.

Frederick Purnell, Jr., RENAISSANCE PHILOSOPHY
Associate Professor of Philosophy, Queens College and the Graduate Center, City University of New York; author of "Jacopo Mazzoni and Galileo" (*Physis, XIV*), "Francesco Patrizi and the Critics of Hermes Trismegistus" (*The Journal of Medieval and Renaissance Studies, V*), "Hermes and the Sibyl: A Note on Ficino's *Pimander*" (*Renaissance Quarterly, XXX*); Chair, Department of Philosophy, Queens College; Fellowship for Independent Study, National Endowment for the Humanities; Fulbright Grantee to Italy; Woodrow Wilson Dissertation Fellow; Associate, Columbia University Seminar on the Renaissance.

Andrew J. Reck, TWENTIETH-CENTURY PHILOSOPHY
Professor and Chairman, Department of Philosophy, and Director, Master of Liberal Arts Program, Tulane University; author of *New American Philosophers, Introduction to William James, Recent American Philosophy, Speculative Philosophy;* editor of *Knowledge and Value* and *George Herbert Mead, Selective Writings;* Past President of Southwestern Philosophical Society, Southern Society for Philosophy and Psychology, and Metaphysical Society of America; currently vice president of the Charles S. Peirce Society.

William L. Reese, GENERAL PHILOSOPHY
Professor of Philosophy and former chairperson at the State University of New York, Albany; former chairperson of the philosophy department at the University of Delaware; author of *The Ascent from Below: An Introduction to Philosophical Inquiry* and the *Dictionary of Philosophy and Religion: Eastern and Western Thought;* co-author of *Process and Divinity* and *Philosophers Speak of God;* general editor of *Philosophy of Science: The Delaware Seminar,* 3 vols.; former co-editor of *Metaphilosophy.*

Abbreviations

abr.	abridged	Lit.	Literature
A.D.	in the year of the Lord	*LJ*	*Library Journal*
AHR	*American Historical Review*	ltd. ed.	limited edition
		MLA	Modern Language Association
Amer.	America(n)		
annot.	annotated	Mod.	Modern
B.C.	before Christ	*N.Y. Herald Tribune*	*New York Herald Tribune*
B.C.E.	before the common era		
bd.	bound	*N.Y. Times*	*New York Times*
bdg.	binding	o.p.	out-of-print
Bk(s).	Book(s)	orig.	original
B.P.	before the present	pap.	paperback
C.E.	of the common era	Pr.	Press
Class.	Classic(s)	pref.	preface
coll.	collected	pt(s).	parts
coll. ed.	collector's ed.	*PW*	*Publishers Weekly*
comp.	compiled, compiler	r.	reigned
corr.	corrected	repr.	reprint
cp.	compare	rev. ed.	revised edition
Ctr.	Center	*SB*	*Studies in Bibliography*
ed.	edited, editor, edition	sel.	selected
Eng.	English	Ser.	Series
enl. ed.	enlarged edition	*SLJ*	*School Library Journal*
fl.	flourished	*SR*	*Saturday Review*
fwd.	foreword	Stand.	Standard
gen. ed(s).	general editor(s)	Supp.	Supplement
ill.	illustrated	*TLS*	*Times Literary Supplement*
imit. lea.	imitation leather		
intro.	introduction	trans.	translated, translator, translation
lea.	leather		
lg.-type ed.	large-type edition	Univ.	University
Lib.	Library	Vol(s).	Volume(s)
lib. bdg.	library binding		

Chronology

Main author entries appear here chronologically by year of birth. Within each chapter, main author entries are arranged alphabetically by surname.

1. **General Philosophy**

2. **Greek and Roman Philosophy**
   Seneca, Lucius Annaeus. c.3 B.C.–A.D. 65
   Lucretius (Titus Lucretius Carus). c.99 B.C.–c.55 B.C.
   Cicero or Tully (Marcus Tullius Cicero). 106 B.C.–43 B.C.
   Epicurus. 341–270 B.C.
   Theophrastus of Eresus. c.372–c.287 B.C.
   Aristotle. 384–322 B.C.
   Plato. 427?–347 B.C.
   Xenophon. c.430–c.355 B.C.
   Socrates. 469 B.C.–399 B.C.
   Heraclitus of Ephesus. fl. c.500 B.C.
   Pythagoras of Samos. c.582–c.507 B.C.
   Marcus Aurelius (Antoninus). A.D. 121–180
   Plotinus. A.D. 205–270

3. **Medieval Philosophy**
   Origen. 185?–254?
   Augustine of Hippo, St. 354–430
   Boethius. c.480–c.524
   Anselm of Canterbury, St. 1033?–1109
   Abelard, Peter. 1079–1142

Bernard of Clairvaux, St. 1090?–1153
John of Salisbury. c.1120–1180
Grosseteste, Robert. c.1168–1253
Albert the Great. 1193–1280
Bacon, Roger. c.1214–c.1294?
Bonaventure of Bagnorea, St. 1221–1274
Thomas Aquinas, St. 1225?–1274
Duns Scotus, John. c.1265–1301
William of Ockham (or Occam). c.1285–c.1349

4. **Renaissance Philosophy**
   Petrarch (Francesco Petrarca). 1304–1374
   Nicholas of Cusa (Nicholas Cusanus). 1401?–1464
   Valla, Lorenzo. c.1407–1457
   Ficino, Marsilio. 1433–1499
   Pomponazzi, Pietro. 1462–1525
   Pico Della Mirandola, Giovanni. 1463–1494
   Erasmus, Desiderius. 1466?–1536
   Cajetan, Cardinal (Thomas De Vio). 1469–1534
   Machiavelli, Niccolò. 1469–1527
   Pico Della Mirandola, Gianfrancesco. 1469–1533

More, Thomas. 1478–1535

Agrippa of Nettesheim, Henry Cornelius. 1486–1535

Vives, Juan Luis. 1492–1540

Paracelsus, Philippus Aureolus (Theophrastus Bombastus von Hohenheim). 1493?–1541

Bodin, Jean. 1530?–1596

Montaigne, Michel Eyquem de. 1533–1592

Bruno, Giordano. 1548–1600

Suárez, Francisco. 1548–1617

Galilei, Galileo. 1564–1642

Campanella, Tommaso. 1568–1639

5. Modern Philosophy, 1600–1900

Bacon, Francis (Baron Verulam, Viscount St. Albans). 1561–1626

Hobbes, Thomas. 1588–1679

Gassendi, Pierre. 1592–1655

Descartes, René. 1596–1650

Pascal, Blaise. 1623–1662

Locke, John. 1632–1704

Spinoza, Baruch (or Benedict). 1632–1677

Malebranche, Nicolas. 1638–1715

Newton, Sir Isaac. 1642–1727

Leibniz (or Leibnitz), Gottfried Wilhelm, Baron von. 1646–1716

Bayle, Pierre. 1647–1706

Vico, Giambattista. 1668–1744

Berkeley, George. 1685–1753

Reid, Thomas. 1710–1796

Hume, David. 1711–1776

Diderot, Denis. 1713–1784

Kant, Immanuel. 1724–1804

Condorcet, Marie Jean Antoine Nicolas Caritat, Marquis de. 1743–1794

Fichte, Johann Gottlieb. 1762–1814

Hegel, Georg Wilhelm Friedrich. 1770–1831

Schelling, Friedrich Wilhelm Joseph von. 1775–1854

Schopenhauer, Arthur. 1788–1860

Comte, Auguste. 1798–1857

Feuerbach, Ludwig Andreas. 1804–1872

Mill, John Stuart. 1806–1873

Kierkegaard, Søren. 1813–1855

Marx, Karl. 1818–1883

Spencer, Herbert. 1820–1903

Dilthey, Wilhelm. 1833–1911

Peirce, Charles Sanders. 1839–1914

James, William. 1842–1910

Nietzsche, Friedrich Wilhelm. 1844–1900

Bradley, F(rancis) H(erbert). 1846–1924

Bosanquet, Bernard. 1848–1923

Royce, Josiah. 1855–1916

Bergson, Henri. 1859–1941

Dewey, John. 1859–1952

Husserl, Edmund. 1859–1938

6. Twentieth-Century Philosophy

Whitehead, Alfred North. 1861–1947

Mead, George Herbert. 1863–1931

Santayana, George. 1863–1952

McTaggart, John McTaggart Ellis. 1866–1925

Shestov, Lev. 1866–1938

Boodin, John Elof. 1869–1950

Russell, Bertrand Arthur William Russell, 3d Earl. 1872–1970

Hocking, William Ernest. 1873–1966

Lovejoy, Arthur Oncken. 1873–1962

Moore, George Edward. 1873–1958

Berdyaev, Nicholas. 1874–1948

Cassirer, Ernst. 1874–1945

Scheler, Max Ferdinand. 1874–1928

Gentile, Giovanni. 1875–1944

Cohen, Morris Raphael. 1880–1947

Sellars, Roy Wood. 1880–1973

Aliotta, Antonio. 1881–1964

Ducasse, Curt John. 1881–1969

Teilhard de Chardin, Pierre. 1881–1955

Maritain, Jacques. 1882–1973

Schlick, Moritz. 1882–1936

Jaspers, Karl. 1883–1969

Lewis, Clarence Irving. 1883–1964

Ortega y Gasset, José. 1883–1955

Bachelard, Gaston. 1884–1962

Brightman, Edgar Sheffield. 1884–1953

Gilson, Étienne. 1884–1978

Bloch, Ernst. 1885–1977

Broad, Charles Dunbar. 1887–1971

Collingwood, Robin George. 1889–1943

Heidegger, Martin. 1889–1976

Marcel, Gabriel. 1889–1973

Wittgenstein, Ludwig Josef Johann. 1889–1951

Gramsci, Antonio. 1891–1937

Blanshard, Brand. 1892–

Langer, Susanne K. 1895–1986

Edman, Irwin. 1896–1954

Hartshorne, Charles. 1897–

Marcuse, Herbert. 1898–1984

Gadamer, Hans-Georg. 1900–

Ryle, Gilbert. 1900–1976

Weiss, Paul. 1901–

Adler, Mortimer J. 1902–

Hook, Sidney. 1902–

Popper, Sir Karl Raimund. 1902–

Adorno T(heodor) W. 1903–1969

Feibleman, James Kern. 1904–

Lonergan, Bernard. 1904–1984

Sartre, Jean-Paul. 1905–1980

Arendt, Hannah. 1906–1975

Goodman, Nelson. 1906–

Merleau-Ponty, Maurice. 1908–1961

Quine, Willard Van Orman. 1908–

Black, Max. 1909–

Ayer, Sir Alfred Jules. 1910–

Austin, John Langshaw. 1911–1960

Malcolm, Norman. 1911–

Sellars, Wilfrid. 1912–

Ricoeur, Paul. 1913–

Buchler, Justus. 1914–

Chisholm, Roderick M. 1916–

Von Wright, Georg H. 1916–

Strawson, Peter Frederick. 1919–

Rawls, John. 1921–

Foucault, Michel. 1926–1984

Habermas, Jürgen. 1929–

Derrida, Jacques. 1930–

Rorty, Richard McKay. 1931–

7. Ancient Religions and Philosophies

8. Eastern Religion and Philosophy

9. Islamic Religion and Philosophy

Muhammad (or Mohammed). 570?–632

Avicenna. 980–1037

Ibn Haym. 994–1064

Ghazālī, al-. 1058–1111

Averroës. 1126–1198

Ibn al-Arabi. 1165–1240

Ibn Tufayl. ?–1185

Rumi. 1207–1273

Ibn Khallikan. 1211–1281

Ibn Khaldun. 1332–1406

Jami. 1414–1492

Jalal al-Din al-Suyuti. 1445–1505

10. Judaism

Philo Judaeus. c.20 B.C.–C.A.D. 50

Josephus Flavius. C.A.D. 38–A.D. 100?

Saadia Gaon (Saadia ben Joseph al-Fayumi). 882–942

Rashi (Solomon ben Isaac). 1040–1105

Judah Ha-Levi. c.1075–1141

Maimonides (Moses ben Maimon). 1135–1204

Kimhi, David. c.1160?–1235?

Nahmanides (Moses ben Nahman, also Rambam). 1194–c.1270

Gersonides (Levi ben Gershon). 1288–1344

Ba'al Shem Tov. c.1700–1760

Nahman of Bratslav. 1772–1811

Hirsch, Samson (ben) Raphael. 1808–1888

Cohen, Hermann. 1842–1918

Baeck, Leo. 1873–1956

Buber, Martin. 1878–1965

Kaplan, Mordecai Menachem. 1881–1983

Rosenzweig, Franz. 1886–1929

Scholem, Gershom. 1897–1982

Soloveitchik, Joseph. 1903–

Heschel, Abraham Joshua. 1907–1972

Fackenheim, Emil. 1916–

Borowitz, Eugene. 1924–

Rubenstein, Richard. 1924–

Waskow, Arthur. 1933–

11. Early Christianity

Tertullian. c.160–c.230

Cyprian of Carthage, St. c.200?/210?–258

Eusebius of Caesarea. c.260–c.340

Basil of Caesarea, St. c.330–379

Ambrose, St. 340?–397

Jerome, St. c.347–419

Chrysostom, St. John. c.354–407

Cassian, St. John. c.365–c.435

Patrick, St. c.390–460

Gregory the Great (Pope Gregory I). c.540–604

Anselm of Canterbury, St. 1033?–1109

Joachim of Fiore. c.1132–1202

Alan of Lille. d.1203

Eckhart, (Johannes) Meister. c.1260–c.1328

Fitzralph, Richard. c.1295–1360

Wyclif, John. c.1330–1384

Hus, John. c.1372–1415

12. Late Christianity

Luther, Martin. 1483–1546

Zwingli, Huldrych (also Huldreick). 1484–1531

Ignatius of Loyola, St. 1491–1556

Menno Simons. 1496?–1561

Calvin, John. 1509–1564

Wesley, John. 1703–1791

Newman, John Henry, Cardinal. 1801–1890

John XXIII, Pope. 1881–1963

Barth, Karl. 1886–1968

Tillich, Paul Johannes. 1886–1965

Niebuhr, Reinhold. 1892–1971

Lewis, C(live) S(taples). 1898–1963

Bonhoeffer, Dietrich. 1906–1945

Merton, Thomas. 1915–1968

Küng, Hans. 1928–

King, Martin Luther, Jr. 1929–1968

13. The Bible and Related Literature

14. Minority Religions and Contemporary Religious Movements

Introduction

Through the years *The Reader's Adviser* has expanded to meet the needs of the reading public. Along with other areas the material on philosophy, religion, and the Bible has been accorded fuller treatment in the successive editions of this major work. In the present thirteenth edition these important areas of human concern have at last been granted a separate volume. With this achievement the entire multivolume work is now able to provide what might be called a map of human culture. The separate volume has made it possible to involve specialists from basic areas of philosophy and religion, providing important information concerning the resources of their special areas. They have brought together a vast panorama of analyses guiding us, the readers of the world, through many problems. I am grateful to them for their evident care and concern.

In some important sense philosophy and religion belong to each other. Their presence in a single volume suggests this special relationship. Indeed, what are now two approaches to life were initially undifferentiated. This common origin can be sensed in Chapter 7, "Ancient Religions and Philosophies," where that period of time is treated prior to the separation of the two approaches. And had the arrangement of the volume been chronological, the study would have begun with Chapter 7. Chapters 8 and 9 provide evidence that the Western separation was exceptional. The East kept its philosophy and religion together. And, of course, there is evidence that even in the West the separation was never complete, certainly not for all philosophers nor for all devotees of religion.

There is no reason why philosophy should occupy the first seven chapters of the volume, approximately, and religion the last seven. That separation obscures the very real interchange between philosophy and religion. For reasons of clarity of exposition, philosophy and religion are treated separately, the story of philosophy in the sweep from Greek to twentieth-century philosophy in Chapters 2 through 6, and that of Christianity in Chapters 11 and 12. Clarity is also served by separate chapters on Islam (Chapter 9), Judaism (Chapter 10), the Bible (Chapter 13), and the movements of minority religions (Chapter 14).

Also, there is an important sense in which philosophy belongs to every volume of *The Reader's Adviser*. For this the Greek philosophers were responsible. Referring to the extensive course of study Plato believed to be necessary in the education of a philosopher, he said: "The process . . . is not the turning over of an oyster-shell, but the turning round of a soul passing from a day which is little better than night to the true day of being, that is, the ascent from below, which we affirm to be true philosophy. . . ." In Plato's scheme of things the neophyte philosopher worked through every field of learning. The study was complete only when "knowledge of the whole" had been gained. The universities in which Plato, Aristotle, and their students sought this knowledge succeeded so well that "knowledge of the whole" finally exceeded human grasp. "Philosophy of" became a practical necessity. Philosophy exists, then, not only in general systems, but in specialized applications to every field of knowledge. For this reason references to philosophy are to be found not only in the seven and one-half chapters devoted to philosophy in this volume, but also, for example, in Chapter 3 of Volume 5 (Philosophy of Science and Pseudoscience). In every discipline treated in this multivolume work the alert reader will be able to discover "philosophy of" material, relating to the specific discipline, a testimony to the continuing vitality of Plato's emphasis on "knowledge of the whole," adapted to the complexity of contemporary knowledge.

William L. Reese

in more than 3500 alphabetically arranged entries" (*QPB Review*). This is the only single volume dictionary with a significant body of material on both Western and Eastern thought.

Ruben, Douglas H., ed. *Philosophy Journals and Serials: An Analytical Guide.* [*Annotated Bibliographies of Serials*] Greenwood 1985 lib. bdg. $35.00. A bibliography of 335 entries, primarily of philosophy journals publishing articles in English. Archives, newsletters, and bulletins are included as well. Location, frequency of publication, price, circulation, purpose, and coverage of the publication provided.

Runes, Dagobert D., ed. *Dictionary of Philosophy.* Philosophical Lib. rev & enl. repr. 1983 $24.95; Rowman rev. & enl. ed. 1984 pap. $10.95. The editor's announced aim is "clear, concise, and correct definitions and descriptions of the philosophical terms throughout the range of philosophic thought." The dictionary's outstanding feature is the analyses of logic by Alonzo Church.

———. *Spinoza: Dictionary.* Greenwood repr. of 1951 ed. 1976 lib. bdg. $29.75. A dictionary related to the understanding of Spinoza, utilizing Spinoza's own discussions of his terms and ideas. The foreword is by Albert Einstein.

Sandeen, Ernest R., and Frederick Hale, eds. *American Religion and Philosophy: A Guide to Information Sources.* [*Amer. Studies Information Guide*] Gale 1978 $62.00. Concentrating primarily on the field of religion, but with three chapters devoted exclusively to philosophy, in 21 chapters and more than 1,600 entries the books, articles, and bibliographical and other relevant source material are presented.

Steenbergen, G. J. *New Encyclopedia of Philosophy.* Trans. by Edmond Van Den Bossche, Philosophical Lib. 1972 $20.00. Contains entries on both terms and principal figures from the Dutch.

Tice, Terrence N., and Thomas P. Slavens. *Research Guide to Philosophy.* [*Sources of Information in the Humanities Ser.*] Amer. Lib. Assn. 1983 lib. bdg. $40.00. A guide to the field of philosophy depicting, according to the authors, "the principal changes since the nineteenth century" and setting forth "the more representative and exemplary literature in each subfield." The material is presented through carefully developed essays.

University of Southern California, Los Angeles. *Catalog of the Hoose Library of Philosophy.* G. K. Hall 6 vols. 1968 $595.00. This catalog of one of the great libraries of philosophy, containing more than 37,000 volumes and representing all fields of philosophy (but with its greatest depth in classical and German philosophy), would be helpful principally to those engaged in library development.

Voltaire. *Philosophical Dictionary.* [*Penguin Class. Ser.*] Trans. by Theodore Besterman, Penguin 1984 pap. $4.95. Although called a dictionary by Voltaire, and arranged in alphabetical form, this work is a compilation of essays by Voltaire on the wide-ranging humanitarian topics of special interest to him. It is, then, like a number of other works on this list carrying the name "dictionary," more of an introduction to the thought of a single philosopher than an introduction to all philosophy. The Voltaire *Philosophical Dictionary* went through numerous editions during Voltaire's lifetime, and it grew in size from edition to edition. As usual with Voltaire's work, it was a bestseller. It was also a target for book burnings.

Wiener, Philip P., ed. *Dictionary of the History of Ideas.* Scribner 5 vols. 1980 pap. $67.50. A cooperative study containing analyses of some 300 basic ideas by almost as many scholars from a variety of fields extending from art to science. A philosophical history of ideas approach is followed in this interdisciplinary volume.

HISTORIES OF PHILOSOPHY

The books in this section, existing in great abundance, deal with the material of philosophy chronologically, showing how a given period or philosophy arose from an earlier one. Encyclopedias and dictionaries epitomize knowledge; histories interpret it. Both are derivative from the writings of the philosophers. A considerable amount of the energy of the philosophical community is dedicated to the work of interpretation, most often showing how philosophical ideas interrelate as philosophies emerge from each other in history, and from their cultures. Between the histories of philosophy and the introductions to philosophy, it is appropriate to mention a number of books that combine history and introduction. Preeminent among these is the much-maligned yet helpful *Story of Philosophy* by WILL DURANT (see Vol. 3). One of the features of the Durant book is its rather great stress on biography to interest the reader in, as well as help him or her to understand, the philosophers. Another feature is the concentration on only the greatest of the philosophers. Included below are books that do one or the other of these things, as well as those that take a unique approach in some other manner.

Alpern, Henry. *March of Philosophy.* Associated Faculty Pr. repr. of 1933 ed. 1968 $24.50. One of the older and well-written histories of philosophy.

Aquila, Richard E. *Rhyme or Reason: A Limerick History of Philosophy.* Univ. Pr. of Amer. 1981 lib. bdg. $14.75 text ed. pap. $5.75. A presentation of philosophy combining rhyme with reason. The 423 limericks about philosophers and philosophy will be of most use to those whose commitment to limericks and philosophy is of equal strength. The value of the work as a teaching instrument may be questionable, since understanding the philosophy is often a condition for understanding the limerick.

Bréhier, Emile. *History of Philosophy.* Univ. of Chicago Pr. 7 vols. 1963–1973 text ed. pap. ea. $5.00–$7.00. From "The Hellenic Age" (Vol. 1) to "Contemporary Philosophy" (Vol. 7). To a greater extent than other historians, Bréhier places the philosophers in their cultural contexts, combining exposition and criticism.

Burley, Walter. *On the Lives and Characters of the Philosophers.* Ed. and trans. by Paul Theiner, Garland 1981 $35.00. An approach that is both philosophical and biographical.

Caponigri, A. Robert. *A History of Western Philosophy.* Univ. of Notre Dame Pr. vols 4–5 1971 ea. $25.00 pap. ea. $4.95. The final two volumes of this set remain in print. Volume 4 deals with the nineteenth century and is titled *The Romantic Age to the Age of Positivism.* Volume 5 deals with the twentieth century and is titled *The Age of Positivism to the Age of Analysis.*

Copleston, Frederick. *History of Philosophy.* Paulist Pr. 9 vols. 1946–74 ea. $19.95. Copleston's goal is to work out the "logical development and inter-connection of philosophical systems." Although he designed the work for "Catholic ecclesiastical seminaries," its acceptance has been very widespread.

Durant, Will. *Story of Philosophy.* Simon & Schuster 1961 pap. $10.95. This immensely successful volume combines philosophy and biography in an appealing manner, but limits consideration to only the most famous philosophers.

Ferm, Vergilius, ed. *History of Philosophical Systems.* [*Essay Index Repr. Ser.*] Ayer 1950 $33.00. Concentrates on metaphysical systems and the differences among them.

Frost, S. E., Jr. *The Basic Teachings of the Great Philosophers*. Darby repr. of 1942 ed. 1980 lib. bdg. $25.00. A compendium of philosophical ideas, on the order of a dictionary, but presented chronologically.

Hartshorne, Charles. *Insights and Oversights of Great Thinkers: An Evaluation of Western Philosophy*. [*Ser. in Systematic Philosophy*] State Univ. of New York Pr. 1983 $39.50 pap. $16.95. Hartshorne confronts the history of philosophy from the standpoint of process philosophy, a position in contrast to the emphasis on substance used by Aristotle.

Hegel, Georg W. *Lectures on the History of Philosophy*. Trans. by E. S. Haldane and F. H. Simson, Humanities 3 vols. repr. of 1896 ed. 1974 text ed. $65.00. It is, indeed, appropriate that there should be a work on the history of philosophy by the philosopher who, more than any other, made history a central philosophical consideration. Hegel applies his triadic method here to show "the necessary development of the successive philosophies from one another," dividing the material into Greek philosophy (the subjective idea), Middle Ages (a period of fermentation and preparation), and German philosophy (the substantial and concrete idea). The third stage is called "the final result." It is "what the World-Spirit has brought before itself in its conscious thinking." This final stage includes, of course, and indeed concludes with, the philosophy of Hegel.

Honderich, Ted, ed. *Philosophy Through Its Past*. [*Pelican Ser.*] Penguin 1984 pap. $7.95. Historical interpretation comes to the fore in this volume.

Jaspers, Karl. *Socrates, Buddha, Confucius and Jesus: Taken from Vol. 1 of the Great Philosophers*. Trans. by Ralph Manheim, Harcourt 1966 pap. $3.95. The only portion now in print of Jaspers' multivolume history of philosophy exemplifies his method of concentrating on principal figures.

Jones, W. T. *A History of Western Philosophy*. Harcourt 5 vols. 1952 o.p. Jones states that he has used a principle of "concentration" since "it is better to understand a few theories than to recognize a great many." He concentrates on major figures, quoting generously from their writings.

Kreyche, Gerald F. *Thirteen Thinkers: A Sampler of Great Philosophers*. Univ. Pr. of Amer. 1976 o.p. An example of the history of philosophy studied through exemplary cases.

Lamprecht, Sterling P. *Our Philosophical Traditions: A Brief History of Philosophy in Western Civilization*. [*Century Philosophy Ser.*] Irvington repr. of 1955 ed. 1980 o.p. A standard history of philosophy with durability, written in an even-handed yet lively manner. Avoids the faults of the usual history.

Lewes, George H. *The Biographical History of Philosophy, from Its Origins in Greece Down to the Present Day*. Arden Lib. repr. of 1862 ed. 1979 lib. bdg. $65.00; Gregg repr. of 1857 ed. text ed. $74.52. An approach to understanding philosophy through biography.

Lloyd, Genevieve. *The Man of Reason: Male and Female in Western Philosophy*. Univ. of Minnesota Pr. 1985 $27.50 pap. $10.95. Not a standard work in the history of philosophy. Lloyd argues that in the history of philosophy reason has been regarded as a male attribute. The philosophers she analyzes in making her case include Plato, Sartre, and Simone de Beauvoir. The distortions she finds suggest that philosophy must proceed differently from now on.

Magill, Frank N., ed. *Masterpieces of World Philosophy in Summary Form*. Harper 1961 $24.50. The emphasis of this book is on detailing the content of a select number of famous philosophical discourses.

Mahowald, Mary B., ed. *Philosophy of Woman: An Anthology of Classic and Current Concepts*. Hackett 1983 $19.50 text ed. pap. $12.50. Essays on the nature of woman, counterbalancing the male-dominated history of Western philosophy.

Marias, Julian. *A Biography of Philosophy*. Trans. by Harold C. Raley, Univ. of Alabama Pr. 1984 $18.75. This "vitalist" Spanish philosopher finds prephilosophical problems in the commonsense world, and traces their evolution into philosophical thought.

Montague, William P. *Great Visions of Philosophy*. [*Paul Carus Lecture Ser.*] Open Court 1950 $29.95. Finding truth in many varieties of speculative thought, Montague ranges here from the Greeks to Bergson.

O'Connor, Daniel J., ed. *A Critical History of Western Philosophy*. Free Pr. 1964 pap. $12.95. A joint effort, chiefly by British authors, with the goal of examining the philosophies of the West from the standpoint of attempting "to bring out whatever may be in them that is of permanent interest."

Oizerman, Theodor. *Problems in the History of Philosophy*. Beekman 1975 $15.00. Imported Pubns. 1973 $7.95. Although many introductions to philosophy center on problems, this is one of relatively few histories to do so.

Ozmon, H. *Twelve Great Western Philosophers*. Oddo 1967 $9.26 pap. $3.94. Here once again the history of philosophy is approached by way of a concentration on "great" figures.

Randall, John H. *The Career of Philosophy*. Columbia Univ. Pr. 3 vols. 1970–77 ea. $32.00–$45.00. Randall takes a cultural approach to philosophy. He begins with the Middle Ages, highlighting the Enlightenment and the Age of Darwin. The contemporary period is called "Philosophy after Darwin."

Ree, J., M. Ayers, and A. Westoby. *Philosophy and Its Past*. Humanities Pr. 1978 o.p. A study in the philosophy of the history of philosophy, bringing historiography into the analysis of the discipline.

Ricoeur, Paul. *Main Trends in Philosophy*. [*Main Trends in the Social and Human Sciences Ser.*] Holmes & Meier 1979 pap. text ed. $26.50. This French philosopher applies his continental approach to the history of philosophy, using phenomenology and hermeneutics (an approach to philosophy that began with the interpretation of texts) as his tools.

Runes, Dagobert D. *Philosophy for Everyman: From Socrates to Sartre*. [*Quality Pap. Ser.*] Littlefield repr. of 1968 ed. 1974 pap. $3.50. Brief synopses of philosophers arranged chronologically.

Russell, Bertrand, ed. *A History of Western Philosophy*. [*Counterpoint Ser.*] Simon & Schuster 1984 pap. $8.95. One of the great histories of philosophy. Each philosopher is praised or criticized from Russell's own perspective. The book is characterized by Russellian humor, insight, and an occasional oversight.

Scharfstein, Ben-Ami. *The Philosophers: Life and Thought*. Oxford 1980 $35.00. A psychoanalytically oriented study of the sources of philosophical systems.

Schlossberg, Edwin, and John Brockman. *The Philosopher's Game: Match Your Wits Against the One Hundred Greatest Thinkers of All Time*. St. Martin's 1977 pap. $6.95. Of the many approaches to the history of philosophy, perhaps the most unusual is this one, in which philosophy is viewed as a game.

Ueberweg, Friedrich. *A History of Philosophy*. Trans. by George S. Morris [*Select Bibliographies Repr. Ser.*] Ayer 2 vols. repr. of 1874 ed. 1977 $48.00. This comprehensive history begins with Thales and continues to the middle of the nineteenth century. It is rich in references to philosophical literature in many languages and contains many scholarly footnotes.

Walsh, Martin J. *A History of Philosophy*. Winston Pr. 1984 pap. $17.95. Walsh succeeded in his goal of producing a "compact textbook or concise reference book" in the history of philosophy. The range is from pre-Socratic philosophy to twentieth-century philosophies of being (the latter largely Thomistic in content).

Webb, Clement C. *A History of Philosophy*. Russell Pr. repr. of 1984 ed. 1985 lib. bdg.

$40.00. A brief history of philosophy written for the British Home University Library series (first edition, 1915), dealing with principal figures and movements in philosophy.

Wedberg, Anders. *A History of Philosophy.* Oxford 3 vols. 1982–84 ea. $24.50–$29.95 ea. pap. $9.95–$13.95. The coverage is from antiquity to Wittgenstein.

Windelband, Wilhelm. *A History of Philosophy.* Trans. by James H. Tufts, Greenwood repr. of 1938 ed. 1979 lib. bdg. $42.50. One of the great nineteenth-century histories, it extends from the Greeks to Nietzsche. It is both problem-oriented and selective, concentrating on prominent philosophers, while relegating the less prominent to its extensive footnotes.

Wolff, Robert P. *Ten Great Works of Philosophy.* New Amer. Lib. 1973 pap. $4.50. Here the principle of concentration is applied to individual philosophical texts rather than to individual philosophers or systems.

INTRODUCTIONS TO PHILOSOPHY

There is, of course, a gradation from works in the history of philosophy to those that serve as introductions to philosophy. Indeed there are two major strategies for introducing the reader to philosophy. One is through a discussion of problems, either by the author or by the philosophers themselves (excerpted in anthologies). The other is through the history of philosophy. Many of the previously mentioned works have also served as introductions to philosophy. Introductions, no less than histories, underline the extent to which philosophy is a teaching discipline. The introductions are most often ordered analytically in terms of problems, not chronologically. As suggested earlier, their deepest motivation is Socratic, although some stress an interest in choice among systems. Both strategies are to be found in the following list. Additional strategies are to be discerned here as well. One of these is the introduction to philosophy through literature. Another is by approaching the problems of philosophy through the eyes of a major philosopher; THOMAS AQUINAS, for example, is sometimes so chosen. One of the works here is subtitled *A Sketch of Aquinate Philosophy.*

The problems approach typically includes consideration of seven or eight topics, among them ethics, epistemology, and the existence of God. Books with this approach differ, however, in that some place their emphasis on questions of value, topics of ethics for example, while others stress questions of logic and epistemology. The same selection of emphasis is to be found in the philosophers writing or editing the books. When philosophy stresses logic and epistemology, it is often called analytic philosophy.

Although the philosophical strategy in use can often be read from the titles, the leaning toward analytic philosophy can seldom be determined in this way. The texts that are heavily analytic have sometimes been so identified; at other times, their preoccupation with questions of logic and epistemology, distinguishing marks of such philosophy, has been noted.

Abel, Reuben. *Man Is the Measure: A Cordial Invitation to the Central Problems of Philosophy.* Free Pr. 1976 pap. $14.95. A book oriented to the problems of philosophy consisting of analyses by the author.

Abelson, Raziel, and Michael Lockwood. *The Philosophical Imagination: An Introduc-*

tion to Philosophy. St. Martin's 1977 text ed. $25.95. Analytically oriented book of readings with introductions. The selections are in five areas, from Eastern philosophers, some from literary sources.

Alston, William P., and Richard Brandt. *The Problems of Philosophy: Introductory Readings.* Allyn & Bacon 3d ed. 1978 text ed. $34.30. An introduction to philosophy designed, say its editors, to present "some of the best discussion" of its major problems; e.g., religious belief, value and obligation, freewill and determinism, the mind-body problem, the foundations of knowledge. Authors with contrasting views are included for each problem, mirroring the philosophical debate.

Armour, Leslie, and Edward T. Bartlett, III. *The Conceptualization of the Inner Life: A Philosophical Exploration.* Humanities Pr. 1981 text ed. $17.50. An introduction to philosophy in the sense that the authors prospect for an appropriate standing ground between "practical human concerns" and the "battleground of metaphysics." The work combines discussions of the nature of argument, metaphysics, and basic concepts ("person," "thing," "dream," "action"), finally providing some coherence between one's inner life and "the whole outside."

Barry, Vincent. *Philosophy: A Text with Readings.* Wadsworth 1980 text ed. $21.95. An approach to philosophy combining text and selections in a single volume.

Beauchamp, Tom L., and Joel Feinberg. *Philosophy and the Human Condition.* Prentice-Hall 1980 text ed. $25.95. A standard anthology presenting contrasting selections on the basic problems of philosophy.

Beck, Robert N. *Perspectives in Philosophy: A Book of Readings.* Henry Holt 3d ed. 1975 o.p. An approach to philosophy through the "isms." Readings on realism, materialism, idealism, positivism, linguistic philosophy, and existentialism.

Bedell, Gary. *Philosophizing with Socrates: An Introduction to the Study of Philosophy.* Univ. Pr. of Amer. 1980 text ed. pap. $9.75. Introduces one to philosophy by way of a study of the six early Socratic/Platonic dialogues (*Protagoras, Meno, Euthyphro, Apology, Crito, Phaedo*). An initial section on Socratic method; the two final sections on the nature of philosophy.

Berman, A. K., and James A. Gould, eds. *Philosophy for a New Generation.* Macmillan 4th ed. 1981 pap. $12.95. A book of readings balanced between relevance and critical analysis of basic topics.

Bochenski, I. M. *Philosophy: An Introduction.* Trans. by William M. Newell, Kluwer Academic 1963 lib. bdg. $16.00. A series of studies of selected philosophical problems and periods. An extensive bibliography of philosophy is included.

Brody, Baruch A. *Beginning Philosophy.* Prentice-Hall 1977 pap. $18.95. Ten analyses of standard problems of philosophy, around 20 pages each, featuring a classical approach to philosophy.

Buford, Thomas O. *Personal Philosophy: The Art of Living.* Holt 1984 text ed. $25.95. A problems approach, its sections initiated by case studies, followed by two opposed positions, and then a mediating position which is that of the author. The objective is to bring philosophy to bear on the issues of life.

Cahn, Steven M., ed. *Classics of Western Philosophy.* Hackett 2d ed. 1985 $30.00 text ed. pap. $19.50. The highlights of Western philosophy anthologized.

——. *A New Introduction to Philosophy.* Univ. Pr. of Amer. repr. of 1971 ed. 1986 text ed. pap. $17.50. A reprint of one of the classic introductions to philosophy.

Capaldi, Nicholas. *An Invitation to Philosophy.* Prometheus Bks. 1981 text ed. pap. $14.95. Combines discussions of the history of philosophy with discussion of basic problems. A chapter on Asian thought is included.

——, and others, eds. *Journeys Through Philosophy.* Prometheus Bks. rev. ed. 1982 text ed. pap. $17.95. Standard readings from Plato to Russell (one-third of the selections are from Plato and Aristotle). A section of medieval philosophy is included; also, a guide to reading philosophy.

Cornman, James W., and others. *Philosophical Problems and Arguments: An Introduction.* Macmillan 3d ed. 1982 o.p. An analytic introduction to philosophy, with analyses by authors, and an extensive bibliography.

Davidson, Robert F. *Philosophies Men Live By.* Holt 2d ed. 1974 text ed. $27.95. Interpretations of hedonism, rationalism, utilitarianism, naturalism, pragmatism, existentialism, and Zen Buddhism, with selected illustrative passages from their chief representatives.

Davis, Thomas D. *Philosophy: An Introduction Through Original Fiction, Discussion and Readings.* Random 2d ed. 1986 text ed. pap. $10.00. A problems approach to philosophy, each problem introduced by one or two fictional stories by Davis, followed by questions on the philosophical themes implicit in the stories, and finally an explicitly philosophical discussion of the topic.

Edwards, James C., and Douglas MacDonald. *Occasions for Philosophy.* Prentice-Hall 1979 pap. $10.95. Readings with the announced goal of Socratic self-knowledge, the first section begins with Socrates (the whole of *Euthyphro* and *Apology*), followed by critical discussions of Socrates' character and mission. Other sections feature personal relations, death and meaningfulness, religion, and philosophy of education.

Edwards, Paul, and Arthur Pap, eds. *Modern Introduction to Philosophy.* Free Pr. 3d ed. 1973 text ed. $18.95. Analytic; substantial readings, placed in context by the editors. Each section ends with an elaborate annotated bibliography.

Ewing, Alfred C. *The Fundamental Questions of Philosophy.* Methuen 1985 pap. $8.95. A distinguished older text dealing with epistemology, matter, mind, space-time, freedom, and God.

Feinberg, Joel. *Reason and Responsibility.* Wadsworth 1980 o.p. Mostly analytic in approach; deals with six problems, including the analytic-synthetic distinction. The selections are ample.

Flew, Antony. *Philosophy: An Introduction.* Prometheus Bks. 1980 text ed. pap. $10.95. A standard introduction covering the customary topics of philosophy by a well-known British philosopher.

Geisler, Norman L., and Paul Feinberg. *Introduction to Philosophy.* Baker Bks. 1980 $16.95. The subtitle is "A Christian Perspective," and the Preface states that the book is "unashamedly" written from that perspective, that the positions compatible with Christianity are presented "as fairly as possible," and that the authors "have tried to refute" anti-Christian views. After an initial section on the nature of philosophy, the volume deals with knowledge, reality, the ultimate, and ethics.

Gould, James A., ed. *Classic Philosophical Questions.* Merrill 1975 o.p. Breaking the basic problems down into subproblems, Gould presents contrasting views from the history of philosophy. For example, in the section on ethics, one of the subproblems is "Is man always selfish?" (Yes—Bernard de Mandeville. No—Joseph Butler). Each chapter concludes with study guide questions and suggested readings.

Grassian, Victor. *Perennial Philosophical Issues.* Prentice-Hall 1984 text ed. $26.95. A problems approach stressing enduring issues.

Halverson, William H. *A Concise Introduction to Philosophy.* Random 1981 $16.95. The work consists of 64 six- to eight-page chapters arguing for various positions.
———. *Concise Readings in Philosophy.* Random 1981 text ed. pap. $11.00. Sixty-four selections correlated to the chapters of the preceding work. Two-thirds are from historical sources.

Harris, William T. *Introduction to the Study of Philosophy.* Ed. by Marietta Kies,

AMS Pr. repr. of 1889 ed. 1976 $21.00. A truly historic introduction to philosophy. Kies produced the book by selecting sufficient material from the work of William T. Harris for a course in philosophy at Mount Holyoke College, Massachusetts. Harris, an idealist and Hegelian, was at the time editor of the *Journal of Speculative Philosophy*. The approach of the book is metaphysical, concluding with "the personality of God" and "the immortality of man."

Hocutt, Max. *First Philosophy: An Introduction to Philosophical Issues*. Krieger 2d ed. repr. of 1980 ed. 1986 lib. bdg. $17.50. An introduction to philosophy through metaphysics.

Hollingdale, R. J. *Western Philosophy: An Introduction*. Taplinger 1983 pap. $5.95. Hollingdale combines an introduction to philosophy and a brief history, first dealing with the problems of logic, epistemology, metaphysics, ethics, aesthetics, and applied philosophy. In part two, he discusses the history of philosophy, divided into Greek philosophy, Catholic philosophy, and modern philosophical movements.

Hollis, Martin. *Invitation to Philosophy*. Basil Blackwell 1985 $24.95 pap. $8.95. Organizing the work around various dichotomies, Hollis invites the student to think along with him about scientific and moral understanding, open and closed questions, vision and reason, inner and outer worlds, subjectivity and objectivity.

Honer, Stanley M., and Thomas C. Hunt. *Invitation to Philosophy*. Wadsworth 4th ed. 1982 pap. $12.95. The authors, presuming a use of primary reading sources, provide a supplement to them in concise discussions of basic philosophical concepts.

Jaspers, Karl. *Way to Wisdom: An Introduction to Philosophy*. Trans. by Ralph Manheim, Yale Univ. Pr. 1960 pap. $6.95. A nonanalytic approach to philosophy by this important German existentialist philosopher. He discusses God, man, science, the world, and the Comprehensive.

Joad, Cyril E. *Guide to Philosophy*. Dover 1936 pap. $9.95. This, one of the older introductions, is by a well-known British philosopher. Joad begins with a discussion of epistemology, which he then applies to metaphysical systems from Plato to Whitehead.

Johnson, Oliver A. *The Individual and the Universe: An Introduction to Philosophy*. Holt 1981 text ed. $29.95. A book of readings on the major fields and central issues of philosophy, beginning with Socrates and concluding with William James.

Klauder, Francis J. *The Wonder of Philosophy*. Philosophical Lib. 1974 $6.95. An outline of the principal positions of Thomistic philosophy, brief survey of the main figures of Western philosophy, a very few pages on Eastern philosophy, and a glossary of terms.

Klemke, E. D., and others, eds. *Philosophy: The Basic Issues*. St. Martin's 1985 text ed. pap. $16.95. A standard anthology treating the problems of philosophy by way of contrasting selections.

Konecsni, Johnemery. *A Philosophy for Living: A Sketch of Aquinate Philosophy*. Univ. Pr. of Amer. 1977 text ed. pap. $11.25. An approach to philosophy through the system of Thomas Aquinas.

Lachs, John, and Charles E. Scott, eds. *The Human Search: An Introduction to Philosophy*. Oxford 1981 text ed. pap. $12.95. A book of selections with introductions of five to six pages, consisting of traditional philosophy, current applications to economics and morals, and literature with philosophic implications.

Ladd, George T. *Introduction to Philosophy: An Inquiry after a Rational System of Scientific Principles in the Relation to the Ultimate Reality*. AMS Pr. repr. of 1890 ed. 1988 $29.50. As the initial reviewer of this book wrote (in 1891), this is a book to be read after, not before, "severe philosophical study." Regarding philosophy as "the science of what is knowable by means of the special sciences," Ladd attempts to reduce this knowledge to system and to provide, along the way, an analysis of philosophical method.

Lazerowitz, M., and A. Ambrose. *Philosophical Theories.* Mouton 1976 text ed. $22.00. These well-known American philosophers deal with topics ranging from epistemology to ethics. Each chapter ends with a section on "doubts and queries." The suggestions for further reading direct one to the more analytic philosophers, such as Moore, Broad, Russell, Howe, and Malcolm.

Levi, Albert W. *Varieties of Experience: An Introduction to Philosophy.* Wiley 1957 o.p. A cultural approach to philosophy in Levi's own voice combining readings and text.

McLaren, Robert B. *The World of Philosophy: An Introduction.* Nelson-Hall 1983 text ed. $23.95 text ed. pap. $11.95. McLaren provides an introduction to philosophy combining discussion of individual philosophers with perennial problems. Its scope is from the ancient world to contemporary times. It is anecdotal, personal, and sometimes analytical; includes a glossary of terms.

Mandelbaum, Maurice, ed. *Philosophic Problems.* Macmillan 2d ed. 1967 o.p. Somewhat analytic.

Marias Aquilera, Julian. *Reason and Life: The Introduction to Philosophy.* Trans. by Kenneth S. Reid and Edward Sarmiento, Greenwood repr. of 1956 ed. 1975 lib. bdg. $24.50. Translated from the Spanish, and dedicated to the author's teacher, Ortega y Gasset, whose thought he follows in his analysis of philosophic problems, including Ortega's emphasis on a "vital reason."

Maritain, Jacques. *An Introduction to Philosophy.* Trans. by E. I. Watkin, Century Bookbindery repr. of 1930 ed. 1983 text ed. $40.00. An approach to philosophy by a famous Catholic philosopher. Maritain combines the history of philosophy with analyses that are Aristotelian or Thomistic (following the thought of Thomas Aquinas).

Mead, Hunter. *Types and Problems of Philosophy.* Irvington 3d ed. 1959 text ed. $27.95. In this classic text, idealism and naturalism are presented as the types of philosophy to be considered, and metaphysics, epistemology, ethics, and aesthetics as the problems. The text is structured around these two decisions. Mead also discusses the origin and development of life.

Minton, Arthur J., and Thomas A. Shipka. *Philosophy: Paradox and Discovery.* McGraw-Hill 2d ed. 1982 text ed. pap. $23.95. Combines discussion of problems with readings.

Mourant, John A., and E. Hans Freund, eds. *Problems of Philosophy.* Macmillan 1964 o.p. A book of readings with ample selections. The authors have added philosophy of science to the more usual topics.

Munitz, Milton K. *The Ways of Philosophy.* Macmillan 1979 o.p. A standard introduction to philosophy by a well-known contemporary philosopher.

Nakhnikian, George. *An Introduction to Philosophy.* T.I.S. 1981 text ed. pap. $9.95. This introduction concentrates on Plato, Descartes, and William James. The text deals with their views and arguments, and is designed to be read along with designated (but not included) readings from these thinkers.

Olen, Jeffrey. *Persons and Their World: An Introduction to Philosophy.* Random 1983 text ed. $15.25..A comprehensive introduction to the basic problems and fields of philosophy, with selections systematically including classical and contemporary philosophers dealing with the same problem.

Olscamp, Paul J. *An Introduction to Philosophy*. Wiley 1971 o.p. A rigorous approach to the basic problems and fields of philosophy approached in the manner of ordinary language philosophers.

Popkin, Richard, and Avrum Stroll. *Philosophy and Contemporary Problems: A Reader*. Holt 1984 text ed. pap. $22.95. Includes classical and contemporary readings, but the latter are emphasized. The approach is problem-centered, and contemporary issues are included, for example, the problems of insanity and abortion.

Purtill, Richard L., and Peter J. Kreeft. *Philosophical Questions: An Introductory Anthology*. Prentice-Hall 1985 text ed. pap. $18.95. Organized around the three Kantian questions—What can we know? What should we do? What can we hope?—the book responds with appropriate selections from both philosophy and literature.

Pustilnik, Jack, and Dale Riepe. *The Structure of Philosophy*. Littlefield 1966 pap. $4.95. A collection of readings on existence, method, and the ideal combining selections from Asian philosophers with those usually included from Western philosophers, and selections from Marxist philosophers alongside the more usually non-Marxist ones. Some contemporaries are included.

Rachels, James, and Frank A. Tillman. *Philosophical Issues: A Contemporary Introduction*. Harper 1972 o.p. A problems approach stressing contemporary issues.

Rader, Melvin. *The Enduring Questions*. Holt 4th ed. 1980 text ed. $29.95. One of the more durable texts. Rader provides unusually ample readings on epistemology, metaphysics, philosophy of religion, and ethics.

Randall, John H., Jr. *Readings in Philosophy*. Harper 3d ed. 1972 pap. $6.95. Selected readings from philosophical classics ranging from Plato to John Dewey.

Randall, John H., Jr., and Justus Buchler. *Philosophy: An Introduction*. Harper rev. ed. 1971 pap. $6.95. A discussion of philosophical topics to be used in conjunction with a book of readings.

Richter, Peyton E., and Walter L. Fogg. *Philosophy Looks to the Future: Confrontation, Commitment and Utopia*. Waveland Pr. 2d ed. repr. of 1978 ed. 1985 text ed. pap. $21.95. A future-oriented approach to philosophy.

Rogers, Jack B., and Forrest Baird. *Introduction to Philosophy: A Case Study Approach*. Harper 1981 text ed. pap. $11.95. A discussion-oriented approach to philosophy through contemporary issues, oriented toward ethics and theology.

Rosenberg, Jay. *The Practice of Philosophy: A Handbook for Beginners*. Prentice-Hall 2d ed. 1984 text ed. pap. $8.95. Discussions of the character of philosophy, the nature of argument, the joys and perils of dialectic, writing four kinds of philosophical essays, six ways to read a philosopher.

Russell, Bertrand. *An Outline of Philosophy*. Allen & Unwin 1979 text ed. $17.95. A classic text dealing with learning, inference, the physical world, and a person's place in the universe.

——. *The Problems of Philosophy*. Century Bookbindery repr. ed. 1983 lib. bdg. $30.00; Oxford repr. of 1912 ed. 1959 pap. $5.95. A text from early in this century, discussing the nature of matter, knowledge by acquaintance and knowledge by description, and other epistemological questions.

Sahakian, William S., and Mabel L. Sahakian. *Realms of Philosophy*. Schenkman 3d ed. 1981 text ed. pap. $10.60

Sanders, Steven, and David Cheny. *The Meaning of Life: Questions, Answers, and Analysis*. Prentice-Hall 1980 text ed. pap. $13.95. Twelve essays on life's meaningfulness (or its contrary) from Tolstoy, Stace, and Camus, as well as contemporary philosophers, including Kurt Baier, Paul Edwards, R. M. Hare, Kai Nielsen, and Richard Taylor.

Scherer, Donald, and Fred Miller. *Introduction to Philosophy: From Wonder to World View*. Prentice-Hall 1979 text ed. $31.95. Begins with a long introductory section on philosophy and logic. Then it deals with seven philosophical problems, each beginning with a piece of fiction; selections from classical philosophers, garnished with cartoons and photographs.

Scriven, Michael. *Primary Philosophy*. McGraw-Hill 1966 text ed. $30.95. In this hard-hitting discussion of philosophical problems, one major goal is to shift the focus of philosophy from God to man. The section on God is especially rigorous, and Scriven's arguments against the possibility of God's existence far outweigh any considerations advanced on the other side.

Snyder, William S., and Eugene A. Troxell. *Making Sense of Things: An Invitation to Philosophy*. St. Martin's 1976 o.p. Designed to convey the message that the history of philosophy is a "storehouse of provocative ideas," the parts of the book are arranged by the nature and attractions of philosophy, five ideas from the philosophical past, and some perspectives from twentieth-century philosophy. Includes a glossary.

Solomon, Robert C. *The Big Questions: A Short Introduction to Philosophy*. Harcourt 2d ed. 1985 text ed. pap. $14.95. A problems-oriented approach to philosophy.

———. *Introducing Philosophy: A Text with Readings*. Harcourt 3d ed. 1985 text ed. pap. $17.95. Combines Solomon's analysis with readings that are ample and well selected. Glossaries of terms conclude each chapter. Biographies of the philosophers.

Sprague, Elmer. *What Is Philosophy: A Short Introduction*. Oxford 1961 pap. $5.95. Deals with philosophic topics from the standpoint of epistemology.

Sprintzen, David A. *The Drama of Thought: An Inquiry into the Place of Philosophy in Human Experience*. Univ. Pr. of Amer. 1978 text ed. pap. $11.25. An approach to philosophy seeking its connections to the rest of life.

Stroll, Avrum, and Richard Popkin. *Introduction to Philosophy*. Holt 3d ed. 1979 text ed. $29.95. No readings, but a solid text on the basic problems of philosophy.

———, eds. *Introductory Readings in Philosophy*. Holt 1972 text ed. pap. $16.95. A set of readings to accompany their (see above), or any other, text on the problems of philosophy.

Struhl, Karsten J., and Paula R. Struhl. *Philosophy Now*. Random 3d ed. 1980 text ed. pap. $13.00. Combines classical and contemporary readings, with emphasis on the latter, and includes such topics as drug experience, the nuclear family, and world revolution, as well as the more usual ones.

Stumpf, Samuel E. *The Elements of Philosophy*. McGraw-Hill 2d ed. 1986 text ed. $28.95. Very short readings accompanying the author's text.

———. *Philosophical Problems*. McGraw-Hill 2d ed. 1983 text ed. pap. $20.95. Substantial readings on five areas of philosophy, with alternate approaches to each, and a selected bibliography.

Titus, Harold, and Marilyn Smith. *Living Issues in Philosophy*. Van Nostrand 7th ed. 1979 o.p. One of the very successful older books. The authors are interested in both problems and systems of philosophy.

Toulmin, Stephen. *Knowing and Acting: An Invitation to Philosophy*. Macmillan 1976 o.p. An epistemological approach to the issues of philosophy.

Trueblood, Elton. *General Philosophy*. [*Twin Brooks Ser.*] Baker Bks. o.p. Another of the very successful older books. The text is in the author's voice, with no accompanying readings. Two appendixes add biographical data on the philosophers discussed and provide a glossary of terms.

Van Croonenburg, Englebert J. *Gateway to Reality: An Introduction to Philosophy*. Univ. Pr. of Amer. repr. of 1963 ed. 1982 text ed. pap. $11.25. An introduction to philosophy from the phenomenological, existentialist point of view. Van Croonenburg is oriented to Gabriel Marcel and the Personalist tradition. The topics include personal vocation, fidelity, death and suffering, and the nature of religious faith.

Wallace, William A. *The Elements of Philosophy: A Compendium for Philosophers and Theologians.* Alba House 1977 pap. $10.95. A concept-oriented approach to philosophy.

Westphal, Fred A. *Activity of Philosophy: A Concise Introduction.* [*Philosophy Ser.*] Prentice-Hall 1969 text ed. pap. $19.95. Westphal has designed this analysis of basic philosophical problems to be used along with one of the anthologies of philosophy.

Wilson, Margaret, and Dan W. Brock. *Philosophy: An Introduction.* Prentice-Hall 1972 o.p. A standard introduction to philosophy.

Windt, Peter Y. *An Introduction to Philosophy: Ideas in Conflict.* West Publishing 1982 text ed. $24.95. Deals with nine problems of philosophy by means of readings, mostly modern. Windt includes appendixes giving advice on the writing of papers in philosophy, biographical notes, and a glossary of terms.

Wolff, Robert P. *About Philosophy.* Prentice-Hall 3d ed. 1986 $25.95. Classical readings and modern applications with respect to ethics, social philosophy, aesthetics, and philosophy of religion.

———. *Philosophy: A Modern Encounter.* Prentice-Hall repr. of 1973 ed. 1976 text ed. pap. $24.95. A standard introduction stressing contemporary issues.

———, ed. *Introductory Philosophy.* Prentice-Hall 1974 text ed. $28.95. A book of readings centering around seven problems with selections from major philosophers. Questions end each selection.

Woodhouse, Mark B. *A Preface to Philosophy.* Wadsworth 3d ed. 1984 pap. $7.75. An analytical approach to recognizing philosophical subject matter and techniques in evaluating ideas and arguments. Woodhouse provides appendixes on the lives and thoughts of great philosophers.

Young, John. *Reasoning Things Out.* Stella Maris Books 1982 pap. $2.50

PHILOSOPHY BY GEOGRAPHIC AREA

This list consists of works that deal with one or another cultural area of the earth. Since in this volume of *The Reader's Adviser* the philosophy and religion of the East have already been separated from those of the West, we shall refrain from mentioning works of Eastern philosophy here. To avoid interfering with the orderly progression from the Greek period to the present, the works of ancient Greek and Roman philosophy will also be avoided. This subsection therefore includes those general works that provide information about philosophy in various areas of the world. Philosophy tends toward universality, and yet, as noted in the Introduction with respect to the contrasts between Anglo-America and the Continent, different styles of philosophizing characterize different areas of the world. Since geographic areas do not fit neatly into the six periods of our division, the philosophy of geographic areas belongs to General Philosophy, with some notable exceptions. One is that British and continental philosophy are subject to discussion under the headings of both modern and twentieth-century philosophy. The other is that because ancient philosophy is virtually identical with the philosophy of ancient Greece and Rome, coverage of these areas will be reserved for the relevant periods.

Africa

Apostel, L. *African Philosophy—Myth or Reality.* [*Philosophy and Anthropology Ser.*] Humanities Pr. 1981 text ed. pap. $45.50. Given the religio-poetic structure of myth and the conceptual structure of philosophy, Apostel discusses the intermediate nature of African thought.

Hountondji, Paulin J. *African Philosophy: Myth and Reality.* Intro. by Irele Abiola [*African Systems of Thought Ser.*] Indiana Univ. Pr. 1983 $18.50 pap. $8.95. Deals with the problem of moving from a mythical form of belief to philosophy. Two philosophies are treated, that of Amo (an eighteenth-century African philosopher) and the "consciencism" of Kwame Nkrumah.

Nkrumah, Kwame. *Consciencism: Philosophy and the Ideology for Decolonization.* Monthly Review repr. of 1965 ed. 1970 pap. $4.50. Nkrumah, adapting Marxism to the African reality, finds in socialism a modern equivalent to African communalism.

Okere, Theophilus. *African Philosophy: A Historico-Hermeneutical Investigation of the Conditions of Its Possibility.* Univ. Pr. of Amer. 1983 text ed. $24.25 text ed. pap. $9.75. An application of hermeneutical techniques to the problem of the possibility of African philosophy.

Teaching and Research in Philosophy: Africa. [*Studies on Teaching and Research in Philosophy Throughout the World*] Unipub 1985 pap. $28.25. A report on the current African situation with respect to philosophical teaching and writing.

Thompson, Robert F. *Flash of the Spirit: African and Afro-American Art and Philosophy.* Random 1984 pap. $9.95. An examination of African culture, including its influence in the Western Hemisphere, through its art, religion, architecture, and artifacts in general.

Wiredu, K. *Philosophy and an African Culture.* Cambridge Univ. Pr. 1980 $39.50 pap. $12.95. A Ghanian philosopher, trained in the analytic tradition, finds a role for technical philosophy in the modernizing nations of Africa, but warns that African philosophers, while filling this role, must not lose their African conscience. Also discusses the role of Marxist thought.

Wright, Richard A., ed. *African Philosophy: An Introduction.* Univ. Pr. of Amer. 3d ed. 1984 text ed. lib. bdg. $26.75 pap. $12.25. A set of essays by experts in the field prospecting for, and considering the possibility of, an African philosophy. There are essays relevant to ancient philosophy, social philosophy, and on time and cause in an African context.

Europe (General)

Bochenski, Innocentius. *Contemporary European Philosophy (Europaische Philosophie der Gegenwart).* Trans. by Donald Nicholl and Karl Aschenbrenner, Greenwood repr. of 1956 ed. 1982 lib. bdg. $35.00; [*California Lib. Repr. Ser.*] Univ. of California Pr. repr. ed. 1974 $13.50 pap. $3.45. A survey of contemporary British and continental philosophy extending into the 1950s.

Perry, Ralph B. *Philosophy of the Recent Past: An Outline of European and American Philosophy Since 1860.* AMS Pr. repr. of 1926 ed. 1982 $29.00. A survey of European and American philosophy from 1860 into the 1920s.

Stromberg, Roland N. *European Intellectual History Since Seventeen Eighty-Nine.*

Prentice-Hall 4th ed. 1986 text ed. $19.95. A survey of European philosophy and letters from 1789 to the present.

FRANCE

Alexander, Ian W. *French Literature and the Philosophy of Consciousness: Phenomenological Essays.* St. Martin's 1985 $25.00. A phenomenological approach to French literature and philosophy.

Chiari, Joseph. *Twentieth-Century French Thought: From Bergson to Levi-Strauss.* Gordian 1975 $18.50. Interesting analyses giving the views of a dozen highly important French philosophers.

Leighton, Walter L. *French Philosophers—New England Transcendentalism.* Greenwood repr. of 1908 ed. 1968 lib. bdg. $15.00. Traces the influence of New England transcendentalism on such important nineteenth-century French philosophers as Cousin and Jouffroy.

Michaud, Regis. *Modern Thought and Literature in France.* [*Essay Index Repr. Ser.*] Ayer repr. of 1934 ed. 1977 $15.75. Explores French thought—"philosophy" in a very general sense—through the work of three early twentieth-century French artists and writers.

Montefiore, Alan, ed. *Philosophy in France Today.* Cambridge Univ. Pr. 1983 $42.50 pap. $11.95. Essays by a dozen well-known French philosophers, interpreting their work to the English-speaking world.

Potts, D. C., and D. G. Charlton, eds. *French Thought Since Sixteen Hundred.* Methuen 1974 pap. $5.95. The philosophical part of a multivolumed work on French culture. The first half of the book is by Potts and deals with the seventeenth- and eighteenth-century philosophers stressing reason, humanity, toleration, romanticism, and materialism. The second half of the book is by Charlton and deals with nineteenth- and twentieth-century French philosophy, including both atheistic and theistic existentialists.

Smith, Colin. *Contemporary French Philosophy: A Study in Norms and Values.* Greenwood repr. of 1964 ed. 1976 lib. bdg. $22.50. A study of recent French thought by an Englishman who finds in it both an emphasis on values and a considerable amount of agreement.

Spink, John S. *French Free Thought from Gassendi to Voltaire.* Greenwood repr. of 1960 ed. 1969 lib. bdg. $65.00. An historical study of French thought from 1619 to 1751.

Wade, Ira O. *Intellectual Origins of the French Enlightenment.* Princeton Univ. Pr. 1971 o.p. Wade states that he wishes to reveal the "true" Enlightenment, and in this volume he concentrates on five freethinkers (Charron, La Mothe Le Vayer, Naude, Patin, and Sorbiere) and five philosophers (Malebranche, Leibniz, Locke, Newton, and Bayle).

GERMANY

Bubner, R. *Modern German Philosophy.* Trans. by Eric Matthews, Cambridge Univ. Pr.1981 $42.50 pap. $13.95. The philosophers who stimulated the development of contemporary philosophy in Britain and America—Frege, Wittgenstein, the members of the Vienna Circle, Popper—are now stimulating philosophy in Germany, influencing thought in numerous areas—phenomenology and hermeneutics, linguistic philosophy, dialectic, and theory of science, among others.

Christensen, Darrel E., and others, eds. *Contemporary German Philosophy.* Pennsylvania State Univ. Pr. 4 vols 1982–85 ea. $22.50. Essays by contemporary German philosophers on topics of interest to them, including their predecessors. Review articles on book-length German philosophy are also included.

Dewey, John. *German Philosophy and Politics*. [*Select Bibliographies Repr. Ser.*] Ayer repr. of 1915 ed. $12.50. An analysis of German character by a famous American philosopher, occasioned by World War I. Dewey argues for a dualism in the German psyche, also discernible in the dualism of German philosophy. In this connection, he offers analyses of Kant, Fichte, and Hegel.

Santayana, George. *Egotism in German Philosophy*. [*Studies in German Lit.*] Haskell repr. of 1916 ed. 1971 lib. bdg. $39.95. A polemic, somewhat dubious philosophically, occasioned, like Dewey's work above, by World War I. Santayana finds German philosophy infected by what we would now term "megalomania."

Stegmueller, Wolfgang. *Main Currents in Contemporary German, British, and American Philosophy*. Kluwer Academic rev. & enl. ed. 1969 lib. bdg. $50.00. A careful and valuable work that assesses not only the contributions of German philosophy to the contemporary world—Kant, Brentano, Husserl, Scheler, Heidegger, Jaspers, N. Hartmann—but also the Austrian contribution—that of Wittgenstein, Carnap, and the Vienna Circle. American philosophy is discussed via Hempel, Oppenheim, Quine, Feigl, Goodman, Pap, and Stevenson; the British are represented by Russell, Broad, and Hare. This work deepens one's appreciation of the debt owed by contemporary philosophy to this part of its European background.

GREAT BRITAIN

Burtt, Edwin A., ed. *The English Philosophers from Bacon to Mill*. Modern Lib. 1939 $11.95. A well-crafted anthology, bringing together the principal works of the British empiricists, most of them reproduced in full.

Grote, Harriet. *Philosophical Radicals of 1832*. Burt Franklin repr. of 1866 ed. 1967 $14.00. A classic, detailing the views of the utilitarian philosophers, especially in relation to the English Reform laws of the 1930s.

Levy, Paul. *Moore: G. E. Moore and the Cambridge Apostles*. Oxford repr. of 1979 ed. 1981 pap. $8.95. A biography and analysis of the life and thoughts of the British philosopher G. E. Moore, including his relationship to The Apostles, a Cambridge intellectual society.

Morris, George S. *British Thought and Thinkers: From John of Salisbury and Roger Bacon to John Stuart Mill and Herbert Spencer*. AMS Pr. repr. of 1880 ed. 1981 $26.00; Gordon Pr. 1977 lib. bdg. $59.95. A survey of British thought from the twelfth to the nineteenth century.

Muirhead, John H. *Platonic Tradition in Anglo-Saxon Philosophy*. [*Muirhead Lib. of Philosophy*] Humanities Pr. repr. of 1931 ed. o.p. A discussion of the idealistic elements in British and American thought from the Cambridge Platonists through Bradley and Royce. Muirhead concludes with an assessment of "what is dead and what is alive in idealism."

GREECE (MODERN)

Cavarnos, Constantine. *Modern Greek Philosophers on the Human Soul*. Inst. Byzantine 1967 repr. 1987 pap. $6.95. A contemporary Greek philosopher finds Platonic themes in modern Greek thought.

———. *Modern Greek Thought*. Inst. Byzantine 1969 repr. 1986 pap. $5.95. An essay discussing the thought of Greek philosophers from the eighteenth century to the present.

ITALY

Kristeller, Paul O. *Eight Philosophers of the Italian Renaissance.* Stanford Univ. Pr. 1964 $15.00 pap. $6.95. Concise discussions of the thought of eight major Renaissance humanists, from Petrarch to Bruno.

POLAND

Jordan, Z. A. *Philosophy and Ideology: The Development of Philosophy and Marxism-Leninism in Poland Since the Second World War.* [*Sovietica Ser.*] Kluwer Academic 1963 lib. bdg. $54.50. This work, tracing the rise, hegemony, and partial decline of Marxism-Leninism in Poland, begins, despite the subtitle, with the development of Marxism from World War I. Part I is titled *Philosophy between the Two Wars.* It details the rise of several schools of Polish philosophy which, following a political decree in 1956, were reduced to the single school of Marxism-Leninism. As the Polish logicians and philosophers criticized the shoddy logic of the official viewpoint, intellectual space appeared, allowing competing schools once more.

Walicki, Andrzej. *Philosophy and Romantic Nationalism: The Case of Poland.* Oxford 1982 $42.00. An expert on Russian and Slavic thought assesses the influence of Hegelian idealism and French revolutionary thought on mid-nineteenth-century Poland, leading to a view that he calls "romantic nationalism." The dissolution of the position after 1848 leads him to examine the views of Marx and Engels on the Polish question.

RUSSIA

Adelmann, F. J. *Philosophical Investigations in the U.S.S.R.* [*Boston College Studies in Philosophy*] Kluwer Academic 1975 pap. $24.00. A compilation of the work of contemporary Soviet philosophers.

Ballestrem, K. G. *Russian Philosophical Terminology.* [*Sovietica Ser.*] Kluwer Academic 1964 lib. bdg. $18.50. As a tool to aid in the interpretation of Russian philosophy, Ballestrem provides English, French, and German equivalents of Russian terms.

Blakeley, T. J. *Soviet Philosophy: A General Introduction to Contemporary Soviet Thought.* [*Sovietica Ser.*] Kluwer Academic 1964 lib. bdg. $18.50. In brief chapters, Blakeley sets forth, often in catalog form, Soviet positions on matter, thought, psychology, logic, historical materialism, ethics, aesthetics, atheism, and the history of philosophy, in addition to the dialectical method.

————. *Soviet Scholasticism.* [*Sovietica Ser.*] Kluwer Academic 1961 lib. bdg. $18.50. Analysis of Soviet philosophical method by a Western Sovietologist as not dialectic at all but hypothetico-deductive, so that Soviet positions become hypotheses from which testable consequences are to be deduced. Soviet philosophers use the method improperly, excluding all the negative cases. The book has been vigorously attacked in the Soviet press.

————, ed. *Themes in Soviet Marxist Philosophy: Selected Articles from the Sovietskaja Enciklopedija.* [*Sovietica Ser.*] Kluwer Academic 1975 lib. bdg. $39.50. Philosophy articles selected from the *Soviet Encyclopedia*, providing an overview of Marxist philosophy.

Bochenski, I. M. *The Dogmatic Principles of Soviet Philosophy (as of 1958): Synopsis of Osnovy Marksistkoj Filosofii.* Trans. by T. J. Blakeley [*Sovietica Ser.*] Kluwer Academic 1963 $16.00. In 78 pages Bochenski summarizes the theses of the 1958 "official" text of Soviet-Marxist philosophy.

————. *Soviet Russian Dialectical Materialism.* Trans. by Nicholas Sollohub, rev. by

T. J. Blakeley, Kluwer Academic rev. ed. 1963 lib. bdg. $18.50. A two-part analysis, the first historical, the second systematic.

Bochenski, I. M., and T. J. Blakeley, eds. *Studies in Soviet Thought.* [*Sovietica Ser.*] Kluwer Academic 1961 lib. bdg. $24.00. A cooperative volume by the Bochenski "Sovietologists" surveying Marxist-Leninist views on logic (formal, mathematical, the principle of contradiction), as well as East-West ideological conflict, and the state of Polish and Czech philosophy in the post-World War II period.

Copleston, Frederick C. *Philosophy in Russia: Herzen to Lenin.* Univ. of Notre Dame Pr. 1985 text ed. $29.95. A history of Russian philosophy by a well-known historian of Western philosophy.

Dobrolyubov, N. A. *Selected Philosophical Russian Contemporary Essays.* Inst. Econ. Pol. 1985 $89.45. A volume extending the historical analyses of this section to the present day.

Edie, James M., and others. *Russian Philosophy.* Univ. of Tennessee Pr. 3 vols. repr. of 1965 ed. 1976 pap. ea. $8.95–$10.95. A historical anthology of works of Russian thinkers especially translated for this publication.

Gavin, William J., and T. J. Blakeley. *Russia and America: A Philosophical Comparison.* [*Sovietica Ser.*] Kluwer Academic 1976 lib. bdg. $24.00. Gavin and Blakeley, finding Russia and America pragmatic as well as mystical, with a frontier mentality and a tolerance for ambiguity, proceed to pair the thinking of Russian and American philosophers—Emerson with Chaadayev, James with Herzen, Royce with Khomyakov, Dewey with Chernyshevsky. The book ends with a consideration of the themes of contemporary Soviet philosophy, and Soviet reactions to American philosophy.

Laszlo, E., ed. *Philosophy in the Soviet Union: A Survey of the Mid-Sixties.* [*Sovietica Ser.*] Kluwer Academic 1967 lib. bdg. $21.00. Essentially an update of the material in the Bochenski and Wetter books in this section: essays on Soviet thought by Western specialists connected with the Fribourg Institute of East European Studies.

Lossky, Nicholas O. *History of Russian Philosophy.* International Univ. Pr. repr. of 1951 ed. 1969 text ed. $40.00 text ed. pap. $12.95. A history of Russian philosophy by a pioneer Russian theologian and philosopher.

Planty-Bonjour, G. *The Categories of Dialectical Materialism: Contemporary Soviet Ontology.* Trans. by T. J. Blakeley [*Sovietica Ser.*] Kluwer Academic 1967 $24.00. An examination of Soviet philosophy from the death of Stalin. Planty-Bonjour finds the dialectic a barrier preventing progress in Soviet thought.

Shein, Louis J., ed. and trans. *Readings in Russian Philosophical Thought.* Mouton 1977 text ed. pap. $13.75. Includes notes and an introductory chapter by Shein.

Somerville, John. *Soviet Philosophy: A Study of Theory and Practice.* Greenwood repr. of 1946 ed. 1968 lib. bdg. $35.00. An introduction to Soviet philosophy by a sympathetic American philosopher. In addition to the usual topics, Somerville includes a chapter on the teaching of philosophy in the Soviet Union.

Swiderski, Edward M., ed. *Philosophical Foundations of Soviet Aesthetics.* [*Sovietica Ser.*] Kluwer Academic 1979 lib. bdg. $34.00 Analysis of Socialist realism both as a theory and as a guide to practice.

Wetter, Gustav A. *Dialectical Materialism.* Trans. by Peter Heath, Greenwood repr. of 1959 ed. 1973 lib. bdg. $49.75. An analysis of dialectical materialism by a German scholar who considers the doctrine apart from political implications utilizing only Soviet writings.

———. *Soviet Ideology.* [*Westview Encore Ed. Ser.*] 1985 pap. $28.50. In this more recent study of Soviet philosophy Wetter considers the topics of dialectical materialism, historical materialism, and capitalism. As in the earlier work (see above), the neo-Thomism of Wetter is sometimes obtrusive.

SCANDINAVIA

Olson, Raymond E., and Anthony M. Paul, eds. *Contemporary Philosophy in Scandinavia.* Johns Hopkins 1972 $37.50. A set of essays by Scandinavian philosophers detailing the contemporary situation in Scandinavian philosophy. The historical section goes back to Kierkegaard and includes the impact of Niels Bohr. Among contributors well known in the West are Von Wright, Hartnack, Hintikka, Naess, and Follesdal.

Skirbekk, Gunnar, ed. *Praxeology: An Anthology.* Universitet 1984 pap. $20.00. A collection of essays turning on the idea of practice by Scandinavian (mostly Norwegian) philosophers. Wittgenstein and philosophy of action are evident influences in these essays that range from aesthetics to politics and conclude with constructivist geometry.

SCOTLAND

Bryson, Gladys. *Man and Society: The Scottish Inquiry of the Eighteenth Century.* Kelley repr. of 1945 ed. 1968 $29.50. Discussion of the eighteenth-century Scottish school of moral philosophers, including Adam Smith and David Hume, which led in the direction of social science.

Grave, S. A. *The Scottish Philosophy of Common Sense.* Greenwood repr. of 1960 ed. 1973 lib. bdg. $22.50. An exposition of the philosophy of common sense from its rise with Thomas Reid and the members of his school, through its international career, to its demise at the hands of John Stuart Mill. Topics treated are skepticism, commonsense, natural signs, sensations, personal identity, morality, and freewill.

Hope, Vincent, ed. *Philosophers of the Scottish Enlightenment.* Columbia Univ. Pr. 1984 $22.50. A set of essays on Scottish philosophy in its best-known period, many by philosophers teaching in Scotland.

Johnston, G. A., ed. *Selections from the Scottish Philosophy of Common Sense.* Open Court 1915 $9.95. Selections from Thomas Reid, Adam Ferguson, James Beattie, and David Stewart, all of whom were responding to David Hume.

McCosh, James. *The Scottish Philosophy, Biographical, Expository, Critical, from Hutcheson to Hamilton.* [*Philosophy in Amer. Ser.*] AMS Pr. repr. of 1875 ed. 1980 $41.50. A comprehensive and classic study of philosophy in Scotland from the end of the seventeenth to the mid-nineteenth century.

Martin, Terence. *Instructed Vision: Scottish Common Sense Philosophy and the Origins of American Fiction.* Kraus repr. of 1961 ed. $16.00. (See under "United States" in this section.)

Robinson, Daniel S., ed. *The Story of Scottish Philosophy: A Compendium of Selections from the Writings of Nine Pre-eminent Scottish Philosophers, with Biobibliographical Essays.* Fwd. by Perry E. Gresham, Greenwood repr. of 1961 ed. 1979 lib. bdg. $24.75. Selections from the writings of the luminaries making up the Scottish Enlightenment.

Seth, Andrew. *Scottish Philosophy.* [*The Philosophy of David Hume Ser.*] Garland 1983 lib. bdg. $33.00. A classic analysis accomplished through comparisons of Hume and Reid, Reid and Kant, Kant and Hamilton, Scottish philosophy and Hegel.

YUGOSLAVIA

Markovic, Mihailo, and Gajo Petrovic, eds. *Praxis*. [*Boston Studies in the Philosophy of Science*] Kluwer Academic 1979 lib. bdg. $55.00 pap. $23.50. Although ostensibly about the social sciences, this volume, comprised of essays by members of a Yugoslavian group called "Praxis," discusses the problem of how to make philosophy practical—that is, a matter of practice (*praxis*). The group, which may be seen as part of the effort of Yugoslavia to find its own road to socialism, has as its goal the development of a social philosophy that will be at the same time a philosophy of liberation.

Latin America

Davis, Harold E. *Latin American Thought: A Historical Introduction*. Free Pr. 1974 text ed. pap. $9.95; Louisiana State Univ. Pr. 1972 $25.00. A balanced analysis of Latin American thought, largely but not exclusively philosophical, from pre-Conquest to the present.

Haddox, John H. *Antonio Caso: Philosopher of Mexico*. [*Texas Pan-Amer. Ser.*] Univ. of Texas Pr. 1971 $8.95. The life and thought of a major twentieth-century Mexican philosopher, with selections from his writings.

Lipp, Solomon. *Three Argentine Thinkers*. Humanities Pr. 1969 text ed. $9.95. Analyses of the views of José Ingenieros, Alejandro Korn, and Francisco Romero.

———. *Three Chilean Thinkers*. Humanities Pr. 1975 text ed. $11.50. Analyses of the views of Francisco Bilbao, Valentin Letelier, and Enrique Molina.

Philosophical Thought in America. OAS 3 vols. 1971–76 pap. ea. $1.00–$3.00. Very brief overviews of major Latin American thinkers.

Romanell, Patrick. *Making of the Mexican Mind: A Study in Recent Mexican Thought*. Fwd. by E. S. Brightman [*Essay Index Repr. Ser.*] Ayer repr. of 1952 ed. 1977 $16.00. Provides not only a history of Mexican thought, including analyses of Antonio Caso and José Vasconcelos, but also describes the impact on Mexico of such figures as Comte, Bergson, Ortega, and the existentialist philosophers.

Vento, Arnold C. *El Hijo Prodijo: A Critical Index of Twentieth-Century Mexican Thought*. Pajarito Pubns. 1978 pap. $5.00. A guide to the resources available in recent Mexican thought.

Weinstein, Michael A. *The Polarity of Mexican Thought*. Pennsylvania State Univ. Pr. 1977 $19.95. Weinstein finds in Mexican philosophy a polarity between instrumentalism and finalism, depending on whether values are viewed as means or ends. Along the way the major Mexican philosophers are discussed.

Zea, Leopoldo. *Latin American Mind*. Trans. by James H. Abbott and Lowell Dunham, Univ. of Oklahoma Pr. 1970 pap. $8.95. This important Mexican philosopher traces the rise of Latin American positivism, following Comte, as a reaction to earlier Latin American philosophies.

United States

American philosophy overlaps the periods of modern and contemporary philosophy. The originators of pragmatism, the principal figures of American philosophy, are treated in Chapters 5 and 6 in this volume. This section lists the general works dealing with the entire area.

Ames, Van Meter. *Zen and American Thought*. Greenwood repr. of 1962 ed. 1978 lib. bdg. $26.50. An American philosopher discusses the similarities between Zen

Buddhism and American thought, going back to Jonathan Edwards and proceeding as far as John Dewey.

Anderson, Paul R., and Max H. Fisch. *Philosophy in America from Puritans to James*. Hippocrene Bks. 1969 lib. bdg. $31.50. An anthology of American philosophy to 1900, accompanied by analyses and notes.

Beaumont, Ernest V. *The Intellectual Cowardice of the American Philosophers*. Amer. Class. College Pr. 1980 $69.75. A criticism of American philosophy based on its aloofness from social issues.

Bertocci, Peter A., ed. *Mid-Twentieth Century American Philosophy: Personal Statements*. Humanities Pr. 1974 text ed. $15.00. Essays by 15 American philosophers in their sixties, invited to sum up their wisdom.

Caws, Peter, ed. *Two Centuries of Philosophy: American Philosophy Since the Revolution—Papers from the Bicentennial Symposium*. [*Amer. Philosophical Quarterly Lib. of Philosophy*] Rowman 1980 $30.00. An overall assessment of American philosophy by a representative group of contemporary philosophers on the occasion of the nation's bicentennial.

Edwards, Rem B. *A Return to Moral and Religious Philosophy in Early America*. Univ. Pr. of Amer. 1982 o.p. An in-depth examination of the thought of Jonathan Edwards, Thomas Jefferson, and Ralph Waldo Emerson, with a view to rediscovering "America in its moral, religious and intellectual dimensions."

Farber, Marvin, ed. *Philosophic Thought in France and the United States: Essays Representing Major Trends in Contemporary French and American Philosophy*. State Univ. of New York Pr. 2d ed. 1968 $47.00. Nearly 40 well-known philosophers discuss the major trends in French and American philosophy.

Fisch, Max H., ed. *Classic American Philosophers*. Prentice-Hall 1966 text ed. pap. $26.95. A classic anthology of selected writings from the work of Peirce, James, Royce, Santayana, Dewey, and Whitehead. Introductory essays by Fisch, Burns, Henle, Kraushaar, Rice, Kennedy, and Lowe.

Gabriel, Ralph H. *American Values: Continuity and Change*. Intro. by Robert H. Walker [*Contributions in Amer. Studies*] Greenwood 1974 lib. bdg. $27.50. Believing the values of a people to be revealed in times of crisis, Gabriel looks for the convictions expressed by American leaders during such times. Writing in the 1950s and 1960s, he suggests that mid-twentieth-century America may represent the "New Enlightenment."

Gavin, William J., and T. J. Blakeley. *Russia and America: A Philosophical Comparison*. [*Sovietica Ser.*] Kluwer Academic 1976 lib. bdg. $24.00. (See under "Europe (General), Russia" in this section.)

Hartshorne, Charles. *Creativity in American Philosophy*. Paragon 1985 pap. $14.95; State Univ. of New York Pr. 1984 $39.50 pap. $16.95. From his own base in process thought, Hartshorne comes to terms with practically the whole of American philosophy. The final chapters deal with some of the younger philosophers, such as Rorty, Neville, and Nozick.

Hook, Sidney. *American Philosophers at Work: The Philosophic Scene in the United States*. Greenwood repr. of 1956 ed. 1968 lib. bdg. $22.25. A mid-century sampling of American philosophy, bringing together representative essays on logic, scientific method, metaphysics, theory of knowledge, ethics, and social philosophy.

Jones, Adam L. *Early American Philosophers*. Ungar 1958 o.p. Analysis of the initial stages of American philosophy.

Kallen, Horace M., and Sidney Hook, eds. *American Philosophy Today and Tomorrow*. [*Essay Index Repr. Ser.*] Ayer repr. of 1935 ed. 1968 $21.50; Irvington repr. of 1935 ed. 1982 lib. bdg. $20.00. Twenty-five representative American thinkers present a cross-section of American philosophical thought in the mid-1930s.

Kolenda, Konstantin, ed. *Person and Community in American Philosophy.* Rice Univ. 1981 pap. $5.50. A cooperative volume turning on the themes of self, society, and community. Most of the essays explicate the views of one of the classical American philosophers, separate essays centering on Peirce, Royce, Santayana, William James, John Dewey, and G. H. Mead.

Kuklick, Bruce. *The Rise of American Philosophy.* Yale Univ. Pr. 1977 pap. $14.95. Illuminates the "history of American thought as a whole" by means of the history of philosophy at Harvard "from the Civil War to the Great Depression." This strategy allows the inclusion of five of the "six classic American philosophers": Peirce, James, Royce, Santayana, and Whitehead. Only Dewey is excluded. The writing is both lively and responsible.

MacKinnon, Barbara. *American Philosophy: A Historical Anthology.* State Univ. of New York Pr. 1985 $49.50 pap. $18.95. A comprehensive anthology of American philosophy, its selections begin with the period of Puritanism and run to the present. In addition to the standard divisions there are sections on Thomism, process philosophy, and phenomenology. Study questions are also a feature of the volume.

Madden, Edward H. *Civil Disobedience and Moral Law in Nineteenth-Century American Philosophy.* Univ. of Washington Pr. 1970 pap. $4.95. An essay in ethics and politics. Madden demonstrates a tradition of civil disobedience theory in America long antedating Thoreau.

Martin, Terence. *Instructed Vision: Scottish Common Sense Philosophy and the Origins of American Fiction.* Kraus repr. of 1961 ed. $16.00. Martin argues that the Scottish common sense philosophy with its distrust of imaginative experience exerted a direct influence on American fiction prior to the 1830s; but at that time the philosophical influence of Carlyle, Coleridge, Cousin, and Kant allowed an escape from the "severities" of the Scottish philosophy.

Miller, Perry G. *Errand into the Wilderness.* Harvard Univ. Pr. 1956 $15.00 pap. $6.95. An interpretation of the sources of American life from the Puritans to Emerson by an expert in American studies.

———. *Nature's Nation.* Harvard Univ. Pr. 1967 $20.00 A companion volume to the preceding entry. Miller discusses here the building and development of America. The title refers to the nation's extension into the West.

Perry, Ralph B. *Philosophy of the Recent Past: An Outline of European and American Philosophy Since 1860.* AMS Pr. repr. of 1926 ed. 1982 $29.00. A discussion of philosophy after Schopenhauer, extending into the 1920s. Organized around the positions of naturalism, idealism, pragmatism, and realism.

Philosophy in America. AMS Pr. 204 vols. 1982–86 $15.00–$74.00. A reprint series whose volumes have various publishing dates, and whose original publication dates reach from the latter part of the nineteenth century to the present. The concentration, however, is later nineteenth to mid-twentieth century. The coverage is of psychology as well as philosophy, especially in areas such as aesthetics and the nature of the mind. There are works on colonial figures, such as Jonathan Edwards, and reprints of the British philosopher F. C. S. Schiller.

Riley, Isaac W. *American Thought from Puritanism to Pragmatism and Beyond: A Greenwood Archival Edition.* Greenwood 2d ed. repr. of 1923 ed. 1970 o.p. A history of American philosophy from Puritanism to critical realism, with a chapter on French influences—i.e., Cousin, Comte, and Bergson.

Rorty, Richard. *Consequences of Pragmatism: Essays 1972–80.* Univ. of Minnesota Pr. 1982 $29.50 pap. $11.95. A collection of recent articles in which Rorty continues his work of probing the interrelationships of established philosophies. Analytic philosophy loses its dominance, and pragmatism is America's most important contribution to human culture, but pragmatism cannot escape the limitations of its own language and history.

Schneider, Herbert W. *A History of American Philosophy*. Orient Bk. Dist. 1969 $12.50. A comprehensive history of American philosophy seen as part of cultural history.

——. *Sources of Contemporary Philosophical Realism in America*. Irvington 1964 text ed. pap. $6.95. A discussion of new and critical realism in America. Includes a bibliography.

Shahan, Robert W., and Kenneth R. Merrill, eds. *American Philosophy: From Edwards to Quine*. Univ. of Oklahoma Pr. 1977 pap. $8.95. Selections from American philosophers from the eighteenth century until the present.

Smith, John E. *The Spirit of American Philosophy*. State Univ. of New York Pr. 1982 $39.50 pap. $10.95. Discusses Peirce, James, Royce, Dewey, and Whitehead. Santayana is omitted as "outside the main drift." The chapter on "Retrospect and Prospect" has been enlarged since the 1963 edition, and a final chapter added on "The New Need for a Recovery of Philosophy."

——, ed. *Contemporary American Philosophy*. [*Muirhead Lib. of Philosophy*] Humanities Pr. 1970 text ed. $18.50. A set of essays from 1970 by well-known American philosophers on their work.

Smith, Thomas V. *Philosophic Way of Life in America*. Associated Faculty Pr. 2d ed. repr. of 1943 ed. 1968 $23.00. Appreciations of Royce, James, Dewey, and Santayana, to which is added Smith's own appreciation of legislative process and the way of compromise.

Townsend, H. G. *Philosophical Ideas in the United States*. 1934. Hippocrene Bks. 1968 lib. bdg. $20.00. Surveys American philosophy from colonial times to John Dewey and includes discussions of empiricism, pluralism, realism, and naturalism.

Weinstein, Michael A. *The Wilderness and the City: American Classical Philosophy as a Moral Quest*. Univ. of Massachusetts Pr. 1982 lib. bdg. $17.50. Treating Royce, Peirce, James, Dewey, and Santayana, the author conducts an "inquest" into "what is still vital" in the American philosophical tradition. Weinstein argues for a "modern individualism" beyond that of pragmatism, characterized by a "deepening of inner tolerance."

Werkmeister, William H. *A History of Philosophical Ideas in America*. Greenwood repr. of 1949 ed. 1981 lib. bdg. $49.75. A comprehensive history of American philosophy running from Puritanism to logical empiricism, naturalism, and the humanism of the 1940s.

White, Morton. *The Philosophy of the American Revolution*. [*Amer. Social Thought Ser.*] Oxford 1978 $22.50 pap. $8.95. Reflections on the philosophy underlying the American Revolution. White often begins with the Declaration of Independence before moving to such topics as self-evident truths, laws of nature, human rights, and "rebellion to tyrants." He also discusses those to whom the Founding Fathers were intellectually indebted, namely, Locke, Hooker, Rousseau.

——. *Science and Sentiment in America: Philosophical Thought from Jonathan Edwards to John Dewey*. Oxford 1972 $25.00. A history of philosophy relating philosophy to questions of general culture. Shows the extent to which American philosophers historically have seen their role as going far beyond philosophy as a technical pursuit.

——, ed. *Documents in the History of American Philosophy: From Jonathan Edwards to John Dewey*. Oxford 1972 text ed. pap. $13.95. Selections from American philosophers from the eighteenth through the middle of the twentieth century.

Wills, Garry, ed. *Values Americans Live By.* Ayer 1974 $35.00. A collaborative volume prospecting for American values.

Winn, Ralph B., ed. *Survey of American Philosophy.* [*Quality Pap. Ser.*] Littlefield repr. of 1955 ed. 1965 pap. $2.95. A cooperative volume on the fields and problems of American philosophy.

COMPARATIVE PHILOSOPHY

The final division of works is comparative philosophy. Some titles of this nature have already appeared: comparisons of American and British philosophy, for example, have been placed in the preceding section. In this section are works comparing three or more areas, as well as general comparisons of Eastern and Western philosophy. From that beginning there is the possible move toward world philosophy, an area pioneered by John Plott. And in one way of looking at it, the most general area would be a philosophy relating to preservation of the ecosystem itself.

East-West

Herman, A. L., and R. T. Blackwood, eds. *Problems in Philosophy: West and East.* Prentice-Hall 1975 $27.95. An anthology of readings that can serve equally well as an introduction to philosophy in general and to comparative philosophy. The selections—on metaphysics, epistemology, theology, and ethics—pair readings from Western and Eastern sources. The reader must surely emerge with a less parochial view than is encouraged by the standard anthology of Western philosophical works.

Moore, Charles A. *Philosophy and Culture, East and West: East-West Philosophy in Practical Perspective.* Univ. of Hawaii Pr. 1962 $25.00. A cooperative volume in which philosophers from East and West are paired in discussing the relation of philosophy and science to practice, and the prospect for world understanding.

———. *Philosophy: East and West.* [*Essay Index Reprint Ser.*] Ayer repr. of 1944 ed. 1977 $24.50. Essays by philosophers from East and West prospecting for a "world philosophy."

Scharfstein, Ben-Ami, ed. *Philosophy East-Philosophy West: A Critical Comparison of Indian, Chinese, Islamic and European Philosophy.* Oxford 1978 $25.00. A cooperative but well-integrated volume by five experts in the field, making cross-cultural comparisons of India, China, and the West, followed by comparisons of Augustine, Descartes, and Shankara; al-Ashari and Spinoza; *li* and "idea"; Berkeley and Vasubandhu; Kant and Nagarjuna, each in relation to a different topic in philosophy.

General Comparative

Burr, John R. *Handbook of World Philosophy: Contemporary Developments Since 1945.* Greenwood 1980 lib. bdg. $65.00 Provides information on philosophic thought and philosophers around the world since 1945.

Copleston, Frederick. *Philosophies and Cultures.* Oxford 1980 $19.95. A significant Western historian of philosophy here extends his range, comparing Western philosophy with that of India and China, including the interrelating of philosophy and religion, different views of the person, of history, and of the history of philosophy.

Hutchison, John A. *Living Options in World Philosophy.* Univ. of Hawaii Pr. 1977 $16.00. Hutchison argues for the possibility of a single world-context, and discusses philosophies from both the Western and Eastern worlds in pointing toward that possibility.

McDermott, Charlene, ed. *Comparative Philosophy: Selected Essays.* Univ. Pr. of Amer. 1983 lib. bdg. $37.50 text ed. pap. $18.50. A cooperative volume on the possibilities and problems of comparative philosophy.

Plott, John C. *Global History of Philosophy.* Asian Humanities Pr. 3 vols. 1980 ea. $11.50–$17.00; Verry 3 vols. 1977–80 text ed. ea. $18.00–$27.00. An approach to philosophy in global terms, developing the thesis that there have been comparable states in the development of philosophy in each of the world's great cultural areas.

Raju, P. T. *Introduction to Comparative Philosophy.* Southern Illinois Univ. Pr. 1970 pap. $9.95. A comparative analysis of philosophy discussing similarities and differences in three great traditions, Western, Chinese, and Indian, by a well-known Indian philosopher who has long taught in the United States.

Stunkel, Kenneth R. *Relations of Indian, Greek and Christian Thought in Antiquity.* Univ. Pr. of Amer. 1979 text ed. pap. $10.75

World Philosophy. Salem Pr. 5 vols. 1982 $250.00. Analyses of 225 major works in philosophy, from East and West, to which are added reviews of scholarly discussions of these works. The analyses run three to five pages in length, and the reviews one to two pages. Western classics predominate, but since the five volumes are organized chronologically, one is able to compare Eastern and Western achievements from the same historical periods.

Zinn, William V. *The Global Philosophy.* Vantage 1983 $10.95. Zinn prospects for an approach to philosophy in global terms.

Ecophilosophy

Skolimowski, Henryk. *Eco-Philosophy.* M. Boyars 1981 $15.00. Arguing that both analytic philosophy and science have lost "values" while concentrating on fact, Skolimowski promotes an ecological approach to the world that will be sensitive to values and consistent with both the sciences and religious aspiration.

CHAPTER 2

Greek and Roman Philosophy

John P. Anton

Socrates: I give you samples of one philosophy after another that you may taste them, and I have the hope that in the end you may come to know your own mind.

—*Theaetetus*

In the last hundred years, modern scholarship has immensely extended the horizon of history... Yet it is even clearer today that this expansion of our intellectual horizon has not altered the central fact: insofar as it is not the history of one particular nation but of a group of nations to which, physically and intellectually, we belong, our history still begins with the Greeks.

—WERNER JAEGER, *Paideia I*

It took many generations of scholars to piece together the history of Greek and Roman philosophy as we have it today. Actually, only fragments have survived of what the early Greeks produced as reflections of their thoughts about the world and the nature of human existence. With few exceptions, as in the case of the writings of PLATO (see also Vol. 3) and ARISTOTLE (see also Vols. 3 and 5), only a fraction of the immense productivity of the Greek mind—be it in philosophy, epic poetry, drama, or history, not to mention art, sculpture, and architecture—exists. But what is extant is of superb quality and still worth studying, not only for the pertinence these monumental achievements have for all ages, but for the training of the mind and perhaps even more for the value they possess in illuminating the problems of our own times.

From what has survived, scholars have been able to piece together not the full story of the emergence and development of philosophy, but what is probably on the whole a reliable account of developments in antiquity. Today, philosophers distinguish between the cultural developments that preceded the emergence of philosophical thinking itself and the diverse phases it exhibited in its development down to the end of the Hellenistic period and the appearance of Christian theology. A close study of these phases permits the division of ancient philosophy into periods. It is customary to use Socrates as a landmark and divide the classical period of Greek philosophy into the pre-Socratic age, the age of the Sophists and Socrates, and then that of Plato and his pupil, Aristotle.

The post-Aristotelian developments form what scholars call the Hellenistic age, which is usually divided into three periods. First comes the early

29

period, with the Stoics, the Epicureans, the Skeptics, and those who continued the traditions Plato and Aristotle had started with the founding of their famous schools. The middle period, which coincided with the expansion of the Roman Empire and the migrations of ideas from east to west and vice versa, led to the rise of strong philosophical interest in Greek thought among the Romans, while it stimulated further explorations and revivals of older movements. The third period, known as the late Hellenistic, witnessed the rise of Neoplatonism—a complex movement, widespread and influential, that made Platonism palatable to the leaders of the growing Christian community, which was becoming increasingly preoccupied with the intellectual problems of their faith. Not least important in this blending of Greek speculation and Eastern religions was the role the writings of Philo Judaeus played in the effort to bring the fruits of Greek logic to bear on the justification of religious beliefs.

As the Greco-Roman civilization was gradually replaced with the steady advent of a culture centered around the fundamental beliefs of the Christian faith, the initial ambivalent responses of the defenders of the new faith withered in favor of a more positive but selective attitude. Once fear and hostility subsided, and Christianity became the official religion of the Roman Empire in the fourth century A.D., the values and achievements of Greece and Rome (at least those that could fit more comfortably into the new way of the future) were eventually given due recognition. It was a long assimilative process, however, and required the passage of centuries before the intellectual and administrative leaders of Christianity could accept the pre-Christian world in the positive light of a great heritage.

The overcoming of initial resistance and the rediscovery and selective assimilation of the classical world of Greece and Rome have marked the phases of growth of the Western world and the passage from the medieval mind through the Renaissance to the great synthesis of the modern world.

What Greece and Rome bequeathed to humanity and to modern Western culture, in particular, is now accepted as a heritage of perennial value and a possession of all mankind. To the Greek developments in philosophy, science, logic, the theater, tragedy, rhetoric, historiography, political freedom, and the idea of democracy, the Romans added the results of their own genius in the great practical arts of administration, public service, and law and government, and although Rome did not produce original philosophies, it proved capable of adding to the spirit of Athens the glory of human virtue under the law of nations and universal peace. Their philosophies continue to provide us today with the foundations and ideals of our humanities.

The bibliography below lists selections of texts in translation, general works covering whole periods or special periods, and works that are mainly treatments of fundamental problems or individual thinkers. Most bibliographical items include a short analytical comment intended as a guide to the main theme of the book. Although this is not the place to treat such items as bibliographies of bibliographies, it is worth mentioning as a matter of practical concern that most items included in this chapter offer select bibliographical lists of books and articles related to their special subject.

Most of the extant texts are now conveniently available in the Loeb editions, with the translation on facing pages. In the last few decades a great number of translations by various hands have appeared in inexpensive editions. It would be burdensome to list all the translations of the writings of such philosophers as Plato and Aristotle that have appeared in paperback. New ones, aspiring to replace the older ones, continue to come out with unusual frequency. Still, it would be difficult to replace such certain venerable translations as Jowett's translation of the Platonic dialogues or W. D. Ross's of Aristotle's works. These continue to hold their own for both elegance and faithfulness to the original. In the case of Plato and Aristotle, one can still recommend with confidence editions that will probably continue to grace any student's collection of masterworks, for instance, *The Collected Dialogues of Plato*, edited by Edith Hamilton and Huntington Cairns (see under Plato in this chapter), and *The Basic Works of Aristotle*, edited by Richard P. McKeon (see under Aristotle in this chapter). The standard *Paperbound Books in Print* (Bowker) offers the interested student all the available inexpensive editions of the philosophical works of the classical philosophers in English translation. Our listings in this chapter are designed to provide bibliographical guidance, first and foremost. (See also Volume 2.)

GENERAL WORKS

Histories and Texts

Armstrong, A. H. *An Introduction to Ancient Philosophy*. [*Quality Pap. Ser.*] Littlefield 3d ed. repr. of 1957 ed. 1981 pap. $7.45. A succinct account of the major thinkers and their ideas, at the introductory level.

Cornford, Francis M. *Before and After Socrates*. Cambridge Univ. Pr. 1932 $29.95 pap. $8.95. A readable account of Greek philosophy; it consists of four lectures on early Greek science as the background to the chapters on Socrates, Plato, and Aristotle.

Diogenes Laertius. *Lives of Eminent Philosophers*. [*Loeb Class. Lib.*] Harvard Univ. Pr. 2 vols. vol. 1 1925 rev. 1938 vol. 2 1925 ea. $13.95. These biographies by a third-century Greek writer are particularly valuable for the quotations from earlier works not preserved by other ancient sources.

Gomperz, Theodor. *Greek Thinkers: A History of Ancient Philosophy*. Humanities Pr. 4 vols. repr. of 1901 ed. 1964 o.p. This work offers a valuable interpretation of the main ideas in early Greek thinkers but it presupposes considerable familiarity with individual philosophers and themes.

Guthrie, William K. *Greek Philosophers: From Thales to Aristotle*. Harper 1951 pap. $5.95. A brief course of lectures "designed for an audience of undergraduates."

———. *A History of Greek Philosophy*. Cambridge Univ. Pr. 6 vols. 1975–81 ea. $69.50–$79.50. Vol. 1, *The Earlier Presocratics and the Pythagoreans;* Vol. 2, *The Presocratic Tradition from Parmenides to Democritus;* Vol. 3, *The Fifth Century Enlightenment;* Vol. 4, *Plato, the Man and His Dialogues, Earlier Period;* Vol. 5, *The Later Plato and the Academy;* Vol. 6, *Aristotle: An Encounter.* In this monumental multivolume study, Guthrie brought together the results of classical scholarship and criticism in a synthetic work already recognized as a landmark. Exhaustive bibliographies in each volume.

Jones, W. T. *A History of Western Philosophy*. Harcourt 2d ed. 5 vols. vols. 1–3 1969 vols. 4–5 1975 pap. ea. $11.95. A readable account of philosophers and schools, with frequent references to the cultural background.

Owens, Joseph. *History of Ancient Western Philosophy*. Prentice-Hall 1959 text ed. $30.00. A learned and well-written account of the major figures, schools, and movements from the beginnings of Greek philosophy to the death of Proclus in A.D. 485.

Robinson, John M. *Introduction to Early Greek Philosophy: The Chief Fragments and Ancient Testimony, with Connecting Commentary*. Houghton Mifflin 1968 text ed. pap. $22.95. Designed primarily as a student's handbook, useful to beginners. Emphasizing the unity of Greek thought, the book states the "main problem" formulated in the earlier stage and proceeds to the "solutions" worked out by the Pluralists and the Sophists.

Special Works

Adkins, Arthur W. *From the Many to the One: A Study of Personality and Views of Human Nature in the Context for Ancient Greek Society Values and Beliefs*. Constable 1970 o.p. This continues the work of Adkins's earlier book (listed below) and concentrates on the portrayal of human nature. Excellent on Plato.

———. *Merit and Responsibility: A Study in Greek Values*. 1960. [*Midway Repr. Ser.*] Univ. of Chicago Pr. 1975 text ed. pap. $20.00. A careful investigation covering the concepts of moral responsibility, moral errors, justice, and the logic of agreements, with extensive discussions on Plato and Aristotle as ethical philosophers.

Anton, John P., and George L. Kustas, eds. *Essays in Ancient Greek Philosophy, Vol. 1*. State Univ. of New York Pr. 1971 $49.50. A selection of the best papers presented at the meetings of the Society for Ancient Greek Philosophy (1954–67) covering all facets and periods of ancient thought.

Anton, John P., and Anthony Preus, eds. *Essays in Ancient Greek Philosophy, Vol. 2*. State Univ. of New York Pr. 1983 $49.50 pap. $22.50. This volume continues the work of the first volume (see above), papers presented at the meetings of the Society for Ancient Greek Philosophy (1968–79) by leading scholars in the field, mostly on Plato and Aristotle.

Auden, W. H., ed. *The Portable Greek Reader*. [*Viking Portable Lib.*] Penguin 1977 pap. $7.95. Selections on significant topics and themes, some from the writings of philosophers, with a useful chronological outline of concurrent thinkers, works, and events.

Baldry, H. C. *The Unity of Mankind in Greek Thought*. Cambridge Univ. Pr. 1965 $39.50. A very readable study from the early Greek poets and the great philosophers to the thinkers after the conquests of Alexander and the rise of Rome.

Beare, J. I. *Greek Theories of Elementary Cognition from Alcmaeon to Aristotle*. [*Classical Studies Ser.*] Irvington repr. of 1906 ed. 1980 o.p. Discusses and documents the physiological and psychological theories of the Greeks on the elementary phenomena of perception, the five senses, and the faculty of sensation in general.

Callahan, John F. *Four Views of Time in Ancient Philosophy*. Greenwood repr. of 1948 ed. 1970 lib. bdg. $22.50. Discusses time and the solutions to the problem of time as developed in the philosophies of Plato, Aristotle, Plotinus, and St. Augustine.

Dodds, Eric R. *The Greeks and the Irrational*. Peter Smith 1986 $16.50; Univ. of

California Pr. 1951 pap. $8.95. A landmark in the interpretation of Greek culture, thought, and literature, with frequent references to philosophy.

Edelstein, Ludwig. *The Idea of Progress in Classical Antiquity.* Johns Hopkins Univ. Pr. 1967 o.p. An important and well-documented analysis of the concept of "progress," which was familiar to the ancient Greeks before its late Hellenistic formulation.

Ferguson, John. *Moral Values in the Ancient World.* Ed. by Gregory Vlastos, Ayer repr. of 1958 ed. 1979 lib. bdg. $19.00. A survey covering the subject of values in ethical pursuits from Homer to the late Hellenistic and early Christian times.

Jaeger, Werner. *Paideia: The Ideals of Greek Culture.* Trans. by Gilbert Highet, Oxford 2d ed. 1986 text ed. pap. $12.95. An excellent study of the cultural ideal as reflected in the writing of poets, historians, orators, and philosophers.

Lloyd, G. E. R. *Magic, Reason and Experience: Studies in the Origin and Development of Greek Science.* Cambridge Univ. Pr. 1979 $62.50 pap. $19.95. Complements other histories of Greek science, assessing the theoretical and practical sides of science and relating both to philosophy. Includes an especially valuable bibliography on the subject.

McMullin, Ernan, ed. *The Concept of Matter in Greek and Medieval Philosophy.* Univ. of Notre Dame Pr. 1965 pap. $8.95. Of special interest are the essays dealing with the conceptions of the material world held by ancient Greek philosophers and scientists.

Murray, Gilbert. *Five Stages of Greek Religion: Studies Based on a Course of Lectures Delivered in April 1912 at Columbia University.* AMS Pr. repr. of 1925 ed. 1980 $12.50; (with the addition of another chapter) Greenwood repr. of 1925 ed. 1976 lib. bdg. $22.50. First published in 1912 as *Four Stages of Greek Religion.* Famous for its chapter "The Failure of Nerve," portraying the breakdown of Greek rationalism in Hellenistic times under the impact of the Oriental cults.

North, Helen. *Sophrosyne: Self-Knowledge and Self-Restraint in Greek Literature.* Cornell Univ. Pr. 1966 o.p. An outstanding treatment of the early meaning of sophrosyne in literature and philosophy, and its subsequent transformation into a Christian virtue.

Onians, Richard B. *The Origins of European Thought about the Body, the Mind, the Soul, the World, Time, and Fate.* Ayer repr. of 1951 ed. 1980 $34.50. The origins of European thought regarding these ideas are traced back to Greek, Roman, Jewish, and Christian concepts and beliefs.

Rohde, Erwin. *Psyche: The Cult of Souls and Belief in Immortality among the Greeks.* [*Select Bibliographies Repr. Ser.*] Ayer repr. of 1920 ed. 1980 $39.95. A classic in the field of ancient views on life.

Sambursky, S. *Physical World of the Greeks.* Trans. by Merton Dagut, Methuen 1956 o.p. A study of the Greek conceptualization of the physical world and how it relates to the modern scientific method and its achievements.

Snell, Bruno. *The Discovery of the Mind in Early Greek Philosophy and Literature.* Dover 1982 pap. $6.00; Peter Smith 1983 $14.00. A collection of essays on mythical thinking and the transition to logical thinking, explaining the relation of literary and intellectual movements to the rise of philosophy and poetry.

Vernant, Jean Pierre. *Myth and Thought among the Greeks.* Routledge & Kegan 1983 $29.95. The original edition (1965) was immediately noticed as a pioneering approach to Greek studies, applying structuralist views to myth, the concept of space, personal identity, reason, work, and technology.

————. *The Origins of Greek Thought.* Cornell Univ. Pr. 1984 $19.95 pap. $6.95. "One of the most stimulating and thoughtful accounts of the invention of philosophy by the Greeks" (*TLS*).

PRE-SOCRATICS

General Works

Barnes, Jonathan. *The Presocratic Philosophers.* [*Arguments of the Philosophers Ser.*] Methuen rev. ed. 1982 pap. $19.95. A lively interpretive work on the rise and development of early Greek speculation on man and nature.

Burnet, John. *Early Greek Philosophy.* Barnes & Noble 4th ed. repr. of 1930 ed. 1963 o.p. One of the most discussed surveys of ancient thought in this century. Very readable and still challenging.

Cornford, F. M. *From Religion to Philosophy: A Study of the Origins of Western Speculation.* Humanities Pr. repr. of 1957 ed. 1979 text ed. pap. $12.50. This work first appeared in 1912 defending the view that science and philosophy could be traced to religious roots through the mythic beginnings of metaphysical concepts.

———. *Principium Sapientiae: The Origins of Greek Philosophical Thought.* Peter Smith o.p. In his last work Cornford brought together his lifelong research into prephilosophical thought, going back to Hesiod and parallel Babylonian sources, to discuss the "nonscientific" nature of early Greek philosophy, making the claim that it relied on inspiration rather than experimentation.

Furley, David J., and R. E. Allen, eds. *Studies in Pre-Socratic Philosophy.* [*International Lib. of Philosophy and Scientific Method*] Humanities Pr. 1970 o.p. Essays by various hands on problems and interlacing themes from the Milesians to the Atomists.

Heidegger, Martin. *Early Greek Thinking: The Dawn of Western Philosophy.* Trans. by Frank Capuzzi, Harper 1975 $7.95 1985 pap. $8.95. Translation into English of four well-known and influential essays by Heidegger on Anaximander (one essay), Heraclitus (two essays), and Parmenides (one essay).

Hussey, Edward. *The Presocratics.* [*Class. Life and Letters Ser.*] Biblio Dist. 1972 $40.50 pap. $13.50; [*Class. Life and Letters Ser.*] Longwood 1972 $40.50 pap. $13.50. A popularized but competent introduction to early Greek thinkers, including the Sophists.

Hyland, D. *The Origins of Philosophy.* Humanities Pr. repr. of 1973 ed. 1984 pap. text ed. $12.95. "Highly recommended to all undergraduate libraries" (*Choice*).

Jaeger, Werner. *The Theology of the Early Greek Philosophers: The Gifford Lectures, 1936.* Trans. by Edward S. Robinson, Greenwood repr. of 1947 ed. 1980 lib. bdg. $55.00. The author seeks to balance the widely held view of the pre-Socratics as scientists and allows them to surface as offerers of remarkable theological insights.

Kirk, G. S., J. E. Raven, and M. Schofield. *The Presocratic Philosophers: A Critical History with a Selection of Texts.* Cambridge Univ. Pr. 1957 2d ed. 1983 pap. $19.95. A long and illuminating introduction sets the pace for this fresh interpretation of the early thinkers of Greece, down to the Atomists, by taking into account the best of recent scholarship; the extant texts are printed with new translations and commentaries.

Mourelatos, Alexander P. D., ed. *The Pre-Socratics: A Collection of Critical Essays.* Doubleday 1974 o.p. Brings together a number of outstanding articles, some written especially for this volume, examining fundamental issues in the pre-Socratic period, with an emphasis on Heraclitus and Parmenides.

Stokes, Michael C. *One and Many in Presocratic Philosophy.* Harvard Univ. Pr. 1971

$22.50. A detailed analysis of the concepts of unity and plurality in the early Greeks, with Xenophanes, Parmenides, and Zeno at the center of the author's interest.

Sweeney, Leo. *Infinity in the Presocratics.* Nijhoff 1972 o.p. Most of the book is on Anaximander's *apeiron* (infinity) and the recent literature on the subject, although attention is given to the views of the other pre-Socratics.

The Milesian Philosophers

Conscious freedom of inquiry had its birthplace in Miletus, a flourishing city in Ionia that had become a cultural and intellectual center. Philosophic thought from its very start took the form of general theories about the nature and origins of reality. The Greeks believed that the first philosopher was Thales of Miletus (fl. 585 B.C.), who attracted others to his views and shared them generously with his fellow citizens.

What is indeed remarkable about Thales and his immediate successors, Anaximander (c.610–546 B.C.) and Anaximenes (fl. 545 B.C.), and the others who came after them with the spread of philosophy to other cities, is the appeal to human reason for explanations of all natural and human events, and even more so the trust they put in reason to discover principles of unity behind the multiplicity of phenomena.

Very few of their writings have come down to us directly; however, later thinkers put together whatever they knew about them and made a commendable effort to preserve their theories. Thus a respectable body of literature grew about the pioneer philosophers of Miletus, and as their fame spread so did the spirit of critical thinking and the desire to come up with better and sounder theories. However different from one another, the answers of later philosophers were all based on the firm belief that nature, whatever it may ultimately be, is intelligible and accessible to human reason.

Kahn, Charles H. *Anaximander and the Origins of Greek Cosmology.* Columbia Univ. Pr. 1964 o.p. Kahn treats Anaximander as the source of the early systems of cosmology; regarded as a model of the study of the extant *testimonia.* The concluding chapter gives a comprehensive view of the Ionian tradition.

Seligman, Paul. *The "Apeiron" of Anaximander: A Study in the Origin and Function of Metaphysical Ideas.* Greenwood repr. of 1962 ed. 1974 lib. bdg. $15.00. A fine addition to the study of early pre-Socratic philosophy and the interpretations of Anaximander's principle of *apeiron* ("Infinity" or "the Indefinite").

Parmenides and the Eleatics

It was actually Xenophanes of Colophon, close in thought to the Milesians and yet one who made daring intellectual leaps in a direction of his own, who founded the Eleatic school and taught Parmenides. Xenophanes was exiled because of his criticisms of popular religious beliefs, that is, for theorizing about the divine in the same way the Milesians theorized about nature. Parmenides (fl. c.485 B.C.), a citizen of the Greek city of Elea in southern Italy, wrote a famous philosophical poem that was destined to become influential and assure him of being "the father of idealism." Ever since the time of Plato, one of whose longest dialogues bears the title *Parmenides*, numerous students of philosophy have essayed to explain his doctrines. He saw the importance of Heraclitus and sought to give a definitive answer to the problem of change by denying that change is essential to understanding being. Reality is one—everlasting, unchangeable, complete, determinate, a well-rounded sphere. His pupils Zeno (fl. c.465–455 B.C.) and Melissus (fifth century B.C.) defended the teachings of their master and developed further the art of logical arguments, insisting that unless one accepts Parmenides' teachings one falls into paradoxical beliefs.

Austin, Scott. *Parmenides: Being, Bounds and Logic.* Yale Univ. Pr. 1986 text ed. $20.00. This "bold exploration of Parmenides' use of language and argument forms . . . a difficult but insightful work" (*Choice*).

Lee, H. D. P. *Zeno of Elea: A Text with Translation and Notes.* Cambridge Univ. Pr. 1936 o.p. A collection of all the textual materials related to Zeno's paradoxes.

Mourelatos, Alexander P. D. *The Route of Parmenides: A Study of Word, Image and Argument in the Fragments.* Yale Univ. Pr. 1970 o.p. A well-known work explaining the grounds for considering the parts of the extant poem continuous, and viewing Parmenides as "the father of Western rationalism."

Taran, Leonardo. *Parmenides: A Text with Translation, Commentary, & Critical Essays.* Princeton Univ. Pr. 1965 o.p. A full as well as impressively technical discussion of the poem of Parmenides.

The Pluralists and Atomists

The fifth century produced a number of outstanding and original thinkers who extended and deepened the work of previous generations. Although only fragments of their writings have survived, we have enough to reconstruct in broad outline their bold theories of nature. Empedocles of Acragas (fifth century B.C.) won fame as philosopher, physician, orator, and statesman. What we have of his two philosophical poems, "On Nature" and "Purifications," shows a profound mind working to understand how the universe can be made intelligible in all its stages when love and strife operate alternately mixing and unmixing the primordial elements of fire, air, water, and earth to produce and dissolve nature as we perceive it now.

Anaxagoras of Clazomenae (500–c.428 B.C.), who is said to have brought philosophy to Athens, taught there for 20 years. He became a member of the Periclean circle in the "golden age" of Greece, only to be accused of impiety and forced to leave Athens to avoid execution. Socrates as a young man sought him out and so did many others who recognized the importance of his theories, especially his views on cosmic reason and on the interpenetration of all elements creating a number of ordered "universes" through an ever-expanding vortex.

Leucippus (fifth century B.C.) and his pupil Democritus of Abdera (494–c.404 B.C.) won their places in the history of science and philosophy with their theory of Atomism, arguing that the building bricks of all things are atoms— indestructible, eternally mobile, endowed with size and shape, moving with different velocities in the void, colliding, hooking together and separating to make and unmake things. Epicurus accepted this theory and turned it into a lasting worldview.

Bailey, Cyril. *Greek Atomists and Epicurus: A Study.* Russell repr. of 1928 ed. 1964 o.p. The author wrote this "as a study of the development of Atomism in Greece and of its embodiment in the comprehensive system of Epicurus" (Preface).

Millerd, Clara E. *On the Interpretation of Empedocles.* Ed. by Leonardo Taran [*Ancient Philosophy Ser.*] Garland 1980 lib. bdg. $16.00. A perceptive work making use of recent philology.

O'Brien, Denis. *Empedocles' Cosmic Cycle: A Reconstruction from the Fragments and Secondary Sources.* Cambridge Univ. Pr. 1969 o.p. An outstanding work on Empedocles' views, based on a firm grasp of the extant fragments, with a fresh interpretation of the role of love and strife.

Schofield, M. *An Essay on Anaxagoras.* Cambridge Univ. Pr. 1980 $29.95. Discussion centers on the doctrines of mind and includes a survey of current research on the fragments of Anaxagoras.

Teodorsson, Sven Tage. *Anaxagoras' Theory of Matter.* Humanities Pr. 1982 text ed. $18.50 pap. $15.00. "Although Anaxagoras' theory of *Nous* has drawn few students in the twentieth century (and no separate study since von Fritz' of 1964), his theory of matter has been the object of study by an impressive series of scholars that begins with Paul Tannery in 1886. The serious student will work his way through this bibliography as diligently as through the original fragments and testimonia" (*Classical Journal*).

Wright, M. R. *Empedocles: The Extant Fragments.* Yale Univ. Pr. 1981 $49.00. A scholarly study with translation of the extant fragments and survey of recent interpretations.

THE SOPHISTS

With the representatives of the Sophist movement and Socrates of Athens in the second half of the fifth century we witness a gradual shift of philosophical interest toward the deepening of an inquiry into the problems of human values, human nature, and political institutions. While there is evidence that the other pre-Socratics also kept in mind the problems of humanity and public conduct, law, and politics, it is with the coming of the great Sophists, Gorgias of Leontini (c.480–380 B.C.), Protagoras of Abdera (c.490–420 B.C.), Hippias, Prodicus, and others that a method gradually emerges and becomes sufficiently refined for the critical analysis of ethical and social values and pursuits. Different positions and theories were adopted, but the great issue that had to be decided was whether it was reasonable to say that universal values and standards for judging human actions could be found. The debate centered around the issue of teaching virtue and who was qualified to do so. The great Sophists took an early lead. Recognizing the importance of the art of the persuasion in maintaining power and controlling public opinion, they developed rhetoric, furthered the logic of arguing in public, and became celebrated teachers. The challenge to their fame and teachings came from a man of humble origins, who made the future of his city his own cause. (See also the main entry for Socrates in this chapter.)

General Works

Guthrie, William K. *The Sophists.* Cambridge Univ. Pr. 1971 pap. $17.95. Originally published as Part I of *A History of Greek Philosophy*, Vol III (1969), this covers "a series of standard topics—nature v. convention, rhetoric and skepticism, social compact theory, 'liberalism'—and then reviews these 'professors' one at a time, including some minor ones (Thrasymachus, Antisthenes, Lycophron)" (*Choice*).

The Older Sophists. A complete translation of the part on the Sophists in *Die Fragmente der Vorsokratiker*, eds. Diels-Kranz. Trans. and ed. by Rosamond Kent Sprague and others. University of South Carolina Pr. 1972 o.p. Brief introductions to each Sophist, including Antiphon and Euthedemus, citing extant fragments and *testimonia* in translation.

Versényi, Laszlo. *Socratic Humanism.* Intro. by Robert S. Brumbaugh, Greenwood repr. of 1963 ed. 1979 lib. bdg. $22.50. An existentialist approach emphasizing the ideal of self-fulfillment and the unity of Socratic views.

HELLENISTIC PHILOSOPHIES

After Alexander's death in 323, a new cultural era begins to emerge as a result of the fusion of ideas and values. Until recently the originality of the philosophical works produced after Plato and Aristotle was seriously disputed. That judgment has now come under criticism and reexamination by philosophers, historians, and philologists who essay to show that the Hellenistic age, rather than being a period of long stagnation and decline, succeeded in making important advances in a number of philosophical and scientific fields. The Hellenistic period appears to fall into an early phase, during which the dominant quest was to secure practical wisdom, and a second phase, characterized by the gradual surge and prevalence of the search for salvational faiths and their justifications.

Texts and Collections

Long, Anthony A., and D. N. Sedley. *The Hellenistic Philosophers.* Cambridge Univ. Pr. 1987 pap. $19.95. Texts of the Stoic, Epicurean, and Skeptical schools in new translations, with material grouped by topic under each school.

Oates, W. J., ed. *The Stoic and Epicurean Philosophers.* Random House 1957 o.p. A representative collection of the writings of Epicurus, Epictetus, Lucretius, and Marcus Aurelius in English translation, with an Introduction and useful notes; included is Cleanthes' "Hymn to Zeus" and Matthew Arnold's essay on Marcus Aurelius.

Shapiro, H., and E. M. Curley. *Hellenistic Philosophy: Selections from Epicureanism, Skepticism, and Neoplatonism.* Modern Lib. 1965 o.p. Brief introductions and selections from Epicurus, Lucretius, Seneca, Epictetus, Marcus Aurelius, Sextus Empiricus, Lucian, Plotinus, and Cicero.

General Works

Armstrong, Arthur H., ed. *The Cambridge History of Later Greek and Early Medieval Philosophy.* Cambridge Univ. Pr. 1967 $82.50. This is the work of several well-known specialists offering a useful summary of this period, for example, Philip Merlan's "Greek Philosophy from Plato to Plotinus" and Henry Chadwick's "Philo and the Beginnings of Christian Thought."

Bevan, E. *Stoics and Skeptics*. Oxford Univ. Pr. 1913 o.p. A stimulating and well-written summary on the rise and development of these schools.

Dudley, D. R. *A History of Cynicism from Diogenes to the Sixth Century A.D.* Ares Pubs. repr. of 1937 ed. 1980 $15.00; Gordon Pr. $69.95. A useful survey of the major phases of Cynicism as a philosophical attitude and way of life.

Hahm, David E. *The Origins of Stoic Cosmology*. Ohio State Univ. Pr. 1977 o.p. Examines critically the sources Stoic thinkers used and extended in creating their own cosmology.

Hicks, Robert D. *Stoic and Epicurean*. Russell repr. of 1910 ed. 1962 $13.00. Three well-organized chapters on Epicurean hedonism, Atomism, and religion; also a fair treatment of Stoicism.

Long, A. A. *Hellenistic Philosophy: Stoics, Epicureans, Skeptics*. [*Class. Life and Letters Ser.*] Biblio Dist. 1974 text ed. pap. $12.00; [*Class. Life and Letters Ser.*] Longwood 2d ed. 1986 $40.50 pap. $12.00. An excellent treatment of these schools, with most attention given to Stoicism; the last chapter discusses the influence of Hellenistic philosophy in later developments and in modern thought.

More, Paul Elmer. *Hellenistic Philosophies*. Greenwood repr. of 1923 ed. o.p. A general discussion with a Platonic bias of later Greek philosophy and its blending with Christian beliefs.

Randall, John H. *Hellenistic Ways of Deliverance and the Making of the Christian Synthesis*. Columbia Univ. Pr. 1970 $28.00. An excellent analysis of the Hellenistic schools of thought—Epicurean, Stoic, and Skeptic—as secular ways; the Roman philosophers; and the turning of Platonism into a religious way of deliverance, preparing the ground for the Christian assimilation of Greek philosophy.

Reale, Giovanni. *The Systems of the Hellenistic Age: A History of Ancient Philosophy*. Trans. by John R. Catan, State Univ. of New York Pr. 1985 $44.50 pap. $14.95. A reliable history of this period from the minor Socratic schools, the Cynics, Cyrenaics, and Megarians down to Cicero and Roman Eclecticism.

The Stoics

The Stoic philosophical school had a long and checkered career, from its founding by Zeno of Citium in Athens late in the fourth century to the Roman era, when Epictetus, a Greek slave, and Marcus Aurelius, an emperor, held Stoic doctrines in the second century A.D. Thus we can speak of a Greek phase of Stoicism and a Roman one, holding essentially the same principles and view of the universe but with different emphases on what the Stoic outlook means when applied to human problems. From the very start we find the Stoics, from Zeno to Cleanthes, combining a revival of Heraclitus's theory of nature and a creative extension of Aristotelian logic, and dividing philosophy into three parts: logic, physics (mixing theology and psychology), and ethics. In certain ways, Stoicism is an eclectic position but not without considerable internal consistency. The fragments we have from Zeno's teachings make difficult any coherent interpretation, but the situation improves with Cleanthes. The third head of the Stoa, he is recognized as the system-builder of Stoicism, defending an ethical thesis that called for submission to the ways of nature, but a nature understood as thoroughly rational and determinate. The Stoics saw the world as being in process, but unfolding a divine and necessary plan, totally logical and intelligible, with human beings capable of rising to ethical completion. Whereas man is a microcosmos of the universe, the universe is the macrocosmos of man: Human reason, being a particular manifestation of the cosmic mind, is a principle that secures the brotherhood and unity of humanity.

Among the important Stoics are Zeno of Citium (c.362/351?–264/259? B.C.), Cleanthes of Assos (c.300–232 B.C.), Chrysippus of Soli (281–201 B.C.), and Epictetus (A.D. 60–138).

Edelstein, Ludwig. *The Meaning of Stoicism.* Harvard Univ. Pr. 1966 $8.95. The Martin Lectures presented at Oberlin along general lines; elliptical but worth reading and typical of the author's learning.

Edelstein, Ludwig, and I. G. Kidd, trans. *Posidonius: The Fragments.* Cambridge Univ. Pr. 1972 $59.00. A new edition of the extant fragments.

Gould, Josiah B. *The Philosophy of Chrysippus.* State Univ. of New York Pr. 1970 o.p. One of the best treatments of this leading Stoic and the climate of opinion in the third century.

Hadas, Moses, ed. *The Essential Works of Stoicism.* Bantam 1961 o.p. A good selection of translated texts from Laertius, Cleanthes, Seneca, Epictetus, and Marcus Aurelius.

Mates, Benson. *Stoic Logic.* Univ. of California Pr. 1953 o.p. Offers a complete description of the propositional logic of the old Stoa; "the most accurate analytical study" (*Journal of Philosophy*).

Oldfather, W. A. *A Bibliography of Epictetus.* Holmes Bk. 1952 $7.00. An exhaustive list of publications of the writings of this Stoic thinker; a helpful guide.

———. *Contributions towards a Bibliography of Epictetus: A Supplement.* Holmes Bk. o.p. Covers additional philological work since the publication of the 1952 item above.

Rist, J. M. *Stoic Philosophy.* Cambridge Univ. Pr. 1969 pap. $13.95. A close and clear examination of the major doctrines and the leading members of the Stoic school and their interlacing concerns and problems, with an emphasis on ethical theory.

———, ed. *The Stoics.* [*Major Thinkers Ser.*] Univ. of California Pr. 1978 pap. $9.95. Thirteen essays by leading authorities in Hellenistic philosophy, all commissioned for this volume, on topics ranging from Stoic grammar to theory of art.

Sambursky, Samuel. *Physics of the Stoics.* Greenwood repr. of 1959 ed. 1973 lib. bdg. $22.50. The author has brought together all the sources available to construct a complete picture of the Stoic conception of nature.

Sandbach, F. H. *The Stoics.* Ed. by M. I. Finley, Norton 1975 o.p. One of the best introductions to the Stoic movement and its major themes, with discussion extending into the Roman phase of Stoicism.

Verbeke, Gerard. *The Presence of Stoicism in Medieval Thought.* Catholic Univ. Pr. 1982 pap. $6.95. A scholarly contribution showing how the views of the Stoics were adapted to medieval thought.

The Skeptics

Skepticism is a post-Aristotelian development formulating its thesis alongside the more positive doctrines of the Epicureans and the Stoics, finally winding up another version of "a way of life." From time to time there appeared thinkers with subtle arguments claiming loyalty to the pursuit of truth but admitting that it was impossible to find. As a result they declared that they had to withhold judgment and remain in intellectual suspension, in *aporia*, without a way out. Some actually advocated abandoning the desire to know, in confidence that complete knowledge was not within human reach. However, this was a conclusion arrived at only after long search and examination of the conditions of knowing; hence the name "Skeptic," that is, a person who takes thinking seriously and accepts the negative consequence. One type of Skepticism originated with Pyrrho of Elis (365–275 B.C.), whose influence extended well into the third century A.D. He concluded that since we cannot have confidence in any scientific theory, the wise man is really wise only when he preserves rational tranquillity by becoming genuinely indifferent to all views. Another trend to Skepticism, less extreme, originated within Plato's Academy and lasted for two centuries (fourth and third); this period is known as the Middle Academy and the New Academy, the representatives being Arkesilaus and Carneades (called the "David Hume" of antiquity). Aenesidemus of Crete in the first century B.C. revived Pyrrhonism but refined it along Academic lines. The last great Skeptic in the tradition of Pyrrho was Sextus Empiricus, a medical doctor, who wrote extensively against the dogmatic teachings of the philosophers. The list given below is merely a selection of representative books.

Burnyeat, M. F., ed. *The Skeptical Tradition*. Univ. of California Pr. 1983 text ed. $40.00 pap. $10.95. "The originality of this book lies in that, for the first time, it gives a quite satisfactory view of the history of skepticism as a tradition stretching from the fourth century B.C. up to Kant" (*Journal of the History of Philosophy*).

Galen. *Three Treatises on the Nature of Science*. Trans. and ed. by R. Walzer and M. Frede, Hackett 1985 text ed. lib. bdg. $17.50 pap. $6.95. In his Introduction Frede offers an excellent discussion of the basic themes in the treatises: On the Sects for Beginners, An Outline of Empiricism, and On Medical Experience.

Hallie, Philip. *Scepticism, Man and God: Selections from the Writings of Sextus Empiricus*. Wesleyan Univ. Pr. 1964 o.p. Representative passages from the text illustrating the concepts involved, accompanied by carefully written annotations.

Patrick, Mary Mills. *The Greek Sceptics*. Columbia Univ. Pr. 1929 o.p. Stimulating and reliable mainly on the connection between later Skepticism and Alexandrian medicine.

Sextus Empiricus. *Against the Musicians (adversus Musicos)*. Trans. by Denise D. Greaves, Univ. of Nebraska Pr. 1986 $15.95. Published here is part of "Against the Mathematicians" and an analysis of the arguments of Sextus Empiricus for and against the nature and value of music.

Stough, Charlotte L. *Greek Skepticism: A Study in Epistemology*. Univ. of California Pr. 1969 $33.00. A systematic exploration of the epistemology of the Greek Skeptics, from Pyrrho to Sextus Empiricus.

Tarrant, Harold. *Scepticism or Platonism: The Philosophy of the Fourth Academy*. Cambridge Univ. Pr. 1985 $39.50. A scholarly reconstruction of the type of Platonism that arose in the first half of the first century B.C. from the mixture of various philosophical traditions, Stoicism, Platonism, and Skepticism.

ARISTOTLE. 384–322 B.C.

One of the great thinkers of all times, Aristotle was born in Stagira in Chalcidice, northern Greece. His father, Nichomachus, was court physician to the king of Macedon. At the age of 17 Aristotle enrolled in Plato's Academy and remained there for 20 years, first as a student and later as a teacher. After Plato's death, accompanied by several close associates he went first to Assos and then to Lesbos, continuing his research and teaching. In 342 he accepted the invitation of King Philip of Macedon to be tutor to his son Alexander. In subsequent years he returned to Athens, where he opened his own school, the Lyceum, also known as the Peripatetic school. He remained there until after the death of Alexander, when the anti-Macedonian party in Athens accused him of impiety. He then fled Athens and died in 322 in the nearby city of Chalkis in Euboea.

Aristotle systematized the available knowledge of his times, and added to it the results of his own original researches to become the founder of most of the sciences. He wrote on logic, rhetoric, literary theory, physics, botany, zoology, psychology, economics, ethics, politics, astronomy, and "first philosophy," or what was later to be named metaphysics. He laid the foundation of scientific methodology and developed further Plato's own ideal of science. Most of his surviving writings are genuine. They became very influential after the Roman conquest of Greece, when Greek scholars edited his manuscripts and wrote extensive commentaries. His philosophy was never eclipsed, although there have been periods of strong reaction against some of his principal doctrines. What has been written about Aristotle is enough to fill the wing of a modern library.

Aristotle sought to bring together within a logical scheme of explanation all the fields of human knowledge, be they about the elements, nature, life or human culture, and political activities. After criticizing his teacher, Plato, for holding that the "Forms" of things are transcendent realities and ideal beings, he argued that forms can exist only as immanent in things and as functional structures determining their kinds and their purposes in each specific case. According to his general theory of life, the structures of living organisms become more complex, from plants to animals to human beings. Organisms develop as distinct individuals completing the cycle of their purpose in life, barring violence or other interruptive factors; but as members of species they remain what they are, untouched by what modern biology was to call "evolution." Human beings possess intelligence, and as they form groups and societies they establish institutions seeking to refine them in the effort to perfect the ways of governing in civilized states. The purpose of human life for Aristotle is the completion of our potential through knowledge and enlightened habits to cope with our emotional and intellectual endowment and to promote cooperation to secure the common good. Thus the highest art for Aristotle was that of intelligent politics and legislation that secures the conditions enabling the citizens to live together in the pursuit of perfectibility and well-being through the habits of practical and intellectual excellence. (See also Volume 3.)

BOOKS BY ARISTOTLE

As in the case of Plato's works, Aristotle's own have been translated and published as individual treatises, as groups of treatises, as the entire corpus, and in selections from representative treatises.

Works: The Oxford Translation. Trans. under the editorship of J. A. Smith and W. D. Ross by J. I. Beare, Ingram Bywater, and others, Oxford 12 vols. 1908–52 ea. $9.95–$19.95. The Oxford Aristotle was issued in parts over a period of years. This monumental translation supersedes all others and contains such great classics as the Jowett "Politics" and the "Poetics" by Bywater.

The Complete Works of Aristotle. Ed. by Jonathan Barnes, Princeton Univ. Pr. 2 vols. 1984 $75.00. A revised edition of the standard Oxford translation of Aristotle's works, with a more comprehensive selection of the fragments.

The Basic Works of Aristotle. Ed. by Richard P. McKeon, Random 1941 $27.95

Works. [*Loeb Class. Lib.*] Harvard Univ. Pr. 23 vols. 1926–70 ea. $13.95. Greek text with translation on the facing pages; competently done by various hands.

The Politics. [*History of Ideas Ser.*] Ayer repr. of 1894 ed. 1976 $39.00; [*Loeb Class. Lib.*] Harvard Univ. Pr. 1932 $13.95; trans. by Ernest Barker, Oxford 1946 pap. $8.95; [*Penguin Class. Ser.*] rev. ed. 1981 pap. $4.95; trans. by L. P. Gerson, Peripatetic Pr. 1986 text ed. lib. bdg $24.00 pap. $12.00; trans. by William Ellis, Prometheus Bks. 1986 text ed. pap. $4.95; trans. by Carnes Lord, Univ. of Chicago Pr. 1984 lib. bdg. $35.00 pap. $9.95

Nicomachean Ethics. Trans. by M. Ostwald, Bobbs-Merrill 1962 o.p.; trans. by Terence Irwin, Hackett 1985 lib. bdg. $19.50 pap. $6.75; ed. by Hugh Tredennick, Penguin 1955 o.p. Important among his more humanistic studies, Aristotle here tries to analyze happiness.

The Ethics of Aristotle. Ed. by John Burnet, Ayer repr. of 1900 ed. 1974 $33.00

The Poetics of Aristotle. Trans. by Preston H. Epps, Univ. of North Carolina Pr. repr. of 1942 ed. 1967 pap. $4.95. Aristotle turns his attention to the arts which he considers a dynamic principle of creativity.

The Rhetoric and the Poetics of Aristotle. Trans. by W. Rhys Roberts and Ingram Bywater, Modern Lib. 1954 $6.95; [*Modern Lib. College Ed. Ser.*] Random 1984 text ed. pap. $4.75. "Aristotle's analysis of the elements of rhetorical discourse (the speaker, the audience, the subject), the kinds of rhetorical discourse (forensic, deliberative, and epideictic), and the modes of persuasion (logical, ethical, and pathetic)" (*Thought*).

Aristotle's De Generatione et Corruptione. Ed. by C. J. F. Williams, Oxford 1982 $32.00 pap. $14.95. Translates as *On Generation and Corruption*, this is Aristotle's treatise on the constantly changing earthly, material bodies.

Aristotle's Eudemian Ethics. Ed. by M. J. Woods, Oxford 1982 pap. $14.95. The editor argues that this work is less mature than the *Nicomachean Ethics;* a valuable commentary.

Aristotle's On the Soul (de Anima). Trans. by H. G. Apostle, Peripatetic Pr. 1982 text ed. $18.00 pap. $9.00. Adequate translation with a brief introduction and comments.

Aristotle's Physics. Trans. by H. G. Apostle, Peripatetic Pr. repr. of 1969 ed. 1980 text ed. $21.60 pap. $10.80; ed. by Edward Hussey, Oxford 1983 pap. $13.95; trans. by Richard Hope, Univ. of Nebraska Pr. 1961 pap. $6.25. These translations are conscientiously done and reflect the effort to remain faithful to the original.

BOOKS ABOUT ARISTOTLE

Ackrill, J. L. *Aristotle on Eudaimonia*. Longwood 1974 pap. $2.50. A leading scholar discusses the arguments that seek to establish "happiness" as the highest value.
———. *Aristotle the Philosopher*. Oxford 1981 text ed. pap. $8.95. A stimulating general introduction emphasizing method, change, science, logic, metaphysics, and the ethics.

Adler, Mortimer J. *Aristotle for Everybody*. Bantam 1980 pap. $4.50. A descriptive outline aimed at introducing Aristotle's philosophy to the casual reader.

Allan, D. F. *Philosophy of Aristotle*. Oxford 2d ed. 1970 pap. $7.95. An excellent introductory work on Aristotle's principal doctrines in metaphysics, ethics, logic, and politics.

Anton, John P. *Aristotle's Theory of Contrariety*. Routledge & Kegan 1957 pap. $12.95. A thorough study of a major theme in Aristotle's philosophical system that is also present in all Greek thinkers.

Barker, Ernest. *Political Thought of Plato and Aristotle*. Dover 1959 pap. $9.95. The second half of this classic work discusses in detail Aristotle's *Politics*.

Barnes, Jonathan. *Aristotle*. Oxford 1982 $13.95 pap. $3.95. Recommended for undergraduates interested in Aristotle's views on science and logic.

Barnes, Jonathan, and Richard Sorabji, eds. *Articles on Aristotle*. St. Martin's 1979 vol. 1 $27.50 vols. 2–4 o.p. Collections of scholarly contributions by specialists covering science (vol. 1), ethics and politics (vol. 2), metaphysics (vol. 3), and psychology and ethics (vol. 4).

Brentano, Franz. *Aristotle and His World View*. Trans. by Roderick Chisholm, Univ. of California Pr. 1978 $25.00 Examines what he found to be the essential features of Aristotle's worldview to show that they constitute a unified system.
———. *On the Several Senses of Being in Aristotle*. Trans. by Rolf George, Univ. of California Pr. repr. of 1975 ed. 1981 $23.00. This was Brentano's doctoral dissertation; important for the influence it had on Heidegger.
———. *The Psychology of Aristotle: In Particular His Doctrine of the Active Intellect with an Appendix Concerning the Activity of Aristotle's God*. Trans. by Rolf George, Univ. of California Pr. 1977 $25.00. The special interest of this work is due to the interpretation Brentano attributes to Aristotle, particularly the doctrine in which Aristotle makes God an active principal in the creation of each human being.

Butcher, S. H. *Aristotle's Theory of Poetry and Fine Art*. Intro. by J. Gassner, Dover 4th ed. 1955 pap. $6.95; Norwood repr. of 1902 ed. 1979 lib. bdg. $50.00. A standard work on the *Poetics*, prefaced by an essay on Aristotelian literary criticism by J. Gassner.

Bywater, Ingram. *Aristotle on the Art of Poetry*. [*Ancient Philosophy Ser.*] Garland 2d ed. 1980 lib. bdg. $53.00; Richart West repr. of 1909 ed. o.p. A readable and influential treatment of Aristotle's aesthetics.

Charles, David. *Aristotle's Philosophy of Action*. Cornell Univ. Pr. 1984 $39.50. Analyzes practical reason and incontinence with frequent reference to recent ethical theorists.

Cherniss, Harold. *Aristotle's Criticism of Presocratic Philosophy*. Hippocrene Bks. 1964 lib. bdg. $32.50. A great critical study, revolutionary and controversial, attacking Aristotle's historiographic method on the ground that Aristotle misunderstood the thought of Plato and thus made it an object of criticism.

Clark, Stephen R. *Aristotle's Man: Speculations Upon Aristotelian Anthropology*. Oxford repr. of 1975 ed. 1983 pap. $13.95. "A unique interpretation of Aristotle . . . which makes the biological conception of devolution—opposed to evolution—crucial to Aristotle's biology" (*Choice*).

Cooper, John M. *Reason and Human Good in Aristotle*. Hackett repr. 1986 text ed. pap. $9.95; Harvard Univ. Pr. 1975 text ed. $17.50. Provides a unifying framework for Aristotle's views on virtue and practical intelligence, basing it on all his ethical writings.

Cooper, Lane. *Aristotelian Theory of Comedy*. Kraus Repr. repr. of 1922 ed. $23.00. An experimental attempt to reconstruct the "lost" part of the *Poetics*.

————. *Poetics of Aristotle*. Cooper Square Pr. repr. of 1930 ed. 1963 $18.50. One of the best books on Aristotle's theory of poetry.

Dancy, R. M. *Sense and Contradiction: A Study in Aristotle*. Kluwer Academic 1975 lib. bdg. $37.00. An outstanding discussion of Aristotle's logic as related to his metaphysics.

During, Ingemar, and G. E. Owens, eds. *Aristotle and Plato in the Mid-Fourth Century*. Humanities Pr. 1960 text ed. $25.00. An excellent collection of essays by different authors setting high standards in recent Aristotelian scholarship.

Edel, Abraham. *Aristotle and His Philosophy*. Univ. of North Carolina Pr. 1982 $27.50 pap. $12.00. A comprehensive work on Aristotle's philosophy, with extensive discussion of its relationship to modern and contemporary systems and ideas.

Elders, L. *Aristotle's Theology: A Commentary on the Book of Metaphysics*. [*Philosophical Texts and Studies Ser.*] Humanities Pr. 1972 text ed. $45.00. An extended analysis of the arguments and the conceptions of theology in Aristotle.

Else, Gerald Frank. *Aristotle's Poetics: The Argument*. Harvard Univ. Pr. 1957 o.p. A monumental work on Aristotle's theory of tragedy, setting forth many original points of interpretation.

————. *Plato and Aristotle on Poetry*. Ed. by Peter Burian, Univ. of North Carolina Pr. 1987 $27.00. A comparative study of the Platonic antecedents of Aristotle's views on poetry.

Evans, J. D. *Aristotle's Concept of Dialectic*. Cambridge Univ. Pr. 1977 $29.95. A competent discussion of the difference between dialectic and demonstrative syllogism.

Ferguson, John. *Aristotle*. [*Twayne's World Authors Ser.*] G. K. Hall 1972 lib. bdg. $13.50. "There is no small compendium to Aristotle in English more useful than this one. It is not intended as a work for scholarly reference. It is written nevertheless, for serious students in the style of a genial teacher, proceeding, text by text, through the entire scope of Aristotle's work" (*Choice*).

Golden, Leon, and O. B. Hardison, Jr. *Aristotle's Poetics: A Translation and Commentary for Students of Literature*. Univ. Presses Fla. 1981 pap. $10.50. A very useful handbook for advanced students in ancient views on tragedy.

Grene, Marjorie. *A Portrait of Aristotle*. Univ. of Chicago Pr. 1979 text ed. pap. $14.00. A sympathetic account, with an emphasis on the scientific side of Aristotle, especially the biological investigations.

Grote, George. *Aristotle*. Ed. by Alexander Bain and C. Croom Robertson, Ayer 2d ed. repr. of 1880 ed. 1974 $37.00. A classic, comprehensive study, still useful.

Hardie, W. F. *Aristotle's Ethical Theory*. Oxford 2d ed. 1981 pap. $29.95. A recent thorough study of Aristotle's ethics.

Heath, Thomas. *Mathematics in Aristotle*. [*Ancient Philosophy Ser.*] Garland 1980 lib. bdg. $36.00. A classic work that collects, translates, and discusses the passages on mathematics.

Hintikka, Jaakko. *Time and Necessity: Studies in Aristotle's Theory of Modality*. Oxford 1973 $42.00. Concentrates on the "logical modalities in Aristotle and their consequences for his ideas on time, determinism and infinity" (Frederick J. Crosson).

Jaeger, Werner. *Aristotle: Fundamentals of the History of His Development*. Oxford 2d ed. 1962 o.p. A landmark in Aristotelian studies seeking to trace the development of his basic ideas through a chronology of his works.

Joachim, H. H. *Aristotle: The Nicomachean Ethics: A Commentary*. Ed. by D. A. Rees, Greenwood repr. of 1951 ed. 1985 lib. bdg. $45.00. Reliable translation with insightful analyses of the major themes and cross-references.

Jones, John. *On Aristotle and Greek Tragedy*. Stanford Univ. Pr. 1962 $20.00 pap. $7.95. This book aims to discover what Aristotle was really saying about the drama in his *Poetics,* and to test these discoveries on plays by Aeschylus, Sophocles, and Euripides.

Kenny, Anthony. *The Aristotelian Ethics: A Study of the Relationship between the Eudemian and Nichomachean Ethics of Aristotle*. Oxford 1978 $42.00. This work challenges the traditional view of the *Eudemian Ethics* as an immature Platonizing treatise written prior to the *Nicomachean Ethics*.

Lear, Jonathan. *Aristotle and Logical Theory*. Cambridge Univ. Pr. 1980 $27.95 1986 pap. $10.95. A scholarly approach describing the dual aspects of Aristotle's syllogistic, in the broad sense of deductive logic and in the narrow sense of isolated formal inferences.

Lloyd, Geoffrey E. *Aristotle: Growth and Structure of His Thought*. Cambridge Univ. Pr. 1968 $44.50 pap. $13.95. A good introduction to Aristotle's development showing the unity and coherence of his philosophy.

Lord, Carnes. *Education and Culture in the Political Thought of Aristotle*. Cornell Univ. Pr. 1982 $24.95. Argues persuasively for Lord's own interpretation of Aristotle's views on art and culture in the context of education.

Lukasiewicz, Jan. *Aristotle's Syllogistic: From the Standpoint of Modern Formal Logic*. Oxford 2d ed. 1957 o.p. A standard work offering a modern interpretation of Aristotle's theory of syllogistic thinking.

Lynch, John Patrick. *Aristotle's School: A Study of a Greek Educational Institution*. Univ. of California Pr. 1972 o.p. Uses archaeological, epigraphical, and literary *testimonia* to reconstruct the founding and history of Aristotle's Peripatetic school.

Monan, J. D. *Moral Knowledge and Its Methodology in Aristotle*. Oxford Univ. Pr. 1968 o.p. A reexamination of the relationship between three ethical works: the *Protrepticus,* the *Eudemian Ethics,* and the *Nicomachean Ethics,* arguing that the *Eudemian* represents Aristotle's mature views.

Mure, G. R. *Aristotle*. Greenwood repr. of 1932 ed. 1975 lib. bdg. $22.50. A comprehensive study of Aristotle's contributions to all branches of knowledge.

Nussbaum, Martha C. *Aristotle's "De Motu Animalium."* Princeton Univ. Pr. 1985 text ed. pap. $17.00. Reliable translation and excellent interpretive essays.

Oates, Whitney J. *Aristotle and the Problem of Value*. Princeton Univ. Pr. 1963 o.p. A general treatment of the Aristotelian aesthetic and conception of culture.

Organ, Troy W. *Index to Aristotle*. Gordian repr. of 1949 ed. 1966 $17.50. A lexicon of the English terminology with references to particular key passages.

Randall, John H. *Aristotle*. Columbia Univ. Pr. 1960 $32.00 pap. $12.50. An important book treating Aristotle as highly relevant to contemporary philosophical pursuits.

Reale, Giovanni. *The Concept of First Philosophy and the Unity of the Metaphysics of Aristotle*. Trans. by John R. Catan, State Univ. of New York Pr. 1980 $58.50 pap. $29.95. Its aim is "to provide the unity of the *metaphysics* and speculative homogeneity" (Introduction); a major work.

Rhodes, P. J. *A Commentary on the Aristotelian Athenaion Politeia*. Oxford 1981 $108.00. "Many scholars have agreed that Aristotle wrote the work . . . but P. J. Rhodes in the philological introduction to this excellent book decides against

Aristotle. . . . As matters stand, uncertainties concerning the authorship do not diminish the significance of the text because, as Dr. Rhodes robustly declares, 'as a historian *A. P.* is mediocre (though by no means useless to us), but as a describer of constitutional practice he is first in the field' " (*Ancient Greece*).

Rorty, Amelie O., ed. *Essays on Aristotle's Ethics.* [*Major Thinkers Ser.*] Univ. of California Pr. 1980 pap. $11.95. A collection of 21 essays by different authors on a broad range of themes on Aristotle's ethical philosophy.

Ross, W. D. *Aristotle.* Barnes & Noble 5th ed. rev. 1964 pap. $6.50. An excellent one-volume introduction to Aristotle's works by one of his outstanding translators and editors in this century.

———. *Aristotle's Prior and Posterior Analytics: A Revised Text with Introduction and Commentary.* [*Ancient Philosophy Ser.*] Garland 1980 lib. bdg. $80.00. An excellent work on the two logical treatises; a valuable contribution to scholarship.

———, ed. *Aristotle: Selections.* Scribner 1971 text ed. pap. $9.95. Representative texts in translation for students' use, with a general introduction.

Schmitt, Charles. *Aristotle and the Renaissance.* Harvard Univ. Pr. 1983 text ed. $18.50. An expert discussion of the postmedieval developments that emerge as novel trends in the encounter of Aristotelianism with new doctrines and the revived tradition.

———. *John Case and Aristotelianism in Renaissance England.* [*Studies in the History of Ideas*] McGill-Queens Univ. Pr. 1983 $35.00. This and the preceding title are among the best accounts of Renaissance Aristotelianism, written by a well-known authority in the history of ideas.

Solmsen, Friedrich. *Aristotle's System of the Physical World.* Johnson Repr. repr. of 1960 ed. $37.00. A detailed treatment by a leading classicist of Aristotle's physical, cosmological, chemical, and meteorological questions, including the connection between his scientific investigations and his theology. A major work.

Sorabji, Richard. *Aristotle on Memory.* Univ. Pr. of New England 1972 $10.00. The best treatment of Aristotle's views on memory, with a translation of *De Memoria.*

———. *Necessity, Cause and Blame: Perspectives on Aristotle's Theory.* Cornell Univ. Pr. 1983 pap. $12.95. An outstanding work on moral conduct to show that Aristotle was an indeterminist.

Stewart, J. A. *Notes on the Nicomachean Ethics of Aristotle.* Ayer repr. of 1892 ed. 1974 o.p. One of the best commentaries on the subject of ethical theory.

Stocks, John L. *Aristotelianism.* Cooper Square Pr. repr. of 1930 ed. 1963 $19.50. One of the best short accounts of Aristotle's ideas and his influence.

Veatch, Henry B. *Aristotle: A Contemporary Appreciation.* Indiana Univ. Pr. 1974 $17.50 pap. $5.95. "Good books for undergraduates on classical philosophy are so rare that this book should probably be acquired by all college libraries" (*Choice*).

Von Fritz, Kurt. *Aristotle's Contribution to the Practice and Theology of Historiography.* Univ. of California Pr. 1957 o.p. A noted classicist defends Aristotle's approach to historical events and theories.

Walsh, James J. *Aristotle's Conception of Moral Weakness.* Columbia Univ. Pr. 1963 o.p. A very useful study of incontinence (*akrasia*) with reference to Socrates and Plato and in relation to Aristotle's own investigations as found in the *Nicomachean Ethics.*

Waterlow, Sarah. *Nature, Change and Agency in Aristotle's Physics: A Philosophical Study.* Oxford 1982 $37.50. Uses the *Physics* to illumine the concept of change and to show how Aristotle constructs the metaphysics of nature.

Wilbur, J. B., and H. J. Allen, eds. *The Worlds of Plato and Aristotle.* Prometheus Bks.

1979 pap. $11.95. A good selection brought together to illustrate the coherence of the systems; informative comments and notes.

Woodbridge, Frederick J. *Aristotle's Vision of Nature.* Ed. by John H. Randall, Jr., Greenwood repr. of 1965 ed. 1983 lib. bdg. $25.00. An impassioned overview of Aristotle's thought and his place in history, based on lectures edited posthumously.

EPICURUS. 341–270 B.C.

Epicurus founded his philosophical school and lived with his friends in his "Garden" in Athens when the city was witnessing the rise of Macedonian dominance and Greek politics reflected the ongoing crisis in values and virtues. Many thinkers felt the growing need for intellectual conservatism and voluntary withdrawal to secure a life of imperturbability. That his school became a model followed in other cities, including Rome, lasting for more than five hundred years, is both testimony to the strong appeal Epicurus's ethical doctrines exerted and a sign of the logical conviction the theory of Atomism generated in his followers. Epicurus, who knew the pre-Socratics well, revived and extended the Atomism of Democritus and Leucippus by finding broader applications for Atomism in psychology, physics, and ethics. Although the principles of the physical teachings of Epicurus were destined for a significant revival and, in certain ways, experimental confirmation in modern times, the special appeal of his philosophy was basically ethical. His physics remains the background to support a way of life aiming at the enhancement of pleasure and avoidance of pain. Epicurus's theories sought to reveal the causes of pain, especially fear, whether fear of death or of divine intervention. He taught that only the acquisition of knowledge helps in the effort to cope with fears and secure a happy life. His influence was felt strongly in Italy and found in Rome an eloquent spokesman in Lucretius, whose masterwork *De Rerum Natura* is by far the most complete exposition of Epicureanism.

BOOKS BY EPICURUS

Epicurea. Ed. by Herman Usener, Irvington repr. of 1887 ed. 1981 lib. bdg. $49.00. The standard collection of sources.

The Philosophy of Epicurus: Letters, Doctrines, and Parallel Passages from Lucretius. Ed. by George K. Strodach, Northwestern Univ. Pr. 1962 o.p. A scholarly collection of Epicurus's writings.

Epicurus: The Extant Remain, with Short Critical Apparatus. Trans. by Cyril Bailey, Hyperion Pr. repr. of 1926 ed. 1980 $32.50. Makes available the writings of Epicurus in English translation, with a guide to the text and the main ideas of Atomism.

BOOKS ABOUT EPICURUS

Asmis, Elizabeth. *Epicurus' Scientific Method.* Cornell Univ. Pr. 1984 $49.50. This work "offers on the whole judicious discussions of Epicurus' theory of perception and of the difficulties confronting his advocacy of the principle that all perceptions are true" (*TLS*).

Bailey, Cyril. *The Greek Atomists and Epicurus: A Study.* Russell repr. of 1928 ed.

1964 o.p. Still a leading study of Greek Atomism, with special attention to Epicurus's philosophy and its originality.

Clay, Diskin. *Lucretius and Epicurus*. Cornell Univ. Pr. 1983 $42.50. An excellent and thorough comparative study of the two philosophers and how Lucretius made innovations.

De Witt, Norman W. *Epicurus and His Philosophy*. Greenwood repr. of 1954 ed. 1973 lib. bdg. $65.00. A strong defense of Epicurus's doctrines concerning "the injustice of the centuries." A very readable account of Epicureanism in antiquity.

Furley, David J. *Two Studies in the Greek Atomists*. Princeton Univ. Pr. 1967 o.p. Two excellent essays, one on indivisible magnitudes and the other a comparative critical analysis of voluntary action in Aristotle and Epicurus, with reference to the earlier Atomists.

Panichas, George A. *Epicurus*. [*Twayne's World Authors Ser.*] G. K. Hall 1970 o.p. A good introduction to Epicurus's times and thought, written for the general reader; also discusses the fluctuations of Epicurus's influence throughout the centuries to recent times.

Rist, J. M. *Epicurus: An Introduction*. Cambridge Univ. Pr. 1972 o.p. A reliable introductory survey of Epicurus's life and doctrines with attention to critical problems.

Sedgwick, Henry D. *Art of Happiness or the Teachings of Epicurus*. [*Essay Index Repr. Ser.*] Ayer repr. of 1933 ed. $17.00. A balanced and sympathetic study of Epicurus's life and ethical goal of happiness.

Strozier, Robert M. *Epicurus and Hellenistic Philosophy*. Univ. Pr. of Amer. 1985 text ed. lib. bdg. $26.00 pap. $11.75. "Based on a reappraisal of Epicurus, this book argues that Epicurean thought underwent a significant development from Epicurus to Lucretius" (*Religious Studies Review*).

Wallace, William. *Epicureanism: Chief Ancient Philosophies*. Darby repr. of 1880 ed. 1980 lib. bdg. $30.00. Presents a sympathetic account of this movement and offers a number of still useful and valuable insights.

HERACLITUS OF EPHESUS. fl. c.500 B.C.

Heraclitus, an Ionian Greek, wrote the book *On Nature* and is credited with writing in a style so difficult that it earned him the reputation of the "dark" thinker. He posed with utter seriousness the problem of change and of an abiding unity that is the hidden "logic" of all reality, its hidden harmony. While strife generates all processes, these are measured and orderly. Nature is basically the element of fire, and so is soul. The extant fragments of his writings continue to perplex their readers, and recent philosophers of Heidegger's stature have found in Heraclitus's vision of reality a source of inspiration and a place to start in the search for wisdom. "Little is known about his life, and the one book he apparently wrote is lost. His views survive in the short fragments quoted and attributed to him by later authors" (*Encyclopaedia Britannica*).

BOOKS ABOUT HERACLITUS

Heidegger, Martin, and Eugen Fink. *Heraclitus Seminar, 1966–1967*. Trans. by Charles H. Seibert, Univ. of Alabama Pr. 1979 $18.75. This work has preserved the record of a seminar on Heraclitus, the unifying theme of which was the distinction of "the one and the many"; fragmentary but interesting.

Kahn, Charles H., ed. *The Art and Thought of Heraclitus: An Edition of the Fragments with Translation and Commentary*. Cambridge Univ. Pr. 1980 $44.50 1981 pap. $18.95. Discusses the thought of Heraclitus, emphasizing the place of logos-reason in nature and man, and offers also a new arrangement of the Diels-Kranz numbering of the fragments.

Kirk, G. S. *Heraclitus: The Cosmic Fragments*. Cambridge University Pr. 1954 $77.50. One of the most important books on Heraclitus to appear in English; especially valuable to readers who have a knowledge of Greek.

Sallis, John, and Kenneth Maly. *Heraclitean Fragments: A Companion Volume to the Heidegger-Fink Seminar on Heraclitus*. Univ. of Alabama Pr. 1980 $18.50. Contains essays on the fragments discussed by Heidegger.

Wheelwright, Phillip E. *Heraclitus*. Greenwood repr. of 1959 ed. 1981 lib. bdg. $22.50. A stimulating account and guide to the extant fragments.

PLATO. 427?–347 B.C.

Plato's real name was Aristocles. He was born into a wealthy, aristocratic Athenian family, and was a blood relation to Pericles and other illustrious Athenians. In his early years he preferred poetry to politics. This changed when he met Socrates, a decisive encounter in his life. Plato, more than any other thinker (with the exception of his pupil Aristotle), influenced profoundly the course of the intellectual history of the Western world. He witnessed the major events of the Peloponnesian War; saw the defeat of Athens, the rise of the Thirty Tyrants in the wake of the Spartan victory and then the return of the Democratic party, and the trial and death of Socrates in 399. He wrote superb dialogues, unsurpassable for content and style, in which Socrates figures as the dominant speaker. The dialogues form three groups: the early, middle, and later dialogues. In the later dialogues, the dramatic setting loses intensity, and the logical and metaphysical themes receive special treatment. They put before the reader the ideal of the life of reason and of responsible discourse in a relentless pursuit of truth. Plato's philosophy is an outgrowth of basic Socratic teachings and covers just about every field of inquiry. His famous theory of the Forms, which asserts the separate existence of transcendent values and universals, has been discussed and criticized or upheld by readers in every generation. We also have a number of letters stating his views in another style. The commentaries, books, and articles still being written on his works and the topics he treated constitute living testimony to the greatness of his thought and its relevance to Western culture. (See also Volume 3.)

BOOKS BY PLATO

The translations of Plato's dialogues, many of them now available in paperback editions, have increased greatly in number in recent decades, and continue to do so. The list given below, while far from being exhaustive, is intended only as a convenience to the interested student.

Opera. Ed. by John Burnet, Oxford 5 vols. 1900–07 vols. 1–4 $14.95 vol. 5 $24.95. The Greek text of the dialogues is available in many editions of individual dialogues. This is presently the authoritative text used by scholars.

Plato's Works. [*Loeb Class. Lib.*] Harvard Univ. Pr. 12 vols. 1914–35 ea. $13.95. This is the Greek text, accompanied by translation into English. All volumes have introductions and notes; the translation is printed on the facing page.

The Collected Dialogues of Plato. Ed. by E. Hamilton and H. Cairns, trans. by various individuals, Pantheon 1961 o.p.; Princeton Univ. Pr. repr. of 1961 ed. 1984 $26.00. Includes the letters. This is the most convenient collection of Plato's dialogues in translation.

Also recommended for their quality are the following translations of individual dialogues or groups of dialogues:

Five Dialogues. [*Philosophical Class. Ser.*] Intro. by Donald J. Zeyl, Hackett 1981 text ed. $12.50 pap. $4.25

The Dialogues of Plato: Euthyphro; Apology; Crito; Meno; Gorgias; Menexenus. Trans. by R. E. Allen, Yale Univ. Pr. 1985 text ed. $32.50. "Excellent individual introductions keyed to the translations" (*Choice*).

Plato's Euthyphro. Intro. by William A. Heidel [*History of Ideas Ser.*] Ayer repr. 1976 $13.00

Plato's Parmenides: Translation and Analysis. Trans. by R. E. Allen, Univ. of Minnesota Pr. 1983 $25.00. An excellent work highly recommended for content and argument, in addition to offering a reliable translation.

The Last Days of Socrates. Trans. by Hugh Tredennick [*Penguin Class. Ser.*] 1954 pap. $3.95

The Trial and Death of Socrates. Trans. by John Warrington, Biblio Dist. repr. of 1963 ed. 1969 $12.95; ed. by Lane Cooper, Burt Franklin repr. of 1941 ed. $14.50; trans. by G. M. Grube, Hackett 1975 pap. $2.25

The Republic. Basic Bks. 1968 text ed. pap. $8.95; trans. by A. D. Lindsay, Biblio Dist. (Everyman's) 1980 pap. $5.95; ed. by James Adam, Cambridge Univ. Pr. 1966 2 vols. text ed. ea. $67.50–$80.00; trans. by A. D. Lindsay, Dutton 1957 pap. $6.75; trans. by G. M. Grube, Hackett 1973 $12.50 text ed. pap. $4.95; trans. by Raymond Larson [*Crofts Class. Ser.*] Harlan Davidson 1979 text ed. $14.95 pap. $6.95; trans. by Benjamin Jowett, Modern Lib. 1982 $7.95; trans. by Francis M. Cornford, Oxford 1945 pap. $4.95; trans. by H. D. Lee [*Penguin Class. Ser.*] 1955 pap. $3.50; trans. by Benjamin Jowett, Random 1955 pap. $3.95. One of the major dialogues of Plato in which he expounds his theories on the structure of justice, of science, and of the soul.

Protagoras. Trans. by C. C. W. Taylor, Oxford 1976 $29.50. "Designed for the Greekless reader. It provides the biographical, historical, and linguistic information requisite for understanding the setting of this important Dialogue, whose themes cover a range of political, cultural, and ethical issues. . . . The translation is in a comfortably modern idiom, with good notes on the more difficult cross-cultural abstractions" (*Choice*).

The Symposium. Trans. by Benjamin Jowett, intro. by F. H. Anderson, Bobbs 1956 pap. $3.00; trans. by Benjamin Jowett, Branden 1983 pap. $3.00; ed. by K. J. Dover Cambridge Univ. Pr. 1980 $39.50 pap. $16.95; trans. by W. Hamilton [*Penguin Class. Ser.*] 1952 pap. $2.95; ed. by John A. Brentlinger, trans. by Suzy Q. Groden, Univ. of Massachusetts Pr. 1970 $12.00 pap. $6.95. An aesthetic and mystical dialogue written at the height of Plato's dramatic power, which records several banquet eulogies of *eros* (desirous love).

The Laws: History. Intro. by E. B. England [*History of Ideas in Ancient Greece Ser.*] Ayer repr. of 1921 ed. 1976 $97.50; trans. by Thomas L. Pangle, Basic Bks. 1979 $26.50 pap. $11.95; trans. by T. J. Saunders [*Penguin Class. Ser.*] 1970 pap. $4.95. "Plato's longest and most intensely practical work contains his ripest utterances on ethics, education, and jurisprudence, as well as his one entirely nonmythical exposition of theology" (*Encyclopaedia Britannica*).

The Platonic Epistles. Trans. by J. Howard [*History of Ideas Ser.*] Ayer repr. of 1932 ed. 1976 $19.00

BOOKS ABOUT PLATO

Annas, Julia. *An Introduction to Plato's Republic.* Oxford 1981 text ed. pap. $10.95. Especially insightful in discussing Plato's distinctions of types of consequences of justice; identifies the dominant moral themes with analytical precision.

Ast, Freidrich. *Lexicon Platonicum Sive Vacum Platonicarum Index, 1835–1838.* Burt Franklin 3 vols. 1969 $89.00. The only available lexicon of Plato's technical vocabulary with reference to key passages in each dialogue.

Barker, Ernest. *Political Thought of Plato and Aristotle.* Dover 1959 pap. $9.95. Traces the origins of political thought in Greece and devotes the first four chapters to Plato and his Socratic predecessors.

Brumbaugh, Robert S. *Plato's Mathematical Imagination: The Mathematical Passages in the Dialogues and Their Interpretation.* Kraus Repr. 1954 $26.00. A competent inquiry into Platonic mathematics "as it is revealed in mathematical imagery," with ample references to recent theories and views.

Burger, Ronna. *The Phaedo: A Platonic Labyrinth.* Yale Univ. Pr. 1984 text ed. $27.50. An interpretive reading of the dramatic structure of this dialogue to show that it corresponds to basic themes and the question of the duality of body and soul in particular.

Burnet, John. *Platonism.* Greenwood repr. of 1928 ed. 1983 lib. bdg. $27.50. A sensitive account of Plato's thought by the eminent editor of the Oxford standard text of Plato's works.

Campbell, Lewis. *The Theaetetus of Plato.* [*Ancient Philosophy Ser.*] Garland 2d ed. 1980 lib. bdg. $43.00. This book is recognized as a landmark for laying the ground for the stylometric tests to decide questions about the chronological order of Plato's dialogues.

Cherniss, Harold F. *Aristotle's Criticism of Plato and the Academy.* Russell repr. of 1944 ed. 1962 $23.00. A challenging work of high scholarship in which the author analyzes the basis for Aristotle's "misguided" criticism of Plato's theory of ideas and numbers.

———. *The Riddle of the Early Academy.* [*Ancient Philosophy Ser.*] Garland 1982 lib. bdg. $18.00. The "riddle" is created by the discrepancy between what Aristotle reports and what Plato writes. Discusses the nature of studies in the Academy and explores the connection between the character of the school and the thought it produced.

Clegg, Jerry S. *The Structure of Plato's Philosophy.* Bucknell Univ. Pr. 1978 $20.00. A close discussion of such central topics as Plato's metaphysics, theory of knowledge, psychology, theory of art, and politics, delineating a unifying structure and consistency in Plato's position.

Cornford, F. M. *Plato and Parmenides.* Routledge & Kegan 1939 o.p. Translation with running commentary tying the logical exercises of the *Parmenides* with that of Parmenides' poem, *Way of Truth.*

———. *Plato's Cosmology.* Routledge & Kegan 1937 o.p. Translation with running commentary offering a comprehensive analysis of Plato's myth on the creation of the physical world.

———. *Plato's Theory of Knowledge: The Theateus and the Sophist of Plato.* Macmillan

1957 text ed. pap. $3.50. Translation with running commentary, displaying the continuity of problems about knowledge and reality in the *Theaetetus* and the *Sophist*.

———. *The Republic of Plato*. Oxford 1941 o.p. Translation with running commentary discussing Plato's political views and method of arguing in defense of their validity.

Crombie, I. M. *An Examination of Plato's Doctrines*. [*International Lib. of Philosophy and Scientific Method*] Humanities Pr. 2 vols. vol. 1 1962 vol. 2 1963 o.p. Volume 1 is on Plato's theories of human nature and society; Volume 2 is a closely and well argued analysis of his theories of reality and knowledge.

———. *Plato: The Midwife's Apprentice*. Greenwood repr. of 1965 ed. 1981 lib. bdg. $22.50. In this shorter work Crombie brings together in highly readable form the conclusions of his two-volume study.

Cushman, Robert E. *Therapeia: Plato's Conception of Philosophy*. Greenwood repr. of 1958 ed. 1976 lib. bdg. $42.50. A challenging book based mainly on the view that Plato understood the problem of man as a plight for which a *therapeia* must be sought. Order in the realm of becoming was to be achieved through a way of life devoted to the search for good and being.

During, Ingemar, and G. E. Owen, eds. *Aristotle and Plato in the Mid-Fourth Century*. Humanities Pr. 1960 text ed. $25.00. An excellent collection of essays by different authors, setting high standards in recent Platonic scholarship.

Elias, Julius A. *Plato's Defence of Poetry*. State Univ. of New York Pr. 1984 $44.50 pap. $17.95. Argues that Plato restored the place of poetry in philosophy and political life—expelled in the *Republic*—by actually conjoining the value of poetry to high-minded myth.

Ficino, Marsilio. *Commentary on Plato's Symposium on Love*. Trans. by Sears Jayne, Spring Pubns. 2d ed. rev. 1985 pap. $18.50. Translation from the Latin text of Ficino's celebrated and influential book on Platonic love.

Field, G. C. *Plato and His Contemporaries*. [*Studies in Philosophy*] Haskell 1974 lib. bdg. $75.00. This well-known book was written as a preliminary to the study of Plato. It describes the times and climate of opinion in Plato's Athens and relates his writings to the literary, historical, and philosophical background.

Gadamer, Hans Georg. *Dialogue and Dialectic: Eight Hermeneutical Studies on Plato*. Intro. by P. Christopher Smith, Yale Univ. Pr. 1980 text ed. $27.50 1983 pap. $8.95. Brings together several studies on basic Platonic topics: dialectic, immortality, truth, reason, poetry, and community, with an emphasis on the dialogue form and the dramatic situation.

———. *The Idea of the Good in Platonic-Aristotelian Philosophy*. Trans. by P. Christopher Smith, Yale Univ. Pr. 1986 $20.00. A series of lectures attempting to show a fundamental agreement between the two philosophers on the concept of the good; the agreement is explained on the basis of their common departure from the moral experience.

Gosling, J. C. *Plato*. [*Arguments of the Philosophers*] Methuen 1984 pap. $9.95. A close analysis of Plato's thesis on method and the theory of Forms.

Grene, David. *Greek Political Theory: The Image of Man in Thucydides and Plato*. Univ. of Chicago Pr. 1965 pap. $1.95. The second part of the book concentrates on Plato as a theorist of politics and a reflective teacher of the art of government.

Grube, G. M. *Plato's Thought*. Intro. by Donald Z. Zeyl, Hackett repr. of 1935 ed. 1980 text ed. $25.00 pap. $9.95. Reissued with new introduction and bibliographic essay. Written with sensitivity to the original texts and the demands of the philosophic issues. One of the best introductions available, with a high degree of faithfulness to Plato's thought.

Gulley, Norman. *Plato's Theory of Knowledge.* Greenwood repr. of 1962 ed. 1986 lib. bdg. $39.75. Traces the development of this theory by discussing in detail Plato's concepts of perception, belief, reason, and sensation, going back to the *Meno* and the *Phaedo* but concentrating mainly on the later Platonic dialogues.

Hall, Robert W. *Plato.* [*Political Thinkers Ser.*] Allen & Unwin 1981 text ed. $24.95 pap. $9.95. Deals with Plato's political and legal views as found in the *Republic,* the *Statesman,* and the *Laws;* also discusses Plato's influence on later thinkers. Lucidly written.

Hare, R. M. *Plato.* [*Past Masters Ser.*] Oxford 1982 $13.95 pap. $4.95. A good general introduction to Plato's major themes.

Havelock, Eric A. *Preface to Plato.* Havard Univ. Pr. 1982 text ed. $8.95. Taking Plato as a point of departure, the discussion leads to early Greek thought to show that it is rooted in the oral tradition.

Joseph, Horace W. *Knowledge and the Good in Plato's Republic.* [*Oxford Classical and Philosophical Monographs*] Greenwood repr. of 1948 ed. 1981 lib. bdg. $22.50. A good account explaining the myth of the sun, the divided line, and the myth of the cave to show how they support the doctrine of the Forms and the way they are interrelated.

Klein, Jacob. *Plato's Trilogy: Theaetetus, the Sophist, and the Statesman.* Univ. of Chicago Pr. 1977 text ed. $16.00 1980 pap. $7.50. A rich discussion of the dramatic quality of the *Meno,* aiming to bring the reader into active participation to view the roles of the interlocutors of Socrates and their ways of embodying virtue.

Koyré, Alexandre. *Discovering Plato.* Trans. by Leonora C. Rosenfield, Columbia Univ. Pr. 1960 o.p. A lively account of select Platonic works to illustrate the method of philosophical dialogue and the range of Plato's doctrines on politics.

Lodge, R. C. *Plato's Theory of Art.* Russell repr. of 1953 ed. 1975 o.p. Uses art in the broadest sense to include the art of politics at the apex of human activity, and shows how for Plato all arts function best in the integrated life of the ideal city.

———. *Plato's Theory of Education.* Russell repr. of 1947 ed. 1970 $21.00. Defends the practical side of Plato's theory of education first as vocational and professional, then leading to political and philosophical leadership.

———. *Plato's Theory of Ethics: The Moral Criterion and the Highest Good.* Shoe String repr. of 1928 ed. 1966 $45.00. Extensive discussion of what Plato proposes as the moral criterion of the highest good as compared with that of the other values.

Lutoslawski, Wincenty. *The Origin and Growth of Plato's Logic: With an Account of Plato's Style and the Chronology of His Writings.* [*Classical Studies Ser.*] Irvington repr. of 1897 ed. 1981 lib. bdg. $59.00. In this important work, the author expanded and elaborated on the findings of Lewis Campbell (see above), using the stylometric method of dating the dialogues.

Lynch, William F. *Approach to the Metaphysics of Plato through the Parmenides.* Greenwood repr. of 1959 ed. 1968 lib. bdg. $15.00. Offers a step-by-step interpretation of the hypotheses in this Platonic dialogue and argues ably that Plato's metaphysics is one of unity in which each form participates in a one-many mode relationship.

McKirahan, Richard D., Jr. *Plato and Socrates: A Comprehensive Bibliography, 1958–1973.* [*Lib. of Humanities Reference Bks.*] Garland 1978 o.p. "Containing 4620 entries culled from hundreds of periodicals and numerous books, the work is divided into 14 subject sections with six on Plato and five on Socrates. The subject arrangements are easy to use and will be a boon to scholars concerned with a specific dialogue or aspect of either philosopher's life and work" (*LJ*).

Moline, Jon. *Plato's Theory of Understanding.* Univ. of Wisconsin Pr. 1981 $27.50.

"Moline's discussion is a rich one, moving from an examination of pre-Platonic philologica and philosophical usage of the term *Episteme* through closely and clearly argued accounts of Plato's dialectic, psychology, epistemology and theory of Forms" (*Choice*).

Moravcsik, Julius, and Phillip Temko, eds. *Plato on Beauty, Wisdom and the Arts.* Rowman 1982 $27.50. Six papers on Plato's theory of art and beauty, aiming at dissolving the paradox of Plato's love of beauty and expulsion of the artist.

More, Paul E. *Platonism.* AMS Pr. 3d ed. repr. of 1931 ed. 1973 $12.75; Greenwood repr. of 1931 ed. 1970 lib. bdg. $22.50. A full survey of Plato's doctrines by a sympathetic follower of Plato in the early part of the twentieth century.

Morrow, Glenn R. *Plato's Slavery in Its Relation to Greek Law.* Ayer repr. of 1939 ed. 1976 o.p. Recognized as an admirable study on the complex issue of Plato's views on slavery and how it compares to current laws in Athens and Attica.

Murdoch, Iris. *The Fire and the Sun: Why Plato Banished the Artists.* Oxford 1977 pap. $6.95. In the Romanes Lecture in 1976, Murdoch reexamines the celebrated question of whether Plato meant to banish all the artists and uses the occasion to discuss Plato's views on beauty in light of comparable theories in modern philosophy and literature.

Nettleship, Richard L. *Lectures on the Republic of Plato.* Folcroft repr. of 1897 ed. 1975 lib. bdg. $47.00; ed. by G. R. Benson, Richard West repr. of 1898 ed. 1976 $49.50. One of the classic treatments of Plato's great work still studied for its balanced interpretation of Plato's conception of political philosophy.

Pater, Walter H. *Plato and Platonism.* Greenwood repr. of 1910 ed. 1970 lib. bdg. $22.50; Richard West repr. of 1910 ed. $35.00. Essays based on a series of lectures to make accessible to the layperson Plato's doctrines by drawing a vivid portrait of the philosopher.

Patterson, Richard. *Image and Reality in Plato's Metaphysics.* Hackett 1985 lib. bdg. $27.50 text ed. pap. $12.75. Examines the concepts of image and model with reference to the sensible world and in the context of the theory of the Forms.

Prior, William J. *Unity and Development in Plato's Metaphysics.* Open Court 1985 $24.95. A useful work for the Greekless reader; it traces the unity of Plato's metaphysics through six dialogues, including the *Timaeus* and the *Sophist*.

Randall, John H. *Plato: Dramatist of the Life of Reason.* Columbia Univ. Pr. repr. of 1970 ed. 1973 o.p. An unconventional but challenging and illuminating interpretation of Plato and his philosophy. The dialogues are presented here as "dramatic portrayals of the life of mind," setting forth a coherent and remarkably complete vision of life, which makes Plato the "dramatist of the life of reason."

Raven, J. E. Earle John. *Plato's Thought in the Making: A Study of the Development of His Metaphysics.* Greenwood repr. of 1965 ed. 1985 lib. bdg. $39.75. Concentrating on the middle dialogues as the ones "of the greatest potential to the non-specialist," the author proceeds with a rigorous treatment of the metaphysical themes in Plato's later works to unravel their conceptual implications.

Robinson, Richard. *Plato's Earlier Dialectic.* [*Ancient Philosophy Ser.*] Garland 2d ed. 1982 lib. bdg. $36.00; Oxford 2d ed. repr. of 1953 ed. 1984 pap. $13.95. Excellent on the method of examination and refutation in the early and middle Platonic dialogues.

Robinson, T. M. *Plato's Psychology.* Univ. of Toronto Pr. 1971 o.p. A thorough discussion of the Platonic views on the human soul in light of what modern authorities have said on the subject. Discounts the late Neoplatonic interpretations.

Rosen, Stanley. *Plato's Sophist: The Drama of Original and Image.* Yale Univ. Pr. 1983 text ed. $30.00 1986 pap. $14.95. A cogent and comprehensive study of Plato's understanding of the difference between the philosopher and the sophist.

————. *Plato's Symposium.* Yale Univ. Pr. 1987 $40.00 pap. $15.95. An important contribution to the literature on this dialogue using the concept of irony to scan the range of the significance of Plato's erotic doctrines.

Ross, W. D. *Plato's Theory of Ideas.* Greenwood repr. of 1951 ed. 1976 lib. bdg. $29.75. Ross advances the position that Plato's development is from the immanence of the Forms toward their transcendence, although Plato himself was never convinced that his theory was completely satisfactory.

Ryle, Gilbert. *Plato's Progress.* Cambridge Univ. Pr. 1966 o.p. Ryle raises anew the question of Plato's development by rejecting the division between "Socratic" and non-Socratic dialogues, a position that has been widely discussed.

Saunders, Trevor J. *Bibliography on Plato's Laws 1920–1970, with Additional Citations through May 1975.* [*History of Ideas Ser.*] Ayer repr. 1976 $21.00. "A list of the books and articles on *Laws* which have appeared since the first publication of E. B. England's *Commentary.* Saunders' work is partially inspired by the reprint of *Commentary* in 1975 (Arno Press)" (*Classical World*).

Sayre, Kenneth M. *Plato's Analytic Method.* Univ. of Chicago Pr. 1969 $17.50. A well-written study on the development of Plato's philosophical methodology as found in the middle dialogues and how it blossoms as the employment of analysis in the *Theaetetus* and the *Sophist.*

Shorey, Paul. *The Unity of Plato's Thought.* [*Ancient Philosophy Ser.*] Garland 1980 lib. bdg. $15.00. "The text of this book is a résumé of the entire body of the Platonic writings. The endeavor has been to omit no significant ideas and to give with every idea enough of the dramatic setting and the over- and undertones of feeling" (Preface).

Sinaiko, Herman L. *Love, Knowledge, and Discourse in Plato: Dialogue and Dialectic in "Phaedrus," "Republic," "Parmenides."* [*Midway Repr. Ser.*] Univ. of Chicago Pr. 1979 text ed. pap. $13.50. Argues that Plato's conception of philosophy required the employment of the dramatic form, and demonstrates this thesis by scrutinizing three dialogues of the middle and late periods, *Phaedrus, Republic,* and *Parmenides.*

Skemp, J. B. *The Theory of Motion in Plato's Later Dialogues.* Coronet repr. of 1942 ed. lib. bdg. $33.00. A comprehensive discussion of the problem of reality and how it should be viewed as including the immovable Forms as well as movement and life. The thesis of this work is that things in motion and in rest as well as the Forms of motion and rest all partake in being.

Solmsen, Friedrich. *Plato's Theology.* Johnson Repr. 1942 $24.00. A careful study centered around Plato's view of the soul as self-moving regarded here as the foundation Plato used for a new cosmic religion beyond civic forms of worship.

Stalley, R. F. *An Introduction to Plato's Laws.* Hackett 1983 text ed. $21.50. Discusses Plato's *Laws* topic by topic to give a unitarian interpretation of his political philosophy.

Stuart, J. A. *The Myths of Plato.* State Mutual Bk. 1983 $60.00. A collection of the major Platonic myths together with an interpretation of their significance from an idealistic point of view.

Taylor, A. E. *Commentary on Plato's Timaeus.* Oxford 1928 o.p. A monumental work discussing every aspect of Plato's views on the creation of the physical universe without ignoring the feature of the *Timaeus* that gives warning of the provisional character of the many theories advanced there.

————. *Plato: The Man and His Work.* Methuen 1960 pap. $16.95. Offers close analyses of all the dialogues, along with very useful commentary, notable for its influence on scholarship.

Tracy, Theodore J. *Physiological Theory and the Doctrine of the Mean in Plato and*

Aristotle. [*Studies in Philosophy*] Mouton 1969 text ed. pap. $28.80. Explores in great detail the doctrine of the mean in Plato, Aristotle, and the Hippocratic writings to show how essential it is to health and intellectual exercise.

Versényi, Laszlo. *Holiness and Justice: An Interpretation of Plato's "Euthyphro."* Univ. Pr. of Amer. 1982 lib. bdg. $24.00 text ed. pap. $11.25. The author takes the position that the *Euthyphro* offers a positive thesis on holiness and knowledge about it; written clearly and with awareness of recent literature.

Vlastos, Gregory. *Platonic Studies.* Princeton Univ. Pr. 2d ed. repr. of 1973 ed. 1981 pap. $16.00. This edition brings together the author's major papers along with several new studies, covering fundamental issues in Plato's metaphysics, ethics, and social philosophy.

————. *Plato's Universe.* Univ. of Washington Pr. 1975 pap. o.p. The John Danz Lectures on the Greek view of the ordered universe and Plato's theories of celestial motion and the constitution of matter.

————, ed. *Plato, One: Metaphysics & Epistemology; a Collection of Critical Essays.* Univ. of Notre Dame Pr. 1978 text ed. pap. $9.95. Both this and the next title contain representative essays by various hands that generated new approaches and explorations reflecting intense interest among European and Anglo-American specialists in ancient philosophy; of the 30 articles included in both collections, only 5 had their first publication here.

————. *Plato, Two: Ethics, Politics, & Philosophy of Art & Religion; a Collection of Critical Essays.* Univ. of Notre Dame Pr. 1978 text ed. pap. $9.95

Voegelin, Eric. *Plato and Aristotle.* Vol. 3 in *Order and History.* Louisiana State Univ. Pr. 1957 $19.95. Part 1 discusses the philosophy of Plato as a precise system of symbols advancing beyond the symbolic framework of the older myth and marking, with Aristotle's system, the high point of philosophy among the Greeks.

Wedberg, Anders. *Plato's Philosophy of Mathematics.* Greenwood repr. of 1955 ed. 1977 lib. bdg. $22.50. An attempt to bring Plato's philosophy of mathematics in line with Aristotle's interpretation of Plato; very technical.

White, Nicholas P. *A Companion to Plato's Republic.* Hackett 1979 text ed. $19.50 pap. $8.50. A readable and reliable guide to the main philosophical issues in Plato's political thought.

————. *Plato on Knowledge and Reality.* Hackett 1976 $30.00 pap. $17.50. The analysis moves progressively through the key dialogues to identify and reconstruct Plato's views on human knowledge of authentic reality and the role of language.

Wild, John. *Plato's Theory of Man.* Hippocrene Bks. 1964 lib. bdg. $27.00. Places in perspective Wild's interpretation of Plato's political philosophy as being in accordance with a coherent theory of natural law.

Woodbridge, F. J. *The Son of Apollo: Themes of Plato.* Biblo & Tannen repr. of 1929 ed. 1972 $12.00. This imaginative and unorthodox view of Plato's writings sees them as the dramatization of the life of reason and illustrates this approach with discussions of Plato's major themes—love, education, politics, and death.

PYTHAGORAS OF SAMOS. c.582–c.507 B.C.

Legend has it that Pythagoras of Samos coined the word *philosophia,* which literally means "love of wisdom." Whereas the Milesians sought a physical element as the origin of all things and proceeded from there to work out a cosmology, their younger contemporary Pythagoras, who was considered one of the wisest and ablest of all Greeks, introduced the idea that the world is made of numbers and that its mathematical structure makes it a harmonious system. He and his disciples—actually one cannot tell them apart—proposed a table of opposites, on which one finds form and matter, limited and unlimited, good and evil, odd and even. One of these Pythagoreans, Philopaus, actually taught that the earth revolves around its axis. Later on, another scientist and astronomer, Aristarchus of Samos, declared in 281 B.C. that the sun is immobile and that all the planets, including the earth, revolve around it. Pythagoras advocated the pursuit of the "philosophical" life to purify the soul in hope of ending its transmigrations or reincarnations.

BOOKS ABOUT PYTHAGORAS OF SAMOS

Burkert, Walter. *Love and Science in Ancient Pythagoreanism.* Trans. by Edwin L. Minar, Jr., Harvard Univ. Pr. 1972 $35.00. An excellent critical study of what is legend and what is reliable evidence about the views held by this school.

Minar, Edwin L., Jr. *Early Pythagorean Politics in Practice and Theory.* Ed. by Gregory Vlastos, Ayer repr. of 1942 ed. 1979 lib. bdg. $12.00. A thoroughly documented account of the religious and political activities related to Pythagorean principles.

Philip, James A. *Pythagoras and Early Pythagoreanism.* [*Phoenix Ser.*] Univ. of Chicago Pr. 1968 pap. $58.00. Drawing chiefly on Aristotelian references, this book argues whether Pythagoras was a shaman or a philosopher.

Raven, J. E. *Pythagoreans and Eleatics: An Account of the Interaction between Two Opposed Schools.* Ares Pubs. 1981 $12.50; Coronet repr. of 1948 ed. lib. bdg. $24.00. An authoritative account of the early phase of the Pythagorean movement and its impact of the rise of the school of Elea in Southern Italy.

SOCRATES. 469 B.C.–399 B.C.

Socrates of Athens developed to a high degree the method of dialectic not only to refute the Sophists but mainly to advance the thesis that universal standards exist. He wrote nothing—his teachings were entirely oral—but he influenced many in his lifetime and those who came after him. Socrates introduced a new, personal approach to philosophy; "know thyself" was his motto.

Socrates was born just a decade after the decisive naval battal of Salamis. He grew up during the Periclean Age and lived through the Peloponnesian Wars. His endurance, valor, and loyalty to his friends are described in detail by Plato and Xenophon. He associated with many of the leading members of the Periclean circle and attempted to train several of the youth in political responsibility, while he himself shunned a political career. His criticisms of public views and policies led to his indictment, and in 399 he was put to death on the charge of corrupting the youth and introducing new deities. To the last day, Socrates continued his quest for the examined life and spent the morning hours with his followers discussing the nature of the soul and the meaning of immortality.

Plato wrote four dialogues in which Socrates is the chief speaker, and these are known as the Socratic dialogues. The *Euthyphro* discusses holiness and piety; the *Apology* is Socrates' defense before his judges; *Crito* is Socrates' answer to a proposal that he attempt escape from jail; *Phaedo* is the story of how Socrates drank the hemlock and died. For the Socratic dialogues, see the books by Plato under Plato's main entry in this chapter. (See also the section on the Sophists in this chapter.)

BOOKS ABOUT SOCRATES

Allen, R. E. *Socrates and Legal Obligation*. Univ. of Minnesota Pr. 1981 $19.50 pap. $8.95. An outstanding examination of the early dialogues of Plato on Socrates' trial.

Dannhauser, Werner J. *Nietzsche's View of Socrates*. Cornell Univ. Pr. 1974 $29.95. "A useful and instructive addition to the growing critical literature on Nietzsche" (*Choice*); it underscores Nietzsche's ambivalent attitude toward Socrates.

Dawson, M. M. *The Ethics of Socrates: A Compilation*. Gordon Pr. $59.95; [*Studies in Philosophy*] Haskell 1974 lib. bdg. $75.00. A convenient sourcebook of *testimonia* bearing on Socrates' distinct ethical theory.

Guthrie, William K. *Socrates*. Cambridge Univ. Pr. 1971 pap. $14.95. Extracted from Volume 3 of his *A History of Greek Philosophy* (see under General Works, Histories and Texts, in this chapter).

Kraut, Richard. *Socrates and the State*. Princeton Univ. Pr. 1984 $45.00 1987 pap. $10.50. A close analysis of Socrates' position as a victim of politics and defender of the law.

O'Brien, Michael J. *The Socratic Paradoxes and the Greek Mind*. Univ. of North Carolina Pr. 1967 o.p. An outstanding work examining closely the paradoxes attending the conceptualization of the relationship between knowledge and virtue.

Santas, Gerasimos X. *Socrates*. [*Arguments of the Philosophers Ser.*] Methuen 1979 $26.95 1982 pap. $10.95. A detailed and absorbing account of views and arguments pertaining mainly to the Socratic method and ethics.

Strauss, Leo. *Socrates and Aristophanes*. [*Midway Repr. Ser.*] Univ. of Chicago Pr. repr. of 1966 ed. 1980 text ed. pap. $18.00. A close reading and interpretation of the comedies of Aristophanes for the light they cast on Socrates' moral and political teachings.

Taylor, A. E. *Socrates*. Greenwood repr. of 1951 ed. 1975 lib. bdg. $22.50; Hyperion Pr. repr. of 1951 ed. 1986 $19.75. Socrates' biography reconstructed on the basis of various reports, especially Plato's.

Vlastos, Gregory, ed. *The Philosophy of Socrates: A Collection of Critical Essays*. [*Modern Studies in Philosophy*] Univ. of Notre Dame Pr. repr. of 1971 ed. 1980 text ed. pap. $9.95. Brings together some previously published and five original essays by various scholars, examining once again the Socratic doctrines.

THEOPHRASTUS OF ERESUS. c.372–c.287 B.C.

Theophrastus assumed the leadership of the Lyceum at Aristotle's death. He was industrious and learned but lacking in originality. His importance lies in carrying on the research Aristotle had firmly established and in attracting numerous students to the school. Diogenes Laertius preserved whatever we know about Theophrastus, especially the long list of his writings—220 titles. Only a few of his treatises survived: *Enquiry into Plants* and *On the Causes of Plants*, a brief philosophical essay known as "Metaphysics," fragments of his *Physical Opinions*, and a literary work titled *Characters*.

Other important members of the Peripatetic school and successors to its leadership were Dikaiarchos of Messene, Aristoxenus, Clearchus, Demetrius of Phaleron, Stration of Lampsakos, Herakleides Ponticus, Eudemus of Rhodes; of special interest are Andronicus of Rhodes (first century B.C.), who edited the works of Aristotle, and Alexander of Aphrodisias (ca. A.D. 200), who wrote important commentaries on Aristotle's *De Anima* and *Metaphysics*.

BOOKS BY THEOPHRASTUS

Metaphysics, trans. and ed. by W. D. Ross and F. H. Fobes. Oxford Univ. Pr. 1929 o.p. An excellent and rare edition, the best available, with introduction and valuable commentary.

The Characters of Theophrastus. Ayer repr. of 1909 ed. 1979 lib. bdg. $19.00. Makes available Theophrastus's collection of 30 brief delineations of typical characters illustrative of Aristotle's pictures of representative kinds of people discussed in the ethics.

BOOKS ABOUT THEOPHRASTUS

Fortenbaugh, William W., ed. *Theophrastus of Eresus: On His Life and Work.* [*Studies in Classical Humanities*] Transaction Bks. 1985 text ed. $49.95. The results of recent work by specialists have been brought together in this collection of essays; an excellent work.

Stratton, G. M. *Theophrastus and the Greek Physiological Psychology before Aristotle.* [*Classical Studies Ser.*] Irvington repr. of 1917 ed. 1981 lib. bdg. $52.00. A fine and dependable account of what has survived of Theophrastus's great work on the history of physics.

XENOPHON. c.430–c.355 B.C.

Socrates' influence grew and a number of "Socratic" schools were formed, each claiming to give an authentic interpretation of his teachings on virtue and dialectic—for example, the Megarians, the Cyrenaics, and the Cynics. Meanwhile, Xenophon, an admirer of Socrates who was more practical than intellectual, preserved a record of what he saw and understood from his association with the "teacher." His writings as historian of both military and cultural events have survived. Xenophon's *Memorabilia, Apology of Socrates*, and *Symposium* give a picture from the common person's point of view that complements that of Aristophanes, the comic poet, whose caricature of Socrates colored the perception of his contemporaries in no small way, as Plato reports in his own *Apology*.

BOOK BY XENOPHON

Memorabilia. Ed. by W. R. Connor, Ayer repr. of 1903 ed. 1979 lib. bdg. $23.00. A convenient and useful edition with informative notes.

BOOKS ABOUT XENOPHON

Anderson, J. K. *Xenophon.* [*Class. Life and Letters Ser.*] Biblio Dist. 1979 $40.50 pap. $12.50. A general introduction to the life and times of Xenophon.

Higgins, W. E. *Xenophon the Athenian: The Problem of the Individual and the Society of the Polis.* State Univ. of New York Pr. 1977 $49.50. Discusses the social and political aspects of Xenophon's writings, especially as they relate to Socrates.

Lander, Mary K. *Index in Xenophontis Memorabilia.* Johnson Repr. repr. of 1900 ed. $12.00. A compilation of lexical uses and themes.

Strauss, Leo. *Xenophon's Socratic Discourse: An Interpretation of the Oeconomicus.* Fwd. by A. Bloom, Cornell Univ. Pr. 1973 pap. $8.95. A chapter-by-chapter discussion of the dialogue to provide a guide to the understanding of Xenophon and the Socratic views he recorded.

ROMAN PHILOSOPHERS

It is not possible to speak of a distinct philosophical school in the case of Rome, but the term *Roman* can be used comprehensively to cover the diverse character of interests and trends Roman thinkers adopted and cultivated with evident fervor and taste. On the whole, it is fair to say that what determined the scope and quality of philosophical activity in Rome was not the Hellenic passion for knowledge but its usefulness for education and public policy. Thus it is no surprise to find that, due to this utilitarian motive, the most popular philosophies were Epicureanism and Stoicism—but without any deep interest in their technical parts. The Epicureans were the first to go to Rome, and their doctrines found in Lucretius a great poetic spokesman. Yet the political climate was such that it made Stoicism more acceptable to the Roman intellectuals and poets, who added to it moral and religious sentiments of their own, resulting thus in a world outlook that was more emphatically eclectic than it was internally coherent. In formulating their eclecticism the Romans were aided by three Greek teachers of philosophy: Panaetius of Rhodes (180–111 B.C.), Posidonius of Apamea (c.135–c.51 B.C.), and Antiochus of Ascalon (128–68 B.C.), the teacher of Cicero. A close reading of Cicero, Seneca, and Marcus Aurelius shows how the Romans' practical experience helped them form their own version of Stoicism, perhaps the only genuine Roman contribution to philosophy. We find here an explicit deification of nature, together with the idea of a universal reason, a view that will reemerge strongly in the philosophies of the eighteenth century.

The Roman mind, seeking to make secure a world in which civilized humanity could be guided by law, duty, and loyalty, found no special appeal in the originality of Greek philosophy or in its devotion to the pursuit of theoretical knowledge. It is not surprising that a version of Stoicism finally prevailed, since it gave the intellectuals what they needed to reflect on the beliefs they already had. (See also Volume 2, Chapter 8, "Latin Literature.")

General Works

Arnold, E. Vernon. *Roman Stoicism: Being Lectures.* [*Select Bibliographies Repr. Ser.*] Ayer facsimile repr. of 1911 ed. $27.50; Irvington repr. of 1911 ed. $26.50; Richard West repr. of 1911 ed. o.p. One of the best earlier attempts to discuss this phase of Stoicism and relate it to modern thought.

Clark, Martin L. *The Roman Mind: Studies in the History of Thought from Cicero to Marcus Aurelius.* Norton 1968 pap. $6.95. "A quite admirable book, distinguished not only by its brevity and lucidity ... but by an incisive historical judgment" (*TLS*).

CICERO or TULLY (MARCUS TULLIUS CICERO). 106 B.C.–43 B.C.

Cicero, Roman orator and statesman, studied philosophy first at Rome under Greek tutors and later visited Greece and attended lectures at the Old Academy in Athens as well as those of Poseidonius, the Stoic. Cicero translated Greek philosophy into Latin, and is responsible for much of the vocabulary transmitted to the West. The philosophical treatises *Academica* and *De Natura Deorum* and the moral writings *De Finibus* and *De Officiis* are renditions and paraphrasings of the Greek philosophies of the time. His most original work is to be found in the political texts *De Republica* and *De Legibus*. (See also Volume 2.)

BOOKS BY CICERO

Works. [*Loeb Class. Lib.*] Harvard Univ. Pr. 28 vols. 1912–58 ea. $12.50. Standard text with translation on the facing page; introductions and useful notes supplied.

Select Letters. Ed. by D. R. Shackleton Bailey, Cambridge Univ. Pr. 1980 $42.50 pap. $15.95; ed. by W. W. How, Oxford 2 vols. 1925–26 vol. 1 Text $18.95 vol. 2 Notes $26.00. In addition to the letters, it offers an informative introduction and useful appendixes.

On Old Age and On Friendship. Trans. by Frank O. Copley, Univ. of Michigan Pr. 1971 pap. $4.50

De Officiis (*On Duties*). Trans. with intro. and notes by H. G. Edinger, Bobbs-Merrill 1974 o.p. This fine edition has a glossary and an index of names.

The Nature of Gods. Trans. by C. P. McGregor, intro. by J. M. Ross, Penguin 1972 pap. $5.95. The best available edition, with a good introduction to Cicero's views on theology and his influence on later writers; glossary, bibliography, and index.

BOOKS ABOUT CICERO

Bailey, D. R. *Cicero.* [*Class. Life and Letters Ser.*] Biblio Dist. 1979 $40.50 pap. $12.00. Reliable and readable treatment of Cicero's works and contributions.

Petersson, Torsten. *Cicero: A Biography.* Biblo & Tannen 1920 $15.00. One of the best standard accounts of Cicero's life.

Rawson, Beryl. *The Politics of Friendship: Pompey and Cicero.* International Specialized Bk. 1978 pap. $17.00 "That politics makes strange bedfellows is nowhere better illustrated than in the case of the political friendship between Pompey and Cicero during the last years of the dying Roman Republic. In her fine, scholarly study, Rawson . . . attempts to analyze and examine critically this case study of political friendship" (*Choice*).

Rawson, Elizabeth. *Cicero: A Portrait.* Cornell Univ. Pr. 1984 $25.00 pap. $9.95. "A full and balanced life of Cicero is not to be written. To say that 'there are gaps in our knowledge particularly at the beginning and the end of his career, where the letters fail us' flatters the biographer's predicament; for the correspondence which lures him to the enterprise scarcely begins until over two thirds of Cicero's life was over, leaving forty-five years of ascent and culmination in silhouette" (*TLS*).

Rolfe, John C. *Cicero and His Influence.* Cooper Square Pr. repr. of 1930 ed. 1963 $18.50. A brief and concise account of Cicero's personal and political career.

Trollope, Anthony. *The Life of Cicero.* Ed. by N. John Hall, Ayer 2 vols. repr. of 1880 ed. 1981 lib. bdg. $90.00

LUCRETIUS (TITUS LUCRETIUS CARUS). c.99 B.C.–c.55 B.C.

We know little of the man. It is certain that he was a contemporary of Cicero and Julius Caesar. He died at the age of 44 leaving only one work, *De Rerum Natura*, a long didactic poem in six books in which he expounds the teachings of Epicurus. Its stated purpose was to describe the real nature of the universe in order to help people learn the truth and thus rid themselves of fears and superstitions about punishments by the gods here or in an afterlife. The Atomic view of the universe and the theory of pleasure in Lucretius's poem reflect in close detail the writings of Epicurus. (See also Volume 2.)

BOOK BY LUCRETIUS

On the Nature of Things. Trans. by W. H. D. Rouse [*Loeb Class. Lib.*] Harvard Univ. Pr. rev. ed. 1975 $12.50; trans. by Frank O. Copley, Norton 1977 $10.95 pap. $3.95. The Loeb offers text and translation on facing pages, with useful marginalia, informative notes, and a brief introduction.

BOOKS ABOUT LUCRETIUS

Clay, Diskin. *Lucretius and Epicurus.* Cornell Univ. Pr. 1983 $39.50. An excellent and thorough comparative study of the two philosophers and how Lucretius made innovations.

Hadzsits, George D. *Lucretius and His Influence.* Cooper Square Pr. repr. of 1930 ed. 1963 $28.50. "The author of this volume is to be congratulated on this sympathetic and perspicacious account of the thought and influence of the Roman poet . . . For him Lucretius lives not only because he turned out a noble collection of vigorous hexameters but also because he gave men a poetic reading of earth that has never been surpassed" (*The American Scholar*).

Minadeo, Richard. *The Lyre of Science: Form and Meaning in Lucretius' De Rerum Natura.* Wayne State Univ. Pr. 1969 $10.95. Emphasizes the literary and poetic features of Lucretius as having been neglected in favor of the philosophical side.

Nichols, James H., Jr. *Epicurean Political Philosophy: The "De Rerum Natura" of Lucretius.* Cornell Univ. Pr. 1976 $22.50. The author undertakes to offer a fuller view of Epicurean thought through a rigorous analysis of Lucretius's *De Rerum Natura.*

Santayana, George. *Three Philosophical Poets.* Cooper Square Pr. repr. of 1910 ed. 1971 lib. bdg. $25.00. An eloquent essay on Lucretius, stressing the poet's ethical naturalism.

MARCUS AURELIUS (ANTONINUS). A.D.121–180

Marcus Aurelius was emperor of Rome from 160 to 180. Although a Roman, he wrote his *Meditations* in Greek, preferring that language for the "propriety and facility of his expressions," since "the Latin tongue in matter of philosophy comes as short of the Greek as the English doth of Latin." Aurelius was a Stoic, and his *Meditations,* composed of 12 books, the only surviving work, was written toward the end of his life during campaigns waged against tribes along the Danube.

BOOKS BY MARCUS AURELIUS

The following titles offer translations by different hands. The introductions vary in length and scope, but all are done by scholars with acknowledged competence.

Meditations. Trans. and ed. by G. M. A. Grube, Hackett 1984 lib. bdg. $15.00 text ed. pap. $4.95; [*Loeb Class. Lib.*] Harvard Univ. Pr. 1916 rev. 1930 $13.95; trans. Maxwell Staniforth [*Penguin Class. Ser.*] 1964 pap. $3.95. "The student who is beginning to explore the humanities, the history of the late empire, and/or ancient philosophy will read the inspiring jottings of Marcus Aurelius and better understand the world in crisis in the second century A.D." (*Classical World*).

Living Stoically: Selections from Marcus Aurelius. Ed. by Roy A. Lawes, State Mutual Bk. 1985 $25.00

The Wisdom of Marcus Aurelius. Ed. by Nathan H. Dole, Foundation for Class. Repr. repr. of 1903 ed. 1985 $117.00

BOOKS ABOUT MARCUS AURELIUS

Bussell, Frederick W. *Marcus Aurelius and the Later Stoics.* Gordon Pr. 1976 lib. bdg. $59.95. "Dr. Bussell's learned and brilliantly able work, closely as it follows the text (all along with exact citations) both of Marcus Aurelius and (on a smaller scale) of his predecessors, Seneca and Epictetus, gives in the end an estimate from a rather special and individual point of view" (*Intl. Journal of Ethics*).

Farquharson, Arthur. *Marcus Aurelius: His Life and His World.* Pref. by D. A. Rees, Greenwood repr. of 1951 ed. 1975 lib. bdg. $22.50. A good survey by the leading authority who wrote a two-volume work on the *Meditations* (1944).

Oliver, James H. *Marcus Aurelius: Aspects of Civic and Cultural Policy in the East.* Amer. School of Classical Studies 1970 pap. $12.50. Views the imperial philosopher in the context of his administration of the Roman Empire.

Sedgwick, Henry D. *Marcus Aurelius: A Biography.* AMS Pr. repr. of 1921 ed. 1974 $21.00. A good account of his life and philosophical outlook.

SENECA, LUCIUS ANNAEUS. c.3 B.C.–A.D.65

Seneca was born in Cordoba, Spain. He received instruction in current eclectic Stoicism. During his career he had the misfortune of suffering banishment by the Emperior Claudius. He served as tutor to the young Nero, later to become his principal adviser. Accused by Nero of involvement in conspiracy against him, he committed suicide at the emperor's command. Seneca wrote moral essays and letters and also nine tragedies. He espoused Stoic doctrines advocating virtue as the only true good and abstinence from materiality and emotions. Life must be ordered to accord with reason and divine will. (See also Volume 2.)

BOOK BY SENECA

The Stoic Philosophy of Seneca: Essays and Letters. Trans. and intro. by Moses Hadas, Norton 1968 pap. $6.95. One of the best collections available, introduced by a learned authority in Latin literature.

BOOKS ABOUT SENECA

Eliot, T. S. *Shakespeare and the Stoicism of Seneca.* Porter 1979 $28.50

Griffin, Miriam D. *Seneca: A Philosopher in Politics.* Oxford 1976 $75.00. An outstanding work on Seneca's career and philosophy; well-documented.

Gummere, Richard M. *Seneca the Philosopher and His Modern Message.* Cooper Square Pr. repr. of 1930 ed. 1963 $18.50. A sympathetic, brief account, useful for its references to how modern literature saw Seneca.

Motto, A. L. *Seneca*. Twayne 1973 o.p. A well-written general introduction to Seneca's life and works, with annotated selected bibliography.

MIDDLE PLATONISM

The period of great historical transitions lasting three centuries, from 80 B.C. to A.D. 220, proved to be as decisive in the transformation of philosophical ideas as it was with regard to military, political, and cultural change. The philosophical activity of the period is highly complex, as recent studies such as John Dillon's have amply demonstrated, and should be reviewed carefully by those who want to undertake serious research into the movement known as Neoplatonism. Elements of Stoicism, Epicureanism, Skepticism, and Aristotelianism are all present in the writings of the Middle Platonists, but the dominant ideas that frame their outlooks and define their philosophical quest are fundamentally Platonic. The Middle Platonists, chief among them Antiochus of Ascalon; the Alexandrians Eudorus and Philo Judaeus; Plutarch of Chaeronia; the leaders of the Athenian School, Nicostratus, Atticus, and Harpocration; plus such thinkers as Gaius, Albinus, Apuleius, and the Neopythagoreans Moderatus, Numerius, and others, together form a wide spectrum of the Platonizing movement that broadened the era's conceptual apparatus to accommodate the claims of religious beliefs to philosophical credibility.

General Works

Billings, Thomas H. *The Platonism of Philo Judaeus*. 1919. Ed. by Leonardo Taran [*Ancient Philosophy Ser.*] Garland 1979 lib. bdg. $18.00. Mainly useful for its careful listing of parallel textual references to Plato's works.

Dillon, John. *The Middle Platonists 80 B.C. to A.D. 220*. Cornell Univ. Pr. 1977 o.p. The best available treatment of a little-known but very influential period, especially as a formative force, with reference to early antecedents but mainly devoted to Philo, the Neopythagoreans, and Antiochus.

Goodenough, Erwin R. *An Introduction to Philo Judaeus*. Allenson 1962 text ed. $11.00. A basic work on Philo's thought.

Sandmel, Samuel. *Philo of Alexandria: An Introduction*. Oxford 1979 pap. $9.95. Covers the main ideas of Philo as thinker and religious leader in Alexandria.

Winston, David, and John Dillon. *Two Treatises of Philo of Alexandria: A Commentary on De Gigantibus and Quod Deus Sit Immutabilis*. [*Brown Class. in Judaica Ser.*] Scholars Pr. GA 1983 pap. $15.00. This edition by two prominent scholars makes accessible the two tracks of Philo's single treatise discussing the immutability of God.

Witt, R. E. *Albinus and the History of Middle Platonism*. Cambridge Univ. Pr. 1937 o.p. A challenging effort to place Albinus in Hellenistic thought.

Wolfson, Harry A. *Philo: Foundations of Religious Philosophy in Judaism, Christianity and Islam*. Harvard Univ. Pr. 2 vols. rev. ed. 1962 $55.00. "We have here not only by far the best and most detailed treatise on Philo that has ever appeared but also an invaluable presentation of the subject matter of the philosophy of religion" (*AHR*).

NEOPLATONISM

The third century A.D. witnessed a new and intensified interest in Platonic thought that both assimilated select elements from the complex tradition of the Middle Platonists and the teachings of the Stoics and tried to provide a philosophical alternative to the recurrent waves of religious movements.

Neoplatonism is a modern term to cover a very complex philosophical movement in later Hellenistic times, one that found adherents not only in Alexandria, where it had its beginnings, but also in many other places, including Athens. Neoplatonism stood for a comprehensive theory of the universe, its ultimate source and the cause of its development, as well as an attitude and a way of life. The divine origin of all things, including humanity, is the One, the perfect and eternal absolute Being or God. Human beings may return to the One only through the path of theoretical knowledge and purity by direct ecstatic experience. For the Neoplatonists each level of reality required the ascent to a higher place of inner consciousness until one finally is united in a timeless moment with the absolute One.

Insofar as Neoplatonism took on the form of a definite system and made use of a philosophical method to articulate its basic thesis and develop distinct arguments to defend it, its real founder is Plotinus, the leading member of the Alexandrian type of Neoplatonism. Alexandrian Neoplatonism was the most influential of the Neoplatonic schools, the others being the Syrian, with I'amblichus its main representative, and the Athenian, led by Proclus (c.410–485), who was also head of the Academy. The Neoplatonism of Athens was still doctrinally alive when the schools of philosophy were closed by order of the Emperor Justinian in 529. Revivals of Platonism, especially in the Renaissance, were actually in the guise of the Neoplatonism of Plotinus.

An excellent and easily accessible survey of the literature on Neoplatonism is available in Wallis's *Neoplatonism*, pp. 185–197, listed below. Later Neoplatonism is discussed by A. C. Lloyd in Armstrong, *The Cambridge History of Later Greek and Early Medieval Philosophy*, Chapters 17–19 (see under Hellenistic Philosophies, General Works, in this chapter).

General Works

Blumenthal, H. J., and A. C. Lloyd, eds. *Soul and the Structure of Being in Late Neoplatonism—Syrianus, Proclus and Simplicius*. Humanities Pr. 1982 text ed. pap. $12.50

Dodds, E. R. *Select Passages Illustrating Neoplatonism*. Ares Pubs. 1980 $12.50. A collection of representative texts from the extant writings of Plotinus, Proclus, and other leading thinkers.

Finamore, John. *Iamblichus and the Theory of the Vehicle of the Soul*. Scholars Pr. GA 1985 pap. $12.95. "This monograph is an important, though naturally limited contribution to the larger topic of the relationship between philosophy and religion" (*Choice*).

Harris, R. Baine, ed. *The Significance of Neoplatonism*. State Univ. of New York Pr. 1976 $34.50. A collection of important papers sampling the significance of Neoplatonism in Western philosophy and culture; organized around three central themes: the sources, the interpretation, and the influence of Neoplatonism.

————, ed. *The Structure of Being: A Neoplatonic Interpretation*. [*Neoplatonism: Ancient and Modern Ser.*] State Univ. of New York Pr. 1981 $44.50 pap. $14.95. A collection of papers delivered at various meetings exploring the strands of logic and ontology in the Neoplatonic movement in contrast to the logic of other ways of philosophizing.

Merlan, Philip. *From Platonism to Neoplatonism*. 2d ed. The Hague 1960. Reliable but dealing often with fine philosophical points and technical matters.

Porphyry. *Porphyry's Isagoge*. Trans., intro., and notes by E. W. Warren, Pontifical Institute of Medieval Studies 1975 pap. Excellent rendition of this influential handbook, with valuable observations in the introduction and notes.

Proclus. *The Platonic Theology* (*Six Books of Proclus on the Theology of Plato*). Pref. by R. Baine Harris [*Great Works of Philosophy Ser.*] Selene Bks. rev. ed. repr. of 1816 ed. 1986 text ed. $35.00 pap. $22.50

Wallis, R. T. *Neoplatonism*. [*Class. Life and Letters Ser.*] Biblio Dist. 1972 text ed. pap. $12.00. An excellent introduction to the Neoplatonic schools from Plotinus to Damascius, written with mastery of the intricacies of the complex history of this movement.

Whittaker, Thomas. *Neo-Platonists*. [*Select Bibliographies Repr. Ser.*] Ayer repr. of 1918 ed. $19.50. A general survey, still useful for its accounts of the background of Neoplatonism, religious developments in later antiquity, and the diverse schools within the movement, and their influence on philosophy and theology.

PLOTINUS. A.D. 205–270

Plotinus studied under Ammonius Sakkas, and later moved to Rome where he continued to develop his views and created a circle of faithful disciples, among them Porphyry the Phoenician (232–304), who edited Plotinus's *Enneads* and wrote works of his own, including *The Life of Plotinus*. Plotinus has been recognized as the last representative of Greek rationalism and one of the great thinkers of all times, having built a system that includes theories of reality, knowledge, ethics, aesthetics, and theology.

BOOKS BY PLOTINUS

Plotinus: Text and Translation. Trans. by A. H. Armstrong [*Loeb Class. Lib.*] Harvard Univ. Pr. 7 vols. 1966–67 ea. $13.95. Armstrong's translation of the *Enneads* supersedes all previous renditions of Plotinus's thought.

Opera: Enneades 1–3. Ed. by H. R. Schwyzer and Paul Henry, Oxford 3 vols. 1964–82 ea. $24.95–$31.00. The definitive text of the *Enneads*, giving precise information on the manuscript tradition and full recording of critical emendations.

The Essential Plotinus: Representative Treatises from the Enneads. Trans. by Elmer O'Brien. Hackett 1975 lib. bdg. $15.00 pap. $4.95. Provides a useful introduction and appendixes with information on readings, glossary, bibliography, and a guide to sources.

The Essence of Plotinus: Extracts from the Six Enneads and Porphyry's Life of Plotinus. Ed. by Grace R. Turnbull, trans. by Stephen Mackenna, Greenwood repr. of 1934 ed. 1977 lib. bdg. $23.75. The editor brings together selections made readable by her corrections of the free translation by Mackenna.

BOOKS ABOUT PLOTINUS

Armstrong, A. H. *The Architecture of the Intelligible Universe in the Philosophy of Plotinus.* Cambridge Univ. Pr. 1940 o.p. One of the standard treatments of Plotinus's philosophy, with an emphasis on the doctrine of the three hypostases.

Atkinson, M. J., ed. *A Commentary on Plotinus: Ennead.* [*Classical and Philosophical Monographs.*] Oxford 1983 $47.50. An excellent and detailed commentary, translation, and bibliography.

Bréhier, Emil. *The Philosophy of Plotinus.* Chicago Univ. Pr. 1958 o.p. A comprehensive yet adequate summary of Plotinus's life, writings, method, and ideas by the distinguished editor of Plotinus's texts in the Budé series.

Inge, W. R. *Philosophy of Plotinus: The Gifford Lectures at St. Andrews, 1917–1918.* Greenwood 2 vols. 3d ed. repr. of 1929 ed. 1968 lib. bdg. $67.50. A landmark in Plotinian studies, still very useful for its comprehensive scope but with an idealist bias.

———. *The Religious Philosophy of Plotinus and Some Modern Philosophies of Religion.* Gordon Pr. 1977 lib. bdg. $59.95. A pioneer interpretation of Plotinus, placing his thought in the context of modern views and religion.

Mead, G. R. *Plotinus.* Holmes Pub. repr. of 1895 ed. 1983 pap. $5.95. An introductory work mainly of historical interest.

Rist, John M. *Eros and Psyche: Studies in Plato, Plotinus, and Origen.* Univ. of Toronto Pr. 1964 o.p. An excellent and thorough treatment of the idea of Platonic love in antiquity.

———. *Plotinus: The Road to Reality.* Cambridge Univ. Pr. 1977 $39.50 pap. $13.95. A comprehensive account of Plotinus's philosophy with valuable excursions into the broader movement of Neoplatonism and its implications; also argues that Plotinus was conscious of his departures from Platonism.

EARLY CHRISTIAN THINKERS

As soon as the religious reform of the Hebraic tradition undertaken by Jesus assumed the form of Christianity, outstanding religious thinkers defended the Lord as *Christos* and mixed Greco-Roman ideas with the new religion. Paul of Tarsus's writings and John's fourth Gospel set the pace and gave direction to the movement, which soon encountered rivalry and antagonisms. During the second century, there was a strong moral interpretation of Christianity aimed at purging the religion of its mystical notions and elements of magic redemption. These moral interpreters of Christianity are the Apologists, with Justin the Martyr and Irenaeus as early spokesmen of this trend. The Alexandrian Platonists—Athanasius, Clement, and Origen— who espoused Christianity were speculative theologians, interested in the philosophical interpretation of the doctrine of the Trinity. While the Western Church Fathers sought to build the body of Christian doctrine on Paul's dualism and his rigorous moralism and on ritual mystery, the Eastern Church Fathers stayed closer to the intellectual and rationalist tradition of the Greek philosophers. Such representatives as Gregory of Nyssa (d.394), Basil the Great (d.379), and Gregory of Nanzianzen (d.390) wrote treatises to explain the fundamentals of faith with the help of philosophical concepts and ideas. The first Westerner to introduce Platonism into Western Christianity was Augustine of Hippo (353–430), who synthesized Greek speculative thought, Hebrew morality, and Roman social experience into a system of faith. (See Chapter 11, "Early Christianity," in this volume.)

General Works

Bigg, Charles. *Christian Platonists of Alexandria: Eight Lectures.* AMS Pr. repr. of 1886 ed. 1980 $27.50. Still useful and informative on the philosophical ideas of Clement, Origen, and others.

Chadwick, H. *Early Christian Thought and the Classical Tradition.* Oxford 1966 pap. $11.50. By a scholar known for his contributions to the Cambridge *History of Greek Philosophy.*

Dodds, E. R. *Pagan and Christian in an Age of Anxiety: Some Aspects of Religious Experience From Marcus Aurelius to Constantine.* Norton repr. of 1965 ed. 1970 pap. $5.95. A judicious and penetrating examination of the conflict between Neoplatonism and Christianity.

Hatch, Edwin. *The Influence of Greek Ideas on Christianity.* 1957. Fwd. by Frederick Grant, Peter Smith 1970 $11.75. A classic in its field tracing the Greek antecedents of Christian thought.

Jaeger, Werner. *Early Christianity and Greek Paideia.* Harvard Univ. Pr. 1985 text ed. pap. $5.95; Oxford repr. of 1965 ed. 1969 pap. $4.95. The Carl Newell Jackson Lectures at Harvard on the historical continuity and the tradition of Greek *paideia* in the centuries of late antiquity.

Jonas, Hans. *The Gnostic Religion.* Beacon 1958 pap. $10.95. Includes chapters on Gnostic and Neoplatonic worldviews; a good introduction to this complex religious movement.

Kerr, H. T. *The First Systematic Theologian, Origen of Alexandria.* Princeton Univ. Pr. 1958 o.p. An excellent introduction to the philosophical ideas of Origen.

Lilla, Salvatore R. *Clement of Alexandria: A Study in Christian Platonism and Gnosticism.* Oxford 1971 o.p. A book based on firsthand knowledge of the sources.

Osborn, E. F. *The Philosophy of Clement of Alexandria.* Kraus Repr. repr. of 1957 ed. $28.00. Continues to be recognized as a useful introduction to Clement's thought.

Tripolitis, Antonia. *The Doctrine of the Soul in the Thought of Plotinus and Origen.* Libra 1977 $6.95. An informative study tracing the background and different orientations of views on the nature of the soul in late antiquity.

CHAPTER 3

Medieval Philosophy

John L. Longeway

For I do not seek to understand that I may believe, but I believe in order to understand. For this also I believe—that unless I believed, I should not understand.

—ANSELM OF CANTERBURY, *Proslogium*

Whenever demonstrative study [i.e., philosophy] leads to any manner of knowledge . . . if the Law [i.e., sacred Scripture] speaks about it . . . [and] there is a conflict, there is a call for interpretation of the Law.

—AVERROËS, *The Decisive Treatise*

Medieval philosophy, beginning with the Fathers of the Church in the second century, and passing over into early modern thought in the seventeenth century, presents the fascinating drama of the growth of a new Christian worldview, defined and justified in a rational tradition notable not only for its philosophical theology but also for rich developments in logic and the philosophy of language. Technically, much of the work is superb. The habit of disputation gave medieval philosophical writing an unmatched density and leanness. In the presentation and refutation of argument, in the precise definition of one's position, in a subtle sense of the distinctions between possible positions, the medieval thinkers excel.

But despite all this, the Middle Ages has had a very bad press. The very name is an insult. The humanists of the Renaissance first began to regard the period as a dark "middle age" between the pristine light of the ancients and the new light of learning in their own time. The Enlightenment converted the insult into a received opinion, dismissing medieval thinkers as worshipers of Aristotelian authority, embroiled in endless disputes over abstruse questions that bore on none of the realities of man's life or the observable universe. All that the antihistorical thinker of the Enlightenment wanted to avoid was attributed to the Middle Ages.

A proper assessment of medieval thought could not begin until a conviction of its intrinsic value arose. This happened among the Thomist scholars of the later nineteenth and early twentieth centuries, who first seriously came to grips with the actual works of the medieval authors in all their complexity and detail, hidden in unreadable manuscripts in the odd corners of old libraries. But for all their scholarship, the Thomists necessarily placed the apex of philosophical achievement in the thirteenth century with

70

their master, St. Thomas Aquinas. They inevitably viewed the later Middle Ages as a period of decay, anticipating the Enlightenment with its empiricist and skeptical movements and its reformist politics. Now their work is supplemented by new scholars with a new set of interests, including especially the Franciscans within the Catholic church, and members of the secular "analytic" school of English-speaking philosophy without. In the past 40 years a whole medieval literature of analysis and logic, empiricism and science, has been brought to light by this new scholarship.

The philosophy of the Middle Ages can be divided fairly naturally into four periods. In the period of the Church Fathers the initial adaptation of Christian doctrine to Platonic and then to Neoplatonic philosophy was accomplished. The school of Clement and Origen, and the work of St. Augustine and Boethius form the landmarks here. In the second period, following the final collapse in the West shortly after Boethius's death, philosophy at first almost entirely disappeared. John Scotus Erigena in the ninth century, and the first truly great philosopher of the Middle Ages proper, and St. Anselm of Canterbury in the eleventh century, are major figures, but philosophy does not really get moving until the twelfth century, with the school of Abelard. By the end of the twelfth century the third period has begun. It is marked by the introduction into the West of Aristotle's works and Arabic commentaries on them, and consequently the importation of the disputes between Neoplatonists and Aristotelians in the Moslem world. Thomas Aquinas was a moderate member of the Aristotelian school. The fourteenth century initiates the fourth and last period of medieval philosophy. It is characterized not only by radical Aristotelianism but also by the nominalism introduced by William of Ockham, a rejection both of Platonic Forms and of "Real Universals" as the object of knowledge, and by an insistence, even among conservatives like John Duns Scotus, that what we speak of and know are individuals alone. The emphasis on the individual in this last period broke down the old accounts of knowledge and encouraged skepticism, while radical political views attacked the power of the Church, and ultimately the power of the king as well. Thus philosophy helped usher in the new worldview of early modern Europe.

ENCYCLOPEDIAS AND GENERAL HISTORIES
OF PHILOSOPHY

Armstrong, D. M. *Cambridge History of Later Greek and Early Medieval Philosophy.* Cambridge Univ. Pr. 1967 $87.50. First rate, but some of the chapters may be too scholarly for one's first encounter with the subject. The book concentrates on the Platonic tradition from Philo through St. Anselm and al-Farabi.

Catholic University of America. *The New Catholic Encyclopedia.* Publishers Guild 17 vols. repr. of 1967 ed. 1981 $750.00. Good articles, with bibliographies, on all the medieval thinkers, and all aspects of medieval thought.

Copleston, F. C. *History of Medieval Philosophy.* Harper 1973 o.p. A good Catholic treatment, more accurate and more balanced than Gilson, but also duller reading.

———. *History of Philosophy.* Vol. 2, *Medieval Philosophy: Augustine to Scotus;* Vol. 3,

Medieval Philosophy: Ockham to Suarez. Doubleday (in one vol.) 1985 pap. $17.95; Paulist Pr. 1976 ea. $19.95. A fuller account than his other history (above), with the same virtues and the same vices.

Edwards, Paul, ed. *The Encyclopedia of Philosophy.* Free Pr. 4 vols. 1973 $260.00. The standard encyclopedia of philosophy in English, carrying articles on all the major thinkers and movements of the Middle Ages. The articles are generally quite good, philosophically sophisticated, and easy to read.

Gilson, Étienne. *History of Christian Philosophy in the Middle Ages.* Christian Classics 1955 o.p. Well written, with a wealth of information and very full bibliographical notes. Gilson's obsessive concern with Thomistic orthodoxy mars the book, and his conviction that skeptical fourteenth-century departures from Thomas's theory of knowledge eventuated in the destruction of true philosophy leads him somewhat to neglect later developments. But even with these flaws, the book is very much worth reading.

Knowles, David. *Evolution of Medieval Thought.* Random 1964 pap. $4.76. An intelligent brief treatment, but densely written.

Kretzmann, Norman, and others. *The Cambridge History of Later Medieval Philosophy: From the Rediscovery of Aristotle to the Disintegration of Scholasticism 1100–1600.* Cambridge Univ. Pr. 1982 $85.00. Deliberately avoids the topics in theology and philosophy of religion interesting to Catholic scholars (and dealt with extensively in other general treatments) to concentrate on secular philosophy, that is, such topics as logic, semantics, epistemology, philosophy of mind, ethics, and political thought. Up-to-date and scholarly, with extensive bibliographies. An excellent survey in the areas it covers.

Leff, Gordon. *Medieval Thought from St. Augustine to Ockham.* Humanities Pr. 1958 text ed. $19.95. A brief treatment, useful to gain a first acquaintance with the subject, but sometimes inaccurate in details.

Marenbon, John. *Early Medieval Philosophy, 480–1150: An Introduction.* Methuen 1983 $19.95. An excellent and up-to-date treatment, and quite readable. Fills in the gap between the two *Cambridge* volumes nicely (see Armstrong and Kretzman above), with some overlap.

Weinberg, Julius R. *Short History of Medieval Philosophy.* Princeton Univ. Pr. 1964 pap. $9.95. A very readable, philosophically sophisticated history, concentrating on the theory of knowledge rather than theology, and giving more favorable attention than usual to the Ockhamist movement and skeptical tendencies. The best short treatment.

COLLECTIONS OF MEDIEVAL PHILOSOPHICAL TEXTS

The collections of texts listed here are much more important as a resource than similar collections in other fields. All the thinkers mentioned below are represented by sizable pieces in them, and often very little of their work is available in English elsewhere.

Fairweather, Eugene R., and John T. McNeill, eds. *Scholastic Miscellany: Anselm to Ockham.* [*Lib. of Christian Class.*] Westminster repr. 1982 pap. $11.95. Attractive translations of theological works, mostly from the early scholastic period of the eleventh and twelfth centuries. Especially see the long pieces from Anselm, and the brief selections from Abelard's theological works.

Grant, Edward. *A Source Book in Medieval Science.* [*Source Books in the History of Science Ser.*] Harvard Univ. Pr. 1974 text ed. $45.00. A very large collection, topically arranged, of selections from the entire period. Well translated, with extensive explanatory material. A wonderful volume to browse in. Much of this material has bearings on what we now call philosophy of science.

Hyman, Arthur, and James J. Walsh, eds. *Philosophy in the Middle Ages: The Christian, Islamic and Jewish Traditions.* Hackett repr. of 1967 ed. 1983 lib. bdg. $30.00 text ed. pap. $15.00. An exceptionally wide-ranging collection with a considerable representation of Jewish and Moslem authors, who are generally slighted in these collections. See especially the "Decisive Treatise" of Averroës on the relation of philosophy to religion. The translations are of uneven quality.

Lerner, Ralph, and Muhsin Mahdi, eds. *Medieval Political Philosophy: A Sourcebook.* [*Agora Pap.*] Cornell Univ. Pr. 1972 pap. $16.95. Long selections from all the more notable works in the Islamic, Jewish, and Latin traditions. Very useful for its Islamic and Jewish sources, many of them unobtainable elsewhere in English.

McKeon, Richard, ed. and trans. *Selections from Medieval Philosophers.* Scribner 2 vols. 1971 o.p. The translations, all by McKeon, are accurate and readable, but wordy. A common theme in these selections is the nature of Truth and the way in which it is known (see the selections from Augustine, Anselm, Thomas Aquinas, and Pseudo-Grosseteste). Especially notable is a selection from Abelard on universals, and the selections from Matthew of Aquasparta, John Duns Scotus, and William of Ockham on knowledge.

Wippel, John F., and Allen B. Wolter, eds. *Medieval Philosophy: From St. Augustine to Nicholas of Cusa.* Free Pr. 1969 text ed. pap. $14.95. A well-translated collection covering the whole period, with a strong Thomist emphasis. See especially the early fourteenth-century treatise on the Agent Intellect.

SPECIAL TOPICS

Bruyne, Edgar de. *The Esthetics of the Middle Ages.* Trans. by Eileen B. Hennessy, Ungar 1969 o.p. Old, but the only general treatment in English, and certainly interesting reading; accessible to those inexpert in philosophy.

Potts, T. C. *Conscience in Medieval Philosophy.* Cambridge Univ. Pr. 1980 $29.95. An introduction and collection of texts on conscience translated from Jerome, Augustine, Peter Lombard, Phillip the Chancellor, Bonaventure, and Aquinas.

Problems of Method in the Study of Medieval Philosophy

The study of medieval philosophy has raised a number of theologically potent questions of method, echoing and extending medieval disputes over the nature of philosophy and its relation to religious belief. Some works reflecting and dealing with these questions are listed below.

Gilson, Étienne. *Spirit of Medieval Philosophy.* Telegraph Bks. repr. of 1949 ed. 1985 lib. bdg. $75.00. Surveys medieval philosophical thought with an eye on the influence of Christian revelation. Gilson argues that a true Christian philosophy limits its aims to a philosophical understanding of Christian dogma, remaining faithful to the dogma within the framework of purely rational speculation. Critics have complained that this is not philosophy at all, but rational theology, and is not, as Gilson claims, what Thomas Aquinas was about.

Harnack, Adolf. *History of Dogma.* Trans. by Neil Buchanan, Peter Smith 7 vols. in 4 $72.00. A classic work on the development of Christian doctrine, rooted in the notion that theological doctrine has developed and changed since the beginnings of Christianity. Catholic scholars have tended to deny that there was or could be any development of a revealed doctrine, but Protestant scholars, for obvious reasons, are far less inclined to take such a position, often speaking of a "progressive" revelation.

Lovejoy, Arthur O. *Great Chain of Being: A Study of the History of an Idea.* [*William James Lectures Ser.*] Harvard Univ. Pr. 1936 $25.00 pap. $8.95. Deals somewhat impressionistically with an interesting topic in Neoplatonic thought, tracing its development from late antiquity through the Middle Ages and into modern thought. The first chapter, "The Study of the History of Ideas," expounds Lovejoy's notion that an idea has a history through which it persists, displaying a life of its own, maintaining its identity in ever new guises, and following its own natural course of development.

Troeltsch, Ernst. *The Social Teaching of the Christian Churches.* Trans. by Olive Wyon, Univ. of Chicago Pr. 2 vols. 1981 pap. ea. $17.00. The best statement of a thesis, critical of Harnack and Lovejoy, that the development of Christian doctrine cannot be understood autonomously, as though it arose from internal forces quite apart from its changing social and cultural setting.

The History of Ideas and Medieval Thought

The works listed below belong to the "history of ideas." They suffer somewhat from a lack of sophistication in philosophy, in which they are only secondarily interested. They are also committed to identifying a single well-defined view of the world characterizing the Middle Ages so they tend to misrepresent the actual variety in the period's thought. They are valuable, however, for their picture of the relation of philosophy to the worldview of the "ordinary" (that is, upper-class, clerical) man.

Artz, Frederick B. *The Mind of the Middle Ages: An Historical Survey, A.D. 200–1500.* Univ. of Chicago Pr. 1980 pap. $16.95. An updating of Taylor. Like Taylor, Artz approaches the period more from the standpoint of literature and the arts than from that of philosophy.

Coulton, G. G. *Studies in Medieval Thought.* Russell repr. 1966 o.p. The most philosophically oriented of these works. Despite its title, the "studies" cohere in a unified account of the whole period.

Southern, R. W. *Medieval Humanism and Other Studies.* Basil Blackwell 1984 pap. $12.95. A collection of articles. Interest in "humanism" in the Middle Ages is in reaction to characterizations of the period as oriented exclusively to the supernatural. Scholars of the Middle Ages are always trying to cut the distinction between their period and the Renaissance down to size.

Taylor, Henry Osborn. *The Medieval Mind.* Harvard Univ. Pr. 2 vols. 1959 o.p. The classic work in this genre. Makes Dante's *Divine Comedy* the centerpiece exhibiting the fully developed medieval worldview.

Averroism and Islamic Thought in the West

Western speculation was strongly influenced by Islamic interpretations of Aristotle. The thought of AVICENNA, whose Neoplatonic reading of the Master provided the backbone for the conservative Franciscan approaches to ARISTOTLE (see also Vols. 3 and 5), was important from early on in the thirteenth century. The much more radical AVERROËS became important in the second half of the thirteenth century. He held that philosophy uncovered a truth that religious doctrine expressed only in metaphors. That was provocative enough, but he coupled this doctrine with a denial of the immortality of the individual soul and of the creation of the world in time. He was the devil himself to the conservative theologians, and the Latin Averroists, beginning with Siger of Brabant, were accused of holding to his heresies. They seem in fact to have held only that his results are what natural reason would prove, and so are "true" in philosophy, but are known through revelation to be false, because God in His power has sometimes set aside the natural laws on which the philosopher relies. Averroist views became quite widespread in the fourteenth and fifteenth centuries, despite conservative Thomistic opposition. (See main entries for Averroës and Avicenna, in Chapter 9 in this volume.)

Fakhry, Majid. *History of Islamic Philosophy*. Columbia Univ. Pr. 1983 2d ed. $29.50. A full account of historical developments in the Middle Ages, though it shows some lack of philosophical sophistication.

Leaman, Oliver. *An Introduction to Medieval Islamic Philosophy*. Cambridge Univ. Pr. 1985 $34.50 pap. $12.95. The most philosophically sophisticated discussion in English, and an excellent book all around, but short on biographical detail, summaries of minor figures, and the like. It is nicely supplemented by the work by Fakhry (above).

MacClintock, S. *Perversity and Error*. Univ. of Indiana Pr. 1956 o.p. A study of the Averroists that takes Steenberghen's work (below) into account, and extends its range beyond the thirteenth century to a consideration of the flourishing Averroism in Italy and France in the fourteenth and fifteenth centuries.

Steenberghen, F. van. *The Philosophical Movement in the Thirteenth Century*. Nelson 1955 o.p. Steenberghen's studies of the Averroistic Aristotelianism of Siger of Brabant in the thirteenth century have freed us from the view of Averroism imposed by its opponents. Steenberghen's Averroists are orthodox, sincere Christians who, unlike Thomas Aquinas, do not think that accurate philosophical thinking leads to the truth. This work and the one above are fundamental not only for the Averroists but also more generally for the introduction of Aristotle to the West. First-rate scholarly studies, but not inaccessible to the general reader who has a little background.

Logic

Boehner, Philotheus. *Medieval Logic: An Outline of Its Development from 1250–1400*. Hyperion Pr. repr. of 1952 ed. 1979 o.p. The best general introduction to new, non-Aristotelian developments in medieval logic from the twelfth century on. These developments have been of the greatest interest to present-day scholars of the Analytic School of philosophy. Very readable.

Kneale, William, and Martha Kneale, eds. *The Development of Logic*. Oxford 1962 $45.00 pap. $14.95. Brief selections from works of logic in translation, including a considerable representation of medieval and ancient writers, with connecting commentary and explanation. A good book to examine after Boehner.

Nuchelmans, G. *Theories of the Proposition*. [*Linguistics Ser.*] Elsevier vol. 1 1973 o.p. vol. 2 1982 o.p. A sophisticated examination of theories of meaning in the Ancient world and the Middle Ages, centering on the meaning of sentences rather than the meaning of words.

Science

Crombie, A. C. *Augustine to Galileo*. Harvard Univ. Pr. 1979 text ed. $27.50. A good introductory treatment; brief, readable, and interesting, but necessarily superficial on many topics.

Grant, Edward. *Physical Science in the Middle Ages*. [*History of Science Ser.*] Cambridge Univ. Pr. 1978 pap. $10.95. A well-written and well-informed brief treatment, suitable for the beginner.

Lindberg, David C., ed. *Science in the Middle Ages*. [*Chicago History of Science and Medicine Ser.*] Univ. of Chicago Pr. 1979 pap. $15.00. A collection of articles by some of the most significant modern scholars. Up-to-date and fascinating.

Maier, Anneliese. *At the Threshold of Exact Science: Selected Writings of Anneliese Maier on Late Medieval Natural Philosophy*. Trans. and ed. by Steven D. Sargent, Univ. of Pennsylvania Pr. 1982 o.p. Maier's extensive German writings provide wonderful reading on all aspects of physical thought in the later Middle Ages. This selection in English provides an excellent introduction to the more detailed study of medieval science.

Thorndike, Lynn. *The First Thirteen Centuries*. Vols. 1 and 2 in *A History of Magic and Experimental Science*. Columbia Univ. Pr. 1923 ea. $75.00. A monumental treatment of medieval science and many aspects of medieval philosophy. It is well worth checking the indexes for the particular philosopher or topic one is interested in.

Politics

Kantorowicz, Ernst H. *The King's Two Bodies: A Study of Medieval Political Theology*. Princeton Univ. Pr. 1981 $58.00 pap. $13.95. On the theory of kingship in the Middle Ages.

Lewis, Ewart. *Medieval Political Ideas*. Cooper Square Pr. repr. of 1954 ed. 1973 lib. bdg. $42.50. A collection of translations from all the major writers, arranged by topic, with an introductory essay on each topic.

Morrall, John B. *Political Thought in Medieval Times*. [*Medieval Academy Repr. for Teaching Ser.*] Univ. of Toronto Pr. 1980 pap. $4.95. A brief introductory treatment.

Ullmann, W. *A History of Political Thought: The Middle Ages*. Penguin 1965 o.p. Another introductory treatment, older but quite competent.

THE PATRISTIC PERIOD

The period from the crystallization of orthodox Christian belief at the end of the first century to the twilight of Rome in the fifth century saw the domestication of philosophy within Christianity. The largely Platonic, and later Neoplatonic, thought of the "Fathers of the Church" is the starting point for philosophy until the introduction of Aristotle in the latter half of the twelfth century. In particular, Augustinian epistemology provided a model for later reflections, and the preservation of ancient elementary logic texts by Boethius provided the groundwork for rich developments in the twelfth century. But the real strength of the Fathers is to be found in their philosophical consideration of religious themes, and here their thought remains influential even today.

Bauer, Walter. *Orthodoxy and Heresy in Earliest Christianity.* Ed. by Robert A. Kraft and Gerharn Krodel, Fortress Pr. 1979 pap. $10.95. An influential work. Argues that the definition of the orthodox position was much looser in the early days of Christianity than later, so that application of later standards of orthodoxy in the discussion of the period is anachronistic and misleading.

Campenhausen, Hans von. *The Fathers of the Greek Church.* A. & C. Black 1963 o.p.

———. *The Fathers of the Latin Church.* Trans. by Manfred Hoffmann, Stanford Univ. Pr. 1964 $32.50. Another edition of this book appeared under the title *Men Who Shaped the Western Church.* Both *The Fathers of the Greek Church* and *The Fathers of the Latin Church* contain perceptive essays on the character, life, and thought of the major church Fathers.

Cassiodorus. *An Introduction to Divine and Human Readings.* Trans. by L. W. Jones, Hippocrene Bks. 1966 lib. bdg. $20.50. Cassiodorus's book laid down the program for the preservation of the classical heritage of Rome and Greece as the chaotic barbarian centuries began, threatening the entire destruction of that heritage.

Chadwick, Henry. *Early Christian Thought and the Classical Tradition: Studies in Justin, Clement, and Origen.* Oxford 1984 text ed. pap. $11.50. A first-rate discussion of Justin Martyr and Clement of Alexandria (late second and early third century) on faith and reason, philosophy, and Christianity. Attractively written and accessible to the beginner.

Cochrane, Charles N. *Christianity and Classical Culture: A Study of Thought and Action from Augustus to Augustine.* Oxford repr. of 1944 ed. 1957 pap. $10.95; Peter Smith 1984 $18.00. A sophisticated discussion of the developments in philosophy of history, political philosophy, and the role and conception of the state in the transformation of the pagan to a Christian empire. Confined largely to Latin writers, but discusses both Christian and pagan authors, beginning with Virgil and Cicero.

Glatzer, Nahum, ed. *The Essential Philo.* Schocken 1970 o.p. A selection from the works of a Jewish Platonistic philosopher of Alexandria who worked from about 20 B.C. to 40 A.D. Philo's adaptation of Platonism to Jewish doctrine formed a model for Christian thinkers of the second and third centuries.

Grant, Robert M. *The Early Christian Doctrine of God.* Univ. Pr. of Virginia 1966 o.p. Covers some of the same ground as Norris, but chiefly interested in the Trinity, the humanity of Christ, and the like concepts, rather than God's relation to the world He created.

———. *Miracle and Natural Law in Graeco-Roman and Early Christian Thought.* Elsevier repr. of 1952 ed. 1981 o.p. Part 1 is on the notions of natural law in late ancient thought, and Part 2 is on the account of miracles in Christianity and its reflection on Christian notions of natural law.

Grant, Robert M., and David Tracy. *A Short History of the Interpretation of the Bible.* Fortress Pr. 1984 2d ed. rev. & enl. pap. $10.95. On scriptural interpretation in general throughout the Middle Ages.

Hatch, Edwin. *The Influence of Greek Ideas on Christianity.* Fwd. by Frederick Grant, Peter Smith 1970 $11.75. A classic work updated. Very much worth reading.

Jonas, Hans. *Gnostic Religion: The Message of the Alien God and the Beginnings of Christianity.* Peter Smith 1970 rev. ed. $18.00. The standard introduction to Gnosticism, the chief opponent to Christianity in the Empire, beautifully written and sympathetic throughout, treating Gnosticism as a religious worldview in its own right, rather than a mere heretical aberration from Christianity. The revised edition adds a chapter on the Nag Hammadi discoveries and a comparison of Gnostic thought to Existentialism and Nihilism.

Justin Martyr. *Complete Writings.* Trans. by T. B. Falls [*Fathers of the Church Ser.*] Catholic Univ. Pr. 1948 $34.95. Justin Martyr, writing in the second century, is the first of the new Christian intellectuals to set himself up as a philosopher. His Platonism is superficial, more a stratagem to get an audience for Christianity than a reflection of genuine philosophical commitments, but many of the themes of his thought nonetheless persisted in Clement and Origen.

Lewis, Clive S. *The Discarded Image: An Introduction to Medieval and Renaissance Literature.* Cambridge Univ. Pr. 1968 pap. $9.95. A very readable introduction to the picture of the world inherited from the fifth century by the later Middle Ages. Nontechnical, with the intention of providing necessary background for the reading of medieval literature.

Norris, Richard A. *God and World in Early Christian Theology.* Seabury 1965 o.p. On the cosmological notions of later Greek antiquity, and the Gnostic and Christian reactions to them. Discusses Justin Martyr, Irenaeus, Tertullian, and Origen.

O'Meara, Dominic J. *Neoplatonism and Christian Thought.* [*Neoplatonism: Ancient and Modern Ser.*] State Univ. of New York 1981 $44.50 pap. $14.95. A collection of articles, most by Catholic scholars, on Neoplatonism in Christian thought from Origen to the twentieth century. For the more sophisticated reader.

Pannenberg, Wolfhart. *Basic Questions in Theology: Collected Essays.* Westminster repr. of 1971 ed. 1983 pap. $12.95. Contains a sophisticated discussion of the adoption into Christianity of the philosopher's notion of God. For someone who wants to go more deeply into the matter.

Pelikan, Jaroslav. *The Christian Tradition: A History of the Development of Doctrine.* Univ. of Chicago Pr. 4 vols. 1971–85 ea. $25.00–$27.50 pap. ea. $10.95–$14.95. A brilliant and comprehensive work. See especially Vol. 1, Chap. 1, on the conflict between Christianity and pagan philosophy. The best general treatment, and superbly written. Should be read first.

——. *The Shape of Death: Life, Death, and Immortality in the Early Fathers.* Greenwood repr. of 1961 ed. 1978 lib. bdg. $22.50. Chapters on Tatian, Clement, Cyprian, Origen, and Irenaeus. Suggestive, brief sketches of their accounts of life after death. Pelikan's scholarship is not trotted about for all to see here, but it thoroughly informs his discussion.

Rand, Edward K. *The Founders of the Middle Ages.* Dover repr. of 1928 ed. 1957 pap. $7.95. A classic study of some early thinkers. Though now outdated, it still provides a nice introduction to late antiquity, discussing the relation of the Church to pagan culture, Ambrose, Jerome, Boethius, Augustine, and Dante. Especially for those who like the elegant style of old books.

Roberts, Alexander, and James Donaldson, eds. *The Ante-Nicene Fathers.* Eerdmans 10 vols. repr. 1951 o.p. A reprint, with additional material, of a major collection of early texts first published in the nineteenth century. See also the entry below for Philip Schaff.

Runciman, Steven. *The Medieval Manichee: A Study of the Christian Dualist Heresy.* Cambridge Univ. Pr. 1982 $39.50 pap. $13.95. Manichaeism was a Gnostic religion influential in St. Augustine's time. Augustine himself was a member as a young man. It continued underground well into the Middle Ages, and was subjected in its different forms to a number of persecutions by the Church.

Sandmel, Samuel. *Philo of Alexandria: An Introduction.* Oxford 1979 pap. $8.95. Updates a classic work by the author's teacher, E. Goodenough, and attempts to clear up its obscurities. Rather more guarded than Wolfson in its assessment of Philo.

Schaff, Philip, and others. *A Select Library of Nicene and Post-Nicene Fathers of the Christian Church.* Eerdmans 28 vols. repr. 1952–56 o.p. A reprint of a collection of translations first published in the late nineteenth century. The translations are often stuffy, and sometimes inaccurate, but these volumes are readily available in libraries. The Ante-Nicene Fathers are those who wrote before the Council of Nicaea in 325, which settled some important theological issues over the divinity of Christ. The Nicene Fathers participated in that council, and the Post-Nicene Fathers wrote afterward.

Turner, Henry E. *The Pattern of Christian Truth: A Study in the Relations between Orthodoxy and Heresy in the Early Church.* AMS Pr. repr. of 1954 ed. 1977 $47.50. Criticizes, with some effectiveness, Bauer's view that there was no established orthodox tradition in the first centuries. In any case, at the end of the second century and the beginning of the third, an orthodoxy became established in response to the problem of sorting out Christians from Gnostics.

Wilken, Robert L., ed. *The Christians as the Romans Saw Them.* Yale Univ. Pr. 1984 $22.50 pap. $7.95. An insightful work, arguing that early Christianity was criticized on essentially religious grounds: it was seen as a secret and private religion in a society depending on a public civic religion for civil unity and moral training. Wilken analyzes the later objections of Galen, Celsus, Porphyry, and the Emperor Julian to Christianity, arguing that many of them were well founded, and that such outside criticisms stimulated Christian theological development.

Wolfson, Harry A. *Philo: Foundations of Religious Philosophy in Judaism, Christianity and Islam.* Harvard Univ. Pr. 2 vols. rev. ed. 1962 $55.00. Argues that Philo first developed the medieval style of Jewish, Arabic, and Christian religious thought through his adaptation of Platonism to the Jewish faith. The resultant notion of God is an uneasy merger of the transcendental Jewish God, completely other than His creation, and the Platonic Logos. This is the God of later Judaism, of Islam, and of Christianity. A big book for the ambitious reader.

———. *Philosophy of the Church Fathers: Faith, Trinity, Incarnation.* Harvard Univ. Pr. 3d rev. ed. 1970 $32.50. A classic discussion by a great scholar, often displaying philosophical sophistication, but sometimes grumpy and idiosyncratic as well. Entertaining reading.

THE PERIOD OF RECOVERY

After Boethius, chaos settled upon the West. It ended only when Charlemagne, who emerged in the latter part of the eighth century as the most powerful ruler in Europe, took an interest in reestablishing learning in his empire. At this time there was still considerable intellectual borrowing from the empire of Byzantium, which was to fade gradually as the West asserted its spiritual independence. The most important philosophical figures of the period are John Scotus Erigena and St. Anselm.

Hornell, W., ed. and trans. *The Rhetoric of Alcuin and Charlemagne.* Princeton Univ. Pr. 1941 o.p. A dialogue between Charles and Albinus. Interesting material on a variety of topics, including justice.

Laistner, Max, and H. H. King. *Thought and Letters in Western Europe, A.D. 500–900.* Cornell Univ. Pr. 2d ed. 1966 pap. $10.95; Gordon Pr. $59.95. An excellent general account of medieval thought in the period of the Dark Ages and the recovery.

O'Meara, John J. *Erigena.* Mercier Pr. 1969 o.p. A brief study of this important figure. Quite readable. John Scotus Erigena, a ninth-century figure, reintroduced the late classical mystical Neoplatonism of Eastern Christianity to the West in translations of Pseudo-Dionysius and Maximus the Confessor. The influence of Erigena's thought on medieval Platonism was great, and he forms an important point of departure for medieval mysticism.

Wallach, Luitpold. *Alcuin and Charlemagne: Studies in Carolingian History and Literature.* Johnson Repr. repr. of 1959 ed. o.p. Interesting for the political side of Carolingian thought.

Wolff, Philippe. *The Awakening of Europe.* Trans. by Anne Carter, Penguin 1968 o.p. Part 1, "The Time of Alcuin"; Part 2, "The Time of Gerbert"; and Part 3, "The Time of Abelard." Alcuin was Charlemagne's "minister of education," responsible for reestablishing learning in his kingdom. Gerbert, in the following century, was interested in scientific matters, and rose to become Pope. A stimulating popular history of the cultural background to philosophy.

THE TWELFTH AND THIRTEENTH CENTURIES

In the twelfth century European philosophy came of age. The ancient texts it had inherited, elementary as they were, posed philosophical questions about the relation of language to reality that were explored in a way going beyond the texts themselves in depth and sophistication. Here Abelard is the outstanding figure. With the introduction of Aristotle's works to the West, along with the Aristotelian philosophies of the Islamic thinkers AVICENNA and AVERROËS, the philosophical scene was transformed. The urgent problem for theologians became the domestication of this foreign giant in the Christian context, and Thomas Aquinas's thought represents the culmination of efforts in this direction.

Aelred of Reivaulx. *Spiritual Friendship.* Cistercian Pubns. 1974 o.p. A charming writer, Aelred (d.1148) here adapts Cicero's *On Friendship* for Christians.

Burr, David. *The Persecution of Peter Olivi.* [*Transaction Ser.*] Amer. Philosophical Society 1976 o.p. Peter Olivi (1248–1298) entered the Franciscan order about 1260, and heard St. Bonaventure teach in 1268. Olivi was forced to retract 22 propositions on monastic poverty in 1283, but this was only his first brush with heresy. He is most noted for arguing that the soul, though it is joined to the body in a substantial unity by inferior forms, is not itself the form of the body. This position was condemned in 1311 at the Council of Vienna. Burr provides a scholarly discussion of both the political and the philosophical-theological issues involved in Olivi's troubles.

Bursill-Hall, G. L. *Speculative Grammars of the Middle Ages: The Doctrine of Partes Orationis of the Modistae.* [*Approaches to Semiotics Ser.*] Moulton 1971 text ed. $44.80. Speculative grammar, which is to medieval logic roughly what Chomskian depth grammars are to modern logic, has captured the interest of modern linguists. This is the best introduction to their account of meaning in English.

Chenu, M. D. *Nature, Man, and Society in the Twelfth Century: Essays on New Theological Perspectives in the Latin West.* Trans. by Lester Little, Univ. of Chicago Pr. 1979 pap. $7.95. A selection of translations from an important French scholar. See especially the essays, "The Renaissance of the Twelfth Century," "The Platonisms of the Twelfth Century," "The Symbolist Mentality," and "The Masters of the Theological Sciences."

Cobban, A. B. *The Medieval Universities.* Methuen 1975 o.p. A good, compact treatment updating Haskins's scholarship.

Gracia, Jorge J. E. *Introduction to the Problem of Individuation in the Early Middle Ages: 500–1200 A.D.* Catholic Univ. Pr. 1984 $54.95. The problem of individuation is the mirror image of the problem of universals. If one assumes, as a Platonist, that universals are more fundamentally real than individuals falling under them, then the problem of the relation between the universal and the individual becomes the problem of how a real universal can come to be many individuals. An excellent study, informed by a thorough knowledge of contemporary discussion of the topic in analytic philosophy.

Haskins, Charles H. *The Renaissance of the Twelfth Century.* Harvard Univ. Pr. 1971 pap. $7.95. A classic, arguing that the twelfth century shares many of the characteristics of the fifteenth-century Renaissance, and ushers in a period of high civilization. It has given rise to much controversy.

———. *The Rise of Universities.* Cornell Univ. Pr. 1957 pap. $4.50. The institution of the university arose in the late twelfth and early thirteenth centuries. Philosophy has taken place largely within the context of the university ever since. This is the standard introduction to this medieval institution.

Hugh of St. Victor. *Discascalicon: A Medieval Guide to the Arts.* Trans. by Jerome Taylor, Columbia Univ. Pr. 1961 o.p. Hugh of St. Victor (1096–1141) was a member of a notable school of mystical thought in the twelfth century. This work is an introduction to the liberal arts and a guide to studies.

John of Paris. *John of Paris on Royal and Papal Power.* Trans. by Arthur P. Monahan, Columbia Univ. Pr. 1974 $27.50. A thirteenth-century defense of the secular power against claims that papal power should absolutely dominate it, suggesting that it is popular consent, rather than the bishop's annointment, that is necessary to legitimize the rule of the king. The view it takes was more radically developed in the course of the fourteenth century.

Kleinz, J. *The Theory of Knowledge of Hugh of St. Victor.* Catholic Univ. Pr. 1978 o.p. Provides a picture of the theory of knowledge in the West before Aristotle intruded on the scene.

Leff, Gordon. *Paris and Oxford Universities in the 13th and 14th Centuries: An Institutional and Intellectual History.* Krieger repr. of 1968 ed. 1975 o.p. Includes accounts of the origin and growth of the two universities and the development of their curricula. The two universities had distinctive intellectual styles, despite their close association with one another, and the root of the split between Anglo-Saxon scientific empiricism and continental humanistic rationalism can be traced in their history.

Llull, Ramon. *Selected Works of Ramon Llull (1232–1316).* Ed. and trans. by Anthony Bonner, Princeton Univ. Pr. 2 vols. 1985 $150.00. A collection of good translations, with ample aids for the reader. Includes Llull's *Ars demonstrativa* and *Ars brevis.* Llull developed an odd sort of logical calculus intended to produce a deduction of every necessary truth, including all the truths of the Christian faith, from the fundamental concepts by which we can classify reality. He thought to use it as a tool for converting the Moslems and Jews. His calculus and the encyclopedic works based on it were influential in the Renaissance reaction against scholastic logic, and some of Leibniz's notions about logic are rooted in Llull's conceptions.

Lynch, John E. *The Theory of Knowledge of Vital du Four.* [*Philosophy Ser.*] Franciscan Institute 1972 $17.00. Vital lived from 1260 to 1327. An excellent survey of the status of theory of knowledge, in particular sense knowledge and knowledge of singulars, just before the great systems of Ockham and Scotus arose, giving insight into the problems that motivated those thinkers.

McKeon, C. K. *A Study of the "Summa philosophiae" of the Pseudo-Grosseteste.* Columbia Univ. Pr. 1948 o.p. This *Summa,* attributed to Robert Grosseteste (c.1175–1253) was in fact written later by an unknown author. It contains a history of philosophy that discusses the work of theology in absorbing Arabian and Greek philosophy and making it Christian; also treatises on truth, on knowledge, on matter and form, on God and His properties, and on psychology and natural science, including light. A kind of encyclopedia, giving a snapshot of the opinions of its time.

Reeves, Marjorie. *The Influence of Prophecy in the Later Middle Ages: A Study of Joachimism.* Oxford 1969 o.p. Joachim of Fiore (c.1135–1202), a mystical philosopher of history, inspired apocalyptic expectations of a new age, often associated with heresy, as late as the sixteenth century.

Smalley, Beryl. *The Becket Conflict and The Schools: A Study of Intellectuals in Politics in the Twelfth Century.* Rowman 1973 o.p. Becket's murder is a dramatic tale often retold in modern literature. Smalley's study gives us another view of it, centered neither in politics nor in dramatic possibilities, but in the role of the intellectual in society.

Thorndike, Lynn, trans. *University Records and Life in the Middle Ages.* [*Columbia Univ. Records of Civilization Ser.*] Norton 1975 o.p. A fascinating collection of documents bearing on every aspect of university life.

Wallace, William A. *Causality and Scientific Explanation: Medieval and Early Classical Science.* Univ. Pr. of Amer. repr. 1981 o.p. Discusses Grosseteste, Aquinas, and a number of other medieval thinkers on philosophy of science, concentrating on their notions about the nature of scientific explanation and its connection to causal accounts of phenomena.

William of St. Thierry. *The Enigma of Faith.* Trans. by John Anderson, Cistercian Pubns. 1974 o.p. William was a contemporary of Bernard of Clairvaux and Abelard. This work is a consideration of the mystical vision and our knowledge of God, culminating in a discussion of the Trinity.

———. *The Golden Epistle: A Letter to the Brethren at Mont Dieu.* Cistercian Pubns. 1971 o.p. A great Cistercian mystic's chief work. William provides here an account of the nature and destiny of man, discussing his animal, rational, and spiritual ends and their relations to one another.

———. *The Mirror of Faith.* Trans. by Thomas X. Davis, Cistercian Pubns. 1979 o.p. William's letters concerning Abelard's errors in theology precipitated the condemnation of Abelard's works at Sens. This antiphilosophical tract reflects a conservative Augustinianism, and emphasizes the need of subjecting reason to Scripture.

William of Sherwood. *Introduction to Logic.* Trans. by Norman Kretzmann, Greenwood repr. 1975 o.p.

———. *William of Sherwood's Treatise on Syncategorematic Words.* Trans. by Norman Kretzmann, Univ. of Minnesota Pr. 1968 o.p. Kretzmann's first-rate translations of William of Sherwood (mid-thirteenth century) provide the best introduction in English to the logic of reference and meaning, and to the analysis of the real logical form of a sentence, developed in the twelfth and thirteenth centuries.

Wippel, John F. *The Metaphysical Thought of Godfrey of Fontaines: A Study in Late Thirteenth-Century Philosophy.* Catholic Univ. Pr. 1981 $31.95. Godfrey was a teacher at the University of Paris who defended the real distinction between being and essence against Henry of Ghent (d.1306?). This is a thorough and scholarly analysis, though it gives little attention to the interests of present-day secular philosophy.

THE LATER MIDDLE AGES

The fourteenth century presents us with philosophy in its vigorous maturity. The task is no longer to absorb and explicate ARISTOTLE (see also Vols. 3 and 5), but to deal with the issues he raises directly on one's own account. The period is marked above all by the final abandonment by Ockham's followers of even the most weakened forms of the theory of real universals, and all schools are impressed with the problem of explaining how knowledge of universal truths, natural laws, and the like can be extorted from our acquaintance with particulars. The followers of Ockham take the most radical view. They argue that we know nothing except our own concepts, which do not resemble the realities they signify, but are connected to them only in that they are caused by them. British empiricism is foreshadowed in this position, and the distinction between English and continental thought is becoming established. The fifteenth century marks the beginning of the Renaissance, but the old medieval schools continue to flourish.

The Fourteenth Century

Buridan, John. *Sophisms on Meaning and Truth.* Trans. by T. K. Scott, Irvington 1966 text ed. pap. $11.95. A fairly accessible translation with notes, but the topic is inaccessible, and the book is only for someone with a knowledge of logic. The sophisms concern various problems with our notions of meaning and reference, including self-referential paradoxes. Buridan, a very influential logician and scientist, died after 1358.

Daly, Lowrie J. *The Political Theory of John Wyclif.* Loyola Univ. Pr. 1962 $4.95. An examination of the radical political thought of Wyclif (1330?–1384), tracing its roots in his intellectual and political background.

Giles of Rome. *De erroribus philosophorum.* Ed. by J. Koch, trans. by J. O. Riedl, Marquette Univ. Pr. 1944 o.p. A work cataloging the errors of excessive Aristotelianism, but do not be fooled, Giles is more an Aristotelian, as well as more skeptical, than Thomas Aquinas.

———. *Theorems on Essence and Existence.* Trans. by M. V. Murray, Marquette Univ. Pr. 1952 o.p. Like Thomas, Giles pins his metaphysical thought on a real distinction between essence and existence, but his view of the distinction is more extreme than Thomas's, emphasizing that only the individual really exists.

Gilson, Étienne. *Dante and Philosophy.* Trans. by David Moore, Peter Smith 1949 $12.75. The foremost study of the topic. One point of controversy is Dante's relation to Averroism, given his praise of Thomas Aquinas's opponent, Siger of Brabant, in *The Divine Comedy.*

Kretzmann, Norman, ed. *Infinity and Continuity in Ancient and Medieval Thought.* Cornell Univ. Pr. 1982 $35.00. A collection of articles in the treatment of infinite divisibility and space and time and the logical problems they give rise to. Somewhat technical, but accessible to the attentive amateur. Wilson's book on Heytesbury (below) is concerned with similar problems as they were dealt with in one of the most influential treatments of the fourteenth century.

Leff, Gordon. *Bradwardine and the Pelagians: A Study of His "De causa Dei" and Its Opponents.* Cambridge Univ. Pr. 1957 o.p. An interesting study of a recurrent theological dispute in Christianity, rooted in Augustine's account of the necessity of God's grace if a man is to do any good or praiseworthy action at all. It is viewed here in the context of the new currents of the fourteenth century.

————. *The Dissolution of the Medieval Outlook: An Essay on Intellectual and Spiritual Change in the Fourteenth Century.* New York Univ. Pr. 1976 o.p. A brief treatment of some of the main themes of fourteenth-century thought, and their effect on the worldview of the Middle Ages. A useful introduction, though the book emphasizes the more radical developments so much that, if taken alone, it gives a false view of the age.

Nicholas of Autrecourt. *The Universals Treatise of Nicholas of Autrecourt.* Trans. by L. A. Kennedy and others, Marquette Univ. Pr. 1971 o.p. Nicholas, an Ockhamist, has been characterized as the "Hume of the Middle Ages." He argues against the possibility of any knowledge of causal relations arising from the senses. A very influential logician and scientist, he died after 1358. See Weinberg's study (below) for his skeptical side. This work places his views on causation in a wider context.

Robson, John A. *Wyclif and the Oxford Schools: The Relation of the "Summa de Ente" to Scholastic Debates at Oxford in the Later Fourteenth Century.* Cambridge Univ. Pr. 1961 o.p. Wyclif was an Oxford Master of the latter half of the century. He was involved in theological controversies, and 45 articles from his works were condemned at the Council of Constance in 1415. In his philosophy and theology he is a fascinating maverick, holding to a form of ultrarealism in reaction to the Ockhamism of his time. He is also the founder of Wyclifism, a heretical reformist movement in Britain. For his political thought see Daly (above).

Weinberg, R. J. *Nicholas of Autrecourt.* Princeton Univ. Pr. 1948 o.p. An excellent study, especially of Nicholas's skepticism. Sophisticated but readable.

Wilson, Curtis. *William Heytesbury: Medieval Logic and the Rise of Mathematical Physics.* Univ. of Wisconsin Pr. 1956 o.p. Heytesbury worked in Merton College from about 1330 (d.1372?–1373?). He wrote on logic, mathematics, and the physical sciences, and this survey of his work is interesting for all three fields. Somewhat technical, but accessible to the attentive reader.

The Fifteenth Century and After

Oakley, Francis. *The Political Thought of Pierre D'Ailly.* Elliots Bks. 1964 $59.50. The Great Schism and the question of the authority of Church Councils versus the authority of the Pope led to some pregnant political thought, identifying the consent of the governed as the source of political authority. D'Ailly provides a good example of this radical strain in fifteenth-century theory.

Oberman, Heiko A. *The Harvest of Medieval Theology: Gabriel Biel and Late Medieval Nominalism.* Labyrinth Pr. repr. of 1963 ed. 1983 pap. $17.50. The Ockhamist thought of Biel (d.1495) is beautifully presented here in its full context. A better account of mature medieval theology on the eve of the Reformation is not to be had. Though scholarly, the book is not technical, philosophically speaking, and is a useful introduction to the fifteenth century.

Skinner, Quentin. *The Foundations of Modern Political Thought: The Renaissance.* Cambridge Univ. Pr. 2 vols. 1978 ea. $54.50 pap. ea. $15.95

Suárez, Francisco. *On Formal and Universal Unity.* Trans. by J. F. Ross, Marquette Univ. Pr. 1964 o.p.

————. *On the Various Kinds of Distinctions.* Trans. by C. Vollert, Marquette Univ. Pr. 1947 o.p.

————. *Suárez on Individuation.* Marquette Univ. Pr. 1982 o.p. Francisco Suárez (1548–1617) is the most important of the sixteenth-century Thomists. His influence on early modern thought, especially on the continent, is very great. These three extensive selections from Suárez's *Metaphysical Disputations* are complex and difficult to follow, coming as they do at the end of a long tradition of discussion of these topics, but worth the reading if one has the time and inclination for it. It is best, of course, to master some of Suárez's tradition first, though Suárez helps by discussing the whole history of each problem he approaches.

ABELARD, PETER. 1079–1142

Abelard studied under the nominalist Roscelin and the realist William of Champeaux. Disagreement with William led him to withdraw to the provinces and set up his own school at Melun in 1104. He returned to Paris in 1116 to teach. His disastrous love affair with the brilliant and sensitive Heloise followed in 1118. Their correspondence is a literary classic. He withdrew to Brittany again after that and wrote the *Theologia summi boni*, which was condemned at Soissons in 1121. When he returned once more to Paris in 1136–1140 to teach, his theology was condemned at Sens, due chiefly to the influence of Bernard of Clairvaux. Peter the Venerable of Cluny mediated the dispute between the two while Abelard was on his deathbed, and Abelard was able to spend his last days peacefully.

BOOKS BY ABELARD

The Letters of Abelard and Heloise. Trans. by Betty Radice, Penguin 1974 $3.95. Includes not only a nice selection from the letters between Peter and Heloise but also Abelard's "Story of My Misfortunes" (*Historia calamitatum*) and the deeply affecting exchange of letters between Heloise and Peter the Venerable on Abelard's death.

Ethics. Ed. and trans. by D. E. Luscombe [*Oxford Medieval Texts Ser.*] 1971 $54.00. A sophisticated argument that a sin resides in one's intention, not in the outward action violating the law.

Abailard's Christian Theology. Trans. by James Ramsay McCullum, Richwood Pub. repr. of 1948 ed. 1976 lib. bdg. $14.50. McCullum includes a good deal of introductory material and commentary. The chief point of Abelard's work is to establish a purely rational understanding of the Trinity, showing that all reasonable men must hold to this tenet of the Christian faith, once it is properly explained and understood.

Sic et non: A Critical Edition. Ed. and trans. by Blanche Boyer and Richard McKeon, Univ. of Chicago Pr. 1976 $130.00. In this work Abelard collects passages from the Fathers on a long list of issues in theology, in each case ranged for and against a stated position. The resolution by the student or commentator of the apparent conflicts was the point of the exercise. The book provides one of the foundations of the scholastic method, though the *Sentences* of Peter Lombard became the standard text of this sort in the universities, a text on which every candidate for a degree in theology was required to comment.

BOOKS ABOUT ABELARD

Luscombe, D. E. *Peter Abelard.* Historical Association 1979 o.p. A brief, but excellent scholarly account of Abelard's life, well written and up-to-date. For those who wonder how much truth there is in Abelard's own rather querulous account of himself.

————. *The School of Peter Abelard: The Influence of Abelard's Thought in the Early Scholastic Period.* Cambridge Univ. Pr. 1969 o.p. Luscombe is able to argue that Abelard's influence was considerable, despite his trouble with Church councils. Especially good for Abelard's theology.

Sikes, J. G. *Peter Abailard.* 1932. Cambridge Univ. Pr. 1965 o.p. The best overall treatment of Abelard's life and thought.

Tweedale, M. *Abailard on Universals.* Elsevier 1976 o.p. Rather technical, but clearly written. A superb book for anyone interested in the problem of universals, making clear the attractiveness of Abelard's sophisticated and influential approach to the question. Full translations of most of the relevant material in Abelard's logical works.

ALBERT THE GREAT. 1193–1280

Albertus Magnus, or Albert the Great, was a Dominican scholar, noted as the teacher of St. Thomas Aquinas. He took roughly the same view of Aristotelianism as his student. His interests, however, extended in other directions, and his reputation is based less on his philosophy than on his work as a naturalist, a dabbler in "natural magic," and an encyclopedic scholar determined to review the whole realm of learning on whatever topic he undertakes. His work is that of a great scholar who helped make the Aristotelian and Arabic traditions available in the West.

BOOK BY ALBERT THE GREAT

The Book of Secrets of Albert Magnus of the Virtues of Herbs, Stones, and Certain Beasts: Also A Book of Marvels of the World. Trans. by Michael R. Best and Frank H. Brightman, Oxford 1973 pap. $7.95. This book is the source of Albert's reputation as a dabbler in "natural magic."

BOOKS ABOUT ALBERT THE GREAT

Kovach, Francis, and Robert Shahan, eds. *Albert the Great: Commemorative Essays.* Univ. of Oklahoma Pr. 1980 $16.95. A collection of essays by Catholic scholars on Albert's metaphysics, including universals, time, being, our knowledge of God, action at a distance, and his opposition to the view of conservative Augustinian scholars of the Franciscan order that all created things are composed from matter and form.

Schwertner, Thomas M. *St. Albert the Great.* Norwood repr. of 1933 ed. lib. bdg. $25.00. An interesting biography of Albert.

ANSELM OF CANTERBURY, ST. 1033?–1109

St. Anselm of Canterbury, far and away the best philosopher of the eleventh century, described his philosophical work as faith seeking understanding. Following Augustine, he argues that without faith he could not find the convincing rational arguments that establish understanding, and that convincing evidence of a contradiction to the faith would invalidate any argument. But nonetheless, faith with understanding is better than faith alone. He avoids the citation of authorities in his writings, using argument alone to establish his points (something for which his teacher Lanfranc chided him), and he insists on answering every possible objection to his views with clear reasons against it. He is but little interested in the task of reconciling authorities, or finding a unity of doctrine in the thought of the various Fathers. However, Augustine is in fact his constant inspiration, providing him even with the dialogue form he uses in his works. Anselm's thought is rooted in dialectical and grammatical technique. He is particularly skilled at resolving difficulties by uncovering the true logical form of expressions with misleading grammatical forms. His writings are without exception a feast for the analytical mind, and yet accessible even to a beginner.

BOOKS BY ST. ANSELM OF CANTERBURY

Saint Anselm: Basic Writings. Intro. by Charles Hartshorne, Open Court 2d ed. 1974 $19.95 pap. $8.95. Contains Anselm's most famous writings. The *Monologium* (c.1070) demonstrates the characteristics of God, while the *Proslogium* (before 1076) is the source of the famous ontological argument for God's existence. *Cur Deus Homo?* (1094–98) is an attempt to establish by reason alone that God must become man to effect the salvation of the human race, and contains fascinating discussions of God's power, freedom of will, evil and its cause, justice and mercy, and any number of other topics. It is a masterpiece of Christian literature.

Anselm of Canterbury. Ed. and trans. by Jasper Hopkins and Herbert Richardson, E Mellen 4 vols. repr. of 1919 ed. 1974–76 $149.95. A translation of most of his important writings. See especially Vol. 3, *Two Letters Concerning Roscelin; The Incarnation of the Word; Why God Became a Man; The Virgin Conception and Original Sin; The Procession of the Holy Spirit; Three Letters on the Sacraments.* Includes two letters on the Trinity against the views of the nominalist Roscelin, who apparently held that, were custom to permit it, we could say there were three Gods. Also, the Epistle on the incarnation of the Word, *On the Virgin Conception and Original Sin, On the Procession of the Holy Spirit, On the Harmony of Foreknowledge, Predestination and the Grace of God with Free Choice,* and letters on the sacraments.

Proslogium. Trans. by M. J. Charlesworth, Univ. of Notre Dame Pr. repr. of 1965 ed. 1979 text ed. $17.95 pap. $6.95. An exemplary analytical and scholarly discussion for the serious student.

The De Grammatico of St. Anselm: The Theory of Paronymy. Trans. by Desmond P. Henry [*Medieval Studies*] Univ. of Notre Dame Pr. 1964 o.p. Of interest to the philosopher of language, this work deals with the meaning and reference of names.

Truth, Freedom, and Evil: Three Philosophical Dialogues. Trans. by Jasper Hopkins and Herbert Richardson, E Mellen 1974 $9.95. Includes *On Truth, On Freedom of Choice,* and *On the Fall of the Devil.* All are clever and fun to read, but the last, an examination of the cause of evil in the world and an attempt to excuse God of any blame, is the most fun.

Why God Became Man and the Virgin Conception and Original Sin. Intro. by Joseph M. Colleran, Magi Bks. 1982 text ed. pap. $4.95; ed. by Herbert Richardson, E Mellen 1980 pap. $7.95

BOOKS ABOUT ST. ANSELM OF CANTERBURY

Barnes, Jonathan. *The Ontological Argument.* St. Martin's 1972 o.p. The most recent discussion of Anselm's famous argument for the existence of God. A sophisticated treatment.

Henry, D. P. *The Logic of St. Anselm.* Oxford 1967 o.p. A general study of Anselm's

theory of meaning and its deployment in argument. Rather technical, but rewarding to someone with a background in logic or in modern analytic philosophy.
————, ed. and trans. *Commentary On "De Grammatico": The Historical-Logical Dimensions of a Dialogue of St. Anselm's.* [*Synthese Historical Lib.*] Kluwer Academic 1973 lib. bdg. $66.00. Both Henry's translation and commentary presuppose a reader with knowledge of modern symbolic logic and an interest in the analytic philosophy of language.
Hopkins, Jasper. *A Companion to the Study of St. Anselm.* Univ. of Minnesota Pr. 1972 $13.95. A great deal of useful information and a thorough bibliography.
Southern, Richard W. *Saint Anselm and His Biographer.* Cambridge Univ. Pr. 2d ed. 1963 o.p. A study of Anselm's thought as well as his life.

AQUINAS, ST. THOMAS. 1225?–1274

[SEE THOMAS AQUINAS, ST. in this chapter.]

AUGUSTINE OF HIPPO, ST. 354–430

St. Augustine was far and away the most important of the Western Fathers. His adaptation of Neoplatonic thought to Christianity, and his forceful defense of his positions in a series of controversies, cast a shadow over the entire Middle Ages, and had a great deal to do with the Reformation. Two noteworthy positions, which define later Augustinianism, are that knowledge only occurs in man due to the illumination of his intellect by God (who acts in this respect more or less like the Platonic Forms), and that perception is an active process of judgment rather than a passive reception of forms. He also held somewhat ambiguously to the view that the will could, in its natural state before original sin, act entirely from itself, without any outside influence. This contrasts with the view that the will is bound to will as it does by one's intellectual view of what is good. On faith and reason, he argues that understanding why a doctrine is true is better than mere belief on faith, and is quite confident that such understanding is attainable by the healthy intellect, at least if it is guided by what it accepts through faith.

BOOKS BY ST. AUGUSTINE OF HIPPO

Works. [*Fathers of the Church Ser.*] Catholic Univ. Pr. 16 vols. 1960–   .
Basic Writings of St. Augustine. Ed. by Whitney J. Oates, Random 2 vols. 1948 o.p. A well-selected collection, including 12 early treatises, the *Confessions*, and extensive selections from *On the Trinity.*
Letters. [*Fathers of the Church Ser.*] Catholic Univ. Pr. 3 vols. 1947–56 ea. $17.95– $29.95. Many of Augustine's letters contain important discussions of doctrine and the relation of faith to reason. This is the best available translation of all the letters in English, but is still, like most older translations of the Fathers, too often garbled and incorrect.
The Confessions. 397–401. [*Fathers of the Church Ser.*] Catholic Univ. Pr. 1953 $34.95; [*Loeb Class. Lib.*] Harvard Univ. Pr. 2 vols. ea. $12.50; trans. by F. J. Sheed, Sheed & Ward 1954 o.p. Sheed's is the best English translation of a masterpiece of Western literature, the first introspective autobiography. See especially the famous discussions of time and eternity in Book XI, and of memory (that is, Platonic *anamnesis* of the Forms) in Book X. Books XII and XIII provide a Platonistic account of creation.

De Dialectica. Ed. by Jan Pinborg, trans. by B. Darell Jackson [*Synthese Historical Lib.*] Kluwer Academic 1975 lib. bdg. $34.00. This early work has been thought inauthentic until recently, but is now generally accepted as Augustine's. This and *On Christian Doctrine* contain some interesting discussions of semantics. See also the articles on Augustine's doctrine of signs in Markus's collection of essays (below).

On Christian Doctrine. Trans. by D. W. Robertson, Jr., Bobbs 1958 pap. $7.20. Especially concerned with the interpretation of Scripture, but also bears on the nature of our mystical knowledge of God.

Against the Academicians. Trans. by Sister M. Patricia Garvey [*Medieval Philosophical Texts in Translation*] Marquette Univ. Pr. 1957 pap. $7.95. The Academicians were pagan philosophers who held that knowledge was impossible, and happiness could be gained most effectively if one recognized this fact and gave up on dogmatic conceptions of the good. Augustine's work against them is interesting in its own right, and provides a source for the renewed examination of skeptical themes in the later Middle Ages; it also established an antiskeptical attitude in Christian philosophy that was to persist until the fourteenth century. Augustinians of the Middle Ages tend to believe that one should be able to prove the propositions of the faith by reason. For the acme of confidence in their ability to do so see St. Anselm.

On Free Choice of the Will. Trans. by A. S. Benjamin and L. H. Hackstaff, Bobbs 1964 pap. $7.20. This is often treated as Augustine's definitive and comprehensive treatment of philosophy; it provides, for instance, the outline for Gilson's book. It deals with the nature of freedom and the effects of original sin on it, the origins of evil, the nature of happiness and the virtues, the relation of the created world to God, and many other topics, all rotating about its central question, how to establish that God is not responsible for evil.

The City of God against the Pagans. 413–426. Doubleday 1958 pap. $5.95; ed. by David Knowles [*Penguin Class. Ser.*] 1984 pap. $2.95. This book discusses political philosophy, in which Augustine takes a radical position on the legitimacy of state power. He argues that it is in the end illegitimate, but that one should obey the ruler for the sake of the limited peace that can be gained if one allows the robbers of the people to be well organized, and protect their victims from competing robbers. Augustine's views of history, also laid out here, represent a radical and self-conscious departure from the cyclical theories implicit in the pagan Platonic worldview.

BOOKS ABOUT ST. AUGUSTINE OF HIPPO

Bonner, Gerald. *St. Augustine of Hippo: Life and Controversies.* AMS Pr. repr. of 1963 ed. 1985 $42.50. A learned and sympathetic survey of Augustine's career and literary productions. Especially good on Augustine and Manichaean dualism, which held that God was balanced in the scheme of things by an equally powerful, but ignorant evil force, and in general on the contrasting religious viewpoints of the time.

Brown, Peter. *Augustine of Hippo: A Biography.* Univ. of California Pr. 1967 pap. $9.95. The standard biography. Well written, thoroughly competent and scholarly, and unusually free from theological bias, Brown's work excels in giving one a sense of Augustine's time and circumstances. His treatment of Augustine's philosophy is nontechnical, concentrating on its religious meaning and its relation to his cultural background.

Chadwick, Henry. *Augustine.* [*Past Masters Ser.*] Oxford 1986 $14.95 pap. $3.95. An excellent brief study, and a good first book on Augustine.

Deane, Herbert A. *The Political and Social Ideas of Saint Augustine.* Columbia Univ. Pr. 1963 pap. $14.00. An honest and hardworking effort to come to terms with Augustine's views.

Evans, G. R. *Augustine on Evil.* Cambridge Univ. Pr. 1983 $34.50. A good complement to Hick's *Evil and the God of Love* (see listing under Origen).

Ferguson, John. *Pelagius: A Historical and Theological Study.* AMS Pr. repr. of 1956 ed. 1979 $27.00. An excellent short account. Pelagius was Augustine's chief opponent on matters concerning grace and free will. The English monk held that men were capable of doing good of their own free will without God's aid, for the only alternative to this would be to deny God's justice in punishing men and in granting grace. Augustine, in his usual combative style, pursued his opponent to the ends of the earth, dispatching dozens of violent tracts against his views. He defended the doctrine of original sin, and the necessity of grace if man is ever to do any good at all, as well as the doctrine that even the Saints are utterly undeserving of salvation. Thus he established a branch of theological controversy that would persist through the Reformation.

Gilson, Étienne. *The Christian Philosophy of St. Augustine.* Hippocrene Bks. repr. of 1960 ed. 1983 lib. bdg. $35.00. The most thorough general account of Augustine's philosophy, and one that comes to grips with the issues, though it must be used with care. Gilson is often too concerned to preserve Augustine's orthodoxy to see his text clearly. Fortunately, the extensive references to Augustine's works make Gilson valuable even when he is wrong.

Markus, Robert A. *Saeculum: History and Society in the Theology of St. Augustine.* Cambridge Univ. Pr. 1970 $54.50. About the best available study on Augustine's views of politics and history.

——, ed. *Augustine: A Collection of Critical Essays.* Doubleday 1972 o.p. A first-rate collection of articles concentrating especially on philosophical as opposed to theological topics. There are articles on Augustine's Platonism, his theory of language and signs, epistemology, philosophy of mind, and his views on God and free will, time and eternity, and political society. The introductory essay by Markus offers a brief but intelligent discussion of the ways in which Augustine was led to consider philosophical issues.

Marrou, H. I. *Augustine and His Influence through the Ages.* Harper 1957 o.p. An excellent brief study by a noted scholar of Augustine's immense influence on the Middle Ages.

O'Connell, Robert J. *Imagination and Metaphysics in St. Augustine.* Marquette Univ. Pr. 1986 $7.95

——. *St. Augustine's Early Theory of Man, A.D. 386–391.* Harvard Univ. Pr. (Belknap Pr.) 1968 text ed. $20.00

——. *St. Augustine's Platonism.* Augustinian Institute 1984 $9.00. Augustine was not at first a Christian, but only converted as a full adult, after first toying with Manichaeism and then committing himself to Neoplatonic philosophy. His knowledge of Plotinus was deep and pervaded his thought. In these three books, reviving the view of the French scholar Prosper Alfaric, O'Connell looks at Augustine's Neoplatonism, and, on the basis of the early philosophical works written after his conversion, argues that his Neoplatonism was not as quickly modified in the direction of orthodoxy as has usually been supposed. A very careful reading of the texts underlies these first-rate studies, a reading free from the usual presuppositions about what Augustine must have meant. The result is a picture of Augustine, even in his maturity, more as a follower of Plotinus, especially in his view of the nature of Christian salvation, than of orthodoxy as it is now conceived. O'Connell is the most intelligent scholar of Augustine on the contemporary scene.

BACON, ROGER. c.1214–c.1294?

Roger Bacon, an Oxford Franciscan, is well known for proposing a grand reform of learning and theology, and for his dabblings in natural science. His vision of science was intensely practical, and he talks much of observation and experiment, and so he has been represented as a precursor of the scientific revolution. Although recent scholarship has considerably deflated his rather exalted view of himself, and undermined the notion that he was some kind of experimentalist or empiricist anticipating the scientific revolution of the sixteenth century, he remains an interesting thinker. He is now viewed as something of an Avicennan conservative, who, like Albert the Great, was impressed by Arabic scientific lore, but began to look old-fashioned with the introduction of a stricter Aristotelianism in the second half of the century. (See also Volume 5.)

BOOKS BY BACON

Opus Maius. 1267–68. Trans. by Robert Belle Burke, Oxford 2 vols. repr. 1962 o.p. Bacon's chief work, proposing his grand reform of learning and theology.

Roger Bacon's Letter Concerning the Marvelous Power of Art and of Nature and Concerning the Nullity of Magic. Trans. by Tenney L. Davis, AMS Pr. repr. of 1923 ed. 1981 $19.50. The source of Bacon's reputation as a proponent of natural science.

BOOKS ABOUT BACON

Bridges, John H. *The Life and Work of Roger Bacon: An Introduction to the Opus Majus.* Ed. by J. Gordon Jones, AMS Pr. repr. of 1914 ed. 1983 $21.50; Richwood Pub. repr. of 1914 ed. lib. bdg. $15.00. A sound work in its time, but Bridges's praise of Bacon as a harbinger of scientific methods of investigation has been considerably moderated in more recent work.

Easton, Stewart C. *Roger Bacon and His Search for a Universal Science.* Greenwood repr. of 1952 ed. 1971 $22.50. The most recent general treatment in English.

BERNARD OF CLAIRVAUX, ST. 1090?–1153

The foremost reformer of his age, Bernard spearheaded the Cistercian movement, reestablishing serious discipline and spirituality in the corrupt Benedictine monasteries. His mystical thought is enormously influential, and deservedly so, but he was also, like many reformers, very much a conservative, who opposed the progressive philosophical movement of his age. This was a time when philosophy was freeing itself from theology, with the establishment of schools of logic and the liberal arts that were no longer under the thumb of the theologians, and whose faculty's interest centered on nontheological issues. Bernard is especially known for his attacks on Abelard and Gilbert de la Porrée (1076–1154).

BOOKS BY ST. BERNARD OF CLAIRVAUX

Treatises II: The Steps of Humility and Pride, on Loving God. Cistercian Pubns. 1974 pap. $5.00. Mystical thought at its best requires a close understanding of human psychology. This work is something of a masterpiece of psychological insight, chastening in its accurate vision of our strategies for avoiding surrender of ourselves to God.

Letters. Ed. by Bruno S. James, AMS Pr. repr. of 1953 ed. 1980 $47.50. Entertaining reading full of wisdom, though there is little philosophy here. Bernard's letters make a nice complement to Abelard's complaint-filled autobiography.

BOOKS ABOUT ST. BERNARD OF CLAIRVAUX

Butler, C. *Western Mysticism: Neglected Chapters in the History of Religion.* Gordon Pr. $69.95. Concerned especially with the practice of mystical prayer and the monastic life. An excellent treatment dealing with St. Bernard at some length.

Evans, G. Rosemary. *The Mind of St. Bernard of Clairvaux.* Oxford 1983 text ed. $30.00. A biography, but one giving due attention to Bernard's intellectual labors. Evans is as favorable as possible to Bernard in his account of the trials of Abelard and Gilbert de la Porrée, arguing that his motives and procedure expressed an understandable concern for the preservation of the integrity of Christian doctrine.

Gilson, Étienne. *The Mystical Theology of St. Bernard.* Trans. by A. H. C. Downes, Sheed & Ward 1940 o.p. Concerned with Christian mystical thought from a theoretical rather than a practical point of view.

Pennington, M. Basil, ed. *St. Bernard of Clairvaux: Essays Commemorating the Eighth Centenary of His Canonization.* Cistercian Pubns. 1977 $14.95. A collection of studies by Catholic scholars. One piece by Joseph Chu-Cong intelligently explores similarities between Far Eastern and Christian mystical experience.

BOETHIUS. c.480–c.524

Born of a distinguished family, Boethius received the best possible education in the liberal arts in Athens, and then entered public life under Theodoric the Ostrogoth, who ruled Italy at that time. He obtained the highest office, but in the end was accused of treason, imprisoned, and executed. His *Consolation of Philosophy* was written while he was in prison. His philosophy, like that of all the Fathers, was Platonistic, but he preserved much of Aristotle's elementary logic, and reported in his commentaries the views of Aristotelians even when they disagreed with his Platonism. Thus he created an interest in Aristotle in subsequent centuries, and provided a basis for the introduction of his works into Europe in the twelfth and thirteenth centuries.

BOOKS BY BOETHIUS

The Consolation of Philosophy. Trans. by Martin F. Tupper, AMS Pr. repr. of 1864 ed. 1985 $34.50; trans. by V. E. Watts [*Penguin Class. Ser.*] 1976 pap. $3.95; ed. by James J. Buchanan, intro. by W. J. Oates [*Milestones of Thought Ser.*] Ungar $7.00 pap. $2.95. Boethius's *Consolation of Philosophy* and short treatises in theology have been among the most popular books in the Western world. *The Consolation* was translated into English first by King Alfred of England, later by Geoffrey Chaucer, and again by Queen Elizabeth I. See especially the discussion of God's foreknowledge.

Tractates, De consolatione philosophiae. Ed. and trans. by E. K. Rand and H. F. Stewart [*Loeb Class. Lib.*] Harvard Univ. Pr. 1973 $12.95. The theological tractates include some interesting work. See especially the tractate on the Trinity, which attempts to reconcile that difficult Christian doctrine with the demands of logic.

BOOKS ABOUT BOETHIUS

Chadwick, H. *Boethius: The Consolations of Music, Logic, Theology and Philosophy.* Oxford 1981 text ed. $42.00. The most thorough and authoritative work on Boethius. Scholarly, and sometimes a bit dry, but on the whole well written and always well thought through. An excellent book.

Reiss, Edmund. *Boethius.* [*Twayne's World Authors Ser.*] G. K. Hall 1982 lib. bdg. $19.95. A good biography providing a less technical consideration of *The Consolation*, as much from a literary as a philosophical point of view.

BONAVENTURE OF BAGNOREA, ST. 1221–1274

A conservative French Franciscan, St. Bonaventure was an active propagandist in the campaign against radical Aristotelianism. He regarded even Thomas Aquinas as too radical, and was the first of a series of Franciscans to oppose the new Aristotle with an older, Avicennan-Augustinian view. He has been a favorite of his order, in part because of his early conservatism, which, in the period following the Reformation, provided the order with a master free from the modernist taint of the fourteenth century. But he is also a talented allegorist and a perceptive spiritual and mystical thinker. His thought is rooted in the Neoplatonic mystical tradition of the twelfth century, but it has been updated under the influence of thirteenth-century Aristotelianism, despite Bonaventure's opposition to the radical side of that movement.

BOOKS BY ST. BONAVENTURE

Breviloquium. Trans. by Erwin E. Nemmers, Herder 1946 o.p. A brief summary of speculative theology, without much argument or discussion of alternative views.

De reductione artium ad theologiam. Trans. by Emma Therese Healy, Franciscan Institute 1955 o.p. On the relation of the arts, in particular philosophy, to theology. The arts should all be used in service of theology, which is the highest science.

Disputed Questions on the Mystery of the Trinity. Trans. by Zachary Hayes, Franciscan Institute 1979 o.p. The best source for Bonaventure's proof of God's existence.

Holiness of Life. Ed. by F. Wilfrid, trans. by Laurence Costello, Herder 1923 o.p. A work full of psychological insight concerning the practice of mystical piety. Bonaventure approaches the topic through a discussion of the mystical virtues: self-knowledge, humility, poverty, silence, prayer, the love of God as inspired by reflection on Christ's sacrifice, and perseverance.

The Mind's Journey to God (Itinerarium mentis in Deum). Trans. by Lawrence S. Cunningham, Franciscan Herald Pr. 1979 $6.95. Usually regarded as Bonaventure's chief work. A treatment of mystical theology, reconciling academic studies and philosophy to a mystical vocation.

BOOKS ABOUT ST. BONAVENTURE

Gilson, Étienne. *The Philosophy of St. Bonaventure.* Franciscan Herald Pr. 1965 $7.50. A classic discussion of the philosopher from a Thomist viewpoint.

Spargo, Emma J. *The Category of the Aesthetic in the Philosophy of St. Bonaventure.* [*Philosophy Ser.*] Franciscan Institute 1953 $8.00. An examination of a Platonic theme—God's beauty reflected in the world—in a great mystical thinker.

DUNS SCOTUS, JOHN. c.1265–1308

Duns Scotus died at about 43 years of age. His thought represents a valiant and subtle effort to meet the new critical tendencies of his times, so apparent in the work of William of Ockham, while yet retaining a recognizable Augustinian realism. The result is a philosophy marked by distinctions sometimes too subtle to be convincing, and a dialectical technique often too complex to follow without close study. But Duns Scotus is by no means a sterile dialectician. His thought is motivated by genuine problems, and he is too much aware of the important considerations on all sides to try to make things appear simple. He lives in a new age, and his response to its contrary and perplexing currents is deep and considered. He is a philosopher worth mastering. Duns Scotus attempted to preserve his Augustinian heritage, particularly the preeminence of the will and its liberty. He argues that the will can command acts of understanding, providing a vision of the good to the intellect, and is not guided, as Thomas Aquinas would have it, entirely by an intellectually provided conception of the good. The will is entirely free. Another important view holds that each individual has a *haecceitas*, a "thisness," which is its form as an individual. Thus individuation is not due to matter or accidents, but to the form of the individual itself. This *haecceitas* is the actuality of the substantial form of the individual, which becomes actual only by becoming individual. Duns Scotus is also known for his proof of God's existence, which is enormously complex because of his sensitivity to the problems with earlier, simpler proofs. It is probably the most sophisticated and complex argument for God's existence ever attempted.

Books by Duns Scotus

Treatise on God as First Principle. Trans. by Allan B. Wolter, Franciscan Herald Pr. 1983 $15.00; *The De Primo Principio of John Duns Scotus.* Ed. and trans. by E. Roche, Franciscan Institute 1949 o.p. The best place to study Scotus's proof of God's existence and the demonstration of His chief properties.

God and Creatures: The Quodlibetal Questions. Trans. by Felix Alluntis and Allan B. Walter, Princeton Univ. Pr. 1975 o.p. Well translated, with a very useful (and, for the technicalities of Scotism, necessary) glossary. Full of interesting discussion, but not for those lacking in courage. In these disputed questions Scotus leaves one both amazed at how relevant seemingly pointless considerations turn out to be, and grasping for some method and plan in his work. This is the inevitable result of the form of the quodlibetal question itself, for the master could be asked anything at all when he undertook a quodlibetal dispute, and had to display both the widest knowledge and the most agile dialectical skill.

Duns Scotus on the Will and Morality. Ed. and trans. by Allan B. Wolter, Catholic Univ. Pr. 1986 $54.95. A collection of texts on the relation of the will to the intellect, the moral law and its relation to God, goodness and the moral and intellectual virtues, and sin. Well selected and translated, with useful notes by the translator.

BOOKS ABOUT DUNS SCOTUS

Bonansea, Bernardino M. *Man and His Approach to God in John Duns Scotus*. Univ. Pr. of Amer. 1983 lib. bdg. $29.75. Discusses especially the primacy of the will and Scotus's opposition to intellectualism, his proof of God's existence, and his notions on predestination and the soul. An excellent treatment, to be studied before going on to more detailed works.

Day, Sebastian. *Intuitive Cognition: A Key to the Significance of the Later Scholastics.* [*Philosophy Ser.*] Franciscan Institute 1947 $4.00. An excellent study of theories of the knowledge of individuals in the fourteenth century, covering Ockham and others as well as Scotus. Essential for an understanding of later medieval epistemology.

Ryan, John K., and Bernardino M. Bonansea, eds. *John Duns Scotus, 1265–1965.* [*Studies in Philosophy and the History of Philosophy*] Catholic Univ. Pr. 1966 o.p. A good collection of essays.

GROSSETESTE, ROBERT. c.1168–1253

Grosseteste was an important figure in the introduction of Aristotle, and the initiator of the Oxford tradition of science later exemplified in Roger Bacon. His thought, which brought a Neoplatonic reading to Aristotle, is old-fashioned by the standards of the latter half of the century. He held many important positions, being one of the first Chancellors of Oxford University, and later Bishop of Lincoln, and was an influential advocate of the Franciscans.

BOOK BY GROSSETESTE

Robert Grosseteste on Light. Trans. by Clare C. Riedl, Marquette Univ. Pr. 1942 o.p. An intriguing blend of Neoplatonic metaphysics and the science of optics, of considerable influence. Grosseteste views light as a self-replicating form that spreads from the sun, losing strength gradually as it moves outward. The entire natural world is the expression of this light informing matter and space.

BOOKS ABOUT GROSSETESTE

Callus, D. A., ed. *Robert Grosseteste: Scholar and Bishop.* Oxford 1955 $22.50. A groundbreaking study that is still useful.

McEvoy, James. *The Philosophy of Robert Grosseteste.* Oxford 1982 $79.00 1986 pap. $19.95. An excellent study of all aspects of Grosseteste's thought, but concentrating especially on his account of knowledge. Thoroughly informed, careful scholarship.

Marrone, Steven P. *William of Auvergne and Robert Grosseteste: New Ideas of Truth in the Early Thirteenth Century.* Princeton Univ. Pr. 1983 $34.50. An excellent study of the difference the introduction of new works by Aristotle made in philosophical thought. Marrone argues that an entirely new approach to the theory of knowledge was established by the introduction of *Posterior Analytics,* on which Grosseteste was the first influential commentator. William of Auvergne represents Western thought on these matters just before the introduction of the new treatise.

JOHN OF SALISBURY. c.1120–1180

John learned about court life as secretary first to Thibaud, and then to Thomas à Becket, both Archbishops of Canterbury. He later became Bishop of Chartres. His books are urbane and clearly written, providing a cultured view of the upper-class society of the twelfth century.

BOOKS BY JOHN OF SALISBURY

Policraticus: The Statesman's Book. Trans. by Murray F. Markland [*Milestones of Thought Ser.*] Ungar 1980 pap. $6.95; *Frivolities of the Courtiers and Footprints of the Philosopher, Being a Translation of the First, Second, and Third Books, and Selections from the Seventh and Eighth Books of the Policraticus of John of Salisbury.* Trans. by Joseph B. Pike, Univ. of Minnesota Pr. 1938 o.p. *Policraticus* provides us with John's political theories. He argues that a king becomes a tyrant if he does not rule in accord with justice and the law, and thus develops a sustained critique of courtly life, which leads men to narcissism and arbitrariness in the exercise of power. He actually goes so far as to commend tyrannicide, but his chief aim is to reform court life so that the characters of rulers will be more virtuous.

The Metalogicon of John of Salisbury: A Twelfth-Century Defence of the Verbal and Logical Arts of the Trivium. Trans. by D. D. McGarry, Greenwood repr. of 1955 ed. 1982 lib. bdg. $39.75. This urbane discussion of the philosophy of the twelfth century is a major source for the period. John heard all the famous masters, and presents all sides to the disputes of the age without taking any, except to advance his own suggestion that universals are in fact concepts, not words or things.

BOOKS ABOUT JOHN OF SALISBURY

Webb, Clement C. J. *John of Salisbury.* Russell repr. of 1931 ed. 1971 o.p. The standard biography of a fascinating man.

Wilks, Michael J., ed. *The World of John of Salisbury.* [*Studies in Church History*] Basil Blackwell 1985 text ed. $45.00 A collection of articles, most in English, by first-rate scholars on all aspects of John's thought, but especially on his political views.

NICHOLAS OF CUSA (NICHOLAS CUSANUS). 1401?–1464

[See Chapter 4 in this volume.]

ORIGEN. 185?–254?

The foremost member of the School of Alexandria, the first school of genuinely philosophical Christian theology. Origen's Platonism is of an older form, uninfluenced by the Neoplatonism of Plotinus, and so his philosophy is quite distinct from that of Augustine on any number of issues, most especially on the issue of original sin and freedom of will, and the justification for God's permitting evil in the world. He became a center of controversy because of his contention that even the Devil would in the end return to God, and he seems to have held that a person enjoys as many successive lives on earth as are needed to return to God after the Fall. But all matters concerning the interpretation of his thought are controversial.

The other members of the school are Clement of Alexandria (c.150–c.213) and Irenaeus of Lyons (died c.202).

BOOK BY ORIGEN

On First Principles: Being Koetschau's Text of the De Principiis. Intro. by H. de Lobac, Peter Smith repr. of 1966 ed. 1973 $12.25. An exciting book, quite controversial in its day, dealing, among other things, with free will and its connection to rationality, the problem of evil, and Christ as the Platonic Logos, the Mind in which the Forms reside. Presents a sweeping cosmological view of world history built around the Fall of God's creatures and their restoration.

BOOKS ABOUT ORIGEN

Bigg, Charles. *The Christian Platonists of Alexandria: Eight Lectures.* AMS Pr. repr. of 1886 ed. 1980 $27.50. Despite its age, perhaps the best single study of Clement and Origen of Alexandria. Argues that their theology is determined by their philosophical views, not the other way around.

Grant, Robert M. *The Letter and the Spirit.* Society for the Propagation of Christian Knowledge 1957 o.p. A good study of the techniques of scriptural exegesis in the Alexandrians. It was necessary, of course, for them to interpret Scripture appropriately if they were to make room for Platonic philosophy in their thought. Allegorical techniques of interpretation were adapted from pagan philosophical treatments of mythology.

Hick, John H. *Evil and the God of Love.* Harper rev. ed. 1977 pap. $6.95. Traces the development of Irenaeus's (2d century) style of theodicy. An excellent book. Most of what it says about Irenaeus bears on Clement and Origen as well, who take a similar approach, one opposed to the usual theodicy in the West, rooted in St. Augustine's thought.

Trigg, Joseph W. *Origen: The Bible and Philosophy in the Third Century Church.* John Knox 1983 pap. $16.95. An excellent intellectual biography, placing Origen's thought in its cultural and historical context. The account is based evenhandedly on both *On First Principles* and the commentaries and homilies, and presents a somewhat less radically Platonistic Origen than is seen by those who rely solely on the former work.

THOMAS AQUINAS, ST. 1225?–1274

Thomas Aquinas, the most noted philosopher of the Middle Ages, was a fairly radical Aristotelian, distinguished from the Augustinians by his rejection of any form of special illumination from God in ordinary intellectual knowledge, and by his view that the soul is the form of the body, the body having no form independent of that provided by the soul itself. He held that the "natural light" of the intellect was sufficient to abstract the form of a natural object from its sensory representations, and so sufficient for natural knowledge without God's special illumination. He asserts that the individual intellect is sufficient in itself for knowledge of the real natures of things, and he rejects the Averroist notion that natural reason might lead us correctly to conclusions that would turn out false when one takes revealed doctrine into account. He is distinguished from later Ockhamists by his "moderate realism": he believed that knowledge arises when the form of a natural object actually enters the intellect, taking on a new manner of being in doing so, so that we actually know the substantial form of a thing as it is in itself. The Ockhamists denied this, holding that we have at best a representation of the form in the intellect, not the form itself, and had to face certain skeptical problems as a result.

BOOKS BY AQUINAS

Basic Writings of St. Thomas Aquinas. Ed. by A. C. Pegis, Random 2 vols. 1945 o.p. Extensive selections from the *Summa Theologiae* and *Summa contra Gentiles.*

Introduction to St. Thomas Aquinas. Ed. by A. C. Pegis [*Modern Lib. College Ed. Ser.*] Random 1965 pap. $3.75. Selections from the two *Summae,* more abbreviated.

St. Thomas Aquinas: Philosophical Texts. Ed. by Thomas Gilby, Labyrinth Pr. 1982 pap. $12.50. (See next entry.)

St. Thomas Aquinas: Theological Texts. Ed. by Thomas Gilby, Labyrinth Pr. 1982 $12.50. These two volumes are composed from many brief selections arranged by topic. Useful for an overview of St. Thomas's opinions, with much that is memorable and quotable, but not a good place to find his reasons, or the more difficult and philosophically subtle points in his thought.

Selected Writings of Thomas Aquinas. Ed. by Robert P. Goodwin, Bobbs 1965 pap. $4.24. A good selection of texts, including *On Being and Essence,* to supplement the *Summae;* well translated.

An Aquinas Reader. Ed. by Mary T. Clark, Doubleday pap. $6.95. Many short selections arranged by topic. Useful for its extensive selections from the commentaries on Aristotle and on Boethius's *On the Trinity.*

On the Truth of the Catholic Faith. Trans. by A. C. Pegis and others, Univ. of Notre Dame Pr. 1975 o.p. This *Summa contra Gentiles,* unlike the *Summa Theologiae,* was intended to proceed as far as possible from reason alone, answering the arguments of pagan, Islamic, and Jewish philosophers against Christian doctrine. It provides an excellent summation of St. Thomas's thought, in a style more congenial to the modern reader than that of the bigger *Summa.*

On Kingship to the King of Cyprus. Trans. by G. B. Phelan, Hyperion Pr. repr. of 1949 ed. 1984 $17.75. Develops a complete theory of kingship rooted as much in Aristotle as Scripture. St. Thomas deals with such issues as the rational justification (abstracting from revelation) of kingship as an institution, the distinction between a tyrant and a king, the nature of the resistance that may lawfully be offered to a tyrant, the supernatural rewards and punishments appropriate to a king, and the kingship of God in the universe.

On the Unity of the Intellect. Trans. by B. Zedler, Marquette Univ. Pr. 1968 o.p. This work was written against the Averroists. It argues that there is no common intellect for all men, so that nature permits individual survival of the soul after death.

On the Eternity of the World. Trans. by Cyril Vollert and others, Marquette Univ. Pr. 1964 o.p. Also directed against Averroism, the issue here is whether natural reason leads us to a conclusion that must be rejected by theology (i.e., that the world is eternal).

Treatise on Separate Substances. Trans. by Francis J. Lescoe, St. Joseph College 1959 o.p. The separate substances are the angels, who are pure intellect, without bodies. A number of questions are posed here about how angels can be contingent, created things if they have no matter, and about the knowledge of angels, which cannot derive from sense perception.

On the Power of God. Trans. by L. Shapcote, Newman repr. 1952 o.p. Especially interesting for its extensive consideration of the problem of evil.

St. Thomas Aquinas: On Spiritual Creatures. Trans. by Mary C. Fitzpatrick and John

J. Wellmuth, Marquette Univ. Pr. 1949 pap. $7.95. Spiritual creatures include both angels and men. Concerns the soul's nature and its immortality, the mind-body problem, and the nature of angels.

On Truth. Trans. by R. W. Mulligan and others, Regnery-Gateway 3 vols. 1952–54 o.p. Deals with all sorts of questions, but especially interesting for the way in which St. Thomas handles Augustinian views.

The Teacher—The Mind. Trans. by James Collins, Regnery-Gateway 1954 o.p. A selection from *On Truth*, dealing with Augustine's notion that only God is truly the teacher when one learns St. Thomas reinterprets Augustine right out of his position, arguing that God illuminates the intellect only by creating it so that it is able to know by its own efforts. He then proceeds to give an account of how we can know the natural world, ourselves, and God.

St. Thomas Aquinas: On Charity. Trans. by Lottie H. Kendzierski, Marquette Univ. Pr. 1960 pap. $7.95. Charity—that is, the love of God—is the most important of the virtues oriented toward the supernatural world rather than toward man's natural ends. The discussion here marks the division of St. Thomas's ethics from Aristotle's, since Aristotle takes no notice of the supernatural.

BOOKS ABOUT AQUINAS

Copleston, Frederick. *Thomas Aquinas*. Barnes & Noble repr. of 1955 ed. 1976 text ed. $24.50; Penguin 1956 pap. $4.95. A brief Catholic treatment, clear and straightforward.

Gilby, Thomas. *The Political Thought of Thomas Aquinas*. Univ. of Chicago Pr. 1958 o.p. An excellent, though complex, study of St. Thomas's theory of law and citizenship, tracing its roots in theology, in ecclesiastical and civil law, in the concerns of the Dominican monk with the status of his vows of poverty, and in Aristotle.

Gilson, Étienne. *The Christian Philosophy of St. Thomas Aquinas*. Hippocrene Bks. repr. of 1956 ed. 1983 lib. bdg. $45.00. A good summary of St. Thomas's thought, scholarly and thoroughly referenced, though one should not expect a critical examination of St. Thomas here.

Kenny, Anthony. *Aquinas*. [*Past Masters Ser.*] Oxford 1980 pap. $3.95. A brief treatment by a sympathetic analytic philosopher. The most sophisticated introduction philosophically, and the best first book on Aquinas.

———. *The Five Ways: St. Thomas Aquinas' Proofs of God's Existence*. Univ. of Notre Dame Pr. 1980 text ed. pap. $4.95. A critical examination of the most famous of St. Thomas's arguments.

———, ed. *Aquinas: A Collection of Critical Essays*. Univ. of Notre Dame Pr. repr. of 1969 ed. 1976 o.p. A collection of essays, very nicely selected, bearing on various philosophical issues approached by St. Thomas. Many fine insights are to be found here.

Lonergan, Bernard. *Verbum: Word and Idea in Aquinas*. Ed. by David B. Burrell, Univ. of Notre Dame Pr. 1967 o.p. Touches on all the central topics in St. Thomas's thought. Difficult reading but it reflects deep consideration and repays the effort.

Roensch, Frederick J. *Early Thomistic School*. Allenson 1964 o.p. Discusses Thomism in England and France, with biographical information on the important Thomists in the 50 years after St. Thomas. Informative discussions of the disputes over the unicity of the substantial form of the real distinction between existence and essence, examining the contribution of a number of important thinkers to each.

Steenberghen, F. van. *Thomas Aquinas and Radical Aristotelianism*. Trans. by Dominic J. O'Meara and others, Catholic Univ. Pr. 1980 $6.95. A penetrating study that forces one to recast the older view of the Aristotelian movement. An excellent survey of the period, as well.

Weisheipl, James A. *Friar Thomas D'Aquino: His Life, Thought, and Work.* Catholic Univ. Pr. repr. of 1974 ed. 1983 pap. $16.95. An excellent up-to-date biography.

Wippel, John F. *Metaphysical Themes in Thomas Aquinas.* [*Studies in Philosophy and the History of Philosophy*] Catholic Univ. Pr. 1984 $31.95. A Catholic work that takes issue with Gilson's interpretation of Aquinas's position on Christian philosophy. The disagreement spreads to the rest of St. Thomas's thought. A first-rate, but noncritical discussion of St. Thomas, insightful but never reaching outside the circles of Catholic scholarship.

WILLIAM OF OCKHAM (or OCCAM). c.1285–c.1349

William of Ockham was a Franciscan at Oxford. He came just short of receiving his theology degree, for he was never able to undertake the necessary year of teaching, due to the long list of those waiting and the opposition of his enemy, John Lutterel. From 1320 to 1324 he taught and wrote at the London *Studium*, the private school of his order. He was summoned to Avignon in 1324 on charges of heresy, and became involved there in the dispute over Franciscan poverty. Ockham fled with Michael of Cesena, General of his order, in 1328, was excommunicated, and took refuge in Munich with Duke Ludwig of Bavaria who had also been excommunicated. He engaged in an extensive polemic against Pope John XXII and his successors from there, writing numerous political works. His philosophy is marked by nominalism. He rejected the notion that we somehow or other get the forms of things themselves into our intellect, attacking especially Scotist attempts to hold on to this view using the "formal distinction," and held that our concepts were like mental words, with a natural capacity to signify their objects, but in no way to be identified with their objects. This led to a strong skeptical current among his followers.

BOOKS BY WILLIAM OF OCKHAM

Philosophical Writings. Ed. and trans. by Philotheus Boehner, Bobbs 1964 o.p. Good brief selections, well translated, from Ockham's works, concentrating on logic and epistemology.

Ockham's Theory of Terms: Part I of the Summa Logicae. 1488. Trans. by Michael J. Loux, Univ. of Notre Dame Pr. 1974 $20.00 pap. $7.95. (See entry below.)

Ockham's Theory of Propositions: Part II of the Summa Logicae. 1488. Trans. by Alfred J. Freddoso and Henry Schuurman, Univ. of Notre Dame Pr. 1980 text ed. $20.00 pap. $7.95. This volume and the one above present the elementary part of Ockham's logic in good translations. Ockham's metaphysics and his logic are closely connected due to his deployment of "Ockham's razor," the notion that we should not suppose that more things exist than are needed to explain the meaning of true sentences. Very often his arguments hang on the logical analysis of a sentence, revealing its logical structure and making it clear that some questionable entity, something other than a word or an individual thing, is not referred to in it.

BOOKS ABOUT WILLIAM OF OCKHAM

Adams, Marilyn McCord. *William of Ockham*. Univ. of Notre Dame Pr. 2 vols. 1986 text ed. $90.00. The definitive general study, sophisticated both in the scholarly and the philosophical sense. Adams is especially interesting on Ockham's views in theology and philosophy of religion.

Boehner, Philotheus, and Eligius Buytaert. *Collected Articles on Ockham*. [*Philosophy Ser.*] Franciscan Institute 1958 $23.00. Boehner is a most important scholar on Ockham. The articles in the latter half of this book, on truth and logic, metaphysics, and political thought, are accessible to the nonspecialist even if those in the first half are not.

Fuchs, Oswald. *The Psychology of Habit According to William Ockham*. [*Philosophy Ser.*] Franciscan Institute 1952 $8.00. "Habit" refers to any disposition that is reinforced by its exercise, and so to knowledge and virtues and vices, as well as habitual inclinations of the will. Fuchs provides a competent study of all these topics.

Leff, Gordon. *William of Ockham: The Metamorphosis of Scholastic Discourse*. Rowman 1975 o.p. A survey of Ockham's thought by way of a detailed summary of his works in their intellectual context. Too often this is rather hard slogging, and Leff is not always insightful in his analyses. It is invaluable, nonetheless, especially for those without Latin, given how little of Ockham's work has been translated into English.

McGrade, A. S. *The Political Thought of William of Ockham*. [*Studies in Medieval Life and Thought*] Cambridge Univ. Pr. 1974 $44.50. A wide-ranging study of Ockham both as a political activist and a theorist. Essentially an exposition of Ockham's views, with only occasional references to his influence, sources, or relation to other thinkers.

Menges, M. C. *The Concept of Univocity Regarding the Predication of God and Creature According to William of Ockham*. [*Philosophy Ser.*] Franciscan Institute 1952 $8.00. An examination of Ockham's contention that God exists in the same sense of the word that we do, opposing the Thomistic view that God is His own existence, and so exists in a different manner.

Moody, Ernest Addison. *The Logic of William of Ockham*. Russell repr. of 1935 ed. 1965 $20.00. Logic plays a greater role in determining Ockham's views than it does in any previous thinker, so this excellent general treatment of his logic is quite important.

———. *Studies in Medieval Philosophy, Science, and Logic*. Univ. of California Pr. 1975 o.p. Good essays on the Ockhamist tradition.

Shapiro, Herman. *Motion, Time and Place According to William Ockham*. [*Philosophy Ser.*] Franciscan Institute 1957 o.p. A detailed discussion of Ockham's work on some topics in Aristotle's *Physics*. Throughout, Ockham's goal is to give an account of motion, time, and place that will exclude any existents other than individuals, and he is aided and abetted by Aristotle in this empiricist aim.

Webering, Damascene. *Theory of Demonstration According to William Ockham*. [*Philosophy Ser.*] Franciscan Institute 1953 $8.00. A very useful study of Ockham's treatment of scientific knowledge, which was conceived as knowledge through "demonstration," as laid out in Aristotle's *Posterior Analytics*. Valuable for Ockham's notions about knowledge of the existence of things and of causal laws.

CHAPTER 4

Renaissance Philosophy

Frederick Purnell, Jr.

> During the Renaissance philosophical thought, without abandoning its theological connections, strengthened its link with the humanities, the sciences, and, we may add, with literature and the arts, thus becoming increasingly secular in its outlook.
> —Paul Oskar Kristeller, *Renaissance Thought and Its Sources*

Although the Renaissance—the era in Western cultural history that extended roughly from 1350 to 1600—may be said not to have produced a philosopher of equal importance to the greatest thinkers of the Middle Ages or the Enlightenment, it was nevertheless an important period in the history of philosophy. One cannot fully appreciate the differences that separate a medieval thinker such as Thomas Aquinas from a modern philosopher such as Descartes (see also Vol. 5) or Locke (see also Vol. 3) without giving due attention to the philosophical changes that took place during the Renaissance, a period best understood as one of transition or fermentation rather than major philosophical synthesis.

One feature of Renaissance culture that influenced the philosophical literature of the period was the rise of humanism. The humanists (whose name derives from an Italian university slang term for a teacher or student of the *studia humanitatis* or "humanities") shared an educational ideal founded on the study of grammar, rhetoric, poetry, history, and moral philosophy. Humanism was thus not a philosophical school or body of teaching akin to Platonism or Stoicism, but a broader cultural movement that profoundly influenced many areas of Renaissance art, literature, and political and social thought and practice.

Humanists displayed attitudes toward philosophy and philosophers ranging from admiration and praise to criticism and outright ridicule, particularly of the "sterile" disputes of the medieval scholastics. At the same time, the humanists' interest in ethics led them to compose moral treatises of their own, both in polished classical Latin and the vernacular languages, and to edit, publish, translate, and comment on the works of ancient philosophers, many of which were unknown or only poorly known to the Middle Ages. Although it would be difficult to identify any single philosophical doctrine that all humanists shared, their ethical writing generally tended to emphasize the individual and the freedom of the human will.

Stimulated in part by the new editions and translations of the humanists and the increased emphasis given to the study of Greek during the fifteenth and sixteenth centuries, Renaissance philosophers devoted their attention to studying and adapting to their own purposes the philosophical heritage of classical antiquity and the medieval period. Platonism had influenced much medieval philosophical speculation, and its influence continued into the Renaissance, but the study of it was now grounded directly on the works of Plato and the principal Platonists to a degree that had been impossible in the Latin world since late antiquity. Marsilio Ficino's Latin translations of the works of PLATO (see also Vol. 3), PLOTINUS, and other important Platonic sources stimulated a resurgence of interest in Plato's thought that was to carry over into the modern period, and his attempt to reconcile Platonism with Christianity would influence the way in which Western philosophers interpreted the Platonic works for centuries.

In similar fashion, the Aristotelian tradition flourished during the Renaissance, giving rise to a multifaceted intellectual movement. Such medieval scholastic-Aristotelian traditions as Thomism and Scotism still found spirited defenders, but alongside these developed a secular Aristotelianism centered in the universities of northern Italy, which sought to interpret Aristotle's teachings outside the framework of Christian faith. Such thinkers as Pietro Pomponazzi, Jacopo Zabarella, and Cesare Cremonini provided an analysis of Aristotle's teachings on such issues as immortality, freedom of the will, and divine providence, which challenged the medieval synthesis of faith and reason.

Beside the attempts to revive the classical philosophical traditions, the Renaissance witnessed efforts by some philosophers to provide an alternative to the authority of the ancients. New philosophies of nature appeared as competitors of the Aristotelian natural philosophy that remained largely dominant in the university faculties of philosophy. The writings of such innovative thinkers as Bernardino Telesio, PARACELSUS (see also Vol. 5), Francesco Patrizi, Tommaso Campanella, Giordano Bruno, and GALILEO (see also Vol. 5) attacked the metaphysical and methodological assumptions underlying the Aristotelian approach to the study of nature, gave new relevance to such alternative ancient traditions as Stoicism, atomism, and skepticism, and prepared the way for the development of mathematical physics in the seventeenth century.

GENERAL BIBLIOGRAPHY

Allen, Don C. *Doubt's Boundless Sea.* Ayer 1979 $25.50. Deals with the revival of the ancient skeptical tradition in the Renaissance and its influence on religious thought.

Ashworth, E. J. *Language and Logic in the Post Medieval Period.* Kluwer Academic 1974 lib. bdg. $53.00. An important study of the development during the Renaissance of late medieval terminist logic, so-called from its emphasis on analyzing the use of terms in sentences.

Baron, Hans. *Crisis of the Early Italian Renaissance: Civic Humanism and Republican Liberty in an Age of Classicism and Tyranny.* Princeton Univ. Pr. 1966 rev. ed. pap. $13.50. This classic study has continued to influence Renaissance intellectual history for more than 30 years. Baron emphasizes the importance, for an understanding of Renaissance political ideals, of what he terms "civic humanism," whose chief proponent was the Florentine republican Leonardo Bruni.

———. *From Petrarch to Leonardo Bruni: Studies in Humanistic and Political Literature.* Univ. of Chicago Pr. 1968 o.p. A collection of some of Baron's most important essays.

Becker, Reinhard P., ed. *German Humanism and Reformation: Selected Writings.* Continuum 1982 $24.50 pap. $10.95. Valuable studies of German humanism.

Bernstein, Eckhard. *German Humanism.* [*World Authors Ser.*] G. K. Hall 1983 lib. bdg. $19.95. Treats the influence of the humanistic movement in the German-speaking lands.

Blau, Joseph L. *The Christian Interpretation of the Cabala in the Renaissance.* Kennikat 1965 o.p. Classic study of the employment of Jewish cabalistic literature by Christian Renaissance thinkers, such as Agrippa, Pico, and Bruno.

Boas, Marie. *The Scientific Renaissance 1450–1630.* Harper 1962 pap. $8.95. A good, general introduction to the scientific achievement of the Renaissance, in which philosophers played a significant role.

Botero, Giovanni. *The Reason of State and the Greatness of Cities.* Routledge & Kegan 1956 o.p. The two principal works of the great sixteenth-century political thinker who opposed Machiavelli's amoral view of politics with a defense of the art of the possible.

———. *A Treatise, Concerning the Causes of the Magnificence and Greatness of Cities.* Walter J. Johnson repr. of 1606 ed. 1979 lib. bdg. $13.00. One of the two works listed above, in a currently available edition.

Bouwsma, William J. *Concordia Mundi: The Career and Thought of Guillaume Postel, 1510–1581.* [*Historical Monographs Ser.*] Harvard Univ. Pr. 1957 $22.50. Excellent treatment of the stormy career of the learned French Orientalist and prophet of universal religious harmony.

———. *The Culture of Renaissance Humanism.* Amer. Historical Assoc. 1973 text ed. pap. $1.50. A brief, but illuminating introduction to the significance of humanism on Renaissance culture.

Bréhier, Emile. *The Middle Ages and the Renaissance.* Vol. 3 in *The History of Philosophy.* Trans. by Wade Baskin, Univ. of Chicago Pr. 1965 text ed. pap. $5.00. Contains an enlightening chapter on major Renaissance thinkers.

Brues, Guy de. *The Dialogues of Guy de Brues: A Critical Edition with a Study in Renaissance Scepticism and Relativism.* Ed. by P. P. Morphos, Johns Hopkins Univ. Pr. 1953 o.p.

Buckley, George T. *Atheism in the English Renaissance.* Russell repr. of 1932 ed. 1965 o.p. Classic study of atheistic tendencies in Renaissance thought and the reaction they evoked in English writers. Traces the influence of French and Italian debates on immortality and political ideas on such authors as Sidney, Bacon, Marlowe, and Walter Raleigh.

Burtt, Edwin A. *The Metaphysical Foundations of Modern Physical Science.* Humanities Pr. 2d ed. 1967 text ed. $29.00 pap. $12.50. A somewhat dated but still stimulating study of the relation between metaphysics and scientific theories. Discusses Copernicus, Kepler, and Galileo, as well as later figures.

Bush, Douglas. *The Renaissance and English Humanism.* Univ. of Toronto Pr. 1939 o.p. A brief, readable survey, stressing the literary aspects of the humanist influence.

Caponigri, A. Robert. *Philosophy from the Renaissance to the Romantic Age.* Vol. 3 in *A History of Western Philosophy.* Univ. of Notre Dame Pr. 1963 o.p. A good general introduction to a selection of the major thinkers of the period.

Cassirer, Ernst. *The Individual and the Cosmos in Renaissance Philosophy.* Trans. by Mario Domandi, Univ. of Pennsylvania Pr. 1972 pap. $10.95. A famous study of Renaissance philosophy in relation to the development of modern thought. Places particular emphasis on Nicholas of Cusa's theory of knowledge as radically distinct from medieval positions. Tends to overstate Cusanus's direct influence on later thinkers.

———, and others, eds. *The Renaissance Philosophy of Man.* Univ. of Chicago Pr. 1956 pap. $10.95. Excellent selection of Renaissance philosophical texts in translation, with important introductory essays. Includes selections from Petrarch, Valla, Ficino, Pico, Pomponazzi, and Vives.

Charron, Jean D. *The Wisdom of Pierre Charron: An Original and Orthodox Code of Morality.* Greenwood repr. of 1961 ed. 1979 lib. bdg. $22.50. An important study of the sixteenth-century French skeptic.

Copleston, Frederick. *History of Philosophy: Late Medieval and Renaissance Philosophy.* Vol. 3 in *History of Philosophy.* Doubleday 1953 pap. $4.95. Long a standard history of philosophy in English. The volumes on the Renaissance are uneven, generally far better on northern European philosophers than on Italian thinkers. Clearly written and accurate.

Costello, Frank B. *The Political Philosophy of Luis De Molina, S.J.* Jesuit Hist. 1974 pap. $18.00. Considers the political thought of the famous Spanish Jesuit theologian.

Davis, J. C. *Utopia and the Ideal Society: A Study of English Utopian Writing, 1516–1700.* Cambridge Univ. Pr. 1981 $59.50 1983 pap. $15.95. Utopian literature flourished during the later Renaissance, with many important philosophers contributing to the genre. This volume discusses English works, concentrating primarily on the seventeenth century.

Debus, A. G. *Man and Nature in the Renaissance.* [*History of Science Ser.*] Cambridge Univ. Pr. 1978 $29.95 pap. $10.95. Fine general introduction to Renaissance science, particularly valuable for its attention to the role of philosophical and mystical patterns of thought in influencing the scientific practices of the day. Amply illustrated.

Dijksterhuis, E. J. *The Mechanization of the World Picture: Pythagoras to Newton.* Fwd. by D. J. Struik, Princeton Univ. Pr. 1986 text ed. $45.00 pap. $14.50. An important and influential study of the emergence of modern physical science.

Fallico, Arturo, and Herman Shapiro, eds. *Renaissance Philosophy.* Modern Lib. 2 vols. 1967–69 o.p. An extensive collection of texts in translation, with brief introductory essays. Particularly valuable for selections from Italian philosophers of nature and northern humanists.

Febvre, Lucien. *The Problem of Unbelief in the Sixteenth Century: The Religion of Rabelais.* Trans. by Beatrice Gottlieb, Harvard Univ. Pr. 1982 text ed. $35.00. A justly famous analysis of skepticism and atheism in the Renaissance, particularly valuable for its treatment of French sources.

Garin, Eugenio. *Astrology in the Renaissance: The Zodiac of Life.* Trans. by June Allen and Carolyn Jackson, Methuen 1983 $21.95 1986 text ed. pap. $9.95. A masterful study by the leading Italian historian of Renaissance thought. Focuses on the debate over the validity and implications of astrology carried on by such philosophers as Pico, Ficino, and Pomponazzi.

———. *Italian Humanism: Philosophy and Civic Life in the Renaissance.* Trans. by Peter Munz, Greenwood repr. of 1965 ed. 1976 lib. bdg. $22.50. Garin views humanism as a broadly philosophical movement, so that his studies embrace much more technical philosophical writing than those of scholars who define the movement more narrowly.

Gilbert, Neal Ward. *Renaissance Concepts of Method.* Columbia Univ. Pr. 1960 o.p. A very important study of a central problem—the development of the concept of *method* in the period leading up to the Scientific Revolution. An excellent survey of Renaissance views on method that traces them to their sources in classical antiquity.

Gilson, Étienne. *History of Christian Philosophy in the Middle Ages.* Random 1955 o.p. The most comprehensive history in English of the works of Christian medieval philosophers. Contains much that is useful for the study of Renaissance figures, particularly those working in the scholastic tradition. Tends to downplay the originality of Renaissance philosophy.

Grant, Edward. *Much Ado about Nothing: Theories of Space and Vacuum from the Middle Ages to the Scientific Revolution.* Cambridge Univ. Pr. 1981 $75.00. Traces the influence of Stoic, atomistic, and Hermetic teachings—the doctrines attributed to the legendary Egyptian sage Hermes Trismegistus—on the development of early modern concepts of space.

Grassi, Ernesto. *Heidegger and the Question of Renaissance Humanism: Four Studies.* Medieval & Renaissance NY 1983 $12.00. Humanism from the perspective of the great modern existentialist philosopher Martin Heidegger.

Gundersheimer, Werner L. *French Humanism: 1470–1600.* Peter Smith 1970 o.p. A series of essays on major topics in French humanism.

Hathaway, Baxter. *The Age of Criticism: The Late Renaissance in Italy.* Greenwood repr. of 1962 ed. 1972 o.p. A basic study.

Heller, Agnes. *Renaissance Man.* Trans. by Richard E. Allen, Schocken 1981 pap. $9.95. A sweeping study of the alteration in man's attitudes toward his place in nature during the Renaissance.

Howell, Wilbur S. *Logic and Rhetoric in England, 1500–1700.* Russell repr. of 1956 ed. 1961 o.p. Important for the philosophical background of the English Renaissance.

Kennedy, Leonard A. *Peter of Ailly and the Harvest of Medieval Philosophy.* E Mellen 1987 text ed. $49.95. Discusses the skeptical implications of the thought of Pierre d'Ailly (1350–1420), a French philosopher and theologian influenced by William of Ockham.

———, ed. *Renaissance Philosophy: New Translations of Lorenzo Valla, Paul Cortese, Cajetan, T. Bacciliere, Juan Luis Vives, Peter Ramus.* Mouton 1973 text ed. pap. $14.00. A good selection of primary sources in translation.

Koenigsberger, Dorothy. *Renaissance Man and Creative Thinking: A History of Concepts of Harmony 1400–1700.* Humanities Pr. 1979 text ed. $28.00. "Provides interesting insights for the scholar who has already developed his own perception of the Renaissance" (*Renaissance Quarterly*).

Kohl, Benjamin G. *Renaissance Humanism 1300–1550: A Bibliography of Materials in English.* [*Reference Lib. of the Humanities*] Garland 1985 $53.00. A basic bibliographic source useful for the study of humanists with philosophical interests.

Koyré, Alexandre. *From the Closed World to the Infinite Universe.* Johns Hopkins Univ. Pr. repr. of 1956 ed. 1968 pap. $6.95; Peter Smith 1983 $13.25. An important and influential study of the development of the doctrine of an infinite universe. Penetrating accounts of premodern cosmologies.

Kristeller, Paul Oskar. *Eight Philosophers of the Italian Renaissance.* Stanford Univ. Pr. 1964 $15.00 pap. $6.95. Fundamental study by the master historian of the Renaissance philosophy. Balanced biographical and expository essays on Petrarch, Valla, Ficino, Pico, Pomponazzi, Telesio, Patrizi, and Bruno.

———. *Medieval Aspects of Renaissance Learning: Three Essays.* Ed. by Edward P.

Mahoney, Duke Univ. Pr. 1974 $17.50. Three important essays on medieval intellectual influences on Renaissance thought.

———. *Renaissance Thought and Its Sources.* Ed. by Michael Mooney, Columbia Univ. Pr. 1979 $39.00 pap. $15.00. An anthology of some of Kristeller's most important studies, including essays on Renaissance humanism, Platonism and Aristotelianism, and Renaissance concepts of man.

———. *Renaissance Thought and the Arts: Collected Essays.* Princeton Univ. Pr. 1980 $25.00 pap. $8.50. More classic studies, including a famous consideration of the development of the modern concept of the arts during the Renaissance.

Levi, A. *French Moralists: The Theory of the Passions 1585–1649.* Oxford 1964 o.p. Considers the importance of the passions in late Renaissance ethical thought.

Lindberg, David. *Theories of Vision from al-Kindi to Kepler.* Univ. of Chicago Pr. 1981 pap. $10.00. The authoritative study of the topic. Essential for an understanding of philosophical discussions of perception in the early modern period.

Lindhardt, Jan. *Martin Luther: Knowledge and Mediation in the Renaissance.* E Mellen 1986 lib. bdg. $49.95. Considers Luther as a representative of Renaissance humanism.

Lockwood, Dean P. *Ugo Benzi, Medieval Philosopher and Physician 1376–1439.* Univ. of Chicago Pr. 1951 o.p. Fundamental study of the famous Italian physician, important for an understanding of the development of medical methodology in an era when philosophy was an integral part of a doctor's training.

Mahoney, Edward P., ed. *Philosophy and Humanism: Renaissance Essays in Honor of Paul Oskar Kristeller.* Columbia Univ. Pr. 1976 $55.00. Wide-ranging anthology of essays in intellectual history by leading American authorities on Renaissance thought.

Manuel, Frank E., and Fritzie P. Manuel. *Utopian Thought in the Western World.* Harvard Univ. Pr. 1979 text ed. $35.00 pap. $12.95. Standard study, valuable for Renaissance utopianism.

Martindale, Joanna, ed. *English Humanism: Wyatt to Cowley.* Longwood 1984 $31.00 pap. $17.50. An anthology of essays that "does much to elucidate . . . the influence of Erasmus on English men of letters" (*Times Educational Supplement*).

Matsen, Herbert S., ed. *Alessandro Achillini (1463–1512) and His Doctrine of Universals and Transcendentals.* Bucknell Univ. Pr. 1975 $30.00. A detailed study of an Italian Aristotelian whose logic and metaphysics show the influence of Ockham's teachings.

Noreña, Carlos G. *Studies in Spanish Renaissance Thought.* Kluwer Academic 1975 lib. bdg. $50.00. "*The* required introduction into this difficult area of the history of philosophy" (*Journal of the History of Philosophy*).

Oberman, Heiko A. *Forerunners of the Reformation: The Shape of Late Medieval Thought.* Trans. by Paul Nyhus, Fortress 1981 pap. $12.95. Emphasizes the importance of late medieval philosophy and theology for an understanding of later controversies.

———. *The Harvest of Medieval Theology: Gabriel Biel and Late Medieval Nominalism.* Labyrinth Pr. repr. of 1963 ed. 1983 pap. $17.50. Biel was a fifteenth-century German philosopher deeply influenced by the writings of predecessors in the nominalistic tradition, such as William of Ockham. Oberman's influential works have stressed the transitional role of late medieval thought in preparing the way for the Protestant Reformation.

Ong, Walter J. *Ramus, Method, and the Decay of Dialogue: From the Art of Discourse to the Art of Reason.* Harvard Univ. Pr. 1983 text ed. pap. $9.95. Masterful study of the fiercely anti-Aristotelian French Calvinist whose attempt to replace traditional logic in the university curriculum aroused heated opposition during the sixteenth century.

Overfield, James H. *Humanism and Scholasticism in Late Medieval Germany.* Princeton Univ. Pr. 1984 text ed. $40.00. Illustrates the interplay of humanism with medieval scholasticism in the German Renaissance.

Padley, G. A. *Grammatical Theory in Western Europe 1500–1700: The Trends in Vernacular Grammar I.* Cambridge Univ. Pr. 1985 $49.50. Detailed study of grammatical theory in the sixteenth and seventeenth centuries.

Partee, Charles, ed. *Calvin and Classical Philosophy.* Heinman 1977 $30.00. Analyzes Calvin's utilization of ancient philosophical doctrines.

Paul of Venice. *Logica Parva.* Trans. by Alan R. Perreiah, Catholic Univ. Pr. 1984 $59.95. Paul was one of the greatest of the long series of logicians who taught at Padua during the fifteenth and sixteenth centuries. His "short logic" became a standard textbook and played an important part in the introduction of late medieval terminist logic—the analysis of the role of terms in sentences—into Italy. It provides a fine example of the approach to logic rejected and ridiculed by the humanists. This careful translation is provided with excellent notes and introductory essays that interpret Paul's work in the light of modern discussions in semantics and the philosophy of language.

Popkin, Richard H. *The History of Scepticism from Erasmus to Spinoza.* Univ. of California Pr. 1979 $37.00 pap. $9.50. "Certain to remain the standard work on the history of early modern scepticism" (*Renaissance Quarterly*).

——, ed. *Philosophy of the Sixteenth and Seventeenth Centuries.* Free Pr. 1966 text ed. pap. $14.95. A good anthology of texts in translation. Renaissance thinkers treated include Vespucci, Erasmus, Luther, Copernicus, Kepler, Galileo, and Montaigne.

Randall, John Herman. *From the Middle Ages to the Enlightenment.* Vol. 1 in *The Career of Philosophy.* Columbia Univ. Pr. 1970 $45.00 pap. $20.00. The strongest treatment of Renaissance thought in a general history of philosophy in English. Presents Randall's argument that the rise of modern scientific method was influenced by the logic of the secular Aristotelians teaching at the University of Padua during the Renaissance.

Reinharz, Jehuda, and Kalman P. Bland, eds. *Mystics, Philosophers, and Politicians: Essays in Jewish Intellectual History in Honor of Alexander Altman.* Duke Univ. Pr. 1982 $36.75. Contains several important essays on Jewish thinkers of the Renaissance.

Reuchlin, Johann. *On the Art of the Kabbalah (De Arte Cabbalistica).* Trans. by Martin Goodman, Abaris Bks. 1983 $20.00. Reuchlin (1455–1522) was the leading Christian Hebraist of his day. His exposition of the Jewish cabala was to prove influential on generations of Christian thinkers who sought to employ its methods in biblical exegesis, philosophy, and magic.

Rice, Eugene F., Jr. *The Renaissance Idea of Wisdom.* Greenwood repr. of 1958 ed. 1973 lib. bdg. $22.50. Traces the progressive secularization of the concept of wisdom during the Renaissance, from Petrarch to Pierre Charron.

Riedl, John O. *A Catalogue of Renaissance Philosophers: 1350–1650.* Coronet Bks. repr. of 1940 ed. lib. bdg. $43.50. A valuable listing of philosophers active during the Renaissance, many little-known and overlooked in standard histories of philosophy.

Robb, Nesca A. *Neoplatonism of the Italian Renaissance.* Hippocrene Bks. 1968 o.p. Although more than 50 years have elapsed since its first appearance, Robb's work remains a valuable introduction to Renaissance Neoplatonism. He analyzes the impact of Neoplatonic sources on Petrarch, Ficino and his Florentine circle, and several important sixteenth-century poets, artists, and philosophers, demonstrating particular sensitivity to the interplay between philosophy and the creative arts.

Rossi, Paolo. *Philosophy, Technology and the Arts in the Early Modern Era.* Trans. by Salvator Attanasio, Harper 1970 o.p. Lucid analysis of the change in attitude toward the mechanical arts during the sixteenth and seventeenth centuries and how it affected the modern view of science.

Santillana, Giorgio de, ed. *The Age of Adventure: The Renaissance Philosophers.* Ayer repr. of 1956 ed. $17.00. A good anthology of writings in translation. Selections from Leonardo, More, Machiavelli, Michelangelo, Erasmus, Copernicus, Montaigne, Kepler, Galileo, and Bruno.

Saunders, Jason L. *Justus Lipsius: The Philosophy of Renaissance Stoicism.* Liberal Arts Pr. 1955 o.p. Lipsius (1547–1606), a Belgian, was one of the greatest humanist scholars of the late sixteenth century. This careful study assesses his central role in the revival of interest in classical Stoicism during the Renaissance.

Schmitt, Charles B. *The Aristotelian Tradition and Renaissance Universities.* Variorum Reprints 1984 o.p. An anthology of essays by a leading historian of Renaissance Aristotelianism. These papers focus on the teaching of philosophy and science in the university curriculum.

———. *Aristotle and the Renaissance.* Harvard Univ. Pr. 1983 text ed. $18.50. An excellent introduction to the many forms of Aristotelianism that flourished during the Renaissance and the many areas of intellectual life they affected.

———. *Cicero Scepticus: A Study of the Influence of the "Academica" in the Renaissance.* Nijhoff 1972 o.p. Traces the role played by Cicero's writings in the Renaissance revival of skepticism.

———. *John Case and Aristotelianism in Renaissance England.* [*Studies in the History of Ideas*] McGill-Queens Univ. Pr. 1983 $35.00. Extensive study of a major English Renaissance philosopher.

———. *Studies in Renaissance Philosophy and Science.* State Mutual Bk. 1981 $70.00. An anthology of Schmitt's most important papers on the relation between philosophy and modern science.

Seigel, J. E. *Rhetoric and Philosophy in Renaissance Humanism: The Union of Eloquence and Wisdom.* Princeton Univ. Pr. 1968 o.p. Good general account of Renaissance humanism.

Skinner, Quentin. *The Foundations of Modern Political Thought: The Renaissance.* Cambridge Univ. Pr. 2 vols. 1978 ea. $54.50 pap. ea. $15.95. The best introduction to the political philosophy of the Renaissance. Provides a lucid interpretation of the writings of all the major political theorists of the fourteenth to the sixteenth centuries and of many lesser-known figures.

Smith, Gerard, ed. *Jesuit Thinkers of the Renaissance.* Marquette Univ. Pr. 1939 $8.95. An anthology of studies of Jesuit scholastics, including Suàrez, Molina, Juan de Mariana, and Cardinal Bellarmine.

Tatarkiewicz, Wladislaw. *Modern Aesthetics.* Vol. 3 in *History of Aesthetics.* Mouton 1974 text ed. $38.40. This volume, from the most comprehensive modern history of the philosophy of art, concentrates on the early modern period to 1700.

Taylor, Henry Osborn. *Thought and Expression in the Sixteenth Century.* Ungar 2 vols. rev. ed. 1930 o.p. A venerable classic, still valuable for its portraits of leading Renaissance men of letters. Compelling account of the humanist influence in literature and philosophy.

Thorndike, Lynn. *A History of Magic and Experimental Science.* Columbia Univ. Pr. 8

vols. 1923–58 ea. $75.00. A treasure trove of information on magic and the occult and their role in the history of science. Volumes 3 to 6 cover the Renaissance period.

———. *Science and Thought in the Fifteenth Century*. Hafner repr. of 1929 ed. 1967 $14.95. An introduction to Renaissance science by the renowned historian of magic.

Toffanin, G. *History of Humanism*. Trans. by E. Gianturco, Latin Amer. Pub. Co. 1954 o.p. Controversial interpretation of humanism as a Catholic reaction to heretical tendencies in thirteenth-century theology and philosophy.

Trinkaus, Charles. *Adversity's Noblemen*. Hippocrene Bks. rev. ed. 1965 lib. bdg. $15.00. Classic study by one of America's leading historians of humanism.

———. *In Our Image and Likeness*. Univ. of Chicago Pr. 2 vols. 1970 $32.50. A masterful analysis of how the Renaissance humanists transformed the concept of human nature inherited from the medieval world. Detailed discussion of numerous thinkers and texts, including works by Petrarch, Salutati, Valla, Ficino, Pico, Manetti, and Pomponazzi.

———. *The Scope of Renaissance Humanism*. Univ. of Michigan Pr. 1983 text ed. $28.50. A collection of essays from various sources.

Walker, D. P. *The Ancient Theology: Studies in Christian Platonism from the Fifteenth to the Eighteenth Century*. Cornell Univ. Pr. 1972 o.p. An indispensable collection of essays on the impact on Renaissance thought of ancient, often spurious, philosophical and theological sources, such as Orpheus, Hermes Trismegistus, and the Chaldaean Oracles.

———. *Spiritual and Demonic Magic from Ficino to Campanella*. Kraus Repr. repr. of 1958 ed. $44.00. A fine account of the theory and practice of magic among Renaissance philosophers.

Wallace, William A. *Causality and Scientific Explanation: Medieval and Early Classical Science*. Univ. Pr. of Amer. 1981 o.p. Important for an understanding of the relation of theories of causation to the rise of modern physical science. Particularly sensitive to the importance of Renaissance philosophical sources in Galileo's intellectual development.

Weiss, Roberto. *Dawn of Humanism in Italy*. Haskell repr. of 1947 ed. 1970 lib. bdg. $22.95. One of the important studies of the origins of humanism.

———. *Humanism in England During the Fifteenth Century*. Oxford 1941 o.p. Documents the spread of humanism from the Continent to England, where it influenced the English Renaissance.

Wolf, Albert. *A History of Science, Technology and Philosophy in the Sixteenth and Seventeenth Centuries*. Peter Smith 2 vols. o.p. Profusely illustrated history of the sciences and their philosophical background in the early years of the Scientific Revolution.

Woodward, William H. *Vittorino Da Feltre and Other Humanist Educators*. Fwd. by E. F. Rice, Jr. [*Classics in Education Ser.*] Teachers College Pr. 1964 o.p. Classic study, first published in 1905, of Vittorino (1378–1446), who founded a famous humanist school in Mantua, and of humanist educational philosophy.

Yates, Frances A. *Occult Philosophy in the Elizabethan Age*. Methuen repr. of 1979 ed. 1983 $21.95 pap. $5.95. Stimulating account of the influence of the Jewish cabala on Christian thinkers in the late fifteenth and early sixteenth centuries. Philosophers and magicians such as Pico, Reuchlin, Agrippa, and John Dee made cabalism an essential component of their studies.

AGRIPPA OF NETTESHEIM, HENRY CORNELIUS. 1486–1535

Born in Cologne, Agrippa lived a life that combined action and adventure with scholarly pursuits. His early career was spent as a secretary and diplomat for the Holy Roman Emperor. Missions to Paris and London brought him into contact with new intellectual movements, and he immersed himself in the study of philosophy and theology, learning Hebrew in order to read the Jewish cabalistic literature. His first great written work, *The Occult Philosophy* (*De occulta philosophia*), completed 1509–10, but not published until 1531–33, is a compendium offering a mystical interpretation of nature through such arcane methods as cabalistic manipulation of Hebrew words and Pythagorean numerology. It quickly established itself as a major handbook of Renaissance magic and was deeply influential on such thinkers as Giordano Bruno.

In the years following the writing of *De occulta philosophia*, Agrippa served as a soldier, lawyer, physician, and theologian. A virulent critic of the clergy and of scholastic theology, he engaged in bitter exchanges with theologically conservative opponents over his religious attitudes. Agrippa's own position lay between the intellectual reformism of Erasmus and the outright break with Catholicism represented by LUTHER. However, Agrippa later moved away from his early confidence in the magical and mystical methods to an unquestioning biblical faith. His most important later work, *Of the Vanitie and uncertaintie of artes and sciences* (*De incertitudine et vanitate scientiarum et artium*), published at Antwerp in 1530, advocates a thoroughgoing rejection of learning and intellectual attainment in favor of a simple religious piety. It came to play an important role in the Renaissance revival of the skeptical tradition of antiquity. Shortly after the appearance of *De incertitudine*, Agrippa was imprisoned for heresy and died in exile in Grenoble, France.

BOOKS BY AGRIPPA

Of the Vanitie and uncertaintie of artes and sciences. 1530. Trans. by James Sandford, ed. by Catherine M. Dunn, California State Univ. Pr. 1974 o.p. The famous Renaissance translation, originally published in London in 1569.

Three Books of Occult Philosophy or Magic. 1531–33. AMS Pr. repr. of 1898 ed. 1981 $39.50

The Philosophy of Natural Magic. Fwd. by Leslie Shepard, Univ. Bks. repr. of 1913 ed. 1974 o.p. A heady dose of Agrippa's magical theory and practice.

BOOKS ABOUT AGRIPPA

Morley, Henry. *Cornelius Agrippa: The Life of Henry Cornelius Agrippa von Nettesheim.* Chapman & Hall 2 vols. 1856 o.p. A dated and somewhat unreliable account of Agrippa's life and works.

Nauert, Charles G., Jr. *Agrippa and the Crisis of Renaissance Thought.* Univ. of Illinois Pr. 1965 o.p. The only comprehensive scholarly account of Agrippa's thought in English. A careful, well-documented study that places Agrippa's work within the intellectual climate of the times.

BODIN, JEAN. 1530?–1596

One of the most influential French philosophers of the sixteenth century, Bodin is known today for his political thought. He received training in law at the University of Toulouse and became an advocate at Paris, where he won the favor of the royal family. His first major work, *Method for the Easy Comprehension of History (Methodus ad facilem historiarum cognitionem)*, published in 1566, provides an overall introduction to his philosophical system. *The Six Bookes of a Commonweale*, which appeared in French in 1576 and later in a Latin version, is in many respects his chief claim to fame as a political philosopher. It contains a strong defense of absolute sovereignty and of monarchy as the best form of government. His *Demonomania*, first published in 1580, is an elaborate account of witchcraft and sorcery intended to assist in the suppression of the black arts. *Theatre of Nature (Universale theatrum naturae)*, printed in 1596, contains his cosmology and his speculations on the nature of the human soul, angels, and the spiritual world. *Colloquy of the Seven (Colloquium heptaplomeres)*, composed in 1588, did not appear in print until the nineteenth century. It takes the form of a dialogue among seven sages of different religions and philosophical persuasions in search of a common creed. Although he was an active and at times controversial writer during the period of France's most bitter religious strife, Bodin seems to have avoided sectarian conflict while maintaining his loyalty to the Catholic church and the monarchy.

BOOKS BY BODIN

Method for the Easy Comprehension of History. 1566. Trans. by Beatrice Reynolds, Russell repr. of 1945 ed. 1985 lib. bdg. $75.00

The Six Bookes of a Commonweale. 1576. Ed. by J. P. Mayer, Ayer repr. of 1962 ed. 1979 lib. bdg. $66.50

Colloquium of the Seven about Secrets of the Sublime. 1857. Ed. and trans. by Marion L. Daniels, Princeton Univ. Pr. 1975 $63.00

BOOKS ABOUT BODIN

Franklin, Julian H. *Jean Bodin and the Rise of Absolutist Theory.* Cambridge Univ. Pr. 1973 $21.95. An excellent account of Bodin's political thought.

———. *Jean Bodin and the Sixteenth-Century Revolution in the Methodology of Law and History.* Greenwood repr. of 1963 ed. 1977 lib. bdg. $22.50. Considers Bodin as legal theorist and philosopher of history.

King, Preston T. *The Ideology of Order: A Comparative Analysis of Jean Bodin and Thomas Hobbes.* Harper 1974 o.p. Bodin's political ideas compared and contrasted with those of the author of *Leviathan.*

Mayer, J. P., ed. *Fundamental Studies of Jean Bodin: An Original Anthology.* [*European Political Thought Ser.*] Ayer 1979 lib. bdg. $46.00. Important collection of basic studies on Bodin.

BRUNO, GIORDANO. 1548–1600

One of the most intriguing characters in late Renaissance thought, Bruno has long held a fascination for historians of science and philosophy. Revered by the nineteenth century as a martyr for the Copernican view of the universe, he has been shown by recent studies to have been far less "modern" in many of his key teachings than previously believed.

His life was a continuous series of conflicts and peregrinations. Born at Nola, near Naples, he entered the Dominican order as a youth but ran afoul of the authorities over the orthodoxy of his beliefs. He fled Italy in 1576 to avoid charges of heresy and made his way to Geneva, where he soon angered the Calvinists, then to Paris, where he lectured on philosophy for a time and published treaties on the art of memory. In 1583 he journeyed to London to join the household of the French ambassador to the English court. There he composed his most important early works, all written in Italian and published surreptitiously in London, the following four in a single year, 1584: (1) *The Ash Wednesday Supper* (*La cena de le ceneri*) contains Bruno's defense of Copernican heliocentrism, conceived as having enormous metaphysical and ethical, as well as merely astronomical, significance; (2) *On the Cause, Principle and One* (*De la causa, principio et uno*) expounds Bruno's metaphysics through the analysis of the notions of cause and principle; (3) *On the Infinite, the Universe and Worlds* (*De l'infinito, universo et mondi*) introduces Bruno's concept of the physical universe as infinite in extent, embracing innumerable finite world-systems; and (4) *The Expulsion of the Triumphant Beast* (*Lo spaccio de la bestia trion fante*) puts forward a heavily symbolic proposal for a reconciliation of religious differences. Other works from the same period deal with Jewish cabala and poetic inspiration.

Bruno's published works reveal him as an innovative thinker who drew his inspiration from ancient philosophical sources as well as from the scientific works of his own time. His bold assertion of the infinity of the physical universe, for example, goes beyond the claims of COPERNICUS (see Vol. 5) or, later, GALILEO (see Vol. 5), but it was not based on any empirical observations or mathematical calculations. Instead it was a logical inference from Bruno's metaphysical assumption that an infinite divine principle could not but produce an infinite effect. His "modern" cosmological views must thus be seen against the background of his absorption with Hermeticism, Neoplatonism, demonic magic, and millenarianism, all of which found other spirited advocates during the Renaissance.

Following his return from England, Bruno traveled in central Europe, teaching and preaching his new vision of the universe to an often hostile audience. In 1591 he accepted an invitation to tutor a Venetian nobleman but was turned over to the Inquisition on charges of heresy. After a long imprisonment in Venice and Rome he was burned alive on the Campo de' Fiori in Rome on February 17, 1600. Though his love of magic and metaphysics may weaken his claim to be viewed as a forerunner of modern science, Bruno remains a legitimate martyr to the principles of free thought and expression.

BOOKS BY BRUNO

The Ash Wednesday Supper. 1584. Trans. by Stanley L. Jaki, Mouton 1975 text ed. $19.60

Cause, Principle, and Unity: Five Dialogues. 1584. Trans. by Jack Lindsay, Greenwood repr. of 1962 ed. 1976 lib. bdg. $22.50

The Expulsion of the Triumphant Beast. 1584. Ed. and trans. by Arthur D. Imerti, Rutgers Univ. Pr. 1964 o.p.

The Heroic Enthusiasts. 1585. Gordon Pr. 1976 lib. bdg. $59.95. One of Bruno's most important "moral" dialogues, dealing with poetic inspiration.

Giordano Bruno's "The Heroic Frenzies." 1585. Trans. by P. E. Memmo, Jr., Univ. of North Carolina Pr. 1964 o.p. Another edition.

BOOKS ABOUT BRUNO

Greenberg, Sidney. *The Infinite in Giordano Bruno: With a Translation of His Dialogue "Concerning the Cause, Principle, and One."* Octagon 1971 lib. bdg. $17.00. An important study of the historical sources of Bruno's concept of the infinite, a central notion in his metaphysics and cosmology.

McIntrye, J. L. *Giordano Bruno.* Macmillan 1903 o.p. One of the earliest attempts to analyze Bruno's philosophical works in a systematic way.

Michel, Paul-Henri. *The Cosmology of Giordano Bruno.* Cornell Univ. Pr. 1973 o.p. Extremely important study of Bruno's account of the physical universe, which views Bruno's philosophy of nature as anticipating modern views.

Nelson, John C. *Renaissance Theory of Love: The Context of Giordano Bruno's "Eroici Furori."* Columbia Univ. Pr. 1958 o.p. Places one of Bruno's most important "moral" dialogues in the context of Platonic treatises on love, a literary-philosophical genre that flourished during the Renaissance.

Paterson, Antoinette M. *The Infinite Worlds of Giordano Bruno.* C. C. Thomas 1970 $23.75. "Succeeds on the whole in making Giordano Bruno relevant enough to our own time and engaging enough to students who might wish to look further into his work" (*Renaissance Quarterly*).

Singer, Dorothea W. *Giordano Bruno, His Life and Thought.* Greenwood repr. of 1950 ed. 1968 lib. bdg. $27.25. The best intellectual biography of Bruno. Contains a valuable translation of Bruno's dialogue "On the Infinite, Universe and Worlds."

Yates, Frances. *Giordano Bruno and the Hermetic Tradition.* [*Midway Repr. Ser.*] Univ. of Chicago Pr. 1979 text ed. pap. $17.00. Ground-breaking study that places Bruno in the tradition of "Hermetic" philosophers, who accepted the authenticity of late ancient texts, falsely attributed to the ancient Egyptian sage Hermes Trismegistus.

——. *Lull and Bruno: Collected Essays.* Methuen 1982 $26.95. A selection of Dame Frances Yates's most important studies of Giordano Bruno and Ramon Lull. Valuable for an understanding of Renaissance occultism and its influence in philosophy, art, and science.

CAJETAN, CARDINAL (THOMAS DE VIO). 1469–1534

The most able and eloquent of the Renaissance followers of the Thomist school of scholastic theology, Thomas de Vio took the name Cajetan from his hometown of Gaeta in Italy. As a youth he entered the Dominican order and, after a rigorous training in philosophy and theology, taught at the University of Padua, then a major center of Aristotelian philosophy, and later at Pavia and Rome. He became master general of the Dominican order in 1508 and a Cardinal in 1517. A mission to Germany (1518–19) brought him into the forefront of the Church's confrontation with MARTIN LUTHER, with whom he engaged in a celebrated theological debate at Augsburg.

In addition to commentaries on works of ARISTOTLE (see also Vols. 3 and 5) and THOMAS AQUINAS, Cajetan composed theological treatises and essays on social philosophy. His most famous work is his massive commentary on Aquinas's *Summa Theologiae*, which played a major role in the development of scholastic theology during the sixteenth century. As a philosopher, Cajetan provided an influential exposition of the concept of analogy and came to reject the possibility of a philosophical proof of the soul's immortality.

BOOKS BY CAJETAN

Cardinal Cajetan Responds: A Reader in Reformation Controversy. Ed. and trans. by Jared Wicks, Catholic Univ. Pr. 1978 o.p. Presents a selection of the great Cardinal's writings on theological issues.

Commentary on Being and Essence. 1508 Ed. and trans. by Lottie H. Kendzierski and Francis C. Wade, S.J., Marquette Univ. Pr. 1964 o.p. This is Cajetan's commentary on St. Thomas's *On Being and Essence.*

The Analogy of Names and the Concept of Being. Ed. and trans. by E. A. Bushinski and H. J. Koren, Duquesne Univ. Pr. 1959 o.p. Cajetan's central metaphysical views are propounded in his analysis of the concepts of being and his development of the Thomist doctrine of analogy.

Aristotle on Interpretation: Commentary by St. Thomas and Cajetan. Trans. by J. T. Oesterle, Marquette Univ. Pr. 1962 o.p. Presents the comments of both Thomas Aquinas and his chief Renaissance expositor on the Aristotelian work *On Interpretation.*

CAMPANELLA, TOMMASO. 1568–1639

A radical and innovative thinker, Campanella lived a stormy life characterized by charges of political intrigue, imprisonment, philosophical speculation, poetic inspiration, and the practice of magic. Today he is best known as a political philosopher, author of the famous utopia, *The City of the Sun.*

Like his older contemporary Giordano Bruno, Campanella emerged from the intellectual milieu of the Dominican order in southern Italy with a philosophical orientation that authorities considered heretical and dangerous. Imprisoned at Naples in 1599, the year before Bruno's execution, on charges of heresy and plotting against Spanish rule, he was not released until 1626. Following another period of imprisonment at Rome and an examination of his views by the Roman Inquisition, he fled Italy in 1634, taking refuge in Paris, where he lived his last years.

Prior to his imprisonment Campanella had been deeply influenced by Bernardino Telesio's defense of a naturalistic, empirically grounded philosophy of nature against the dominant Aristotelianism of the university curriculum. From Telesio he adopted the notions of heat and cold as active principles operative on matter, space, and time as prior to and independent of bodies, and the concept of spirit as a corporeal power responsible for sensation and distinct from the intellective mind infused into man by God. These doctrines gave a strongly naturalistic character to Campanella's concept of nature and man, but they were combined with an interest in magic that had its origins in ancient Neoplatonism and Hermeticism.

The City of the Sun portrays a highly ordered communistic state in which political power and religious authority are united in a controlling priesthood.

BOOKS BY CAMPANELLA

The City of the Sun: A Poetical Dialogue. 1623. Ed. by Daniel J. Donno, Univ. of California Pr. 1981 $21.50 pap. $4.95; Riverrun 1985 pap. $4.50. Beautifully presented bilingual edition of Campanella's great dialogue. Superb introduction.

The Defense of Galileo. 1616. Trans. by Grant McColley, Ayer repr. of 1937 ed. 1975 $14.00; Richwood Pub. repr. of 1937 ed. 1976 lib. bdg. $14.50. Campanella's *Apologia* on behalf of the great scientist's defense of Copernicanism.

BOOK ABOUT CAMPANELLA

Bonansea, Bernardino M. *Tommaso Campanella: Renaissance Pioneer of Modern Thought.* Catholic Univ. Pr. 1969 $19.95. "A balanced and informative discussion of three of the most important studies made by Campanella—epistemology, metaphysics, and ethico-political theory" (*Renaissance Quarterly*).

ERASMUS, DESIDERIUS. 1466?–1536

The most renowned scholar of his time, Erasmus was a leading proponent of what has been termed "Christian humanism," the mastery of the humanities and classical studies coupled with a devotion to Christian piety. Born in Rotterdam, Holland, Erasmus received his early training at the famous school of the Brethren of the Common Life at Deventer where Nicholas of Cusa had studied earlier. He entered the Augustinian order and in 1492 was ordained a priest. A period at Paris devoted to the study of philosophy and theology was followed by a series of journeys to England and Italy, which brought him into contact with many of the leading humanists in Europe. During an extended visit in England (1509–14) he stayed for a time with THOMAS MORE (see also Vol. 1), to whom he dedicated his famous *Praise of Folly* (*Moriae encomium*) in 1509. He was appointed Professor of Greek and Divinity at Cambridge, where he prepared his influential edition of the New Testament. Returning to the Continent, he devoted the remainder of his life to his writing, editing, and correspondence.

A prolific writer, Erasmus serves as a prime example of the tremendous influence a Renaissance man of letters could attain through the medium of print. His editions of classical and early Christian authors formed the patrimony of generations of subsequent scholars. His open criticism of the hypocrisy and venality of the Churchmen of his day sounded a chord that Luther was to echo and doubtless aided in the progress of the Protestant Reformation. But Erasmus himself was no Protestant. Though he advocated reform, he remained within the Catholic Church, openly attacking Luther's position on the will in his treatise *On Free Will* (*De libero arbitrio*) of 1524.

Like many of his humanist contemporaries, Erasmus did not compose formal philosophical treatises but presented his thoughts on ethics, religion, and society in polished literary essays or in his voluminous correspondence. Particularly important for an understanding of his thought are the

Colloquies (1516), *The Handbook of a Christian Soldier (Enchiridion militis christiani)* (1503), and *The Praise of Folly.*

BOOKS BY ERASMUS

The Essential Erasmus. Ed. and trans. by John P. Dolan, New Amer. Lib. 1964 pap. $3.95. A handy selection of texts, including *The Praise of Folly* and *The Handbook of the Militant Christian.*

Christian Humanism and the Reformation: Selected Writings with the Life of Erasmus by Beatus Rhenanus. Ed. by John C. Olin, Peter Smith 1973 $11.25

Desiderius Erasmus Concerning the Aim and Method of Education. Ed. by William H. Woodward, fwd. by Craig R. Thompson [*Classics in Education Ser.*] Teachers College Pr. 1964 o.p. A classic study of Erasmus's educational philosophy, accompanied by a selection of his writings on education. Extensive bibliography.

Enchiridion Militis Christiani (An English Version). 1503. Trans. by Anne O'Donnell [*Early English Text Society Ser.*] Oxford 1981 text ed. $42.00

Adages. 1508. Ed. and trans. by Margaret M. Phillips and R. A. Mynors, Univ. of Toronto Pr. 1982 $65.00. One of Erasmus's most influential works, an extensive collection of Latin proverbs with his exposition and comments.

Erasmus on His Times: A Shortened Version of the Adages of Erasmus. Ed. by Margaret M. Phillips, Cambridge Univ. Pr. 1967 pap. $9.95. A concise version of *Adages.*

The Praise of Folly. 1509. Ed. by Leonard F. Dean, Hendricks House 1983 $4.95; trans. by Betty Radice, Penguin 1971 pap. $4.95; trans. by Hoyt H. Hudson, Princeton Univ. Pr. 1941 $23.50 pap. $6.95; Univ. of Michigan Pr. 1958 pap. $5.95; ed. and trans. by Clarence H. Miller, Yale Univ. Pr. 1979 text ed. $25.00 pap. $7.95

Education of a Christian Prince. 1516. Trans. by Lester K. Born, Hippocrene Bks. 1965 lib. bdg. $27.50. An extensive introduction complements a careful translation of this classic of Christian humanism. Good bibliography.

Colloquies of Erasmus. 1516. Trans. by Craig R. Thompson, Univ. of Chicago Pr. 1965 $45.00

Ten Colloquies. 1516. Trans. by Craig R. Thompson, Bobbs 1957 pap. $7.20

Discourse on Free Will. 1524. Ed. and trans. by Ernst F. Winter [*Milestones of Thought Ser.*] Ungar 1961 pap. $6.95. Contains selections from Erasmus's *De libero arbitrio* and Luther's *De servo arbitrio.*

Ciceronianus: Or, A Dialogue on the Best Style of Speaking. Trans. by Izora Scott [*Columbia Univ. Teachers College Contributions to Education*] AMS Pr. repr. of 1908 ed. 1982 $22.50. Important for an understanding of Erasmus's dedication to humanist rhetorical ideals.

On Copia of Words and Ideas. Ed. and trans. by Donald B. King and H. David Rix, Marquette Univ. Pr. 1963 o.p. Erasmus's influential textbook for rhetorical training. It profoundly influenced Renaissance literary style and education.

BOOKS ABOUT ERASMUS

Allen, Percy S. *Age of Erasmus.* Russell repr. of 1914 ed 1963 o.p. *Age of Erasmus* and the following title are standard studies of Erasmus's life and times.

———. *Erasmus: Lectures and Wayfaring Sketches.* Oxford 1934 o.p.

Bainton, Roland. *Erasmus of Christendom.* Crossroad 1982 pap. $12.95; Scribner 1969 $20.00. Masterful intellectual biography.

Bouyer, Louis. *Erasmus and His Times.* Trans. by F. X. Murphy, Newman 1959 o.p.

Translation of the French edition. A good general introduction to Erasmus's place in the history of Renaissance humanism.

Boyle, Marjorie O. *Christening Pagan Mysteries: Erasmus in Pursuit of Wisdom.* Univ. of Toronto Pr. 1981 $22.50. "Excellent, learned, and useful" (*Renaissance Quarterly*).

Dorey, T. A., ed. *Erasmus.* Univ. of New Mexico Pr. 1970 o.p. "This volume by British and Canadian scholars 'contains chapters on the importance of Erasmus as an interpreter of the Classics, as a satirist, and as a writer of letters. There is an account of his work as a Biblical scholar and religious reformer, an examination of his linguistic style, and a discussion of the Medieval background and the significance of Erasmus to our own times' " (Introduction).

Huizinga, Johan. *Erasmus and The Age of Reformation.* Harper 1957 o.p. "Excellent intellectual biography" (*Encyclopedia of Philosophy*).

Phillips, Margaret M. *Erasmus and the Northern Renaissance.* Rowman 1981 o.p. Excellent introduction to Erasmus's works, summarizing the results of recent scholarship.

Rabil, Albert. *Erasmus and the New Testament: The Mind of a Christian Humanist.* Trinity Univ. Pr. 1972 o.p.

Smith, Preserved. *Erasmus: A Study of His Life, Ideals and Place in History.* 1923. Dover 1962 o.p. Standard biography.

FICINO, MARSILIO. 1433–1499

The leading figure in the Renaissance revival of Platonism, Marsilio Ficino profoundly influenced the philosophical thought of his own and following centuries. Born near Florence, the son of a physician, Ficino received his early training in philosophy, medicine, and theology and devoted himself to the study of Greek. His learning attracted the attention of one of his father's eminent patients, Cosimo de' Medici, of the powerful Florentine banking family, and in 1462 Cosimo established him at a villa and supplied him with Greek manuscripts for translation. Here Ficino set up his famous Florentine Academy, devoted to the study and celebration of Plato's teachings. He continued to receive the active support of the Medici until their expulsion from Florence in 1494.

Ficino's labors as a translator provided his Greekless contemporaries with access to the greatest works of the ancient Platonic tradition. His Latin version of PLATO's (see also Vol. 3) dialogues, published in 1484, made the entirety of Plato available for the first time in translation. Ficino also prepared translations of other important sources such as the Neoplatonist PLOTINUS, Proclus, Iamblichus, pseudo-Dionysius the Areopagite, and the Greek works attributed to Hermes Trismegistus (a fabled Egyptian priest supposedly contemporary with Moses).

To Ficino, the Platonic tradition represented an ongoing heritage of divinely inspired ancient wisdom reconcilable with Christian revelation. His reading of Plato in the light of late Neoplatonists, such as Plotinus and Proclus, survived long after the Renaissance and remained the prevalent interpretation of Plato's thought until comparatively recent times. His chief philosophical work, *Platonic Theology* (1482), represents an attempt to demonstrate the immortality of the human soul on Platonic grounds in a way consistent with Christian doctrine. It represents reality as a hierarchy, from

God down to material bodies, with rational soul, the level proper to man, as a mean that participates in the characteristics of both higher and lower beings. This scheme, derived with important modifications from Plotinus, was to influence many later Platonists, including Ficino's younger friend and colleague Giovanni Pico della Mirandola.

Ficino's devotion to Platonism must thus be seen within the context of his Christianity. He was ordained priest in 1437 and later served as a canon of the Florentine cathedral. His intellectual synthesis of Platonism and Christianity, however, so powerfully appealing to the Medici circle, was a far cry from the reformist zeal of Savonarola, whose rise to power in 1494 saw Ficino enter into a quiet retirement until his death.

In addition to the titles listed below, see also the books by Garin, Kristeller, Robb, and Walker in the General Bibliography at the beginning of this chapter.

BOOKS BY FICINO

Commentary on Plato's Symposium on Love. 1469. Trans. by Sears R. Jayne, Spring Pubns. 2d rev. ed. 1985 pap. $18.50. Careful translation of one of Ficino's most influential works, a classic in the rich Renaissance philosophical literature on love.

The Letters of Marsilio Ficino. 1495. Schocken 3 vols. 1985 ea. $18.95–$23.50. Carefully executed translation from Ficino's published correspondence, a rich source for his philosophical teachings.

The Book of Life. Trans. and intro. by Charles Boer, Spring Pubns. 1980 pap. $12.50. First English translation of Ficino's important treatise on medicine and natural magic.

Marsilio Ficino and the Phaedran Charioteer. Ed. and trans. by Michael J. B. Allen, Univ. of California Pr. 1981 o.p. Masterly translation and introduction to the various texts in which Ficino discusses the enduring Platonic image of the rational soul as charioteer in the *Phaedrus.*

Marsilio Ficino: The 'Philebus' Commentary. Ed. and trans. by Michael J. B. Allen, Univ. of California Pr. 1975 o.p. Careful translation and study of Ficino's great commentary on Plato's *Philebus.*

BOOKS ABOUT FICINO

Allen, Michael J. B. *The Platonism of Marsilio Ficino: A Study of His Phaedrus Commentary, Its Sources and Genesis.* Univ. of California Pr. 1984 text ed. $33.00. A rich and learned account of Ficino's Platonism, centering on the *Phaedrus* commentary. An essential work.

Collins, Ardis B. *The Secular Is Sacred: Platonism and Thomism in Marsilio Ficino's Platonic Theology.* Nijhoff 1974 o.p. Emphasizes Ficino's debt to Thomas Aquinas.

Jayne, Sears R. *John Colet and Marsilio Ficino.* Greenwood repr. of 1963 ed. 1980 lib. bdg. $24.75. Discusses Ficino's influence on English humanism.

Kristeller, Paul Oskar. *The Philosophy of Marsilio Ficino.* Peter Smith 1964 $12.75. Long a classic, this is still the best general study of Ficino. The English version lacks the comprehensive annotation of the Italian and German editions.

GALILEI, GALILEO. 1564–1642

Galileo, the great astronomer and physicist whose researches played so crucial a role in the history of science, also occupies an important place in the history of philosophy for his part in overthrowing the predominant Aristotelian concept of the nature of the universe. Galileo considered himself a philosopher and referred to himself as such on the title pages of his most influential works. Much recent research has been devoted to examining both the philosophical background of Galileo's scientific achievements and the philosophical implications of his scientific method.

Born in Pisa, the eldest son of a famous music theorist, Galileo entered on the study of medicine at the University of Pisa but quickly shifted his interest to mathematics. From 1589 to 1592, he taught mathematics at Pisa while studying independently with Jacopo Mazzoni, a distinguished professor of philosophy. His earliest scientific works, directed against ARISTOTLE'S (see also Vols. 3 and 5) account of freely falling bodies, date from this period. In 1592 he moved to Padua, where he lectured on mathematics and astronomy, and by 1597 he was defending the Copernican helicocentric theory of the universe in a letter to his friend Mazzoni.

When, in 1609, he learned of the invention of the telescope in Holland, Galileo quickly designed an improved version of the instrument for his own astronomical observations. His startling discoveries—including the satellites of Jupiter—were revealed in 1610 in his *Starry Messenger* (*Sidereus nuncius*), which led to his appointment as mathematician and philosopher to the Grand Duke of Tuscany. On a visit to Rome in 1611 he demonstrated the power of his instrument and defended the Copernican worldview in learned circles.

Church authorities were divided on the question of whether the Copernican theory was consistent with scriptural accounts of the cosmos, and Galileo's position was attacked on theological grounds. He defended himself eloquently in his famous *Letter to the Grand Duchess Christina* (1615), arguing for the independence of scientific inquiry from theological constraints. Nevertheless, in the following year he was forbidden to hold or teach the Copernican view. Retiring to Florence to pursue his scientific researches, Galileo let the Copernican question lie until a new Pope, Urban VIII, seemed to offer a more favorable reception to his views. In 1632 he brought out his great *Dialogue Concerning the Two Chief World Systems*, a presentation of the Ptolemaic-Aristotelian and Copernican systems heavily weighted in favor of the scientific superiority of the latter. In spite of the support of his Florentine and Roman friends, Galileo was tried and forced to recant his defense of helicocentrism under threat of torture; the *Dialogue* was placed on the *Index of Prohibited Books* and its author sentenced to house arrest for life. Galileo's last years were spent in scientific investigations that culminated in the publication of his *Discourses on Two New Sciences* (1638).

Galileo's legacy as a philosopher lies in his outspoken defense of the autonomy of scientific investigation from philosophical and theological authority, and his conviction that mathematical proofs can and should be sought in physical science, that celestial and terrestrial phenomena can be accounted for by a single set of scientific laws, and that scientific explanations cannot be divorced from direct empirical observation of phenomena.

In addition to the titles listed here, see also the books by Boas, Burtt, Dijksterhuis, Koyré, Randall, and Wallace in the General Bibliography at the beginning of this chapter. (See also Volume 5.)

BOOKS BY GALILEO

Galileo's Early Notebooks: The Physical Questions. Trans. by William A. Wallace, Univ. of Notre Dame Pr. 1977 text ed. $24.95. Reveals Galileo's early dependence on scholastic sources.

Discoveries and Opinions of Galileo. Doubleday 1957 pap. $5.95. Includes *The Starry Messenger* (1610), *Letter to the Grand Duchess Christina* (1615), and excerpts from *Letters on Sunspots* (1613) and *The Assayer* (1623).

Dialogue Concerning the Two Chief World Systems, Ptolemaic and Copernican. 1632. Trans. by Stillman Drake, Univ. of California Pr. 2d. rev. ed. 1967 pap. $11.95

Two New Sciences: Including "Centers of Gravity" and "Force of Percussion." 1638. Ed. and trans. by Stillman Drake, Univ. of Wisconsin Pr. 1974 o.p.

On Motion and On Mechanics. Ed. and trans. by I. E. Drabkin and Stillman Drake [*Publications in Medieval Science*] Univ. of Wisconsin Pr. 1960 o.p. Galileo's early treatise on motion (c.1590), criticizing Aristotle's theories, and his treatise on mechanics (c.1600), both with valuable introductions.

BOOKS ABOUT GALILEO

Butts, Robert E., and Joseph C. Pitt, eds. *New Perspectives on Galileo.* Kluwer Academic 1978 lib. bdg. $39.50 pap. $15.80. An important collection of recent studies.

Clavelin, Maurice. *The Natural Philosophy of Galileo: Essay on the Origins and Formation of Classical Mechanics.* Trans. by A. J. Pomerans. MIT 1974 o.p. Influential study of the philosophical background of Galileo's scientific work.

Drake, Stillman. *Galileo at Work: His Scientific Biography.* Univ. of Chicago Pr. 1978 $30.00 1981 pap. $9.95. Important, if somewhat controversial, portrait of Galileo's scientific career. Emphasizes the study of the great scientist's research techniques, rather than his finished works.

————. *Galileo Studies: Personality, Tradition, and Revolution.* Univ. of Michigan Pr. 1970 o.p. Valuable series of papers on Galileo's scientific achievements, emphasizing his associates and opponents in his physical and astronomical investigations.

Finocchiaro, Maurice A. *Galileo and the Art of Reasoning: Rhetorical Foundations of Logic and Scientific Method.* Kluwer Academic 1980 lib. bdg. $42.00 pap. $21.00. "Finocchiaro certainly succeeds in making his point that the *Dialogue* makes a splendid work-book for anyone who wants to see critical reason in action. . . . The book will be very useful for anyone who is working with the complex argument of the *Dialogue*" (*Renaissance Quarterly*).

Geymonat, Ludovico. *Galileo Galilei: A Biography and Inquiry into His Philosophy of Science.* Ed. and trans. by Stillman Drake, McGraw-Hill 1965 o.p. Influential intellectual biography of Galileo, carefully tracing the development of his scientific works and his ongoing battle with ecclesiatical authorities.

Golino, Carlo L., ed. *Galileo Reappraised.* Univ. of California Pr. 1966 $28.00. Five papers by leading Galileo scholars on a range of topics, including his role as a man of letters, his religious views, and so on.

Koyré, Alexandre. *Galileo Studies.* Trans. by J. Mephem, Humanities Pr. 1978 o.p.

Discusses Galileo's achievement from a philosophical perspective. Koyré emphasizes the "Platonic" character of Galileo's view of reality.

McMullin, Ernan. *Galileo Man of Science.* Basic Bks. 1967 o.p. Includes a comprehensive bibiliography of works on Galileo (1940–64).

Ronan, Colin A. *Galileo.* Putnam 1974 o.p. Nicely illustrated, readable account of Galileo's overall achievement.

Shapere, Dudley. *Galileo: A Philosophical Study.* Univ. of Chicago Pr. 1974 pap. $2.95. Fundamental study by a distinguished philosopher of science.

Shea, William R. *Galileo's Intellectual Revolution: Middle Period, 1610–1632.* Watson Pub. Intl. 1977 pap. $8.95. "An informative and illuminating contribution to Galileo studies . . . concise and well written" (*Renaissance Quarterly*).

Wallace, William A. *Galileo and His Sources.* Princeton Univ. Pr. 1984 text ed. $42.50. Emphasizes Galileo's dependence on scholastic Aristotelian sources, showing his ties to thinkers such as Christopher Clavius and Jacopo Mazzoni.

———. *Prelude to Galileo: Essays on Medieval and Sixteenth-Century Sources of Galileo's Thought.* Kluwer Academic 1981 o.p. "Required reading for the expert, the early chapters particularly provide a lucid introduction to that cloudy world of science from the High Middle Ages through the 17th Century" (*Choice*).

MACHIAVELLI, NICCOLO. 1469–1527

Machiavelli was a Florentine diplomat, political theorist, and man of letters whose name has become synonymous with political amorality and opportunism as a result of his candid and uncompromising portrayal of the effective ruler in *The Prince.* From 1498 to 1512, during the period of republican government in Florence, Machiavelli enjoyed a successful career as public servant and diplomat, but on the reinstatement of the Medici he was dismissed and sent into exile. Frustrated by his enforced absence from political life, he turned his attention to a serious study of the classics. The perspective gained from this reading, coupled with his reflection on his own experiences and observations of political events, formed the basis for his writings.

The Prince, written in 1513 but published posthumously in 1532, was dedicated to Lorenzo de' Medici, ruler of Florence. It is a handbook for successful rule, predicated on the assumptions that human nature is constant, that the political skill (virtù) exhibited by successful rulers in the past in dealing with adverse fortune can be drawn on to instruct a contemporary prince in similar circumstances, and that only such a prince—able to be ruthless when necessary—will be strong enough to unite Italy and free her from foreign dominion. This represents a bold departure from the standard handbooks on the education of princes, which emphasized the moral improvement of the people through the example of a morally superior ruler.

Machiavelli's other works include the *Discourses on Livy* (1532), *The Art of War* (1521), *History of Florence* (1532), and a popular comedy, *La Mandragola* (1524). His correspondence is filled with witty and often irreverent reflections on contemporary events and personalities. (See also Volume 3.)

BOOKS BY MACHIAVELLI

The Portable Machiavelli. Ed. by Peter Bondanella and Mark Musa, Penguin 1979 pap. $7.95. Excellent selection from the full range of Machiavelli's writings.

The Discourses. 1532. Trans. by Leslie J. Walker, Methuen 2 vols. 1975 set $45.00 ea. $24.50; ed. by Bernard Crick, Penguin 1984 pap. $4.95. Machiavelli's masterly exposition and commentary on Livy, essential for an understanding of his political thought.

The Art of War. 1521. Trans. by Ellis Farnesworth, Bobbs 1965 o.p. Machiavelli's learned treatise on the theory and practice of warfare.

The Prince. 1532. Ed. by Daniel Donno, Bantam 1981 pap. $1.95; ed. and trans. by Thomas G. Bergin [*Crofts Class. Ser.*] Harlan Davidson 1947 text ed. pap. $3.50; ed. and trans. by Robert M. Adams, Norton 1977 $19.95 pap. $6.95; ed. and trans. by Peter Bondanella and Mark Musa, Oxford 1984 pap. $2.25; trans. by George Bull, Penguin 1961 pap. $2.25; trans. by Harvey C. Mansfield, Jr., Univ. of Chicago Pr. 1985 lib. bdg. $18.00 pap. $5.95

BOOKS ABOUT MACHIAVELLI

Gilbert, A. H. *Machiavelli's "Prince" and Its Forerunners.* Barnes & Noble repr. 1968 o.p. Seminal study that views *The Prince* against the background of traditional "advice to princes" literature. Includes a detailed commentary on *The Prince.*

Mansfield, Harvey C., Jr. *Machiavelli's New Modes and Orders: A Study of the "Discourses on Livy."* Cornell Univ. Pr. 1979 $45.00. Controversial study that gives an unorthodox interpretation of the *Discourses.*

Pitkin, Hanna F. *Fortune Is a Woman: Gender and Politics in the Thought of Niccolò Machiavelli.* Univ. of California Pr. 1984 $27.50. "Wide-ranging and deep-reaching study on the psychological and political problem of 'autonomy.' . . . Filled with insights, broad learning, and wisdom"(*Renaissance Quarterly*).

Ridolfi, Roberto. *The Life of Niccolò Machiavelli.* Trans. by C. Grayson, Univ. of Chicago Pr. 1963 o.p. Comprehensive biography by a leading Machiavelli scholar.

Ruffo-Fiore, Silvia. *Niccolò Machiavelli* [*World Authors Ser.*] G. K. Hall 1982 lib. bdg. $15.95. Good general introduction to Machiavelli's life and works.

Strauss, Leo. *Thoughts on Machiavelli.* Univ. of Chicago Pr. 1984 text ed. pap. $13.00. Original and controversial account of Machiavelli's politics.

MONTAIGNE, MICHEL EYQUEM DE. 1533–1592

Montaigne, the great French essayist, was not a systematic philosopher. Yet his *Essays*, published in three editions between 1580 and 1595, exercised a powerful influence in philosophical circles with their acute reflections on customs, biases, and the human condition. Born to an aristocratic family near Bordeaux, Montaigne enjoyed a life of relative retirement, devoted to his writings. His tolerance and lack of dogmatism enabled him to avoid the religious controversies raging in France, and apart from a visit to Italy and a period of service as mayor of Bordeaux, his time was largely given over to his intellectual pursuits.

The main subject of Montaigne's *Essays* was himself, with all his foibles. His preoccupation with himself reflects a tendency present in many Renaissance humanists, beginning with Petrarch, to make the individual with his personal peculiarities an object of study. Yet with Montaigne this is no mere literary concern, but the starting point of a philosophical employment of introspection that would lead ultimately to DESCARTES' (see also Vol. 5) method of doubt.

It cannot be said that a consistent philosophical position runs through the *Essays.* Knowing Montaigne, we should not expect one. But patterns of thought emerge, recurring themes from Stoic and Epicurean sources, as well as an abiding skepticism. The most sustained presentation of his skepticism may be found in his essay *Apology for Raymond Sebonde,* where he expresses his concern for the inability of human reason to arrive at knowledge by its own devices.

In addition to the titles listed here, the reader should consult Richard H. Popkin, *The History of Scepticism from Erasmus to Spinoza,* in the General Bibliography at the beginning of this chapter. (See also Volume 2.)

BOOKS BY MONTAIGNE

The Complete Works of Montaigne: Essays, Travel Journal, Letters. Trans. by Donald M. Frame, Stanford Univ. Pr. 1957 $42.50. Most accurate and readable modern English translation of Montaigne. "Contains Montaigne's famous 'Essays,' written from 1572 to 1592; the 'Travel Journal,' an account of his trip to Germany, Switzerland and Italy in 1580; and the thirty-nine 'Letters,' most of which were written when Montaigne was mayor of Bordeaux from 1581 to 1585" (*N.Y. Herald Tribune Bk. Review*).

The Complete Essays of Montaigne. 1580–95. Trans. by Donald M. Frame, Stanford Univ. Pr. 1958 $35.00 pap. $15.95. Frame's great translation is a model of accuracy and eloquence.

BOOKS ABOUT MONTAIGNE

Brush, Craig. *Montaigne and Bayle: Variations on the Theme of Skepticism.* Nijhoff 1966 o.p. Evaluates Montaigne's role in the skeptical tradition. "[Brush] has succeeded marvellously well" (*Journal of the History of Philosophy*).

Frame, Donald M. *Montaigne: A Biography.* North Point Pr. repr. of 1965 ed. 1984 pap. $15.00. Outstanding life by the leading American authority on Montaigne.

——. *Montaigne's Discovery of Man: The Humanization of a Humanist.* Greenwood repr. of 1955 ed. 1983 lib. bdg. $32.50. Classic study of Montaigne's humanism.

Hallie, Philip P. *The Scar of Montaigne: An Essay in Personal Philosophy.* Wesleyan Univ. Pr. 1966 $16.00. "Brings philosophical as well as literary discipline to bear primarily on the skeptical aspects of Montaigne's thinking. The result is a sympathetic and penetrating analysis" (*Choice*).

La Charité, Raymond. *The Concept of Judgment in Montaigne.* Nijhoff 1968 o.p. Provides a close analysis of Montaigne's use of the concept of judgment in relation to allied notions such as "understanding," "reason," and "knowledge."

Regosin, Richard. *The Matter of My Book: Montaigne's "Essais" as the Book of the Self.* Univ. of California Pr. 1977 $22.00. "One of the best recent books on Montaigne" (*Renaissance Quarterly*).

Sayce, R. A. *The Essays of Montaigne: A Critical Exploration.* Northwestern Univ. Pr. 1972 $19.95. "This book takes as its starting-point . . . [Montaigne's] contradictions . . . and aims at a total picture of the Essais, their thought and form, which will not throw one side into relief by suppressing another. The contradictions are examined in detail and through them the elements of a final unity emerge" (Publisher's note).

MORE, THOMAS. 1478–1535

Humanist, statesman, martyr, and saint, Thomas More was one of the leading figures of the English Renaissance. Educated at Oxford, he combined the study of law with a mastery of Greek and an interest in the humanistic disciplines. In 1497 he met and befriended Erasmus, who later dedicated his *Praise of Folly* to him. More was also influenced by Giovanni Pico della Mirandola and composed a biography of the Italian Platonist that he published with a translation of some of his works.

More's most influential work was his *Utopia*, published in Louvain in 1516. It is a fanciful depiction of an island whose inhabitants practice community of goods, religious toleration, and control of man's baser instincts. More's utopian creation was intended as both a stinging critique of the social evils of contemporary England and as an image for his own society to reflect on.

Like Erasmus, More was not led to religious schism by his reformist ideas. His decision to engage in political life in a time of religious confrontation led to his martyrdom. While serving as Lord Chancellor under Henry VIII, More opposed the King's divorce of Catharine of Aragon, was removed from office, and later tried and executed for refusing to swear allegiance to the King as head of the Church of England. He composed *A Dialogue of Comfort against Tribulation* (1534) during his imprisonment.

In addition to the titles listed here, see also the books by Davis, Manuel and Manuel, and Skinner in the General Bibliography in this chapter. (See also Volume 1.)

BOOKS BY MORE

Utopia. 1516. Trans. by John Donnelly, Marquette Univ. Pr. 1984 pap. $4.95; ed. by John Dolan and James Greene, New Amer. Lib. 1984 pap. $4.95; ed. and trans. by Robert M. Adams, Norton 1976 $12.95 text ed. pap. $4.95; trans. by Paul Turner, Penguin 1965 pap. $2.95; trans. by Peter K. Marshall, Washington Square Pr. pap. $2.95; ed. by Edward Surtz, Yale Univ. Pr. 1964 $20.00 pap. $5.95

A Dialogue of Comfort against Tribulation. 1534. Ed. by Louis L. Martz and Frank Manley, Yale Univ. Pr. 1976 $77.00. More's consolatory piece penned during his imprisonment. The Yale edition is definitive.

BOOKS ABOUT MORE

Chambers, Raymond W. *The Place of St. Thomas More in English Literature and History.* Haskell repr. of 1937 ed. 1969 lib. bdg. $75.00

———. *Thomas More.* Univ. of Michigan Pr. 1958 o.p. A standard work, still valuable.

Hexter, Jack H. *More's Utopia: The Biography of an Idea.* [*History of Ideas Ser.*] Greenwood repr. of 1952 ed. 1976 lib. bdg. $22.50. Justifiably famous analysis of the methods and motives that underlie More's great work.

Kautsky, Karl. *Thomas More and His Utopia.* Humanities Pr. 1980 o.p.

Logan, George M. *The Meaning of More's Utopia.* Princeton Univ. Pr. 1983 $31.00. "This informed and humane work is . . . among the *optimi* I have seen on Utopia" (*Renaissance Quarterly*).

Marius, Richard. *Thomas More: A Biography.* Knopf 1984 $22.95. Outstanding new biography, essential to an understanding of a complex and often enigmatic figure.

Surtz, Edward L. *The Praise of Pleasure: Philosophy, Education, and Communism in More's "Utopia."* Harvard Univ. Pr. 1957 o.p. "The book is well worth the attention of readers who desire to penetrate beneath the surface of such a world-classic as 'Utopia' and the age which produced it" (*LJ*).

NICHOLAS OF CUSA (NICHOLAS CUSANUS). 1401?–1464

Churchman, humanist, and philosopher, Nicholas was born in Kues (Latin, Cusa), Germany, and educated at the famous school of the Brethren of the Common Life in Deventer, Holland. Following university training in philosophy, theology, and canon law he entered on a career as a legal adviser to Church officials. He served on several important embassies as papal representative and was made a Cardinal in 1448.

Nicholas's philosophical works are characterized by their concern with the problem of knowledge. *On Learned Ignorance* (*De Docta Ignorantia*) and *On Conjectures* (*De conjuncturis*), both written in 1440, emphasize the limitation placed on human reason by its need to extend its knowledge through a comparison of the unknown with the known. Since absolute precision can never be attained by a finite comparative power, the absolute truth is unattainable by rational means. Wisdom thus consists in recognizing the approximate, conjectural character of all rational theories, and Nicholas was hopeful that reflection on the limits of rational investigation would serve to banish dogmatism from philosophical and theological disputes.

In his cosmological speculations he asserted the indeterminacy of the physical universe, and hence denied that the earth could be located precisely at the center of the cosmos. He thus represents a step toward a more open-ended view of the universe, and was doubtless influential on later cosmologists such as Bruno.

BOOKS BY NICHOLAS OF CUSA

On Learned Ignorance. 1440. Trans. by Germain Heron, Hyperion repr. of 1945 ed. 1982 $19.25

Nicholas of Cusa On Learned Ignorance: A Translation and an Appraisal of De Docta Ignorantia. 1440. Trans. and commentary by Jasper Hopkins, Banning Pr. 2d ed. 1985 text ed. $23.00. pap. $10.00. Cusanus's most important early work, here with a close philosophical commentary.

Nicholas of Cusa's Debate with John Wenck: A Translation and an Appraisal of De Ignota Litteratura and Apologia Doctae Ignorantiae. 1449. Trans. and commentary by Jasper Hopkins, Banning Pr. 2d ed. 1984 text ed. $23.00. Presents Wenck's attack on Cusanus's *On Learned Ignorance* with Nicholas's reply.

Idiota de mente (The Layman: About Mind). 1450. Trans. by Clyde Lee Miller, Abaris Bks. 1979 o.p.

Nicholas of Cusa's Dialectical Mysticism: Text, Translation, and Interpretive Study of De Visione Dei. 1453. Trans. and commentary by Jasper Hopkins, Banning Pr. 1985 text ed. $25.00 pap. $10.00

Nicholas of Cusa On God as Not-Other: A Translation and an Appraisal of De Li Non Aliud. 1462. Trans. and commentary by Jasper Hopkins, Banning Pr. 2d ed. text ed. 1983 $20.00. "Provide[s] students of Cusanus with the opportunity of studying his later philosophical ideas more fully than before" (*Renaissance Quarterly*).

Nicholas of Cusa's Metaphysic of Contradiction. Trans. by Jasper Hopkins, Banning Pr. 1983 text ed. $23.00. Nicholas's *De dato patris luminum* (*On the Gift of the Father of Lights*).

BOOKS ABOUT NICHOLAS OF CUSA

Bett, Henry. *Nicholas of Cusa.* [*Great Medieval Churchmen Ser.*] Richwood Pub. repr. of 1932 ed. 1976 lib. bdg. $17.50. Long a standard account of Cusanus's life and work.

Hopkins, Jasper. *A Concise Introduction to the Philosophy of Nicholas of Cusa.* Banning Pr. 3d ed. 1986 text ed. $20.00. "Offers . . . not only an introductory essay on Cusanus's life, some problems of interpretation, and some of Cusanus's important philosophical ideas, but also an English translation of *De possest* (1460) alongside its Latin text" (*Renaissance Quarterly*).

Sigmund, Paul E. *Nicholas of Cusa and Medieval Political Thought.* Harvard Univ. Pr. 1963 o.p. Considers the Cardinal as a political philosopher against the background of his times.

Watts, Pauline Moffit. *Nicholaus Cusanus: A Fifteenth-Century Vision of Man.* Brill 1982 o.p. The best overall account of Cusanus's philosophy in English.

PARACELSUS, PHILIPPUS AUREOLUS (THEOPHRASTUS BOMBASTUS VON HOHENHEIM). 1493?–1541

Swiss physician, chemist, alchemist, and mystic, Paracelsus spent his life traveling, healing, teaching, and writing. The son of a physician, he was early attracted to the study of metallurgy and his medical practice emphasized the use of chemical over herbal remedies. Paracelsus rejected the traditional medical authorities of Greek and Arabic science such as Galen, Celsus (his name can be interpreted to mean "beyond Celsus"), and Avicenna. Instead he steeped himself in the alchemical and Hermetic literature (the body of works attributed to the fabulous Hermes Trismegistus), developing a full-blown philosophy grounded on the alchemical theory of man as the microcosm, and of the identity of man's constituent humors with the essential chemical principles of nature. Paracelsus's teachings thus juxtapose originality and innovation with acceptance of arcane and occult beliefs and practices, a combination encountered in many Renaissance thinkers. (See also Volume 5.)

BOOKS BY PARACELSUS

Selected Writings. Ed. by Jolande Jacobi, trans. by Norbert Guterman [*Bollingen Ser.*] Princeton Univ. Pr. 2d ed. 1958 $32.50. Basic collection of Paracelsus's most important works.

The Hermetic and Alchemical Writings of Paracelsus. Trans. by A. E. Waite, Shambhala 2 vols. repr. of 1894 ed. 1976 o.p. Old but still useful selection of works in translation. A glossary of alchemical terminology is appended.

The Archidoxes of Magic. c.1524. Trans. by Robert Turner, Weiser 1975 pap. $9.95. A facsimile reprint of the 1656 edition, originally entitled *Of the Supreme Mysteries of Nature.*

Coelum Philosophorum: Or, the Book of Vexations. Trans. by A. E. Waite, Holmes Pub. repr. of 1894 ed. 1984 pap. $2.95

BOOKS ABOUT PARACELSUS

Debus, Allen G. *The Chemical Philosophy: Paracelsian Science and Medicine in the Sixteenth and Seventeenth Centuries.* Science History Pubns. 1977 o.p. A comprehensive study of the ancient and medieval alchemical background to Paracelsus's work, his original contributions as chemist and philosopher, and the influence of his work on later figures. Illustrated.

Pachter, Henry M. *Magic into Science: The Story of Paracelsus.* Arden Lib. repr. of 1951 ed. 1982 lib. bdg. $35.00

Pagel, W. *Paracelsus.* S. Karger 2d ed. 1982 $77.25. Authoritative account of Paracelsus's work and its significance.

Stillman, John M. *Theophrastus Bombastus von Hohenheim Called Paracelsus.* AMS Pr. repr. of 1920 ed. 1982 $34.50

PETRARCH (FRANCESCO PETRARCA). 1304–1374

The great Italian poet and scholar Petrarch has been called the father of humanism and the first modern man. Renowned today chiefly for his Italian verses, Petrarch was famous in his own time for his Latin writings, which included orations, letters, and moral treatises. Many of the attitudes he expressed and the sources he cited came to exercise great influence on his many humanist successors.

Petrarch rejected the scholasticism of the medieval period as sterile and barbarous, preferring the elevated and refined classical works of such authors as CICERO (see also Vol. 2) and SENECA (see also Vol. 2) to the empty theological subtleties of the schoolmen. He admired ARISTOTLE (see also Vols. 3 and 5), who was venerated by the scholastics, but he preferred PLATO (see also Vol. 3). His favorite Christian author was ST. AUGUSTINE, from whom he adopted the use of pagan learning and eloquence to support a Christian ideal of life. One of his important treatises, *On the Secret Conflict of My Worries* (*Secretum*, 1358), takes the form of a dialogue between himself and the Saint.

Petrarch was born in Arezzo but lived most of his life at Avignon until returning to Italy in 1353. Among his most important writings on philosophical ideas are *On the Solitary Life* (1356), *On the Remedies of Good and Bad Fortune* (1366), *On His Own Ignorance and That of Many Others* (1367), and *The Ascent of Mount Ventoux.* (See also Volume 2.)

BOOKS BY PETRARCH

Letters on Familiar Matters: Rerum Familiarum Libri. Trans. by Aldo S. Bernardo, Johns Hopkins Univ. Pr. 3 vols. 1982–85 text ed. ea. $35.00. First full translation into English of 350 letters written by Petrarch between 1325 and 1366.

The Life of Solitude. 1356. Trans. by Jacob Zertlin, Hyperion repr. of 1924 ed. 1985 $29.50. Petrarch's famous defense of the solitary life, a reminder that not all humanists preferred the active life over the contemplative.

Petrarch's Secret: Or, the Soul's Conflict with Passion. c.1358. Trans. by William H. Draper, Hyperion repr. of 1911 ed. 1983 $21.45

Four Dialogues for Scholars. 1366. Ed. and trans. by Conrad H. Rawski, Case Western 1967 o.p. Includes four dialogues from *On the Remedies of Good and Bad Fortune.*

BOOKS ABOUT PETRARCH

Baron, Hans. *Petrarch's "Secretum": Its Making and Its Meaning.* Medieval Acad. 1985 $22.00. "Anyone who works on the *Secretum* in the future must take his start from Baron's careful and perceptive treatment of it" (*Renaissance Quarterly*).

Bergin, Thomas G. *Petrarch*. G. K. Hall o.p. Excellent introduction to the life and works by the eminent Italianist.

Foster, Kenelm. *Petrarch: An Introduction to the Canzoniere*. Columbia Univ. Pr. 1984 $14.00. Provides a background to the study of Petrarch's poetic masterpiece.

Mann, Nicholas. *Petrarch*. [*Past Masters Ser.*] Oxford 1984 $13.95 pap. $3.95. "An excellent introduction" (*Renaissance Quarterly*).

Trinkaus, Charles. *The Poet as Philosopher: Petrarch and the Formation of Renaissance Consciousness*. Yale Univ. Pr. 1979 text ed. $25.00. "Beginning with what has frequently been taken as Petrarch's solipsism, Trinkaus cogently describes how Petrarch generalized his own subjective experience. . . . The rich variety of secondary themes and striking insights cannot even be catalogued" (*Renaissance Quarterly*).

Wilkins, Ernest H. *The Making of the "Canzoniere" and Other Petrarchan Studies*. Folcroft repr. of 1951 ed. 1977 lib. bdg. $50.00. Important series of papers by the dean of American Petrarch scholars.

————. *Studies in the Life and Works of Petrarch*. Medieval Acad. repr. of 1955 ed. 1977 $12.00

PICO DELLA MIRANDOLA, GIANFRANCESCO. 1469–1533

Not to be confused with his celebrated uncle, Giovanni (see his biography below), the younger Pico played a very different role in Renaissance thought. Deeply influenced by the zealous piety of Savonarola, he adopted a skeptical attitude toward the claims of reason and philosophy that stands in bold contrast to the intellectual optimism of his uncle. Pico's chief work, *On the Vanity of Pagan Learning* (*Examen vanitatis doctrinae gentium*), appeared in 1520. It defends a fideistic position—affirming the superiority of faith—and declares that only by depending on faith can man's reason arrive at truth or wisdom. As the first Renaissance work to employ in a serious way the arguments of the great ancient skeptic Sextus Empiricus, it occupies an important place in the history of skepticism. In addition to the title listed here, the reader should consult Richard H. Popkin, *The History of Scepticism from Erasmus to Spinoza*, in the General Bibliography in this chapter.

BOOK BY GIANFRANCESCO PICO

On the Imagination. 1500. Ed. and trans. by Harry Caplan, Greenwood repr. of 1930 ed. 1971 lib. bdg. $22.50. Gianfrancesco draws his inspiration in this work from Aristotle's discussion of imagination in his treatise *On the Soul*.

BOOK ABOUT GIANFRANCESCO PICO

Schmitt, Charles B. *Gianfrancesco Pico della Mirandola (1469–1533) and His Critique of Aristotle*. Nijhoff 1967 o.p. Only comprehensive account in English of Gianfrancesco's major work. Emphasizes his place in the skeptical tradition and his importance as a source of skeptical ideas in later thinkers. Comprehensive bibliography.

PICO DELLA MIRANDOLA, GIOVANNI. 1463–1494

The Count of Mirandola and Concordia, a small state not far from Florence, Giovanni Pico was the exemplification of the brilliant Renaissance philosopher-prince. As a youth he came to Florence and entered into the circle of Marsilio Ficino's Platonic Academy. He studied philosophy at the University of Padua, a center of Aristotelian thought, and in Ferrara and Paris. As a result, his writings show a more positive assessment of Aristotelianism and the scholastics than do Ficino's, even though Pico was strongly influenced by the great Platonist's theories. In 1486 Pico published at Rome his famous collection of 900 *Conclusions* that he hoped to defend in a public disputation against all comers. A papal commission found several of the conclusions of dubious orthodoxy, however, and the debate was canceled. Pico composed an *Apology* (1487) in defense of his views but was forced to flee to France in an attempt to avoid arrest. Imprisoned briefly, he was released through the intervention of his Florentine patron, Lorenzo de' Medici. Pico died in his thirty-second year in 1494, the year the Medici were expelled from Florence.

The most arresting statement of Pico's philosophical aims is found in the famous *Oration* intended to open the defense of his 900 *Conclusions* in 1486. Frequently referred to as the *Oration on the Dignity of Man*, the work begins with a praise of man's miraculous nature. Against the background of a Neoplatonic view of reality derived from Ficino, Pico singles out man as unique in the universe, having been endowed by God with the seeds of all sorts of beings, from the highest to the lowest, in his soul. Through his freewill man is able to adopt for himself the nature he chooses; by his choices he can live the life of a beast, a rational thinker, or a god. No more eloquent defense of man's capacity for self-perfection was penned in the Renaissance.

Pico advocated an eclectic approach to the study of philosophy, refusing to limit himself to a single school or tradition in his search for truth. He attempted to reconcile the views of Plato and Aristotle where they appeared to differ, and though he accepted the validity of Christianity he did not hesitate to employ Islamic and Jewish sources in his studies. His use of Jewish cabalistic writings was particularly significant. Among his important works are the treatise *On Being and the One* (1491), *Heptaplus* (1489), an allegorical interpretation of the biblical account of creation, and his unfinished *Disputation against Astrology* (1496). In addition to the titles listed here, the reader should consult the books by Blau, Garin, Walker, and Yates in the General Bibliography in this chapter.

BOOKS BY GIOVANNI PICO

On the Dignity of Man, On Being and the One, Heptaplus. 1489–96. Trans. by Charles G. Wallis and others, Bobbs 1965 pap. $7.87

Commentary on a Canzone of Benivieni. 1486. Trans. by Sears R. Jayne, Peter Lang 1984 $32.00. An example of the way in which Florentine Platonists drew philosophical inspiration from poetic works.

Heptaplus, or Discourse on the Seven Days of Creation. 1489. Trans. by Jessie B. McGraw, Philosophical Lib. 1977 o.p. Pico's allegorical and philosophical interpretation of the creation reveals his dependence on ancient Platonic sources and Jewish cabala.

Of Being and Unity. 1491. Trans. by Victor M. Hamm, Marquette Univ. Pr. 1943 pap.

$5.95. The only surviving portion of Pico's attempt to reconcile the views of Plato and Aristotle. Reveals his originality within the Florentine Platonic Academy.

BOOKS ABOUT GIOVANNI PICO

Dulles, Avery. *Princeps Concordiae: Pico della Mirandola and the Scholastic Tradition.* Harvard Univ. Pr. 1941 o.p. Stresses Pico's use of scholastic sources. He was more influenced by the Latin scholastics than was Ficino.

Kibre, Pearl. *The Library of Pico della Mirandola.* AMS Pr. repr. of 1936 ed. 1977 $17.50. This valuable reconstruction of Pico's library reveals his wide reading and eclectic tastes. Essential for an appreciation of his intellectual background.

POMPONAZZI, PIETRO. 1462–1525

The leading Aristotelian philosopher of his day, Pomponazzi is an excellent example of the new "secular" interpreters of ARISTOTLE (see also Vols. 3 and 5) who became influential during the Renaissance. These thinkers provided a distinctly different reading of Aristotle's views from that of the medieval scholastic theologians and were less hesitant in stressing the issues on which he differed from Christian doctrine.

A native of Mantua, Pomponazzi studied philosophy and medicine at the University of Padua and taught there from 1488 to 1509. In the latter year he moved to the University of Ferrara, then to Bologna in 1512. In 1516 he published his controversial *Treatise on the Immortality of the Soul (Tractatus de immortalitate animae)*, which immediately gave rise to a storm of protest. In it he rejected the Thomistic defense of human immortality as inconsistent with the principles of Aristotle's philosophy. Although the immortality of the soul could be accepted on faith, it could not be defended by reference to Aristotle or human reason, both of which clearly argued that the soul dies with the body.

Pomponazzi's analysis in the *Tractatus* raised questions about his candor in professing to accept on faith what could be shown to be inconsistent with reason. Similar questions arise in regard to his other works, especially *On Enchantments (De incantationibus)* and *On Fate, Free Will and Predestination (De fato, libero arbitrio et praedestinatione)*, both of which, though composed around 1520, were published only posthumously, the former in 1556, the latter in 1567. In any case his lead was followed by later secular Aristotelians, and his strict separation of the realms of faith and reason may be said to anticipate in some ways the philosophical attitudes of the Enlightenment.

Pomponazzi's works are generally unavailable in English; however, a translation of his *Tractatus* may be found in Ernst Cassirer and others, *The Renaissance Philosophy of Man*, listed in the General Bibliography in this chapter.

BOOK ABOUT POMPONAZZI

Douglas, Andrew H. *The Philosophy and Psychology of Pietro Pomponazzi.* Ed. by C. Douglas and R. P. Hardie, Coronet Bks. repr. of 1910 ed. lib. bdg. $57.50. An old classic; out-of-date in many respects, it is still valuable for the light it sheds on this important philosopher.

SUÁREZ, FRANCISCO. 1548–1617

Suárez, the leading Jesuit philosopher and theologian of the Counter Reformation, was born in Granada, Spain, and studied law at the University of Salamanca. He joined the Jesuits in 1564 and pursued studies in philosophy and theology that led to his appointment as professor at several Spanish and Portuguese universities and the Jesuit College at Rome. His career centered on his teaching and writing until his retirement shortly before his death.

Suárez was a metaphysician of the first order, and his views influenced such later philosophers as DESCARTES (see also Vol. 5) and Leibniz. His *Metaphysical Disputations* (*Disputationes metaphysicae*), 1597, shows the influence of THOMAS AQUINAS, although Suárez rejected key Thomistic doctrines, such as the real distinction between essence and existence in creatures. He showed his independence particularly in his philosophy of law, developing an account of legal obligation founded on the primacy of will rather than reason. His legal writings have won him a prominent place among theorists of international law.

BOOKS BY SUÁREZ

Selections from Three Works of Francisco Suárez. 1612–21. Ed. by J. B. Scott, Oxford 2 vols. 1944 o.p. Selections (Vol. 1, in Latin; Vol. 2, in English translation) from Suárez's chief works—*De legibus, Defensor fidei,* and *De triplici virtute theologica*—dealing with international law.

On Formal and Universal Unity. Trans. by J. R. Ross, Marquette Univ. Pr. 1964 o.p. Central to an understanding of Suárez's metaphysics and theology.

On the Various Kinds of Distinctions. Trans. by Cyril Vollert, Marquette Univ. Pr. 1947 pap. $7.95. How Suárez applies distinctions to the solution of metaphysical problems.

On the Essence of Finite Being as Such, on the Existence of the Essence, and Their Distinction. Trans. by Norman J. Wells, Marquette Univ. Pr. 1983 pap. $24.95. Expounds Suárez's views on the key metaphysical problem of the relation of essence to existence in finite beings.

BOOKS ABOUT SUÁREZ

Fichter, Joseph Henry. *Man of Spain: A Biography of Francis Suárez.* Macmillan 1940 o.p. "An enthusiastic and very readable story of his life, written because the author thinks, not without reason, that the great Spanish scholar who was addressed even before his death by a Roman Pontiff as Doctor *eximius et pius* deserves of posterity a more popular place than has been accorded him" (*America*).

Mullaney, T. *Suárez on Human Freedom.* Johns Hopkins Univ. Pr. 1950 o.p.

VALLA, LORENZO. c.1407–1457

A distinguished historian, humanist, and classical scholar, Lorenzo Valla was also the author of several works of philosophical importance. Born in Rome, he counted among his teachers Leonardo Bruni and the great humanist educator Vittorino da Feltre. He was ordained a priest in 1431, taught rhetoric briefly, then traveled through northern Italy before accepting a position as secretary to Alfonso I, King of Naples, with whom he remained for more than a decade. In 1448 he moved to Rome and accepted a position as a papal notary.

Valla's most renowned scholarly accomplishment was his exposure of the famous "Donation of Constantine" as a forgery. This document had long been cited in support of papal claims to temporal authority in Italy; Valla's careful analysis showed it to be spurious. His *Elegantiae*, composed in 1435 through 1444 and first published in 1471, set the standard of correct Latin style for generations. As a philosopher he is remembered for the dialogue *On Pleasure*, also known as *On the True Good* (c.1434), which defends pleasure—interpreted as the beatitude to be enjoyed by Christians in the life to come—as the highest good, rejecting the Stoic ideal of virtue. His *On Free Will* deals with the apparent conflict between divine foreknowledge and human freedom, rejecting the standard medieval solution derived from BOETHIUS and proposing Valla's own, which LEIBNIZ would later praise. He criticizes scholastic theology and expresses reservations about reason's capacity to provide answers to ultimate metaphysical questions. In his *Dialectical Disputations* Valla mounted an attack on Aristotelian logic and put forward his own novel alternative based on classical Latin usage. Valla serves as an example of a Renaissance humanist whose philosophical interests carried him beyond a merely stylistic rejection of medieval scholasticism. (*The Renaissance Philosophy of Man*, edited by ERNST CASSIRER and others, contains a translation of Valla's *On Free Will* [see the General Bibliography in this chapter].)

BOOKS BY VALLA

De Voluptate (On Pleasure). c.1434. Trans. by Maristella Lorch and A. Kent Heiatt, Abaris Bks. 1978 $20.00. "The translators are to be commended both for treating the original faithfully and for rendering Valla's lively Latin into a brisk and idiomatic modern English" (*Renaissance Quarterly*).

"The Profession of the Religious" and the Principal Arguments from "The Falsely-Believed and Forged Donation of Constantine." Ed. and trans. by Olga Z. Pugliese [*Renaissance and Reformation Texts in Translation*] Univ. of Toronto Centre for Reformation and Renaissance Studies 1985. Two of Valla's most famous works, his dialogue on the religious orders and his skillful unmasking of the forged "Donation of Constantine."

VIVES, JUAN LUIS. 1492–1540

Spanish humanist and outspoken critic of scholasticism, Vives spent most of his career in northern Europe. Born in Valencia, he left Spain as a youth to study at the University of Paris and then settled in Bruges, Belgium. Vives found the university faculty in Paris strongly dominated by adherents of late medieval terminist logic, devoted to the analysis of the use of terms in sentences; in his treatise *Against the Pseudo Dialecticians* (*Adversus pseudodialecticos*) of 1520, he rejected their attempt to employ the methods and distinctions of logical analysis in treating philosophical and theological questions.

Vives taught for a time in Louvain where he became friends with Erasmus, whose aim of combining classical learning and Christian piety he shared. He also taught at Oxford, and while in England served as adviser to Queen Catherine of Aragon, whom he supported during Henry VIII's divorce proceedings. Returning to Bruges, he devoted the remainder of his life to teaching and writing.

Vives shared the general humanist disdain for scholastic theology, though his objections went beyond questions of style. Like ST. AUGUSTINE, he preferred self-analysis and moral improvement to the scientific study of nature. His *On the Soul and Life* (1538) stressed the empirical study of the self. Although he rejected key elements of Platonism, Vives was thoroughly conversant with the writings of the Florentine Platonists. His delightful *Fable about Man* expresses, through allegory, Giovanni Pico's view of man as uniquely capable of determining his own nature. (*The Renaissance Philosophy of Man*, edited by ERNST CASSIRER and others, contains a translation of Vives's *Fable about Man* [see the General Bibliography in this chapter].)

BOOKS BY VIVES

Juan Luis Vives Against the Pseudodialecticians: A Humanist Attack on Medieval Logic. 1520. Trans. and ed. by Rita Guerlac, Reidel Pub. 1979 o.p. An excellent translation of one of Vives's most important attacks on scholasticism.

Vives On Education: A Translation of the "De Tradendis Disciplinis" of Juan Luis Vives. 1531. Intro. by Foster Watson, fwd. by Francesco Cordasco, Rowman repr. of 1913 ed. 1971 o.p. Sets forth Vives's program for humanist education.

BOOKS ABOUT VIVES

Noreña, Carlos G. *Juan Luis Vives.* Nijhoff 1970 o.p. "This is an important book, and clearly the best introduction to Vives" (*Renaissance Quarterly*).

Tobriner, Marian Leona. *Vives' Introduction to Wisdom: A Renaissance Textbook.* Fwd. by Lawrence A. Cremin [*Classics in Education Ser.*] Teachers College Pr. 1968 o.p. Contains a translation of Vives's handbook for the humanist seeker after truth, with a careful analytic introduction by the translator.

CHAPTER 5

Modern Philosophy, 1600–1900

Richard H. Popkin

There are more things in heaven and earth, Horatio, than are dreamt of in your philosophy.
—SHAKESPEARE, *Hamlet*

How beauteous mankind is! O brave new world, that hath such people in't.
—SHAKESPEARE, *The Tempest*

Modern philosophy covers the period from the late Renaissance to the beginning of the twentieth century. The great intellectual upheavals of the Renaissance and the Reformation had a significant effect on people's attitudes toward traditional knowledge. The all-encompassing authority for determining what was true in religious knowledge was challenged by the Reformers. Subjects and methods taught in the universities were questioned by the humanistic scholars. The rediscovery of so much forgotten data and of so many different outlooks from the ancient worlds of Greece, Rome, Palestine, and early Christendom raised radical new possibilities for understanding the present, and for questioning previous understandings. The wealth of new data garnered from the voyages of exploration, from new astronomical, physical, chemical, and medical research, made previous theories untenable. All of this, coupled with the rediscovery of ancient Greek skepticism, created one of the greatest intellectual crises encountered in Western thought.

The dramatic attempts to create new philosophies were efforts to overcome the erosion of confidence in a previous intellectual and theological understanding, and to develop a new basis for the emerging scientific picture of the world. The seventeenth century began with the bold attempt of FRANCIS BACON (see also Vol. 1) to offer a new method for finding all the truths about the world, and with the bolder attempt of RENÉ DESCARTES (see also Vol. 5) to find a method for discovering truth so certain that no skeptical doubts could shake it. This certain truth would lead finally to an understanding of the cosmos in mathematical terms. Descartes offered a new metaphysical basis of knowledge, and his proposed solution became the source of the basic questions that philosophy dealt with during the next three centuries. Gassendi, Spinoza, Malebranche, LOCKE (see also Vol. 3), and Berkeley all tried to show the weaknesses in Descartes's system, and to offer instead their own philosophies as the basis for understanding the newly discovered scientific world. Hume and Kant tried to show the narrow

135

limits of what could be known according to the new philosophy and the new science.

In the nineteenth century fresh attempts were made to overcome the difficulties, and to broaden our understanding as biology, psychology, and the social sciences contributed new data and perspectives. German metaphysics, Marxism, British empiricism, the "Darwinism" of Nietzsche and Spencer, all set forth new ways of understanding man and nature. By the end of the nineteenth century the more practical American thinkers began to see the great quest for certainty and overall understanding that ran from Bacon and Descartes to Nietzsche and Spencer as both impracticable and undesirable. Instead, the American pragmatists set forth a more down-to-earth way of seeing and evaluating intellectual problems.

This section covers the works of the main philosophers of this three-century period, and writings about them. First we will begin with general works about the period.

GENERAL BIBLIOGRAPHY

Aiken, Henry D., ed. *The Age of Ideology: The Nineteenth-Century Philosophers.* [*Essay Index Repr. Ser.*] Ayer repr. of 1956 ed. $19.00; New Amer. Lib. 1956 pap. $4.95. Selected readings from various nineteenth-century thinkers, such as Kant, Fichte, Hegel, Schopenhauer, Comte, John Stuart Mill.

Beck, Lewis W., ed. *Eighteenth-Century Philosophy.* Free Pr. 1966 text ed. pap. $13.95. A selection of readings from Newton, Locke, Berkeley, Hume, Reid, Leibniz, Wolff, Lessing, and Kant.

Bréhier, Emile. *History of Philosophy.* Trans. by Wade Beskin, Univ. of Chicago Pr. vols. 4–7 1966–73 text ed. pap. ea. $5.00. Vol. 4, *Seventeenth Century;* Vol. 5, *Eighteenth Century;* Vol. 6, *The Nineteenth Century: Period of Systems, 1800–1850;* Vol. 7, *Contemporary Philosophy since 1850.* Portions of a massive and comprehensive history of philosophy by a leading French authority.

Bronowski, Jacob, and Bruce Mazlish. *The Western Intellectual Tradition: From Leonardo to Hegel.* [*Essay Index Repr. Ser.*] Ayer repr. of 1960 ed. $37.00; Harper 1962 pap. $8.95. A general survey of the development of the modern intellectual world.

Burtt, Edwin A., ed. *The English Philosophers from Bacon to Mill.* Modern Lib. 1939 $11.95. Lengthy selections from Bacon, Hobbes, Locke, Hume, and Mill.

———. *The Metaphysical Foundations of Modern Physical Science.* [*International Lib. of Psychology, Philosophy, and Scientific Method*] Humanities Pr. 1967 text ed. $29.00 pap. $12.50. A work on the mystical, metaphysical, alchemical, and astrological ideas that played a role in the background of the rise of modern science.

Caponigri, A. Robert. *Philosophy from the Romantic Age to the Age of Reason.* Vol. 4 in *A History of Western Philosophy.* Univ. of Notre Dame Pr. 1971 $25.00 pap. $4.95. "Its focus is . . . primarily on the 19th century. . . . While selective as any history must be, the volume is a good manual on 19th-century thought. Lists of readings, name index, and subject index" (*Choice*).

Collins, James D. *God in Modern Philosophy.* Greenwood repr. of 1959 ed. 1978 lib. bdg. $32.75. A study of how the conception of God changed in modern thought.

———. *Interpreting Modern Philosophy.* Princeton Univ. Pr. 1972 $46.50 pap. $14.50. An excellent exposition of the role of the history of philosophy in understanding philosophy.

Copleston, Frederick. *Modern Philosophy: The French Enlightenment to Kant.* Vol. 6 pt. 2 in *A History of Philosophy.* Doubleday 1985 pap. $4.50. Part of an important nine-volume comprehensive history of philosophy by a leading English Catholic thinker.

———. *Seventeenth and Eighteenth Century British Philosophers.* Vol. 5 in *A History of Philosophy.* Doubleday 2 vols. 1985 pap. ea. $3.95. One of the volumes in a "remarkable history of Western philosophy" (*Choice*).

Edwards, Paul, ed. *The Encyclopedia of Philosophy.* Free Pr. 4 vols. 1973 $260.00. Contains articles on all of the main movements and thinkers of the period by a wide variety of scholars from the United States and Europe. The articles include basic bibliographical materials for further reading.

Feyeraband, Paul. *The Rise of Western Rationalism.* [*Philosophy Now Ser.*] Humanities Pr. 1978 o.p. A provocative picture of how modern thought developed.

Flower, Elizabeth, and Murray G. Murphey. *A History of Philosophy in America.* Hackett 2 vols. 1975 ea. $17.50. A careful scholarly history; the most complete available.

Funkenstein, Amos. *Theology and the Scientific Imagination from the Middle Ages to the Seventeenth Century.* Princeton Univ. Pr. 1986 text ed. $39.50. A brilliant new interpretation of the role of theology in the rise of scientific ideas.

Gardiner, Patrick, ed. *Nineteenth-Century Philosophy.* Free Pr. 1969 text ed. pap. $14.95. "One of an eight-volume series of readings covering the span of Western philosophy, it solves the problem of selection by limiting itself to 13 writers (Fichte, Hegel, Schopenhauer, Feuerbach, Stirner, Marx, Kierkegaard, Nietzsche, Comte, Whewell, Mill, Mach, Bradley), and choosing from each a series of short extracts on issues which are alive and moot in contemporary philosophy" (*Choice*).

Gay, Peter. *The Enlightenment: An Interpretation.* Simon & Schuster rev. ed. 1985 $15.95. A major overall study by a leading intellectual historian.

Hacking, Ian. *The Emergence of Probability: A Philosophical Study of Early Ideas about Probability, Induction, and Statistical Inference.* Cambridge Univ. Pr. 1984 pap. $12.95. An important controversial monograph about how probability and induction developed as kinds of reasoning.

Hampshire, Stuart, ed. *Age of Reason: The Seventeenth-Century Philosophers.* New Amer. Lib. 1984 pap. $2.95. "[A] volume in the Great Ages of Western Philosophy Series. It includes a general introduction, and selections from the writings of Bacon, Galileo, Hobbes, Descartes, Pascal, Spinoza, and Leibniz" (*Jewish Social Studies*).

Hartshorne, Charles. *Insights and Oversights of Great Thinkers: An Evaluation of Western Philosophy.* State Univ. of New York Pr. 1983 $39.50 pap. $16.95. A discussion by a leading American philosopher of what we can learn from past thinkers.

Hazard, Paul. *European Thought in the Eighteenth Century: From Montesquieu to Lessing.* Peter Smith 1973 $16.50. A survey of Enlightenment thought by one of the best French historians of ideas.

Höffding, Harald, and B. E. Meyer. *A History of Modern Philosophy: A Sketch of the History of Philosophy from the Close of the Renaissance to Our Own Day.* Folcroft repr. of 1908 ed. 2 vols. 1985 o.p. A still basic history of modern thought, covering material through the nineteenth century.

Jones, W. T. *Hobbes to Hume.* Vol. 3 in *A History of Modern Philosophy.* Harcourt 2d ed. 1969 text ed. pap. $11.95

———. *Kant and the Nineteenth Century.* Vol. 4 in *A History of Modern Philosophy.* Harcourt 2d rev. ed. 1975 text ed. pap. $11.95

Kaufmann, Walter. *From Shakespeare to Existentialism.* Princeton Univ. Pr. 1980 $29.50 pap. $11.50

Koestler, Arthur. *Sleepwalkers*. Putnam 1963 o.p. "I think Mr. Koestler has two basic motives: (1) He wants to show that the great inventors were not rational, totally lucid minds, but passionate, confused, lyrical and, most often, religious. They were 'sleepwalkers,' in the sense that they stumbled forward, sometimes not even recognizing their most important discoveries. (2) He wants to heal the gap he sees between science and religious belief by arguing that the basic impulse behind the two phenomena is the same" (*20th Century*).

————. *The Watershed: A Biography of Johannes Kepler*. Fwd. by John Durston, Univ. Pr. of Amer. 1985 text ed. pap. $12.25. The selection from *Sleepwalkers* containing the story of Kepler. "This is as entertaining as Nancy Mitford's account of Voltaire and Mme. du Châtelet" (*20th Century*).

Koyré, Alexandre. *From the Closed World to the Infinite Universe*. Johns Hopkins Univ. Pr. repr. of 1956 ed. 1968 pap. $6.95. Important study of the philosophical assumptions involved in the beginnings of modern science.

Lamprecht, Sterling P. *Our Philosophical Traditions: A Brief History of Philosophy in Western Civilization*. [*Century Philosophy Ser.*] Irvington repr. of 1955 ed. 1980 o.p. A good general introductory history of philosophy.

Levi, Albert W. *Philosophy and the Modern World*. [*Midway Repr. Ser.*] Univ. of Chicago Pr. repr. of 1959 ed. 1977 text ed. pap. $16.00. "The most interesting and informative general interpretation of twentieth-century philosophy that has been written" (Huston Smith, *Saturday Review*).

Lewes, George H. *The Biographical History of Philosophy from Its Origin in Greece down to the Present Day*. Gregg repr. of 1857 ed. 1979 text ed. $74.52. A well-known mid-nineteenth century work, giving the lives of famous philosophers.

Loeb, Louis E. *From Descartes to Hume: Continental Metaphysics and the Development of Modern Philosophy*. Cornell Univ. Pr. 1981 $32.50. A history of seventeenth- and eighteenth-century thought seen from the perspective of contemporary analytic philosophy.

Lossky, Nicholas O. *The History of Russian Philosophy*. International Univ. Pr. 1969 text ed. $40.00 pap. $12.95. An excellent study of Russian thought by one of the leaders of the Russian Orthodox Seminary in Paris.

Lovejoy, Arthur O. *Great Chain of Being: A Study of the History of an Idea*. [*William James Lectures Ser.*] Harvard Univ. Pr. 1936 $25.00 pap. $8.95. This work traces a central metaphysical idea from antiquity to the nineteenth century.

Lukàcs, Georg. *History and Class Consciousness*. Trans. by Rodney Livingstone, MIT repr. of 1923 ed. 1971 pap. $7.95. A major Marxist study of the rise of modern philosophy.

Mandelbaum, Maurice. *History, Man, and Reason: A Study in Nineteenth-Century Thought*. Johns Hopkins Univ. Pr. 1971 o.p. Available through University Microfilms. Important study by a leading authority on the development of the philosophy of history.

Mandrou, Robert. *From Humanism to Science, 1480 to 1700*. Trans. by Brian Pearce [*History of European Thought Ser.*] Penguin 1986 pap. $6.95. A survey of modern thought by a leading French intellectual historian.

Marias, Julian. *History of Philosophy*. Dover 22d ed. 1966 pap. $8.50. Important history of philosophy from the pre-Socratics to Heidegger and Ortega by a leading twentieth-century Spanish thinker.

Merz, John Theodore. *A History of European Thought in the Nineteenth Century*. Peter Smith 1976 repr. 4 vols. ea. $16.50. One of the finest histories of the period.

O'Connor, Daniel J., ed. *A Critical History of Western Philosophy*. Free Pr. 1985 pap. $13.95. A collection of essays by different British and American scholars on various philosophers. Their views are presented and examined in terms of analytic philosophy.

Popkin, Richard H. *The High Road to Pyrrhonism.* Ed. by R. A. Watson and J. E. Force [*Studies in Hume and Scottish Philosophy*] Austin Hill Pr. 1980 $25.00 pap. $10.00. A collection of essays on the role of skepticism in modern thought, written over 25 years, dealing with Bayle, Berkeley, Hume, and the development of modern racism.

————. *The History of Scepticism from Erasmus to Spinoza.* Univ. of California Pr. 1979 $37.00 pap. $9.50. Basic study of the revival of ancient skepticism in the Renaissance and Reformation, and its influence on the development of modern thought.

————. *Philosophy of the Sixteenth and Seventeenth Centuries.* Free Pr. 1966 text ed. pap. $14.95. Selected readings from Renaissance authors and Bacon, Descartes, Gassendi, Hobbes, Pascal, Spinoza, Malebranche, Leibniz, and Bayle.

Randall, John H. *The Career of Philosophy.* Columbia Univ. Pr. 2 vols. 1970 pap. ea. $19.00–$20.00. Vol. 1, *From the Middle Ages to the Enlightenment;* Vol. 2, *From the German Enlightenment to the Age of Darwin.* Randall's monumental history of modern philosophy is a most ambitious project that reinterprets most of the philosophers.

————. *The Making of the Modern Mind: A Survey of the Intellectual Background of the Present Age.* Columbia Univ. Pr. rev. ed. 1976 $55.00 pap. $20.00. An important survey by Randall, written over 60 years ago, showing how the modern intellectual world began.

————. *Philosophy after Darwin: Chapters for the Career of Philosophy and Other Essays.* Ed. by Beth J. Singer, Columbia Univ. Pr. 1977 $34.00. The unfinished remainder of Randall's history of modern philosophy.

Ree, J. *Philosophy and Its Past.* Humanities Pr. 1978 $20.00 pap. $9.75. Essays on the value of the history of philosophy by M. R. Ayers, J. Ree, and A. Westoby.

Rosenfield, Leonora. *From Beast Machine to Man Machine: Animal Soul in French Letters from Descartes to La Mettrie.* Hippocrene Bks. 1968 o.p. Important study of the materialistic, biological, and psychological theories in France from Descartes to the mid-eighteenth century.

Russell, Bertrand. *A History of Western Philosophy.* [*Counterpoint Ser.*] Simon & Schuster 1984 pap. $8.95. A lively, although not always accurate, survey by one of the leading twentieth-century thinkers.

Sellars, Wilfrid. *Philosophical Perspectives: History of Philosophy.* Ridgeview 1979 text ed. lib. bdg. $23.00 pap. $6.50. Essays on philosophical topics, using historical settings, by a leading contemporary American thinker.

Smith, Thomas V., and Marjorie Grene, eds. *Philosophers Speak for Themselves: Berkeley, Hume, and Kant.* Univ. of Chicago Pr. 2d ed. 1957 pap. $7.50

————. *Philosophers Speak for Themselves: From Descartes to Locke.* Univ. of Chicago Pr. 2d ed. 1957 $25.00 pap. $11.00

Spink, John S. *French Free-Thought from Gassendi to Voltaire.* Greenwood repr. of 1960 ed. 1969 lib. bdg. $65.00. A useful study of irreligious skeptical thought from 1650 to 1750 in France.

Ueberweg, Friedrich. *A History of Philosophy.* Trans. by George S. Morris [*Select Bibliographies Repr. Ser.*] Ayer repr. of 1874 ed. 2 vols. $48.00. Volume 2 is *History of Modern Philosophy.*

Weinberg, Julius R. *Ockham, Descartes, and Hume: Self-Knowledge, Substance, and Causality.* Ed. by William J. Courtenay, Univ. of Wisconsin Pr. 1977 $30.00. A collection of essays by a leading American historian of philosophy on medieval and modern thinkers, emphasizing epistemological themes.

Wiener, Philip. *Evolution and the Founders of Pragmatism*. Fwd. by John Dewey, Univ. of Pennsylvania Pr. repr. of 1949 ed. 1972 pap. $9.95. A study of the role of the theory of evolution in the development of pragmatic philosophy in the nineteenth century.

————, ed. *Dictionary of the History of Ideas*. Scribner 5 vols. 1980 pap. $67.50. A topical collective work, covering many important general themes about modern philosophy, such as "Modern Skepticism," "Religious Tolerance," etc. Written by noted scholars from different disciplines.

Windelband, Wilhelm. *A History of Philosophy: With Especial Reference to the Formation and Development of Its Problems and Conceptions*. Trans. by James H. Tufts, Greenwood repr. of 1938 ed. 1979 lib. bdg. $42.50. One of the most important nineteenth-century German histories of philosophy.

Yolton, John W. *Perceptual Acquaintance from Descartes to Reid*. Univ. of Minnesota Pr. 1984 $32.50 pap. $13.95. Theories about the role of perception in human knowledge in Descartes, the Cartesians, and the British empiricists up to Thomas Reid.

————. *Thinking Matter: Materialism in Eighteenth-Century Britain*. Univ. of Minnesota Pr. 1984 $29.50 pap. $12.95. A scholarly study of the controversy over whether thinking can be a material process, and the implications of such a theory.

SEVENTEENTH CENTURY

BACON, FRANCIS (BARON VERULAM, VISCOUNT ST. ALBANS). 1561–1626

Francis Bacon is chiefly known for his early advocacy of empirical philosophy and science. He was educated at Trinity College, Cambridge, later studied law, and was elected to Parliament in 1584. Under Queen Elizabeth I and King James I he was an important civil servant who became solicitor-general in 1607, attorney-general in 1613, and lord chancellor in 1618. Bacon was usually on the king's side in the struggles between the Crown and Parliament. His political career came to an end in 1621 when he was convicted of taking bribes, and was imprisoned for a short time.

His major works, most of which he wrote while active in government affairs, are his *Essays* (1597), *The Advancement of Learning* (1605), *The New Atlantis* (1627), and his program for a complete reform of knowledge by empirical means, published as the *Novum Organum* and *The Great Instauration*, in 1620. After his political disgrace, he continued writing scientific and philosophical works, and is reported to have died because of his empirical scientific research: He developed bronchitis after performing an experiment in refrigeration that involved stuffing snow into a chicken.

Recently some hitherto unknown manuscripts of Bacon have been discovered that suggest he might have had a more positive theory about the nature of the world than appears in his printed works. A new edition of his writings is now being undertaken, which may lead to some reevaluation and reinterpretation of his philosophy. (See also Volume 1.)

BOOKS BY BACON

Works of Francis Bacon. Ed. by J. Spedding and others, Scholarly repr. of 1858–74 ed. 15 vols. 1988 lib. bdg. $1,295.00. The only complete edition of Bacon's works.

Philosophical Works of Francis Bacon. [*Select Bibliographies Repr. Ser.*] Ayer repr. of 1905 ed. $38.00

The Physical and Metaphysical Works of Lord Bacon, Including the Advancement of Learning and Novum Organum. Scholarly repr. 1976 $55.00

Essays. 1597–1625. Intro. by Geoffrey Grigson, AMS Pr. repr. of 1940 ed. 1988 $31.50; annot. by Richard Whately [*Essay Index Repr. Ser.*] Ayer repr. of 1861 ed. 5th ed. rev. $29.50; ed. by John Pitcher [*Penguin Class. Ser.*] 1986 pap. $4.95. Essays modeled on Montaigne's, dealing with a wide range of topics—literary, philosophical, political, and so on.

The Advancement of Learning. 1605. Ed. by G. W. Kitchin, Biblio Dist. 1981 $15.00 pap. $7.95. A statement of Bacon's plans for improving knowledge.

Great Instauration and New Atlantis. 1617, 1620. Ed. by J. Weinberger [*Croft Class. Ser.*] Harlan Davidson 1980 text ed. $12.95 text ed. pap. $3.95. Bacon's fundamental theory for changing the way of gaining knowledge, and his utopian picture of how this would work out.

Novum Organum and Related Writings. Ed. by Thomas Fowler, Arden Lib. repr. of 1889 ed. 1979 $100.00; ed. by Fulton H. Anderson, Bobbs 1960 $9.63. Bacon's theory of knowledge, and methodology.

Francis Bacon: A Selection of His Works. Ed. by Sidney Warhaft [*College Class. in Eng. Ser.*] Odyssey Pr. 1965 pap. $13.24

BOOKS ABOUT BACON

Anderson, Fulton H. *Francis Bacon: His Career and His Thought.* Greenwood repr. of 1962 ed. 1978 lib. bdg. $28.50. A standard intellectual biography.

Craik, George L. *Bacon: His Writings and His Philosophy.* Arden Lib. repr. of 1860 ed. 1983 lib. bdg. $85.00. A general survey, written in the 1840s, of Bacon's views.

Farrington, Benjamin. *Francis Bacon: Philosopher of Industrial Science.* [*Eng. Biographies Ser.*] Haskell repr. 1973 lib. bdg. $75.00; 1950 Hippocrene Bks. repr. 1979 lib. bdg. $18.00. An influential Marxist interpretation of Bacon's thought.

———. *The Philosophy of Francis Bacon.* Univ. of Chicago Pr. 1967 pap. $1.95. "Farrington has translated three works of Bacon available previously only in their original Latin for the classicists or in fragmented and inadequate translations. . . . The translations are felicitous. . . . The writing is clear, the thoughts penetrating, and no educated person can read these little-known pieces without recognition of Bacon's genius" (*Science & Society*).

Jardine, Lisa. *Francis Bacon: Discovery and the Art of Discourse.* Cambridge Univ. Pr. 1975 $39.50. An important study examining Bacon's theory of discovery in terms of Renaissance ideas.

Rossi, Paolo. *Francis Bacon: From Magic to Science.* Trans. by Sacha Rabinovitch [*Midway Repr. Ser.*] Univ. of Chicago Pr. repr. of 1968 ed. 1978 text ed. pap. $14.00. "A first-rate translation of what has become a Baconian classic. . . . Rossi's study is also a compendium of rare titles and authors of the English and European Renaissance to which scholars and graduate students will refer again and again" (*Choice*).

Vickers, Brian. *Francis Bacon and Renaissance Prose.* Cambridge Univ. Pr. 1968 $59.50. An important study by a scholar well versed in the intellectual background of the Renaissance.

————, ed. *Essential Articles for the Study of Francis Bacon.* [*Essential Articles Ser.*] Shoe String 1968 $32.50. This brings together much important recent research and reinterpretation.

Wallace, Karl R. *Francis Bacon on the Nature of Man.* Univ. of Illinois Pr. 1967 $19.95. A study of Bacon's views about man's intellectual, volitional, and emotive faculties.

Weinberger, Jerry. *Science, Faith, and Politics: Francis Bacon and the Utopian Roots of the Modern Age.* Cornell Univ. Pr. 1985 text ed. $32.50. A commentary on Bacon's *The Advancement of Learning.*

BAYLE, PIERRE. 1647–1706

Bayle was the son of a French Protestant minister. Forced to flee to Holland in 1681 because of the persecution of the Huguenots, he lived there the rest of his life. Bayle wrote a very large number of works attacking all kinds of theories in theology and philosophy, and opposing all kinds of intolerance, and edited one of the first major philosophical journals. His most famous work is his immense four-folio *Historical and Critical Dictionary* (1697–1702), in which he developed a complete skepticism against "everything that is said, and everything that is done." This work, considered the "Arsenal of the Enlightenment," greatly influenced Berkeley, Hume, and VOLTAIRE (see Vol. 2).

BOOK BY BAYLE

Historical and Critical Dictionary: Selections. 1697. Trans. by Richard H. Popkin, Bobbs 1965 o.p.

BOOKS ABOUT BAYLE

Labrousse, Elisabeth. *Bayle.* [*Past Masters Ser.*] Oxford 1983 $12.95. A short introduction to Bayle's thought and influence by the leading scholar of his work.

Sandberg, Karl C. *At the Crossroads of Faith and Reason: An Essay on Pierre Bayle.* Univ. of Arizona Pr. 1966 $6.00. An intriguing essay arguing that Bayle was a serious religious believer.

THE CAMBRIDGE PLATONISTS

The Cambridge Platonists were a group of seventeenth-century religious philosophers whose leading members were Henry More (1614–87) and Ralph Cudworth (1617–88). They accepted the new science, but sought to ground it in a metaphysics based on a revised form of Platonism and the theories of Plotinus. Moderates in the quest for certainty, they developed a theory of limited certainty in religious and scientific matters. Many of them were active in the Royal Society, and influenced ISAAC NEWTON (see also Vol. 5), who had studied with them and was then their colleague.

BOOKS ABOUT THE CAMBRIDGE PLATONISTS

Cassirer, Ernst. *The Platonic Renaissance in England.* Gordian repr. of 1954 ed. 1970 $19.50. A basic study by one of the most important historians of modern philosophy.

Colie, Rosalie L. *Light and Enlightenment: A Study of the Cambridge Platonists and the Dutch Arminans.* Cambridge Univ. Pr. 1957 o.p. An excellent study, showing the development of similar ideas in England and Holland, and the influence groups in each country had on those in the other.

Conway, Anne. *The Principles of the Most Ancient and Modern Philosophy.* Kluwer Academic 1982 $35.00. A remarkable work by a disciple and friend of Henry More, criticizing the views of Hobbes, Descartes, and Spinoza. This book influenced Leibniz.

More, Henry. *A Collection of Several Philosophical Writings.* Ed. by René Wellek, Garland 2 vols. 2d ed. 1978 lib. bdg. set $101.00. A reprint of a group of More's main philosophical works, put together in the late seventeenth century by the author himself. It includes his writings against Descartes.

——. *Philosophical Writings of Henry More.* Ed. by Flora I. MacKinnon, AMS Pr. repr. of 1925 ed. 1978 $26.00. Selections from some of More's works. The excerpts do not give the full flavor of his idiosyncratic views.

Powicke, Frederick J. *The Cambridge Platonists.* Greenwood repr. of 1926 ed. 1971 lib. bdg. $22.50. A standard authority.

DESCARTES, RENE. 1596–1650

René Descartes was born in the Touraine district in France. He received his education at the newly established Jesuit college at La Flèche, but claimed later that he had learned little there that was useful or important. In 1618 he moved to Holland, where he met various mathematicians and scientists. During the early campaigns of the Thirty Years War, Descartes was an officer in the Dutch army. He became renowned in intellectual circles for his discovery of a branch of mathematics called analytic geometry. After a visit to Paris in 1628, Descartes retired to Holland to work out his philosophical system, seeking a completely certain basis for knowledge that could not be challenged by any skeptical objections. His solution was first presented in the *Discourse on Method* (1637), and more fully developed in his *Meditations on First Philosophy* (1641). The latter work was published together with objections to Descartes's philosophy by such thinkers as Arnauld, Gassendi, and Hobbes, and with replies by Descartes. In 1644 he published his *Principles of Philosophy*, developing both his philosophical theory and its application to the sciences. He also published shorter works on human psychology and biology. Descartes quickly became famous for his new system of ideas. In 1649, Queen Christina of Sweden invited him to join the intellectual court she had established in Stockholm; he went there in the fall of 1649, and died during the winter of 1650.

Descartes is called the father of modern philosophy because he created the first full-scale system of thought to replace Scholasticism. Many of the philosophers who followed built on Descartes's views, and sought to overcome problems that had been found in his system. For more than three centuries the central problems dealt with by most philosophers in Europe and America have derived from Descartes's efforts.

The complete works of Descartes have never been translated into English, although gradually more of them are appearing. A full collection of his writings, including his large correspondence, was edited and published in France early in the twentieth century, in the original French and Latin, edited by Adam and Tannery. (See also Volume 5.)

BOOKS BY DESCARTES

Philosophical Writings. Ed. and trans. by Elizabeth Anscombe and Peter T. Geach, Bobbs 1971 pap. $7.20; (under the title *Philosophical Works*) ed. and trans. by E. S. Haldane and G. R. Ross, Cambridge Univ. Pr. 2 vols. 1967 $57.50 pap. ea. $14.95; trans. by John Cottingham and Dugald Murdoch, Cambridge Univ. Pr. 2 vols. 1985 ea. $44.50 pap. ea. $12.95. A new translation that includes some works not available in earlier translations, bibliographical references, and index.

Descartes' Conversation with Burman. Oxford 1974 o.p. Burman was a philosophy student who visited Descartes and asked him various questions about his philosophy. The text is Burman's, and if correct, gives some interesting answers to problems Descartes's views have raised.

Discourse on Method. 1637. Trans. by Laurence J. LaFleur, Bobbs 1960 pap. $5.44; ed. and trans. by Donald A. Cress, Hackett 1980 text ed. pap. $2.45; trans. by John Veitch, Open Court 1962 $8.95 pap. $3.95. This was Descartes's systemization of how one arrives at truth. "The method which Descartes proposed to apply to every sphere of knowledge was that which was best exemplified in analytical geometry. The stages and procedure used in a geometrical problem could surely be made to yield results of equal certitude in the sphere of metaphysics, logic, and ethics" (E. W. F. Tomlin).

Meditations on First Philosophy. 1641. Trans. by Ronald Rubin, Arete Pr. 1986 text ed. pap. $3.95; trans. by Laurence J. LaFleur, Bobbs 2d ed. 1960 pap. $4.24; trans. by Donald A. Cress, Hackett 1979 text ed. pap. $2.95. "Extensive metaphysical, heuristic work; his major opus" (Tice and Slavin, *Research Guide to Philosophy*, ALA, 1983).

Principles of Philosophy. 1644. Trans. by Reese P. Miller and Valentine R. Miller, Kluwer Academic 1983 lib. bdg. $59.00. A new complete translation, with annotations of this statement of Descartes's system.

Philosophical Letters. Ed. and trans. by Anthony Kenny, Univ. of Minnesota Pr. 1981 pap. $11.95. A selection of important letters dealing with basic philosophical topics.

Treatise of Man. Trans. with commentary by Thomas S. Hall [*Monographs in the History of Science Ser.*] Harvard Univ. Pr. 1972 $16.50. Descartes's posthumously published study on man as a biological entity.

BOOKS ABOUT DESCARTES

Balz, Albert G. *Descartes and the Modern Mind.* Shoe String repr. of 1952 ed. 1967 $37.50. A by now classic study of Descartes and his role in the formulation of modern thought.

Beck, Leslie J. *The Metaphysics of Descartes: A Study of the Meditations.* Greenwood repr. of 1965 ed. 1979 lib. bdg. $25.00. A careful examination of this text by a well-known Descartes commentator.

Blom, John J. *Descartes: His Moral Philosophy and Psychology.* New York Univ. Pr. 1978 $35.00. A 100-page study of Descartes's moral and psychological views, plus translations of some of his letters from 1641 to 1649 to document the study.

Caton, Hiram. *The Origin of Subjectivity: An Essay on Descartes.* Yale Univ. Pr. 1972 o.p. "A knowledge of Descartes and the problems his writings have raised is essential; advanced undergraduates will understand Caton and enjoy his references" (*Choice*).

Chomsky, Noam. *Cartesian Linguistics: A Chapter in the History of Rationalist Thought.* Univ. Pr. of Amer. repr. of 1966 ed. 1983 text ed. pap. $7.75. An attempt by one of the leading theorists in contemporary linguistics to show that the roots of his own nonbehavioral theory of linguistics go back to certain followers of Descartes at the end of the seventeenth century.

Curley, E. M. *Descartes against the Skeptics.* Harvard Univ. Pr. 1978 $17.50. A careful examination of Descartes's arguments against skepticism, and an evaluation of his system in terms of contemporary analytic philosophy.

Gaukroger, Stephén, ed. *Descartes: Philosophy, Mathematics and Physics.* [*History of Science and Philosophy Ser.*] Barnes & Noble 1980 $30.00. An interesting collection of essays by leading scholars on Descartes's work in each of these fields. The emphasis is on his mathematical and scientific activities, which are too often neglected in considering his philosophy.

Gilson, Étienne. *Index Scholastico-Cartesian.* Burt Franklin repr. of 1913 ed. 1964 $28.50. First work to show significant similarities and differences between Descartes's work and the Scholasticism of his times.

Gueroult, Martial. *Descartes' Philosophy Interpreted According to the Order of Reasons: The Soul and God.* Trans. by Roger Ariew, Univ. of Minnesota Pr. 1984 $35.00 pap. $15.95. An interpretation by one of the most important Descartes scholars in France in recent years. It is the only one of Gueroult's works to be translated so far.

Hooker, Michael, ed. *Descartes: Critical and Interpretive Essays.* Johns Hopkins Univ. Pr. 1978 text ed. pap. $9.95. "The Hooker collection emphasizes formal logical tools more than the other collections and it focuses on the concept of method in the *Meditations* and body-mind duality" (*Choice*).

Joachim, Harold L. *Descartes' Rules for the Direction of the Mind.* Ed. by Errol E. Harris, Greenwood repr. of 1957 ed. 1979 lib. bdg. $22.50. A very careful commentary on this early work of Descartes.

Keeling, Stanley Victor. *Descartes.* Greenwood repr. of 1934 ed. o.p. "First published in 1934, this standard work is still extremely valuable for all students of Descartes. . . . Some notice of Cartesian studies since 1934 is made, but no references are included to treatments of Cartesian themes by recent analytic philosophers" (*Choice*).

Maritain, Jacques. *Three Reformers: Luther, Descartes, Rousseau.* Associated Faculty Pr. 1970 pap. $16.00; Greenwood repr. of 1950 ed. 1979 lib. bdg. $22.50. A comparison by one of the leading philosophers.

Popkin, Richard H. *History of Scepticism from Erasmus to Descartes.* [*Philosophical Texts and Studies Ser.*] Humanities Pr. rev. ed. 1964 text ed. $26.25. A study showing how Descartes's attempt to answer skepticism grew out of the revival of ancient skepticism.

Rosenfield, Leonora. *From Beast Machine to Man Machine: Animal Soul in French Letters from Descartes to La Mettrie.* Hippocrene Bks. 1968 o.p. A study of how Descartes's theory about beasts and machines developed into a mechanistic theory of man.

Roth, Leon. *Descartes' Discourse on Method.* Folcroft repr. of 1937 ed. 1975 lib. bdg. $25.00. A careful examination of Descartes by an important scholar of modern philosophy.

Sebba, Gregor. *Bibliographia Cartesiana: A Critical Guide to the Descartes Literature*

(1800–1960). Heinman 1964 o.p. An indispensable guide to all of the literature on Descartes up to 1960. Covers materials in most languages, with evaluative comments. A supplement covering subsequent material by V. Chappell and W. Doney, *Twenty-Five Years of Descartes Scholarship, 1960–1984: A Bibliography*, will be published by Garland (1987).

Smith, Norman. *Studies in the Cartesian Philosophy*. Telegraph Bks. repr. of 1902 ed. 1985 lib. bdg. $95.00. Still valuable interpretation of Descartes's theory.

Spinoza, Baruch de. *The Principles of Descartes' Philosophy*. Trans. by Halbert Hains Britan, Open Court 1978 pap. $6.75. Spinoza's first published work, which is, in part, a commentary on Descartes's views.

Talmor, Ezra. *Descartes and Hume*. Pergamon 1980 $23.00. Author tries to show how Hume saved Cartesianism from its own contradictions.

Vartanian, Aram. *Diderot and Descartes: A Study of Scientific Naturalism in the Enlightenment*. [*History of Ideas Ser.*] Greenwood repr. of 1953 ed. 1975 lib. bdg. $22.50. A basic study of the biological theories of Descartes and Diderot, showing Diderot's contribution.

Vendler, Zeno. *Res Cogitans: An Essay in Rational Psychology*. [*Contemporary Philosophy Ser.*] Cornell Univ. Pr. 1972 $27.50. On Descartes's theory of the mind.

Watson, Richard A. *The Breakdown of Cartesian Metaphysics*. Humanities Pr. 1986 $35.00. An expanded and revised version of an earlier study on what happened to Descartes's philosophy in the latter half of the seventeenth century.

———. *Downfall of Cartesianism*. [*International Studies in the History of Ideas*] Austin Hill Pr. o.p. "An intellectual history informed by analytic interests . . . explains the 'downfall of Cartesianism' . . . as due to the inability to handle an ontology of mind and extension" (Tice and Slavin, *Research Guide to Philosophy*, ALA, 1983).

Williams, Bernard. *Descartes: The Project of Pure Enquiry*. Penguin 1978 pap. $4.95. An interpretation and analysis by one of the leading present-day English thinkers.

Wilson, Margaret D. *Descartes*. [*Arguments of the Philosophers Ser.*] Methuen 1978 pap. $9.95. An important presentation of Descartes's philosophy, interpreted by a leading American analytic historian of philosophy. "The focus is on *Meditations*, I and II . . . as a choice among more recent books on Descartes's *Meditations*, Wilson lags behind Curley [and] Bernard A. O. Williams' *Descartes: The Project of Pure Enquiry*" (*Choice*).

GASSENDI, PIERRE. 1592–1655

Pierre Gassendi, a Catholic priest, was a leading skeptic regarding the possibility of gaining actual knowledge of reality, and an advocate of Epicurean physics as the best way to explain natural phenomena. Beginning his intellectual career by teaching and writing against Aristotelianism, he became the Royal Professor of Mathematics at the Collège de France, and wrote extensively about Epicurean science. Gassendi was a leading opponent of alchemy, astrology, the Rosicrucians, and Descartes. His scientific theories rivaled those of Descartes during the seventeenth century.

BOOKS BY GASSENDI

Pierre Gassendi's Institutio Logica. 1658. Ed. by Howard Jones, Humanities Pr. 1981 text ed. pap. $18.50. A posthumous work of Gassendi, which is the best presentation of his theory of knowledge.

Selected Works. Trans. by Craig B. Brush, Johnson Repr. 1972 $45.00. A collection of Gassendi's writings on philosophy, science, and religion.

BOOK ABOUT GASSENDI

Egan, Howard T. *Gassendi's View of Knowledge: A Study of the Epistemological Basis of His Logic.* Univ. Pr. of Amer. 1984 lib. bdg. $27.00 text ed. pap. $13.50

HOBBES, THOMAS. 1588–1679

Thomas Hobbes was born at Malmesbury, England, during the attack of the Spanish Armada on England. He came from a poor family, but received an education and taught Latin and Greek. After receiving his bachelor's degree from Oxford in 1608, he became a tutor to the son of William Cavendish, Earl of Devonshire. In this capacity he traveled in Europe, and met Galileo and many of the leading scientists in France and Italy. Through the Earl of Devonshire he also met leading English figures, including Francis Bacon.

During the Puritan Revolution, Hobbes fled to Paris, where he stayed from 1640 to 1651. He was part of the circle of philosophers and scientists around Father Mersenne, a central figure in European intellectual life who corresponded with people all over Europe. While in Paris Hobbes wrote and published *De Cive* (1642), his reply to Descartes, and developed most of what appeared in the *Leviathan* (1651). In the late 1640s he became tutor to the exiled son of the king, the future Charles II. The publication of his political theory in *Leviathan* led to his estrangement from the royalists, and to his return to England, where he spent the rest of his long life. Hobbes was constantly engaged in quarrels with theologians, politicians, philosophers, scientists, and mathematicians, and was regularly accused of antireligious and even atheistic views. In his later years he wrote several controversial works defending himself against his many opponents. After the Restoration, Charles II awarded him a pension, but the religious establishment considered him a heretic. His political theory on the basis of sovereignty and political obligation has had great influence and is still much studied and debated.

BOOKS BY HOBBES

The English Works of Thomas Hobbes. Ed. by William Molesworth, Adler's 11 vols. 1966 $863.00. The only complete edition of Hobbes's works in English.

De Cive or the Citizen. 1642. Ed. by Sterling P. Lamprecht, Greenwood repr. of 1949 ed. 1982 lib. bdg. $28.25; (with the title *De Cive: The English Version*) ed. by Howard Warrender, Oxford 1983 $67.00. Warrender's version is the initial volume of the new Clarendon edition of the philosophical works of Hobbes. *De Cive* is Hobbes's first published version of his political theory, intended as one part of his overall philosophy dealing with the social body.

Elements of Law: Natural and Politic. 1650. Ed. by Ferdinand Tonnies, Biblio Dist. 2d ed. rev. 1969 $35.00. The earliest formulation of Hobbes's political theory.

Leviathan. 1651. Ed. by Herbert W. Schneider, Bobbs 2 pts. 1958 pap. $9.08; ed. by Michael Oakeshott, Macmillan 1962 pap. $3.95; ed. by C. B. Macpherson, Penguin 1982 pap. $5.95; ed. by Francis B. Randall, Washington Square Pr. 1969 pap. $.90. The most complete statement of Hobbes's philosophy, especially of his political theory.

Man. 1658. (and *Citizen.* 1651). Ed. by Bernard Gert, Peter Smith repr. 1978 $16.75. Hobbes's theory of living bodies, especially of man.

Behemoth: The History of the Causes of the Civil Wars in England and of the Counsels and Artifice by Which They Were Carried On. 1682. Ed. by William Molesworth, Burt Franklin repr. of 1840 ed. 1962 $22.50. Hobbes's interpretation of the Puritan period.

Dialogue between a Philosopher and a Student of the Common Laws of England. Ed. by Joseph Cropsey, Univ. of Chicago Pr. 1971 lib. bdg. $16.00. "Cropsey has in effect given Hobbes scholars a new dimension in interpreting his theory of politics and has provided a lengthy and lucid introduction which students of politics, philosophy, and law should find provocative" (*Choice*).

Thomas White's De Mundo Examined in First English Translation. Trans. by H. W. Jones, Beekman 1976 o.p. This is a hitherto unknown writing of Hobbes—probably his earliest philosophical work—discovered in manuscript in Paris in the 1950s.

BOOKS ABOUT HOBBES

Balz, Albert G. *Idea and Essence in the Philosophies of Hobbes and Spinoza.* AMS Pr. repr. of 1918 ed. 1983 $17.00

Brown, K. C. *Hobbes Studies.* Basil Blackwell 1965 o.p. Contains articles by several leading scholars including Leo Strauss, A. E. Taylor, and Keith Thomas.

Gauthier, David P. *Logic of Leviathan: The Moral and Political Theory of Thomas Hobbes.* Oxford 1969 $12.95. A careful analytic study of Hobbes's basic argument.

Goldsmith, Maurice. *Hobbes's Science of Politics.* Columbia Univ. Pr. 1966 o.p. "Goldsmith's well written, lucid, sensible, and comprehensive analysis of Hobbes' political philosophy, his careful examinations of rival interpretations, and his full and useful bibliography and footnotes undoubtedly make his book the most valuable single work on Hobbes for the undergraduate library" (*Choice*).

Hinnant, Charles H. *Thomas Hobbes.* [*Twayne's Eng. Authors Ser.*] G. K. Hall 1977 o.p. "The reader looking for a straightforward guide to Hobbes's life and doctrines will find this study of use" (*LJ*).

MacPherson, Crawford B. *The Political Theory of Possessive Individualism: Hobbes to Locke.* [*Oxford Pap. Ser.*] 1962 pap. $7.95. "MacPherson's Marxian presuppositions may discourage some readers from close study of his book. Yet the serious student of the Stuart period should not neglect this provocative and often penetrating analysis" (*American Historical Review*).

Mintz, Samuel I. *Hunting of Leviathan.* Cambridge Univ. Pr. 1962 o.p. On the critics of Hobbes in the late seventeenth century.

Oakeshott, Michael. *Hobbes on Civil Association.* Univ. of California Pr. 1975 o.p. Four essays by Oakeshott, a leading Hobbes scholar, on Hobbes and interpretations of him. "Oakeshott's measured admiration for Hobbes is expressed with the grace, buoyancy, and insight that make this essay required reading for all students of Hobbes, if not of modernity itself. . . . A classic in its field" (*Choice*).

Peters, Richard S. *Hobbes.* Greenwood repr. of 1956 ed. 1979 lib. bdg. $39.75. "The author notes the manifold source of Hobbes' outlook: the Baconian concept of knowledge as the ability to manipulate nature to human goals; the Cartesian belief that a sound scientific method is the key which opens the secrets of man and nature; the then widespread belief in the values of the geometric approach as solving all problems from epistemology to ethics, i.e., an approach which started from self-evident deductive principles and concluded in a philosophy of civilization logically proceeding from such axioms" (*Science & Society*).

Raphael, D. D. *Hobbes: Morals and Politics.* [*Political Thinkers Ser.*] Allen & Unwin 1977 text ed. $19.95. "Intended as a handbook for students unfamiliar with the moral and political philosophy of Hobbes. . . . It provides an introduction to most of the major issues raised in Hobbes's philosophy as well as . . . interpretations of some of those issues" (*Choice*).

Reik, Miriam. *The Golden Lands of Thomas Hobbes*. Wayne State Univ. Pr. 1977 text ed. $25.00. A study of Hobbes's development as a writer, historian, and political theorist.

Rogow, Arnold A. *Thomas Hobbes: Radical in the Service of Reaction*. Norton 1986 $19.95. "Rogow's thesis is that Hobbes's pessimistic depiction of man's state of nature as one of timidity, insecurity, distrust, and ambition has its psychological origins in Hobbes's own character, particularly as a result of his formative years in Malmesbury. . . . An informative work for scholars and students" (*LJ*).

Ross, Ralph, and others, eds. *Thomas Hobbes in His Time*. Univ. of Minnesota Pr. 1975 o.p. A series of articles on Hobbes, including one by John Dewey.

Sacksteder, William. *Hobbes Studies Bibliography: 1879–1979*. Bowling Green Univ., Philosophy Documentation Center 1982 $18.50. The most complete available bibliography on Hobbes.

Shapin, Steven, and Simon Schaffer. *Leviathan and the Air Pump: Hobbes, Bayle, and the Experimental Life*. Princeton Univ. Pr. 1985 $60.00. An attempt to place Hobbes in the development of the science of his time.

Spragens, Thomas A., Jr. *The Politics of Motion: The World of Thomas Hobbes*. Univ. Pr. of Kentucky 1973 $20.00. On Hobbes's science and politics.

Stephen, Sir Leslie. *Hobbes*. 1904. Univ. of Michigan Pr. 1961 o.p. "One cannot read Sir Leslie Stephen's book without appreciating that, apart altogether from the circumstance that English moral philosophy shaped itself—and, for the most part, frankly—as an answer to Hobbes' daring system, Hobbes for his own sake makes a charming study" (*Intl. Journal of Ethics*).

Strauss, Leo. *Political Philosophy of Hobbes: Its Basis and Its Genesis*. Trans. by Elsa M. Sinclair, Univ. of Chicago Pr. 1984 pap. $10.00. "The strengths of the book include the availability of the essays under a single cover, the systematic introduction, and the thorough chronological bibliography. [Hilail] Gildin's introduction is a valuable summary of Strauss' thought and contains some interesting observations on historicism and positivism" (*Choice*).

Von Leyden, W. *Hobbes and Locke: The Politics of Freedom and Obligation*. St. Martin's 1982 $25.00. Important comparative study by a leading authority on seventeenth-century English thought.

Warrender, Howard. *The Political Philosophy of Hobbes: His Theory of Obligation*. Oxford 1957 o.p. A now classic study of Hobbes's thought. "Partly because of [the] wise limitation of his objective, but chiefly because of the natural clarity of Mr. Warrender's style and his high standards of exposition, this is probably the clearest and most readable account yet to appear of Hobbes's political philosophy" (*Hibbert Journal*).

Watkins, J. W. N. *Hobbes's System of Ideas*. Hilary House Pubs. 1965 o.p. "Mr. Watkins suggests that while Hobbes did derive his prescriptions from factual premises, he did not commit a logical fallacy, because 'his prescriptions are not *moral* prescriptions—they are more like doctor's orders of a peculiarly compelling kind' " (*English Historical Review*).

LEIBNIZ (or LEIBNITZ), GOTTFRIED WILHELM, BARON VON. 1646–1716

Leibniz, one of the last real polymaths (one of encyclopedic learning), was born in Leipzig. Educated there and at the universities at Jena and Altdorf, he then served as a diplomat for the Elector of Mainz, and was sent to Paris, where he lived for a few years and came into contact with leading scientists, philosophers, and theologians. During a trip to England he was elected to the Royal Society; he made a visit to Holland to meet Spinoza. Back in Germany he became librarian to the Duke of Brunswick, whose library was the largest in Europe outside the Vatican. From there he became involved in government affairs in Hanover, and later settled in Berlin at the court of Queen Sophie Charlotte of Prussia. Leibniz was involved in the diplomatic negotiations that led to the Hanoverian succession to the English throne.

From his university days he showed an interest in mathematics, logic, physics, law, linguistics, and history, as well as theology and practical political affairs. He discovered calculus, independent of Newton, and had a protracted squabble about which of them should be given credit for the achievement. The developer of much of what is now modern logic, he discovered some important physical laws, and offered a physical theory that is close to some twentieth-century conceptions. Leibniz was interested in developing a universal language, and tried to master the elements of all languages.

He corresponded widely with scholars all over Europe, and with some Jesuit missionaries in China. His philosophy was largely worked out in answer to those of other thinkers, such as LOCKE (see also Vol. 3), Malebranche, Bayle, and Arnauld. Although he published comparatively little during his lifetime, Leibniz left an enormous mass of unpublished papers, drafts of works, and notes on topics of interest. His library, which has been preserved, contains annotations, analyses, and often refutations of works he read. The project of publishing all of his writings, undertaken in the 1920s by the Prussian Academy, was delayed by World War II but was resumed thereafter, and now more than 60 (of a projected 100) volumes have appeared. It is not likely that the project will be completed in the twentieth century. So far, very few of Leibniz's writings have been translated into English, although he has greatly influenced English and American thinkers.

BOOKS BY LEIBNIZ

Discourse on Metaphysics, Correspondence with Arnauld, Monadology. Trans. and ed. by George R. Montgomery, Open Court 2d ed. 1973 $18.95 pap. $6.95. Some of the best short statements of Leibniz's philosophy, and his defense and explanation of it in answer to Arnauld.

Discourse on the Natural Theology of the Chinese. Trans. by Henry Rosemont, Jr., and Daniel J. Cook [*Society for Asian and Comparative Philosophy*] Univ. of Hawaii Pr. 1977 text ed. pap. $8.00. One of the first attempts by a Western thinker to figure out what Oriental philosophy is about, and how it relates to the concerns of Western thinkers. Leibniz got most of his information from Jesuit missionaries.

The Leibniz-Arnauld Correspondence. Ed. and trans. by H. T. Mason, intro. by G. H. Parkinson [*Philosophy of Leibniz Ser.*] Garland 1985 lib. bdg. $30.00. An important discussion of some of Leibniz's key ideas in letters to one of his critics.

Logical Papers: A Selection. Trans. by G. H Parkinson, Oxford 1966 $32.50. Some of Leibniz's writings that relate to modern symbolic logic and mathematics.

New Essays Concerning Human Understanding. Ed. by Peter Remnant and Jonathan Bennett, Cambridge Univ. Pr. 1981 $90.00 pap. $24.95 abr. ed. 1982 $13.95. This is a new translation of Leibniz's answer to John Locke.

The Monadology and Other Philosophical Writings. Ed. by R. C. Sleigh [*Philosophy of Leibniz Ser.*] Garland 1985 lib. bdg. $55.00. A new edition of some of Leibniz's central metaphysical texts.

Leibniz's Philosophical Writings. Ed. by G. H. Parkinson, trans. by Mary Morris, Biblio Dist. 1983 pap. $7.00; Rowman 1973 $13.50. Some basic essays on the metaphysics of Leibniz.

Philosophical Papers and Letters. Ed. by Leroy E. Loemker, Humanities Pr. 1970 o.p. The largest group of writings presently available in English.

Political Writings of Leibniz. Ed. by Patrick Riley [*Cambridge Studies in the History and Theory of Politics*] 1981 pap. $16.95. These writings are interesting in themselves, and also in relation to Leibniz's political activities in European dynastic politics, and to efforts by the Lutherans to reunite the Christian churches.

BOOKS ABOUT LEIBNIZ

Adams, Robert M., and others, eds. *Essays on the Philosophy of Leibniz.* [*Rice Univ. Studies*] 1978 pap. $10.00. A group of essays by a variety of contemporary scholars.

Barber, W. H. *Leibniz in France—From Arnauld to Voltaire: A Study in French Reactions to Leibnizianism, 1670–1760.* Ed. by R. C. Sleigh, Jr. [*Philosophy of Leibniz Ser.*] Garland 1985 lib. bdg. $40.00. A reprint of an important study of Leibniz's personal activities in France, and of his influence, positive and negative, in the Enlightenment.

Brown, Stuart C. *Leibniz.* Univ. of Minnesota Pr. 1985 $35.00 pap. $12.95. "The book proceeds by briefly discussing the important topics to be found in Leibniz's philosophy, and it sets these topics in a developmental framework. . . . Thus it concentrates on the *Discourse on Metaphysics* and the *New System* and does not more than mention the *New Essays on Human Understanding* or *Theodicy*" (*Choice*).

Dewey, John. *Leibniz's New Essays Concerning the Human Understanding: A Critical Exposition.* Gordon Pr. 1977 lib. bdg. $59.95. One of Dewey's first philosophical works was this critique and commentary on Leibniz's response to Locke's *Essay*.

Hooker, Michael, ed. *Leibniz: Critical and Interpretive Essays.* Univ. of Minnesota Pr. 1982 pap. $12.95. A collection of essays by various scholars on Leibniz. "The essays are of high quality and deal with epistemological and logical issues . . . also contains a useful and extensive bibliography by John Kish" (*Choice*).

Jolley, Nicholas. *Leibniz and Locke: A Study of the New Essays and Human Understanding.* Oxford 1984 $39.95. An examination of Leibniz's critique of Locke's *Essay*.

Leclerc, Ivor, ed. *The Philosophy of Leibniz and the Modern World.* Vanderbilt Univ. Pr. 1973 $17.95. Ten papers by Leroy E. Loemker, and four by M. Capek, I. Leclerc, N. Rescher, and N. L. Wilson.

Loemker, Leroy E. *Struggle for Synthesis: The Seventeenth-Century Background of Leibniz's Synthesis of Order and Freedom.* Harvard Univ. Pr. 1972 $22.50. "This substantial study of Leibniz goes beyond its title to consider many related topics and writers. . . . Not only is the author at home with the well-known theological, literary, and scientific works closely related to Leibniz, but he also introduces unfamiliar writers and works, adding to this study's value" (*Choice*).

Martin, Gottfried. *Leibniz: Logic and Metaphysics.* Ed. by R. C. Sleigh, Jr. [*Philosophy of Leibniz Ser.*] Garland 1985 lib. bdg. $30.00. Translation of an important German study on Leibniz.

Merz, John T. *Leibniz.* Arden Lib. repr. of 1901 ed. 1978 lib. bdg. $35.00. A still valuable study of Leibniz's thought.

Meyer, R. W. *Leibniz and the Seventeenth-Century Revolution.* Ed. by R. C. Sleigh, Jr.

[*Philosophy of Leibniz Ser.*] Garland 1985 lib. bdg. $35.00. Leibniz seen in terms of the political, intellectual, and religious crisis of his time.

Mungello, David E. *Leibniz and Confucianism: The Search for Accord.* Univ. of Hawaii Pr. 1977 text ed. $14.00. On Leibniz's interpretations of Chinese thought.

Ortega y Gasset, José. *The Idea of Principle in Leibnitz and the Evolution of Deductive Theory.* Norton 1971 o.p. "Although the matter is highly technical, the manner is brilliantly compelling even to the lay reader—in Ortega's own estimate, this is 'something presented as literature which results in philosophy.' Obligatory reading for all students of 20th-Century thought" (*LJ*).

Parkinson, G. H. *Logic and Reality in Leibniz's Metaphysics.* Ed. by R. C. Sleigh, Jr. [*Philosophy of Leibniz Ser.*] Garland 1985 lib. bdg. $30.00. An examination of the relation of logic to metaphysics and theology in Leibniz.

Rescher, Nicholas, ed. *Leibniz: An Introduction to His Philosophy.* Univ. Pr. of Amer. repr. of 1979 ed. 1986 text ed. pap. $10.75. A short technical presentation of Leibniz by a leading American philosopher.

Russell, Bertrand. *A Critical Exposition of the Philosophy of Leibniz.* Humanities Pr. 1958 o.p. Russell, at the end of the nineteenth century, was one of the first to read Leibniz's mathematical-logical manuscripts and to see their relevance to contemporary thought. Russell became convinced there must have been two Leibnizes: one who wrote popular metaphysical theory, and another who was a great mathematical logician far in advance of his time.

Yost, Robert. *Leibniz and Philosophical Analysis.* Ed. by R. C. Sleigh, Jr. [*Philosophy of Leibniz Ser.*] Garland 1985 lib. bdg. $30.00. A study of the relation of Leibniz's views and those of contemporary philosophical analysis.

LOCKE, JOHN. 1632–1704

Locke grew up during the Puritan revolution, which his father supported, and was sent up to Oxford where he was trained as a medical doctor. Although he did not practice, he worked with some of the important doctors of the time (and wrote the preface to Sydenham's *Treatise on Smallpox*). Locke traveled abroad as private secretary to the powerful Earl of Shaftesbury and tutor to the earl's son; in the early 1680s Locke had to flee to the Continent with Shaftesbury because of the latter's political opposition to James II. In Holland, Locke became involved with liberal Dutch and Huguenot theologians and philosophers, and some of his basic theories were worked out in discussions with them. In 1688, when the Glorious Revolution brought William of Orange to the throne, Locke returned to England, where he quickly became a leading spokesman for the new constitutional monarchy and the theoretician for a liberal democratic government. His writings on political philosophy, *Two Treatises of Government*, begun before his exile and completed and published in 1690, became one of the basic justifications for democratic systems of government (and greatly influenced the development of the governments in the American colonies and in the United States).

Locke had started writing a book on the origin, extent, and certainty of knowledge early in his career. It was brought almost to completion in Holland, and was published in England in 1690 as *An Essay Concerning Human Understanding*, which is perhaps *the* fundamental statement of the empirical theory of knowledge. In it he sought to explain and justify the empirical science of the Royal Society, of which he was a member.

When his *Essay* appeared, Locke was attacked as too skeptical, too inconsistent, and too much like Spinoza. Edward Stillingfleet, the bishop of Worcester, saw that Locke's empirical method, if applied to religion, would lead to doubts about Christianity. Others saw Locke's contention that matter may be able to think as a disguised version of Spinoza's philosophy. And Leibniz, in his *New Essays*, tried to show the inconsistencies in Locke's view (as did Berkeley a few years later). Locke's work, quickly translated into French, had a very great influence on the *philosophes*.

Since World War II, an enormous collection of Locke's manuscripts, the Lovelace Papers, has become available, containing drafts of his writings, notes, letters, and so on. His library, with his marginal notes, has also been preserved. Oxford has undertaken a reediting of his works on the basis of this material. Locke's letters have now been published, many of them for the first time (with English translations when necessary), and the new Oxford Clarendon Press edition of his writings has appeared; others are in preparation. (See also Volume 3.)

BOOKS BY LOCKE

Works. Adler's 10 vols. repr. of 1823 ed. 1963 $524.00; [*Select Bibliographies Repr. Ser.*] Ayer 2 vols. $56.00. A new edition of the works of John Locke is presently being prepared by scholars. This is to be published by the Oxford Clarendon Press (John Locke, *A Paraphrase and Notes on the Epistles of St. Paul*, ed. by Arthur W. Wainwright, 2 vols., 1987), based on much new manuscript material, plus material from Locke's library.

Correspondence of John Locke. Ed. by E. S. De Beer and Gavin R. De Beer, Oxford 8 vols. 1976–87 ea. $110.00–$119.00. First complete edition of Locke's letters, with translations of Latin ones.

An Essay Concerning Human Understanding. 1690. Ed. by A. O. Woozley, New Amer. Lib. 1974 pap. $8.95; ed. by Peter H. Nidditch [*Works of John Locke*] Oxford 1975 $79.00 1979 text ed. pap. $14.95; ed. by Alexander Campbell Fraser, Peter Smith 2 vols. 1959 set $33.50

A Letter Concerning Toleration. Ed. by Patrick Romanell, Bobbs 2d ed. 1955 pap. $3.56; ed. by James Tully [*Philosophical Class. Ser.*] Hackett 1983 text ed. pap. $3.45. Locke's important statement on the reasons for tolerating diverse opinions in religion.

The Reasonableness of Christianity and A Discourse of Miracles. Ed. by I. T. Ramsey, Stanford Univ. Pr. 1958 pap. $6.95. Locke's moderate views on religious questions.

The Second Treatise of Civil Government. Prometheus Bks. 1986 pap. $3.95. Locke's most important statement of his theory of democratic government.

The Second Treatise of Government and A Letter Concerning Toleration. Ed. by J. W. Gough, Barnes & Noble 3d ed. repr. of 1966 ed. 1976 o.p.; Prometheus Bks. 1986 pap. $3.95. Text of two of Locke's important essays.

Two Tracts on Government. Ed. by Philip Abrams, Cambridge Univ. Pr. 1967 $42.50. A critical edition of Locke's two main writings on political theory. "Readily intelligible to undergraduate students of political philosophy. Most important and highly recommended" (*Choice*).

BOOKS ABOUT LOCKE

Aaron, Richard I. *John Locke*. Oxford 3d ed. 1971 $42.00. A basic commentary on Locke's philosophy. "Although the book does not argue a revisionist or reworked thesis, it remains, in its bibliographically updated edition, one of the best surveys of Locke's general philosophy and impact. A fine introduction to Locke which even the specialist will value" (*Choice*).

Alexander, Peter. *Ideas, Qualities and Corpuscles: Locke and Bayle on the External World*. Cambridge Univ. Pr. 1985 $44.50. A careful new study of Locke and Bayle on knowledge of the external world.

Alexander, Samuel. *Locke*. Associated Faculty Pr. repr. of 1908 ed. 1970 $15.00. An evaluation of Locke by an important speculative metaphysician.

Brandt, Reinhard, ed. *John Locke Symposium*. De Gruyter 1980 text ed. $35.75. A series of important essays on Locke.

Christophersen, Hans O. *Bibliographical Introduction to the Study of John Locke*. [*Bibliography and Reference Ser.*] Burt Franklin repr. of 1930 ed. 1969 $18.50. Important bibliography, now somewhat out of date.

Cranston, Maurice. *John Locke: A Biography*. Ed. by J. P. Mayer [*European Political Thought Ser.*] Ayer repr. of 1957 ed. 1979 lib. bdg. $34.50. This is now the standard biography.

Dewhurst, Kenneth. *John Locke: Physician and Philosopher*. Garland 1985 lib. bdg. $40.00. Emphasizes Locke's medical works and concerns. Includes Locke's medical notes.

Dunn, John. *Locke*. [*Past Masters Ser.*] Oxford 1984 pap. $3.95. "John Dunn has done an excellent job in relating the different parts of Locke's writing to one another and, in addition, his book is highly readable and has an agreeable reflective melancholy of its own" (*The Listener*).

——. *The Political Thought of John Locke: An Historical Account of the Argument of the 'Two Treatises of Government.'* Cambridge Univ. Pr. 1983 pap. $14.95. A very careful attempt to place Locke's political writings in their historical setting; based on access to the Locke manuscripts.

Filmer, Robert. *Patriarchia and Other Political Works of Sir John Filmer*. [*Philosophy of John Locke Ser.*] Garland 1985 lib. bdg. $40.00. A reprint of one of the main works Locke was attacking in his writings on political philosophy.

Franklin, Julian H. *John Locke and the Theory of Sovereignty: Mixed Monarchy and the Right of Resistance in the Political Thought of the English Revolution*. [*Cambridge Studies in the History and Theory of Politics*] 1981 pap. $10.95. A study of Locke's unique contribution to the modern theory of sovereignty.

Fraser, Alexander C. *Locke*. Telegraph Bks. repr. of 1907 ed. 1985 lib. bdg. $50.00. Important nineteenth-century interpretation of Locke.

Gay, Peter, ed. *John Locke on Education*. [*Classics in Education Ser.*] Teachers College Pr. 1964 text ed. $10.00

Gibson, James. *Locke's Theory of Knowledge and Its Historical Relations*. Cambridge Univ. Pr. 1968 o.p. A fundamental study of Locke.

Green, Thomas Hill. *Hume and Locke*. Peter Smith 1968 $9.00. "A 19th-century philosopher, now much too neglected, offers a penetrating critique of the empirical tradition in British philosophy" (*N.Y. Times Bk. Review*).

Hall, Roland, and Roger Woodhouse. *Eighty Years of Locke Scholarship, 1900–1980: A Bibliographic Guide*. Columbia Univ. Pr. 1983 $20.00. Basic bibliographical guide for twentieth-century writing on Locke.

Jenkins, J. J. *Understanding Locke*. Columbia Univ. Pr. 1983 $15.00. An introduction to philosophy through Locke's *Essay*. "The book is full of arguments for and against Lockean positions, and the clear and lively style makes it a joy to read. . . . Excellent bibliography" (*Choice*).

Jolley, Nicholas. *Leibnitz and Locke: A Study of the New Essays and Human Understanding.* Oxford 1984 $39.95. A study of Leibniz's critique of Locke.

Kendall, Willmoore. *John Locke and the Doctrine of Majority Rule.* Peter Smith 1965 o.p. "The work under review is heartily to be welcomed. For Professor Kendall is concerned, not simply with the theory of majority decision, but rather with a complex of ideas which together constitute the philosophy of majority-rule democracy" (*American Political Science Review*).

King, Peter. *The Life and Letters of John Locke, with Extracts from His Journals and Common-place Books.* Garland 1984 lib. bdg. $66.00. The earliest biographical work on Locke.

Lough, John. *Locke's Travels in France, 1675–1679: As Related in His Journals, Correspondence and Other Papers.* Garland 1984 lib. bdg. $45.00. Interesting in terms of the leaders in science and philosophy Locke met in France at the time.

Mackie, J. L. *Problems from Locke.* Oxford 1976 text ed. $29.95 text ed. pap. $12.95. Discussion of several basic epistemological issues based on Locke's account of knowledge.

MacPherson, Crawford B. *The Political Theory of Possessive Individualism: Hobbes to Locke.* [*Oxford Pap. Ser.*] 1962 pap. $7.95. An important Marxist interpretation of Hobbes and Locke.

Morris, Charles R. *Locke, Berkeley, Hume.* Greenwood repr. of 1931 ed. 1979 lib. bdg. $22.50. A significant study by a leading American pragmatist.

Norris, John. *Christian Blessedness, with Reflections upon a Late Essay Concerning Human Understanding.* Ed. by René Wellek, Garland repr. of 1690 ed. 1978 lib. bdg. $51.00. An evaluation of Locke by the leading English follower of Malebranche.

Romanell, Patrick. *John Locke and Medicine.* Prometheus Bks. 1984 $23.95. A thorough study of the philosophical aspects of Locke's medical writings and activities.

Schouls, Peter A. *The Imposition of Method: A Study of Descartes and Locke.* Oxford 1980 text ed. $45.00. A comparison of the methodology employed by the two thinkers.

Sergeant, John. *Solid Philosophy Asserted against the Fancies of the Idealists: Or, the Method to Science Farther Illustrated; with Reflexions on Mr. Locke's Essay Concerning Human Understanding.* Garland 1984 lib. bdg. $60.00. Important criticism of Locke by one of the leading Catholic philosophers of his time.

Squadrito, Kathleen M. *John Locke* [*Twayne's Eng. Authors Ser.*] G. K. Hall 1979 $13.50. Good general presentation of Locke's views on theory of knowledge, religion, ethics, education, and political philosophy.

———. *Locke's Theory of Sensitive Knowledge.* Univ. Pr. of Amer. 1978 text ed. pap. $11.50. A careful study of Locke's account of knowledge by direct experience.

Steinberg, Jules. *Locke, Rousseau, and the Idea of Consent: An Inquiry into the Liberal-Democratic Theory of Political Obligation.* [*Contributions in Political Science*] Greenwood 1978 lib. bdg. $29.95. A comparison and contrast of these two theoreticians of liberal democratic theory.

Tarcov, Nathan. *Locke's Education for Liberty.* Univ. of Chicago Pr. 1984 lib. bdg. $22.00

Vaughn, Karen I. *John Locke: Economist and Social Scientist.* Univ. of Chicago Pr. 1980 lib. bdg. $13.50 pap. $6.50. A study of Locke's economic theory, which is usually ignored.

Von Leyden, W. *Hobbes and Locke: The Politics of Freedom and Obligation.* St. Martin's 1982 $25.00. A very good study by one of the leading scholars of seventeenth-century English thought.

Wood, Neal. *The Politics of Locke's Philosophy: A Social Study of "An Essay Concerning Human Understanding."* Univ. of California Pr. 1983 $29.00. An attempt to interpret Locke's *Essay* in terms of the politics of the time. "Wood's work is an exploration of the social and political views of Locke and his age, based on Locke's *Essay*. Neither the subject matter nor the author's language will raise any difficulties for a typical undergraduate" (*Choice*).

Woolhouse, R. S. *Locke.* [*Philosophers in Context Ser.*] Univ. of Minnesota Pr. 1983 $35.00 1985 pap. $12.95. An attempt to put the basic ideas of Locke's *Essay* in their historical context. "The background information and quotations are used judiciously and always with an eye toward illuminating the central ideas in Locke's *Essay*" (*Choice*).

Yolton, J. W. *John Locke: An Introduction.* Basil Blackwell 1985 $29.95 pap. $9.95. A general presentation of Locke's views by a leading contemporary Locke scholar.

———. *John Locke and the Way of Ideas.* AMS Pr. repr. of 1956 ed. 1987 $29.50. Represents the same kind of historical-philosophical study as his *Locke and the Compass of Human Understanding.*

———. *Locke and the Compass of Human Understanding.* Cambridge Univ. Pr. 1970 $34.50. A selective commentary of themes in Locke's views by a leading Locke scholar.

MALEBRANCHE, NICOLAS. 1638–1715

Malebranche, a priest of the Catholic order of the Oratorians, became very excited when he first came across a book by Descartes. For ten years he studied Descartes's system, and then wrote his major works as a defense of Cartesianism, slightly amended by the influence of St. Augustine. He defended his version of Cartesian-Augustinianism and its application to theology against the orthodox Cartesians, against Leibniz and Bayle, and against the Jansenist leader Antoine Arnauld. Malebranche was accused by the Jesuits of being heretical, especially on the question of the causes of evil actions. His works were translated into English at the end of the seventeenth century, and greatly influenced both Berkeley and Hume. His complete works have recently been published in a scholarly French edition.

BOOKS BY MALEBRANCHE

Dialogues on Metaphysics. Trans. by Willis Doney, Abaris Bks. 1980 $20.00. A popular presentation of Malebranche's central theories.

The Search after Truth and Elucidations of the Search after Truth (*De la recherche de la vérité and éclaircissements*). 1674. Trans. by Paul J. Olscamp, Ohio State Univ. Pr. 1980 $50.00. This is Malebranche's first and major statement of his philosophy, along with his answers to some of his Cartesian opponents, who had attacked him for deviating from the master's views on some points. This is the first new translation since 1704.

BOOKS ABOUT MALEBRANCHE

Church, Ralph W. *A Study in the Philosophy of Malebranche.* Associated Faculty Pr. repr. of 1931 ed. 1970 $28.50. An important work in bringing Malebranche to the attention of the English-language reading public.

Hobart, Michael E. *Science and Religion in the Thought of Nicolas Malebranche.* Univ.

of North Carolina Pr. 1982 $19.95. A study of Malebranche's influence on the last of the Cambridge Platonists and on Berkeley and Hume. An interesting appendix considers Malebranche's influence on colonial American thought.

Walton, Craig. *De la recherche du bien: A Study of Malebranche's Science of Ethics.* Kluwer Academic 1972 o.p. An examination of a side of Malebranche's work that is too often neglected.

NEWTON, SIR ISAAC. 1642–1727

Newton studied at Cambridge University, and became a Fellow of Trinity College. His early scientific work and his discovery of calculus led to his appointment as Lucasian Professor of Mathematics. Newton and Leibniz had a long acrimonious dispute as to which of them properly deserved credit for the discovery. In 1687 Newton published his most important scientific work, *Principia Mathematica* (*The Mathematical Principles of Natural Philosophy*), in which he presented his theory of the physical universe, his laws of motion, and the principle of universal gravitation. Newton later became director of the Royal Mint and president of the Royal Society. His employment of the empirical method gave great impetus to its use in other areas of research, and he became a leading force in Enlightenment science. Publicly Newton appeared as the greatest scientist of his age. In private he was carrying on alchemical researches, and drafting long works on theology, especially on the prophecies in the biblical books of Daniel and Revelation. He kept his alchemical and theological work secret from all but a few trusted disciples, especially since his views on religion were considered heretical. Most of his alchemical and theological writings have not been published. Several recent studies try to come to grips with the many sides of Newton's work. (See also Volume 5.)

BOOKS BY NEWTON

Sir Isaac Newton's Mathematical Principles of Natural Philosophy and His System of the World. 1687. Trans. by Andrew Motte, Greenwood 1962 lib. bdg. $32.50

Newton's Philosophy of Nature. Trans. by H. Standish Thayer [*Lib. of Class. Ser.*] Free Pr. 1974 pap. $12.95; Hafner 1953 text ed. pap. $7.95. Excerpts from Newton's scientific writings that indicate his philosophy and that played an important role in Enlightenment thought.

Certain Philosophical Questions: Newton's Trinity Notebook. Ed. by J. E. McGuire and Martin Tamny, Cambridge Univ. Pr. 1983 $90.00. A careful scholarly edition of the notebook Newton kept when he first went to college, indicating the interest he had at the time in the theories of the Cambridge Platonists.

BOOKS ABOUT NEWTON

Christianson, Gale E. *In the Presence of the Creator: Isaac Newton and His Times.* Free Pr. 1984 $27.50. "While not the scholarly tour-de-force of Richard Westfall's definitive biography *Never at Rest*, Christianson's account . . . provides a reliable and captivating study" (*LJ*).

Dobbs, Betty J. *The Foundations of Newton's Alchemy: Or "The Hunting of the Greene Lyon."* [*Cambridge Pap. Lib.*] 1983 pap. $17.95. "Dobbs's study of Newton's alchemical manuscripts now shows us yet another side of this complex genius. Through deep and careful research she has established that Newton was not only curious about alchemy but that he studied the subject intensely and believed he had succeeded in carrying through alchemical transformations" (*Choice*).

Force, James E. *William Whiston: Honest Newtonian.* Cambridge Univ. Pr. 1985 $37.50. On Newton's chosen successor, who was a religious millenarian and antitrinitarian.

Hurlbutt, Robert H. *Hume, Newton, and the Design Argument.* Univ. of Nebraska Pr. rev. ed. 1985 $24.95. An examination of the design or teleological argument about the existence of God as presented by Newton and criticized by Hume.

Manuel, Frank E. *The Religion of Isaac Newton: The Fremantle Lectures 1973.* Oxford 1974 $24.95. Attempts to give a psychological explanation of Newton's religious views; includes the publication of one of his manuscripts on religion.

Westfall, Richard S. *Never at Rest: A Biography of Isaac Newton.* Cambridge Univ. Pr. 1981 $75.00 1983 pap. $24.95. A prize-winning work that attempts to give an overall interpretation of Newton as scientist, alchemist, and theologian.

PASCAL, BLAISE. 1623–1662

Blaise Pascal was born in Clermont-Ferrand, France, raised in Paris (where his father was a government official), and educated privately. Pascal discovered mathematics independently, and as a child started working out mathematical theories. At 16 he completed a work on conic sections, and at 19 invented the first adding machine. (The principle on which his machine was based led recently to the development of the computer language called "Pascal.") Pascal next joined the contemporary scientific community, many members of which were friends of his father. In his early twenties, he wrote on the nature of the vacuum, and in 1648 made the crucial experiment of carrying an inverted tube of mercury (a barometer) up a mountain, thus obtaining measurements from which he evolved the theory of atmospheric pressure.

Pascal's family was involved with the Augustinian reform movement within the Catholic Church, called Jansenism. After an overpowering mystical experience, Pascal devoted himself chiefly to religious writings and activities, often withdrawing to the Jansenist monastery at Port-Royal outside Paris. There he wrote his *Provincial Letters* (1656), a satirical defense of Jansenism against the Jesuit opposition, and also the fragments that comprise his masterpiece, the *Pensées* (*Thoughts*) (1670), which present his views on philosophy, religion, and morality. Left unfinished at his death, this work is still being revised and reordered on the basis of continued scholarly examination of the actual fragments and new information about Pascal's last years.

BOOKS BY PASCAL

Great Short Works of Pascal. Trans. and ed. by John Blackenagel and Emile Caillet, Greenwood repr. of 1948 ed. 1974 $15.00. Pascal's scientific, mathematical, and short religious writings.

The Provincial Letters. 1656. Penguin 1982 pap. $4.95. Pascal's scathing, satirical attack on the Jesuits.

Pensées. 1670. Trans. by A. J. Krailsheimer [*Penguin Class. Ser.*] 1966 pap. $3.95. A new translation based on the reordering of Pascal's text.

BOOKS ABOUT PASCAL

Davidson, Hugh M. *Blaise Pascal.* [*Twayne's World Authors Ser.*] G. K. Hall 1983 lib. bdg. $16.95. An overall presentation of Pascal's thought in science, religion, and philosophy, and an examination of him as a writer.

———. *The Origins of Certainty: Means and Meanings in Pascal's Pensées."* Univ. of Chicago Pr. 1979 lib. bdg. $16.00. Attempt to show Pascal's method, and how it leads to religious certainty.

Goldmann, Lucien. *Hidden God.* Trans. by Philip Thody [*International Lib. of Philosophy and Scientific Method Ser.*] Humanities Pr. 1976 o.p. An intriguing interpretation by a leading French Marxist thinker.

Rescher, Nicholas. *Pascal's Wager: A Study of Practical Reasoning in Philosophical Theology.* Univ. of Notre Dame Pr. 1985 text ed. $19.95. An examination of the kind of reasoning involved in Pascal's wager (his conclusion that since one cannot prove or disprove God's existence, one may lose by not believing and can only gain by believing), and an evaluation of what it establishes, by a leading contemporary thinker.

SPINOZA, BARUCH (or BENEDICT). 1632–1677

Spinoza was born in Amsterdam, the son of Portuguese Jewish refugees who had fled from the persecution of the Spanish Inquisition. Although raised in the Jewish community, he rebelled against its religious views and practices, and in 1656 was formally excommunicated from the Portuguese-Spanish Synagogue of Amsterdam, and thus effectively cast out of the Jewish world. He joined a group of nonconfessional Christians (although he never became a Christian), the Collegiants, who professed no creeds or practices but shared a spiritual brotherhood. He was also apparently involved with the Quaker mission in Amsterdam. Spinoza eventually settled in The Hague where he lived quietly, studying philosophy, science, and theology, discussing his ideas with a small circle of independent thinkers, and earning his living as a lens grinder. He corresponded with some of the leading philosophers and scientists of his time, and was visited by Leibniz and many others. He is said to have refused offers to teach at Heidelberg, or to be court philosopher for the Prince of Conde. During his lifetime he published only two works, *The Principles of Descartes' Philosophy* (1666) and the *Theological Political Tractatus* (1670). In the first his own theory began to emerge as the consistent consequence of that of Descartes. In the second, he gave his reasons for rejecting the claims of religious knowledge, and elaborated his theory of the independence of the state from all religious factions. After his death (probably caused by consumption due to glass dust), his major work, the *Ethics,* appeared in his *Opera Posthuma,* and presented the full metaphysical basis of his pantheistic view. Spinoza's influence on the Enlightenment, on the Romantic Age, and on modern secularism has been tremendous. There has been an increase of interest in his views in the last decade, and a complete new translation of his works is presently in progress.

BOOKS BY SPINOZA

The Collected Works of Spinoza. Ed. by Edwin Curley, Princeton Univ. Pr. 1985 text ed. vol. 1 $47.50. This is the first volume (of an expected two-volume set) in the complete new translation presently underway (the former one, more than a century old, is not complete). Volume 1 contains the *Ethics* and *On the Correction of the Understanding*. It is very carefully done, with much scholarly explanation of the problems involved.

The Works of Spinoza. Trans. by R. H. Elwes, Peter Smith 2 vols. 1951 $29.50. Although it does not contain all the works, and the translation is no longer adequate, this is the most complete collection of Spinoza's writings presently available. Volume 1 includes the *Theological Political Treatise* and the *Political Treatise*. Volume 2 contains the *Ethics*, the *Improvement of the Understanding*, and selected letters.

Earlier Philosophical Writings: The Cartesian Principles and Thoughts on Metaphysics. Trans. by F. A. Hayes, Irvington repr. of 1963 ed. 1973 o.p. The first work published by Spinoza, not included in *Works*.

The Ethics and Selected Letters. Trans. by Samuel Shirley, Hackett 1982 text ed. lib. bdg. $19.50 pap. $4.95. A lively new translation of this portion of Spinoza's work.

Algebraic Calculations of the Rainbow and the Calculation of Chances. Ed. by Michael Petry, Kluwer Academic 1986 lib. bdg. $44.50. A careful critical edition of a work that was believed lost.

Books about Spinoza

Allison, Henry E. *Benedict De Spinoza*. [*Twayne's World Authors Ser.*] G. K. Hall 1975 o.p. A good general introduction to the thought of Spinoza.

Balz, Albert G. *Idea and Essence in the Philosophies of Hobbes and Spinoza*. AMS Pr. repr. of 1918 ed. 1983 $17.00. A good basic study by an important American historian of philosophy.

Bennett, Jonathan. *A Study of Spinoza's Ethics*. Hackett 1984 lib. bdg. $25.00 text ed. pap. $13.75. This provocative examination of Spinoza's text by a leading contemporary linguistic philosopher has stirred much debate.

Caird, John. *Spinoza*. [*Select Bibliographies Repr. Ser.*] Ayer repr. of 1888 ed. $21.00. A still interesting presentation by a leading English historian of philosophy of the last century.

Collins, James, ed. *Spinoza on Nature*. Southern Illinois Univ. Pr. 1984 $32.50. One of the last works by this important historian of philosophy.

Delahunty, R. J. *Spinoza*. [*Arguments of the Philosophers Ser.*] Methuen 1985 $49.95. A recent detailed presentation of the various aspects of Spinoza's thought.

Den Uyl, Douglas J. *Power, State, and Freedom: An Interpretation of Spinoza's Philosophy*. Longwood 1983 text ed. pap. $13.00. An interpretation of Spinoza's political thought in terms of present issues.

Duff, Robert A. *Spinoza's Political Philosophy*. Kelley repr. of 1903 ed. 1970 $37.50. A classic study of Spinoza's views about man and society.

Feuer, Lewis S. *Spinoza and the Rise of Liberalism*. Greenwood repr. of 1958 ed. 1983 lib. bdg. $39.75. One of the most stimulating books about Spinoza's political thought and its relation to historical developments.

Freeman, Eugene, and Maurice Mandelbaum, eds. *Spinoza: Essays in Interpretation*. Open Court 1975 pap. $8.95. A collection of articles by 14 different English and American scholars, with a most useful bibliography by E. M. Curley.

Giancotti, Emilia, ed. *Proceedings of the First Italian International Congress on Spinoza*. Humanities Pr. 1985 $60.00. One of the three volumes resulting from congresses in commemoration of the three-hundred-fiftieth anniversary of Spinoza's birth. (The others were held in Amsterdam and in Wolfenbuttel, West Germany, respectively.) These congresses brought together scholars from all over the world to share their interests and findings about Spinoza, and the resulting volumes contain some very worthwhile papers.

Grene, Marjorie, ed. *Spinoza: A Collection of Critical Essays*. [*Modern Studies in Philosophy*] Univ. of Notre Dame Pr. repr. of 1973 ed. 1979 text ed. $18.95 pap. $9.95. "These essays on Spinoza deal with his method, with his metaphysics, and with his views on man and society. . . . With a teacher's help the essays can provide undergraduates with a valuable source of critical commentary" (*Choice*).

Grene, Marjorie, and Debra Nails, eds. *Spinoza and the Sciences*. Kluwer Academic 1986 $54.50. An important collection of articles by various Spinoza scholars on the connection between his work and the development of physical and social science in his time and now.

Hampshire, Stuart. *Spinoza*. Penguin 1952 pap. $4.95. One of the best introductions to and surveys of Spinoza's thought; well written, by one of England's leading philosophers.

Hart, Alan. *Spinoza's Ethics: A Platonic Commentary*. Humanities Pr. 1983 text ed. $25.00. An interesting commentary on Books I and II.

Hessing, Siegfried, ed. *Speculum Spinozanum: 1677–1977*. Fwd. by Huston Smith, Methuen 1978 o.p. This collection of 32 essays, some by Hessing and others by an international group of scholars, issued for the three-hundredth anniversary of Spinoza's death, was the first of several such collective volumes that have greatly revived interest in Spinoza's thought, and have even led to the publication of a journal of Spinoza studies, *Studia Spinozanum*. Hessing stresses the relation of Spinoza's thought to mysticism, Buddhism, and the Kabbala.

Jaspers, Karl. *Spinoza*. Trans. by Ralph Manheim [*Great Philosophers Ser.*] Harcourt 1974 pap. $2.95. An exposition of Spinoza's thought by one of the leading German existentialists.

Kashap, S. Paul, ed. *Studies in Spinoza: Critical and Interpretive Essays*. Univ. of California Pr. 1973 pap. $10.95. A collection of essays by 14 different Spinoza scholars from Europe to America. "[This volume] will be welcomed by all serious Spinoza students, particularly so because, while some of these articles are frequently cited, the original publications are scattered and often difficult to obtain" (*LJ*).

Kennington, Richard, ed. *The Philosophy of Baruch Spinoza*. [*Studies in Philosophy and the History of Philosophy*] Catholic Univ. Pr. 1980 $26.95. A group of 16 studies on Spinoza by various scholars, including Paul Weiss, Michael Hooker, Willis Doney, José Benardete. "The titles [of the essays] give a fair indication of the topics treated, and as they show, the collection is balanced, first of all, in the obvious sense of including a cross section of major issues in Spinoza's philosophy" (*Review of Metaphysics*).

Kline, George L. *Spinoza in Soviet Philosophy: A Series of Essays*. Hyperion Pr. repr. of 1952 ed. 1981 $19.75. A fundamental study of the importance of Spinoza's views in Russian Communist thought.

Lucas, Jean M. *The Oldest Biography of Spinoza*. Ed. by Abraham Wolf, Associated Faculty Pr. repr. of 1927 ed. 1970 $21.50. This work, dating from the late seventeenth or early eighteenth century, is the first known biography of Spinoza, and contains many of the stories about him that have become legendary. It, along with the first published biography (by Colerus), established the saintly image of Spinoza. Only in recent years has information come to light that makes one doubt some of the picture. The Lucas biography, first published in 1719, was presumably written by a follower of Spinoza. It circulated in manuscript, often together with a work called *The Spirit of M. Spinoza, Or the Three Imposters*,

Moses, Jesus, and Mohammed, whose authorship is still unknown, although a good deal of the text is drawn from Spinoza's published works.

Mark, Thomas C. *Spinoza's Theory of Truth.* Columbia Univ. Pr. 1972 o.p. A prize-winning dissertation that gave rise to a reevaluation of Spinoza's epistemology.

Martineau, James. *A Study of Spinoza.* [*Select Bibliographies Repr. Ser.*] Ayer repr. of 1895 ed. $23.50. Evaluation of Spinoza by a leading British idealist.

Naess, Arne. *Freedom, Emotion and Self-Substance: The Structure of a Central Part of Spinoza's Ethics.* Universitet 1975 text ed. pap. $11.00. Naess, one of Scandinavia's leading philosophers, stresses the importance of Spinoza's conception of man and the world for the environmentalist concerns being voiced today.

Nau, Jerome. *Emotions, Thought and Therapy: A Study of Hume and Spinoza and the Relationship of Philosophical Theories of the Emotions to Psychological Theories of Therapy.* Univ. of California Pr. 1977 $30.00. Interesting consideration of the therapeutic value of the theories of Spinoza and Hume about human emotions.

Oko, Adolph S. *A Spinoza Bibliography.* G. K. Hall 1970 o.p. Oko built up the two great Spinoza collections that are at Columbia University and Hebrew Union College, Cincinnati. His bibliography is invaluable for doing research on Spinoza. A privately printed catalog exists of the Abraham Wolf Spinoza Collection, which is now in Special Collections at the University of California, Los Angeles. In addition to these bibliographies, there is an immense, two-volume *Lexicon* of all of the words and terms that appear in Spinoza's writings, by Boscherini, available from Kluwer Academic. It treats the terms only in their original languages.

Pollack, Frederick. *Spinoza: His Life and Philosophy.* Gordon Pr. repr. of 1880 ed. $59.95; Irvington repr. of 1880 ed. 1981 $47.00. This was the standard work on Spinoza available in English a century ago. Much of it is still interesting and useful.

Roth, Leon. *Spinoza.* Hyperion Pr. repr. of 1954 ed. 1986 $21.45. A clear, careful presentation of Spinoza's philosophy seen in terms of the ideas of his time.

———. *Spinoza, Descartes and Maimonides.* Russell 1963 o.p. An important work, comparing these three philosophers on basic metaphysical and epistemological issues. Since Spinoza attacked Maimonides so often, it is interesting to see how their views actually compare.

Shehan, Robert, and J. J. Biro. *Spinoza: New Perspectives.* Univ. of Oklahoma Pr. 1977 $15.00. A small collective volume gathered together for the three-hundredth anniversary of Spinoza's death. Contains articles on different topics.

Strauss, Leo. *Spinoza's Critique of Religion.* Trans. by E. M. Sinclair, Schocken 1982 pap. $8.50. Written in Germany before Hitler, this study by one of the most stimulating political theorists of modern times attempts to show what Spinoza was really driving at in his *Tractatus Theologico-Politicus.* Erudite and provocative.

Sullivan, Celestine J. *Critical and Historical Reflections on Spinoza's "Ethics."* Univ. of California Pr. 1958 o.p. Some considerations on Spinoza by a Catholic thinker.

Wetlesen, Jon. *The Sage and the Way: Studies in Spinoza's Ethics of Freedom.* Humanities Pr. 1979 text ed. $55.00. Interprets Spinoza in the light of Buddhist thought.

Wienpahl, Paul. *The Radical Spinoza.* New York Univ. Pr. 1979 $32.50. A strong statement of the view, first offered at the end of the seventeenth century by Pierre Bayle, that Spinoza's thought is a kind of Oriental philosophy.

Willis, R. *Spinoza: His Life, Correspondence and Ethics.* Gordon Pr. 1977 lib. bdg. $76.95. A work of a century ago, giving the background of Spinoza, information about his milieu, his influence to the mid-nineteenth century, and the text of his correspondence and *Ethics.*

Wolf, Abraham, ed. *Correspondence of Benedict De Spinoza*. Biblio Dist. 1966 o.p. The complete correspondence of Spinoza (except for a recently discovered additional letter), this volume also provides information about the various correspondents.

Wolfson, Harry A. *The Philosophy of Spinoza: Unfolding the Latent Processes of His Reasoning*. Harvard Univ. Pr. 1983 text ed. pap. $15.00. This masterful commentary tries to show how Spinoza developed his theory. Wolfson stresses the role of medieval arguments, especially among the Jewish commentators known to Spinoza, and claims that Spinoza was both the last of the medieval thinkers and the first of the modern ones.

Zweig, Arnold. *The Living Thoughts of Spinoza*. Century Bookbindery repr. of 1939 ed. 1986 lib. bdg. $20.00. Selections from Spinoza of contemporary relevance.

EIGHTEENTH CENTURY

BERKELEY, GEORGE. 1685–1753

Berkeley was born and raised in Ireland, studied at Trinity College, Dublin, and then became a Fellow there. While still a Fellow he worked out most of his philosophic theories. He published his first work, *Essay Towards a New Theory of Vision*, in 1709, and the first part of his *Treatise Concerning the Principles of Human Knowledge* in 1710. When these works were not successful in convincing the philosophical world of his views, he wrote and published the more popular *Three Dialogues between Hylas and Philonous* in 1713. Berkeley was made Dean of Derry in 1724, and in 1734 Bishop of Cloyne, Ireland, a post he held until his retirement, when he moved to Oxford. In 1728 he embarked on a voyage to America, hoping to establish a college in Bermuda. Although this proved infeasible, he stayed for two years in Newport, Rhode Island, where he wrote *Alciphron* (1732), a defense of religion. He had a great influence on early American education, both through his gift of books to the library at Yale and through his philosophy, which was adopted by SAMUEL JOHNSON (see Vol. 1), later to become the first president of King's College (now Columbia University). Berkeley, California, is named for him in honor of his poem predicting the development of civilization and culture in America.

BOOKS BY BERKELEY

Berkeley's Philosophical Writings. Ed. by David M. Armstrong, Macmillan 1965 pap. $5.95. A collection of all the main philosophical works of Berkeley.

Philosophical Works including the Works of Vision. Ed. by M. R. Ayers, Biblio Dist. 1975 $20.00 pap. $8.95. Berkeley's main philosophical works, plus the works on vision, the philosophical commentaries, and his correspondence with Johnson.

Philosophical Writings. Ed. by T. E. Jessop, Greenwood repr. of 1953 ed. 1983 lib. bdg. $22.50. A collection of Berkeley's texts by one of the editors of his complete works.

Principles, Dialogues and Philosophical Correspondence. Ed. by Colin M. Turbayne, Macmillan 1965 o.p. Berkeley's two main philosophical works plus his correspondence with the American Samuel Johnson.

A Treatise Concerning the Principles of Human Knowledge. 1710. Ed. by Colin M. Turbayne, Bobbs 1957 pap. $4.79; ed. by Kenneth Winkler [*Philosophical Class. Ser.*] Hackett 1982 lib. bdg. $15.00 text ed. pap. $3.45; ed. by G. J. Warnock, Open Court 1985 pap. $7.95

Three Dialogues between Hylas and Philonous. 1713. Ed. by Colin M. Turbayne, Bobbs 1954 pap. $5.99; ed. by Robert M. Adams, Hackett 1979 lib. bdg. $15.00 text ed. pap. $3.45; ed. by Thomas J. McCormack, Open Court 1969 pap. $4.95

Works on Vision. Ed. by Colin M. Turbayne [*Lib. of Liberal Arts*] Greenwood repr. of 1963 ed. 1981 lib. bdg. $22.50. Relevant texts on vision, plus discussions of the topic from other works of Berkeley.

BOOKS ABOUT BERKELEY

Bracken, Harry M. *Berkeley.* St. Martin's 1975 $19.95. A new interpretation of Berkeley by one of the most careful contemporary scholars.

———. *The Early Reception of Berkeley, 1710–1733* Kluwer Academic 1965 o.p. A study of the first reactions to Berkeley's philosophy.

Broad, C. D. *Berkeley's Argument.* [*Studies in Philosophy*] Haskell 1975 lib. bdg. $22.95. Examination of Berkeley's central epistemological arguments by one of England's expositors of philosophy.

Jessop, Thomas E. *Bibliography of George Berkeley.* [*Bibliography and Reference Ser.*] Burt Franklin repr. of 1934 ed. 1968 $14.50. Bibliography of Berkeley's published works and manuscripts, and writings about him. A revised, enlarged edition published by Nijhoff, The Hague, 1973.

Luce, A. A. *The Life of George Berkeley, Bishop of Cloyne.* Greenwood repr. of 1949 ed. $17.50. The most complete biography yet done, by a leading interpreter and defender of Berkeley.

Rand, Benjamin. *Berkeley's American Sojourn.* AMS Pr. repr. of 1932 ed. 1987 $8.50. The information available about Berkeley's trip to America, whom he met and what he did.

Steinkraus, Warren E., ed. *New Studies in Berkeley's Philosophy.* Univ. Pr. of Amer. repr. of 1966 ed. 1982 text ed. lib. bdg. $27.75 pap. $12.75. A collection of articles by different scholars.

Turbayne, Colin M., ed. *Critical and Interpretive Essays.* Univ. of Minnesota Pr. 1982 pap. $10.95. A variety of essays on Berkeley by 20 different scholars.

Urmson, J. O. *Berkeley.* [*Past Masters Ser.*] Oxford 1982 $13.95 1983 pap. $3.95. An exposition of Berkeley's thought by one of the best linguistic philosophers of English.

Warnock, G. J. *Berkeley.* Univ. of Notre Dame Pr. 1983 $14.95 pap. $7.95. A survey of Berkeley's views by a leading English contemporary philosopher.

CONDORCET, MARIE JEAN ANTOINE NICOLAS CARITAT, MARQUIS DE. 1743–1794

Condorcet was the last of the *philosophes*, a disciple of d'Alembert and Turgot, and was still alive and active during the French Revolution. After serving in both the *Académie des Sciences* and the *Académie Française*, Condorcet became involved in various reform projects during the revolution. He offered plans for reforming education and health services, and for eliminating slavery, and in 1793 wrote a draft of a liberal constitution. Forced into hiding by the shifts in political fortune during the Reign of Terror, he wrote his masterpiece, *The Sketch for a Historical Picture of the Progress of the Human Mind* (1795). He died in prison after being captured in 1794.

BOOK BY CONDORCET

The Sketch for a Historical Picture of the Progress of the Human Mind. 1795. Trans. by June Barraclough, intro. by Stuart Hampshire, Hyperion Pr. repr. of 1955 ed. 1985 $22.00. Condorcet's classic presentation of his theory of the infinite perfectibility of mankind.

BOOKS ABOUT CONDORCET

Baker, Keith M. *Condorcet: From Natural Philosophy to Social Mathematics.* Univ. of Chicago Pr. 1982 $17.00. Basic study of how Condorcet developed the tools for dealing with social problems.

Rosenfield, Leonora C., ed. *Condorcet Studies I.* Humanities Pr. 1984 o.p. A collection of articles by American and European scholars on Condorcet's life and his reform projects in law, government, and education, as well as his philosophical and scientific views.

DIDEROT, DENIS. 1713–1784

Diderot was one of the most prolific writers of the Enlightenment. He is known for writing plays, novels, art criticism, and philosophical works, and, most important, for editing the great encyclopedia that brought together the learning and the critical, rational philosophy of the *philosophes*. It was probably the most important achievement of the French Enlightenment. Diderot worked on the *Encyclopédie* from 1751 to 1772. It was published in 28 volumes originally, later supplemented with 6 volumes and 2 volumes of tables. (See also Volume 2.)

BOOKS BY DIDEROT

Diderot, Interpreter of Nature: Selected Writings. Ed. by Jonathan Kemp, trans. by Jean Stewart, Hyperion Pr. repr. of 1937 ed. 1981 $29.15. Fine translations of Diderot's chief philosophical works.

Diderot's Early Philosophical Works. Ed. by Margaret Jourdain, AMS Pr. repr. of 1916 ed. 1981 $15.00; Burt Franklin 1972 lib. bdg. $20.50. Contains his *Philosophic Thoughts, Letter on the Blind* and its additions, and *Deaf and Dumb.*

The Letter on the Blind for the Benefit of Those Who See. 1749. Amer. Class. College Pr. 1983 $66.85. An important scientific and epistemological study by Diderot.

A Pictorial Encyclopedia of Trades and Industry. 1751–52. Ed. by Charles C. Gillespie, Dover 2 vols. 1959 ea. $25.00. Some of the articles from the *Encyclopedia* on this subject.

Rameau's Nephew and D'Alembert's Dream. 1796. [*Penguin Class. Ser.*] 1976 pap. $5.95. Diderot's most famous philosophical stories.

Diderot's Thoughts on Art and Style. Trans. by Beatrix Tollemache [*Philosophy Monographs Ser.*] Burt Franklin repr. of 1893 ed. 1971 lib. bdg. $17.00. Diderot's writings on art criticism.

BOOKS ABOUT DIDEROT

Brenner, Geoffrey. *Order and Chance: The Pattern of Diderot's Thought.* Cambridge Univ. Pr. 1983 $42.50. A new study presenting a central thread of Diderot's ideas.

Cru, R. Loyalty. *Diderot as a Disciple of English Thought.* [*Columbia Univ. Studies in Romance Philology and Literature*] AMS Pr. repr. of 1925 ed. 1981 $33.75. Diderot's use of English ideas from Locke onward.

France, Peter. *Diderot*. [*Past Masters Ser.*] Oxford 1983 $12.95 pap. $3.95. A general presentation of Diderot's thought.

Gordon, Douglas H., and Norman L. Torrey. *The Censoring of Diderot's Encyclopedia and the Reestablished Text*. AMS Pr. repr. of 1947 ed. 1981 $15.00. An account of what was removed by censors from the *Encyclopedia*.

Morley, John. *Diderot and the Encyclopedists*. Richard West repr. of 1878 ed. 1975 2 vols. $19.25. A classic study of Diderot's role in the Enlightenment.

Schwartz, Leon. *Diderot and the Jews*. Fairleigh Dickinson Univ. Pr. 1981 $22.50. "This good, well-written, scholarly work focuses on Diderot's attitude to Jews and Judaism. Schwartz disagrees with the broad scholarly opinion that Diderot was anti-Semitic. . . . [Diderot's] occasional anti-Jewish remarks, Schwartz argues, are to be taken with consideration of an evaluation of Diderot's views toward toleration" (*Choice*).

Vartanian, Aram. *Diderot and Descartes: A Study of Scientific Naturalism in the Enlightenment*. Greenwood repr. of 1953 ed. 1975 $19.25. A comparison of Diderot's and Descartes's biological views, showing what is new in Diderot.

Wilson, Arthur M. *Diderot*. Oxford 1972 $45.00. This is now the standard biography of Diderot in English.

THE ENLIGHTENMENT

Altmann, Alexander. *Moses Mendelssohn: A Biographical Study*. Univ. of Alabama Pr. 1973 o.p. A monumental study of Mendelssohn's role in the German Enlightenment and the Jewish world of the time.

Beck, Lewis W., ed. *Eighteenth-Century Philosophy*. Free Pr. 1966 text ed. pap. $13.95. Includes selections from Rousseau, Condillac, Holbach, Voltaire, Wolff, and Lessing as well as the major European philosophers of the time.

Becker, Carl. *The Heavenly City of the Eighteenth Century Philosophers*. Yale Univ. Pr. 1932 pap. $5.95. On the utopian expectations of some of the leading eighteenth-century thinkers.

Cassirer, Ernst. *The Philosophy of the Enlightenment*. Trans. by J. Pettegrove, Princeton Univ. Pr. 1951 pap. $9.95. An important comprehensive survey by one of the leading historians of philosophy. Emphasizes the Enlightenment in Germany.

Crocker, Lester G. *An Age of Crisis: Man and World in Eighteenth-Century French Thought*. [*Goucher College Ser.*] Johns Hopkins Univ. Pr. 1959 o.p. An overall interpretation of the Enlightenment by an important scholar of the history of ideas in France.

Frankel, Charles. *The Faith of Reason*. Hippocrene Bks. repr. of 1948 ed. 1969 lib. bdg. $17.00. Important study on the idea of progress in the Enlightenment.

Herder, Johann von. *Reflections on the Philosophy of the History of Mankind*. Univ. of Chicago Pr. 1968 o.p. Basic work by one of the leading German thinkers of the late eighteenth century.

Hertzberg, Arthur. *The French Enlightenment and the Jews*. Columbia Univ. Pr. 1968 o.p. A study of the conflict between the tolerant theoretical views of the *philosophes* and their actual views about Jewish emancipation.

Mendelssohn, Moses. *Jerusalem; or, On Religious Power and Judaism*. Trans. by Allan Arkush, Univ. Pr. of New England 1983 $20.00 pap. $10.00. Mendelssohn's defense of freedom of religion and explanation of the uniqueness of Judaism.

————. *Moses Mendelssohn: Selections from His Writings*. Ed. by Alfred Jospe, Viking 1975 o.p. Contains *Jerusalem* and several essays and letters on religion, tolerance, and Judaism.

————. *Phaedon; or, The Death of Socrates*. [*Jewish People Ser.*] Ayer repr. of 1789 ed.

1973 $22.00. Mendelssohn's version, in Enlightenment terms, of the evidence of the immortality of the soul.

Schwab, Richard, and Walter Rex, trans. and eds. *Preliminary Discourse to the Encyclopedia of Diderot*. Macmillan 1963 o.p. This is the famous statement of d'Alembert.

FICHTE, JOHANN GOTTLIEB. 1762–1814

From a poor family, Fichte was first instructed privately, and then attended the academy at Pforta and the University of Jena. He was very much influenced by Lessing, Spinoza, and Kant, the last of whom he visited in 1791. The next year he wrote his *Critique of All Revelation;* it was published anonymously, and many people attributed the work to Kant. When his authorship became known, Fichte was hailed and appointed professor at Jena; however, his orthodoxy was challenged and he had to give up his post. Appointed professor and rector at the newly established University of Berlin, he became the leading spokesman for German nationalist resistance to Napoleon. His *Addresses to the German Nation* (1808) rallied German opposition to the French Emperor and became a seminal statement of German nationalism, often appealed to later by the Nazis. Fichte's metaphysical system, in which the creative ego is the center, made him a major figure in the German idealist movement. He died caring for wounded soldiers in the struggle against Napoleon.

BOOKS BY FICHTE

Fichte's Critique of All Revelation. 1792. Trans. by G. D. Green, Cambridge Univ. Pr. 1978 $34.50. Fichte's extension of Kant's view of religion to revealed religion.

Characteristic of the Present Age. 1794. Univ. Pr. of Amer. repr. of 1899 ed. 1978 $30.00. Subtitled "The way toward the blessed life; or the doctrine of religion."

The Science of Knowledge: With First and Second Introductions. 1794. Trans. by John Lachs, Cambridge Univ. Pr. 1982 $42.50 pap. $14.95. The basic statement of Fichte's metaphysical system.

The Vocation of Man. 1800. Trans. by William Smith, Bobbs 1956 pap. $5.99; trans. by E. Ritchie, Open Court 1965 $12.95 pap. $5.95. Fichte's popular presentation of his philosophy.

Addresses to the German Nation. 1808. Ed. by George Kelly, Harper o.p. Fichte's rallying call to the Germans to resist Napoleon and French influences.

BOOKS ABOUT FICHTE

Englebrecht, Helmuth C. *Johann Gottlieb Fichte*. AMS Pr. repr. of 1926 ed. 1971 $14.50. On Fichte's political writings and his nationalism.

Hegel, Georg W. *The Difference between Fichte's and Schelling's System of Philosophy*. Trans. by Jere Sirber, Ridgeview 1978 $23.00 pap. $6.50. An evaluation by Fichte's successor in German philosophy.

HUME, DAVID. 1711–1776

David Hume was born in Edinburgh to a minor Scottish noble family, raised at the estate of Ninewells, and attended the University of Edinburgh for two years until he was 15. Although his family wished him to study law, he found himself unsuited to this. He studied at home, tried business briefly, and after receiving a small inheritance traveled to France, settling at La Flèche, where Descartes had gone to school. There he completed his first and major philosophical work, *A Treatise of Human Nature* (1739–40), published in three volumes. Hume claimed on the title page that he was introducing the experimental method of reasoning into moral subjects, and further that he was offering a new way of seeing the limits of human knowledge. Although his work was largely ignored, Hume gained from it a reputation as a philosophical skeptic and an opponent of traditional religion. (In later years he was called "the great infidel.") This reputation led to his being rejected for professorships at both Edinburgh and Glasgow. To earn his living he served variously as the secretary to General St. Clair, as the attendant to the mad Marquis of Annandale, and as the keeper of the Advocates Library in Edinburgh. While holding these positions he wrote and published a new version of his philosophy, the two *Enquiries*, and many essays on social, political, moral, and literary subjects. He also began his six-volume *History of England from the Roman Invasion to the Glorious Revolution* (1754–62), the work that made him most famous in his lifetime. Having now become well known in literary and political circles, he was appointed secretary to the British ambassador in Paris, where he was for a time in charge of the embassy. He was on friendly terms with many of the leading figures in the French Enlightenment, but had a disastrous friendship with ROUSSEAU (see also Vol. 3), who visited England under his sponsorship. Hume served as secretary of state in the British government in 1767–68, but lost his position when the government fell because of its policy toward the American colonies. After seeking other positions, Hume retired from public life and settled in Edinburgh, where he was the leading figure in Scottish letters and a good friend to many of the leading intellectuals of the time, including ADAM SMITH (see Vol. 3) and BENJAMIN FRANKLIN (see Vols. 3 and 5). During this period, he completed the *Dialogues Concerning Natural Religion*, which he had been working on for more than 25 years. Hume first worked on the *Dialogues* in the middle of his career, but put them aside as too provocative. In his last years he finished them and they were published posthumously in 1779. They are probably his best literary effort, and have been the basis for continuous discussion and debate among philosophers of religion. Toward the end of Hume's life, his philosophical work began to be taken seriously, and the skeptical problems he had raised were tackled by philosophers in Scotland, France, and finally Germany, where Kant claimed that Hume had awakened him from his dogmatic slumbers.

Hume was one of the most influential philosophers of modern times, both as a positive force on skeptical and empirical thinkers and as a philosopher to be refuted by others. Interpreters are still arguing about whether he should be seen as a complete skeptic, a partial skeptic, a precursor of logical positivism, or even a secret believer.

BOOKS BY HUME

The Letters of David Hume. Ed. by J. Y. Greig, Garland 2 vols. 1983 lib. bdg. $121.00.
    This is a reprint of the edition done over 50 years ago. Many letters have been discovered since this publication. Because the volume includes only Hume's

letters and not those written to him, it is often difficult (without using Burton, listed below) to follow what is being discussed

The New Letters of David Hume. Ed. by Ernest C. Mossner, Garland 1983 lib. bdg. $33.00. This volume includes letters discovered after Greig's edition. Other letters that have since been found appear in various journals. No complete edition of Hume's correspondence is in the offing.

Philosophical Works. Ed. by Thomas H. Green and Thomas H. Grose, Adler's 4 vols. repr. of 1882 ed. 1964 set $382.25. This, the closest there is to a "complete works" of Hume, does not include any of his *History of England*, the recently discovered works, or the philosophical correspondence. An edition of Hume's philosophical writings is presently being prepared for the Princeton University Press by David Fate Norton (4 volumes of text, 4 volumes of concordance; due 1989–99).

A Treatise of Human Nature. 1739–40. Ed. by P. H. Nidditch, Oxford 1978 text ed. pap. $10.95; ed. by Ernest C. Mossner [*Penguin Class. Ser.*] 1986 pap. $6.95. The Oxford edition is the best available one of Hume's first and fullest statement of his philosophy. Nidditch has included corrections found in Hume's hand in copies of the original printing; unfortunately, however, they are in an appendix and have not been integrated into the text.

Abstract of a Treatise of Human Nature, 1740: A Pamphlet Hitherto Unknown. Ed. by P. Sraffa, intro. by John Maynard Keynes, Shoe String 1965 o.p. A pamphlet by Hume, apparently his own review of his *Treatise of Human Nature.*

An Enquiry Concerning Human Understanding: And Letter from a Gentleman to His Friend in Edinburgh. 1748. Ed. by Eric Steinberg, Hackett 1977 text ed. lib. bdg. $15.00 pap. $2.95. The *Letter from a Gentleman* is a recently discovered pamphlet in which Hume defended his views from charges made against them when he was being considered for a professorship at the University of Edinburgh. The pamphlet, apparently put together from letters Hume had sent to Lord Kames, may also be the basis of his revised presentation of his philosophy in *Enquiry.*

Enquiries Concerning Human Understanding and Concerning the Principles of Morals. 1751. Ed. by P. H. Nidditch, Oxford 3d ed. 1975 text ed. pap. $9.95. "It is the first edition of either Enquiry to contain extended scholarly annotations (40 pages worth) and it claims more accuracy than the modern American-style versions edited by C. W. Hendel.... authoritative and very readable" (*Choice*).

An Enquiry Concerning the Principles of Morals. 1751. Ed. by J. B. Schneewind [*Philosophical Class. Ser.*] Hackett 1983 lib. bdg. $15.00 text ed. pap. $3.45. "Though there may be some contradictions in Hume's philosophy (and in some cases he was well aware of them himself), there is more consistency in his approach to morals as related to his approach to cognizance than would seem on the surface.... In the analysis of moral judgment, Hume finds that it too is ultimately founded not on reason but on a sentiment. Though Hume refrains from referring to this statement as skeptical, we are entitled to conclude that in a sense it amounts to skepticism. On the other hand, this sentiment is a fundamental working factor in human life" (*Ethics*).

History of England: From the Invasion of Julius Caesar to the Revolution of 1688. 1754–62. Ed. by Rodney W. Kilcup [*Classics of British Historical Literature Ser.*] Univ. of Chicago Pr. 1975 text ed. $30.00

The Natural History of Religion. 1755. (and *Dialogues Concerning Natural Religion*). Ed. by A. Wayne Colver and Vladimir Price, Oxford 1976 $49.95; ed. by H. E. Root, Stanford Univ. Pr. 1957 pap. $4.95. A critical edition of these two works with extensive annotations.

Dialogues Concerning Natural Religion. 1779. Ed. by Norman Kemp Smith, Bobbs 1947 pap. $8.40; ed. by Nelson Pike [*Text and Critical Essays Ser.*] Bobbs 1970 pap. $9.63; ed. by Richard H. Popkin, Hackett 1980 lib. bdg. $15.00 text ed. pap. $2.95; ed. by Henry D. Aiken [*Lib. of Class. Ser.*] Hafner 1970 text ed. pap. $7.95. The text in Popkin's edition has been checked against Hume's original manuscript, and is accompanied by two of his other posthumously published essays, "On Suicide" and "On the Immortality of the Soul." Kemp Smith's text is accompanied by a lengthy commentary showing the order in which the work was written, and dating the later additions; it also includes the text of Hume's last conversation with Boswell. Pike's edition includes critical essays on the text by various philosophers of religion.

Of the Standard of Taste and Other Essays. Ed. by John W. Lenz, Bobbs 1965 pap. $7.97. Some of Hume's writings on aesthetics.

Writings on Economics. Ed. by Eugene Rotwein [*Essay Index Repr. Ser.*] Ayer repr. of 1955 ed. $22.00. Hume's writings on banking, public credit, trade, and so forth.

BOOKS ABOUT HUME

Anderson, Robert F. *Hume's First Principles.* Univ. of Nebraska Pr. 1966 $16.50. An examination of the kind of metaphysical first principles Hume seems to have accepted.

Ayer, A. J. *Hume.* Oxford 1980 pap. $3.95. Sprightly presentation of Hume by one of the best-known English analytic philosophers.

Beauchamp, Tom L., and Alexander Rosenberg. *Hume and the Problem of Causation.* Oxford 1981 $29.95. A very carefully argued attempt to resolve the problem of causation as raised by Hume.

Berry, Christopher J. *Hume, Hegel and Human Nature.* Kluwer Academic 1983 lib. bdg. $41.50. A striking comparison of the views of Hume and Hegel considered in their contemporary settings.

Burton, John H. *The Life and Correspondence of David Hume.* Garland 1983 lib. bdg. $110.00. The first basic collection of data about Hume's life.

Capaldi, Nicholas. *David Hume: The Newtonian Philosopher.* [*Twayne's World Authors Ser.*] G. K. Hall 1975 o.p. A fine survey of Hume's views, presenting him in the traditional Newtonian experimental philosophy.

Chappell, V. C., ed. *Hume: A Collection of Critical Essays.* Univ. of Notre Dame Pr. 1968 $18.95 1974 pap. $9.95. Essays on various aspects of Hume's thought by a wide range of scholars.

Church, Ralph W. *Hume's Theory of the Understanding.* Greenwood repr. of 1935 ed. 1980 lib. bdg. $22.50. One of the first works of new scholarship about Hume's philosophy.

Flew, Antony. *Hume's Philosophy of Belief.* Humanities Pr. 1965 o.p. A very careful examination of this aspect of Hume's theory.

Fogelin, Robert J. *Hume's Skepticism in the Treatise of Human Nature.* [*International Lib. of Philosophy*] Methuen 1985 $25.00. A well-argued case for interpreting Hume as a thoroughgoing skeptic.

Forbes, Duncan. *Hume's Philosophical Politics.* Cambridge Univ. Pr. 1975 $57.50 1985 pap. $14.95. A careful examination of Hume's political thought in terms of the issues of his time.

Green, Thomas Hill. *Hume and Locke.* Peter Smith o.p. A work by a nineteenth-century British idealist who was very influential in reviving interest in Hume's philosophy and was one of the editors of Hume's *Philosophical Works.*

Hall, Roland. *Fifty Years of Hume Scholarship.* Columbia Univ. Pr. 1979 $12.50. This work supplements Jessop's bibliography (see below) and covers almost all the books and articles on Hume in the period. The bibliography is kept up-to-date by addenda published in journals.

Hendel, Charles W. *Studies in the Philosophy of David Hume*. Garland 1983 lib. bdg. $55.00. A reprint of one of the basic studies of the naturalist side of Hume's thought.

Hurlbutt, Robert H. *Hume, Newton, and the Design Argument*. Univ. of Nebraska Pr. rev. ed. 1985 $24.95. A study of Newton's presentation of the design or teleological argument, and Hume's criticism of it.

Jessop, T. E. *A Bibliography of David Hume and of Scottish Philosophy from Francis Hutcheson to Lord Balfour*. Garland 1983 lib. bdg. $36.00 Reprint of the basic bibliographical reference work about Hume.

Jones, Peter. *Hume's Sentiments: Their Ciceronian and French Context*. Columbia Univ. Pr. 1982 $24.00. A new interpretation of the context of Hume's views that is causing much discussion.

Kemp Smith, Norman. *The Philosophy of David Hume*. Greenwood repr. 1983 $55.00. In this work, Kemp Smith sets forth his interpretation of Hume as a naturalist rather than a skeptic, which was the dominant reading for quite a while.

Laird, John. *Hume's Philosophy of Human Nature*. Garland 1983 lib. bdg. $42.00. A very careful commentary on Hume's views and writings.

Leroy, Andre L. *David Hume*. Trans. by J. P. Mayer [*European Political Thought Ser.*] Ayer repr. of 1953 ed. 1979 lib. bdg. $25.50. A presentation and interpretation of Hume's views by the leading French Hume scholar (and translator of Hume into French).

Livingston, Donald W. *Hume's Philosophy of Common Life*. Univ. of Chicago Pr. 1985 lib. bdg. $30.00 pap. $13.95. This important recent work on Hume shows that his positive writings on moral and social topics are consistent with his skepticism.

Mackie, J. L. *Hume's Moral Theory*. [*International Lib. of Philosophy and Scientific Method*] Methuen 1980 $26.95 pap. $10.95. A good presentation and examination of Hume's moral theory.

Merrill, Kenneth R., and Robert W. Shahan, eds. *David Hume: Many-Sided Genius*. Univ. of Oklahoma Pr. 1976 pap. $8.95. A group of essays by Hume scholars in connection with the bicentennial of his death.

Morice, G. P., ed. *David Hume: Bicentenary Papers*. Univ. of Texas Pr. 1977 o.p. Another collection of essays for the two-hundredth anniversary of Hume's demise.

Morris, Charles R. *Locke, Berkeley, Hume*. Greenwood repr. of 1931 ed. 1979 lib. bdg. $22.50. A comparison of the so-called British empiricists by a leading American pragmatist.

Mossner, Ernest C. *The Forgotten Hume, Le Bon David*. AMS Pr. repr. of 1943 ed. 1967 $10.00. A ground-breaking study of Hume's role as a literary critic of his contemporaries.

———. *The Life of David Hume*. Oxford 2d ed. 1980 $59.00. The most comprehensive biography of Hume to date. The second edition includes new material discovered in the last 25 years.

Norton, David F. *David Hume: Common Sense Moralist, Sceptical Metaphysician*. Princeton Univ. Pr. 1982 $32.00 1984 pap. $14.50. An attempt to reconcile Hume's positive naturalistic moral theory with his skeptical theory of knowledge.

Norton, David F., and Nicholas Capaldi, eds. *McGill Hume Studies*. Austin Hill Pr. 1979 $22.50 pap. $8.95. Selected papers from the Hume commemoration at McGill University.

Noxon, James. *Hume's Philosophical Development: A Study of His Methods*. Oxford

1973 $27.95. An attempt to show how Hume's philosophy developed, against interpreters who say he had the same theory all his life.

Passmore, John. *Hume's Intentions.* Longwood repr. of 1968 ed. 1980 $26.50. Examination of what Hume was trying to achieve, and the weakness of his reasoning in so doing.

Popkin, Richard H. *The High Road to Pyrrhonism.* Ed. by R. A. Watson and J. E. Force, Austin Hill Pr. 1980 $25.00 pap. 10.00. A collection of the author's essays, many on Hume, which started the modern interpretation of Hume as a complete skeptic.

Price, Henry H. *Hume's Theory of the External World.* Greenwood repr. of 1940 ed. 1981 lib. bdg. $25.00. A very careful discussion of the texts in Hume dealing with our knowledge of the external world.

Seth, Andrew. *Scottish Philosophy.* Garland 1983 lib. bdg. $33.00. Important nineteenth-century survey of the eighteenth-century Scottish thinkers, including Hume.

Stove, D. C. *Probability and Hume's Inductive Skepticism.* Oxford 1973 $22.50. Applies the modern theory of induction to Hume's analysis and argues that some of Hume's skeptical conclusions are not warranted.

Stroud, Barry. *Hume.* [*Arguments of the Philosophers Ser.*] Methuen repr. of 1977 ed. 1981 pap. $10.95. Presents Hume's skepticism in terms of contemporary analytic thought.

Talmor, Ezra. *Descartes and Hume.* Pergamon 1980 $23.00. Author tries to show how Hume saved Cartesianism from its own contradictions.

Taylor, A. E. *David Hume and the Miraculous.* Folcroft 1927 lib. bdg. $10.00. Hume contended that the occurrence of miracles is inherently implausible and cannot be accepted by reasonable people. This work, which should be compared with C. S. Lewis's *Miracles,* claims that Hume's conclusion is unjustified.

Todd, William B., ed. *Hume and the Enlightenment: Essays Presented to Ernest Campbell Mossner.* Univ. of Texas, Harry Ransom Humanities Research Center 1974 $12.95. A festschrift volume.

Zabeeh, Farhang. *Hume: Precursor of Modern Empiricism.* Humanities Pr. rev. ed. 1973 $12.75. An attempt to interpret Hume in terms of modern logical empiricism.

KANT, IMMANUEL. 1724–1804

The son of a saddler, and probably the grandson of a Scottish immigrant, Kant was born and educated in Königsberg, Germany, graduating from the university there in 1746. A tutor for several years, he began teaching at the University of Königsberg in 1755, initially instructing in several different fields, including physics, mathematics, geography, and philosophy. His first writings were on scientific subjects; one was an important work in 1755 on the nature of the heavens, offering a theory of how the universe began. In 1770, Kant was appointed to the chair of logic and metaphysics. He worked slowly on his major philosophical theory, the *Critique of Pure Reason,* which set forth his "Copernican Revolution" regarding the nature of human knowledge; it was not published until 1781, when he was in his late fifties. Kant had been raised in the German metaphysical tradition of Leibniz and Wolff. As a result of reading Hume, Kant said he was awakened from his dogmatic slumber and saw that a new examination of the nature of human knowledge had to be undertaken. Leibniz had intellectualized appearances and

Locke had sensualized concepts. Hume took both views to their extreme and advanced a complete skepticism. Kant sought to show how there could be necessary and universal knowledge without claiming that one could actually know reality. Most of Kant's friends and contemporaries were bewildered by the difficulty of his argument. As a result, he wrote a simpler version, the *Prolegomena to Any Future Metaphysics* (1783), and a second, much revised edition of the *Critique* (1787) to answer questions and objections that had been raised. These works were followed, in the second and third critiques, by an extension of his views to include morality and aesthetics. By the end of the eighteenth century, Kant had become one of the era's most important thinkers, initiating a whole new approach to philosophical problems. His work has led to a wide range of developments, some pursuing aspects of his theory, others combating them. Neo-Kantianism has been a force well into our own day, and leading philosophers of opposing movements still find it necessary to come to terms with Kant's views, proving the acuteness of his prediction that all future philosophers would either have to accept his views or refute them.

Kant himself spent his whole life in Königsberg, following a precise routine and keeping a daily account of his activities. Only two events are supposed to have upset his schedule: One was when he first heard about the French Revolution; the other when he received and immediately read a copy of ROUSSEAU's *Emile* (see also Vol. 3).

BOOKS BY KANT

Kant's Cosmogony: As in His Essay on Retardation of the Rotation of the Earth. 1755. Trans. by W. Hastie [*Contributions in Philosophy*] Greenwood 1968 lib. bdg. $29.95. One of Kant's earliest writings, on how the cosmos began in terms of the nebular hypothesis.

Inaugural Dissertation of 1770. Ed. by William J. Eckoff, AMS Pr. repr. of 1894 ed. 1974 $11.50. Kant's address on being appointed a professor at Königsberg.

Critique of Pure Reason. 1781. Biblio Dist. 2d ed. 1978 pap. $4.95; Doubleday 1966 pap. $7.95; trans. by Norman Kemp Smith, St. Martin's 1969 pap. $14.95. This is the first of Kant's three *Critique*'s dealing with human knowledge. The Kemp Smith translation is the best known and best regarded of those that are easily available.

Prolegomena to Any Future Metaphysics. 1783. Bobbs rev. ed. 1950 pap. $5.99; trans. by Paul Carus, Hackett 1977 $16.50 pap. $3.45; intro. by Lewis W. Beck, Open Court 1985 pap. $4.95

Fundamental Principles of the Metaphysics of Morals. 1785. Trans. by Thomas K. Abbott, Bobbs 1949 pap. $4.24. A simplified version of the *Critique of Practical Reason.*

Critique of Practical Reason. 1788. Trans. by Lewis W. Beck, Bobbs 1956 pap. $7.20. Kant's second *Critique*, dealing with moral reasoning.

Critique of Judgment. 1790. Trans. by J. H. Bernard [*Lib. of Class. Ser.*] Hafner 1970 text ed. pap. $12.95; trans. by J. C. Meredith, Oxford 1952 pap. $10.95. This is Kant's third *Critique*, dealing with aesthetics.

First Introduction to the Critique of Judgment. Trans. by James Haden, Irvington 1965 text ed. pap. $7.95. A new translation of this important statement of Kant's aesthetics.

Religion within the Limits of Reason Alone. 1793. Harper 1960 pap. $8.95. Kant's important essay on rational religion.

Perpetual Peace. 1795. Trans. by Campbell Smith, Amer. Class. College Pr. 1983 $69.85. Kant's plan for a peaceful world based on international law.

Perpetual Peace and Other Essays on Politics, History, and Moral Practice. Trans. by Ted Humphrey [*Philosophical Class. Ser.*] Hackett 1983 lib. bdg. $16.50 text ed. pap. $3.95. A new translation of several of Kant's social and political essays.

Education. Univ. of Michigan Pr. 1960 pap. $6.95. Kant's essay on the subject, in terms of his philosophy.

Foundations of the Metaphysics of Morals (and *What Is Enlightenment?*). Trans. by Lewis W. Beck, Bobbs 1959 pap. $4.79; ed. by Robert P. Wolff [*Text and Critical Essays Ser.*] Bobbs 1969 pap. $10.28. *What Is Enlightenment?* is an important contribution to Kant's philosophy of history. The Wolff volume contains an interesting collection of essays by different scholars on Kant's moral theory.

Grounding for the Metaphysics of Morals. Trans. by James W. Ellington [*Philosophical Class. Ser.*] Hackett 1981 lib. bdg. $16.50 text ed. pap. $3.45. Same as the *Foundations* (see above) in a new translation.

On History. Ed. and trans. by Lewis W. Beck, Bobbs 1963 pap. $5.99

Kant's Inaugural Dissertation and Early Writings on Space. Trans. by John Handyside, Hyperion Pr. repr. of 1929 ed. 1984 $15.00. "It makes available in a competent translation and convenient form some of Kant's early writings, much needed fully to understand his later work and the morphology of his mind. There are selected passages from his *Thoughts on the True Estimation of Living Force* (1747), his essay *On the First Ground of the Distinction of Regions in Space* (1768), and finally his *Dissertation on the Form and Principles of the Sensible and Intelligible World* (1770)" (*Ethics*).

Kant's Introduction to Logic and His Essay on the Mistaken Subtilty of the Four Figures. Trans. by Thomas K. Abbott, Greenwood repr. 1963 lib. bdg. $22.50. Kant's views on logic, with some notes by S. T. Coleridge.

Lectures on Ethics. Trans. by Louis Infield, Hackett repr. of 1979 ed. 1980 text ed. pap. $6.95. "This book represents an attempt toward the construction of a text of Kant's class lectures on ethics from three students' notebooks. . . . The editor presents the book, then, as substantially the lectures of Kant between the years 1775 and 1781. . . . These lectures will lessen the notion that the earlier Kant was greatly influenced by Shaftesbury and other English moralists of the same school" (*American Journal of Sociology*).

Lectures on Philosophical Theology. Trans. by Gertrude M. Clark, Cornell Univ. Pr. 1978 text ed. $24.50 1986 pap. $7.95. A translation, with notes by Allan Wood, of Kant's lectures on the subject.

Moral Law: Kant's Groundwork for the Metaphysics of Morals. Trans. by H. J. Paton, Barnes & Noble repr. of 1948 ed. 1978 pap. $11.95. Translated with analysis and notes by one of the leading English Kant scholars.

Observations on the Feeling of the Beautiful and Sublime. Ed. by John T. Goldthwait [*California Lib. Repr. Ser.*] Univ. of California Pr. repr. of 1960 ed. 1981 $14.50. The early versions of Kant's aesthetic theories.

Kant's Political Writings. Ed. by H. Reiss, Cambridge Univ. Pr. 1970 pap. $13.95. A new translation of Kant's main political writings.

Philosophical Correspondence. Trans. by Arnulf Zweig, Univ. of Chicago Pr. 1967 o.p. Selections from Kant's correspondence about his philosophy from 1759 to 1799.

Universal Natural History and Theory of the Heavens. Trans. by W. Hastie, ed. by Milton K. Munitz [*Ann Arbor Paperbacks Ser.*] Univ. of Michigan Pr. 1969 o.p. Two of Kant's important scientific essays.

BOOKS ABOUT KANT

Adickes, Erich. *German Kantian Bibliography*. Burt Franklin repr. of 1896 ed. 1967 $40.50. By one of the leading German scholars of Kant.

Allison, Henry E. *Kant's Transcendental Idealism: An Interpretation and Defense*. Yale Univ. Pr. 1984 $33.50. A scholarly interpretation of Kant's basic theory.

Aquila, Richard E. *Representational Mind: A Study of Kant's Theory of Knowledge*. [*Studies in Phenomenology and Existential Philosophy Ser.*] Indiana Univ. Pr. 1984 $22.50. A study of Kant's theory of knowledge in terms of intentionality.

Arendt, Hannah. *Lectures on Kant's Political Philosophy*. Univ. of Chicago Pr. 1982 o.p. Discussions of Kant's political theory by one of the twentieth century's best analysts of political thought.

Aschenbrenner, Karl. *A Companion to Kant's Critique of Pure Reason: Transcendental Aesthetic and Analytic*. Univ. Pr. of Amer. 1983 lib. bdg. $30.00 text ed. pap. $13.50. A helpful commentary on Kant's difficult text.

Aune, Bruce. *Kant's Theory of Morals*. Princeton Univ. Pr. 1980 o.p. An examination of Kant's argument on morality in terms of analytic philosophy.

Beck, Lewis W. *A Commentary to Kant's "Critique of Practical Reason."* [*Midway Repr. Ser.*] Univ. of Chicago Pr. repr. of 1960 ed. 1984 text ed. pap. $15.00. By America's leading authority on Kant.

———. *Early German Philosophy: Kant and His Predecessors*. Harvard Univ. Pr. (Belknap Pr.) 1969 $35.00. A very important background book, giving a much-needed picture of the state of German philosophy before Kant, and of how Kant's philosophy related to that of earlier German thinkers.

———. *Essays on Kant and Hume*. Yale Univ. Pr. 1978 $22.50. A group of essays by Beck on the two philosophers.

———. *Studies in the Philosophy of Kant*. [*Essay and Monograph Ser.*] Greenwood repr. of 1965 ed. 1981 lib. bdg. $25.00. A group of 13 studies by Beck on Kant and his influence.

———, ed. *Kant Studies Today*. Open Court 1969 $29.95. A collective volume giving an interesting picture of what is being studied about Kant by present-day scholars.

———. *Kant's Theory of Knowledge: Selected Papers*. Kluwer Academic 1974 pap. $16.00. A fine collection of rather recent Kant scholarship.

Bennett, Jonathan. *Kant's Analytic*. Cambridge Univ. Pr. 1966 $44.50 pap. $13.95. A provocative book by one of the leading analytic philosophers.

———. *Kant's Dialectic*. Cambridge Univ. Pr. 1974 pap. $13.95. A companion work to *Kant's Analytic* (see above).

Broad, C. D. *Kant: An Introduction*. Ed. by C. Lewry, Cambridge Univ. Pr. 1978 pap. $15.95. Broad was one of the most careful expositors and critics of philosophical ideas and arguments. His presentation of Kant's thought is most helpful.

Caird, Edward. *The Critical Philosophy of Immanuel Kant*. Kraus Repr. 2 vols. repr. of 1889 ed. 1968 $58.00. The first important volume on Kant in English.

Cassirer, Ernst. *Kant's First Critique: An Appraisal of the Significance of Kant's Critique of Pure Reason*. Humanities Pr. repr. of 1954 ed. 1978 o.p. By one of the leading neo-Kantian philosophers of the twentieth century.

———. *Kant's Life and Thought*. Trans. by James Haden, Yale Univ. Pr. 1981 $36.00 pap. $12.95. "A clear and readable account of Kant's intellectual development. . . . In spite of its age, there is now no better treatment in English of Kant's thought than this; it will doubtless become, and remain for some time, the standard work in English on Kant's life and thought. This is an intellectual biography, written as an introduction to the reading of Kant's philosophical works" (*Choice*).

Ewing, Alfred C. *Short Commentary on Kant's Critique of Pure Reason.* Univ. of Chicago Pr. 2d ed. 1967 pap. $9.00. One of the helpful commentaries for people beginning their study of Kant's difficult text.

Findlay, John N. *Kant and the Transcendental Object.* Oxford 1981 $29.95. Important study by a leading interpreter of German thought.

Gram, Moltke S. *The Transcendental Turn: The Foundation of Kant's Idealism.* Univ. Pr. of Florida 1985 $30.00. A provocative interpretation.

———, ed. *Interpreting Kant.* Univ. of Iowa Pr. 1982 text ed. $16.00. A collective volume of mainly new interpretations.

Hendel, Charles W. *The Philosophy of Kant and Our Modern World.* Greenwood repr. of 1957 ed. 1981 lib. bdg. $19.75. A still valuable exposition by an expert on many aspects of eighteenth-century thought.

Jaspers, Karl. *Kant.* Trans. by Ralph Manheim, Harcourt 1966 pap. $4.95. An introductory presentation by one of Germany's prominent philosophers.

Kaufmann, Walter. *Discovering the Mind.* McGraw-Hill 1980 $14.95. A well-written presentation by a leading expositor and commentator on German thought.

Kemp Smith, Norman. *Commentary to Kant's Critique of Pure Reason.* Humanities Pr. 1923 2d ed. $30.50. Perhaps the most widely studied commentary on Kant in English.

Lindsay, Alexander D. *Kant.* Richard West repr. of 1934 ed. 1978 lib. bdg. $40.00. A still valuable presentation of Kant's thought.

Mohanty, J. N., and Robert W. Shahan, eds. *Essays on Kant's Critique of Pure Reason.* Univ. of Oklahoma Pr. 1982 $17.50. A collective volume of some recent interesting pieces about Kant's first *Critique.*

Murphy, Jeffrie G. *Kant: The Philosophy of Right.* [*Philosophers in Perspective Ser.*] St. Martin's 1970 pap. $7.95. A brief presentation of Kant's theory of principles of moral rectitude of actions.

Paton, Herbert J. *The Categorical Imperative: A Study in Kant's Moral Philosophy.* Univ. of Pennsylvania Pr. 1971 pap. $10.95. One of Paton's excellent studies on a central theory of Kant.

———. *Kant's Metaphysics of Experience.* [*Muirhead Lib. of Philosophy*] Humanities Pr. 2 vols. repr. of 1961 ed. 1976 text ed. pap. $40.00. An important study by one of the leading English expositors of Kant.

Prichard, H. A. *Kant's Theory of Knowledge.* Ed. by Lewis W. Beck, Garland repr. of 1909 ed. 1977 lib. bdg. $32.00. One of the ground-breaking studies of its day, and still worth reading.

Rescher, Nicholas. *Kant's Theory of Knowledge and Reality: A Group of Essays.* Univ. Pr. of Amer. 1983 lib. bdg. $26.00 text ed. pap. $11.25. Examination of Kant's epistemology and metaphysics by a leading contemporary philosopher.

Riley, Patrick. *Kant's Political Philosophy.* [*Philosophy and Society Ser.*] Rowman 1983 text ed. $31.50. A presentation of Kant's political views by a leading historian of political philosophy.

Schilpp, Paul A. *Kant's Pre-Critical Ethics.* Ed. by Lewis W. Beck, Garland repr. of 1960 ed. 2d ed. 1977 $29.00. Main study on this topic.

Scruton, Roger. *Kant.* [*Past Masters Ser.*] Oxford 1982 $12.95 pap. $3.95. A survey of Kant's views by a controversial contemporary philosopher.

Seth, Andrew. *The Development from Kant to Hegel, with Chapters on the Philosophy of Religion.* Ed. by Lewis W. Beck, Garland repr. of 1882 ed. 1976 lib. bdg. $24.00. A classic work tracing this side of Kant's philosophy and its immediate influence on German thought.

Sidgwick, Henry. *Lectures on the Philosophy of Kant and Other Philosophical Lectures*

and Essays. Ed. by James Ward, Kraus Repr. repr. of 1905 ed. 1968 $32.00.
Lectures by one of England's leading authorities on the history of ethics.

Strawson, P. F. *The Bounds of Sense: An Essay on Kant's Critique of Pure Reason.*
Methuen 1966 pap. $14.95. An interesting interpretation of Kant by one of England's leading metaphysical thinkers.

Walsh, W. H. *Kant's Criticism of Metaphysics.* Columbia Univ. Pr. 1975 $20.00; Univ.
of Chicago Pr. 1976 pap. $4.50. A new evaluation of Kant's views on metaphysics.

Watson, John. *Kant and His English Critics: A Comparison of Critical and Empirical Philosophy.* Ed. by Lewis W. Beck, Garland repr. of 1881 ed. 1976 lib. bdg. $45.00. A still valuable work.

———. *The Philosophy of Kant Explained.* Arden Lib. repr. of 1908 ed. 1981 lib. bdg. $50.00. A still useful commentary.

Werkmeister, William H. *Kant: The Architectonic and Development of His Philosophy.*
Open Court 1980 pap. $9.95. An exposition of Kant by a leading interpreter in America.

———. *Reflections of Kant's Philosophy.* Univ. Pr. of Florida 1975 $8.00. Considerations about Kant by one of his leading interpreters.

Wolff, Robert Paul. *Kant's Theory of Mental Activity: A Commentary on the Transcendental Analytic of the Critique of Pure Reason.* Peter Smith repr. 1973 $18.00. An interesting work by one of the liveliest of the present generation of Kant scholars.

———, ed. *Kant: A Collection of Critical Essays.* Univ. of Notre Dame Pr. 1968 $9.95.
A collective volume by various scholars.

Yovel, Yirmiahu. *Kant and the Philosophy of History.* Princeton Univ. Pr. 1979 $42.00. A valuable study by one of Israel's leading philosophers.

REID, THOMAS. 1710–1796

Thomas Reid was born near Aberdeen, where he later went to college. His philosophy of common sense, a special faculty that all people have that he took to be more reliable than any philosophical reasoning, was developed as an answer to Hume and Berkeley. He started a school of Scottish philosophers that included James Beattie, Dugald Stewart, and Sir William Hamilton. Reid and his followers had a great influence on American thought in the first half of the nineteenth century.

BOOKS BY REID

Essays on the Active Powers of Man. 1788. Ibis Pub. VA repr. of 1788 ed. 1986 lib. bdg. $35.00 text ed. pap. $20.00. This and the next title are Reid's lectures, which he organized in these two works after he retired from teaching.

Essays on the Active Powers of the Human Mind. Intro. by B. Brody, MIT 1969 pap. $7.95

Thomas Reid's Inquiry and Essays. Ed. by Ronald E. Beanblossom and Keith Lehrer [*Philosophical Class. Ser.*] Hackett repr. of 1975 ed. 1983 lib. bdg. $16.50 text ed. pap. $6.95. Reid's major works, his answer to Hume, and his lectures.

BOOKS ABOUT REID

Daniels, Norman. *Thomas Reid's Inquiry: The Geometry of Visibles and the Case for Realism.* Fwd. by Hilary Putman, Burt Franklin 1974 lib. bdg. $14.95. A study of Reid's theory of perception and its relation to present-day realist theories.

Grave, S. A. *The Scottish Philosophy of Common Sense.* Greenwood repr. of 1960 ed.

1973 $17.25. A basic study of the philosophical basis of the Scottish common sense philosophy.

Hope, Vincent, ed. *Philosophers of the Scottish Enlightenment*. Columbia Univ. Pr. 1984 $22.50. A new study of the eighteenth-century Scottish thinkers.

Jessop, T. E. *A Bibliography of David Hume and of Scottish Philosophy from Francis Hutcheson to Lord Balfour*. Garland 1983 lib. bdg. $36.00. The most complete bibliography on Scottish philosophy, including Reid's work.

McCosh, James. *The Scottish Philosophy, Biographical, Expository, Critical, from Hutcheson to Hamilton*. [*Philosophy in Amer. Ser.*] AMS Pr. repr. of 1875 ed. 1980 $41.50. An exposition of Scottish common sense philosophy by one of its best adherents.

Marcil-Lacoste, Louise. *Claude Buffier and Thomas Reid: Two Common Sense Philosophers*. [*Studies in the History of Ideas*] McGill-Queens Univ. Pr. 1982 $27.50. Comparative study of a French and Scottish version of the common sense theory of philosophy.

Priestley, Joseph. *An Examination of Dr. Reid's Inquiry into the Human Mind*. Ed. by René Wellek, Garland repr. of 1774 ed. 1978 lib. bdg. $51.00. One of the first criticisms of Reid's theory.

Selby-Bigge, L. A., ed. *British Moralists: Being Selections from Writers Principally of the Eighteenth Century*. Ibis Pub. VA repr. of 1897 ed. 1986 lib. bdg. $45.00 text ed. pap. $25.00. A still basic collection of texts of eighteenth-century British thinkers.

Seth Pringle Pattison, Andrew. *Scottish Philosophy: A Comparison of the Scottish and German Answers to Hume*. Burt Franklin repr. of 1890 ed. 1971 $20.50. A classic study by an expert on Scottish philosophy, showing the similarities and differences in the Scottish and German answers to Hume.

VICO, GIAMBATTISTA. 1668–1744

Vico, an Italian jurist and philosopher, was born in Naples and studied at the university there. He then became a tutor and later, in 1699, a professor of rhetoric. He began publishing in 1710, writing works on law. In 1725 he published the *Principles of a New Science*, his theory of history. A much-revised edition appeared in 1730, and in 1735 he was appointed historiographer royal to King Charles of Naples.

His work, written in Italian, was little known in the eighteenth century, but became influential when translated into other European languages in the nineteenth century. His theory of history—that each culture expresses its history in its art, literature, and mythology, and can be understood in terms of its imaginative productions, rather than its strict chronological developments—has attracted widespread attention, and his work is being studied and commented on more and more. (See also Volume 2.)

BOOKS BY VICO

Vico: Selected Writings. Trans. and ed. by Leon Pompa, Cambridge Univ. Pr. 1982 $39.50 pap. $14.95. Texts from essays and lectures by Vico and from *The New Science*.

The New Science of Giambattista Vico. 1725. Trans. by Thomas G. Bergin and Max H. Fisch, Cornell Univ. Pr. 1984 pap. $12.95. Vico's major work on the philosophy of history.

The Autobiography of Giambattista Vico. 1725–31. Trans. by Thomas G. Bergin, Cornell Univ. Pr. 1963 pap. $7.95. Includes Vico's story of his life, plus that of his last years by the Marquis of Villarosa.

BOOKS ABOUT VICO

Berlin, Isaiah. *Vico and Herder: Two Studies in the History of Ideas.* Viking 1976 o.p. By one of England's most renowned historians of ideas.

Caponigri, A. Robert. *Time and Idea: The Theory of History in Giambattista Vico.* Univ. of Notre Dame Pr. 1968 pap. $6.95. An important study of Vico's philosophy of history.

Grimaldi, Alfonsina A. *The Universal Humanity of Giambattista Vico.* Vanni 1958 $12.50. A scholarly study of Vico's conception of humanity.

Manson, Richard. *Theory of Knowledge of Giambattista Vico: On the Method of the New Science Concerning the Common Nature of the Nations.* Shoe String 1969 $16.50. A brief, careful analysis of Vico's epistemology.

Mooney, Michael. *Vico in the Tradition of Rhetoric.* Princeton Univ. Pr. 1985 text ed. $26.00. Vico seen in the tradition of ancient Renaissance and modern rhetoric.

Pompa, Leon. *Vico: A Study of the New Science.* Cambridge Univ. Pr. 1975 $34.50. A detailed study by a leading Vico expert.

Stephenson, Charles L. *Giambattista Vico and the Foundations of a Science of the Philosophy of History.* Amer. Class. College Pr. 1982 $69.85. A scholarly study of Vico's theory and its relation to the development of the philosophy of history.

Tagliacozzo, Giorgio, ed. *Vico and Contemporary Thought.* Humanities Pr. 1979 text ed. $20.00. Essays by 20 European and American scholars.

———. *Vico and Marx.* Humanities Pr. 1983 text ed. $35.00. A collective volume of essays by various scholars.

———. *Vico: Past and Present.* Humanities Pr. 1981 o.p. Two volumes of essays on Vico by a large number of European and American scholars.

Tagliacozzo, Giorgio, and Donald Verene, eds. *Giambattista Vico's Science of Humanity.* Johns Hopkins Univ. Pr. 1976 $39.50. A collection of essays by European and American scholars. "The essays contain seeds for overcoming the antithesis between the natural and social sciences, for a philosophical grasp of the whole which could deepen the self-understanding of modern man. The comprehensive list of works on Vico published in English or in English translation is a valuable research tool for Vico scholarship" (*LJ*).

———. *New Vico Studies.* Humanities Pr. 1985 text ed. pap. $15.00. A collection of articles by a group of scholars in Europe and America.

Verene, Donald P. *Vico's Science of Imagination.* Cornell Univ. Pr. 1981 $24.95. An examination of the role imagination plays in Vico's *New Science.*

NINETEENTH CENTURY

BERGSON, HENRI. 1859–1941 (NOBEL PRIZE 1927)

Born in Paris of Jewish parents, Bergson received his education there and then taught philosophy. He was appointed professor of philosophy at the Collège de France in 1900, and elected a member of the French Academy in 1914. Bergson developed his philosophy by stressing the biological, evolutionary elements involved in thinking, reasoning, and creating. He saw the vitalistic dimension of man as being of the greatest importance. His various writings received great acclaim both in France and throughout the learned world, and in 1927 he was awarded the Nobel Prize for Literature (there is no Nobel Prize for philosophy). In defiance of the Nazis after their conquest of France, he insisted on wearing a yellow star to show his solidarity with other French Jews, and shortly before he died, he gave up all his positions and renounced his many honors in protest at the discrimination against Jews by the Nazis and the Vichy French regime.

BOOKS BY BERGSON

Time and Free Will. 1889. [*Muirhead Lib. of Philosophy*] Humanities Pr. 1971 $31.75. Bergson's development of the notion of real duration and its relation to human freedom.

Matter and Memory. 1896. [*Muirhead Lib. of Philosophy*] Humanities Pr. 1978 o.p. Bergson's theory of mind and body.

Laughter: An Essay on the Meaning of the Comic. 1901. Trans. by Cloudesley Brereton and Fred Rothwell, Richard West repr. of 1921 ed. 1977 lib. bdg. $35.00. One of the few philosophical works on this subject.

Creative Evolution. 1907. Trans. by Arthur Mitchell, Telegraph Bks. repr. of 1911 ed. 1981 lib. bdg. $50.00; Univ. Pr. of Amer. 1984 text ed. pap. $13.50. Bergson's most famous work on the development of man and the cosmos.

The Two Sources of Morality and Religion. 1932. Greenwood repr. of 1935 ed. 1974 lib. bdg. $25.00; trans. by Carter W. Horsfall, Univ. of Notre Dame Pr. 1977 text ed. pap. $8.95. Bergson's attempt to develop an evolutionary ethics and religion.

The Creative Mind: An Introduction to Metaphysics. 1934. Citadel Pr. 1974 pap. $3.95; (under the title, *An Introduction to Metaphysics: The Creative Mind*) [*Quality Pap. Ser.*] Littlefield repr. of 1965 ed. 1975 pap. $5.95. On man's role in the evolutionary world.

BOOKS ABOUT BERGSON

Capek, M. *Bergson and Modern Physics: A Reinterpretation and Reevaluation.* [*Synthese Lib.*] Kluwer Academic 1971 $42.00. A careful consideration of Bergson's views by a philosopher of science, who relates them to the changes in physics in the twentieth century.

Dodson, George R. *Bergson and the Modern Spirit.* Gordon Pr. 1976 lib. bdg. $59.95

Kumar, Shiv K. *Bergson and the Stream of Consciousness Novel.* Greenwood repr. of 1963 ed. 1979 lib. bdg. $24.75. Relation of Bergson's philosophy to new twentieth-century novel style.

Maritain, Jacques. *Bergsonian Philosophy and Thomism.* Greenwood repr. of 1955 ed. 1968 lib. bdg. $29.75. A consideration of Bergson's views by the leading French Catholic philosopher of the twentieth century.

Pilkington, A. E. *Bergson and His Influence.* Cambridge Univ. Pr. 1976 $49.50. Attempt to evaluate what Bergson's impact has been.

Russell, Bertrand. *The Philosophy of Bergson.* Folcroft repr. of 1914 ed. 1980 lib. bdg. $25.00. Russell's very interesting critique of his contemporary.

BOSANQUET, BERNARD. 1848–1923

Bosanquet was educated at Harrow and at Balliol College, Oxford, where he subsequently taught ancient history from 1871 to 1881. He then moved to London, became involved in social causes, and translated some of the works of the German idealists Hegel and Lotze. A major figure in the British idealist movement, Bosanquet wrote on a wide range of subjects. He has been described as more Hegelian than his contemporary, Francis Herbert Bradley, and also less skeptical. He gave the Gifford lectures in 1912.

BOOKS BY BOSANQUET

Knowledge and Reality: A Criticism of F. H. Bradley's "Principles of Logic." 1885. Kraus Repr. 1968 $31.00. Bosanquet's indication of his differences with Bradley.

Logic, or the Morphology of Knowledge. 1888. Kraus Repr. 1968 2 vols. in 1. 2d ed. $46.00. A working out of his differences with Bradley.

A History of Aesthetic. 1892. Ibis Pub. VA 1986 $30.50 pap. $15.00. One of the first studies on the development of the subject, plus Bosanquet's aesthetic theory.

The Philosophical Theory of the State. 1899. Ibis Pub. VA 1986 $25.00 pap. $14.00. An idealistic justification of the state.

The Essentials of Logic: Being Ten Lectures on Judgment and Inference. 1895. Kraus Repr. 1968 $18.00

The Principle of Individuality and Value. 1911. [*Gifford Lectures*] Kraus Repr. 1968 $29.00. On the nature of human beings.

The Value and Destiny of the Individual. 1913. [*Gifford Lectures*] Kraus Repr. 1968 $32.00. On the nature of the self and soul.

Social and International Ideals: Being Studies in Patriotism. 1917. Kraus Repr. 1968 $31.00. A collection of essays on social questions.

Some Suggestions in Ethics. 1918. Kraus Repr. 1968 $23.00. Discussions on practical moral issues.

Implication and Linear Inferences. 1920. Kraus Repr. 1968 $15.00. Interesting work of the period on logic.

Three Chapters on the Nature of the Mind. 1923. Ed. by Helen Bosanquet, Kraus Repr. 1968 $18.00. From an unfinished work.

Croce's Aesthetics. Gordon Pr. 1974 $59.95. Presentation of Croce's important ideas for the English-language audience.

BRADLEY, F(RANCIS) H(ERBERT). 1846–1924

Bradley, the son of an evangelical clergyman, was educated at Oxford, became a fellow of Merton College, and remained there for the rest of his life. He was the leading English advocate of Hegel's philosophy and argued strongly for it against such figures as WILLIAM JAMES (see also Vol. 3) and BERTRAND RUSSELL (see also Vol. 5). His book *Appearance and Reality* (1893) was the most important statement of the case for the English Hegelians.

BOOKS BY BRADLEY

Appearance and Reality: A Metaphysical Essay. 1893. Oxford repr. of 1897 ed. 1930 $42.00

Collected Essays. Greenwood 2 vols. repr. of 1935 ed. 1968 $31.75; Oxford 1935 $52.00. Some of the articles on philosophical subjects Bradley published in different journals.

BOOK ABOUT BRADLEY

Manser, Anthony. *The Philosophy of F. H. Bradley.* Oxford 1984 $34.50. The best available study of Bradley.

COMTE, AUGUSTE. 1798–1857

Comte, a French philosopher, began and developed the philosophy called "positivism." He held that all previous philosophies could be described and classified according to which of three historical stages they belonged to—the supernatural, the metaphysical (or abstract), or the positive (or scientific) stage. The positive or scientific stage allowed for a science of human society—sociology—that described human development from the primitive or religious to the positive stage. Comte is often considered the founder of sociology. To replace the supernatural and metaphysical religions, Comte introduced a religion of humanity, which had some of the trappings of a church but was devoted to humanistic approaches to human problems. His organization still exists in France, but has few followers, having been superseded by other ideologies.

BOOKS BY COMTE

Auguste Comte and Positivism: The Essential Writings. Ed. by Gertrud Lenzer, Harper 1975 o.p. Selections that give a picture of Comte's views.

A General View of Positivism. [*Reprints in Sociology Ser.*] Irvington repr. of 1848 ed. 1971 lib. bdg. $39.50. An overall presentation of Comte's philosophy.

The Positive Analysis of Social Phenomena. Amer. Class. College Pr. 1983 $97.75. One of Comte's systematic statements of his philosophy.

Positive Philosophy. Trans. by Harriet Martineau, AMS Pr. repr. of 1855 ed. 1977 $38.50. The central statement of Comte's theory. A condensation of Comte's six-volume French presentation.

System of Positive Polity. 1851. Burt Franklin 4 vols. repr. of 1875 ed. 1973 set $115.00. A late massive formulation of Comte's views.

BOOKS ABOUT COMTE

Caird, Edward. *Social Philosophy and Religion of Comte.* Kraus Repr. repr. of 1885 ed. 1968 $23.00. A Victorian evaluation of Comte by a leading historian of philosophy of the time.

Lévy-Bruhl, Lucien. *The Philosophy of Auguste Comte.* Gordon Pr. repr. of 1903 ed. 1976 lib. bdg. $59.95. A presentation of Comte's views by one of the leading French social theorists of the following generation.

Mill, John Stuart. *Auguste Comte and Positivism.* Univ. of Michigan Pr. 1961 o.p. Still one of the best presentations and analyses of Comte's system, by the leading British empiricist of the time.

Sokoloff, Boris. *The Mad Philosopher: Auguste Comte.* Greenwood repr. of 1961 ed. 1975 lib. bdg. $22.50. Stresses the eccentricities of Comte and his philosophy, as well as its antidemocratic tendencies.

DEWEY, JOHN. 1859–1952

John Dewey, one of the most important philosophers and educators of the United States, was born in Vermont. He studied at Johns Hopkins, and taught at the universities of Michigan and Minnesota before settling at the University of Chicago in 1894. During his ten years there, Dewey began to publish a series of works on human psychology and reasoning, and on the ways people learn. These works put him quickly in the forefront of philosophers and psychologists of education. He developed a kind of social pragmatic theory that he called "instrumentalism," showing how people learn by doing. In 1904, he moved to Columbia University, where he remained for the rest of his academic career—the dominant figure in the philosophy department and its chairman for many years, and the guiding influence on Teachers College, Columbia's school of education. In a very full series of works, Dewey sought to show how his instrumentalist theory could explain the thinking process and the way people deal with problems, and how both could be improved by the application of scientific methods and knowledge. Dewey's program included both educational reform (he was the theoretician of the progressive education movement that children should learn by doing) and reform of the intellectual process. His books *The Quest for Certainty* and *Reconstruction in Philosophy*, both from the 1920s, showed how intellectuals had tried to achieve too much in the quest for unattainable goals, and how, by restricting the intellectual quest to attainable goals, the growing results of science could be continuously applied to the solution of human problems. For Dewey, the pragmatic interpretation of human intellectual activity was more a social matter than an individual one, as William James had construed it. Dewey stressed the social needs and the social goals that could be achieved. Society would be improved and better able to deal with its problems through a better educated citizenry. Society itself, as Dewey saw it, should be organized to best deal with problem solving. Such an organization would involve a thoroughly democratic political structure emphasizing social needs.

Dewey was an important figure in movements to develop social democracy and to strengthen democratic institutions. Throughout his long career he emphasized the importance of the practical, and the role of theory as an aid to solving practical problems. He was opposed by those adhering to various metaphysical traditions and by the logical positivists and analytic philosophers, who thought he had grossly underestimated the role of abstract thinking, and that his theory could not really encompass the results of modern logic. Dewey's thought was extremely influential in the first half of this century, but has gradually been eclipsed by interest in other philosophical theories, especially analytic philosophy and recent Continental philosophy.

Dewey was one of the most prolific writers in philosophy. The project of publishing his complete works in chronological order is now nearing completion. (See also Volume 3.)

BOOKS BY DEWEY

The Early Works of John Dewey, 1882–1898. Ed. by Jo Ann Boydston, Southern Illinois Univ. Pr. 5 vols. 1967–72 ea. $17.50–$19.95 pap. ea. $6.95–$8.95. This collection and the subsequent volumes listed below are sponsored by the Cooperative Research on Dewey Publications Program at Southern Illinois University.

The Middle Works of John Dewey, 1899–1924. Ed. by Jo Ann Boydston, Southern Illinois Univ. Pr. 15 vols. 1976–83 ea. $19.95–$25.00

The Later Works of John Dewey, 1925–1953. Southern Illinois Univ. Pr. 5 vols. 1981–84 ea. $22.50–$30.00

The School and Society. 1899. Intro. by Joe R. Burnett, Southern Illinois Univ. Pr. 1980 pap. $5.95. Early statement of Dewey's philosophy of education.

How We Think: A Restatement of the Relation of Reflective Thinking to the Educative Process. 1909. Heath 1933 text ed. $16.95. Early study in the psychology of logic.

Reconstruction in Philosophy. 1920. Beacon 1957 pap. $10.95. Lectures Dewey gave in Tokyo, presenting his survey of modern philosophy and how it can be saved.

Human Nature and Conduct. 1922. Century Bookbindery repr. of 1922 ed. 1986 lib. bdg. $40.00; Modern Lib. 1935 $3.95. One of Dewey's basic works on ethics.

Experience and Nature. 1925. Dover repr. of 1929 ed. 1958 pap. $6.95; Open Court repr. of 1925 ed. 1971 rev. ed. $19.95 pap. $6.95. The Carus Lectures, Dewey's "metaphysics."

Democracy and Education: An Introduction to the Philosophy of Education. 1916. Darby repr. of 1932 ed. 1982 lib. bdg. $30.00; Free Pr. 1966 pap. $10.95. The role of an improved educational process in a democratic society.

A Common Faith. Yale Univ. Pr. 1934 pap. $3.95. Dewey's philosophy of religion.

Logic: The Theory of Inquiry. 1938. Irvington 1960 o.p. Dewey's mature examination of the reasoning process.

Theory of Valuation. [*Foundations of the Unity of Science Ser.*] Univ. of Chicago Pr. 1939 pap. $4.00. Dewey's instrumentalist explanation of values.

Philosophy of Education. 1946. [*Quality Pap. Ser.*] Littlefield repr. of 1958 ed. 1971 pap. $4.95

On Education. Intro. by Reginald D. Archambault, Univ. of Chicago Pr. 1974 pap. $11.00. A reprint of one of Dewey's important statements on his views.

Experience and Education. Macmillan (Collier Bks.) 1963 pap. $3.95; Peter Smith 1983 $12.50. A lecture by Dewey.

The Influence of Darwin on Philosophy and Other Essays. Peter Smith repr. 1951 $11.50. Some of Dewey's early influential essays.

Problems of Men. 1946. Greenwood repr. of 1946 ed. 1968 lib. bdg. $29.75. A collection of essays and addresses.

The Public and Its Problems: An Essay in Political Inquiry. Ohio Univ. Pr. 1954 pap. $5.95; Telegraph Bks. repr. of 1946 ed. 1987 lib. bdg. $30.00. Dewey's instrumentalism applied to the political process.

Studies in Logical Theory. AMS Pr. repr. of 1903 ed. 1975 $34.50. One of Dewey's first examinations of the psychology of logic.

The Theory of Moral Life. Irvington repr. of 1960 ed. 1980 text ed. pap. $9.95. Another statement of Dewey's ethical views.

(and Arthur F. Bentley). *Knowing and the Known.* Greenwood repr. of 1949 ed. 1976 lib. bdg. $25.00. Dewey's last work, done with his friend Bentley, on epistemology.

BOOKS ABOUT DEWEY

Bernstein, Richard J. *John Dewey.* Ridgeview repr. of 1966 ed. 1981 lib. bdg. $24.00 text ed. pap. $8.50. Focuses on Dewey's views on experience and nature, his metaphysics.

Blewett, John, ed. *John Dewey: His Thought and Influence.* Fwd. by John S. Brubacher, Greenwood repr. of 1960 ed. 1973 lib. bdg. $22.50. A collection of essays by various Catholic scholars, including James Collins.

Boydston, Jo Ann, ed. *A Guide to the Works of John Dewey.* Southern Illinois Univ. Pr. 1972 pap. $7.95. An indispensable research tool for studying Dewey's philosophy.

Cahn, Steven M., ed. *New Studies in the Philosophy of John Dewey.* Univ. Pr. of New England 1977 pap. $9.00. A collective volume of recent Dewey scholarship.

Coughlan, Neil. *Young John Dewey: An Essay in American Intellectual History.* Univ. of Chicago Pr. 1975 $13.00. A study of Dewey's early intellectual life.

Dicker, George. *Dewey's Theory of Knowledge.* Temple Univ. Pr. 1976 pap. $19.95. A study of Dewey's epistemology.

Dykhuizen, George. *Life and Mind of John Dewey.* Intro. by Harold Taylor, Southern Illinois Univ. Pr. 1973 $22.50 1978 pap. $5.95. The most complete scholarly intellectual biography of John Dewey, representing many years of careful research.

Geiger, George R. *John Dewey in Perspective.* Greenwood repr. of 1958 ed. 1974 lib. bdg. $22.50. A pragmatist's evaluation of Dewey's achievement.

Gouinlock, James. *John Dewey's Philosophy of Value.* Humanities Pr. 1972 text ed. $15.00. An important study of this aspect of Dewey's thought.

Handlin, Oscar. *John Dewey's Challenge to Education: Historical Perspectives on the Cultural Context.* Greenwood repr. of 1959 ed. 1972 lib. bdg. $22.50. Interesting pictures of Dewey's role written by one of the best American social and intellectual historians.

Hook, Sidney. *John Dewey: An Intellectual Portrait.* Greenwood repr. of 1939 ed. 1976 lib. bdg. $19.75. A picture of Dewey by one of the next generation of American pragmatists.

———, ed. *John Dewey: Philosopher of Science and Freedom.* Greenwood repr. of 1950 ed. 1976 lib. bdg. $29.00. A collective volume mainly by Dewey's students.

Lamont, Corliss, ed. *Dialogue on John Dewey.* Horizon Pr. 1981 pap. $4.95. A tribute by some of Dewey's friends and students.

McDermott, John J., ed. *The Philosophy of John Dewey.* Univ. of Chicago Pr. 2 vols. 1981 pap. $14.00. Selected texts.

Moore, Edward C. *American Pragmatism: Peirce, James and Dewey.* Greenwood repr. of 1961 ed. 1984 lib. bdg. $45.00. Basic comparative study of the three leading American thinkers.

Morganbesser, Sidney. *Dewey and His Critics.* Hackett 1977 $30.00 pap. $12.50. A collection of articles raising critical points about Dewey's philosophy.

Nathanson, Jerome. *John Dewey: The Reconstruction of the Democratic Life.* Ungar 1967 o.p. An excellent summary of Dewey's ideas in his role as philosopher, psychologist, educator, and social theorist.

Philosopher of Common Man. Greenwood 1968 $22.50. Contributions by many of Dewey's students and colleagues.

Thayer, Horace S. *Logic of Pragmatism: An Examination of John Dewey's Logic.* Greenwood repr. of 1952 ed. 1970 lib. bdg. $22.50. A study of Dewey's views on logic and the reasoning process.

Thomas, Milton H. *John Dewey: A Centennial Bibliography.* Univ. of Chicago Pr. rev. ed. 1962 $12.50. This bibliography of writings about Dewey first appeared in 1929. A second edition was put out ten years later, and the third carried the project up to 1960.

White, Morton G. *Origin of Dewey's Instrumentalism.* Hippocrene Bks. 1964 lib. bdg. $16.50. A reprint of this prize-winning work, tracing the roots of Dewey's philosophy.

DILTHEY, WILHELM. 1833–1911

Dilthey was a German philosopher concerned with the epistemological analysis of human studies, especially history. The son of a clergyman, Dilthey studied theology at Heidelberg. He then held chairs at Basel, Kiel, Breslau, and finally at the University of Berlin. His main theory dealt with the "philosophy of life"—philosophy as lived, experienced. This has had a great influence on the contemporary concern with hermeneutical philosophy.

BOOKS BY DILTHEY

The Essence of Philosophy. Trans. by Stephen A. Emery and William T. Emery, AMS Pr. repr. of 1954 ed. 1976 $27.00; Greenwood repr. of 1954 ed. $22.50. First work of Dilthey's to appear in English.

Poetry and Experience. Vol. 5 in *Selected Works of Dilthey.* Trans. and ed. by Rudolf A. Makkreel and Frithjof Rodi, Princeton Univ. Pr. 1985 $32.50. The first edition of Dilthey's selected works to appear, giving a good indication of his method of analysis.

BOOKS ABOUT DILTHEY

Hodges, Herbert A. *The Philosophy of Wilhelm Dilthey.* [*International Lib. of Sociology and Social Reconstruction*] Greenwood repr. of 1952 ed. 1974 lib. bdg. $22.50. The first attempt to explain Dilthey's philosophy in English.

Makkreel, Rudolf A. *Dilthey: Philosopher of the Human Studies.* Princeton Univ. Pr. 1975 $49.00 pap. $16.00. A comprehensive reinterpretation of Dilthey's philosophy as well as a study of its development.

FEUERBACH, LUDWIG ANDREAS. 1804–1872

Ludwig Feuerbach was born in Bavaria and studied theology at Heidelberg and Berlin, and philosophy at Erlangen. He was very much influenced by Hegel and especially by radical interpretations of his theory. Feuerbach became involved with some radical publications, but dropped out when KARL MARX (see also Vol. 3) participated, because of his opposition to Marx's views and politics. Feuerbach was an active participant in some of the liberal factions in the 1848 revolution, and retired when the revolution failed to produce any results. He was one of the leaders of the group called "the radical Hegelians," who found themselves denounced by Marx and his followers. Feuerbach's most important work was *The Essence of Christianity* (1841), an attempt to present Christianity entirely in naturalistic and humanistic terms.

BOOKS BY FEUERBACH

The Essence of Christianity. 1841. Fwd. by H. Richard Niebuhr, Peter Smith 1958 $18.25; fwd. by H. Richard Niebuhr, Harper 1987 pap. $7.95; trans. and ed. by E. Graham Waring and F. W. Strothmann, Ungar 1975 pap. $3.45. Feuerbach's most influential text, arguing for a completely humanistic interpretation of Christianity.

Thoughts on Death and Immortality. Trans. by James A. Massey, Univ. of California Pr. 1981 $33.00 pap. $6.95. Feuerbach's first work, which treated Christianity as an egoistic and inhumane religion.

BOOKS ABOUT FEUERBACH

Engels, Friedrich. *Ludwig Feuerbach and the End of Classical German Philosophy.* Imported Pubns. 1969 pap. $.75. On the role played by Feuerbach in influencing the philosophy of Marx and Engels.

Marx, Karl, and Friedrich Engels. *Feuerbach: Opposition of Materialistic and Idealis-*

tic Outlook. Beekman 1970 $9.95. Evaluation of Feuerbach's view from a Marxist perspective.

Wartofsky, Marx. *Feuerbach.* Cambridge Univ. Pr. 1977 $32.50 1982 pap. $16.95. Important contemporary reexamination and reevaluation of Feuerbach.

HEGEL, GEORG WILHELM FRIEDRICH. 1770–1831

Hegel was born in Stuttgart in Württemberg, Germany, in 1770 and was educated there before going to the university at Tübingen. There he studied theology as well as science, philosophy, and classics from 1788 to 1793. At the university, he became a close friend of the poet HÖLDERLIN (see Vol. 2) and the philosopher Schelling. Hegel was a tutor for several years before being appointed to the faculty of the University of Jena. His early publications indicate that at this period he was greatly influenced by Kant, Fichte, and Schelling as well as by Greek philosophy and the revived philosophy of Spinoza. Hegel and Schelling published a philosophical journal together. In 1807 Hegel completed his first major work, *The Phenomenology of Mind* (or *Spirit*), on the development of spirit or mind in the world. He became rector of a gymnasium at Nuremberg, a professor at Heidelberg, and then finished his career as professor of philosophy at the University of Berlin, succeeding Fichte in that position. During his career as a teacher he published his *Science of Logic* (1812–16), *Encyclopedia of the Philosophical Sciences* (1817), and the *Outlines of the Philosophy of Right* (1821). After his death, his students collected his lectures and notes and published a number of volumes based on them. Hegel's system as it appeared in his writings and in the posthumous works dominated the philosophical scene in Germany for several decades, and had great influence in the rest of Europe and even in the United States, where the St. Louis Hegelians spread his views. His ideas comprise one of the most studied and criticized of modern metaphysical systems. The study of Hegel has been revived in Europe since World War I, and his work has been reexamined as a source of Marxism, of phenomenology, and of existentialism. An enormous amount of literature about Hegel continues to appear, as well as new translations of his works.

BOOKS BY HEGEL

The Phenomenology of Mind. 1807. Trans. by James B. Baillie, intro. by George Lichtheim, Harper 1967 pap. $11.50; [*Muirhead Lib. of Philosophy*] Humanities Pr. 1966 text ed. $35.00; (under the title, *The Phenomenology of the Spirit*), trans. by A. V. Miller and J. N. Findlay, Oxford 1977 $32.50 pap. $12.95. The Miller and Findlay translation is the first new translation of this all-important work. This is Hegel's first major work, developing his theory of the nature of mind and reality.

Hegel's Logic: Being Part One of the Encyclopedia of Philosophical Sciences. 1817. Trans. by William Wallace, Oxford 3d ed. 1975 $42.00 text ed. pap. $8.95. Part of the encyclopedia Hegel wrote at Heidelberg in 1817.

Lectures on the Philosophy of Religion. 1832. Ed. by Peter Hodgson, Univ. of California Pr. 1984 $38.50. Hegel's lectures, published only after his death.

Aesthetics: Lectures on Fine Art. 1835–38. Trans. by T. M. Knox, Oxford 2 vols. 1975 $125.00. Hegel's lectures on the subject, published posthumously.

The Introduction to Hegel's Philosophy of Fine Art. Trans. by Bernard Bosanquet, Gordon Pr. 1976 lib. bdg. $59.95. Bosanquet was a leading figure among the English Hegelians at the end of the nineteenth century.

Lectures on the History of Philosophy. 1833–36. Trans. by F. H. Simson, Humanities Pr. 3 vols. repr. of 1896 ed. 1974 text ed. $65.00. These are based on student notes, but give an important picture of Hegel's interpretation of various philosophers, ancient and modern.

Lectures on the Philosophy of History. 1837. Intro. by Carl J. Friedrich, Dover 1956 text ed. pap. $6.50. This work consists of lecture notes collected by Hegel's students after his death.

Early Theological Writings. Ed. by T. M. Knox and R. Kroner [*Works in Continental Philosophy Ser.*] Univ. of Pennsylvania Pr. repr. of 1948 ed. 1971 pap. $12.95. First publication in English of these early essays.

The Essential Writings. Ed. by Frederick G. Weiss, Harper 1974 pap. $9.95. Selections from many of Hegel's writings.

Hegel's First Principle. Trans. by William T. Harris, Gordon Pr. 1976 lib. bdg. $59.95. Harris was one of the St. Louis Hegelians, the group that introduced Hegel's philosophy to America. A portion of Hegel's *Logic.*

Lectures on the Philosophy of World History: Reason in History. Ed. by H. B. Nisbet [*Cambridge Studies in the History and Theory of Politics*] 1981 $37.50 pap. $16.95. Lectures Hegel gave on the subject, translated from a new German edition.

The Letters. Trans. by Clark Butler and Christine Deiler, Indiana Univ. Pr. 1985 $47.50. Over 750 pages of letters of Hegel.

Natural Law. Ed. by T. M. Knox, Univ. of Pennsylvania Pr. 1975 pap. $9.95. A new translation of Hegel's views on the subject.

The Philosophy of Hegel. Ed. by Carl J. Friedrich [*Modern Lib. College Ed. Ser.*] Random 1965 text ed. pap. $4.00. Selections from a range of Hegel's texts.

The Philosophy of History. Trans. by J. Sibree, Arden Lib. repr. of 1900 ed. $45.00; Peter Smith 1956 $15.50. Lectures collected after Hegel's death.

Hegel's Philosophy of Mind. Trans. by William Wallace, Gordon Pr. 1976 lib. bdg. $59.95. The last part of Hegel's philosophical encyclopedia.

Political Writings. Trans. by T. M. Knox, Garland repr. of 1964 ed. 1984 lib. bdg. $40.00. A collection of essays on political affairs of the early nineteenth century.

Reason in History: A General Introduction to the Philosophy of History. Trans. by Robert S. Hartman, Bobbs 1953 pap. $5.99. Hegel's lecture on the nature of history in a new translation.

Three Essays, 1793–1795: The Tübingen Essay, Berne Fragments, the Life of Jesus. Trans. and ed. by John Dobbins, Univ. of Notre Dame Pr. 1984 text ed. $18.95. Quite interesting material about the early Hegel.

BOOKS ABOUT HEGEL

Althusser, Louis. *Politics and History: Montesquieu, Rousseau, Hegel, Marx.* Schocken repr. of 1972 ed. 1978 pap. $7.95. Very interesting comparative work by a leading European political philosopher.

Avineri, Shlomo. *Hegel's Theory of the Modern State.* [*Cambridge Studies in the History and Theory of Politics*] 1973 $39.50 pap. $13.95. Excellent analysis by a leading Israeli political philosopher.

Baillie, James B. *The Idealistic Construction of Experience.* Garland 1984 $45.00. By one of the first persons to translate Hegel into English.

Caird, Edward. *Hegel.* AMS Pr. repr. of 1883 ed. 1971 $22.50. An important presentation of Hegel at its time, and still interesting.

Cohen, Robert S., and Marx Wartofsky, eds. *Hegel and the Sciences.* Kluwer Academic 1984 lib. bdg. $61.50. A series of essays on Hegel by scholars from Europe and America.

Cook, Daniel. *Language in the Philosophy of Hegel.* Mouton 1973 text ed. pap. $18.00. On Hegel's view of the importance of language in philosophy, and the role language played in his thought.

Croce, Benedetto. *What Is Living and What Is Dead in the Philosophy of Hegel.* Trans. by Douglass Ainslee, Univ. Pr. of Amer. repr. of 1915 ed. 1985 text ed. $10.50; Garland 1984 lib. bdg. $30.00. Very influential writings by one of the twentieth-century philosophers most influenced by Hegel.

Fackenheim, Emil L. *The Religious Dimension in Hegel's Thought.* Peter Smith 1984 $16.25; Univ. of Chicago Pr. repr. of 1967 ed. 1982 pap. $10.00. This work is the result of years of study and analysis and seeks to show that Hegel offers a basis for religion in the modern world.

Findlay, John N. *Hegel: A Re-examination.* [*Muirhead Lib. of Philosophy*] Humanities Pr. repr. of 1958 ed. 1964 text ed. $17.50; Oxford repr. of 1958 ed. 1976 pap. $6.95. A very important reevaluation of Hegel, after all of the criticism of his thoughts by the positivists and analytic philosophers.

Gadamer, Hans Georg. *Hegel's Dialectic: Five Hermeneutical Studies.* Trans. by P. Christopher Smith, Yale Univ. Pr. repr. of 1976 ed. 1982 $18.50 pap. $6.95. Significant interpretation by one of the leading contemporary German hermeneutical philosophers.

Gray, Jesse G. *Hegel's Hellenic Ideal.* Garland 1984 $25.00. An interesting study about Hegel's debt to Greece and his conception of the Greek contribution to the world.

Harris, Errol E. *An Introduction to the Logic of Hegel.* Univ. Pr. of Amer. 1984 $27.75. Useful introduction by one of the best present-day Hegel scholars.

Harris, H. S. *Hegel's Development: Night Thoughts, Jena 1801–1806.* Oxford 1983 $66.00

———. *Hegel's Development: Toward the Sunlight, 1770–1801.* Oxford 1972 $64.00. These two volumes present a striking interpretation of how Hegel's philosophy arose and developed.

Hegel Society of America. *Hegel's Social and Political Thought: The Philosophy of Objective Spirit—Proceedings of the 1976 Hegel Society of America Conference.* Ed. by Donald Philip Verene, Humanities Pr. 1980 text ed. $19.95. Collection of papers given by various Hegel scholars at this conference.

Heidegger, Martin. *Hegel's Concept of Experience.* Octagon repr. of 1970 ed. 1983 $17.50. An interpretation of Hegel by one of the most important twentieth-century philosophers.

Hobhouse, Leonard T. *The Metaphysical Theory of State: A Criticism.* Greenwood repr. of 1918 ed. 1984 lib. bdg. $25.00. A classic critical analysis of Hegel's political theory.

Hook, Sidney. *From Hegel to Marx: Studies in the Intellectual Development of Karl Marx.* Univ. of Michigan Pr. 1962 pap. $6.95. A most important study, focused primarily on Marx, but describing those elements in Hegel that Marx took over.

Hyppolite, Jean. *Genesis and Structure of Hegel's Phenomenology of Spirit.* Trans. by Samuel Cherniak and John Heckman [*Studies in Phenomenology and Existential Philosophy Ser.*] Northwestern Univ. Pr. 1974 text ed. $29.95. pap. $13.95. This work was one of the major ones in reviving interest in and concern about Hegel's thought in France in the post–World War II years. It was most influential in Europe and the United States.

Kain, Philip J. *Schiller, Hegel and Marx: State, Society and the Aesthetic Ideal of Ancient Greece.* McGill-Queens Univ. Pr. 1982 $25.00. A comparison of the evaluations of the artistic and political ideals of ancient Greece by these three important German thinkers.

Kaufmann, Walter. *Hegel: A Reinterpretation.* Univ. of Notre Dame Pr. 1978 o.p. A lively commentary by one of the leading interpreters of nineteenth-century German philosophy.

Lauer, Quentin. *Essays in Hegelian Dialectic.* Fordham Univ. Pr. 1977 $22.50 pap. $9.00. Eleven essays on a range of topics concerning Hegel's philosophy, theology, and influence.

———. *Hegel's Concept of God.* State Univ. of New York 1982 $44.50 pap. $16.95. Analysis of this central concept in Hegel's system by a prominent Catholic philosopher.

———. *Hegel's Idea of Philosophy.* Fordham Univ. Pr. 2d ed. 1983 pap. $7.50. A brief introduction to Hegel, plus a new translation of his introduction to the history of philosophy.

Lowenberg, Jacob. *Hegel's Phenomenology: Dialogues on the Life of the Mind.* Open Court 1965 o.p. A lively presentation of Hegel's thought by one of his leading admirers during the twentieth century in the United States.

Lowith, Karl. *From Hegel to Nietzsche.* Garland 1984 lib. bdg. $55.00. An important study in intellectual history.

Lukàcs, Georg. *The Young Hegel: Studies in the Relations between Dialectics and Economics.* Trans. by Rodney Livingstone, MIT 1975 pap. $12.50. A basic study by one of the most important Marxist theorists in the twentieth century. Influenced the reexamination of both Hegel and Marx throughout Europe.

MacIntyre, Alasdair, ed. *Hegel: A Collection of Critical Essays.* [*Modern Studies in Philosophy*] Univ. of Notre Dame Pr. repr. of 1972 ed. 1976 text ed. $19.95 pap. $6.95. A collective volume put forth as a possible antidote to the revival of interest in Hegel and Hegelian themes.

McTaggart, John M. *Commentary on Hegel's Logic.* Russell repr. of 1910 ed. 1964 $18.00. A most careful commentary by one of the last of the English Hegelians.

———. *Studies in the Hegelian Dialectic.* Russell repr. of 1922 ed. 2d ed. 1964 $20.00. Another fine work by McTaggart, a very rigorous thinker.

Marcuse, Herbert. *Reason and Revolution: Hegel and the Rise of Social Theory.* Humanities Pr. repr. of 1941 ed. 2d ed. 1983 text ed. pap. $15.00. An important study by one of the leaders of the Frankfurt School on how radical social analysis developed out of Hegel's ideas. This work was very influential in the 1960s and 1970s among left-wing thinkers.

Marx, Karl. *Critique of Hegel's "Philosophy of Right."* Ed. by J. O. O'Malley, Cambridge Univ. Pr. 1970 $34.50. One of the seminal works of Karl Marx, clearly indicating his break with Hegel.

Marx, Werner. *Hegel's Phenomenology of Spirit.* Harper 1975 o.p. A useful commentary and interpretation.

Mure, Geoffrey R. *An Introduction to Hegel.* Greenwood repr. of 1950 ed. 1984 $29.75. Presenting Hegel in terms of his views on Aristotle, and how these clarify Hegel's philosophy.

Popper, Karl R. *Open Society and Its Enemies.* Princeton Univ. Pr. 2 vols. 5th rev. ed. 1966 $36.00 pap. $9.95. One of the most critical attacks on Hegel by one of the leading present-day philosophers.

Rosen, Stanley. *G. W. F. Hegel: An Introduction to the Science of Wisdom.* Yale Univ. Pr. 1974 pap. $8.95. A thorough, sympathetic presentation of Hegel for the modern audience.

Schacht, Richard. *Hegel and After: Studies in Continental Philosophy between Kant and Sartre.* Univ. of Pittsburgh Pr. 1975 pap. $12.95. An attempt to provide the background of Continental philosophy for an English-language audience.

Singer, Peter. *Hegel.* [*Past Masters Ser.*] Oxford 1983 $12.95 pap. $3.95. A brief discussion of a few themes in Hegel.

Solomon, Robert C. *In the Spirit of Hegel: A Study of G. W. F. Hegel's "Phenomenology of Spirit."* Oxford 1983 $32.50 pap. $14.95. A commentary by one of the leading present-day interpreters of Continental philosophy.

Stace, Walter T. *The Philosophy of Hegel: A Systematic Exposition.* Dover repr. of 1924 ed. 1955 text ed. pap. $8.95. For years one of the clearest expositions of Hegel available in English.

Stirling, J. H. *The Secret of Hegel: Being the Hegelian System in Origin Principle Form and Matter.* [*Reprints in Philosophy Ser.*] Irvington repr. of 1898 ed. 1981 2d ed. rev. lib. bdg. $49.00. One of the first expositions of Hegel for the English-language audience. It was said when it came out that the author kept Hegel's secret very well.

Taylor, C. *Hegel.* Cambridge Univ. Pr. 1975 $65.00 pap. $19.95. An exposition of Hegel's thought that "admirably combines detailed criticisms and intimacy with the subject" (Stuart Hampshire Olsen).

Verene, Donald P. *Hegel's Recollection: A Study of Images in the Phenomenology of Spirit.* State Univ. of New York 1985 $44.50 pap. $16.95. Examination of Hegel's imagery by a leading Vico scholar.

Wallace, William. *Prolegomena to the Study of Hegel's Philosophy, and Especially of His Logic.* Russell repr. of 1894 ed. 2d ed. 1968 $12.00. By one of the first translators of Hegel into English.

HUSSERL, EDMUND. 1859–1938

Edmund Husserl was originally a mathematician and then became a philosopher. He was a professor at the universities of Halle, Göttingen, and Freiburg in Germany. As a Jew, he was mistreated by the Nazis after they came to power; even Husserl's successor and protégé, MARTIN HEIDEGGER, rector at Freiburg under the Nazis, refused to let Husserl use the library. He published few works during his lifetime, but left an enormous amount of manuscript writing, which was fortunately saved by his students and is gradually being edited, published, and translated into various languages.

Husserl is the founder of the movement known as phenomenology, which tries to base knowledge on pure experience. Its central ideas appeared in his *Logical Investigations* (1900–01) and *Ideas: General Introduction to Pure Phenomenology* (1913). These views were developed by a group of his students, including Martin Heidegger, Merleau-Ponty, and Levin, among others.

BOOKS BY HUSSERL

Cartesian Meditations: An Introduction to a Phenomenology. 1932. Kluwer Academic 1977 pap. $13.00. These are lectures Husserl gave in Paris, introducing his views to the French philosophical public. They are published in the phenomenology series started by the Dutch publisher Martinus Nijhoff (now part of Kluwer Academic), originally edited by L. Van Breda, who along with several of his students had helped save Husserl's papers. The series contains a great many works by and about Husserl in German, French, and English.

The Crisis of European Sciences and Transcendental Phenomenology: An Introduction to *Phenomenological Philosophy.* Trans. by David Carr [*Studies in Phenomenology and Existential Philosophy Ser.*] Northwestern Univ. Pr. 1970 $28.95 pap. $11.95. This work was written two or three years before Husserl's death, and contains the final version of his view.

Ideas Pertaining to a Pure Phenomenology and to a Phenomenological Philosophy. 1913. Trans. by Fred Kersten, Kluwer Academic 1983 text ed. pap. $19.50

Phenomenology and the Foundation of the Sciences. Trans. by Ted Klein and William Polin, Kluwer Academic 1980 $29.00. Part of the continuing publication of Husserl's writings in English.

BOOKS ABOUT HUSSERL

Bachelard, Suzanne. *Study of Husserl's Formal and Transcendental Logic.* Trans. by Lester E. Embree [*Studies in Phenomenology and Existential Philosophy Ser.*] Northwestern Univ. Pr. 1968 $15.95. By one of France's most brilliant logicians.

Derrida, Jacques. *Speech and Phenomena: And Other Essays on Husserl's Theory of Signs.* Trans. by David B. Allison, pref. by Newton Garver [*Studies in Phenomenology and Existential Philosophy Ser.*] Northwestern Univ. Pr. 1973 text ed. $18.95 pap. $7.95. By the leading figure in the deconstructionalist movement.

Dreyfus, Hubert L., and Harrison Hall, eds. *Husserl: Intentionality and Cognitive Science.* MIT 1982 $35.00 pap. $9.95. A collection of writings by various authors.

Gurwitsch, Aron. *Studies in Phenomenological Psychology.* Northwestern Univ. Pr. 1966 o.p. By one of the first members of the phenomenological movement to come to the United States.

Ingarden, Ramon. *On the Motives Which Led Husserl to Transcendental Idealism.* Kluwer Academic 1975 o.p. Ingarden developed an important center of phenomenological thought at the University of Krakow.

Kockelmans, Joseph J. *Edmund Husserl's Phenomenological Psychology.* [*Psychology Ser.*] Humanities Pr. repr. of 1967 ed. 1978 text ed. $17.50. A study of Husserl's psychology, its role and influence.

Levinas, Emmanuel. *The Theory of Intuition in Husserl's Phenomenology.* [*Studies in Phenomenology and Existential Philosophy Ser.*] Northwestern Univ. Pr. repr. of 1973 ed. 1985 pap. $10.95. Levinas was one of Husserl's most important and original students.

Natanson, Maurice. *Edmund Husserl: Philosopher of Infinite Tasks.* [*Studies in Phenomenology and Existential Philosophy Ser.*] Northwestern Univ. Pr. 1973 $22.95 pap. $8.95. A presentation of Husserl's ideas by a leading American phenomenologist.

Sokolowski, Robert. *Husserlian Meditations: How Words Present Things.* [*Studies in Phenomenology and Existential Philosophy Ser.*] Northwestern Univ. Pr. 1974 $22.95 pap. $11.95. An exposition and commentary on Husserl's work.

Spiegelberg, Herbert. *The Context of the Phenomenological Movement.* Kluwer Academic 1981 $29.50. A collection of studies by Spiegelberg on Husserl and his influence.

———. *The Phenomenological Movement.* Kluwer Academic 1981 3d ed. rev. & enl. $106.00. An all-important history of the phenomenological movement by one of its early members. A fourth edition will be published shortly.

Willard, Dallas. *Logic and the Objectivity of Knowledge: Studies in Husserl's Early Philosophy.* [*Ser. in Continental Thought*] Ohio Univ. Pr. 1984 text ed. $29.95. A scholarly exposition of Husserl's early philosophical writings.

JAMES, WILLIAM. 1842–1910

William James, the leading figure of the movement in American philosophy called "pragmatism," was born in New York. He was the son of Henry James, Sr., a minor New England transcendentalist, who was one of the leading advocates of Emmanuel Swedenborg's Church of the New Jerusalem (a movement to which the English poet WILLIAM BLAKE [see Vol. 1] also belonged). William James was also the brother of HENRY JAMES (see Vol. 1), and it was often said that William wrote philosophy books as if they were novels, and Henry wrote novels as if they were philosophy books. Thus the easy style of William is contrasted with the ponderous one of Henry. William was educated in the United States and in Europe. He studied painting, science, and medicine, taking a medical degree at Harvard in 1869. He took part in Louis Agassiz's expedition to Brazil and also did advanced scientific and medical study in Germany. He was then appointed an instructor in anatomy and physiology at Harvard in 1872, moved on to become an assistant professor of psychology, and from 1880 a professor of philosophy. He gave the Gifford Lectures in Edinburgh in 1901 and 1902. His first major publication was his *Principles of Psychology* (1890). Building on his psychological researches and his discussions in a philosophy club with Charles Sanders Peirce and Chauncey Wright, he began developing a theory about how human beings think, and what forms the bases for their beliefs. He characterized this with a term he borrowed from Peirce, "pragmatism." As he devoted more and more of his time to developing his philosophical approach, and teaching philosophy, he expounded the pragmatic theory in a series of books and essays that have provided the fundamental statement of the view. William James, possibly from his parental upbringing, had a religious temperament, unlike many of his tough-minded scientific colleagues. Using both his pragmatic method and his psychological researches, he sought to defend some kind of religious attitude in his essay "The Will to Believe" (1897) and in his book *The Varieties of Religious Experience* (1902). As the leading spokesman for pragmatism, he defended this theory against idealistic opponents in the United States, and against more positivistic thinkers like BERTRAND RUSSELL. (See also Volume 3.)

BOOKS BY JAMES

The Writings of William James. Ed. by John M. McDermott, Univ. of Chicago Pr. 1978 pap. $20.00. A collection of selections from James's main works.

Collected Essays and Reviews. Ed. by Ralph B. Perry, Russell repr. of 1920 ed. 1969 $20.00. Thirty-nine articles from 1869 to 1910.

The Works of William James. Harvard Univ. Pr. 1975–88 17 vols. $35.00–$40.00

Essays in Pragmatism. Ed. by Alburey Castell, Free Pr. 1974 pap. $8.95; Hafner 1970 $8.95. Seven of James's best-known philosophical essays.

Essays in Psychology. Ed. by Frederick Burkhardt, Fredson Bowers, and Ignas K. Skrupskelis, intro. by William R. Woodward [*Works of William James*] Harvard Univ. Pr. 1983 text ed. $40.00. This is Volume 13 of *The Works of William James.*

Essays in Radical Empiricism and a Pluralistic Universe. 1912. Harvard Univ. Pr. 1976 $25.00; Peter Smith repr. 1967 $19.00. Two of the most basic statements of the pragmatic theory of knowledge and of the nature of the world.

Essays in Religion and Morality. Harvard Univ. Pr. 1981 text ed. $25.00. Collection of essays on these subjects.

The Principles of Psychology. 1980. Dover 2 vols. 1950 text ed. pap. ea. $9.95; Harvard Univ. Pr. 1981 $27.50 1983 pap. $17.50; Peter Smith 2 vols. 1950 $33.50. James's first major work. "This critical text of the preeminent classic of American psychology incorporates the results of the highest standards of textual scholarship to present James's intentions in a definitive edition.... Awarded the Seal of the Center for Scholarly Editions" (*Choice*).

The Will to Believe and Human Immortality. 1897. Dover 1956 pap. $5.95; Peter Smith 1956 $15.75. A pragmatic defense of some kind of religious belief.

The Varieties of Religious Experience: A Study in Human Nature. 1902. [*Works of William James*] Harvard Univ. Pr. 1985 text ed. $45.00; Modern Lib. 1936 $6.95; New Amer. Lib. 1958 pap. $4.50; [*Penguin Amer. Lib. Ser.*] 1982 pap. $4.95. James's major work on the study of religion, its effect on people and its value.

Pragmatism. 1907. Ed. by Ralph Barton Perry, New Amer. Lib. 1965 pap. $6.95. Paperback edition of this basic work, edited by one of James's leading students.

Pragmatism: A New Name for Some Old Ways of Thinking. 1907. Ed. by Frederick Burkhardt, Harvard Univ. Pr. 1976 $27.50. Reissue of James's immensely popular and influential work. "In addition to the 'clear text,' it provides a splendid historical, philosophical, and biographical introduction by H. S. Thayer, notes on the text with full bibliographical data, a complete account of the textual history and critical apparatus (including four appendixes of documents related to the text), and a complete index" (*Choice*).

The Meaning of Truth: A Sequel to Pragmatism. 1909. Ed. by Frederick Burkhardt, Fredson Bowers, and Ignas K. Skrupskelis, Harvard Univ. Pr. 1976 text ed. $25.00. Reissue of James's defense of pragmatism against such early critics as Bradley and Russell.

Some Problems of Philosophy: A Beginning of an Introduction to Philosophy. Greenwood repr. of 1911 Ed. 1968 lib. bdg. $22.50; Harvard Univ. Pr. 1979 text ed. $30.00. James's last work, unfinished, contains his theory of perception.

A Pluralistic Universe. 1909. Folcroft repr. of 1912 ed. 1973 lib. bdg. $40.00; Harvard Univ. Pr. 1977 $30.00; Norwood repr. of 1912 ed. 1980 lib. bdg. $45.00. James's criticism of idealism challenges Hegel, Fechner, and Bergson.

Memories and Studies. 1911. Ed. by Henry James, Folcroft repr. of 1911 ed. 1973 lib. bdg. $30.00; Greenwood repr. of 1911 ed. 1968 lib. bdg. $22.50; Scholarly repr. of 1911 ed. 1971 $15.00. Fifteen popular essays and addresses, chosen by his son, Henry James.

Pragmatism and The Meaning of Truth. Intro. by A. J. Ayer, Harvard Univ. Pr. 1978 $25.00 pap. $8.95. Two of James's most important statements of, and defenses of, his philosophy.

Pragmatism and Other Essays. Ed. by J. L. Blau, Washington Square Pr. 1983 pap. $4.95. A collection of some of James's essays edited by a leading historian of American philosophy.

William James on Psychical Research. Ed. by Gardner Murphy and Robert Ballou, Kelley repr. of 1960 ed. 1979 $27.50. "This book, ably compiled and edited, contains lectures, articles, letters, and a detailed account of sittings with the medium Mrs. Piper, in whom James was interested from 1885 right up to the time of his death in 1910" (*New Statesman*).

The Letters of William James. Ed. by Henry James, Kraus Repr. 2 vols. in 1 1920 o.p. James's correspondence edited by his son.

BOOKS ABOUT JAMES

Ayer, Alfred J. *Origins of Pragmatism: Studies in the Philosophy of Charles Sanders Peirce and William James.* Freeman Cooper 1968 $12.50. A lively discussion of the two philosophers, and of pragmatism in general, by one of England's leading analytic philosophers.

Barzun, Jacques. *A Stroll with William James.* Harper 1983 $19.45; Univ. of Chicago Pr. 1984 pap. $10.95. An interesting and witty appreciation of James as a person and as a thinker by one of America's best intellectual historians and literary critics.

Brennan, Bernard P. *William James.* [*Twayne's U.S. Authors Ser.*] New College & Univ. Pr. 1968 pap. $8.95. A general presentation of James's philosophy.

Corti, W. *The Philosophy of William James.* Adler's 1977 pap. $25.90. Proceedings of an international conference evaluating James's philosophy.

Flournoy, T. *Philosophy of William James.* [*Select Bibliographies Repr. Ser.*] Ayer repr. of 1917 ed. 1978 $22.00. A presentation of James's philosophy by this Swiss philosopher.

Ford, Marcus P. *William James's Philosophy: A New Perspective.* Univ. of Massachusetts Pr. 1982 lib. bdg. $13.50. "This book is concerned with James's thought overall. . . . [Ford] believes that James's theory of truth is a confused form of the correspondence theory of truth and that James was, for the most part, a panpsychist" (Publisher's note).

James, William. *In Commemoration of William James, 1842–1942.* AMS Pr. repr. of 1942 ed. 1981 $18.00. A volume of addresses made by various scholars in honor of the one-hundredth anniversary of James's birth at celebrations held by the Conference on Methods in Philosophy and the Sciences, the Eastern Division of the American Philosophical Association, and the Western Division of the American Philosophical Association.

Kallen, Horace M. *William James and Henri Bergson: A Study in Contrasting Theories.* AMS repr. of 1914 ed. 1975 $24.50. Kallen was one of the best pragmatists trained at Harvard in James's time.

Levinson, Henry S. *The Religious Investigations of William James.* [*Studies in Religion*] Univ. of North Carolina Pr. 1981 $27.50. "A first-class analysis of James, sustaining the high level in making clear relations with other systems and figures of James's lifetime and the implications of positions and currents" (*Choice*).

Marcell, David W. *Progress and Pragmatism: James, Dewey, Beard and the American Idea of Progress.* [*Contributions in Amer. Studies*] Greenwood 1974 lib. bdg. $29.95. A comparative study of these three thinkers in relation to the American view of progressive development.

Moore, Edward C. *American Pragmatism: Peirce, James and Dewey.* Greenwood repr. of 1961 ed. 1984 lib. bdg. $45.00. This volume has become one of the standard presentations and evaluations of the subject.

Perry, Ralph B. *Annotated Bibliography of the Writings of William James.* Folcroft repr. of 1920 ed. 1972 lib. bdg. $22.50; Norwood repr. of 1920 ed. 1980 lib. bdg. $15.00; Verbeke 1968 $12.50

———. *The Thought and Character of William James.* Greenwood 2 vols. repr. of 1935 ed. 1974 lib. bdg. $78.00. An excellent intellectual biography by one of James's leading students.

Reck, Andrew J. *Introduction to William James: An Essay and Selected Texts.* Indiana Univ. Pr. 1967 o.p. A fine essay on James, plus some important texts; "gives the broad outline of James's philosophy . . . [stressing its] contemporary relevance" (*LJ*).

Vanden Burgt, Robert J. *The Religious Philosophy of William James*. Nelson-Hall 1981 text ed. $19.95 pap. $9.95. "On the whole Vanden Burgt's study . . . makes a unique and valuable contribution. [He] has written in clear, nontechnical language an introduction to the religious philosophy of James and has done it in such a way as to set James within the context of contemporary discussions in theology and the philosophy of religion" (*Christian Century*).

Wild, John D. *The Radical Empiricism of William James*. Greenwood repr. of 1969 ed. 1980 lib. bdg. $37.50. The relation of James's thought to modern Continental philosophy and such philosophers as Heidegger, Merleau-Ponty, and Husserl.

KIERKEGAARD, SØREN. 1813–1855

Kierkegaard, a great Danish philosopher and theologian, was hardly known outside his homeland until the twentieth century. His striking critical attack on traditional philosophy (especially the German idealism accepted by many of his countrymen) and his advocacy of acceptance of beliefs on pure faith became the basis of the modern philosophy called "existentialism."

Kierkegaard was born and raised in Copenhagen. He studied philosophy and theology, writing a master's essay on Socrates' concept of irony, a notion that obviously played a role in his own writing. He was trained in Hegelian philosophy and in liberal, critical interpretation of Christianity and the Bible. He went to Germany to continue his studies, and a brief acquaintance with the actual world of German idealism led him to rebel. He began publishing a series of strange and somewhat baffling works, attributed to pseudonymous authors. Some were fictional, such as the famous *Either/Or* (1843). Some were religious rhapsodies, such as the *Edifying Discourses* (1847). A central group were philosophical-theological writings starting with the *Philosophical Fragments* (1844), a short, incisive presentation of Kierkegaard's alternative to traditional philosophizing and liberal Christianity. This was followed by a massive sequel, *The Concluding Unscientific Postscript* (1846), which is in part an extremely critical attack on Hegelianism and on the German idealistic enterprise of system building. A group of works such as *Fear and Trembling* (1843) and *The Sickness unto Death* (1848) apply the Kierkegaardian approach to specific problems of human existence. The highly polemical *Training in Christianity* (1850) attacks any effort at constructing a rational basis for Christian religious belief. The last phase of Kierkegaard's work consists of tirades against Christianity as it was practiced in his day, what he called an assault on Christianity. These works were apparently written by a bewildering assortment of pseudonymous authors, who take different positions and argue with each other. Finally some of the works are put forth with the claim that "S. Kierkegaard" is responsible for their publication, and finally that S. Kierkegaard is their author. The interpretation of the authorships has been a continuing attempt to unravel what Kierkegaard was doing. He himself said he could not just present his views directly, but had to use indirect discourse, which the authorships represent in differing ways. Various scholars have offered theories, usually contending there was a definite plan in choosing the pretended authors. Some have seen it as an attempt to make clear to his rejected fiancée why he could not marry her, but had to go his lonely way attacking the philosophical and religious establishment. Others have seen it as a way of building up from a philosophical critique to a very personal and individualistic statement of the meaning of religious belief, a statement that could emerge only from this dialogue of many kinds of authors, at various stages of intellectual and spiritual quest that Kierkegaard himself had undertaken.

Kierkegaard was regarded as a crank in the Denmark of his day, and was considered much like Hans Christian Andersen's ugly duckling. His work was practically unknown outside Scandinavia. However, in the beginning of the twentieth century, his writings were discovered by both French and German thinkers, translated, and much discussed; he was discovered in the United States a couple of decades later. His defense of religion by stressing its irrational character was pursued by various neo-orthodox theologians, and by the Russian Orthodox theorist Lev Chestov. His critique of accepted philosophy, and his emphasis on the personal need to make a commitment in order to find a way of life even though the commitment could not be justified, were taken up by the group of European thinkers who became known as existentialists. Some shared Kierkegaard's religious quest, others (such as JEAN-PAUL SARTRE [see also Vol. 2] and ALBERT CAMUS [see Vol. 2]), offered an atheistical version. Since World War II most of Kierkegaard's writings have been translated, and there is an ever-growing body of literature about him and his theories.

BOOKS BY KIERKEGAARD

Kierkegaard Anthology. Modern Lib. 1959 $3.95. A well-rounded collection of selections from the various sides of Kierkegaard's writing.

The Concept of Irony: With Constant Reference to Socrates. 1841. Trans. by Lee M. Cappel [*Midland Bks.*] Indiana Univ. Pr. 1968 pap. $7.95. This is Kierkegaard's master essay. Cappel's introduction is illuminating.

Either/Or. Trans. by Walter Lowrie, Princeton Univ. Pr. 2 vols. 1971 pap. ea. $7.95

Diary of a Seducer. Trans. by Gerd Gillhoff, Ungar 1966 text ed. $7.95. One of the main stories is *Either/Or.*

Fear and Trembling. 1843. Trans. by Alastair Hanny [*Penguin Class. Ser.*] 1986 pap. $3.95

Philosophical Fragments. 1844. Trans. by David Swenson, ed. by Niels Thulstrup [*Amer.-Scandinavian Foundation Ser.*] Princeton Univ. Pr. 2d ed. 1962 o.p. In addition to many notes, this edition contains a commentary on the work.

The Concluding Unscientific Postscript. 1846. Trans. by Walter Lowrie [*Amer.-Scandinavian Foundation Ser.*] Princeton Univ. Pr. 1941 pap. $10.50

Works of Love: Some Christian Reflections in the Form of Discourses. 1847. Trans. by Howard V. Hong and Edna H. Hong, Harper 1964 pap. $7.95; Peter Smith 1962 $17.75. Kierkegaard's important discussion of Christian ethics.

Christian Discourses. 1848. Trans. by Walter Lowrie, Princeton Univ. Pr. 1971 pap. $10.50. Some religious discussions on various themes.

The Sickness unto Death: A Christian Psychological Exposition for Upbuilding and Awakening. 1848. Trans. by Howard V. Hong and Edna H. Hong, Princeton Univ. Pr. 1980 $27.50 pap. $9.50. Discussion of the meaning of life.

Attack upon "Christendom." 1854–55. Trans. by Walter Lowrie, Princeton Univ. Pr.

1944 pap. $8.50. These are Kierkegaard's polemical writings against the religious establishment and the comfortable believers, written at the end of his life.

The Concept of Anxiety. Trans. by Howard V. Hong and Edna H. Hong, Princeton Univ. Pr. 1980 $29.50 pap. $7.95. A psychological study of sin.

Purity of Heart. Trans. by Douglas Steere, Harper 1956 pap. $7.95. On the nature of spiritual life.

Training in Christianity. 1850. Trans. by Walter Lowrie [*Amer.-Scandinavian Foundation Ser.*] Princeton Univ. Pr. 1944 $31.00 pap. $7.95. One of the major "indirect" statements of Kierkegaard's theology.

Two Ages: The Age of Revolution and the Present Age. Trans. by Howard V. Hong and Edna H. Hong, Princeton Univ. Pr. 1978 text ed. $22.50. This work started out as a book review and became an important essay about literature.

Søren Kierkegaard's Journals and Papers. Trans. by Howard V. Hong and Edna H. Hong, Indiana Univ. Pr. 7 vols. 1967–78 ea. $30.00–$60.00. An all-important source for following Kierkegaard's development and interpreting his ideas.

BOOKS ABOUT KIERKEGAARD

Arbaugh, George E., and George B. Arbaugh. *Kierkegaard's Authorship: A Guide to the Writings of Kierkegaard.* Augustana College 1968 $6.95. A useful guide to unraveling the various pseudonymous authors used by Kierkegaard.

Collins, James. *The Mind of Kierkegaard: With a New Preface and Updated Bibliographical Notes.* Princeton Univ. Pr. repr. of 1965 ed. 1983 $29.00 pap. $9.50. Important study of Kierkegaard by the leading Catholic historian of philosophy in America.

Diem, Hermann. *Kierkegaard's Dialectic of Existence.* Trans. by Harold Knight, Greenwood repr. of 1959 ed. 1978 lib. bdg. $22.50. A critique of much modern Kierkegaard interpretation, with a presentation of an alternative reading.

Elrod, J. W. *Being and Existence in Kierkegaard's Pseudonymous Works.* Princeton Univ. Pr. 1975 $30.50. A very careful examination of a key thread in Kierkegaard's thought.

———. *Kierkegaard and Christendom.* Princeton Univ. Pr. 1981 $30.50. A study of Kierkegaard's actual relation to the Christian world.

Hannay, Alstair. *Kierkegaard.* [*Arguments of the Philosophers Ser.*] Methuen 1982 $29.95. Kierkegaard presented by a leading exponent of contemporary linguistic philosophy.

Lebowitz, Naomi. *Kierkegaard: A Life of Allegory.* Louisiana State Univ. Pr. 1985 text ed. $25.00. A very sensitive analysis by a literary critic.

Lowrie, Walter. *Kierkegaard.* Peter Smith 2 vols. repr. 1970 $28.50. Lowrie's complete biography, plus his interpretation of Kierkegaard's thought. This was the first work to give the English language audience a large picture of Kierkegaard's philosophy.

———. *Short Life of Kierkegaard.* Princeton Univ. Pr. 1942 pap. $8.95. The first biography available in English.

Mackey, Louis. *Kierkegaard: A Kind of Poet.* Univ. of Pennsylvania Pr. 1971 $26.25 pap. $11.95. Argues that Kierkegaard was neither a theologian nor a philosopher, but a poet.

McKinnon, Alastair, ed: *Computational Analysis of Kierkegaard's Samlede Vaerker.* Princeton Univ. Pr. 6 vols. 1979 $495.00. A concordance of all the words that appear in Kierkegaard's writings, done by computer analysis. Very helpful if one wants to follow Kierkegaard's use of certain concepts.

Perkins, Robert L., ed. *Kierkegaard's Fear and Trembling: Critical Appraisals.* Univ. of

Alabama Pr. 1981 text ed. $24.75 pap. $14.75. A collection of evaluations of this great work of Kierkegaard by different scholars.

Sontag, Frederick. *A Kierkegaard Handbook.* John Knox 1980 pap. $7.25. A reference guide for leading ideas in Kierkegaard. "Rather than presenting an overall systematic development of Kierkegaard's thought, Sontag concentrates on complementary categories such as 'happy/unhappy,' 'inwardness/communication,' 'necessity/possibility,' 'repetition/freedom,' which nevertheless lead to a unifying comprehension of Kierkegaard's total work" (*LJ*).

Stack, George J. *Kierkegaard's Existential Ethics.* [*Studies in Humanities*] Univ. of Alabama Pr. 1977 $15.00 pap. $5.50. An attempt to find a central focus in Kierkegaard's thought.

———. *On Kierkegaard: Philosophical Fragments.* [*Eclipse Bks.*] Humanities Pr. 1976 text ed. pap. $9.95. A commentary on this important, basic work.

Taylor, Mark C. *Kierkegaard's Pseudonymous Authorship: A Study of Time and Self.* Princeton Univ. Pr. 1975 $45.00. A careful examination of these themes as they develop in the pseudonymous works.

Thompson, Josiah. *Kierkegaard.* Knopf 1973 o.p. This is one of the best surveys of Kierkegaard's views.

———. *Kierkegaard: A Collection of Critical Essays.* Doubleday 1972 o.p. An excellent collection of articles on Kierkegaard by several scholars, dealing with many aspects of Kierkegaard's thought. Unfortunately it is out of print.

Thulstrup, Niels. *Kierkegaard's Concluding Unscientific Postscript.* Trans. by Robert J. Widenmann, Princeton Univ. Pr. 1984 $60.00. The commentary is most helpful with this central and difficult text of Kierkegaard.

———. *Kierkegaard's Relation to Hegel.* Trans. by George Stengren, Princeton Univ. Pr. 1980 $40.00 pap. $17.00. An important study. One of the key focuses of Kierkegaard's point of view.

MARX, KARL. 1818–1883

Karl Marx was born in Trier, Germany. His father was a lawyer who had converted from Judaism to Lutheranism during the reaction after Napoleon's fall. Marx studied at the universities of Bonn and Berlin. He wrote various radical publications and had to leave Germany for Paris and Brussels because of his political activities. He met FRIEDRICH ENGELS (see Vol. 3), the son of an English factory owner, and together in 1847 they wrote *The Communist Manifesto* and then in the following year became involved in the 1848 revolution. After the revolution's failure, Marx moved to England with his family, remaining there the rest of his life. He did hack writing to support himself and his family, and was also partially supported by Engels. Much of his time was spent in the British Museum, writing his great work, *Das Kapital* (1867–69), which was still not completed at the time of his death. Marx was active in starting what became the Communist movement, and wrote many works to further the cause. He is now regarded as the basic philosopher of Communism, or of its theory, Marxism. He is also considered one of the most influential thinkers who ever lived. As the bibliography below indicates, there has been more interest in recent years in his early philosophical writings than in his later economic and political ones. (See also Volume 3.)

BOOKS BY MARX

Writings of the Young Marx on Philosophy and Society. Ed. and trans. by Lloyd D. Easton and Kurt H. Guddat, Doubleday 1967 o.p. A collection of the early writings of Marx.

The Portable Karl Marx. Ed. by Eugene Kamenka, Penguin 1983 pap. $6.95. A collection of Marx's writings by a leading historian of social philosophy.

Economic and Philosophy Manuscripts. 1844. Ed. by Dirk Struik, Intl. Pubs. Co. 1964 $3.25. The so-called early Marx writings, which precede the more systematic formulation of his views.

The Communist Manifesto. 1848. Intl. Pubs. Co. 1983 $3.25; [*Crofts Class Ser.*] Harlan Davidson 1955 text ed. pap. $3.25; New York Labor News 7th ed. 1968 $1.25; pref. by Leon Trotsky, Path Pr. 1968. $.95; intro by A. J. P. Taylor, Penguin (Pelican) 1968 $2.25; Regnery-Gateway 1982 pap. $3.95; ed. by D. Ryazanoff, Russell repr. of 1930 ed. 1963 $18.00; ed. by Joseph Katz, trans. by Samuel Moore, intro. by F. B. Randall, Washington Square Pr. pap. $2.95

Capital. 1867–69. Ed. by Friedrich Engels, Intl. Pubs. Co. 3 vols. 1967 $35.00; trans. by Ben Fowkes and David Fernbach, Random (Vintage) 3 vols. 1977–82 pap. ea. $7.95–$10.95. A standard edition of Marx's major economic-philosophical theory.

(and Friedrich Engels). *Feuerbach: Opposition of Materialistic and Idealistic Outlook.* Beekman 1970 $9.95. Marxist criticism of Feuerbach.

(and Friedrich Engels). *On Historical Materialism.* Beekman 1972 $18.00; Intl. Pubs. Co. 1975 pap. $4.25. A statement of Marxist materialist metaphysics.

BOOKS ABOUT MARX

Avineri, Shlomo. *Varieties of Marxism.* Kluwer Academic 1977 o.p. An interesting study by one of Israel's leading political theorists.

Berlin, Isaiah. *Karl Marx: His Life and Environment.* Oxford 4th ed. 1978 pap. $7.95. A superb picture of the world Marx grew up in and how he developed intellectually.

Bottomore, Tom, ed. *Modern Interpretations of Marx.* Basil Blackwell 1981 o.p. A collection of essays giving a range of contemporary interpretations of Marx.

Garaudy, Roger. *Karl Marx: Evolution of His Thought.* Trans. by Nan Apotheker, Greenwood repr. of 1967 ed. 1976 lib. bdg. $27.50. By a philosopher who used to be a leading theoretician for the French Communist Party.

Gould, Carol C. *Marx's Social Ontology: Individuality and Community in Marx's Theory of Social Reality.* MIT 1978 pap. $6.95. A careful study of Marx's view of man and society.

Hook, Sidney. *From Hegel to Marx: Studies in the Intellectual Development of Karl Marx.* Univ. of Michigan Pr. 1962 pap. $6.95. An important examination of how Marx's theory developed.

McMurty, John. *The Structure of Marx's World-View.* Princeton Univ. Pr. 1978 $27.50 pap. $7.95. An attempt to put Marx's views in terms of an ontological framework.

Moore, Stanley. *Marx on the Choice between Socialism and Communism.* Harvard Univ. Pr. 1980 $12.50. "Moore . . . concludes that Marx's historical materialism does account for the transition of a socialist economy with exchange, but that the alleged superiority of a communist economy without exchange is based on arguments derived from Hegel and Feuerbach, not historical materialism" (*LJ*).

Singer, Peter. *Marx.* [*Past Masters Ser.*] Oxford 1980 pap. $3.95. "Singer deftly sorts out key ideas and explains clearly even the most difficult of them, e.g., Marx's concept of alienation. His is as good an introduction to Marx as any I know" (*LJ*).

Tucker, Robert C. *Philosophy and Myth in Karl Marx*. Cambridge Univ. Pr. 2d ed. 1972 $44.50 pap. $12.95. An examination of how Marx's thought developed, and a critical reinterpretation of it.

Wood, Allen. *Karl Marx*. [*Arguments of the Philosophers Ser.*] Methuen 1981 $26.95 1985 pap. $14.95. "Pays meticulous attention both to Marx's own pronouncements and to the philosophical milieu from which Marx's philosophy arose. Marx scholars and neophytes alike will profit from this superb book" (*Choice*).

MILL, JOHN STUART. 1806–1873

John Stuart Mill was the son of James Mill, a philosopher and psychologist, who was the leading disciple of the English utilitarian JEREMY BENTHAM (see Vol. 3). Young Mill was a prodigy who was raised by his father according to Bentham's principles of education. By the time he was eight years old, he was reading Greek and Latin and was given the task of tutoring his sister in various academic subjects. While he was a teenager, Mill began publishing serious learned articles in magazines like the *Edinburgh Review*. By the time he was 20, he was one of the leading spokesmen for utilitarianism. He suffered a breakdown, and realized that his strict and isolated upbringing had had a dehumanizing effect on him, so he began to broaden his interests and developed a modified version of his original views. His *Autobiography* (1873) poignantly describes his intellectual and emotional development. He fell in love with Harriet Taylor, the wife of a Unitarian minister, who refused to give her a divorce. Mill realized through his association with Mrs. Taylor the legal plight of women and wrote on their behalf to try to change the situation. He married Harriet Taylor after her husband died, but she died soon afterward. Mill attributed his mature views, which appear in his great political classic *On Liberty* (1859) and his largest philosophical writing, the *System of Logic* (1843), to his intellectual companionship with Harriet Taylor. In 1865 Mill was elected to Parliament for one term and tried to act solely from philosophical examinations of the issues. As a result, some of his constituents rejected him in the subsequent election. Toward the end of his life, Mill became sympathetic to the democratic socialism that was then being developed by Robert Owen. He is regarded as one of the most important theorists of British empiricism and one of the classical advocates of civil liberties and democratic government. (See also Volume 3.)

BOOKS BY MILL

Collected Works. Univ. of Toronto Pr. 1963– ea. $45.00–$175.00. This scholarly edition is still in progress; several volumes have already appeared. Includes letters, autobiographies, and literary essays.

An Examination of Sir William Hamilton's Philosophy. Ed. by J. M. Robson, intro. by Alan Ryan, Univ. of Toronto Pr. 1979 $45.00. Mill's careful discussion of the philosophy of common sense.

System of Logic: Ratiocinative and Inductive. 1843. Ibis Pub. VA repr. of 1872 ed. 8th ed. 1986 lib. bdg. $40.00 text ed. pap. $25.00; ed. by J. M. Robson, Univ. of Toronto Pr. 2 vols. 1974 $85.00

On Liberty. 1859. Ed. by Currin V. Shields, Bobbs 1956 pap. $5.99; ed. by Alburey Castell [*Crofts Class. Ser.*] Harlan Davidson 1947 text ed. pap. $3.50; ed. by David Spitz [*Norton Critical Eds.*] 1975 text ed. pap. $5.95; Penguin 1982 pap. $3.95; Prometheus Bks. 1986 pap. $3.95

Utilitarianism. 1863. Ed. by Oskar Piest, Bobbs 1957 pap. $4.24; [*Fount Religious Pap. Ser.*] Collins 1976 pap. $2.95; ed. by George Sher, Hackett 1979 text ed. pap. $2.50; ed. by Samuel Gorovitz [*Text and Critical Essays Ser.*] Macmillan 1971 pap. $15.12. Mill's statement and defense of a modified version of Bentham's original theory.

(and Harriet T. Mill). *The Subjection of Women.* 1869. Ed. by Sue Mansfield [*Crofts Class. Ser.*] Harlan Davidson 1980 text ed. $12.95 pap. $3.95; Merrimack 1983 pap. $6.95; MIT 1970 pap. $4.95. One of the seminal works showing the condition of women, the supposed justifications of that condition, and needed reforms.

The Autobiography of John Stuart Mill. 1873. Columbia Univ. Pr. 1924 pap. $12.00; ed. by Jack Stillinger, Houghton Mifflin 1964 pap. $5.95

Three Essays on Religion. AMS Pr. repr. of 1874 ed. 1974 $23.45; Greenwood repr. of 1874 ed. 1969 lib. bdg. $37.50. These essays are one of the best statements of agnosticism.

Representative Government and the Degeneration of Democracy. Inst. Econ. Pol. 2 vols. 1985 $187.95. Important study of the theory of representative governments, and their faults in practice.

BOOKS ABOUT MILL

Bain, Alexander. *John Stuart Mill: A Criticism with Personal Recollections.* Kelley repr. of 1882 ed. 1969 $22.50; Richard West repr. of 1882 ed. 1973 $10.00. An important intellectual biography of Mill by an empiricist of the following generation in England.

Duncan, G. *Marx and Mill: Two Views of Social Conflict and Social Harmony.* Cambridge Univ. Pr. 1973 $44.50 pap. $12.95. A comparative study of these two contemporary political philosophers.

Ellery, John B. *John Stuart Mill.* [*Eng. Authors Ser.*] G. K. Hall 1970 o.p. A good general presentation of J. S. Mill's contributions in philosophy and politics.

Halevy, Elie. *The Growth of Philosophical Radicalism.* Faber 3d ed. 1972 o.p. The best history of the philosophical movement that runs from Bentham to J. S. Mill.

Hayek, Friedrich A. von, ed. *John Stuart Mill and Harriet Taylor: Their Friendship and Subsequent Marriage.* Kelley repr. of 1951 ed. 1969 o.p.; Richard West repr. of 1951 ed. 1979 lib. bdg. $40.00. A study by one of the leading economic theorists of the twentieth century.

Lane, Michael. *Bibliography of the Works of John Stuart Mill.* Univ. of Toronto Pr. 1982 $35.00

Marcuse, Herbert. *A Critique of Pure Tolerance.* Beacon 1969 $6.95. One of the strongest attacks on Mill's view of civil liberties by a leading Marxist thinker.

Neff, Emery. *Carlyle and Mill.* Hippocrene Bks. 1964 lib. bdg. $26.00. An interesting picture of these two brilliant intellectuals who were originally friends and became advocates of completely opposing philosophies.

Spencer, Herbert. *John Stuart Mill: His Life and Works.* Folcroft repr. of 1873 ed. 1976 lib. bdg. $17.50. By those who considered themselves Mill's disciples, written shortly after his death.

Stephen, Leslie. *The English Utilitarians: Jeremy Bentham, James Mill, John Stuart*

Mill. Peter Smith 3 vols. in 1 repr. 1950 $24.00. An excellent study of these thinkers, by a leading intellectual historian at the end of the nineteenth century.

NIETZSCHE, FRIEDRICH WILHELM. 1844–1900

Nietzsche was born in 1844 in Röcken, Germany, the son of a Lutheran pastor of Polish ancestry. He was raised in Prussia, where he attended a military academy, and then studied classics, theology, and philosophy at the universities of Bonn and Leipzig. At the age of 25, he was appointed professor at the University of Basel in Switzerland. There he lectured on classical and ancient philosophy. Nietzsche briefly served as a medical orderly in the German army in the Franco-Prussian war, during which he was badly injured. In 1872, he published his first important work, *The Birth of Tragedy Out of the Spirit of Music.* Although this work was much influenced by his admiration for RICHARD WAGNER (see Vol. 3) and Schopenhauer, by 1878 Nietzsche had broken with both of them. He resigned from the University of Basel that year because of bad health. For the next ten years, he lived in retirement, writing the books for which he is most famous, including *Thus Spake Zarathustra* (1883-91), *Beyond Good and Evil* (1886), and the *Genealogy of Morals* (1887). He wrote nothing further. At the beginning of 1889, he became insane and was institutionalized until his death in 1900. His sister was responsible for publishing material that existed in manuscript, including his autobiography, *Ecce Homo, The Antichrist, Nietzsche Contra Wagner,* and a patchwork of his notes, *The Will to Power.* Nietzsche was not recognized as a serious thinker and writer until the onset of his illness, when the Danish critic Georg Brandes lectured on his work. His ideas influenced many in different directions. He was a hero to the Nazis, while others claim that he was misunderstood and misrepresented by them. Nietzsche was against German nationalism and anti-Semitism, but his sister edited some of his work to disguise this. His works are now considered classics, whose messages of biological humanism, the joy and importance of creativity, and the possibility that values and religion are just human creations have to be taken seriously as key parts of modern ideology.

As James Gutman wrote in *The Nation* (1968), "Nietzsche's thoughts and visions are increasingly relevant. His analyses of human weakness and his vision of the possibilities of human power, his awareness of the dissolution of traditional values of Christendom, his sense of urgency of a revaluation of traditional values, and the almost apocalyptic anticipation of wars to come make his writings singularly topical."

BOOKS BY NIETZSCHE

Complete Works. Ed. by Oscar Levy, Gordon Pr. 18 vols. $1,800.00. The only complete edition in English.

Basic Writings of Nietzsche. Ed. and trans. by Walter Kaufmann Modern Lib. 1968 $9.95. The best available collection of some of the most important of Nietzsche's writings.

The Portable Nietzsche. Ed. and trans. by Walter Kaufmann [*Viking Portable Lib.*] Penguin 1977 pap. $7.95. Contains new translations by Kaufmann of some of the major works: *Thus Spake Zarathustra; Twilight of the Idols; The Antichrist; Nietz-sche Contra Wagner.*

A Nietzsche Reader. Trans. by R. J. Hollingdale [*Penguin Class Ser.*] 1978 pap. $4.95. A good collection of different texts of Nietzsche.

The Birth of Tragedy. 1872 Gordon Pr. 1974 $100.00; trans. by Walter Kaufmann, Random (Vintage) 1967 pap. $4.95. Nietzsche's first important work.

The Birth of Tragedy (and *The Genealogy of Morals*). Trans. by Francis Golffing, Doubleday 1956 pap. $5.95. Nietzsche's first works, which combined his philology and philosophy.

Thus Spake Zarathustra. 1883–91. Gordon Pr. 1974 lib. bdg. $100.00; trans. by Thomas Common, Modern Lib. 1982 $6.95. Nietzsche's best-known work. His philosophy is set forth in literary parables.

Beyond Good and Evil. 1886. Gordon Pr. 1974 lib. bdg. $100.00; trans. by R. J. Hollingdale [*Penguin Class. Ser.*] 1973 pap. $3.50; trans. by Walter Kaufmann, Random (Vintage) 1966 pap. $3.95; trans. by Marianne Cowan, Regnery-Gateway 1955 pap. $6.50. A more didactic presentation of Nietzsche's view.

On the Genealogy of Morals. 1887. Trans. by Walter Kaufmann, Random (Vintage) 1967 pap. $4.76. Nietzsche's great work on how values developed.

The Will to Power. 1901. Gordon Pr. 2 vols. 1974 lib. bdg. $200.00; trans. by Walter Kaufmann, Random (Vintage) 1968 pap. $10.95. A work put together by Nietzsche's sister from unfinished fragments. Very influential on antidemocratic forces in the twentieth century.

Ecce Homo. 1908. Trans. by R. J. Hollingdale, Penguin 1979 pap. $3.95. Nietzsche's autobiography.

The Antichrist. Ayer repr. of 1930 ed. 1972 $13.00

The Gay Science. Trans. by Walter Kaufmann, Random 1974 $6.95. Nietzsche's enthusiastic evolutionary study of values.

The Joyful Wisdom. Gordon Pr. 1974 lib. bdg. $100.00; trans. by Thomas Common, Ungar 1981 pap. $6.95. This is the same work as *The Gay Science.*

Nietzsche: A Self-Portrait from His Letters. Ed. by Peter Fuss and Henry Shapiro, Harvard Univ. Pr. 1971 o.p. This out-of-print work is available through University Microfilms. The letters really give remarkable insight into Nietzsche's personality, and his final collapse into insanity.

BOOKS ABOUT NIETZSCHE

Brandes, Georg. *Friedrich Nietzsche.* Haskell repr. of 1914 ed. 1972 $49.95. By the first critic to recognize Nietzsche's importance and his genius.

Clive, Geoffrey. *The Philosophy of Nietzsche.* New Amer. Lib. 1984 pap. $4.95. A good presentation of Nietzsche's views by a leading interpreter of nineteenth-century thought.

Copleston, Frederick. *Friedrich Nietzsche: Philosopher of Culture.* Barnes & Noble 2d ed. 1975 o.p. An interesting appreciation of Nietzsche by the leading English Catholic historian of philosophy.

Danto, Arthur. *Nietzsche as Philosopher.* Columbia Univ. Pr. repr. of 1965 ed. 1980 pap. $11.00; Macmillan 1965 $9.95 pap. $2.45. A lively, critical evaluation by a leading contemporary analytic philosopher.

Guppy, Robert, ed. *Index to Nietzsche.* Trans. by Paul V. Cohn, Gordon Pr. 1974 lib. bdg. $100.00

Jaspers, Karl. *Nietzsche: An Introduction to His Philosophical Activity.* 1936. Trans. by Charles F. Wallrof and Frederick J. Schmitz, Regnery-Gateway 1969 o.p. One of Germany's leading thinkers of the twentieth century presents Nietzsche's basic theories.

Kaufmann, Walter. *Nietzsche: Philosopher, Psychologist, Antichrist.* Princeton Univ. Pr. 4th ed. 1975 pap. $11.95. A well-written presentation by a scholar who devoted many years to comprehending Nietzsche's achievements.

Magnus, Bernd. *Nietzsche's Existential Imperative.* [*Studies in Phenomenology and Existential Philosophy Ser.*] Indiana Univ. Pr. 1978 $20.00. "Although not meant as an introduction to Nietzsche's thought, the book is more insightful than Walter Kaufmann's general overview ([in his translation of Nietzsche's] *Beyond Good and Evil,* 1966), though less detailed than Karl Jaspers' work (*Nietzsche*). Its attention to both logical and existential aspects should make it a touchstone for future studies" (*LJ*).

Mann, Heinrich. *The Living Thoughts of Nietzsche.* Ed. by Arthur O. Mendel, Century Bookbindery repr. of 1939 ed. 1981 $20.00

Mencken, Henry L. *The Philosophy of Friedrich Nietzsche.* Noontide 1982 pap. $7.00

Morgan, George A., Jr. *What Nietzsche Means.* Greenwood repr. of 1943 ed. 1975 lib. bdg. $24.00. An early attempt to make clear that Nietzsche was not the philosopher the Nazis had made of him.

Peters, Hans F. *Zarathustra's Sister: The Case of Elizabeth and Friedrich Nietzsche.* Wiener repr. of 1977 ed. 1985 pap. $9.95. The role Nietzsche's sister played in the editing and publishing of his works.

Rosenberg, Alfred. *Nietzsche.* Gordon Pr. 1975 lib. bdg. $59.95. The Nazi theoretician's version of the philosopher's thoughts.

Salomé, Lou A. *Nietzsche.* Trans. by Siegfried Mandel [*Austrian-German Culture Ser.*] Black Swan 1986 $22.50. Lou Andreas-Salomé was a young Finnish woman who played a fateful part in Nietzsche's life; she was interested in his intellectual pursuits, but not in marriage to him.

Schacht, Richard. *Nietzsche.* [*Arguments of the Philosophers Ser.*] Methuen 1983 $35.00 pap. $17.50. A good sympathetic presentation.

Shestov, Lev. *Doestoevsky, Tolstoy and Nietzsche.* Trans. by Bernard Martin and E. Spencer, Ohio Univ. Pr. 1969 o.p. A leading thinker of the Russian Orthodox Church compares and evaluates the religious views of the three thinkers.

Solomon, Robert C., ed. *Nietzsche: A Collection of Critical Essays.* [*Modern Studies in Philosophy*] Univ. of Notre Dame Pr. repr. of 1973 ed. 1980 text ed. pap. $9.95. "Contains 21 interpretive and evaluative essays, seven of which were written especially for this volume. There are original pieces by Philippa Foot, Ivan Soll, Arnold Zuboff, the editor, et al., and excerpts from works by Walter Kaufmann, Martin Heidegger, Karl Jaspers, Thomas Mann, G. B. Shaw, Herman Hesse, et al."(*LJ*).

Steiner, Rudolf. *Friedrich Nietzsche: Fighter for Freedom.* Intro. by Paul M. Allen [*Spiritual Science Lib.*] Garber Comm. repr. of 1960 ed. 1985 2d rev. ed. lib. bdg. $15.00. By the leading twentieth-century theosophist.

Stern, J. P. *A Study of Nietzsche.* [*Major European Authors Ser.*] Cambridge Univ. Pr. 1979 $39.50 1982 pap. $14.95. A good overall presentation of Nietzsche's views.

PEIRCE, CHARLES SANDERS. 1839–1914

Peirce was the son of the eminent mathematician and Harvard professor Benjamin Peirce. The young Peirce attended Harvard, where he studied science, mathematics, and philosophy. For 30 years he worked for the U.S. Geodetic Survey. Because of personal difficulties, he taught only briefly as a lecturer at Harvard (1864–65, 1869–71) and at Johns Hopkins (1879–84). Peirce greatly influenced such contemporaries as William James and Josiah Royce. He wrote no books and published very little during his lifetime—

mostly articles and encyclopedia entries—but many collections of his articles and unpublished papers have appeared. Peirce was a brilliant logician and creative metaphysician. His papers, many published long after his death, are of great importance in the philosophical literature.

BOOKS BY PEIRCE

Collected Papers of Charles Sanders Peirce. Ed. by Charles Hartshorne, Paul Weiss, and Arthur Burks, Harvard Univ. Pr. 8 vols. 1960 ea. $55.00–$60.00. This edition is arranged by topics.

Writings of Charles S. Peirce: A Chronological Edition. Ed. by Max Fisch and Christian Kloesel, Indiana Univ. Pr. 3 vols. 1982–84 ea. $32.50–$40.00. A new edition undertaken to place Peirce's writings and papers in their proper chronological sequence.

Philosophical Writings of Peirce. Ed. by Justus Buchler, Dover 1940 pap. $6.50. A selection of 28 essays by Peirce on a wide range of topics.

Selected Writings. Ed. by Philip P. Wiener, Dover 1966 text ed. pap. $8.95. Subtitled "Values in a Universe of Chance."

Chance, Love, and Logic. Century Bookbindery repr. of 1923 ed. 1980 lib. bdg. $50.00. A collection of essays on various subjects.

BOOKS ABOUT PEIRCE

Apel, Karl-Otto. *Charles Sanders Peirce: From Pragmatism to Pragmaticism.* (*Der Denkweg Von Charles Sanders Peirce*). Trans. by John M. Krois, intro. by Richard J. Bernstein, Univ. of Massachusetts Pr. 1981 lib. bdg. $22.50. An evaluation by a leading contemporary European philosopher.

Ayer, Alfred J. *Origins of Pragmatism: Studies in the Philosophy of Charles Sanders Peirce and William James.* Freeman, Cooper 1968 $12.50. An insightful examination of these two major American thinkers by one of the leading British analytic philosophers.

Bernstein, Richard J., ed. *Perspectives on Peirce: Critical Essays on Charles Sanders Peirce.* Intro. by Paul Weiss, Greenwood repr. of 1965 ed. 1980 lib. bdg. $22.50. Essays by Paul Weiss, Rulon Wells, Norwood Hanson, R. Bernstein, and John E. Smith.

Buchler, Justus. *Charles Peirce's Empiricism.* Hippocrene Bks. 1966 lib. bdg. $24.00. A basic study by an important American pragmatist.

Freeman, Eugene, ed. *The Relevance of Charles Peirce.* Hegeler Inst. 1983 $29.95. A collection of essays by present-day scholars on Peirce's importance today.

Gallie, W. B. *Peirce and Pragmatism.* Greenwood repr. of 1966 ed. 1975 lib. bdg. $22.50. One of the basic studies of Peirce's thoughts.

Moore, Edward C. *American Pragmatism: Peirce, James and Dewey.* Greenwood repr. of 1961 ed. 1985 lib. bdg. $45.00. "A discussion of American pragmatism as it is found in the writings of its three major advocates" (Preface).

Murphey, Murray G. *Development of Peirce's Philosophy.* Harvard Univ. Pr. 1961 o.p. Basing his book on unpublished Peirce manuscripts, Murphey sought insight into Peirce's thought through the events of the philosopher's life. This fine study is now out of print, but can be obtained from University Microfilms.

ROYCE, JOSIAH. 1855–1916

Royce was the leading idealistic philosopher in the United States during the period of the development of American pragmatism. Born in Grass

Valley, California, he was educated in San Francisco and at the University of California. After his graduation in 1873, he studied in Germany for a year at Heidelberg, Leipzig, and Göttingen. He then returned to the United States and took a doctorate at Johns Hopkins. He taught English composition at the University of California, and in 1882 was invited to Harvard to "fill in" for William James. He was appointed to an assistant professorship at Harvard in 1885 and remained there for the rest of his career. Influenced by Hegel, Royce developed his own philosophy of absolute or objective idealism, in which it is necessary to assume that there is an "absolute experience to which all facts are known and for which all facts are subject to universal law." He published his major works from 1885 onward, including his Gifford Lectures, *The World and the Individual* (1900–01). Along with James, Royce had a great influence on the advanced students who were to become the next generation of American philosophers.

BOOKS BY ROYCE

Basic Writings of Josiah Royce. Ed. by John J. McDermott, Univ. of Chicago Pr. 2 vols. 1969 ea. $30.00. "Stresses the relevance for today of Royce's belief that true individualism is possible only as part of life in a community" (*LJ*).

The Spirit of Modern Philosophy. 1892. Dover repr. of 1892 ed. 1983 pap. $8.95; Richard West repr. of 1892 ed. 1977 lib. bdg. $25.00. Royce's evaluation of some of the many thinkers from Spinoza onward, and the problems they were dealing with.

The World and the Individual. 1900–01. Peter Smith 2 vols. repr. 1976 $21.50. The Gifford Lectures, containing the most extended presentation of Royce's views.

The Conception of Immortality. 1900. Greenwood repr. of 1900 ed. 1968 $15.00. Royce's discussion of what can be permanent in human existence.

Race Questions, Provincialism, and Other American Problems. 1908. [*Essay Index Repr. Ser.*] Ayer repr of 1908 ed. 1967 $18.00. Essays on some American social problems.

The Problems of Christianity. 1913. Univ. of Chicago Pr. 1968 $25.00. A fuller development of the themes in *The Philosophy of Loyalty*. Royce's last major work.

Fugitive Essays. 1920. [*Essay Index Repr. Ser.*] Ayer repr. of 1920 ed. $21.50. A wide range of essays on various philosophers and philosophical problems, and on religion.

Letters of Josiah Royce. Ed. by John Clendenning, Univ. of Chicago Pr. 1970 $25.00. Careful edition of the available correspondence.

The Philosophy of Josiah Royce. Intro. by John K. Roth, Hackett repr. of 1971 ed. 1982 lib. bdg. $18.50 text ed. pap. $9.95. Selections from representative works, with a good introduction.

The Philosophy of Loyalty. Hafner repr. of 1908 ed. 1971 $20.95; Richard West 1985 lib. bdg. $30.00 Royce's basic moral theory.

The Religious Philosophy of Josiah Royce. Ed. by Stuart G. Brown, Greenwood repr. of 1952 ed. 1976 lib. bdg. $22.50. Excerpts from Royce's major works, with a brief introduction.

Sources of Religious Insight. Octagon 1977 $20.00. Lectures given in 1911 evaluating the role of religious insight in human life.

BOOKS ABOUT ROYCE

Buranelli, Vincent. *Josiah Royce.* [*Twayne's U.S. Authors Ser.*] New College & Univ. Pr. 1964 pap. $8.95. A presentation of Royce not only as a philosopher, but as a novelist, essayist, and social critic as well.

Clendenning, John. *The Life and Thought of Josiah Royce.* Univ. of Wisconsin Pr. 1985 text ed. $27.50. A genuinely comprehensive intellectual biography of Royce, from his family background to his intellectual struggles at Harvard. An excellent scholarly work.

Fuss, Peter L. *The Moral Philosophy of Josiah Royce.* Harvard Univ. Pr. 1965 o.p. This first full-scale study of Royce's ethics both carefully and critically exposits Royce's views and traces their development.

Marcel, Gabriel. *Royce's Metaphysics.* Trans. by Gordon Ringer, Greenwood repr. of 1956 ed. 1975 lib. bdg. $22.50. A presentation, interpretation, and evaluation of Royce's philosophy and religious views by one of the leading French Catholic existentialist thinkers.

Robinson, Daniel S. *Royce and Hocking: American Idealists.* Chris Mass 1968 $6.95. An introduction to the philosophy of these two American idealists, with selected letters.

———, ed. *Royce's Logical Essays.* Chris Mass 1971 $10.00. A collection of the essays on traditional and symbolic logic by Royce.

Singh, Bhagwan B. *The Self and the World in the Philosophy of Josiah Royce.* C. C. Thomas 1973 o.p. Royce's thought compared with Indian philosophy.

Smith, John E. *Royce's Social Infinite: The Community of Interpretation.* Shoe String repr. of 1950 ed. 1979 $17.50. Important study of this aspect of Royce's view by one of the leading historians of American philosophy.

SCHELLING, FRIEDRICH WILHELM JOSEPH VON. 1775–1854

Schelling was one of the major German idealist philosophers. He first studied theology, and through his friendship with his student Hegel (and the romantic poet Hölderlin), he became interested in the philosophies of Spinoza, Kant, and Fichte. In 1798, Schelling became professor at Jena, where Fichte was a colleague. Schelling and Hegel edited a philosophical journal together from 1803 to 1806. Schelling taught at various universities in Germany, and developed his own philosophy, which he called the "Philosophy of Nature," followed by the "Philosophy of Identity." In his later years, he worked primarily on the philosophy of history. He wrote extensively. His complete works in German have appeared in two editions, one of 14 volumes and the other of 8 volumes. A bibliographical index of his writings by Fritz Marti will appear shortly.

BOOKS BY SCHELLING

The Unconditional in Human Knowledge: Four Early Essays, 1794–1796. Ed. and trans. by Fritz Marti, Bucknell Univ. Pr. 1976 $35.00. These essays show Schelling going beyond Kant. Excellent introductory materials.

Of Human Freedom. 1809. Trans. by James Gutmann, Open Court 1985 pap. $8.95. Schelling's explanation of the problem of evil.

The Ages of the World. 1854. Trans. by Frederick D. Bolman, AMS Pr. repr. of 1942 ed. 1981 $21.00. Schelling's philosophy presented in terms of the evolution of the divine principle in history.

BOOKS ABOUT SCHELLING

Brown, Robert F. *The Later Philosophy of Schelling: The Influence of Boehme on the Works of 1809–1815.* Bucknell Univ. Pr. 1976 $25.00. Interesting study of the influence of the seventeenth-century German mystic on Schelling's later works.

Esposito, Joseph L. *Schelling's Idealism and Philosophy of Nature.* Bucknell Univ. Pr. 1978 $24.50. A good exposition of Schelling's metaphysical system.

Heidegger, Martin. *Schelling's Treatise on the Essence of Human Freedom.* Trans. by Joan Stambaugh [*Continental Thought Ser.*] Ohio Univ. Pr. 1985 text ed. $26.95 pap. $14.95. An evaluation of one of Schelling's great works by a leading German thinker of the twentieth century.

Marx, Werner. *The Philosophy of F. W. J. Schelling: History, System, and Freedom.* Trans. by Thomas Nenon. Indiana Univ. Pr. 1984 $24.95. The most complete examination of Schelling's thought available in English.

Tillich, Paul. *Mysticism and Guilt-Consciousness in Schelling's Philosophical Development.* Trans. by Victor Nuovo, Bucknell Univ. Pr. 1975 $16.50. An examination of religious themes in Schelling by one of the most important twentieth-century theologians.

SCHOPENHAUER, ARTHUR. 1788–1860

Schopenhauer is one of the best-known German philosophers. He was very hostile to the German metaphysicians of his time, especially Hegel, whom he believed to be a charlatan. His first writings examined the bases of metaphysical reasoning, starting with the *On the Fourfold Root of the Principle of Sufficient Reason* (1813) and the *World as Will and Idea* (1818). Schopenhauer followed the antirational tendencies in post-Kantian philosophy, as well as ideas he derived from the recently discovered texts of Indian mysticism. The result was a very pessimistic outlook, resulting from recognizing that the will is the fundamental feature of the universe, forcing people to strive for the unattainable. Through recognition of the purposelessness of it all, one could try to quiet the endless volitional drives through the methods of the Oriental thinkers, and through art. On the positive side, Schopenhauer's ideas have been influential in aesthetics. His pessimism had a vogue at the end of the nineteenth century. It apparently influenced young Wittgenstein.

BOOKS BY SCHOPENHAUER

On the Fourfold Root of the Principle of Sufficient Reason. 1813. Trans. by E. F. J. Payne, Open Court 1974 $13.95 pap. $8.95

The World as Will and Idea. 1818. Trans. by R. B. Haldane and J. Kemp, AMS Pr. 3 vols. repr. of 1896 ed. 1978 $87.50; Dover 2 vols. 1966 text ed. pap. ea. $8.95

On the Basis of Morality. 1841. Ed. by E. F. J. Payne, Macmillan 1965 o.p. Schopenhauer's attack on Kantian ethics, which the author said on the title page was *not* awarded a prize by the Royal Danish Society of Scientific Studies.

Parerga and Paralipomena: Short Philosophical Essays. 1851. Trans. by E. F. J. Payne, Oxford 2 vols. 1974 $115.00 pap. $39.50. A collection of essays and aphorisms by Schopenhauer.

Counsels and Maxims. Scholarly repr. of 1899 ed. 1981 lib. bdg. $29.00. Schopenhauer's epigrams and advice.

Religion: A Dialogue, and Other Essays. [*Essay Index Repr. Ser.*] Ayer 3d ed. repr. of

1891 ed. 1980 $13.00; trans. by T. Bailey Saunders, Greenwood repr. of 1899 ed. 1973 lib. bdg. $25.00. Another collection of some of Schopenhauer's most negative views.

Studies in Pessimism. Scholarly repr. of 1903 ed. $39.00. Some of Schopenhauer's most pessimistic essays.

The Will to Live: Selected Writings of Arthur Schopenhauer. Ed. by Richard Taylor, Ungar 1967 pap. $5.95. A collection of representative texts by Schopenhauer.

The Wisdom of Life: Being the First Part of Aphorismen zur Lebenswiesheit. Amer. Class. College Pr. 1985 $97.85; trans. by T. Bailey Saunders [*Essay Index Repr. Ser.*]. Ayer repr. of 1890 ed. 1972 $12.00. One of the first works of Schopenhauer to be widely read in English.

The World as Will and Representation. 1818. Trans. by E. F. J. Payne, Peter Smith 2 vols. 1966 set $33.50. Another translation of Schopenhauer's major contribution, *The World as Will and Idea.*

BOOKS ABOUT SCHOPENHAUER

Copleston, Frederick. *Arthur Schopenhauer: Philosopher of Pessimism.* Barnes & Noble repr. of 1946 ed. 1975 o.p. By a leading English Catholic historian of philosophy.

Dauer, Dorothea W. *Schopenhauer as Transmitter of Buddhist Ideas.* [*European Univ. Studies*] Peter Lang 1969 $6.55. A brief study of Schopenhauer's role in making Europe aware of Buddhism.

Hamlyn, D. W. *Schopenhauer.* [*Arguments of the Philosophers Ser.*] Methuen 1980 $26.95 1985 pap. $14.95. An examination of Schopenhauer's main philosophical writings.

Magee, Bryan. *The Philosophy of Schopenhauer.* Oxford 1983 $29.95. A new general presentation of Schopenhauer's views for a contemporary audience.

Mann, Thomas. *The Living Thoughts of Schopenhauer.* Arden Lib. repr. of 1939 ed. 1983 lib. bdg. $25.00. A selection of Schopenhauer's ideas by one of the greatest twentieth-century German novelists.

Nietzsche, Friedrich. *Schopenhauer as Educator.* Regnery Bks. 1965 pap. $3.95. Nietzsche was originally very impressed by Schopenhauer, but then decided his views were too negative. Schopenhauer is also attacked in Nietzsche's *Human, All Too Human.*

Wallace, William. *Life of Arthur Schopenhauer.* Scholarly repr. of 1890 ed. 1971 $29.00. One of the first works to make the English public aware of Schopenhauer.

SPENCER, HERBERT. 1820–1903

Herbert Spencer, born in Derby, England, is remembered for applying the theory of evolution to all of the branches of human knowledge. Never formally educated, he was privately taught, and trained himself in many subjects. He first became a schoolmaster, and then a civil engineer. In 1848 he was appointed a subeditor of the journal *The Economist.* Spencer began publishing his views in 1851, in the work *Social Statics.* This was followed in 1855 by his *The Principles of Psychology.* After the appearance of DARWIN'S (see Vol. 5) work, Spencer became one of the leading advocates of social Darwinism. He tried to incorporate all of human knowledge into what he called "Synthetic Philosophy." He had a great vogue in the late nineteenth century, especially in the United States. (See also Volume 3.)

BOOKS BY SPENCER

Works. Adler's 21 vols. repr. of 1884 ed. 1966 $1,360.00. The only complete edition of his writings.

Essays on Education and Kindred Subjects. 1861. AMS Pr. repr. of 1911 ed. 1977 $21.50; Biblio Dist. repr. of 1911 ed. 1976 $12.95; Telegraph Bks. repr. of 1911 ed. 1986 lib. bdg. $40.00. Four articles by Spencer on types of education.

Herbert Spencer on Social Evolution. Ed. by J. D. Peel [*Heritage of Sociology Ser.*] Univ. of Chicago Pr. 1975 pap. $15.00. Selections from Spencer on how societies evolve.

Social Statics; or, The Conditions Essential to Human Happiness Specified, and the First of Them Adopted. 1851. Gregg repr. of 1851 ed. 1969 text ed. $49.68; Kelley repr. of 1851 ed. 1969 $35.00; Schalkenbach repr. of 1850 ed. 1970 $6.00. Spencer's answer to Comte, contending that society should be reorganized by effects of habit on character.

The Principles of Sociology. 1876–96. Greenwood 3 vols. repr. 1975 lib. bdg. $90.00; Shoe String (Archon) repr. of 1868 ed. 1969 $49.50. Spencer's immense work in which he examines the data of social theory, and the laws of social development.

The Principles of Psychology. 1855, rev. ed. 1870–72. Gregg repr. of 1855 ed. text ed. $62.10; Longwood 2 vols. repr. of 1881 ed. 1977 lib. bdg. $70.00, Spencer's analysis of how the human mind works.

The Evolution of Society: Selections from Herbert Spencer's "Principles of Sociology." Ed. by Robert L. Carneiro [*Midway Repr. Ser.*] Univ. of Chicago Pr. repr. of 1967 ed. 1974 pap. $10.50. A selection of texts from Spencer's three volumes, giving the core of his study.

The Principles of Ethics. 1879–93. Intro. by Tibor Machan, Liberty Fund 2 vols. repr. of 1897 ed. 1978 $20.00 1980 pap. $8.00. Spencer's statement of social Darwinism.

BOOKS ABOUT SPENCER

Hudson, W. H. *The Philosophy of Herbert Spencer.* [*Studies in Philosophy*] Haskell 1974 lib. bdg. $75.00. A short introductory presentation of Spencer's thought.

Royce, Josiah. *Herbert Spencer: An Estimate and Review Together with a Chapter of Personal Reminiscences.* Ayer 1955 $13.00. An evalution by a leading contemporary opponent.

Wiltshire, David. *The Social and Political Thought of Herbert Spencer.* Oxford 1978 $29.95. An evaluation a century later of Spencer's contribution.

CHAPTER 6

Twentieth-Century Philosophy

Andrew J. Reck

Speculative Philosophy is the endeavor to frame a coherent, logical, necessary system of general ideas in terms of which every element of our experience can be interpreted.

—ALFRED NORTH WHITEHEAD

An outstanding feature of twentieth-century philosophy, of whatever sort, has been the growth of its self-consciousness. . . . This does not preclude the elaboration of a world view, though philosophical system-building has gone almost wholly out of fashion.

—ALFRED JULES AYER

Philosophy entered the twentieth century divided, for the most part, between an idealism that was allied with religion and a naturalism that marched with science. The idealism, which in the nineteenth century had found its leading champion in HEGEL, maintained that the key to the nature of reality was to be found in characteristic features and operations of the human mind; it favored a spiritualistic interpretation of the world. The dominant form of idealism in the nineteenth century was absolute idealism; it posited the existence of an absolute mind. But personalistic idealists rose up on behalf of the primacy of finite personal selves. John McTaggart and Edgar Sheffield Brightman are distinct but exemplary representatives of personalism in the twentieth century. By contrast with idealism, naturalism took its inspiration from the great progress the sciences were making. Measuring the impact of Darwinian evolution on the inherited conceptions of man and human values, philosophical naturalism was initially a deterministic materialism. However, it differed from its antecedents by assuming the form of evolutionism, and it underscored the employment of the scientific method as the sole route to reliable belief or knowledge.

In the early years of the century two movements emerged to challenge the regnant schools of idealism and naturalism. Realism had its roots in earlier philosophy, especially the Scottish commonsense realism of THOMAS REID in the eighteenth and James McCosh in the nineteenth century. Whereas idealism had held that the object of cognition does not exist independently of the knowing mind, the realists asserted its independent reality. As the nineteenth century ended, the leading idealists, such as F. H. BRADLEY at Oxford and JOSIAH ROYCE at Harvard, were targets for criticism by a broad spec-

212

trum of thinkers on this epistemological thought. G. E. Moore at Cambridge and the new realists in America, such as R. B. Perry at Harvard, were in the vanguard of the assault against idealism in behalf of realism. Subsequently new realism was challenged by critical realism. Although the critical realists concurred with the new realists in affirming the independent existence of the objects of knowledge, they affirmed that knowledge of them is indirect, that it is mediated by representations in the mind. Critical realists in turn divided into two camps: those who held that mind is directly cognizant of essences, which have a distinct ontological status, as George Santayana argued, and those who contended that the mental representations of objects consist of sense data, which are located in the mind, as Roy Wood Sellars and A. O. Lovejoy maintained.

Pragmatism, originating in the thought of Charles Sanders Peirce and popularized by WILLIAM JAMES (see also Vol. 3), came to the fore in the late nineteenth century, but it flourished in the first quarter of the twentieth century, fed by the works of JOHN DEWEY (see also Vol. 3), GEORGE HERBERT MEAD (see Vol. 3), C. I. Lewis, and Sidney Hook. Whatever the differences among the pragmatists, and these differences were considerable, their common ground was the theme that thought is intimately linked to action and that meaningful theory is grounded in experience.

Meanwhile, the naturalism inspired by science began to split up and move in almost opposite directions. Attention to the development of the categories of natural science, particularly in the wake of the acceptance of the Darwinian principle of evolution in biology and of the quantum theory and relativity in physics, inspired speculations in philosophical cosmology, represented by John Elof Boodin and, far more famously, by Alfred North Whitehead. Indeed, Whitehead offered the last great speculative system to receive a wide hearing. Although Whitehead called his system the philosophy of organism, it has generally been accepted as process philosophy. The most recent expression of process philosophy, with special reference to theology, has been in the works of Charles Hartshorne. Clearly a characteristic theme of process philosophy in its most influential recent formulation is theism, in contradistinction to the regnant scientific naturalism, which is sometimes atheistic and professedly humanist.

While process philosophy grew out of naturalism, in particular evolutionism, to propose a doctrine of God in opposition to atheism and secular humanism, another school of thought widespread in the mid-twentieth century sprang up under the aegis of the Roman Catholic church. In 1879, Pope Leo XIII urged the devoted study of the philosophy and theology of St. Thomas Aquinas, but he explicitly admonished that the revival of Thomism be consistent with the discoveries made since the saint's own time. Neo-Thomism became a major intellectual force from the time of World War I until well after World War II, persuasively presented in the works of Jacques Maritain, Étienne Gilson, and, in a singular way, by Mortimer J. Adler, since he is not a professed Roman Catholic. In recent decades neo-Thomism has receded, persisting in Roman Catholic thought in the guise of transcendental Thomism, articulated by such thinkers as the Jesuit Bernard Lonergan.

Science, not religion, has been the most prestigious cultural institution in the twentieth century. Early in the century the investigations of BERTRAND RUSSELL (see also Vol. 5) and Alfred North Whitehead on the nature of mathematics bore fruit with the presentation of the formalist theory. This theory maintained that the foundations of mathematics are in logic; it consequently transformed logic so that it came to resemble mathematics in its symbolic representation. Further investigations into the nature of formal statements in logic and mathematics led to the theory, advocated by Ludwig Wittgenstein, that these statements say nothing about the world, that they are tautologies. This conception, allied with the requirement of scientific method that concepts and theories be testable experimentally or within experience in order to be cognitively meaningful, constituted the core of the movement known as logical positivism, originating in Vienna in the 1920s and spreading to the English-speaking world. Logical positivism broadened into logical empiricism, perhaps the dominant philosophical attitude in American philosophical thought today, poses an antimetaphysical stance; it is nonetheless fundamentally naturalistic. Logical empiricism is the movement out of which a whole generation of leading American philosophers has sprung, including W. V. Quine, Nelson Goodman, Wilfrid Sellars, and Roderick Chisholm.

In Great Britain Wittgenstein had begun in the 1930s to turn his attention from investigations into the formal languages of logic and mathematics exclusively. Such investigations had been the focus of his early work and had proved to be central to logical positivism. They continued to be pursued with vigor by Rudolf Carnap. Wittgenstein, on the other hand, then inspired the examination of ordinary language. Carried on at Oxford by Gilbert Ryle, John Austin, and P. F. Strawson, to a degree independently of each other, these investigations gave rise to a kind of analytic philosophy which, in contrast with the emphasis of logical empiricism on formal language, has been termed "linguistic analysis."

While logical empiricism and linguistic analysis constituted the movement of analytic philosophy that embraced most academic philosophers, mainly in the English-speaking world, events outside the academy had shaken the foundations of Western culture. Many philosophers addressed themselves to the problems of value and the philosophy of culture. Ernst Cassirer, Ortega y Gassett, and Miguel de Unamuno are three who come to mind.

More pervasive still was the movement of philosophers toward a renewed emphasis on subjectivity that led to the rise of existentialism. Foreshadowed by Kierkegaard's religious and cultural investigations and by Nietzsche's poetic, aphoristic essays concerning man, morals, and culture in the nineteenth century, existentialism dominated philosophical thought in the mid-twentieth century on the European continent and in literary circles everywhere. It had found its philosophical method in the phenomenology of Edmund Husserl. In the hands of Max Scheler, Martin Heidegger, Karl Jaspers, and later JEAN-PAUL SARTRE (see also Vol. 2) and Maurice Merleau-Ponty, phenomenology has been extended to examine value-laden areas of human experience and action beyond simply the cognitive states of consciousness. This expanded line of exploration, concentrating on the moral and social problems and breakdowns in twentieth-century Western civilization, naturally led existentialists to confront the challenges of Marxism.

With the establishment of the U.S.S.R. and its advocacy of Marxism as the official ideology, the study of Marxism took on a new seriousness. European intellectuals found the humanistic character of the early Marx more appealing than the historical or economic determinism of his later pronouncements. Their Marxism consequently took on a different guise, attending more to matters of art and culture than to economics. Thus critical theory, associated with the Frankfurt School, came into being.

Philosophy today consists of the rivalry of all these schools, further complicated by the existence of independent minds. Although the speculative system building exemplified by the works of Whitehead and Santayana in the first third of this century has indeed receded, it still is represented by the prodigious work of a singular thinker like Paul Weiss. However, the preoccupation with philosophical method, conspicuous in the writings of analytic philosophers at midcentury, remains a prevalent trait of current philosophical thinking, but it has taken a "postanalytic" turn with the emergence of the hermeneutics of Hans-Georg Gadamer and the deconstructionism of MICHEL FOUCAULT (see also Vols. 2 and 5) and Jacques Derrida.

BIBLIOGRAPHY

Aune, Bruce A. *Rationalism, Empiricism, and Pragmaticism: An Introduction.* Random 1970 text ed. pap. $8.00. A textbook in theory of knowledge that translates classical theories in modern philosophy into the contemporary idiom of analytic philosophy.

Ayer, Alfred Jules. *Logical Positivism.* Free Pr. 1966 pap. $14.95. "A well selected collection of 17 very important essays. . .plus a valuable historical orientation in the form of an introduction by the editor" (Ernest Gellner, *Guardian*).

———. *Philosophy in the Twentieth Century.* Random 1983 pap. $8.95. Presents "brief explanations of some main issues in this century's critical and speculative Western philosophy, primarily of the Anglo-American varieties" (*LJ*).

Ballard, Edward G. *Philosophy at the Crossroads.* Louisiana State Univ. Pr. 1971 $30.00. A sensitive and scholarly interpretation of the turn in modern philosophy toward phenomenology and existentialism; particularly good on Husserl and Heidegger.

Barnes, Hazel E. *Existentialist Ethics.* 1967. Univ. of Chicago Pr. 1985 pap. $16.00. Barnes first "expands on the need for an ethic that will allow existentialist thinking to be applied to ordinary life decisions, [then] she contrasts existential thinking—usually Sartre's brand of existential philosophy—with the other current intellectual fashions (beatniks and hipsters, the New Left, and various Eastern philosophies) and then attempts to outline the life responsibilities of anyone who claims to be an existentialist" (*PW*). A "highly critical work" (*LJ*).

Barrett, William. *The Illusion of Technique: A Search for Meaning in a Technological Civilization.* Doubleday 1978 pap. $6.95. "In this survey of twentieth-century philosophy, Barrett concentrates on the thought of Ludwig Wittgenstein, Martin Heidegger, and William James" (*Bk. Review Digest*).

———. *Irrational Man: A Study in Existential Philosophy.* Doubleday 1958 pap. $5.95; Greenwood repr. of 1958 ed. 1977 lib. bdg. $29.75. "Barrett is very clever and clear in following the thread of [existentialism] down through the ages. But he is perhaps at his best in the chapters in which he describes the individual contributions of such men as Kierkegaard, Nietzsche, and Heidegger" (*Kirkus*).

Bernstein, Richard J. *Philosophical Profiles: Essays in a Pragmatic Mode*. Univ. of Pennsylvania Pr. 1986 $25.00 pap. $10.95. Penetrating essays on leading contemporary European thinkers by a brilliant American commentator.

———. *Praxis and Action: Contemporary Philosophies of Human Activity*. Univ. of Pennsylvania Pr. 1971 pap. $11.95. "Without denying the obvious divergence of contemporary philosophical movements—Marxism, existentialism, pragmatism, and analytic philosophy—Bernstein claims that a common ground for comparison can be found in the notion of action, broadly conceived" (*LJ*).

Bertocci, Peter A., ed. *Mid-Twentieth Century American Philosophy: Personal Statements*. Humanities Pr. 1974 text ed. $15.00. Intellectual creeds of 15 prominent American philosophers including Brand Blanshard, Charles Hartshorne, Stephen Pepper, Roy Wood Sellars, and Paul Weiss.

Blackham, Harold John. *Six Existentialist Thinkers*. Methuen 1983 pap. $8.95. A trustworthy handbook.

Bochenski, Innocentius Marie. *Contemporary European Philosophy*. Trans. by Donald Nicholl and Karl Aschenbrenner, Greenwood repr. of 1956 ed. 1982 lib. bdg. $35.00. A selective survey of twentieth-century philosophy. Distinguishes seven main systems: empiricism, idealism, life, philosophy, phenomenology, existentialist philosophy, and the philosophy of being. It treats the contributions of individual philosophers within the framework of this classification.

———. *The Methods of Contemporary Thought*. Trans. by Peter Caws, Kluwer Academic 1965 lib. bdg. $22.50. An essay on contemporary philosophical methodology by an internationally famous logician and historian of philosophy.

Boyer, David L., and others, eds. *The Philosopher's Annual*. Rowman vol. 1 1978 $25.00 pap. $12.50 vol. 2 1979 $25.00; Ridgeview vols. 3–5 1980–82 lib. bdg. ea. $24.00 text ed. pap. ea. $8.50. Each volume contains a selection of outstanding articles by distinguished philosophers published during the year.

Brown, S. C., and Wolf Mays, eds. *Linguistic Analysis and Phenomenology*. Bucknell Univ. Pr. 1972 $26.50. "This volume contains the proceedings of the six symposia of the 'Philosophers into Europe' conference held under the joint auspices of the Royal Institute of Philosophy and the British Society for Phenomenology at the University of Southampton in September 1969. The object was to bring together English and continental philosophers in an interchange of views. An attempt was made to find a bridge between linguistic philosophy and phenomenology and to see if these two styles of philosophy could be unified" (*Bk. Review Digest*).

Burr, John R., ed. *Handbook of World Philosophy: Contemporary Developments since 1945*. Greenwood 1980 lib. bdg. $65.00. This is "a one-volume survey attempting to provide an internationally representative sample. . .of the character, directions, wealth, and varieties of the reflections and activities called 'philosophic' as described. . .by philosophers particularly knowledgeable about the region or country being discussed" (*LJ*).

Butler, Christopher. *Interpretation, Deconstruction, and Ideology: An Introduction to Some Current Issues in Literary Theory*. Oxford 1984 $24.95 pap. $10.95. This book "will be useful to those who feel they have not yet grasped the grounds of the various oppositional modes in criticism, and the differences in their oppositions" (Cairns Craig, *TLS*).

Callinicos, Alex. *Marxism and Philosophy*. Oxford 1983 $19.95 pap. $7.95. "Callinicos attempts an overview of Marxist philosophy, especially its status as a philosophy.... The book has four parts: the Hegelian and Fregean traditions from which spring Marxism and analytic philosophy; Marxism from Marx to Lukács, Adorno, and Althusser; the sense in which Marxism is a materialism (both a naturalism and a realism); and questions of ideology and language" (*Choice*).

Caton, Charles E. *Philosophy and Ordinary Language.* Univ. of Illinois Pr. 1963 o.p. "An anthology presenting 12 essays on language by philosophers of the 'ordinary-language' movement, so called because the distinguishing characteristic of this group of analytic philosophers is their taking special and systematic account of the role played by ordinary language in the genesis and resolution of philosophical problems" (*LJ*).

Cell, Edward. *Language, Existence and God: Interpretations of Moore, Russell, Ayer, Wittgenstein, Wisdom, Oxford Philosophy and Tillich.* Humanities Pr. repr. of 1971 ed. 1978 text ed. $17.50. "Cell has provided a needed addition to the literature on religious language; a competent intermediate-level critical survey of major problems in the field, combined with some positive suggestions worthy of consideration by all" (*Choice*).

Chiari, Joseph. *Twentieth Century French Thought from Bergson to Levi-Strauss.* Gordian 1975 $18.50. The author assesses the work of such French philosophers as Merleau-Ponty, Sartre, Marcel, Lavelle, Maritain, Camus, Weil, Teilhard de Chardin, Bachelard, Foucault, and Althusser.

Chisholm, Roderick M., ed. *Realism and the Background of Phenomenology.* Ridgeview 1981 text ed. lib. bdg. $24.00 pap. $8.50. An anthology prepared by a leading American thinker, this contains an erudite introduction and 12 selections from such thinkers as Brentano, Husserl, Prichard, the American new realists, Samuel Alexander, Russell, Lovejoy, and G. E. Moore.

Christensen, Darrel E., and others, eds. *Contemporary German Philosophy.* [*Contemporary German Philosophy Ser.*] Pennsylvania State Univ. Pr. 4 vols. 1982–85 ea. $22.50. This series is "projected as a yearbook following volumes reviewing the 1960–80 period. CGP [*Contemporary German Philosophy*] is to be devoted to making available in English contributions to philosophical comprehension originating in German" (*The Philosopher's Index*).

Cobb, John B., Jr., and W. Widick Schroeder, eds. *Process Philosophy and Social Thought.* Ctr. Sci. Study 1981 $24.95 pap. $11.95. Eighteen essays that explore the influence of process philosophy on social and political thought, "divided into three parts, dealing with process thought and social theory, social ethics, and liberation theology, respectively" (Marjorie Suchocki, *Journal of Religion*).

Collins, James D. *The Existentialists: A Critical Study.* Greenwood repr. of 1952 ed. 1977 lib. bdg. $22.50. "A carefully thought out, straightforward analysis of existentialism, the most discussed and controversial philosophy of the twentieth century. It should be of value to all who are interested in modern philosophy" (*Kirkus*).

Copleston, Frederick Charles. *Bergson to Sartre.* Vol. 9, Part II in *History of Philosophy.* Doubleday 1977 pap. $4.50. The second half of the final volume of Copleston's monumental history of philosophy is devoted to French philosophy in the twentieth century. "Copleston shows himself to be one of the finest, clearest expositors of philosophers and philosophical theories or themes writing today" (*Choice*).

———. *Contemporary Philosophy: Studies of Logical Positivism and Existentialism.* Search Pr. 1956 o.p. An introductory survey of two rival contemporary philosophical movements by the foremost Roman Catholic historian of philosophy.

Cunningham, Gustavus W. *Idealistic Argument in Recent British and American Philosophy.* [*Essay Index Repr. Ser.*] Ayer repr. of 1933 ed. 1977 $27.50; Greenwood repr. of 1933 ed. 1970 lib. bdg. $22.50. "An excellent statement of the development of idealistic philosophy in England and America since 1800" (M. H. Moore, *Journal of Religion*).

Durfee, Harold A. *Analytic Philosophy and Phenomenology.* Kluwer Academic 1976 pap. $42.00. An attempt to uncover the common principles of the two rival philosophical methods dominant today.

Flew, Antony G., ed. *Logic and Language Second Series.* Basil Blackwell 1973 pap. $11.95. An anthology similar to Flew's 1951 *Essays on Logic and Language.* It represents the latest developments in Anglo-American analytic philosophy.

Floistad, Guttorn, ed. *Contemporary Philosophy: A New Survey.* Martinus Nijhoff 5 vols. 1981–87 lib. bdg. ea. $58.50–$82.50 vol. 1, *Philosophy of Language, Philosophical Logic;* vol. 2, *Philosophy of Science;* vol. 3, *Philosophy of Action;* vol. 4, *Philosophy of Mind;* vol. 5, *Africa.* "A continuation of two earlier series of chronicles, *Philosophy in the Midcentury* (1958–59) and *Contemporary Philosophy* (1968)" (Preface).

Friedman, George. *The Political Philosophy of the Frankfurt School.* Cornell Univ. Pr. 1981 $29.95. This book treats "the ideas of the German scholars and social critics associated with the Frankfurt School (Benjamin, Adorno, Horkheimer, Marcuse). . .[it studies] the origins of their thought, the manner in which they perceived the problems of modern society, and the way they sought to solve these problems" (Publisher's note).

Friedman, Maurice, ed. *The Worlds of Existentialism: A Critical Reader.* Univ. of Chicago Pr. 1973 pap. $13.50. "A lively introduction. . . . There is no book of introductory readings that is so versatile, cosmopolitan and exhaustive. . . . Recommended generally" (R. L. Perkins, *LJ*).

Garcia, Jorge J., and others, eds. *Philosophical Analysis in Latin America.* Kluwer Academic 1984 lib. bdg. $55.00. An anthology of articles by Latin American analytic philosophers demonstrating that interest in "scientific philosophy" is established in Latin America.

Geuss, R. *The Idea of a Critical Theory: Habermas and the Frankfurt School.* [*Modern European Philosophy*] Cambridge Univ. Pr. 1981 $27.95 pap. $8.95. Geuss gives "an excellent discussion of the various meanings attributed to the concept of ideology. . . . Strongly recommended for scholars" (*Choice*).

Grene, Marjorie. *Introduction to Existentialism.* Univ. of Chicago Pr. 1984 text ed. pap. $7.00. A lucid exposition and critical evaluation of existentialism by an expert in the history of philosophy.

Hancock, Roger N. *Twentieth Century Ethics.* Columbia Univ. Pr. 1974 $26.00. "This book surveys the main types of twentieth-century Anglo-American metaethical theories, questions the rigid separation of metaethics from normative ethics, and defends a naturalistic metaethics" (Robert Hoffman, *LJ*).

Hanfling, Oswald. *Logical Positivism.* Columbia Univ. Pr. 1981 $26.00. Hanfling "attempts to delineate the philosophical problems, and preferred solutions to those problems, that gave rise to. . .logical positivism. . . . [He describes] the problems and positions of logical positivism [and treats]. . .the positivistic problematic ranging from epistemology to ethics" (*Choice*).

Harlow, Victor E. *Bibliography and Genetic Study of American Realism.* Kraus Repr. repr. of 1931 ed. $15.00. A pioneer historical, critical, and bibliographic account of new realism and critical realism in American philosophy.

Held, David. *Introduction to Critical Theory: Horkheimer to Habermas.* Univ. of California Pr. 1980 $42.00 pap. $14.00. "Mr. Held's purpose in his introduction to critical theory is to determine its historical context, to express its empirical and theoretical concerns, and to discuss and evaluate the work of its key figures.

Two branches of critical theory are distinguished: (1) the Frankfurt School, which includes Horkheimer, Adorno, and Marcuse, and (2) Jürgen Habermas" (*Philosopher's Index*).

Holt, Edwin B., and others. *New Realism: Cooperative Studies in Philosophy.* Kraus Repr. repr. of 1912 ed. $36.00. This is the classic cooperative volume, which contains the program of and essays by the American new realists.

Hook, Sidney, ed. *Art and Philosophy: A Symposium.* New York Univ. Pr. 1966 o.p. Proceedings of a conference consisting of brief addresses, followed by comments and replies on the part of leading experts in aesthetics and philosophy of art, organized by the editor.

———. *Determinism and Freedom in the Age of Modern Science: A Philosophical Symposium.* New York Univ. Pr. 1958 o.p. In the same format as above, a profound record of the issues of freedom and determinism at the cutting edge of contemporary philosophical research.

———. *Human Values and Economic Policy: A Symposium.* New York Univ. Pr. 1967 $25.00. In the same format as above, a good starting point for persons interested in situating economic value in the general scheme of values.

———. *Language and Philosophy: A Symposium.* New York Univ. Pr. 1969 o.p. A valiant effort to bring together leading philosophers on the nature and function of language.

———. *Law and Philosophy: A Symposium.* New York Univ. Pr. 1964 o.p. An early symposium on the philosophy of law.

———. *Philosophy and History: A Symposium.* New York Univ. Pr. 1963 o.p. Leading philosophers reflect on history and on each other's views.

———. *Psychoanalysis, Scientific Method and Philosophy: A Symposium.* New York Univ. Pr. 1959 $25.00. A tough-minded series of examinations and critiques on whether psychoanalysis is scientifically valid.

———. *Religious Experience and Truth: A Symposium.* New York Univ. Pr. 1961 $25.00. This is one of the volumes, some listed above, that reprint the proceedings of a series of important symposia held under the auspices of New York University's Institute of Philosophy.

International Philosophy Year Conferences, Brockport. *Contemporary Philosophic Thought.* Ed. by Howard E. Kiefer and Milton K. Munitz, State Univ. of New York Pr. 4 vols. 1970 vols. 1 & 3 o.p. vol. 2 $44.50 vol. 4 $35.50. The collected papers presented at a conference on the status of philosophy internationally.

Joergensen, Joergen. *Development of Logical Empiricism.* [*Foundations of the Unity of Science Ser.*] Johnson Repr. repr. of 1951 ed. 1978 $12.00; Univ. of Chicago Pr. 1951 pap. $2.50. A monograph in the *Encyclopedia of Unified Science*, this work traces the development of logical empiricism, focusing on the Vienna Circle.

Jones, William Thomas. *The Twentieth Century to Wittgenstein and Sartre.* Vol. 5 in *A History of Western Philosophy.* Harcourt 2d rev. ed. 1975 text ed. pap. $11.95. M. R. Gabbert said in his review of the first edition of this standard textbook: "Three main principles guide the writer: (1) concentration upon major figures; (2) extensive quotation from sources; and (3) full presentation of cultural background" (*Annals of the Amer. Academy*).

Kallen, Horace M., and Sidney Hook, eds. *American Philosophy Today and Tomorrow.* [*Essay Index Repr. Ser.*] Ayer repr. of 1935 ed. 1968 $21.50; Irvington repr. of 1935 ed. 1982 lib. bdg. $20.00. "The aim of this philosophic symposium is to present the views of 25 representative American thinkers on the problems with which the times confront the American philosopher, and the solutions which Americans must find for tomorrow" (*Boston Transcript*).

Kaufmann, Walter. *From Shakespeare to Existentialism: Essays on Shakespeare and*

Goethe; Hegel and Kierkegaard; Nietzsche, Rilke, and Freud; Jaspers, Heidegger, and Toynbee. Princeton Univ. Pr. 1980 $29.50 pap. $11.50. Lucid and witty, Kaufmann uncovers the "hidden meanings" in Heidegger.

Kingston, Frederick T. *French Existentialism: A Christian Critique.* Univ. of Toronto Pr. 1961 o.p. A sensible and sensitive essay favoring Marcel over Sartre.

Krikorian, Yervant H., ed. *Naturalism and the Human Spirit.* Columbia Univ. Pr. 1944 $36.00. A collection of 15 original essays, including one by John Dewey, articulating the philosophy of naturalism.

Kuklick, Bruce. *The Rise of American Philosophy: Cambridge, Massachusetts, 1860–1930.* Yale Univ. Pr. 1977 pap. $14.95. A gossipy history of the Harvard philosophy department, which included such greats as James, Royce, Santayana, C. I. Lewis, and A. N. Whitehead, as well as such lesser figures as Ralph Barton Perry and William Ernest Hocking.

Laszlo, Ervin. *Introduction to Systems Philosophy—Toward a New Paradigm of Contemporary Thought.* Gordon & Breach 1972 $49.95. A zealous advocacy of a holistic systems approach in contradistinction to the allegedly outmoded atomistic approach of modern science.

Lewis, H. D., ed. *Contemporary British Philosophy.* Humanities Pr. 1978 o.p. A collection of original essays by contemporary British philosophers.

Lingis, Alphonso. *Libido: The French Existential Theories.* [*Studies in Phenomenology and Existential Philosophy Ser.*] Indiana Univ. Pr. 1986 $22.50. The best introduction of French existential and neo-Freudian psychoanalytic theory to English readers.

Llewelyn, John. *Beyond Metaphysics? The Hermeneutic Circle in Contemporary Continental Philosophy.* Humanities Pr. 1985 text ed. $21.95. A penetrating, although sometimes obscure, investigation of "the end of philosophy."

Lucas, George R., Jr. *The Genesis of Modern Process Thought: A Historical Outline with Bibliography.* Scarecrow Pr. 1983 $20.00. The best bibliography of process philosophy in print.

Lucey, Kenneth, and Tibor Machan. *Recent Work in Philosophy.* Rowman 1983 text ed. $38.95. Slanted to social, political, and economic philosophy, with a libertarian bias.

Macquarrie, John. *Existentialism.* Penguin 1973 pap. $4.95. "A reader who has knowledge of some existentialists and who wants to fill in the gaps and to gain a more adequate, comprehensive view of existentialism will find this volume eminently useful" (C. S. Milligan, *Christian Century*).

———. *Twentieth Century Religious Thought: The Frontiers of Philosophy and Theology, 1900–1980.* Macmillan rev. ed. 1983 text ed. pap. $19.95. A perceptive and scholarly survey by a leading theologian.

Magill, Frank N., ed. *World Philosophy: Essays and Reviews of 225 Major Works.* Salem Pr. 5 vols. 1982 $250.00. Volumes 4 and 5 cover the period 1896–1971; each major work is summarized, followed by a summary of leading critical works on it and a selective annotated bibliography.

Mehta, Ved. *Fly and the Fly-Bottle: Encounters with British Intellectuals.* Columbia Univ. Pr. 1983 $32.00 pap. $12.00. "A report of the author's interviews with British historians and philosophers. These include discussions with Bertrand Russell, Ernest Gellner, A. J. Ayer, Iris Murdoch, A. J. P. Taylor, Lewis Namier, and others. The material in the book originated in *The New Yorker*" (*Bk. Review Digest*).

Merrell, Floyd. *Deconstruction Reframed.* Purdue Univ. Pr. 1985 $18.50. A scholarly study of deconstruction, mainly for literary criticism.

Montefiore, Alan, ed. *Philosophy in France Today.* Cambridge Univ. Pr. 1983 $42.50

pap. $11.95. "Editor Alan Montefiore attempts to reveal the philosophical climate of France today by presenting 11 original essays by contemporary French philosophers. Written especially for this. . .publishing venture, the essays are aimed at an English-speaking public. They include Jacques Derrida's 1980 defense of his *thèse d'état*. The other philosophers included are Pierre Bourdieu, Jacques Bouveresse, Jean-Toussaint Desanti, Vincent Descombes, Claude Lefort, Emmanuel Levinas, Jean-François Lyotard, Pierre Macherey, Louis Maren, and Paul Ricoeur" (*Choice*).

Morris, Charles. *Logical Positivism, Pragmatism and Scientific Empiricism*. AMS Pr. repr. of 1937 ed. 1979 $20.00. A lucid exposition and evaluation of the common features of three main tendencies in twentieth-century philosophy.

————. *The Pragmatic Movement in American Philosophy*. Braziller 1970 pap. $3.25 "This is the clearest explanation of American pragmatism ever written. Morris's study. . .is so pellucid and insightful that his little book must be greeted as a classic presentation and advocacy of pragmatism, a fresh restatement as living thought" (Robert Ginsburg, *Annals of the Amer. Academy*).

Munitz, Milton K. *Contemporary Analytic Philosophy*. Macmillan 1981 text ed. pap. $20.50. A critical exposition of analytic philosophy, in reference to basic topics and issues as well as to the major figures. An indispensable overview for the advanced student.

Norris, Christopher. *The Contest of Faculties: Deconstruction, Philosophy and Theory*. Methuen 1985 $32.00 pap. $12.95. A brilliant study of deconstructionism by a leading expert in literary criticism and philosophy.

————. *Deconstruction: Theory and Practice*. Methuen 1982 $25.00 pap. $11.95. "Norris' remarkable success at presenting a clear and critical picture of central issues without jargon and partisanship makes this book especially valuable to students of modern criticism and philosophy" (Richard Kuez-Rowski, *LJ*).

————. *The Deconstructive Turn: Essays in the Rhetoric of Philosophy*. Methuen 1984 pap. $11.95. "By revealing the common philosophical assumptions that underlie both deconstruction and some strains of analytic philosophy, Norris hopes to show the affinities between these supposedly hostile philosophies and thus, by implication, the mainstream position of deconstructivist practice. By, at the same time, deconstructing the texts of some of the. . .analytic philosophers, i.e., Ryle, Wittgenstein, and Austin, Norris hopes to show the superiority of Derrida's reading of the theory of philosophy" (*Choice*).

Pap, Arthur. *Elements of Analytic Philosophy*. Hafner repr. of 1949 ed. 1972 $19.95. A classic textbook by a brilliant young practitioner summing up the issues and topics of analytic philosophy, mainly logical empiricism, as matters were at midcentury.

Passmore, John. *A Hundred Years of Philosophy*. Penguin 2d ed. 1967 pap. $5.95. "Starting with John Stuart Mill's *System of Logic* (1843) he carries his survey down to embrace logical positivism, semantics [and] existentialism. . . . He restricts 'philosophy' to epistemology, logic and metaphysics [and writes] mainly from an English point of view, [treating] American and Continental philosophers" (Publisher's note).

————. *Recent Philosophers*. Open Court 1985 $23.95. "This new work, a worthy successor to *A Hundred Years of Philosophy*, gives a clear description of major trends and personalities. Philosophers discussed prominently include Chomsky, Davidson, Dennett, Derrida, Dummet, Feyerabend, Goodman, Mary Hesse, Kripke, David Lewis, Montague, Putnam, and Rorty" (Publisher's note).

Perry, Ralph Barton. *Philosophy of the Recent Past: An Outline of European and American Philosophy since 1860*. AMS Pr. repr. of 1926 ed. 1980 $29.00. "Taking as its point of departure philosophy in 1860, Professor Perry's volume treats post-Schopenhauerean thought, English, American and Continental, with special regard to the development of its four main tendencies: naturalism, idealism, pragmatism, and realism" (*Lit. Review*).

————. *Present Philosophical Tendencies.* Greenwood repr. of 1955 ed. 1968 lib. bdg. $22.50. Idealism, naturalism, pragmatism, and realism are the four tendencies presented in Perry's book. "Its conciseness and admirable lucidity suit it to educated readers possessing slight knowledge of formulated philosophy" (ALA, *Booklist*).

Poster, Mark. *Existential Marxism in Postwar France: From Sartre to Althusser.* Princeton Univ. Pr. 1975 $42.00 pap. $11.50. The scholarly classic on the topic.

Rajchman, John, and Cornell West, eds. *Post-Analytic Philosophy.* Columbia Univ. Pr. 1985 $37.00 pap. $15.50. "There is a diversity in philosophy today that contrasts with the uniformity of logical positivism and analytic philosophy, the programs which formed these philosophers, but from which, in various ways and to various degrees, they have all departed" (Preface). Among the philosophers included are Richard Rorty, John Rawls, and Richard J. Bernstein.

Randall, John H., Jr. *Philosophy after Darwin: Chapters for the Career of Philosophy and Other Essays.* Ed. by Beth J. Singer, Columbia Univ. Pr. 1977 $34.00. "The volume is remarkable for its lucid, penetrating taxonomy of what Randall deems the chief ingredients of 'modern philosophy.' It is essential for all graduate and undergraduate libraries" (*Choice*).

Reck, Andrew J. *The New American Philosophers: An Exploration of Thought since World War II.* Louisiana State Univ. Pr. 1968 o.p. The new American philosophers are C. I. Lewis, Stephen Pepper, Brand Blanshard, Ernest Nagel, John Hermann Randall, Jr., Justus Buchler, Sidney Hook, F. C. S. Northrop, James Kern Feibleman, John Wild, Charles Hartshorne, and Paul Weiss. "What history will do with these men is not yet clear, but Professor Reck has declared himself at this point. The essays in the volume are of relatively equal length, survey the basic positions of each of the writers, never enter into long criticism and analysis" (*LJ*).

————. *Recent American Philosophy: Studies of Ten Representative Thinkers.* Pantheon 1964 o.p. Ralph Barton Perry, William Ernest Hocking, George Herbert Mead, John Elof Boodin, Wilbur Marshall Urban, Dewitt H. Parker, Roy Wood Sellars, Arthur O. Lovejoy, Elijah Jordan, and Edgar Sheffield Brightman are the ten thinkers discussed. "The book will likely remain standard for some time. Recommended for colleges and large city libraries" (R. L. Perkins, *LJ*).

Ricoeur, Paul. *Main Trends in Philosophy.* [*Main Trends in the Social and Human Sciences Ser.*] Holmes & Meier 1979 text ed. pap. $26.50. A leading French philosopher offers an interpretive survey.

Robinson, Daniel Sommer, ed. *An Anthology of Recent Philosophy: Selections for Beginners from the Writings of the Greatest 20th Century Philosophers.* Telegraph Bks. repr. of 1929 ed. 1972 lib. bdg. $125.00. "A book of selected readings, for beginners, from recent philosophic literature. The excerpts are arranged in groups according to the chief types and problems of philosophy. Each selection is preceded by an analysis and followed by suggestions and questions" (*Bk. Review Digest*).

Rorty, Richard McKay, ed. *The Linguistic Turn: Recent Essays in Philosophical Method.* Univ. of Chicago Pr. 1971 pap. $12.00. This anthology, whose title caught on as the name for the development of Anglo-American philosophy, consists of 37 selections from twentieth-century philosophers and an erudite 40-page introduction by the editor.

Ryan, Michael. *Marxism and Deconstruction: A Critical Articulation.* Johns Hopkins

Univ. Pr. 1982 text ed. pap. $8.95. Ryan presents a "comparison of deconstruction and marxism (endeavoring to) relate deconstruction to the dialectical tradition in philosophy and (to) demonstrate how deconstruction can be used in the critique of ideology. . . . Ryan proposes a deconstructive marxism, lacking the metaphysical underpinnings of conservative 'scientific' marxist theory and employing deconstructive analysis both for marxist political criticism and to further current antimetaphysical developments within marxism" (Publisher's note).

Schaub, Edward L., ed. *Philosophy Today: Essays on Recent Developments in the Field of Philosophy.* [*Essay Index Repr. Ser.*] Ayer repr. of 1928 ed. 1979 $25.00. "Essays on contemporary English and American, French, German, Russian, Scandinavian and South American philosophy, reprinted from the *Monist*" (*Bk. Review Digest*).

Schneider, Herbert W. *Sources of Contemporary Philosophical Realism in America.* Irvington 1964 text ed. pap. $6.95. A survey of American realism, new and critical, discussing the issues and the figures, and providing bibliography, by the historian of American philosophy.

Sciacca, Michele F. *Philosophical Trends in the Contemporary World.* Trans. by Attilio M. Salerno, Irvington 1964 text ed. $49.50 pap. $19.95. A survey of the main trends in philosophy in midcentury by a leading Italian philosopher.

Silverman, Hugh J., and Don Ihde, eds. *Hermeneutics and Deconstruction: Selected Studies in Phenomenology and Existential Philosophy.* State Univ. of New York Pr. 1985 $44.50 pap. $19.95. An anthology of essays by academic experts on the subject.

Smith, John E., ed. *Contemporary American Philosophy: Second Series.* Humanities Pr. 1971 o.p. The book "contains contributions from teachers of philosophy in American universities. . .[discussing] their own work and that of their teachers and colleagues" (*Choice*).

Solomon, Robert C. *Existentialism.* Modern Lib. 1974 pap. $7.00; Random 1974 text ed. pap. $6.50. An excellent selection of writings by a leading scholar on existentialism.

――――. *Introducing the Existentialists.* Hackett 1981 text ed. pap. $3.95. Well-written, witty, informative introductory text.

Spiegelberg, Herbert. *The Phenomenological Movement: An Historical Introduction.* Kluwer Academic 3d ed. rev. and enl. ed. 1982 lib. bdg. $84.50 text ed. pap. $32.50. The classic survey of the main figures and topics in phenomenology.

Stegmueller, W. *Main Currents in Contemporary German, British and American Philosophy.* Kluwer Academic rev. and enl. ed. 1969 lib. bdg. $50.00. A thorough and demanding survey of the main figures and significant philosophical theories in twentieth-century philosophy.

Taylor, Mark C., ed. *Deconstruction in Context: Literature and Philosophy.* Univ. of Chicago Pr. 1986 text ed. $45.00 pap. $16.95. A collection of critical essays for the advanced student.

Thayer, H. S. *Meaning and Action: A Critical History of Pragmatism.* Hackett 1981 text ed. $30.00 pap. $15.00. "For any collection on American philosophy this volume will be an essential addition, because of its comprehensiveness, scholarly competence, and sound judgments. The bibliography is most scholarly" (B. P. Brennan, *LJ*).

――――, ed. *Pragmatism: The Classic Writings.* Hackett 1982 text ed. lib. bdg. $18.50 pap. $8.50. An anthology to match the book listed above.

Urmson, J. O. *Philosophical Analysis: Its Development Between the Two World Wars.* Oxford 1956 $19.95. A survey of the genesis of linguistic analysis from the earlier twentieth-century forms of analytic philosophy represented by G. E. Moore, Bertrand Russell, C. D. Broad, and the early Wittgenstein.

Wachterhauser, Brice R., ed. *Hermeneutics and Modern Philosophy*. State Univ. of New York Pr. 1986 $49.50 pap. $16.95. A collection of scholarly essays for the advanced student.

Wahl, Jean A. *A Short History of Existentialism*. Greenwood repr. of 1949 ed. 1972 lib. bdg. $22.50; Richard West repr. of 1949 ed. 1979 lib. bdg. $15.00. A facile but insightful sketch of the development of existentialism by a leading French philosopher.

Warnock, Geoffrey J. *English Philosophy since 1900*. Greenwood repr. of 1969 ed. 1981 lib. bdg. $25.00. A concise but reliable history.

Warnock, Mary. *Existentialism*. Oxford 1970 text ed. pap. $5.95. "This useful and modest little book...guides the nonspecialist through existentialism, shows that this philosophy is really no more difficult than any other serious intellectual movement, and that the problems of these thinkers have much in common with those of other philosophic schools" (P. J. W. Miller, *Mod. Language Journal*).

Wedberg, Anders. *A History of Philosophy: From Bolzano to Wittgenstein*. Oxford 1984 text ed. $29.95 pap. $13.95. "This third and final volume of Wedberg's *History of Philosophy* traces the development of European philosophy from the beginning of the nineteenth century through the mid-twentieth century. Like its predecessors, its scope is limited to logical, epistemological, and ontological questions presented from an analytical perspective" (*Choice*).

Weitz, Morris. *Twentieth-Century Philosophy: The Analytic Tradition*. Free Pr. 1966 text ed. pap. $14.95. A useful anthology.

White, Morton. *Pragmatism and the American Mind: Essays and Reviews in Philosophy and Intellectual History*. Oxford 1973 pap. $5.95. This "collection of essays and critical reviews by one of America's most able analytic philosophers [treats] a wide range of topics in American intellectual history" (*Choice*).

——. *Toward Reunion in Philosophy*. Atheneum 1963 pap. $1.65. A brilliant attempt by one of America's leading philosophers to uncover the common ground of pragmatism and analytic philosophy.

——, ed. *Age of Analysis: Twentieth Century Philosophers* [*Essay Index Repr. Ser.*] Ayer 1955 $19.00; NAL 1955 repr. 1986 $3.95. "It is not simply an anthology. It is an anthology plus.... The 'plus' consists in the introduction to the collection and to each of the thinkers presented" (Jerome Nathanson, *N.Y. Herald Tribune*).

ADLER, MORTIMER J. 1902–

Born in New York City, Mortimer Adler was educated at Columbia University, where as a philosophy instructor he taught in a program focused on the intellectual foundations of Western civilization. Called to the University of Chicago in 1927 by President Robert Hutchins, he played a major role in renovating the undergraduate curriculum to center on the great books. His philosophical interests, committed to the dialectical method, crystallized in a defense of neo-Thomism. But he never strayed far from concerns with education and other vital public issues.

From 1942 to 1945 Adler was director of the Institute for Philosophical Research, based in San Francisco, California. Since 1945, he has served as associate editor of Great Books of the Western World series, and in 1952 he published *Syntopicon*, an analytic index of the great ideas in the great books. In 1966 he became director of the editorial planning for the fifteenth edition of the *Encyclopaedia Britannica,* and in 1974, chairman of its editorial board.

Adler has been devoted in recent years to expounding his interpretations of selected great ideas and to advocating his *Paideia Proposal,* a program that would require that all students receive the same quantity and quality of education, and that would concentrate on the study of the great ideas expressed in the great books, a study conducted by means of the dialectical method. In 1977 he published his autobiography, *Philosopher at Large.*

BOOKS BY ADLER

(and Jerome Michael). *Crime, Law, and Social Science.* 1933. [*Criminology, Law Enforcement, and Social Problems Ser.*] Patterson Smith repr. of 1971 ed. 1984 $15.00. A sound textbook on criminology that is sensitive to ethical principles.

Art and Prudence. Ed. by Garth S. Jowett, Ayer repr. of 1937 ed. 1978 lib. bdg. $59.50. A comprehensive and penetrating study of the authority of morals over art.

How to Read a Book. Simon & Schuster repr. of 1938 rev. ed. 1972 pap. $8.95. A useful, unrivaled guide.

St. Thomas and the Gentiles. Marquette Univ. Pr. 1938 $7.95. A concise statement of neo-Thomism.

(and Robert Hutchins, eds.). *Great Books of the Western World.* 1952. Ency. Brit. 54 vols. lib. bdg. $999.00. A collection of the great books in well-bound standard editions in the English language.

(and Louis O. Kelso). *The Capitalist Manifesto.* Greenwood repr. of 1958 ed. 1975 $29.75. The case for capitalism, an antidote to communism and socialism.

(and Milton Mayer). *Revolution in Education.* Univ. of Chicago Pr. 1958 $15.00. The argument on behalf of great books, great ideas, and dialectic in education.

(and Louis O. Kelso). *The New Capitalists.* Greenwood repr. of 1961 ed. 1975 $22.50. Additional investigations of how capitalism flourishes.

Freedom: A Study of the Development of the Concept in the English and American Traditions of Philosophy. Magi Bks. 1968 pap. $.50. An example of dialectic applied to the idea of freedom.

(ed.). *Annals of America: 1493–1973.* Ency. Brit. 23 vols. 1976 lib. bdg. $459.00. A collection of basic American works.

(and Robert Hutchins, eds.). *The Great Ideas Anthologies.* Ayer 4 vols. 1976 lib. bdg. $84.00. The 100 great ideas illustrated by selections of passages in which they are expressed.

Some Questions about Language. Open Court 1976 $19.95. Raises questions about the validity of linguistic philosophy.

(and Charles Van Doren). *Great Treasury of Western Thought: A Compendium of Important Statements on Man and His Institutions by the Great Thinkers in Western History.* Bowker 1977 $37.50. A selection of passages of wisdom on all the fundamental topics that concern human beings.

Aristotle for Everyone: Difficult Thought Made Easy. (Under title of *Aristotle for Everybody*) Bantam 1980 pap. $3.95; Macmillan 1978 $11.95. A lucid introduction to the difficult philosophy of Aristotle, which Adler espouses.

How to Think about God: A Guide for the Twentieth-Century Pagan. Macmillan 1980 $10.95. A provocative, but very clear, essay.

The Angels and Us. Macmillan 1982 $11.95. Adler takes angels seriously and indicates why.

The Paideia Proposal: An Educational Manifesto. Macmillan 1982 $7.95 pap. $3.95. A
    proposal for an educational program based on great ideas and dialectic.
How to Speak and How to Listen: A Guide to Pleasurable and Profitable Conversation.
    Ed. by B. Lippman, Macmillan 1983 $12.95 pap. $5.95. A useful guide.
Paideia Problems and Possibilities. Macmillan 1983 $7.95 pap. $3.95. A continuation
    of the discussion posed by *The Paideia Proposal.*
The Paideia Program: An Educational Syllabus. Macmillan 1984 $8.95 pap. $4.95. The
    proposal for implementing *The Paideia Proposal.*
Six Great Ideas: Truth, Goodness, Beauty, Liberty, Equality, Justice. Macmillan 1984
    pap. $5.95. A clear and concise discussion of these ideas.
A Vision of the Future: Twelve Ideas for a Better Life and a Better Society. Macmillan
    1984 $14.95. A sane futurist vision based on traditional notions.
Ten Philosophical Mistakes. Macmillan 1985 $12.95. A facile, but illuminating, philo-
    sophical essay.
A Guidebook to Learning: For the Lifelong Pursuit of Wisdom. Macmillan 1986 $13.95.
    A handy manual.
We Hold These Truths. Macmillan 1987 $14.95. Incisive analysis and defense of the
    principles that underlie the American political system, focused on the Constitu-
    tion.

ADORNO, T(HEODOR) W. 1903–1969

A leading member of the Institute for Social Research at the University of
Frankfurt founded in 1923, commonly known as the Frankfurt School, Adorno
shared with Max Horkheimer, Walter Benjamin, and Herbert Marcuse the
conviction that a critical theory of Marxism, opposed to all forms of positivism
in social science and to all interpretations of Marxism burdened with dogmatic materialism, was indispensable for the constitution and reconstruction
of democracy. He took up the cudgels against positivism and advocated the
method of dialectics grounded in a critical rationalism that propelled him into
intellectual conflict with Hegel, Heidegger, and Heideggerian hermeneutics.
A neo-Marxist, he examined the aesthetics of a mass society without the economic reductionism that rendered so much Marxist criticism sterile. Pessimistic about the prospects for art in contemporary society, he was nevertheless
particularly distinguished in his philosophy and criticism of music.

A refugee from Nazi Germany, Adorno resided in Los Angeles from late
1941 to the fall of 1949, when he returned to Germany to participate in the
resurrection of the Frankfurt School. During exile, however, Adorno continued to write, some of his most significant work being produced in these
years.

BOOKS BY ADORNO

The Positivist Dispute in German Sociology. 1969. Gower 1981 pap. $12.50. A critique
    of positivism.
The Jargon of Authenticity. Trans. by Knut Tarnowski and Frederic Will, Methuen
    1986 pap. $10.95; Northwestern Univ. Pr. 1973 $17.95 pap. $7.95. An abstruse
    dialectical study of the language of morals.
Negative Dialects. Continuum 2d ed. 1973 pap. $14.95. A probing investigation of
    dialectic as a method of inquiry.
Philosophy of Modern Music. Continuum 1973 $12.50 rev. ed. 1980 pap. $10.95. An
    original study of the nature, function, and uses of modern music.

(and Max Horkheimer). *Dialectic of Enlightenment*. Trans. by John Cumming, Continuum 1975 pap. $9.95. A penetrating critique of the Enlightenment from the standpoint of critical theory.

Introduction to the Sociology of Music. Trans. by E. B. Ashton, Continuum 1976 $16.95. A basic work in the field.

Minima Moralia: Reflections from a Damaged Life. Trans. by E. F. Jephcott, Schocken 1978 $11.95. An abstruse but profound treatise on the ethical issues confronting a human being living in the present century.

In Search of Wagner. Schocken 1981 $14.50. A contribution to the philosophy of music.

Prisms. Trans. by Samuel Weber and Sherry Weber, MIT 1982 pap. $7.95. An essay in aesthetics and culture.

Against Epistemology—A Metacritique: Studies in Husserl and the Phenomenological Antinomies. Trans. by Willis Domingo, MIT 1983 $32.50 pap. $8.95. A profound contribution to contemporary theory of knowledge and phenomenology.

(and Else Frenkel-Brunswik). *The Authoritarian Personality*. Norton abr. ed. 1983 pap. $12.95. A basic work on the topic.

Aesthetic Theory. Trans. by G. Lenhardt, Methuen 1984 $49.95 1986 pap. $17.95. The most comprehensive and systematic statement of Adorno's philosophy of art and aesthetics.

BOOK ABOUT ADORNO

Jay, Martin. *Adorno*. Harvard Univ. Pr. 1984 text ed. $15.00 pap. $5.95. An account of Adorno's Marxism, his aesthetic modernism, his cultural conservatism, his anticipation of deconstructionism, and his self-conscious Jewishness. "For those interested in the Frankfurt School's positions on music, culture, art, and politics, Jay's study is useful and enriching reading" (*Choice*).

ALIOTTA, ANTONIO. 1881–1964

Born in Salerno, Aliotta taught at the Universities of Padua and Naples in Italy. After publishing studies in experimental psychology, he authored in 1912 a vast critical analysis of contemporary philosophy in which he defended a theistic idealism. This work was translated into English and published in 1914. As the neo-Hegelian idealism of CROCE (see Vol. 2) and Gentile became ascendant in Italy, Aliotta sided with its opponents, drawing for his support on philosophical developments outside Italy; in particular he embraced pragmatism, realism, and relationism.

BOOK BY ALIOTTA

The Idealistic Reaction against Science. 1912. Trans. by Agnes McCaskill [*History, Philosophy and Sociology of Science*] Ayer repr. of 1914 ed. 1975 lib. bdg. $37.50. A classic work defending philosophical idealism in contemporary science.

ARENDT, HANNAH. 1906–1975

A refugee from Nazi Germany, Hannah Arendt had studied with Martin Heidegger and Karl Jaspers. In the United States she taught at the University of Chicago and the New School for Social Research in New York City. Her field became cultural criticism. She was one of the most eminent political theorists of her time and the author of penetrating studies of political action, totalitarianism, democracy, morality and the life of mind, anti-Semitism, and modernity. Her pioneering work on totalitarianism appeared in 1951.

Arendt's book *The Human Condition* appeared in 1958. Exploring the human triad of labor, work, and action, she displayed in this work a singular mastery of the categories of philosophical anthropology and social philosophy in a distinctive style that draws on ancient ideas and ideals.

Arendt proceeded to apply her remarkably critical mind to the characteristic experiences, events, and persons of her times. She was especially concerned with the status of Jewishness in the contemporary world. But she never abandoned investigations into the history of philosophy and other basic philosophical topics, as her posthumous publications reveal. (See also Volume 3.)

BOOKS BY ARENDT

The Origins of Totalitarianism. 1951. Harcourt 3 vols. 1968 pap. $3.95–$4.95 vol. 1, *Antisemitism;* vol. 2, *Imperialism;* vol. 3, *Totalitarianism.* A classic in the field, this work established Arendt's reputation. It reveals psychological and social causes for the formation of human personalities compatible with and supportive of political dictatorships.

Rachel Vernhagen: The Life of a Jewish Woman. 1957. Trans. by Richard Winston and Clara Winston, Harcourt 1974 pap. $7.95. A biography of a Jewish woman illustrating feminism and the struggles against anti-Semitism.

The Human Condition. Peter Smith 1958. $17.00; Univ. of Chicago Pr. 1970 pap. $12.95. A profound philosophical work.

Between Past and Future: Eight Exercises in Political Thought. 1961. Penguin enl. ed. 1977 pap. $6.95; Peter Smith 1983 $12.50. An insightful exploration of issues in political philosophy and practical politics.

Eichmann in Jerusalem: A Report of the Banality of Evil. 1963. Penguin repr. of rev. ed. 1977 pap. $6.95; Peter Smith 1972 $17.00. Originally published in *The New Yorker,* this profile is widely known.

On Revolution. 1963. Greenwood 1982 lib. bdg. $35.00; [*Pelican Ser.*] Penguin repr. of 1963 ed. 1977 pap. $6.95; Peter Smith 1973 $14.25. A philosophical theory of revolution, comparing and contrasting the American, French, and Russian revolutions.

Men in Dark Times. 1968. Harcourt 1970 pap. $8.95. A collection of studies of men confronting difficult political situations.

Crises of the Republic. Harcourt 1972 pap. $5.95. A collection of articles on pressing problems.

The Life of the Mind. 1978. Harcourt 1981 pap. $9.95. Posthumously published, unfinished work of systematic philosophy.

Lectures on Kant's Political Philosophy. Ed. by Ronald Beiner, Univ. of Chicago Pr. 1982 $17.50. Posthumously published university lectures delivered by Arendt.

BOOKS ABOUT ARENDT

Kateb, George. *Hannah Arendt: Politics, Conscience, Evil.* [*Philosophy and Society Ser.*] Rowman & Allanheld 1984 $26.50. An expository and sympathetically critical examination of the body of Arendt's work.

May, Derwent. *Hannah Arendt.* Penguin 1986 $4.95. An accessible and accurate account of her life and work.

Tolle, Gordon J. *Human Nature under Fire: The Political Philosophy of Hannah*

Arendt. Univ. Pr. of Amer. 1982 text ed. lib. bdg. $27.75 pap. $11.50. A penetrating but limited scholarly study.

Whitfield, Stephen J. *Into the Dark: Hannah Arendt and Totalitarianism.* Temple Univ. Pr. 1980 $29.95. Focuses on Arendt's treatments of totalitarianism and Eichmann. Whitfield "has provided a valuable assessment of her explanation of totalitarianism" (Michael Curtis, *AHR*).

Young-Bruehl, Elisabeth. *Hannah Arendt: For Love of the World.* Yale Univ. Pr. 1982 $35.00 1983 pap. $14.95. Based on Arendt's papers and correspondence, the author's personal acquaintance with Arendt, and interviews with Arendt's family and friends, this book relates Arendt's childhood and adolescence, her friendship with Karl Jaspers, and her love affair with Martin Heidegger.

AUSTIN, JOHN LANGSHAW. 1911–1960

Educated at Shrewsbury School and Balliol, Oxford, Austin became a fellow at Oxford in 1933, where he taught, except during World War II, until his death in 1960. At Oxford he was appointed White professor of moral philosophy in 1952. A prominent figure in the development of British analytic philosophy, Austin emphasized the value of ordinary language in illuminating and resolving philosophical problems. He preferred to do philosophy by attending to the way words function in ordinary language.

Austin's methods and results are contained in numerous papers and two succinct books. His major achievements in the school of linguistic analysis include (1) his theory of elocutionary forces in language usage, which overhauled the distinctions between performatives and constatives, and (2) his critique of sense-datum theory in the light of his linguistic discoveries.

BOOKS BY AUSTIN

Philosophical Papers. 1961. Ed. by James Urmson and Geoffrey Warnock, Oxford 3d ed. 1979 text ed. pap. $22.00. A collection of Austin's published articles; for advanced scholars only.

How to Do Things with Words. Oxford 1962 o.p. An introduction to Austin's theory of language and his method of linguistic analysis.

Sense and Sensibilia. Ed. by Geoffrey Warnock, Oxford 1962 pap. $7.95. This work contains Austin's devastating critique of the sense-datum theory in epistemology.

BOOK ABOUT AUSTIN

Fann, K. T., ed. *Symposium on J. L. Austin.* [*International Lib. of Philosophy and Scientific Method*] Humanities Pr. repr. of 1969 ed. 1979 text ed. $32.50. A collection of 28 essays by prominent Anglo-American analytic philosophers on Austin's conception of philosophy, on specific points raised in his papers, on his critique of sense-datum theory, and on his theory of linguistic meaning and speech acts.

AYER, SIR ALFRED JULES. 1910–

After education at Eton and Oxford, Ayer studied philosophy at the University of Vienna, where he affiliated with the Vienna Circle, the school of logical positivism led by MORITZ SCHLICK (see also Vol. 5). On his return to England, he accepted an appointment in 1933 as lecturer at Oxford, and, except for his military service during World War II, he has been writing and teaching philosophy ever since. In 1946 he was appointed Grote professor at the University of London and in 1959 Wykeham professor at Oxford.

His fame was established with the publication of his first book, *Language, Truth and Logic*, in 1936. This work introduced logical positivism to the English-speaking world in a clear, vigorous, and persuasive style. Building on the thought of RUSSELL (see also Vol. 5) and Wittgenstein, Ayer sharpened their theses, boldly revealing the affiliations of logical positivism with traditional British empiricism, particularly the work of DAVID HUME.

For his contributions to philosophy Ayer was knighted by the British Crown. He has provided an account of his life, at least of its professional and philosophical sides, in two volumes of autobiography, listed below.

BOOKS BY AYER

Language, Truth and Logic. 1936. Dover 1956 pap. $2.75; Peter Smith repr. of 1946 ed. 2d ed. 1952 $13.50. Brilliant, vigorous introduction of logical positivism to English readers.

Philosophical Essays. Greenwood repr. of 1954 ed. 1980 lib. bdg. $27.50. A collection of Ayer's previously published essays in epistemology and the philosophy of mind.

Problem of Knowledge. Penguin 1957 pap. $4.95. An elementary presentation of the epistemology of logical positivism.

Logical Positivism. Free Pr. 1966 pap. $14.95; Greenwood repr. of 1959 ed. 1978 lib. bdg. $32.50. A book of readings from the logical positivists with an introduction by the editor.

Origins of Pragmatism: Studies in the Philosophy of Charles Sanders Peirce and William James. Freeman, Cooper 1968 $12.50. Commentaries on themes in the philosophies of Peirce and James relevant to logical empiricist issues.

Russell and Moore: The Analytical Heritage. [*William James Lectures Ser.*] Harvard Univ. Pr. 1971 $16.50. Appreciative but critical account of the contributions of Russell and Moore.

Bertrand Russell as a Philosopher. Longwood 1972 pap. $2.25. On Russell in the same vein as the volume listed above.

Part of My Life. Oxford 1978 pap. $7.95. The first volume of Ayer's autobiographical reflections.

Probability and Evidence. Columbia Univ. Pr. 1979 $21.00 pap. $11.00. A technical investigation of problems in epistemology and inductive logic.

Hume. Oxford 1980 pap. $3.95. A critical appreciation of the Scottish empiricist.

Philosophy in the Twentieth Century. Random 1983 pap. $8.95. A critical history from the standpoint of a leading practitioner of philosophical analysis.

Freedom and Morality and Other Essays. Oxford 1984 $22.50. A collection of Ayer's previously published essays, mostly on moral and practical topics.

More of My Life. Oxford 1984 o.p. The second volume of memoirs.

Wittgenstein. Random 1985 $19.95; Univ. of Chicago Pr. 1986 pap. $8.95. A critical appreciation of the contributions of this major twentieth-century philosopher.

Voltaire. Random 1986 $19.95. A critical appreciation of the French *philosophe*, with excerpts from his writings.

BACHELARD, GASTON. 1884–1962

Born in Bar-sur-Aube, France, Bachelard received his doctorate in 1927, became professor of philosophy at the University of Dijon in 1930 and held the chair in the history and philosophy of science at the University of Paris from 1940 to 1954.

In epistemology and philosophy of science Bachelard espoused a dialectical rationalism, or dialogue between reason and experience. Rejecting the Cartesian conception of scientific truths as immutable, he insisted on experiment as well as mathematics in the development of science and described the cooperation between the two as a philosophy of saying "no," of being ever ready to revise or abandon the established framework of scientific theory to express the new discoveries.

In addition to his contributions to the epistemological foundations of science, he explored the role of reverie and emotion in the expressions of both science and more imaginative thinking. His psychological explanations of the four elements—earth, air, fire, water—illustrate this almost poetic aspect of his philosophy.

BOOKS BY BACHELARD

Psychoanalysis of Fire. 1932. Trans. by A. C. Ross, Beacon Pr. 1964 pap. $5.95. The first of his imaginative psychological explanations of the elements.

The New Scientific Spirit. 1934. Trans. by Arthur Goldhammer, Beacon Pr. 1985 $22.95 1986 pap. $9.95. The introduction to his dialectical interpretation of science in which experiment and imagination are as significant as reason.

Water and Dreams: An Essay on Imagination of Matter. 1942. Trans. by Edith R. Farrell, Dallas Institute 1983 $25.00. An exploration of the role of dreams in the formation of the scientific theory of matter.

Poetics of Space. Trans. by Maria Jolas, Beacon Pr. 1969 pap. $7.95. The geometry of space approached and construed as imaginative poetry.

Poetics of Reverie: Childhood, Language and Cosmos. Beacon Pr. 1971 pap. $8.95. A late work tracing Bachelard's themes back to the mental life of children.

BOOKS ABOUT BACHELARD

Smith, Roch C. *Gaston Bachelard.* [*Twayne's World Authors Ser.*] G. K. Hall 1982 lib. bdg. $17.95

Tiles, Mary. *Bachelard: Science and Objectivity.* [*Modern European Philosophy*] Cambridge Univ. Pr. 1985 $34.50 pap. $12.95. This introduction to Bachelard's basic ideas on epistemology and philosophy of science discusses his theory of conceptual change and compares his approach to that characteristic of analytic philosophers.

BERDYAEV, NICHOLAS. 1874–1948

The great Russian Orthodox religious philosopher was born in Kiev. After the revolution he founded the Free Academy of Spiritual Culture and was given the chair of philosophy at the University of Moscow. He was imprisoned for his defense of religion and was driven into exile, first to Berlin (1922), then to Paris (1934).

Though Berdyaev's early interest was in Marxism, "it was a deviation from orthodox Marxism in that it insisted that only transcendental critical idealism can solve the problem of truth" (Louis J. Shein, *Readings in Russian Philosophical Thought*). He later became interested in mystical and religious ideas and developed a process cosmology and theology.

His last testament, *The Realm of Spirit and the Realm of Caesar*, found after his death and put into publishable form by a group of his friends, shows "no sign of decay of mental power or spiritual force." His "lucid thought and luminous style give his work an almost compulsive force."

BOOKS BY BERDYAEV

The Russian Revolution. 1933. Univ. of Michigan Pr. 1960 o.p. Perceptive explanation of the world-shaking event by an ambivalent Russian émigré.

Solitude and Society. 1938. Trans. by George Reavey, Greenwood 1976 lib. bdg. $25.00. An exemplary presentation of the reflective nature of this intensely religious but heterodox philosopher.

Leontiev. 1940. Academic International Pr. 1968 pap. $15.00; Arden Lib. repr. of 1940 ed. 1978 lib. bdg. $25.00. A concise critical biography.

The Russian Idea. 1948. Trans. by R. M. French, Greenwood 1979 lib. bdg. $37.50. A probing attempt to elicit the essence of Russia.

The Beginning and the End. 1952. Trans. by R. M. French, Greenwood 1976 lib. bdg. $35.00. A profound essay on the eschatological aspects of cosmology and theology.

The Realm of Spirit and the Realm of Caesar. 1953. Trans. by Donald A. Lowrie, Greenwood 1975 lib. bdg. $55.00. Posthumously published work exhibiting Berdyaev's final struggles with the political and religious conflicts of his life and times.

The Destiny of Man. 1954. Trans. by Natalie Duddington, Hyperion 1979 $25.85. A process metaphysics of man's nature, status, and function in the cosmos.

BOOKS ABOUT BERDYAEV

Allen, E. L. *Freedom in God: A Guide to the Thought of Nicholas Berdyaev.* Arden Lib. 1978 lib. bdg. $12.00; Folcroft 1980 lib. bdg. $12.50. A handy manual on a central theme.

Lowrie, Donald A. *Rebellious Prophet: A Life of Nicolai Berdyaev.* Greenwood repr. of 1960 ed. 1974 lib. bdg. $35.00. The author was a close associate of Berdyaev during the Russian thinker's 24-year exile in Paris. "Utilizing unrivaled opportunities for an intimate knowledge of his subject, Lowrie has produced a book which may be confidently regarded as Berdyaev's definitive biography—at least for a long time to come" (Matthew Spinka, *Christian Century*).

Seaver, G. *Nicolas Berdyaev.* Gordon Pr. 1979 $59.95. A reliable critical biography.

Wernham, James C. S. *Two Russian Thinkers: An Essay in Berdyaev and Shestov.* Univ. of Toronto Pr. 1968 o.p. A scholarly comparative study.

BLACK, MAX. 1909–

Max Black was born in Baku, Russia, received his B.A. in mathematics from Cambridge University, studied at Göttingen, and received his Ph.D. in philosophy from the University of London in 1939. Migrating to the United States in 1940, he became an American citizen in 1948. After teaching at the University of Illinois, he was appointed professor of philosophy at Cornell in 1948.

Black has been an influential analytic philosopher, introducing to American students the scientific and analytic modes of philosophizing associated with C. D. Broad, G. E. Moore, and Ludwig Wittgenstein. He has been especially prominent in the pursuit of problems raised by Wittgenstein, and he has stressed the importance of the linguistic method in philosophical thought.

BOOKS BY BLACK

Nature of Mathematics. [*Quality Pap. Ser.*] Littlefield repr. of 1930 ed. 1965 pap. $3.95. An early critical exposition of the major theories of the nature of mathematics.

Language and Philosophy: Studies in Method. Greenwood repr. of 1949 ed. 1981 lib. bdg. $27.50. A collection of essays illustrating Black's method of linguistic analysis.

(ed.). *Philosophical Analysis: A Collection of Essays*. [*Essay Index Repr. Ser.*] Irvington repr. of 1950 ed. 1984 lib. bdg. $49.00 pap. $14.95. A basic collection of essays on the topic.

Critical Thinking. Prentice-Hall 2d ed. 1952 text ed. $25.95. A widely used textbook in college courses on elementary logic.

Problems of Analysis: Philosophical Essays. Greenwood repr. of 1954 ed. 1971 lib. bdg. $22.50. A collection of previously published essays for the advanced student.

Models and Metaphors: Studies in Language and Philosophy. Cornell Univ. Pr. 1962 $27.50. The same type of collection as the title above.

A Companion to Wittgenstein's "Tractatus." Cornell Univ. Pr. 1964 $42.50. A handbook in the form of partial commentary to Wittgenstein's major but obscure book.

Caveats and Critiques: Philosophical Essays in Language, Logic, and Art. Cornell Univ. Pr. 1975 $27.50. A collection of previously published essays.

(ed.). *The Social Theories of Talcott Parsons: A Critical Examination*. [*Arcturus Bks. Paperbacks*] Southern Illinois Univ. Pr. 1976 pap. $8.95. A collection of essays critically treating Parsons's social theories; for the advanced students.

The Prevalence of Humbug and Other Essays. Cornell Univ. Pr. 1983 $19.95 pap. $7.95. A collection of essays, some revealing Black's playfulness.

BLANSHARD, BRAND. 1892–

Brand Blanshard is an American philosopher who studied at Oxford as a Rhodes scholar. The Oxford method of education and the philosophical style of idealism (or rationalism) that flourished there during the period around World War I have profoundly influenced his career as a teacher and philosopher in America. He received his American degrees from the University of Michigan, Columbia University, and Harvard University, and he has taught at Swarthmore College and Yale University.

His two-volume work *The Nature of Thought* (1939) is a critical survey of the theories of mind and knowledge that prevailed during the first half of the twentieth century and is also a constructive argument for the nature of reason as sovereign. In his Gifford lectures at St. Andrews and his Carus lectures before the American Philosophical Association, Blanshard argued against what he has considered the detractors of reason—moral relativism and noncognitivism, existentialism, and analytic philosophy in its various forms—and he published these lectures in expanded and revised form in the trilogy on reason listed below.

BOOKS BY BLANSHARD

The Nature of Thought. 1939. [*Muirhead Lib. of Philosophy*] Humanities 2 vols. 1964 text ed. $45.00

On Philosophical Style. Greenwood repr. of 1954 ed. lib. bdg. $22.50. An elegant essay on the importance of clarity in philosophy.

(ed.). *Education in the Age of Science.* [*Essay Index Repr. Ser.*] Ayer 1959 $20.00. A collection of essays defending liberal education.

Reason and Goodness. [*Gifford Lectures*] Open Court 1961 o.p.

Reason and Analysis. [*Paul Carus Lecture Ser.*] Open Court 2d ed. 1962 $11.95

The Uses of a Liberal Education and Other Talks to Students. Open Court 1973 $17.95. A collection of very readable essays on education.

Reason and Belief. [*Gifford Lectures*] Yale Univ. Pr. 1974 $28.75

Four Reasonable Men: Aurelius, Mill, Renan, Sidgwick. Wesleyan Univ. Pr. 1984 $25.00 pap. $9.95. Beautifully written studies of four moralists whose lives and works exemplify the significance of reason.

BOOK ABOUT BLANSHARD

Schilpp, Paul Arthur, ed. *The Philosophy of Brand Blanshard.* [*Lib. of Living Philosophers*] Open Court 1980 $39.95. This volume consists of Blanshard's autobiography, 30 critical essays, Blanshard's replies to his critics, and his bibliography.

BLOCH, ERNST. 1885–1977

Bloch ranks as a major German Marxist philosopher. Beginning his career as author and teacher during World War I, he moved in the orbit of Marxist thought during the 1920s. In 1933 he left Germany and eventually found his way to the United States, where he created his major work, *The Principle of Hope.* After World War II, he settled in East Germany, where from 1948 to 1957 he was professor at the University of Leipzig. His work eventually aroused the hostility of the authorities, and in 1961 he was granted political asylum in West Germany.

Block departed from orthodox Marxism by attending to the problem of intellectual culture and refraining from treating it merely as superstructure determined by the materialist elements of political economy. Stressing the role of hope—as an inner drive or hunger in material human beings—for a possible ideal future order, Bloch's thought may be described as utopian, involving the realization of a religious community, akin to the kingdom of God, where men are no longer exploited but are free. His style echoes recent expressionism and is also rich in mystical overtones of biblical origin.

BOOKS BY BLOCH

The Principle of Hope. 1954–59. Trans. by Neville Plaice and others, MIT 3 vols. 1986 $95.00. Bloch's proud, comprehensive treatise on hope; a major work in the history of philosophy.

Natural Law and Human Dignity. 1960. Trans. by Dennis J. Schmidt, MIT 1985 text ed. $25.00. Bloch's examination of the nature of man and of law.

Essays on the Philosophy of Music. Trans. by P. Palmer, Cambridge Univ. Pr. 1985 $49.50 pap. $14.95. A collection of essays on the philosophy and aesthetics of music.

BOODIN, JOHN ELOF. 1869–1950

Born in Sweden, Boodin immigrated to the United States in 1887. He studied at Brown University and Harvard University, and he taught at Grinnell College, the University of Kansas, Carleton College, and the University of California at Los Angeles. He was an original thinker who sought to construct a system of philosophy in the light of the theory of evolution and relativity physics. His theory of cosmic evolution was both empirical and idealist, and he applied his theory to religion and social philosophy.

BOOKS BY BOODIN

Time and Reality. [*Philosophy in Amer. Ser.*] AMS Pr. repr. of 1904 ed. 1980 $20.00. A metaphysical essay on the negativity of time.

God and Creation. AMS Pr. 2 vols. repr. of 1934 ed. 1970 $67.50. A comprehensive theory of cosmic evolution with a survey of rival theories.

The Social Mind: Foundations of Social Philosophy. [*Philosophy in Amer. Ser.*] AMS Pr. repr. of 1939 ed. 1980 $43.00. A philosophical treatise on the nature, status, and functions of social mind.

Religion of Tomorrow. AMS Pr. repr. of 1943 ed. 1981 $14.00. A concise preview of the future of religion from the standpoint of a cosmic evolutionist.

BRIGHTMAN, EDGAR SHEFFIELD. 1884–1953

Educated at Brown University and at Boston University, Brightman became Borden Parker Bowne professor of philosophy at Boston University in 1919. He was the leading exponent of philosophical personalism in America during his lifetime. Among the personalist school of thinkers he was best known for his advocacy of the thesis that God is finite. Otherwise, he contended, the existence of evil is inexplicable or God is not benevolent.

BOOKS BY BRIGHTMAN

Religious Values. Kraus Repr. repr. of 1925 ed. 1968 $29.00. A basic compendium of religious values and their definitions from the standpoint of personalism.

The Problem of God. [*Philosophy in Amer. Ser.*] AMS Pr. repr. of 1930 ed. 1978 $27.50. Brightman's theory of the finitude of God and his reasons.

Moral Laws. Kraus Repr. repr. of 1933 ed. 1968 $23.00. A treatise in which moral principles are formulated on the basis of religion.

Personality and Religion. [*Philosophy in Amer. Ser.*] AMS Pr. repr. of 1934 ed. 1981 $20.00. An appealing interpretation of personality as the key to religion.

Philosophy of Religion. Greenwood repr. of 1940 ed. 1984 lib. bdg. $29.75. A reliable and useful textbook for college students.

The Spiritual Life. [*Philosophy in Amer. Ser.*] AMS Pr. repr. of 1942 ed. 1981 $27.50. A personalistic essay on the spiritual.

(ed.). *Personalism in Theology.* [*Philosophy in Amer. Ser.*] AMS Pr. repr. of 1943 ed. 1978 $24.50. A collection of essays by experts with an introduction by the editor.

BROAD, CHARLES DUNBAR. 1887–1971

Born in a suburb of London and educated at Cambridge, Broad taught at several universities before returning to Cambridge, where he reluctantly became Knightbridge professor of moral philosophy in 1933. During the period between the two world wars Broad was the clear and meticulous advocate of the traditional academic philosophy. In epistemology he defended the doctrine of representative perception; in metaphysics, the doctrine of mind-body dualism; and in moral philosophy, the objectivity of value and the cognitive character of moral judgments.

BOOKS BY BROAD

Five Types of Ethical Theory. 1920. [*International Lib. of Philosophy and Scientific Method*] Humanities Pr. 8th ed. 1978 text ed. $35.00. Lucid analyses of great ethical theories, such as those of Spinoza, Kant, and John Stuart Mill.

Examination of McTaggart's Philosophy. Hippocrene Bks. 3 vols. repr. of 1933–38 ed. 1972 lib. bdg. $92.00. Intensive commentary of the singular metaphysical idealism of the Cambridge philosopher.

Hume's Doctrine of Space. Longwood 1961 pap. $2.25. A penetrating and lucid examination of the Scottish philosopher's concept of space.

Lectures on Psychical Research. [*International Lib. of Philosophy and Scientific Method*] Humanities Pr. 1962 text ed. $32.50. Brilliantly cogent essays on the paranormal in psychology and spiritualism.

Induction, Probability and Causation: Selected Papers. [*Synthese Library*] Kluwer Academic 1968 lib. bdg. $34.00. A collection of technical papers for the advanced student.

Berkeley's Argument. [*Studies in Philosophy*] Haskell 1975 lib. bdg. $22.95. A concise but probing essay on the Jewish philosopher's idealism.

(and C. Lewy). *Leibniz: An Introduction.* Cambridge Univ. Pr. 1975 $32.50. A standard account of Leibniz's works.

Ethics. Ed. by C. Lewy, Kluwer Academic 1985 lib. bdg. $49.00. A collection of papers by Broad on ethics for advanced students.

BOOK ABOUT BROAD

Schilpp, Paul Arthur, ed. *The Philosophy of C. D. Broad.* [*Lib. of Living Philosophers*] Open Court 1959 $34.95. This book contains Broad's autobiography, critical essays on his work by various philosophers, his reply to his critics, and his bibliography.

BUCHLER, JUSTUS. 1914–

Born in New York City, Justus Buchler studied at City College and Columbia University, where he taught until his appointment as distinguished professor of philosophy at the State University of New York at Stony Brook. An influential interpreter of the pragmatic philosophy of Charles Peirce, Buchler has subscribed to the philosophical naturalism associated with Columbia University in midcentury, a naturalism led by JOHN DEWEY (see also Vol. 3) and George Santayana. Buchler has sought to modify this naturalism in order to accommodate humanistic concerns. He has propounded a singular metaphysical system for the sake of his intellectual aims.

BOOKS BY BUCHLER

Charles Peirce's Empiricism. Hippocrene Bks. repr. of 1939 ed. 1966 $24.00. A scholarly dissertation focusing on Peirce's conceptions of scientific methodology and of knowledge.

Toward a General Theory of Judgment. Dover repr. of 1951 ed. 1980 pap. $6.95. A prolegomenon to an original theory of judgment.

Nature and Judgment. Univ. Pr. of Amer. repr. of 1955 ed. 1985 text ed. pap. $9.75. An advanced essay on the naturalistic framework of human judgment.

The Concept of Method. Univ. Pr. of Amer. repr. of 1961 ed. 1985 text ed. pap. $9.75. A theory of method by reference to theories of method held by important philosophers.

Metaphysics of Natural Complexes. Columbia Univ. Pr. 1966 o.p. A treatise on basic philosophical categories.

The Main of Light. Oxford 1974 o.p. Buchler's philosophy of poetry.

Books about Buchler

Ross, Stephen David. *Transition to an Ordinal Metaphysics.* State Univ. of New York Pr. 1980 $44.50 pap. $16.95. Ross offers a metaphysical system that he explicitly erects on the basis of the ontological categories Buchler expounds in his *Metaphysics of Natural Complexes.* While Ross offers a critical exposition of Buchler's thought, he also indicates how and why he feels compelled to modify it.

Singer, Beth J. *Ordinal Naturalism: An Introduction to the Philosophy of Justus Buchler.* Bucknell Univ. Pr. 1983 $27.50. A lucid and comprehensive account of Buchler's philosophy by a devoted disciple.

CASSIRER, ERNST. 1874–1945

Cassirer, a German neo-Kantian philosopher, taught at several European universities before coming to the United States and teaching at Yale (1941–44) and at Columbia. A prolific historian of philosophy, Cassirer was influenced by Kant and Hegel but originated his own distinctive doctrine. The centerpiece of Cassirer's thought is his theory of symbolic forms. He construed representation, the ground of symbolic form, to be essentially symbolic, fusing perceptual materials with conceptual meanings. Man, he taught, is essentially a symbolizing animal. Symbolic forms, he maintained, are manifest in different modes—language, myth, art, science, and religion. Cassirer utilized his theory of symbolic forms in the elaboration of a flexible philosophy of culture.

Books by Cassirer

Symbol, Myth, and Culture: Essays and Lectures by Ernst Cassirer 1935–1945. Ed. by Donald P. Verene, Yale Univ. Pr. 1979 $38.50 pap. $11.95. A collection of previously unpublished essays with an erudite introduction by the editor.

The Problem of Knowledge: Philosophy, Science, and History since Hegel. 1906–20. Trans. by W. H. Woglom and C. W. Hendel, Yale Univ. Pr. 1950 $17.50 pap. $9.95. Cassirer's presentation of the problem of knowledge by means of historical studies.

Substance and Function and Einstein's Theory of Relativity. 1910. Trans. by W. C. Swabey and M. C. Swabey, Dover 1953 pap. $7.95; Peter Smith 1949 $10.75. A probing and speculative philosophical examination of scientific concepts.

Kant's Life and Thought. 1918. Trans. by James Haden, Yale Univ. Pr. 1981 text ed. $40.00 pap. $13.95. An influential intellectual biography.

The Philosophy of Symbolic Forms. 1923–29. Trans. by Ralph Manheim, Yale Univ. Pr. 3 vols. 1953–57 pap. ea. $10.95–$11.95 vol. 1, *Language;* vol. 2, *Mythical*

Thought; vol. 3, *The Phenomenology of Knowledge.* Cassirer's comprehensive masterwork, presented with unsurpassed philosophical scholarship and brilliance.

Language and Myth. 1925. Trans. by Susanne K. Langer, Dover repr. of 1946 ed. 1953 pap. $2.50; Peter Smith 1950 $13.50. A concise, lucid theory of language and myth with reference to symbolic form.

The Individual and the Cosmos in Renaissance Philosophy. 1927. Trans. by Mario Domandi, Univ. of Pennsylvania Pr. 1972 pap. $10.95. A clear, scholarly essay on a central theme in Renaissance thought.

The Philosophy of the Enlightenment. 1932. Trans. by F. Koelin and J. Pettegrove, Princeton Univ. Pr. 1951 pap. $9.95. One of the great works of scholarship on the Enlightenment.

The Platonic Renaissance in England. 1932. Gordian repr. of 1954 ed. 1970 $19.50. An engaging historical study of an intellectual episode in England.

An Essay on Man: An Introduction to a Philosophy of Human Culture. Yale Univ. Pr. repr. of 1944 ed. 1962 pap. $7.95. Philosophical anthropology elucidated within the framework of symbolic form theory.

The Myth of the State. Ed. by C. W. Hendel, Greenwood repr. of 1946 ed. 1983 lib. bdg. $29.75; Yale Univ. Pr. repr. of 1946 ed. 1961 pap. $8.95. A timely and provocative theory of politics.

(and others, eds.). *Renaissance Philosophy of Man.* Univ. of Chicago Pr. 1956 pap. $10.95. A collection of essays and selections from original sources.

BOOKS ABOUT CASSIRER

Itzkoff, Seymour W. *Ernst Cassirer: An Annotated Bibliography.* Garland 1986 lib. bdg. $35.00. The standard Cassirer bibliography.

——. *Ernst Cassirer: Scientific Knowledge and the Concept of Man.* Univ. of Notre Dame Pr. 1971 o.p. "An exposition and extension of the philosophy of Ernst Cassirer, especially as that philosophy is set forth in the philosophy of symbolic forms" (*Choice*).

Lipton, David R. *Ernst Cassirer: The Dilemma of a Liberal Intellectual in Germany, 1914–33.* Univ. of Toronto Pr. 1978 $22.50. "Lipton examines Cassirer's thought during the war and Weimar years, discussing both its internal development and how this development was. . .related to political events in Germany. Thus Cassirer's work becomes a case study for an analysis of German liberalism, its relation to Kantian and neo-Kantian thought, and how this relationship. . .entailed ideological and electoral weakness" (*LJ*).

Schilpp, Paul Arthur, ed. *The Philosophy of Ernst Cassirer.* [*Lib. of Living Philosophers*] Open Court repr. of 1949 ed. 1973 $42.95 pap. $22.95. A critical survey of Cassirer's life and thought, containing 23 essays by contemporary philosophers, an essay by Cassirer, and a bibliography of his work.

CHISHOLM, RODERICK M. 1916–

Educated at Brown and Harvard, Chisholm has taught at many universities in America and abroad, but throughout his long career his permanent position has been at his alma mater, Brown University. His work has been influenced by the luminaries in twentieth-century analytic philosophy, but he has perhaps studied Thomas Reid, Franz Brentano, and G. E. Moore most closely. His 1957 work *Perceiving* established his reputation as a meticulous analyst who diligently discloses the philosophical puzzles that arise when we think and talk about perception and who constructively shows how these may be resolved. Although he has labored long and hard on epistemological questions, Chisholm has also probed fundamental metaphysical problems, such as the nature of the self.

BOOKS BY CHISHOLM

(ed.). *The Vocation of Man: Fichte.* Macmillan 1956 text ed. pap. $5.50. English translation of the nineteenth-century German idealist's major work, with a scholarly introduction by the editor.

Perceiving: A Philosophical Study. [*Contemporary Philosophy Ser.*] Cornell Univ. Pr. 1957 $24.95. Sharply analytic monograph on the puzzles associated with discourse about perceiving.

The Problem of the Criterion. Marquette Univ. Pr. 1973 $7.95. A carefully wrought lecture in the analytic vein on a central theme in classic theory of knowledge.

Theory of Knowledge. Prentice-Hall 2d ed. 1977 text ed. pap. $13.95. A basic textbook presenting a major philosophical discipline in analytically elegant prose.

Person and Object: A Metaphysical Study. [*Paul Carus Lecture Ser.*] Open Court 1979 pap. $16.95. Fundamental metaphysics in defense of the substance concept.

The First Person: An Essay on Reference and Intentionality. Univ. of Minnesota Pr. 1981 $22.50 1982 pap. $10.95. A major contemporary contribution to metaphysics and philosophy of mind.

(ed.). *Realism and the Background of Phenomenology.* Ridgeview 1981 text ed. lib. bdg. $24.00 pap. $8.50. An anthology containing an erudite introduction and 12 selections from such thinkers as Brentano, Husserl, Prichard, the American new realists, Samuel Alexander, Russell, Lovejoy, and G. E. Moore.

Brentano and Meinong Studies. Humanities Pr. 1982 text ed. pap. $12.50. Philosophical scholarship at its best, for advanced students.

The Foundations of Knowing. Univ. of Minnesota Pr. 1982 pap. $10.95. The essentials for a theory of knowledge elegantly but technically formulated by a contemporary leader in the field.

BOOK ABOUT CHISHOLM

Bogdan, Radu J., ed. *Roderick M. Chisholm.* Kluwer Academic 1986 lib. bdg. $59.50. A volume in the Profile series, it contains Chisholm's intellectual autobiography and original articles by experts on various aspects of his philosophy.

COHEN, MORRIS RAPHAEL. 1880–1947

Cohen, who taught philosophy at the City College of New York and who began life as the son of Russian-Jewish immigrants, was one of the foremost Jewish intellectuals in America during the first half of this century. He expounded a philosophy of rationalism and realism in step with contemporary science and relevant to the social issues of his times and, through his books and teaching, had a widespread influence.

In a review of *A Dreamer's Journey* (1949), Cohen's autobiography, Perry Miller wrote in *The Nation:* "It is both ironic and fitting that with the posthumous publication of his autobiography, even though it was left unfinished and the last chapters are fragments, there appears the book by which Morris Cohen will be longest and most widely remembered. It will demand a permanent place among the classics of immigrant narrative, and one not too far behind the greater classics of intellectual biography. And because it reveals in human terms, with humility and yet with a touch of vanity, the sources from which his strength is gathered, it explains why he conspicuously succeeded in writing philosophy that can be read as literature."

BOOKS BY COHEN

Reason and Nature: An Essay on the Meaning of Scientific Method. Dover 1978 pap. $7.50; Folcroft repr. of 1931 ed. 1985 lib. bdg. $65.00. Clear exposition and critique of the central concepts in science by a proponent of the parity of reason with experiment.

Law and the Social Order: Essays in Legal Philosophy. Shoe String repr. of 1933 ed. 1967 $39.50; (and *Moral Aspects of Criminal Law*) Transaction Bks. 1982 pap. $19.95. An early investigation of legal theory by an American philosopher.

(and Ernest Nagel). *An Introduction to Logic and Scientific Method.* Darby repr. of 1934 ed 1982 lib. bdg. $50.00; (first part only, with the title *An Introduction to Logic*) Harcourt 1962 pap. $6.95. A basic textbook for college undergraduates.

A Preface to Logic. 1944. Dover 1977 pap. $5.95. An introduction to symbolic logic and scientific methodology facilely expressed.

The Faith of a Liberal. Ayer repr. of 1946 ed. $26.00. Persuasively written political and social creed of an American Jewish intellectual of the first rank.

The Meaning of Human History. 1947. [*Paul Carus Lecture Ser.*] Open Court 2d ed. 1968 $11.95 pap. $4.95. Unfinished treatise on the philosophy of history.

(and Israel Drabkin). *A Source Book in Greek Science.* [*Sourcebooks in the History of the Sciences Ser.*] Harvard Univ. Pr. 1948 text ed. $35.00. An anthology of selections from original sources in an impeccable English translation.

A Dreamer's Journey: The Autobiography of Morris Raphael Cohen. [*Modern Jewish Experience*] Ayer repr. of 1949 ed. 1975 $30.00

BOOK ABOUT COHEN

Delaney, Cornelius. *Mind and Nature: A Study on the Naturalistic Philosophies of Cohen, Woodbridge and Sellars.* Univ. of Notre Dame Pr. 1969 $9.95. A work of outstanding scholarship accessible to readers who are not advanced students of philosophy.

COLLINGWOOD, ROBIN GEORGE. 1889–1943

Collingwood was a remarkable thinker who sought to bridge the gulf that DARWIN'S (see Vol. 5) discoveries appeared to have set up between science and religion in the nineteenth century. He began to study Latin at age four, Greek at six, and the natural sciences shortly afterward. He attended Oxford University, where he studied philosophy, classics, archaeology, and history; later he taught philosophy there. Participation in numerous archaeological excavations allowed him to see, he said, "the importance of the questioning activity in life," and he became a respected scholar on the subject of Britain under the Roman conquest. In fact, Collingwood's sense of history was unparalleled among his contemporaries. His first-rate work in archaeology resulted in a number of books—*Roman Britain* (1921), *The Archaeology of Roman Britain* (1930, with Ian Richmond), *Roman Britain and the English Settlements* (1937, with J. N. Myres), and *Roman Inscriptions of Britain* (1965, with R. P. Wright)—testifying to his excellence in the field.

But he was also an artist by nature—a fine, disciplined writer who was actively interested in music and the pictorial arts. He deplored the divisiveness of increasing specialization and sought a philosophy that would harmonize all knowledge, and a religion "scientific" in nature in which faith and reason each played a role. He felt that the Renaissance had mistakenly drawn lines of separation among the various disciplines of study, and that a close unity existed among them.

He began as an idealist, and his thought reflects the influence of individual idealists, in the case of art, for example, the influence of CROCE (see Vol. 2). But more important than recent philosophers to the shaping of his thought were PLATO (see also Vol. 3) and HEGEL, especially as regards the dialectical method. In his mature period Collingwood sought to ground all the special sciences on idealist foundations, to ascertain within the dialectical function of mind the unity of religion, science, history, art, and philosophy. In his last years, however, Collingwood became critical of idealism. His ethical and political views grew somber, and pessimism seemed to overwhelm him.

BOOKS BY COLLINGWOOD

Speculum Mentis, or The Map of Knowledge. Greenwood repr. of 1924 ed. 1982 lib. bdg. $39.75. Original idealist treatise on the branches of human knowledge and cultural fields, magisterially composed.

Outlines of a Philosophy of Art. Somerset Pub. repr. 1925 $39.00. A useful guide to the basic principles and problems in the field.

An Essay on Philosophical Method. Oxford 1933 $39.95. A lucid, concise presentation of Collingwood's critical method.

Human Nature and Human History. [*Studies in Philosophy*] Haskell repr. of 1936 ed. 1972 lib. bdg. $39.95. An essay on philosophical anthropology marking a shift from idealism to pessimism on the author's part.

The Principles of Art. Oxford repr. of 1938 ed. 1958 $13.75 pap. $9.95. Basic work on the philosophy of art; highly readable.

An Autobiography. Oxford 1939 $14.95. The author's intellectual development concisely and wittily related.

An Essay on Metaphysics. Univ. Pr. of Amer. repr. of 1940 ed. 1984 pap. $10.50. A critical theory of metaphysics as the study of presuppositions.

The New Leviathan: Man, Society, Civilization and Barbarism. AMS Pr. repr. of 1942 ed. 1984 $40.00; Greenwood repr. of 1942 ed. 1984 lib. bdg. $47.50. A gloomy treatise on the state of politics and civilization, provoked in part by the times.

The Idea of Nature. Oxford repr. of 1945 ed. 1960 pap. $8.95. An imaginative, critical, and speculative survey of the idea of nature in the history of thought.

The Idea of History. Ed. by T. M. Knox, Oxford 1946 pap. $9.95. A novel philosophy of history elaborated systematically and by studies of historians and philosophers, and their methods.

Essays in the Philosophy of History. Ed. by Robin W. Winks, Garland 1985 lib. bdg. $25.00. A collection of essays by Collingwood, of interest to the specialist.

BOOKS ABOUT COLLINGWOOD

Donagan, Alan. *The Later Philosophy of R. G. Collingwood.* Univ. of Chicago Pr. repr. of 1962 ed. 1986 pap. $20.00. A critical study attributing Collingwood's later pessimism to his mental condition.

Ketner, Kenneth L. *An Emendation of Collingwood's Doctrine of Absolute Presupposi-*

tions. Texas Tech Pr. 1973 pap. $2.00. A narrow, technical essay on a central topic in Collingwood's methodology.

Kraus, Michael, ed. *Critical Essays in the Philosophy of Robin George Collingwood*. Oxford 1972 $49.95. "The essays are serious studies of Collingwood's ideas—not mere 'appreciation'.... This is a useful volume, one which ought to introduce Collingwood to readers in many fields other than philosophy" (*Virginia Quarterly Rev.*).

Russell, Anthony F. *Logic, Philosophy and History: A Study in the Philosophy of History Based on the Work of R. G. Collingwood*. Univ. Pr. of Amer. 1984 text ed. lib. bdg. $84.00 pap. $20.75. "This book aims to evaluate R. G. Collingwood's claim that the method proper to history is a heretofore underdeveloped logic of questioning and problem-solving" (*The Philosopher's Index*).

DERRIDA, JACQUES. 1930–

Derrida is the leading figure in the current movement in philosophy and literary criticism known as "deconstructionism." His philosophy has grown out of the phenomenological tradition and the work of Martin Heidegger. He esteems this tradition as the culmination of Western philosophy, which he interprets as grounding meaning in "presence"—some self-authenticating experience that reveals the meaning of signs. He denies the possibility of "presence" in this sense. He arrives at his position by a critique of the role of language—especially writing—and argues that the "differance" between the sign and its object undermines the possibility of "presence." Thus a "deconstruction" is tantamount to the dismantling of metaphysics and literature by revealing its presuppositions, presuppositions that are contradictory since the representation of thought in language, while it appeals to presence, rests upon "differance."

BOOKS BY DERRIDA

Speech and Phenomena: And Other Essays on Husserl's Theory of Signs. Trans. by David B. Allison [*Studies in Phenomenology and Existential Philosophy Ser.*] Northwestern Univ. Pr. 1973 text ed. $18.95 pap. $7.95. A collection of critical and imaginative essays by the French deconstructionist on the founder of phenomenology.

Of Grammatology. Trans. by C. Gayati Spivak, Johns Hopkins Univ. Pr. 1977 pap. $9.95. Presentation of a new theory of language, in part by means of provocative commentary on the theories of others, such as Rousseau.

Writing and Difference. Trans. by Alan Bass, Univ. of Chicago Pr. 1978 lib. bdg. $25.00 1980 pap. $12.00. Basic work on the nature of language and writing, fundamental to the understanding of deconstructionism.

Positions. Trans. by Alan Bass, Univ. of Chicago Pr. 1981 $11.95 pap. $5.00. Exceptionally brilliant, though idiosyncratic, essay.

Spurs: Nietzsche's Styles. Trans. by Barbara Harlow, Univ. of Chicago Pr. 1981 pap. $6.95. Commentaries at their puzzling best.

Margins of Philosophy. Trans. by Alan Bass, Univ. of Chicago Pr. 1983 lib. bdg. $25.00 pap. $12.95. Racy, titillating, teasing comments on philosophy and literature.

Signesponge-Signsponge. Trans. by Richard Rand, Columbia Univ. Pr. 1984 lib. bdg.

$24.00 pap. $13.00. Literary exercises, sometimes exasperating, sometimes obfuscating, but always rewarding.

Memoires for Paul De Man. Columbia Univ. Pr. 1986 $17.50. Art commentary of interest mainly to those who are concerned.

The Post Card: From Socrates to Freud and Beyond. Trans. by Alan Bass, Univ. of Chicago Pr. 1987 lib. bdg. $46.00 pap. $18.95. "A mock-epistolary account of the scholarly debate over the value and authenticity of Plato's 'letters'. . .a deconstructive reading of *Beyond the Pleasure Principle,* and a critique of Lacan" (Publisher's note).

BOOKS ABOUT DERRIDA

Harvey, Irene E. *Derrida and the Economy of Differance.* [*Studies in Phenomenology and Existential Philosophy Ser.*] Indiana Univ. Pr. 1986 $24.95. "The aim of this text is to situate the work of Jacques Derrida within the tradition of Continental Philosophy and to show his responses to this tradition. Derrida's notions of *differance,* metaphysics and deconstruction are analysed as philosophical strategies which together form an economy" (*The Philosopher's Index*).

Kerrigan, William, and Joseph H. Smith, eds. *Taking Chances: Derrida, Psychoanalysis, and Literature.* Johns Hopkins Univ. Pr. 1984 $20.00. A scholarly collection of essays by specialists.

Llewelyn, John. *Derrida on the Threshold of Sense.* St. Martin's 1986 $27.50 pap. $10.95. Perceptive commentary on the theory of meaning and truth.

Megill, Allan. *Prophets of Extremity: Nietzsche, Heidegger, Foucault, Derrida.* Univ. of California Pr. 1985 $24.95. "The book portrays Nietzsche, Heidegger, Foucault, and Derrida as participants in a single tradition of 'crisis thought.' Articulated against the background of Kant, Hegel, and nineteenth-century Romanticism, this tradition sees the modern world as existing in a state of moral, intellectual, and political crisis. Participants in the tradition appeal to aesthetic categories as refuge or remedy for the alleged crisis, with Derrida finally turning this 'aestheticism' against crisis thought itself" (*The Philosopher's Index*).

Nordquist, Joan, ed. *Jacques Derrida: A Bibliography.* Ref. Rsch. Serv. 1986 text ed. pap. $15.00. Useful bibliography of writings by and about Derrida.

Norris, Christopher. *Content of Faculties: Philosophy and Theory after Deconstruction.* Methuen 1982 $25.00 pap. $11.95. "This book is addressed to philosophers and literary theorists. It applies some of the insights of deconstructionist criticism to problems in the fields of epistemology, philosophical semantics, narrative theory and legal hermeneutics" (*The Philosopher's Index*).

Sallis, John, ed. *Deconstruction and Philosophy: The Texts of Jacques Derrida.* Univ. of Chicago Pr. 1986 $24.95. "Bringing together the essays by twelve leading Derridean scholars on an important paper by Derrida (previously unpublished in English), the collection retrieves the significance of deconstruction for philosophy" (Publisher's note).

Staten, Henry. *Wittgenstein and Derrida.* Univ. of Nebraska Pr. 1984 $19.95 pap. $7.95. "The concept of *differance* is examined in relation to the classical philosophical concepts of *eidos, logos,* and the object-in-general, in the context of the problem of time. Deconstruction sees syntax as radically temporal. Wittgenstein's 'zigzag' writing in the *Investigations* is then interpreted as deconstructive syntax, directed, like Derrida's work, against the dominance of the philosophical preoccupation with the form of entity, of an object-in-general" (*The Philosopher's Index*).

DUCASSE, CURT JOHN. 1881–1969

Born in France, Ducasse immigrated to the United States in 1900. A graduate of the University of Washington and Harvard, where he served as the assistant of Josiah Royce, he taught at the University of Washington and Brown. Although Ducasse maintained that philosophy is a science in its method, it differs from the other sciences in regard to its subject matter. He also insisted on the universality of causation, denying that chance or indeterminism can exist. At the same time he held that mind is not a part of nature, and throughout his career he investigated and wrote about the "wild facts" of mental telepathy, clairvoyance, and precognition.

BOOKS BY DUCASSE

Nature, Mind and Death. [*Paul Carus Lecture Ser.*] Open Court 1951 $19.95. Cogent and coherent treatise in metaphysics.

Paranormal Phenomena, Science and Life after Death. Parapsych. Foundation 1969 pap. $4.00. Wise probings into "wild facts."

Critical Examination of the Belief in a Life after Death. C. C. Thomas 1974 pap. $35.75. Concise but thorough investigation of the belief in life after death approached partly by consideration of historical perceptions but essentially by reference to logic and evidence.

BOOK ABOUT DUCASSE

Hare, Peter H., and Edward H. Madden. *Causing, Perceiving and Believing: An Examination of the Philosophy of C. J. Ducasse.* [*Philosophical Texts and Studies Ser.*] Kluwer Academic 1975 lib. bdg. $37.00. A scholarly treatise on the crucial theme of Ducasse's philosophy.

EDMAN, IRWIN. 1896–1954

Professor of philosophy at Columbia, Irwin Edman was a very popular philosopher, much in demand on the lecture circuit. *Philosopher's Holiday* (1938), an autobiography of a sort, made the author well known to the general reading public. His love of music, travel, and poetry, and his unusual contacts with curious human beings, "philosophers without portfolios," give his books a wide interest. He followed in the direction of WILLIAM JAMES (see also Vol. 3) and JOHN DEWEY (see also Vol. 3), guided by Platonism.

BOOKS BY EDMAN

Human Traits and Their Social Significance. Arden Lib. repr. of 1919 ed. 1978 lib. bdg. $30.00. A doctoral dissertation in philosophical anthropology and social philosophy, remarkable for its readability.

Adam, the Baby, and the Man from Mars. [*Essay Index Repr. Ser.*] Ayer repr. of 1929 ed. 1968 $20.00. Witty essayistic observations on contemporary humanity.

The Contemporary and His Soul. Kennikat repr. of 1931 ed. 1975 $18.50. Urbane, sensitive, humorous commentary on contemporary man.

Arts and the Man. Norton repr. of 1939 ed. 1960 pap. $5.95. Informed, cosmopolitan interpretation and criticism of the arts.

Philosopher's Quest. Greenwood repr. of 1947 ed. 1973 lib. bdg. $18.00. Highly readable and humorous account of the goal and methods of the philosopher personally illustrated.

FEIBLEMAN, JAMES KERN. 1904–

James Kern Feibleman is a prolific philosophical author, who has published nearly 50 books of poetry, novels, autobiography, but mostly serious philosophy. A native New Orleanian, he has taught at Tulane University, where he chaired the department of philosophy from 1952 to 1969. His major endeavor has been to formulate a system of philosophy that rests on the ontological foundations of realism that harks back to PLATO (see also Vol. 3) but that accommodates modern science. The outline of Feibleman's system is expounded in his massive *Ontology* (1951), but it is elaborated in a number of volumes in special areas such as aesthetics, ethics, political philosophy, legal philosophy, and so on. Feibleman has also published several books of popular philosophy.

BOOKS BY FEIBLEMAN

Christianity, Communism, and the Ideal Society: A Philosophical Approach to Modern Politics. AMS Pr. repr. of 1937 ed. 1978 $38.00. Reflective assessment of the promises and the defects of rival ideologies.

Philosophers Lead Sheltered Lives: A First Volume of Memoirs. AMS Pr. repr. of 1952 ed. 1979 $27.50. Sensitive autobiography of the philosopher's early years.

Religious Platonism. Greenwood repr. of 1959 ed. 1971 lib. bdg. $22.50. Insightful scholarly monograph on the references to religion in Plato and their subsequent uses in the history of thought.

Collected Poems. Horizon Pr. 1974 $8.95. Philosophical poetry at its best.

Understanding Civilizations: The Shape of History. Horizon Pr. 1975 $8.95. Popular presentation of philosophy of culture by means of historical survey of leading theories.

Understanding Oriental Philosophy. New Amer. Lib. repr. of 1976 ed. 1984 pap. $9.95. A compact handbook introducing Oriental philosophies.

New Proverbs for Our Day. Horizon Pr. 1978 $7.95 pap. $3.95. Witty and wise aphorisms.

Understanding Human Nature: A Popular Guide to the Effects of Technology on Man and His Behavior. Horizon Pr. 1978 $8.95. Lucid and cogent treatment of the nature of man.

Ironies of History. Horizon Pr. 1980 $9.95. Popular study.

Conversations: A Kind of Fiction. Horizon Pr. 1982 $15.95. A philosophical dialogue mythically based on a round table of faculty members and administrators who lunched together regularly at Tulane University.

From Hegel to Terrorism and Other Essays on the Dynamic Nature of Philosophy. Humanities Pr. 1985 text ed. $15.00. Provocative essays intending to show how terrorism is the practical implication of Hegel's thought.

Justice, Law, and Culture. Kluwer Academic 1985 $28.00. Realistic philosophy of law.

Education and Civilization. Kluwer Academic 1987 $30.00. Philosophy of education with thoughtful applications.

BOOK ABOUT FEIBLEMAN

Whittemore, Robert C., ed. *The Reach of Philosophy, Essays in Honor of James Kern Feibleman*. Tulane Univ. Pr. 1977 $10.00. This festschrift consists of ten essays by scholars who discuss all areas of Feibleman's thought. It also contains a bibliography of his philosophical writings through 1976.

FOUCAULT, MICHEL. 1926–1984

Foucault held the chair in the history of systems of thought at the Collège de France and was the reigning Parisian intellectual when he died. Foucault's influential theory of knowledge is historically oriented. It is an "archaeology" that lays bare the conceptual scheme that preconditions the rise and development of the particular sciences, especially the human sciences of biology, economics, and language, during a given period. Further, the conceptual schemes are themselves the products of an infrastructure that is determined not so much by means of reason as by the power relations that prevail. Foucault's thought has affinities to both Nietzsche and to MARX (see also Vol. 3).

Foucault pursued his philosophical method by undertaking historical (or "archaeological") investigations in regard to institutions and cultural phenomena in the West that traditional historians have neglected—medicine, madness, the prison, sexuality.

"Foucault has an original analytical mind with a fascination for facts. He is adept at reorganizing past events to rethink the present. He engagingly turns familiar truths into doubt or chaos. . . . Foucault is one of many who want a new conception of how power and knowledge interact" (Ian Hacking, *N.Y. Review of Bks.*). (See also Volumes 2 and 5.)

BOOKS BY FOUCAULT

Birth of the Clinic: An Archaeology of Medical Perception. Pantheon 1973 $8.95; Random 1974 pap. $3.95. A unique history of medicine illustrating Foucault's theses about the efficacy of concealed power relations.

Madness and Civilization: A History of Insanity in the Age of Reason. Random 1973 pap. $4.95. A singular history of what constitutes insanity, reveals the intention of control.

The Order of Things: An Archaeology of the Human Sciences. Random 1973 pap. $5.95. Foucault's most fundamental text on theory of knowledge.

Language, Counter-Memory, Practice: Selected Essays and Interviews. Ed. by Donald F. Bonchard, trans. by Simon Sherry, Cornell Univ. Pr. 1977 $29.95 1980 pap. $8.95. A collection of Foucault's essays and interviews of particular interest to the specialist.

The History of Sexuality: An Introduction. Vol. 1 in *The History of Sexuality*. Trans. by Robert Hurley, Pantheon 1978 $8.95; Random 1980 pap. $4.95. First volume of a monumental, but idiosyncratic, history of sex in Foucault's mode; two other volumes listed below.

Discipline and Punish: The Birth of the Prison. Trans. by Alan Sheridan, Random 1979 pap. $7.95. A remarkable history of human conceptions and the purposes of the penal system.

Power-Knowledge: Selected Interviews and Other Writings 1972–1977. Pantheon 1981 $12.95 pap. $5.95. A brilliant selection of Foucault's provocative pronouncements.

This Is Not a Pipe. Illus. by René Magritte, trans. by James Harkness, Univ. of California Pr. 1982 $16.50 pap. $5.95. Playful, imaginative, exciting piece.

The Uses of Pleasure. Vol. 2 in *The History of Sexuality.* Trans. by Robert Hurley, Pantheon 1985 $17.95. The second volume of Foucault's historical investigations of sexuality.

Death and the Labyrinth: The World of Raymond Roussell. Trans. by Charles Ruas, Doubleday 1986 pap. $15.95. Art criticism, sometimes exasperating, but more often informative.

The Care of the Self. Vol. 3 in *The History of Sexuality.* Trans. by Robert Hurley, Pantheon 1987 $18.95. Posthumously published third volume of Foucault's comprehensive, historical study of sexuality.

BOOKS ABOUT FOUCAULT

Cooper, Barry. *Michel Foucault: An Introduction to the Study of His Thought.* E Mellen 1982 $39.95. A scholarly monograph with illuminating discussion of Foucault's thought.

Dreyfus, Hubert L., and Paul Rabinow. *Michel Foucault: Beyond Structuralism and Hermeneutics.* Univ. of Chicago Pr. 1983 lib. bdg. $25.00 pap. $10.95. This book is "a study of the major work of Michel Foucault." It interprets him "on human discourse in relation to history and the various disciplines which attempt to elucidate it" (*The Philosopher's Index*).

Hoy, David. *Foucault: A Critical Reader.* Basil Blackwell 1986 $45.00 pap. $14.95. A collection of scholarly essays and commentary.

Menson, Jeffrey. *Genealogies of Morals: Nietzsche, Foucault, Donzelot and the Eccentricity of Ethics.* St. Martin's 1986 $27.50. Seeks to evaluate Nietzsche's and Foucault's contribution to a selected set of issues relating to social policy and administration, the status of the person, and political values. It also attempts "to illustrate the productiveness of some aspects of Foucault's 'genealogical perspectives' " (*The Philosopher's Index*).

Nordquist, Joan, ed. *Michel Foucault: A Bibliography.* Ref. Rsch. Serv. 1986 $15.00. The bibliography with which the serious research on Foucault must begin.

Rajchman, John. *Michel Foucault: The Freedom of Philosophy.* Columbia Univ. Pr. 1985 $22.00 1986 pap. $12.50. Perceptive, informative, sometimes obscure commentary on central themes in Foucault's thought.

GADAMER, HANS-GEORG. 1900–

Professor emeritus at the University of Heidelberg, Gadamer is one of the founding fathers of contemporary hermeneutics. He has constructed a general theory of hermeneutics that has been hailed for liberating the humanistic enterprise of interpretation from the confining strictures of science. At the same time Gadamer has faced the problem of truth for investigations in which conclusions may radically differ. In seeking universals he has formulated a kind of logic of interpretation, the criterion for which is for the most part the subject matter being interpreted.

Gadamer has illustrated his hermeneutical theory by authoring numerous studies in the history of philosophy. PLATO (see also Vol. 3), ARISTOTLE (see also Vol. 3), Hegel, and others have been his subjects. These hermeneutical essays in the history of philosophy have been welcomed by scholars for the new light they cast on their subjects. For example, by Gadamer's methods, Plato is demythologized, and the upshot is a philosophy similar to Aristotle's, although ironically Aristotle, who criticized Plato severely, stressed the mythological cast of Plato's philosophical reflection.

BOOKS BY GADAMER

Philosophical Hermeneutics. Univ. of California Pr. 1976 pap. $8.95. Introduction to Gadamer's method, his theory of interpretation.

Dialogue and Dialectic: Eight Hermeneutical Studies on Plato. Trans. by P. Christopher Smith, Yale Univ. Pr. 1980 $27.50 1983 text ed. pap. $8.95. A major contribution to Plato scholarship and to contemporary theories of interpretation.

Hegel's Dialectic: Five Hermeneutical Studies. Trans. by P. Christopher Smith, Yale Univ. Pr. 1982 $18.50 pap. $6.95. Highly interpretive studies of central themes in the philosophy of the nineteenth-century German idealist.

Reason in the Age of Science. Trans. by Frederick G. Lawrence, MIT 1982 text ed. $22.50 pap. $7.95. Penetrating critique of scientific method.

Truth and Method. Continuum 1982 pap. $16.95. Profound epistemological inquiry into the status of truth as regards science and humanistic scholarship.

Philosophical Apprenticeships. Trans. by Robert R. Sullivan, MIT 1985 $17.50. Hermeneutical investigations of philosophical influences.

The Idea of the Good in Platonic-Aristotelian Philosophy. Trans. by P. Christopher Smith, Yale Univ. Pr. 1986 $20.00. "The task Gadamer sets himself is to explain how it is that Aristotle offers serious criticisms of Plato's theory of ideas, and yet essentially accepts the doctrine, including the idea of the good, which plays a central role in the philosophy of both Plato and Aristotle" (*Review of Metaphysics*).

BOOKS ABOUT GADAMER

Palmer, Richard E. *Hermeneutics: Interpretation Theory in Schleiermacher, Dilthey, Heidegger, and Gadamer.* [*Studies in Phenomenology and Existential Philosophy Ser.*] Northwestern Univ. Pr. 1969 $9.95. Scholarly dissertation on the main influential recent theories of interpretation for the advanced student.

Weinsheimer, Joel C. *Gadamer's Hermeneutics: A Reading of "Truth and Method."* Yale Univ. Pr. 1985 $20.00. "A detailed, comprehensive, and now controversial exposition of *Truth and Method* in a form accessible to the nonspecialist reader. . . . The opening chapter focuses on Gadamer's objections to the monopoly on truth often imputed to scientific method, and yet suggests some affinities of hermeneutics with mathematical logic" (*The Philosopher's Index*).

GENTILE, GIOVANNI. 1875–1944

One of the major figures in the rise of idealism in Italy during the early twentieth century, Gentile regarded the present act of thinking to be the foundation of everything else. His idealism was therefore absolutely subjective, although he preferred to regard it as an actualism. In 1922 Gentile was appointed minister of education in Mussolini's cabinet and in 1924 the first president of the National Fascist Institute of Culture. He remained a loyal Fascist to the bitter end: When Mussolini fell, Gentile retired briefly, then actively supported the Fascist Social Republic the Germans established. He was killed in Florence on April 15, 1944, by Italian Communist partisans.

BOOKS BY GENTILE

Reform of Education. Trans. by Dino Bigongiari [*Studies in Fascism: Ideology and Practice*] AMS Pr. repr. of 1922 ed. 1981 $25.00. The classic document delineating and establishing the Fascist theory and system of education.

Genesis and Structure of Society. Trans. by H. S. Harris, Univ. of Illinois Pr. 1966 pap. $8.95. Philosophical sociology on an authoritarian basis; excellent translation.

Theory of the Spirit and the Egocentric Propensities of Man. Foundation for Class. Repr. 2 vols. 1986 $237.45. Original statement of Gentile's idealism systematically presented.

BOOKS ABOUT GENTILE

Holmes, Roger W. *The Idealism of Giovanni Gentile*. [*Studies in Fascism: Ideology and Practice*] AMS Pr. repr. of 1937 ed. 1982 $29.50. "Mr. Holmes has written a clear and competent account of Gentile's technical philosophy and those seeking knowledge of the Italian's thought will find this book a useful introduction" (Eliseo Vivas, *The Nation*).

Romanell, Patrick. *Croce versus Gentile: A Dialogue on Contemporary Italian Philosophy*. [*Studies in Fascism: Ideology and Practice*] AMS Pr. repr. of 1947 ed. 1979 $18.00. Polemical contrast of the views of two influential twentieth-century thinkers, exposed by a leading scholar in the field.

Smith, William A. *Giovanni Gentile on the Existence of God*. Ed. by S. A. Matczak [*Philosophical Questions Ser.*] Learned Pubns. 1970 $18.00. A careful study of a central theological theme in Gentile's thought.

GILSON, ETIENNE. 1884–1978

Born in Paris, Gilson was educated at the University of Paris. He became professor of medieval philosophy at the Sorbonne in 1921, and in 1932 was appointed to the chair in medieval philosophy at the Collège de France. In 1929 he cooperated with the members of the Congregation of Priests of St. Basil, in Toronto, Canada, to found the Pontifical Institute of Medieval Studies in association with St. Michael's College at the University of Toronto. Gilson served as professor and director of studies at the institute.

Like his fellow countryman Jacques Maritain, Étienne Gilson was a neo-Thomist for whom Christian revelation is an indispensable auxiliary to reason, and on faith he accepted Christian doctrine as advocated by the Roman Catholic church. At the same time, like THOMAS AQUINAS, he accorded reason a wide compass of operation, maintaining that it could demonstrate the existence of God and the necessity of revelation, with which he considered it compatible.

Why anything exists is a question that science cannot answer and may even deem senseless. Gilson found the answer to be that "each and every particular existing thing depends for its existence on a pure Act of existence." God is the supreme Act of existing. An authority on the Christian philosophy of the Middle Ages, Gilson lectured widely on theology, art, the history of ideas, and the medieval world.

Books by Gilson

Index Scholastico-Cartesian. B. Franklin repr. of 1913 ed. 1964 $28.50. Thorough index of basic concepts in Descartes's writings.

The Philosophy of St. Thomas Aquinas. 1919. Ed. and trans. by G. A. Ebrington and Edward Bullough, Ayer repr. of 1937 ed. 1982 $26.50. Sympathetic exposition of St. Thomas Aquinas's thought, lucidly presented.

The Christian Philosophy of St. Augustine. 1929. Hippocrene Bks. repr. of 1960 ed. 1980 lib. bdg. $35.00. Clear presentation of Christian themes in St. Augustine's thought.

The Spirit of Medieval Philosophy. 1932. Telegraph Bks. repr. of 1949 ed. 1985 lib. bdg. $75.00. Magisterial interpretation of medieval philosophy.

The Unity of Philosophical Experience. Christian Classics repr. of 1937 ed. 1982 pap. $15.00. Acute argumentative tract on philosophy, demonstrating the superiority of St. Thomas Aquinas.

God and Philosophy. Yale Univ. Pr. 1941 pap. $6.95. Incisive narration of the leading early Christian, Moslem, and medieval conceptions of the basis of theological beliefs.

History of Philosophy and Philosophical Education. Marquette Univ. Pr. 1947 $7.95. Lucid demonstration of the role of the history of philosophy in philosophical understanding by a leading historian.

Wisdom and Love in St. Thomas Aquinas. Marquette Univ. Pr. 1951 $7.95. Scholarly elucidation of central themes in Thomas Aquinas's thought.

The Christian Philosophy of St. Thomas Aquinas. Hippocrene Bks. repr. of 1956 ed. 1983 lib. bdg. $35.00. St. Thomas Aquinas presented as a Christian thinker by a devoted adherent to his philosophy.

Elements of Christian Philosophy. Greenwood repr. of 1960 ed. 1978 lib. bdg. $35.00. A handbook of essentials.

Heloïse and Abelard. Univ. of Michigan Pr. 1960 pap. $7.95. The scholarly study of a legendary relationship that has excited the imaginations of romantics for centuries.

From Aristotle to Darwin and Back Again: A Journey to Final Causality, Species, and Evolution. Trans. by John Lyon, Univ. of Notre Dame Pr. 1984 text ed. $22.95 1986 pap. $11.95. Profound, if controversial, interpretation of Western philosophical thought.

Thomist Realism. Trans. by A. Mark Wauck, Ignatius Pr. 1986 pap. $9.95. Systematic presentation of neo-Thomist philosophy, by a leading figure in the movement.

Books about Gilson

O'Neil, Charles J., ed. *An Etienne Gilson Tribute.* Univ. of Toronto Pr. 1959 o.p. "Twenty-one contributions on 21 phases of philosophical thought form this tribute. Each is an expression of the esteem held for Étienne Gilson by his students from the Pontifical Institute of Medieval Studies over 30 years" (Publisher's note).

Shook, Lawrence K. *Etienne Gilson.* Humanities Pr. 1984 text ed. $29.95. An invaluable introductory survey of Gilson's life and works.

GOODMAN, NELSON. 1906–

Goodman is a prominent and influential American philosopher, who has taught at the University of Pennsylvania, Brandeis, and Harvard. His early publications grew out of his reflections on and revisions of the logical positivism of Rudolf Carnap. His work in the philosophy of science has been most appreciated for his original treatment of induction. His work in the philosophy of language contains several important elements that have been at the forefront of recent philosophical discussion in the English-speaking world: structural simplicity, constructionalism, phenomenalism, and nominalism. Indeed, Goodman has been the most original nominalist in twentieth-century philosophy, although his sense of nominalism is most sophisticated.

Goodman's later work has been directed to an investigation of representationalism. Although representation in the first instance comes to attention in language, Goodman has investigated this principle as it is involved in different philosophical systems.

BOOKS BY GOODMAN

The Structure of Appearance. [*Synthese Library*] Kluwer Academic repr. of 1951 ed. 1977 lib. bdg. $42.00 pap. $11.00. Technical treatise on language-based phenomenalism and ontology, influenced by Carnap's logical empiricism.

Fact, Fiction and Forecast. 1954. Harvard Univ. Pr. 4th ed. 1983 text ed. $10.00 pap. $4.95. Original theory of induction.

Languages of Art. 1968. Hackett 2d new ed. 1976 text ed. $19.50 pap. $9.95. Analytic philosophy of art at its best.

Problems and Projects. 1972. Hackett 1973 text ed. $19.50 pap. $9.95. Logically elegant formulations of issues at the frontiers of contemporary analytic philosophy.

Ways of Worldmaking. Hackett 1978 $15.00 pap. $5.95. Pluralist theory of philosophical systems logically defined and defended.

Of Mind and Other Matters. Harvard Univ. Pr. 1984 text ed. $17.50. Collection of essays on philosophy of mind and other metaphysical, epistemological, and aesthetic themes, elaborated with unmatched logical precision.

BOOKS ABOUT GOODMAN

Elgin, Catherine A. *With Reference to Reference.* Hackett 1982 text ed. lib. bdg. $27.50 pap. $12.75. This book "weaves Goodmanian insights into a comprehensive, extensional theory of reference.... It shows how distinctions Goodman draws in aesthetic contexts can account for the ways symbols function elsewhere—in science, mathematics, etc." (*The Philosopher's Index*).

Martin, R. M. *Pragmatics, Truth, and Language.* [*Boston Studies in the Philosophy of Science*] Kluwer Academic 1979 lib. bdg. $42.00 pap. $14.50. Technical critique of Goodman's epistemology for advanced students, presented by a prominent logician.

GRAMSCI, ANTONIO. 1891–1937

Founder of the Italian Communist party in 1921, Gramsci was a man of action who also ranks as a man of thought. Imprisoned by the Fascists in 1926 and not released until a week before his death, Gramsci overcame oppressive prison conditions to write thousands of pages on philosophy and politics. After World War II selections from his writings were published, and these were widely read by those who formed the New Left in Western Europe, contributing immeasurably to the development of neo-Marxism.

Gramsci rejected the idea that the Communist revolution could be achieved without philosophy by political action alone. The task, he felt, was to transform Marxist theory from ideas in individual minds into mass beliefs. The philosophy that could effectuate this task was for him tantamount to a new ethic. Seeking to construct a philosophy appropriate to the intellectual and cultural forms dominant in the Italy of his time, Gramsci blended Crocean idealism with Marxism. While he defended Leninism and the importance of political organization and action, he held that the adoption of the new ethic, reinvigorating Marxist philosophy, was necessary if the revolution was to be achieved.

BOOKS BY GRAMSCI

The Modern Prince and Other Writings. International Pubns. 1959 pap. $2.95. Gramsci's renovation of Machiavellianism and his critique of Fascism.

Prison Notebooks: Selections. Trans. by Quentin Hoare and Geoffrey N. Smith, International Pubns. 1971 pap. $7.25. Selections from voluminous politico-philosophical writings composed by the Italian Marxist during his imprisonment by the Fascists, inspired by his expressed purpose: "It would be important to do something for eternity."

Antonio Gramsci: Selections from Political Writings, 1910–1920. Beekman 1978 pap. $19.95; International Pubns. 1977 $13.50 1978 pap. $6.95. Collection of articles, many of which had appeared in the Socialist newspaper *Avanti.* Sequel volume of political writings, 1921–26, is out of print.

Selections from Cultural Writings. Ed. by David Forgacs and Geoffrey N. Smith, trans. by William Boelhower, Harvard Univ. Pr. 1985 text ed. $20.00. The book "consists of writings by Gramsci on such topics as theatre criticism, literary criticism, aesthetics, language, popular literature, journalism, Italian Catholic writers, Dante, Pirandello, and Manzoni" (*Review of Metaphysics*).

BOOKS ABOUT GRAMSCI

Boggs, Carl. *Gramsci's Marxism.* Longwood 1976 pap. $6.75. Critical evaluation of Gramsci's renovated Marxism.

———. *The Two Revolutions: Antonio Gramsci and the Dilemmas of Marxism.* South End Pr. 1984 $20.00 pap. $9.50. Appreciation of Gramsci's role in neo-Marxism and the theory of revolution.

Cammett, John M. *Antonio Gramsci and the Origins of Italian Communism.* Stanford Univ. Pr. 1967 $25.00. This book "represents a substantial contribution to the growing body of literature dealing with a critical phase of modern European history; moreover, there is no satisfactory account of Gramsci's thought and role in English" (*Choice*).

Cavalcanti, Pedro, and Paul Piscone, eds. *History, Philosophy and Culture in the Young Gramsci.* Telos Pr. 1975 $12.00. Collection of scholarly essays on the early development of Gramsci from idealism to Marxism.

Davis, John A., ed. *Gramsci and Italy's Passive Revolution.* Barnes & Noble 1979 text ed. $28.50. Collection of historical essays focused on Gramsci's influence over Italian communism.

Entwistle, Harold. *Antonio Gramsci: Conservative Schooling for Radical Politics.* Methuen 1979 pap. $9.50. "The book is readable and should be of interest for students of educational, political, and social theory" (*Choice*).

Fernia, Joseph V. *Gramsci's Political Thought: Hegemony, Consciousness, and the Revolutionary Process.* Oxford 1981 $29.95. Expert analysis of Gramsci's political theory and its practical application; indispensable for the understanding of Gramsci.

Joll, James. *Antonio Gramsci.* [*Modern Masters Ser.*] Viking 1978 $9.95. Gramsci is recognized by some "as the most important European communist since Lenin. Joll, in [attempting to make] this clear, considers his political journalism as well as his. . . theoretical contributions" (*LJ*).

Kiros, Teodros. *Toward the Construction of a Theory of Political Action.* Univ. Pr. of Amer. 1985 text ed. lib. bdg. $29.50 pap. $14.50. Limited scholarly dissertation, for the advanced student.

Salamini, Leonardo. *The Sociology of Political Praxis: An Introduction to Gramsci's Theory.* Methuen 1981 $28.95. Well-written, comprehensive, penetrating study.

Sassoon, Anne S. *Approaches to Gramsci.* Writers & Readers 1982 $14.95 pap. $7.95. An elementary guide to a complex thinker.

HABERMAS, JÜRGEN. 1929–

Professor of philosophy at the University of Frankfurt, Habermas is the leading figure in contemporary critical theory, a neo-Marxist philosophy that grew out of the Frankfurt School. Habermas's own version of critical theory may be distinguished from the earlier Frankfurt School of Horkheimer, Adorno, and Marcuse. These philosophers and social scientists, while Marxist, adhere to a notion of critique that stems from Kant and Hegel, as well as Marx, and they share the conviction that, despite the historical conditioning of knowledge, reason possesses a measure of autonomy in the moment of criticism.

In the 1950s Habermas set out to analyze contemporary society by means of the methods of empirical science, but at the same time he stressed that the critique be undertaken from a historical and practical standpoint. He stood against Marxists on the one hand and positivists on the other. In the course of furthering his critique of society he has engaged in a cluster of research projects, which have been published in separate works: a general theory of communication, which he calls "universal pragmatics"; a theory of how human beings are socialized to acquire the competence to communicate; and a theory of social evolution, which he maintains is a renovated historical materialism.

BOOKS BY HABERMAS

Knowledge and Human Interests. Trans. by Jeremy J. Shapiro, Beacon Pr. 1971 pap. $10.95. Obscurely written but profound theory of knowledge, requisite to an understanding of Habermas's program.

Toward a Rational Society: Student Protest, Science, and Politics. Trans. by Jeremy J. Shapiro, Beacon Pr. 1971 pap. $6.95. A tract for the understanding of the student movement in the 1960s from the standpoint of critical theory.

Theory and Practice. Trans. by John Viertel, Beacon Pr. 1973 pap. $10.95. The essentials of the philosophy of action.

Legitimation Crisis. Trans. by Thomas McCarthy, Beacon Pr. 1975 pap. $7.95. The probing critique of the claims to authority by the establishment.

Communication and the Evolution of Society. Trans. by Thomas McCarthy, Beacon Pr. 1979 pap. $8.95. Habermas's account of the role of language in society, preliminary to his later masterpiece.

Philosophical-Political Profiles. Trans. by Frederick Lawrence, MIT 1983 text ed. $27.50. Essays, sympathetic and critical, of leading twentieth-century thinkers.

Reason and the Rationalization of Society. Vol. 1 in *The Theory of Communicative*

Action. Trans. by Thomas McCarthy, Beacon Pr. 1985 $35.00 pap. $14.95. The first volume, though obscurely composed, of Habermas's most significant, mature work.

BOOKS ABOUT HABERMAS

Bernstein, Richard, ed. *Habermas and Modernity.* MIT 1985 $20.00 pap. $8.95. Collection of essays by experts, edited and introduced by a leading American philosophical scholar.

Geuss, Raymond. *The Idea of a Critical Theory: Habermas and the Frankfurt School.* [*Modern European Philosophy*] Cambridge Univ. Pr. 1981 $27.95 pap. $8.95. Important scholarly study, indispensable to the serious student of critical theory.

Held, David. *Introduction to Critical Theory: Horkheimer to Habermas.* Univ. of California Pr. 1980 $42.00 pap. $14.00. "Mr. Held's purpose in his introduction to critical theory is to determine its historical context, to express its empirical and theoretical concerns, and to evaluate the work of its key figures"—Horkheimer, Adorno, Marcuse, and Habermas (*The Philosopher's Index*).

Keat, Russell. *The Politics of Social Theory: Habermas, Freud, and the Critique of Positivism.* Univ. of Chicago Pr. 1981 $25.00 pap. $9.00. Probing examination of central concerns in the Habermas program.

McCarthy, Thomas A. *The Critical Theory of Jürgen Habermas.* MIT 1978 pap. $13.50. A standard work of exposition and criticism of Habermas's philosophy.

Thompson, John B., and David Held. *Habermas: Critical Debates.* MIT 1982 text ed. $37.50 pap. $12.50. This is "an impressive series of essays on various features of Habermas's social theory, together with a substantial and fair-minded—though not always very convincing—'Reply to My Critics'—by Habermas himself" (Quentin Skinner, *N.Y. Review of Bks.*).

HARTSHORNE, CHARLES. 1897–

Hartshorne was educated at Harvard University where he coedited with Paul Weiss the first six volumes of *The Collected Papers of Charles Sanders Peirce* (1931–36) and became associated with Alfred North Whitehead. He has taught at Harvard, the University of Chicago, Emory, and the University of Texas-Austin. Hartshorne is the undisputed leader in the development of process philosophy and theology since the death of Whitehead.

A consummate metaphysician, Hartshorne has resurrected the ontological argument for the existence of God, reframing it in terms of contemporary modal logic. He has espoused a doctrine of panpsychism, according to which mind (with feeling) permeates all things, and has defended the compatibility of this doctrine with contemporary physics. A pantheist, Hartshorne has proposed a complex theory of God, which views divinity as a relative, processional kind of being, with an abstract eternal nature and a concrete nature subject to change and suffering. He has presented his process theology in his widely read book *The Divine Relativity*.

In addition to his labors as teacher and philosophical author, Hartshorne is an avid birdwatcher and has written a prizewinning book, *Born to Sing: An Interpretation and World Survey of Bird Song* (Indiana Univ. Pr. 1973 o.p.).

BOOKS BY HARTSHORNE

The Philosophy and Psychology of Sensation. Telegraph Bks. repr. of 1934 ed. 1985 lib. bdg. $95.00. Comprehensive general theory of sensation, carefully constructed, supporting the claims of panpsychism.

Beyond Humanism: Essays in the Philosophy of Nature. Peter Smith repr. of 1937 ed. 1975 $11.50. A collection of essays demonstrating that the twentieth-century revolution in science supports a new natural theology.

The Divine Relativity: A Social Conception of God. Yale Univ. Pr. 1948 o.p. The basic text of process theology.

(and William L. Reese, eds.). *Philosophers Speak of God.* 1953. [*Midway Repr. Ser.*] Univ. of Chicago Pr. 1976 $22.00. Selections from the history of thought on the nature of God; comprehensive and readable.

A Natural Theology for Our Time. Open Court 1967 pap. $9.95. Sketch of process theology and its ground in the science of nature.

Whitehead's Philosophy: Selected Essays, 1935–1970. [*Landmark Ed.*] Univ. of Nebraska Pr. 1972 pap. $19.50. Essays on Whitehead by one of his leading followers and commentators.

Anselm's Discovery: A Re-Examination of the Ontological Proof for God's Existence. Open Court 1973 $23.95 pap. $11.95. Readable interpretation of Anselm's profound and obscure argument for the existence of God.

The Logic of Perfection and Other Essays in Neoclassical Metaphysics. Open Court 1973 pap. $8.95. Remarkable for its reformulation of the ontological argument for the existence of God in the symbolic calculi of mathematical logic.

Aquinas to Whitehead: Seven Centuries of Metaphysics of Religion. Marquette Univ. Pr. 1976 $7.95. Insightful elaboration of a central theme in philosophy and religion.

Creative Synthesis and Philosophic Method. Univ. Pr. of Amer. 1983 text ed. pap. $15.25. A major treatise on Hartshorne's method in philosophy.

Insights and Oversights of Great Thinkers: An Evaluation of Western Philosophy. State Univ. of New York Pr. 1983 $39.50 pap. $16.95. Idiosyncratic but illuminating interpretations of the history of philosophy.

Omnipotence and Other Theological Mistakes. State Univ. of New York Pr. 1983 $34.50 pap. $9.95. Acute critique of conventional features of traditional conceptions of God.

Creativity in American Philosophy. Paragon 1985 pap. $26.95; State Univ. of New York Pr. 1984 $39.50 pap. $16.95. Original and controversial interpretation of American philosophy and its essential themes.

BOOKS ABOUT HARTSHORNE

Cobb, John B., Jr., and Franklin I. Gramwell, eds. *Existence and Actuality: Conversations with Charles Hartshorne.* Univ. of Chicago Pr. 1985 $22.00 pap. $9.95. This collection "contains Hartshorne's short autobiographical sketch, 'How I Got That Way,' and nine critical and appreciative essays, with his response to each" (A. J. Reck, *Ethics*).

Devaney, Sheila G. *Divine Power: A Study of Karl Barth and Charles Hartshorne.* Fortress Pr. 1986 pap. $16.95. Scholarly comparative study of two outstanding twentieth-century theologians.

Goodwin, George L. *The Ontological Argument of Charles Hartshorne.* Scholars Pr. GA 1978 pap. $9.95. Limited by thorough examination of Hartshorne's favorite argument for the existence of God.

Gragg, Alan. *Charles Hartshorne*. Ed. by Bob E. Patterson, Word Bks. new ed. 1973 $8.95. Unfinished monograph on Hartshorne's life and works.

Gunton, Coline E. *Becoming and Being: The Doctrine of God in Charles Hartshorne and Karl Barth*. Oxford 1978 text ed. $39.95. Scholarly comparative study of the theology of two prominent twentieth-century thinkers.

Maskop, John C. *Divine Omniscience and Human Freedom: Thomas Aquinas and Charles Hartshorne*. Mercer Univ. Pr. 1984 $14.95. Dissertation comparing and criticizing the doctrines of rival theologians set apart by the centuries.

Minor, William S., ed. *Charles Hartshorne and Henry Nelson Wieman*. Univ. Pr. of Amer. 1983 text ed. pap. $8.75. Collection of scholarly papers on two contemporary philosophical theologians edited by a disciple.

———. *Directives from Charles Hartshorne and Henry Nelson Wieman Critically Analyzed*. Foundation for Philosophy of Creativity 1969 pap. $5.00. Minor's meticulous analysis of correspondence he received, for the most part, as founder and president of the Foundation for Philosophy of Creativity.

Peters, Eugene H. *Hartshorne and Neoclassical Metaphysics: An Interpretation*. Univ. of Nebraska Pr. 1970 $12.95. Concise, thorough, lucid estimation of Hartshorne's place in the history of metaphysics.

Reese, William L., and Eugene Freeman, eds. *Process and Divinity: The Hartshorne Festschrift*. Open Court 1964 $32.95. A collection of papers by former students and colleagues of Hartshorne on different aspects of his work.

Viney, Donald W. *Charles Hartshorne and the Existence of God*. [*Philosophy Ser.*] State Univ. of New York Pr. 1984 $39.50 pap. $14.95. A critical interpretation of a central question in Hartshorne's philosophy.

Whitney, Barry L. *Evil and the Process God: The Problem of Evil in Charles Hartshorne's Thought*. [*Toronto Studies in Theology*] E Mellen 1985 $49.95. Dissertation on a crucial theme in Hartshorne's thought.

Wood, Forrest, Jr., and Michael DeArmey, eds. *Hartshorne's Neo-Classical Theology*. Tulane Studies in Philosophy 1986 $10.00. Proceedings of a conference on Hartshorne held at the University of Southern Mississippi in April 1985, it contains six essays by prominent scholars, an original essay by Hartshorne, and an excellent introduction by the editors.

HEIDEGGER, MARTIN. 1889–1976

Although Heidegger's early education was in scholastic philosophy, he became interested in HUSSERL's phenomenology. Whereas Husserl's phenomenological investigations centered on cognition and bracketed existence, Heidegger expanded the subject matter for phenomenology, examining such noncognitive states as anxiety. Moreover, he employed the phenomenological method to illuminate ontology and resolve questions of existence.

After teaching at Marburg, Heidegger went to Freiburg as successor to Husserl. In 1933 he became the first National Socialist rector at Freiburg. Esteemed by many as the foremost twentieth-century philosopher, Heidegger has been tainted by his association with the Nazis. At Freiburg he concluded his lectures with the declaration: "Heil Hitler!" Nevertheless, during his final years he was described as "everyman's conception of a German philosopher: ascetic, withdrawn, a trifle eccentric and virtually impossible to understand . . . [a] mixture of scholar and Black Forest peasant and he still favors breeches and heavy woolen stockings. From time to time he shows up at the University of Freiburg to hold crowd-attracting lectures. . . . Almost a recluse, Heidegger has been known to abuse callers who have gotten him on the phone, and to follow it up with an unfriendly letter. This does not happen often because Heidegger has no phone of his own" (*N.Y. Times*).

Heidegger distinguished *Sein* (Being) from *Dasein* (Being there). *Dasein* implies that "man is possibility, he has the power to be. His existence is in his choice of the possibilities which are open to him, and since this choice is never final, once for all, his existence is indeterminate because not terminated. . . . The mode of existence of the human being . . . is being-in-the-world . . . the being of a self in its inseparable relations with a not-self, the world of things and other persons in which the self always and necessarily finds itself inserted" (H. J. Blackham, *Six Existentialist Thinkers*. Methuen 1983 pap. $8.95). This stark view of individual man confronting absolute nothingness has been paradigmatic for twentieth-century atheistic existentialism. The later Heidegger, with his mystical references to the concealment of Being, has opened the door to theism.

Heidegger's philosophy has been advanced by means of a reinterpretation of the entire Western philosophical tradition since the pre-Socratics. Despite the opposition of specialist scholars, his work has been received as an achievement of contemporary hermeneutics. Meanwhile his own mode of expression, intermixing philosophical jargon with the German slang of his time, has inspired countless commentaries. No twentieth-century philosopher has been the subject of as many books, monographs, and articles as Martin Heidegger, whose *Sein und Zeit* (1927) was carried in the knapsack of many German soldiers as they marched to the Eastern front.

BOOKS BY HEIDEGGER

Basic Writings. Ed. by David F. Krell, Harper 1977 pap. $10.95. An anthology of selections from Heidegger; a good place to begin.

Being and Time. 1927. Trans. by John Macquarrie and Edward Robinson, Harper 1962 $24.45. This is the first translation into English of a book often called untranslatable. *Sein und Zeit* is one of the great classics of modern philosophy and a basic work in existentialism. It is a very difficult book even for a German reader, "full of coined expressions, puns, and resurrected obsolete terms. Nevertheless, the translation accurately reflects the original style and spirit as well as the substance, with a marked consistency of vocabulary aided by a glossary of German expressions and several indexes" (*LJ*).

Existence and Being. Regnery-Gateway 1949 pap. $5.95. A collection of essays that, in English translation, introduced Heidegger to an Anglo-American audience.

An Introduction to Metaphysics. 1953. Trans. by Ralph Manheim, Yale Univ. Pr. 1959 pap. $7.95. This reworked text of lectures delivered at the University of Heidelberg in 1935 contains two favorable allusions to nazism.

What Is Philosophy? Trans. by William Kluback and Jean T. Wilde, New College & Univ. Pr. 1956 pap. $4.95. Metaphilosophy in the puzzling mode of questioning.

The Question of Being. Trans. by William Kluback and Jean T. Wilde, New College & Univ. Pr. 1958 pap. $4.95. Basic ontology with a tendency to obscurantism.

Nietzsche. 1961. Harper 3 vols. 1979–84 ea. $18.45–$19.45 vol. 1, *The Will to Power as Art*, trans. by David F. Krell; vol. 2, *The Eternal Recurrence of the Same*, trans. by David F. Krell; vol. 3, *The Will to Power as Knowledge and as Metaphysics*, ed. by

David F. Krell, trans. by Joan Stambaugh and Frank A. Capuzzi; vol. 4, *Nihilism*, trans. by Frank A. Capuzzi. Voluminous investigations that convey more about the thinking of the author than of his subject.

What Is a Thing? Trans. by W. B. Barton, Jr., and Vera Deutsch, Regnery-Gateway 1968 pap. $5.95; Univ. Pr. of Amer. 1985 text ed. pap. $8.75. "The book is quite important in its own right, without reference to the clarification on the history of Heidegger's thought which it can provide: the sorts of 'thing' he investigates include tools, man, works of art, the state, and the world" (*LJ*).

Discourse on Thinking. Trans. by John M. Anderson and E. Hans Freund, Harper 1969 pap. $5.95. "Can be recommended to the lay reader who wants a brief introduction to Heidegger" (*LJ*).

Hegel's Concept of Experience. Hippocrene Bks. repr. of 1970 ed. 1983 lib. bdg. $17.50. Heideggerian hermeneutics at its problematic best.

What Is Called Thinking? Trans. by J. Glenn Gray and Fred D. Wieck, Harper 1972 pap. $7.95. "A translation of lectures from 1952 that are as near a definitive statement of Heidegger's new period that can be found. . . . A careful reading of this [wise] work can reveal far more to the philosophically uninitiated . . . than can most of his other works" (*LJ*).

Poetry, Language and Thought. Trans. by Albert Hofstadter, Harper 1975 pap. $6.95. This is an "indispensable addition to Heidegger in English and required reading for anyone interested in philosophy. . . . Heidegger, in short, is here not merely philosophizing but thinking. The translation is adequate and at times insightful and felicitous" (*Choice*).

On Time and Being. Trans. by Joan Stambaugh, Harper 1977 pap. $4.95. This book "contains four items: a 1962 lecture, 'Time and Being'; a seminar report on it by Alfred Guzzani; a 1969 lecture, 'The End of Philosophy and the Task of Thinking'; a 1963 festschrift essay, 'My Way to Phenomenology' " (*LJ*).

The Question Concerning Technology and Other Essays. Trans. by William Lovitt, Harper 1977 pap. $7.95; Garland 1978 lib. bdg. $24.00. Influential work contributing to the current hostility by humanistic intellectuals toward technology.

The Basic Problems of Phenomenology. Trans. by Albert Hofstadter [*Studies in Phenomenology and Existential Philosophy*] Indiana Univ. Pr. 1982 $32.50. Authoritative, if abstruse, work in excellent English translation.

On the Way to Language. Ed. by J. Glenn Gray and Fred D. Wieck, trans. by Peter Hertz, Harper 1982 pap. $8.95. Preliminary to the understanding of language in the Heideggerian mode.

The Metaphysical Foundations of Logic. Trans. by Michael Heim [*Studies in Phenomenology and Existential Philosophy*] Indiana Univ. Pr. 1984 $25.00. Obscurantist critique of logic in good translation.

Early Greek Thinking: The Dawn of Western Philosophy. Trans. by David F. Krell and Frank A. Capuzzi, Harper 1985 pap. $8.95. Controversial interpretation of the pre-Socratics.

Schelling's Treatise on the Essence of Human Freedom. Trans. by Joan Stambaugh [*Continental Thought Ser.*] Ohio Univ. Pr. 1985 text ed. $26.95 pap. $14.95. Heideggerian hermeneutics exercised on the nineteenth-century German romantic idealist's most coherent major tract.

BOOKS ABOUT HEIDEGGER

Blitz, Mark. *Heidegger's "Being and Time" and the Possibility of Political Philosophy.* Cornell Univ. Pr. 1981 $27.50. Finely honed analytic examination of a crucial Heideggerian concern.

Bove, Paul A. *Destructive Poetics: Heidegger and Modern American Poetry.* Columbia Univ. Pr. 1980 $23.50. Critical examination of Heidegger's influence on contemporary American poetry.

Caputo, John D. *The Mystical Element in Heidegger's Thought.* Fordham Univ. Pr. rev. ed. 1986 pap. $12.50; Ohio Univ. Pr. 1978 $28.95. Splendid disquisition of Heidegger's mysticism.

Demske, James M. *Being, Man and Death: A Key to Heidegger.* Univ. Pr. of Kentucky 1970 o.p. This book "is nearly indispensable for the serious student of Heidegger and will be useful for the beginner despite its limited focus and theme. Good bibliography of the relevant works in German and English.... Certainly belongs in all libraries" (*Choice*).

Fell, Joseph P. *Heidegger and Sartre: An Essay on Being and Place.* Columbia Univ. Pr. 1983 $32.00 pap. $17.00. Acute, scholarly comparative study, intended for advanced students.

Fynsk, Christopher. *Heidegger: Thought and Historicity.* Cornell Univ. Pr. 1986 text ed. $24.95. Lucid and coherent monograph on Heidegger's conception of history and its relation to philosophical thought.

Gillespie, Michael A. *Hegel, Heidegger, and the Ground of History.* Univ. of Chicago Pr. 1984 lib. bdg. $22.00 1986 pap. $8.95. Brilliantly executed scholarly commentary on historicist themes in Hegel and Heidegger.

Goldmann, Lucien. *Lukács and Heidegger: Towards a New Philosophy.* Trans. by William Q. Boelhower, Methuen 1985 pap. $8.95. Comparative study by a major French literary critic.

Guignon, Charles B. *Heidegger and the Problem of Knowledge.* Hackett 1983 text ed. $27.50 pap. $12.75. Perceptive discussion of the epistemological problems in Heidegger's philosophy.

Halliburton, David. *Poetic Thinking: An Approach to Heidegger.* Univ. of Chicago Pr. 1982 lib. bdg. $22.50. Engrossing approach through poetry and the German philosopher's use of language, of special interest to students of literary criticism.

Heine, Steven. *Essential and Ontological Dimensions of Time in Heidegger and Dogen.* State Univ. of New York Pr. 1986 $44.50 pap. $16.95. Sheer, unadulterated metaphysics.

Kockelmans, Joseph J. *Heidegger and Science.* Univ. Pr. of Amer. 1985 text ed. lib. bdg. $29.50 pap. $14.50. The German philosopher's critique of science and scientific reason examined definitively by a distinguished scholar.

———. *On the Truth of Being: Reflections on Heidegger's Later Philosophy.* [*Studies in Phenomenology and Existential Philosophy*] Indiana Univ. Pr. 1985 $24.95. Reflective investigations on key elements in Heidegger's post-World War II thinking.

———, ed. *A Companion to Martin Heidegger's "Being and Time."* Univ. Pr. of Amer. 1986 text ed. lib. bdg. $26.50 pap. $14.25. A helpful handbook, especially for the beginner.

Kolb, David. *The Critique of Pure Modernity: Hegel, Heidegger, and After.* Univ. of Chicago Pr. 1986 lib. bdg. $25.00. Scholarly interpretation of the responses to modernity by the dominant modes of idealism and existentialism in recent thought.

Krell, David F. *Intimations of Mortality: Time, Truth, and Finitude in Heidegger's Thinking of Being.* Pennsylvania State Univ. Pr. 1986 $22.50. Probing examination of Heideggerian ethics.

Langan, Thomas. *The Meaning of Heidegger: A Critical Study of an Existentialism Phenomenology.* Greenwood repr. of 1959 ed. 1983 lib. bdg. $35.00. Brilliant introductory exposition and commentary.

Macomber, W. B. *Anatomy of Disillusion: Martin Heidegger's Notion of Truth.* [*Studies in Phenomenology and Existential Philosophy*] Northwestern Univ. Pr. 1967 $19.95. A thorough and sometimes technical monograph.

Macquarrie, John. *Martin Heidegger.* John Knox 1968 pap. $3.95. A reliable overview.

Marx, Werner. *Heidegger and the Tradition.* [*Studies in Phenomenology and Existential Philosophy*] Northwestern Univ. Pr. 1971 $19.95 pap. $11.95. Profound but often puzzling interpretation by an influential contemporary German thinker.

———. *Heidegger Memorial Lectures.* Humanities 1982 $12.50. Commentary for the specialist.

———. *Is There a Measure on Earth?* Trans. by T. J. Nenon and Reginald Lilly [*Foundations for Nonmetaphysical Ethics*] Univ. of Chicago Pr. 1987 $22.95. "Distinguished philosopher Werner Marx provides a close reading, critique, and *Weiterdenken,* or further thinking, of Martin Heidegger's later work on death, language, and poetry" (Publisher's note).

Murray, Michael, ed. *Heidegger and Modern Philosophy.* Yale Univ. Pr. 1978 pap. $10.95. A collection of essays by and for experts.

Poggeler, Otto. *Martin Heidegger's Path of Thinking.* Trans. by Dan Margushak and Sigmund Barber, Humanities 1986 text ed. $45.00. Laborious investigation of an obscure but basic theme.

Richardson, Joseph. *Heidegger.* Kluwer Academic 3d ed. 1974 lib. bdg. $50.00. Monumental commentary, second to none in the field.

Robinson, James M., and John B. Cobb, Jr., eds. *The Later Heidegger and Theology.* Greenwood repr. of 1963 ed. 1979 lib. bdg. $22.50. A collection of scholarly essays examining Heidegger's early atheism and later theism.

Schalow, Frank. *Imagination and Existence: Heidegger's Retrieval of the Kantian Ethic.* Univ. Pr. of Amer. 1986 text ed. lib. bdg. $24.75 pap. $11.75. A readable dissertation contrasting Cassirer and Heidegger on Kant.

Schmitt, Richard. *Martin Heidegger on Being Human: An Introduction to Sein und Zeit.* Peter Smith repr. of 1969 ed. 1976 $11.25. A good place for the young student of Heidegger to start.

Scott, Charles E. *The Language of Difference.* Ed. by John Sallis, Humanities Pr. 1986 $35.00. A Vanderbilt philosopher makes plain some abstruse language.

Shahan, Robert W., and J. N. Mohanty. *Thinking about Being: Aspects of Heidegger's Thought.* Univ. of Oklahoma Pr. 1985 $18.95. A collection of articles originally published in the *Southwestern Journal of Philosophy.*

Spanos, William D., ed. *Martin Heidegger and the Question of Literature: Toward a Postmodern Literary Hermeneutics.* [*Studies in Phenomenology and Existential Philosophy*] Indiana Univ. Pr. 1980 $20.00. Aimed at specialists in the theory of literary criticism.

Steiner, George. *Martin Heidegger.* [*Modern Masters Ser.*] Penguin 1980 pap. $4.95. Brilliant interpretation by a stellar literary critic.

Theunissen, Michael. *The Other: Studies in the Social Ontology of Husserl, Heidegger, Sartre, and Buber.* Trans. by Christopher Macann, MIT 1984 text ed. $45.00 1986 pap. $13.50. Existentialist social psychology and philosophy critically explored.

Vail, I. M. *Heidegger and Ontological Difference.* Pennsylvania State Univ. Pr. 1972 $24.50. A monograph for specialists.

White, David A. *Heidegger and the Language of Poetry.* Univ. of Nebraska Pr. 1978 $19.95. Of particular interest to students of poetry and literary criticism.

———. *Logic and Ontology in Heidegger.* Ohio State Univ. Pr. 1986 $22.50. Insightful specialist monograph on major Heideggerian concerns.

Williams, John R. *Martin Heidegger's Philosophy of Religion.* Humanities Pr. 1977 text ed. pap. $9.25. Introductory investigation of an aspect of Heidegger's thought that is often neglected.

Zimmerman, Michael. *Eclipse of the Self: The Development of Heidegger's Concept of Authenticity.* Ohio Univ. Pr. rev. ed. 1986 text ed. $22.95 pap. $12.95. Well-written dissertation on Heidegger's philosophy of mind, pertinent to existential psychoanalytic theory.

————, ed. *The Thought of Martin Heidegger.* Tulane Studies in Philosophy 1985 $10.00. A collection of perceptive essays by sympathetic experts.

HOCKING, WILLIAM ERNEST. 1873–1966

Influenced by both WILLIAM JAMES (see also Vol. 3) and JOSIAH ROYCE, as well as by early initiation into science and engineering, Hocking described his philosophical thinking as composed of "realism . . . mysticism . . . idealism also, its identity not broken." "I wish," he once said, "to discern what character our civilizations, now unsteadily merging into a single world civilization, are destined to take in the foreseeable future, assuming that we have a foreseeable future."

The Harvard "President's Report" (1965–66) said of him: "William Ernest Hocking, Alford Professor of Natural Religion, Moral Philosophy and Civil Polity, *Emeritus*, died June 12, 1966, in his ninety-third year. Professor Hocking, like R. B. Perry, was a scholar who bridged the years from the admired era of Santayana, Palmer, Royce and James to our own times. His school of thought has been called objective idealism or, in his own words 'non-materialistic realism,' a kind of blend of the pragmatic and the idealistic. His first book, *The Meaning of God in Human Experience* (1912), established his reputation and became a classic in the region between philosophy and theology. This was the beginning of a long line of books and articles which for half a century brought his characteristic 'warmth, clarity and insight' (in the words of a colleague) to a variety of human problems ranging from ethics to education. A sampling of [his] titles will suggest the reach of his ecumenical temper. . . . Mr. Hocking graduated from the College in 1901 and took his doctorate in 1904. After a period at Berkeley and at New Haven, he returned here as Professor of Philosophy in 1914 and five years later was elected to the Alford chair. Although he became *Emeritus* in 1943, he remained active and intellectually alert to the end of his life, conducting a large and lively correspondence with friends, colleagues and students the world over and lending the kindly sagacity of a great teaching mind to countless admiring younger men and women."

BOOKS BY HOCKING

The Meaning of God in Human Experience. Yale Univ. Pr. 1912 o.p. Influential American work in the philosophy of religion drawing on James's pragmatism and Royce's idealism.

Man and the State. Elliots Bks. repr. of 1926 ed. 1958 $24.00; Shoe String repr. of 1926 ed. 1968 $35.00. Elegantly written, systematic idealist political philosophy.

Present Status of the Philosophy of Law and of Rights. Rothman repr. of 1926 ed. 1986 lib. bdg. $22.50. Critical monograph of contemporary legal theory as bearing on rights.

The Self, Its Body, and Freedom. AMS Pr. repr. of 1928 ed. 1980 $13.00. Idealist metaphysics, clearly written but profound in content.

Human Nature and Its Remaking. 1923. AMS Pr. repr. of 1929 ed. 1982 $37.00. Highly original philosophy of man, stressing the primacy of will.

The Lasting Elements of Individualism. AMS Pr. repr. of 1937 ed. 1980 $14.00. Vigorous defense of liberalism against the then ascendant totalitarianisms.

Living Religions and a World Faith. [*Hibbert Lecture Ser.*] AMS Pr. repr. of 1940 ed. 1980 $28.50. Comparative studies in search of common religious ground by an authentically sympathetic and ironic thinker.

What Man Can Make of Man. AMS Pr. repr. of 1942 ed. 1980 $18.00. Concise essay on human possibilities optimistically appreciated.

Freedom of the Press. [*Civil Liberties in Amer. History*] Da Capo repr. of 1947 ed. 1974 lib. bdg. $29.50. Comprehensive treatment of the topic.

The Meaning of Immortality in Human Experience, Including Thoughts on Life and Death. Greenwood repr. of 1957 ed. rev. ed. 1982 lib. bdg. $27.50. Imaginative metaphysical essays, containing proofs of man's immortality.

BOOKS ABOUT HOCKING

Robinson, Daniel S. *Royce and Hocking: American Idealists.* Chris Mass 1968 $6.95. Sympathetic portrait of two Harvard idealists by a disciple.

Rouner, Leroy S. *Within Human Experience: The Philosophy of William Ernest Hocking.* Harvard Univ. Pr. 1969 text ed. $20.00. Rouner compresses "into one book the essence of Hocking's 17 books and 270 essays. The result, exhibiting a methodology similar to Hocking's own style of announcing and elaborating ideas rather than constructing systematic defenses of them, is a fairly readable introduction to this Weltanschauung" (*Choice*).

HOOK, SIDNEY. 1902–

Hook was born and educated in New York City and taught, very early in his career, in the city's public schools. Morris Cohen (see above) was among his teachers at City College; he later studied under JOHN DEWEY (see also Vol. 3) at Columbia University, where he received his Ph.D. in 1927. He immediately began teaching at New York University, where he subsequently served as chairman of the philosophy department at the Washington Square College, head of the graduate department, and head of the all-university department, retiring from this post in May 1968. On that occasion one of his colleagues recalled Hook's remark, "I've had a wonderful week, a fight every day" (*N.Y. Times*). Brand Blanshard has called Hook "that inexhaustible geyser of books, lectures, and essays, a philosopher who scents the smell of battle from afar and is soon in the midst of it, giving as well as he gets, and usually somewhat better."

An early Marxist in his fervent desire for social reform, Hook was deeply impressed by his teachers Cohen and Dewey. He still passionately espouses a form of Marxism that is a "democratic socialism," but of his own brand; he early denounced communism as practiced in the Soviet Union and remains one of its most dogged and vocal opponents.

"As a philosopher, Hook's most distinctive contribution is his theory of democracy.... On occasions too numerous to count Hook has attempted to elucidate the objective meaning of democracy, to canvas the objections raised against it, to marshal the arguments in its behalf, and, as behooves the philosopher, to examine the kinds of theoretical justifications which from time to time come forth in its support.... His early books, *Towards the Understanding of Karl Marx* and *From Hegel to Marx,* are by far the best expository, interpretive, historical, and critical studies of MARX's (see also Vol. 3) thought ever written by an American philosopher.... Persistently criticizing the historical determinism of orthodox Marxism, Hook argues that history contains the contingent and the unforeseen and, further, that individual men play important roles in the making of history" (Reck, *The New American Philosophers*). *The Hero in History* concerns this idea.

The *N.Y. Times* said of him: "A pragmatist who believes that all viable reform must come from within, he has had few rivals in his ability to launch and sustain a dialogue on the great issues of our time. He has made those dialogues memorable for their fireworks, whether the subject was nuclear physics or psychoanalysis, civil disobedience or the Bill of Rights— or a new form of tyranny over the mind of man." He recently defended the right of the scholar to remain "disengaged" in his search for truth, and attacked Herbert Marcuse for what Hook considers a new dogmatism.

Professor Hook received Guggenheim Fellowships in 1928 and 1953 to study European philosophy, traveling to Russia and Germany, and was granted a Ford Foundation Fellowship in 1958 to study Asian philosophy and culture. A fellow of the American Academy of Arts and Sciences, he was president of the Eastern Division of the American Philosophical Association in 1959. As founder of New York University's Institute of Philosophy, he has edited a series of volumes recording the symposia it conducted, symposia on the cutting edge of philosophical research (see above under "Bibliography"). Hook has served as Thomas Jefferson lecturer at the Library of Congress, the most distinguished appointment in the humanities to be offered by the federal government of the United States.

BOOKS BY HOOK

The Metaphysics of Pragmatism. AMS Pr. repr. of 1927 ed. 1982 $20.00. Dissertation on the fundamental categories implicit in Deweyan pragmatism.

From Hegel to Marx: Studies in the Intellectual Development of Karl Marx. Univ. of Michigan Pr. repr. of 1936 ed. 1978 $6.95. In-depth essays on the German thinkers who led up to Marx from Hegel, organized around the theme of Marx's own development.

John Dewey: An Intellectual Portrait. Greenwood repr. of 1939 ed. 1973 lib. bdg. $22.50. A readable interpretation of Dewey's philosophy by a disciple who emphasized its affinity to Marxism.

Marx and the Marxists: The Ambiguous Legacy. Krieger repr. of 1955 ed. 1982 pap. $8.50. Probes ways the humanism of Marx has been betrayed by Soviet communism.

Common Sense and the Fifth Amendment. Constructive Action repr. of 1957 ed. 1963 pap. $1.75. Polemic tract during the McCarthy era that was critical of the invocation of the Fifth Amendment by persons questioned by Congressional committees.

The Quest for Being and Other Studies in Naturalism and Humanism. Greenwood repr. of 1961 ed. 1971 lib. bdg. $22.50. A materialistic naturalist objects to fashionable modes of metaphysical thinking, illustrated by Heidegger.

Religion in a Free Society. Univ. of Nebraska Pr. 1967 $10.95. The perspective on religion by an acute and articulate secular humanist.

The Paradoxes of Freedom. Greenwood repr. of 1970 ed. 1984 lib. bdg. $25.00. Provocative essay by an American Marxist-pragmatist, who became the favorite intellectual of conservatives during the Nixon administration.

Education and the Taming of Power. Open Court 1973 $9.95. Educational theory, with practical consideration of student unrest and its destructive impact on academic freedom.

Revolution, Reform and Social Justice: Studies in the Theory and Practice of Marxism. New York Univ. Pr. 1975 $25.00. Advanced studies, weighing the advantages of democratic reform over violent revolution in the attainment of social justice.

Philosophy and Public Policy. Southern Illinois Univ. Pr. 1980 $19.50 pap. $10.95. Pioneering investigation of the interplay of philosophy and public affairs.

BOOKS ABOUT HOOK

Kurtz, Paul. *Sidney Hook and the Contemporary World: Essays on the Pragmatic Intelligence.* Harper 1968 o.p. A collection of essays in honor of Hook on his sixty-fifth birthday, edited by a disciple who is also the leading American humanist.

———. *Sidney Hook: Philosopher of Democracy and Humanism.* Prometheus Bks. 1982 $20.95. "A wide-ranging collection of essays in honor of Sidney Hook's eightieth birthday. The topics include socialism and marxism, democracy and equality, the ontology of pragmatism, the philosophy of liberal education, and the ethics of humanism. Among the 20 contributors are Richard Rorty, Lewis Feuer, Ernest Nagel, David Sidorsky, Anthony Flew, Marvin Kohl, Nicholas Capaldi. There is a complete bibliography of works by and about Hook" (*The Philosopher's Index*).

Reck, Andrew J. *The New American Philosophers.* Louisiana State Univ. Pr. 1968 o.p. Contains a full-length chapter exploring Hook's synthesis of Marxism and pragmatism.

JASPERS, KARL. 1883–1969

Karl Jaspers was one of the originators of German existentialism. He began his career as a psychiatrist, but was increasingly concerned about philosophical and moral issues. His was "a lucid and flexible intelligence in the service of a genuine and passionate concern for mankind." Removed from his professorship at the University of Heidelberg by the Nazis in 1937, he was reinstated in 1945 on the approval of the American Occupation Army. In 1949 he went to the University of Basel. The *N.Y. Times* wrote of him in his lifetime: "Jaspers shows himself . . . to be one of the most diligent and sensitive students of contemporary history. He has a good eye for the present because he knows what to fear in it—particularly the loss of individual freedom."

Jaspers was deeply concerned about the fate of man, and in his book *The Future of Mankind*, entitled in its updated edition *The Atom Bomb and the Future of Man*, he attempted to arouse conscience in the face of the deadly danger of atomic warfare "at the same time . . . attempt[ing] to apply the principles of his philosophy to a new field, and to lay the foundations of a political philosophy" (*TLS*). After the German publication of this book, Jaspers was awarded the German Peace Prize at the 1958 Frankfurt Book Fair. Hannah Arendt, who had been his student and a translator of some of his works, made the presentation.

The obituary of Jaspers in the *N.Y. Times* commented on his great personal courage: "As professor of philosophy at the University of Heidelberg he was outspoken against Hitlerism. The Nazis retired him in 1937, but they could not silence him short of killing him. And this they planned to do. Indeed, on the eve of the departure of Jaspers and his wife for a concentration camp, they were saved by the American Army's capture of Heidelberg in 1945. Restored to his professorship after the war, he was unsparing in criticism of Germans for their war guilt and for their genocidal campaigns against Jews and other minorities. . . . As for moral guilt, he argued that every individual is morally accountable for his deeds. 'It is never simply true that orders are orders,' he declared. . . . Dr. Jaspers' wife was Gertrud Mayer, whom he married in 1910. She was a Jew, and her husband's refusal to part from her was among the Nazis' indictments of Dr. Jaspers." The *Times* said in assessing him: "With SØREN KIERKEGAARD, Martin Heidegger and Jean-Paul Sartre, Karl Jaspers was one of the makers and shapers of existentialist philosophy. For almost 50 years, in books, essays and lectures, he strove to give a personalist answer to modern man's questions about his own nature and the nature of existence."

BOOKS BY JASPERS

Karl Jaspers: Basic Philosophical Writings. Ed. by Leonard Ehrlich and others, Ohio Univ. Pr. 1986 text ed. $55.00 pap. $26.95. A worthwhile anthology, selecting representative writings, recommended as the text for a seminar on Jaspers.

General Psychopathology. 1922. Trans. by J. Hoenig and W. Hamilton, Univ. of Chicago Pr. 1963 $55.00. Authoritative textbook for its time.

Man in Modern Age. 1931. AMS Pr. repr. of 1933 ed. 1978 $28.50. Incisive critique of civilization in the aftermath of World War I; early analysis of alienation.

The Perennial Scope of Philosophy. Trans. by Ralph Manheim, Shoe String repr. of 1949 ed. 1968 $22.50. Brilliant, if controversial, essay on the nature and function of philosophy.

The Way to Wisdom: An Introduction to Philosophy. Trans. by Ralph Manheim, Yale Univ. Pr. repr. of 1951 ed. 1960 pap. $6.95. A summary of his philosophical beliefs, "a beautiful and puzzling book" (*LJ*).

Reason and Anti-Reason in Our Time. Trans. by Stanley Godman, Shoe String repr. of 1952 ed. 1971 $17.50. Time-honored theme treated with an eye to contemporary relevance.

Tragedy Is Not Enough. Trans. by H. A. Reiche and others, Shoe String repr. of 1952 ed. 1969 $17.50. Passionate commentary on human self-destructiveness and guilt.

The Origin and Goal of History. Trans. by Michael Bullock, Greenwood repr. of 1953 ed. 1977 lib. bdg. $35.00. Perplexing but profound metaphysics of history.

Truth and Symbol. New College & Univ. Pr. 1959 pap. $4.95. Surprisingly readable monograph on meaning and knowledge.

The Great Philosophers. Ed. by Hannah Arendt, trans. by Ralph Manheim, Harcourt 2 vols. 1962–66 o.p. Vol. 1, *The Foundations;* Vol. 2, *The Original Thinkers.* Harvest Bks. pap. eds. of some separate chapters of each volume are available:

from Vol. 1, *Kant* ($4.95); *Plato and Augustine* ($4.95); *Socrates, Buddha, Confucius, and Jesus* ($3.95). From Vol. 2, *Spinoza* ($2.95). "This is a major work, a brilliant book, difficult in parts, and to be recommended for all libraries except the very small." It is not a history of philosophy. "Jaspers defends the unity of philosophy and his aim is to make philosophy available to all, to provide the serious reader with a guide 'to the thinking of the great philosophers and to a personal encounter with them.' " The second volume "consists of long essays on the pre-Socratics, Plotinus, Anselm, Nicholas of Cusa, Spinoza, the Chinese Lao Tzu and the Indian Nagarjuna. Jaspers' own ideas are found in the brief introduction. . . . This book is original, difficult and important. It will appeal to both the professional philosopher and to the student of thought and culture" (*LJ*).

Philosophy. Trans. by E. B. Ashton, Univ. of Chicago Pr. 3 vols. 1969–71 ea. $14.00–$21.00. Jaspers "takes his place among the major expositors of existential philosophy on the American scene" (*Choice*).

Philosophy of Existence. Trans. by Richard F. Grabau, Univ. of Pennsylvania Pr. 1971 $17.50 pap. $9.95. Excellent translation of basic work on existentialism.

The Atom Bomb and the Future of Man. Trans. by E. B. Ashton, Univ. of Chicago Pr. 1984 pap. $10.95. Updated edition of *The Future of Mankind.*

Nietzsche: An Introduction to the Understanding of His Philosophical Activity. Trans. by Charles F. Wallraff and Frederick J. Schmitz, Univ. Pr. of Amer. 1985 text ed. pap. $17.75. Highly personal interpretation of Nietzsche's life and work.

BOOKS ABOUT JASPERS

Ehrlich, Leonard H. *Karl Jaspers: Philosophy as Faith.* Univ. of Massachusetts Pr. 1975 $20.00. "Ehrlich carefully delineates Jaspers' notion of philosophical faith and religious faith, and then mirrors Jaspers' basic concepts in the thought of religious thinkers such as Buber and Tillich" (*LJ*).

Schilpp, Paul Arthur, ed. *The Philosophy of Karl Jaspers.* [*Lib. of Living Philosophers*] Open Court 1957 2d ed. 1981 $39.95. This volume consists of Jaspers's philosophical autobiography, 24 essays by prominent philosophers on different aspects of Jaspers's thought, his reply to comments and criticism, and his bibliography.

Wallraff, Charles F. *Karl Jaspers: An Introduction to His Philosophy.* Princeton Univ. Pr. 1970 $27.50 pap. $10.50. An accessible overview of Jaspers's philosophy, perhaps the best intellectual biography of the German philosopher in English.

Young-Bruehl, Elisabeth. *Freedom and Karl Jaspers' Philosophy.* Yale Univ. Pr. 1981 $20.00. "The author shows an admirable mastery of Jaspers' thought. This is a scholarly, demanding work—in keeping with its subjects—and very worthwhile" (L. H. Brody).

LANGER, SUSANNE K. 1895–1986

As friend and pupil of Alfred North Whitehead, Susanne Langer was led into a long and profound study of symbolic logic. From the beginning of her career as a philosophical author of the first rank Langer was committed to the role of philosophy as the systematic study of meanings, and she studied symbols and feelings not only in regard to their intrinsic form but also in the broader context of their many relations and functions within civilization and culture. Her thesis in her magnum opus, *Mind: An Essay on Human Feeling,* is that the mind's "function is possessed to a greater or lesser extent by all organic life, from the unicellular organism to man, and that all life is permeated with acts that are influenced by it. . . . Professor Langer propounds two opposed and complementary functional principles by which organic life proceeds—individuation and involvement. A cell or an organ inhibits its own growth at a certain point. This is an example of individuation. On the other hand, involvement has been present in organic life since the very beginning. Not only are cells involved with other cells but all acts are to some extent involved with other acts. And acts tend to recur, forming rhythmic patterns. Professor Langer is fascinated by rhythm—by what she refers to as 'dialectical concatenation into rhythmic series,' which is to be observed in the acts of organisms. She even suggests a rhythmic origin for life . . . though she quickly dismisses this idea as speculative. . . . The references to art are also continually cropping up. Growth—the perpetual trend of life—is compared with melody, which always moves (or, rather, grows) to its point of climax and then recedes, often to gather impetus toward a succeeding climax. In our apprehension of the world around us, 'feeling' is basic. 'Where nothing is felt,' Professor Langer states (and few would disagree), 'nothing matters' " (Winthrop Sargeant, *The New Yorker*).

BOOKS BY LANGER

Introduction to Symbolic Logic. 1937. Dover 3d ed. 1967 text ed. pap. $6.50. A standard textbook.

Philosophy in a New Key: A Study in the Symbolism of Reason, Rite and Art. 1942. Harvard Univ. Pr. 3d ed. 1957 $20.00 pap. $6.95. Influential original essay on the nature and significance of language for philosophy.

Feeling and Form: A Theory of Art. Macmillan repr. of 1953 ed. 1977 text ed. pap. $10.50. Philosophy of art systematically and lucidly presented.

Problems of Art. Macmillan repr. of 1957 ed. 1977 text ed. pap. $10.50. Ten philosophical lectures.

(ed.). *Reflections on Art: A Source Book of Writings by Artists, Critics and Philosophers.* Ayer repr. of 1958 ed. 1979 $30.00. Sensitive and sensible anthology recommended for college courses in the field.

Mind: An Essay on Human Feeling. Johns Hopkins Univ. Pr. 3 vols. 1967–82 pap. $34.50. "The study traces the continuous evolution of life from its simplest forms to the most complex phenomena of mind. . . . For advanced students of philosophy of biology, aesthetics, and philosophy of mind" (*Choice*).

LEWIS, CLARENCE IRVING. 1883–1964

C. I. Lewis ranks among the most influential American academic philosophers. He spent most of his long career at Harvard University, guiding the education of many graduate students who later held faculty positions at American colleges and universities. As a very young professor, first at the University of California-Berkeley and later at Harvard, Lewis established a national and international reputation in symbolic logic, to which he had been introduced in the early years of the century by his mentor Josiah Royce. Lewis wrote one of the early histories of symbolic logic, *A Survey of Symbolic Logic* (1918). Of more importance his dissatisfaction with the principle of material implication presented by RUSSELL (see also Vol. 5) and Whitehead in *Principia Mathematica* inspired him to construct a system of strict implication, one of the earliest forms of modal logic. He presented this theory in a book he coauthored with Cooper Harold Langford, *Symbolic Logic* (1932).

Lewis is most famous for his articulation of a form of pragmatism known as conceptual pragmatism. A close student of KANT, he was impressed with the role of a priori concepts in the interpretation of experience and the formation of knowledge. Critical of what he regarded as the neglect of formal conceptual structures by such philosophers as JAMES (see also Vol. 5) and DEWEY, he upheld a doctrine of the a priori, but, unlike Kant, he stressed its pragmatic character. His epistemology of conceptual pragmatism was unfolded in his book *Mind and the World-Order* (1929).

When the American Philosophical Association met in 1945 for the first time after World War II, Lewis was invited to deliver its most prestigious lectures—the Paul Carus lectures. He addressed himself to the epistemological and valuational issues raised by the rising tide of logical positivism. He defended and elaborated a theory of meaning that denied its reducibility to the syntax of language. He drew sharp distinctions between the analytic and synthetic and articulated a theory of formal and empirical judgments. Against the noncognitivists he expounded a naturalistic theory of value judgments. In published form Lewis's lectures prompted discussions in the professional journals of a quantity and quality that had never before been equaled in American philosophy.

BOOKS BY LEWIS

Collected Papers of Clarence Irving Lewis. Ed. by John D. Goheen and John L. Mothershead, Stanford Univ. Pr. 1970 $32.50. Scholarly edition of Lewis's papers, published for the most part in technical journals.

Analysis of Knowledge and Valuation. 1947. [*Paul Carus Lecture Ser.*] Open Court 1981 $19.95 pap. $7.95. Critical and systematic presentation of theory of knowledge and value theory; an American classic.

Values and Imperatives: Studies in Ethics. Ed. by John Lange, Stanford Univ. Pr. 1969 $17.50. Lewis's writings on ethics; cogent and Kantian.

BOOKS ABOUT LEWIS

Rosenthal, Sandra. *The Pragmatic A Priori.* Fireside Bks. 1975 $10.00. Dissertation on Lewis's theory of necessary knowledge.

Schilpp, Paul Arthur, ed. *The Philosophy of C. I. Lewis.* [*Lib. of Living Philosophers*], Open Court 1968 $29.95. This volume contains Lewis's philosophical autobiography, essays in various aspects of his philosophy by distinguished philosophers, his reply to his critics, and his bibliography.

LONERGAN, BERNARD. 1904–1984

A Roman Catholic priest, Rev. Bernard Lonergan, S.J., was born in Buckingham, Quebec, and educated at Loyola College in Montreal, Heythrop College (London), the University of London, and the Gregorian University in Rome. Among his many teaching positions in Canada, Europe, and the United States, he taught at the Gregorian University in Rome from 1953 to 1965 and has served as Stielman professor at the Harvard Divinity School. He was esteemed by many to have been the leading figure in the turn of neo-Thomism from a rigid scholastic Aristotelianism into a flexible mode of thinking that absorbs the insights of Kant and post-Kantian thought. His kind of Thomism is commonly referred to as transcendental Thomism.

BOOKS BY LONERGAN

Subject. Marquette Univ. Pr. 1968 $7.95. A lecture on the nature, status, and function of the subject.

Doctrinal Pluralism. Marquette Univ. Pr. 1971 $7.95. Theology at its purest.

A Second Collection. Westminster 1975 $12.00. A collection of essays, always profound and perplexing.

Insight: A Study of Human Understanding. Harper 1977 pap. $15.95. Lonergan's masterpiece, unfolding his transcendental Thomism.

Method in Theology. Harper 1979 pap. $11.50. The delineation of Lonergan's sophisticated methodology; not easy to read.

BOOKS ABOUT LONERGAN

Crowe, Frederick E. *The Lonergan Enterprise*. Cowley Pubns. 1980 pap. $6.00. A sympathetic commentary by a Lonergan disciple.

Lamb, Matthew L., ed. *Creativity and Method: Studies in Honor of Rev. Bernard Lonergan, S.J.* Marquette Univ. Pr. 1981 $29.95 pap. $19.95. A collection of studies by leading experts specializing in Lonergan's thought.

Meynell, Hugo A. *The Theology of Bernard Lonergan*. [*Studies in Religion*] Scholars Pr. GA 1986 text ed. $15.95 pap. $11.95. A scholarly dissertation for specialists.

LOVEJOY, ARTHUR ONCKEN. 1873–1962

Lovejoy, who was educated at the University of California-Berkeley and Harvard, taught at several American universities before going in 1910 to Johns Hopkins, where he taught until his retirement in 1938. His major contributions were in epistemology and the history of ideas, although he should also be counted as a man of action, having been one of the organizers of the Association of American University Professors.

Lovejoy's earliest philosophical interests were in epistemology and metaphysics. In metaphysics he was a temporalist, and many of his writings are devoted to the nature of time and to the doctrines of philosophers and scientists on time. He firmly believed in the reality of time, including the reality of past time.

Epistemologically Lovejoy was a critical realist. In this regard he was one of seven philosophers who contributed to *Essays in Critical Realism* (1920), a major cooperative effort signaling a school of thought that held that knowledge is about an independent reality but is mediated by representations or ideas. This view involves an epistemological dualism, and Lovejoy's book, *The Revolt against Dualism* (1930), is the most penetrating critique of such philosophers as Whitehead and Russell who attempted to supplant dualism with monism. It also presents a systematic defense of epistemological dualism and, further, of mind-body or psychophysical dualism.

Lovejoy was a pioneer in the field of intellectual history. Indeed, he was founding editor of the *Journal of the History of Ideas*. Lovejoy defined ideas as unit principles that persist through history and that ramify in a variety of fields, requiring cross-disciplinary studies. He himself was an expert practitioner of the method, his own book, *The Great Chain of Being* (1936), remaining a classic of which even contemporary scholars in the field must take account.

BOOKS BY LOVEJOY

The Revolt against Dualism: An Inquiry Concerning the Existence of Ideas. 1930. [*Paul Carus Lecture Ser.*] Open Court 2d ed. 1960 $21.95 pap. $8.95. Devastating critique of the various monisms of the new realists, Bertrand Russell, A. N. Whitehead, and others, and a plausible defense of dualism.

(and George Boas). 1933. *Primitivism and Related Ideas in Antiquity.* Hippocrene Bks. repr. of 1935 ed. 1965 lib. bdg. $39.75. First volume in a series that has been discontinued; the intersection of the history of ideas and anthropology at its best.

The Great Chain of Being: A Study of the History of an Idea. [*William James Lectures Ser.*] Harvard Univ. Pr. 1936 $25.00 pap. $8.95. Classic interpretation of a major theme in Western philosophy.

Essays in the History of Ideas. Greenwood repr. of 1948 ed. 1978 lib. bdg. $29.50. Collection of previously published essays illustrating Lovejoy's unsurpassed erudition.

The Reason, the Understanding, and the Time. Johns Hopkins Univ. Pr. 1961 o.p. Inimitable exploration of metaphysical themes in philosophy during the eighteenth and nineteenth centuries, illuminating Kant, Hegel, and Bergson.

Reflections on Human Nature. Johns Hopkins Univ. Pr. 1961 pap. $6.95. Study of moral philosophy during the seventeenth and eighteenth centuries as the background for understanding the works of the American founding fathers.

The Thirteen Pragmatisms and Other Essays. Greenwood repr. of 1963 ed. 1983 lib. bdg. $21.95. A collection of scholarly essays by Lovejoy, published mainly during his early period when pragmatism was the primary target of his criticism.

BOOKS ABOUT LOVEJOY

Wilson, Daniel J. *Arthur O. Lovejoy: An Annotated Bibliography.* Garland 1982 lib. bdg. $36.00. Useful and authoritative; indispensable to research on Lovejoy.

———. *Arthur O. Lovejoy and the Quest for Intelligibility.* Univ. of North Carolina Pr. 1980 $20.00. "This biography focuses on Lovejoy's intellectual development and on the connections among the facets of his career. . . . [Lovejoy] believed that only reason could order and make intelligible the experienced world without destroying its reality" (*The Philosopher's Index*).

MCTAGGART, JOHN MCTAGGART ELLIS. 1866–1925

McTaggart was a British metaphysician who taught at Cambridge from 1897 to 1923. He was one of the main figures in the school of Hegelianism that flourished in Great Britain from the third quarter of the nineteenth century well into the first quarter of the twentieth century. Though he ranks beside F. H. BRADLEY and BERNARD BOSANQUET, McTaggart espoused a peculiar brand of Hegelian idealism. On HEGEL he was a superb commentator, but never a slavish expositor. While he believed that reality is essentially spiritual, his idealism retreated from conjuring up absolutes. Rather he insisted on the primacy of finite individual persons. His denial of the existence of time has continued to intrigue philosophers, and his *Nature of Existence* has incited the extensive critique of C. D. Broad, in what is perhaps the most celebrated instance in twentieth-century philosophy of an exceptionally prominent and influential thinker painstakingly and at length commenting on the work of another.

BOOKS BY MCTAGGART

Some Dogmas of Religion. Kraus Repr. repr. of 1906 ed. 1962 $23.00. Highly original, beautifully composed essays undermining the foundations of Christian theism.

Commentary on Hegel's Logic. Russell repr. of 1910 ed. 1964 $18.00. Clearest introduction to Hegel's "greater logic" ever written.

Human Immortality and Pre-Existence. Kraus Repr. repr. of 1916 ed. 1964 $23.00. Idiosyncratic but cogent case for the transmigration of souls and reincarnation.

Studies in Hegelian Cosmology. Ibis Pub VA repr. of 1918 ed. 1978 text ed. lib. bdg. $25.00 pap. $13.00; Garland 1984 $38.00. Brilliant, innovative interpretations of Hegel's philosophy, replacing the notion of the Absolute with the idea of the all-inclusive spiritual community.

The Nature of Existence. Scholarly 2 vols. repr. of 1921–27 ed. 1968 $68.00. Systematic treatise of metaphysics, clearly expounded and cogently argued, containing such startling theses as the unreality of time.

Studies in Hegelian Dialectic. Russell repr. of 1922 ed. 2d ed. 1964 $20.00. Further original commentary on Hegel, focused on the German's methodology.

Philosophical Studies. Ed. by S. V. Keeling, Ayer repr. of 1934 ed. 1977 $17.75. Posthumously published collection of McTaggart's essays on a variety of philosophical topics.

BOOK ABOUT MCTAGGART

Geach, P. T. *Truth, Love, and Immortality: An Introduction to McTaggart's Philosophy.* Univ. of California Pr. 1979 $25.50. Keenly analytical monograph on perplexing themes in McTaggart composed subtly by a prominent British philosopher with the intention of providing an introduction.

MALCOLM, NORMAN. 1911–

Born in Kansas, Malcolm studied with O. K. Bouwsma at the University of Nebraska, and later at Harvard. He studied at Cambridge University (1938–39), where he was influenced by G. E. Moore but even more profoundly by Ludwig Wittgenstein. He taught at Cornell University, where he played a major role as host in the visits to the United States by Moore and Wittgenstein after World War II, and in the subsequent triumph of their kind of analytic philosophy in the United States.

Malcolm has been one of the most illustrious practitioners of the method of linguistic analysis with its emphasis on ordinary language, a method introduced by Wittgenstein. He has applied this method effectively to traditional metaphysical topics such as the ontological argument for the existence of God and to epistemological questions concerning dreaming. Malcolm has written extensively in the fields of epistemology and philosophy of mind, and his works have had a wide audience among British and American academic philosophers.

BOOKS BY MALCOLM

Ludwig Wittgenstein, a Memoir. 1958. Oxford 2d ed. 1984 pap. $6.95. Well-written reminiscences of the famous Cambridge philosopher by a devoted disciple.

Dreaming. Humanities 1962 text ed. pap. $7.95. Sophisticated analytic theory of
what the language of dreaming means.
Memory and Mind. Cornell Univ. Pr. 1977 $24.95. Conceptual analysis at the highest
level.
Thought and Knowledge: Essays. Cornell Univ. Pr. 1977 $22.50. A collection of Mal-
colm's papers in theory of knowledge and philosophy of mind previously published in specialist professional journals.
Nothing Is Hidden: Wittgenstein's Criticism of His Early Thought. Basil Blackwell
1986 text ed. $34.95. Controversial but stimulating commentary on Wittgenstein's
alleged change of mind by one who should know.

BOOK ABOUT MALCOLM

Ginet, Carl, and Sydney Shoemaker, eds. *Knowledge and Mind: Philosophical Essays.*
Oxford 1983 $34.95. A collection of essays by philosophers in honor of Malcolm.
The essays treat philosophical topics of the kind to which Malcolm's own work
is devoted.

MARCEL, GABRIEL. 1889–1973

Marcel has been described as a theistic or Christian existentialist. Born in
Paris of Protestant parents, he converted to Roman Catholicism in 1924.
Prior to his conversion, he had immersed himself in idealism, as his first
book, a study of ROYCE's metaphysics, reveals. Before Jaspers and Heidegger
were known to French intellectuals, Marcel had written about themes central to existentialism, but with a religious twist. He had acknowledged
concern for the vitality and pervasiveness of religious experience, and, like
MARTIN BUBER, he had pointed to the sociality of human experience, which
bears witness to the presence of the Divine.

For Marcel, Being involves participation. No man can be separated from
the whole of Being to which he is related. Nor can he be reduced to merely a
facet of Being; for he is a concrete individual, his experience is immediate,
spontaneous, unpredictable. Though entranced by the mystery of existence,
man may illuminate it by means of philosophical reflection.

BOOKS BY MARCEL

Being and Having: An Existentialist Diary. 1935. Trans. by Katherine Farrer, Peter
Smith repr. of 1949 ed. 1957 $11.25. The intimate record of one man's experi-
ence of his personal participation in fundamental Being.
Creative Fidelity. Trans. by Robert Rosthal, Crossroad NY repr. of 1949 ed. 1982 pap.
$9.95. Inspiring, Christian existentialist essay on being creative yet faithful.
Philosophy of Existence. Trans. by Manya Harai [*Essay Index Repr. Ser.*] Ayer repr. of
1949 ed. 1978 $14.25. Introduces existentialism from the Christian standpoint.
Homo Viator: Introduction to a Metaphysic of Hope. Trans. by Emma Craufurd, Peter
Smith repr. of 1951 ed. 1962 $16.75. Christian existentialist theory of man,
stressing hope instead of despair; an inspiration.
The Mystery of Being. Trans. by Ren Hague [*Gifford Lectures*] AMS Pr. 2 vols. repr. of
1951 ed. 1976 $44.50; Univ. Pr. of Amer. 2 vols 1984 text ed. pap. ea. $7.75–
$8.50. Ontology demonstrating the limits of reason and the need for faith.
Royce's Metaphysics. Trans. by Virginia Ringer and Gordon Ringer, Greenwood repr.
of 1956 ed. 1981 lib. bdg. $22.50. A profound dissertation on idealism.
The Philosophy of Existentialism. Citadel Pr. 1961 pap. $3.95. Restatement of Mar-

cel's "philosophy of existence," contrasted with opposing or rival types of existentialism.

Man against Mass Society. Univ. Pr. of Amer. repr. of 1962 ed. 1985 text ed. pap. $7.75. Eloquent plea for the individual person against inimical tendencies in contemporary civilization.

Philosophical Fragments: 1901–1914 and the Philosopher and Peace. Univ. of Notre Dame Pr. 1965 pap. $3.95. Early philosophical reflections that throw light on the philosopher's development from idealism to existentialism.

Tragic Wisdom and Beyond. Trans. by Stephen Jolin and Peter McCormick [*Studies in Phenomenology and Existential Philosophy Ser.*] Northwestern Univ. Pr. 1973 text ed. $19.95 pap. $10.95. Excellently translated treatise on the interconnection of the moral and the metaphysical in human existence.

BOOKS ABOUT MARCEL

Cain, Seymour. *Gabriel Marcel.* Regnery-Gateway 1979 pap. $4.50. Readable, reliable portrait of Marcel's thought.

Gallagher, Kenneth T. *The Philosophy of Gabriel Marcel.* Fwd. by Gabriel Marcel, Fordham Univ. Pr. rev. ed. 1975 pap. $9.00. Marcel was for nearly four decades one of the world's most influential thinkers, "underivative and unclassifiable though he may be. This book is the first study in the U.S. of Marcel's work in its entirety. Marcel himself, in the foreword, approves Gallagher's results, especially the latter's identification of 'participation' as the leitmotif of his thought" (*LJ*).

Lapointe, François H., and Claire C. Lapointe. *Gabriel Marcel and His Critics: An International Bibliography (1935–1976).* [*Reference Lib. of the Humanities*] Garland 1977 lib. bdg. $39.00. Authoritative bibliography that is indispensable for research on Marcel.

McCown, Joe. *Availability: Gabriel Marcel and the Phenomenology of Human Openness.* Scholars Pr. GA 1978 pap. $9.95. Doctoral dissertation on a central theme in Marcel's philosophy.

Schilpp, Paul Arthur, and Lewis E. Hahn, eds. *The Philosophy of Gabriel Marcel.* [*Lib. of Living Philosophers*] Open Court 1984 pap. $39.95. "The work . . . permits Marcel to reply to some of his major critics. Scholars from Austria, England, France, Germany, Italy, Spain, and the United States put to him searching questions and seek clarification of his major theses. . . . The volume also includes a bibliography of Marcel's writings prepared by François Lapointe and an intensely personal intellectual autobiography" (*The Philosopher's Index*).

MARCUSE, HERBERT. 1898–1984

Marcuse once lauded the graffiti of French students in May 1968 as an incisive slogan for his own vision of revolution: "All power to the imagination!" and "Be reasonable: ask the impossible." Described in the *N.Y. Times* as "dapper, relaxed and [radiating] philosophical benignity," he was blamed by many for the worldwide wave of student rebellion in the 1960s—Angela Davis was his most notorious student.

Born in Germany, Marcuse attended the Universities of Freiburg and Berlin. A Social Democrat in Germany, he migrated to the United States in 1934, became a citizen in 1940, and served as a high United States government consultant during World War II. He lectured at Harvard and Columbia and taught philosophy and political science at Brandeis. At the end of his life he was a professor of philosophy at the University of California at San Diego.

The *N.Y. Times* said of him: "Dr. Marcuse is a professed philosophical Marxist, in that he sees contemporary life as a class struggle in which suppressed and exploited segments of society should act to revamp the socio-economic order. . . . Soviet spokesmen, however, disown and denounce Dr. Marcuse because he rejects KARL MARX's (see also Vol. 3) cherished 'working class' as the instrument of revolutionary change and thinks it must come from groups like oppressed minorities and freethinking youth." Marcuse himself said, "I have tried to show that any change would require a total rejection or, to speak the language of the students, a perpetual confrontation of [contemporary] society." By late 1968 Professor Marcuse had become, again according to the *N.Y. Times*, the "idol" of "restive college students from Berkeley to Bologna" and an apostle of the "New Left." "He tears us apart if we don't think analytically," said his students at the time. "If we come out sounding like Marcuse. . . . He insists on the questioning spirit."

Marcuse was in his lifetime the most famous exponent of critical theory, the neo-Marxism associated with the Frankfurt School of Horkheimer and Adorno and now headed by Habermas. His work provoked vehement opposition from conservatives, liberals, and radicals of the Right and the Left. His book *One Dimensional Man* (1964) is a "critique of modern technological societies. . . . One-dimensionality refers to a tendency to flatten our diverse and conflicting levels of existence and experience and make them consistent. . . . Art and literature no longer provide a refuge for oppositional personalities who do not fit into the dominant scheme of things; even the most avant-garde and 'shocking' cultural products are accepted by the benign establishment. They not only siphon off discontent, they too have market value. Since all forms of potential opposition can be accepted within the status quo, their revolutionary and critical character is deflated. In a series of brilliant analyses that probe deeply into language, popular culture, science, and philosophy, Marcuse traces how multi-dimensional criticism has been collapsed into one-dimensional ideology" (Robert Blauner, *Transaction*). In this work Marcuse indicts both the United States and the Soviet Union, but the United States more harshly.

Marcuse incited the ire of critics who objected to his intolerance of rival positions. Thus Sidney Hook accused Marcuse of wanting to deny freedom of speech to extremists, or even to those who would "choose 'middle-class values.' He replied [said Hook]: 'Well, since I have already gone out on a limb, I may as well go all the way, I would prefer that they did not have the right to choose wrongly.' " From Marcuse's point of view Germany during the Weimar Republic made Hitler's rise to power possible because it granted him too much freedom.

In an article that appeared in the *N.Y. Times Magazine* (October 27, 1968) there is reported an interview by three French journalists in which Marcuse defined what he believed was his relationship to the student movement. Some sympathizers with the students deplored their use of violence; the reporters questioned Marcuse on this point:

Reporters: "And to try to destroy this society which is guilty of violence, you feel that violence is both legitimate and desirable. Does this mean that you think it is impossible to evolve peacefully and within the democratic framework toward a nonrepressive, freer society?"

Marcuse: "The students have said it: a revolution is always just as violent as the violence it combats. I believe they are right."

Reporters: "But you still think it is possible, in spite of the judgment of FREUD (see Vols. 3 and 5), to whom you refer frequently in *Eros and Civilization*, to create a free society. Doesn't this betray a remarkable optimism?"

Marcuse: "I am optimistic, because I believe that never in the history of humanity have the resources necessary to create a free society existed to such a degree. I am pessimistic because I believe that the established societies—capitalist society in particular—are totally organized and mobilized against this possibility."

BOOKS BY MARCUSE

Reason and Revolution: Hegel and the Rise of Social Theory. 1941. Humanities Pr. repr. of 2d ed. 1983 text ed. pap. $15.00. Influential study of Hegel, contributing to the restoration of his reputation as a positive force in free society.

Eros and Civilization: A Philosophical Inquiry into Freud. 1955. Beacon Pr. 1974 pap. $10.95. Revolutionary synthesis of Freud and Marx; the basic work of the American New Left.

One Dimensional Man: Studies in the Ideology of Advanced Industrial Society. 1964. Beacon Pr. 1966 pap. $6.95. "His virtuoso presentation spans a remarkably wide range of thinking—the social sciences, philosophy (especially philosophy of science and logic), linguistics, and literature and the arts. . . . A brilliant book" (*LJ*).

An Essay on Liberation. Beacon Pr. 1969 pap. $5.95. "In this explorative essay he presses beyond Marxist 'critical analysis' to offer utopian speculations made necessary by the inchoate anarchism of student 'activists' who know what they are against but need a vision of a truly free society to sustain them in a long struggle against overwhelming odds. Marcuse only approximates that vision, at best. . . . But his critique of the brutalizing effects of what he considers our conservative-capitalist Establishment is powerful. [The] book may in time prove a prophetic and noble statement" (*PW*).

Counterrevolution and Revolt. Beacon Pr. 1972 $6.95. "Marcuse brings together aesthetics, the study of nature, and the prospects of world revolution" (*Christian Century*).

(and Karl Popper). *Revolution or Reform: A Confrontation.* New Univ. Pr. 1976 $14.95. Polemical exchange between two giants of twentieth-century thought.

The Aesthetic Dimension: Toward a Critique of Marxist Aesthetics. Beacon Pr. 1978 pap. $4.95. Basic text on art and aesthetics, not always easy going, but most rewarding to the specialist.

From Luther to Popper: Studies in Critical Philosophy. Schocken 1984 pap. $7.95. A meritorious venture in intellectual history, but uneven in quality.

BOOKS ABOUT MARCUSE

Alford, C. Fred. *Science and the Revenge of Nature: Marcuse and Habermas.* Univ. Pr. of Florida 1985 $24.50. Scholarly interpretation of the critique of science in the critical theories of Marcuse and Habermas.

Line, Peter. *Marcuse and Freedom: The Genesis and Development of a Theory of Hu-*

man Liberation. St. Martin's 1985 $27.50. Monograph evaluating the liberation theme in Marcuse, which has been influential in the New Left.

Lipshires, Sidney. *Herbert Marcuse: From Marx to Freud and Beyond.* Schenkman 1974 text ed. pap. $8.95. Intellectual portrait of Marcuse, especially good on the background of his thought.

Lukes, Timothy J. *The Flight into Inwardness: Herbert Marcuse and Liberatory Aesthetics.* Susquehanna Univ. Pr. 1985 $24.50. Highly interpretive essay on the confluence of art and the theme of freedom in Marcuse's thought.

MacIntyre, Alasdair. *Herbert Marcuse: An Exposition and a Polemic.* [*Modern Masters Ser.*] Viking 1970 $9.95. Brilliant critical portrait by a prominent moral philosopher; forcefully written.

Pippin, Robert, and others. *Marcuse: Critical Theory and the Promise of Utopia.* Bergin & Garvey 1986 $34.95 pap. $16.95. A collection of specialist essays on Marcuse's revolutionary and utopian thought.

Schoolman, Morton. *The Imaginary Witness: The Critical Theory of Herbert Marcuse.* Free Pr. 1980 $24.95; New York Univ. Pr. 1984 pap. $13.50. Judicious investigation and evaluation of Marcuse's critical theory.

Stenernagel, Gertrude A. *Political Philosophy as Therapy: Marcuse Reconsidered.* Greenwood 1979 lib. bdg. $29.95. Provocative criticism, written with verve.

Woddis, Jack. *New Theories of Revolution: A Commentary on the Views of Franz Fanon, Regis Debray and Herbert Marcuse.* Intl. Pubs. Co. 1972 $10.00 pap. $4.00. The author "seeks to show that Fanon, Debray and Marcuse . . . grossly underestimate the importance of the working class" (*Choice*).

MARITAIN, JACQUES. 1882–1973

T. S. ELIOT (see Vol. 1) once called Maritain "the most conspicuous figure and probably the most powerful force in contemporary philosophy." His wife and devoted intellectual companion, the late Raissa Maritain, was of Jewish descent but joined the Catholic Church with him in 1906. Maritain studied under Bergson but was dissatisfied with his teacher's philosophy, eventually finding certainty in the system of ST. THOMAS AQUINAS. He lectured widely in Europe, in North and South America, and lived and taught in New York during World War II. Appointed French ambassador to the Vatican in 1945, he resigned in 1948 to teach philosophy at Princeton, where he remained until his retirement in 1953. He was prominent in the Catholic intellectual resurgence. He had a keen perception of modern French literature and a definite political philosophy. Although Maritain regarded metaphysics to be central to civilization and metaphysically his position was Thomism, he took full measure of the intellectual currents of his time and articulated a resilient and vital Thomism, applying the principles of scholasticism to contemporary issues.

In November 1963, Maritain was honored by the French literary world with the national Grand Prize for letters; the *N.Y. Times* reported that he "learned of the award at his retreat in a small monastery near Toulouse where he has been living in ascetic retirement for the last few years." In 1967 the publication of *The Peasant of the Garonne* disturbed the French Roman Catholic world. In it, Maritain attacked the "neo-modernism" that he had seen developing in the church "in the past decade or two and especially in the years since the Second Vatican Council. . . . He laments that in avant-garde Roman Catholic theology today he can 'read nothing about the redeeming sacrifice or the merits of the Passion.' In his interpretation, the whole of the Christian tradition has identified redemption with the sacrifice of the cross. But now all of that is being discarded, along with the idea of hell, the doctrine of creation out of nothing, the infancy narratives of the Gospels, and belief in the immortality of the human soul" (Jaroslav Pelikan, SR).

BOOKS BY MARITAIN

Art and Scholasticism: With Other Essays. Trans. by J. F. Scanlon [*Essay Index Repr. Ser.*] Ayer repr. of 1930 ed. 1980 $13.00. Influential, insightful, informed account of the status, nature, and functions of art in neo-Thomist perspective.

An Introduction to Philosophy. Trans. by E. I. Watkin, Century Bookbindery repr. of 1930 ed. 1984 text ed. $40.00. A basic textbook for neo-Thomism.

The Things That Are Not Caesar's. Telegraph Bks. repr. of 1930 ed. 1983 lib. bdg. $40.00. Persuasive lecture on the supreme matters of morals and religion.

Art and Scholasticism and the Frontiers of Poetry. 1935. Trans. by Joseph W. Evans, Univ. of Notre Dame Pr. 1974 pap. $6.95. An edition of the first item listed above; contains Maritain's theory of poetry.

Freedom and the Modern World. Trans. by Richard O'Sullivan, Gordian repr. of 1936 ed. 1971 $15.00. A tract for the times when totalitarianisms were on the rise threatening all freedom and when the liberal democracies mistook individual license for genuine freedom.

True Humanism. Trans. by M. R. Adamson, Ayer repr. of 1938 ed. $22.00; Greenwood repr. of 1941 ed. 3d ed. 1983 lib. bdg. $35.00. Emphasis on religion and spirituality to distinguish Maritain's humanism from secular humanism.

A Christian Looks at the Jewish Question. Ayer repr. of 1939 ed. 1981 $17.00. An attack on anti-Semitism.

A Preface to Metaphysics: Seven Lectures on Being. Ayer repr. of 1939 ed. 1983 $15.00. Readable, concisely written introduction to Maritain's neo-Thomism.

Scholasticism and Politics. [*Essay Index Repr. Ser.*] Ayer repr. of 1940 ed. 1983 $15.00. Political philosophy in a neo-Thomist framework directed against the causes of World War II.

Ransoming the Time. Trans. by Harry L. Binsse, Gordian repr. of 1941 ed. 1972 $25.00. Sensitively composed essay on the temporalism of modernism and the Catholic remedy.

The Living Thoughts of St. Paul. Arden Lib. repr. of 1942 ed. 1983 lib. bdg. $20.00. A caring selection with illuminating comments.

Saint Thomas and the Problem of Evil. Marquette Univ. Pr. 1942 $7.95. Stimulating lecture on a contemporary problem pertinent to the philosophy of St. Thomas.

Education at the Crossroads. 1943. [*Terry Lectures Ser.*] Yale Univ. Pr. 1960 pap. $4.95. The case for neo-scholasticism forcefully argued.

Rights of Man and Natural Law. Gordian repr. of 1943 ed. 1971 $17.50. Human rights interpreted in the framework of natural law; a classic in the field.

Christianity and Democracy. Trans. by Doris C. Anson [*Essay Index Repr. Ser.*] Ayer repr. of 1944 ed. 1972 $15.00; (and *Rights of Man and Natural Law)* Ignatius Pr. 1968 pap. $9.95. Delineates clearly the Christian bases of democracy.

Three Reformers: Luther, Descartes, Rousseau. Greenwood repr. of 1950 ed. 1982 lib. bdg. $22.50; Kennikat 1970 pap. $16.00. In-depth studies of three major modern thinkers, who are sympathetically but critically examined by one who rejected modernity.

Man and the State. 1951. Univ. of Chicago Pr. 1956 pap. $4.45. Received the Catholic Literary Award (1952); neo-Thomist political philosophy on the grand scale.

Creative Intuition in Art and Poetry. [*Bollingen Ser.*] Princeton Univ. Pr. 1952 pap. $14.95. Brilliant widely received philosophy of art aesthetics.

Approaches to God. Trans. by Peter O'Reilly, Greenwood repr. of 1954 ed. 1978 lib. bdg. $32.50. Persuasive, clear-headed descriptions of how God can be reached.

Bergsonian Philosophy and Thomism. Greenwood repr. of 1955 ed. 1968 lib. bdg. $29.75. English translation of Maritain's doctoral dissertation, in which he rejected the temporalist, evolutionist philosophy of his teacher, Bergson, for the Roman Catholic philosophy of St. Thomas Aquinas.

On the Philosophy of History. Kelley repr. of 1957 ed. 1979 $19.50. A lecture transformed into a monograph presenting the Roman Catholic theory of history harking back to St. Augustine's *City of God.*

Reflections on America. Gordian repr. of 1958 ed. 1975 $17.50. An optimistic tribute to the American way.

On the Use of Philosophy: Three Essays. Greenwood repr. of 1961 ed. 1982 lib. bdg. $22.50. Persuasive arguments for the importance of philosophy.

The Responsibility of the Artist. Gordian repr. of 1962 ed. 1972 $12.50. On the relationship between art and morality.

The Person and the Common Good. Univ. of Notre Dame Pr. 1966 pap. $4.45. Essential to an understanding of Maritain's neo-Thomist social thought and his concern for social justice.

The Education of Man: Educational Philosophy. Ed. by Donald Gallagher and Idella Gallagher, Greenwood repr. of 1967 ed. 1981 lib. bdg. $22.50. A collection of Maritain's essays on the theory of education.

On the Church of Christ: The Person of the Church and Her Personnel. Trans. by Joseph W. Evans, Univ. of Notre Dame Pr. 1973 text ed. $24.95. Roman Catholic interpretation of Christianity.

Science and Wisdom. Telegraph Bks. repr. 1980 lib. bdg. $25.00. Profound, abstruse, technical treatise on his theory of knowledge that is intended for advanced students.

Notebooks. Trans. by Joseph W. Evans, Magi Bks. 1984 $12.95. A saintly man's jottings lovingly translated and posthumously published.

BOOKS ABOUT MARITAIN

Allard, Jean-Louis. *Education for Freedom: The Philosophy of Education of Jacques Maritain.* Trans. by Ralph C. Nelson, Univ. of Notre Dame Pr. 1982 text ed. pap. $8.95. Scholarly monograph on a practically significant aspect of Maritain's thought.

Doering, Bernard. *Jacques Maritain and the French Catholic Intellectuals.* Univ. of Notre Dame Pr. 1983 text ed. pap. $22.95. Investigative reconstruction of Maritain's French milieu.

Fecher, Charles A. *Philosophy of Jacques Maritain.* Greenwood repr. of 1953 ed. 1981 lib. bdg. $22.50. A careful, well-written intellectual portrait.

Griffin, John H., and Yves R. Simon. *Jacques Maritain: Homage in Words and Pictures.* Magi Bks. 1974 $12.95. Celebratory collection; primarily of human interest.

Jung, Hwa Jol. *The Foundation of Jacques Maritain's Political Philosophy.* Univ. of Florida Pr. 1960 pap. $3.50. Scholarly monograph focused critically on Maritain's political philosophy.

Smith, B. W. *Jacques Maritain, Antimodern or Ultramodern?* Greenwood 1976 $25.00.

Thoughtful essay, slanted toward the theme of ultramodernity in Maritain's thought.

MEAD, GEORGE HERBERT. 1863–1931

Mead was a leading figure in the development of pragmatism. He joined the faculty of the University of Chicago at the invitation of JOHN DEWEY (see also Vol. 3) and, after Dewey's departure for Columbia, he became chairman of its philosophy department.

Mead's influence has extended beyond philosophy to psychology and sociology. He presented a theory of the emergence of the human mind in the evolutionary social process and of the development of individual personality that is known as social behaviorism. He also probed the metaphysical issues raised by pragmatism and the advances of science in regard to evolution and relativity physics as well as in regard to the formulation of scientific method. He proposed a philosophy of the present according to which the past is interpreted (construed) from the standpoint of the present. At the time of his death he was at work on a cosmology in which the act is the central category. During his lifetime Mead published numerous articles articulating every aspect of his thought but never published a book-length work. He was nevertheless esteemed as a seminal thinker of the first rank, and his lecture notes were posthumously published as books. (See also Volume 3.)

BOOKS BY MEAD

Selected Writings. Ed. by Andrew J. Reck, Univ. of Chicago Pr. 1981 $30.00 pap. $10.95. A representative selection of 25 articles Mead published in his lifetime.

Mind, Self, and Society: From the Standpoint of a Social Behaviorist. 1934. Ed. by Charles W. Morris, Univ. of Chicago Pr. 1967 lib. bdg. $30.00 pap. $7.00. Splendidly edited lecture notes from Mead's famous course on social psychology.

The Philosophy of the Act. 1938. Ed. by Charles W. Morris and David L. Miller, Univ. of Chicago Pr. 1972 pap. $3.95. Lecture notes and other notes and papers by Mead on his fundamental philosophy.

The Philosophy of the Present. Ed. by Arthur E. Murphy [*Paul Carus Lecture Ser.*] Open Court repr. of 1939 ed. 1959 $14.95; Univ. of Chicago Pr. 1980 pap. $5.95. Unpublished Carus lectures, supplemented by published papers, presenting Mead's novel theory of time.

George Herbert Mead on Social Psychology. Ed. by Anselm Strauss [*Heritage of Sociology Ser.*] Univ. of Chicago Pr. 1964 $22.50 pap. $12.00. A selection from Mead's published writings intended as an introductory text.

The Individual and the Social Self: Unpublished Work of George Herbert Mead. Ed. by David L. Miller, Univ. of Chicago Pr. 1982 text ed. lib. bdg. $26.00 pap. $12.95. New light is cast on the development of Mead's social psychology by this collection prepared by a devoted disciple.

BOOKS ABOUT MEAD

Aboulafia, Mitchell. *The Mediating Self: Mead, Sartre, and Self-Determination.* Yale Univ. Pr. 1986 $16.50. Imaginative and suggestive scholarly monograph.

Baldwin, John D. *George Herbert Mead: A Unifying Theory for Sociology.* Sage 1986 text ed. pap. $8.95. Readable account of Mead for sociologists.

Corti, Walter R. *The Philosophy of George Herbert Mead.* Adler's 1977 pap. $17.75. Proceedings of an international conference on Mead.

Hanson, Karen. *The Self Imagined: Philosophical Reflections on the Social Character of Psyche.* Methuen 1986 $26.95. Sensitive essay on the nature of the self, inspired in large part by Mead's social psychology.

Joas, Hans. *G. H. Mead, a Contemporary Re-Examination of His Thought.* Trans. by Raymond Meyer, MIT 1985 text ed. $30.00. Best account of Mead in relation to German thought.

Kang, W. *G. H. Mead's Concept of Rationality: A Study of the Use of Symbols and Other Implements.* Mouton 1976 text ed. $25.60. Probing but sympathetic critique of Mead's concept of mind.

Lewis, J. David, and Richard L. Smith. *American Sociology and Pragmatism: Mead, Chicago Sociology and Symbolic Interaction.* Univ. of Chicago Pr. 1981 lib. bdg. $30.00. Forcefully argues that metaphysical realism is the basis of Mead's social psychology, a basis ignored by his heirs in the Chicago School to their detriment.

Miller, David L. *George Herbert Mead: Self Language and the World.* Univ. of Chicago Pr. 1980 pap. $7.95. A comprehensive and sympathetic interpretation of Mead's thought by a former student who later became a distinguished professor of philosophy at the University of Texas-Austin.

Pfuetze, Paul. *Self, Society, Existence, Human Nature and Dialogue in the Thought of George Herbert Mead and Martin Buber.* Greenwood repr. of 1961 ed. 3d ed. 1973 lib. bdg. $22.50. A penetrating, although sometimes pedestrian, comparative study.

Schellenberg, James A. *Masters of Social Psychology: Freud, Mead, Lewin, and Skinner.* Oxford 1978 text ed. $10.95 pap. $5.95. An excellent book to begin the study of Mead's contribution in relation to those of other prominent twentieth-century psychologists.

MERLEAU-PONTY, MAURICE. 1908–1961

Appointed professor at the Collège de France in 1952, Merleau-Ponty was a most highly esteemed professional philosopher because of his technical works in phenomenology and psychology, but he was also an activist commentator on the significant cultural and political events of his time, as well as a collaborator with JEAN-PAUL SARTRE (see also Vol. 2) and SIMONE DE BEAUVOIR (see Vol. 2) in the founding and editing of *Les Temps modernes* in Paris immediately after World War II.

Besides being influenced by HUSSERL and Heidegger, Merleau-Ponty also assimilated the contributions of experimental psychology and Gestalt psychology to focus on perception and behavior. His work on the structure of behavior appeared in 1942, and although it centered on the body, it presented an interpretation of the distinctions between the mental, the vital (biological), and the physical that ruled out the reductionist inclinations of behaviorism. With the appearance of his work on the phenomenology of perception in 1945, his position as a philosopher ranking beside Heidegger and Sartre was established. He unveiled a theory of human subjectivity similar to theirs but with greater technical precision. From the standpoint of an existentialist thinker whose conception of subjectivity stressed the primacy of freedom, he examined Marxism and the political factions and movements fostered in MARX's (see also Vol. 3) name. The resulting studies, always insightful and provocative, satisfied neither the Right nor the Left.

In the foreword to the English translation of Merleau-Ponty's inaugural lecture at the Collège de France, John Wild and James Edie praised him for having made "important contributions to the phenomenological investigation of human existence in the life-world and its distinctive structures. He was a revolutionary, and his philosophy, even more than that of his French contemporaries, was a philosophy of the evolving, becoming 'historical present.' Merleau-Ponty views man as an essentially historical being and history as the dialectic of meaning and non-meaning which is working itself out through the complex, unpredictable interaction of men and the world. Nothing historical ever has just one meaning; meaning is ambiguous and is seen from an infinity of viewpoints. He has been called a philosopher of ambiguity, of contradiction, of dialectic. His search is the search for 'meaning' " (Foreword to *In Praise of Philosophy*).

BOOKS BY MERLEAU-PONTY

The Structure of Behavior. 1942. Trans. by Alden Fischer, Duquesne Univ. Pr. 1983 pap. $12.50. Here the philosopher shows "that man relates to his own existence as a totality which moves from this wholeness in ways which favor his own particular growth tendencies rather than as a mere reactor to the world as an imposer of determined responses" (*LJ*).

The Phenomenology of Perception. 1945. Trans. by Colin Smith, Humanities Pr. rev. ed. 1962 text ed. pap. $22.50. Conceptually complex and original synthesis of Gestalt psychology and experimental psychology in conformity with the phenomenological method.

Humanism and Terror: An Essay on the Communist Problem. 1947. Beacon Pr. 1969 pap. $11.95; Greenwood repr. of 1969 ed. 1980 lib. bdg. $27.50. "Merleau-Ponty has a faith in the proletariat that is beautiful in the abstract but that sees in the revolutionary reality what simply isn't there" (*America*).

Sense and Non-Sense. 1948. Trans. by Hubert L. Dreyfus [*Studies in Phenomenology and Existential Philosophy Ser.*] Northwestern Univ. Pr. 1964 $19.95 pap. $8.95. Seminal work on the meaning of meaning and meaninglessness.

Adventures of the Dialectic. 1955. Trans. by Joseph J. Bien [*Studies in Phenomenology and Existential Philosophy Ser.*] Northwestern Univ. Pr. 1973 text ed. $21.95 pap. $9.95. Incisive critique and interpretation of Hegelian and Marxist themes.

Signs. 1960. Trans. by Richard C. McCleary [*Studies in Phenomenology and Existential Philosophy Ser.*] Northwestern Univ. Pr. 1964 $24.95 pap. $10.95. "In *Signs* he leaves no important area of inquiry untouched—the philosophical, political, anthropological, the sociological or the artistic—in his search for that which can be understood from within even as 'personal intentions' are tending toward progresses which are themselves 'mediated by things.' The mythical is not a past fact, but a means 'of resolving some local, present tension, and is re-created in the dynamics of the present' " (*LJ*).

The Primacy of Perception. Trans. by William Cobb and others, ed. by James M. Edie [*Studies in Phenomenology and Existential Philosophy Ser.*] Northwestern Univ. Pr. 1964 $21.95 pap. $8.95. "In *The Primacy of Perception* he uses the phenomenological approach to reexamine the basis of humanity: 'humanity relations are able to grow, to change their avatars to lessons, to pick out the truth of their past in the present, to eliminate certain mysteries which render them opaque and thereby make themselves more translucent.' Of special significance is the correlation which Merleau-Ponty finds between the linguistic phenomenon and the emergence of the sense of self-identity" (*LJ*).

The Visible and the Invisible. Trans. by Alphonso Lingis [*Studies in Phenomenology and Existential Philosophy Ser.*] Northwestern Univ. Pr. 1969 $22.95 pap. $11.95. Foray into fundamental metaphysics.

Consciousness and the Acquisition of Language. Trans. by Hugh J. Silverman [*Studies in Phenomenology and Existential Philosophy Ser.*] Northwestern Univ. Pr. 1973 text ed. $19.95 pap. $8.95. The author "synthesizes the works of Paul Guillaume, Edmund Husserl, and Max Scheler, and then ... [attacks] Piaget's approach. Many American scholars would view this material as a strange blend of philosophy and psychology" (*Choice*).

The Prose of the World. Trans. by John O'Neill, ed. by Claude Lefort [*Studies in Phenomenology and Existential Philosophy Ser.*] Northwestern Univ. Pr. 1973 text ed. $19.95 pap. $10.95. Posthumously published work that illuminates Merleau-Ponty's understanding and employment of language.

BOOKS ABOUT MERLEAU-PONTY

Barral, Mary R. *The Body in Interpersonal Relations: Merleau-Ponty*. Univ. Pr. of Amer. 1984 text ed. pap. $14.50. Scholarly monograph focused on Merleau-Ponty's theory of the body in psychology; for the advanced student.

Cooper, Barry. *Merleau-Ponty and Marxism: From Terror to Reform*. Univ. of Toronto Pr. 1979 $30.00. Accurate evaluation of the French philosopher's relation to Marxism.

Hadreas, Peter J. *In Place of the Flawed Diamond: An Investigation of Merleau-Ponty's Philosophy of Perception*. P. Lang Pubs. 1986 text ed. $30.30. An examination of Merleau-Ponty's phenomenology of perception for specialists.

Kruks, Sonia. *The Political Philosophy of Merleau-Ponty*. Humanities Pr. 1981 text ed. $28.50. Reliable overview of Merleau-Ponty's philosophy of politics.

Lapointe, François H., and Claire C. Lapointe. *Maurice Merleau-Ponty and His Critics: An International Bibliography, 1942–76*. [*Reference Lib. of the Humanities*] Garland 1976 lib. bdg. $25.00. Authoritative bibliography as far as it goes; a good place for the researcher to begin.

O'Neill, John. *Perception, Expression and History: The Social Phenomenology of Maurice Merleau-Ponty*. Northwestern Univ. Pr. 1970 $12.95. Highly interpretive but rewarding monograph.

Sheridan, James. *Once More from the Middle: A Philosophical Anthropology*. Ohio Univ. Pr. 1973 $10.00. Somewhat loose-jointed but insightful work.

MOORE, GEORGE EDWARD. 1873–1958

G. E. Moore was one of the giants in the formation of analytic philosophy in the English-speaking world. During most of his professional life he was affiliated with Cambridge University—as a student and as a fellow at Trinity from 1892 to 1896 and from 1898 to 1904 respectively; as a university lecturer from 1911 to 1925; as a professor of mental philosophy and logic from 1925 until his retirement in 1939.

Moore's philosophical contributions touch on three areas: philosophical method, moral philosophy, and theory of knowledge. His philosophical method is exhibited in his unrelenting effort to discover and elucidate the meanings of philosophical concepts and in his appeal to common sense. This method is evident in his work in ethics and epistemology. *Principia Ethica* (1903) established him as the foremost critic of ethical naturalism; his conceptions of goodness as an indefinable quality and of intrinsic value as organic unity were influential not only in philosophical circles but also among the artists and writers that comprised the Bloomsbury group. Moore's work in epistemology is spread out in a large number of articles distinguished for the nicety of analysis; these articles span six decades, revealing a thinker who moved out of idealism into realism and then moved back and forth among the varieties of realism on such questions as the status of sense data—i.e., whether they exist, and if they exist, whether they are physical parts of things or are mental representations only.

BOOKS BY MOORE

Early Essays. Ed. by Tom Regan, Temple Univ. Pr. 1986 $29.50. An excellent edition of Moore's early writings, mainly on epistemology and ethics.

Philosophical Papers. [*Muirhead Lib. of Philosophy*] Humanities Pr. repr. of 1959 ed. 1977 text ed. $25.00. "The selection was made evidently by Moore himself. Included are 'A Defence of Common Sense' and 'Proof of an External World,' two works essential to an understanding of Moore's thought, and Moore's careful notes on the 1930–33 lectures of Wittgenstein. . . . Hence this volume will be of real use to students of Moore—which is to say, to anyone seriously interested in philosophy itself" (V. C. Chappell, *Ethics*).

Principia Ethica. 1903. Cambridge Univ. Pr. 1959 $37.50 pap. $12.95. Most influential work in the English language on ethics in the twentieth century.

BOOKS ABOUT MOORE

Ayer, Alfred J. *Russell and Moore: The Analytical Heritage.* [*William James Lectures Ser.*] Harvard Univ. Pr. 1971 $16.50. Critical estimations of the works of two of England's most famous twentieth-century philosophers by an equally famous one.

Klemke, E. D. *Epistemology of G. E. Moore.* Northwestern Univ. Pr. 1969 $15.95. Solid critical monograph.

Levy, Paul. *G. E. Moore and the Cambridge Apostles.* Oxford 1981 pap. $8.95. Witty historical account of Moore and the celebrated Cambridge club to which he belonged as an undergraduate.

Lewy, C. *G. E. Moore on the Naturalistic Fallacy.* Longwood 1964 $2.25. Acute analytic study.

O'Connor, David. *The Metaphysics of G. E. Moore.* Kluwer Academic 1982 $34.95. Systematic interpretation and commentary.

Regan, Tom. *Bloomsbury's Prophet: G. E. Moore and the Development of His Moral Philosophy.* Temple Univ. Pr. 1986 $29.95. Well-researched interpretation of Moore's moral philosophy in connection with the famous Bloomsbury Circle, which included Virginia Woolf.

Schilpp, Paul Arthur, ed. *The Philosophy of G. E. Moore.* [*Lib. of Living Philosophers*] Open Court 2 vols. 1968 $29.95 pap. $14.95. Collection of original critical essays by prominent thinkers on Moore and his replies; a scholar's treasure.

White, Alan R. *G. E. Moore: A Critical Exposition.* Greenwood repr. of 1969 ed. 1980 lib. bdg. $24.75. Thoughtful and well-written critical study.

ORTEGA Y GASSET, JOSÉ. 1883–1955

Essayist and philosopher, a thinker influential in and out of the Spanish world, Ortega was professor of metaphysics at the University of Madrid from 1910 until the outbreak of the Spanish Civil War in 1936. *The Revolt of the Masses* (1930), his most famous work, owes much to post-Kantian schools of thought, especially to NIETZSCHE and BERGSON. Ortega's predominant thesis is the need of an intellectual aristocracy governing in a spirit of enlightened liberalism. Although Franco, after his victory in the civil war, offered to make Ortega Spain's "official philosopher" and to publish a deluxe edition of his works—with certain parts deleted—the philosopher refused. Instead, he chose the life of a voluntary exile in Argentina, and in 1941 he was appointed professor of philosophy at the University of San Marcos in Lima, Peru. He returned to Spain in 1945 and died in Madrid.

Ortega's reformulation of the Cartesian *cogito* displays the fulcrum of his thought. While Descartes declared *"Cogito ergo sum"* (I think, therefore I am), Ortega maintained *"Cogito quia vivo"* (I think because I live). He subordinated reason to life, to vitality. Reason becomes the tool of man existing biologically in a given time and place, rather than an overarching sovereign. Ortega's philosophy consequently discloses affinities in its metaphysics to both American pragmatism and European existentialism in spite of its elitism in social philosophy.

BOOKS BY ORTEGA Y GASSET

Man and Crisis. 1922. Trans. by Mildred Adams, Norton 1958 pap. $6.95. "This book will not only be widely read. It will also be remembered" (*N.Y. Times*).

The Modern Theme. 1923. Trans. by James Cleugh, Darby repr. of 1931 ed. 1981 lib. bdg. $35.00. Vitalistic interpretation of intellectual and cultural tendencies in the early decades of the twentieth century.

History as a System. 1924–39. Norton 1962 pap. $5.95; (and *And Other Essays toward a Philosophy of History)* Greenwood repr. of 1961 ed. 1982 lib. bdg. $25.00. Ortega's suggestive existentialist statement.

The Revolt of the Masses. 1930. Trans. by the author, Norton 1932 $7.95 1964 pap. $3.95; trans. by Anthony Kerrigan, ed. by Kenneth Moore, Univ. of Notre Dame Pr. 1985 $20.00. Most famous and influential work; required reading for persons interested in the nature of civilization.

Man and People. 1957. Trans. by Willard R. Trask, Norton 1963 pap. $6.95. "The book will remain a vivid recounting of some of the chief features of the topography, flora and fauna of live human experience" (*N.Y. Herald Tribune*).

What Is Philosophy? 1958. Trans. by Mildred Adams, Norton 1964 pap. $6.95. Charming if biased essay.

The Origin of Philosophy. Trans. by Tony Talbot, Norton 1967 pap. $4.95. "Stimulating insights sparkle here like gems; that philosophy was a fruit of the entrance of Greece into a period of freedom, that freedom involves enlargement of the circle of possibilities beyond immediate needs, that contact with foreigners expands the circles of one's choices, that 'vital wealth' results in part from emancipation from myth and tradition" (*LJ*).

Some Lessons in Metaphysics. Norton 1970 pap. $5.95. A master's pronouncements on fundamental philosophy.

Phenomenology and Art. Trans. by Philip W. Silver, Norton 1975 $8.95. Theory of art, with the phenomenology rendered tractable.

Historical Reason. Trans. by Philip W. Silver, Norton 1984 $19.95. Profound, but readable.

An Interpretation of Universal History. Trans. by Mildred Adams, Norton 1984 pap. $7.95. Philosophy of history in the grand manner, seeking to delineate patterns of meaning in the plethora of events.

BOOKS ABOUT ORTEGA Y GASSET

McClintock, Robert. *Man and His Circumstances: Ortega as Educator.* Trans. by Frances M. Lopez-Morrillas, Teachers College Pr. 1971 text ed. $22.95. Scholarly monograph on Ortega's educational theory, illustrated by his career.

Niedermayer, Franz. *José Ortega y Gasset.* Trans. by Peter Tirner [*Lit. and Life Ser.*] Ungar 1973 $14.95. Reliable account of his life and works.

Ourmette, Victor. *José Ortega y Gasset.* [*Twayne's World Authors Ser.*] G. K. Hall 1982 lib. bdg. $16.95. Straightforward portrayal of Ortega's principal works.

Raley, Harold. *José Ortega y Gasset: Philosophy of European Unity.* Univ. of Alabama Pr. 1971 $17.50. Scholarly monograph on a major theme in Ortega's thought.

Silver, Philip W. *Ortega as Phenomenologist.* Columbia Univ. Pr. 1978 $25.00. Sophisticated interpretation of Ortega's work, written for the advanced student.

Wiegert, Andrew J. *Life and Society: A Meditation on the Social Thought of José Ortega y Gasset.* Irvington 1983 text ed. $29.95. Suggestive and illuminating essay.

POPPER, SIR KARL RAIMUND. 1902–

Born in Vienna, Popper was associated with the Vienna Circle of logical positivism; although never a member, he shared common interests with those who were and exerted considerable influence over some of them. The publication of his *Logik der Forschung* (1935) marked a major turn in the development of logical positivism. Whereas logical positivism (empiricism) had adopted as the "verification criterion" for the meaning of a statement the possibility of its being verified in experience or the process of its being verified in experience, Popper advanced a "falsification criterion" according to which a statement is empirically meaningless unless it can be conceived how it may be tested and falsified.

From this early work Popper went on to advance original and comprehensive theories about the nature of science, its methodology and epistemology. Meanwhile with Europe caught up in the throes of nazism, Popper left Austria for teaching positions in Australia, New Zealand, and England, eventually occupying chairs at the University of London and Oxford. In 1945, as World War II drew to a close, Popper published his penetrating critique of PLATO (see also Vol. 3), Hegel, and MARX (see also Vol. 3) as progenitors of totalitarian society and made a cogent and persuasive case for the values and principles of liberal society. This work plunged Popper in the midst of sometimes rancorous controversies with scholars who wished to defend Plato, Hegel, and Marx. Whatever the validity of Popper's scholarship, the work nonetheless won for him the esteem of those who appreciated his commitment to liberalism. With the publication of *The Poverty of Histori-*

cism (1961) Popper's reputation as a defender of the concept of human freedom was further enhanced by his assault on the sort of determinism fostered by social science and supported by historicism. The British Crown knighted Popper for his contributions to philosophy.

BOOKS BY POPPER

Popper Selections. Ed. by David Miller, Princeton Univ. Pr. 1985 $12.95 pap. $8.95. A good place for the beginner to start.

Logic of Scientific Discovery (Logik der Forschung). Harper rev. ed. of 1935 ed. 1968 pap. $9.95. Major work in the development of logical empiricism.

The Open Society and Its Enemies. 1945. Princeton Univ. Pr. 2 vols. 5th rev. ed. 1966 vol. 1 $34.00 pap. $9.95 vol. 2 $38.00 pap. $9.95. Controversial but widely read; Popper's most famous work among the public at large.

The Poverty of Historicism. 1961. Harper 1977 pap. $5.95. Criticism at its destructive best.

Conjectures and Refutations: The Growth of Scientific Knowledge. Harper 1968 pap. $8.95. Original treatise on scientific method.

Objective Knowledge: An Evolutionary Approach. Oxford 1972 text ed. pap. $9.95. Realist theory of knowledge brought up to date.

The Open Universe: An Argument for Indeterminism. Ed. by W. W. Bartley, III, Rowman 1982 $29.50 pap. $10.95. A splendid collection of Popper's essays bearing on the free will versus determinism argument.

Quantum Theory and the Schism in Physics. Ed. by W. W. Bartley, III, Rowman 1982 $31.50 1984 pap. $10.95. A collection of Popper's essays, technical in character for the most part.

Realism and the Aim of Science. Ed. by W. W. Bartley, III, Rowman 1983 text ed. $38.50 1985 pap. $12.95. A collection of Popper's essays pertinent to his scientific realism.

The Subtle Connection between the Theory of Experience and the Logic of Science. Foundation for Class. Repr. 2 vols 1985 $167.50. Specialized investigation into the relations of experience and theory in science.

Unended Quest: An Intellectual Autobiography. Open Court rev. ed. 1985 $12.95 pap. $8.95. The first edition of the inspiring work appeared in Paul Arthur Schilpp, ed., *The Philosophy of Karl Popper* [*Lib. of Living Philosophers*] Open Court 1978.

BOOKS ABOUT POPPER

Berkson, William, and John Wettersten. *Learning from Error: Karl Popper's Psychology of Learning.* Open Court 1984 $16.95. Specialist monograph on an aspect of Popper's thought.

Burke, T. E. *The Philosophy of Popper.* Longwood 1983 pap. $12.50. "This is a critical study of Popper's most original and influential ideas—on philosophy, science, pseudo-science, historicism, freedom" (*The Philosopher's Index*).

Levinson, Paul, ed. *In Pursuit of Truth: Essays on the Philosophy of Karl Popper on the Occasion of His 80th Birthday.* Humanities Pr. 1982 text ed. $25.00. The essays in this volume, written by internationally distinguished scholars, introduce, explain, critique, and defend "Popper's philosophy of science, social science, and mind and matter, and explore. . .its applications to education, technology, literary criticism and art" (*The Philosopher's Index*).

O'Hear, Anthony. *Karl Popper.* Methuen 1982 pap. $10.95. "This book is concerned mainly with Popper's epistemology. . . . [It] is clearly written and competent" (*LJ*).

QUINE, WILLARD VAN ORMAN. 1908–

Quine, a professor of philosophy at Harvard University, has been one of the most respected academic American philosophers since the end of World War II. An accomplished and creative mathematical logician, he has written textbooks that generations of philosophy students have used in their classes. Quine's lasting contribution to philosophy, however, lies in the fields of epistemology and ontology. Using the rigorous tools of formal logic but expressing himself in a fine prose style, Quine has analyzed the nature and function of language and has found that the epistemological principles on which logical positivism (empiricism) rests are defective. He has undermined the sharp distinction between analytic and empirical statements. He has also brought into question the empiricist program of reducing empirical statements for meaningfulness into direct and unequivocal reports describing what is given in experience. He has shown instead the indeterminacy of translation, stressing the dependence of empirical meanings on the conceptual structures to which they belong. His holistic approach to the web of knowledge has simultaneously been accompanied in ontology by an early commitment to nominalism. However, his nominalistic program, at first denying the need to posit any abstract entities, has been modified in later years. Although Quine presented his highly influential views in articles that subsequently were collected and published together in various volumes, in 1960 he provided a coherent and systematic statement of his thought in his book *Word and Object.*

BOOKS BY QUINE

Word and Object. MIT pap. $9.95. Quine's most systematic work; a classic in recent American analytic philosophy.

From a Logical Point of View: Nine Logico-Philosophical Essays. Harvard Univ. Pr. 2d rev. ed. 1961 $14.00 pap. $5.95. A collection of his previously published essays, containing his famous paper "Two Dogmas of Empiricism."

Ontological Relativity and Other Essays. Columbia Univ. Pr. 1969 pap. $11.00. A collection of essays pertinent to such central theses of Quine as the primacy of language for metaphysics.

Philosophy of Logic. 1969. Harvard Univ. Pr. 2d ed. 1986 text ed. pap. $6.95. Exploratory essay on the foundations of logic.

The Roots of Reference. [*Paul Carus Lecture Ser.*] Open Court 1973 $16.95. Penetrating investigation of the basic ideas of language and meaning.

The Ways of Paradox and Other Essays. Harvard Univ. Pr. 1976 $22.50 pap. $8.95. A collection of essays previously published in specialist journals.

(and J. S. Ullian). *The Web of Belief.* Random 2d ed. 1978 text ed. pap. $7.00. A lucid presentation of the holistic theory of knowledge.

Theories and Things. Harvard Univ. Pr. 1981 text ed. $15.00 1986 pap. $6.95. Language and ontology reviewed by Quine, who offers clearer statements but no change of view.

The Time of My Life: An Autobiography. MIT 1986 $19.95. A record distinguished by its mentions of persons and places.

BOOKS ABOUT QUINE

Dilman, Ilham. *Quine on Ontology, Necessity and Experience.* State Univ. of New York Pr. 1984 $39.50 pap. $14.95. A severely critical study of Quine's metaphysics.

Gibson, Roger F. *The Philosophy of W. V. Quine: An Expository Essay.* Univ. Pr. of Florida 1982 $22.00 1986 pap. $12.00. A sympathetic introduction to Quine's philosophy.

Gochet, Paul. *Ascent to Truth: A Critical Examination of Quine's Philosophy.* Philosophia Pr. 1986 $35.00 pap. $29.00. Scholarly monograph by a leading European follower of Quine.

Hahn, Lewis, and Paul Arthur Schilpp, eds. *The Philosophy of W. V. Quine.* [*Lib. of Living Philosophers*] Open Court 1986 $49.95 pap. $24.95. A collection of original articles by the leading experts on Quine's philosophy, preceded by Quine's intellectual autobiography and followed by his responses to his critics. The volume concludes with a bibliography of Quine's writings.

Shahan, Robert W., and Chris Swoyer, eds. *Essays on the Philosophy of W. V. Quine.* Univ. of Oklahoma Pr. 1979 $15.00. A collection of articles by prominent philosophers that originally appeared in the *Southwest Journal of Philosophy.*

RAWLS, JOHN. 1921–

John Rawls, professor of philosophy at Harvard University, had published a number of articles on the concept of justice as fairness before the appearance of his magnum opus, *A Theory of Justice* (1971). While the articles had won for Rawls considerable prestige, the reception of his book thrust him into the front ranks of contemporary moral philosophy. Presenting a Kantian alternative to conventional utilitarianism and intuitionism, Rawls offers a theory of justice that is contractual and that rests on principles that he alleges would be accepted by free, rational persons in a state of nature—i.e., of equality. The chorus of praise was loud and clear. Stuart Hampshire acclaimed it as "the most substantial and interesting contribution to moral philosophy since the war" (*N.Y. Review of Books*). And H. A. Bedau declared: "As a work of close and original scholarship in the service of the dominant moral and political ideology of our civilization, Rawls's treatise is simply without a rival" (*The Nation*). Rawls historically achieved two important things: (1) he articulated a coherent moral philosophy for the welfare state, and (2) he demonstrated that analytic philosophy was most capable of doing constructive work in moral philosophy.

BOOK BY RAWLS

A Theory of Justice. Harvard Univ. Pr. 1971 $25.00 pap. $9.95. Most influential work in political, legal, and social philosophy by an American author since World War II.

BOOKS ABOUT RAWLS

Blocker, H. Gene, and Elizabeth H. Smith, eds. *John Rawls' Theory of Social Justice: An Introduction.* Ohio Univ. Pr. 1980 text ed. $29.95 pap. $14.95. A collection of essays for the serious student.

Mason, David T., and J. H. Wellbank. *John Rawls and His Critics: A Bibliography.* Garland 1982 lib. bdg. $91.00. A good place for the serious researcher to begin.

Wolff, Robert P. *Understanding Rawls: A Reconstruction and Critique of a Theory of*

Justice. Princeton Univ. Pr. 1977 $27.50 pap. $10.00. Outstanding interpretation by a prominent philosopher.

RICOEUR, PAUL. 1913–

Professor of philosophy at the University of Paris and the University of Chicago, Ricoeur has been described as "possibly the only younger philosopher in Europe whose reputation is of the magnitude of that of the old men of existentialism—Marcel, Jaspers, Heidegger, and SARTRE [see also Vol. 2].... [His] is the most massive accomplishment of any philosopher of Christian faith since the appearance of Gabriel Marcel" (Sam Keen, *Christian Century*).

A practitioner of the phenomenology of HUSSERL mediated by a return to Kant—in that things in themselves, though unknowable, are not excluded by bracketing existence but are acknowledged as the necessary conditions for the possibility of human experience—Ricoeur has examined those parts of experience—faulty, fallible, and susceptible of error and evil—that other phenomenologists, interested primarily in the cognitional, have neglected. In this respect he follows in the footsteps of Heidegger and Sartre, but he goes beyond them in his discovery of principles transcending human subjectivity that are amenable to spiritual interpretation. Here Ricoeur steps within the contemporary hermeneutic circle of Heidegger and Gadamer, on whom he has written. Ricoeur's hermeneutical method however has much in common with the methods of biblical exegesis, and in this respect his works should be especially appealing to seminarians and ministers.

BOOKS BY RICOEUR

The Philosophy of Paul Ricoeur: An Anthology of His Work. Ed. by Charles E. Reagan and David Stewart, Beacon Pr. 1978 pap. $9.95. This anthology includes selections from Ricoeur's "hermeneutic writings on the will, phenomenology, religion, faith, philosophy of language, and Freud" (*LJ*).

History and Truth. [*Studies in Phenomenology and Existential Philosophy Ser.*] Northwestern Univ. Pr. 1965 $25.95 pap. $12.95. Deeply metaphysical treatise in quest of transcendent principles within the course of events.

Fallible Man: Philosophy of the Will. 1966. Fordham Univ. Pr. rev. ed. 1986 $25.00 pap. $10.00. The first part of Ricoeur's *Philosophie de la volonté* to be translated into English.

Freedom and Nature: The Voluntary and Involuntary. Trans. by E. V. Kohak [*Studies in Phenomenology and Existential Philosophy Ser.*] Northwestern Univ. Pr. 1966 $29.95 pap. $13.95. Advanced phenomenology pertinent to the problem of free will versus scientific determinism.

Husserl: An Analysis of His Phenomenology. Trans. by Edward G. Ballard and Lester Embree [*Studies in Phenomenology and Existential Philosophy Ser.*] Northwestern Univ. Pr. 1967 $21.95 pap. $10.95. Ricoeur's works of translation and commentary "have made him the foremost authority of all French commentators on Husserl" (J. M. Edie, *Journal of Philosophy*).

Symbolism of Evil. Trans. by Emerson Buchanan, Beacon Pr. 1969 pap. $10.95. Compelling interpretation; hermeneutics at its best.

Freud and Philosophy: An Essay on Interpretation. Trans. by Denis Savage [*Terry Lectures Ser.*] Yale Univ. Pr. 1970 pap. $15.95. Ricoeur "examines the validity of the psychoanalytical interpretation of culture, particularly as expressed in Freud's writings on art, morality, and religion" (*TLS*).

The Conflict of Interpretations: Essays on Hermeneutics. Ed. by Don Ihde [*Studies in Phenomenology and Existential Philosophy Ser.*] Northwestern Univ. Pr. 1974 text ed. $26.95 pap. $13.95. This collection contains 22 essays written from 1960 to 1969. It is "an attempt at redefining the Greek and Biblical hermeneutic patterns by 'grafting' them onto phenomenology" (*Choice*).

Interpretation Theory: Discourse and the Surplus of Meaning. Texas Christian Univ. Pr. 1976 pap. $8.00. A monograph to make hermeneutics plain.

The Rule of Metaphor: Multi-Disciplinary Studies of the Creation of Meaning in Language. Trans. by Robert Czerny, Univ. of Toronto Pr. 1977 pap. $15.95. An "examination of the philosophy of metaphor from Aristotle to the present" (Publisher's note).

Main Trends in Philosophy. Holmes & Meir 1979 text ed. pap. $26.50. An overview of philosophy in midcentury.

Essays on Biblical Metaphor. Ed. by Lewis S. Mudge, Fortress Pr. 1980 pap. $8.95. A collection of Ricoeur's writings, especially recommended for clergy.

Time and Narrative. Trans. by Kathleen McLaughlin and David Pellaner, Univ. of Chicago Pr. 2 vols. 1984–86 $22.50–$25.00. This work "introduces Ricoeur's theory of the interdependence of temporality and narrative order" (*LJ*).

Lectures on Ideology and Utopia. Ed. by George Taylor, Columbia Univ. Pr. 1986 $30.00. Rewarding reflections on politics.

BOOKS ABOUT RICOEUR

Klemm, David E. *The Hermeneutical Theory of Paul Ricoeur: A Constructive Analysis.* Bucknell Univ. Pr. 1983 $22.50. "The book analyzes Ricoeur's hermeneutical method of textual understanding and the possibility that Ricoeur's philosophy is equivalent to theological hermeneutics" (*The Philosopher's Index*).

Skousgaard, Stephen. *Language and the Existence of Freedom: A Study in Paul Ricoeur's Philosophy of Will.* Univ. Pr. of Amer. 1979 o.p. "This book locates contemporary man's experience of the perennial philosophical issue of 'freedom versus determinism.' " It utilizes "Ricoeur's early philosophical work" (*The Philosopher's Index*).

Van den Hengel, John W. *The Home of Meaning: The Hermeneutics of the Subject of Paul Ricoeur.* Univ. Pr. of Amer. 1982 text ed. lib. bdg. $33.00 pap. $15.75. "The work. . .analyzes the outcome of subjectivity in the philosophy of Paul Ricoeur" (*The Philosopher's Index*).

RORTY, RICHARD MCKAY. 1931–

Richard Rorty was educated at the University of Chicago and Yale. He taught at Princeton University and in 1981 was named university professor at the University of Virginia. In 1981 he was awarded a five-year fellowship by the MacArthur Foundation.

Rorty first attracted the attention of the international community of philosophers with the publication of *The Linguistic Turn* (1967). Containing 37 selections from twentieth-century philosophers, it opens with Rorty's 40-page introduction. The volume shows "the ways in which language problems have invaded the province of philosophy, the kinds of solutions which the linguistic philosophers have advanced, and the probable pattern of linguistic philosophizing for the future" (LJ). Rorty's anthology has become a classic introduction to analytic philosophy, and the title phrase has caught on as the name of an era of philosophy.

However, Rorty had no sooner published this work than he suffered misgivings about the future of analytic philosophy. Mastering the developments in hermeneutics and in deconstructionism in European philosophy and returning to his roots in the pragmatism of WILLIAM JAMES (see also Vol. 3) and JOHN DEWEY (see also Vol. 3), Rorty came to doubt the epistemological foundations of analytic philosophy. This doubt, sustained by detailed analyses of the works of contemporary analytic philosophers, was generalized to include the entire tradition of Western philosophy since PLATO (see also Vol. 3). The upshot was the publication of *Philosophy and the Mirror of Nature* (1979). This work announces the death of philosophy as a kind of higher knowledge but recommends its continuance as edification, a literary and intellectual achievement. The reviewers, even those who objected to its central theses, admired the work for its style and boldness. The review in *Choice* concisely stated the case: "Rorty is one of the most erudite among philosophers now writing, at ease in both history of philosophy and in contemporary analytic thought. . . . The arguments advanced in course of discussion will doubtless be submitted to close scrutiny and much criticism, but this bold and provocative book is bound to rank among the most important of the decade. The writing is superb."

BOOKS BY RORTY

(ed.). *The Linguistic Turn: Recent Essays in Philosophical Method.* 1967. Univ. of Chicago Pr. 1971 pap. $12.00. An anthology second to none in its field.

Philosophy and the Mirror of Nature. Princeton Univ. Pr. 1979 $37.00 pap. $8.95. Humorous, subtle, and revolutionary.

Consequences of Pragmatism: Essays 1972–1980. Univ. of Minnesota Pr. 1982 $29.50 pap. $11.95. Consisting of 12 previously published essays, together with a new introduction, the volume shows how Rorty, a major voice in analytic thought, draws on such postmodern European thinkers as Heidegger and appeals to American pragmatism in continuing the arguments presented in *Philosophy and the Mirror of Nature.*

(and others, eds.). *Philosophy in History: Essays on the Historiography of Philosophy.* Cambridge Univ. Pr. 1984 $42.50 pap. $9.95. New series of innovative volumes devoted to new ways to do philosophy in regard to its history.

RUSSELL, BERTRAND ARTHUR WILLIAM RUSSELL, 3D EARL.
1872–1970 (NOBEL PRIZE 1950)

Of Bertrand Russell his publishers have written: "It has been said that 'his admirable and lucid English style may be attributed to the fact that he did not undergo a classical education at a public school.'" As an English stylist Lord Russell had the extraordinary gift of understanding and pioneering in the most abstruse fields of human knowledge and of being able to make at least their broader outlines crystal clear to the layperson. (In this connection he described the title of a course he wished to give at an American university as "Words and Facts." But not until he had made the title five times as long and heavy with philosophic jargon did he feel it would be acceptable to the authorities.) Though a mathematical logician, Russell lived a life that was political and passionate. To disagree on occasion with his political judgment and even to deplore some of his personal foibles is not inconsistent with recognizing him as a person with one of the greatest logical minds as well as one of the warmest hearts mankind has produced. In the first volume of his *Autobiography* he said: "Three passions, simple but overwhelmingly strong, have governed my life: the longing for love, the search for knowledge, and unbearable pity for the sufferings of mankind." And elsewhere: "Often I feel that religion, like the sun, has extinguished the stars of less brilliancy but not less beauty, which shine upon us out of the darkness of a godless universe. The splendour of human life, I feel sure, is greater to those who are not dazzled by the divine radiance; and human comradeship seems to grow more intimate and more tender from the sense that we are all exiles on an inhospitable shore."

After a lonely childhood Russell went to Cambridge, the university with which he was chiefly associated throughout his long productive life. Although he succeeded to an earldom in 1931 and then took his seat in the House of Lords, he was imprisoned during World War I as a pacifist.

Russell wrote his greatest work, *Principia Mathematica* (3 vols. 1910–13), in collaboration with Alfred North Whitehead. It demonstrated that mathematics rests on logical foundations, and it formulated logical expressions in a symbolic calculus to reveal logical structures concealed by ordinary grammar. The impact of this work was to transform logic as a philosophical discipline. The subject-predicate form and the syllogisms ARISTOTLE (see also Vols. 3 and 5) had discovered yielded center stage to a symbolic logic of relations and quantification. The "unofficial parts" of *Principia* (the parts written in English) are attributed to Russell, while Whitehead is credited with composing the symbolic calculi. In these "unofficial" parts key notions such as material implication, existential quantification, descriptions, and the theory of types are introduced. Discussions of these notions dominated philosophy of logic and epistemology for a half century thereafter, and Russell's theories, presented in articles and books, were the normal starting point for these discussions.

Russell's serious philosophical works after *Principia* were in epistemology and philosophy of mind. He strove to overcome the Cartesian dualisms of both the epistemological and the psychophysical kinds. His theory of knowledge then was very close to new realism, although in his later work he lapsed into phenomenalism. On the mind-body dualism he expounded a neutral monism, mind and matter being functional distinctions drawn in regard to a stuff that was in itself neither mental nor physical.

After World War I Russell came under the influence of Wittgenstein, whose *Tractatus Logico-Philosophicus* he introduced to English readers. During this period Russell expounded a theory of logical atomism. In 1940 he lectured at the University of Chicago, Harvard University, and the University of California; that year he was appointed professor of philosophy at the

College of the City of New York, but the appointment was later revoked by a Supreme Court justice on the ground that certain passages in his books carried moral contamination for the youth of New York City. (See *The Bertrand Russell Case*, listed below.) He returned to England in 1944 as fellow and lecturer at Trinity College, Cambridge. Here he completed his "philosophical testament," *Human Knowledge* (1948), a book of enormous scope. "All the central issues in contemporary philosophy, from the theory of meaning to the nature of space-time are discussed with. . .characteristic incisiveness, technical skill and imagination" (Sidney Hook). A rationalist, a materialist, a great mathematician, to him science was truth. His books were always provocative and highly personal, reflecting his immense knowledge and zest for life. He was awarded the 1950 Nobel Prize for literature, sharing it with the novelist WILLIAM FAULKNER (see Vol. 1).

Always a crusader for pacificism, his dread of nuclear war colored his attitude in most of his later writings. In *Unarmed Victory* (1963) he tried to influence leaders and public opinion on both sides. In 1967 Russell sponsored, but did not attend, a "Vietnam war crimes tribunal," which he declared to be in the legal tradition of the international trials at Nuremberg after World War II. This tribunal examined America's use of antipersonnel bombs in raids on North Vietnam, heard accounts from North Vietnamese victims of bombs and chemical warfare, and saw films of bombed areas. Accused of genocide, the United States refused to comment on the tribunal's conclusion. His own articles on the general subject, *War Crimes in Vietnam*, were published in 1967. Early in 1969 a conference called by the Bertrand Russell Peace Foundation (again without the philosopher in attendance) found the Soviet Union similarly blameworthy for its 1968 invasion of Czechoslovakia.

The first two volumes of his *Autobiography* have sometimes been found frivolous and "scrappy" but by most critics are admired as the eminently readable—and often very funny—outline of an incredibly rich experience of a fearless iconoclast, in constant contact with the great and near-great, who often found himself discharged or willingly let go for his unorthodox activities and opinions—particularly in this country—and often in financial straits as a result. Malcolm Muggeridge said in *Esquire:* "The second volume is even better than the first. . . . Russell is an authentic hero of our time, and posterity will value, as we do, his honest, truthful and accomplished account of himself," a sentiment echoed many times over. He wrote an average of a letter every 30 hours of his life and some 100,000 of these (mostly to other great or powerful men of his age) were privately sold in summer 1967, together with some 400 manuscripts. This treasure trove has yet to be published—books by Russell, therefore, may be expected to appear for a generation or more to come. Because of his longevity, his acquaintances spanned nearly a century. He "debated philosophy with Wittgenstein and fiction with CONRAD (see Vol. 1) and D. H. LAWRENCE (see Vol. 1), he. . .argued economics with Keynes and civil disobedience with Gandhi, his open letters. . .provoked STALIN (see Vol. 3) to a reply and Lyndon Johnson to exasperation" (George Steiner, *The New Yorker*). (See also Volume 5.)

BOOKS BY RUSSELL

The Basic Writings of Bertrand Russell 1903–1959. Ed. by Robert E. Egner and Lester E. Dennon, preface by the author, Simon & Schuster 1967 pap. $13.95. "This anthology, authorized and introduced by the author himself, consists of 81 essays and chapters or passages from longer works and has been selected to represent Lord Russell as philosopher, mathematician, man of letters, historian and analyst of international affairs." The book is addressed to the informed layman and the "selections, in addition to illustrating the astounding range of Lord Russell's interest and knowledge, demonstrate his 'ability to discuss any problem in a scientific, objective and dispassionate way.' " (*LJ*).

Logic and Knowledge: Essays 1901–50. Ed. by Robert Charles Marsh, Allen & Unwin 1977 text ed. $18.95. A selection of Russell's most significant essays on the technical subjects of logic and epistemology, prepared for the serious student.

The Principles of Mathematics. 1903. Norton repr. of 1930 ed. 1964 pap. $4.95. Introductory work presenting Russell's revolutionary theory that logic is the basis of mathematics.

(and Alfred North Whitehead). *Principia Mathematica.* 1910–13. Cambridge Univ. Pr. 3 vols. 2d ed. 1925–27 $400.00. Monumental treatise on the foundations of mathematics; a classic for all time, though accessible only to the expert.

The Problems of Philosophy. 1912. Oxford 1959 pap. $5.95. Classic introduction to philosophy for the educated layperson.

Mysticism and Logic and Other Essays. 1918. Barnes & Noble 1981 pap. $8.95. A collection of stimulating essays that have been influential beyond the limited circle of academic philosophers.

Introduction to Mathematical Philosophy. 1919. Simon and Schuster 1971 pap. $8.50. Elementary restatement of the theory of mathematics based on logic.

Bolshevism: Practice and Theory. Ayer repr. of 1920 ed. 1978 $17.00. Journalistic account of the Soviet Union in its early days by a sympathetic visitor who turned critical.

The Analysis of Mind. Humanities Pr. repr. of 1921 ed. 1978 $17.50. Profound but lightly written theory demolishing the substance concept of mind.

The Problems of China. Allen & Unwin 1922 text ed. $9.95. Journalistic account of China from an enlightened visitor.

Icarus on the Future of Science. West repr. of 1924 ed. 1977 lib. bdg. $17.50. Playful essay.

The ABC of Relativity. 1925. New Amer. Lib. rev. ed. 1970 pap. $4.50. Philosophical analysis of the scientific theory; good exposition.

What I Believe. Darby repr. of 1925 ed. 1983 lib. bdg. $15.00. A credo for the humanist, the naturalist, the empiricist, and the liberal.

Our Knowledge of the External World. 1926. Humanities Pr. repr. of rev. ed. 1972 text ed. $25.00. Original theory of knowledge unfolding the perspectival theory of perception.

Sceptical Essays. 1928. Allen & Unwin repr. of 1935 ed. 1960 pap. $4.95. Popular and stimulating.

The Conquest of Happiness. 1930. Liveright 1971 pap. $6.95. Ethics intended for the educated layperson.

Education and the Social Order. 1932. Allen & Unwin 1980 pap. $4.95. A monograph in Russell's clear style presenting his theory of education.

In Praise of Idleness and Other Essays. 1935. Allen & Unwin 1981 pap. $3.95. Imaginative popular essays.

Power. 1938. Norton 1969 pap. $6.95. Ambitious though superficial endeavor to plumb the root principle of politics.

An Inquiry into Meaning and Truth. 1940. Allen & Unwin 1980 $17.95 pap. $6.95. Technical work in philosophical semantics during the early period of the field's development.

A History of Western Philosophy: And Its Connection with Political and Social Circumstances from the Earliest Times to the Present Day. 1945. Simon & Schuster 1984 pap. $8.95. Classic yet popular work; the best history of philosophy written by a great twentieth-century philosopher.

Authority and the Individual. 1949. Allen & Unwin 1977 pap. $3.95. Reith lecture, vaunting individual freedom.

Unpopular Essays. 1951. Simon & Schuster 1969 pap. $8.70. Popular collection, prepared as many of Russell's collections were, in order to make money.

Human Society in Ethics and Politics. Allen & Unwin 1954 text ed. $18.50. Superficial reflections.

Bertrand Russell's Best. Ed. by R. E. Egner, New Amer. Lib. 1958 repr. 1986 pap. $3.95. Selection of Russell's witticisms.

Common Sense and Nuclear Warfare. AMS Pr. repr. of 1959 ed. 1979 $18.00. A "Better Red Than Dead" tract.

My Philosophical Development. 1959. Allen & Unwin 1975 pap. $3.95. An intellectual autobiography—beginning when he was 16 and written with his usual clarity and wit. With an appendix, "Russell's Philosophy," by Alan Wood.

Bertrand Russell Speaks His Mind. Greenwood repr. of 1960 ed. 1974 lib. bdg. $22.50. Selection of Russell's provocative statements on the issues of the day.

Has Man a Future? Greenwood repr. of 1962 ed. 1984 lib. bdg. $27.50.

The Scientific Outlook. Norton 1962 pap. $6.95. Well-written statement of the role of science in civilization.

The Art of Philosophizing and Other Essays. 1968. Littlefield 1977 pap. $5.95. "The three essays in this book, "The Art of Rational Conjecture," "The Art of Drawing Inferences," and "The Art of Reckoning," were written in 1942 for Hademan-Julius and are now printed in book form for the first time. The pieces respectively tell how to be a philosopher, a logician, and a mathematician" (*LJ*).

The Autobiography of Bertrand Russell. Allen & Unwin 3 vols. repr. of 1970 ed. 1981 ea. $17.95

The Collected Papers of Bertrand Russell. Ed. by Kenneth Blackwell and others, Allen & Unwin 7 vols. 1983–84 $55.00–$75.00. "The editorial task has been discharged with exemplary thoroughness and efficiency. The entire series of volumes, when completed, will be indispensable to a thorough study of the intellectual development of one whose influence on the philosophy of his and our time has perhaps been greater than that of any other single individual" (P. F. Strawson, *TLS*). The set is expected to run to 28 volumes.

Bertrand Russell. Ed. by Ann Redpath, Creative Education 1985 lib. bdg. $8.95. Readable selections providing a partial picture of Russell's educational theory.

BOOKS ABOUT RUSSELL

Ayer, A. J. *Bertrand Russell as a Philosopher.* Longwood 1972 pap. $2.25. Sympathetic interpretation of Russell by a leading English philosopher.

———. *Russell and Moore: The Analytical Heritage.* [*William James Lectures Ser.*] Harvard Univ. Pr. 1971 $16.50. Brilliant comparative study illuminating the background of Russell's thought.

Clark, Ronald. *Bertrand Russell and His World.* Thames & Hudson 1981 $14.95. Outstanding, comprehensive biography by an accomplished author.

Dewey, John, and H. M. Kallen, eds. *The Bertrand Russell Case.* Da Capo repr. of 1941 ed. 1972 lib. bdg. $29.00. The report on Russell's academic freedom case against the City College of New York prepared by two famous American philosophers.

Eames, Elizabeth R. *Bertrand Russell's Theory of Knowledge.* Braziller 1969 $6.00. A scholarly monograph on a central preoccupation of Russell.

Gottschalk, Herbert. *Bertrand Russell: A Life.* Allen & Unwin 1967 pap. $2.95. A straightforward and readable appraisal.

Hardy, Godfrey H. *Bertrand Russell and Trinity: A College Controversy of the Last War.* Ed. by Walter P. Metzger, Ayer repr. of 1942 ed. 1983 lib. bdg. $14.00. An investigative record of Russell's loss of his position at Cambridge during World War I because of his pacificism, including accounts of the villainous role played by McTaggart.

Killiminister, C. W. *Russell.* St. Martin's 1984 $27.50. A critical evaluation of Russell's work.

Kuntz, Paul G. *Bertrand Russell.* [*Twayne's Eng. Authors Ser.*] G. K. Hall 1986 lib. bdg. $14.95. Well-researched, well-written study prepared by an outstanding scholar that is an excellent place to start the study of Russell.

Sainsbury, Mark. *Russell.* [*Arguments of the Philosophers Ser.*] Methuen 1979 $36.00 pap. $14.95. Acute analytic critique of Russell's thought for the advanced student.

Schilpp, Paul A., ed. *The Philosophy of Bertrand Russell.* [*Lib. of Living Philosophers*] Open Court 4th ed. 1980 o.p. Collection of original critical essays, preceded by Russell's intellectual biography and followed by his responses to his critics. The volume closes with a bibliography of Russell's writings.

Vellacott, J. O. *Bertrand Russell and the Pacifists in the First World War.* St. Martin's 1981 $26.00. Careful reconstruction of an important moment in Russell's life; very readable social history.

RYLE, GILBERT. 1900–1976

Ryle exerted an influence over academic philosophers in the English-speaking world almost without equal at midcentury. As Waynefleet professor of philosophy at Oxford and as G. E. Moore's successor to the editorship of *Mind,* the most prestigious philosophical journal in Great Britain, Ryle shaped the orientation of philosophical discussion for more than a decade. Independently of Wittgenstein he invented a philosophical method of linguistic analysis, maintaining indeed that systematic confusions in theory stemmed from misleading grammatical expressions.

Ryle's most remarkable contribution to philosophy, however, was in the area of philosophy of mind. His crowning achievement was *The Concept of Mind* (1949). Utilizing his method of linguistic analysis on discourse about mind and the mental, he maintained that the radical distinction between mind and body, Cartesian dualism, stemmed from category mistakes. A felicitous writer with a distinctively colloquial style free of jargon, Ryle invented phrases—such as "the ghost in the machine" to indicate supposed Cartesian mental substance—which still reverberate in the literature of philosophy and psychology.

BOOKS BY RYLE

The Concept of Mind. 1949. Univ. of Chicago Pr. 1984 pap. $10.95. Most influential work in the philosophy of mind by a British author to appear after World War II.

Dilemmas. Cambridge Univ. Pr. 1954 pap. $9.95. "From the first page to the last the argument is easily followed and brilliantly illustrated by example" (Stuart Hampshire, *New Statesman and Nation*).

Plato's Progress. Cambridge Univ. Pr. 1966 o.p. "Professor Ryle presents an original, indeed revolutionary account of Plato's development" (*TLS*).

On Thinking. Rowman 1980 $20.00. A monograph displaying Ryle's characteristic conceptual verve.

BOOKS ABOUT RYLE

Kolenda, Konstantin, ed. *Studies in Philosophy: A Symposium on Gilbert Ryle.* Rice Univ. 1972 pap. $10.00. A collection of original critical essays on Ryle by prominent philosophers.

Lyons, William. *Gilbert Ryle: An Introduction to His Philosophy.* Humanities Pr. 1980 text ed. $30.00. "This book is an introduction to the work of Gilbert Ryle. . . . It lays bare the central themes in Ryle's work, shows how they knit together, and critically discusses his arguments when pursuing those themes. . . . It contains a short biography of Ryle, a bibliography, and an index" (*The Philosopher's Index*).

SANTAYANA, GEORGE. 1863–1952

A gentle philosopher-poet, born and reared in Spain, educated at Harvard and later professor of philosophy there, Santayana resided in England, France, and Italy after 1914. At the beginning of World War II he entered the nursing home in Rome managed by nuns known as the Blue Sisters and remained there until his death. He was still a Spanish subject. His last book, *The Poet's Testament* (1953), contains a few unpublished lyrics, several translations, and two plays in blank verse. The title comes from the poem read at his funeral, which begins: "I give back to the earth what the earth gave/ All to the furrow, nothing to the grave."

Santayana wrote philosophy in an inimitable prose, enriched with imagery and metaphor. His meanings were always complex and often ironic. In this style, so untypical of the professionalized philosophy that sprang up in the English-speaking world during his lifetime, Santayana nevertheless articulated an epistemological critical realism and an ontology of essence and matter that drew the attention and admiration of philosophers and scholars.

His first published philosophical book, *The Sense of Beauty* (1896), was an important contribution in aesthetics, a classic text that is still in use. His multivolume work *The Life of Reason* expresses his naturalistic philosophy of history and culture. It states the essence of his attitude toward nature, life, and society. *Scepticism and Animal Faith* (1923) presents his theory of knowledge and also serves as an introduction to his system of philosophy, *Realms of Being* (1927–40). The titles of the separate volumes of this remarkable work, now out of print, reveal the lineaments of his system: *Realm of Essence* (1927), *Realm of Matter* (1930), *Realm of Truth* (1937), and *Realm of Spirit* (1940). His ideas were "popularized" in his only novel, *The Last Puritan*, which became a surprise bestseller overnight. "He came into a changing American scene with a whole group of concepts that enormously enriched our thinking. He gave a moving vitality to what had often been obscure abstractions. . . . he made the whole relationship of reason and beauty, each to the other, come alive and stay alive" (*N.Y. Times*). Although Santayana's *Complete Poems* (1975) is out of print, several volumes of his poetry are available and are listed below. A critical edition of Santayana's complete writings under the general editorship of Herman Saatkamp is in progress.

BOOKS BY SANTAYANA

Birth of Reason and Other Essays. Ed. by Daniel Cory, Columbia Univ. Pr. 1968 $30.00. Excellent collection of Santayana's essays introducing his thoughts, prepared by his former secretary.

Little Essays Drawn from the Writings of George Santayana. Ed. by L. P. Smith, Ayer repr. of 1920 ed. 1978 $20.00. Excerpts from Santayana's writings, especially from *The Life of Reason;* very well done.

The Idler and His Works. Ed. by Daniel Cory, Ayer repr. of 1957 ed. 1975 $15.00. Scintillatingly popular.

Physical Order and Moral Liberty. Ed. by John Lachs and Shirley Lachs, Vanderbilt Univ. Pr. 1969 $15.95. Previously unpublished essays.

The Sense of Beauty: Being the Outline of Aesthetic Theory. 1896. Dover repr. of 1938 rev. ed. 1955 pap. $3.95; Peter Smith 1952 $14.00. Highly influential masterpiece in the history of aesthetics.

Interpretations of Poetry and Religion. 1900. Peter Smith 1958 $11.25. Original work demonstrating the symbolic affinity of art and religion.

The Life of Reason. 1905–06. Dover 1980–83 pap. $4.50–$6.00; Peter Smith 1982–83 $12.50–$14.50. Vol. 1, *Reason in Common Sense;* Vol. 2, *Reason in Society;* Vol. 3, *Reason in Religion;* Vol. 4, *Reason in Art;* Vol. 5, *Reason in Science.* Magisterial masterpiece on the role of reason in culture, unrivaled in twentieth-century thought.

Three Philosophical Poets. Cooper Sq. repr. of 1910 ed. 1971 lib. bdg. $25.00. Dante, Shakespeare, and Goethe are construed in terms of the philosophies they project.

Egotism in German Philosophy. Haskell repr. of 1916 ed. 1971 lib. bdg. $39.95. Polemical monograph against German idealism as causative of World War I.

Scepticism and Animal Faith: Introduction to a System of Philosophy. 1923. Dover 1955 text ed. pap. $6.00; Peter Smith 1950 $14.75. The best formulation of the theory of knowledge of critical realism, and a sketch of the realms of being.

The Genteel Tradition at Bay. 1931. Haskell 1977 lib. bdg. $75.00. Collection of incisive essays on literature and culture.

Some Turns of Thought in Modern Philosophy. Ayer repr. of 1933 ed. 1972 $11.00. Collection of inimitable essays interpreting recent philosophy.

The Last Puritan: A Memoir in the Form of a Novel. Scribner 1936 $25.00. Bestselling novel expressing Santayana's evaluation of America.

The Idea of Christ in the Gospels; or God in Man, a Critical Essay. AMS Pr. repr. of 1946 ed. 1979 $30.00. Santayana's critical interpretation of Christianity.

Dominations and Powers: Reflections on Liberty, Society and Government. 1951. Kelley repr. of 1954 ed. 1975 $37.50. Masterful political philosophy with comments relevant to the international situation immediately after World War II.

Persons and Places: The Autobiography of George Santayana. Ed. by Herman J. Saatkamp, Jr., and William G. Holzberger, MIT 1986 text ed. $25.00. Critical edition of the first volume of Santayana's autobiography.

BOOKS ABOUT SANTAYANA

Arnett, Willard Eugene. *Santayana and the Sense of Beauty*. Peter Smith repr. of 1955 ed. 1984 $12.00. A discerning analysis of Santayana as artist-philosopher.

Munson, T. N. *The Essential Wisdom of George Santayana*. Greenwood repr. of 1962 ed. 1983 lib. bdg. $29.75. Scholarly interpretation of Santayana's thought, stressing the doctrine of essence.

Saatkamp, Herman J., Jr., and John Jones. *George Santayana: A Bibliographical Checklist, 1880–1980*. Philos. Document. 1982 $25.50. Authoritative bibliography indispensable to the serious researcher.

Singer, Beth. *The Rational Society: A Critical Reading of Santayana's Social Thought*. UPB 1970 $10.00. Invaluable analytic monograph on a central aspect of Santayana's work.

Singer, Irving. *Santayana's Aesthetics*. Greenwood repr. of 1957 ed. 1973 lib. bdg. $22.50. Solid investigation and detailed criticism distinguish this scholarly monograph.

Sprigge, Timothy. *Santayana: An Examination of His Philosophy*. [*Arguments of the Philosophers Ser.*] Methuen 1974 $20.00. Penetrating critical evaluation of Santayana, insightfully rendered in the current philosophical idiom.

Stallknecht, Newton P. *George Santayana*. [*Pamphlets on Amer. Writers Ser.*] Univ. of Minnesota Pr. 1971 pap. $1.25. Sensitive introductory study.

SARTRE, JEAN-PAUL. 1905–1980

Sartre was the chief prophet of atheistic existentialism, that bleak philosophy of despair that grew from the defeat of France. When the intellectuals of the Left Bank felt abandoned and helpless, it offered both a personal and a social answer. There are two types of existentialists, those who follow the mystical Danish pastor of the nineteenth century, SØREN KIERKEGAARD, and Sartre's atheistic followers, who reject Kierkegaard's belief in God but accept his idea of man's existence in a hostile, disordered world, trying to make the best of things, fulfilling his life and achieving final freedom. In *Existentialism*, Sartre denied that his philosophy is one of despair, and said: "Man is nothing else but what he makes of himself. You're free, choose, that is, invent." But many find his formula full of paradoxes. *Being and Nothingness* (1943), the *Critique of Dialectical Reason* (1960), and *Search for a Method* (1957) provide the core of his thought and its development. In the latter two volumes he answered his critics by setting the existentialist "man alone" in his social and world context.

For 13 years Sartre was an obscure teacher of philosophy. Mobilized as a private at the beginning of the war, he was taken prisoner and spent nine months in a German war prison. When released, he returned to Paris to take an active part in the Communist resistance organization. He abandoned teaching for writing and formulated his philosophy. In Paris he was the leader of a brilliant and creative group of writers that included Maurice Merleau-Ponty, ALBERT CAMUS (see Vol. 2), and SIMONE DE BEAUVOIR (see Vol. 2).

In a review of the English translation of Sartre's *Literary and Philosophical Essays*, William Barrett wrote: "It isn't usual that you can say of an acknowledged playwright or novelist that a book of his essays may be as valuable as anything he has done. But Sartre has always seemed to me an idea man, an intellectual first, only afterward an artist; his novels and plays come alive where he touches upon the idea, where the idea is directly on stage or hanging around very close in the wings; the center of his power as a writer is neither in philosophy nor literature separately, but in their curious point of intersection" (*N.Y. Times*).

In 1964 Sartre published the autobiography of his early years, *The Words* (1964), and in the same year was offered the Nobel Prize for literature, which he refused. Sartre's achievements as a man of letters rival his contributions to philosophy. He is known for such novels as *Nausea* (1938), *The Age of Reason*, and *Troubled Sleep*, the plays *No Exit* (1944), *The Flies* (1943), and the short story "The Wall." He also wrote penetrating works of literary and philosophical criticism on GENET (see Vol. 2), FLAUBERT (see Vol. 2), and BAUDELAIRE (see Vol. 2). (See also Volume 2.)

BOOKS BY SARTRE

The Philosophy of Jean-Paul Sartre. Ed. by R. D. Cumming, Random 1972 pap. $4.95. Selections from 15 of Sartre's works arranged in logical order—"the only single-volume compendium of Sartre's work available"—brings together "the basic ideas heretofore scattered in many volumes and covering an astonishing variety of subjects. In the process Dr. Cumming has offered a particularly lucid introduction, has organized the material under clarifying subject headings (often provided by himself), and has attempted to reach a standard usage for Sartre's difficult and highly semantic vocabulary" (*LJ*).

The Transcendence of the Ego: An Existentialist Theory of Consciousness. 1937. Ed. and trans. by Forrest Williams and Robert Kirkpatrick, Farrar 1957 pap. $3.95; Octagon 1972 lib. bdg. $12.00. First published in France in 1937, this marks Sartre's break with the German phenomenological movement originating with Husserl, by which he had been greatly influenced, and led to the full existentialist expression of *Being and Nothingness.* A "brilliant polemic against the pure Ego" (*Journal of Philosophy*).

Being and Nothingness. 1943. Trans. by Hazel E. Barnes, Philos. Lib. 1956 $9.95; Washington Square Pr. 1983 pap. $6.95. This work is basic to the understanding of atheistic existentialism.

Existentialism and Human Emotions. Citadel Pr. 1971 pap. $3.95; Philos. Lib. 1947 pap. $3.95. Contains *Existentialism* as well as parts of *Being and Nothingness.*

Existentialism and Humanism. 1947. Haskell 1977 lib. bdg. $29.95. Defines existentialism as humanism.

What Is Literature? 1947. Peter Smith 1958 $13.50. Stresses the importance of the commitment of the writer.

Anti-Semite and Jew. 1948. Schocken 1965 $5.00 pap. $4.95. Controversial existentialist analysis of anti-Semitism.

Existential Psychoanalysis. 1953. Trans. by Hazel E. Barnes, Regnery-Gateway 1962 pap. $4.95. A new psychoanalysis based on the principles of existentialism.

Search for a Method. 1957. Trans. by Hazel E. Barnes, Vintage 1968 pap. $4.95. Sartre clarifies his view of the nature of history and its effect on the individual's search for freedom and rediscovery of himself, both central concerns of existentialism. This provides an introduction to Sartre's second great philosophical work after *Being and Nothingness*—the *Critique of Dialectical Reason*—and demonstrates how Sartre reconciled his existentialism with Marxism as aspects of the same worldview.

Imagination: A Psychological Critique. Trans. by Forrest Williams, Univ. of Michigan Pr. 1962 o.p. In this book, of great importance to philosophers and psychologists and of interest to the informed layperson, Sartre continued his examination of the bases of psychology-philosophy with studies of images and imagination.

Literature and Existentialism. 1962. Trans. by Bernard Frechtman, Citadel Pr. 1980 pap. $3.95. Reiteration of paramount value of commitment on the part of the author for significant literature.

Essays in Aesthetics, Art and Philosophy: An Existentialist Approach. Trans. by Wade Baskin, Ayer 1963 $12.00; Citadel Pr. 1967 pap. $5.95. A collection of Sartre's essays on art and philosophy, some having appeared in *Les temps modernes,* which he founded and edited with Simone de Beauvoir and Maurice Merleau-Ponty.

Essays in Existentialism. Ed. by Wade Baskin, Citadel Pr. 1967 pap. $5.95. A useful collection of readable essays.

Psychology of Imagination. Greenwood 1978 lib. bdg. $32.50. Significant phenomenological investigation.

The Emotions: Outline of a Theory. Trans. by Bernard Frechtman, Citadel Pr. 1984 pap. $3.95. Influential phenomenological study.

The War Diaries of Jean-Paul Sartre: November 1939 to March 1940. Pantheon 1985 $17.95. Historically invaluable personal record.

Thoughtful Passions: Jean-Paul Sartre's Intimate Letters to Simone de Beauvoir. Macmillan 1986 $22.95. Letters illuminating the early phase of his lifelong relationship with Simone de Beauvoir.

BOOKS ABOUT SARTRE

Anderson, Thomas C. *The Foundation and Structure of Sartrian Ethics.* Univ. Pr. of Kansas 1979 $22.50. An analytic critique of existential ethics.

Aronson, Ronald. *Jean-Paul Sartre: Philosophy in the World.* Schocken 1980 $9.95. A sympathetic portrait of Sartre as world thinker.

Barnes, Hazel E..*Sartre and Flaubert.* Univ. of Chicago Pr. 1982 $25.00 pap. $10.95. Scholarly, literary study by Sartre's translator.

Brosman, Catherine. *Jean-Paul Sartre.* [*Twayne's World Authors Ser.*] G. K. Hall 1983 lib. bdg. $13.50 1984 pap. $5.95. Concise, comprehensive treatment of Sartre's life and work; a good introduction.

Catalano, Joseph S. *A Commentary on Jean-Paul Sartre's Critique of Dialectical Reason: Theory of Practical Ensemble.* Univ. of Chicago Pr. 1987 text ed. $45.95 pap. $19.95. Useful guide to the understanding of Sartre's systematically dialectical work on Marxism and existentialism.

———. *Commentary on Sartre's Being and Nothingness.* Univ. of Chicago Pr. 1985 text ed. pap. $13.00. Helpful elementary critical reading of Sartre's obscure masterpiece in existential ontology.

Caws, Peter. *Sartre.* [*Arguments of the Philosophers Ser.*] Methuen 1979 $26.95 1984 pap. $10.50. Acute elucidation and critique of the cogency of Sartre's philosophy.

Cohen-Solal, Annie. *Sartre: A Life.* Pantheon 1987 $24.95. This "long, careful and loving portrait of Sartre turns a remote and puzzling mandarin into a true existential being, warts and all" (*Time*).

De Beauvoir, Simone. *Adieux: A Farewell to Sartre.* Trans. by Patrick O'Brien, Pantheon 1984 $19.45 1985 pap. $8.95. Loving personal salute, sometimes bittersweet, from Sartre's lifelong lover.

Desan, Wilfrid. *The Marxism of Jean-Paul Sartre.* Peter Smith repr. of 1965 ed. 1974 $11.50. "Professor Desan's [study of Sartre's *Critique of Dialectical Reason*] is not only a brilliant analysis of Sartre's work, but is invaluable for its exposition of Marxism in several manifestations, its practical application to questions such as the Negro revolution, and for its meticulous and always scrupulous objections to the Sartrean position as regards Marxism" (*LJ*).

Fell, Joseph P., III. *Emotion in the Thought of Sartre.* Columbia Univ. Pr. 1965 $28.00. "Professor Fell draws primarily from Sartre's *The Emotions: Outline of a Theory* and *Being and Nothingness.* In the second part of the book he analyzes Sartre's idea in the light of other theories—those of William James, Janet, and others— and shows Sartre's specific innovations and his debts to Hegel" (*LJ*).

———. *Heidegger and Sartre: An Essay on Being and Place.* Columbia Univ. Pr. 1983 $32.00 pap. $17.00. Scholarly monograph intended for specialists.

Greene, Norman N. *Jean-Paul Sartre: The Existentialist Ethic.* Greenwood repr. of 1960 ed. 1982 lib. bdg. $22.50. Capable critical study focused on ethical themes.

Grene, Marjorie. *Sartre.* Univ. Pr. of Amer. 1983 text ed. pap. $14.00. Outstanding intellectual portrait by a leading philosophical scholar.

Hartmann, Klaus. *Sartre's Ontology: A Study of Being and Nothingness in the Light of Hegel's Logic.* [*Studies in Phenomenology and Existential Philosophy Ser.*] Northwestern Univ. Pr. 1966 $19.95 pap. $9.95. "An outstanding interpretation of Sartre for specialists" (*LJ*).

King, Thomas M. *Sartre and the Sacred.* Univ. of Chicago Pr. 1974 $17.00. Scholarly monograph on a neglected theme, profoundly puzzling.

Manser, Anthony. *Sartre: A Philosophic Study.* Greenwood repr. of 1966 ed. 1981 lib. bdg. $29.75. "The work manifests an almost intuitive awareness of the vital meaning of Sartre's words; yet this is not a matter of easy insight, but of serious, painstaking study, into which the reader is carefully drawn. Perhaps the only full-length study of Sartre in English, which begins adequately to judge Sartre as a philosopher, and at the same time place him literarily" (*Choice*).

Natanson, Maurice. *A Critique of Jean-Paul Sartre's Ontology.* [*Studies in Philosophy*] Haskell repr. of 1950 ed. 1972 lib. bdg. $39.95. Careful exposition and criticism, highly compressed, good to have at hand when reading *Being and Nothingness.*

Poster, Mark. *Sartre's Marxism.* Cambridge Univ. Pr. 1982 $15.95. Positively merits being the last word on the subject.

Rahv, Betty T. *From Sartre to the New Novel.* Kennikat 1974 $21.95. Literary history for literary critics.

Salvan, Jacques. *To Be and Not to Be: An Analysis of Jean-Paul Sartre's Ontology.* Wayne State Univ. Pr. 1962 pap. $6.95. Compared to Natanson's monograph, Salvan's is more imaginative.

Schilpp, Paul A., ed. *The Philosophy of Jean-Paul Sartre.* [*Lib. of Living Philosophers*] Open Court 1981 $29.95. A collection of original essays by leading experts on all aspects of Sartre's thought.

Scriven, Michael. *Sartre's Existential Biographies.* St. Martin's 1984 $21.95. An Australian analytic philosopher of science changes course and comes up with a winner.

Suhl, Benjamin. *Jean-Paul Sartre: The Philosopher as a Literary Critic.* Columbia Univ. Pr. 1973 $26.00 pap. $13.00. "One of the best books on Sartre" (*Choice*).

SCHELER, MAX FERDINAND. 1874–1928

Born in Munich, Scheler was a pupil of Rudolf Eucken. Afterward he taught at the Universities of Jena, Munich, and Cologne. In 1910 he retired from teaching to live in Berlin and pursue an independent career as a philosophical author. Under the influence of HUSSERL, he adopted the phenomenological method. Useful in the descriptive analysis of subjective mental processes, the phenomenological method was employed by Scheler for the examination of value experiences, such as the experiences involved in social institutions and religion. Scheler's main contributions were to the fields of philosophy and sociology. He is credited with having influenced Martin Heidegger, Ernst Cassirer, Gabriel Marcel, and Ortega y Gasset.

Scheler has been viewed as a symbol of European intellectual unrest before and after World War I; his personal life was stormy—for example, he had three wives. Yet in the midst of internal and external unrest and turmoil Scheler persisted in his philosophical labors. Between 1913 and 1916 he published what is regarded as his major work; it is devoted to a phenomenological investigation of ethical values. His conversion to Roman Catholicism in 1920 was widely interpreted as a manifestation of the spiritual and intellectual vitality of the church. An account of his conversion is given in his book *On the Eternal in Man* (1921). Scheler's later writings concentrate on social philosophy and the sociology of knowledge.

BOOKS BY SCHELER

Formalism in Ethics and Non-Formal Ethics of Values: A New Attempt toward the Foundations of Ethical Personalism. 1913–16. Trans. by Manfred S. Frings and Roger L. Funk [*Studies in Phenomenology and Existential Philosophy Ser.*] Northwestern Univ. Pr. 1973 text ed. $29.95 pap. $13.95. Scheler's major work; an ambitious endeavor to articulate a phenomenology of ethical values.

On the Eternal in Man. 1921. Trans. by Bernard Noble, Shoe String repr. of 1960 ed. 1972 $35.00. Scheler's book is "one of the clearest and most comprehensive discussions of the approach to theistic philosophy. . . . [It] shows a remarkable combination of observation with metaphysical acumen" (*TLS*).

Man's Place in Nature. 1928. Trans. by Hans Meyerhoff, Farrar 1962 pap. $5.25. Philosophical anthropology in the service of the metaphysically transcendent, stirringly eloquent for a philosopher's work.

Selected Philosophical Essays. Trans. by David Lachterman [*Studies in Phenomenology and Existential Philosophy Ser.*] Northwestern Univ. Pr. 1973 $13.95. "These [essays]. . .are closely connected to Scheler's master work, *Formalism in Ethics and Non-Formal Ethics of Values*" (*LJ*).

Problems of a Sociology of Knowledge. Ed. by Kenneth Strikkers, trans. by Manfred S. Frings [*International Lib. of Sociology*] Methuen 1980 $25.00. Scheler's pioneering writing in a field that came into existence, partly through his efforts, but after his death.

BOOKS ABOUT SCHELER

Nota, John H. *Max Scheler: The Man and His Works.* Franciscan Herald Pr. 1983 $12.00. An appreciation.

Schneck, Stephen F. *Person and Polis: Max Scheler's Personalism as Political Theory.* State Univ. of New York Pr. 1986 $34.50 pap. $10.95. A scholarly monograph that assumes some knowledge of Scheler's work.

Staude, J. R. *Max Scheler, 1874–1928: An Intellectual Portrait.* Free Pr. 1967 $10.95. "A good introductory study" (*Choice*).

SCHLICK, MORITZ. 1882–1936

Schlick studied at Berlin under Max Planck and received his Ph.D. in physics in 1904. He taught at Rostock and Kiel before joining the faculty at Vienna in 1922. His early work *General Theory of Knowledge* (1918) reveals his commitment to realism and to the experimental method in scientific and philosophical knowledge. At Vienna he led the Vienna Circle of logical positivism and was instrumental in recruiting Rudolf Carnap. The publication of Ludwig Wittgenstein's *Tractatus Logico-Philosophicus* (1921) influenced radically the subsequent development of his thought. Increasingly he stressed the empirical verification criterion for truth and meaning and became severely critical of statements in philosophy and elsewhere that could not meet this criterion. Hence the logical positivists whom he led became notorious for their thesis that metaphysics is non-sense. His mature epistemology was presented in the publication of the second edition of his *General Theory of Knowledge* (1925). He also advanced a noncognitivist theory of ethical statements in his book *Problems of Ethics* (1939).

BOOK BY SCHLICK

General Theory of Knowledge. 2d ed. 1925. Trans. by A. E. Blumberg [*Lib. of Exact Philosophy*] Open Court 1985 pap. $12.95; Springer-Verlag 1974 $52.00

SELLARS, ROY WOOD. 1880–1973

Professor of philosophy at the University of Michigan, Sellars was a major figure in the rise of American critical realism. While Santayana was the most famous member of the movement, remarkable for his doctrine of essence, Sellars, along with Lovejoy, articulated a critical realist epistemology without invoking the doctrine of essence. Perhaps the most sober of all the critical realists in his adherence to the results of the natural sciences, he expounded, in his books *Evolutionary Naturalism* (1922) and *The Philosophy of Physical Realism* (1933), a systematic philosophy of evolutionary naturalism and physical realism. Sellars was a materialist in fundamental ontology, a democratic socialist in political theory and practice, and a humanist in religion.

BOOKS BY ROY WOOD SELLARS

The Essentials of Philosophy. AMS Pr. repr. of 1917 ed. 1974 $21.00. "This book. . .is one of the most acceptable introductory texts that has come under his (the reviewer's) notice" (A. G. Balz, *Journal of Philosophy*).

The Next Step in Religion: An Essay toward the Coming Renaissance. AMS Pr. repr. of 1918 ed. 1974 $24.50. "An honest book is the noblest work of the pen, and this is an honest book. This writer is certainly grim and iconoclastic, but his purpose is to lay the foundation for a new and better structure" (*Boston Transcript*).

Religion Coming of Age. AMS Pr. repr. of 1928 ed. 1974 $20.50. "Professor Sellars raises the traditional theological questions. In answering them, he comes to the conclusion that there is no reason for belief in immortality and that man has no cosmic 'comparison'. . . . The result is a view of the universe which provides the outlines at least of that synthesis of modern thought and knowledge which has been so long needed" (Granville Hicks, *The Nation*).

BOOK ABOUT ROY WOOD SELLARS

Delaney, Cornelius. *Mind and Nature: A Study in the Naturalistic Philosophies of Cohen, Woodbridge and Sellars.* Univ. of Notre Dame Pr. 1969 $19.95. Scholarly monograph on philosophical naturalism; contains chapters of exposition and criticism of Sellars's thought.

SELLARS, WILFRID. 1912–

Wilfrid Sellars has taught at the University of Minnesota, Yale University, and the University of Pittsburgh. The son of Roy Wood Sellars, he won early fame at Minnesota as the coeditor of two volumes, one on logical analysis, the other on ethical theory, that introduced a generation of American students to the problems and issues of analytic philosophy. Sellars's early articles, influenced by the logical atomism of Wittgenstein and RUSSELL (see also Vol. 5), reveal an inquisitive metaphysician who was also a careful student of the great figures in the history of philosophy. As Sellars matured, his work took a turn in the direction of KANT and PEIRCE. From Kant he derived his sense of the role of conceptual structure—in the contemporary term, language—in shaping experience, so that there is no absolute given. From Peirce he gained insight into the normative aspect of all beliefs, including science. However, Sellars does not merely follow his sources. A profoundly original metaphysician, he has transformed all these conceptions in the articulation of a philosophical system distinctively his own.

BOOKS BY WILFRID SELLARS

(and Herbert Feigl, eds.). *Readings in Philosophical Analysis.* 1949. Ridgeview 1981 lib. bdg. $25.00 text ed. pap. $15.00. A whole generation of students, from which come the present faculties of philosophy in our colleges and universities, learned the problems and issues in analytic philosophy from this influential anthology.

(and John Hospers, eds.). *Readings in Ethical Theory.* 1952. Prentice-Hall 2d ed. 1970 text ed. $35.95. The first edition received the following praise: "This reviewer finds the volume intellectually exciting. . . . This result was achieved by a rigorous restriction in the range of material used and in a happy and entirely rational collocation of it. The selections are at a uniformly high level: they reveal competent ethicists at work, writing for philosophically literate readers" (E. W. Hall, *Ethics*).

Science and Metaphysics: Variations on Kantian Themes. 1968. Humanities 1982 text ed. pap. $15.00. "Although Professor Sellars's philosophical writings make difficult reading, their content is rewarding. . . . What distinguishes [his] scientific realism from older and modern versions of scientism is his emphasis on the normative aspects of both practical and theoretical thinking" (*TLS*).

Philosophical Perspectives: History of Philosophy. Ridgeview 1979 lib. bdg. $23.00 text ed. pap. $6.50. Collection of Sellars's essays on important past philosophers and topics.

Philosophical Perspectives: Metaphysics and Epistemology. Ridgeview 1979 lib. bdg. $23.00 text ed. pap. $6.50. Collection of Sellars's essays on philosophy.

Naturalism and Ontology. Ridgeview 1980 lib. bdg. $24.00 text ed. pap. $7.50. A treatise in metaphysics.

Pure Pragmatics and Possible Worlds: The Early Essays of Wilfrid Sellars. Ed. by Jeffrey Sicha, Ridgeview 1980 lib. bdg. $24.00 text ed. pap. $9.50. A collection of Sellars's early essays.

BOOKS ABOUT WILFRID SELLARS

Delaney, C. F., and others. *The Synoptic Vision: Essays on the Philosophy of Wilfrid Sellars.* Notre Dame Univ. Pr. 1977 text ed. $17.95. "This book is intended as a general introduction to the philosophy of Wilfrid Sellars. There are chapters on his 'Theory of Knowledge,' 'Ontology,' 'Philosophy of Science,' 'Philosophy of Mind' and 'Ethical Theory.' In addition to systematizing Sellars' thought in these various ideas, an effort is made to exhibit the overall unity in Sellars' philosophical orientation" (*The Philosopher's Index*).

Evans, Joseph Claude, Jr. *The Metaphysics of Transcendental Subjectivity: Descartes, Kant and W. Sellars.* Benjamins North Am. 1984 $26.00. "The last chapter deals with Sellars' transformation of Kant" (*The Philosopher's Index*).

Pitt, Joseph C. *Pictures, Images and Conceptual Change: An Analysis of Wilfrid Sellars' Philosophy of Science.* [*Synthese Library*] Kluwer Academic 1981 $34.00. "This essay is an analysis of the problems undermining an adequate account of conceptual change as found in the work of W. Sellars, Goodman and Quine" (*The Philosopher's Index*).

SHESTOV, LEV. 1866–1938

Shestov belongs in the stream of the religious existentialists and was deeply interested in the work of NIETZSCHE and KIERKEGAARD; he knew and was close to Berdyaev and in touch with HUSSERL, Heidegger, and BUBER. In his own strong voice, however, deeply reliant on the God not of the conventional churches, but of the Old Testament as he interpreted it, he denounced conventional metaphysics and the domination of a rigidly structured worldview in which man is governed by Necessity. Men, he cried, have fettered themselves with crutches and limits and made themselves puny; we must seek a new God—with God "all things are possible." His most important early "existential" work, an attack on traditional metaphysics, was *The Apotheosis of Groundlessness* (1905, entitled in English translation *All Things Are Possible*), to which D. H. LAWRENCE (see Vol. 1) provided the introduction. The novelist wrote: 'Everything is possible,' this is his really central cry. It is not nihilism. It is only a shaking free of the human psyche from old bonds. The positive central idea is that the human psyche or soul, really believes in itself. . . . No ideal on earth is anything more than an obstruction, in the end, to the creative issue of the spontaneous soul." In a brilliant introduction to *Athens and Jerusalem* (1966), Bernard Martin says, "Shestov suggests. . .that modern man can perhaps reach the God of the Bible only by first passing through the experience of his own nothingness, and by coming to feel, as Nietzsche did, that God is not. . . . 'Sometimes [says Shestov] this is the sign of the end and of death. Sometimes of the beginning and of life. As soon as man feels that God is not, he suddenly comprehends the frightful horror and the wild folly of human temporal existence. . .[and] awakens. . . . Was it not so with Nietzsche, SPINOZA, PASCAL, LUTHER, AUGUSTINE, even with St. Paul?' "

The son of Jewish parents, Shestov studied at Kiev and the University of Moscow. He received the title candidate of laws from the University of Kiev, but was denied the doctor of law title because his dissertation on the Russian working class was judged "revolutionary" by the Committee of Censors in nineteenth-century Moscow. Working for awhile in his father's textile firm, he began writing for avant-garde periodicals in Kiev. In 1898 his first book appeared: *Shakespeare and His Critic Brandes,* in which he attacked the positivism and skeptical rationalism of the famous Danish critic and essayist in the name of a vague moral idealism.

Shestov spent a number of years abroad—in Switzerland or Germany—before World War I. In 1918–19 he taught Greek philosophy at the People's University of Kiev, but, dissatisfied with the Bolshevik regime, he settled in Paris in 1920, where he taught at the Sorbonne and moved in a circle of Russian émigrés, including Berdyaev. He became increasingly interested in religion and the work of the great religious philosophers. Shestov was deeply concerned philosophically with Russian literature—particularly DOSTOEVSKY (see Vol. 2) and CHEKHOV (see Vol. 2)—and wrote many essays on the subject.

BOOKS BY SHESTOV

All Things Are Possible and Penultimate Words and Other Essays. Ohio Univ. Pr. 1977 $16.00. A collection of the most important of Shestov's essays; an excellent introduction to his thought.

Chekhov and Other Essays. 1908. Univ. of Michigan Pr. 1966 o.p. Contents: "Anton Chekhov"; "The Gift of Prophecy [Dostoyevsky]"; "Penultimate Words"; "The Theory of Knowledge."

Potestas Calvium. 1919. Trans. by Bernard Martin, Ohio Univ. Pr. 1978 $15.00. A "striking assault on rationalist metaphysics" (*PW*).

Athens and Jerusalem. Trans. by Bernard Martin, Ohio Univ. Pr. 1966 o.p. Written in 1938, first published in Paris in 1951, this translation includes a lengthy, "brilliant" (*LJ*) introduction by Bernard Martin. "In this long, closely-reasoned examination of the roots and development of the Judaeo-Christian tradition, Shestov makes clear his passionate anti-rationalism, persuasively denying the claims to truth made by speculative philosophy (Athens)" (*LJ*).

Dostoyevsky, Tolstoy and Nietzsche. Trans. by Bernard Martin and Spencer E. Roberts, Ohio Univ. Pr. 1969 $18.00. Literary criticism in the service of religion.

In Job's Balances: On the Sources of Eternal Truths. Trans. by Camilla Coventry and C. A. Macartney, Ohio Univ. Pr. 1975 $20.00. Profoundly mystical.

Speculation and Revelation. Trans. by Bernard Martin, Ohio Univ. Pr. 1982 lib. bdg. $32.95. Singular mystical response to the time-honored controversy between reason and revelation or faith.

BOOK ABOUT SHESTOV

Wernham, James C. *Two Russian Thinkers: An Essay in Berdyaev and Shestov.* Univ. of Toronto Pr. 1968 o.p. Wernham emphasizes the two philosophers' "common bond as existentialist thinkers under a strong influence of Dostoevski and their common concern for religious metaphysics. He shows Shestov as having had the sharper critical faculty" (*LJ*).

STRAWSON, PETER FREDERICK. 1919–

An Oxford philosopher, Strawson has been a prominent member of the circle of "ordinary language philosophers," although his interests have, during the course of his long and productive career, shifted from ordinary language analysis to metaphysics.

Strawson's first book, *Introduction to Logical Theory* (1952), makes the case for ordinary language over formal language by showing that symbolic calculi do not capture the rich complexity of ordinary language. It contains an extensive and sophisticated defense of Aristotelian logic against RUSSELL (see also Vol. 5) and the symbolic logic that is widely held to have replaced Aristotelian logic.

With the appearance of *Individuals* (1959) Strawson presented his descriptive metaphysics; he proposed that the concept of the person be taken as a primitive concept in order to avoid, on the one hand, the incoherence produced by Cartesian dualism of mind and body and, on the other hand, its opposite, the claim that states of consciousness just are and have no owner. As Strawson has expounded his position, it is a form of Aristotelianism, modified however by a Kantian method of approach. His book on KANT in turn retrieves the basic theme of an a priori structure operative in knowledge and experience, but dismisses the transcendental psychology and instead identifies this structure with language.

BOOKS BY STRAWSON

Introduction to Logical Theory. 1952. Methuen 1963 pap. $13.95. "Nowhere before have the problems of interpreting as opposed to doing formal logic been so fully and so seriously treated" (*New Statesman & Nation*).

Individuals: An Essay in Descriptive Metaphysics. 1959. Methuen 1964 pap. $12.95. Masterpiece of descriptive metaphysics in linguistic philosophy.

The Bounds of Sense: An Essay on Kant's Critique of Pure Reason. Methuen 1966 pap. $14.95. "Lucid and well argued, this book is sure to become a classic" (*Choice*).

(ed.). *Philosophical Logic.* Oxford 1967 pap. $8.95. A collection of learned papers on logical theory; well edited from the linguistic point of view.

Logico-Linguistic Papers. Methuen 1974 pap. $14.95. A collection of Strawson's papers on logic and language.

Subject and Predicate in Logic and Grammar. Methuen 1974 pap. $13.95. The book treats traditional concepts of predication and naming. The author also "introduces what he calls 'perspicuous grammar,' which is a set of universal requirements that rules must satisfy to qualify as rules of grammar" (*LJ*).

Freedom and Resentment and Other Essays. Methuen 1976 pap. $12.95. A collection of 12 essays. "Strawson emerges as an academic philosopher—albeit an extremely able one" (L. J. Cohen, *TLS*).

Skepticism and Naturalism: Some Varieties. Columbia Univ. Pr. 1984 $18.50. Woodbridge lectures at Columbia University, where the Oxford philosopher subtly put down skepticism in favor of naturalism.

BOOKS ABOUT STRAWSON

Tiles, J. E. *Things That Happen.* Ed. by Andrew Brennan and William E. Lyons, Humanities 1981 text ed. $25.00; Pergamon 1981 $9.00. "This monograph examines Strawson's claim that a language could be used to talk about material objects without its speakers having the capacity to talk about events, and concludes that Strawson's claim is insupportable" (*The Philosopher's Index*).

Van Straaten, Zak, ed. *Philosophical Subjects: Essays Presented to P. F. Strawson.* Oxford 1980 $39.95. "This anthology [of 12 original essays] reflects Strawson's broad philosophical interests, which range from moral issues and aesthetics to topics in the philosophy of mind and descriptive metaphysics" (*The Philosopher's Index*).

TEILHARD DE CHARDIN, PIERRE. 1881–1955

Pierre Teilhard de Chardin was a Jesuit priest who also was an accomplished paleontologist. As a young man he conducted anthropological research in China, and *Early Man in China*, one of his writings from his period as a scientist, is still available.

Teilhard de Chardin's lively mind moved beyond science to speculative cosmology. He ranks as an interpreter of naturalistic evolution within a broadened framework of spirituality. During his lifetime his writings were disapproved by the authorities in his order and the church; however, their posthumous publication in the wake of Vatican II catapulted Teilhard into the very center of attention by intellectuals and philosophers throughout the world. Although his views seem insupportable to many more cautious minds, they have been taken seriously and have stimulated considerable discussion.

Teilhard's system of philosophy has been ably epitomized by J. E. Bruns in his review of *Phenomenon of Man:* " 'The story of life is no more than a movement of consciousness veiled by morphology.' These words of the author, referring to consciousness as related to organic structure, express the essential theme of his book. . . . Evolution has not run its course. Geogenesis led to biogenesis, 'which turned out in the end to be nothing else than psychogenesis. . . . Psychogenesis has led to man. Now it effaces itself, relieved or absorbed by another and a higher function—the engendering and subsequent development of all the stages of the mind, in one word *noogenesis.*' Noogenesis implies the production of a 'superabundance of mind' and looks forward to the ultimate earth, a 'universe of conscious substance.' Teilhard envisions mankind, through an ever increasing psychosocial unity, concentrating on the transcendent center of this psychic convergence—God—until it reaches the 'Omega point,' the 'fulfillment of the spirit of the earth,' a detachment of the mind from its material matrix and an abandonment of its organoplanetary foothold" (*Catholic World*).

BOOKS BY TEILHARD DE CHARDIN

Early Man in China. AMS Pr. repr. of 1941 ed. 1975 $22.00. Scientific record of the discovery of "Peking man."

Phenomenon of Man. Trans. by Bernard Wall, Harper 1960 pap. $7.95. Philosophical anthropology within a spiritual cosmic framework; the key to Teilhard's thought.

Divine Milieu: An Essay on the Interior Life. Harper 1961 pap. $5.95. Almost mystical rhapsodic description and speculation on the pervasiveness of the divine mind.

Future of Man. 1964. Harper 1969 pap. $6.95. Visionary hypothesis of where evolution leads.

Hymn of the Universe. 1965. Harper 1969 pap. $5.95. Poetic prose to report the spiritual unity of the universe.

Activation of Energy. 1971. Trans. by René Hague, Harcourt 1972 pap. $6.95. Spiritualistic theory of the source of physical energy.

Christianity and Evolution. 1971. Harcourt 1974 pap. $6.95. Synthesis of traditional religion and biological science.

Human Energy. 1971. Harcourt 1972 pap. $3.95. Plumbs the spiritual depths of human effort.

Toward the Future. 1975. Harcourt 1984 pap. $4.95. Hopeful and aspiring essay.

The Heart of the Matter. Trans. by René Hague, Harcourt 1979 $8.95 1980 pap. $5.95. Confession of the primacy of the spiritual in all union and affection.

On Love and Happiness. Harper 1984 $9.45. Lucid moral essay grounded in the principles of a cosmic religion.

BOOKS ABOUT TEILHARD DE CHARDIN

Birx, H. James. *Pierre Teilhard de Chardin's Philosophy of Evolution.* C. C. Thomas 1972 $19.50. Scholarly monograph restricted to a critical interpretation of Teilhard on evolution.

Culliton, Joseph T. *A Processive World View for Pragmatic Christians.* Philos. Lib. 1975 $13.95. Jumps off from Teilhard's thought to propose process theology for Christianity.

Dodson, E. O. *The Phenomenon of Man Revisited: A Biological Viewpoint on Teilhard de Chardin.* Columbia Univ. Pr. 1984 $26.50. Outstanding work of scholarship; the best yet to appear on Teilhard.

Farcy, Robert S. *The Spirituality of Teilhard de Chardin.* Harper 1981 pap. $5.95. Sympathetic introduction to Teilhard's religiosity.

Grau, Joseph A. *Morality and the Human Future in the Thought of Teilhard de Chardin: A Critical Study.* Fairleigh Dickinson Univ. Pr. 1976 $28.50. Narrow scholarly monograph, useful for an understanding of Teilhard's moral philosophy.

Gray, Donald P. *A New Creation Story: The Creative Spirituality of Teilhard de Chardin.* Anima Pubns. 1979 pap. $2.00. Uncritical laudatory essay.

Grim, John, and Mary E. Grim. *Teilhard de Chardin: A Short Biography.* Anima Pubns. 1984 pap. $2.00. Concise, covers the basic facts.

King, Thomas M. *Teilhard's Mysticism of Knowing.* Harper 1981 $14.95. Well-written study, illuminates crucial aspects of Teilhard's thought.

King, Thomas M., and James F. Salmon, eds. *Teilhard and the Unity of Knowledge.* Paulist Pr. 1983 pap. $6.95. Collection of essays by sympathetic scholars.

King, Ursula. *Towards a New Mysticism: Teilhard de Chardin and Eastern Religion.* Harper 1980 pap. $8.95. Appreciative assessment of Teilhard's mysticism, with special reference to Eastern religion.

Klauder, Francis J. *Aspects of the Thought of Teilhard de Chardin.* Chris Mass 1971 $6.95. Perceptive commentary.

Kraft, R. Wayne. *Reason to Hope: A Synthesis of Teilhard de Chardin's Vision and Systems Thinking.* Intersystems 1983 pap. $12.95. Special plea for a dubious synthesis.

Kropf, Richard W. *Teilhard, Scripture, and Revelation: Teilhard de Chardin's Reinterpretation of Pauline Themes.* Fairleigh Dickinson Univ. Pr. 1980 $29.50. Excellent but limited scholarly monograph.

Lukas, Mary, and Ellen Lukas. *Teilhard.* McGraw-Hill 1981 pap. $6.95. Worthy intellectual, spiritual portrait.

Lyons, J. A. *The Cosmic Christ in Origen and Teilhard de Chardin.* Ed. by Maurice Wiles, Oxford 1982 $34.95. Invaluable contribution to the history of Christology.

Neilson, Francis. *Teilhard de Chardin's Vision of the Future.* Revisionist Pr. 1979 lib. bdg. $39.50. Sympathetic, persuasively written work.

Sethna, K. D. *The Spirituality of the Future: A Search Apropos of R. C. Zaehner's Study in Sri Aurobindo and Teilhard de Chardin.* Fairleigh Dickinson Univ. Pr. 1981 $32.50. Scholarly monograph, commenting on a commentator.

Tucker, Mary E. *The Ecological Spirituality of Teilhard.* Anima Pubns. 1985 pap. $2.00. A follower's sympathetic account.

UNESCO Colloquium. *Science and Synthesis: An International Colloquium Organized by UNESCO on the Tenth Anniversary of the Death of Albert Einstein and Teilhard de Chardin.* Trans. by B. M. Crook, Springer-Verlag 1971 $29.00. Record of the proceedings, containing the addresses and comments of leading scholars in the field.

TOYNBEE, ARNOLD JOSEPH. 1889–1975

[SEE VOLUME 3.]

UNAMUNO, MIGUEL DE. 1864–1936

[SEE VOLUME 2.]

VON WRIGHT, GEORG H. 1916–

A Finnish philosopher, Von Wright has had joint appointments at the University of Helsinki and Cambridge University, and Helsinki and Cornell University. Arriving at Cambridge in 1939, he soon came under the spell of Wittgenstein. Nevertheless, he is a most original neo-Wittgensteinian. Famous for his pioneer work in the development of deontic logics, he has investigated in original ways other philosophical topics, such as the epistemological distinction between explanation and understanding and the significance of this distinction for such problems as the nature of causation and the differences between the natural and the social sciences.

BOOKS BY VON WRIGHT

Explanation and Understanding. Ed. by Max Black [*Contemporary Philosophy Ser.*] Cornell Univ. Pr. 1971 $24.95. Original treatise in theory of knowledge, basic to the conception of the division between natural sciences and "social sciences."

Logic and Philosophy. Kluwer Academic 1980 lib. bdg. $25.00. A work of genius.

Wittgenstein. Univ. of Minnesota Pr. 1982 $29.50 pap. $13.95. A memoir of the great philosopher by a devoted student.

Philosophical Papers. Cornell Univ. Pr. 2 vols. 1983 $27.50–$29.50. A collection of Von Wright's previously published papers.

BOOK ABOUT VON WRIGHT

Hahn, Lewis E., ed. *The Philosophy of Georg Henrik von Wright* [*Lib. of Living Philosophers*] Open Court 2 vols. 1986 $64.95–$89.95. Contains original critical essays by prominent scholars, preceded by Von Wright's intellectual autobiography and followed by his reply to his critics. The work concludes with a bibliography of Von Wright's writings.

WEISS, PAUL. 1901–.

Educated at the City College of New York and Harvard University, where he prepared his doctoral dissertation under the supervision of Alfred North Whitehead, Paul Weiss has taught at Bryn Mawr, Yale, and the Catholic

University of America. Founding editor of the *Review of Metaphysics* and founding first president of the Metaphysical Society of America, Weiss has been the leading advocate of speculative philosophy in the English-speaking world since World War II.

His work may be divided into three stages. During the first stage Weiss labored as a logician whose earliest publications were devoted to the nature of systems as logical wholes. During this period he coedited with Charles Hartshorne *The Collected Papers of Charles Sanders Peirce* (1931–58). As he matured, however, he became increasingly interested in metaphysical and ethical questions, as manifest in his books *Reality* (1938), *Nature and Man* (1947), and *Man's Freedom* (1950). The concern with ethical questions caused him to revise radically his early metaphysics. This led to the second stage of his development, capped with the publication of *Modes of Being* (1958). In his modal philosophy Weiss presented and justified dialectically four modes of being: actuality, ideality, existence, and God. Thereafter he explored the concrete manifestations and interplay of these modes in history, art, education, sport, and so forth.

As Weiss progressed in these investigations, he entered the third stage of his development—the postmodal phase in which he revised the modal metaphysics by acknowledging additional principles. His books *Beyond All Appearances* (1974) and *First Considerations* (1977) are landmarks in this final stage. During Weiss's latest period he has further advanced his investigations into the realities and norms for persons and the social order.

Weiss's multivolume *Philosophy in Process*, a remarkable document in which the philosopher reveals how he thinks about the topics and themes as he writes the books on them, shows the intellectual wrestlings of an important thinker at work.

BOOKS BY WEISS

Philosophy in Process. Southern Illinois Univ. Pr. 7 vols. 1966–1978 ea. $25.00; State Univ. of New York Pr. vol. 7, pt. 2 1985 $44.00 pap. $24.50 vols. 8–9 1984–86 $49.50 pap. $24.50

Reality. 1938. [*Arcturus Bks. Paperbacks*] Southern Illinois Univ. Pr. 1967 pap. $8.95. Original metaphysics of the highest quality, influenced by Aristotle and Whitehead.

Nature and Man. 1947. Univ. Pr. of Amer. 1983 text ed. pap. $13.50. Naturalistic theory of man as the basis for an ethics.

Man's Freedom. 1950. [*Arcturus Bks. Paperbacks*] Southern Illinois Univ. Pr. 1967 pap. $8.95. Theory of human freedom in a distinctly novel metaphysical framework.

Modes of Being. Southern Illinois Univ. Pr. 1958 lib. bdg. $19.95 [*Arcturus Bks. Paperbacks*] 1968 pap. $11.95. A dialectical classic of ontology, depicting the modes of actuality, ideality, existence, and God.

Our Public Life. 1959. Southern Illinois Univ. Pr. 1966 $10.95 [*Arcturus Bks. Paperbacks*] pap. $7.95. A concise and original theory of law and of politics.

History: Written and Lived. Southern Illinois Univ. Pr. 1962 $6.95. Philosophy of history as an application of a metaphysics.

Religion and Art. Marquette Univ. Pr. 1963 $7.95. Lecture on the interplay of two major cultural institutions.

God We Seek. Southern Illinois Univ. Pr. 1964 $10.95 [*Arcturus Bks. Paperbacks*] 1973 pap. $7.95. Profound, original work, indispensable to the theologian or the clergy.

World of Art. [*Arcturus Bks. Paperbacks*] Southern Illinois Univ. Pr. 1964 pap. $5.95. Philosophy of art, unfolding the basic categories.

Nine Basic Arts. [*Arcturus Bks. Paperbacks*] Southern Illinois Univ. Pr. 1966 pap. $5.95. Investigation of the individual arts, complementing the *World of Art.*

Making of Men. Southern Illinois Univ. Pr. 1967 $10.95 1969 pap. $7.95. Lucid philosophy of education.

Sport: A Philosophic Inquiry. Southern Illinois Univ. Pr. 1969 $24.95 1971 pap. $12.95. Philosophy of sport; original but readable by anyone.

Beyond All Appearances. Southern Illinois Univ. Pr. 1974 $18.95. Penetrating postmodal metaphysics, marking change in Weiss's ontology.

(and Jonathan Weiss). *Right and Wrong: A Philosophical Dialogue between Father and Son.* [*Arcturus Bks. Paperbacks*] Southern Illinois Univ. Pr. 1974 pap. $5.95. "Its only precedent may be *De Magistro* (*On Teaching*), a dialogue recorded in A.D. 389 between St. Augustine and his brilliant fifteen-year-old illegitimate son, Adeodatus" (*Time*).

Cinematics. Southern Illinois Univ. Pr. 1975 $9.95. Philosophy of the cinema; of universal interest.

First Considerations: An Examination of Philosophical Evidence. Southern Illinois Univ. Pr. 1977 $13.85. Stresses "the transition from appearances and actualities to ultimate conditioning realities—finalities" (Weiss). Contains comments by critics and Weiss's replies.

You, I, and the Others. Southern Illinois Univ. Pr. 1980 $25.95. "Studies the fundamental dimensions and roles of the individual human actuality" (Krettek).

Privacy. Southern Illinois Univ. Pr. 1983 $30.00. Probing investigation of interior humanity.

Toward a Perfected State. State Univ. of New York Pr. 1986 $44.50 pap. $18.95. The work "addresses the metaphysical principles that underlie social and political philosophy" and "traces the interconnections of particular practical issues with speculative topics in ontology and epistemology" (*Ethics*).

BOOK ABOUT WEISS

Krettek, Thomas, ed. *Creativity and Common Sense: Essays in Honor of Paul Weiss.* State Univ. of New York Pr. 1987 $44.50 pap. $14.95. "This collection makes a significant contribution to the development of Weissian scholarship and to the growing appreciation of the significance of his thought for the discussions of contemporary philosophy" (Publisher's note).

WHITEHEAD, ALFRED NORTH. 1861–1947

Whitehead, who began his career as a mathematician, ranks as the foremost philosopher in the twentieth century to construct a speculative system of philosophical cosmology. After his graduation from Cambridge, he lectured there until 1910 on mathematics. Like BERTRAND RUSSELL (see also Vol. 5), his most brilliant pupil, Whitehead viewed philosophy at the start from the standpoint of mathematics, and, with Russell, he wrote *Principia Mathematica* (1910–13). This work established the derivation of mathematics from logical foundations and has transformed the philosophical discipline of logic. From his work on mathematics and its logical foundations Whitehead proceeded to what has been regarded as the second phase of his career. In 1910 he left Cambridge for the University of London, where he lectured until he was appointed professor of applied mathematics at the Imperial College of Science and Technology. During his period in London Whitehead produced works on the epistemological and metaphysical principles of science. The major works of this period are *An Enquiry Concerning the Principles of Natural Knowledge* (1919), *The Concept of Nature* (1920), and *The Principle of Relativity* (1922).

In 1924, at age 63, he retired from his position at the Imperial College and accepted appointment as professor of philosophy at Harvard University where he began his most creative period in speculative philosophy. In *Science and the Modern World* (1925) Whitehead explored the history of the development of science, examining its foundations in categories of philosophical import, and remarked that with the revolutions in biology and physics in the nineteenth and early twentieth centuries a revision of these categories was in order. Whitehead unveiled his proposals for a new list of categories supporting a comprehensive philosophical cosmology in *Process and Reality* (1929), a work hailed as the greatest expression of process philosophy and theology. *Adventures of Ideas* (1933) is an essay in the philosophy of culture; it centers on what Whitehead considered the key ideas that have shaped Western culture.

BOOKS BY WHITEHEAD

(and Bertrand Russell). *Principia Mathematica.* 1910–13. Cambridge 3 vols. 2d ed. 1925–27 $400.00. Classic work demonstrating the logical foundations of mathematics; for the expert only.

Introduction to Mathematics. 1911. Oxford repr. of 1948 ed. rev. ed. 1959 pap. $8.95. For the intelligent reader, who need not be a mathematician.

The Organization of Thought, Educational and Scientific. Greenwood repr. of 1917 ed. 1974 lib. bdg. $22.75. Systematically illuminating work.

An Enquiry Concerning the Principles of Natural Knowledge. 1919. Dover 1982 pap. $5.95. Original investigation into the cognitive grounds of science.

The Concept of Nature. Cambridge repr. of 1920 ed. 1975 pap. $12.95. Brilliant but technical attack against dualism.

Science and the Modern World. 1925. Free Pr. 1967 pap. $9.95; Irvington 1987 text ed. $29.50 pap. $8.95; Philos. Lib. 1984 pap. $7.50. History of science at the highest level of suggestiveness; most widely read of Whitehead's books.

Religion in the Making. 1926. New Amer. Lib. 1960 pap. $5.95. Process philosophy of religion; recommended to theologians and clergy.

Symbolism: Its Meaning and Effect. 1927. Fordham Univ. Pr. 1985 $12.50 pap. $7.50. Whitehead's basic principles of knowledge and meaning, concisely presented.

The Aims of Education. 1928. Free Pr. 1967 pap. $9.95. Theory of education; invaluable for educators.

The Function of Reason. 1929. Beacon Pr. 1958 pap. $6.95. Beautifully written and profound monograph on the speculative and practical uses of reason.

Process and Reality: An Essay in Cosmology. 1929. Free Pr. corr. ed. 1978 $16.95 text ed. pap. $9.95. Greatest and most influential work in English on speculative systematic philosophy in the twentieth century.

Adventures of Ideas. 1933. Free Pr. 1967 text ed. pap. $9.95; Macmillan 1933 $14.95. Breezy philosophy of civilization by elucidation of key ideas.

Nature and Life. Greenwood repr. of 1934 ed. 1980 lib. bdg. $22.50. Brief presentation of the basic categories in Whitehead's system of process metaphysics.

Modes of Thought. 1938. Free Pr. 1968 pap. $9.95. Abstruse but fundamental.

Science and Philosophy. 1947. Philos. Lib. 1984 pap. $7.50. Collection of Whitehead's essays.

Essays in Science and Philosophy. Greenwood repr. of 1947 ed. 1968 lib. bdg. $37.50. Reissue of title above.

BOOKS ABOUT WHITEHEAD

Alfred North Whitehead: A Primary-Secondary Bibliography. Philos. Document. 1977 $23.50. A good place for the researcher to start.

Belaief, Lynn. *Toward a Whiteheadian Ethics.* Univ. Pr. of Amer. 1985 lib. bdg. $26.00 text ed. pap. $12.75. Essayistic and suggestive.

Blyth, John W. *Whitehead's Theory of Knowledge.* Kraus Repr. repr. of 1941 ed. 1973 $18.00. A doctoral dissertation.

Brumbaugh, Robert S. *Whitehead, Process Philosophy, and Education.* State Univ. of New York Pr. 1982 $42.50 pap. $18.95. Monograph on process philosophy of education by a Whiteheadian.

Cappon, Alexander P. *About Wordsworth and Whitehead.* Philos. Lib. 1982 $14.95. Whitehead's chapter on the romantic revolt in *Science and the Modern World* inspires this literary study.

Christian, William A. *An Interpretation of Whitehead's Metaphysics.* Greenwood repr. of 1959 ed. 1977 lib. bdg. $35.00. Based mainly on the later writings, beginning with *Science and the Modern World* (1925), this work discusses theological implications.

Code, Murray. *Order and Organism: Steps toward a Whiteheadian Philosophy of Mathematics and the Natural Sciences.* State Univ. of New York Pr. 1985 $44.50 pap. $17.95. Scholarly monograph.

Eisendrath, Craig R. *Unifying Moment: The Psychological Philosophy of William James and Alfred North Whitehead.* Harvard Univ. Pr. 1971 $22.50. Imaginative endeavor to demonstrate common ground for Whitehead and James.

Fitzgerald, Janet A. *Alfred North Whitehead's Early Philosophy of Space and Time.* Univ. Pr. of Amer. 1979 $12.25. Investigation of concepts in Whitehead's writings before his migration to the United States.

Ford, Lewis S. *The Emergence of Whitehead's Metaphysics, 1925–29.* State Univ. of New York Pr. 1984 $49.50 pap. $19.95. Careful historical reconstruction of Whitehead's preparation for *Process and Reality* by a disciple.

Ford, Lewis S., and George L. Kline, eds. *Explorations in Whitehead's Philosophy.* Fordham Univ. Pr. 1983 $35.00 pap. $20.00. Collection of essays by experts.

Hall, David L. *The Civilization of Experience: A Whiteheadian Theory of Culture.* Fordham Univ. Pr. 1973 $25.00. Brooding speculative essay on any aspect of Whitehead's thought; highly recommended.

Hartshorne, Charles. *Whitehead's Philosophy: Selected Essays, 1935–70.* [*Landmark Ed.*] Univ. of Nebraska Pr. 1972 $19.50. Collection of insightful essays on Whitehead by the leading process theologian.

Hartshorne, Charles, and Creighton Peden. *Whitehead's View of Reality.* Pilgrim Pr. 1981 pap. $6.95. Concise overview.

Hendley, Brian. *Dewey, Russell, Whitehead: Philosophers as Educators.* Southern Illinois Univ. Pr. 1985 text ed. $19.95 pap. $9.95. Informative.

Kuntz, Paul G. *Alfred North Whitehead.* [*Twayne's Eng. Authors Ser.*] G. K. Hall 1984 lib. bdg. $19.95. Excellent intellectual portrait by a distinguished scholar.

Lambert, Jean C. *The Human Action of Forgiving: A Critical Application of the Meta-physics of Alfred North Whitehead*. Univ. Pr. of Amer. 1985 lib. bdg. $26.00 text ed. pap. $14.50. A caring extension of Whitehead's thought.

Lango, John W. *Whitehead's Ontology*. State Univ. of New York Pr. 1972 $34.50. Analysis of Whitehead's basic categories.

Lawrence, Nathaniel. *Whitehead's Philosophical Development*. Greenwood repr. of 1956 ed. 1968 lib. bdg. $22.50. Exceptional scholarly investigation, indispensable to an understanding of Whitehead.

Leclerc, Ivor. *Whitehead's Metaphysics: An Introductory Exposition*. Univ. Pr. of Amer. 1986 text ed. pap. $11.00. Brilliant monograph, recommended for all readers of Whitehead.

Lee, Otis H., ed. *Philosophical Essays for Alfred North Whitehead*. Russell repr. of 1936 ed. 1967 $8.50. A festschrift containing papers illuminating Whitehead's thought.

Lowe, Victor. *Alfred North Whitehead: The Man and His Work, Vol. 1: 1861–1910*. Johns Hopkins Univ. Pr. 1985 $27.50. The first volume of the definitive biography of Whitehead by the leading authority.

————. *Understanding Whitehead*. Johns Hopkins Univ. Pr. 1962 pap. $7.95. The author of this book has been "remarkably successful in helping the more general reader to understand Whitehead's philosophy. . . . The opening chapter entitled 'Whitehead's Way' serves as a general introduction. Successive chapters on the first, second, and third periods of Whitehead's work grow increasingly complex but never incomprehensible" (*LJ*).

Lowe, Victor, and others. *Whitehead and the Modern World: Science, Metaphysics, and Civilization*. [*Essay Index Repr. Ser.*] Ayer repr. of 1950 ed. 1977 $15.00. A collection of original essays.

Lucas, George R. *Two Views of Freedom in Process and Thought*. Scholars Pr. GA 1979 $14.00 pap. $9.95. Specialized commentary.

Mack, Robert D. *Appeal to Immediate Experience*. [*Essay Index Repr. Ser.*] Ayer repr. of 1945 ed. 1976 $14.00. Scholarly monograph on the method of Bradley, Dewey, and Whitehead.

Mason, David K. *Time and Providence: An Essay Based on an Analysis of the Concept of Time in Whitehead and Heidegger*. Univ. Pr. of Amer. 1982 lib. bdg. $37.25 text ed. pap. $19.50. Suggestive doctoral dissertation.

Neilson, Francis. *Alfred North Whitehead*. Revisionist Pr. 1979 lib. bdg. $39.95. Intellectual portrait.

Nobo, Jorge L. *Whitehead's Metaphysics of Extension and Solidarity*. State Univ. of New York Pr. 1986 $49.50 pap. $24.50. Scholarly commentary on difficult topics.

Palter, Robert M. *Whitehead's Philosophy of Science*. Univ. of Chicago Pr. 1960 $16.00. Sometimes technical examination of the central concepts in Whitehead's philosophy of science.

Pols, Edward. *Whitehead's Metaphysics: A Critical Examination of Process and Reality*. Southern Illinois Univ. Pr. 1967 $8.95. Profound commentary by a creative philosopher.

Reese, William L., and Eugene Freeman, eds. *Process and Divinity: The Hartshorne Festschrift*. Open Court 1964 $32.95. Contains essays illuminating Whitehead's philosophy.

Ross, Stephen D. *Perspective in Whitehead's Metaphysics*. State Univ. of New York Pr. 1983 $49.50 pap. $19.50. Buchler's creative disciple has prepared an enlightening interpretation of Whitehead.

Schilpp, Paul A. *The Philosophy of Alfred North Whitehead*. [*Lib. of Living Philoso-*

phers Ser.] Open Court 1971 o.p. This contains the only existing Whitehead autobiography, critical essays, and bibliography of his works.

Sherburne, Donald W., ed. *A Key to Whitehead's "Process and Reality."* Univ. of Chicago Pr. 1981 pap. $10.00. Useful handbook.

Wallack, F. Bradford. *The Epochal Nature of Process in Whitehead's Metaphysics.* State Univ. of New York Pr. 1980 $44.50 pap. $16.95. Scholarly monograph on a crucial point.

Wilmot, Laurence. *Whitehead and God: Prolegomena to Theological Reconstruction.* Humanities Pr. 1979 text ed. $17.25. Casts light on Whitehead's theology.

Wood, Forrest, Jr. *Whiteheadian Thought as a Basis for the Philosophy of Religion.* Univ. Pr. of Amer. 1986 lib. bdg. $19.50 text ed. pap. $8.75. Persuasive essay, recommended to the clergy.

WITTGENSTEIN, LUDWIG JOSEF JOHANN. 1889–1951

Born in Vienna, Wittgenstein was educated at Linz and Berlin. In 1908 he went to England, registering as a research student in engineering at the University of Manchester. There he studied BERTRAND RUSSELL'S (see also Vol. 5) *Principles of Mathematics* by chance, and decided to study with Russell at Cambridge. From 1912 to 1913 he studied under Russell's supervision and began to develop the ideas that crystallized in his *Tractatus*. With the outbreak of World War I he returned home and volunteered in the Austrian Army. During his military service he prepared the book published in 1921 as the *Tractatus*, first translated into English in 1922 by C. K. Ogden. Wittgenstein emerged as a philosopher whose influence spread from Austria to the English-speaking world.

Perhaps the most eminent philosopher during the second half of the twentieth century, Wittgenstein had an early impact on the members of the Vienna Circle, with which he was associated. The logical atomism of the *Tractatus*, with its claims that propositions of logic and mathematics are tautologous and that the cognitive meaning of other sorts of scientific statements is empirical, became the fundamental source of logical positivism, or empiricism. Bertrand Russell adopted it as his position, and A. J. Ayer was to accept and profess it 15 years later.

From the end of World War I until 1926, Wittgenstein was a schoolteacher in Austria. In 1929, his interest in philosophy renewed, and he returned to Cambridge. His lectures aroused the interest of his auditors. Even G. E. Moore came under Wittgenstein's spell. At Cambridge Wittgenstein began a new wave in philosophical analysis distinct from the *Tractatus*, which had inspired the rise of logical positivism. Whereas the earlier Wittgenstein had concentrated on the formal structures of logic and mathematics, the later Wittgenstein attended to the fluidities of ordinary language. His lectures, remarks, conversations, and letters made lasting imprints on the minds of his most brilliant students who have long since initiated the unending process of publishing them. During his lifetime Wittgenstein himself never published another book after the *Tractatus*. However, he was explicit that the work disclosing the methods and topics of his later years be published. This work, *Philosophical Investigations* (Macmillan

1953 o.p.), is esteemed to be his most mature expression of his philosophical method and thought.

BOOKS BY WITTGENSTEIN

Tractatus Logico-Philosophicus. 1921. Trans. by D. F. Pears and B. F. McGuinness, Humanities Pr. 1972 text ed. $17.50 pap. $7.95; trans. by C. K. Ogden, Methuen 1981 pap. $7.95. The most influential work in the development of logical positivism.

Remarks on the Foundations of Mathematics. 1956. Trans. by G. E. M. Anscombe, ed. by G. H. Von Wright and R. Rhees, MIT 1983 text ed. pap. $12.50. Reflections critical of formalism in mathematics marking a breakthrough in the field.

The Blue and Brown Books: Preliminary Studies for the Philosophical Investigations. 1958. Harper 2d ed. 1969 pap. $5.95. Notes of Wittgenstein's lectures, circulated originally among his students, revealing his shift of methods.

Notebooks 1914–1916. Trans. by G. E. M. Anscombe, ed. by G. E. M. Anscombe and G. H. Von Wright, Univ. of Chicago Pr. repr. of 1961 ed. 1980 lib. bdg. $20.00 1984 pap. $8.50. Observations preliminary to the *Tractatus Logico-Philosophicus*.

Lectures and Conversations on Aesthetics, Psychology, and Religious Belief. Ed. by Cyril Barret, Univ. of California Pr. 1967 pap. $3.50. "In 1938 Wittgenstein delivered a short course of lectures on aesthetics to a small group of students at Cambridge. The present volume has been compiled from notes taken down at the time by three of the students. . .supplemented by notes of conversations on Freud. . .and by notes of some lectures on religious belief" (Publisher's note).

Zettel. Trans. by G. E. M. Anscombe, ed. by G. E. M. Anscombe and G. H. Von Wright, Univ. of California Pr. 1967 pap. $8.95. Notes on the ontological foundations of logic.

On Certainty. Harper 1972 pap. $5.95. Lectures on the theory of knowledge.

Philosophical Grammar. Trans. by A. J. Kenny, Univ. of California Pr. 1974 $9.95. Lectures on the logic of ordinary language.

(and Paul Englemann). *Letters from Ludwig Wittgenstein*. Trans. by L. Furtmuller, Horizon Pr. 1974 pap. $2.95. The letters from Wittgenstein are accompanied by Englemann's memoir of him.

Philosophical Remarks. 1975. Ed. by Rhees Rush and others, Univ. of Chicago Pr. 1980 pap. $8.95. Taken from Wittgenstein's lectures and seminars.

Remarks on Colour. Trans. by Linda McAlister and Margarete Schattle, ed. by G. E. M. Anscombe, Univ. of California Pr. 1977 $23.00 pap. $3.45. How questions about colors are questions about the usage of words about color.

Remarks on Frazer's Golden Bough. 1979. Trans. by A. C. Miles and R. Rhees, Humanities 1983 text ed. pap. $7.95. Comments on a masterpiece of cultural anthropology.

Culture and Value. Trans. by Peter Winch, ed. by G. H. Von Wright, Univ. of Chicago Pr. 1980 $20.00 pap. $7.95. Remarks on the language of anthropology.

Remarks on the Philosophy of Psychology. Trans. by C. G. Luckhardt and A. E. Aue, ed. by G. H. Von Wright and others, Univ. of Chicago Pr. 2 vols. 1980 lib. bdg. vol. 1 $40.00 vol. 2 $27.50. Taken from Wittgenstein's lectures; particularly interesting on William James.

Last Writings, Preliminary Studies for Part Two Philosophical Investigations. Trans. by C. G. Luckhardt and A. E. Aue, Univ. of Chicago Pr. 1982 lib. bdg. $28.50. Posthumously published incomplete second part of *The Philosophical Investigations*.

Wittgenstein's Lectures, Cambridge 1930–32: From the Notes of John King and Desmond Lee. Ed. by Desmond Lee [*Phoenix Ser.*] Univ. of Chicago Pr. 1982 pap. $5.50. Noteworthy for marking the shift from the formal language emphasis of the *Tractatus* to the ordinary language analysis of *The Philosophical Investigations.*

Wittgenstein's Lectures, Cambridge 1932–35. Ed. by Margaret Macdonald and Alice Ambrose [*Phoenix Ser.*] Univ. of Chicago Pr. 1982 pap. $6.95. Witness to the emerging development of Wittgenstein's later method of ordinary language analysis.

BOOKS ABOUT WITTGENSTEIN

Anscombe, G. E. M. *Introduction to Wittgenstein's Tractatus.* Univ. of Pennsylvania Pr. 1971 pap. $10.95. Well-done commentary by the only woman allegedly allowed into his seminars by Wittgenstein.

Ayer, A. J. *Wittgenstein.* Univ. of Chicago Pr. 1986 pap. $8.95. Compact intellectual portrait by a leading English philosopher.

Baker, G. P., and P. M. Hacker. *Wittgenstein: Meaning and Understanding—Essays on the Philosophical Investigations.* Univ. of Chicago Pr. 1986 pap. $14.95. Logically subtle commentary.

Bartley, W. W., III. *Wittgenstein.* Open Court 1985 pap. $9.95. This "is a sensitive and exceptionally interesting account of a philosopher even more enigmatic than Sartre. . . . Bartley's emphasis on the moral thrust of the philosophy provides a new perspective, as does the apparently well-documented description of Wittgenstein's experience as a schoolteacher in lower Austria. His treatment is nontechnical, lucid, and concise" (*LJ*).

Black, Max. *A Companion to Wittgenstein's "Tractatus."* Cornell Univ. Pr. 1964 $40.00. Almost a handbook by the distinguished Cornell analytic philosopher.

Block, Irving, ed. *Perspectives on the Philosophy of Wittgenstein.* MIT 1982 text ed. $32.50 pap. $9.95. A collection of specialist essays.

Bloor, David. *Wittgenstein and Social Theory.* Columbia Univ. Pr. 1983 $27.50. Scholarly monograph on the impact of ordinary language analysis on social science.

Bolton, Derek. *An Approach to Wittgenstein's Philosophy.* Humanities 1979 text ed. $28.50. One easy way.

Bouwsma, O. K. *Wittgenstein: Conversations, 1949–1951.* Ed. by J. L. Craft and Ronald E. Hustwit, Hackett 1986 pap. $4.95. A record of private conversations of a philosophical nature by a midwestern disciple.

Cavell, Stanley. *The Claim of Reason: Wittgenstein, Skepticism, Morality, and Tragedy.* Oxford 1979 pap. $9.95. A Harvard philosopher's musings on Wittgenstein and the end of philosophy.

Fann, K. T. *Ludwig Wittgenstein: The Man and His Philosophy.* Humanities rev. ed. 1978 text ed. pap. $9.95. An introduction to the work of Wittgenstein.

Finch, Henry L. *Wittgenstein, the Early Philosophy: An Exposition of the Tractatus.* Humanities 1982 text ed. $17.50. Elementary interpretation.

———. *Wittgenstein, the Later Philosophy: An Exposition of the Philosophical Investigations.* Humanities 1977 text ed. $17.50. Introductory analysis.

Findlay, J. N. *Wittgenstein: A Critique.* Methuen 1985 $29.95. Biting critique by a distinguished British philosopher who did not capitulate.

Fogelin, Robert J. *Wittgenstein.* [*Arguments of the Philosophers Ser.*] Methuen 1986 text ed. pap. $12.95. Sharp analysis of Wittgenstein's logic in support of his methods.

Hacker, P. M. *Insight and Illusion: Wittgenstein on Philosophy and the Metaphysics of Experience.* Oxford 1972 pap. $6.95. "Hacker's analysis is thorough and probably the most sympathetic we have to date. The book is brilliantly written and is an excellent companion guide to and beyond the writings of Wittgenstein" (*LJ*).

Hallett, Garth. *A Companion to Wittgenstein's "Philosophical Investigations."* Cornell Univ. Pr. 1977 $55.00. Thorough commentary by a Roman Catholic priest.

Hardwick, Charles S. *Language Learning in Wittgenstein's Later Philosophy.* Mouton 1971 text ed. pap. $11.60. "A clearly written critical work on the later Wittgenstein's doctrines of language and learning" (*Choice*).

Hartnack, Justus. *Wittgenstein and Modern Philosophy.* Trans. and ed. by Maurice Cranston, Univ. of Notre Dame Pr. 2d ed. 1985 text ed. $11.95 pap. $5.95. The Danish Professor Hartnack "analyzes the key ideas found in the *Tractatus Logico-Philosophicus* and *Philosophical Investigations* and traces Wittgenstein's influence on the schools of logical positivism and analytical philosophy and some contemporary British philosophers" (*LJ*).

Hintikka, Merrill B., and Jaakko Hintikka. *Investigating Wittgenstein.* Basil Blackwell 1986 $39.95. Rewarding studies.

Hunter, J. M. *Understanding Wittgenstein: Studies of Philosophical Investigations.* Basil Blackwell 1986 $39.95; Columbia Univ. Pr. 1985 $35.00. Probing and insightful book.

Kenny, Anthony. *The Legacy of Wittgenstein.* Basil Blackwell 1984 text ed. $24.95 pap. $12.95. Assessment of Wittgenstein's influence on philosophy.

———. *Wittgenstein.* Harvard Univ. Pr. 1974 pap. $5.95. This book "is a masterpiece of both scholarship and criticism. It tracks the development and interplay of the many themes that have given Wittgenstein a central place in contemporary philosophy" (*Choice*).

Kerr, Fergus. *Theology after Wittgenstein.* Basil Blackwell 1986 text ed. $45.00. Assessment of the post-Wittgensteinian status of theology.

Lapointe, François H., comp. *Ludwig Wittgenstein: A Comprehensive Bibliography.* Greenwood 1980 lib. bdg. $45.00. A good place for the serious researcher to begin.

Lazerowitz, Morris. *The Language of Philosophy.* Kluwer Academic 1978 lib. bdg. $31.50 pap. $18.50. Philosophical analysis that owes as much to Freud as to Wittgenstein.

Luckhardt, C. Grant, ed. *Wittgenstein: Sources and Perspectives.* Cornell Univ. Pr. 1978 $35.00. An informative collection.

McDonough, Richard. *The Argument of the "Tractatus": Its Relevance to Contemporary Theories of Logic, Language, Mind, and Philosophical Truth.* State Univ. of New York Pr. 1986 $39.50 pap. $12.95. Good on tracing the implications of Wittgenstein's early thought.

McGinn, Colin. *Wittgenstein on Meaning.* Basil Blackwell 1985 lib. bdg. $29.95. Specialist monograph.

McGuinness, Brian, ed. *Wittgenstein and His Times.* Univ. of Chicago Pr. 1982 lib. bdg. $15.00. Excellent collection illuminating Wittgenstein's background.

Malcolm, Norman. *Nothing Is Hidden: Wittgenstein's Criticism of His Early Thought.* Basil Blackwell 1986 text ed. $34.95. Penetrating subtle interpretation of the philosopher's self-criticism.

Morawetz, Thomas. *Wittgenstein and Knowledge: The Importance of "On Certainty."* Humanities Pr. 1980 text ed. pap. $7.95; Univ. of Massachusetts Pr. 1978 lib. bdg. $10.00. Highly specialized but crucial to an understanding of Wittgenstein's theory of knowledge.

Morick, Harold, ed. *Wittgenstein and the Problem of Other Minds.* Humanities 1981 text ed. pap. $7.95. A collection of essays by experts on Wittgenstein's philosophy of mind.

Mounce, H. O. *Wittgenstein's Tractatus: An Introduction.* Univ. of Chicago Pr. 1981 lib. bdg. $19.00 text ed. pap. $7.95. No better work on Wittgenstein's *Tractatus* in print.

Peterson, Thomas D. *Wittgenstein for Preaching: A Model for Communication.* Univ. Pr. of Amer. 1980 text ed. pap. $11.25. Relevant to the clergy.

Pitkin, Hanna F. *Wittgenstein and Justice: On the Significance of Ludwig Wittgenstein for Social and Political Thought.* Univ. of California Pr. repr. of 1972 ed. 1985 $30.00. "Though both title and subtitle mention Wittgenstein, this book is more broadly based on Wittgensteinianism as developed not only by Wittgenstein but by such philosophers as Austin, Ziff and Cavell—the last being quoted almost as much as the master himself. . . . The book requires some sophistication from its readers. . . . It is recommended as a good, clear survey of the Wittgensteinian position for qualified students" (*Choice*).

Rhees, Rush, ed. *Ludwig Wittgenstein: Personal Recollections.* Rowman 1981 $28.50. Recollections of Wittgenstein by prominent disciples.

Richardson, John T. *The Grammar of Justification: An Interpretation of Wittgenstein's Philosophy of Language.* St. Martin's 1976 $25.00. A major contribution to the understanding of Wittgenstein.

Rubenstein, David. *Marx and Wittgenstein: Social Praxis and Social Explanation.* Methuen 1981 $27.95. Brilliant comparative study; of special interest to Marxists.

Shanker, Stuart G., ed. *Ludwig Wittgenstein: Critical Assessments.* Longwood 4 vols. 1986 $431.00. Massive collection of critical articles on Wittgenstein.

Shanker, Stuart G., and V. A. Shander, eds. *A Wittgenstein Biography.* Vol. 5 in *Ludwig Wittgenstein: Critical Assessments.* Longwood 1986 $52.00. A collection of memoirs of Wittgenstein.

Staten, Henry. *Wittgenstein and Derrida.* Univ. of Nebraska Pr. 1984 $19.95 pap. $7.95. A study of deconstructionist technique in Wittgenstein.

Stenius, Erik. *Wittgenstein's Tractatus: A Critical Exposition of its Main Lines on Thought.* Greenwood repr. of 1964 ed. 1982 lib. bdg. $25.00. A classic commentary.

Vander Verr, Garret L. *Philosophical Skepticism and Ordinary Language Analysis.* Univ. Pr. of Kansas 1978 $29.95. Construes Wittgenstein and his disciples as philosophical skeptics.

Vesey, Godfrey. *Understanding Wittgenstein.* Cornell Univ. Pr. 1976 pap. $10.95. Introductory work by a professor in the British Open University.

Von Wright, G. H. *Wittgenstein.* Univ. of Minnesota Pr. 1982 $29.50 pap. $13.95. Recollections of Wittgenstein by a distinguished philosopher.

Waissmann, Friedrich. *Ludwig Wittgenstein and the Vienna Circle: Conversations Recorded by Friedrich Waissmann.* Trans. by Joachim Schulte and Brian McGuinness, ed. by Brian McGuinness, Barnes & Noble 1979 text ed. $28.50. Noteworthy record that is indispensable to an understanding of the rise of logical positivism.

Westphal, Jonathan. *Colour: Some Philosophical Problems from Wittgenstein.* Basil Blackwell 1987 text ed. $45.00. Carefully wrought analytic commentary.

CHAPTER 7

Ancient Religions and Philosophies

Gregory D. Alles

The real history of [hu]man[kind] is the history of religions.
—F. Max Müller

This device was the silliest in all history, especially because the Greeks have been from very ancient times distinguished from the barbarians by superior sagacity and freedom from foolishness.
—Herodotus

In the sentence quoted immediately above, Herodotus (see Vol. 3) is preparing the reader for a strange story. He is about to tell how Pisistratus became tyrant of Athens for the second time (mid-sixth century b.c.e.). Pisistratus, the story goes, entered into an alliance by marrying the daughter of his former enemy, Megacles. Once allied, these two crafty rogues set to work. They hunted up a beautiful woman six feet tall, dressed her in full armor, and placed her in a chariot with Pisistratus at her side. Then they sent heralds ahead of the chariot to proclaim that Athena herself, the patroness of Athens, was escorting the former tyrant back to her city. The ruse is supposed to have worked. "The rumor spread throughout the countryside that Athena was bringing back her favorite, and those in the city, convinced that the woman really was the goddess, worshiped her and welcomed Pisistratus" (Herodotus 1.60).

Herodotus's tale and his preface to it are in a way analogous to the materials covered in this chapter and the average reader's likely reaction to them. This chapter discusses what may loosely be called "ancient religions and philosophies." It contains three main blocks of material: (1) prehistoric religions and philosophies (from the rise of humanity to the invention of writing); (2) the religions and philosophies of the ancient urban civilizations, both the civilizations of the Mediterranean region and of Middle and South America; and (3) the religions and philosophies of the tribal peoples of Oceania, Australia, Africa, and the Americas.

In part, the title has been adopted simply for editorial convenience. First, it is rarely necessary to distinguish philosophy from religion for any of these peoples. Among them, philosophy as a major, autonomous tradition of thought is found only in ancient Greece and its cultural legacy (see Chapter 2, "Greek and Roman Philosophy," in this volume). Ordinarily, the chapter will simply speak of religion. Furthermore, prehistoric and tribal religions are not usually considered "ancient religions," but these religions are ex-

322

tremely important, and they deserve a place in *The Reader's Adviser*. As a result, the religions in this chapter are ancient only in a rather vague sense: They do not as such play major roles in what Europeans and North Americans call "the modern world."

It is futile to try to identify common traits that distinguish these religions from the kinds of religions discussed in other chapters. What they share the most is perhaps the analogy to Herodotus and his story. Unlike many of the religions of Asia, or Judaism, Christianity, and Islam, these ancient religions do not often convey to the average American reader the metaphysical profundity or moral rigor that evokes our admiration, if at times our confused admiration. Moreover, the social, economic, political, cultural, and psychological circumstances in which these religions flourished are, unlike those of minority religions in the United States, usually too remote for us to have a ready, possibly intuitive grasp of the needs that these beliefs, practices, and institutions satisfied. It is easy to admire Egyptian or Greek or Aztec "advances" in science or politics or literature. The average reader is likely to look on the religions of these peoples—the worship of the sun, heart sacrifice—as so much foolishness and superstition.

This chapter begins with a section on the study of religions. Several books here do not discuss ancient religions at all. Nevertheless, discerning readers can learn from them strategies and techniques that they can use to make (some) sense of the religions that follow. They will discover that these are the same strategies and techniques that the best books on ancient religions—and other religions—employ.

GENERAL BIBLIOGRAPHY

A few books and multivolume collections are invaluable for studying many or all ancient religions, and in some cases all religions. Among them are the following.

Adams, Charles J., ed. *A Reader's Guide to the Great Religions*. Free Pr. 2d ed. 1977 $24.95. Bibliographical essays by leading experts; beginning to become dated, but still extremely useful.

Brandon, S. G. F., ed. *A Dictionary of Comparative Religion*. Scribner 1970 $50.00. Contains some longer, discursive articles on religious traditions and concepts, with brief suggestions for further reading.

A Dictionary of Non-Christian Religions. Westminster 1973 $10.95. For quick references on names; illustrated, but no suggested readings.

Eliade, Mircea. *From Primitives to Zen: A Thematic Sourcebook in the History of Religions*. Harper 1978 $12.00. Snippets from the full range of religions, arranged by topics.

———. *A History of Religious Ideas*. Trans. by Willard Trask and Diane Apostolos Cappadona, Univ. of Chicago Pr. 3 vols. 1979–85 ea. $25.00–$27.50. An articulate and insightful survey by a master; full bibliographies that tend toward older works.

———, ed. *Encyclopedia of Religion*. Macmillan 16 vols. 1986 $1,100.00. Up-to-date articles in English by an international team of authors; articles vary in quality, but some are real gems.

Encyclopaedia Britannica. Encyclopaedia Britannica 32 vols. 1987 $1,049.00. Solid
   articles on all religions.
Hastings, James, ed. *The Encyclopedia of Religion and Ethics*. Fortress Pr. 12 vols.
   1926 $599.95. Older, but many articles are still helpful, if used with care.
Smart, Ninian, and Richard D. Hecht. *Sacred Texts of the World: A Universal Anthology*. Crossroad NY 1984 pap. $16.95. Variety of well-known and lesser-known
   texts—the majority not "ancient"—informed by Ninian Smart's six-dimensional
   notion of religion.

RELIGIONS AND THE STUDY OF RELIGIONS

In many cases, the ways in which different scholars study religions reflect
the history of their disciplines, especially from the Enlightenment to the
present. There is no entirely satisfactory history of these developments, but
the following books are helpful.

De Vries, Jan. *Perspectives in the History of Religions*. Intro. by Kees W. Bolle, Univ.
   of California Pr. 1977 pap. $3.65. A confirmed romantic's history of significant
   movements; screeches to a halt in the mid-twentieth century.
Jordan, Louis Henry. *Comparative Religion: Its Genesis and Growth*. Scholars Pr. GA
   repr. of 1905 ed. 1986 pap. $19.50. Often verbose and vapid; a mine of informa-
   tion on the nineteenth century for the more serious reader.
Sharpe, Eric J. *Comparative Religion: A History*. Open Court 1986 $31.95 1987 pap.
   $14.95. Interesting stories about influential persons, as well as summaries of
   their ideas.

Problems of Definition and Origin

Nonspecialists occasionally ask scholars of religions two basic questions that
they cannot answer: What is religion, and where does—or did—religion come
from?

Many different definitions of religion have been proposed. Some suggest
that scholars should work with a commonsense notion of religion (see Spiro
in the entry for Banton below). Others formulate definitions that reflect
more sophisticated theories about religion and culture (see Tillich, also
Geertz, in the entry for Banton below). Still others advocate describing the
"family resemblances" that most religions more or less share (see Rudolph
and Smart below).

None of these proposals is entirely satisfactory, and for a good reason.
Religion is an English word that grew up in the climate of Judaism, Islam,
and especially Christianity. It is in many ways well suited to express the
kinds of phenomena that are encountered in these traditions, but cultural
phenomena in other parts of the world often do not conform to the Judeo-
Christian-Islamic model. Traits that English-speaking people are accustomed to associate with religion may be entirely lacking elsewhere, and
many languages do not even have a word for religion. As a result, scholars
generally find it more fruitful *not* to define religion. Instead, they use religion as a rough label and try to develop categories that are appropriate to
the purposes and materials they are studying.

Every now and then, the question of the definition of religion gives a little kick. The question of the origin of religion seems to have died. The last half of the nineteenth century was a time of intense fervor about evolution. At that time several theories of the origin of religion were born. The names of some of these theories are still well known, and occasionally they put in an appearance in introductory textbooks, but the theories themselves lost their power to animate scholarly discussions long ago.

"Animism" (formulated by E. B. Tylor) suggested that religion began with the belief that spirits hidden in all sorts of objects were responsible for life and events. "Preanimism" (formulated by R. R. Marett) focused on the emotional encounter with *mana*, a fluid, nonpersonal, powerful but dangerous substance that early humans found they could not manipulate with magic. "Totemism" (formulated by J. F. McLennan) centered on the relations between social groups such as clans and animal species that were thought to be their eponymous ancestors. Sir James Frazer conceived of religion as a response of submission before natural phenomena when attempts at magical control had failed.

One occasionally reads that speculations about the origin of religion ceased when scholars discovered they could not refute a very surprising theory, the theory of "original monotheism" (formulated especially by Wilhelm Schmidt beginning in 1912). What actually happened was that scholarly presuppositions and concerns changed, and the question of the origin of religion gradually went out of fashion. After years of exposure, European and American eyes began to adjust to the unfamiliar light of the rest of the world. Scholars began to write about particular cultures instead of "culture" and particular religions instead of "religion." They also began to search for complex sociological and psychological forces hidden beneath the surface of appearances that were responsible for religious ideas and behavior. At the same time, many who specialized in the study of religion became fascinated with ideas first developed by Friedrich Schleiermacher in the early nineteenth century. They looked on each religion as expressing a unique and incomparable experience of the sacred, to be understood and respected in its own right. All of these concerns directed scholarly attention away from any search for the origin of religion.

Since the 1960s interest has grown in the science of ethology (the study of animal behavior). Scholars have begun to note parallels between patterned animal behavior and human religious rituals (see, for example, Walter Burkert under Greek Religion below). There may be seeds here for a new theory of the origin of religion, but a sustained and vigorous argument has not yet been published.

Baird, Robert D. *Category Formation and the History of Religions*. Mouton 1971 text ed. $20.50. Eventually endorses Tillich's "ultimate concern"; philosophical discussion probably too complex for the average reader.

Banton, Michael, ed. *Anthropological Approaches to the Study of Religion*. Methuen 1968 pap. $13.95. Contains two now classic definitions, Melford Spiro's definition of religion in terms of culturally postulated superhuman beings, and Clifford Geertz's notion of religion as a cultural system.

Rudolph, Kurt. *Historical Fundamentals and the Study of Religions*. Macmillan 1985

$17.95. Argues against a philosophically postulated notion of religion; contains Rudolph's own "descriptive circumscription."

Sharpe, Eric J. *Understanding Religion.* St. Martin's 1984 $19.95. Proposes a fourfold alternative to Smart's six dimensions (see below).

Smart, Ninian. *The Religious Experience of Mankind.* Scribner 3d ed 1984 text ed. $30.00 pap. $17.95. An introductory textbook; toward the beginning gives Smart's now well-known "six dimensions of religion."

Smith, Wilfred C. *The Meaning and End of Religion.* Fwd. by John Hick, Harper 1978 pap. $9.95. Useful discussion of the term *religion* and the problems with it; Smith's solution—"faith" and "cumulative tradition"—has its own drawbacks.

Tillich, Paul. *Systematic Theology.* Univ. of Chicago Pr. 3 vols. in 1 1967 $37.50. A major work in philosophical theology that advances a popular definition—religion as the state of being grasped by an "ultimate concern"—in the opening pages to volume one.

Ways to Study Religions

For a general introduction to the many different ways of studying religions, the following anthologies are helpful.

Capps, Walter H. *Ways of Understanding Religion.* Macmillan 1972 o.p. Illustrates seven different ways of understanding religion (e.g., searching for the origin, describing the structure, analyzing symbols) with short selections from the writings of scholars who have applied a given approach.

Morris, Brian. *Anthropological Studies of Religion: An Introductory Text.* Cambridge Univ. Pr. 1987 $42.50 pap. $12.95. Descriptive introduction to modern theories—mostly sociological, psychological, and anthropological—from G. W. F. Hegel and Karl Marx to Claude Lévi-Strauss and other structuralists.

Waardenburg, Jacques. *Classical Approaches to the Study of Religion: Aims, Methods and Theories of Research.* Mouton 2 pts. 1973–74 text ed. pt. 1 $47.50 pt. 2 $58.50. First part contains small selections from a wide variety of influential scholars of religions, beginning in the mid-nineteenth century; Part 2 is a bibliography.

Whaling, Frank, ed. *Contemporary Approaches to the Study of Religion.* Mouton 2 vols. 1984 vol. 1 $39.95 vol. 2 $29.95. Intended as a companion to Waardenburg (above); a survey of current scholarship.

THEOLOGICAL (CHRISTIAN)

Within a particular religious tradition, there are many possible approaches to other religions. They form a spectrum between two extremes: assimilating one religion to another (because they are thought to be complementary or identical) and polemics (attacking other religions as erroneous and threatening). In the ancient Mediterranean world, the first extreme was by far the more common. The second was the approach that Christians preferred. Christianity made claims that were unusually exclusive: At most its ancient adherents considered non-Christian beliefs and practices to be "preparation for the gospel."

Today, many practicing Christians still engage in polemics. As a result, some denominational publications on non-Christian religions are misleading or simply erroneous. But many thinkers in mainline Protestant denominations and in the Roman Catholic church have adopted more moderate positions. For example, the well-known Catholic theologian Karl Rahner called devout adherents of other religions "anonymous Christians"—Christians who had not heard the name of Christ. In the late nineteenth century and in the twentieth century a movement arose within Christianity that strove to overcome the divisions between the various Christian bodies. This "ecumenical" movement has now spilled over into more open relations with, and a genuine interest in, other religions. The basic method, "interreligious dialogue," assumes many forms.

Cobb, John B., Jr. *Beyond Dialogue: Toward a Mutual Transformation of Christianity and Buddhism.* Fortress Pr. 1982 pap. $8.95. A Christian theologian formulates his faith, as transformed by his encounter with Buddhism, and witnesses to the Christian truth he finds in Buddhism, all under the patronizing gaze of the philosopher Alfred North Whitehead.

Ingram, Paul O., and Frederick J. Streng, eds. *Buddhist-Christian Dialogue: Mutual Renewal and Transformation.* Univ. of Hawaii Pr. 1986 text ed. pap. $10.00. For an introduction to one of the most vibrant and thoughtful interreligious conversations taking place today.

Kraemer, Hendrik. *The Christian Message in a Non-Christian World.* Harper 1938 o.p.; Westminster 1960 o.p. An older, articulate statement of the position, influenced by Karl Barth, that the Gospel of Christianity is qualitatively different from religion, human striving to reach God.

Rahner, Karl. *Concerning Vatican Council II.* Vol. 6 in *Theological Investigations.* Crossroad NY 1973 $24.50. Contains Rahner's essay "Anonymous Christians."

Smart, Ninian. *A Dialogue of Religions.* Greenwood repr. of 1960 ed. 1981 lib. bdg. $22.50. More in the age-old tradition of philosophical dialogue, as in Lessing's *Nathan the Wise,* itself based on an earlier Jewish model.

Smith, Wilfred Cantwell. *Towards a World Theology: Faith and the Comparative History of Religion.* Westminster 1981 $20.00. Attempts to formulate a theological view rooted in the unity that the author perceives in all human religious history.

SOCIAL-SCIENTIFIC

The social sciences represent a different approach to religions that has at times been openly antagonistic. This approach seeks to explain certain religious phenomena, and sometimes all religion, in terms of psychological and/or sociological forces. Those who wrote groundbreaking studies at the beginning of the twentieth century are still highly influential: for the psychology of religion, SIGMUND FREUD (see Vols. 3 and 5), CARL G. JUNG (see Vol. 5), and WILLIAM JAMES (see also Vols. 3 and 5); and for the sociology of religion, KARL MARX (see also Vol. 3), MAX WEBER (see Vol. 3), and EMILE DURKHEIM (see Vol. 3). All of these thinkers belong to what might be called the "grand theoretical tradition" of the social sciences. Much less grand, much more concrete, but no less dispensable are those social scientists who use statistical methods to address specific problems.

PSYCHOLOGICAL

Freud, Sigmund. *The Future of an Illusion.* Ed. by James Strachey, Norton 1975 $10.95 pap. $2.95. Freud's analysis of the conscious and unconscious personality led him eventually to diagnose religion as a neurotic illusion.

————. *Moses and Monotheism.* Trans. by James Strachey, Norton 1962 $3.95. A psychological explanation of the origins of monotheism.

————. *Totem and Taboo.* Trans. by James Strachey, Norton 1962 pap. $3.95; trans. by Abraham A. Brill, Random 1960 pap. $2.95. Religion derives from the guilt brothers feel when, in the primal horde, they kill the father who has been keeping all women for himself; terrible history, more interesting as psychology.

Homans, Peter. *Theology after Freud: An Interpretive Inquiry.* Irvington 1970 $29.50. Uses neo-orthodox Protestant theology and Freud's psychoanalysis to explore the relations of theology and psychology and more generally the problems of secularization.

James, William. *The Varieties of Religious Experience: A Study in Human Nature.* Intro. by John E. Smith, Harvard Univ. Pr. 1985 text ed. $45.00; ed. by Martin Marty, Penguin 1982 pap. $4.95. A leading, early American psychologist examines extreme manifestations of religious experience.

Jung, Carl G. *Mandala Symbolism.* Trans. by R. F. Hull [*Bollingen Ser.*] Princeton Univ. Pr. 1972 pap. $8.95. Explores the themes of the "mandala" symbol in various cultures; profusely illustrated; a brief look at Jung at work.

————. *Psyche and Symbol: A Selection from the Writings of C. G. Jung.* Doubleday 1958 pap. $6.50. A reasonable selection of essays that can serve as an introduction to Jung's thought. Jung sought to identify the shared images or "archetypes" that constitute the collective unconscious.

Kakar, Sudhir. *Shamans, Mystics, and Doctors: A Psychological Inquiry into India and Its Healing Practices.* Beacon Pr. 1983 pap. $10.95; Knopf 1982 $15.00. An insightful application of psychological method beyond the Euro-American sphere.

Van Herik, Judith. *Freud on Femininity and Faith.* Univ. of California Pr. 1982 $32.50. An exploration that finds misogyny and androcentrism underlying Freud's critical thought; focuses on Freud's critique of religion in *Moses and Monotheism* and *Totem and Taboo.*

Sociological

Bellah, Robert. *Beyond Belief: Essays on Religion in a Post-Traditional World.* Harper 1976 text ed. pap. $7.95. Essays on religion in modern society and the problems of modernization in the Western and non-Western world.

Berger, Peter L. *The Sacred Canopy: Elements of a Sociological Theory of Religion.* Doubleday repr. of 1967 ed. 1969 pap. $4.50. Religion in terms of a society's "world-construction" and "world maintenance," with a close look at secularization.

Blasi, Anthony J., and Michael W. Cuneo, eds. *Issues in the Sociology of Religion: A Bibliography.* Garland 1984 $53.00. Probably too technical for most "general" readers.

Durkheim, Emile. *The Elementary Forms of the Religious Life.* Trans. by Joseph W. Swain, Free Pr. 1965 text ed. pap. $14.95. Uses Australian "totemism" to discuss religion as the objectification of cohesive social forces.

Marx, Karl. *On Religion.* [*Classics in Religious Studies*] Scholars Pr. GA repr. of 1964 ed. 1982 $10.50. A useful anthology; for Marx, religion is part of an ideological superstructure built on the ground of an economic infrastructure characterized by class struggle.

Weber, Max. *The Protestant Ethiç and the Spirit of Capitalism.* [*Counterpoint Pap. Ser.*] Allen & Unwin 1985 pap. $8.95; Peter Smith 1984 $15.50; Scribner rev. ed. repr. of 1930 ed. 1977 pap. $8.95. Perhaps the most accessible way to approach Weber's thought on religion; stands Marx on his head to examine the ways in which economic systems are conditioned by religious ethics.

Wilson, Bryan. *Religion in Sociological Perspective.* Oxford 1982 pap. $7.95. By a modern-day Weberian who has been especially interested in sectarianism.

HISTORICAL-INTERPRETIVE

The social-scientific and theological approaches are most often applied to contemporary religions. Those who study ancient religions usually take an approach that can be called "historical-interpretive." Three broad historical-interpretive disciplines can be distinguished on the basis of the "interpretive framework" that each uses to understand religions.

1. History in the narrow sense—critical history—examines documents in order to construct both narratives about past events and accounts of past structures. Occasionally history is informed by insights from psychology, sociology, and other reflective disciplines, but many historians who have written about ancient religions think that simple accuracy is their goal. As a result, their accounts are often informative but unsophisticated. The operative interpretive framework for such historians is generally an "area" defined by the limits of space and time, for example, Republican Rome.

2. Anthropology has tended to explore contemporary tribal peoples through the method of ethnography. It interprets religious phenomena as one component of human culture, its interpretive framework. Anthropologists write accounts of cultural structures and of the forces that impel them to change. During the twentieth century, anthropological studies have become increasingly sophisticated, and anthropologists frequently invoke insights developed in the social sciences.

3. A third discipline, the "history of religions," technically investigates religious structures and events in terms of a different interpretive framework: religion as a global phenomenon. Historians of religions have tended to be suspicious of the social sciences, accusing them of "reducing" (or ignoring) what makes religion distinctive. In recent usage, the term *history of religions* has almost become synonymous with the ideas of a single, influential scholar, MIRCEA ELIADE (see Vol. 2).

The historical-interpretive study of religions has passed through various phases, as have all humanistic studies, for during different periods scholars use different models or "paradigms" to help them study and make sense of religions. After World War I, scholars of religions tended to look on religions as sets of meanings. In the neoromantic view, these meanings were conceived of as expressions of religious experiences. In a more modern vein, they were thought to derive from the place that religious phenomena occupied in language-like codes. In an extreme form, the investigation of these codes became known as "structuralism."

During the late 1960s and early 1970s, structuralism became something of a fad in American and British colleges and universities. But a structuralist study of religions has several disadvantages. First, this approach is entirely static or "synchronic." It identifies codes, but cannot explain why codes change. Second, such a study tends to divorce codes from their context in action. For example, some scholars have written as if the purpose of a ritual were to communicate a code, when in fact the ritual communicated the code only to the scholar who did not know it; for the participants, the ritual did something quite different. Third, such an approach tends to emphasize the normative and elite at the expense of other facets and members of a society. Finally, it ignores other components of religions besides meaning, or else it tries to assimilate all of religion to meaning.

Today, much creative scholarship seems to be taken up with redressing these deficiencies. Some conceive of their activity as filling out the paradigm of meaning. Others see themselves struggling to replace it. Studies written over the past 15 years have tended to focus on topics such as religious change, religions of women and oppressed minorities, religion and power, and the place of the physical body in religion.

Atkinson, Clarissa W., and Margaret B. Miles, eds. *Immaculate and Powerful: The Female in Sacred Image and Social Reality.* Beacon 1985 $21.95 1987 pap. $12.95. Good essays that center primarily, though not exclusively, on the Christian West.

Bynum, Caroline Walker, and others. *Gender and Religion: On the Complexity of Symbols.* Beacon Pr. 1986 $25.00. Ten articles, plus introduction; geographically wide-ranging and mature.

Eliade, Mircea. *Patterns in Comparative Religion.* NAL 1958 pap. $9.95; Peter Smith $16.00. A systematic attempt to identify the various forms according to which the sacred manifests itself.

———. *The Sacred and the Profane: The Nature of Religion.* Trans. by Willard Trask, Harcourt repr. of 1959 ed. 1968 pap. $4.95; Peter Smith 1983 $13.75. Perhaps the most accessible route to this leading scholar's thought: discusses sacred space, sacred time, sacred dimensions of nature and of life.

Evans-Pritchard, E. E. *Theories of Primitive Religion.* Greenwood 1985 $29.75. A historical survey by the former leading British anthropologist.

Geertz, Clifford. *The Interpretation of Cultures.* Basic Bks. 1973 pap. $11.95. Influential essays on interpretive anthropology, including Geertz's notions of "thick description" and "religion as a cultural system."

Haddad, Yvonne Yazbeck, and Ellison Banks Findly, eds. *Women, Religion, and Social Change.* State Univ. of New York Pr. 1985 $49.00 pap. $19.50. Essays on women and social change with a much more global perspective than Atkinson (above).

Lessa, William A., and Evon Z. Vogt. *Reader in Comparative Religion: An Anthropological Approach.* Harper 4th ed. 1979 text ed. pap. $31.50. For years and through successive editions, a very useful anthology of the study of religion primarily by anthropologists.

Lévi-Strauss, Claude. *Structural Anthropology.* Basic Bks. 1963 $11.95. Outlines Lévi-Strauss's structuralist method in several famous essays.

———. *Tristes Tropiques.* Adler's Foreign Bks. rev. ed. 1984 $9.00; Washington Square Pr. 1982 pap. $4.95. A delightful, autobiographical account of ethnological experiences, primarily in South America; with a few hints of its author's theories.

Lincoln, Bruce, ed. *Religion/Rebellion/Revolution: An Interdisciplinary and Cross-Cultural Collection of Essays.* St. Martin's 1985 $27.50. Interesting essays on a wide variety of topics by solid but creative scholars.

Long, Charles H. *Significations: Signs, Symbols, and Images in the Interpretation of Religion.* Fortress Pr. 1986 $12.95. Collected essays on religious meanings informed by both hermeneutical ("interpretive") and critical thought.

Otto, Rudolf. *Idea of the Holy: An Inquiry into the Non-Rational Factor in the Idea of the Divine and Its Relation to the Rational.* Trans. by John W. Harvey, Oxford 2d ed. 1950 pap. $8.95. Classic analysis of the nonrational side of religion as an experience of a *mysterium tremendum et fascinans* (a mystery that evokes both fear and fascination).

Ricoeur, Paul. *Interpretation Theory: Discourse and the Surplus of Meaning.* Texas Christian Univ. Pr. 1976 pap. $8.00. A short but difficult book by the leading contemporary philosopher of interpretation.

Rudolph, Kurt. *Historical Fundamentals and the Study of Religions.* Macmillan 1985 $17.95. A good representative of a strong European current that insists the study of religions should be rooted in history.

Smart, Ninian. *Concept and Empathy: Essays in the Study of Religion.* Ed. by Donald Wiebe, New York Univ. Pr. 1986 $35.00. Collected essays on the philosophy and comparative study of religion by a leading British-American thinker who prefers to label his subject of study "worldviews."

Smith, Jonathan Z. *Imagining Religion: From Babylon to Jonestown.* Univ. of Chicago Pr. 1982 $17.50. Stimulating, well-written essays that question some of the basic assumptions and categories of Eliade's work; an insightful final essay on the Jonestown mass suicide.

Smith, Wilfred Cantwell. *Faith and Belief.* Princeton Univ. Pr. 1979 $33.50. A scholar who prefers to talk about "faith" rather than "religion" examines Buddhist, Hindu, Islamic, and Roman Catholic faith, as well as the English meanings of related terms.

Wach, Joachim. *The Comparative Study of Religions.* [*Lectures on the History of Religions*] Columbia Univ. Pr. 1958 $30.00 pap. $12.00. An older work in the history of religions that discusses religion in terms of experience and three kinds of expression: in thought, in action, and in social grouping.

General Phenomena

In studying religions, it is often helpful to have some ideas about the kinds of phenomena one will encounter. One genre of scholarly literature attempts to identify the general phenomena that make up all religions. This genre is known rather loosely as the "phenomenology of religion." The most frequently cited example is probably *Religion in Essence and Manifestation,* by the Dutch scholar Gerardus van der Leeuw (Princeton Univ. Pr. 1986 $60.00).

But treatments in this and similar broad overviews tend to be rather vague and generic. It is usually more beneficial to examine one particular kind of phenomenon more intensively. Several different phenomena that occupy prominent places in ancient religions have received intense scrutiny and discussion. The bibliographies that follow will introduce the reader to the major lines of inquiry.

MYTH

Average readers are likely to look on myths as so much literary nonsense, pleasant stories with little religious importance and no truth. In the twentieth century, scholars of religions of every disciplinary persuasion have begun to take myths very seriously. If we define myth as a sacred narrative that expresses the most profound religious truth, regardless of historical accuracy or logical consistency, it is possible to call the creation stories in

Genesis and the stories about the life of Jesus myths, regardless of our personal convictions.

Views on and theories about myth are as varied as the different sorts of scholars who study religions. Among the more important have been: studies in the early part of this century that explored the relations between myth and ritual; the work of Mircea Eliade, which emphasizes the cosmogonic myth as a means to return to and recreate the original conditions of the cosmos; the structuralist school of CLAUDE LÉVI-STRAUSS (see Vol. 3) and his successors, which reads myths in terms of embedded codes based on binary oppositions (yes/no; black/white; and so on); and psychological interpretations based either on the work of CARL G. JUNG (see Vol. 5) (myths as expressions of unconscious archetypes) or SIGMUND FREUD (see Vols. 3 and 5) (myths as projections of repressed psychological tensions).

COLLECTIONS

Long, Charles H. *Alpha: The Myths of Creation.* Scholars Pr. GA repr. of 1963 ed. 1983 $13.50. A seminal study of cosmogonic myths.

Sproul, Barbara C. *Primal Myths: Creating the World.* Harper 1979 pap. $9.95. More myths than Long's book, but much less insightful analysis.

STUDIES

Campbell, Joseph. *The Masks of God.* Penguin 4 vols. 1976 pap. ea. $7.95; Viking 1968 $19.95. A major collection by a well-known American thinker; applies Jungian insights in a rather eclectic fashion.

Doty, William G. *Mythography: The Study of Myths and Rituals.* Univ. of Alabama Pr. 1986 $28.50. An extensive discussion of the various approaches to mythology; good for orientation.

Dundes, Alan, ed. *Sacred Narrative: Reading in the Theory of Myth.* Univ. of California Pr. 1984 $42.00 pap. $11.95. A selection of readings from a wide range of scholars of myth, both classical and contemporary.

Eliade, Mircea. *Cosmos and History: The Myth of the Eternal Return.* Ed. by Robin W. Winks [*History and Historiography Ser.*] Garland 1985 lib. bdg. $25.00. Eliade's major study of the cosmogonic myth.

———. *Myth and Reality.* Harper 1963 pap. $5.95. A concise, easy-to-read statement of Eliade's views on myth.

———. *Myths, Dreams and Mysteries: The Encounter between Contemporary Faiths and Archaic Realities.* Harper 1967 pap. $5.95. How myth (in Eliade's sense) infects the modern world.

Jung, Carl G., and Carl Kerenyi. *Essays on a Science of Mythology: The Myths of the Divine Child and the Mysteries of Eleusis.* [*Bollingen Ser.*] Princeton Univ. Pr. rev. ed. 1963 pap. $6.95. Easy access to Jung's ideas on myth, together with application to Greek religion by a prominent follower.

Kramer, Samuel Noah, ed. *Mythologies of the Ancient World.* Doubleday 1961 pap. $6.95. Useful essays on mythology throughout the ancient world.

Lévi-Strauss, Claude. *From Honey to Ashes: An Introduction to a Science of Mythology.* Hippocrene Bks. repr. of 1973 ed. 1980 lib. bdg. $34.50; trans. by Doreen Weightman, Univ. of Chicago Pr. 1973 pap. $13.00. Applies Lévi-Strauss's ideas to South American mythology.

———. *Structural Anthropology.* Basic Bks. 1963 $11.95. Outlines Lévi-Strauss's structuralist method in several famous essays.

SACRIFICE

The practice of sacrifice, the ritual killing of animals, is likely to strike most modern readers as somewhat peculiar. Scholars have proposed several theories to try to understand it.

The two oldest theories are the gift theory and the communion theory. Both were given classical form toward the end of the nineteenth century. The gift theory (expressed by the British anthropologist E. B. Tylor) is encapsulated in an old Latin saying addressed to the god: *do ut des*, "I give so that you will give." The communion theory, as formulated by William Robertson Smith, envisions sacrifice as originating when members of a clan celebrated their common ancestry by killing and eating the animal who represented their ancestor (their "totem"). Two French sociologists, Henri Hubert and Marcel Mauss, formulated a more sophisticated notion of sacrifice as communion. Through the consecration and mediation of the victim, the sacrificer comes into contact with the world of the sacred.

More recent scholars have formulated other theories to account for sacrifice. One theory, working with the interaction of myth and ritual, sees sacrifice as the ritual expression of a mythical view according to which the world or life derived from the division of a primal being (compare with Jensen below). Another theory suggests that sacrifice is a means to redirect social aggression from members of society onto a harmless victim (Girard below). Still another, more psychological theory views sacrifice as a ritual means of dealing with the anxiety that accompanies the act of killing (compare with Burkert below).

None of these theories has achieved universal acclaim, but the last two, being more recent, are probably receiving the most attention.

Bourdillon, M. F. C., and Meyer Fortes, eds. *Sacrifice.* Academic Pr. 1980 $43.00. Essays from a variety of viewpoints; unfortunately, the book lacks unity.

Burkert, Walter. *Homo Necans: The Anthropology of Ancient Greek Sacrificial Ritual and Myth.* Trans. by Peter Bing, Univ. of California Pr. 1983 $33.00 pap. $10.95. A study by a brilliant master that uses primarily Greek material to advance the notion of sacrifice as a reaction to anxiety.

Evans-Pritchard, E. E. *Theories of Primitive Religion.* Greenwood repr. of 1965 ed. 1985 lib. bdg. $29.75; Oxford 1965 pap. $9.95. Useful comments on the study of sacrifice and other topics; for a detailed account of sacrifice among an African people, see this author's *Nuer Religion* (see under Religions of Africa below).

Girard, Rene. *Violence and the Sacred.* Trans. by Patrick Gregory, Johns Hopkins Univ. Pr. 1977 text ed. $27.50 pap. $9.95. The sacrifice as a social mechanism redirecting violence onto a scapegoat—for Girard, the source of the sacred itself.

Hubert, Henri. *Sacrifice: Its Nature and Function.* Trans. by W. D. Halls, Univ. of Chicago Pr. 1964 pap. $11.00. A classic study of Hebraic and Vedic sacrifice; application to tribal peoples questionable.

Jensen, Adolf E. *Myth and Cult among Primitive Peoples.* Univ. of Chicago Pr. 1963 $10.00. Traces the origin of sacrifice to the ritual reenactment of myths among early planters; a difficult but worthwhile book.

RITES OF PASSAGE

Rites of passage are the very common rituals that accompany transitions through significant stages of life, especially birth, puberty, marriage, and death. Since 1909, the common model for understanding these rituals has been the sequence of events proposed by Arnold van Gennep. Van Gennep applied this schema to both rites of passage and rites marking transitions in the course of the year (new year, solstices, equinoxes). According to him, these rites take place in three stages: (1) preliminal rites or rites of separation, (2) liminal rites or rites of transition, and (3) postliminal rites or rites of reintegration ("liminal," from Latin *limen*, "threshold").

Since van Gennep's time, several scholars have expanded on certain facets of his schema. The most influential of these attempts was the work of the anthropologist Victor Turner. Turner utilized the "liminality" found at the center of Arnold van Gennep's analysis to explore all sorts of "antistructural" conditions and situations, such as groups on the fringes of societies.

In recent years, scholars have begun to devote more attention to women's rites of passage, which had been unduly neglected.

Bettelheim, Bruno. *Symbolic Wounds: Puberty Rites and the Envious Male*. Free Pr. 1954 o.p. Well-known psychological study of mutilation, a common facet in rites of passage.

Douglas, Mary. *Purity and Danger: An Analysis of the Concepts of Pollution and Taboo*. Methuen repr. of 1966 ed. 1984 pap. $6.95. Influential structuralist analysis of impurity as that which falls outside society's categories.

Eliade, Mircea. *Birth and Rebirth: Rites and Symbols of Initiation*. Harper 1958 $4.95. Explores religious significance of rites of passage.

Fried, Martha N., and Morton H. Fried. *Transitions: Four Rituals in Eight Cultures*. Norton 1980 $14.95; Penguin 1981 pap. $7.95. Examines birth, puberty, marriage, and death ceremonies in tribal and Asian cultures, and, most interestingly, in socialist societies.

Gennep, Arnold van. *The Rites of Passage*. Trans. by Monika B. Vizedon and Gabrielle L. Caffee, Univ. of Chicago Pr. 1960 $10.00 1961 pap. $6.00. The classic study.

Lincoln, Bruce. *Emerging from the Chrysalis: Studies in Rituals of Women's Initiation*. Harvard Univ. Pr. 1981 text ed. $17.50. Women's initiation in several societies, with an assessment of van Gennep's theory.

Turner, Victor W. *The Ritual Process: Structure and Anti-Structure*. Cornell Univ. Pr. 1977 pap. $8.95; De Gruyter 1969 lib. bdg. $27.95. The most accessible source for Turner's notions of liminality and *communitas* (the social correlate to liminality, where people encounter each other directly rather than in roles defined by status).

SHAMANISM

Several types of religious specialists are found among the religions discussed in this chapter, including priests and sacred kings. One type of specialist that has received intense scholarly scrutiny is the shaman.

The word *shaman* is derived from the Tunguz language in Asia. Defined strictly, shamanism is a phenomenon of Siberia and central Asia, but shamanism in this narrow sense has strong affinities to rituals and beliefs found in other parts of the globe, especially among the tribal peoples of North and South America.

Significant shamanic traits include an ecstatic, trancelike state, at times induced by drugs, that is interpreted as the wandering of the shaman's soul from his or her body; dramatic rituals (and magic tricks) that allow the community to participate in the shaman's wanderings and to receive their benefits; the invocation of spirits, at times in animal form, as the shaman's assistants; and severe initiatory experiences, often associated with physical and mental illness, conceived in terms of death and rebirth.

In Siberia and central Asia, the shaman is primarily a healer. Shamans are also said to meet with the celestial gods, escort the souls of the dead to their new homes, and gain esoteric knowledge from their travels in the spirit world.

Dioszegi, Vilmos, and M. Hoppal, eds. *Shamanism in Siberia*. International Pubns. 1978 $53.00; State Mutual Bk. 1978 $150.00. Much material on Asian shamanism.

Duerr, Hans P. *Dreamtime: Concerning the Boundary between Wilderness and Civilization*. Basil Blackwell 1985 $24.95 1987 pap. $12.95. A wide-ranging and provocative essay, with voluminous notes, on general phenomena such as witchcraft and shamanism.

Eliade, Mircea. *Shamanism: Archaic Techniques of Ecstasy*. Trans. by Willard R. Trask [*Bollingen Ser.*] Princeton Univ. Pr. 1964 $47.50 pap. $11.95. Full discussion of what Eliade calls the "shamanic ideology" over a wide expanse of the globe; full bibliography to date of composition.

Grim, John A. *The Shaman: Patterns of Siberian and Ojibway Healing*. [*Civilization of the Amer. Indian Ser.*] Univ. of Oklahoma Pr. 1983 pap. $19.95. A clear and concise discussion.

Harner, Michael. *The Way of the Shaman: A Guide to Power and Healing*. Bantam 1982 text ed. pap. $4.50. Something of a "how-to" book, with much useful material.

Reichel-Dolmatoff, Gerardo. *The Shaman and the Jaguar: A Study of Narcotic Drugs among the Indians of Colombia*. Temple Univ. Pr. 1975 $29.95. Explores shamans and a common South American shamanic image, the jaguar, among a northwest Amazonian tribe, as well as the shamans' use of hallucinogens.

PREHISTORIC RELIGIONS

The term *prehistoric religions* embraces the immense expanse of religious activity that extends from the rise of humanity over a million years ago to the founding of the first major urban civilizations in the Ancient Near East around 3000 B.C.E. The designation identifies not so much a coherent group of religious beliefs, practices, and institutions as it does the problem researchers face when trying to study these religions. The mute physical remains that alone survive from this period provide little definite information about prehistoric beliefs and institutions or even about the particular rituals of which they are the remnants. In fact, there is no evidence at all for religion throughout most of prehistory. Some date evidence for religious beliefs and practices back as early as 100,000 B.P. (before the present), but such a date is very bold and probably much too early.

In trying to overcome these difficulties, scholars have traveled one of two roads. Some prefer a high road that others find too airy and speculative. The former assume that there is a clear and uniform relationship between cultural patterns, especially means of livelihood, and certain religious beliefs, practices, and institutions. Then they try to elucidate the religions of prehistoric peoples through analogies with similar contemporary or near-contemporary peoples. These scholars usually associate the religion of hunters and gatherers with some sort of "otiose" supreme being and a quasi-divine master of animals. The next major stage is the religion of agriculturalists, with its themes of sexuality and death. Then, at the end of the prehistoric period, come cities with their gods, temples, and perhaps sacred kings.

The alternate approach to prehistoric religions avoids speculation and stays much closer to the actual, physical remains. Those who travel this "low road" provide us with detailed and occasionally interesting descriptions of artifacts and the locations where they were found. Unfortunately, all too often they can tell us very little about the religious significance of these artifacts. Still, many prefer an honest admission of ignorance to bolder and less certain speculations.

This section is arranged under three main headings: Paleolithic Period, Neolithic Religion, and Indo-European Religions. The religion of the prehistoric Indo-Europeans is particularly susceptible to reconstruction on the basis of traditions preserved among later historic peoples.

Bonser, Wilfrid. *A Prehistoric Bibliography*. Ed. by June Troy, Basil Blackwell 1976 $75.00. Nine thousand books and articles, but unfortunately now over a decade old.

Dahlberg, Frances. *Woman the Gatherer*. Yale Univ. Pr. 1981 $22.50. Eight contributors attempt to redress the androcentric orientation of many books on prehistory.

Daniel, Glyn E. *Short History of Archaeology*. [*Ancient People and Places Ser.*] Thames & Hudson 1981 $19.95 1983 pap. $8.95. A beautifully illustrated, readable survey of the development of an important scholarly tool; deals with virtually all areas of archaeology, including prehistoric.

Hawkes, Jacquetta, ed. *Atlas of Ancient Archaeology*. McGraw-Hill 1974 o.p. A very useful tool designed for the general reader. Maps and drawings with commentary, region by region; Europe predominates.

Jensen, Adolf E. *Myth and Cult among Primitive Peoples*. Trans. by Marianna Choldin and Wolfgang Wiessleder, Univ. of Chicago Pr. 1963 $10.00. Heavy reading, tightly theoretical; very significant in critiquing categories often applied to prehistoric religions.

Maringer, Johannes. *The Gods of Prehistoric Man*. Knopf 1960 o.p. Older but useful: period-by-period survey of evidence, with a synthesis on religions of hunters and early farmers.

Renfrew, Colin. *Before Civilization*. Cambridge Univ. Pr. 1979 pap. $9.95. Archaeological methods and their application to significant periods and artifacts in European prehistory.

Roe, Derek. *Prehistory: An Introduction*. Univ. of California Pr. 1972 pap. $6.95. Heavy on the British Isles.

Wenke, Robert J. *Patterns in Prehistory: Mankind's First Three Million Years*. Oxford 2d ed. 1984 $35.00 pap. $16.95. An account from the beginnings to the complex civilizations of the Old and New Worlds; tries to work out a deterministic, evolutionistic picture.

Paleolithic Period

The Paleolithic period (the "Old Stone Age") ended in Europe about 10,000 B.P. It provides several kinds of evidence that are suggestive of religion but by no means definitive. All dates are only approximate.

Burials, which begin in the Middle Paleolithic (50,000 B.P.?), form part of the earliest evidence. Certain features hint at a belief in life after death: careful placement and orientation of the body, the use of red ocher (as a symbol of life?), and the presence of grave goods, which become increasingly numerous toward the end of the Paleolithic period.

Some scholars see evidence of animal sacrifice in deposits of bones near burial sites and of hunting rituals in what would appear to be the careful treatment of bear skulls and longbones (from about 50,000 B.P.). There is no evidence of human sacrifice before the Neolithic period and the rise of agriculture.

Much more suggestive of religion are various forms of representational art. Cave paintings begin about 30,000 B.P. They are found in an area that stretches from the Ural Mountains to the Atlantic, but they are concentrated in southern France and northern Spain. The most frequent subjects are carefully drawn animals, such as reindeer. Some features suggest shamanistic practices: For example, one famous drawing portrays a supine, ithyphallic man with what appears to be a bird-headed staff by his side.

Slightly later (28,000 B.P.?) female figurines begin to appear. Some are stylized carvings of bone, others slightly more realistic, but all emphasize powers of regeneration and nurture: the hips, belly, and breasts. These figurines seem to be connected with some sort of fertility cult, but their religious significance remains obscure.

Breuil, Henri, and Raymond Lantier. *The Men of the Old Stone Age: Palaeolithic and Mesolithic.* Trans. by B. B. Rafter, Greenwood repr. of 1965 ed. 1980 lib. bdg. $32.50. Careful introduction to a wide range of material; good discussion of art; final chapters on funerary customs and religious practices.

LeRoi-Gourhan, André. *The Dawn of European Art: An Introduction to Palaeolithic Cave Painting.* Cambridge Univ. Pr. 1982 $27.95. Beautiful color illustrations and artistic analysis by one of the world's leading authorities.

Soffer, Olga. *The Upper Paleolithic of the Central Russian Plain.* Academic Pr. 1985 $49.95 pap. $24.95. For those who want to see detailed archaeology in action; conclusions are readable.

Ucko, Peter, and Andree Rosenfeld. *Paleolithic Cave Art.* McGraw-Hill 1967 o.p. Indispensable for its critical discussions of different scholars' approaches.

White, Randall. *Dark Caves, Bright Visions: Life in Ice Age Europe.* Norton 1986 $35.00. Beautifully illustrated. From an exhibition of the American Museum of Natural History; see especially its Chapter 4, "World of Ideas and Symbolic Expression."

Wymer, J. J. *The Paleolithic Age.* St. Martin's 1982 $35.00. A detailed, but still readable, discussion of evidence; for those who want more than a general survey of trends.

Neolithic Religion

The Neolithic began with a revolution: the discovery of agriculture in Europe and Southeast Asia about 10,000 B.P. Other significant discoveries gave this period a distinctive character: the domestication of animals such as dogs, sheep, and goats; the development of pottery and metallurgy; and a shift to a sedentary way of life. At the near end of the period, the Neolithic gives way to large-scale urbanization and the invention of writing, that is, to the historic civilizations of the Ancient Near East that came into existence about 5000 B.P.

The shift to agriculture may have resulted in significant religious developments, such as a new concern for the symbolic significance of the earth. Nevertheless, there was no uniform Neolithic religious complex. When the Neolithic began around 10,000 B.P., there were only isolated settlements. During the next three thousand years, Neolithic cultures were active and expanding in the Near East and southeast Europe. After about 7000 B.P. intense Neolithic activity began in other parts of the globe, such as North Africa and southwest Europe.

The best known Neolithic religious complexes are those of the Near East (for example, Jericho and Catal Huyuk) and of southeast Europe (for example, Lepenski Vir). The religion of the Neolithic Near East centered on the sexual aspects of agriculture, chthonic cults, death, and ancestor cults. It had distinctive house shrines that became completely separated from dwellings by the end of this period. The religion of Neolithic southeast Europe appears to have been somewhat different. Sites there show little concern for death and ancestor cults and few indisputable shrines. Instead, the cult seems to have centered on the domestic hearth, which was carefully laid out. Southeast Europe has also provided scholars with a large number of very suggestive Neolithic figurines.

During the last couple decades, nonspecialists have been intensely interested in at least some features of another Neolithic development. About the fifth millennium B.C.E., processes began that led eventually to the construction of impressive megaliths in west and northwest Europe. The best known of these monuments is, of course, Stonehenge, first built about 3800 B.P. during the Late Neolithic in Britain.

Burl, Aubrey. *Rites of the Gods*. Biblio Dist. 1981 text ed. $26.50. British prehistory to 43 C.E., by periods; very readable, with black-and-white photos.

Gimbutas, Marija. *The Goddesses and Gods of Old Europe, 7000 to 3500 B.C.: Myths, Legends, and Cult Images*. Univ. of California Pr. 1982 pap. $14.95. Insightful look at sculptural types and their possible religious significance; too speculative for some.

Krupp, E. C., ed. *In Search of Ancient Astronomies: Stonehenge to Von Daniken, Archaeoastronomy Discovers Our Sophisticated Ancestors*. McGraw-Hill 1979 pap. $6.95. Articles on the "astronomy" of Neolithic Britain, along with other areas and periods: North America, Mesoamerica, and Egypt.

Marshack, Alexander. *The Roots of Civilization: The Cognitive Beginnings of Man's First Art, Symbol, and Notation*. McGraw-Hill 1972 o.p. A reflective, speculative encounter with the evidence.

Michell, John. *Megalithomania: Artists, Antiquarians and Archaeologists at the Old Stone Monuments*. Cornell Univ. Pr. 1982 $22.50. Profusely illustrated account of modern humanity's love affair with the megaliths, by one of the lovers.

Milisauskas, Sarunas. *European Prehistory*. Academic Pr. 1979 $29.50. Economic, sociopolitical, settlement, and ritual organizations of Europe in the Neolithic, Bronze, and Iron ages.

Redman, Charles L. *The Rise of Civilization: From Early Farmers to Urban Society in the Ancient Near East.* W. H. Freeman 1978 o.p. On the rise of agriculture and urbanization.

Trump, D. H. *The Prehistory of the Mediterranean.* Yale Univ. Pr. 1981 $36.00. pap. $8.95. Millennium by millennium, from the development of agriculture to the beginning of the classical world; highly descriptive.

Twohig, Elizabeth See. *The Megalithic Art of Western Europe.* Oxford 1981 $145.00. A good introduction to the megaliths and their context.

Indo-European Religions

Before the onset of modern European colonization, the family of Indo-European languages stretched from the west coast of Europe to Iran, South Asia, and, through central Asia, to a small portion of Asian Pacific coast. The original, prehistoric ancestors of these peoples and the language that they spoke are known as "proto-Indo-European."

It is impossible to determine whether the proto-Indo-Europeans were a single, unified community. Evidence for their existence is linguistic, and it has always been difficult to associate these peoples with any particular archaeological remains. Many regions have been proposed as the original proto-Indo-European homeland. The most widely accepted view today is that advanced by Marija Gimbutas. Gimbutas has identified the proto-Indo-Europeans with a people she calls the Kurgan culture after the local name for the kinds of mounds these people built. The Kurgan people originally lived in the South Russian steppe between the Dneper river and the Ural mountains, north of the Caucasus. They began expanding outward during the first half of the fourth millennium B.C.E.

For other Indo-European religions besides those discussed in this section, see below under Ancient Urban Civilizations: Religions of the Ancient Mediterranean World—Iranian, Hittite and Canaanite, Greek, and Roman religions; and Chapter 8, "Eastern Religion and Philosophy," in this volume.

PROTO-INDO-EUROPEANS

Through comparative lexicography and mythology, it is possible to reconstruct both the society and the religion of the proto-Indo-Europeans with some success. The most important contribution in this century has been made by the French scholar Georges Dumézil.

The proto-Indo-Europeans were seminomadic pastoralists whose most important herds consisted of cattle. According to Dumézil, both their pantheon and their society were stratified in a three-tiered hierarchy that resembled the three upper classes (the three twice-born *varnas*) in traditional Hindu society. Dumézil has described this system of classification as an ideological structure, independent of social and religious organizations but ordering them. The ideology is composed of three functions (hence its common designation, "the tripartite ideology"). The first function is priestly regal; it includes both cosmic rule and social sovereignty, frequently represented by two distinct figures. The second function is military, the prowess of the warrior. The third function is productive; it is often associated with twins, and its concern is with nourishment, health, wealth, and well-being.

A few recent writings have explored aspects of Indo-European religion that stand outside Dumézil's model. Among the most interesting is the notion, first articulated by Bruce Lincoln and Jaan Puhvel, that the Indo-Europeans shared a cosmogony according to which the world came into existence through the division of a primal person, as in the famous Indian *Purusha-sukta* (*Rigveda* 10.90). The model has several possible implications, among them the potential for elucidating the common Indo-European heritage of sacrifice and the frequent myths of the periodic disintegration and reconstitution of the universe.

Benveniste, Emile. *Indo-European Language and Society.* Trans. by Elizabeth Palmer, Univ. of Miami Pr. 1973 $29.50. Indispensable study of Indo-European institutions through comparative philology.

Dumézil, Georges. *The Destiny of the Warrior.* Trans. by Alf Hiltebeitel, Univ. of Chicago Pr. 1971 $15.00. Two specific studies. Unfortunately, Dumézil's magisterial summary, *L'ideologie tripartie des Indo-Europeens* (1958) has not been translated.

Lincoln, Bruce. *Myth, Cosmos, and Society: Indo-European Themes of Creation and Destruction.* Harvard Univ. Pr. 1986 $22.50. Insightful study by an author always worth reading; sensitive to religious issues.

———. *Priests, Warriors and Cattle: A Study in the Ecology of Religions.* [*Hermeneutics Studies in the History of Religions*] Univ. of California Pr. 1981 $40.00. Argues for a common religious structure for Indo-European and East African peoples, resulting from a way of life centered on cattle herding.

Littleton, C. Scott. *The New Comparative Mythology: An Anthropological Assessment of the Theories of Georges Dumézil.* Univ. of California Pr. 1980 $9.95. The best way for an English reader to approach Dumézil's thought; by a disciple.

Oosten, Jarich G. *The War of the Gods: The Social Code in Indo-European Mythology.* [*International Lib. of Anthropology*] Methuen 1985 $32.50. Applies structuralist methods to view Indo-European myths as cognitive structures; for those who want to go beyond description to more sophisticated analysis.

Polome, Edgar C. *Language, Society, and Paleoculture: Essays by Edgar C. Polome.* Ed. by Anwar S. Dil, Stanford Univ. Pr. 1982 $32.50. Essays by a leading thinker on the reconstruction of ancient cultures from languages.

CELTIC RELIGION

The Celts were Indo-European inhabitants of the continent of Europe and the British Isles. Their civilization climaxed during the fourth century B.C.E. Later, they were displaced from much of continental Europe and England by their distant Germanic cousins. Our knowledge of Celtic religions is based on Celtic literature from Ireland, descriptions of Celtic beliefs and practices by Greek and Roman writers (especially JULIUS CAESAR [see Vol. 3], who called them "Gauls"), some sculpture, and a few inscriptions.

The religious ideas and the deities of the Celts remain somewhat obscure. Their great god, known in Ireland as Lug Lamfota (called Mercury by Caesar), was a patron of the arts. Other gods included Taranis/Jupiter, a god of the sky and thunder; Teutates/Mars, perhaps a tutelary god of the tribe; and the horned Cernunnos, some of whose representations recall the Indian god

Shiva Pasupati (and the "horned god" from Indus Valley seals) and who seems to have been a sort of Master of Animals.

The details of Celtic worship are also obscure. There are many references to human sacrifice. Irish sources tell us that the year was divided in half by major festivals on May 1 (Beltine) and November 1 (Samain). These days are, of course, still associated with celebrations: Mayday and Halloween. Before the Roman period, the Celts seem to have worshiped in forest sanctuaries rather than in temples. Their priests were the well-known Druids, who preserved their lore by committing verses to memory, refusing to write it down. The Celts also made use of seers, both men and women, who practiced their art by interpreting the flights of birds and the bodies of slain animals.

Gray, Elizabeth A. *Cath Maige Tuired: The Second Battle of Mag Tuired.* Irish Texts Society 1982 o.p. An important mythological text.

MacCana, Proinsias. *Celtic Mythology.* [*Lib. of the World's Myths and Legends*] Bedrick Bks. 1985 $18.95. A brief, illustrated survey.

Nagy, Joseph Falaky. *The Wisdom of the Outlaw: The Boyhood Deeds of Finn in Gaelic Narrative Tradition.* Univ. of California Pr. 1985 $35.00. Uses modern mythological theory to explore an important Irish cycle; for the dedicated student.

Piggott, Stuart. *The Druids.* Thames & Hudson 1985 $10.95. A readable account of the Celtic priests.

Powell, T. G. E. *The Celts.* 1958. Pref. by Stuart Piggott [*Ancient People and Places Ser.*] Thames & Hudson repr. of 1980 ed. 1983 pap. $10.95. A readable, illustrated overview of the Celts; one of the four chapters is on religion.

Ross, Anne. *The Pagan Celts: The Creators of Europe.* Barnes & Noble 1986 $29.95. A well-written and illustrated overview of Celtic life, including religion and art.

GERMANIC RELIGION

The Germanic peoples inhabited the broad expanse of land and islands between the Black Sea and Greenland just prior to the Christianization of northern Europe. Features of their religion are described by classical and medieval Latin authors, such as TACITUS (see Vol. 3). Their religion is also known from archaeological remains in Scandinavia, and runic inscriptions that begin about the first century C.E. The best source of information, especially about myths, is lengthy Old Norse compositions that originated in Iceland from the twelfth to fourteenth centuries, the Eddas and the scaldic poems.

At the center of the Germanic world was the world tree, an evergreen ash known as Yggdrasil. Beneath it was a well, the well of wisdom. The gods were divided into two major families that at one time had done battle with one another: the Aesir, for the most part gods of battle, and the Vanir, gods of fertility and riches. Among the former were several well-known deities: Odin (god of occult wisdom), Thor (god of order), Balder (in West Norse, the innocent, suffering god), and Loki (a changer of shape who deceived and cheated the gods). The Germans also knew a host of other beings: elves, dwarfs, spirits, and guardians.

The Germans seem to have had no universal beliefs about the afterlife.

Many modern readers will be familiar with the notion of Valhalla, but it does not seem to have been widespread among the Germanic peoples. Another distinctive and familiar notion is that of the *Ragnarok*, a time in the future at which the gods and demons will fight to mutual annihilation, with the result that the world will be destroyed. Some traditions suggest that a new world will arise after this destruction, but they may result from Christian influence.

Many sagas, Eddas, and other texts are conveniently available in English translation from Penguin Classics.

Bauschatz, Paul C. *The Well and the Tree: World and Time in Early Germanic Culture.* Univ. of Massachusetts Pr. 1982 lib. bdg. $25.00. A scholarly exploration of early Germanic cosmology.

Davidson, Hilda R. Ellis. *Gods and Myths of Northern Europe.* Penguin 1965 $4.95. Readable and informative account of Germanic mythology, but occasionally unreliable.

Dumézil, Georges. *Gods of the Ancient Northmen.* Trans. by Einar Haugen, Univ. of California Pr. 1974 $34.00 pap. $8.95. The Germanic gods in comparative perspective (for Dumézil, see under Proto-Indo-Europeans, above).

Turville-Petre, E. O. G. *Myth and Religion of the North.* Greenwood repr. of 1964 ed. 1975 lib. bdg. $49.75. A full and reliable account of Germanic religion.

Ward, Donald. *The Divine Twins: An Indo-European Myth in Germanic Tradition.* Univ. of California Pr. 1968 o.p. Detailed study of an important Indo-European theme; for the serious reader.

ANCIENT URBAN CIVILIZATIONS: RELIGIONS OF THE ANCIENT MEDITERRANEAN WORLD

The word *civilization* does not imply increased mental capabilities or more complex thought. It refers instead to innovations in patterns of settlement and technology. In general, civilizations are characterized by urbanization, technological progress, occupational specialization, social stratification, political organization, and literacy.

The development of civilizations and city life is a complex and debated question. The best case for the role of religion has been made by the geographer Paul Wheatley. According to Wheatley the ceremonial center was the focus around which urbanization first occurred.

Urbanization seems to have arisen independently in several areas that are here called areas of "primary urbanization," among them Egypt, Mesopotamia, Mesoamerica, and the Peruvian highlands. Areas that adopt "civilized" ways of life as the result of diffusion are here called "secondary centers of civilization."

This chapter discusses the ancient urban civilizations of both the Ancient Mediterranean World and the Americas. For the ancient civilizations of India and China, see Chapter 8, "Eastern Religion and Philosophy," in this volume.

Adams, Robert. *Evolution of Urban Society: Early Mesopotamia and Prehispanic Mexico.* De Gruyter 1966 text ed. $22.95. A fascinating account that uses anthropological categories to draw parallels.

Childe, V. Gordon. *New Light on the Most Ancient East.* Norton 4th ed. 1969 pap. $4.95. No longer all that new, but by a leading theorist of the development of civilization; looks at Egypt, Mesopotamia, and the Indus valley.

Fustel de Coulanges, Numa Denis. *The Ancient City: A Study on the Religion, Laws, and Institutions of Greece and Rome.* Johns Hopkins Univ. Pr. 1980 $7.95. A nineteenth-century classic; this edition contains a helpful foreword by two outstanding modern scholars, Arnaldo Momigliano and S. C. Humphreys.

Hammond, Mason. *The City in the Ancient World.* Ed. by Lester Bartson, Harvard Univ. Pr. 1972 $35.00. The city in the ancient Mediterranean from its emergence to the early medieval period; extensive annotated bibliography.

Mumford, Lewis. *The City in History: Its Origins, Its Transformations, and Its Prospects.* Harcourt 1968 pap. $9.95. A classic study.

Rykwert, Joseph. *The Idea of a Town: The Anthropology of Urban Form in Rome, Italy, and the Ancient World.* Princeton Univ. Pr. 1976 $54.00. Attempts to identify the conceptual model underlying the building of Roman towns; sets this model in comparative context.

Wheatley, Paul. *Pivot of the Four Quarters: A Preliminary Inquiry into the Origins and Character of the Ancient Chinese City.* Beresford Bks. 1971 $22.95. A remarkable study of immense comparative breadth; looks well beyond the Chinese city.

Ancient Mediterranean Civilizations

One scholar in particular, Cyrus H. Gordon, has sought to identify the common features of the ancient Mediterranean civilizations, or to be more precise, the civilizations of the Ancient Near East. Gordon's syntheses are fascinating for the general reader, but in the scholarly world he has remained something of a lone wolf. Most scholars find his characterizations both too vague and too general to be genuinely distinctive and too inattentive to differences between various regions and religions. They prefer to limit their investigations to various aspects of particular times and places.

There are, however, a few books and series that are very useful in studying several or all of the religions of the ancient Mediterranean. The general reader should be aware of the following titles.

Cambridge Ancient History. Cambridge Univ. Pr. 12 vols. and 5 vols. of plates ea. $62.50–117.50. Detailed scholarly essays on every aspect of ancient Mediterranean history; third edition is most recent.

Doria, Charles, and Harris Lenowitz. *Origins: Creation Texts from the Ancient Mediterranean.* AMS Pr. 1976 $32.50. A brief introduction, then a wide variety of translated texts, arranged topically by methods of creation (rising, falling, dividing, creation through verbal proclamation).

Finegan, Jack. *Archaeological History of the Ancient Middle East.* Westview Pr. 1979 $42.50. Concentrates on Egypt and Mesopotamia; ignores other peoples; peculiarly deferential to traditions about Israel.

Frankfort, Henri, and William A. Irwin. *The Intellectual Adventure of Ancient Man: An Essay on Speculative Thought in the Ancient Near East.* Univ. of Chicago Pr. repr. of 1946 ed. 1977 pap. $12.95. Brilliant interpretive essays on the mythic worldviews of Egyptians, Mesopotamians, Hebrews, and Greeks.

Gaster, Theodor H. *Thespis: Ritual, Myth, and Drama in the Ancient Near East.* Fwd. by Gilbert Murray, Gordian 2d ed. rev. 1975 $35.00. An impressive, speculative account of seasonal rituals and myths and their literary survivals; not to everyone's taste.

Gordon, Cyrus H. *Before the Bible.* [*Essay Index Repr. Ser.*] Ayer repr. of 1962 ed. 1973 $24.00. A broader view of the ancient Mediterranean than is usually given.

Kramer, Samuel Noah, ed. *Mythologies of the Ancient World.* Doubleday 1961 pap. $6.95. Useful essays on mythology throughout the ancient world.

Ochshorn, Judith. *The Female Experience and the Nature of the Divine.* Indiana Univ. Pr. 1981 o.p. Vulnerable but useful; stresses Israelites as unusually misogynistic.

Oxford Classical Dictionary. Ed. by N. G. Hammond and H. H. Scullard, Oxford Univ. Pr. 2d ed. 1970 $49.95. Shorter articles on subjects pertaining to Greece, Rome, and the Hellenistic-Roman world.

Pritchard, James B., ed. *Ancient Near East in Pictures Relating to the Old Testament.* Princeton Univ. Pr. 2d ed. 1969 $75.00. A useful companion to the texts (below). The *Supplement* is out of print.

———. *Ancient Near Eastern Texts Relating to the Old Testament* (and *The Ancient Near East in Pictures Relating to the Old Testament*). Princeton Univ. Pr. 1969 $147.00. Standard collection of texts in less than fluent translations from all over the ancient Near East.

Areas of Primary Urbanization

EGYPT

The religion of ancient Egypt is remarkable on several accounts. First, it persisted for a very long time relatively undisturbed by foreign influences. Second, at its center stood several distinctive concepts: The world was considered to be an eternal unity; it was presided over by the king (in later times called the pharaoh) as the living embodiment of the god; and the king's primary function was to ensure the continuance of order (*ma'at*) against chaos by performing the daily and seasonal rituals.

Despite the major position of funerary texts and monuments in our knowledge of ancient Egypt, the Egyptians were hardly morbid pessimists. The texts reveal an optimistic attitude toward life, of which death was simply an inevitable part.

The Egyptian gods readily combined the animal and the human, the material and the abstract. For example, the falcon-headed Horus was identified with the reigning king. Each locality had its own system of gods, whose personalities were somewhat fluid.

During the Old Kingdom (dynasties 3–6, roughly 2700–2200 B.C.E.) Egyptian religion was primarily a state religion with little interest in the private concerns of individuals. During this period, the famous pyramids were built as funerary monuments to the king. Later, in less stable times, the Egyptians began to discuss such topics as human responsibility and the possibility of an afterlife for others besides the king. During the New Kingdom (dynasties 18–20, roughly 1600–1100 B.C.E.) the supremacy of the Egyptian empire under the watchful eye of Amon-Re was celebrated in stone with massive, impressive temples at Thebes.

One series of events has long fascinated modern readers. Amenhotep IV (r.c.1360–1344 B.C.E.) changed his name to Akhenaton, moved his capital to Amarna, and imposed what looks to some like a monotheism centered on the noon sun, Aton. Akhenaton's attempt was as much a political as a religious maneuver; in Egypt the two were hardly distinct. Akhenaton's movement died with the pharaoh himself, and later generations obliterated Akhenaton's name from Egypt's monuments.

TEXTS

Lichtheim, Miriam. *Ancient Egyptian Literature: A Book of Readings.* Univ. of California Pr. 3 vols. 1973–80 pap. ea. $9.95. Good translations from a wide variety of texts plus brief commentary.

Simpson, William K., ed. *The Literature of Ancient Egypt: An Anthology of Stories, Instructions, and Poetry.* Trans. by W. K. Simpson, Yale Univ. Pr. 1973 pap. $11.95. Selected translations by leading scholars.

STUDIES

Cerny, Jaroslav. *Ancient Egyptian Religion.* 1952. Greenwood repr. of 1957 ed. 1979 lib. bdg. $50.00. Popular treatment; general but useful.

David, A. Rosalie. *The Ancient Egyptians: Religious Beliefs and Practices.* [*Religious Beliefs and Practices Ser.*] Methuen 1982 $26.00 pap. $10.00. A history of Egyptian religion from the earliest times to the end of the New Kingdom.

———. *A Guide to Religious Ritual at Abydos.* Humanities Pr. 1981 text ed. pap. $40.00. Line drawings of ritual scenes from the temple at Abydos, with informative commentary.

Frankfort, Henri. *Ancient Egyptian Religion: An Interpretation.* Harper 1961 $7.95. Speculative treatment of selected topics; emphasizes themes of unity and static eternality.

———. *Kingship and the Gods: A Study of Ancient Near Eastern Religion as the Integration of Society and Nature.* Pref. by Samuel N. Kramer, Univ. of Chicago Pr. repr. of 1948 ed. 1978 pap. $14.95. Contrasts the divine king of Egypt with human rulers of Mesopotamia; a classic text, but needs some modification.

Hornung, Erik. *Conceptions of God in Ancient Egypt.* Cornell Univ. Pr. 1982 $29.95. Insightful study of the interaction of polytheism and unity in the Egyptian view of god.

Morenz, Siegfried. *Egyptian Religion.* Cornell Univ. Pr. 1973 $39.95. Best recent, general survey.

Redford, Donald B. *Akhenaton: The Heretic King.* Princeton Univ. Pr. 1984 text ed. $42.50 1987 pap. $14.50. A careful study of the pharaoh and his movement by a scholar thoroughly familiar with the evidence.

Romer, John. *Ancient Lives: Daily Life in Egypt of the Pharaohs.* Holt 1984 $18.45. From a television series; centers on daily life in a village of Egyptian artisans.

Sauneron, Serge. *The Priests of Ancient Egypt.* Grove repr. of 1960 ed. 1980 pap. $3.50. Useful information on Egyptian rituals not readily available elsewhere; readable style.

Trigger, B. G., and others. *Ancient Egypt: A Social History.* Cambridge Univ. Pr. 1983 $57.50. pap. $19.95. An informed, easily read overview of Egyptian history, with bibliographical essays for those interested in further reading.

MESOPOTAMIAN RELIGIONS

Unlike ancient Egypt, ancient Mesopotamia (the land between the Tigris and Euphrates rivers) confronts the modern reader with a bewildering array of different peoples. Among them, the most important were the Sumerians, early inhabitants of the south, those who spoke Akkadian, later Semitic invaders. The Semites were eventually divided into two major groups, the Babylonians in the south and the Assyrians in the north. At different times in the second and first millennia B.C.E. the Assyrians and Babylonians managed to conquer and rule the entire region.

Mesopotamian gods generally represented the forces and objects of nature. They dwelt in temples, where their presence was usually symbolized with a sacred image. Temple complexes often included a stepped pyramid or ziggurat, but the precise significance of the ziggurats is disputed.

At the temples, human servants tended to the god's daily needs. They fed, clothed, bathed, and entertained the god; took him or her out for walks; woke the god up and put him or her to bed. On special festal occasions, such as the famous Akitu festival, the god might be carried in procession through the town or from one residence to another. Mesopotamian myths often attribute human existence to the gods' desire for servants so that they themselves would not have to work.

The Mesopotamians developed complex arts of astronomy and divination through dreams and hepatoscopy (the examination of livers of sacrificed animals). Remnants of a well-developed literature survive in cuneiform writing on clay tablets that include fragments of the well-known epic Gilgamesh and the cosmogonic hymn *Enuma Elish*, sung in praise of Marduk, god of Babylon.

TEXTS

Gilgamesh. Trans. by John Gardner and John R. Maier, Knopf 1984 $18.95; Random House 1985 pap. $9.95. An author and a scholar team up to produce a readable, tablet-by-tablet translation of this famous epic.

Heidel, Alexander. *The Babylonian Genesis: The Story of Creation.* Univ. of Chicago Pr. 2d ed. 1963 $6.00. Translations of *Enuma Elish* and other creation texts; with commentary and remarks on parallels with the Hebrew Bible.

Lambert, William G. *Babylonia Wisdom Literature.* Oxford 1960 $55.00. A standard, massive tome on the subject; for those who want to see what scholars work with; introduction, text, and translation.

Wolkstein, Diane, and Samuel Noah Kramer. *Inanna: Queen of Heaven and Earth.* Harper 1983 $16.30 pap. $8.95. Illustrated, poetic retelling of the myths and hymns of Inanna, with commentary; scholars may fret, but very good for the nonspecialist.

STUDIES

Frankfort, Henri. *Kingship and the Gods: A Study of Ancient Near Eastern Religion as the Integration of Society and Nature.* Pref. by Samuel N. Kramer, Univ. of Chicago Pr. repr. of 1948 ed. 1978 pap. $14.95. Contrasts the divine king of Egypt with human rulers of Mesopotamia; a classic text, but needs some modification.

Hooke, S. H. *Babylonian and Assyrian Religion.* Univ. of Oklahoma Pr. 1975 o.p. Older study by a member of the myth-and-ritual school.

Jacobsen, Thorkild. *The Treasures of Darkness: A History of Mesopotamian Religion.* Yale Univ. Pr. 1976 pap. $9.95. The best recent, general survey; outlines successive stages through which Mesopotamian religion passed.

Kramer, Samuel Noah. *From the Poetry of Sumer: Creation, Glorification, Adoration.* Univ. of California Pr. 1979 $27.50. An overview, with excerpts, of Sumerian literature, organized around the three themes of the subtitle.
———. *History Begins at Sumer: Twenty-Seven Firsts in Man's Recorded History.* Univ. of Pennsylvania Pr. 1981 $35.00. A survey of Sumerian life and achievements; the rhetorical device—"first achievements"—is at times strained.
———. *In the World of Sumer: An Autobiography.* Wayne State Univ. Pr. 1986 $37.50. A personal look at the life of the century's leading Sumerologist.
———. *Sumerian Mythology.* Univ. of Pennsylvania Pr. 1972 o.p. An examination of important Sumerian texts, with many lengthy quotes.
Lloyd, Seton. *The Archaeology of Mesopotamia: From the Old Stone Age to the Persian Conquest.* Thames & Hudson rev. ed. 1984 pap. $10.95. Profusely illustrated and lucidly written overview, organized chronologically.
Oppenheim, A. Leo. *Ancient Mesopotamia: Portrait of a Dead Civilization.* Univ. of Chicago Pr. 2d rev. ed. 1977 $25.00 pap. $15.00. With an essay on the dangers of trying to write an overview of Mesopotamian religion.
Pallis, Svend A. *The Babylonian Akitu Festival.* AMS Pr. repr. of 1926 ed. 1982 $42.50. Older scholarly study of perhaps the most famous Babylonian ritual.
Ringgren, Helmer. *Religions of the Ancient Near East.* Trans. by John Sturdy, Westminster 1972 $7.50. Survey of Sumerian, Babylonian-Assyrian, and Canaanite religions, with an eye to Old Testament parallels.

Secondary Centers of Civilization

IRANIAN RELIGIONS

The religious traditions of Iran prior to the advent of Islam in the seventh century C.E. have been extremely influential in the history of the world's religions. Unfortunately, our literary sources are fragmentary, not infrequently inconsistent, and at times written in a language that is tremendously difficult to construe.

In origin, the Iranians are Indo-European peoples with close affinities to the Aryans in India. From hints in later writings and from comparative evidence, it seems that these people worshiped a multitude of gods, divided into ashuras and daevas (cp. Sanskrit *asura* and *deva*), through libations and animal sacrifices administered by a class of priests. Followers of Georges Dumézil (see above under Proto-Indo-Europeans) have detected his tripartite ideology in the old Iranian pantheon: the first function represented by Mithra and Ahura Mazda (cp. Sanskrit Mitra and, perhaps, Varuna), the second by Verethraghna (cp. Sanskrit Vritrahan, an epithet of Indra), the third by Anahita, Nanhaithya, and Atar.

The major event in Iranian religions was the reform of Zarathustra, who lived in the eastern part of the region sometime during the first half of the first millennium B.C.E. Zarathustra rejected the sacrifice of animals and formulated an ethical monotheism focused on Ahura Mazda, the "wise lord." The choice between good and evil was reflected in two opposed spirits, twin sons of Ahura Mazda: Spenta Mainyu and Aura Mainyu. Zarathustra's teachings are difficult to locate geographically during the early period. For example, the Achaemenids, the Persian rulers conquered by Alexander the Great, may or may not have been Zoroastrian. The religion of

Zarathustra's followers—Zoroastrianism—is characterized by several distinctive traits: fire rather than animal sacrifice, a dualistic struggle between good and evil in which human beings participate, an apocalyptic vision in which god intervenes at the end of history to vindicate the good, the belief that upon death human beings must successfully negotiate the "bridge of the requiter," and the exposure of corpses to be stripped of their flesh by vultures and other animals, a practice taken from the Magi (pre-Zoroastrian and then Zoroastrian priests of the Medes in western Iran). The Zoroastrian scriptures, the Avesta, contain poems (*Gathas*) attributed to Zarathustra.

The influence of Iranian religions is difficult to gauge. Significant features of Judaism, Christianity, and Shi'ite Islam seem to derive from Iranian influence. In addition, Iran contributed significant movements to the Hellenistic and Roman worlds: Mithraism (a mystery religion) and Manichaeism (a gnostic religion of salvation). Zoroastrianism still persists today, most notably among the Parsis in India.

TEXTS

Boyce, Mary. *Textual Sources for the Study of Zoroastrianism*. Barnes & Noble 1984 $23.50. Texts from a variety of periods and sources.

Henning, M., trans. *Avesta: The Hymns of Zarathustra*. Hyperion 1985 $21.00. Readable translations of the *Gathas* attributed to Zarathustra.

Malandra, William W. *An Introduction to Ancient Iranian Religions: Readings from the Avesta and Achaemenid Inscriptions*. Univ. of Minnesota Pr. 1983 $29.50. A wide range of readings, organized by topic, with an introduction.

STUDIES

Boyce, Mary. *A History of Zoroastrianism*. Brill 1982 o.p. The now-standard English-language history of the movement, with material on pre-Zoroastrian background.

——. *Zoroastrians: Their Religious Beliefs and Practices*. Methuen 1985 $9.95. A popular account of medieval and modern Zoroastrianism.

The Cambridge History of Iran. Cambridge Univ. Pr. 3 vols. 1983 vol. 1 $87.50 vol. 2 $100.00 vol. 3 $162.50. Several solid scholarly articles on Zoroastrianism and related subjects.

Duchesne-Guillemin, Jacques. *The Western Response to Zoroaster*. Greenwood 1973 $27.50. A critical survey of much of Western Zoroastrian scholarship by a leading figure in the field.

Hinnells, John R. *Persian Mythology*. [*Lib. of the World's Myths and Legends*] Bedrick Bks. 1985 $18.95. A useful presentation of both pre-Zoroastrian and Zoroastrian mythology, tastefully illustrated with black-and-white and some color photographs.

——. *Zoroastrianism and the Parsis*. State Mutual Bk. 1985 $13.00. A popular, informative account of the Parsis.

HITTITE AND CANAANITE RELIGIONS

The best-known religion of ancient Asia Minor (Turkey) is that of the Hittites. The Hittites were Indo-European peoples who settled in the center of the region and ruled from about 1700 to 1200 B.C.E. Their archives have been discovered at Bogazkoy (ancient Hattusa).

Literary remains are too fragmentary to provide any full information on the myths of these people. Their gods, who were treated as monarchs or masters, lived in temples, from which they occasionally departed if they were displeased. The causes of divine displeasure were discerned through divination. Archaeologists have uncovered prayers by Hittite kings that confess faults to the gods and seek to make expiation. Among the Hittite gods were Tarhun, a weather god associated with a sacred bull, and his wife, the sun goddess Arinnitti. The Hittite goddess Kubaba appears to have become the Hellenistic Cybele, but the precise manner in which this transformation took place is not known.

Of ancient Syria and Palestine, the best-known religion (apart from the religion of ancient Israel) is the religion of the Canaanites. The Canaanites were Semitic-speaking, allegedly pre-Israelite inhabitants of Palestine, with close cultural affinities to ancient Syrian peoples. They are known from the Hebrew Bible and from texts discovered at the site of ancient Ugarit (fl. c. 1450–1200 B.C.E.; north coast of Syria). Excavations at Ebla (fl. especially c.2600–2250; northwest Syria) during the last two decades have also provided us with texts, but the interpretation of these texts is hotly disputed.

The Canaanites worshiped a variety of deities, among them El, king and creator; Dagon, an obscure god associated with fertility; Baal ("Lord") Hadad, a storm god who figures in myths of death and resurrection; Asherah, the consort of El; Anath, the consort of Baal who resembles the Indian goddess Kali; and Astarte, goddess of love and war. Canaanite myths from Ugarit show strong affinities to the narratives of the Hebrew Bible. Canaanite sacrificial rituals are little known, but seem to have resembled those of ancient Israel. Similarly, it is presumed that the Canaanites had three agricultural festivals similar to the festivals to which the later Israelites gave a historical interpretation: Passover, Pentecost, and Booths.

Many scholars approach Canaanite religions from the perspective of later Judaism and Christianity. Even with the best of intentions, they often reflect the much too exaggerated distinction between Canaanites and Israelites that was propounded by the Hebrew Bible after the fact and for ideological reasons. *Caveat lector.*

HITTITES—STUDIES

Alexander, Robert L. *The Sculpture and Sculptors of Yazilikava.* Univ. of Delaware Pr. 1986 $29.50. An architectural historian, whose primary interest is America, examines a major, late, Hittite outdoor sanctuary (fourteenth century—twelfth century B.C.E.).

Gurney, O. R. *Some Aspects of Hittite Religion.* Longwood 1976 $10.25. One of the very few book-length studies of Hittite religion written in English; discusses pantheon, cult, magical formulae.

Macqueen, J. G. *The Hittites and Their Contemporaries in Asia Minor.* Thames & Hudson rev. ed. 1986 $22.50. Illustrated and readable account of several aspects of Hittite life, including religion.

CANAANITES—TEXTS

Cassuto, Umberto. *The Goddess Anath: Canaanite Epics of the Patriarchal Age.* Eisenbrauns repr. of 1951 ed. 1971 $30.00. The "sub-subtitle" is *Texts, Hebrew Transla-*

tion, Commentary, and Introduction; primarily for scholars; perhaps useful for the serious reader undeterred by the trappings of scholarship.

Coogan, Michael D., ed. and trans. *Stories from Ancient Canaan.* Westminster 1978 pap. $7.95. Translations of a variety of Ugaritic texts, with introductions; intended for the general reader; a valuable tool.

Driver, G. R. *Canaanite Myths and Legends.* Rev. by J. C. L. Gibson, Allenson 1950 o.p. Introduction, texts, and translations; more imposing than Coogan, not so imposing as Cassuto; indispensable for the serious reader.

CANAANITES—STUDIES

Albright, William F. *Yahweh and the Gods of Canaan: An Historical Analysis of Two Contrasting Faiths.* Eisenbrauns repr. of 1968 ed. 1976 $12.00. See especially its Chapter 3, "Canaanite Religion in the Bronze Age."

Gerstenblith, Patty. *The Levant at the Beginning of the Middle Bronze Age.* Eisenbrauns 1983 $15.00. For archaeological data.

Kapelrud, Arvid S. *The Ras Shamra Discoveries and the Old Testament.* Trans. by G. W. Anderson, Univ. of Oklahoma Pr. 1963 o.p. On the Ugaritic texts and their religion (deities and cult).

Pettinato, Giovanni. *The Archives of Ebla: An Empire Inscribed in Clay.* Doubleday 1981 $17.95. By the epigrapher of the expedition; reconstructions, readings, and conclusions are disputed, but no better book is available on the Ebla texts.

Ringgren, Helmer. *Religions of the Ancient Near East.* Trans. by John Sturdy, Westminster 1972 $7.50. Survey of Sumerian, Babylonian-Assyrian, and Canaanite religions, with an eye to Old Testament parallels.

Young, Gordon Davis, ed. *Ugarit in Retrospect: Fifty Years of Ugarit and Ugaritic.* Eisenbrauns 1981 text ed. $15.00. Collected articles, mostly in English and mostly technical.

GREEK RELIGION

During the second millennium B.C.E. two different cultural traditions inhabited mainland Greece and the Aegean. The Cretan-based Minoans dominated during the first half of the millennium. They are well known for frescoes depicting a sport of bull-jumping and for a great female deity, depicted with bare breasts, flounced skirt, and snakes in her hands. The mainland-based Mycenaeans dominated during the second half of the millennium. They were Greek-speaking people whose tablets, in a script known as Linear B, have revealed the names of many later Greek gods: the supreme male god Zeus, Hera, Potnia (Athena), and several others, including Dionysus.

"Classical Greece" (more accurately, archaic and classical Greece) refers to the civilization associated with Greek-speaking city-states (*poleis*) and peoples or regions (*ethnē*) in the eastern and central Mediterranean prior to the conquests of Philip II and his son Alexander "the Great" of Macedon (mid-fourth century B.C.E.). The religious patterns of classical Greece were established in the eighth and early seventh centuries B.C.E., when the polis and Greek literacy developed.

Normative religious structures included activities on three levels: (1) cults of the individual household; (2) the festivals of the polis; and (3) celebrations at pan-Hellenic sanctuaries such as Delphi, Dodona, and Delos.

The activities of poets such as Homer and Hesiod systematized the Greek pantheon and myths to some extent, but each polis had its own deities, myths, and festivals. Those of Athens are the best known.

In addition, the Greeks knew several religious practices that stood at more or less distance from the normative observances. Mysteries were secret, initiatory rituals connected with agriculture rather than social structures. The worship of Dionysus celebrated the sacred as destructive of normal order, often in images of bands (*thiasoi*) of raging women (*maenads*) ripping apart animals and eating raw flesh (*omophagia*). Orphism, a nebulous movement, stood at the opposite extreme from Dionysiac movements. It promised a blessed destiny for the soul after death through a life of purification and vegetarianism.

At times the polis appropriated the first two types of observance for itself. The best examples are the mysteries of Eleusis and the festivals of Dionysus at Athens. Orphism remained the preserve of itinerant, charismatic ascetics.

TEXTS

Most Greek texts are conveniently available, with facing-page English translation, in the Loeb Classical Library, Harvard University Press, at $13.95 per volume.

Rice, David G., and John E. Stambaugh, eds. *Sources for the Study of Greek Religion.* Scholars Pr. GA 1979 $8.75. Topically arranged selections, with brief commentary.

STUDIES

Boardman, John, and David Finn. *The Parthenon and Its Sculptures.* Univ. of Texas Pr. 1985 $35.00. A highly readable and visually pleasing treatment of this most famous of Greek temples by a leading authority.

Burkert, Walter. *Greek Religion.* Trans. by John Raffan, Harvard Univ. Pr. 1985 text ed. $30.00 1987 pap. $9.95. Best single volume currently available.

———. *Homo Necans: The Anthropology of Ancient Greek Sacrificial Ritual and Myth.* Trans. by Peter Bing, Univ. of California Pr. 1983 $27.50. Emphasizes continuity from early hunting traditions and the anxiety of killing.

Chadwick, J. *The Mycenaean World.* Cambridge Univ. Pr. 1976 $52.50 pap. $13.95. A readable, well-illustrated account of the Mycenaeans on the basis of the Linear B tablets, by one of the scholars who deciphered them; a chapter on religion.

Detienne, Marcel. *The Creation of Mythology.* Univ. of Chicago Pr. 1986 $25.00. An imaginative look at Greek myths through the eyes of a creative and alluring French writer.

Dodds, E. R. *The Greeks and the Irrational.* Univ. of California Pr. 1951 pap. $8.95. A classical study of Greek psychology.

Fontenrose, Joseph. *The Delphic Oracle: Its Responses and Operations, with a Catalog of Responses.* Univ. of California Pr. 1978 pap. $10.95. A full catalog of responses; debunks ancient and modern rumors.

Garland, Robert. *The Greek Way of Death.* Cornell Univ. Pr. 1985 text ed. $24.50. A brief but informative study of the average Greek's encounter with death.

Guthrie, W. K. C. *The Greeks and Their Gods.* Beacon Pr. 1955 $8.95. Somewhat dated, but good on the distinction between Olympian and chthonic ritual (rituals devoted to spirits of the earth and underworld).

Harrison, Jane E. *Prolegomena to the Study of Greek Religion.* [*Ancient Religion and Mythology Ser.*] Ayer repr. of 1922 ed. 1976 $57.50; Humanities Pr. 1981 o.p. A classic; uses outdated anthropological theories, but readable, enjoyable, and informative.

Kerenyi, Karoly. *The Religion of the Greeks and Romans*. Greenwood repr. of 1962 ed. 1973 lib. bdg. $24.75. By a scholar much indebted to Jung.

Linforth, Ivan M. *The Arts of Orpheus*. Ayer repr. of 1941 ed. 1977 $24.50. Hypercritical; refreshing for an occasional shot of academic sobriety.

Mylonas, George E. *Eleusis and the Eleusinian Mysteries*. Princeton Univ. Pr. 1961 o.p. Careful discussion of Eleusinian history on the basis of archaeology; weaker on ritual.

Nilsson, Martin P. *Greek Folk Religion*. Intro. by A. D. Nock, Univ. of Pennsylvania Pr. 1972 pap. $10.95. An often neglected topic; for years Nilsson was "the" expert; his many books are still useful.

Parke, H. W. *Festivals of the Athenians*. [*Aspects of Greek and Roman Life Ser.*] Cornell Univ. Pr. 1977 $26.50 1986 pap. $8.95. A reliable, month-by-month survey; little interpretation.

Pomeroy, Sarah B. *Goddesses, Whores, Wives and Slaves: Women in Classical Antiquity*. [*Studies in the Life of Women*] Schocken 1976 pap. $7.95. The first book to read on women in the ancient world.

Vernant, Jean Pierre. *The Origins of Greek Thought*. Cornell Univ. Pr. 1984 pap. $7.95. A small book on the shift from Mycenaean kingship to polis organizations by a major contemporary scholar of Greece.

Vidal-Naquet, Pierre. *The Black Hunter: Forms of Thought and Forms of Society in the Greek World*. Trans. by Andrew Szegedy Maszak, Johns Hopkins Univ. Pr. 1986 text ed. $28.50. Assorted essays, challenging but stimulating, by a leading French scholar.

ROMAN RELIGION

Rome is said to have been founded April 21, 753 B.C.E. as a Latin settlement on the Palatine Hill. It was governed by a king until 509, when a republic was established. The power of the Roman Republic gradually expanded to encompass much of the Mediterranean world, but republican government collapsed during civil wars in the mid-first century B.C.E. It was replaced by an empire, established about 30 B.C.E. under the beneficent tutelage of Augustus, its "first citizen" or princeps.

Roman religion can be characterized by three distinctive traits. First, the Roman gods were identified not by mythology, which Rome essentially lacked, but by their distinctive functional activities. At times, functional specialization produced a great number of minor deities, each of whom presided over one minute aspect of an entire endeavor. Second, the Romans were religiously conservative. They carefully preserved the ways of the past, even when they had forgotten their meaning or purpose. Third, the Romans readily supplemented their own traditions with the gods and rituals of others. They rarely, however, allowed these new cults inside the sacred boundary of the old city, the pomerium.

The Romans worshiped their gods as necessary to success in any endeavor. During the Republic, several significant developments took place in this worship. Through Greek influence, the Roman gods were given human-like personalities and identified with Greek gods (Jupiter-Zeus; Juno-Hera;

Minerva-Athena). Greek influence also led to the adoption of new kinds of rituals for these gods.

Religious functionaries held prominent positions in Roman society, and during the Republic, importance gradually shifted away from the old functionaries of the monarchy (the *rex sacrorum*—"king of the rites"—and the flamines) toward the *pontifex maximus* (the "highest priest") and several priestly associations or "colleges," such as the college of augurs, from whom officials had to secure divine sanction before undertaking any official act. Originally these offices were the prerogative of the aristocratic or patrician class, but gradually they became open to the people (the "plebs").

TEXTS

Most Latin texts are conveniently available, with facing-page English translation, in the Loeb Classical Library, Harvard University Press, at $13.95 per volume.

Grant, Frederick C., ed. *Ancient Roman Religion*. Bobbs 1957 o.p. A very useful collection of sources, divided more or less by historical periods; scanty on commentary.

STUDIES

Connor, W. R. *Roman Augury and Etruscan Divination*. [*Ancient Religion and Mythology Ser.*] Ayer 1976 $14.00

Crawford, Michael. *The Roman Republic*. Harvard Univ. Pr. 1982 text ed. pap. $6.95. For those whe want a good, recent history.

Dumézil, Georges. *Archaic Roman Religion*. Trans. by Philip Krapp, Univ. of Chicago Pr. 2 vols. 1971 $45.00. The major study of Roman religion from an Indo-European perspective; lively, detailed arguments against the views of other scholars.

———. *Camillus: A Study of Indo-European Religion as Roman History*. Trans. by James Needham, Univ. of California Pr. 1980 $24.00. Examines the way in which ancient Roman historians allegedly reflected Indo-European mythic themes.

Fowler, W. Warde. *The Roman Festivals of the Period of the Republic*. Gordon Pr. 1977 $59.95. A turn-of-the-century, month-by-month account; helpful for data, but depends on outmoded notions of early religion and society.

Henig, Martin. *Religion in Roman Britain*. St. Martin's 1984 $29.95. Roman religion in a province where remains are very accessible.

Liebeschuetz, J. H. W. G. *Continuity and Change in Roman Religion*. Oxford 1979 text ed. $65.00. A very scholarly study of the interaction of political and religious change.

Ogilvie, R. M. *The Romans and Their Gods in the Age of Augustus*. Norton 1970 pap. $5.95. Religion at a time when Romans were conservatively turning to the ways of the past; depends heavily on literary evidence.

Scullard, H. H. *Festivals and Calendars of the Roman Republic*. Cornell Univ. Pr. 1981 $32.50. Month-by-month, day-by-day; more up to date than Fowler, but the weight of sheer description overwhelms any sense of what it was all about.

The Mediterranean "Oikoumene": Religions of the Hellenistic World and the Roman Empire

By the time Alexander the Great died in 323 B.C.E., he had overrun the Persian Empire and territories to the east as far as the Indus River. When

Rome annexed Egypt almost 300 years later, it had no control over the eastern parts of Alexander's territories, but it joined the rest of Alexander's lands to its own holdings to form a unified, civilized world (in Greek, an "oikoumene") that filled the entire Mediterranean basin. The result was a common, hybrid culture, shared by diverse peoples who were united by two linguae francae, Greek in the east and Latin in the west.

In this oikoumene, the old religious orders—religions of particular peoples and places—remained, but they merely existed, they did not often live. Several changes overwhelmed them. (1) The new oikoumene dispersed peoples and their religions throughout the "world," and distinctions born from local conceit—Greek/barbarian, Jew/Gentile—gave way to a sophisticated cosmopolitanism. (2) Religions tended to address the needs not of communities but of individuals; as religions of conviction, they promised converts individual rewards, such as a blessed afterlife. (3) The dominant form of religious society was not the community of one's birth but the voluntary association.

A general tolerance marked most of the religious movements and trends of the period, and this tolerance often led to accommodation. Romans adopted Greek rituals and Greek names for their gods. Magical formulae frequently linked the god of the Greeks and the god of the Jews, Zeus and Yahweh (YHWH). Only two exclusive movements violated the general rule of tolerance while otherwise conforming to "ecumenical" patterns: Judaism and Christianity. When Constantine made Christianity essentially the state religion of the Roman Empire in 324 C.E., he effectively sounded the death knell for this vibrant period in the history of religions.

The best brief introduction to these religions is not a book but an article that uses categories ultimately derived from the history of Judaism to elucidate all religions of the time: Jonathan Z. Smith's "Hellenistic Religions" in *Encyclopaedia Britannica*, 15th ed., vol. 8.

TEXTS

Austin, M. M. *The Hellenistic World from Alexander to the Roman Conquest: A Selection of Ancient Sources in Translation.* Cambridge Univ. Pr. 1981 $72.50 pap. $22.95. Includes 279 selections, many from ancient historians, organized by geography and chronology; suggested readings, but few comments.

Bagnall, Roger, and Peter Derow. *Greek Historical Documents: The Hellenistic Period.* Scholars Pr. GA 1981 text ed. pap. $10.95. Inscriptions and papyri, organized topically, with a heavy emphasis on Egypt; 20 documents on religion in Greek cities and Ptolemaic Egypt.

Grant, Frederick C., ed. *Hellenistic Religions: The Age of Syncretism.* Bobbs 1953 pap. $13.24. Useful older collection of sources pertaining to institutional religion, newer cults, religious ideas of the philosophers, and the critique of religion.

Koester, Helmut. *History, Culture and Religion of the Hellenistic Age.* Vol. 1 in *Introduction to the New Testament.* De Gruyter 1982 $32.95. A full survey of the times, but less on Hellenistic religions than one might imagine or desire.

STUDIES

Brown, Peter. *Society and the Holy in Late Antiquity.* Univ. of California Pr. 1982 $30.00. Masterful essays on both method and selected topics of late antiquity; highly recommended.

Cumont, Franz. *Oriental Religions in Roman Paganism.* Intro. by G. Showerman, Dover repr. of 1911 ed. 1956 pap. $5.95. Older but still valuable study; examines the spread of the gods of Asia Minor, Egypt, Syria, and Persia, as well as astrology and magic.

Dodds, E. R. *Pagan and Christian in an Age of Anxiety: Some Aspects of Religious Experience from Marcus Aurelius to Constantine.* Norton repr. of 1965 ed. 1970 pap. $5.95. Attempts to look at psychological causes for the material and spiritual changes that occurred roughly in the third century C.E.

Ferguson, John. *The Religions of the Roman Empire.* [*Aspects of Greek and Roman Life Ser.*] Cornell Univ. Pr. 1985 text ed. $34.50 pap. $8.95. Discursive description of Roman religion around the year 200 C.E.

McCormack, Sabine G. *Art and Ceremony in Late Antiquity.* Univ. of California Pr. 1981 $45.00. Detailed, readable, and intelligent study of the art and ceremony of the imperial court after Diocletian; illustrated, but not so well as one would like.

MacMullen, Ramsay. *Paganism in the Roman Empire.* Yale Univ. Pr. 1981 text ed. $30.00 pap. $8.95. By a scholar who has been pioneering new approaches to the subject.

Nock, Arthur D. *Essays on Religion and the Ancient World.* Ed. by Zeph Stewart, Oxford 1986 $98.00. Articles by a scholar of formidable stature on a wide variety of subjects; difficult, but indispensable for the serious reader.

Teixidor, Javier. *The Pagan God: Popular Religion in the Greco-Roman Near East.* Princeton Univ. Pr. 1977 o.p. A useful study of common religious patterns based on inscriptions; intended to supplement ordinary scholarly discussions of the period.

Walbank, F. W. *The Hellenistic World.* [*Fontana History of the Ancient World Ser.*] Univ. of California Pr. 1984 $60.00. For those who want a recent survey; readable and reliable.

MYSTERIES

Mysteries derive their name from the manner in which their most sacred rituals and narratives were performed: in secret celebrations to which only initiates were admitted. They also often included other acts, such as processions, that were performed publicly. Many but not all mysteries had their roots in seasonal, agricultural celebrations. By Hellenistic and Roman times they had been individualized and interiorized. Their common concern was with the fate of the individual after death, generally the fate of the individual soul.

There were many different mystery religions, each with its own deity, rituals, and class of worshipers. The Great Mother of Phrygia, Cybele, was worshiped particularly by craftsmen. Her priests publicly castrated themselves in imitation of her young lover Attis. The most popular mysteries were the mysteries of Isis, originally connected with the funerary rites of the dead Egyptian king. Her mysteries were practiced especially by the lower classes in seaport and trading towns. Especially popular with Roman soldiers and administrators was the god Mithras, originally an Indo-Iranian god, who created life by capturing and slaying a bull. The mysteries of Sol Invictus, the Syrian sun-god whose birthday was celebrated on December 25, were eventually assimilated with the mysteries of Mithras. They were very popular during the third century C.E., and for a time they were promoted as the official religion of the Roman Empire.

During the second century Christianity came to be practiced as a mystery cult; for example, only initiates were allowed to be present at the celebration of the Eucharist. Christianity still retains many features derived from the mysteries, such as occasional liturgical references to Christ as the Sun (Sol) and the celebration of his birth on December 25. Many Gnostic movements also adopted the trappings of the mystery cults.

Campbell, Joseph, ed. *The Mysteries*. Princeton Univ. Pr. 1955 $13.50. Jungian essays that start with, but are not limited to, Hellenistic and Roman mysteries.

Cumont, Franz. *The Mysteries of Mithra*. Trans. by Thomas J. McCormack, Dover 2d ed. repr. of 1911 ed. 1956 pap. $5.95. An older, useful account of the growth of Mithraism and its teachings, practices, and institutions.

Godwin, Joscelyn. *Mystery Religions in the Ancient World*. Harper 1981 pap. $9.95. Probably the best introduction for the average reader; illustrated.

Nilsson, Martin P. *The Dionysiac Mysteries of the Hellenistic and Roman Age*. [*Ancient Religion and Mythology Ser.*] Ayer repr. of 1957 ed. 1976 $13.00. A readable, illustrated essay, with occasional terms in Greek, by a reliable and respected scholar.

Solmsen, Friedrich. *Isis among the Greeks and Romans*. Harvard Univ. Pr. 1979 $14.00. An interesting study of a limited topic: the assimilation of Isis to classical traditions.

Vermaseren, Maarten J. *Cybele and Attis: The Myth and the Cult*. Thames & Hudson 1977 o.p. A well-illustrated survey, organized by both geography (Greece, Rome, provinces) and by topic (art, literature, mythology, cults, and festivals).

HEALERS, MAGICIANS, AND DIVINE MEN

Even before the oikoumene the peoples of the Mediterranean were familiar with the arcane arts of the Middle East. Etruscan haruspicy seems to have been indebted to Babylonian divination, while the skills and lore of the Magi, priests of the Medes, had become legendary among the Greeks. The cosmopolitan culture of the oikoumene gave the practitioners of arcane arts a wide territory in which to display their talents. In the first two centuries of the Roman Empire, charismatic individuals of all sorts—prophets, magicians, and healers—abounded.

Astrology was extremely fashionable during this period. In fact, it was during the Hellenistic period that astrology as ordinarily practiced—with signs of the zodiac, planets and their houses, and correspondences between the heavens and the human body—was invented. Theorists conflated Babylonian and Egyptian astral lore with Greek observations and theories to produce the astrological synthesis.

During the same period, the resort to magicians and magical formulae was common on every level of society. Disease was often attributed to the influence of demons. As a result, magicians were often summoned to identify the offending demons and order them to depart. The ability to perform magical acts might not simply be a sign of special skills. Those who performed wonders were at times endowed with an aura of divinity. They were "divine men."

These last characteristics have, of course, a certain affinity to the person of Jesus. A more pagan example might be Apollonius of Tyana, a wandering ascetic and teacher in the neo-Pythagorean tradition. Apollonius is alleged to have performed miracles of healing, including resuscitating the dead. Apollonius's biography is, however, late, and it was probably distorted in the interests of anti-Christian propaganda.

Betz, Hans Dieter, ed. *The Greek Magical Papyri in Translation, including the Demonic Spells.* Univ. of Chicago Pr. 1986 lib. bdg. $39.95. Translation, with full scholarly apparatus, of very important documents for the study of ancient magic.

Corrington, Gail Peterson. *The "Divine Man": His Origin and Function in Hellenistic Popular Religion.* Peter Lang 1986 $35.00. Tries to see divine men against a popular rather than literary or philosophical background.

Cumont, Franz. *Astrology and Religion among the Greeks and Romans.* Dover 1912 pap. $3.50. The best book on Greek astrology is even older and in French. This will do as an introduction.

Hadas, Moses, and Morton Smith. *Heroes and Gods: Spiritual Biographies in Antiquity.* [*Essay Index Repr. Ser.*] Ayer repr. of 1965 ed. $19.00. General study of "aretalogies" (accounts of miraculous deeds) from the Greek heroes to Christian martyrs, with translations and summaries of more notable texts (including the Gospel of Luke).

Luck, Georg. *Arcana Mundi: Magic and the Occult in the Greek and Roman Worlds.* Johns Hopkins Univ. Pr. 1985 text ed. $32.50 pap. $12.95. Primarily literary texts, a few formulaic papyri, with sometimes lengthy introduction, pertaining to magic, miracles, demonology, divination, astrology, and alchemy.

Smith, Morton. *Jesus the Magician.* Harper 1982 pap. $12.95. Stimulating if controversial argument that Jesus used magical methods, that he appeared as a magician to outsiders, and that the canonical Gospels deliberately took issue with and suppressed this charge.

IMPERIAL CULT

The modern secular state is a new star that arose on the horizon of history during the Enlightenment. Before then, religion and politics were generally intertwined, often in very complicated ways.

In the first two centuries of the Roman Empire, the relation between religion and politics took a form that we are likely to misread as a cheap political trick: worship of the emperor. Different scholars trace the imperial cult to different origins. Alexander the Great, never given to modesty, had himself proclaimed the son of Zeus Ammon. The practice offended his Greek soldiers but not the conquered peoples, who were accustomed to associate their rulers with the divine. The cult of the ruler continued among Alexander's successors. As Rome expanded, victorious generals and provincial governors found themselves accorded divine honors in the east. When JULIUS CAESAR (see Vol. 3) was apotheosized by the Senate, his adopted son, the emperor Augustus, erected temples dedicated to both Rome (whose protective spirits had long been worshiped) and the divine Julius.

The cult of the emperor took many forms: cults fostered by the imperial government, cults granted by individual municipalities, and cults established by private individuals and corporations. In the Augustan period, worship was directed to Rome and Augustus jointly—in Italy, to the genius (life spirit) of Augustus and the guardians of the crossroads. Later emperors were worshiped in association not with Rome but with the collective body of emperors, or else simply individually. In Rome, an emperor generally did not receive divine honors until after his death. Recent scholarship has begun to note that the emperor, although divine, was not given quite the same honor or status as the other, traditional gods.

The imperial cult waned in the third century. It was replaced by the view that the emperor ruled on the basis of divine appointment.

Fears, J. Rufus. *Princeps A Diis Electus: The Divine Election of the Emperor as a Political Concept at Rome.* Pennsylvania State Univ. Pr. 1977 $38.00. Religious and historical assessment—for the serious student.

Millar, Fergus. *The Emperor in the Roman World.* [*Aspects of Greek and Roman Life Ser.*] Cornell Univ. Pr. 1977 $62.50. General discussion, with occasional references to religious aspects.

Price, S. R. F. *Rituals and Power: The Roman Imperial Cult in Asia Minor.* Cambridge Univ. Pr. 1984 $52.50 1986 pap. $14.95. A careful study that reassesses the nature of the emperor's divinity in Asia Minor; difficult for the average reader, but worth it.

GNOSTICISM

The name *Gnosticism* derives from the Greek word *gnosis*, "knowledge." It refers to a variety of movements in the late ancient world that shared one fundamental trait: in them, a person was said to be saved by esoteric knowledge. The origins of Gnosticism and its precise relation to Christianity—was it a heresy or an independent movement?—are disputed. In any case, Gnosticism was flourishing by the second century C.E.

Gnosticism never had an organized hierarchy to insist on a uniform set of beliefs or practices. The typical organization was that of an elite teacher with a select band of followers. Gnosticism also did not have a universally accepted set of sacred writings. Instead, Gnostics wrote their own rather obscure compositions and used allegory to read the scriptures of many different religions in a peculiarly gnostic manner. Similarly, Gnostics often borrowed and adapted cultic observances from other religious traditions, although they considered some practices, such as baptism and the Christian Eucharist, suspect.

The Gnostics were dualists. They sharply distinguished light from darkness and spirit from matter. On their view, the world was not created by the supreme god, the absolute good spirit. Rather, the world was basically a mistake that came into existence through division, a fall, or the agency of a lesser demiurge, often identified with the Jewish god Yahweh (YHWH). But Gnosticism also taught that human beings were intrinsically related to the supreme "unknown God." They contained a certain divine spark, and it was the purpose of Gnosticism to liberate this divine spark through knowledge revealed by a divine emissary or redeemer.

The apostolic tradition of Christianity vigorously attacked Gnosticism, and in doing so developed many significant Christian features: a canon of Scripture, a creed, episcopal authority, and the beginnings of systematized Christian thought. For centuries Gnosticism was known primarily from the writings of its Christian enemies. In 1945, a large number of writings, many of them Gnostic, were discovered at Nag Hammadi in Egypt. Scholars are still editing these writings and assessing their implications.

TEXTS

Foerster, Werner, ed. *Gnosis: A Selection of Gnostic Texts.* Oxford 2 vols. 1971 o.p. A useful and important collection of a wide range of texts in translation: Coptic, Mandaean, and pertinent collections from early Christian writers.

Grant, Robert M., ed. *Gnosticism: A Source Book of Heretical Writings from the Early Christian Period.* AMS Pr. 1961 $32.50. A convenient selection from Gnostic texts.

Robinson, James M. *The Nag Hammadi Library.* Harper 1978 $23.00 pap. $11.95. Accessible translations with brief introductions of writings that contribute significantly to our knowledge of Gnosticism.

STUDIES

Hedrick, Charles W., and Robert Hodgson, eds. *Nag Hammadi, Gnosticism, and Early Christianity.* Hendrickson 1986 $14.95. Collection of articles by leading scholars that reflects the current state of thought.

Jonas, Hans. *The Gnostic Religion: The Message of the Alien God and the Beginnings of Christianity.* Peter Smith 1961 $18.00. For years the standard book with which to begin studying Gnosticism.

Pagels, Elaine. *The Gnostic Gospels.* Random 1979 $14.95 1981 pap. $3.95. A scholarly study that has not met with uniform assent.

Rudolph, Kurt. *Gnosis: The Nature and History of Gnosticism.* Trans. by P. W. Coxon, K. H. Kuhn, and R. M. Wilson, Harper 1982 $28.45 pap. $14.95. The best current, comprehensive survey; discusses sources, general structure, and history of Gnosticism.

Walker, Benjamin. *Gnosticism: Its History and Influence.* Borgo Pr. 1986 lib. bdg. $24.95. Use with caution; an idiosyncratic presentation.

ANCIENT URBAN CIVILIZATIONS: RELIGIONS OF THE NEW WORLD

For years many scholars of prehistoric America believed that human beings had lived in the New World much earlier than the available evidence indicated. In recent years, dramatic discoveries have begun to confirm that suspicion. An example from North America is the Meadowcroft Rock Shelter in Pennsylvania, with finds datable roughly to 20,000 B.P.

But compared with the Old World, civilizations in the New World developed rather late, for the American environment posed different challenges from those of Europe, Asia, and North Africa. For example, the inhabitants of the Americas needed to develop to a high degree the cultivation of several different crops (corn, beans, squash) that they could plant concurrently before a large population could be sustained in a small area. As early as 6500 B.C.E., inhabitants of the New World began to domesticate plants, but two important crops, maize and then beans, appear not to have been domesticated until as many as 3,000 years later. Village settlements began to appear in Mesoamerica and Peru sometime around 2000 B.C.E. We can begin to detect the rise of urban civilizations in these regions from about 1200 B.C.E. from the remains of monumental traditions of temple architecture and sculpture.

Jennings, Jesse D., ed. *Ancient North Americans*. W. H. Freeman 1983 text ed. $29.95
———. *Ancient South Americans*. W. H. Freeman 1983 text ed. $29.95. This and the volume listed above are two regional surveys by experts. The volume on North America includes Mesoamerica.
Shutler, Richard, Jr., ed. *Early Man in the New World*. Sage 1983 $29.95 pap. $16.95. Scholarly articles on all areas of the New World, with a report on Meadowcroft Rock Shelter and a summary of developments (1970–80).

Religions of Mesoamerica

THE MAYAN REGION

In Mesoamerica, civilization first developed in the alluvial lowlands of Tabasco and the Yucatan peninsula. The earliest civilization is associated with people known as the Olmecs, whose remains have been found at such sites as San Lorenzo and La Venta (late second to mid-first millennium B.C.E.). The Olmecs were succeeded by the Maya, who flourished in the Yucatan lowlands especially from 300 to 900 C.E. After this "classical period," the Maya did not disappear. Their descendants survive to this day, practicing a variety of Christianity that integrates many native elements.

The interpretation of Olmec religious monuments is a particularly vexing problem. Religion seems to have centered on complex rites performed in temples for the sake of both cosmic and sociopolitical well-being. On one account, Olmec iconography utilized especially two different figures: a Dragon (crocodile-eagle-jaguar-human-serpent) as a deity of an elite, and a Bird Monster (eagle-mammal-reptile) associated with agriculture and mind-altering substances. Some have suggested that these two figures were predecessors of Maya and Aztec deities, but not all have accepted this idea.

The Mayan religion continued features found earlier among the Olmecs: temples as the ceremonial centers of settlements, elaborate rituals performed by a priesthood, and perhaps the androgynous creator god known to the Maya as Itzamna. During the classical period, the Maya practiced human sacrifice, especially by decapitation. They learned heart sacrifice from the peoples of the Mexican highlands between the tenth and the thirteenth centuries C.E.

The most impressive achievement of Mayan religion is its calendar. The Maya developed an elaborate calendar that consisted of two separate, concurrent cycles: a 260-day cycle of 20 13-day "weeks," and a 365-day cycle of 18 20-day "months," supplemented by 5 intercalary days. In the Mayan calendar, each day was associated with particular aspects of particular deities. As a result, the Maya could identify with precision the forces at work on any given day. Specific conjunctions of the two cycles would recur after an interval of 52 years. The great 52-year "Calendar Round" began on the conjunction of the first days of both cycles. It marked the periodic dissolution and recreation of the world.

OLMECS

Benson, Elizabeth P. *The Olmecs and Their Neighbors: Essays in Memory of Matthew W. Stirling.* Dumbarton Oaks 1981 $30.00. Essays on a wide variety of subjects.

Bernal, Ignacio. *The Olmec World.* Trans. by Fernando Horcasitas, Univ. of California Pr. 1969 pap. $12.95. A general cultural survey, with some illustrations, that includes a brief section on Olmec religion.

Coe, Michael D., and Richard A. Diehl. *In the Land of the Olmec.* Univ. of Texas Pr. 2 vols. 1980 $100.00. Volume 1 is a report on excavations at San Lorenzo; Volume 2 is an ethnography of the people of the region, together with the region's history.

Luckert, Karl W. *Olmec Religion: A Key to Middle America and Beyond.* [*Civilization of the Amer. Indian Ser.*] Univ. of Oklahoma Pr. 1976 $14.95. Unorthodox methods and conclusions but stimulating.

Nicholson, H. B., ed. *Origins of Religious Art and Iconography in Preclassic Mesoamerica.* Univ. of Southern California Lat. Amer. Ctr. 1976 o.p. Contains a definitive paper on the Dragon and Bird Monster by Peter Joralemon.

Soustelle, Jacques. *The Olmecs: The Oldest Civilization in Mexico.* Trans. by Helen R. Lane, Doubleday 1984 $17.95; Univ. of Oklahoma Pr. 1985 pap. $10.95. An up-to-date synthesis.

MAYA

Aveni, Anthony F. *Skywatchers of Ancient Mexico.* [*Texas Pan-Amer. Ser.*] Univ. of Texas Pr. 1980 text ed. $30.00 1983 pap. $17.50. Something of a classic text by a leader in the study of archaeoastronomy; well worth reading.

Hammond, Norman. *Ancient Maya Civilization.* Rutgers Univ. Pr. 1982 pap. $14.00. A recent survey, for the general reader, of Mayan history and way of life, with a short chapter on religion.

Hammond, Norman, and Gordon R. Willey, eds. *Maya Archaeology and Ethnohistory.* [*Texas Pan-Amer. Ser.*] Univ. of Texas Pr. 1979 text ed. $30.00. Papers from a scholarly symposium discuss physical evidence, interpretations, and contemporary Maya peoples.

Henderson, John S. *The World of the Maya.* Cornell Univ. Pr. 1983 $14.95. An illustrated survey, organized more or less chronologically, with a nice chapter on the Maya worldview.

Pearce, Kenneth. *The View from the Top of the Temple: Ancient Maya Civilization and Modern Maya Culture.* Univ. of New Mexico Pr. 1984 $24.95 pap. $12.95. Attempts to show continuity in contemporary Maya practices with those of ancient Maya civilization, especially in matters of religion; organized as a traveler might encounter the region today.

Tedlock, Barbara. *Time and the Highland Maya.* Univ. of New Mexico Pr. 1981 pap. $10.95. Divination and the calendar among contemporary Maya.

Tedlock, Dennis. *Popol Vuh: The Definitive of the Mayan Book of the Dawn of Life and the Glories Gods and Kings.* Simon & Schuster 1985 $19.95 1986 pap. $9.95. An important Mayan text, with notes, glossary, and an extensive introduction.

Thompson, J. Eric S. *Maya History and Religion.* [*Civilization of the Amer. Indian Ser.*] Univ. of Oklahoma Pr. repr. of 1970 ed. 1976 $24.95. In-depth but readable accounts of such topics as the use of tobacco, patterns of worship, the major and lesser gods, and creation myths.

THE MEXICAN HIGHLANDS

Civilization in the drier highlands of central Mexico began later than in the moister lowlands, but it followed similar patterns, probably inherited from the Olmecs.

The most significant early settlement was the city of Teotihuacan, about 30 miles northeast of Mexico City. The city flourished especially between 100 and 650 C.E.; it was later regarded as a mythical, perfect city by both Toltecs and Aztecs. Teotihuacan is especially notable for the care with which it was laid out. The city was divided into quarters by two broad avenues that crossed at right angles. The Avenue of the Dead, the major north-south avenue one-and-a-half miles long, connected the pyramid of the moon at its north with the temple of Quetzalcoatl at its south. Along the east side of the avenue was a complex containing the pyramid of the sun.

After the decline of Teotihuacan, the Toltecs were the next major group to dominate the region. They founded the city of Tula about 50 miles north of Mexico City. According to legend, the Toltecs had been led to Tula by a priest named Quetzalcoatl, from whom they had received all good things. This priest advocated the worship of an androgynous god, supreme and benevolent. His teachings were also associated with the abolition of human sacrifice and a god who regularly sacrificed himself by letting blood.

The last of the great civilizations of the Mexican highlands was that of the Aztecs, who called themselves Mexica. At the direction of their patron deity, the Aztecs built their city, Tenochtitlan, in 1325 on an island in the center of a lake, today the site of Mexico City.

The Aztecs preserved the elaborate spatial and temporal arrangement of their Mesoamerican predecessors. They worshiped several gods in anthropomorphic form, who show iconographical similarities with the gods of earlier peoples. Among their gods were Huitzilopochtli, their patron; the celestial androgyne Omoteotl; and his/her four offspring: Tezcatlipoca (the arch-sorcerer), Quetzalcoatl (the feathered serpent god), Xiuhtecuhtli (the sacred fire), and Tlaloc (god of rain and fertility).

Aztec religion attempted to maintain the orders of the universe and of society by imitating the creative sacrifice of the gods. The most notorious and typical of Aztec rituals was the heart sacrifice, practiced assiduously at the Templo Mayor, recently unearthed in the center of Mexico City, primarily for the purpose of nourishing the sun.

Aztec domination collapsed before the onslaught of the Spaniard Hernán Cortés in the period from 1519 to 1521. Native traditions have continued primarily in a loose syncretism with Christianity.

TEOTIHUACAN

Miller, Mary E. *The Art of Mesoamerica.* [*World of Art Ser.*] Thames & Hudson 1986 pap. $9.95. A beautiful book that discusses the layout of Teotihuacan, as well as Olmec, Maya, and Aztec art.

TOLTECS

Davies, Nigel. *The Toltec Heritage: From the Fall of Tula to the Rise of Tenochtitlan.* Univ. of Oklahoma Pr. 1980 $29.50

————. *The Toltecs, Until the Fall of Tula.* Univ. of Oklahoma Pr. 1977 o.p. Both volumes immerse the reader in the many problems that arise in studying the Toltecs. The first is a close look at a very obscure period.

Diehl, Richard A. *Tula: The Toltec Capital of Ancient Mexico.* Thames & Hudson 1983 $27.50. A profusely and beautifully illustrated book, discussing the excavations at Tula and the Toltec culture, by the director of the excavations; little specifically on religion.

AZTECS

Aveni, Anthony F. *Skywatchers of Ancient Mexico.* [*Texas Pan-Amer. Ser.*] Univ. of Texas Pr. 1980 text ed. $30.00 1983 pap. $17.50. Something of a classic text by a leader in the study of archaeoastronomy; well worth reading.

Brundage, Burr C. *The Fifth Sun: Aztec Gods, Aztec World.* [*Texas Pan-Amer. Ser.*] Univ. of Texas Pr. 1979 pap. $8.95. Perhaps the best book with which to start; focuses on myths and worldview.

————. *The Jade Steps: A Ritual Life of the Aztecs.* Univ. of Utah Pr. 1985 $22.50. A detailed and sophisticated examination of Aztec ritual with some sophistication.

Carrasco, David. *Quetzalcoatl and the Irony of Empire.* Univ. of Chicago Pr. 1984 $25.00. A masterful, lucidly written study of the religious significance of the ceremonial center at Tenochtitlan and its mythic paradigms.

Conrad, Geoffrey W., and Arthur A. Demarest. *Religion and Empire: The Dynamics of Aztec and Inca Expansion.* Cambridge Univ. Pr. 1984 $69.50. Seeks to demonstrate that changes in traditional religion were crucial to the rise and decline of both the Aztecs and the Incas; for the serious reader.

Davies, Nigel. *The Aztecs: A History.* Univ. of Oklahoma Pr. repr. of 1973 ed. 1980 pap. $12.95. For those who want a general, historical overview.

Leon-Portilla, Miguel. *Aztec Thought and Culture: A Study of the Ancient Nahuatl Mind.* Trans. by Jack E. Davis [*Civilization of the Amer. Indian Ser.*] Univ. of Oklahoma Pr. repr. of 1963 ed. 1982 $19.95. An attempt to describe the "philosophy" of the Nahuatl-speaking peoples of the Valley of Mexico prior to the arrival of the Spanish.

Pasztory, Esther. *Aztec Art.* Abrams 1983 $60.00. Treatment of Aztec art sensitive to its religious significance.

Townsend, Richard F. *State and Cosmos in the Art of Tenochtitlan.* Dumbarton Oaks 1979 pap. $8.00. A study sensitive to religion.

Inca Religion

When the Spaniards first came to the Andes in 1527, the Incas were the dominant power. Their empire was relatively new—they had started to expand about a century earlier—and they had been preceded by several civilizations in the region. Unfortunately, we have no written records from the Incas or any other pre-Columbian Andean peoples (as we do for the Maya and Aztecs in Mesoamerica). Our knowledge of their religion is limited.

Among the gods of the Incas were Viracocha, a creator and culture-hero; Inti, the sun, the supreme god; Apu Illapu, the giver of rain; and Mama-Kilya, the goddess of the moon. The Incas built temples for these gods, often in the form of stepped pyramids, the most famous of which is the temple of the sun at Cuzco. In addition, there were many smaller shrines and sacred places.

The temples housed not only the images of the gods but also priests and "chosen women" dedicated to temple service. Typical Inca religious practices included sacrifice, in times of extreme need human sacrifice, and (like the Romans) the resort to divination before every official activity. The Inca calendar had 12 months of 30 days each. It identified both religious and agricultural occasions.

Brundage, Burr C. *Empire of the Inca.* Intro. by Arnold J. Toynbee [*Civilization of the Amer. Indian Ser.*] Univ. of Oklahoma Pr. 1985 pap. $10.95. A highly readable account of Inca history, sensitive to religious beliefs and practices.

Conrad, Geoffrey W., and Arthur A. Demarest. *Religion and Empire: The Dynamics of Aztec and Inca Expansion.* (See the entry under The Mexican Highlands, Aztecs, in this section.)

Lumbreras, Luis G. *The Peoples and Cultures of Ancient Peru.* Smithsonian 1974 pap. $13.95. A careful archaeological survey from 21,000 B.C.E. to 1532 C.E.; for the serious reader only.

Morris, Craig, and Donald E. Thompson. *Huanuco Pampa: An Inca City and Its Hinterland.* Fwd. by Donald E. Thompson [*Ancient People and Places Ser.*] Thames & Hudson 1985 $29.95. A perceptive study, using literary and archaeological evidence, of an administrative outpost of the Inca empire; beautiful photographs; with a discussion of ritual activities.

Osborne, Harold. *Indians of the Andes: Incas, Aymaras, and Quechuas.* Gordon Pr. 1977 $59.95. A readable narrative survey, from the beginnings of human habitation to the present, with occasional discussions of religion.

Urton, Gary. *At the Crossroads of the Earth and the Sky: An Andean Cosmology.* [*Latin Amer. Monographs*] Univ. of Texas Pr. 1981 text ed. $30.00. Fieldwork among a contemporary Andean people (at Misminay) reveals astronomical beliefs and practices strongly reminiscent of the ancient Incas.

TRIBAL RELIGIONS

Tribal religions are ancient religions only in a very loose sense of the term. For example, one might say that a native American ritual belongs to "the religion of the ancients," but such a phrase is misleading. It tempts us to view tribal practices as both age-old and irrelevant to modern life. The truth is that tribal religions have never been static. They are not fossils preserved from the Stone Age. Like the religions of urban civilizations, they can and do change with time, sometimes dramatically. Furthermore, inherited tribal traditions still can and still do influence contemporary life, even in "modern" settings.

The number of different tribal religions is immense. For example, it is estimated that there are as many as 700 different tribal religions in sub-Saharan Africa alone. Obviously, this chapter cannot begin to provide references to them all, but tribal religions tend to show regional similarities. Therefore, this section is divided along broad geographical lines: the religions of Australia and Oceania, of Africa, and of the Americas.

There is danger in this approach. In some sense, continental regions are still too broad. The best works on tribal religions tend to be focused much more narrowly. They usually deal only with the beliefs, practices, and institutions of a particular people. Limitations of space do not permit a more detailed treatment here. A few general titles are mentioned, along with some more famous or more recent special studies. The interested reader should consult the bibliographies in the books listed below and in the reference works cited in the introduction to this entire chapter.

Two other topics deserve special attention in this section. Tribal religions have often been called "nonliterate religions," for the peoples who practice them have not traditionally had means of writing. There has been considerable discussion recently of the scholarly problems posed by orality. Some of the more important contributions are listed below under Orality and Literacy. In addition, the modern West has had an immense impact on most tribal societies, including their religions. The confrontation with the West forms the last topic of this chapter.

Orality and Literacy

Discussions of the peculiar nature of oral traditions are at least as old as 1762. In that year, the Scottish poet James McPherson published what he claimed were translations of orally transmitted poems by the Scottish Gaelic poet Ossian (third century C.E.). His claim stirred up storms of controversy over all of Europe for the next century. During the romantic period, there was a great deal of interest in collecting folklore of all sorts. This movement was stimulated by J. G. Herder, who insisted that poetry derived from feelings human beings had when they encountered the world and that these feelings were best expressed not in literate poetry but in oral folk songs.

In the last few decades, discussions have focused on the conditions that orality imposes on nonliterate cultures. One major hypothesis suggests that oral compositions, especially poetry, are constructed from a traditional store of formulaic phrases and themes. This hypothesis was developed by Milman Parry and his student, Albert Lord, on the basis of contemporary Yugoslav and ancient Homeric poetry. A bolder theory suggests that the technology of communication (oral, literate, electronic) inevitably conditions the nature of thought. This suggestion was made most notoriously by Marshall McLuhan; among more professional scholars the view has been advanced best by the anthropologist Jack Goody, among students of antiquity by Eric Havelock. Both theories are suggestive, but neither has found universal assent. It has become clear that the distinction between orality and literacy is complex and related to many other distinctions, for example, elite and popular.

Especially during the last ten years, scholars have begun to think not only about conditions orality imposes on the societies they study but also about the conditions it imposes on their own work. There has been a particular interest in the possibility of using oral sources to write history, as well as or even instead of written documents.

Finnegan, Ruth. *Oral Poetry: Its Nature, Significance and Social Context*. Cambridge Univ. Pr. 1980 pap. o.p. The best single-volume introduction to oral poetry.

Foley, John M. *Oral-Formulaic Theory and Research: An Introduction and Annotated Bibliography*. [*Reference Lib. of the Humanities*] Garland 1984 lib. bdg. $48.00. Indispensable bibliographical guide to work done on the Parry-Lord hypothesis.

Goody, Jack, ed. *The Domestication of the Savage Mind*. Cambridge Univ. Pr. 1977 $34.50 pap. $12.95. The effects of literacy on an oral culture, by the leading anthropological theorist.

Havelock, Eric A. *The Literate Revolution in Greece and Its Cultural Consequences*. Princeton Univ. Pr. 1982 $29.00 pap. $12.95. Assorted essays that reflect on and refine the author's earlier views.

———. *Preface to Plato*. Harvard Univ. Pr. 1982 text ed. $8.95. Emphasizes the oral aspect of early Greek thought, beginning with the "Homeric Encyclopedia."

Henige, David. *Oral Historiography*. Longman 1982 text ed. pap. $8.95. On gathering historical materials through oral interrogation; good bibliography.

Lord, Albert B. *The Singer of Tales*. Harvard Univ. Pr. 1981 text ed. pap. $8.95. The classic statement of the Parry-Lord hypothesis.

Ong, Walter J. *Orality and Literacy: The Technologizing of the World*. Methuen 1982 $18.95 pap. $10.95. A concise statement of the view that orality and literacy produce certain structures of consciousness.

Parry, Milman. *The Making of Homeric Verse*. Ed. by Adam Parry, Oxford 1971 o.p. Collected papers, with an extensive introduction, from a scholar who died young but left as a legacy the building blocks of the oral-formulaic theory.

Stock, Brian. *The Implications of Literacy: Written Language and Models of Interpretation in the Eleventh and Twelfth Centuries*. Princeton Univ. Pr. 1987 $50.50. Argues that the development of literacy in Europe leads to a new interdependence between oral and written discourse; a modification of earlier, simpler views.

Religions of Oceania and Australia

The religions of Oceania (the islands of the southwest Pacific) present several common features. The behavior of the peoples in this region is governed to a great degree by status or rank (expressed in Polynesian by the terms *mana* and *tapu*). Status derives in turn largely from owning and successfully tending plots of land.

The peoples of Oceania account for the objects and events of the world by invoking two classes of beings: (1) gods who have never been human, among them an "otiose" creator and culture heroes who are active in cosmogonic myths; and (2) the sacred dead, who inhabit a distant, often indistinct land. As a result, most of these peoples have careful and elaborate rituals for disposing of corpses.

The inhabitants of this region conceive of the divine as being able to take up temporary residence in small, carved, human-shaped figurines (*tiki*). In cases of need, they frequently have recourse to diviners, often women. Most of the region is now nominally Christian, but traditional features are often evident beneath a very thin Christian veneer.

The religions of aboriginal Australia have been well preserved in the northern and central parts of the continent. Central to and distinctive of all Australian religions is the way in which Australians conceive of the sacred: "the Dreaming."

The Dreaming is the time when mythical beings first emerged from the formless chaos and created the world as it is today. When these beings departed, they left some of their sacredness behind, especially in particular sacred places.

The religious life of the Australians consists essentially of the interrelations between people and the sacred as manifested in the Dreaming. At times these relations occur naturally. For example, conception and birth result when a spirit animates a new human being. These relations also occur in rituals, some of which are open to all members of the community, others restricted to one sex or the other. Because the most spectacular rituals are performed by men in secret, earlier scholars concluded that women had no secret sacred knowledge or activities. Later research, especially by women in the field, has proved them wrong.

Australian rituals often recreate the myths of the Dreaming, using special vehicles to indicate the presence of deities, such as the bull-roarer (an object that is attached to a string and whirs as it is swung in a circle) or the *tjurunga* (a sacred, decorated board).

OCEANIA

Alpers, Antony. *The World of the Polynesians Seen through Their Myths and Legends, Poetry, and Art.* Oxford 1986 $10.95. An attractive collection of Polynesian bits and pieces with some introduction; fun to browse.

Bateson, Gregory. *Naven: A Survey of the Problems Suggested by a Composite Picture of the Culture of a New Guinea Tribe Drawn from Three Points of View.* Stanford Univ. Pr. 2d ed. 1958 $35.00 pap. $10.95. Theoretically ground-breaking ethnographic account that begins with a study of a ritual known as *naven;* for the serious reader.

Firth, Raymond. *Rank and Religion in Tikopia.* Allen & Unwin 1970 $37.95. The last of three studies of Tikopia religion by a master ethnographer; focuses on religious leadership, spirits and mediumships, and the advance of Christianity.

Leenhardt, Maurice. *Do Kamo: Person and Myth in the Melanesian World.* Univ. of Chicago Pr. 1979 $18.00. An epoch-making study that helped clarify differences between Melanesian and European ways of thinking.

Malinowski, Bronislaw. *Argonauts of the Western Pacific.* Pref. by James Frazer, Waveland Pr. repr. of 1961 ed. 1984 text ed. pap. $10.95

———. *Coral Gardens and Their Magic: A Study of the Methods of Tilling the Soil and of Agricultural Rites in the Trobriand Islands.* Dover 1978 $12.95. This and the previous title are reprints of classic, delightfully readable texts by an author who pioneered both ethnographic method and functionalist theory.

———. *Magic, Science and Religion and Other Essays.* Greenwood repr. of 1948 ed. 1984 lib. bdg. $35.00. A collection of Malinowski's most important theoretical essays.

Meigs, Anna S. *Food, Sex and Pollution: A New Guinea Religion.* Rutgers Univ. Pr. 1984 text ed. $22.50. Fascinating study of a religion of the New Guinea highlands not in terms of gods, spirits, and beliefs but as a "religion of the body."

Sahlins, Marshall. *Island of History.* Univ. of Chicago Pr. 1985 $22.50. A sophisticated reflection on history, using Hawaii as the example; a stimulating book, but only for the most serious readers.

AUSTRALIA

Bell, Diane. *Daughters of the Dreaming*. Allen & Unwin 1984 text ed. pap. $14.95. A descriptive account of women and their rituals from fieldwork in north-central Australia.

Charlesworth, Max, and Kenneth Maddock, eds. *Religion in Aboriginal Australia: An Anthology*. Univ. of Queensland Pr. 1984 text ed. $39.50. Essays by fieldworkers on a wide range of topics.

Eliade, Mircea. *Australian Religions: An Introduction*. Ed. by Victor Turner [*Symbol, Myth and Ritual Ser.*] Cornell Univ. Pr. 1973 o.p. An influential historian of religions reflects on Australian religions.

Kaberry, Phyllis M. *Aboriginal Women, Sacred and Profane*. Gordon Pr. $69.95. A groundbreaking study of aboriginal women, including their religion.

Maddock, Kenneth. *The Australian Aborigines: A Portrait of Their Society*. Penguin 1975 o.p. A general study, with occasional references to religion.

Religions of Africa

Several traits characterize most, if not all, of the traditional religions of sub-Saharan Africa. These people generally know a supreme god, but this god is usually remote from human beings and their concerns. As a result, he receives no cult. Instead, the events of daily life are the preserve of various kinds of lesser deities and of the ancestors, who receive the appropriate ritual attention.

African religions take a great deal of interest in misfortunes. Human sickness and suffering are attributed to one of two causes: (1) they are either caused by spirits or ancestors offended by a person's actions or inattention or (2) they are the result of sorcery practiced by one's personal enemies.

In the case of either of these events, the sufferers and their families will consult a specialist: a priest or diviner or medium. These specialists identify the cause of the misfortune and prescribe its ritual cure. Offended spirits or ancestors are generally palliated by an offering, usually animal sacrifice.

For most Africans, the individual person is a composite of many souls. A person's life proceeds along several fixed stages, generally marked by rites of passage. The last stage of life occurs after death, when the once living person becomes an ancestor.

Booth, Newell S. *African Religions: A Symposium*. NOK 1977 text ed. $21.50. Articles on various aspects of African religions, including African religions in the Americas and Christianity and Islam in Africa.

Deng, Francis Mading. *Dinka Folktales: African Stories from the Sudan*. Fwd. by Michael Reisman, Holmes & Meier 1974 text ed. $39.50. A collection of tales with a brief (too brief) introduction.

Evans-Pritchard, E. E. *Nuer Religion*. Oxford 1956 $10.95. A fieldwork classic, especially valuable for its discussion of spirits and the practice of sacrifice.

Fortes, Meyer. *Oedipus and Job in West African Religion*. [*Cambridge Studies in Social Anthropology*] Cambridge Univ. Pr. 1984 $32.50 pap. $9.95; Hippocrene Bks. repr. of 1959 ed. 1980 lib. bdg. $15.50. An extended essay on fate in West African religions.

Karp, Ivan, and Charles S. Bird, eds. *Explorations in African Systems of Thought.* [*African Systems of Thought Ser.*] Indiana Univ. Pr. 1980 $25.00; Smithsonian rev. ed. repr. of 1980 ed. 1987 pap. $14.95. Essays on a variety of topics, loosely organized as modes of thought, images of social experience, cultural dynamics, and comparison.

Lewis-Williams, J. *The Rock Art of Southern Africa.* Cambridge Univ. Pr. 1983 $27.95. A sensitive study with beautiful illustrations.

Lienhardt, Godfrey. *Divinity and Experience: The Religion of the Dinka.* Oxford 1961 $45.00. Another fieldwork classic from the Sudan; organized in terms of types of divinities and techniques for controlling experience.

MacGaffey, Wyatt. *Religion and Society in Central Africa: The Bakongo of Lower Zaire.* Univ. of Chicago Pr. 1986 lib. bdg. $45.00 text ed. pap. $16.95. A readable account, from the perspective of the anthropology of religion, of cosmology, ritual and power, and continuity and change.

Mbiti, John S. *Introduction to African Religion.* Heinemann 1975 text ed. pap. $12.50. A topical overview intended for general readers with no previous knowledge of the subject.

Parrinder, Geoffrey. *African Traditional Religion.* Greenwood 3d ed. 1976 lib. bdg. $25.00. Popular for years; discusses African worldviews, gods, rituals, sociological aspects, sorcery, and the fate of the soul.

Ranger, T. O., and I. N. Kimambo, eds. *The Historical Study of African Religion.* [*Lib. Repr. Ser.*] Univ. of California Pr. 1976 o.p. A valuable collection of essays on various types of religious phenomena and on developments in the last two hundred years.

Turner, Victor. *The Forest of Symbols: Aspects of Ndembu Ritual.* Cornell Univ. Pr. 1970 pap. $12.95. An influential study of ritual symbolism.

Zahan, Dominique. *The Religion, Spirituality, and Thought of Traditional Africa.* Trans. by Lawrence M. Martin, Univ. of Chicago Pr. repr. of 1970 ed. 1979 lib. bdg. $17.00 pap. $9.95. A stimulating attempt to discover the principle that animates African life; not to everyone's taste.

Zuesse, Evan. *Ritual Cosmos: The Sanctification of Life in African Religions.* Ohio Univ. Pr. 1980 $21.95 1985 pap. $12.95. Attempts to combine anthropology and religious studies to elucidate the spiritual universe underlying African symbols and practices.

Religions of the Americas

In the New World, there are several very different regions and religions. Inasmuch as these regions and religions are likely to be of more immediate interest to the (North) American readers for whom this bibliography is intended, it seems best to comment not on the New World as a whole but briefly on each of its subdivisions.

North American religions (occasionally called "Native American religions") know a variety of gods and spirits. Among them the most common are a sky-god as the supreme deity; a trickster figure who, as a culture hero, is prominent in myths; and among hunting peoples animal-shaped guardians that are obtained in visions, often visions brought on by severe fasting. Rituals in this region tend to be very elaborate, consisting of long sequences of prayers, offerings, and dances. Their goal is to maintain a balance in relations with gods and spirits. A common figure in North America is the medicine man or shaman, a visionary who, along with other powers, has the power to heal.

Mesoamerica has as a region been heavily Christianized from the days of the Spanish conquest, but as mentioned above, the Christianity of the Indian peoples often retains many pre-Columbian elements. Among the strongest of these elements are an intense concern with cosmology that sees earthly order as a replication of heavenly order; shamans who often use hallucinogens—still indispensable but now outside the bounds of acceptable society; and the ancient cult of the dead. Perhaps the best example of Mesoamerican syncretism is the widespread veneration of the Virgin of Guadalupe. The story is that the Virgin Mary manifested herself in Indian form in Guadalupe in December 1531, and since that time she has been venerated, in a form distinct from the Spanish Catholic Mary, under the name of the Aztec goddess Tonantzin.

South America has a wide variety of religious traditions, ranging from the descendants of the ancient Andean civilizations to simpler tribes in the eastern lowlands. As in many other tribal religions, most indigenous peoples of this region know of a supreme creator god, but this god remains without a cult, except in the Andes. Of more direct significance, especially among hunting peoples, are different types of masters of animals. A common religious symbol in this region is the jaguar, and the jaguar is in turn connected at times with the shaman. In South America shamans were very widespread, and they frequently used mind-altering drugs to supplement their other arts.

The best known of the pre-Columbian Caribbean religions are those of two peoples: the Island Arawak and the Island Carib. Both peoples knew a high god who was of little practical importance. Rituals were generally directed instead to spirits (*zemii*), often embodied in conical objects, and among the Arawak to the ancestors. Both peoples made ritual use of tobacco, narcotics, and stimulants, but the Caribbean region is most noted for one ritual that was certainly practiced and for another that may be only legendary. The Caribs practiced a ritual known as couvade: in imitation of their wives' labor, new fathers were isolated for 40 days and nights. From the word Carib (in Spanish, Caribal) derives the English word "cannibal." Some have recently suggested that the Caribs never practiced cannibalism. Even if they did, they would have done so only on infrequent ritual occasions.

NORTH AMERICA

Brown, Joseph Epes. *The Spiritual Legacy of the American Indian*. Crossroad Publishing 1984 $8.95. Essays on a wide variety of topics; concerned with the interaction of religion and culture and the fundamental principles of North American religions.

Driver, Harold E. *Indians of North America*. Univ. of Chicago Pr. 2d ed. rev. 1969 pap. $16.95. Comprehensive, comparative overview by topic; see especially its Chapter 8, "Social and Religious Aspects of Subsistence," and Chapter 23, "Religion, Magic, and Medicine."

Gill, Sam D. *Native American Religions: An Introduction*. Wadsworth 1981 text ed.

pap. $15.25. A good general introduction; tends to focus on the author's specialty, the Southwest.

Grim, John A. *The Shaman: Patterns of Siberian and Ojibway Healing.* [*Civilization of the Amer. Indian Ser.*] Univ. of Oklahoma Pr. 1983 pap. $19.95. A clear and concise discussion.

Handbook of North American Indians. Smithsonian 20 vols. 1978–86 prices vary. Variously in and out of print. Organized primarily by region, then by tribe. Information specifically on religion may be hard to get.

Howard, James H. *Shawnee: The Ceremonialism of a Native Indian Tribe and Its Cultural Background.* Ohio Univ. Pr. 1981 $28.95 pap. $14.95. Historical and cultural account of a tribe originally in the east; much on ritual practices.

Hultkrantz, Ake. *Belief and Worship in Native North America.* Ed. by Christopher Vecsey, Syracuse Univ. Pr. 1981 $30.00. Collected essays on belief and myth, worship and ritual, ecology, and persistence and change.

———. *The Religions of the American Indians.* [*Hermeneutics Studies in the History of Religions*] Univ. of California Pr. 1979 $20.95 pap. $9.95. Topical treatment intended as a general survey; heavy on North America, with chapters on the ancient civilizations.

———. *The Study of American Indian Religions.* Scholars Pr. GA 1983 $12.95. Six essays for those who want to put various scholars into historical perspective.

Kroeber, Karl, ed. *Traditional Literatures of the American Indians: Texts and Interpretations.* Univ. of Nebraska Pr. 1981 $16.50 pap. $5.95. Collections of texts with critical introductions; allegedly intended for nonspecialists.

Underhill, Ruth M. *Red Man's Religion: Beliefs and Practices of the Indians North of Mexico.* Univ. of Chicago Pr. 1972 pap. $10.00. Very readable study by a well-known scholar.

Walker, James R. *Lakota Belief and Ritual.* Ed. by Raymond J. Demallie and Elaine A. Jahner, Univ. of Nebraska Pr. 1980 $21.50 1983 pap. $14.95

———. *Lakota Myth.* Univ. of Nebraska Pr. 1983 $29.95 pap. $14.95. This and the preceding title are excellent editions of fieldwork dating from 1896 to 1914; for those who want to brush up against "raw data."

MESOAMERICA

Dow, James. *The Shaman's Touch: Otomi Indian Symbolic Healing.* Univ. of Utah Pr. 1986 $13.95. A recent report on field experience; in places reads somewhat uneven.

Fontana, Bernard L. *Taramuhara: Where Night Is the Day of the Moon.* Northland 1979 o.p. Beautiful, strikingly vivid color photographs; text based primarily on secondary sources.

Handbook of Middle American Indians. Univ. of Texas Pr. 16 vols. and suppls. 1964–76 various prices. See especially Vol. 6, *Social Anthropology,* for articles on religion.

Myerhoff, Barbara. *Peyote Hunt: The Sacred Journey of the Huichol Indians.* Cornell Univ. Pr. 1976 pap. $9.95. Well-known description of the peyote hunt and reflections on its significance.

Pearce, Kenneth. *The View from the Top of the Temple: Ancient Maya Civilization and Modern Maya Culture.* (See the entry under Religions of Mesoamerica, The Mayan Region, Maya, in this chapter.)

Taggart, James M. *Nahuat Myth and Social Structure.* [*Texas Pan-Amer. Ser.*] Univ. of

Texas Pr. 1983 text ed. $25.00. A somewhat technical account of traditional cosmology and society in the valley of Mexico.

Tedlock, Barbara. *Time and the Highland Maya*. (See the entry under Religions of Mesoamerica, The Mayan Region, Maya, in this chapter.)

Vogt, Evon Z. *Tortillas for the Gods: A Symbolic Analysis of Zinacanteco Rituals*. Harvard Univ. Pr. 1976 $18.00. A sophisticated study of all sorts of rituals in Zinacanteco culture, aiming at a symbolic decoding.

SOUTH AMERICA

Handbook of South American Indians. Cooper Square Pr. 7 vols. 1957 o.p. Old, but nothing more recent is comparable; by region.

Lévi-Strauss, Claude. *From Honey to Ashes: An Introduction to a Science of Mythology*. Hippocrene Bks. repr. of 1973 ed. 1980 lib. bdg. $34.50; trans. by Doreen Weightman, Univ. of Chicago Pr. 1973 pap. $13.00. Applies Lévi-Strauss's ideas to South American mythology.

Nimuendaju, Curt. *The Eastern Timbira*. Ed. by Robert H. Lowie, AMS Pr. repr. of 1946 ed. 1984 $74.50. By an ethnologist who was adopted into a Brazilian tribe.

Osborne, Harold. *South American Mythology*. [*Lib. of the World's Myths and Legends*] Bedrick Bks. 1986 $18.95. The best general overview of the subject.

Reichel-Dolmatoff, Gerardo. *Amazonian Cosmos: The Sexual and Religious Symbolism of the Takano Indians*. Trans. by Gerardo Reichel-Dolmatoff, Univ. of Chicago Pr. repr. of 1971 ed. 1974 pap. $7.95. A fine study of the world of thought of the Desana, a subgroup of the Takano tribe.

———. *The Shaman and the Jaguar: A Study of Narcotic Drugs among the Indians of Colombia*. Temple Univ. Pr. 1975 $29.95. Explores shamans and a common South American shamanic image, the jaguar, among a northwest Amazonian tribe, as well as the shamans' use of hallucinogens.

Sullivan, Lawrence. *South American Religions: An Orientation to Meaning*. Macmillan 1987 $35.00. A good overview from the perspective of the study of religions.

Urton, Gary, ed. *Animal Myths and Metaphors in South America*. Univ. of Utah Pr. 1985 pap. $17.50. Several authors use South American material to discuss a vexing anthropological problem: the relations other peoples postulate between themselves and animals.

Wilbert, Johannes, and Karin Simoneau, eds. *Folk Literature of the Tehuelche Indians*. UCLA Lat. Amer. Ctr. 1976–85 ea. $25.00–$37.00. Several volumes, all of whose titles begin *Folk Literature of* . . . For those who want collections of folklore.

CARIBBEAN

Alegria, Ricardo E. *Ball Courts and Ceremonial Plazas in the West Indies*. Yale Univ. Anthro. 1983 pap. $12.50. Scholarly study of a very common ritual setting in the Americas.

Arens, W. *The Man-Eating Myth: Anthropology and Anthropophagy*. Oxford 1979 $19.95 pap. $8.95. Takes a critical view—perhaps a too critical view—of all reports of cannibalism.

Layng, Anthony. *The Carib Reserve: Identity and Security in the West Indies*. Fwd. by Leo A. Despres, Univ. Pr. of Amer. 1983 text ed. lib. bdg. $27.50 pap. $12.00. A descriptive ethnographic account, with chapters on setting, social structure, religion and education, and the local economy.

Olsen, Fred. *On the Trail of the Arawaks*. [*Civilization of the Amer. Indian Ser.*] Univ. of Oklahoma Pr. 1975 $21.95 pap. $11.95. A very readable and well-illustrated account, occasionally rich in autobiographical narrative and reflection.

The Confrontation with the Modern West

The European colonial powers were vastly superior to tribal peoples in terms of their material possessions, technological abilities, and capabilities for war. When tribal groups were not simply killed off, they were severely disadvantaged economically, politically, and culturally under colonial rule. They were also subjected to intense pressures to adopt European Christianity that, whatever the intentions of the missionaries, were experienced as an extension of colonial policy. In this situation, traditional religions, which usually sought to provide well-being in the world, were severely strained.

Many tribal peoples found the pressures to adopt Christianity irresistible, for a variety of reasons, but they often transformed the "white man's" religion drastically. Ecstatic-emotional Christianity (Pentecostal movements)—in some sense a critique of normative Christianity—has been popular among some native North Americans and Australians. The Christianity of contemporary Mesoamerican Indians has preserved many traditional elements (see above under Religions of the Americas). In Africa, many churches have either seceded from the churches of their former rulers or been founded quite independently by African prophets such as Simon Kimbangu and Isaiah Shembe.

Other tribal peoples adjusted their traditions to the changing world, not infrequently in an attempt to do what sheer physical force could not do: drive out or destroy the white invaders or, failing that, in an attempt to preserve some amount of independent integrity. Among such movements are the Ghost Dances, Sun Dances and Peyote movements of the North American Indians, the neo-traditional movements in Africa, and neo-African movements in the Caribbean such as voodoo, Santería, and Shango.

Perhaps the most famous of these movements are the cargo cults of Melanesia. These cults attempt to induce the gods to send to the natives massive amounts of European goods, and they arouse in their followers the conviction that just such cargo is about to arrive. Political motives for the cargo cults cannot be discounted, but not all cargo cults have involved hostility toward Europeans. According to traditional beliefs, the gods are ultimately the source of all material well-being. Cargoists seem to be using these traditional beliefs to interpret and respond to the immense material disparity between themselves and the European colonizers.

Aberle, David F. *The Peyote Religion among the Navaho.* Univ. of Chicago Pr. 1982 $35.00. A sound treatment of the peyote cult among a particular people.

Barrett, Leonard E. *The Rastafarians: Sounds of Cultural Dissonance.* Beacon 1977 pap. $9.95. For a look at the religiopolitical movement most familiar to American readers from its association with reggae (music of Jamaican origin).

Burridge, Kenelm. *New Heaven, New Earth: A Study of Millenarian Activities.* Basil Blackwell 1969 text ed. pap. $12.95. A careful analysis of millennial movements that finds at the core a prophet who redresses imbalances created when a community living under one symbolic code moves to another.

Fernandez, James W. *Bwiti: An Ethnography of the Religious Imagination in Africa.* Princeton Univ. Pr. 1982 $97.50 pap. $28.00. A lengthy examination of "world reconstruction" in the equatorial villages of the Gabon Republic, peppered with allusions to Coleridge's *Kubla Khan.*

Jorgenson, Joseph G. *The Sun Dance Religion: Power for the Powerless.* Univ. of Chicago Pr. 1972 $12.50. About an old hunting ritual that was transformed by the wretched experience of reservation life and continues as a dominant religious form to this day.

Kolig, Erich. *Silent Revolution: The Effects of Modernization on Australian Aboriginal Religion.* Institute for the Study of Human Issues 1981 text ed. $27.50. Discusses the transformation of aboriginal religious life that has resulted from the impact of Western economics; based on fieldwork in the Fitzroy area of northern Western Australia.

LaBarre, Weston. *The Peyote Cult.* Shoe String 1975 $27.50. For an introduction to the peyote cult in general.

Laitin, David D. *Hegemony and Culture: Politics and Religious Change among the Yoruba.* Univ. of Chicago Pr. 1986 $30.00 pap. $13.95. The interaction of culture and politics in the Yoruba religious conflict; very self-conscious about the Western tradition of analyzing both.

Lawrence, Peter. *Road Belong Cargo: A Study of the Cargo Movement in the Southern Madang District New Guinea.* Fwd. by J. K. McCarthy, Humanities Pr. 1967 text ed. pap. $12.50. Emphasizes the role of the native view of the world in examining a particular cargo cult in Papua New Guinea.

MacGaffey, Wyatt. *Modern Congo Prophets: Religion in a Plural Society.* Indiana Univ. Pr. 1983 $22.50. A sensitive, sophisticated account.

Metraux, Alfred. *Voodoo in Haiti.* Schocken 1972 pap. $8.95. If you read only one book on voodoo, read this one; it is the best general introduction.

Simpson, George E. *Black Religions in the New World.* Columbia Univ. Pr. 1978 $40.00. Black religions in the Caribbean, South America, and North America, presented by an anthropologist who has been writing on the subject for 40 years.

Sundkler, B. G. M. *Zulu Zion and Some Swazi Zionists.* Oxford 1976 o.p. South African prophets and their movements, as described by an expert on independent South African Christianity.

Turner, Harold. *Bibliography of New Religious Movements in Primal Societies.* G. K. Hall 1977 o.p. A helpful guide into literature that is increasing at an immense rate.

Walker, Sheila S. *The Religious Revolution in the Ivory Coast: The Prophet Harris and the Harris Church.* [*Studies in Religion*] Univ. of North Carolina Pr. 1983 $29.95. An informative account of the early history and development of an independent African church (1913–73).

Worsley, Peter. *The Trumpet Shall Sound: A Study of Cargo Cults in Melanesia.* Schocken 1968 pap. $8.95. A historical survey of the cargo cults, informed by the sociology of Max Weber and his disciples.

CHAPTER 8

Eastern Religion and Philosophy

Norman J. Girardot

The Orient is not only adjacent to Europe; it is also the place of Europe's greatest and richest and oldest colonies, the source of its civilizations and languages, its cultural contestant, and one of its deepest and most recurring images of the Other.

—EDWARD SAID, *Orientalism*

[Since] the peoples of the West are no longer the only ones to "make" history, their spiritual and cultural values will no longer enjoy the privileged place, to say nothing of the unquestioned authority, that they enjoyed some generations ago.

MIRCEA ELIADE, *The Quest*

Eastern philosophy and religion is in many ways an impossibly amorphous and misleading category. The subject matter of Eastern philosophy and religion represents, however, only a subset of a broader "Eastern," "Oriental," or "non-Western" classification system that maps a very important, though shifting, imaginary universe. Indeed, the generalized concept of the East has commonly been used as a convenient, though falsely monolithic, label for everything beyond the known landscape of European or Western consciousness. The common divisions of Near, Middle, Central, Extreme, or Far East, therefore, tended to define aspects and phases of the history of the West's own self-understanding as much as they described actual geographic and cultural entities.

The particular encounter with, and understanding of, diverse Eastern philosophies and religions is, moreover, especially expressive of the overall "orientalist" legacy. Thus it was primarily the provocative "otherness" of Eastern religions and philosophies that directly challenged the singular authoritative logic of Western philosophic and religious truth. One reaction to this kind of confrontation was to ignore or denigrate Eastern traditions so that, for example, from the one-sided evolutionary perspective of nineteenth-century historiography, Eastern thought was uniformly seen as essentially retarded, prephilosophical, or superstitious. Directly counterpunctual to these rationalistic evaluations was the persuasive Romantic conviction in the superiority of a pan-Eastern pure mythopoetic religiosity, mystical spirituality, or "perennial philosophy."

These antithetical views are equally reductionistic and beguiling, but unfortunately both perspectives still influence, in varying degrees, the popular

375

understanding of Eastern traditions. It is finally the case, then, that the recalcitrant otherness of diverse non-Western traditions prevents the easy application of any single interpretive principle. In fact, the study of these traditions explicitly calls into question the universality of Western judgments concerning the very definition, and compartmentalized nature, of "religion" and "philosophy."

Despite the continuing authority of various orientalist preconceptions, much progress has been made in recent decades toward the unbiased study and explication of different Eastern religions and philosophies, although comparative philosophical studies are still relatively less developed than the comparative history of world religions. One of the strongest outcomes of this comparative work is the affirmation of the distinctive cultural, intellectual, and religious integrity of the various so-called Eastern, Oriental, non-Western, or Asian traditions. It must be understood, therefore, that the category of "Eastern philosophy and religion" used in this chapter represents only a loose bibliographic grouping of traditions located across a very broad cultural and geographic spectrum. No intrinsic intellectual or religious unity is implied.

While the diversity and complexity of these traditions must be respected, it should nevertheless be noted that some of the traditions are regionally and historically interconnected and share numerous cultural, linguistic, intellectual, and religious features—not the least of which are those that came about through the coercive influence of the Western world. In this chapter, these roughly interrelated cultural units are indicated by particular geographically contiguous groupings—such as the convenient use of "East Asian," "South," and "Southeast Asian" regional categories.

Given the unavoidable global implications of contemporary history, a respect for, and an accurate knowledge of, the philosophic and religious framework of Eastern traditions, no matter how loosely categorized, becomes especially acute. The irony of the situation today is, in fact, suggested by East Asia's accelerated impingement on the West which, as exemplified most dramatically by Japan's challenge to American economic superiority, starts to reverse the pivot of otherness. At the very least, these developments question some of the hoariest and most cherished categories of understanding. As both Western and Eastern traditions become fully oriented to the circular reality of truth and the world, what then can either the concept of the East or the West, Orient or Occident, mean?

EAST ASIAN TRADITIONS

"East Asia" is a regional classification that comprises the traditions of China, Japan, Korea, and, to a lesser extent, Tibet. Each of these traditions has its own unique cultural configuration, but the general influence of Chinese civilization on the development of the younger Japanese and Korean traditions represents an important unifying factor. It is in this way that specific Chinese religious and philosophical traditions—as well as many other intellectual, artistic, and social aspects of Chinese civilization—were imported into, and adapted to, the Korean and Japanese cultures. Confucianism and Buddhism, in both their philosophical and religious sense, may, in fact, be said to be the most significant common factors throughout the whole East Asian region.

Chinese Traditions

The origins of Chinese civilization go back to the rise of neolithic farming communities now dated to the third, and perhaps, fourth millennium B.C.E. It is within those archaic cultural enclaves, and then more explicitly within the first city-state tradition known as the Shang dynasty, that the foundational social, intellectual, and religious traits of a coherent civilization emerge. The most distinctive and far reaching of these were the characteristic ritual patterns of divination and ancestor worship. From roughly the time of the feudal kingdoms of the sixth century B.C.E. down to the early imperial period of the Former Han dynasty (second to first centuries B.C.E.), the earliest forms of Confucianism and Taoism, as well as other contending traditions, emerged to give expression to philosophical, moral, and religious ideas that would become integral to Chinese culture. Despite the differences among the early schools of thought, the *tao/yin-yang/wu-hsing* theory of the naturalistic universe came to be generally accepted, and, in fact, continued as the basic cosmological framework for all thought and action down to modern times.

Confucianism and Taoism, though greatly altered in succeeding periods, constitute, along with Mahayana Buddhism, the traditional "three religions" of China. Buddhism was originally foreign to China and its great success after the breakup of the Han dynasty must be seen in relation to how it was transformed within the Chinese milieu while, at the same time, contributing many new intellectual and religious ideas. Alongside these three literate traditions, and often interacting with them, were multifarious forms of popular religion.

It is, in fact, important that the characteristic syncretistic interpenetration of the so-called three religions and popular religious forms be taken into account throughout the history of Chinese religions. Recent developments in the nineteenth and twentieth centuries, especially since the Chinese Communist revolution, have profoundly altered, if not totally done away with, many of these age-old habits of practice and belief. Finally, it should be noted that, in contrast to the long-standing study and appreciation of the Classics and early Confucianism, the full scholarly investigation of religious Taoism, Chinese Buddhism, neo-Confucianism, and popular religion has only emerged in recent decades.

REFERENCE WORKS AND ANTHOLOGIES

Adams, Charles J., ed. *A Reader's Guide to the Great Religions*. Free Pr. 2d ed. 1977 $24.95. See particularly the chapter by W. A. C. H. Dobson, "The Religions of China (Excepting Buddhism)," which is a balanced and concisely annotated survey of scholarly works that has not been sufficiently updated in the second edition.

Chan, Wing-tsit. *Source Book in Chinese Philosophy*. Princeton Univ. Pr. 1963 $60.50 pap. $12.50. An excellent compilation of primary source readings from the major philosophical and religious traditions by the dean of contemporary commentators on Chinese philosophy. Faithful translations and helpful introductions to the various texts.

De Bary, William Theodore, and others, eds. *Sources of Chinese Tradition*. Columbia Univ. Pr. 2 vols. 1960 pap. ea. $14.00–$16.00. Along with Chan's *Source Book*, the best collection of primary readings on Chinese philosophy and religion. Introductory discussions to the various texts and traditions are especially valuable.

Eliade, Mircea, ed. *Encyclopedia of Religion*. Macmillan 16 vols. 1986 $1,100.00. Entries on various aspects of Chinese religious tradition represent accessible surveys of recent scholarship. Most authoritative and up-to-date general reference source.

Fu, Charles Wei-hsun, and Chan, Wing-tsit. *Guide to Chinese Philosophy*. G. K. Hall 1978 o.p. Though skewed in the direction of Confucian and neo-Confucian thought, this work is an authoritative and useful annotated bibliography of Chinese philosophical tradition.

Thompson, Laurence G. *Chinese Religion in Western Languages: A Comprehensive and Classified Bibliography of Publications in English, French, and German Through 1980*. [*Monograph of the Assn. for Asian Studies*] Univ. of Arizona Pr. 1985 $19.95. Exhaustive compilation of Western scholarship by one of the best, and most comprehensively informed, scholars of Chinese religion. Very accurate listing of many obscure publications, but not annotated.

———. *The Chinese Way in Religion*. [*Religious Life of Man Ser.*] Dickenson 1973 pap. $10.95. Interesting and worthwhile compilation of primary and secondary source readings with excellent contextual discussions. In contrast with the Chan and De Bary sourcebooks, this work includes important materials on popular tradition. Companion volume to *Chinese Religion in Western Languages* (above).

Yu, David C. *Guide to Chinese Religion*. G. K. Hall 1985 lib. bdg. $45.00. Somewhat eccentric in its organization and annotations, but covers many important, and relatively ignored, studies found in specialized journals. Complements Fu and Chan's *Guide to Chinese Philosophy*.

GENERAL WORKS

Baird, Robert D., and Alfred Bloom. *Religion and Man: Indian and Far Eastern Religious Traditions*. Harper 1972 text ed. pap. $14.95. Popular textbook introduction from a historical perspective. Bloom's discussions of East Asian traditions are particularly informative and well executed.

Chai, Chu, and Winberg Chai. *The Story of Chinese Philosophy*. Greenwood repr. of 1961 ed. 1975 lib. bdg. $22.50. Semipopular and now somewhat out-of-date presentation of the development of Chinese philosophy. Most authoritative on Confucian tradition.

Christie, Anthony. *Chinese Mythology*. [*Lib. of the World's Myths and Legends*] P. Bedrick Bks. 1985 $18.95. Fascinating nonscholarly discussion of both classical and popular mythology.

Creel, Herrlee G. *Chinese Thought from Confucius to Mao Tse-tung*. Univ. of Chicago Pr. 1971 pap. $8.95. Readable and generally reliable popular discussion that reflects Creel's special strengths in the ancient period.

De Groot, J. J. *The Religious System of China*. Oriental Bk. Store 6 vols. repr. of 1892–1910 ed. 1982 $130.00. Early and still valuable general study of the "system" of Chinese religion as related to its archaic origins. Especially noteworthy for its copious use of primary sources and illustrative materials.

Feibleman, James K. *Understanding Oriental Philosophy.* New Amer. Lib. 1984 pap. $9.95. Competent introductory discussion that places Eastern thought in relation to Western philosophical issues.

Fung, Yu Lan. *A History of Chinese Philosophy.* Trans. by Derk Bodde, Princeton Univ. Pr. 2 vols. 1952 pap. ea. $15.95–$20.95. Classic work by one of the leading contemporary Chinese philosophers. A basic starting point for any consideration of Chinese philosophical and religious thought. However, Fung's later retractions and Maoist modifications of his views should be noted.

Hackett, Stuart C. *Oriental Philosophy: A Westerner's Guide to Eastern Thought.* Univ. of Wisconsin Pr. 1979 pap. $10.95. Concise introduction to the philosophical implications of Eastern thought.

Hinnells, John R., ed. *A Handbook of Living Religions.* Penguin 1984 pap. $7.95. The chapter on "Chinese Religions" by Michael Saso is a good general introduction to the overall tradition.

Jochim, Christian. *Chinese Religions.* Prentice-Hall 1986 text ed. pap. $13.95. Thematic introduction to Chinese religious traditions as related to a broad cultural framework. Synthetically draws on recent specialized scholarship.

Kitagawa, Joseph M. *Religions of the East.* Westminster enl. ed. 1968 pap. $7.95. Popular thematic appraisal of Chinese religion from the sociology of religions viewpoint of Joachim Wach.

Koller, John M. *Oriental Philosophies.* Scribner 2d ed. 1985 text ed. pap. $12.95. Good introductory analysis from a comparative philosophical point of view.

Moore, Charles A., ed. *The Chinese Mind: Essentials of Chinese Philosophy and Culture.* Univ. of Hawaii Pr. 1967 text ed. pap. $8.95. Interesting, though disjointed and now dated, collection of articles from various comparative perspectives.

Needham, Joseph. *Science and Civilisation in China.* Cambridge Univ. Pr. 6 vols. to date 1954–87 ea. $67.50–$170.00. A modern classic that traces the history of Chinese science in its close relationship to religious and philosophical thought. Especially provocative and controversial with respect to its discussions of Taoism. Technical and scholarly, though written with graceful style and telling insight.

Overmyer, Daniel L. *The Religions of China.* Harper 1986 pap. $6.95. Brief, and sometimes overly terse, synthetic history that is noteworthy for its integrated discussion of popular religious currents. Digests the best of current specialized research.

Smith, D. Howard. *Chinese Religions.* Holt 1968 o.p. Somewhat dated with respect to recent scholarship concerning Taoism, neo-Confucianism, Buddhism, and popular religion; but still helpful for its appraisal of the ancient tradition.

Thompson, Laurence G. *Chinese Religion: An Introduction.* Wadsworth 3d ed. 1979 text ed. o.p. Probably the best general introductory text specifically devoted to Chinese religion. Thematically organized and based on available scholarship. Effectively integrates elite and popular traditions within the total Chinese cultural milieu.

Weber, Max. *Religion of China.* Free Pr. 1968 text ed. $14.95. Early synthetic study by one of the great masters of comparative sociological analysis. Though based on secondary, and sometimes untrustworthy and dated, scholarship, it is still worth consulting for its methodological implications.

Yang, C. K. *Religion in Chinese Society: A Study of Contemporary Social Functions of Religion and Some of Their Historical Factors.* Univ. of California Pr. 1961 o.p. Neo-

Weberian sociological discussion that is important for its revisionist demonstration of the religious nature of Confucianism and the general Chinese tradition.

ANCIENT TRADITION AND THE CLASSICS

The ancient religious tradition primarily refers to the various beliefs and practices associated with the development of a coherent Chinese civilization during the first millennium B.C.E. It is in this period that ancestral ritual, along with its related ideas of the afterlife and divination practices of communication with the dead and other spirits, takes shape as a fundamental expression of Chinese tradition. Also evident in the earliest periods are the characteristic Chinese understanding of the bureaucratic ordering of life on earth and in the heavens and the basic emphasis on the king or emperor's interrelated political and religious responsibilities for insuring the harmonious relation between the human and spirit realms.

It is, in fact, the so-called Classics—those semisacred scriptures that primarily included the *Book of History, Book of Songs, Spring and Autumn Annals, Book of Rites,* and the *Book of Changes*—that record the righteous ways of past Sage kings and constitute a kind of permanent guide to civic life (especially as it came to be interpreted by the Confucian tradition). The Classics, therefore, represent an attempt to determine and inculcate a standardized understanding of the meaning of human existence and may be said to be concerned with three basic principles: (1) the importance of a common ritualized pattern of life, (2) the significance of the political-theological theory of the "mandate of Heaven," which insured the divine legitimacy of a ruling house (and in the early Chou period probably involved quasimonotheistic belief in an all powerful sky deity known as T'ien or Shang Ti), and (3) the dynamic interrelatedness of all aspects of space and time as expressed by the key ideas of *tao* as the ultimate principle, of *yin* and *yang* as the complementary opposites of existence, and of *Wu Hsing* as the "five phases" that qualitatively characterize all change.

Eliade, Mircea. *From Gautama Buddha to the Triumph of Christianity.* Volume 2 in *A History of Religious Ideas.* Trans. by William R. Trask, Univ. of Chicago Pr. 1982 $25.00. See particularly the chapter "The Religions of Ancient China." Compact general discussion of the historical development of ancient Chinese religion from the standpoint of Eliade's distinctive comparative concern for the paradigmatic nature of myth, ritual, and symbol. Sometimes too reliant on the speculative scholarship of C. Hentze and Marcel Granet.

Field, Stephen, trans. *Tian Wen: A Chinese Book of Origins.* New Directions 1986 $22.95 pap. $8.95. Important, although enigmatic and terse, collection of ancient mythic fragments in interrogatory form. Skillfully translated and supplemented with notes sensitive to the mythological and ritual background.

Granet, Marcel. *The Religion of the Chinese People.* Trans. by Maurice Freedman, Harper 1977 pap. $5.95. Popular synthetic discussion by one of the great French sinological scholars. Controversial conclusions and now somewhat out-of-date, but still important for its use of a speculative Durkheimian method that stressed the origins of classical religion within ancient social traditions.

Laufer, Berthold. *Jade: A Study in Chinese Archaeology and Religion.* Dover repr. of 1912 ed. 1975 pap. $6.95; Kraus repr. of 1912 ed. $41.00; Peter Smith Repr. $15.25. Classic study that is still useful for its impressive command of ancient archaeological and textual sources as they bear on the religious import of jade implements.

Legge, James, trans. *The Sacred Books of China.* [*Sacred Bks. of the East Ser.*] Humanities Pr. 6 vols. $90.00; Krishna 6 vols. $600.00; Peter Smith 2 vols. $28.50. Faithful translation of the most important ancient classics with copious philological notes by the greatest of the nineteenth-century Protestant missionary scholars. Though stilted in a Victorian manner, still the standard Western versions of the Classics. Legge's introductory discussions are now dated in terms of modern scholarship.

Loewe, Michael. *Chinese Ideas of Life and Death.* Allen & Unwin 1982 text ed. $25.00

———. *Ways to Paradise: The Chinese Quest for Immortality.* Allen & Unwin 1979 text ed. $34.00. This and the title above are important general discussions of Han dynasty religious beliefs, symbolism, and practices by one of the leading experts.

Munro, Donald J. *The Concept of Man in Early China.* Stanford Univ. Pr. 1969 $22.50. Technically proficient and deftly written analysis of early Confucian and Taoist thought that is notable for its reference to comparable Western ideas.

Rubin, Vitaly A. *Individual and State in Ancient China: Essays on Four Chinese Philosophers.* Trans. by Steven I. Levine, Columbia Univ. Pr. 1976 $25.00. Concise and readable account of Confucius, Chuang Tzu, Mo-tzu, and Shang Yang as related to political philosophy by an accomplished Russian scholar.

Schwartz, Benjamin I. *The World of Thought in Ancient China.* Harvard Univ. Pr. 1985 text ed. $27.50. Impressive, and elegantly written, recent synthesis by one of the most respected intellectual historians of China. Incorporates the best of contemporary sinological scholarship but tends to neglect perspectives coming from the comparative history of religions.

Waley, Arthur, trans. *The Nine Songs: A Study of Shamanism in Ancient China.* City Lights 1973 o.p. Important early observations on ecstatic practices in the ancient southern state of Ch'u.

———. *Three Ways of Thought in Ancient China.* Stanford Univ. Pr. 1939 pap. $7.95. Felicitous translations of, and brief commentary on, Mencius, Chuang Tzu, and Legalist (or "Realist" as Waley prefers) texts.

Wilhelm, Richard, and C. F. Baynes, trans. *The I Ching or Book of Changes.* [*Bollingen Ser.*] Princeton Univ. Pr. 3d ed. 1967 $16.50. Sinologically sound, though "scriptural," translation of the Classic that influenced the thought of Carl Jung and became something of a cult classic in the 1960s and 1970s.

CONFUCIUS AND CONFUCIANISM

Confucius (traditional dates, 551–479? B.C.) was born during the Chou period when the feudal order was disintegrating. It was Confucius's genius as China's "first teacher" and greatest sage to establish a method for bringing harmony and stability back into political and personal life. He stressed, therefore, an education in the ritual principles (*li*) and moral principles (especially *jen* or "benevolence") as codified in the ancient Classics. Through the propriety of ritual and the progressive cultivation of morality within the family and state all men could achieve the nobility of a virtuous (*te*) life.

While Confucius himself was not successful in impressing his ideas on the ruling powers of his day, his later disciples—especially the "second sage" known as Mencius (who emphasized the original goodness of human nature) and others like the tough-minded Hsun Tzu—went on to develop and apply his thought in ways that would ultimately influence all of Chinese tradition. The triumph of the tradition, in fact, came about initially during the early Han dynasty (first two centuries B.C.E.) when Confucianism was established as official state doctrine. In subsequent periods, especially after the breakup of the Han dynasty and the special appeal of Buddhism and religious Taoism during the fragmentation and turmoil of the Six Dynasties period, Confucian tradition was largely moribund.

After the reestablishment of a unified Chinese empire in the T'ang dynasty, a newly vital form of Confucianism, known as neo-Confucianism, sought to revise the ancient tradition (especially in a Mencian spirit) by incorporating some of the more sympathetic intellectual and religious aspects of Buddhism and Taoism. In the great figure of Chu Hsi (1130–1200), neo-Confucianism became a total synthetic system of cosmological thought (e.g., the idea of the *t'ai-chi* or "great ultimate" and its inner moral rule of *li* or cosmic "principle"), political action, social reciprocity, and personal moral-spiritual cultivation. There were other important developments of neo-Confucian thought as seen in the almost Chan-like works of Wang Yang-ming (see below), but it was essentially Chu Hsi's version that became the orthodox tradition down until the beginning of the twentieth century.

Chai, Chu, and Winberg Chai. *Confucianism.* Barron 1974 o.p. Competent popular discussion of the development of Confucian tradition.

Chan, Wing-tsit, trans. *Instructions for Practical Living and Other Neo-Confucian Writings by Wang Yang-ming.* Columbia Univ. Pr. 1963 o.p. This and the title below are the best available translations, and introductory discussions, of Chu Hsi and Wang Yang-ming—the two greatest figures associated respectively with the Schools of Reason and Mind in neo-Confucianism.

———. *Reflections on Things at Hand: The Neo-Confucian Anthology Compiled by Chu Hsi and Lu Tsu-ch'ien.* Columbia Univ. Pr. 1967 $36.00 pap. $16.00

Chang, Carsun. *The Development of Neo-Confucian Thought.* Greenwood repr. of 1957 ed. 1977 lib. bdg. $26.75; New College & Univ. Pr. 1957 pap. $10.95. Important, although rather turgid, historical treatment of neo-Confucian philosophy. Should be considered in the light of more recent scholarship.

Creel, Herrlee G. *Confucius: The Man and the Myth.* Greenwood repr. of 1949 ed. 1973 lib. bdg. $23.00. Well-executed general study of Confucius and the development of Confucian tradition from the standpoint of ancient Chinese intellectual history.

De Bary, William Theodore. *Neo-Confucianism Orthodoxy and the Learning of the Mind and Heart.* Columbia Univ. Pr. 1981 $30.00. Gracefully written and learnedly temperate study of neo-Confucianism by a leading scholar.

———, ed. *The Unfolding of Neo-Confucianism.* [*Neo-Confucianism Ser. and Studies in Oriental Culture*] Columbia Univ. Pr. 1975 $38.00 pap. $18.50. Important scholarly collection that reflects the revived interest and appreciation of the rich philosophical and religious complexity of neo-Confucianism.

Fingarette, Herbert. *The Secular as Sacred.* Harper 1972 $5.95. Provocative new interpretation of the Confucian *Analects* by a nonsinologist. Accessible to a general audience and noteworthy for its treatment of Confucius's abiding philosophical and religious significance.

Hall, David L., and Ames, Roger T. *Thinking Through Confucius.* State Univ. of New York Pr. 1987 pap. $12.95. Whiteheadian or "process" interpretation of Confucius by a professional philosopher and sinologist. Argument for the continuing relevance of Confucianism.

Lau, D. C., trans. *Confucius: The Analects.* [*Class. Ser.*] Penguin 1979 o.p. Along with Waley's version, the best available translation of the *Analects.*

———. *Mencius.* [*Class Ser.*] Penguin 1970 pap. $5.95. First-rate translation and commentary.

McNaughton, William, ed. *The Confucian Vision.* Univ. of Michigan Pr. 1974 $8.50 pap. $2.95. Short allusive introduction and suggestive compilation of various Confucian texts under key topical headings. Popular in format but at times too fragmentary.

Shryock, John K. *The Origin and Development of the State Cult of Confucius.* Paragon repr. of 1932 ed. 1966 o.p. Still the only available work that specifically treats the transformation of early Confucianism into the civic religion of traditional China. Scholarly historical study.

Taylor, Rodney L. *The Cultivation of Sagehood as a Religious Goal in Neo-Confucianism: A Study of Selected Writings of Kao P'an-lung (1562–1626).* Scholars Pr. GA 1978 pap. $10.25

———. *The Way of Heaven: An Introduction to the Confucian Religious Life.* Heinman 1986 pap. $29.50. This and the title above are important for their innovative delineation of the religious nature of Confucianism as a system of "self-transformation."

Tu, Wei-ming. *Confucian Thought: Selfhood as Creative Transformation.* State Univ. of New York Pr. 1985 pap. $14.95

———. *Humanity and Self-Cultivation: Essays in Confucian Thought.* Humanities Pr. 1980 o.p. Tu is perhaps the most knowledgeable and sensitive contemporary interpreter of the Confucian tradition. Many of these collected essays here and the book above represent minor classics in the modern reassessment of Confucianism. Balanced appreciation of the philosophical, ethical, and religious implications.

Waley, Arthur D. *The Analects of Confucius.* Random 1966 o.p. Very readable, and generally trustworthy, translations of Confucius—although Waley is sometimes too confident in his attempt to determine the "original" *Analects.* Also to be recommended for its introductory discussion of the cultural and intellectual context.

Watson, Burton, ed. and trans. *Basic Writings of Mo Tzu, Hsun Tzu, and Han Fei Tzu.* [*Records of Civilization, Sources and Studies*] Columbia Univ. Pr. 1967 $20.00. Fluid and reliable modern translation.

Wright, Arthur F., ed. *Confucianism and Chinese Civilization.* Stanford Univ. Pr. 1964 $27.50 pap. $10.95. Helpful, though rather technical, collection of diverse scholarly articles.

EARLY TAOIST CLASSICS AND THE TAOIST RELIGION

The ultimate roots of the Taoist tradition go back to the turmoil of the late Chou period (sixth through third centuries B.C.E.) and are especially associated with the semihistorical figure known as Lao Tzu or the "Old Master." At more or less the same time, another shadowy sage known as Chuang Tzu was also teaching, like Lao Tzu, an enigmatic philosophy that challenged the ritualized public morality of the Confucians. Early so-called "classical" or "philosophical" Taoism is, then, not so much a distinct school of thought but rather a convenient label for the basically similar mystical visions found in the ancient texts attributed to Lao Tzu (the *Tao Te Ching* or the Classic of the Tao and its Power) and Chuang Tzu (the composite text known as the *Chuang Tzu*). These texts generally emphasized the need for a mystical return to a union with the unsullied dynamic principle of natural life known as the *Tao.* Rejecting the ritual propriety and civic righteousness of Confucianism, they recommended the method of *Wu-wei* or "non[competitive] action" as the way to reactivate the inner power (*te*) and spontaneous freedom (*tzu-jan*) of the *Tao.*

In the early Han period (second and first centuries B.C.E.) the thought of Lao Tzu and Chuang Tzu was loosely incorporated into popular movements that stressed the salvational goal of physical immortality as associated with the figure of the *hsien* (Taoist immortal, saint, or holy man). It was, therefore, the popular cult of immortality, and various messianic movements during the breakup of the later Han dynasty (especially the movements identified with the new revelations of the semilegendary Chang Tao-ling—the first "heavenly master" of religious Taoism), that gave rise to the organized Taoist religion. The Six Dynasties Period of political disunity (second through sixth centuries C.E.) saw the greatest efflorescence of sectarian forms of religious Taoism and produced various complex ecclesiastical, theological, liturgical, and scriptural (culminating in the so-called Taoist canon or *Tao Tsang*) institutions. Religious Taoism retained some of the ancient mystical and individualistic spirit of Lao Tzu and Chuang Tzu (Lao Tzu, in fact, became a kind of salvational deity associated with the highest trinity of Taoist gods), but more fundamentally functioned as a popular vehicle for ritually insuring the periodic renewal of corporate life, especially at the village level.

Blofeld, John. *Taoism: The Road to Immortality.* Shambhala 1978 pap. $9.95. Knowledgeable and fascinating, though rather uncritical, popular discussion of religious Taoism. As a self-styled insider, Blofeld reinforces the hermetic "magic garden" image of religious Taoism.

Chang, Chung-yuan. *Creativity and Taoism.* Harper repr. of 1963 ed. 1970 pap. $6.95. Informed and graceful essays on the various cultural and artistic embodiments of the Taoist tradition. Written for a general audience.

Cleary, Thomas, trans. *The Inner Teachings of Taoism.* Shambhala 1986 pap. $9.95. Knowledgeable translation of, and brief contextual commentary on, some of the esoteric texts of religious Taoism. Popular format.

Feng, Gia-fu, and Jane English, trans. *Lao Tzu: Tao Te Ching.* Random 1972 o.p. Fluent new translation that is noteworthy for its use of images that complement the text. Popular format.

Girardot, N. J. *Myth and Meaning in Early Taoism: The Themes of Chaos (hun-tun).* [*Hermeneutics Studies in the History of Religions*] Univ. of California Pr. 1983 $39.50. Comparative analysis of the mythological and symbolic context for understanding the early Taoist texts.

Graham, A. C., trans. and ed. *Chuang Tzu: The Inner Chapters.* Allen & Unwin 1987 pap. $7.95. Innovative scholarly translation and sinuously intelligent commentary by one of the most gifted of contemporary scholars. Along with Watson's rendition (see below), the best available modern translation.

Hoff, Benjamin. *The Tao of Pooh.* Dutton 1982 $8.95; Penguin 1983 pap. $4.95. Pooh bear as Lao Tzu! Introduction to Taoist philosophy via the medium of the popular children's story. Often effective and entertaining, but in places overly precious and misleading.

Kaltenmark, Max. *Lao Tzu and Taoism.* Trans. by Roger Greaves, Stanford Univ. Pr. 1969 $15.00 pap. $5.95. Best available semipopular introduction to classical Taoism (Lao Tzu and Chuang Tzu), along with a brief section devoted to later religious Taoism, by one of the most accomplished modern French scholars.

Lau, D. C., trans. *Lao Tzu: Tao Te Ching.* Penguin 1963 o.p. Excellent modern scholarly translation that stresses the philosophical-political implications of the text more than the religious-mystical aspects.

McNaughton, William, ed. *Taoist Vision.* Univ. of Michigan Pr. 1971 $7.95. Semipopular work that gathers short passages from various Taoist texts, and related materials, under topical headings. Helpful, though brief, introductory discussion; readable though at times eccentric translations.

Maspero, Henri. *Taoism and Chinese Religion (Le taoisme et les religions Chinoises).* Trans. by Frank A. Kierman, Jr., intro. by Timothy Barrett, Univ. of Massachusetts Pr. 1981 lib. bdg. $40.00. Important collection of scholarly essays by the eminent French sinologue. Includes Maspero's groundbreaking early work on religious Taoism.

Morgan, Evan, trans. *Tao: The Great Luminant—Essays from Huai-nan-tzu.* Coronet repr. of 1935 ed. $24.00. Still the only available partial translation of the important, and little known, synthetic Taoist text of the Han period. Translations are overly effusive and not always very accurate, but the sense of the text comes through.

Rawson, Philip, and Laslo Legeza. *Tao: The Eastern Philosophy of Time and Change.* Crown 1974 o.p. Popular discussion of the cosmological and metaphysical implications of Taoism. Knowledgeable and worthwhile, but rather esoteric at times. Especially valuable for its abundant color plates and thematic illustrations.

Saso, Michael R. *Taoism and the Rite of Cosmic Renewal.* Washington State Univ. Pr. 1972 pap. $4.00. Short ethnographic discussion of the living tradition of liturgical Taoism on Taiwan by one of the leading scholars of religious Taoism. Semipopular in format, but sometimes overly technical and confusing.

Smullyan, Raymond M. *The Tao Is Silent.* Intro. by Martin Gardner, Harper 1977 $8.95 pap. $4.95. Delightful, and thought provoking, popular musings on the meaning and contemporary significance of Taoist thought. At times, however, more "Smullyanism" than Taoism.

Waley, Arthur. *The Way and Its Power: A Study of the Tao Te Ching and Its Place in Chinese Thought.* Grove 1958 pap. $4.95. Valuable translation, intrepretive commentary, and introduction that emphasize the mystical (or early "Taoist yoga") implications of the text.

Ware, James R., trans. *Chinese Alchemy, Medicine, and Religion in the China of A.D. 320: The Nei P'ien of Ko Hung (Pao-p'u tzu).* Dover 1981 $7.50. Complete accurate translation of an important Taoist text that stresses the esoteric methods of alchemical "immortality." The translation of individual terms are sometimes idiosyncratic and misleading.

Watson, Burton, trans. *Chuang Tzu: Basic Writings.* Columbia Univ. Pr. 1964 o.p. Along with Graham's version (see above), the best available modern translation.

Welch, Holmes. *Taoism: The Parting of the Way.* (Orig. title: *Parting of the Way*) Beacon Pr. 1966 pap. $6.95. Very readable popular work that is especially valuable for its suggestive discussion of the original meaning and modern significance of *Tao-te-ching.* Discussion of later religious Taoism is now dated.

Wilhelm, Richard, trans. *Lao Tzu: Tao Te Ching.* Methuen 1985 pap. $5.95. Good scholarly translation, helpful notes, general introduction, and contextual essay that stress the metaphysical and religious implications of the text.

Wu, Kuang-Ming. *Chuang Tzu: World Philosopher at Play.* Crossroad NY 1982 $12.95; Scholars Pr. GA 1982 $12.95. Engaging phenomenological analysis of the interrelated philosophical, religious, and social meaning of Chuang Tzu.

CHINESE BUDDHISM

Buddhism entered China during the second century C.E. and during the Six Dynasties period (second through sixth centuries C.E.) became fully integrated within Chinese tradition (e.g., the idea of Karma or moral retribution became an accepted part of popular Chinese tradition at this time). The development of Buddhism during this period primarily concerns the intellectual and practical adaptation of Buddhism to its Chinese environment, its struggle with the indigenous traditions of Taoism and Confucianism, and the emergence of various synthetic scriptural schools (such as T'ien-T'ai and Hua Yen Buddhism) and the more popular, influential, and uniquely Chinese forms known as Pure Land and Ch'an, or Zen, Buddhism.

In general, it was the Mahayana form of Buddhism that entered China and such distinctive Mahayana doctrines as the role of the savior Bodhisattva and the "emptiness" of existence are especially prominent in the Pure Land and Ch'an traditions.

Pure Land was especially the religion of the masses and promised salvation in a Pure Land heaven through faith and devotion to the Bodhisattva A-mi-t'o-fo (Amitabha Buddha). Ch'an Buddhism, more of an elitist school that showed the special influence of Taoism, stressed the discipline of meditation (*ch'an* = *dhyana*) as the basic way to experience the "empty" truth of everyday life.

Blofeld, John. *Bodhisattva of Compassion: The Mystical Tradition of Kuan Yin.* Shambhala 1978 pap. $9.95. Informative study of the most important Chinese Buddhist savior figure. Sometimes idiosyncratic interpretations.

————. *The Jewel in the Lotus: Outline of Present Day Buddhism in China.* [*China Studies*] Hyperion Pr. repr. of 1948 ed. 1986 $20.50. Minor popular classic on the modern practice of Chinese Buddhism. Knowledgeable, but not always reliable from a strict scholarly standpoint.

Chang, Chung-yuan, ed. *The Original Teachings of Ch'an Buddhism.* Grove 1982 pap. $9.95. Helpful contextual discussion and good translations of important, yet little known, works associated with the Chinese origins of Ch'an (or Zen) Buddhism.

Ch'en, Kenneth. *Buddhism in China: A Historical Survey.* [*Studies in History of Religion*] Princeton Univ. Pr. 1974 pap. $13.50. Scholarly, though not overly technical, discussion of Chinese Buddhism by one of the leading modern experts. Most reliable general historical survey.

Robinson, Richard H., and Willard L. Johnson. *The Buddhist Religion: A Historical Introduction.* Wadsworth 3d ed. 1982 text ed. pap. $11.25. Informative introductory text to overall tradition with good concise chapters on East Asian Buddhism. Digests best of modern technical scholarship.

Welch, Holmes. *The Practice of Chinese Buddhism, 1900–1950.* Harvard Univ. Pr. 1967 pap. $10.95. Definitive descriptive presentation of modern Chinese Buddhist customs. Scholarly format.

Wright, Arthur F. *Buddhism in Chinese History.* Stanford Univ. Pr. 1959 $13.50 pap. $6.95. Short semipopular synthesis that stresses the historical, cultural, and intellectual aspects of the tradition.

POPULAR RELIGION

Ahern, Emily M. *Cult of the Dead in a Chinese Village.* Stanford Univ. Pr. 1973 $22.50. Important interpretive study of modern ancestral practices from an anthropological perspective.

Dennys, N. B. *The Folk-Lore of China: And Its Affinities with That of the Aryan and Semitic Races.* Ayer repr. of 1876 ed. 1972 $20.00; Gale repr. of 1876 ed. 1972 $43.00. Theoretical perspective outmoded, but still a valuable descriptive study of south Chinese folklore.

Eberhard, Wolfram. *Chinese Fairy Tales and Folk Tales.* Folcroft 1937 lib. bdg. $32.50

————. *Chinese Festivals.* [*Asian Folklore and Social Life Monograph*] Oriental Bk. Store 1972 $25.00. This title and the one above, both by Eberhard, are semipopular discussions by one of the most knowledgeable modern experts on Chinese popular customs.

Hsu, Francis L. *Under the Ancestors' Shadow: Kinship, Personality and Social Mobility in China.* Stanford Univ. Pr. repr. of 1948 ed. 1967 $27.50 pap. $7.95. Fascinating scholarly analysis of modern village ancestral tradition from a comparative social-psychological perspective.

Jordan, David K. *Gods, Ghosts, and Ancestors: The Folk Religion of a Taiwanese Village.* Univ. of California Pr. 1972 o.p. Notable anthropological study of current practices on Taiwan.

Jordan, David K., and Daniel L. Overmyer. *The Flying Phoenix: Aspects of Chinese*

Sectarianism in Taiwan. Princeton Univ. Pr. 1986 text ed. $39.50. Effectively integrated scholarly study of the historical and ethnographic aspects of contemporary Taiwanese sects.

Palmer, Martin, trans. *T'ung Shu.* Shambhala 1986 pap. $7.95. Intriguing discussion and partial translation of a typical folk almanac. Popular format that follows illustrative style of a traditional almanac.

Wagner, Rudolf G. *Reenacting the Heavenly Vision: The Role of Religion in the Taiping Rebellion.* Univ. of California IEAS 1984 pap. $12.00. Short, lucid, scholarly analysis of the religious nature of the most important nineteenth-century revolutionary movement.

Waley, Arthur, trans. *Monkey, Folk Novel of China.* Grove 1958 pap. $8.95. Engaging partial translation of a work that represents a fascinating compendium of popular religious lore.

Yu, Anthony. *The Journey to the West.* Univ. of Chicago Pr. 4 vols. 1977–83 lib. bdg. ea. $35.00. Elegant and authoritative complete translation of *Monkey,* the great folk classic that describes the fantastic travels of a motley group of Buddhist pilgrims searching for salvation.

FOREIGN INFLUENCES AND THE MODERN ERA

Briere, O. *Fifty Years of Chinese Philosophy: Eighteen Ninety-Eight to Nineteen Fifty.* Pref. by E. R. Hughes, Greenwood repr. of 1956 ed. 1979 lib. bdg. $22.50. Brief, rather disjointed, descriptive account of the struggles of traditional Chinese thought with Western tradition.

Bush, Richard C., Jr. *Religion in Communist China.* Abingdon 1970 o.p. Informed general appraisal of religion, both traditional and non-Chinese, during the Maoist period. Needs revision in light of the post-Maoist era.

Chan, Wing-tsit. *Religious Trends in Modern China.* Hippocrene Bks. repr. of 1953 ed. 1970 o.p. Interesting and still important discussion of the impact of Western ideas and modernization.

Cohen, Paul A. *China and Christianity: The Missionary Movement and the Growth of Chinese Antiforeignism, 1860–1870.* Harvard Univ. Pr. 1963 $27.50. Important for its descriptive analysis of the nineteenth-century antimissionary movements. Scholarly format.

Dunne, George H. *Generation of Giants.* Univ. of Notre Dame Pr. 1962 $19.95. Semipopular narrative history of the Jesuit missionary experience in China.

Fairbank, John K., ed. *The Missionary Enterprise in China and America.* [*Studies in Amer. East Asian Relations*] Harvard Univ. Pr. 1974 text ed. $25.00. Significant scholarly essays on various nineteenth- and early twentieth-century missionary topics.

Gernet, Jacques. *China and the Christian Impact: A Conflict of Cultures.* Trans. by Janet Lloyd, Cambridge Univ. Pr. 1985 $49.50 pap. $17.95. Brilliant and groundbreaking analysis of the religious and intellectual conflict between Jesuit and Confucian scholars. Scholarly but accessible.

Latourette, Kenneth S. *History of Christian Missions in China.* Russell repr. of 1929 ed. 1967 $22.50. Important, and generally balanced, historical study of missionary tradition by the leading Protestant scholar of his day.

Levenson, Joseph R. *Confucian China and Its Modern Fate: A Trilogy.* Univ. of California Pr. 1968 $34.00 pap. $12.95. Minor scholarly classic by one of the great modern exponents of Chinese intellectual history.

Lifton, Robert J. *Revolutionary Immortality: Mao Tse-tung and the Chinese Revolution.* Peter Smith o.p. Fascinating psychological interpretation of the religious functionality of Maoism.

Metzger, Thomas A. *Escape from Predicament: Neo-Confucianism and China's Evolving Political Culture.* Columbia Univ. Pr. 1986 $13.00. Controversial revisionist discussion of the role of neo-Confucianism in the modern period.

Welch, Holmes. *Buddhism Under Mao.* Harvard Univ. Pr. 1972 o.p. Careful descriptive study of the political and religious status of Buddhism. Readable scholarly work.

Japanese and Korean Traditions

Japan and Korea, though each represents a distinctive tradition, may be linked because of certain shared linguistic similarities (i.e., common affinities with the Altaic language family) and because of their interrelated history of cultural borrowings from the more ancient Chinese legacy. In fact, many of the appropriations from China, particularly Confucian political and ethical thought and Buddhism, were initially transmitted to Japan through the medium of early Korean tradition. Given the impact of China on these traditions, it is especially important to examine the manner in which Chinese elements (e.g., the Chinese written script, Confucian political and social institutions, the *yin-yang* cosmological system, and various Buddhist sectarian traditions) were adapted and transformed by the unique cultural geniuses of Japan and Korea. Another critical consideration concerns the way indigenous pre-Chinese religious elements developed in the face of the foreign influx—that is, the continuation of ancient shamanistic practices of Korea, the emergence of Shinto in Japan, and, finally, the overall nature and significance of folk practices in both Korea and Japan.

In the modern period, the influence of Western tradition must be taken into account, especially in relation to the spectacular rise of "new religions" and the Westernization of philosophical, social, and political thought. Finally, it should be noted that Korean religious and intellectual tradition has still not been sufficiently studied.

REFERENCE WORKS AND ANTHOLOGIES

Adams, Charles J., ed. *A Reader's Guide to the Great Religions.* Free Pr. 2d ed. 1977 $24.95. See especially Joseph M. Kitagawa's chapter, "The Religions of Japan." Excellent annotated compilation of scholarly books and articles.

Earhart, H. Byron. *The New Religions of Japan: A Bibliography of Western Language Materials.* G. K. Hall o.p. Comprehensive annotated survey of materials by one of the leading experts on new religious movements.

———. *Religion in the Japanese Experience.* Dickenson 1973 text ed. pap. $10.95. Interesting popular collection of primary and secondary source readings that complements Earhart's *Japanese Religion* (see next section under General Works).

Holzman, Donald, and Yukihiko Motoyama. *Japanese Religion and Philosophy.* Greenwood repr. of 1959 ed. 1975 lib. bdg. $22.50. Useful, though now dated, survey of both religious and philosophical materials.

Itasaka, Gen, and Maurits Dekker, eds. *Encyclopedia of Japan.* Kodansha 9 vols. 1983 set $620.00. Concise, authoritative, and up-to-date basic reference source for many topics related to both religion and philosophy.

Lancaster, Lewis R., ed. *The Korean Buddhist Canon: A Descriptive Catalogue.* [*Center for Korean Studies*] Univ. of California Pr. 1980 $60.00. First Western presentation of the overall contents and distinctive features of the Buddhist patrology within Korean religious history.

Schwade, Arcadio. *Shinto-Bibliography in Western Languages: Bibliography on Shinto and Religious Sects, Intellectual Schools and Movements Influenced by Shintoism.* Heinman 1986 pap. $26.95. Helpful recent compilation that includes many obscure, yet valuable, scholarly publications.

Silberman, Bernard S. *Japan and Korea: A Critical Bibliography.* Greenwood repr. of 1962 ed. 1982 lib. bdg. $27.50. Needs revision in light of recent scholarship, but still useful for its annotated comments on materials up to the 1960s.

Tsunoda, Ryusaku, and others. *Sources of Japanese Tradition.* Columbia Univ. Pr. 1958 o.p. Like De Bary's *Sources of Chinese Tradition* (see under East Asian Traditions, Chinese Traditions, Reference Works and Anthologies, in this chapter). This is an expertly produced anthology of representative primary texts accompanied by succinct introductory discussions.

GENERAL WORKS

Anesaki, Masaharu. *History of Japanese Religion.* Tuttle repr. of 1930 ed. 1963 $23.50. General historical overview by one of Japan's leading scholars. Still an important source, but somewhat stilted in style and dated in content and method.

Benedict, Ruth. *Chrysanthemum and the Sword: Patterns of Japanese Culture.* New Amer. Lib. 1967 pap. $7.95. Fascinating and controversial World War II analysis of Japanese tradition by a leading cultural anthropologist that includes many topics directly bearing on religious issues.

Earhart, H. Byron. *Japanese Religion: Unity and Diversity.* [*Religious Life of Man Ser.*] Dickenson 2d ed. 1974 pap. $3.95; Wadsworth 3d ed. 1982 text ed. pap. $11.25. "Suitable for an undergraduate survey course or for an introductory approach to religious thought and practice. Excellent footnotes; annotated bibliography; and index. The table of religious history, introduction, and presentation of themes prepare the reader for the history and themes of three major periods" (*Choice*).

———. *Religions of Japan: Many Traditions Within One Sacred Day.* [*Religious Traditions of the World Ser.*] Harper 1984 $6.95. Balanced introductory appraisals of religion that draw on the best of specialized scholarship. Popular textbook format.

Ellwood, Robert S., Jr. *An Invitation to Japanese Civilization.* Wadsworth 1980 pap. $11.25. Well-written general introduction that brings out the diffuse interrelation of culture, religion, and philosophy in Japan.

Hinnells, John R., ed. *A Handbook of Living Religions.* Penguin 1984 pap. $7.95. The chapter devoted to Japanese religions provides an excellent, and concise, overview of the tradition.

Il-ch'ol Sin, and others. *Main Currents of Korean Thought.* [*Korean Art, Folklore, Language, and Thought Ser.*] Pace Intl. Res. 1983 $25.00. Collection of diverse articles on philosophical and religious topics by leading authorities.

Kitagawa, Joseph M. *Religion in Japanese History.* Columbia Univ. Pr. 1966 $33.00. Scholarly study that stresses the sociological significance of the history of Japanese religions. Especially strong on Buddhist tradition.

Moore, Charles A., ed. *Japanese Mind: Essentials of Japanese Philosophy and Culture.* Univ. of Hawaii Pr. 1967 text ed. pap. $6.95. Interesting, though uneven, collection of articles from a comparative philosophical perspective.

Nakamura, Hajime. *Ways of Thinking of Eastern Peoples: India, China, Tibet, Japan.* Ed. by Philip P. Wiener, Univ. of Hawaii Pr. rev. ed. 1964 text ed. pap. $10.95. Tantalizing, although controversial, comparative analyses of the distinctive linguistic and intellectual traits of Asian traditions that is especially authoritative concerning Japan. Contextual considerations for both philosophy and religion.

Piggott, Juliet. *Japanese Mythology.* [*Lib. of the World's Myths and Legends*] P. Bedrick Bks. rev. ed. 1984 $18.95; [*Lib. of the World's Myths and Legends*] Creative Education repr. of 1968 ed. 1982 $16.95. Good semipopular presentation of both elite and popular mythology.

ANCIENT TRADITION AND SHINTO IN JAPAN

After a long period of prehistoric development, Japanese civilization starts to emerge as a self-consciously coherent tradition in the sixth century C.E. Through the coalescence of various clans under a single ruling house, the ancient Japanese tradition was clearly influenced via Korea by Confucianism concerning state polity and public morality and by Buddhism concerning religious matters. The most important expression of the ancient imperial tradition is found in the composite texts known as the *Nihongi* and *Kojiki* (dating to roughly the eighth century C.E., but drawing on earlier oral tradition) that articulate the official story of the divine origins of Japan. From the mythic perspective of these works (much of it adapted from Chinese and other sources), Japanese imperial tradition was understood as a direct inheritance from the sacred foundational actions of the gods (the *kami* spirits), especially the sun goddess Amaterasu-omi-kami. Shinto as the "Way of the Kami" represents the semi-organized and syncretistic expression (institutionalized Shinto clearly betrays Buddhist influence) of the national mythology and primarily involves ritual traditions of purification and worship designed to maintain a balanced and reciprocal relationship with the *kami* spirits. During World War II, Shinto became the nationalistic state religion; but even after its official disestablishment in 1945, it continues as a significant expression of Japanese indigenous culture and tradition.

Aston, W. G. *Nihongi: Chronicles of Japan from the Earliest Times to A.D. 697.* Tuttle 1971 pap. $10.50. Only available complete rendition of the ancient sacred classic of Shinto and the imperial cult. Dated, but reliable scholarly translation.

———. *Shinto: The Ancient Religion of Japan.* Telegraph Bks. 1982 o.p. Still helpful, though methodologically dated, early study by a leading scholar of the time.

Chamberlain, Basil Hall, trans. *Ko-ji-ki, or Records of Ancient Matters.* Asia Society repr. of 1882 ed. 1973 o.p. Early complete scholarly translation, with copious notes, of one of the semisacred scriptures of Shinto and the imperial tradition. Dated in style and method, but still a standard and reliable source.

Ono, Sokyo. *Shinto: The Kami Way.* Tuttle 1962 $8.50. Interesting popular introductory treatment by a Shinto priest.

Ross, Floyd H. *Shinto: The Way of Japan.* Greenwood repr. of 1965 ed. 1983 lib. bdg. $35.00. Semipopular and readable thematic history.

JAPANESE AND KOREAN BUDDHISM

Buddhism, particularly sinified forms of Mahayana coming from Korea, entered Japan during the formative period of the sixth century C.E. and by the Nara period (710–784) was primarily represented by six philosophical and monastic centers closely associated with the imperial tradition. Later in the Heian and Kamakura periods (eighth to fourteenth centuries), Buddhism became more fully assimilated into the native tradition in ways that resulted in such syncretistic forms as Ryobu Shinto. More important, however, were the important Bajrayana esoteric sect of Shingon founded by the brilliant Kobo Daishi (also known as Kukai), the philosophical school of Tendai (= the Chinese T'ien-t'ai), and the more popular Pure Land (Jodo) traditions of Honen and Shinran, the Rinzai (stressing *koan* practice) and

Soto (stressing sitting meditation) Zen traditions, and the evangelical *Lotus Sutra* sect founded by the messianic Nichiren (1222–82). Given its powerful appeal to the common people, Pure Land tradition and its devotion to the Bodhisattva Amida Buddha was the most popular of these developments; but Zen Buddhism, especially in relation to the distinctive Soto Zen thought of Dogen, had a pervasive impact on Japanese art and culture (e.g., such characteristic "do" arts as the tea ceremony, gardening, theater, haiku poetry, and so on).

Anesaki, Masaharu. *Nichiren: The Buddhist Prophet.* Peter Smith 1916 $11.25. General historical study of the founder of one of the most important, and distinctive, Buddhist sects.

Bloom, Alfred. *Shinran's Gospel of Pure Grace.* [*Assn. for Asian Studies Monograph*] Univ. of Arizona Pr. 1965 pap. $4.50. Short, interestingly written, scholarly study of the founder of the pietist True Pure Land sect. Pure Land Buddhism is a kind of Mahayana that stresses the salvation of the common person through faith in the power of the Bodhisattva deity known as Amida Buddha.

Buswell, Robert E. *The Korean Approach to Zen: The Collected Works of Chinul.* Univ. of Hawaii Pr. 1983 text ed. $29.95. Valuable scholarly study of the distinctive, and little known, aspects of Korean Zen as expressed in the work of the monk Chinul.

Castile, Rand. *The Way of Tea.* Weatherhill 1971 $27.50. Excellent semipopular description of the tea cult that treats its historical, religious, philosophical, and aesthetic aspects.

Dumoulin, Heinrich. *History of Zen Buddhism.* Trans. by Paul Peachey, Beacon Pr. repr. of 1963 ed. 1969 o.p. Minor modern classic that concisely and authoritatively lays out the general history of Zen in China and Japan. Comparative discussion of Christian and Zen mystic experience colored by apologetic concerns.

Hoover, Thomas. *Zen Culture.* Random 1977 o.p. Best popular discussion of the influence of Zen on various aspects of Japanese culture and art.

Kapleau, Philip. *The Three Pillars of Zen: Teaching, Practice, Enlightenment.* Doubleday 1980 pap. $9.95. Intelligent and well-written discussion of the nature of Rinzai Zen by a leading American master. Rinzai Zen stresses sudden enlightenment by means of *koan* practice.

Kim, Hee-Jin. *Dogen Kigen: Mystical Realist.* [*Assn. for Asian Studies Monograph*] Univ. of Arizona Pr. 1975 pap. $8.95. Significant scholarly study of the most brilliant exponents of Soto Zen. Soto Zen stresses enlightenment via *shikau taya* or "seated meditation alone."

O'Neil, Kevin. *An Introduction to Nichiren Shoshu Buddhism.* Crises Research Pr. 1980 pap. $5.00. Popular discussion of the history of Nichiren sectarian Buddhism with an emphasis on the modern period. Nichiren emphasized the importance of the *Lotus Sutra* and the relationship between the state and religion.

Robinson, Richard, and Willard L. Johnson. *The Buddhist Religion.* [*Religious Life of Man Ser.*] Dickenson 2d ed. 1977 pap. $8.95. Informative textbook introduction to the overall tradition with good concise chapters on East Asian Buddhism. Digests best of modern technical scholarship.

Sen, Soshitsu. *Tea Life, Tea Mind.* Weatherhill 1979 pap. $7.50. Interesting reflections on the philosophical and religious nature of the tea cult.

Starr, Frederick. *Korean Buddhism: History-Condition-Art: Three Lectures.* AMS Pr. repr. of 1918 ed. 1981 $25.00. Very general and dated, but still helpful early work on a little studied tradition.

Sunim, Kusan. *The Way of Korean Zen.* Intro. by Stephen Batchelor, Weatherhill 1985 pap. $12.50. Knowledgeable descriptive presentation.

Suzuki, D. T. *Zen and Japanese Culture.* [*Bollingen Ser.*] Princeton Univ. Pr. 1959 $52.00 pap. $10.95. Entertaining popular essays on the Zen arts, especially samurai swordsmanship, by the most famous Zen apostle to the West.

POPULAR TRADITIONS IN JAPAN AND KOREA

Blacker, Carmen. *The Catalpa Bow: A Study of Shamanistic Practices in Japan.* Allen & Unwin 2d ed. 1986 pap. $14.95. Brilliant interpretive study, from both a historical and ethnographic point of view, of the important role of shamanism in Japan.

Burma, Ian. *Behind the Mask: On Sexual Demons, Sacred Mothers, Transvestites, Gangsters and Other Japanese Cultural Heroes.* New Amer. Lib. 1985 pap. $8.95. Fascinating popular study of the archetypal and mythic context for contemporary Japanese popular culture.

Covell, Alan C. *Ecstasy: Shamanism in Korea.* Hollym Intl. 1983 $19.50. General analysis of the nature and function of shamanistic practices within Korean tradition.

Dorson, Richard M., ed. *Studies in Japanese Folklore.* [*Folklore of the World Ser.*] Ayer repr. of 1963 ed. 1980 lib. bdg. $34.50. Important collection of varied articles by leading authorities. Especially helpful for drawing out the religious implications of folklore.

Hearn, Lafcadio. *Kokoro: Hints and Echoes of Japanese Inner Life.* Greenwood repr. of 1896 ed. 1970 lib. bdg. $25.00; Tuttle 1972 pap. $6.50. Engaging meditations by the famous literary eccentric. Hearn (1850–1904) was a journalist, essayist, and novelist of Irish-Greek extraction who emigrated to the United States and then to Japan in 1890. Fascinated with the exotic and strange, he wrote extensively on Japanese culture, religion, and legends. Known as Koizumi Yakumo in Japan, he taught literature at the Imperial University in Tokyo from 1896 to 1903.

Hori, Ichiro. *Folk Religion in Japan: Continuity and Change.* Ed. by Joseph M. Kitagawa and Alan L. Miller [*Haskell Lectures Ser.*] Univ. of Chicago Pr. 1983 text ed. pap. $15.00. Compilation of important articles by one of the leading Japanese historians of religion.

Huhm, Halla Pai. *Kut: Korean Shamanist Rituals.* Hollym Intl. 1980 o.p. Engaging popular discussion of contemporary practices.

In-Sob, Zong, trans. *Folk Tales from Korea.* Grove 1979 o.p. Popular representative collection.

Janelli, Roger L., and Dawnhee Y. Janelli. *Ancestor Worship and Korean Society.* Stanford Univ. Pr. 1982 $27.50. Social-scientific study of a rural Korean village that stresses the relationship of kinship and ancestral traditions. Helpful is the description of the role of neo-Confucian institutions and indigenous shamanistic type rituals.

Kendall, Laurel. *Shamans, Housewives and Other Restless Spirits: Women in Korean Ritual Life.* Univ. of Hawaii Pr. 1985 $20.00. An ethnographic study of feminine and shamanistic village practices that raises important issues concerning the nature and significance of the role of women in the history of Korean religion.

Mayer, Fanny H., ed. and trans. *Ancient Tales in Modern Japan: An Anthology of Japanese Folk Tales.* Indiana Univ. Pr. 1985 $27.50. Well-translated collection of exemplary folktales.

Smith, Robert J. *Ancestor Worship in Contemporary Japan.* Stanford Univ. Pr. 1974 o.p. Important scholarly analysis of ancestral tradition from both a historical and ethnographic viewpoint.

FOREIGN INFLUENCES AND THE MODERN ERA IN JAPAN AND KOREA

Bellah, Robert N. *Tokugawa Religion: The Values of Pre-Industrial Japan.* Free Pr. 1959 pap. $9.95. Minor modern classic study from the standpoint of the sociology of religion.

Boxer, C. R. *The Christian Century in Japan: 1549 to 1650.* Univ. of California Pr. repr. of 1967 ed. 1974 $49.50. Historical survey of Roman Catholicism in Japan with translated documents.

Clark, Donald N. *Christianity in Modern Korea.* Univ. Pr. of Amer. 1986 lib. bdg. $12.75 text ed. pap. $4.75. Descriptive study of the influential role of Christian groups on modern day Korea.

Davis, Winston. *Dojo: Magic and Exorcism in Modern Japan.* Stanford Univ. Pr. 1980 $27.50 pap. $9.95. Fascinating sociological analysis of a new religion known as Sukyo Mahikari that stresses Meuling magic and ritual.

De Bary, William Theodore, and Jahyun K. Haboush, eds. *The Rise of Neo-Confucianism in Korea.* Columbia Univ. Pr. 1985 $40.00. Collection of articles by a group of international scholars on the generally neglected topic of neo-Confucianism in Korean tradition. Technical and topically fragmented in nature, but important as an initial survey of issues related to Korean neo-Confucianism.

Endo, Shusoku. *Silence.* Taplinger 1980 pap. $6.95. Haunting historical novel of the clash between traditional Japanese values and Christianity.

Hardacre, Helen. *The Religion of Japan's Korean Minority: The Preservation of Ethnic Identity.* [*Korea Research Monographs*] Univ. of California IEAS 1984 text ed. pap. $12.00. Groundbreaking study of the distinctive Buddhist and shamanistic nature of religion among ethnic Korean groups in Japan.

McFarland, H. Neill. *Rush Hour of the Gods: A Study of the New Religious Movements in Japan.* Macmillan 1967 $11.95. Balanced popular appraisal of five new religions.

Nishitani, Keiji. *Religion and Nothingness.* Intro. by Winston L. King, Univ. of California Pr. 1982 $35.95 pap. $10.95. Translation of one of the key works of the most famous contemporary Japanese philosopher. Existentialist and Buddhist in tone.

Nosco, Peter, ed. *Confucianism and Tokugawa Culture.* Princeton Univ. Pr. 1984 $32.50. Significant compilation of scholarly articles on neo-Confucianism's broad influence during the Tokugawa period.

Phillips, James M. *From the Rising of the Sun: Christians and Society in Contemporary Japan.* Orbis Bks. 1981 pap. $14.95. Popular study of the place of Christianity in contemporary Japan.

Piovesana, G. *Recent Japanese Philosophical Thought, 1862–1962.* Sophia Univ. Pr. 1968 o.p. Competent survey of the diverse influence of Western thought on modern Japanese philosophy.

Tibetan Traditions

Although uniquely sequestered by its mountainous geography, Tibet was greatly influenced by both the Indian and Chinese cultural traditions. In terms of regional history, it may be most appropriately considered in relation to those East and West Asian traditions that interacted with Chinese civilization. With regard to religion, however, Tibet was most intensely affected by South Asian currents of Buddhism and Hinduism. Thus aside from the earliest forms of indigenous religious practice and belief, known as *Bon*, Tibetan religious and intellectual life came to be dominated by a distinctive theocratic form of Buddhism, sometimes called Lamaism. Besides shamanistic and ritualistic contributions coming from the indigenous *Bon* tradition, Tibetan Buddhism is primarily a Vajrayana ("thunderbolt vehicle") form of Mahayana that involves a complex demonology and stresses liturgical practices, magical techniques, devotional practices to various bodhisattva deities, and esoteric forms of meditation involving the prominent use of *mandala* imagery. In spite of, and perhaps to some degree because of, its relative isolation and esoteric religious proclivities, Tibet has often exerted a special fascination on Western observers. For this reason, there is a considerable popular and scholarly literature on Tibetan religious tradition, though it is sometimes overly romanticized and occultish in nature.

Chang, Garma C., trans. *Hundred Thousand Songs of Miarepa.* Harper 1970 o.p. Annotated translation of the poetic work of the exceptional eleventh-century Buddhist poet, magician, and mystic.

Eliade, Mircea. *From Muhammad to the Age of Reforms.* Volume 3 in *A History of Religious Ideas.* Trans. by Alf Hiltebeitel and Diane Apostolos-Cappadona, Univ. of Chicago Pr. 1985 $27.50. See especially the chapter on "Tibetan Religions." Helpful overview of Tibetan religious history from Eliade's comparative perspective. Good annotated bibliography.

Guenther, Herbert V. *Tibetan Buddhism in Western Perspective.* Dharma 1977 pap. $8.95. General descriptive analysis that is, at times, overly technical.

Gyatso, Geshe K. *Buddhism in the Tibetan Tradition: A Guide.* Methuen 1984 pap. $9.95. Semipopular historical survey.

Gyatso, Tenzin. *The Buddhism of Tibet and the Precious Garland.* Allen & Unwin 1983 pap. $12.50. Interesting and authoritative descriptive study with a discussion of key texts.

Hoffmann, Helmut. *The Religions of Tibet.* Greenwood repr. of 1961 ed. 1979 lib. bdg. $24.75. Distinguished scholarly study that covers pre-Buddhist, as well as Buddhist, traditions.

Hopkins, Jeffrey, and Ann Klein. *Compassion in Tibetan Buddhism.* Ed. by Elizabeth Napper, Snow Lion 2d ed. 1980 pap. $10.95. Semipopular account of the principle of compassion by two leading Buddhist scholars.

Sierksma, F. *Tibet's Terrifying Deities: Sex and Aggression in Religious Acculturation.* Tuttle 1967 o.p. Fascinating psychosocial analysis of Tibetan religious symbolism. Scholarly format.

Sopa, Geshe Lhundup, and Jeffrey Hopkins. *The Practice and Theory of Tibetan Buddhism.* Grove 1976 pap. $4.95. Useful popular introduction by two authoritative commentators.

Trungpa, Chogyam. *Cutting Through Spiritual Materialism.* Shambhala 1973 pap. $8.95. Transcriptions of lectures applying Buddhist thought to modern American life by a noted Tibetan master.

Wentz, Walter Yeeling Evans, trans. *Bardo Thodol: The Tibetan Book of the Dead.* Oxford 1957 o.p. Complete translation of the celebrated esoteric Buddhist text that recounts the journeys of the soul after death.

SOUTH AND SOUTHEAST ASIAN TRADITIONS

South Asia refers to the Indian subcontinent of Asia that in recent history embraces, besides the political entity of India itself, the peripheral countries of Sri Lanka, Pakistan, Nepal, Bhutan, and Bangladesh. Culturally this is a region that is primarily defined by the rise and spread of the ancient Indian civilization. India and China were the oldest and most fertile civilizations in all of Asia and were, consequently, the two most important radiating centers for the cultural development, respectively, of the various South and East Asian traditions.

Despite the prevailing popular impression of a monolithic Asia, it is important to recognize that India and China, and so also their related South and East Asian spheres of influence, represent distinctly different cultural realms. In fact, the significant cultural differences between India and China are strongly reflected in their quite dissimilar religious and intellectual heritages. Thus ancient Indian Vedic culture with its growing emphasis on religious asceticism is quite foreign to the early Chinese this-worldly affirmation of life. Indeed, classical India's passionate and meticulous quest for the timeless apart from the weary cycles of incarnate life contrasts strongly with ancient China's general acceptance of the temporal rhythms of the cosmos.

It is true that in the course of Asian history both India and China came to share aspects of Buddhist tradition as a common denominator—although Buddhism, it should be noted, was eventually overwhelmed in India, the land of its origin, by Hinduism and Islam. But this observation must be tempered with the realization that Buddhism, in either its Theravada or Mahayana forms (and more so than is seen in the career of "Roman" Christianity in Europe), characteristically adapted itself to its host culture in ways that resulted in strikingly distinctive regional variants. Regardless of the nominal pan-Asian ecumenism of Buddhism, therefore, Indian—and more generally South and Southeast Asian—religion and philosophy must be viewed in terms of their own unique character.

Ironically, it may even be argued that to some degree India and the West possess more of a cultural affinity than do India and China. This is a result of the so-called Indo-European theory that through the comparative philological analysis of European languages and Sanskrit came the conclusion that both the ancient West and ancient India shared a common Aryan ancestry; and this was a hypothesis that accounted not only for various linguistic similarities but also for many general aspects of culture and religion. In fact, it was the Indo-European theory—developed in the eighteenth and nineteenth centuries through the work of Sir William Jones, Franz Bopp, and Max Mueller—that was at the heart of the development of a comparative historiographic method that sought to uncover the hidden universal traits of world culture.

(*The author acknowledges the assistance of Michael Winston in the preparation of the section devoted to South and Southeast Asia.*)

South Asian Traditions of India

South Asia, and to a great extent Southeast Asia, are primarily characterized by Indian tradition, especially in terms of its ancient political civilization, Sanskrit literature, and religion. It is important, then, that an understanding of Indian tradition be approached in a way that respects its rich complexity and diversity. This refers to an appreciation of the complicated intermingling of pre-Aryan (going back to the Indus valley civilization of the third millennium) and Indo-Aryan factors (entering northwest India around 1500 B.C.E.) that gave rise to classical Hindu civilization as the most representative expression of the Indian cultural and religious genius.

However, this is only part of the picture, since Hinduism is itself a lushly variegated tradition at both the elite and popular levels of culture and only represents one, albeit dominant, facet of the overall history of Indian religion. Thus an investigation of Indian religiosity must also take into account such important movements as Jainism, Buddhism, and Sikhism that, at different moments, creatively dissented from orthodox Hinduism. In addition to these groups, the highly significant role of Islam (especially in relation to the Sikh tradition and the creation of Pakistan and Bangladesh) and the Indian Zoroastrians known as the Parsis must be considered, as well as the influence of Christianity throughout the modern period. Despite this plurality of religious history, it can nevertheless be said that Hinduism and Buddhism represent the two most original Indian contributions to the overall history of world religions.

REFERENCE WORKS AND ANTHOLOGIES

Adams, Charles J., ed. *A Reader's Guide to the Great Religions.* Free Pr. 2d ed. 1977 $24.95. Comprehensive annotated bibliographies pertinent to South Asian tradition are found in Chapter 3 on "Hinduism" and Chapter 4 on "Buddhism."

De Bary, William Theodore, ed. *Sources of Indian Tradition.* Columbia Univ. Pr. 2 vols. 1964 vol. 1 pap. $16.00 vol. 2 pap. $15.00. Includes helpful background discussions of the major traditions and a good selection of classical religious and philosophical texts.

Eliade, Mircea. *A History of Religious Ideas.* Trans. by Willard R. Trask, Univ. of Chicago Pr. 2 vols. 1979–84 vol. 1 $25.00 pap. $16.95 vol. 2 $27.50 pap. $16.95. Concise coverage of basic religious themes, persons, and sects from a comparative perspective.

————, ed. *Encyclopedia of Religion.* Macmillan 16 vols. 1986 $1,100.00. Up-to-date and authoritative general entries on the most important aspects of Indian tradition.

Frazier, Allie M., ed. *Readings in Eastern Religious Thought.* Westminster 3 vols. 1969 pap. ea. $4.95. Volumes 1 and 2 are devoted to representative Hindu and Buddhist writings. (Volume 3 deals with Chinese and Japanese religions.) Helpful introductions.

Mueller, Max F. *The Sacred Books of the East.* Oxford 50 vols. 1879–1910 o.p. Classic sourcebook for translations of important Vedic and Upanishadic texts by various scholars. Helpful, though somewhat dated, introductions; copious notes. This work was a formative influence on the emergence of the comparative discipline of the history of religions.

Radhakrishnan, Sarvepalli, and Charles A. Moore, eds. *Sourcebook in Indian Philosophy.* Princeton Univ. Pr. 1957 $53.00 pap. $12.95. Comprehensive selection of basic texts with excellent introductions.

Reynolds, Frank E., John Holt, and John Strong. *Guide to Buddhist Religion.* G. K. Hall 1981 lib. bdg. $57.50. Useful up-to-date annotated bibliography.

Sharma, Jagdish S. *Encyclopedia of India.* Asia Bk. 2 vols. 2d ed. rev. 1981 $195.00. Concise entries on basic aspects of religion and philosophy.

GENERAL WORKS

Baird, Robert D., and Alfred Bloom. *Religion and Man: Indian and Far Eastern Religious Traditions.* Harper 1972 text ed. pap. $14.95. Concise and balanced introductory text.

Barth, A. *Religions of India.* Trans. by J. Wood, Asia Bk. 6th ed. repr. of 1880 ed. 1980 $23.95; Coronet 1980 text ed. $22.00; State Mutual Bk. $25.00. Early, but still worthwhile, compendium.

Basham, A. L., ed. *A Cultural History of India.* Oxford 1975 $29.95. Succinctly written and authoritative discussion of the interrelationship of religion and culture.

———. *The Wonder That Was India: A Survey of the Culture of the Indian Subcontinent Before the Coming of the Muslims.* Grove 1959 o.p. Classic introduction to pre-Muslim India. Indian tradition treated as a whole, integrating the different cultural elements of religion, society, art, and language.

Bhattacharyya, and others, eds. *The Cultural Heritage of India.* Vedanta Pr. 6 vols. 1937–86 ea. $39.95. Volumes 3 and 4 focus on philosophy and religion.

Bowker, John. *Problem of Suffering in the Religions of the World.* Cambridge Univ. Pr. 1970 $47.50 pap. $10.95. Interesting introduction to the major world religions and the way each deals with the problem of suffering. Helpful discussion of Hinduism and Buddhism.

Brown, Norman. *Man in the Universe: Some Cultural Continuities in Indian Thought.* Univ. of California Pr. 1970 o.p. Brilliant synthetic presentation of key ideas that have shaped Indian tradition.

Burghart, Richard, and Audrey Cantlie, eds. *Indian Religion.* St. Martin's 1985 $27.50. Good recent topical overview of Indian traditions.

Dasgupta, S. N. *A History of Indian Philosophy.* Orient Bk. Dist. 5 vols. 1952–55 $56.00. Authoritative survey of Indian philosophical systems from the Vedas to the modern period. Discusses the Jain and Buddhist philosophies as well as the six orthodox philosophical systems of Hinduism.

Hinnells, John R., ed. *A Handbook of Living Religions.* Penguin 1984 pap. $7.95. The sections on Hinduism, Sikhism, Jainism, and Buddhism are excellent and up-to-date survey discussions.

Hopkins, Edward W. *The Religions of India.* Longwood repr. of 1895 ed. 1979 lib. bdg. $65.00. Informative early work that surveys the major religious traditions.

Koller, John M. *The Indian Way.* Macmillan 1982 pap. $16.00. Excellent interpretive introduction to religious and philosophical aspects of Indian tradition.

Moore, Charles A., ed. *The Indian Mind: Essentials of Indian Philosophy and Culture.* Univ. of Hawaii Pr. 1967 o.p. Valuable general discussions of various philosophical, religious, social, and ethical topics by leading Western and Indian authorities.

Mueller, Friedrich M. *Lectures on the Origin and Growth of Religion, as Illustrated by the Religions of India.* AMS Pr. repr. of 1882 ed. 1976 $34.50. Presentation of Mueller's classic, though controversial and now largely discredited, theory of religious origins as related to Indo-European tradition. Mueller is regarded as the father of the comparative history of religions.

Schweitzer, Albert. *Indian Thought and Its Development.* Peter Smith 1962 $11.00. Interesting discussion by the famous Christian theologian and humanitarian.

Smith, Huston. *The Religions of Man.* Harper 1964 o.p. Balanced and well-written introduction to major world religions with especially effective discussions of Hinduism and Buddhism. Popular format.

Zimmer, Heinrich. *Philosophies of India.* Ed. by Joseph Campbell [*Bollingen Ser.*] Princeton Univ. Pr. 1969 $51.00 pap. $12.50. Good semipopular treatment of the major religions and philosophies of India.

THE ANCIENT HERITAGE: PRE-ARYAN AND VEDIC TRADITIONS

The pre-Aryan Indus Valley civilization of the third millennium B.C.E. reveals traits (e.g., seals depicting a goddess, images of a male god seated in a yogic posture somewhat like the later Hindu Shiva, ritual purification using water) that strongly suggest a linkage with some of the central aspects of classical Hinduism. However, the arrival of the seminomadic Indo-European tribes in the middle of the second millennium is considerably more important for the actual development of Hindu tradition. The Vedic religion of the earliest Indo-Aryans was a complex polytheistic ritual tradition structured on a tripartite caste system (which is the basis for the traditional Indian caste society).

A special group of priest-poets produced a collection of ritual texts known as the *Vedas* (works of "divine knowledge") that preserve the official core of the ancient religion and, at the same time, constitute the most sacred scriptures of the later Hindu tradition. The oldest of the *Vedas* was the *Rig-Veda*, a priestly collection of sacrificial hymns in praise of the gods. Other *Vedas* include the *Atharva-Veda*, which concerned the domestic cult and the somewhat later *Brahmanas* that were priestly commentaries of the sacrificial ritual and included explicit ideas of ascetic practice and meditation.

The most important stage in the evolution of the ancient Vedic religion toward Hinduism is found in the last of the Vedas known as the Upanishads. Here the emphasis decisively shifts from communal ritual to a personal quest for union with a monistic divinity known as Brahman. The religious philosophy of the Upanishads articulates for the first time what will become the key principles of Hinduism—i.e., the theory of *samsara* (wheel of life and cycle of rebirth), the idea of *karma* (the accountability of action), the theory of the human self (*atman*), and the ascetic methods of liberation (*moksha*) from the world of *samsara* and *karma.* In later tradition, the commentaries on the Upanishads by Shankara (788–820) and Ramanuja (1017–1137) represent literary and philosophical classics that are especially connected with the important Vedantic school of Hinduism (especially emphasizing a nondualist or modified nondualist understanding of deity). It was, in fact, Vedanta that especially influenced Western "perennial philosophy" thinkers like ALDOUS HUXLEY (see Vol. 1) and CHRISTOPHER ISHERWOOD (see Vol. 1).

Bhagat, M. G. *Ancient Indian Asceticism.* Orient Bk. Dist. 1976 $20.00; South Asia Bks. 1976 $18.50. Study of the development of the dominant ascetic tendencies within early Indian tradition.

Das, A. C. *Rigvedic India.* Orient Bk. Dist. 2 vols. 1971 $29.50. Scholarly presentation of Vedic culture and religion.

Drekmeier, Charles. *Kingship and Community in Early India.* Stanford Univ. Pr. 1962 $27.50. Analysis of the traditions of sacral kingship. Scholarly format.

Dutt, Romesh C. *A History of Civilisation in Ancient India.* Orient Bk. Dist. 2 vols. repr. of 1888 ed. 1972 $29.50. Still valuable historical study by an important early scholar.

Fairservis, Walter A., Jr. *The Roots of Ancient India: The Archaeology of Early Indian Civilization.* Univ. of Chicago Pr. 2d rev. repr. ed. 1975 pap. $7.95. Best available general discussion of pre-Aryan civilization.

Gonda, Jan. *Vision of the Vedic Poets.* Mouton 1963 text ed. $28.80. Excellent scholarly analysis of the visionary core of Vedic religion.

Heesterman, J. C. *The Inner Conflict of Tradition: Essays in Indian Ritual, Kingship and Society.* Univ. of Chicago Pr. 1985 lib. bdg. $32.00 pap. $14.95. Significant scholarly study of the interrelationship between religion and society.

Hume, Robert E., trans. *The Thirteen Principal Upanishads.* Oxford rev. 2d repr. of 1931 ed. 1984 pap. $16.95. Important early translation of the principal Upanishads.

Keith, Arthur B. *The Religion and Philosophy of the Veda and Upanishads.* Greenwood 2 vols. repr. of 1925 ed. 1971 lib. bdg. $34.00; Orient Bk. Dist. 2 vols. repr. ed. 1976 $42.00. Classic authoritative analysis by one of the greatest of the early Indologists. Copious technical annotations.

Mascaro, Juan, trans. *Upanishads.* [*Class. Ser.*] Penguin 1965 pap. $2.95. Effective modern translation of seven Upanishads and portions of others. Helpful introduction.

O'Flaherty, Wendy D. *The Rig Veda: An Anthology.* [*Class. Ser.*] Penguin 1982 pap. $5.95. Readable, reliable, and representative collection of Vedic hymns with excellent introductory discussions.

Otto, Rudolf. *Mysticism East and West.* Macmillan 1970 pap. $2.95; trans. by Richenda C. Payne, Theos. Pub. House repr. of 1932 ed. 1987 pap. $8.75. Important exposition of the mysticism in the Upanishads as interpreted by Shankara, the most famous philosopher of the Vedanta school of Hinduism and who emphasized a strict nondualistic monism. Discusses parallels and contrasts with the Christian mystic-philosopher Meister Eckhart.

Panikkar, Raimundo. *The Vedic Experience: Mantramanjari.* Auromere 1983 $28.50. Fascinating collection of various Vedic texts with insightful interpretive commentary.

Radhakrishnan, Sarvepalli. *The Principle Upanishads.* Humanities Pr. repr. of the 1953 ed. 1978 o.p. Important and readable translation by a well-known scholar and statesman. Good introduction to philosophical Hinduism.

Renou, Louis. *Religions of Ancient India.* Coronet repr. of 1953 ed. 1972 text ed. $19.95. Synthetic semipopular presentation of early religious development by a leading French Indologist.

Wheeler, Mortimer. *Indus Civilization.* Cambridge Univ. Pr. 3d ed. 1968 pap. $12.95. Important scholarly presentation of pre-Aryan Indian tradition. Not as balanced and up-to-date as Fairservis (see above).

HINDUISM

Probably the oldest living major religion, Hinduism is a social and religious system that is tremendously complex. Today it includes some 500 million adherents who make up more than four-fifths of the total population of India. Permeating throughout almost all aspects and levels of Indian life and society, Hinduism embraces a hierarchical caste social structure; a profound intellectual, philosophical, and literary tradition; and an incredibly diverse iconographical devotional structure that involves many different, and fluid, understandings of divinity.

The Upanishads, 108 Vedic works composed in Sanskrit between 600 B.C.E. and 300 B.C.E., represent the formative scriptural works of Hinduism. Building on the Upanishadic foundation and organically incorporating all sort of additional devotional beliefs, practices, and scriptures, classical Hinduism appears as a distinct tradition in the period roughly from 500 B.C.E. to 500 C.E. One of the most important aspects of this development, and in fact something that characterizes the major strains of modern-day Hinduism, was the emergence of an intense devotional (*bhakti*) theism loosely centered on either Vishnu (and his *avatars* or "down comings" like Krishna) or Shiva (associated also with the important mother goddess cult of Durga-Parvati). The primary sources for these popular developments are found in the two great epics known as the *Ramayana* and the *Mahabharata* (especially the section known as the *Bhagavadgita* or "Song of the Lord [Krishna]") and the mythic *Puranas.*

Bowes, Pratima. *The Hindu Tradition: A Philosophical Approach.* Routledge & Kegan 1977 o.p. Excellent introductory survey and critical analysis.

Carpenter, K. *Theism in Medieval India.* South Asia Bks. 1977 $22.50. Interesting historical analysis of Hindu devotional doctrine of god.

Chaudhuri, Nirad C. *Hinduism: A Religion to Live By.* Oxford 1979 pap. $9.95. Engaging and sensitive portrait of Hinduism as a practical way of life. Popular format.

Eck, Diana L. *Darsan: Seeing the Divine Image in India.* Anima Pubns. 2d ed. enl. 1985 pap. $5.95. Engaging popular study of Hindu iconology.

Eliade, Mircea. *Yoga: Immortality and Freedom.* Trans. by Willard R. Trask [*Bollingen Ser.*] Princeton Univ. Pr. 1970 $42.50 pap. $11.50. Classic study of the development and significance of yoga by the famous historian of religions.

Embree, Ainslie T., ed. *The Hindu Tradition—Readings in Oriental Thought.* Random 1972 pap. $5.95. Representative collection of primary sources showing religious and cultural developments of the Hindu religion arranged chronologically.

Gonda, J. *Visnuism and Sivaism: A Comparison.* Longwood 1970 $38.50; Orient Bk. Dist. 1976 $12.50. Scholarly study of the two major forms of Hindu devotion.

Hiltebeitel, Alf. *The Ritual of Battle: Krishna in the Mahabharata.* Cornell Univ. Pr. 1975 o.p. Important scholarly analysis of the great Indian epic work.

Hopkins, Thomas J. *The Hindu Religious Tradition.* Dickenson 1971 o.p. Concise textbook discussion of the diverse elements of the Indian tradition from the early Aryans to modern Hindu reform. Stresses the ritual structure of Hindu tradition.

Kinsley, David. *Hinduism: A Cultural Perspective.* Prentice-Hall 1982 $17.00. Fine introductory text that views religion as a cultural system that interacts with historical, intellectual, and social forms.

———. *The Sword and the Flute-Kali and Krsna: Dark Visions of the Terrible and the Sublime in Hindu Mythology.* Univ. of California Pr. 1975 pap. $7.95. Fascinating study of the deities Krishna and Kali.

Klostermeier, K. *Mythologies and Philosophies of Salvation in the Theistic Traditions of India.* Humanities Pr. 1984 text ed. pap. $23.95. Excellent, though technical, study of Hindu theism.

Mascaro, Juan. *The Bhagavad Gita.* [*Class. Ser.*] Penguin 1962 pap. $3.50. Good recent translation of one of the great classics of Hindu spirituality.

O'Flaherty, Wendy, trans. *Hindu Myths: A Sourcebook Translated from the Sanskrit.* [*Class. Ser.*] Penguin 1975 pap. $5.95. Delightful collection of tales about Hindu gods and demons. Convenient source for the most important myths of the major and minor gods of classical Hinduism.

———. *Karma and Rebirth in Classical Indian Traditions.* Univ. of California Pr. 1980 $41.00. Enlightening scholarly study of two key concepts.

Radhakrishnan, Sarvepalli. *The Hindu View of Life.* Allen & Unwin 1980 pap. $4.95. Authoritative and readable introduction to Hindu religion with excellent explication of the Hindu idea of Dharma (i.e., duty, law, truth, morality).

Singer, Milton B., ed. *Krishna: Myths, Rites, and Attitudes.* Fwd. by Daniel H. Ingalls, Greenwood repr. of 1966 ed. 1981 lib. bdg. $27.50; Univ. of Chicago Pr. 1969 pap. $12.00. Accessible anthropological study of Bhakti devotion and the Krishna/

Vaishnava religious movements down to the present. Bhakti is the key idea of "loving devotion" toward a savior deity (especially Krishna as an *avatar* of the god Vishnu) found especially among the Vaishnavas or followers of Vishnu. The American Hari Krishna movement is a contemporary descendant of these traditions.

Zaehner, Robert C. *Hinduism*. Oxford repr. of 1962 ed. pap. $8.95. Very readable and knowledgeable, though sometimes eccentric, introductory discussion. Emphasis is on the doctrine of the *avatar*.

JAINISM AND EARLY BUDDHISM

Rising out of, and selectively reacting against, Upanishadic speculation and practice of the sixth century B.C.E. were two distinctive religious movements: Jainism and Buddhism. The first of these was founded by the older contemporary of Buddha, Mahavira (traditionally dated as 540–468 B.C.E.). As the "great hero" of Jainism, Mahavira stressed an extreme version of the Upanishadic ascetic way of life, and most notably, gave special prominence to *ahimsa*, the principle of nonviolence toward all living creatures. Jainism claims to have grown out of the teachings of 24 Jinas ("conquerors") or Tirthankaras ("makers of the ford") that culminated in Mahavira's radical monastic asceticism. Rejecting a belief in a supreme deity, Jains seek liberation from Karma and transmigration through a strict life of self-denial and nonviolence. Today there are several million Jain believers in India.

The second, and greater tradition in terms of world history, was the movement stemming from the spiritual insights of Siddhartha Gautama, the "enlightened one" or Buddha, who is said to have been the son of a rich king in a town in northern India. Rejecting the world and practicing forms of renunciation and asceticism for six years, Siddhartha eventually found the traditional Upanishadic practices to be profitless. Enlightened to a new and more universally applicable method of salvation (understood as a radical freedom from rebirth known as *nirvana*), Siddhartha as the Buddha stressed a *middle* path between the extremes of sense, desire, and indulgence on the one hand, and extreme asceticism and self-denial on the other hand. The Buddha also rejected the Upanishadic ideas of the soul or self (*atman*) as well as all traditional notions of god. Most fundamentally, the "middle path" of Buddhism involves the Noble Truths of suffering and its causation and the holy eightfold path that leads to liberation from rebirth. As a method of salvation open to all men and women regardless of ethnic caste or cultural origin, the way of the Buddha, in either its Theravada or Mahayana forms, eventually went on to encompass the entire Asian world.

Theravada (the "school of the elders," also known from a Mahayana perspective as Hinayana or the "small vehicle" of liberation) is the primary tradition within South and Southeast Asia and characteristically stresses an individualistic monastic path of salvation and rejects the significance of devotional practices. Mahayana (the "great vehicle") started to distinguish itself from Theravada at about the time of the rise of Christianity and is predominantly found within East Asian tradition. Mahayana basically emphasizes the salvation of all beings through the compassionate power of the bodhisattvas, popular devotional practices, the identity of *samsara* and *nirvana* as expressed in the doctrine of *sunyata* or "emptiness," and the continuing revelation of Buddhist wisdom in the sutra literature (especially significant is the famous *Lotus Sutra*).

Berry, Thomas. *Buddhism*. Anima 1967 pap. $5.95. Brief popular overview of Buddhist tradition with insightful comparative discussions.

Bhargava, Dayanand. *Jaina Ethics*. Orient Bk. Dist. 1968 o.p. Concise and sensitive presentation.

Bist, Umrao S. *Jaina Theories of Reality and Knowledge*. South Asia Bks. 1985 $6.50. Knowledgeable analysis of the philosophical basis of Jain doctrine.

Byron, Thomas. *The Dhammapada: The Sayings of the Buddha*. Random 1976 pap. $5.95. Effective rendering of an important early work.

Chatterjee, Asim K. *A Comprehensive History of Jainism, 1000 AD to 1600 AD*. South Asia Bks. 1984 $28.50. Competent overview of Jain origins and later development.

Conze, Edward. *Buddhism: Its Essence and Development*. Harper 1982 pap. $6.95; Peter Smith $17.50; State Mutual Bk. 1975 $25.00. Classic popular introduction by one of the greatest Buddhist scholars.

———. *Buddhist Texts Through the Ages*. Harper 1964 o.p. An excellent collection of early Buddhist texts translated from the Pali and Sanskrit.

———. *Buddhist Thought in India*. Univ. of Michigan Pr. 1967 pap. $8.95. Scholarly study of early Buddhist developments in India.

Coomaraswamy, Ananda K. *Buddha and the Gospel of Buddhism*. Coronet 1975 text ed. $17.00. A good overview of Buddha's life and teachings. Interesting comparison of Buddhism and Christianity.

———. *Hinduism and Buddhism*. Greenwood repr. of 1943 ed. 1971 lib. bdg. $22.50. Fascinating comparative study.

Davids, Thomas W. *Buddhist India*. [*Select Bibliographies Repr. Ser.*] Ayer repr. of 1903 ed. $28.00. Early, though still interesting, discussion.

De Bary, William Theodore. *The Buddhist Tradition in India, China and Japan*. Random 1972 o.p. Representative and reliably translated selection of Theravada and Mahayana writings with a good treatment of early Buddhism in India.

Dutt, Nalinaksha. *Buddhist Sects in India*. Orient Bk. Dist. 1978 pap. $7.50; South Asia Bks. 2d ed. 1977 $9.00. Authoritative study of important sectarian developments within Buddhism.

Gard, Richard A., ed. *Buddhism*. [*Great Religions of Modern Man Ser.*] Braziller 1976 $8.95. Competent topical collection that covers the breadth of Buddhist tradition.

Hesse, Hermann. *Siddhartha*. Bantam 1982 pap. $2.95; Buccaneer Bks. repr. ed. 1983 lib. bdg. $16.95; New Directions 1951 $16.95 pap. $3.00. Provocative fictional reworking of the story of Siddhartha Gautama that expresses Hesse's synthetic understanding of Eastern thought and religion. Hesse's story is essentially a tale of Siddhartha's quest for self-awareness that runs from his experiments with the ascetic denial of the world, his involvement in the world and sexuality, and finally to his ultimate acceptance of the unity of spirit and matter.

Hindery, Roderick. *Comparative Ethics in Hindu and Buddhist Traditions*. Orient Bk. Dist. 1978 $18.95. Useful descriptive presentation.

Jacobson, Nolan P. *Understanding Buddhism*. Southern Illinois Univ. Pr. 1985 text ed. $19.95 text ed. pap. $10.95. Effective interpretive study.

Jaini, Padmanabh S. *The Jaina Path of Purification*. Univ. of California Pr. 1979 $35.95. Best overall presentation of the Jain understanding of life. Scholarly, yet accessible to the general reader.

Janai, Jagmandar. *Outlines of Jainism*. Ed. by F. W. Thomas, Hyperion Pr. repr. of 1940 ed. 1981 $21.00. Concise treatment by an insider to the tradition.

Janai, Manak C. *Life of Mahavira*. South Asia Bks. 1986 $8.00. Biographical portrait of the Jain founder.

Jayatilleke, K. *Early Buddhist Theory of Knowledge*. South Asia Bks. 1981 $22.00. Important philosophical analysis of Buddhist epistemology. Scholarly format.

Johansson, Rune. *The Dynamic Psychology of Early Buddhism*. [*Scandinavian Insti-*

tute of Asian Studies Monographs] Humanities Pr. 1979 text ed. pap. $15.00. Interesting study of the psychological implications of Buddhist theory.

Kalupahana, David J. *Buddhist Philosophy: A Historical Analysis.* Univ. of Hawaii Pr. 1976 text ed. pap. $4.95. Well-written brief presentation of basic principles in early Buddhism and the emergence of Theravada and Mahayana.

——. *Causality: The Central Philosophy of Buddhism.* Univ. of Hawaii Pr. 1975 o.p. Significant interpretive analysis by a leading contemporary Buddhologist. Technical in format, though accessible.

King, Winston L. *Theravada Meditation: The Buddhist Transformation of Yoga.* Pennsylvania State Univ. Pr. 1980 $22.75. Stresses the Hindu contributions to the development of Buddhist meditation. Scholarly format.

Ling, Trevor. *The Buddha: Buddhist Civilization in India and Ceylon.* Scribner 1973 o.p. Scholarly, though accessible, historical and sociological treatment of Buddhist tradition, especially concerning India and Ceylon.

Rahula, Walpola. *What the Buddha Taught.* Grove 1974 o.p. Insightful popular introduction to the Buddha's teaching from the perspective of Theravada tradition.

Robinson, Richard H., and Willard L. Johnson. *The Buddhist Religion: An Historical Introduction.* Wadsworth 3d ed. 1982 $11.25. Popular introductory text that includes excellent coverage of the origins and early Indian development of Buddhism.

Ross, Nancy W. *Buddhism: A Way of Life and Thought.* Knopf 1980 $12.95; Random 1981 pap. $6.95. Well-written and popular introduction to Buddhism. Somewhat romanticized at times.

Stcherbatsky, T. *Central Conception of Buddhism and the Meaning of the Word Dharma.* Orient Bk. Dist. repr. ed. 1979 $12.50; Verry 1961 $10.00. Classic early philosophical study of Buddhist thought by a leading Russian scholar.

Varma, V. P. *Early Buddhism and Its Origin.* Coronet 1973 o.p. Competent discussion of the Indian context for the origins of Buddhism.

Warder, A. K. *Indian Buddhism.* Orient Bk. Dist. 2d ed. rev. 1980 text ed. $22.00. Descriptive historical overview of Buddhist history within India.

SIKHISM AND PARSIISM

Sikhism is a religion of the Punjab region of India that grew out of a sect of dissenters from orthodox Hinduism. Formally established by Guru Nanak in the fifteenth century, Sikhism embodies its founder's open-minded conviction that all men, regardless of caste, were worthy to seek god. Nanak popularized the notion of guruship and stressed a monotheistic understanding of god that reveals both Hindu and Islamic traits. It was Nanak's successor, Angad, who composed the Adi Granth or holy scripture of Sikhism by combining Nanak's teachings with his own religious insights on the tradition of the gurus and the union with the Divine. Originally pacifist in orientation, Sikhs suffered extreme persecution under the Moghul emperors of the seventeenth century and in response developed distinctive methods of self-defense. In the modern period Sikhism has experienced continued waves of repression but has managed to become one of the most active and progressive groups in South Asia. The Sikh religious center is the famous Golden Temple at Amritsar.

The Parsis (from the root *pars* for Persia) are the Indian descendants of the ancient Zoroastrian tradition. Primarily entering India during the eighth century after the Muslim conquest of Persia, the Parsis are traditionally centered in the Bombay area of India. While basically adhering to the ancient Zoroastrian faith, Parsiism also betrays the influence of various Hindu beliefs and practices. Though only a small minority group, the Parsis have had considerable influence in modern Indian history.

Archer, John C. *Sikhs in Relation to Hindus, Moslems, Christians and Ahmadiyyas: A Study in Comparative Religion.* Russell repr. of 1946 ed. 1971 o.p. Authoritative scholarly study.

Cole, W. Owen. *The Guru in Sikhism.* South Asia Bks. 1984 pap. $7.00. Important scholarly discussion of the key idea of guruship.

————. *Sikhism and Its Indian Context, 1469–1708.* South Asia Bks. 1984 $38.50. Learned treatment of the vicissitudes of Sikh history.

————. *The Sikhs.* Methuen 1986 pap. $14.95. Semipopular overview of Sikh tradition by a leading scholar.

Cole, W. Owen, and Piara Sambhi. *The Sikhs: Their Religious Beliefs and Practices.* [*Lib. of Religious Beliefs and Practices*] Methuen 1986 text ed. pap. $14.95. Very good and balanced presentation of Sikh daily life, worship, ceremonies, theology, and ethics.

Gill, Pritam S. *Concepts of Sikhism.* Orient Bk. Dist. 1979 $10.00. Informative and concise discussion of the most important Sikh doctrines.

Haug, Martin. *The Parsis.* Orient Bk. Dist. repr. of 1878 ed. 1978 $25.00. Dated, but still helpful, historical study.

Hinnells, John. *Zoroastrianism and the Parsis.* State Mutual Bk. 1985 $13.00. Popular discussion by a leading scholar.

Jain, Nirmal K. *Sikh Religion and Philosophy.* Orient Bk. Dist. 1979 text ed. $12.50. Instructive analysis by a knowledgeable commentator.

Juergensmeyer, Mark, and Gerald Barrier, eds. *Sikh Studies: Comparative Perspectives of a Changing Tradition.* Humanities Pr. 1980 $16.00. Important scholarly collection of articles that stresses the social and political involvement of the tradition in the modern world.

Karaka, Dosabhai F. *History of the Parsis.* AMS Pr. 2 vols. repr. of 1884 ed. 1977 $70.00. Important early scholarly study. Treatment of historical developments during the medieval period is especially valuable.

McLeod, W. H. *Guru Nanak and the Sikh Religion.* Oxford 1968 o.p. Best and most reliable introduction to the life of the founder of Sikhism.

Moulton, James H. *Treasure of the Magi: A Story of Modern Zoroastrianism.* AMS Pr. repr. of 1917 ed. 1975 $21.75. Early work that is still useful for its discussion of Indian Parsiism.

Singh, Daljeet. *Sikhism.* Orient Bk. Dist. 1979 text ed. $17.95. Readable insider's portrait of the tradition.

Singh, Wazir. *Philosophy of Sikh Religion.* Intro. by Pritam Singh, Asia Bk. 1981 $13.95. Competent discussion of the philosophical implications of Sikh tradition.

POPULAR RELIGION

Amore, Roy C. *Lustful Maidens and Ascetic Kings: Buddhist and Hindu Stories of Life.* Oxford 1981 text ed. $21.95 pap. $6.95. Engaging popular collection of significant folktales and themes. Helpful contextual introductions.

Ayyar, P. V. *South Indian Customs.* South Asia Bks. repr. ed. 1986 $18.00. Valuable collection of ethnographic materials.

Clothey, Fred W. *Rhythm and Intent: Ritual Studies from South India.* South Asia Bks. 1984 $15.00. Interpretive analysis of popular ritual traditions.

Coomaraswamy, Ananda K., and M. E. Noble. *Myths of the Hindus and Buddhists.* Dover repr. of 1913 ed. 1967 pap. $6.95; Peter Smith $15.25. Popular representation of some of the most widespread myths and folktales.

Dumont, Louis. *Homo Hierarchicus: The Caste System and Its Implications.* Trans. by Basia Gulati, Univ. of Chicago Pr. rev. ed. 1981 $36.00 pap. $17.00. Brilliant sociological analysis of the caste system.

Meyer, J. J. *Sexual Life in Ancient India*. Orient Bk. Dist. 1971 $12.50. Discusses sexual customs in relation to religious tradition.

Oman, John C. *Cults, Customs, and Superstitions of India: Being a Revised and Enlarged Edition of Indian Life, Religious and Social*. AMS Pr. repr. of 1908 ed. 1982 $36.00. Useful early compendium of popular practices and beliefs.

Sharma, B. N.. *Festivals of India*. South Asia Bks. 1978 $30.00. Descriptive discussion of the background and nature of some of the most common festival traditions.

Thurston, Edgar. *Omens and Superstitions of Southern India*. Folcroft repr. of 1912 ed. 1979 lib. bdg. $40.00. Semipopular discussion of folk traditions.

Welbon, Guy, and Glen Yocum, eds. *Festivals in South India and Sri Lanka*. South Asia Bks. 1982 $25.00. Important topical collection of articles by leading scholars.

Whitehead, Henry. *The Village Gods of South India*. South Asia Bks. repr. ed. 1986 $15.00. Interesting presentation of beliefs concerning local deities.

FOREIGN INFLUENCES AND THE MODERN ERA

Throughout its long history, and in fact going back to the time of the Indo-Aryan invasions, India experienced many incursions of foreign political rule and alien religious influence. The influx of Islam represents the most conspicuous example of these vicissitudes during the medieval period; and from the eighteenth century until 1947, India was subject to British dominion and the general influence of Western thought and religion. Despite the denigrating impact of Western ideas and religion on the native tradition, many modern Indian philosophers and religious thinkers sought to universalize and rejuvenate the indigenous culture and, in fact, eventually acted as agents that brought Indian religious thought to the West. Thus, a consideration of modern Indian thought and religion must take into account not only the presence of Christianity and currents of Western style secularization but also the vital rethinking of Hinduism by such important figures as Ramakrishna, Vivekananda, Aurobindo, and Gandhi.

Mohandas Karamchand Gandhi (1869–1948), later known as Mahatma or "great soul," deserves to be particularly noted for his combination of religious principles and effective political action. Studying law in London and fighting for Indian rights in South Africa, Gandhi returned to India to lead the independence movement against the British rule. Drawing on a theory of nonviolence eclectically inspired by Hinduism (especially as expressed in the *Bhagavad-Gita*), Jainism, Christianity, and Tolstoy, Gandhi practiced the "soul force" protest methods of *satyagraha* and sought to democratize the Hindu caste system. Gandhi was assassinated by Hindu extremists only a year after his instrumental role in achieving Indian independence, but the continuing inspiration of his life and thought is seen in such important events as the American black liberation movement led by MARTIN LUTHER KING, JR.

Ashby, Philip H. *Modern Trends in Hinduism*. [*Lectures in the History of Religions*] Columbia Univ. Pr. 1974 $22.50. Helpful discussion of religious and philosophical developments in relation to social change.

Aurobindo, Sri. *The Mind of Light*. Dutton 1971 o.p. Best introductory statement of Aurobindo's revisionist thought. Aurobindo Ghose (1872–1950) was a modern-day visionary philosopher who emphasized a new kind of integral yoga that led to union with the Divine.

Baba, Meher. *The Mastery of Consciousness: An Introduction and Guide to Practical Mysticism and Methods of Spiritual Development*. Ed. by Allan Y. Cohen, Harper 1977 o.p. Overview of the life and teachings of Meher Baba, an important avataric figure of the twentieth century who developed a new approach to philosophical Hinduism and Sufism.

Chatterjee, Margaret. *Gandhi's Religious Thought*. Notre Dame Univ. Pr. 1983 $19.95. Important new study that brings out the Hindu and Christian aspects of Gandhi's thought.

Datta, Dhirendra M. *Philosophy of Mahatma Gandhi*. Fwd. by A. Garnett, Univ. of Wisconsin Pr. 1953 pap. $10.95. Brief readable descriptive study.

Gandhi, Mohandas K. *An Autobiography: Or the Story of My Experiments with Truth*. Dover repr. of 1948 ed. 1983 pap. $6.95; trans. by Mahadev Desai, Greenleaf Bks. 2d ed. 1983 $8.00 1984 pap. $4.50. Autobiographical account that provides important insight into Gandhi's social and philosophical outlook.

Isherwood, Christopher. *Ramakrishna and His Disciples*. Vedanta Pr. repr. of 1965 ed. 1980 pap. $8.95. Fascinating, though subjective, account of Ramakrishna's life and the spread of his Vedanta teachings to the West.

Juergensmeyer, Mark. *Fighting with Gandhi*. Harper 1984 $12.95. Engaging and insightful discussion of Gandhi's idea of nonviolence and the methods of *satyagraha* or "grasping onto principles." Popular format.

Krishnamurti, Jiddu. *Commentaries on Living*. Ed. by D. Rajagopal, Theos. Pub. House 3 vols. 1967 pap. ea. $4.75–$5.50. Collection of syncretistic religious writings that were influential in the West.

Lutyens, Mary. *Krishnamurti: The Years of Fulfillment*. Avon 1984 pap. $4.95; Farrar 1983 $15.50. Well-written biographical account outlining Krishnamurti's career in Asia and the West.

Mahesh Yogi, Maharishi. *The Science of Being and Art of Living*. Signet 1969 o.p. Religious and philosophical reflections by the founder of the influential "transcendental meditation" movement.

Mujeeb, M. *The Indian Muslims*. McGill-Queens Univ. Pr. 1967 o.p. Comprehensive discussion of Islamic life in India.

Neill, Stephen. *A History of Christianity in India 1707–1858*. Cambridge Univ. Pr. 1985 $79.50. Authoritative discussion of the important impact of Christianity on Indian tradition.

Nikhilananda, Swami, trans. *Gospel of Sri Ramakrishna*. Fwd. by Aldous Huxley, Ramakrishna 1984 $19.95 abr. ed. 1980 $8.50. A firsthand account of the teachings of Ramakrishna.

Rajneesh, Bhagwan Shree. *The Great Challenge*. Grove 1982 o.p. Good introduction to the teachings of the controversial present-day philosopher and mystic.

Rama, Swami. *Living with the Himalayan Masters*. Himalayan Intl. Inst. 1978 o.p. Discussion of the religious teachers of modern India from the perspective of an Indian philosopher and scholar.

Rao, K. L. *Mahatma Gandhi and Comparative Religion*. South Asia Bks. 1979 $15.00. Interesting study of Gandhi in relation to the history of religions.

Rolland, Romain. *Life of Ramakrishna*. Vedanta Pr. 1930 pap. $5.95. Well-written and engaging hagiography.

Smith, W. C. *Modern Islam in India: A Social Analysis*. AMS Pr. repr. of 1946 ed. 1974 $23.00; South Asia Bks. repr. of 1946 ed. 1985 $18.50. Descriptive study of the problems of Indian Islam within the modern period.

Srivastava, H. C. *Intellectuals in Contemporary India*. South Asia Bks. 1979 $11.50. Informative portraits of modern religious, philosophical, and secular thinkers.

Southeast Asia

Southeast Asia is a regional classification that includes Vietnam, Laos, Cambodia, Thailand, Burma, and Malaya, as well as the insular countries of

Indonesia and the Philippines. Despite the complexity of these diverse national heritages, there is a common cultural heritage that was primarily due to the historical impact of the older Indian and Chinese civilizations. In fact, Southeast Asia was commonly known as Indo-China, a label descriptive of the formative influence of the two ancient traditions to the west and north. Southeast Asia was, indeed, a kind of geographical crossroads at which many different cultural and religious traditions came together.

Indian Hinduism and Theravada Buddhism were especially influential in the shaping of the cultures of Laos, Cambodia, Thailand, and Burma. Chinese tradition was also a sporadic political and cultural factor within those traditions, but the greatest impress of traditional Chinese culture—including Confucianism, Taoism, and Sinitic forms of Mahayana Buddhism—was on the Vietnamese tradition. Another important ingredient in this mix of cultural factors in Southeast Asia was the strong missionizing influx of Islam and Christianity (especially in terms of the role of Islam in Malaya and Indonesia, and Christianity in the Philippines). In each case, however, the religious contributions coming from India and China, and to a lesser extent from Islam and Christianity, were distinctively transformed in relation to the genius of the indigenous local tradition. Thus, the important and largely dominant religious role of Buddhism in the majority of Southeast Asian countries must be seen in terms of how official forms of Buddhism were popularly adapted to the folk culture and religion.

GENERAL WORKS

Cadet, J. M. *Ramakien: The Thai Epic*. Kodansha 1970 $35.00. Readable and competent translation of an important religious and political work.

Desai, Santosh N. *Hinduism in Thai Life*. Asia Bk. 1980 $23.95. Descriptive study of the important influence of Hinduism on Thai tradition.

Heine-Geldern, Robert. *Conceptions of State and Kingship in Southeast Asia*. Cornell SE Asia 1956 pap. $3.50. Important brief discussion of the interrelationship between religion and politics from the standpoint of comparative cultural history.

Hooker, A. Thomas, ed. *Islam in South East Asia*. Humanities Pr. 1983 $39.95. Collection of scholarly articles on the role and significance of Islam in Southeast Asia.

Smith, Bardwell L., ed. *Religion and Legitimation of Power in Thailand, Laos and Burma*. Anima Pubns. 1978 pap. $7.95. Valuable symposium on various historical and thematic aspects of religion and politics. Scholarly format.

Von der Mehden, Fred. *Religion and Modernization in Southeast Asia*. Syracuse Univ. Pr. 1986 $29.95. Scholarly analysis of the modern significance of religion.

POPULAR RELIGION

Anuman, Rajadhon Phraya. *Life and Ritual in Old Siam: Three Studies of Thai Life and Customs*. Ed. by William J. Gedney, Greenwood repr. of 1961 ed. 1979 lib. bdg. $24.75. Valuable ethnographic study.

Htin, Aung U. *Folk Elements in Burmese Buddhism*. Greenwood repr. of 1962 ed. 1978 lib. bdg. $22.50. Important descriptive study of popularized Buddhism.

Kirsch, Thomas. *Feasting and Social Oscillation: A Working Paper on Religion and Society in Upland Southeast Asia*. Cornell SE Asia 1984 $5.00. Interpretive analysis of feasting ritual from a social-anthropological perspective.

Scanlon, Phil, Jr. *Southeast Asia: A Cultural Study Through Celebration*. Intro. by Robert H. McKinley [*Northern Illinois Univ. Center for Southeast Asian Studies*]

Cellar 1985 pap. $14.00. Interesting study of the ritual context for Southeast Asian tradition. Scholarly format.

Tambiah, S. J. *Buddhism and the Spirit Cults in Northeast Thailand.* Cambridge Univ. Pr. 1970 pap. $19.95. Excellent anthropological study of popular Buddhist practices. Technical, yet very readable, scholarship.

———. *The Buddhist Saints of the Forest and the Cult of Amulets: A Study in Charisma, Hagiography, Sectarianism and Millennial Buddhism.* Cambridge Univ. Pr. 1984 $57.50 pap. $18.95. Insightful reflections on the interactions between Buddhism and popular tradition.

Wales, Q. *Divination in Thailand.* Humanities Pr. 1983 text ed. $10.50. Informative descriptive study of divinatory practices.

Young, Ernest. *The Kingdom of the Yellow Robe: Being Sketches of the Domestic and Religious Rites and Ceremonies of the Siamese.* AMS Pr. repr. of 1898 ed. 1982 $31.00. Early, though still valuable, compendium of ethnographic observations.

BUDDHIST TRADITIONS

Bunnay, Jane. *Buddhist Monk, Buddhist Layman.* Cambridge Univ. Pr. 1973 o.p. A basic source for understanding Buddhist life in Thailand from the perspectives of the monastic and lay communities.

Goldstein, Joseph. *The Experience of Insight.* Shambhala 1987 pap. $10.95. Lucid popular exposition of the Burmese method of Vipassana meditation (a kind of self-insight technique).

Ishii, Yoneo. *Sangha, State, and Society: Thai Buddhism in History.* Trans. by Peter Hawkes, Univ. of Hawaii Pr. 1985 text ed. $25.00 pap. $16.00. Important scholarly study that stresses the social and political role of Buddhism.

Lester, Robert C. *Theravada Buddhism in Southeast Asia.* Univ. of Michigan Pr. 1973 $7.95. Effective overview of Buddhism stressing its social organization and cultural life. Includes a helpful general exposition of Buddhist philosophy.

Ray, Nihar Ranjan. *An Introduction to the Study of Theravada Buddhism in Burma: A Study of Indo-Burmese Historical and Cultural Relations from the Earliest Times to the British Conquest.* AMS Pr. repr. of 1946 ed. 1982 $25.00. Authoritative descriptive presentation of Burmese Buddhist tradition.

Spiro, Melford E. *Buddhism and Society: A Great Tradition and Its Burmese Vicissitudes.* Univ. of California Pr. 2d ed. rev. 1982 $40.00 pap. $10.95. Significant sociological analysis of the transformations of Buddhism within Burmese tradition. Scholarly, yet accessible.

Suksamran, Somboon. *Buddhism and Politics in Thailand.* Gower 1982 text ed. pap. $25.00. Knowledgeable discussion of the modern political significance of Buddhism.

———. *Political Buddhism in Southeast Asia: The Role of the Sangha in the Modernization of Thailand.* St. Martin's 1977 $20.00. Informed analysis by a leading scholar.

Swearer, Donald K. *Buddhism and Society in Southeast Asia.* [*Focus on Hinduism and Buddhism Ser.*] Anima Pubns. 1981 pap. $4.95. Insightful discussion of Buddhism in a Southeast Asian village and urban traditions. Popular format.

———. *Secrets of the Lotus: Studies in Buddhist Meditation.* Ed. by C. Alexandre, Macmillan 1971 $6.95 pap. $1.95. Informed and sensitive introduction to Buddhist meditation as practiced in Burma.

Wells, Kenneth E. *Thai Buddhism: Its Rites and Activities.* AMS Pr. repr. of 1960 ed. 1982 $34.50. Competent descriptive overview of the distinctive aspects of ritual practice.

CENTRAL ASIAN, MIDDLE EASTERN, AND NORTH AFRICAN TRADITIONS (EXCLUSIVE OF JUDAISM, CHRISTIANITY, AND ISLAM)

This category can only be considered an extremely arbitrary grouping that loosely brings together all those traditions that fall between the cultural and historical brackets of the West and the major Far Eastern civilizations of China and India. Having been lost within the shadows cast by the extreme polarities of West and East, this diverse body of traditions has been largely neglected or, when studied, often only appreciated as the backdrop for the rise and triumphant expansion of the dominant biblical and Koranic faiths.

Thus the study of ancient Babylonian, Semitic, and Persian religions was especially promoted by the light such investigations might throw on the rise and development of Judaism and Christianity. In a similar fashion, studies of Central, North, and Western Asia—sometimes collectively called "Eurasia"—frequently have been concerned with how those traditions were influenced by Islam (and Buddhism) or with how they reflected back on the hypothetical Indo-European homeland. By virtue of its antiquity, monumental nature, and intimate association with the central concerns of the overall civilization, Egyptian religious thought and practice have captivated Western observers in a special way. This interest, therefore, has given rise to an abundance of popular and scholarly works.

Central, North, and West Asian Traditions

Dioszegi, V., ed. *Popular Beliefs and Folklore Tradition in Siberia.* [*Uralic and Altaic Ser.*] Mouton 1968 text ed. $40.80. Collection of scholarly articles that stress important aspects of traditional Siberian religion.

Eliade, Mircea. *From Muhammad to the Age of Reforms.* Volume 3 in *A History of Religious Ideas.* Trans. by Alf Hiltebeitel and Diane Apostolos-Cappadona, Univ. of Chicago Pr. 1985 $27.50. See the chapter on "The Religion of Ancient Eurasia: Turko-Mongols, Finno-Ugrians, Balto-Slavs." Readable synthetic discussion that fits these traditions into the overall history of world religions. Excellent annotated bibliography.

Heissig, Walther. *The Religions of Mongolia.* Trans. by Geoffrey Samuel, Univ. of California Pr. 1980 $31.00. Accessible scholarly presentation of Mongolian religious history.

Keary, Charles F. *Outlines of Primitive Belief among the Indo-European Races.* Longwood repr. of 1882 ed. 1977 lib. bdg. $50.00. Dated, but still helpful, descriptive treatment.

Moses, Larry, and Stephen A. Halkovic, Jr. *Introduction to Mongolian History and Culture.* [*Uralic and Altaic Ser.*] Indiana Univ. Research Inst. for Inner Asian Studies 1985 pap. $20.00. Recent scholarly overview of Mongolian tradition that includes useful discussions of religion.

Pozdneyev, Aleksei M. *Religion and Ritual in Society: Lamaist Buddhism in Late 19th-Century Mongolia (Ocherki byta buddiiskikh monastyrei).* Ed. by John R. Krueger, trans. from the Russian by Alo Raun and Linda Raun, Mongolia 1978 o.p. Scholarly study by a distinguished Russian expert.

Shirokogorov, Sergei M. *Psychomental Complex of the Tungus.* AMS Pr. repr. of 1935 ed. 1982 $120.00. Classic psychoanalytic analysis of Siberian shamanism. Important from both a descriptive and methodological perspective.

Middle Eastern Traditions

ASSYRO-BABYLONIAN AND SEMITIC TRADITIONS

Eliade, Mircea. *From the Stone Age to the Eleusinian Mysteries.* Volume 1 in *A History of Religious Ideas.* Trans. by Willard R. Trask, Univ. of Chicago Pr. 1979 $25.00. See the chapters on "The Mesopotamian Religions" and "The Religions of the Hittites and the Canaanites." Readable and up-to-date surveys with valuable bibliographic essays.

Farnell, Lewis R. *Greece and Babylon: A Comparative Sketch of Mesopotamian, Anatolian, and Hellenic Religions.* Gordon Pr. 1977 lib. bdg. $59.95. Authoritative comparative study by a brilliant classical scholar.

Frankfort, Henri. *Kingship and the Gods: A Study of Ancient Near Eastern Religion as the Integration of Society and Nature.* Pref. by Samuel N. Kramer, Univ. of Chicago Pr. repr. of 1948 ed. 1978 pap. $12.95. Very readable minor classic by an outstanding oriental scholar.

Gibson, John C. *Canaanite Myths and Legends.* Fortress Pr. 1978 $32.95. Accessible and reliable scholarly presentation that digests specialized research.

Jacobsen, Thorkild. *The Treasures of Darkness: A History of Mesopotamian Religion.* Yale Univ. Pr. 1976 pap. $9.95. Fascinating interpretations by one of the leading experts in Mesopotamian tradition.

Kramer, Samuel N. *Sumerian Mythology.* Univ. of Pennsylvania Pr. 1972 pap. $10.95. Authoritative translations and discussions of the most important myths concerning the origin of man, the great flood, and the descent to the underworld.

Sanders, N. K. *The Epic of Gilgamesh.* [*Class. Ser.*] Penguin 1966 pap. $2.50. Readable semipopular redacted translation with helpful introduction and notes.

Sayce, Archibald H. *Lectures on the Origin and Genesis of Religion as Illustrated by the Religion of the Ancient Babylonians.* AMS Pr. repr. of 1888 ed. 2d ed. 1980 $47.00. Important work in the history of scholarship but now dated in terms of method and content.

PERSIAN ZOROASTRIANISM

Zoroastrianism is the religion founded by the Persian prophet Zoroaster/Zarathustra (traditionally dated c.628–c.551 B.C.E.) and, in subsequent periods, was spread throughout the ancient Persian empire by the Magi priests. Zoroaster's teachings are thought to be preserved in the *Gathas*, which constitute the oldest sections of the Zoroastrian scriptures known as the *Avesta*. Zoroaster basically accomplished a sweeping reform of ancient Persian polytheism that was rooted ultimately in Indo-European tradition and showed similarities with the Aryan religion on Vedic India. The essence of Zoroaster's message was his revelation of a supreme deity known as Ahura Mazda who demands an ethical life for salvation.

Many aspects of ancient Zoroastrianism—its ethical monotheism and dualistic conception of good and evil forces, its emphasis on free will, its belief in heaven and hell, its conviction in the future appearance of a messianic savior, and so on—influenced the development of Judaism and Christianity. After the conquest of Persia by Islam, Zoroastrianism declined in the land of its birth to the extent that today the largest number of Zoroastrians are to be found in India as the Parsis.

Boyce, Mary. *Zoroastrians: Their Religious Beliefs and Practices.* Methuen 1985 o.p. Comprehensive presentation that draws on the best of current scholarship. Scholarly, yet accessible.

Dawson, Miles M. *Ethical Religion of Zoroaster.* AMS Pr. repr. of 1931 ed. 1983 $22.50. Worthwhile early study.

Dhalla, Maneckji N. *Zoroastrian Theology from the Earliest Times to the Present Day.* AMS Pr. repr. of 1914 ed. 1974 $30.00. Somewhat apologetic, though still valuable, early historical discussion.

Duchesne-Guillemin, J. *The Hymns of Zarathustra.* Beacon Pr. 1963 o.p. Authoritative translation of the oldest sections of the *Zend Avesta* (the Zoroastrian scriptures). Semipopular in format.

Eliade, Mircea. *A History of Religious Ideas.* Trans. by Willard R. Trask, Univ. of Chicago Pr. 2 vols. 1979–84 vol. 1 $25.00 pap. $16.95 vol. 2 $27.50 pap. $16.95. See particularly the chapter in Volume 1 on "Zarathustra and the Iranian Religion," and in Volume 2 on "New Iranian Synthesis." Helpful overview that stresses the general significance of Zoroastrian tradition within the history of world religions.

Hinnells, John R. *Persian Mythology.* [*Lib. of the World's Myths and Legends*] P. Bedrick Bks. 1985 $18.95. Semipopular presentation that includes translated mythic materials and contextual discussion.

North African Traditions: Ancient Egypt

Allen, George, trans. *Book of the Dead; Or, Going Forth by Day: Ideas of the Ancient Egyptians Concerning the Hereafter as Expressed in Their Own Terms.* [*Studies in Ancient Oriental Civilization Ser.*] Univ. of Chicago Pr. 1974 text ed. pap. $20.00. Recent authoritative translation and discussion. Scholarly, yet accessible.

Armour, Robert. *Gods and Myths of Ancient Egypt.* Columbia Univ. Pr. 1986 pap. $15.00. Scholarly analysis that draws on current specialized research.

Breasted, James. *The Development of Religion and Thought in Ancient Egypt.* Intro. by John A. Wilson, Univ. of Pennsylvania Pr. repr. of 1912 ed. 1972 pap. $12.95. Minor scholarly classic by one of the great early Egyptologists.

Budge, Ernest A. Wallis, trans. *The Book of the Dead.* Citadel Pr. 1984 pap. $12.95; intro. by David Lorimer, Methuen 1985 pap. $9.95; Univ. Bks. 1960 $25.00

———. *Egyptian Magic.* Dover repr. of 1899 ed. 1971 pap. $4.00; Methuen 1979 pap. $6.95; Peter Smith $14.25

———. *Egyptian Religion.* Methuen repr. of 1972 ed. 1979 pap. $6.95. All three of the titles by Budge are dated and sometimes unreliable, but still useful semipopular works by a knowledgeable early scholar.

Cerny, Jaroslav. *Ancient Egyptian Religion.* Greenwood repr. of 1957 ed. 1979 lib. bdg. $50.00. Important synthetic study by a distinguished European scholar.

David, A. Rosalie. *The Ancient Egyptians: Religious Beliefs and Practices.* Methuen 1982 $26.00 pap. $10.00. Good up-to-date scholarly study.

Eliade, Mircea. *From the Stone Age to the Eleusinian Mysteries.* Volume 1 in *A History of Religious Ideas.* Trans. by Willard R. Trask, Univ. of Chicago Pr. 1979 $25.00. See the chapter on "Religious Ideas and Political Crises in Ancient Egypt." Readable synthesis along with helpful annotated bibliography.

Frankfort, Henri. *Ancient Egyptian Religion: An Interpretation.* Harper 1961 pap. $7.95; Peter Smith $16.00. Valuable semipopular work by a leading expert.

Ions, Veronica. *Egyptian Mythology.* [*Lib. of the World's Myths and Legends*] P. Bedrick Bks. rev. ed. 1983 $18.95; [*Lib. of the World's Myths and Legends*] Creative

Education repr. of 1968 ed. 1982 $16.95. Convenient and generally reliable collection with helpful commentary.

Morenz, Siegfried. *Egyptian Religion.* Cornell Univ. Pr. 1973 $39.95. Brilliant synthetic work. Scholarly yet accessible format that sets Egyptian religion within the context of the overall history of religions.

Murnane, William J. *The Penguin Guide to Ancient Egypt.* Penguin 1983 pap. $12.95. Semipopular and comprehensive work that includes excellent discussions of religion.

Seligman, Charles G. *Egypt and Negro Africa: Study in Divine Kingship.* AMS Pr. repr. of 1934 ed. 1978 $21.50. Interesting and insightful comparative study. Scholarly format.

Shorter, A. W. *The Egyptian Gods: A Handbook.* Methuen 1978 pap. $7.50. Recent survey of basic information on the Egyptian pantheon.

CHAPTER 9

Islamic Religion and Philosophy

Leo Hamalian

Islam endures. It grows. It changes. Islam is a potent force in the world of today. We of the West may be appreciably aware of these facts without suspecting the moving causes which underlie them. We desire, however, to know these causes. We ought to know them.
—JOHN CLARK ARCHER, *Mystical Elements in Mohammad*

By a conservative estimate, more than 600 million people profess the faith of Islam, with the number steadily increasing. Through warfare, proselytizing, and the influence of its great medieval scholars, the religion founded by Muhammad has had, from its very beginning in the seventh century A.D. to the present, an enormous impact on the Western world.

Islam emphasizes a strict monotheism and uncompromising adherence to certain religious practices. Although the history of Islam produced many sects and movements, its followers (known as Muslims or Mussulmen) were traditionally bound by a common faith and a sense of belonging to a single community. Recently the political strife and armed clashes between Sunni and Shiite sects throughout the Muslim world have shaken that sense of common unity to its very foundation. These unfolding disturbances along with a militant "reawakening" among the religious, especially in parts of the Middle East, both threaten and strengthen Islam anew.

Whatever differences political tensions may create among Muslims, the basic beliefs necessary to the faithful continue to be contained in the Five Doctrines: (1) there is only one true God, Allah; (2) there are angels, including Gabriel and a fallen angel, *iblis* (Satan or Shatin), whose minions are the *djinn* (demons or genies) with supernatural power over human beings; (3) there are four inspired books: the Torah, the Psalms of David, the Evangel of Jesus, and the Koran (Qur'an), which contains Allah's final message and which is therefore supreme among the four; (4) there are 28 prophets including Adam, Noah, Abraham, Moses, Jesus, and John the Baptist, but the greatest and the last is Muhammad; (5) there will be an end of this world, a bodily resurrection, and a final judgment (in some sects this salvation is immediately available to anyone who falls in defense of the faith). The doctrine of *kismet* (fate, or whatever is destined or inevitably decreed) is also taught but not as necessary to faith.

The faithful believer responds to Allah by the Five Pillars of Faith: (1) the profession of faith: "There is no god but Allah and Muhammad is his Prophet"

413

recited correctly and feelingly at least once in his or her lifetime; (2) prayer five times a day facing Mecca; (3) the giving of alms to the needy; (4) fasting from daybreak to sundown during the holy month of Ramadan; and (5) pilgrimage (*hadj*) to Mecca through which one becomes a *hadji* or a person of honor. The development of Muslim thought has been marked by countless complex theological differences, often accentuated by bitter political dissension intensified by many factors—politics toward Israel, expanding populations, economic pressures created by fluctuating petroleum prices, and the influence of revolutionary thought and modern technology on traditional mores and customs.

The major schism has been between the Sunni orthodoxy (the term *sunnah* refers to the "well-trodden path of the consolidated majority") and the Shiah, the followers of Ali, the fourth caliph and son-in-law of the Prophet, who was murdered by the Kharijites (a secessionist sect in favor of a radically democratic and puritanical reform community) for accepting arbitration with Muawiya, the founder of the Umayyad dynasty. In contrast to the open profession, pragmatism, and consensual nature of Sunni belief, the Shiah emphasize transcendentalism, dissimulation, and emotionalism. The violent demise of Husayn (in 680), son of Ali, is celebrated, especially in Iran, with orations, passion plays (known in Afghanistan and on the Indian subcontinent as *ta'ziyahs*), and processions in which the celebrants, worked up to a frenzy, beat themselves with heavy chains and sharp instruments, inflicting bodily wounds in imitation of Husayn's death at the hands of Umayyad troops (these ceremonies are not practiced in Egypt or elsewhere in North Africa). While Shiism claims only about 50,000,000 adherents (mainly in Iran, where it has been the official religion since the sixteenth century), its doctrines have profoundly influenced Sunni Muslims, especially in the way they venerate Ali and his family, and in the respect they show his descendants, known as *sayyids* in the East and *asharifs* in North Africa.

Shiism has produced several "extremist" sects, most notably the Ismailis (found mainly in East Africa, Pakistan, India, and Yemen), who instead of recognizing Musa as the seventh imam (spiritual leader) as do most Shiites, upheld the claims of his elder brother Ismail. Another subdivision of the Shiites is that of the Imamites or "Twelvers," who supported the descendants of al-Kadim, brother of Ismail the seventh imam. Ever since their twelfth imam, al-Mahdi, reportedly disappeared, they have believed that he is still living and that he will appear again to restore justice to the world. Sufism, or Islamic mysticism, which emerged out of Shiism, stresses asceticism, ecstasy, and intuitive knowledge as bulwarks against the overworldliness and legalist tendencies that constantly endanger the Muslim community. The Mawlawiyah order of Muslims, founded by the famed Persian mystic Rumi and now popularly known in the West as the Dancing or Whirling Dervishes, is a Turkish version of Sufism, in which the symbolism of the dancer's robes and headdress is as central to the mysteries of the order as its texts.

Islam appears to be revitalized in many parts of the world, and is attracting new adherents, especially in places distant from its traditional centers, such as the Philippines, Indonesia, central Asia, black Africa, and black America.

ANTHOLOGIES, DICTIONARIES, ENCYCLOPEDIAS, AND HANDBOOKS

Adams, Charles J., ed. *A Reader's Guide to the Great Religions*. Free Pr. 2d ed. 1977 $24.95. Of the eight essays, Adams's long overview of Islam is among the best. Adams was Director of Islamic Studies at McGill University, Canada.

Archer, John Clark. *Faiths Men Live By*. Ayer repr. of 1934 ed. 1977 $25.50. Thirty-five pages and a "student's manual and study guide" devoted to Islam.

Ballou, Robert O. *The Portable World Bible*. [*Viking Portable Lib.*] Penguin 1977 pap. $6.95. This volume contains sacred and traditional writing of the world's eight basic source religions, with excellent introductions to each section. A glossary and an index are included.

Brandon, S. G. *A Dictionary of Comparative Religion*. Scribner 1970 lib. bdg. $50.00. "This authoritative work, which fills the need for an up-to-date concise dictionary of the subject . . . is very highly recommended" (*LJ*).

Browne, Lewis, comp. *The World's Greatest Scriptures: An Anthology of the Sacred Books of the Ten Principal Religions*. Macmillan 1962 o.p. Historical introductions; interpretive comments; decorations and maps for the scriptures of Babylonia, Egypt, Hinduism, Buddhism, Confucianism, Jainism, Zoroastrianism, Judaism, Christianity, and Islam.

Clarke, James Freeman. *Ten Great Religions*. 1871. Houghton Mifflin o.p. A dated but very readable chapter on Islam.

Davidson, Gustav. *A Dictionary of Angels: Including the Fallen Angels*. Free Pr. 1972 $22.95 pap. $11.95. An illustrated sourcebook containing 3,000 entries that identify and describe the angels of Judaism, Christianity, and Islam. "The discipline of angelology . . . has just received a shot in the arm in the form of this unique reference work that the devotees of erudition will have a hard time putting down" (*LJ*).

A Dictionary of Comparative Religion. Scribner 1970 o.p. Furnishes data on beliefs, deities, and practices of religions worldwide.

Eastman, Roger, ed. *The Ways of Religion*. Harper 1975 text ed. pap. $21.95. An anthology in comparative religion that combines pertinent and interesting primary sources and expository materials for each of the major religions.

Editors of Life. *The World's Great Religions*. Western Pub. 1957 o.p. The late Dr. Paul Hutchinson says in his introduction: "In this presentation of the great living religions . . . there is no attempt to force the faiths into ideological compartments that can be more deceptive than informative. What is here being sought is to show them as their followers know and practice them, with enough reference to the contents of the holy books, the sacred legends and myths and their traditional teachings which lie behind these practices to make them intelligible." Almost half of this book is devoted to Christianity, but Islam is presented thoroughly by beautiful color photography and a carefully chosen anthology drawn from scriptural writings. The book makes a great plea for religious tolerance: "In their religious aspirations men [and presumably women] do not differ much from one another, no matter where they live or when."

Ellwood, Robert S. *Historical Atlas of the Religions of the World*. Ed. by Isma'il Ragi al Farugi, Macmillan 1974 $15.00. The 65 maps "cover such subjects as origins and distributions of religions, spread of the sects, and locations of shrines and temples, sites and cities, as well as unusual topics such as stimulants and narcotics in religious use and pilgrim traffic to Mecca" (*LJ*).

Gard, Richard A. *Great Religions of Modern Man*. Braziller 6 vols. 1961 o.p. Rituals, prayers, and dogmas with commentaries of the great world religions. The section on Islam is edited by John Alden Williams.

Gaskell, G. A. *Dictionary of All Scriptures and Myths*. Crown 1960 o.p. Deals with the sacred language of the various world religions—the origin, nature, and meaning of the scriptures and myths attached to them. Entries are arranged conveniently for the general reader.

Gibb, Hamilton A., and J. H. Kramers, eds. *The Shorter Encyclopedia of Islam*. Cornell Univ. Pr. 1957 $85.00. Emphasis on religion and canonical law.

Great Religions of the World. Ed. by Huston Smith and others, National Geographic 1971 o.p. Stunning color illustrations for two crisp and authoritative essays, Edward Jurji's "Mohammad Is His Prophet" and Thomas Abercrombie's "The Sweep of Islam." Also a selection of sacred texts.

Hastings, James, ed. *Encyclopedia of Religion and Ethics*. Fortress 13 vols. $599.95. Indispensable for reliability and comprehensiveness, this vast work of 10,000 pages presents articles on all religions of the world and on all the great systems of ethics. The entries embrace the range of biography, theology, philosophy, and related disciplines.

Head, Joseph, and S. L. Cranston, eds. *Reincarnation: An East-West Anthology*. Theos. Pub. House 1968 pap. $5.50. "This noble anthology proves that belief in reincarnation or some transformation after death is, or has been, held in all parts of the world, from the most primitive times. . . . The quotations, many of considerable length, begin in the East with excellently chosen passages from the Buddhist, Hindu, Sikh, Egyptian, Judaic and other scriptures or from pertinent commentaries. Then follow Christian, Mohammedan, and other texts, including the early Christian, the Druses [an Islamic sect based in Syria and Lebanon], and those of other faiths. Part II is devoted to Western thinkers on reincarnation. Part III comprises quotations from scientists and psychobiologists on the subject. . . . An essential item for all large religious collections and useful in a library of any size, this book should be invaluable to clergymen and to professional writers and speakers" (*LJ*).

Hinnells, John R., ed. *The Penguin Dictionary of Religions*. [*Reference Ser.*] Penguin 1984 pap. $6.95. Contains brief entries on sects and practices, with a particularly good bibliography.

Hughes, Thomas P. *A Dictionary of Islam*. Gordon Pr. repr. of 1885 ed. 2 vols. 1980 lib. bdg. $199.95; Irvington lib. bdg. $34.00; Orient Bk. Dist. repr. of 1885 ed. 1977 $48.00. A nineteenth-century work, which is, as its subtitle says, an "encyclopedia of the doctrines, rites, ceremonies, and customs, together with the technical and theological terms of the Muhammedan religion."

Jeffery, Arthur. *A Reader on Islam*. Ayer repr. of 1962 ed. 1980 lib. bdg. $50.00. Substantial study from original sources illustrating beliefs and practices.

Kritzeck, James, ed. *Anthology of Islamic Literature: From the Rise of Islam to Modern Times*. New Amer. Lib. 1975 pap. $10.95. The more than 40 selections include newly translated sections of the Koran and essays, poetry, and proverbs on the favorite Islamic themes of love, beauty, death, and God. Ranges from the Age of Caliphs (the more or less political counterparts of the imams) to the Mughal poetry of India and the Ottoman poetry at the end of the eighteenth century. The editor is a professor of Oriental Studies at the University of Notre Dame.

———. *Modern Islamic Literature: From 1800 to the Present*. New Amer. Lib. 1972 o.p. The book jacket reads: "Assembled here for the first time are selections from the best and most important Moslem writers of modern times. Although regarded as masters of literary style in their own countries, many of them are virtually unknown to readers of English. Some are being introduced to Western audiences in their first translations; others are represented by excerpts from influential works that have generally escaped the attention of critics outside the Islamic world." Included are masterpieces of fiction by Tewfiq al-Hakim, Mahmud Taymur, and Sadegh Hedayat.

Landis, Benson Y. *World Religions: A Brief Handbook for the Layman.* 1957. Dutton rev. ed. 1965 o.p. Landis, of the National Council of Churches, has edited a most useful reference work. According to *Library Journal*, the revised edition does "not outdate your copy of the first edition . . . only the statistics have been updated."

Lewis, Bernard, and others. *The Encyclopaedia of Islam.* Macmillan new ed. 5 vols. to date 1965–1986 set $871.00. Brings together in a projected ten-volume set the religious and political life of the Islamic community. The arrangement of articles according to the Arabic alphabet and language makes its use somewhat awkward for the unpracticed Western reader. Though still incomplete, this monumental new edition is authoritative and expansive on almost anything related to Muslim life and Islamic doctrine.

Mandelbaum, Bernard. *Choose Life.* Bloch 1972 pap. $5.95. An attempt to illuminate human life by drawing on many sources of wisdom, including Islamic lore.

Parrinder, Geoffrey. *A Dictionary of Non-Christian Religions.* Westminster 1973 $10.95. "A timely and authoritative dictionary" (*LJ*).

Robinson, Francis. *Atlas of the Islamic World Since 1500.* Facts on File 1982 $35.00. Best collection of maps available.

Williams, John A., ed. *Themes of Islamic Civilization.* Univ. of California Pr. 1971 $43.00 pap. $8.95. Employing original texts, Williams examines Islamic ideas on the community, political and individual freedom, law, holy war, and mysticism.

Zaehner, Robert C., ed. *Concise Encyclopedia of Living Faiths.* Beacon 1967 pap. $16.95. A large, scholarly, well-illustrated description of the world's major religions. Islam is included in the prophetic group (as contrasted to the mystical or immanent group).

GENERAL HISTORIES AND COMPARATIVE STUDIES

Ahmad, Aziz. *Islamic Modernism in India and Pakistan.* Oxford 1967 o.p. Not intended as a comprehensive or detailed survey, this introduction to the landmarks of political thought in Islamic India and Pakistan deals mainly with individual thinkers and their works.

Ajami, Fouad. *The Vanished Imam: Musa al Sadr and the Shia of Lebanon.* Cornell Univ. Pr. 1986 text ed. $17.95. A fascinating analysis and clarification of the religious and political issues at stake in the present-day civil war in Lebanon, written by a Lebanese Shiite. "May give Western readers the clearest picture yet of the heritage of suffering and betrayal embedded in Shia Islam" (*Atlantic Monthly*).

Akhavi, Shahrough. *Religion and Politics in Contemporary Iran.* State Univ. of New York Pr. 1980 $44.50 pap. $16.95. Along with studies of Keddie and Mottahedeh, this book gives one a good picture of the Islamic revolution in Iran during the 1970s.

Aletrino, L. *Six World Religions.* Trans. by Mary Foran, Morehouse 1969 pap. $4.95.

"An objective analysis by a well-known Dutch journalist of the major non-Christian religions of the world" (*PW*).

Allen, Henry E. *Turkish Transformation: A Study in Social and Religious Development.* Greenwood repr. of 1935 ed. 1968 lib. bdg. $22.50. Impact of modernism on the Islamic tradition in Turkey.

Amir, Ali Syed. *The Spirit of Islam: A History of the Evolution and Ideals of Islam with a Life of the Prophet.* Methuen 1865 o.p.

Arnold, Thomas W. *The Preaching of Islam: A History of Propagation of the Muslim Faith.* 1896. [*Mid-East Studies*] AMS Pr. repr. of 1913 ed. 1983 $27.50. A classic study of the missionary aspect of Islam.

Arnold, Thomas W., and A. Guillaume, eds. *The Legacy of Islam.* 1960. Gordon Pr. repr. 1976 lib. bdg. $75.00. A series of authoritative articles on Islam as a socioreligious and cultural force, reprinted often.

Bach, Marcus. *Had You Been Born in Another Faith.* Prentice-Hall 1961 o.p. This is a useful, popular guide, not intended as a profound study. It gives the general reader an accurate, simply and agreeably written account of the major religions.

Batatu, John. *The Old Social Classes and the Revolutionary Movements of Iraq.* [*Princeton Studies on the Near East*] 1979 $125.00 pap. $34.50. Although the title suggests a limited scope, this impressive work uses Iraq as a case study in exploring the relationship among ideology, social structure, and tradition in the Arab-Islamic context.

Bennigsen, Alexandre. *Mystics and Commissars.* Univ. of California Pr. 1985 $32.00. Emphasizes the struggle of Sufism in the Soviet Union and gives considerable space to the conflict of cultures in the Afghanistan War.

Bishai, Wilson B. *Islamic History of the Middle East.* Foreword by Richard Frye, Allyn & Bacon 1968 o.p. "Dr. Bishai's book . . . was written mainly for college students. He describes the chronological sequence of events but more is added to the bare bones of events and dates. Reasons for the fall of a dynasty or a change in outlook are given to the reader who is invited to consider further implications of the great periods of Islamic history. . . . The glossaries of terms and unfamiliar words, especially for students, and the bibliographies are well balanced for more reading."

Blunt, Wilfred Scawen. *The Future of Islam.* Kegan Paul 1882 o.p. An early classic by a brilliant English writer who lived among the Muslims and traveled throughout Saudi Arabia. A collection of essays from *Fortnightly Review*, this prophetic little book urges Western readers to change their attitudes toward Islam that date back to the Crusades or to watch both Africa and southern Asia fall under its sway.

Boer, Tjitze J. De. *The History of Philosophy in Islam.* Scholarly repr. of 1903 ed. $39.00. A valuable brief account.

Bouquet, A. C. *Comparative Religion.* Penguin 1973 o.p. This fine study is by an outstanding authority in the field.

Bowker, John. *Problems of Suffering in the Religions of the World.* Cambridge Univ. Pr. 1975 $47.50 pap. $12.95. According to *Library Journal*, a "penetrating and moving study" that devotes a chapter to how Islam copes with anguish in the lives of its devotees.

Bradley, David G. *A Guide to the World's Religions.* Spectrum Bks. 1962 o.p. A superb job of condensation and clarification, this little book is both sympathetic and measured; an excellent quick reference, with a very useful bibliography of paperbound books on the world's religions.

Braude, Benjamin, and Bernard Lewis, eds. *Christians and Jews in the Ottoman*

Empire: The Functioning of a Plural Society. Holmes & Meier 2 vols. 1982 text ed. $94.50. For hundreds of years the Muslim Ottomans ruled a territory of great ethnic and religious diversity. How did this vast empire, stretching from the Caucasus to the Sahara and from the Carpathians to the Zagros, endure for so long? The contributors to this work examine the political and social arrangements that made possible the effective functioning of a polyethnic, multireligious society for more than 400 years. Written by eminent scholars, these essays weigh the fundamental question of religion and community in the Middle East. The topics include the nature of contact between Muslims and non-Muslims.

Bravmann, Rene A. *African Islam.* Smithsonian 1984 pap. $16.95. Selection of essays that explore the social and historical dynamics as well as the aesthetic response of Africans to the appearance of Islam south of the Mediterranean littoral. Focus is on the author's personal experience with Islamic thought and art.

Brockelmann, C. *History of the Islamic People.* Methuen 1980 $26.95 pap. $15.00. A general introduction, useful for identifying many people and groups.

Browne, Lewis. *This Believing World.* Macmillan 1944 $9.95 pap. $2.95. A simple account of the great religions of mankind.

Bush, Richard C. *Religion in Communist China.* Abingdon 1970 o.p. "A well-researched book and nowhere else can one become familiar with so many facets of the religious problems of the world's most populous nation" (*Critic*).

Cash, Wilson W. *The Expansion of Islam: An Arab Religion in the Non-Arab World.* Columbia Univ. Pr. 1928 o.p. A general history of Islam as it related to other cultures and responded to Western ideas. Bibliography and maps.

Comstock, Richard, and others. *Religion and Man: An Introduction.* Harper 1971 $12.95. "Six areas of religion are analyzed for the reader with limited religious background" (*Wilson Library Bulletin*).

Cragg, Kenneth. *The Call of the Minaret.* Orbis Bks. 2d ed. rev. & enl. 1985 pap. $13.95. Interesting study of the contrast between Christianity and Islam.

———. *The House of Islam.* [*Religious Life of Man Ser.*] Dickenson 2d ed. 1975 text ed. pap. $10.95. "A valuable supplementary text . . . strongly recommended as a follow-up to Gibb" (*Choice*).

Curtis, Michael, ed. *Religion and Politics in the Middle East.* [*Westview Special Studies on the Middle East*] Westview 1982 pap. $14.95. Reliable and reasonably current collection of essays by authorities in the field.

Daniel, Norman A. *Islam and the West.* Columbia Univ. Pr. 1960 $26.00. Seeks to correct erroneous ideas many Europeans have about Islam.

Dann, Uriel, ed. *The Great Powers in the Middle East, 1919–1939.* Holmes & Meier 1984 $39.50. Perhaps the most critical period in the development of modern Middle Eastern politics came between the two world wars. Britain and France vied for influence and control in this predominantly Muslim region by making conflicting promises to the leaders of the emergent Arab nationalism as well as to the Zionists. These essays by a distinguished roster of international contributors provide an account of how the great powers acted to advance their own national interests in the Middle East and how those actions influenced the nations and issues in the area so that they still hold center stage in world politics today.

Dekmejian, Hrair. *Islam in Revolution: Fundamentalism in the Arab World.* [*Contemporary Issues in the Middle East Ser.*] Syracuse Univ. Pr. 1985 text ed. $28.00 pap. $13.95. "One of the strengths of the work lies in its emphasis on fundamentalist movements beginning from the very inception of Islam as a world religion. In this manner, the author shows that Islamic resurgence does not simply mean a "rediscovery" of the religion by Moslems, but rather a reappropriation for a new purpose. For believers, Islam has a renewed appeal as a familiar and culturally authentic idiom of political protest" (Massoud Javadi, *Ararat*).

Donner, Fred M. *The Early Islamic Conquests*. [*Princeton Studies on the Near East*] 1981 $44.00 pap. $19.95. "This book represents a description and interpretation of the early Islamic conquest movement, from its beginnings under the Prophet Mohammad . . . through the conquest of the Fertile Crescent" (Preface).

Endress, Gerhard. *An Introduction to Islamic History*. Columbia Univ. Pr. 1986 $16.00

Esposito, John L. *Islam and Politics*. Syracuse Univ. Pr. 1984 $28.00. Most of the book deals with events and developments since 1979 when the Islamic storm broke in full fury with the birth of the Islamic republic in Iran. Esposito believes that the "ripple effect of Islamic resurgence" was badly misunderstood in the West.

———, ed. *Islam and Development: Religion and Sociopolitical Change*. [*Contemporary Issues in the Middle East Ser.*] Syracuse Univ. Pr. 1980 text ed. pap. $9.95. Helpful and basically reliable collection.

Esslemont, J. E. *Baha'u'llah and the New Era: An Introduction to the Baha'i Faith*. Baha'i 5th rev. ed. 1980 pap. $4.50. Founded by Mirza Husayn Ali, known as the Baha'u'llah ("Glory of God"), the Baha'i religion stems from the Babi faith, a revolutionary offshoot of Shiah Islam. This book is the classic introduction to the Baha'i faith, giving a general view of its history and teachings. (For Baha'i, see Chapter 14 in this volume.)

Farah, Caesar E. *Islam: Beliefs and Observances*. Barron rev. ed. 1970 text ed. pap. $6.50. "It is the author's wish that the reader will acquire a more accurate perspective of what Islam stands for today. . . . To help him towards that end, a conscious attempt has been made to simplify as much as is reasonable the most important ingredients of Islamic religion and to show the range of their impact on the lives of its adherents" (Preface). Contains a useful glossary and annotated bibliography.

Faruqi, al Isma'il Ragi. *Islam*. Argus Comm. 1979 o.p. In recent years introductions to Islam written by Muslims have become increasingly available to English-reading audiences. Anyone wishing to understand the meaning of Islamic tradition for Muslims should utilize these important sources. Among the best is this very readable discussion by a Sunni thinker with considerable teaching experience in the West.

Finegan, J. *Archaeology of World Religions*. Princeton Univ. Pr. 1952 o.p. Treats primitive religions for the scholar and the general reader.

Gabrieli, Francesco. *The Arab Revival*. Random 1961 o.p. Useful opening chapter on "The Glorious Past."

Gaer, Joseph. *What the Great Religions Believe*. New Amer. Lib. 1964 pap. $3.95. In a readable and understandable style, Gaer explains the major beliefs of 11 religions, Islam prominent among them. Following the explanations or brief biography of the founder of each religion, he presents selections from its sacred literature.

Gaudefroy-Demombynes, Maurice. *Muslim Institutions*. Greenwood repr. of 1950 ed. 1984 lib. bdg. $35.00. Describes principal institutions of Islam from original sources.

Geertz, Clifford. *Islam Observed: Religious Development in Morocco and Indonesia*. Univ. of Chicago Pr. repr. of 1968 ed. 1971 pap. $6.00. This study lays out a general framework for the comparative analysis of religion and applies it to the development of a supposedly single creed, Islam, as it influences two contrasting civilizations. This work has shaped many analyses of Islam in general and Muslim fundamentalism in particular.

Gibb, Hamilton A. *Modern Trends in Islam*. Hippocrene Bks. repr. of 1947 ed. 1971 lib. bdg. $18.50. Presents a critique of Islamic modernist thought that shaped both Muslim and non-Muslim views in the following years. Though now outdated, this study continues to provide an important framework for analysis and study.

———. *Mohammedanism: An Historical Survey*. Oxford 2d ed. repr. of 1953 ed. 1962 pap. $5.95. A penetrating study of Islam, regarded by many as the classic exposition by a Western author.

———. *Studies in the Civilization of Islam*. Ed. by William R. Polk and Stanford J. Shaw, Princeton Univ. Pr. repr. of 1962 ed. 1982 pap. $11.95. Sir Hamilton Gibb was a world-renowned authority on Islam at Harvard University. This book contains 15 major essays on Islamic history and culture selected by his assistants. Among them is an important essay by Gibb, "Arab-Byzantine Relations Under the Umayyad Caliphate."

Gibb, Hamilton A., and Harold Bowen. *Islamic Society and the West*. Oxford 2 vols. 1957 o.p. A study of the impact of Western civilization on Muslim culture in the Near East. Although strongly criticized in recent years, this book remains a valuable reference, especially in its coverage of the eighteenth century in special areas (see also Naff and Owen below).

Glubb, John Bagot. *The Great Arab Conquests*. Prentice-Hall 1963 o.p. The term "Arab Empire," besides its limited reference to the Arabs of Arabia known to have migrated into various regions of the Middle East after the rise of Islam, also refers to the vast majority of the original inhabitants of these regions who became Arabized by conversion to Islam as well as by the adoption of Arabic as a mother tongue. Glubb, who once served as commander of the Jordanian Army, describes how Islam followed wherever the Arabs went.

Goldhizer, Ignaz. *Introduction to Islamic Theology and Law*. Trans. by Andras Hamori and Ruth Hamori, Princeton Univ. Pr. 1981 o.p. Historical perspective needs to be supplemented by an understanding of the intellectual content of Islam. This recently translated "classic" admirably serves that purpose.

———. *Muslim Studies*. Allen & Unwin 2 vols. 1967 o.p. Originally published in German in 1890, still an excellent source of study on Hadith (the corpus of Muhammad's sayings).

Guillaume, Alfred. *Islam*. Penguin 2d ed. 1961 o.p. Published in 1954 as *Traditions of Islam*, this excellent brief survey for the reader new to the subject is based partially on Goldhizer's works. Guillaume is a respected authority on Arabic studies.

Hackin, J., and others. *Asiatic Mythology*. Crowell 1963 o.p. An account of the various religions, sects, and mythologies outlined and explained within their historical setting.

Haddad, Robert M. *Syrian Christians in Muslim Society: An Interpretation*. [*Princeton Studies on the Near East*] Greenwood repr. of 1970 ed. 1981 lib. bdg. $22.50. "A significant contribution to several areas. The summing-up is an interpretive essay which will be well used by those studying minority groups, whether within or without the Middle East" (*Choice*).

Haddad, Yvonne Yazbeck. *Contemporary Islam and the Challenge of History*. State Univ. of New York Pr. 1982 $49.50 pap. $19.95. Analyzes "the forces and events of the twentieth century, both within and without the Islamic community, that have made it necessary for Muslims to redefine and articulate their understanding of Islam" (Prologue).

Hawting, G. R. *The First Dynasty of Islam: The Umayyad Caliphate A.D. 661–750*. Southern Illinois Univ. Pr. 1986 text ed. $24.95. The Umayyad period was a crucial one for the development of Islam. At the outset of the 90-year Umayyad rule over the Middle East, the region had just been conquered by the Arabs, and there is little unambiguous data about the development of Islam during that era. By the time the dynasty was overthrown, the Arabic languages and culture had made substantial progress among the non-Arab conquered peoples, many of the religious features distinctly Islamic had begun to crystallize, and large numbers of subject people became converts. Hawting, who lectures in the history of the Near and Middle East at the School of Oriental and African Studies in London, provides an introductory survey of this period. After discussing the problem of source material, he enters the continuing debate about the place of the Umayyads in Islamic history.

Hayes, John R. *The Genius of Arab Civilization: Source of Renaissance*. MIT 2d ed. 1983 text ed. $35.00 pap. $11.95. In his introduction, R. B. Winder says that this book aims to introduce the general reader to "the cultural achievements and heritage of the Arabs." This goal is met in a format that combines more than 80 full-color illustrations with a group of scholarly essays by outstanding authorities on the subject. Among them is Majid Fakhry on philosophy and history and John Badeau on the Arab role in Islamic culture. Ibrahim Madkour, formerly president of the Academy of Arabic Language in Cairo, surveys Arab civilization, past and present, and ventures some predictions about its future.

Hitti, Philip K. *History of the Arabs*. St. Martin's 10th ed. 1970 o.p. Among the best references on the historical development of Islam.

———. *Islam: A Way of Life*. Regnery 1971 pap. $7.50. A readable little volume by one of the world's experts in Arab affairs.

Hodgson, Marshall G. *Venture of Islam: Conscience and History in World Civilization*. Univ. of Chicago Pr. 3 vols. 1975 ea. $30.00. It is helpful to have access to a general interpretation of the whole sweep of Islamic history. Perhaps the most significant such study in recent years, the successor to Brockelmann, is this book. "This is a nonpareil work, not only because of its command of its subject, but also because it demonstrates how, ideally, history should be written" (*The New Yorker*).

Holt, P. M., and others, eds. *Cambridge History of Islam*. Cambridge Univ. Pr. 2 vols. 1977–78 $250.00 pap. $90.00. The society and civilization of the central Islamic lands and the further Islamic lands; particularly good are three chapters on Islam in Southeast Asia. Among the best and most authoritative of the surveys.

Idowu, E. Bolaji. *African Traditional Religion*. Orbis Bks. 1973 o.p. "This important book is the first to place the study of African religion in the larger context of religious studies. The author is well qualified by his competence in the history of religions, Christian theology, and the religion of the Yoruba [some of whom are Muslim]" (*Choice*).

Iqbal, Mohammad. *The Reconstruction of Religious Thought in Islam*. Kazi 1970 $14.50. Penetrating attempt at a modern rethinking of Islam.

Israeli, Raphael, ed. *The Crescent in the East: Islam in Asia Major*. State Mutual Bk. 1981 $30.00. An anthology by the author of *Muslims in China*, which in condensed form appears as the final essay, is created around the idea that though the political, spiritual, and economic core of Islam has been geographically located in the Middle East, the large masses of believers dwell further to the

East in Asia and constitute by sheer weight of numbers the numerical heartland of Islam.

Itzkowitz, Norman. *Ottoman Empire and Islamic Tradition.* Univ. of Chicago Pr. repr. of 1972 ed. 1980 pap. $6.00. A brief, clear, and precise history of the pre-nineteenth-century Ottoman Empire and its interaction with Islam. Itzkowitz is a professor of Near Eastern Studies at Princeton University.

Jansen, Godfrey. *Militant Islam.* Harper 1980 pap. $4.95. Jansen examines the militancy of Islam from 1800 to the present, emphasizing its resurgence in the last decades. He analyzes the position of traditionalists, like Ayatollah Khomeini of Iran and General Zia of Pakistan, who advocate strict adherence to Koranic precepts, the religious figures eager to maintain the status quo, and the reformers trying to adapt the faith to the demands of the modern world. The book concludes with a survey of the many views of what a modern Islamic order should be and assesses Islam's future in the last part of this century. Perhaps the best journalistic treatment among the recent paperbacks.

Kaba, Lansine. *Wahhabiyya: Islamic Reform and Politics in French West Africa.* [*Studies in African Religion*] Northwestern Univ. Pr. 1974 $17.95. "A significant addition to the literature on African Islam" (*Choice*).

Kahn, Margaret. *Children of the Jinn: In Search of the Kurds and Their Country.* Putnam repr. 1980 o.p. A popular introduction to contemporary Islamic societies.

Katsh, Abraham I. *Judaism and the Koran.* A. S. Barnes 1962 o.p. The biblical and Talmudic backgrounds in Surahs 2 and 3 of the Koran.

Keddie, Nikki R. *Religion and Politics in Iran: Shi'ism from Quietism to Revolution.* Yale Univ. Pr. 1983 text ed. $28.50 1984 pap. $9.95. An excellent study, complements Akhavi and Mottahedeh.

Keen, Sam, ed. *Voices and Visions.* Harper 1976 o.p. "Nine prominent 'gurus' explain different ways of understanding altered consciousness and the transformations they have undergone in their quest for comprehension" (*Booklist*).

Kelly, Marjorie. *Islam: The Religious and Political Life of a World Community.* Praeger 1984 $42.95 pap. $16.95. A collection of essays that seeks to reveal "the dynamism and diversity of Islam in today's world" (Preface).

Kepel, Gilles. *Muslim Extremism in Egypt: The Prophet and the Pharaoh.* Pref. by Bernard Lewis, Univ. of California Pr. 1986 $18.95. Using chiefly Arab and French sources, Kepel takes up "the challenge to Western categories of thought posed by contemporary Islam in its most spectacular, most monstrous manifestations" (Introduction).

Kettani, M. Ali. *Muslim Minorities in the World Today.* Mansell 1986 $56.00. In the words of the author, this book recounts "the long, continuous and glorious epic of the struggle for survival against heavy odds of minority Muslim communities in the different parts of the world." Though highly partisan, its up-to-date census of Muslim populations throughout the world makes it the most useful book on the subject.

Kitagawa, Joseph M. *Religions of the East.* Westminster 1960 enl. ed. 1968 pap. $7.95

Kitagawa, Joseph M., and Charles H. Long, eds. *History of Religions: Essays on the Problem of Understanding.* Univ. of Chicago Pr. 1967 $17.50. When this volume was first published in 1935, *Library Journal* said "[it] consists of 11 essays on the problem of religious understanding or hermeneutics [the study of the principles of methodology applied to sacred texts] as seen by a group of specialists in the history of religions. . . . Very well written."

Koller, John M. *Oriental Philosophies.* Macmillan 2d ed. 1985 text ed. pap. $12.95. "While a certain exuberance allied with an over-reliance on Western or 'Westernized' Asian source material flaws the author's attempt at a complete summary of Asian philosophical-religious thought, Koller's approach has nobility and a valuable distinction—he has a gift for succinct definition that most readers will appreciate" (*PW*).

Lammens, Henri. *Islam: Beliefs and Institutions.* Trans. by E. Denison Ross, Coronet repr. of 1929 ed. $23.50; Gordon Pr. 1976 lib. bdg. $59.95. Despite its hypercritical skepticism, one of the early classics on the subject and an indispensable source of reference.

Lapidus, Ira M. *Contemporary Islamic Movements in Historical Perspective.* [*Policy Papers in International Affairs*] Univ. of California, Institute of International Studies 1983 pap. $4.95. Policy papers in international affairs involving Islam.

Laroui, Abdallah. *The History of the Maghrib: An Interpretive Essay.* Trans. by Ralph Manheim [*Studies on the Near East*] Princeton Univ. Pr. 1977 $48.50. Useful and thought-provoking interpretation of Islam's role in North Africa by an authority in the studies of the area.

Levonian, Lufty. *Islam and Christianity.* Allen & Unwin 1941 o.p. A study of the relationship of two major religions, in psychological and historical terms, by an authority who was Dean of the School of Theology in Beirut.

Levtzion, Nehemia, ed. *Conversion to Islam.* Holmes & Meier 1979 text ed. $39.50. The essays in this volume span the 13 centuries of Islamic history. They range from analyses of historical processes to a review of modern European and Muslim interpretations of conversions, from anthropological studies to literary analyses of local myths, chronicles, and didactic literature.

Lewis, Bernard. *The Jews of Islam.* Princeton Univ. Pr. 1984 $17.50. Lectures delivered at Hebrew Union College in Cincinnati developed into a definitive analysis of the Jewish preserve in the Arab world.

————. *Race and Color in Islam.* Hippocrene Bks. repr. 1980 o.p. Lewis writes in his preface: "Describing the evidence of prejudice and discrimination in the Islamic countries, I have tried to correct the false pictures drawn by the myth makers, the picture of the total absence of such evils. [But] at no time did the Islamic world ever practice the kind of racial discrimination which we find in the Republic of Africa or which existed until recently in parts of the United States."

————. *Semites and Anti-Semites: An Inquiry into Conflict and Prejudice.* Norton 1986 $18.95. A Princeton specialist in the Near East, Professor Lewis explains that for centuries Christian and Muslim attitudes toward Jews diverged: Christians vilified Jews as people who had refused Christ, while Muslims regarded Jews as insignificant losers (Muhammad had beaten three Jewish tribes) and focused their hostility on Christians. Lewis, after tracing its evolution in Europe, shows how anti-Semitism was imported into the Middle East. At present, the media in the Muslim Middle East claim that John Wilkes Booth and Al Capone were Jews and evoke the memory of "that great man Hitler." Even so, Lewis contends that this insanity has not permeated Islamic society. A peaceful settlement between Israel and its neighbors would arrest the spread of the disease, says Professor Lewis.

Lewis, I. M., ed. *Islam in Tropical Africa.* Indiana Univ. Pr. 2d ed. 1980 $25.00 pap. $10.95. A classic text in a revised, updated edition that presents 14 specialist studies on the history and sociology of the Muslim communities of sub-Saharan Africa.

Lichtenstadter, Ilse. *Islam and the Modern Age.* Irvington 1958 text ed. $29.00. Because Lichtenstadter lived in Egypt and Pakistan, she is in a good position to appraise the problems and perplexities that confront Muslims at the opening of the atomic age. Foreword by Sir Mohammed Zafulla Khan, vice president of the International Court of Justice.

Lincoln, C. Eric. *The Black Muslims in America*. Beacon 1961 o.p. A study of the Black Muslim movement in America. The *Atlanta Journal-Constitution* commented: "Dr. Lincoln not only has produced the only definitive book on the rituals, beliefs, and accomplishments of the Muslims, but he has done a beautiful job of placing the movement within its psychological and sociological context."

Ling, Trevor. *A History of Religion East and West: An Introduction and Interpretation*. Harper 1970 o.p. "This book will be most helpful to the nonspecialist. What it lacks in depth and variety of interpretation it provides in scope and general information" (*Choice*).

Lings, Martin. *A Sufi Saint of the Twentieth Century: Shaikh Ahmad al-'Alawi, His Spiritual Heritage and Legacy*. Univ. of California Pr. 1972 $30.00 pap. $4.95. The first edition of this book, *A Moslem Saint in the Twentieth Century*, was described by the *Journal of Near Eastern Studies* as "one of the most thorough and intimately engaging books on Sufism to be produced by a Western scholar."

Macdonald, Duncan B. *Aspects of Islam*. [*Select Bibliographies Repr. Ser.*] Ayer repr. of 1911 ed. 1971 $25.50. Concentrates on the theological education and training of Muslim missionaries.

Margoliouth, David S. *The Early Development of Mohammedanism*. AMS Pr. repr. of 1914 ed. 1979 $22.50. Helpful study of the formulation of Islamic doctrine, by Oxford University don and author of the primer, *Mohammedanism*.

Marshall, Richard H., Jr., and others, eds. *Aspects of Religion in the Soviet Union, 1917–1967*. Univ. of Chicago Pr. 1971 $35.00. This collection of essays enhances our understanding of religion in the Soviet Union, especially of the growing Muslim population in the Adzhar Republic.

Maududi, Abdul A. *Towards Understanding Islam*. Trans. by Khurshid Ahmad, Kazi 1963 pap. $5.50; New Era Publications 1985 pap. $5.95. This basic introduction by a leading South Asian Muslim fundamentalist thinker of the twentieth century has gone into many editions.

Metcalf, Barbara Daly. *Islamic Revival in British India: Deoband, 1860–1900*. Princeton Univ. Pr. 1982 $31.50. Describes one of the major movements of religious renewal in British India, that of the reformist 'ulama (the religious scholars) of the late nineteenth century.

Mitchell, Richard P. *Society of the Muslim Brothers*. [*Middle Eastern Monographs Ser.*] Oxford 1969 o.p. There are several important studies that have helped to shape contemporary awareness of the style of Islam called "fundamentalist." A work of critical significance, this book is even accepted by many members of the Muslim Brotherhood as the standard authority on the history of the organization.

Morgan, Kenneth W., ed. *Islam: The Straight Path—Islam Interpreted by Muslims*. Ronald 1958 o.p. Skillfully meshed interpretations of various aspects of Islam by 11 outstanding scholars, among them the Chinese Muslim Dawood C. M. Ting. Morgan was Director of the Fund for the Study of Great Religions at Colgate University, Hamilton, New York.

Mottahedeh, Roy. *The Mantle of the Prophet: Religion and Politics in Modern Iran*. Pantheon 1986 pap. $9.95; Simon & Schuster 1985 $17.95. Deals with the revival of religious enthusiasm in late twentieth-century Iran. The author, a MacArthur Fellow, writes·like a novelist. Highly recommended.

Naff, Thomas, and Roger Owen, eds. *Studies in Eighteenth-Century Islamic History*. Southern Illinois Univ. Pr. 1977 $24.95. Despite its importance for Islamic history, the eighteenth century only recently has received the attention it deserves.

This is perhaps the best collection of materials illustrating the main lines of contemporary scholarship in this period.

Naipaul, V. S. *Among the Believers: An Islamic Journey.* Knopf 1981 $15.00; Random 1982 pap. $6.95. A fascinating account of a journey to three Islamic nations by a novelist and travel writer of major stature. Highly recommended as an introduction to the realities of modern Islamic society as seen by a sophisticated Western observer.

Nasr, Seyyed H. *Ideals and Realities of Islam.* Allen & Unwin 1983 pap. $6.95. An introduction written from the perspective of modern philosophical Sufism within the Shiite tradition.

Needleman, Jacob, and Dennis Lewis, eds. *Sacred Tradition and Present Need.* Viking 1975 o.p. "These essays . . . present authoritative spokesmen for Christianity . . . Samkhya of India, Vedanta, mythology, and Sufism. The book aims to show that traditional religions . . . are more reliable guides for today's spiritual questing than substitute panaceas" (*LJ*).

Neill, Stephen. *Christian Faiths and Other Faiths.* Inter-Varsity 1984 pap. $7.95. Intended for the Christian understanding of, and dialogue with, other religions.

Noss, John B. *Man's Religions.* Macmillan 5th ed. 1974 text ed. $15.95. A most valuable book that offers a fine sympathetic introduction to all major religions.

Oded, Arye. *Islam in Uganda.* Transaction Bks. 1974 $19.95. This case history studies Islamization through a centralized state in pre-Colonial East Africa. It investigates the penetration and expansion of Islam in Buganda, examines the patterns of Islamization in that kingdom compared with other regions, and analyzes the causes that facilitated and enhanced the diffusion of Islam as well as those that hindered its progress.

Parrinder, Edward G. *Book of World Religions.* Dufour 1967 $12.50. "This book by an eminent British authority on the comparative study of religions is divided into four parts—'Men at Prayer,' 'The Founders,' 'Holy Books and Their Teachings,' and 'Growth and Present State of Religions' with many cross-references" (*LJ*). To add to the value of this volume there are maps and charts, an outline of religious teachers and their writings, dates and statistics of the world's religions, symbols for each sect, and numerous photographs.

Peretz, Don, Sofia Mohsen, and Richard W. Moench. *Islam: Legacy of the Past, Challenge of the Future.* New Horizon Pr. 1984 $12.95. Recent developments in Islam and their relationship to civil law, socialism, education, and so forth.

Pullapilly, Cyriac K., ed. *Islam in the Contemporary World.* Crossroad 1980 o.p. Short but perceptive discussions of the major Islamic minorities.

Qutb, Sayyid. *This Religion of Islam.* New Era Pubns. 1977 pap. $2.95. Originally in Arabic, this introduction by one of the major scholars in the Muslim Brotherhood of Egypt exists in many editions. Qutb was executed during the Nasser era, but his works remain widely read in Egypt and throughout the Islamic world.

Rahman, Fazlur. *Islam.* Univ. of Chicago Pr. 2d ed. 1979 pap. $9.95. Professor Rahman was the Director of the Central Institute for Islamic Research, in Karachi, Pakistan, and his works have exerted a significant influence on the thought of Western scholars. His perspective is that of a contemporary modernist within the Sunni tradition. "The best general introduction to, and interpretation of, the Islamic religion which has yet been written" (Professor James Kritzeck, University of Notre Dame).

Roberts, Dennis. *Islam: A Concise Introduction.* Harper 1982 pap. $7.95. Written in clear, simple English, this book covers Muhammad's life, his marriage, Islamic law, society, politics, family, and domestic relations, as well as theology. "The intention is not to examine Islam through a telescope made in Christendom, but to try to see Islam as it sees itself" (Introduction).

Rosenthal, Erwin I. *Islam in the Modern National State.* Cambridge Univ. Pr. 1966 o.p. "A thorough, competent study based upon firsthand acquaintance with the people, and with leaders and native scholars in each country. For the specialist and advanced student" (*LJ*).

————. *Political Thought in Medieval Islam: An Introductory Outline.* Greenwood repr. of 1958 ed. 1985 lib. bdg. $47.50. An excellent study of the ways in which Islamic political thought has developed and of the reasons for the course it has taken.

Ruthven, Malise. *Islam in the World.* Oxford 1984 $27.95 pap. $8.95. An editor with the BBC's Arabic Service, Ruthven attempts a "comprehensive account of the Islamic *Weltanschauung*," something he thinks books by both Muslim and non-Muslim specialists in the field of Islamic studies fail to do. He shows how Islam's "continuous political manifestations fall within tradition of political activism going back nearly fourteen hundred years" (Preface). Albert Hourani said this book is "full of original ideas and judgments based on wide reading and personal observations."

Said, Edward W. *Covering Islam: How the Media and the Experts Determine How We See the Rest of the World.* Pantheon 1981 $10.95 pap. $4.95. Brilliant, often controversial interpretation by a Palestinian teaching at Columbia University, almost indispensable to a balanced view of the Middle East.

Savory, Roger M., ed. *Introduction to Islamic Civilization.* Cambridge Univ. Pr. 1976 $49.50 pap. $16.95. A challenging collection of essays ranging in time from the pre-Islamic to the modern era and showing the interaction between Christian West and Islamic East from the Crusades down to the encroachment of the West on the Muslim world. Fully illustrated.

Schact, Joseph, and C. E. Bosworth, eds. *The Legacy of Islam.* Oxford 2d ed. 1974 text ed. $29.95 pap. $8.95. This work "has a two-fold purpose: to analyze the contribution of Islamic civilization to the achievements of mankind and to depict the contacts of Islam with the non-Islamic world" (*Choice*).

Schimmel, Annemarie, and Abdolajawad Falaturi, eds. *We Believe in One God: The Experience of God in Christianity and Islam.* Crossroad 1979 o.p. Nine leading Christian and Muslim theologians exchange ideas on a broad range of theological, social, and political issues.

Schoeps, Hans-Joachim. *The Religions of Mankind.* Trans. by Richard Winston and Clara Winston, Doubleday 1966 o.p. Schoeps is a widely recognized authority in the field of comparative religion. "A smoothly flowing translation, the book reads well and easily, furthered by Dr. Schoeps' decision to concentrate on the broad sweep rather than the minute details of historical development. . . . This book should become a basic work" (*LJ*).

Schuon, Frithjof. *Dimensions of Islam.* Trans. by P. N. Townsend, Preface by Seyyed Hossein, Allen & Unwin 1970 o.p. Schuon "has rendered an invaluable service . . . by making transparent the religious forms and practices of the most diverse traditions, thereby revealing the transcendent unity that lies behind their forms." (Preface).

————. *Understanding Islam.* Trans. by D. M. Matheson, Allen & Unwin 1976 pap. $5.95. A closely argued commentary "designed to explain why the Moslems believe [in Islam]" (*LJ*).

Slater, Robert H. *World Religions and World Community.* [*Lectures on the History of*

Religions] Columbia Univ. Pr. 1963 $28.00. An examination of the major religions, their common elements and differences, and the contributions they may make toward the survival of the race.

Smith, Wilfred C. *Islam in Modern History.* Princeton Univ. Pr. 1957 $37.00 pap. $10.50. "This work will fail if it does not enable non-Muslims to understand better the behavior of Muslims that they observe, books by Muslim authors that they read, and Muslims that they meet" (Preface). A challenging and controversial study of Islam in a state of flux.

Spencer, Robert F., ed. *Religion and Change in Contemporary Asia.* Univ. of Minnesota Pr. 1971 o.p. "This book is rather remarkable for the consistent clarity and in-depth approach of all its essays" (*LJ*).

Stewart, Desmond. *Early Islam.* [*Great Ages of Man*] Silver Burdett 1967 o.p. "Stewart, who has lived and taught in the Middle East, accomplishes what is an extremely difficult task—presenting the background and early theological and political development of Islam coupled with a series of chapters devoted to the culture, science and art of the early Islamic world" (*LJ*).

Stoddard, Lothrop. *The New World of Islam.* Scribner 1921 o.p. Calling the rise of Islam "the most amazing event in human history," the author explains why. Stoddard is highly critical of women's role in Islam and tends to see Islam as a threatening force, but he provides a good picture of Islamic dynamism during and immediately after World War I.

Stoddard, Philip, and others, eds. *Change and the Muslim World.* [*Contemporary Issues in the Middle East Ser.*] Syracuse Univ. Pr. 1981 text ed. pap. $11.95. Based on papers presented at a two-day conference in Washington, D.C., in 1980, this volume discusses religious and political issues that concern the Islamic world from Morocco to Indonesia.

Sweetman, James W. *Islam and Christian Theology: A Study of the Interpretations of Theological Ideas in the Two Religions.* 1947. Gordon Pr. 3 vols. 1980 lib. bdg. $229.95. The only work that sets out to explore this area thoroughly, and hence an instructive aid to the serious student who wishes to understand Islamic thought in relation to that of the West. Not for the impatient, however.

Trimingham, J. Spencer. *The Influence of Islam upon Africa.* Praeger 1968 o.p. "Dr. Trimingham, former head of the Department of Arabic and Islamic Studies at the University of Glasgow, describes the penetration of Islam into the African continent, interpreting the implications of this still unfinished process upon the life and thought of Africa" (*PW*). This is a revised and condensed version of Trimingham's previous books about Islam in the Sudan, Ethiopia, and West Africa.

Voll, John O. *Islam: Continuity and Change in the Modern World.* Westview 1983 text ed. pap. $14.50. Explores the broad dimensions of Islam, looking at the vitality of the main elements of the faith across the centuries and finding the basis of today's Islamic resurgence in the continuing interaction of varying styles of Islam—fundamentalist, conservative, and individualist—and in the way each meets the challenge of the modern era.

Von Grunebaum, Gustave E. *Medieval Islam: A Study in Cultural Orientation.* Univ. of Chicago Pr. 2d ed. 1961 pap. $5.95. A general overview of Muslim culture during the Middle Ages by an outstanding scholar in the field.

Watt, W. M. *The Influence of Islam upon Medieval Europe.* Columbia Univ. Pr. 1973 pap. $10.00. Fine short history of an important crossing of cultures.

Wright, Robin. *Sacred Rage: The Crusade of Modern Islam.* Simon & Schuster 1985 $16.95 1986 pap. $7.95. Especially useful in covering the religious aspects of terrorism and violence in the Middle East with candor and penetration.

Ye'or, Bat. *The Dhimmi: Jews and Christians under Islam.* Trans. by David Maisel and others, Fairleigh Dickinson 1985 $25.00 pap. $9.95. Ye'or, an Egyptian Jew, analyzes the historical realities faced by the *dhimmi*, people (Jews and Christians) who were subjected to Muslim domination.

Zaehner, Robert C. *Concordant Discord: The Interdependence of Faiths.* Oxford 1970 $15.00. "Zaehner's jumping from one cultural-religious expression to another is fascinating although sometimes disconcerting. His radical interpretations are refreshing and intriguing" (*Choice*).

ISLAMIC MYSTICISM, PHILOSOPHY, AND THEOLOGY

Arberry, Arthur J. *The Doctrine of the Sufis.* Cambridge Univ. Pr. 1977 pap. $13.95. Sufism is the name commonly given to the mystical tradition in Islam that arose from Shiite belief. It has been marked by extensive borrowing from other mystical religious practices—Christian, Buddhist, and Neoplatonic—and by the great literary flowering it inspired. Many of the most famous Persian poets (see biographical entries for Jami and Rumi) were Sufis, as were some of Islam's most important philosophers (see entries for al-Ghazālī and ibn al-Arabi). Arberry is a leading Western expert on Sufism, and this brief account, with translated examples, is highly recommended.

———. *Revelation and Reason in Islam.* AMS Pr. repr. of 1957 ed. 1982 $20.00. The problem of the "sublime dilemma" as it affects Islam. Challenging, clear, and comprehensive treatment of a difficult subject.

Arjomand, Said A. *The Shadow of God and the Hidden Imam: Religion, Political Order and Societal Change in Shi'ite Iran from the Beginning to 1890.* Univ. of Chicago Pr. 1984 lib. bdg. $28.00. A study of the intellectual, historical, theological, and social foundations of Shiite Islam in Iran.

Arnold, T. W. *The Preaching of Islam.* Apt Bks. repr. of 1913 ed. 1984 text ed. $50.00; Kazi 1956 $35.00. A history of the propagation of the Muslim faith, emphasizing its missionary nature.

Attar, Farid. *Muslim Saints and Mystics: Episodes from the Tadhkirat Al-Auliya (Memorial of the Saints).* Trans. by Arthur J. Arberry, Methuen 1979 pap. $8.95. A prose work by one of the great poets of thirteenth-century Islamic literature. This is "the first volume of a series aimed at making major works of Persian literature more generally available to the interested Western reader" (*LJ*). Bibliography. In the UNESCO Collection of Representative Works.

Birge, John K. *The Bektashi Order of Dervishes.* AMS Pr. repr. of 1937 ed. 1982 $35.00. Detailed full treatment of the order, history, and doctrine.

Bravmann, M. M. *The Spiritual Background of Islam.* Brill 1972 o.p. The customs and concepts of the ancient Arabs that were absorbed into later religious doctrine. Particularly good on the interrelationship of the spiritual and the social.

Brown, J. P. *The Dervishes, or Oriental Spiritualism.* Ed. by H. A. Rose, F Cass 1968 o.p. Originally published in 1868, this book remains one of the best treatments of the subject. "All that the Editor has been able to do in the way of research has but served to confirm the scholarly accuracy of Brown's work" (Introduction). Brown takes the reader on a journey through the various orders—the Rifa'ia (Howling Dervishes), the Baqtashis, the Malamiyun (or Hamzawis), the Malavi (Whirling Dervishes), the Naqshbandis, the hashish-imbibing dervishes of northern Iran (Hashshashin), the wandering dervishes of India, and the real and false dervishes.

Copleston, Frederick. *Religion and the One: Philosophies East and West [Gifford Lec-*

tures] Crossroad 1981 $17.50. A study of the idea, in Eastern metaphysics, of the One as the source of the many and as the ultimate reality.

Cragg, Kenneth. *The Pen and the Faith: Eight Modern Muslim Writers and the Qur'an.* Foreword by Sam Bhajjan, Allen & Unwin 1985 text ed. $16.00. A selection from contemporary Muslim writers who wish to illuminate "the diversity of Quaranic understanding and to indicate how Quaranic guidance is discerned and applied to critical situations in the modern world." Sam Bhajjan, who wrote the foreword, is Director of the Henry Martin Institute of Islamic Studies in Hyderabad.

Craig, William L. *The Kalam Cosmological Argument.* Barnes & Noble 1979 text ed. $28.50. Examines one particular "proof" for the existence of God: the Kalam cosmological argument, originated with medieval Arab theologians and bequeathed to the West, where it became the center of a hotly disputed controversy (more or less over free will).

Donaldson, Dwight M. *The Shi'ite Religion: A History of Islam in Persia and Iraq.* AMS Pr. repr. of 1933 ed. 1980 $49.50. A thorough but not critical study.

Fakhry, Majid. *A History of Islamic Philosophy.* Univ. of Chicago Pr. 2d ed. 1983 $29.50. An excellent account of the historical unfolding, rather than of the conceptual complexities, of Islamic thought.

Franzius, Enno. *The History of the Order of Assassins.* Funk & Wagnalls 1969 o.p. The term "assassins" identifies members of the Ismaili sect, founded by Hasan Sabbah, who at the end of the eleventh century chose Nizar as their imam and who in the twelfth century accepted the Aga Khan as such. The sect began when Sabbah seized a mountain fortress in northern Persia and made it the headquarters of his secret religious and political group that for two centuries spread terror from India to Egypt. Determined to conquer the entire Middle East, he planned the murder of prominent Muslim leaders. His corps of hashish-inspired devotees (hence their name "Hashshashin," or the Westernized "assassin") carried out his orders as a sacred religious duty.

Hatcher, William S., and Martin J. Douglas. *The Bahai Faith: The Emerging Global Religion.* Harper 1985 $14.45. Attempts to examine the wide range of teachings of Bahaism, "an independent religion on a par with Christianity and other recognized world religions" (Introduction).

Hitti, Philip K. *The Origins of the Druze People and Religion, with Extracts from Their Sacred Writings.* AMS Pr. repr. of 1928 ed. 1981 $19.00. Though written 60 years ago, this study remains authoritative and revealing.

Hodgson, Marshall G. *The Order of the Assassins.* AMS Pr. repr. of 1955 ed. 1978 $46.50. A collection of translations of various authors, perhaps the most complete on the subject.

Hourani, George F. *Reason and Tradition in Islamic Ethics.* Cambridge Univ. Pr. 1985 $39.50. Islamic traditionalism has provided much of the strength and, paradoxically, the flexibility of the faith. This work deals with an aspect of its longstanding contest with a powerful current of potentially corrosive philosophical rationalism.

———, ed. *Essays on Islamic Philosophy and Science.* State Univ. of New York Pr. 1974 $49.50. A first-rate collection that illuminates many aspects of Muslim thought, by one of the great Arab scholars in the world.

Kasravi, Ahmad. *On Religion.* Trans. by M. R. Ghanoonparvar, ed. by Mohammad Ali Jazayery, Univ. of Texas Pr. 1986 pap. $11.00. Scholar, historian, and journalist, Kasravi became a student of Shi'a theology at an early age but later turned into an outspoken critic of the clerical establishment and was assassinated in 1946 by Islamic fundamentalists. This volume, the first of several devoted to his religious proclamations, introduces two of his most celebrated and controversial works: *On Islam* and *Shi'ism*.

Keddie, Nikki R., ed. *Scholars, Saints, and Sufis: Muslim Religious Institutions Since 1500*. Peter Smith 1983 $14.50; Univ. of California Pr. 1972 pap. $9.95. In this anthology on Muslim religious institutions in the modern Middle East, B. G. Martin's "A Short History of the Khalwati Order of Dervishes" is outstanding.

Leaman, Oliver. *An Introduction to Medieval Islamic Philosophy*. Cambridge Univ. Pr. 1985 $34.50 pap. $12.95. Intelligent, thorough, and highly recommended, perhaps the best work of its kind available.

Lewis, Bernard. *The Origins of Isma'ilism: A Study of the Historical Background of the Fatimid Caliphate*. AMS Pr. repr. of 1940 ed. 1974 $22.50. A basic work on this important sect.

Lings, Martin. *What Is Sufism?* Univ. of California Pr. 1975 o.p. "The basic themes of Sufism are brought out in a way that considers its historical development, its ties with Islam, and its mysticism. A substantive introduction which will not only expand the reader's spiritual awareness, but also widen his perspective of the Islamic world" (*LJ*).

Macdonald, Duncan B. *Religious Attitude and Life in Islam*. AMS Pr. repr. of 1909 ed. 1970 $20.50. These Haskell lectures in comparative religion delivered at the University of Chicago in 1906, reprinted in Beirut, remain for some specialists an excellent insight into Islam at work. Gibb's *Modern Trends* supplements this work.

MacEoin, Denis, and Ahmed al-Shahi, eds. *Islam in the Modern World*. St. Martin's 1983 $25.00. "There are three themes that run through these [eleven] essays: encounters between the Islamic and Western worlds; Sufism in contemporary Islam; and the current wave of Islamic resurgence. . . . The special facility of British scholarship with historico-descriptive data makes the work rewarding background reading on some of the most important aspects of contemporary Islam. . . . The book collectively presents a comprehensive overview and a lucid explanation of current religio-political concerns of the Muslim world, and is a welcome addition to the growing literature on the subject" (*Middle East Journal*).

Massé, Henri. *Islam*. Trans. by Halide Edib, Putnam 1938 o.p. Intended as a corrective to the "limited aims" of Gaudefroy-Demombynes and the "dogmatic accounts" of Goldhizer and Lammens.

Morewedge, Parviz, ed. *Islamic Philosophical Theology*. State Univ. of New York Pr. 1979 $35.00. "Unquestionably a major contribution to an understanding of Islamic philosophical theology. It is comprised of 11 substantive essays written by internationally recognized authorities (e.g., L. Gardet, W. C. Smith, F. E. Peters, R. M. Frank, and G. F. Hourani). . . . Notes on each essay and the provision of an index enhance the usefulness of the collection" (*Choice*).

———. *Islamic Philosophy and Mysticism*. [*Studies in Islamic Philosophy and Science*] Caravan 1981 $45.00. Both *Islamic Philosophical Theology* and *Islamic Philosophy and Mysticism* by Morewedge contain a number of excellent essays

Nasr, Seyyed H. *Knowledge and the Sacred*. Crossroad 1982 $17.50. A series of lectures by a specialist in Sufi doctrines that explores the intellectual and spiritual chaos of modern times.

Nicholson, Reynold A. *The Mystics of Islam: An Introduction to Sufism*. Schocken 1975 pap. $5.95. The "best single study on the subject" (Caesar Farah).

Parrinder, Geoffrey. *Mysticism in the World's Religions*. Oxford 1976 text ed. pap. $6.95. Clarifies the claims of mysticism in various faiths.

Rescher, Nicholas. *The Development of Arabic Logic*. Univ. of Pittsburgh Pr. 1964 o.p. An instructive history of the subject.

Shafii, Mohammed. *Freedom from the Self: Sufism, Meditation, and Psychotherapy*. Human Sciences Pr. 1985 $29.95. Shafii compares modern psychoanalytic theory with Sufism. He maintains that, as the spiritual and psychological core of Islam, Sufism has evolved a holistic concept of human development built on basic personality structures strikingly similar to those in psychoanalysis and ego psychology. He believes that the Sufis have developed insightful psychotherapeutic methods of remedying emotional suffering and personality fragmentation, techniques that stress an intense psychomystical relationship between the seeker and the Sufi guide, or *Pir*, a relationship he regards as parallel in many respects to that between Western psychotherapists and their patients. The book discusses the seven stages of human development according to Sufi doctrine and provides ample references to original Sufi stories, anecdotes, poetry, and other works.

Shah, Idries. *The Sufis*. Institute for the Study of Human Knowledge repr. of 1963 ed. 1983 $19.95. A popular treatment, with a wonderful introduction by Robert Graves, the English poet. Excellent and entertaining annotations and anecdotes from the life of Masrudin.

———. *Tales of the Dervishes: Teaching-Stories of the Sufi Masters over the Past Thousand Years*. Dutton 1970 pap. $6.95. "An anthology of translations [that] contains tales used by the Sufi masters to initiate the seekers and novices and help them along to reach the stages of perfection on their way to knowing the divine Reality. . . . With meaning and depth on several levels, the book will be enjoyed by a spectrum of readers from the teen-ager to the scholar" (*LJ*).

Trimingham, J. Spencer. *The Sufi Orders in Islam*. Oxford 1973 o.p. "This book contains a very valuable account of the historical development of the Islamic, mystic, Sufi orders. . . . Until a more adequate historical account is written, this work is the most informative text available in English" (*Choice*).

Tritton, Arthur S. *Islam: Belief and Practice*. Hutchinson House 1951 o.p. A short account of the essentials of Islam. "Muslims do not like to be called Mohammedans because the name suggests that they worship their prophet" (Preface).

———. *Muslim Theology*. Hyperion Conn. repr. of 1947 ed. 1980 $22.00. Useful reference to various aspects of doctrinal development.

Watt, W. M. *The Formative Period of Islamic Thought*. Columbia Univ. Pr. 1973 $22.50. The first chapter is an excellent treatment of the Kharijite movement and the development of its doctrines. The final chapter on the chief Sunnite theologians is especially useful for specialists.

———. *Islamic Philosophy and Theology*. Aldine 1962 o.p. In Islam, as in most Eastern thought, the division between philosophy and religion cannot be clearly drawn. This book provides an excellent introduction to Islamic speculation, with a necessarily strong emphasis on its theological side, stressing in particular the early opposition between the Sunnite orthodoxy and the rationalist Mutazilites.

Wensinck, Arent J. *The Muslim Creed: Its Genesis and Historical Development*. Coronet repr. of 1932 ed. $22.00. Critical study of the rise of the orthodox view.

Williams, Jon Alden. *Islam*. Braziller 1962 o.p. A coherent and comprehensive anthology covering important aspects of Islam.

AVERROËS. 1126–1198

Averroës is the name in the West of Abu al-Walid Muhammed ibn-Ahmad ibn-Rushd al-Qurtubi, an influential Muslim thinker who integrated Islamic tradition with Greek philosophy. Educated in Muslim religious, medical, and philosophical studies, he became the chief judge of Córdoba (where he was born) and later personal physician to two caliphs. He wrote a series of summaries and commentaries on ARISTOTLE (see also Vols. 3 and 5) and on PLATO's (see also Vol. 3) *Republic*, as well as attacks on Avicenna's view of existence. Western Christian philosophers drew inspiration from his interpretation of Aristotle, especially his assertion that reason and philosophy are superior to faith and knowledge founded on faith. He died in Marrakesh in Morocco.

BOOK BY AVERROËS

Averroës on Plato's "Republic." Trans. by Ralph Lerner, Cornell Univ. Pr. 1974 pap. $6.95. Particularly interesting for the light it sheds on the problems encountered by an Islamic thinker as he tries to come to terms with early Western political thought.

BOOKS ABOUT AVERROËS

Kogan, Barry S. *Averroës and the Metaphysics of Causation.* State Univ. of New York Pr. 1985 $44.50 pap. $16.95. A study of Averroës's response to the philosophical views of the Ash'arites.

Mohammad, Ovey N. *Averroës' Doctrine of Immortality: A Matter of Controversy.* Humanities Pr. 1984 text ed. pap. $11.00. It is generally considered that Averroës did not believe in the survival of the individual self after death, though he did hold that our being also consists of an immortal, immaterial intelligence, resembling the soul in Plato. This work by Mohammad argues against that view, and supplies an interesting, if unconventional, reading of Averroës.

AVICENNA. 980–1037

The most famous of the philosopher-scientists of Islam, Abu Ali al-Husayn ibn-Abd Allah ibn-Sina, known in the West as Avicenna, was born in Bukhara, Persia, and died in Hamadan. After a long period of wandering through Persia, he became the court physician of Shams al-Dawlah in Hamadan and composed the *Kitab ash-shifa* (The Book of Healing), a vast philosophical and scientific encyclopedia, and the *Canon of Medicine*, among the most famous books in the history of medicine. He was also a Neoplatonic thinker whose influence was felt throughout the Christian West during the Middle Ages. Medieval thought reacted powerfully to the rediscovery, in the twelfth and thirteenth centuries, of the work of ARISTOTLE (see also Vols. 3 and 5), which had been exercising the intellects of Islamic thinkers for some time already. Hence, many of the doctrinal disputes that arose in Europe in the course of the late thirteenth and early fourteenth centuries reflect the opposing views of Arab thinkers, notably those of Averroës and Avicenna. Avicenna's thought itself had been developed out of a variety of sources. In addition to PLATO (see also Vol. 3), there were influences of Stoic logic and earlier Islamic theological philosophers. One of his more important beliefs was that God is the "Necessary Existent," the necessary ground from which all existent things proceed. In themselves, he argued, no things that exist do so necessarily, that is, they may or may not be. Everything that exists must therefore have a cause, and the chain of such causality would be an infinite regression without God, the one necessary being. God is thus in himself the cause of all existence and of all things being as they are. This "necessitarian" limitation provoked a severe reaction among Western thinkers who saw it as a limitation placed on God's freedom.

BOOKS BY AVICENNA

Avicenna's Psychology. Ed. by F. Rahman, Hyperion Conn. repr. of 1952 ed. 1984 $15.00. As in much early Greek philosophy, "psychology" refers to the soul, not the mind.

The Metaphysics. Trans. by Parviz Morewedge, Columbia Univ. Pr. 1973 o.p. The "Book of the Wisdom of Allah."

BOOKS ABOUT AVICENNA

Afnan, Soheil M. *Avicenna: His Life and Works.* Greenwood repr. of 1958 ed. 1980 lib. bdg. $27.50. The place to start for the student first approaching Avicenna.

Corbin, Henry. *Avicenna and the Visionary Recital.* Trans. by Willard R. Trask, Spring Pubns. 1980 pap. $14.50. Avicenna's mystical doctrines and their development in the context of the Sufi tradition.

Gohlman, William. *The Life of the Sina.* State Univ. of New York Pr. 1974 o.p. A critical edition and annotated translation.

Nasr, Seyyed H. *Three Muslim Sages: Avicenna, Suhrwardi, Ibn-'Arabi.* Caravan 1976 text ed. pap. $10.00. Views of Islamic thought in its mystical and rationalist aspects.

GHAZĀLĪ, AL-. 1058–1111

Abu Hamid Muhammed ibn-Muhammed a-tusi al-Ghazālī began an academic career in Baghdad, but abandoned it after a spiritual crisis in 1095. He became a Sufi mystic and, after years of wandering, settled in Tus, Persia (his birthplace), where he and his followers took up a monastic life. After visiting Mecca, Alexandria, and Jerusalem (which he left just before it was captured by the Crusaders), he resumed teaching in Nishapur until his death. Ironically considered by Europeans as the disciple of Avicenna (because he was best known in the West through a translation of his detailed presentation of Avicenna's philosophy), al-Ghazālī had actually summarized and explained Avicenna in order to attack him. In keeping with his mystical point of view, al-Ghazālī contested Avicenna's rationalist emphasis on the superiority of philosophical knowledge to religious belief, a disagreement that found multiple echoes in Western medieval debates over the relative place of faith and reason. It was through his writing that Sufism, long regarded as a heretical doctrine in Iran, was made acceptable to the orthodox. Though his works are not widely available in translation, they exerted a tremendous influence on all later Persian thought.

BOOKS BY AL-GHAZĀLĪ

The Incoherence of the Philosophers (Tahāfut al-Falāsifah). Orientalia $8.25. All philosophical systems are attacked, from those of Plato and Aristotle to those of his own day. This work was answered by Averroës.

The Book of Knowledge. Orientalia 1970 $15.00. A translation of al-Ghazālī's *Book of Fear and Hope*, which was his most influential work.

The Faith and Practice of al-Ghazali. Trans. by W. Montgomery Watt, Longman 2d ed. 1963 o.p. Al-Ghazālī describes how he examined Kalam (orthodox Muslim scholasticism), Falsafa (metaphysics based on Greek thought), and T'lim (the doctrine of those who accept uncritically the teaching of an infallible imam) before choosing Sufism.

BOOKS ABOUT AL-GHAZĀLĪ

Ormsby, Eric. *Theodicy in Islamic Thought*. Princeton Univ. Pr. 1984 text ed. $30.00. As the title indicates, this is a study of the controversy stirred up by al-Ghazālī's belief that the world, being the creation of a perfect god, must itself necessarily be the best of all possible worlds—a point of view that found Western expression during the Enlightenment and that Voltaire mocked in *Candide*.

Watt, W. Montgomery. *Muslim Intellectual: A Study of al-Ghazali*. Edinburgh Univ. Pr. 1963 o.p. The most informative study of the man and his environment.

IBN AL-ARABI. 1165–1240

Muhammad ibn-'Ali Ibn al-Arabi, also called Muhyi al-Din, was the celebrated Muslim philosopher who first formulated the esoteric mystical dimension of Islamic thought. Born in Murcia, Spain, he devoted 30 years to the study of traditional Islamic sciences in Seville. After traveling extensively in the East, he settled in Damascus, where he spent his last days in contemplation, teaching, and writing. Ibn al-Arabi composed two great mystical treatises, *The Meccan Revelations* and *Wisdom of the Prophets (Fusus al-Hikam)*. Completed in Damascus, *The Meccan Revelations* is a personal encyclopedia of 560 chapters extending over all the esoteric sciences in Islam as he knew them, combined with valuable autobiographical information. *Wisdom* contains only 27 chapters, but as the mature expression of ibn al-Arabi's mystical thought, it is regarded as one of the most important documents of its kind. However, he is best known for his mystical odes, wherein, like all Sufis, he expresses his longing for union with God in terms of passionate human love (in Mecca, he fell in love with a young beauty who came to personify wisdom for him). It is not clear whether his poetry is religious or erotic, an ambiguity also characteristic of the work of the great Persian lyricist Hafiz. Critics have found in ibn al-Arabi's poetry, as in most Sufi verse, elements of Muslim orthodoxy, Manichaeanism, Gnosticism, Neoplatonism, and Christianity.

BOOKS BY IBN AL-ARABI

Philosophy of Plato and Aristotle. Free Pr. 1962 o.p.
Tarjuma'n Al-Ashwa'q. Theosophical Publishing House $14.25
Wisdom of the Prophets. Trans. by Titus Burckardt, Weiser 1976 pap. o.p.

Books about Ibn al-Arabi

Affifi, Abul E. *The Mystical Philosophy of Muhyid Din-Ibnul 'Arabi.* AMS Pr. repr. of 1939 ed. 1977 $12.00. Courageous attempt to reduce a difficult subject to order.
Nicholson, Reynold A. *Studies in Islamic Mysticism.* Cambridge Univ. Pr. 1979 pap. $16.95

IBN HAZM. 994–1064

'Ali ibn-Ahmad, known in the West as Ibn Hazm, is among the greatest Arab writers. The grandson of a Spanish convert to Islam, he served as the chief minister at Córdoba until forced to withdraw from public life as a result of the odium created by his bitter attacks on his theological opponents. Though he began as a poet, he developed into the outstanding figure in eleventh-century Hispano-Arab prose literature through his renowned book on chivalric love, *Tauq al-Hamama (The Ring of the Dove).* This vivid picture of life in Muslim Spain, describing some of the more intimate experiences of Ibn Hazm himself, is thought to have had an important influence on Provençal poetry. Ibn Hazm belonged to the Zahiri school of Islamic thought, a strict sect that interpreted the Koran literally, recognizing no precedent except that based either on the Koran or well-verified customs of the Prophet. He wrote an influential tract on comparative religion, *The Book of Religious and Philosophical Sects,* wherein he analyzes and rejects the claims made by the various non-Muslim faiths, exposing at some length the inconsistencies in the Old and New Testaments. Because he attacked many of the most revered authorities of Islam, his books were once publicly burned in Seville.

Book by Ibn Hazm

The Ring of the Dove: A Treatise on the Art and Practice of Arab Love. Trans. by Arthur J. Arberry, AMS Pr. repr. of 1953 ed. 1978 $34.50

Book about Ibn Hazm

Nicholson, L. H. *The Heterodoxies of the Shi'ites According to Ibn Hazm.* Yale Univ. Pr. 1909 o.p.

IBN KHALDUN. 1332–1406

'Abd al-Rahman ibn-Muhammad, known as Ibn Khaldun, the Arab philosopher and historian, was born in Tunis to an aristocratic family long resident in Muslim Spain. He was educated well and given various official posts in North Africa and Spain. After serving as the Sultan of Granada's ambassador to the court of Pedro the Cruel in Castile, he retired to Egypt, where he became chief judge. Before he died in Cairo, he went on an embassy to Tamerlane, described in his autobiography. *The Book of Examples,* a general history of the Muslims, especially the North African dynasties, is regarded as his principal work, but his reputation really rests on his introduction to it, the first systematic treatise on the philosophy of history.

BOOK BY IBN KHALDUN

The Muqaddimah. Ed. by N. J. Dawood, trans. by Franz Rosenthal [*Bollingen Ser.*] abr. ed. Princeton Univ. Pr. 1967 $25.00 pap. $12.95; 3 vols. 2d ed. 1967 $160.00. In this introduction to his multivolume history, Ibn Khaldun criticizes the view that history is a mere record of events, and presents his own view of how it must be pursued and of how societies have developed. We must, he says, investigate the sources of our information carefully and evaluate them critically; we must consider the larger social context within which historically relevant events occur, and we must seek to understand their causes. Ibn Khaldun sees human beings as social animals, conditioned by their surroundings and the climate they live in. They start as nomads, of pure and simple manners, loyal to the tribe, but in time they settle down to a sedentary, urbanized existence. This development has both negative and positive aspects—though the arts and sciences can flourish only in urban communities, the townsfolk lose the virtues of the nomad, and their tribal spirit turns into nationalism. Nations become corrupted by luxury, and eventually ruder, more vigorous people sweep them away. As the city grows in size, the ruler must devote more and more attention to maintaining peace and justice, and as the realm expands, it requires increasingly the unifying force of religion. Ibn Khaldun concludes that a dynasty normally endures for four generations. The introduction ends with an account of the various Muslim systems of government and a short survey of the arts and sciences, education, magic, and literature, which in effect summarizes the knowledge of the period.

BOOKS ABOUT IBN KHALDUN

Fischel, W. J. *Ibn Khaldun and Tamerlane: Their Historic Meeting in Damascus.* Univ. of California Pr. 1952 o.p.

Mahdi, Muhsin. *Ibn Khaldun's Philosophy of History: A Study in the Philosophic Foundation of the Science of Culture.* Univ. of Chicago Pr. 1964 o.p.

IBN KHALLIKAN. 1211–1281

The great biographer, Ahmad ibn-Muhammad, known as Ibn Khallikan, was born in Arbela (in present-day Iraq), studied there and in Aleppo, and then went to Egypt, where he became deputy judge and professor. In 1261, he was promoted to chief judge of Damascus, but after ten years was dismissed and returned to his professorship in Egypt. He was reappointed to Damascus about seven years later, but was again dismissed shortly before his death. In studies of the Prophet, great importance had been attached from the start to the men who reported, directly or indirectly, his words and acts. Muslim historians also included information concerning notable men of Islam in their chronicles, inasmuch as they were the spiritual heirs of the Prophet. Frequently they added obituaries of those who had died in a given year as an appendix to the annals of that year. Often such information was arranged in separate biographical dictionaries dealing with specific professions. Ibn Khallikan occupies the leading place in this literary genre.

BOOK BY IBN KHALLIKAN.

Ibn Khallikan's Biographical Dictionary. International Bk. Ctr. 4 vols. $110.00. This great work took 18 years to complete. It is the most comprehensive biographical dictionary in Arab literature, with hundreds of entries, arranged alphabetically, relating to rulers, soldiers, scholars, judges, statesmen, and poets. It is enriched by many entertaining and informative anecdotes of Muslim life.

IBN TUFAYL. ?–1185

Though known in his day as a philosopher, some of whose views were criticized by Averroës, Ibn Tufayl is today remembered as the author of the philosophical novel, *Hayy ibn Yaqzan*. An allegory of the conflict between reason and religion, the story traces the intellectual development of a man secluded on a desert island who, through his own unaided efforts, arrives at knowledge of the divine. Later, he encounters a wise man of religion, who is astonished to discover that, despite all his training and knowledge of doctrine, he knows no more than the untutored hermit.

BOOK BY IBN TUFAYL

Hayy ibn Yaqzan. Trans. by Lenn E. Goodman, Gee Tee Bee 1983 $29.95 pap. $16.95. The fascination with man in a state of nature has a long history in European literature—from Montaigne's "On Cannibals," to Shakespeare's *Tempest,* and such later examples as *Robinson Crusoe.* Ibn Tufayl's novel on this theme was widely translated in Europe during the seventeenth century and enjoyed considerable popularity, often with some such title as *The Self-Taught Philosopher.*

JALAL AL-DIN AL-SUYUTI. 1445–1505

Abd-Fadl Abd-Arrahman ibn-Abi Bakr Jalal al-Din al-Suyuti was an Egyptian author who wrote about everything of importance to Islam, especially the religious sciences. The son of a judge, he was tutored by a Sufi friend of his father. In 1486 he was given a chair in the mosque of Babybars in Cairo. His attempt to reduce the stipends of Sufi scholars at the mosque precipitated a revolt in which he was almost killed. He was placed on trial, and afterward put under house arrest on the island of Rawda, where he worked in seclusion until his death. With Jala ad-Din al-Mahalli, he coauthored a word-by-word commentary on the Koran (o.p.).

BOOK ABOUT JALAL

Sartain, E. M. *Jalal Al-Din Al-Suyuti.* Cambridge Univ. Pr. 2 vols. 1975 ea. $44.50– $52.50 set $86.00. Volume 1 is a biographical and intellectual study with notes on Jalal's autobiography. Volume 2 is the Arabic text of the autobiography, appearing here in complete form for the first time. In the tradition of the *tarjama,* or biographical notice written by learned men about their own careers for inclusion in their various bibliographical compendiums, this is not autobiography in the Western sense of the word, but it is an authoritative document about religious life in fifteenth-century Egypt.

JAMI. 1414–1492

Nur ad-Din Abd ar-Rahman, known as Jami, was a Persian poet, scholar, and mystic, and the last great figure of the Golden Age of Persian literature. He studied for a theological career at Samarkand before entering the mystical life. Sultan Husayn Bayqara, the Timurid ruler of Herat, founded a college especially for him, where he achieved enormous fame and authority as teacher, writer, and proponent of the mystical way.

BOOK BY JAMI

Edward FitzGerald's Salaman and Absal. Arthur J. Arberry. Cambridge Univ. Pr. 1956 $37.50. Jami's *Haft Aurang* [*the seven thrones*] is a set of seven long poems. Two of them, one of which is *Salaman and Absal,* expound through allegorical love stories the mystic's quest for God. The second and more celebrated is "Yusef and Zulaykha."

BOOK ABOUT JAMI

Davis, F. Hadland. *Jami: The Persian Mystic and Poet.* Sunwise Turn. 1981 pap. $3.25

MUHAMMAD (or MOHAMMED). 570?–632

The Arabs of pre-Islamic times needed a hero capable of assuming a tripartite role. First, he had to be a political leader in order to establish a united Arab nation; second, he had to be a military genius who could transform the Arab raiding capacity into a fighting force capable of advancing the Arabs as a whole; and third, he had to be a religious leader with divine authority to receive support beyond tribal boundaries.

When Muhammad was born in Mecca, that great trade center was already the focus of religious piety attached to the Kaaba, the Holy Rock, and its pantheon of tribal deities, of whom Allah was one. The future Prophet of Islam was orphaned at an early age, and was raised by his grandfather and uncle, both of whom were prominent members of the Quraysh, the tribe responsible for maintaining the Kaaba and its lands and sacred well. Under their guardianship, Muhammad grew up in an atmosphere of religious excitement.

Possibly from Jews and Christians who visited or dwelt in Mecca, possibly from contacts made with them on his travels, Muhammad learned something of the biblical faith. In his twenties, he married the wealthy widow Khadijah, who freed him from financial concern, supported his meditations, bore him seven children, and became his first and most fervent follower. In a cave on Mount Hira near Mecca, where Muhammad often withdrew for meditation, he experienced a vision of the angel Gabriel calling him to prophesy. When he felt convinced that the revelation was genuine, Muhammad began to preach, proclaiming Allah as the one true God, the same God who had revealed himself to Abraham, Moses, and Jesus. It was his monotheism that aroused the fury of the inhabitants of Mecca, whose livelihood depended in part on pilgrims who came to worship the gods of the Kaaba.

Muhammad was forced to flee Mecca in 622. From this event, known as the Hegira, Islam dates its calendar. It marks the beginning of the Muhammadan era. The Prophet found refuge in Medina and there established his theocracy. There too he began to develop his theory of Holy War (*jihad*). He assembled an army, and in 630 marched against Mecca. He easily conquered the city, purged the Kaaba of pagan gods, and pronounced the brotherhood of all who became Muslims. He was well on his way to unifying the divergent Arab tribes when he died suddenly of an unknown cause (according to one legend, poisoned by a woman who sought to test his ability to prophesy the future).

The sacred book of Islam, the Koran, is written in classical Arabic and considered to be the most influential book in the world after the Bible. The faithful believe that it was revealed by God to his Prophet Muhammad, who in turn revealed it to his adherents. The 114 separate Surahs, or chapters, which make up the book are said to have been written down first on pieces of paper (papyrus), stones, palm leaves, rib bones, pieces of leather, "as well as upon the hearts of men." After the Prophet's death, the book was edited and arranged by Muhammad's secretary, Zaid ibn Thabit, on the orders of the caliph Abu Bakr.

BOOKS BY MUHAMMAD

The Koran. Ed. and trans. by J. M. Rodwell, Biblio Dist. 1978 pap. $3.50; trans. by George Sale, Warne 1983 pap. $8.95. Rodwell's translation was the first translation with the Surahs arranged in chronological order. Sale's translation first appeared in 1734 and has passed through many editions. It has become something of a classic and is still regarded as useful in many respects though later translations have more or less supplanted it. The notes in particular are out-of-date.

The Quran. Ed. by E. H. Palmer [*Sacred Books of the East*] Asian Humanities Pr. 2 vols. ea. $15.00. An early translation that supplements Sale's of 1734.

The Meaning of the Glorious Koran. Trans. by M. M. Pickthall, New Amer. Lib. 1963 pap. $4.50. For the first time, the sacred book of Islam, translated by an Englishman who became a Muslim, is true to the spirit and meaning of the Arabic. With a foreword by Pickthall.

The Qur'an: A New Translation with a Critical Rearrangement of the Surahs. Trans. by Richard Bell, Fortress 2 vols. ea. $14.95; trans. by N. J. Dawood, Penguin 1956 pap. $3.95. The Dawood translation is for those who only want a taste of the whole. Bell's text, although a radical departure from the traditional arrangement, is perhaps more appealing to the average non-Muslim Western reader.

The Koran Interpreted. Trans. by Arthur J. Arberry, Macmillan 1964 pap. $13.95. Professor Arberry of Cambridge University aims "to present to English readers what Muslims the world over hold to be the meaning of the words of the Koran, and the nature of that Book, in not unworthy language and concisely, with a view to the requirements of English Muslims." Highly esteemed by Muslims for its precise rendering of Koranic style.

BOOKS ABOUT THE KORAN

Ayoub, Mahmoud M. *The Qur'an and Its Interpreters.* State Univ. of New York Pr. 1984 $29.50. First of a series of commentaries covering the entire Koran, whose purpose is to introduce English readers to the Koran as Muslims have understood it. Key sources are Arabic.

Bell, Richard. *Introduction to the Qur'an.* Edinburgh Univ. Pr. 1958 o.p. Intended to accompany Bell's translation of the Koran. Clarifies his sometimes misunderstood views of the Surahs on which his analysis was based.

Cragg, Kenneth. *The Event of the Koran: Islam and Its Scripture.* Allen & Unwin 1972 o.p. Examines the Koran as "a fusion, unique in history, of personal *charisma*, literary fascination, corporate possession, and imperative religion" (Introduction).

Jeffery, Arthur. *Materials for the History of the Text of the Qur'an.* AMS Pr. repr. of 1937 ed. 1979 $57.50. Handy for a critical study of the Koran.

———. *The Qur'an As Scripture.* AMS Pr. repr. of 1952 ed. 1980 $18.00; Ayer 1979 lib. bdg. $12.00. Deals with the Koran's view of its own function.

Kassis, Hanna E. *A Concordance of the Qur'an.* Univ. of California Pr. 1984 $95.00.

Based on Arberry's translation, this work comprises the *Concordance* proper and an extensive index of all the English words that occur as translations of the Arabic in the Koran. Arranged alphabetically, the index consists of two parts, one devoted to the divine name of Allah and the other to the remaining vocabulary.

Stanton, H. U. *The Teaching of the Qur'an, with an Account of Its Growth.* Biblo & Tannen repr. 1969 $15.00. Summarizes the essence of Koranic doctrine.

BOOKS ABOUT MUHAMMAD

Abbott, Nabia. *Aishah: The Beloved of Mohammad.* Arno Pr. repr. of 1942 ed. 1973 $18.00. The Prophet married many women after his move to Medina, not limiting himself to four (a variety of motives are given—some political, some personal, some humanitarian), but while his beloved Aisha was alive, he took no other woman. This is an account of that remarkable relationship.

Ali, Syed A. *The Spirit of Islam: A History of the Evolution and Ideals of Islam with a Life of the Prophet.* Hilary House Pubs. 1922 o.p. "An account of the history and evolution of Islam as a world religion, its rapid spread and remarkable hold it obtained over the conscience and minds of millions of people within a short space of time" (Preface). The life of the Prophet is based on *Sirat-ur-Rasul* of Ibn Hasham (829 A.D.), supplemented by Ibn ul-Athir's *Chronicles of Tabari* and the *Sirat ul-Halabia* of al-Halabi. Contains valuable discussion of al-Ghazālī and As-Sarraz, two thinkers who systematized Sufistic philosophy.

Andrae, Tor. *Mohammed: The Man and His Faith.* Trans. by T. Menzel, Ayer repr. of 1936 ed. 1979 $19.00. Standard biography by a Lutheran bishop, scholarly yet simple and vital.

Archer, John Clark. *Mystical Elements in Mohammed.* AMS repr. of 1924 ed. 1981 $22.50. "We have not chosen to examine herein either the Faith or the record of its development. Mohammed alone engages us. Nor is it the whole of his life our present concern, but only an aspect and portion which seems not yet to be understood in full measure . . . Mohammed the mystic" (Preface).

Azzam, Abd-al-Rahman. *The Eternal Message of Muhammad.* Devin 1964 $9.50. This study, by the former first Secretary General of the Arab League, emphasizes Islam as both a culture and a religion; a life of the Prophet is included.

Balyuzi, M. M. *Mohammed and the Course of Islam.* Oxford 1976 o.p. Balyuzi candidly states his belief in the God-given mission of Muhammad and thinks such belief is a necessary antidote to Western scholars whose skepticism precludes the recognition of Muhammad as the messenger of God. He maintains that his book corrects the "grotesquely distorted" portraits of Muhammad that popular writers have created.

Bey, Essad. *Mohammed.* 1936. Trans. by Helmut Ripperger, State Mutual Bk. 1985 $50.00. "Mohammed launched the idea of a state of God into the world. What happened to the idea?" Bey asks and attempts to answer the question by providing a historical context for the development of the idea.

Carlyle, Thomas. *On Heroes, Hero Worship, and the Heroic in History.* Ed. by Carl Niemeyer, Univ. of Nebraska Pr. 1966 pap. $6.95. The Scottish writer's assessment of Muhammad is contained in the second chapter of this classic.

Dibble, R. F. *Mohammed.* Viking 1926 o.p. A popular and readable biography, sympathetic, often witty, and occasionally overwritten. The large type makes it particularly useful to senior citizens.

Gabrieli, Francesco. *Muhammad and the Conquests of Islam.* Trans. by Virginia Luling and Rosamund Linell, McGraw-Hill 1968 o.p. Gabrieli is an Italian specialist on Islam. "His style is compact and economical and the translation reads well. The story is well connected and impressive without a burdensome emphasis on dates and historical background" (*LJ*). Contains a great bibliography, along with great photographs.

Glubb, John B. *The Life and Times of Muhammad*. Stein & Day 1970 o.p. This book "should have a special place among the biographies of Muhammad since its author [Glubb Pasha] is thoroughly familiar with Bedouin Arabs, having lived among them a good portion of his life. This familiarity with the setting ... makes the work particularly valuable" (*Choice*).

Ibn-Hisham. *The Life of Muhammad*. Trans. by Alfred Guillaume, Oxford 1955 o.p. The standard original account with useful notes.

Lings, Martin. *Muhammad*. Inner Traditions International 1983 $24.95. A thorough, scholarly work based on the writings of Muslim historians of the eighth and ninth centuries.

Margoliouth, David S. *Mohammed and the Rise of Islam*. AMS Pr. repr. of 1905 ed. 1973 $30.00; Ayer repr. of 1905 ed. 1973 $34.00. Margoliouth approaches Muhammad as "a great man who solved a political problem of appalling difficulty—the construction of a state and an empire out of the Arab tribes" (Preface).

Muir, William. *The Life of Mohammad from Original Sources*. Ed. by Thomas H. Weir, AMS Pr. new rev. ed. repr. of 1923 ed. 1978 $57.50. Detailed and thorough.

Rodinson, Maxime. *Muhammad*. Trans. by Anne Carter, Pantheon 1980 pap. $5.95. "On the basis of the same facts, each generation writes history afresh," says Rodinson. This is a French version of the Prophet in light of recent scholarship. Among the best of the recent biographies of a man who "turned the world upside down."

Schimmel, Annemarie. *And Muhammad Is His Messenger: The Veneration of the Prophet in Islamic Piety*. Univ. of North Carolina Pr. 1985 $32.00 pap. $9.95. "Schimmel conveys to the reader a sense of what the figure of the Prophet—that unrivalled exemplar of human perfection—means to hundreds of millions of Muslims" (R. J. Zwi Werblowsky, Hebrew University of Jerusalem).

Watt, W. Montgomery. *Muhammad at Mecca*. Oxford 1953 o.p. This book deals with the first part of the Prophet's career, paying special attention to the economic and sociological background.

——. *Muhammad at Medina*. Oxford repr. of 1956 ed. 1981 $39.95. A study of the second part of the Prophet's career from the standpoint of a modern historian (a sequel to an earlier volume, see above).

——. *Muhammad: Prophet and Statesman*. Oxford 1961 pap. $7.95. Essentially an abridgment of the author's *Muhammad at Mecca* and *Muhammad at Medina*. "Western scholarship's last word to date on the Prophet of Islam. Watt deserves credit for his methodical revaluation of Islamic tradition ... and for having used Andrae's [see above] comparative research combined with sociological principles to explain the success of Muhammad's message" (Francesco Gabrieli, *Muhammad and the Conquests of Islam*).

RUMI. 1207–1273

Rumi is the West's name for Jalal ud-Din, known also as "Mawlana" or "Our Master," the great Persian mystic and founder of the Mawlawiyah or Mevlevi order of the so-called Dancing Dervishes. Born in Balkh in northern Afghanistan, an important center of Arab learning, while still young he fled with his father before the Mongol invasion of Jenghiz Khan. After much wandering, they settled in Konya (formerly called Iconium or Rum, from which his name derives), capital of a Seljuk sultanate in Asia Minor. Rumi succeeded his father as professor of theology and like him became a renowned public preacher. He first probed the secrets of the mystic way under the guidance of an old student of his father's, but his real conversion did not come until his encounter with the spiritual director Shams al-Din of Tabriz, to whom he became passionately devoted. This relationship unleashed a series of rapturous lyrics, many inspired by al-Din, whom Rumi saw as the reflection of the Godhead. Rumi was buried alongside his father in Konya, and his shrine remains a revered place of pilgrimage in modern-day Turkey.

BOOKS BY RUMI

Open Secret: Versions of Rumi. Trans. by Coleman Barks and John Moyne, Threshold 1984 pap. $7.00. "Barks and Moyne offer felicitous new translations of Rumi. . . . These reflections on love, the dance of selves, happiness, acceptance of life's sorrows, and the transitory nature of joy are touchingly sensitive in their search for philosophical peace of mind" (*LJ*).

The Mathnawi of Jalalu'ddin Rumi. Trans. by R. A. Nicholson, State Mutual Bk. 3 vols. 1985 $175.00. The most recent translation of Rumi's great work in some 27,000 couplets. According to one scholar, it is "an unsystematized 3-volume exposition in fables, stories, and reflections cast in highly poetical language of the basic ideas of mysticism."

The Discourses of Rumi. Ed. by A. J. Arberry, Weiser 1977 o.p. Seventy-one of his short prose meditations on the mystical life, recorded by one of his disciples.

Mystical Poems of Rumi. Trans. by Arthur J. Arberry, Univ. of Chicago Pr. 1974 pap. $7.95

Mystical Poems of Rumi: Second Selection. Trans. by Arthur J. Arberry, Caravan 1983 $20.00. A reprint of the pioneering inexpensive edition of 1974 published by the University of Chicago Press (see above).

Rumi: Poet and Mystic. Trans. by R. A. Nicholson, Allen & Unwin 1978 pap. $6.50

BOOK ABOUT RUMI

Iqbal, Afzal. *The Life and Work of Muhammed Jalal-ud-Din Rumi.* Inst. for the Study of Human Knowledge 1983 $29.95. This promises to become the standard scholarly work on the great poet.

CHAPTER 10

Judaism

Richard E. Cohen and Jacob Neusner

For as wisdom grows, vexation grows;
to increase learning is to increase heartache.
—ECCLESIASTES 1:18, TRANS. OF *Tanakh*

Jews form one of humanity's older enduring groups. In the nature of things, the longer a group exists, the more interesting its history, the more diverse its culture, the more complex its society. In the case of the Jews, who look back on 4,000 years of continuous history, matters are made still more complicated by dispersion throughout Europe, Asia, North and South Africa, North and Latin America, and Australasia. Consequently, although a small group, Jews have written a large history for themselves. Since Christianity and Islam share the Hebrew Scriptures or Old Testament, and since all parties take for granted that today's Jews form the descendants of the "Israel" of those Scriptures, considerable interest attaches to Jews and what they do and are. The more we know, the more complicated we realize is the history of the Jews, on the one side, and the history of Judaism, on the other.

The complication is the same for both religion and society. Jews from 586 B.C. onward have not lived in a single country, but in many lands. The condition of dispersion is normal. Furthermore, while Jews appeal to the Hebrew Bible as the authority and source of theology and law alike, nonetheless, through time, Jews have formed a variety of Judaic religious systems, not one Judaism but many Judaisms. There have been many Judaisms, each autonomous, every one identifying an urgent question and offering a self-evidently valid answer. These Judaisms are not coherent with one another and do not form a linear chain back to Scripture. In antiquity, we realize, a range of Judaic systems—worldviews, ways of life, each addressed to distinct definition of a social entity called an "Israel"— flourished. The Essene community of Qumran, for example, constitutes one such Judaic religious system, not to be treated as harmonious with, or a linear development of, any other Judaism either contemporary with, or prior to, itself. Since every Judaic system takes up a distinctive, urgent question and presents an answer found by its adherents to be self-evidently true, we realize that the questions found urgent and the answers deemed self-evident will prove diverse among the various Judaisms. Along these same lines, there has been not one linear and unitary "Jewish history." Since Jews lived in various places, in diverse political and cultural circumstances, they have also worked out various histories. Jews' histories are not continuous with one another and do not form a single linear chain, a unitary "Jewish history," any more than the various Judaisms all grow out of one another, or, all together, out of Scripture (except after the fact). It follows that the more we know about the Jews as a group and about their religion, the more complex matters appear to be.

This bibliography lays forth, in all its complexity, the history, religion, and culture of Judaism. It distinguishes between the history of the Jews as a group of people and the history of Judaism as a religion. Within the category of Judaism, it distinguishes between personal ideology and institutionalized movements. The bibliography begins with general works; subsequent sections divide Judaism into ancient, medieval, and modern historical periods, with subsections devoted to specific aspects of Jewish life and experience.

GENERAL BIBLIOGRAPHY

Surveys and Encyclopedias of Jewish History

While people take for granted that there is a single Jewish "people" with one unitary history, the Jews have, in fact, formed diverse groups over time, each such group in its particular location living out a distinct history of its own. The Jews in ancient Egypt had their own history, which moved along its own lines, different from the history of the Jews in the Land of Israel ("Palestine"), and the Jews in Babylonia had yet another distinct history. In a few ways, these historical entities shared common traits, but they do not represent a single history. Hence one-volume histories of the Jews, while popular, give a sense of unity and cogency that, in fact, the evidence does not support. Still, these histories are an excellent way of gaining a perspective on the long and diverse histories of Jews in various places and times, and they provide a good introduction to a subject far more complex than people realize. Comprehensive works propose to link Jews' histories in different times and places into the history of the Jews, treating as one the various diverse groups. These works tend to take a diachronic view, joining data from a long span of time, but selecting only facts deemed continuous and understood as incremental. The alternative (the synchronic) view sees Jews in particular times and places and describes them within the encompassing framework of ·the age under discussion. The former approach is more popular, because it tells a sustained narrative, beginning to end, and gives readers the sense that they know pretty much the whole story. The latter approach presents difficulties, because it maintains there really is no "whole story." The general works listed here carefully define and delineate matters so that there is no oversimplification or harmonization of diverse facts into a single fictive picture.

The histories that follow, whether by one author or many, tend to telescope much into a small framework. Nonetheless, all provide valuable introductions to individual topics and problems. Furthermore, in the case of the Jews and Judaism efforts to interpret facts into meaningful patterns fall into the category of theology, and thus histories of the Jews, which teach lessons and draw meaningful conclusions, form the counterpart, for Judaism, of theology in Christianity.

Two large and important encyclopedias, one outdated but still useful, should also be consulted. *The Jewish Encyclopedia* (1901–1906) contains many classic articles, although of course knowledge has grown, and the twentieth century is omitted. The *Encyclopedia Judaica* (1972), while flawed, is the single best introduction to most of the topics it covers, and it can be read sequentially for the vast information it contains.

Ausubel, Nathan, and David C. Gross. *Pictorial History of the Jewish People: From Biblical Times to Our Own Day throughout the World*. Crown rev. ed. 1984 $19.95. Gross has updated Ausubel's one-volume illustrated work, originally published in 1953. More than 1,000 photographs and short essays cover many details of Jewish history from biblical events to the present.

Baron, Salo W. *The Jewish Community: Its History and Structure to the American Revolution*. Greenwood 3 vols. repr. of 1942 ed. 1972 lib. bdg. $53.50. Detailed study of Jewish political and religious institutions from antiquity until the early modern period.

———. *A Social and Religious History of the Jews*. Columbia Univ. Pr. 18 vols. 1952–83 2d ed. rev. & enl. ea. $45.00. This monumental work of scholarship, covering all aspects of Jewish history from antiquity through the medieval period, is an indispensable reference work for any major library.

Baron, Salo W., and others. *Economic History of the Jews*. Ed. by Nahum Gross, Schocken 1976 pap. $5.50. A broad range of articles, originally published in the *Encyclopedia Judaica*, on Jewish economic history, from agriculture in ancient Israel to department stores in America.

Ben-Sasson, Haim, ed. *A History of the Jewish People*. Harvard Univ. Pr. 1985 pap. $18.95. A comprehensive survey with articles written by scholars at the Hebrew University of Jerusalem. The selection and treatment of topics often reflect an Israeli perspective.

Biale, David. *Power and Powerlessness in Jewish History*. Schocken 1986 $18.95. Effort to dispel the myth of Jewish political passivity and ineptitude. Considers activities and ideologies of the Jewish community from the Middle Ages to the present.

Bridger, David, and Samuel Wolk, eds. *The New Jewish Encyclopedia*. Behrman rev. ed. 1976 $14.95. A good one-volume encyclopedia, designed for young readers.

Conway, Joan. *The Diaspora Story: The Epic of the Jewish People among the Nations*. Random 1980 o.p. An overview of Jewish history, full of photos, paintings, maps, and charts.

Dimont, Max I. *Jew, God and History*. New Amer. Lib. 1972 pap. $4.95. A novel approach to Jewish history with many original, far-fetched theories about the survival and influence of Jews over the centuries. A blurb on the back cover claims that "it reads like a detective story."

Eban, Abba. *Heritage: Civilization and the Jews*. Summit 1986 pap. $16.95. Attractive coffee-table book, with photographs, illustrations, and maps. Gives a superficial account of Jewish history and culture through the ages, based on the popular Public Broadcasting System television series.

————. *My People: The Story of the Jews*. Random 1984 pap. $14.95. A sounder treatment of Jewish history than the preceding work, especially the sections on modern Israeli politics.

Encyclopedia Judaica. Macmillan 16 vols. 1972 o.p. Excellent articles by important scholars on every imaginable topic on Jews and Judaism.

Finkelstein, Louis, ed. *The Jews: Their History, Culture and Religion*. Greenwood 2 vols. 3d ed. repr. of 1960 ed. 1979 o.p. A comprehensive survey of Jewish history with articles on each period by noted scholars.

Grayzel, Solomon. *A History of the Jews*. Jewish Pubns. rev. ed. repr. of 1947 ed. 1968 $12.95; New Amer. Lib. 1968 pap. $4.95. A popular and readable one-volume history of the Jews that is frequently uncritical and apologetic.

The Jewish Encyclopedia. Gordon Pr. 12 vols. repr. of 1901–06 ed. 1976 $998.95. Documents the state of Jewish knowledge at the turn of the century. Many of these articles are still the authoritative statement on their subjects.

Kedourie, Elie, ed. *The Jewish World: History and Culture of the Jewish People*. Abrams 1979 o.p. A richly illustrated introduction to Jewish civilization by various scholars.

Kobler, Franz, ed. *Letters of Jews through the Ages*. Hebrew Pub. 2 vols. 1978 pap. ea. $7.95. Vol. 1, *From Biblical Times to the Renaissance*; Vol. 2, *From the Renaissance to the Emancipation*. These collections of private letters give a view of the everyday world of Jews, often very different from the view afforded by religious texts and public documents. Kobler places the letters in context with informative introductions.

Lewis, Bernard. *The Jews of Islam*. Princeton Univ. Pr. 1984 $42.50 1987 pap. $8.95. A scholarly analysis of the close cultural interchange between Arabs and Jews over 14 centuries, by one of the foremost authorities on Islam.

Margolis, Max, and Alexander Marx. *History of the Jewish People*. Atheneum 1969 text ed. pap. $10.95. A collection of the basic facts about the Jews' histories in various times and places.

Meyer, Michael A., ed. *Ideas of Jewish History*. [*Lib. of Jewish Studies*] Behrman 1974 $15.95. Documents the various ways Jews throughout the ages have understood their own particular historical experience.

Raphael, Chaim. *The Road from Babylon: The Story of Sephardic and Oriental Jews*. Harper 1986 $22.45. This attractive and readable book presents an overview of the history of Jewish communities in non-Western countries, from their origins to the twentieth century.

Roth, Cecil. *A History of the Jews: From Earliest Times throughout the Six Day War*. Schocken rev. ed. 1970 pap. $8.95. A concise and readable survey that views the Jews in relationship to the cultural and historical contexts in which they have lived.

Schwarz, Leo W., ed. *Great Ages and Ideas of the Jewish People*. Modern Lib. 1956 $7.95. This popular collection of essays by noted scholars emphasizes the cultural and religious history of the Jews in each period, from ancient Israel to the "American Experience."

Seltzer, Robert M. *Jewish People, Jewish Thought: The Jewish Experience in History*. Macmillan 1980 $29.95. Surveys Jewish religious and intellectual development in the contexts of changing social and political circumstances.

Shenker, Israel. *Coat of Many Colors: Pages from Jewish Life*. Doubleday 1985 $19.95. A journalist examines that broad category, the Jews—"a singular confusion." Discusses with wit and insight the features of religion, language, and attitudes that make Jews a distinct group.

Silver, Daniel J., and Bernard Martin. *A History of Judaism.* Basic Bks. 2 vols. 1974 $40.00. A good introduction to the history of Judaism, which occasionally touches on the social and political history of the Jews.

Werblowsky, Zwi, and Geoffrey Wigoder, eds., *The Encyclopedia of the Jewish Religion.* Adama 1986 $39.95. Nontechnical, one-volume encyclopedia of Jewish beliefs and practices and key figures in the history of Judaism.

Yerushalmi, Yosef H. *Zakhor: Jewish History and Jewish Memory.* [*Stroum Lectures in Jewish Studies*] Univ. of Washington Pr. 1982 $17.50. A philosophic history of Jewish historiography. Argues that memory has always held a central place in Judaism, but that historians have played an uncertain and ambiguous role.

Judaism

The religion, Judaism, comprises a sizable family of related but essentially independent Judaic systems. For a very long time, a single paramount system existed. Because it appealed to the myth that at Sinai God revealed the Torah to Moses in two media, writing and memory, it is called the Judaism of the dual Torah. That single system defines the canon on the basis of which people write books on the philosophy and theology of Judaism, the ethics of Judaism, the religious practices, including the liturgy, of Judaism, and the like. There is, of course, no such thing as a single, uniform "Judaism." Quite to the contrary, history yields many Judaisms, each with its own worldview, way of life, and definition of who and what is "Israel." Any picture that claims to encompass all Jews and to deal with every important document is, by definition, making selections—selections that are guided by a prior criterion for what is going to matter. That is why, to understand the Jewish worldview, the reader moves from history to theology, to efforts to explain and account for the whole, viewed all together and all at once. Theology in the form of reflection on the past, present, and future character and condition of the Jews need not deal in particular with the proof and definition of God. Rather, much of it addresses the condition of "Israel," the holy people. Discourse shades off into sociology and even ethnography. The main thrust of works on the Jewish worldview, however, is the effort to see things whole and in a cogent way.

What has been said about the Jewish worldview applies equally to the Judaic way of life. True, Scripture assigns to Israel, the Jewish people, certain religious duties. As diverse Judaisms read Scripture, however, each one made its choices concerning which, among the truths of Scripture, proved relevant to the system at hand. Any account of the Jewish way of life today will address the way of life required by the Judaism of the dual Torah, oral and written, which is explained presently. It will cover the liturgy and holy way of life of that particular Judaism. It will describe the holy days and festivals as these are designated and observed by that Judaism. Such an account will not take up issues of the sociology of Jews in the modern world, indicators of behavior that today are deemed distinctive to Jews. Judaism in the form of the dual Torah is what tells us about the Judaic way of life.

GENERAL

Bamberger, Bernard J. *The Story of Judaism*. Schocken 3d ed. 1964 pap. $9.95. A well-written history of Jewish ideas, practice, and institutions.

Birnbaum, Philip. *Encyclopedia of Jewish Concepts (A Book of Jewish Concepts)*. 1964. Hebrew Pub. rev. ed. 1979 $25.00 pap. $14.95. A useful resource with short articles on Jewish terms and concepts, listed alphabetically by transliterated Hebrew words.

Davies, W. D., ed. *The Cambridge History of Judaism*. Cambridge Univ. Pr. 1979 $62.50. Collections of essays of uneven quality on various topics. While not continuous and coherent, the essays include a few classic statements.

Glatzer, Nahum N. *The Judaic Tradition*. Behrman 1982 text ed. pap. $9.95

Jacobs, Louis. *The Book of Jewish Belief*. Behrman 1984 text ed. pap. $7.95. Very light reading. A basic, and at times superficial, introduction to Jewish thought, with illustrations.

Lewisohn, Ludwig. *What Is This Jewish Heritage?* B'nai B'rith 1954 o.p. A powerful, brief statement of why young Jews should affirm their Jewish roots.

Neusner, Jacob. *Between Time and Eternity: The Essentials of Judaism*. Dickenson 1975 pap. $10.95. An introduction to the fundamentals of Judaism.

———. *Life of Torah: Readings in the Jewish Religious Experience*. Wadsworth 1984 o.p. An anthology of modern classical writings on the principal aspects of Judaic religious life.

———. *Self-Fulfilling Prophecy: Exile and Return as the History of Judaism*. Beacon Pr. 1987 $25.00. Offers the encompassing theory that all Judaic systems refer back to the pattern of exile and return to make sense of the world.

———. *The Way of Torah: An Introduction to Judaism*. [*Religious Life of Man Ser.*] Wadsworth 4th ed. 1988 $11.50. A simple introduction to the history and beliefs of Judaism, from the beginning to the present; a widely used textbook.

Petuchowski, Jacob J. *Heirs of the Pharisees*. Univ. Pr. of Amer. repr. of 1970 ed. 1986 text ed. pap. $12.00. Examines the worldview and way of life of the ancient Pharisees as a model for contemporary Judaism.

Prager, Dennis, and Joseph Telushkin. *The Nine Questions People Ask about Judaism*. Simon & Schuster 1981 $14.95 1986 pap. $7.95. This book, written for skeptical Jews and curious Christians, answers, in a controversial style, such common questions as "How can I believe in God after the Holocaust?" and "Why shouldn't I intermarry?"

Roth, Leon. *Judaism: A Portrait*. Schocken repr. of 1961 ed. 1972 pap. $4.95. A fluent introduction to Judaism by a traditionally minded philosopher.

Steinberg, Milton. *Basic Judaism*. 1947. Aronson 1987 $22.00; Harcourt 1965 pap. $3.95. This compact book remains one of the best introductions to Jewish thought, practice, and institutions.

Wouk, Herman. *This Is My God*. Doubleday 1959 $14.95; Pocket Bks. 1983 pap. $4.95. For those interested in a readable, one-volume introduction to Judaism, this is it.

ART AND MUSIC

While many people suppose that the commandment against making a graven image prevented Jews from developing an artistic tradition, the opposite is true. From antiquity to the present, Jews have decorated synagogues, made objects for cultic and ritual use, and otherwise fostered a graphic and tactile artistic tradition. Moreover, a musical tradition began with the requirement that synagogue liturgy be sung, and, still more important, for the Torah to be read aloud in accord with a fixed pattern of cantillation. Thus, in both art and music, a long tradition of expression has marked the history of Judaism.

Kanof, Abram. *Jewish Art and Religious Observance*. Abrams 1980 o.p. Historical pictorial overview of Jewish observance at home and in the synagogue. Beautiful presentation of ceremonial art objects with an analysis of their relationship to Judaism.

Krinsky, Carol Herselle. *Synagogues of Europe: Architecture, History, Meaning*. Architectural History Foundation 1985 $50.00 1987 pap. $25.00. An attractive and thorough treatment of the architecture, history, and meaning of the synagogue, from antiquity to the twentieth century. Synagogues are placed in the context of the various Jewish communities that built and prayed and lived in them.

Landsberger, Franz. *A History of Jewish Art*. Kennikat 1973 o.p. An excellent introduction to Jewish art through the ages.

Roth, Cecil. *Jewish Art: An Illustrated History*. New York Graphic Society 1971 o.p. Revised and updated by Bezalel Narkiss. Survey of Jewish art culled from many contexts.

Ungerleider-Mayerson, Joy. *Jewish Folk Art: From Biblical Days to Modern Times*. Summit 1986 $50.00. A contemporary scholar of Jewish art presents a survey of the creations of folk artists.

Werner, Eric. *The Sacred Bridge: Liturgical Parallels in Synagogue and Early Church*. [*Music Repr. Ser.*] Da Capo repr. of 1959 ed. 1979 lib. bdg. $65.00; Ktav 1985 $29.50; State Mutual Bk. 1981 $60.00. The classic account of the music of Judaism and of the synagogue, and the cross-influences of Jewish and Christian liturgical music over the centuries, by the leading musicologist of Judaism in the twentieth century.

Wigoder, Geoffrey, ed. *Jewish Art and Civilization*. Walker 1972 $150.00. Richly illustrated survey of Jewish civilization arranged chronologically by country.

————. *The Story of the Synagogue: A Diaspora Museum Book*. Harper 1986 $35.00. Coffee-table book displaying the art and architecture of synagogues throughout the world and throughout history, from the remnants and replicas in Tel Aviv's Diaspora Museum. Portrays the synagogue as a community center, school, and place of worship.

ETHICS

The ethics of Judaism is a complex subject that encompasses various ways of thinking about ethical problems, from the Scripture's prophetic injunctions through the philosopher's efforts at generalization and the defense of inclusive principles of conduct. Although the importance of ethics to Judaism makes the subject urgent, systematization of thought has always competed with more fragmentary ways of stating matters, such as the use of apothegms. The ethical tradition reaches expression at every period in the history of Judaism—scriptural, Talmudic, medieval, modern—and in every medium of Judaic discourse, from the received holy books through the liturgy.

Bleich, J. David. *Contemporary Halakhic Problems*. [*Lib. of Jewish Law and Ethics*] Ktav 1977–83 2 vols. $20.00 pap. ea. $14.95. Recommended as a view of the typical Orthodox mode of discussing Jewish law.

Borowitz, Eugene B. *Choosing a Sex Ethic: A Jewish Inquiry*. Schocken 1970 pap. $5.95. A Reform rabbi outlines his approach to sexuality and ethical decisions in general. He outlines four levels of sexual ethics, the highest of which is abstinence before marriage. (See Borowitz's main listing in this chapter.)

Dan, Joseph. *Jewish Mysticism and Jewish Ethics.* Univ. of Washington Pr. 1986 $20.00. Explains how the Jewish mystical tradition has informed, and should continue to inform, Jewish ethics.

Feldman, David M. *Birth Control in Jewish Law: Marital Relations, Contraception, and Abortion as Set Forth in the Classic Texts of Jewish Law.* Greenwood repr. of 1968 ed. 1980 lib. bdg. $27.50; Schocken repr. of 1968 ed. 1974 pap. $8.95. An analysis of traditional Jewish mores concerning sexuality and contraception, with a comparison to Christianity. The discussion on abortion provides a good introduction to the way rabbis and scholars approach issues of Jewish law (Halakhah).

———. *Health and Medicine in the Jewish Tradition: The Pursuit of Wholeness.* Crossroad NY 1986 $15.95. Short book on traditional Jewish mores concerning health and medical practice.

Freehof, Solomon Benner. *New Reform Responsa.* Hebrew Union College Pr. 1980 o.p. The latest in a series of volumes in which a Reform rabbi responds to such ethical questions as conversion, burial, and artificial insemination.

Kelner, Menachem Marc, ed. *Contemporary Jewish Ethics.* Sanhedrin 1978 o.p. Somewhat dated collection of essays by various authors, reprinted from other sources, that reflects mainstream and traditional perspectives. For example, feminism and homosexuality appear in the section on "sexual equality and sexual deviance."

Klagsbrun, Francine. *Voices of Wisdom: Jewish Ideals and Ethics for Everyday Living.* Jonathan David 1986 $16.95; Pantheon 1980 $17.95. An anthology of inspiring Jewish quotations from sources ranging from the Bible to twentieth-century works, selected for a contemporary audience and arranged by topic.

Leiman, Sid Z., ed. *Jewish Moral Philosophy.* Behrman 1979 o.p. A collection of essays on the theory of Jewish ethics.

Novak, David, ed. *Halakhah in a Theological Dimension: Essays on the Interpretation of Law and Theology in Judaism.* Scholars Pr. GA 1985 $19.75. Derives theological principles from Jewish law and looks to these principles, rather than to the details of Jewish law, for answers to such contemporary ethical and religious issues as drug abuse, nuclear disarmament, and whether women should be rabbis.

LITURGY

The liturgy is received and classic, that is, Judaic worship conforms to received patterns. It is not subject to daily invention and does not require a direct and immediate revelation from God or call from God to say prayers. The liturgy is divided into two parts—that covering ordinary days, Sabbaths, and festivals, and that covering the Days of Awe or High Holy Days (the New Year and the Day of Atonement) in autumn. The prayer book follows a fixed pattern of worship, although all modern Judaic religious groups have made additions, revisions, and deletions.

Agnon, S. Y. *Days of Awe.* Schocken 1948 o.p. The great novelist here introduces the High Holy Days, guiding the reader through the main beliefs in a compelling manner.

Arzt, Max. *Justice and Mercy.* Hartmore 1963 $12.50. An introduction to the liturgy for the High Holy Days that leads the reader through the principal prayers.

Birnbaum, Philip, ed. and trans. *The Birnbaum Haggadah.* Hebrew Pub. 1976 $5.95 pap. $3.95. A good translation of the Passover Haggadah, with Hebrew and English on facing pages and a running English commentary.

———. *Hasiddur Hashalem: Daily Prayer Book.* Hebrew Pub. 1977 pap. $9.95. In this version of the traditional weekly prayer book, the English translation faces the original Hebrew and Aramaic. Footnotes give biblical references and background information for the most important prayers.

——. *Mahzor Hashalem: High Holyday Prayer Book.* Hebrew Pub. 5 vols. 1971 $58.00. This traditional prayer book for the High Holy Days is designed for practical use as well as for study.

Bronstein, Herbert, ed. *A Passover Haggadah.* Central Conference of Amer. Rabbis 1982 $27.50 pap. $9.95. Published by the Reform movement, this Haggadah avoids sexist language.

Cardozo, Arlene Rossen. *Jewish Family Celebrations: Shabbat, Festivals and Traditional Ceremonies.* St. Martin's 1982 $17.50 1985 pap. $6.95. A guidebook for beginners, dealing with Jewish holidays, Bar/Bat Mitzvahs, weddings, and births.

Donin, Hayim H. *To Pray as a Jew.* Basic Bks. 1980 $17.95. Walks readers through a traditional synagogue service, part by part, presenting historical background and practical instructions.

Gaster, Theodor H. *Festivals of the Jewish Year: A Modern Interpretation and Guide.* Morrow 1971 pap. $7.95; Peter Smith 1962 $18.75. A simple account of the festivals of Judaism, what they mean, and how they are observed.

Goodman, Philip, ed. *Hanukkah Anthology.* Jewish Pubns. 1976 $15.95. This and the following books edited by Goodman provide useful guides for the celebration of the major Jewish festivals. Each volume contains approximately 400 pages of readings from biblical, Rabbinic, and modern sources as well as information on related art, music, children's stories, and activities.

——. *Passover Anthology.* Jewish Pubns. 1961 $14.95

——. *Purim Anthology.* Jewish Pubns. 1949 $7.50

——. *Rosh Hashanah Anthology.* Jewish Pubns. 1970 $10.95

——. *The Shavuot Anthology.* Jewish Pubns. 1975 $9.95

——. *The Sukkot and Simhat Torah Anthology.* Jewish Pubns. 1973 o.p.

——. *Yom Kippur Anthology.* Jewish Pubns. 1971 $9.95

Idelsohn, A. Z. *Jewish Liturgy and Its Development.* Schocken 1967 o.p. A classic account of the development of Jewish liturgy from antiquity through the nineteenth century.

Kadushin, Max. *Worship and Ethics: A Study in Rabbinic Judaism.* 1964. Bloch 1975 pap. $8.95. Explains the theory that Judaic liturgy expresses principles of ethical behavior.

Martin, Bernard. *Prayer in Judaism.* Basic Bks. 1968 o.p. A good introduction to the content of Jewish liturgy and its function in Jewish life.

Neusner, Jacob. *The Enchantments of Judaism.* Basic Bks. 1987 $15.95. A theology of Judaism based on the liturgical life of observance, showing how life is transformed through the right words said in the right way.

Petuchowski, Jakob J., ed. *Understanding Jewish Prayer.* Ktav 1972 pap. $7.95. An introduction to the Judaic prayer book and its main prayers.

Raphael, Chaim. *A Feast of History: Passover through the Ages as a Key to Jewish Experience.* Simon & Schuster 1972 $12.50. A beautiful collection of photographs enhances this popular book on the historical development of the Passover seder. Presents the entire Hebrew Haggadah with an English translation.

Schauss, Hayyim. *The Jewish Festivals: From Their Beginnings to Our Own Day.* 1938. UAHC rev. ed. 1969 $8.00. A classic introduction to the High Holy Days and how they are observed.

——. *The Lifetime of a Jew: Throughout the Ages of Jewish History.* 1950. UAHC rev. ed. 1976 pap. $7.95. Reviews the life-cycle celebrations of Judaism, birth through death, and spells out the practices and their meanings.

Stern, Chaim, ed. *Gates of Prayer for Weekdays and at a House of Mourning.* Central

Conference of Amer. Rabbis 1975 $20.00 pap. $2.75. The recently revised daily prayer book of the Reform movement. An interesting contrast to the Birnbaum version in terms of style and content.

————. *Gates of Repentance*. Central Conference of Amer. Rabbis 1978 $16.00. The recently revised High Holy Day prayer book of the Reform movement.

Strassfeld, Michael. *The Jewish Holidays*. Harper 1985 $24.45 pap. $15.95. Traditional approaches and contemporary reinterpretations of Jewish holidays by a leader of the Havurah fellowship movement. Designed for observant Jews interested in keeping holidays in the fullness of tradition.

Waskow, Arthur I. *Seasons of Our Joy: A Handbook of Jewish Festivals*. Summit 1986 $17.95. Traditional and innovative approaches to Jewish holidays with practical information on how to prepare for each festival. Discusses the special prayers, songs, food, and background readings for each holiday.

PHILOSOPHY

Jewish philosophy is mainly a medieval phenomenon, beginning with the Muslim conquest of the Middle East and the introduction of the great tradition of Greek philosophy into the world of Judaism (and, later, Christianity). As a result, Judaic thinkers, starting with Saadya in ninth-century Baghdad, faced the problem of harmonizing rationalism with revelation, reason with Scripture. For the next 500 years, there was a continuous philosophical tradition, mainly in the Muslim world. Then, in the nineteenth century, a new philosophical tradition began in Germany, a tradition whereby Reform Judaic thinkers accommodated Judaic thought to the systems of KANT and HEGEL. This modern tradition has continued in the United States as well.

Blau, Joseph L. *The Story of Jewish Philosophy*. Ktav 1971 $8.95. Presents an overview of Jewish thought throughout the ages for readers without a background in philosophy.

Guttmann, Julius. *Philosophies of Judaism: The History of Jewish Philosophy from Biblical Times to Franz Rosenzweig*. 1964. Schocken 1973 pap. $13.50. A good, descriptive introduction to the major philosophical systems of medieval and modern Judaism.

Katz, Steven T. *Jewish Philosophers*. Bloch 1975 $10.95 pap. $8.95. A summary of Jewish thought from antiquity to the present, with individual essays on more than 30 major figures. Primarily an adaptation of articles appearing in the *Encyclopedia Judaica*.

Petuchowski, Jakob J. *Ever since Sinai: A Modern View of Torah*. Arbit 3d ed. 1979 text ed. pap. $5.95. A popular introductory textbook on the theology of Judaism.

Schoeps, Hans Joachim. *The Jewish-Christian Argument: A History of Theologies in Conflict*. Holt 1963 o.p. Covers both sides of the dispute from the beginnings of the church until the twentieth century.

Talmage, Frank, ed. *Disputation and Dialogue: Readings in the Jewish-Christian Encounter*. Ktav 1975 pap. $14.95. An excellent anthology of theological disputes between Jews and Christians during the last two millennia. Arranged by topic with clearly written introductions.

RELIGIOUS LITERATURE

These books offer an introduction to Judaic religious literature from biblical times to the present. Constant study of the classic writings is regarded as a religious duty. There is nothing secular in the literary act of writing a holy book.

Frank, Ruth S., and William Wolheim. *The Book of Jewish Books: A Readers' Guide to Judaism.* Harper 1986 $15.95 pap. $8.95. A useful reference book for anyone interested in building a Jewish library. Contains interesting reviews on all types of literature, from Jewish history and philosophy to children's books, cookbooks, and introductory essays for the uninitiated.

Holtz, Barry, ed. *Back to the Sources: Reading the Classic Jewish Texts.* Summit 1984 $19.95. A readable introduction with chapters on ten different forms of Jewish religious literature, from biblical narrative, law, and poetry to the teachings of Hasidic masters. Each chapter includes extensive citations, commentaries, and a bibliography.

Zinberg, Israel. *A History of Jewish Literature.* Ktav 1971–78 12 vols. ea. $22.50. Comprehensive survey of Jewish literature, with emphasis on the medieval period.

RELIGIOUS PRACTICE

Judaic religious practice involves a variety of everyday religious duties, which sanctify the Jewish people and make their lives conform to God's will. These religious duties, called *mitzvot* (often translated as commandments), require that certain things be done or not done. They affect every aspect of life from eating to sexual conduct; they also order the division of time into ordinary and holy days, as well as prescribing conduct for the latter. The following books present diverse authoritative accounts of the holy way of life of Judaism.

Bial, Morrison D. *Liberal Judaism at Home: The Practices of Modern Reform Judaism.* UAHC rev. ed. repr. of 1967 ed. 1971 pap. $5.00. "For Jews who are orthodox or conservative in their practice, this book will give some insight into Reform ritual. The author also seems to be interested in convincing Reform Jews that rituals are not reactionary" (*Choice*).

Diamant, Anita. *The New Jewish Wedding.* Summit 1985 $16.95 1986 pap. $8.95. Both a practical guide for planning a wedding and a historical study of the development of Jewish marriage customs.

Dobrinsky, Herbert. *A Treasury of Sephardic Laws and Customs.* Ktav 1986 text ed. $29.50 pap. $16.95. A comprehensive compendium of laws and customs of the four main Sephardic Jewish communities of North America—Syrian, Moroccan, Judeo-Spanish, and Spanish-Portuguese.

Donin, Hayim. *To Be a Jew: A Guide to Jewish Observance in Contemporary Life.* Basic Bks. 1972 $17.95. Detailed reference on orthodox practice, daily life, holidays, and rites of passage.

Klein, Isaac. *A Guide to Jewish Religious Practice.* [*Moreshet Ser.*] Ktav 1979 $20.00. A comprehensive code of Jewish law designed for Conservative Jews, dealing with daily prayers, the holidays, dietary laws, and marriage.

Lamm, Maurice. *Jewish Way in Death and Mourning.* Jonathan David rev. ed. 1972 pap. $7.95. A historical account and practical guide to the traditional Jewish understanding of and customs relating to death and mourning.

———. *The Jewish Way in Love and Marriage.* Harper 1982 pap. $9.95. An Orthodox perspective on sexual ethics and marital customs.

Latner, Helen. *Your Jewish Wedding.* Doubleday 1985 pap. $4.95. A handbook on the details of planning a wedding, from selecting a caterer to arranging the place settings.

Maslin, Simeon J., ed. *Shaarei Mitzvah: Gates of Mitzvah.* Central Conference of Amer. Rabbis 1979 $9.95 pap. $7.95. Guide to Reform Jewish practices at each rite of passage from birth to death.

Strassfeld, Michael, and Richard Siegel, comps. *The Jewish Catalog: A Do-It Yourself*

Kit. Jewish Pubns. 1973 pap. $8.95. An introduction for the uninitiated and a reference book for the well informed. Full of interesting information and playful illustrations on traditional Jewish observance.

————. *The Second Jewish Catalog: Sources and Resources.* Jewish Pubns. 1976 $8.95. Companion volume to the preceding book. Provides background information and readings on various aspects of Jewish observance.

Strassfeld, Michael, and Sharon Strassfeld, eds. *The Third Jewish Catalogue: Building Community.* Jewish Pubns. 1980 $9.95. The final volume of the trilogy focuses on Jewish communal responsibility, discussing charity, social action, ecology, Zionism, and much more. Includes an index to all three volumes.

Trepp, Leo. *The Complete Book of Jewish Observance.* Behrman 1980 $16.50. A comprehensive guide to the Orthodox, Conservative, and Reform practices, with discussion of the theories behind each custom.

ANCIENT JUDAISM

Ancient Judaism covers the period from the formation of the Pentateuch, the Five Books of Moses, as we now have it, in the fifth century B.C. (c.450 B.C.), to the Muslim conquest of the Near and Middle East in the middle of the seventh century A.D. (c.640). During that period of a thousand years, Jews in the Roman Empire witnessed three important turning points: the incorporation of the Land of Israel into the Roman Empire in the century from 140 to 40 B.C., the destruction of the Temple in Jerusalem in A.D. 70, and the establishment of Christianity as the religion of the Roman Empire in the fourth century (from the edict of toleration of 312 to the conversion of Constantine just before his death in 337). The first of these events joined the Jews of the Land of Israel to the larger world of cosmopolitan Rome. The second marked a massive change in the religious world in which Judaism would flourish. The third redefined the political conditions in which Jews would live from the fourth to the nineteenth centuries. The meaning of the first—the inclusion of the Land of Israel in the Roman Empire—was that the Jews would participate in the cultural life of the Greco-Roman world as part of the Greek- and Aramaic-speaking East. The weight of the second— the destruction of the Temple—bore heavily for the next century, as a new mode of worship of, and relationship to, God had to be worked out. The meaning of the establishment of Christianity as the definitive force in the politics and culture of the West was ambiguous. On the one hand, Jews lost their long-established rights and immunities, being merely tolerated (and sometimes not even tolerated), pending the second coming of Christ and their final conversion. On the other, hand, Jews' fundamental view of themselves, as stated by their Holy Scriptures, found reinforcement in Christianity's adoption of those same Scriptures. A shared reading of the revelation, or Torah, of ancient Israel lent to Jews' holy books an importance and a general currency not earlier known. As a result, Jews' sense of themselves as a special and distinctive group was confirmed by the politics and culture of the West.

History of the Jews

SECOND TEMPLE PERIOD

The Jews between 450 B.C. and A.D. 70 lived throughout the Roman Empire, in the Land of Israel, Egypt, Syria, Asia Minor, Greece, Italy, as well as in Babylonia, the western satrapy of the Iranian Empire, at the confluence of the Tigris and Euphrates rivers in present-day Iraq. Much information is available on the Jews in the Land of Israel and Egypt, less on their histories in other parts of the Roman and Iranian empires. The sole continuous history concerns the Jews in the Land of Israel and rests on the narrative composed by a Jewish general and historian, Josephus, who wrote after the destruction of the Temple in 70 to explain the tragic event and to provide, for ancient readers, a positive view of the Jews as loyal citizens, despite the actions of those he represented as a radical and extreme group. Histories of Jews in other parts of the world, even in Egypt, where Greek-speaking Jews produced a sizable corpus of writings, are episodic and not continuous. For the Jews in the Iranian empire, we have only bits and pieces of stories.

Alon, Gedalyahu. *Jews, Judaism and the Classical World: Studies in Jewish History in the Times of the Second Empire and Talmud*. Trans. by Israel Abrahams, Humanities Pr. 1977 text ed. $38.50. Alon's studies on religion and history are original and important landmarks.

Bickerman, Elias. *From Ezra to the Last of the Maccabees: Foundations of Post-Biblical Judaism*. Schocken 1962 pap. $5.95. This brief work is a classic account, pulling together the major trends in Judaism and the Jews' history in the Land of Israel in a brief and insightful account. The best small book on the subject.

Bickerman, Elias, and Morton Smith. *The Ancient History of Western Civilization*. Harper 1976 $17.50. This important textbook places the Jews and the Land of Israel into the much broader context of ancient history and culture from the beginnings to the end of antiquity. It is literate and readable, and covers every conceivable topic in a remarkably succinct way. The two best historians of the period collaborated on this classic.

Büchler, Adolph. *Studies in Jewish History*. Oxford 1956 o.p. These specialist essays on particular topics show us the finest work of the major historian of Talmudic Judaism of the early part of the twentieth century.

Hengel, Martin. *Judaism and Hellenism: Studies in Their Encounter in Palestine during the Early Hellenistic Period*. Trans. by John Bowden, Fortress 1981 o.p. The definitive work on the relationship between Judaism and the surrounding Hellenistic world, this covers every subject with full bibliography, notes, and a judicious, compelling account of the whole. The single most important work on the subject.

Jagersma, Henk. *A History of Israel from Alexander the Great to Bar Kochba*. Fortress 1986 pap. $12.95. A good and reliable one-volume history.

Jeremias, Joachim. *Jerusalem in the Time of Jesus: An Investigation into Economic and Social Conditions during the New Testament Period*. Fortress 1975 pap. $7.95. This work concentrates on aspects of social life and culture, describing the everyday life of the time and place. It is colorful and engaging.

Klausner, Joseph. *The Messianic Idea in Israel*. Macmillan 1955 o.p. Klausner surveys the doctrines concerning the Messiah stated in various Judaic writings from biblical times to the end of antiquity. This is the classic survey.

Neusner, Jacob. *First-Century Judaism in Crisis: Yohanan ben Zakkai and the Renaissance of Torah*. Ktav 1981 $14.95. A popular account of what happened in Judaism before and after the destruction of the Temple. Very readable.

Neusner, Jacob, and Ernest S. Frerichs, eds. *Goodenough on the History of Religion and on Judaism*. Scholars Pr. GA 1986 pap. $29.95. The most important essays on Judaism and on history of religion by America's foremost historian of religion.

Oesterley, William O. *From the Fall of Jerusalem: 586 B.C. to the Bar-Kakhba Revolt, A.D. 135*. Vol. 2 in *A History of Israel*. Oxford 1932 o.p. An old, but still useful, detailed survey.

Pfeiffer, Robert H. *History of New Testament Times*. Greenwood repr. of 1949 ed. 1972 lib. bdg. $23.00. Pfeiffer's account is rich in bibliography and presents essays on many important topics.

Radin, Max. *The Jews among the Greeks and Romans*. Ayer repr. of 1915 ed. 1973 $33.00. This old but still valuable book is a pioneering work on its subject.

Reicke, Bo. *The New Testament Era: The World of the Bible from 500 B.C. to A.D. 100*. Fortress 1974 pap. $8.95. Yet another one-volume history of the Jews and Judaism in the setting of the interests of the New Testament; this remains a reliable and valuable account.

Reinhold, Meyer. *Diaspora: The Jews among the Greeks and Romans*. Samuel-Stevens 1983 $24.95. A useful and attractively presented short collection of primary sources describing all aspects of Jewish life outside the Land of Israel during the Greek and Roman periods.

Russell, David S. *Between the Testaments*. Fortress 1960 o.p. A brief account of the Judaisms of the period between Ezra and the first century.

———. *The Jews from Alexander to Herod*. Oxford 1967 pap. $13.95. A history of the Jews in the period from the third to the first century B.C.

Sandmel, Samuel. *Herod: A Profile of a Tyrant*. Lippincott 1967 o.p. A biography, restating the received narratives of Josephus, together with materials deriving from Roman writings and archaeology, on the most important Jewish ruler in the first century B.C.

Schürer, Emil. *The History of the Jewish People in the Age of Jesus Christ: A New English Edition*. Rev. and ed. by Geza Vermes, Fergus Millar, and Pamela Vermes, Fortress 4 vols. 1973– ea. $34.95–$44.95. Three volumes have already appeared. Covering all topics of history, politics, religion, and culture, with thorough updating of bibliographies as well as scholarly presentation, these are the starting point for all research on ancient Judaism.

Segal, Alan F. *Rebecca's Children: Judaism and Christianity in the Roman World*. Harvard Univ. Pr. 1986 text ed. $20.00. A well-written summary of recent scholarship on Judaism and Christianity from the destruction of the first Temple to the end of the first century of the common era, with anthropological comparisons to present-day religions.

Tcherikover, Victor. *Hellenistic Civilization and the Jews*. Atheneum repr. of 1959 ed. 1970 pap. $9.95. A classic of scholarship, this work covers the relationship of Jews to the larger Greek-speaking world in which they lived. Regarded as the best work in English to its time, but superseded by Hengel.

Whittaker, Molly. *Jews and Christians: Graeco-Roman Views*. Cambridge Univ. Pr. 1985 $47.50 pap. $18.95. Collects Greek and Latin sources from 200 B.C.E. to 200 C.E. on Jews and Christians written by others.

Zeitlin, Solomon. *The Rise and Fall of the Judean State: A Political, Social and Religious History of the Second Commonwealth*. Jewish Pubns. 3 vols. 1968–78 ea. $10.00–$12.50. The author did not accept the testimony, for late antiquity, of the Dead Sea Scrolls, finding them a medieval forgery. As a result, his work is idiosyncratic and important only for completeness in large research collections. He has won no substantial hearing for his ideas on any subject.

———. *Studies in the Early History of Judaism*. Ktav 4 vols. 1973–78 ea. $49.50–

$59.50. The studies are erudite but uncritical, with the result that the proposed theses cannot be evaluated by the normal standards of the humanities. Important only for completeness in large collections.

RABBINIC PERIOD

The Rabbinic Period is so named because during that time, from 70 to 640, the Jewish leaders in both the Land of Israel and Babylonia bore the title "rabbi," meaning "my lord" or "sir." Rabbis were sages, who both mastered the Torah, written and oral, and participated in the Jews' government—autonomous regimes recognized by the two world empires (Rome for the Land of Israel, Iran for Babylonia) as part of their systems of governing diverse populations, so far as possible, under their own local authorities. For the Land of Israel, Jewish self-government came to an end in the early fifth century, as the now Christian Roman government withdrew recognition from the autonomous administration that had flourished for 400 years. For Babylonia, the same pattern repeated itself in the sixth century. By the rise of Islam in the seventh century, Jews in both empires found themselves in far less suitable circumstances than they had known earlier.

Avi-Yonah, Michael. *The Holy Land from the Persian to the Arab Conquests 536 B.C.– A.D. 640: A Historical Geography.* Baker Bk. 1966 o.p. An important complement to the next entry, necessary for the study of history and politics.
——. *The Jews under Roman and Byzantine Rule: A Political History of Palestine from the Bar-Kokhba War to the Arab Conquest.* Schocken repr. 1984 $23.00. The best single one-volume history of the Jews in the Land of Israel from the second through the seventh centuries; reliable and complete.
Goodman, Martin. *State and Society in Roman Galilee, A.D. 132–212.* Rowman 1983 text ed. $33.95. Extensively notated study of Jewish communal and political institutions.
Lieberman, Saul. *Greek in Jewish Palestine: Studies in the Life and Manners of Jewish Palestine in the II–IV Centuries C.E.* Feldheim 1965 $13.95. A collection of discrete observations on Greek words and phrases in Talmudic literature, not coherent and without any thesis, but important for lexicographical purposes.
——. *Hellenism in Jewish Palestine: Studies in the Literary Transmission, Beliefs and Manners of Palestine in the I Century B.C.E.–IV Century B.C.E.* Ktav 1962 o.p. Another collection like the foregoing.
Neusner, Jacob. *A History of the Jews in Babylonia.* Humanities Pr. 5 vols. 1965–70 o.p. Note that Vol. 1, *The Parthian Period,* has been reprinted in paperback by Scholars Pr. GA.
——. *Israel and Iran in Talmudic Times: A Political History.* [*Studies in Judaism*] Univ. Pr. of Amer. 1987 lib. bdg. $27.50 text ed. pap. $14.75. A reproduction of the important chapters concerning politics of the author's *History of the Jews in Babylonia II–V.*
——. *Israel's Politics in Sasanian Iran: Jewish Self-Government in Talmudic Times.* [*Studies in Judaism*] Univ. Pr. of Amer. 1987 lib. bdg. $24.75 text ed. pap. $12.25. A reproduction of the important chapters concerning the Jews' institution of self-government of the author's *History of the Jews in Babylonia II–V.*
——. *Judaism, Christianity, and Zoroastrianism in Talmudic Babylonia.* [*Studies in Judaism*] Univ. Pr. of Amer. 1987 lib. bdg. $26.50 text ed. pap. $13.50. A reproduction of the important chapters concerning the history of the religions of Babylonia of the author's *History of the Jews in Babylonia II–V.*

Source Material

LITERATURE

JEWISH LITERATURE IN GREEK

During the Hellenistic period, the Jewish cultural elite was thoroughly conversant with Greek language and thought. Greek was the language of commerce, politics, and culture for Jews in the Land of Israel and the Diaspora (itself a Greek word). In fact, many faithful Jews relied on the Septuagint, the Greek translation of the Bible (third century B.C.), because they did not understand Hebrew. The extant Jewish literature in Greek is limited primarily to the works of two authors, Philo and Josephus. For the influence of Greek language and thought on Palestinian Jewish religious literature, see the works by Saul Lieberman listed above. (See also Josephus's and Philo's main entries in this chapter.)

Belkin, Samuel. *In His Image: The Jewish Philosophy of Man as Expressed in Rabbinic Tradition.* Greenwood repr. of 1960 ed. 1979 lib. bdg. $27.50. A thoughtful introduction to the life and system of Philo.

Feldman, Louis H. *Scholarship on Philo and Josephus, 1937–1962.* [*Studies in Judaica Ser.*] Bloch 1962 o.p. The classic bibliography by the leading bibliographer of Philo and Josephus and the foremost Josephus scholar of the day.

Jews in the Hellenistic World: Josephus, Aristeas, The Sibylline Oracles, Eupolemus. Cambridge Univ. Pr. 1985 $42.50 pap. $12.95. An illustrated presentation of Greek literature dealing with Hellenistic Jewish life.

TARGUMS

Targums are translations of the Hebrew Bible into Aramaic, the language common among Jews in Palestine, Syria, and lands east. The best-known targums were preserved among Jewish scholars down through the centuries: Targum Onkelos, the so-called Fragmentary Targums, and Targum (Pseudo-) Jonathan—all translations of the Pentateuch, and Targum Jonathan to the Prophets and the Writings. These texts, along with Targum Neofiti to the Pentateuch, were probably completed between 300 and 700 C.E., but scholars are certain that they also contain some material that reflects the thinking of earlier periods. In general, targums provide a fairly literal rendering of the Hebrew text into Aramaic. They tend to follow the Hebrew text closely, although the translators often add a word or two to the literal rendition. In addition to the trend of literal translation, however, the targums occasionally contain sizable augmentations to the literal text. These expansions—and to a lesser extent the translation material—reveal information concerning the use of Scripture by the translators. This information is used by modern scholars—most frequently New Testament scholars—to discover the way Scripture was understood by the Jews in Palestine.

Bowker, John W. *The Targums and Rabbinic Literature.* Cambridge Univ. Pr. 1969 $67.50. An introduction to some of the targums together with an account of some Rabbinic writings; not very well informed on the latter subject.

Chilton, Bruce D. *A Galilean Rabbi and His Bible: Jesus' Use of the Interpreted Scripture of His Time.* [*Good News Studies Ser.*] M. Glazier 1984 $7.95. A thoughtful attempt to use the later targums to illuminate the interpretations of the Hebrew Scriptures placed into Jesus' mouth by the Gospel writers.

———. *Targumic Approaches to the Gospels: Essays in the Mutual Definition of Judaism and Christianity.* Univ. Pr. of Amer. 1987 lib. bdg. $24.75 text ed. pap.

$12.25. An engaging collection of essays on targumic interpretations of Scripture and their relationship to interpretations found in the Gospels.

Etheridge, J. W., trans. *Targums of Onkelos and Jonathan Ben Uzziel on the Pentateuch with the Fragments of the Jerusalem Targum from the Chaldee.* 1862. Ktav repr. of 1865 ed. 1969 $59.50. The only complete English translation of either targum.

Hayward, Robert. *Divine Name and Presence: The Memra.* Allanheld 1981 $25.50. An interesting and readable study of the targumic term *memra*, which is used by the targums instead of God's name.

Levey, Samson H. *The Messiah: An Aramic Interpretation.* Ktav 1974 $20.00. A collection and discussion of passages from many different targums that concern the Messiah. Draws few conclusions.

McNamara, Martin. *From Targum to Testament.* Eerdmans 1972 o.p. An outdated introduction to the targums by a New Testament scholar who has a strong interest in linking targum materials to sayings of Jesus.

Smolar, Leivy, and Pinchas Churgin. *Studies in Targum Jonathan to the Prophets.* Ktav 1983 $59.50. Philologically based studies of the history, geographical allusions, and matters of Jewish law found in the targum to the prophets.

RABBINIC LITERATURE

From the second to the seventh century, Jewish sages, who addressed each other by the title "rabbi," composed a number of documents in Palestine and Babylonia. These books, which came to be called Rabbinic literature, became canonized as a sacred body of literature, along with the Hebrew Bible. This corpus contains a variety of literary genres, including legal codes, biblical interpretation, legends, moral exhortations, and philosophic discussions. The documents were written at different times, in different places, in different languages (Hebrew and Aramaic), by different people, for different purposes. Each document has distinct characteristics that distinguish it from other documents, but all books of the Rabbinic canon exhibit certain common features, such as the frequent reference to the statements and actions of rabbis and the division of the text into discrete and compact discussions. For material on the religious movement reflected in this body of literature, see under Ancient Judaism: Rabbinic Judaism in this chapter.

Ginzberg, Louis. *Legends of the Jews.* Jewish Pubns. 7 vols. 1956–62 set $8.00 ea. $11.95. This work anthologizes Rabbinic comments on the Hebrew Scriptures from a variety of books and periods. The materials are homogenized and removed from context so the work cannot be used for critical purposes, but as an anthology of how various persons in the history of Judaism read various biblical stories, it is engaging and readable.

Green, William S. *Approaches to Ancient Judaism: Theory and Practice.* Scholars Pr. GA 3 vols. 1983–85 pap. ea. $15.00–$17.25. Collections of original and important articles on ancient Judaism.

Mielziner, Moses. *Introduction to the Talmud.* Bloch 4th ed. repr. of 1925 ed. 1969 $17.95 pap. $12.95. With a new bibliography (1925–67), by Alexander Guttmann. An old but still useful bibliographic study, together with a summary of basic facts about Talmudic literature.

Montefiore, C. G., and H. Loewe, eds. *A Rabbinic Anthology.* Schocken 1970 pap. $16.95. The best single anthology of Talmudic and Midrashic writings, organized around topics of theological interest. For the study of Judaic religious thought, a necessary item.

Neusner, Jacob. *Genesis and Judaism: The Perspective of Genesis Rabbah, An Analyti-*

cal Anthology. Scholars Pr. GA 1985 $28.95 pap. $22.95. An anthology, arranged by important topics, of the Rabbinic reading of Genesis.

———. *The Oral Torah: The Sacred Books of Judaism, An Introduction*. Harper 1985 $19.45. An introduction to principal documents of the oral Torah, together with an account of the theory of how these writings form part of the Torah.

———. *Scriptures of the Oral Torah: Sanctification and Salvation in the Sacred Books of Judaism*. Harper 1987 consult publisher for information. An anthology to illustrate and amplify the preceding item.

———, ed. *The Study of Ancient Judaism*. Ktav 2 vols. 1982 ea. $37.50. Vol. 1, *Mishnah, Midrash, Siddur;* Vol. 2, *The Palestinian and Babylonian Talmuds*. Bibliographic essays by various scholars, introducing studies of the named documents. The essays on the two Talmuds, by Baruch M. Bosker and David Goodblatt, respectively, are regarded as classics in the genre of bibliographic essays and cover all topics pertinent to Talmudic literature, history, and exegesis.

Nickelsburg, George W. E. *Jewish Literature between the Bible and the Mishnah: A Historical and Literary Introduction*. Fortress 1981 $19.95. A good introduction to the Jewish literature of the Hellenistic and early Roman periods organized according to historical occurrences.

Petuchowski, Jakob J. *Our Masters Taught Rabbinic Stories and Sayings*. Crossroad NY 1982 $10.95. A short collection of citations arranged by topic on theological and ethical subjects. Serves a broader audience than Montefiore and Loewe (see above).

Strack, Hermann L. *Introduction to the Talmud and Midrash*. 1931. Atheneum 1969 text ed. pap. $8.95. Completed a half century ago, this work remains an excellent bibliographic summary of the nineteenth- and early twentieth-century scholarly literature on all important topics.

THE MISHNAH AND TOSEFTA

The earliest extant document of the Rabbinic corpus is the Mishnah, a philosophic law code, compiled at the beginning of the third century but also containing material from the previous two centuries. In large part, the Mishnah provides a utopian picture of the way Jews should act in a perfect world. It is a sizable document consisting of six divisions, divided into 63 tractates, each containing a number of chapters. The Mishnah represents the first statement of Rabbinic Judaism, the movement that provided the foundation of practically all subsequent forms of Judaism. The Tosefta (c.300) is a commentary on the Mishnah. Like the Mishnah, it contains material presumably preserved from the preceding centuries. In general, the Tosefta is less tightly reasoned and composed than the Mishnah.

Blackman, P., trans. *Mishnayoth*. Judaica Pr. 6 vols. 1964 o.p. A popular collection that juxtaposes the original Hebrew text and the English translation. Contains extensive notation and introductions that make the text more accessible to the uninitiated.

Brooks, Roger. *Support for the Poor in the Mishnaic Law of Agriculture: Tractate Peah*. Scholars Pr. GA 1983 pap. $21.00. A systematic translation and interpretation of the Mishnah's and the Tosefta's tractate on the stated subject.

Danby, Herbert, trans. *The Mishnah*. Oxford 1933 $45.00. The first English translation. This handy one-volume work is a generally reliable translation.

Eilberg-Schwartz, Howard. *The Human Will in Judaism: The Mishnah's Philosophy of Intention*. Scholars Pr. GA 1986 $31.95. A monograph of considerable interest on the role of intentionality in the working of the Judaic religious system presented by the Mishnah; readable and interesting.

Haas, Peter J. *A History of the Mishnaic Law of Agriculture: Tractate Maaser Sheni.*
   Scholars Pr. GA 1980 $15.00. A systematic translation and interpretation of the
   Mishnah's and the Tosefta's tractate on second tithe, that is, a portion of the
   crop to be set aside and eaten in Jerusalem.
Jaffee, Martin S. *Mishnah's Theology of Tithing: A Study of Tractate Maaserot.* Scholars Pr. GA 1981 text ed. pap. $15.00. A systematic translation and interpretation
   of the Mishnah's and the Tosefta's tractate on tithing.
Mandelbaum, Irving J. *A History of the Mishnaic Law of Agriculture: Kilayim.* Scholars Pr. GA 1981 text ed. pap. $18.00. A systematic translation and interpretation
   of the Mishnah's and the Tosefta's tractate on the taboo against mixing distinct
   classifications of materials, for example, mixed seeds, linen and wool, and the
   like.
Neusner, Jacob. *Judaism: The Evidence of the Mishnah.* Univ. of Chicago Pr. 1981
   $25.00 pap. $15.95. An account of the religious system of the Mishnah, the first
   document of the Judaism of the dual Torah, read as a distinct but comprehensive statement of a worldview.
———. *Method and Meaning in Ancient Judaism.* Scholars Pr. GA 3 vols. 1979–83
   pap. ea. $13.50–$27.50. Collections of essays on special topics pertinent to the
   Mishnah and correct methods for studying it.
———. *The Tosefta: Its Structure and Sources.* Scholars Pr. GA 1986 pap. $39.95.
   Classifies and analyzes the various types of material in the Tosefta in terms of
   literary form and relationship to the Mishnah.
———, trans. *The Mishnah: A New Translation.* Yale Univ. Pr. 1988 consult publisher
   for information. The result of a 30-volume study on this central document of
   Rabbinic Judaism. This is the first translation that separates the text into cogent units of discourse (comparable to verses in the Bible) and that follows the
   carefully patterned literary forms of the original.
———. *The Tosefta Translated from the Hebrew.* Ktav 6 vols. 1977–85 ea. $45.00. The
   only English translation.
Newman, Louis E. *The Sanctity of the Seventh Year: A Study of Mishnah Tractate
   Shebiit.* Scholars Pr. GA 1983 pap. $12.00. A systematic translation and interpre-
   tation of the Mishnah's and the Tosefta's tractate on the prohibition of agricultural work in the Land of Israel in the seventh year.

MIDRASHIC COMPILATIONS

   Midrash, meaning "investigation," refers to the interpretation of the Hebrew Bible. The word also has come to describe those documents composed from the third
century on that contain discussion of Scripture. These documents discuss the Bible
through paraphrase, exegesis, philological analysis, and imaginative embellishment.
The documents arrange material in a variety of ways. For example, Genesis Rabbah
provides a verse-by-verse analysis of the book of Genesis whereas Pesikta deRab
Kahana presents topical discussions related to the weekly lections.

Braude, William G., and Israel J. Kapstein, trans. *Pesikta De-Rab Kahana: R. Kaha-
   na's Compilation of Discourses for Sabbath and Festival Days.* Jewish Pubns. 1975
   $23.95. A literate and attractive rendition, not at all close to the Hebrew text.
———. *Pesikta Rabbati: Homiletical Discourses for Festal Days and Special Sabbaths.*
   [*Judaica Ser.*] Yale Univ. Pr. 2 vols. 1968 $85.00. An excellent translation, faith-
   ful to the Hebrew and easily read.
Glatzer, Nahum N., ed. *Hammer on the Rock: A Midrash Reader.* Schocken 1962 pap.
   $4.95. An anthology of Midrashic literature accomplished with taste and charm.
Goldin, Judah. *The Living Talmud: The Wisdom of the Fathers.* New Amer. Lib. 1957

pap. $3.95. A translation of "The Fathers" (Mishnah-tractate Avot) together with a commentary, readily accessible to the American reader.

——. *The Song at the Sea.* Yale Univ. Pr. 1971 o.p. A translation of part of a Rabbinic commentary on the book of Exodus, rich in erudite observations.

——, trans. *The Fathers According to Rabbi Nathan.* Schocken 1974 o.p. A literate translation, lacking reference system and critical apparatus, of an important text, which amplifies and contains numerous stories about the sages listed in "The Fathers" (Mishnah-tractate Avot).

Hammer, Reuven, trans. *Sifre: A Tannaitic Commentary on the Book of Deuteronomy.* [*Judaica Ser.*] Yale Univ. Pr. 1986 text ed. $45.00. A good translation, but lacking all analytical apparatus, it can be used only to survey the contents—not to conduct studies—of the original text. A new translation of the same document is under way to meet the need for a usable translation for analytical purposes.

Handelman, Susan A. *The Slayers of Moses: The Emergence of Rabbinic Interpretation in Modern Literary Theory.* [*Modern Jewish Lit. and Culture Ser.*] State Univ. of New York Pr. 1982 $49.50 pap. $18.95. Argues that Modern Jews—Freud, Derrida, and Bloom—advocate approaches akin to the supposed "intertexuality" of Midrash, a dubious, unproven assumption about the character of Rabbinic literature. Difficult to read.

Hartman, Geoffrey, and Sanford Budick. *Midrash and Literature.* Yale Univ. Pr. 1986 $28.50. A collection of essays on the relationship between Judaic biblical exegesis and contemporary literary criticism.

Lauterbach, Jacob Z., trans. *Mekilta De-rabbi Ishmael.* [*Lib. of Jewish Class.*] Jewish Pubns. 3 vols. 1976 pap. $19.95. A model of first-class translation and presentation of an important document, with a complete analytical program.

Neusner, Jacob. *Invitation to Midrash: The Working of Rabbinic Bible Interpretation.* Harper 1988 consult publisher for information. A systematic account of the character of Rabbinic Midrash, and of the distinctive viewpoints and traits of its principal documents.

——. *Judaism and Scripture: The Evidence of Leviticus Rabbah.* Univ. of Chicago Pr. 1986 $50.00. An account of how the Rabbinic mode of interpreting Scripture presents not merely comments on verses but systematic propositions and arguments.

——. *What Is Midrash?* Fortress 1987 pap. $5.95. A simple definition of the types of Midrash-writing produced in diverse Judaic circles and in Christianity.

——, trans. *The Fathers According to Rabbi Nathan: An Analytical Translation and Explanation (Version A).* Scholars Pr. GA 1986 $41.95. An analytical translation, with form-critical comments and introduction, stressing a close and literal reading of the text and a systematic account of the viewpoints stressed by the commentators who expanded and amplified "The Fathers" (Mishnah-tractate Avot).

——. *Genesis Rabbah. The Judaic Commentary to the Book of Genesis: A New American Translation.* Scholars Pr. GA 1985 $35.75 pap. $29.55. An analytical translation, with form-critical comments and introduction, stressing a close and literal reading of the text and a systematic account of the viewpoints stressed by the fourth-century exegetes.

——. *Pesiqta deRab Kahana: An Analytical Translation.* Scholars Pr. GA 2 vols. 1987 ea. $34.95. A very literal and analytical translation stressing a close reading of the text and a systematic account of the viewpoints stressed by the exegetes.

——. *Sifre to Numbers: An American Translation.* Scholars Pr. GA 2 vols. 1986 text ed. ea. $24.95–$27.95 pap. ea. $19.95–$22.95

——. *Torah from Our Sages: Pirke Avot.* Rossel Bks. 1986 $18.95 pap. $9.95. A new commentary to the classic, stressing issues of an intellectual character, specifically explaining how the document's editors present a cogent system of Judaism through their layout of sayings.

Neusner, Jacob, and Roger Brooks, trans. *Sifra. The Rabbinic Commentary on Leviticus: A New Translation.* Scholars Pr. GA 1985 $22.95 pap. $18.25. A partial translation (approximately 15 percent of the whole) of the Rabbinic commentary to Leviticus; further parts of the document are being translated at this time.

Neusner, Jacob, and Anthony J. Saldarini. *Scholastic Rabbinism: A Literary Study of the Fathers According to Rabbi Nathan.* Scholars Pr. GA 1982 text ed. pap. $12.00. A careful study of an alternative text of the classic document.

Porton, Gary G. *Understanding Rabbinic Midrash: Texts and Commentary.* Ktav 1985 $14.95. A full and systematic introduction to sample Midrash texts, with commentary and bibliography.

Sanders, James A. *Torah and Canon.* Fortress 1972 pap. $5.95. An account of how the formation of the canon of the Hebrew Scriptures itself constituted a commentary or Midrash on Scripture; a classic work.

TALMUD

Two vast commentaries to the Mishnah, called Talmuds, were created, one in the Land of Israel (c.400), bearing the title of the Talmud of the Land of Israel or the Palestinian Talmud (in Hebrew, the Yerushalmi), the other in Babylonia (c.600), called the Talmud of Babylonia (in Hebrew, the Bavli). The latter is a larger work containing a significant amount of Midrashic material as well as commentary on the Mishnah. The Talmud of Babylonia is assumed to be the consummate text of Rabbinic Judaism, melding together the various strains of material into one conclusive statement.

Jacobs, Louis. *The Talmudic Argument: A Study in Talmudic Reasoning and Methodology.* Cambridge Univ. Pr. 1984 $44.50. Continues the interest of the foregoing, now with attention to the larger traits of argument.

Neusner, Jacob. *Invitation to the Talmud.* Harper rev. ed. 1984 $19.45. Presents a passage as it unfolds in the Mishnah, Tosefta, Talmud of the Land of Israel, and Talmud of Babylonia, with attention to the larger historical and social context taken for granted in that passage.

———. *Judaism in Society: The Evidence of the Yerushalmi. Toward the Natural History of a Religion.* [*Chicago Studies in the History of Judaism*] Univ. of Chicago Pr. 1984 lib. bdg. $25.00. An account of the social and historical context presupposed by the literary traits of the Talmud of the Land of Israel.

———. *Judaism: The Classical Statement, the Evidence of the Bavli.* Univ. of Chicago Pr. 1986 $37.00. Explains the relationship of the Talmud of Babylonia to all of the prior documents of the Judaism of the dual Torah and shows why that particular book turned out to be authoritative.

———, ed. *Our Sages, God and Israel: An Anthology of the Jerusalem Talmud.* Rossel Bks. 1985 $19.95. An anthology, with special attention to issues drawn from religion, of the foregoing.

———, trans. *The Talmud of Babylonia: An American Translation.* [*Brown Judaic Studies.*] Scholars Pr. GA 1985 $29.95 pap. $23.00. This new American translation emphasizes analytical traits, which permits us to read the document as any modern writing is read, in paragraphs, with clear indications of the continuities and breaks in thought and argument.

———. *The Talmud of the Land of Israel: A Preliminary Translation and Explanation.*

Univ. of Chicago Pr. 35 vols. 1982–84 various prices. The only translation of the first of the two Talmuds, about A.D. 400.

———. *The Talmud of the Land of Israel: A Preliminary Translation and Explanation. Vol. 35: Introduction, Taxonomy.* Univ. of Chicago Pr. 1984 $19.00. An introduction to the internal evidence for the literary and formal character of the Talmud of the Land of Israel, explaining how that document takes up a position separate from prior writings.

Steinsaltz, Adin. *The Essential Talmud.* Basic Bks. 1982 pap. $8.95. An uncritical account of Babylonian Talmudic values and ideals, viewed as part of an ongoing tradition continuous with present-day Orthodox Judaism.

MATERIAL EVIDENCE: ART AND ARCHAEOLOGY

Art and archaeology frequently provide a very different perspective on the world of late antiquity than do written sources. Literary evidence often represents the idealistic views of the intellectual and religious elite who had the capacity and desire to express themselves through the written word. Such material often presents a harmonious and homogeneous picture of a religious system. In reality, however, religious practices and beliefs vary even within a small community of coreligionists. The visual evidence of wall paintings, mosaics, and decorative arts focuses on a different range of symbols from those we find in the extant literature. For example, the artwork on the wall of the synagogue at Dura-Europos (on the Euphrates in Babylonia) from the middle of the third century portrays Greco-Roman images banned in Rabbinic literature. Archaeology also provides information on the daily life, economy, and social structure of Jewish communities. In the upper Galilee, for example, archaeologists have recently unearthed some information that corroborates the view of Jewish life found in the Talmud (e.g., ritual baths and study houses) and some information that calls it into question (e.g., pig bones and burial tombs).

Brooten, Bernadette J. *Women Leaders in Ancient Synagogues: Inscriptional Evidence and Background Issues.* Scholars Pr. GA 1982 pap. $20.00. A fresh look at inscriptions from the first six centuries A.D. reveals that women took on a greater role in the synagogue than was previously thought.

Chiat, Marilyn. *Handbook of Synagogue Architecture.* [*Brown Judaic Studies.*] Scholars Pr. GA 1982 pap. $20.00. A compendium of information about ancient synagogues discovered throughout the Near East. Describes the layout, ornamentation, inscriptions, and coins found at each site.

Goldman, Bernard. *The Sacred Portal: A Primary Symbol in Ancient Judaic Art.* [*Brown Class. in Judaica Ser.*] Univ. Pr. of Amer. repr. of 1966 ed. 1986 text ed. pap. $15.75. An interpretation, in the tradition of Goodenough, of an important piece of ancient Judaic art.

Goodenough, Erwin R. *Jewish Symbols Abridged.* Ed. by Jacob Neusner, Princeton Univ. Pr. 1988 $29.50. An abridgment of the next title.

———. *Jewish Symbols in the Greco-Roman Period.* [*Bollingen Ser.*] Princeton Univ. Pr. 13 vols 1953–69 o.p. The classic work on the interpretation of the art of Judaism, revealed in archaeology in particular. Demonstrates the confluence of Hellenistic and Jewish images and ideas. Richly illustrated and well written, for a wide audience.

Gutmann, Joseph. *Beauty in Holiness: Studies in Jewish Ceremonial Art and Customs.* Ktav 1970 $50.00. The foremost contemporary scholar of art in Judaism presents some of his major conclusions.

————, ed. *Ancient Synagogues: The State of Research*. Scholars Pr. GA 1981 pap. $14.00. A collection of clearly written articles on the symbolism, architecture, and function of ancient synagogues.

————. *The Synagogue: Studies in Origins, Archaeology, and Architecture*. Ktav 1974 $35.00. Reproduction of scholarly articles on the material and literary evidence of ancient synagogues.

Kraeling, Carl H. *The Synagogue*. Ktav rev. ed. 1979 $100.00. A report on the art and architecture of the synagogue excavated at Dura-Europos, Mesopotamia (present-day Syria), the most important synagogue find in modern times; one wall was completely intact, and covered with representational art. Kraeling's original report is reprinted with the illustrations.

Levine, L. I. *Ancient Synagogues Revealed*. Wayne State Univ. Pr. 1982 o.p. A survey of known discoveries, conveniently summarized, with essays by noted scholars.

Yadin, Yigael. *Massada: Herod's Last Fortress and the Zealot's Last Stand*. Random 1966 $25.00. Yadin tells the story of the Zealots' last stand and collective suicide of 73 C.E. in the war against Rome. He vividly describes the process of excavation and the archaeological finds, which are also presented in pictures.

Religious Movements

FIRST-CENTURY SECTS

No single orthodoxy in the early centuries A.D. characterized all the Jews all over the world. Those in Egypt spoke Greek; those in the Land of Israel, Greek and Aramaic and, possibly, Hebrew as well; those in Babylonia one kind of Aramaic, those in the Land of Israel, a different kind. Furthermore, the Greek-speaking Jews, represented by Philo of Alexandria, read Scripture within the categories of the Greek-speaking world, while those who spoke Hebrew produced a different reading altogether. Still, among the common theology of the Jews in late antiquity we should point to important—indeed definitive—components, such as Scripture, read in diverse ways, to be sure; reverence for the Temple and its sacrificial system—more important to those nearby, less so for those at a distance; and above all identification within a common social entity, "Israel." That identification bore so many differing elements among diverse groups, however, that to seek a single orthodox "Judaism" produces frustration. Harmonizing all the different viewpoints into a single orthodoxy distorts the evidence and yields only misinterpretation, out of all context. Against the background of a common culture prevailing in one place, namely, the Land of Israel, however, a number of small groups, each with its own special points of emphasis and interest, may be described. These are called sects.

GENERAL

Kraft, Robert A., and George W. E. Nickelsburg. *Early Judaism and Its Modern Interpreters*. Scholars Pr. GA 1986 $24.95 pap. $19.50. A systematic and thorough presentation of recent scholarship on the Judaisms of the period from 500 B.C. to A.D. 70. Reliable and judicious.

Neusner, Jacob. *Judaism in the Beginning of Christianity*. Fortress 1984 pap. $5.95. A brief and popular account of what is known about first-century Judaism in the Land of Israel.

Nickelsburg, George W. E., and Michael E. Stone. *Faith and Piety in Early Judaism: Texts and Documents*. Fortress 1983 $19.95. An excellent collection of sources in translation, introduced and properly presented.

Simon, Marcal. *Jewish Sects at the Time of Jesus*. Trans. by James H. Farley, Fortress

1980 o.p. A good summary of what is known about the sects mentioned in the New Testament and in the writings of Josephus.

Stone, Michael E. *Scripture, Sects and Visions: A Profile of Judaism from Ezra to the Jewish Revolts.* Fortress 1980 $11.95. A collection of essays, not sustained or systematic but interesting in spots.

PHARISEES

The Pharisees, well known because of their prominent position in the Gospels of Matthew, Mark, and Luke, are described in two further bodies of sources: the writings of Josephus and the Rabbinic literature of the second and later centuries. The writings of Josephus, first in order of composition, identify the Pharisees as a political party in the time of the Hasmonean rulers of the first century B.C., and also as a philosophical group with certain distinctive ideas concerning, for example, free will, the life of the soul after death, and so forth. Next in line, the Gospels represent the Pharisees in part as a political group, in part as people who kept certain aspects of the law with special care. These aspects of the law cover three main matters: Sabbath observance, purity laws, and tithing of foods. Purity laws applied in the Temple and protected the cult and the priesthood and offering from those sources of contamination specified in the books of Leviticus and Numbers. Pharisees—so the Gospels portray them—kept those same laws at home. They therefore sought to live a holy way of life even outside the Temple and to identify with the cult and the priesthood the table of the family at home. Tithing laws affect the disposition of crops and the preparation of food—hence were also a kind of dietary rule. The later Rabbinic writings include many sayings assigned to authorities before 70 B.C., and some of those authorities are identified by Josephus or New Testament writers with Pharisees. These sayings assigned to pre-70 figures who may have been Pharisees deal with the same issues as are prominent in the Gospels' accounts of the matter.

Baeck, Leo. *Pharisaism in the Making: Selected Essays.* Ktav 1972 o.p. The issues are theological, not historical. An apologetic work, reacting to the Christian prejudices against the Pharisees.

——. *The Pharisees.* Schocken 1947 o.p. A theological work, in which the historical Pharisees are not the center of interest.

Büchler, Adolph. *Studies in Sin and Atonement.* [*Lib. of Biblical Studies Ser.*] Ktav 1967 o.p. Büchler's theological studies rest on the premise that whatever is assigned to a given authority was really said by that authority, and whatever anyone said, without regard to that person's dates, represents opinion held in the first century. The studies therefore comprise a collection on a common theme.

Finkelstein, Louis. *The Pharisees: The Social Background of Their Faith.* Jewish Pubns. 2 vols. 3d ed. 1962 o.p. A socioeconomic interpretation of the Pharisees as plebeians, against upper-class Sadducees; very popular in its day, long since rendered a mere curiosity.

Neusner, Jacob. *From Politics to Piety: The Emergence of Pharisaic Judaism.* Ktav 1978 pap. $9.95. A summary of the distinct sources that refer to the Pharisees and an analysis of the viewpoint of each.

ESSENES

The Essenes, another small group or sect, are known from references among ancient writers, in particular Josephus, and also from the Dead Sea library found at Qumran. Josephus portrays them within the same pattern as applies to the Pharisees, but the Dead Sea Scrolls present a much more elaborate and detailed picture.

In that picture the Essenes bear affinities to the Pharisees, in their interest in sanctification in general and the holy meal in particular, and also to the Christians, in
their concern for salvation overall, and the meaning of history and the end of time.
Later on, in the writings of Rabbinic Judaism of the fourth through seventh centuries, these same concerns for sanctification now, attained through living a holy war
of life, and salvation at the end of time, would come to a fresh statement. The
structure, however, remained constant.

Ringgren, H. *The Faith of Qumran*. Fortress 1963 o.p. A systematic account of the
    religious viewpoint of the Judaism of Qumran.
Roth, Cecil. *The Historical Background of the Dead Sea Scrolls*. Blackwell 1958 o.p. A
    rather idiosyncratic effort to identify the opaque references of some of the Dead
    Sea documents with various known persons and events. Never gained much
    scholarly credence.
Vermes, Geza. *The Dead Sea Scrolls in English: Qumran in Perspective*. Fortress repr.
    of 1978 ed. 1981 pap. $8.95; Penguin 1962 pap. $4.95. The classic survey of the
    first 25 years of research; the starting point for all work.

SADDUCEES

What is known about the Sadducees comes from the Gospels' references, on the
one side, and statements in Josephus's writings, on the other. No writings deriving
from Sadducees come down from ancient times, with the result that knowledge of
the group and its place in the larger Judaic world is slight. Josephus represents the
group within his established pattern, a political party of philosophical opinion, and
the Gospels' references conform also to their larger scheme, presenting an organized
group, with some political influence, opposed to Jesus. For information on the Sadducees, see Religious Movements: First-Century Sects, General.

EARLY CHRISTIANS

A sizable and important literature treats Christianity within the Judaic context in
which it came to original expression. Since all of the earliest Christians were Jews
and saw their community as an "Israel," the prevailing approach is sensible. Quite
what it means to see Christianity as a Judaism, however, is not entirely worked out
as yet. The important continuities between the earliest Christian writings and the
Hebrew Scriptures or Old Testament, registered forcefully by the First Gospel, for
example, form an important starting point. Vast tracts of the Gospels cannot be
grasped without a detailed knowledge of Judaic belief and behavior, and, we also
stress, the Gospels form the principal source (along with Josephus) for our understanding of Jews' worldviews and ways of life in the Land of Israel in the first
century.

Barrett, C. K. *The Gospel of John and Judaism*. Trans. by D. M. Smith, Fortress 1975
    $3.95. A fine example of how knowledge derived from various Judaic documents
    facilitates the understanding of a Gospel.
———, ed. *New Testament Background: Selected Documents*. Harper 1961 pap. $6.95.
    Among the documents are samples of Judaic writings.
Bultmann, Rudolf. *Primitive Christianity: In Its Contemporary Setting*. Trans. by Regi-
    nald H. Fuller, Fortress repr. of 1956 ed. 1980 pap. $8.95. Surveys the various
    groups that comprise Judaism. This account of Judaism is ignorant and bigoted.
    A bad work by a good scholar.

Davies, W. D. *Jewish and Pauline Studies*. Fortress 1983 text ed. $29.95. Studies by Davies extending the method and findings of the work listed below.

———. *Paul and Rabbinic Judaism: Some Rabbinic Elements in Pauline Theology*. Fortress 1983 text ed. $29.95. The best account of how knowledge of Judaic sources leads us to a deeper understanding of Paul.

Kee, Howard C. *Christian Origins in Sociological Perspective: Methods and Resources*. Westminster 1980 pap. $9.95. Includes substantial and highly competent treatment of the Judaic setting, in society, of earliest Christianity.

———. *The Origins of Christianity: Sources and Documents*. Prentice-Hall 1973 o.p. A valued reader for the topic, including good treatment of Judaism.

Sanders, E. P. *Jesus and Judaism*. Fortress 1985 $19.95. The best account of the relationship of certain sayings and actions of Jesus to the Judaism of the time and place.

———. *Paul and Palestinian Judaism: A Comparison of Patterns of Religion*. Fortress 1977 $32.95 pap. $19.95. Places Paul in the context of the Dead Sea Judaism and the Judaism represented by later Judaic writings of rabbis and pursues a systematic theology to prove that the Judaism of the day focused on convenantal nomism.

Stendahl, Krister. *Paul among Jews and Gentiles*. Fortress 1976 o.p. Argues that Paul's primary concern was the relationship between Jews and gentiles, and that his idea of justification by faith can be understood only as a reflection of this concern.

Theissen, Gerd. *The Social Setting of Pauline Christianity: Essays on Corinth*. Trans. by John H. Schutz, Fortress 1982 $19.95. Includes much about Judaism, but the sources are used uncritically and the author knows very little about the problems of studying ancient Judaism or about the sociology of the Jewish world.

———. *The Sociology of Early Palestinian Christianity*. Trans. by John Bowden, Fortress 1978 pap. $5.95. The same criticism applies to this work as to the previous entry.

Vermes, Geza. *Jesus and the World of Judaism*. Fortress 1984 pap. $10.95. Collection of essays on Jesus in the Jewish cultural milieu, with emphasis on the evidence from the Dead Sea Scrolls.

———. *Jesus the Jew: A Historian's Reading of the Gospels*. Collins 1977 pap. $4.95; Fortress repr. of 1973 ed. 1981 pap. $9.95; Macmillan 1974 $6.95. A rather private vision of Jesus, in which a highly selective view of what he really did and said produces the picture of a Galilean pietist.

SAMARITANS

After the reigns of David and Solomon, the ancient people of Israel split in two—the northern kingdom comprising ten tribes in Samaria and the southern kingdom comprising two tribes in Judea. In 722 B.C.E., the Assyrians conquered the north and forced the deportation of the ten tribes (the famous ten lost tribes of Israel). The leadership of the Judeans, centered in Jerusalem, subsequently warned against contact with the Israelites from Samaria, arguing that the Samaritans had intermarried with non-Israelites and had forgotten the Torah. The Samaritans continued to live as a distinct group in the Land of Israel, parallel to and part of the Jewish people. Unlike the Jews, who ceased conducting sacrifices after the destruction of the Temple in Jerusalem, the Samaritans continued cultic practices at their temple at Mount Gezirim. Another difference is that the Samaritans know of no oral Torah

to supplement their Scriptures, which are almost identical to the Jewish Pentateuch. A small community of Samaritans remains today in the State of Israel.

Bowman, John. *The Samaritan Problem: Studies in the Relationship of Samaritanism,
Judaism, and Early Christianity.* Trans. by Alfred M. Johnson, Jr. [*Pittsburgh
Theological Monographs*] Pickwick 1975 pap. $8.75. Study of the Samaritans in
antiquity and their relationship to the New Testament Gospels and the Dead
Sea Scrolls.

——, ed. and trans. *Samaritan Documents: Relating to Their History, Religion and
Life.* [*Pittsburgh Original Texts and Translations Ser.*] Pickwick 1977 pap. $11.50.
The standard anthology of extant Samaritan writings.

Coggins, R. J. *Samaritans and Jews: The Origins of Samaritanism Reconsidered.* John
Knox 1975 o.p. Argues that the relations of Samaritans and Jews prior to the
Christian era were closer and more complex than previously believed.

Gaster, Moses. *The Samaritans: History, Doctrines and Literature.* Gordon Pr. 1976
lib. bdg. $134.95; Kraus Repr. 1923 pap. $28.00. This work remains a good
general survey.

Purvis, James D. *The Samaritan Pentateuch and the Origin of the Samaritan Sect.* Harvard Univ. Pr. 1968 o.p. The classic introduction to the origin of the Samaritans.

Wright, G. E. *Shechem: Biography of a Biblical City.* McGraw-Hill 1965 o.p. Follows
the development of Shechem and its central place in early Samaritan history.

RABBINIC JUDAISM

Rabbinic Judaism is that Judaism which maintains the story of the dual Torah.
Specifically, when Moses ascended to Mount Sinai to receive the Torah, it came to
him in two media, writing and memory. The written Torah comprises the Five
Books of Moses or Pentateuch, that is, Genesis, Exodus, Leviticus, Numbers, and
Deuteronomy. The oral Torah consisted of sayings or "traditions" handed on not in
writing but through oral formulation and oral transmission—hence, memory. This
oral, or memorized, Torah then came to be written down in diverse documents
produced by sages, or rabbis, in late antiquity.

To spell these matters out in some detail: The writings produced by sages, or
rabbis, of late antiquity in the Land of Israel ("Palestine") and Babylonia fall into
two groups, each with its own plan and program; one produced in the second and
third centuries, the second in the fourth and fifth. The first of these groups of
writings begins with the Mishnah, a philosophical law book brought to closure A.D.
200, and later called the first statement of the oral Torah. In its wake, the Mishnah
drew tractate Abot, c.A.D. 250, a statement concluded a generation after the Mishnah
on the standing of the authorities of the Mishnah; Tosefta, c.A.D. 300, a compilation
of supplements of various kinds to the Mishnah; and three systematic exegeses of
books of Scripture or the written Torah, Sifre to Leviticus, Sifre to Numbers, and
Sifre to Deuteronomy, of indeterminate date but possibly concluded by A.D. 300.
Overall these books form one stage in the unfolding of the Judaism of the dual
Torah, a stage that stressed issues of sanctification of the life of Israel, the people, in
the aftermath of the destruction of the Temple of Jerusalem in A.D. 70, in which, it
was commonly held, Israel's sanctification came to full realization in the bloody
rites of sacrifice to God on high. We call this system a Judaism without Christianity,
because the issues found urgent in the documents representative of this phase address questions not pertinent to the Christian challenge of Israel.

The second set of these writings begins with the Talmud of the Land of Israel, or
Yerushalmi, generally supposed to have come to a conclusion around A.D. 400; Genesis Rabbah, assigned to about the next half century; Leviticus Rabbah, c.A.D. 450;

Pesiqta deRab Kahana, c.a.d. 450–500; and, finally, the Talmud of Babylonia or Bavli, assigned to the late sixth or early seventh century, c.a.d. 600. The two Talmuds systematically interpret passages of the Mishnah, and the other documents, as is clear, do the same for books of the written Torah. Some other treatments of biblical books important in synagogue liturgy, particularly the Five Scrolls, e.g., Lamentations Rabbati, Esther Rabbah, and the like, are supposed also to have reached closure at this time. This second set of writings introduces, alongside the paramount issue of Israel's sanctification, the matter of Israel's salvation, with doctrines of history and the Messiah given prominence in the larger systemic statement.

The first of the two stages in the formation of the Judaism of the dual Torah exhibits no sign of interest in, or response to, the advent of Christianity. The second, from the Yerushalmi forward, lays points of stress and emphasis that, in retrospect, appear to respond to and to counter the challenge of Christianity. The point of difference, of course, is that from the beginning of the legalization of Christianity in the early fourth century to the establishment of Christianity at the end of that same century, Jews in the Land of Israel found themselves facing a challenge that, prior to Constantine, they had found no compelling reason to consider. The specific crisis came when the Christians pointed to the success of the church in the politics of the Roman state as evidence that Jesus Christ was king of the world, and that his claim to be Messiah and King of Israel had now found vindication. When the Emperor Julian, 361–363, apostasized and renewed state patronage of paganism, he permitted the Jews to begin to rebuild the Temple, part of his large plan of humiliating Christianity. His prompt death on an Iranian battlefield supplied further evidence for heaven's choice of the church and the truth of the church's allegations concerning the standing and authority of Jesus as the Christ. The Judaic documents that reached closure in the century after these events attended to those questions of salvation—for example, the doctrine of history and of the Messiah, the authority of the sages' reading of Scripture as against the Christians' interpretation, and the like—that had earlier not enjoyed extensive consideration. In all, this second Judaism, which the author characterizes as a Judaism despite Christianity, met the challenge of the events of the fourth century. The Judaic system of the dual Torah, expressed in its main outlines in the Yerushalmi and associated compilations of biblical exegeses concerning Genesis, Leviticus, and some other scriptural books, culminated in the Bavli, which emerged as the authoritative document of the Judaism of the dual Torah from then to now.

Adler, Morris. *The World of the Talmud.* Schocken 2d ed. 1963 pap. $4.95. A very brief and popular description of Talmudic beliefs, readable and attractive.

Bamberger, Bernard. *Proselytism in the Talmudic Period.* Hebrew Union College Pr. 1939 o.p. A survey of references in Talmudic literature to conversion to Judaism.

Bonsirven, Joseph. *Palestinian Judaism in the Time of Jesus Christ.* Holt 1964 o.p. Originally published in French (1934–35). This is a counterpart, by a French Jesuit, to Moore's picture of the Judaism of the Land of Israel in the first centuries B.C. and A.D. It is informed and thoughtful.

Cohen, Abraham. *Everyman's Talmud.* Schocken 1975 pap. $11.25. An early effort at presenting a topical anthology of Talmudic literature. Still useful, although not so accessible as *A Rabbinic Anthology*, by Montefiore and Loewe, listed above under Rabbinic Literature.

Finkelstein, Louis. *Akiba: Scholar, Saint and Martyr.* Atheneum 1970 text ed. pap. $6.95; Jewish Pubns. 1962 pap. $6.95. An imaginative semifictional biography, paraphrasing and amplifying stories in the Talmudic literature about the most important rabbi of the founding generation of Judaism.

Ginzberg, Louis. *Students, Scholars, and Saints.* 1928. Univ. Pr. of Amer. 1985 text ed. pap. $12.75. Classic and masterful essays on fundamental topics in the biography of important Judaic sages.

Glatzer, Nahum N. *Hillel the Elder: The Emergence of Classical Judaism.* B'nai B'rith 1959 o.p. A brief retelling of Talmudic tales about Hillel in the form of a semifictional biography.

Kadushin, Max. *Worship and Ethics: A Study in Rabbinic Judaism.* Bloch 1975 pap. $8.95. A brilliant and systematic effort to show the value system implicit in the liturgy of Judaism; the most successful study on its subject ever written.

Landman, Leo, ed. *Messianism in the Talmudic Era.* Ktav 1979 $59.50. A survey of writings on the topic of the Messiah.

Marmorstein, Arthur. *Doctrine of Merits in Old Rabbinical Literature.* Ktav 1969 o.p. A collection of sayings and stories relevant to the doctrine that the merits of one's ancestors serve as a treasury of virtue against which one can draw, for example, for forgiveness in time of suffering.

———. *The Old Rabbinic Doctrine of God.* 1927–37. Gregg repr. of 1937 ed. text ed. $74.52. A collection of sayings and stories on the conception of God in various Rabbinic writings, topically organized.

Moore, George Foot. *Judaism in the First Centuries of the Christian Era.* Harvard Univ. Pr. 1954 o.p. The classic work of historical theology on Judaism in late antiquity, organized in accord with the categories of Protestant theology. While not historical in any sense, it is a sound composition of diverse sayings forming a coherent picture.

Neusner, Jacob. *The Foundations of Judaism.* Fortress 3 vols. 1983–85 ea. pap. $6.00. An account of the historical development of the exegesis of Scripture in Rabbinic Judaism called Midrash, the concept of the Messiah and the doctrine of history, and the symbol of the Torah and the doctrine of the dual Torah.

———. *From Testament to Torah: An Introduction to Judaism in Its Formative Age.* Prentice-Hall 1987 $14.67. A summary of the author's general theory of the formation of Judaism in late antiquity, for college students.

———. *Judaism and Christianity in the Age of Constantine: Issues of the Initial Confrontation.* Univ. of Chicago Pr. 1987 $29.95. A general theory of the formative history of Judaism.

———. *Judaism and Story: The Evidence of the Fathers According to Rabbi Nathan.* Univ. of Chicago Pr. 1988 consult publisher for information. An account of how the story began to serve as a medium for conveying important values of formative Judaism.

———. *Judaism in the Matrix of Christianity.* Fortress 1986 pap. $12.95. A series of essays that collectively point to the fourth century as the point at which the indicator traits of the Judaism of the dual Torah first reached literary expression.

———. *Torah from Our Sages: Pirke Avot.* Rossel Bks. 1986 $18.95 pap. $9.95. A popular commentary and theological exercise, attached to the definitive document, Mishnah tractate "The Fathers."

———. *Vanquished Nation, Broken Spirit: The Virtues of the Heart in Formative Judaism.* Cambridge Univ. Pr. 1987 $24.95. A systematic account of the doctrine of emotions and right attitudes laid forth in formative Judaism.

———, ed. *Judaisms and Their Messiahs in the Beginning of Christianity.* Cambridge Univ. Pr. 1987 consult publisher for information. A dozen scholars discuss the role of the Messiah in various Judaic systems in antiquity, including Christianity.

Schechter, Solomon. *Some Aspects of Rabbinic Theology.* Behrman 1936 o.p. A classic and elegant essay on basic theological beliefs of the Judaism of the dual Torah; best of its genre.

Schiffman, Lawrence H. *Who Was Jew: Rabbinic and Halakhic Perspectives on the Jewish-Christian Schism.* Ktav 1985 $14.95 pap. $8.95. Discusses Jewish self-definition during the early years of Christianity. Uncritically assumes that documents from the third to seventh centuries accurately report the situation in the first century.

Spiegel, Shalom. *The Last Trial: On the Legend and Lore of the Command to Abraham to Offer Isaac as a Sacrifice—The Akedah.* [*Jewish Legacy Ser.*] Behrman 1979 pap. $7.95. An account of how Judaism read and interpreted the story of the binding of Isaac.

Steinberg, Milton. *As a Driven Leaf.* Behrman 1939 o.p. Historical fiction, based on Talmudic literature, about Rabbi Elisha ben Abuyah and his search for faith. A wonderful way to learn about the world of the sages.

MEDIEVAL JUDAISM

History of the Jews

The beginning of medieval history for Jews in Christendom is marked by the recognition, in the fourth century, that Christianity was the religion of the state. Henceforth, the West became Christian, and the conditions in which Jews would work out their histories were defined. In the case of the territories conquered in the seventh and later centuries by Muslim armies, medieval history begins with the rise of Islam. For Jews medieval history in the Christian West ended with the secularization of politics, beginning first with the U.S. Constitution in 1787 and the French Revolution in 1789. From the fourth to the nineteenth centuries, no important political changes essentially reshaped the conditions of the histories of Jews. For Jews in the Muslim world, the turning point came in 1948, with the creation of the State of Israel. Until that time whatever political changes took place in Muslim countries, the situation and position of the Jews remained essentially constant. Jews in various countries and regions, in Europe west and east, North Africa, and the Middle East, participated in the history of those areas. No single or linear path joins the discrete histories of various groups of Jews into a single unified history. Certain problems do, however, find a place in common among those histories. For example, Jews were minorities in both Muslim and Christian countries, although the rules for treating minorities differed from country to country, as well as from Christendom to Islam. Furthermore, Jews maintained contact with one another, forming one important means by which trade and culture were mediated between the two worlds of medieval times. Many important books trace the history of Jews in particular countries or regions, Spain and North Africa, for example, or France or England. Others survey matters of culture, as these proved uniform for Jews in Christian or in Muslim countries. Still others treat ideas that shaped peoples' thinking throughout the Jewish world, both Christian and Islamic.

GENERAL

Abrahams, Israel. *Jewish Life in the Middle Ages.* 1932. Atheneum 1969 text ed. pap. $7.95. Remains a good introduction to the social life of Jews in medieval Christendom. Discusses economics, home life, slave trade, social mores, synagogue activities, and much more.

Blumenthal, David R. *Approaches to Judaism in Medieval Times.* Scholars Pr. GA 2 vols. 1978–85 vol. 1 pap. $14.95 vol. 2 pap. $18.95. Essays on medieval Jewish literature, philosophy, and religion.

Chazan, Robert, ed. *Medieval Jewish Life: Studies from the Proceedings of the American Academy for Jewish Research.* Ktav 1974 o.p. Eclectic collection of essays by noted scholars on political, social, and intellectual history.

Finkelstein, Louis. *Jewish Self-Government in the Middle Ages.* Jewish Sem. 1924 o.p. The classic study of medieval Jewish political institutions.

Lazar, Moshe. *The Sephardic Tradition: Ladino and Spanish-Jewish Literature.* Norton 1972 o.p. An excellent complement to the Marcus volume, this anthology presents English translations of Spanish and Ladino (a Spanish dialect written with Hebrew characters) literature from Jewish communities in Muslim and Christian countries of the fifteenth to nineteenth centuries.

Marcus, Jacob R., ed. *The Jew in the Medieval World: A Source Book, 315–1791.* Atheneum 1969 text ed. pap. $10.95; Greenwood repr. of 1938 ed. 1975 lib. bdg. $22.50. Extensive collection of documents from late antiquity to the early modern period, on the social, political, and religious history of the Jews in Islamic and Christian countries. Portrays the attitude of the non-Jewish world toward the Jews and the internal developments within the Jewish community itself.

JEWS IN CHRISTIAN LANDS

The Latin Christian West began in Italy, Spain, and France, and only gradually made its way into Germany, Poland, and southeastern Europe, meeting the Greek-speaking Christian East as it came north and west from Byzantium into the Ukraine and Russia, Greece and Bulgaria, and what is now Yugoslavia. The two great Christian civilizations encompassed large Jewish populations. The histories of Jews in those Christian kingdoms and empires varied. From the Crusades onward, the Western Latin kingdoms—Spain, France, Germany, and England—became less and less tenable for Jewish life. The advances toward the east, particularly in Poland, Lithuania, and White Russia, by contrast, opened new territories for Jewish settlement, and the (relative) toleration accorded by the Polish and Lithuanian monarchies attracted Jews driven out of England, France, and Germany from the twelfth century onward.

Baer, Yitzhak. *History of the Jews in Christian Spain.* Jewish Pubns. 2 vols. 1966 pap. ea. $6.95. In-depth study of Spanish Jewry from the Christian reconquest of the Iberian peninsula to the expulsion and forced conversion of the Jews. Includes extensive quotations of primary sources.

Berger, David, trans. and ed. *The Jewish-Christian Debate in the High Middle Ages.* Jewish Pubns. 1978 o.p. Translation (with the original Hebrew) of an anonymous Jewish polemic against Christianity.

Bowman, Steven B. *The Jews of Byzantium, 1204–1453.* [*Judaic Studies Ser.*] Univ. of Alabama Pr. 1985 $42.50. Detailed studies of the internal structure of the medieval Jewish community in Asia Minor and its relationship to other Jewish communities.

Chazan, Robert. *Medieval Jewry in Northern France: A Political and Social History.*

Johns Hopkins Univ. Pr. 1973 o.p. The standard work on the political and social history of medieval French Jewry.

————, ed. *Church, State and Jew in the Middle Ages.* [*Lib. of Jewish Studies*] Behrman 1979 text ed. pap. $9.95. Studies Jewish life from the eleventh to the thirteenth centuries, a time in which Jews became subject to new restrictions and special policies. Discusses how religious and political officials frequently condoned the persecution of the Jews, even when official church and state policy guaranteed protection to the Jewish community.

Cohen, Jeremy. *The Friars and the Jews: The Evolution of Medieval Anti-Judaism.* Cornell Univ. Pr. 1984 pap. $10.95. Careful analysis of church history and the complex role that Jews and Judaism played in medieval Christian theology. The first study of the attitudes of Dominican and Franciscan friars toward Judaism in the twelfth and thirteenth centuries.

Cutler, Allan H., and Helen E. Cutler. *The Jew as Ally of the Muslim: Medieval Roots of Anti-Semitism.* Univ. of Notre Dame Pr. 1985 text ed. $50.00. Well-documented study of how Christians portrayed Jews as an internal threat, allied with the powerful Muslim empire beyond the borders, from the eleventh to fourteenth centuries. This question of divided loyalties remains a source of present-day anti-Semitism.

Eidelberg, Shlomo, ed. and trans. *The Jews and the Crusaders: The Hebrew Chronicles of the First and Second Crusades.* Univ. of Wisconsin Pr. 1977 $23.50. Eyewitness accounts of the devastation inflicted by Christian zealots.

Glückel of Hameln. *The Memoirs of Glückel of Hameln.* Trans. by Marvin Lowenthal, intro. by Robert Rosen, Schocken 1977 pap. $7.95. Written by a seventeenth-century woman to inform her children about her personal, familial, and communal background. Excellent source on the world of seventeenth-century German Jewry.

Grayzel, Solomon. *The Church and the Jews in the Thirteenth Century: A Study of Their Relations during the Years 1198–1254 Based on the Papal Letters and the Conciliar Decrees of the Period.* Dropsie College 1933 o.p. Collection of more than 100 official documents of the Catholic Church from a century in which Jews took on new roles in European society as the social, political, and religious order shifted from feudal to more centralized organization.

Hanover, Nathan. *The Abyss of Despair.* Intro. by William B. Helmreich, Transaction Bks. 1983 pap. $14.95. Eyewitness accounts of the Chmielnicki Massacres of 1648 to 1652, which had a devastating effect on East European Jewry.

Katz, Jacob. *Exclusiveness and Tolerance: Studies in Jewish-Gentile Relations in Medieval and Modern Times.* Oxford 1961 o.p. Widely cited study of the position of Jews in European society during a period of radical change.

————. *Tradition and Crisis: Jewish Society at the End of the Middle Ages.* Free Pr. 1961 o.p. Excellent survey on European Jewry at the threshold of modernity. Discusses the organization of the Jewish community and cultural trends in eastern and central Europe from 1500 to 1800.

Maccoby, Hyam, ed. *Judaism on Trial: Jewish-Christian Disputations in the Middle Ages.* [*Littman Lib. of Jewish Civilization*] Oxford 1982 $34.00. The best account of the medieval "disputations," in which Judaic and Christian theologians would defend their own faith, respectively, and criticize the other. Tells the story in clear and accessible form.

Pollack, Herman. *Jewish Folkways in Germanic Lands (1648–1806): Studies in Aspects of Daily Life.* MIT 1971 o.p. A well-documented study of everyday life, with chapters on folk medicine, synagogue activity, rites of passage, and dietary habits. Includes illustrations.

Richardson, Henry G. *The English Jewry under Angevin Kings.* Greenwood repr. of 1960 ed. 1983 lib. bdg. $35.00. Details state policy toward the Jews and the actual circumstances of Jewish life in England until the expulsion of the Jews in 1290. Includes the 60 pages of original documents.

Richardson, Henry G., Diane K. Roskies, and David G. Roskies. *The Shtetl Book.* Ktav 1979 o.p. This book on small-town Jewish life in eastern Europe contains many photographs and personal accounts. In contrast to the Zborowski and Herzog volume (see below), the authors of this book state, "We were determined not to make do with generalizations and sentimentalism. Our book is about real places and people."

Roth, Cecil. *A History of the Jews in England.* Oxford 3d ed. 1979 $13.50. Continuous story from the earliest Jewish settlement in Roman times through the expulsion in 1290 and down to the readmission of the Jews in 1654 and their life in Britain to recent times.

——. *A History of the Jews in Venice.* Jewish Pubns. 1930 o.p. Classic study of the Jews of Venice, a small population of less than 5,000 souls that had an important impact on that city for centuries.

——. *A History of the Jews of Italy.* Jewish Pubns. 1946 o.p. The first history ever written on the Jews in Italy as a whole, this study covers the period from late antiquity to World War I.

——. *A History of the Marranos.* [*Modern Jewish Experience*] Ayer facsimile repr. of 1932 ed. 1975 $35.50; Schocken 1974 pap. $10.95. The classic scholarly treatment of the "Marranos" (probably derived from the word for "pig"), the Jews forced to hide their identity during the Spanish Inquisition.

——. *The Jews of the Renaissance.* Jewish Pubns. 1959 o.p. Traces the influence the Jews had on the Italian Renaissance in art, medicine, music, literature, ethics, and biblical studies.

Ruderman, David B. *The World of a Renaissance Jew: The Life and Thought of Abraham ben Mordecai Farissol.* Ktav 1981 $20.00. The intellectual biography of a prominent figure who lived in Renaissance Italy from 1452 to 1528. His life is placed in context of Jewish and general social, cultural, and religious trends.

Schoenfeld, Joachim. *Shtetl Memories: Jewish Life in Galicia under the Austro-Hungarian Empire and in the Reborn Poland, 1898–1938.* Ktav 1985 text ed. $17.50. Standard collection of first-person accounts.

Trachtenberg, Joshua. *The Devil and the Jews: The Medieval Conception of the Jew and Its Relation to Modern Anti-Semitism.* 1943. Jewish Pubns. 1983 pap. $6.95. This important book traces the development of the mythology of Jews as demons, sorcerers, and heretics, derived in part from a misconception of Jewish mysticism.

Twersky, Isadore, ed. *Studies in Medieval Jewish History and Literature.* [*Judaic Monographs*] Harvard Univ. Pr. 1979 text ed. $25.00; [*Judaic Monographs*] Harvard Univ. Center for Jewish Studies 1985 text ed. $25.00. Technical essays on Jewish religious life and literature.

Weinryb, Bernard. *The Jews of Poland: A Social and Economic History of the Jewish Community in Poland from 1100–1800.* Jewish Pubns. 2d ed. 1973 o.p. Traces the growth of the Polish Jewish population from a few individuals to over a million. In addition to the topics announced in the title, this book discusses religious trends, especially mysticism and Hasidism.

Yerushalmi, Yosef Hayim. *From Spanish Court to Italian Ghetto: Isaac Cardoso, A Study in Seventeenth-Century Marranism and Jewish Apologetics.* Univ. of Washington Pr. repr. of 1971 ed. 1981 pap. $12.50. In-depth biography of an individual who lived as a nominal Christian in Spain at a time when anti-Judaism forced Jews underground, then moved to Italy in 1648, becoming a prominent member and defender of the Jewish community.

Zborowski, Mark, and Elizabeth Herzog. *Life Is with People: The Culture of the Shtetl.* Intl. Univ. Pr. 1962 text ed. $45.00; intro. by Margaret Mead, Schocken 1962 pap. $8.95. Popular and sentimental account of the daily life and spirituality of small-town Jewish life in eastern Europe. Written in a style that captures the spirit of the Yiddish language.

JEWS IN MUSLIM LANDS

The Muslim conquest encompassed large Jewish populations in Babylonia (present-day Iraq), settled there from 586 B.C. The end of Iranian (Zoroastrian) rule was greeted with relief, since its final century had been marked by unstable government. The Muslim conquest of Syria, Palestine, and much of Asia Minor drove out the Roman (Christian) government, and, as the Muslim armies swept into Egypt, what is now Libya, Tunisia, Algeria, and Morocco, the old Roman colonies rapidly adopted Islam and gave up Christianity. The Jewish communities remained stable. Islam accorded to Jews the status of *dhimmi*, protected "people of the book"; Jews were tolerated and not required to accept Islam, although they were also treated as subordinate persons. The general policy of toleration was occasionally set aside here and there, but overall no sustained attacks, expulsions of entire populations, or vigorous persecution of Jews characterized Muslim rule.

Adler, Elkan N., ed. *Jewish Travellers in the Middle Ages: Nineteen Firsthand Accounts.* Dover repr. of 1930 ed. 1987 pap. $8.95. A good source of information about the everyday life of Jews throughout the medieval world.

Ashtor, Eliyahu. *The Jews of Moslem Spain.* Trans. by Jenny M. Klein, Jewish Pubns. 1985 $19.95. In-depth account of the prosperous Spanish Jewish community in its "Golden Age," from 711 until the Christian conquest of the Iberian peninsula. This social, political, religious, and cultural history makes extensive use of Jewish and Muslim sources.

Cohen, Amnon. *Jewish Life under Islam: Jerusalem in the Sixteenth Century.* Harvard Univ. Pr. 1984 text ed. $30.00. Well-documented, clearly written study of the Jews in Jerusalem, at the beginning of Ottoman rule, who were tolerated as a "protected people" under Islam.

Cohen, Mark R. *Jewish Self-Government in Medieval Egypt: The Origins of the Office of the Head of the Jews.* [*Princeton Studies on the Near East*] 1981 $41.00. A study of the establishment of centralized Jewish communal institutions in Egypt at a time of cultural and economic prosperity, based on the analysis of two hundred *geniza* documents. Although Jews could not participate fully in the political affairs of the Muslim state, they were granted a degree of autonomy over their own affairs.

Goitein, Shlomo Dov. *Jews and Arabs: Their Contacts through the Ages.* Schocken 3d ed. 1974 pap. $6.95. Excellent short introduction to the social and intellectual interaction of the two communities from before the advent of Islam through the thirteenth century. Examines the legal status, cultural milieu, and influence of the Jews in Arab lands.

———. *Letters of Medieval Jewish Traders.* Princeton Univ. Pr. 1974 o.p. A huge depository of literature (called a *geniza*) was discovered in a Cairo synagogue in the nineteenth century. Among the important finds were letters from traders that reveal details about the economic activity of Mediterranean Jews during the medieval period.

———. *A Mediterranean Society: The Jewish Communities of the Arab World as Por-*

trayed in the Documents of the Cairo Geniza. Univ. of California Pr. 5 vols. 1967–
85 ea. $42.00–$48.00. Vol. 1, *Economic Foundations;* Vol. 2, *Community;* Vol. 3,
Family; Vol. 4, *Daily Life;* Vol. 5, *The Individual.* Makes some of the voluminous
finds of the Cairo synagogue accessible to those interested in everyday Jewish
life during the medieval period. The final volume studies the conception of the
person, as reflected in the *geniza* documents, in the context of medieval thought
in general.

Mann, Jacob. *The Jews in Egypt and in Palestine under the Fatimid Caliphs, with
Preface and Reader's Guide by Shlomo Dov Goitein.* Ktav 1970 o.p. Analyzes the
Cairo synagogue *geniza* fragments to paint a picture of Jewish political and
communal life in Egypt and Palestine from 969 to 1204.

Stillman, Norman A. *The Jews of Arab Lands: A History and Source Book.* Jewish
Pubns. 1979 $10.95. An extensive collection of Jewish and Muslim documents,
from the origins of Islam until the nineteenth century, set in historical context.
A balanced treatment, displaying the mix of prosperity and persecution Jews
faced under Islamic rule.

Jewish Thought

In contrast to the wide diversity of Jewish movements and philosophies
that have existed in ancient and modern times, Judaism remained relatively uniform during the medieval period. Except for the major schism
with the Karaites (see under Religious Movements below), all Jewish movements and thinkers followed the Judaism of the dual Torah established in
late antiquity. Judaism, however, did not stand still. Jewish thinkers established new modes of thought—often in dialogue or disputation with their
Muslim and Christian counterparts—in legal codification, biblical commentary, philosophy, and mysticism. These categories frequently overlap, but
we shall treat them separately for the sake of convenience.

LEGAL CODIFICATION AND COMMENTARY

The compilation of the Babylonian Talmud marked the culmination of the development of the oral Torah. The medieval Jewish authorities who saw themselves as
the continuators of this tradition faced the task of adapting and interpreting this
body of literature to address new circumstances and problems. During the latter
part of the first millennium, Jews from throughout the world appealed to the
Goanim, legal experts in Babylonia, for advice in applying the laws of the Talmuds
to everyday life. This exchange of letters is called the Responsa Literature. The
codifications of Jewish law, compiled during the first centuries of the second millennium, represent the other major body of legal literature from the medieval period.
These codifications arranged laws according to topics in order to provide a convenient reference manual. The authoritarian code of religious law for Orthodox Jewry
was the product of Joseph Karo (c.1488–1574). Born in Toledo, Karo moved with his
family to Turkey after the 1492 expulsion of Jews from Spain. He eventually settled
in Safed, Palestine, where he wrote the Shulhan Arukh, the systematic compilation
of Jewish law—from Rabbinic sources and subsequent tradition—that remains cen-
trally important to this day.

When published in 1864, Solomon Ganzfried's abridgment of the Shulhan Arukh soon gained widespread acceptance among Orthodox Jews. It remains the only version translated into English that contains all parts of the code. (See Maimonides' main listing in this chapter.)

Abraham Ibn Daud. *Sefer ha-Qabbalah: The Book of Tradition.* Trans. by Gerson D. Cohen, Jewish Pubns. 1967 o.p. Written in 1161 to disprove the claims of the Karaites, this historical narrative attempts to establish the continuity of the Rabbinic legal tradition from the biblical period until the twelfth century.

Appel, Gersion. *The Concise Code of Jewish Law: Daily Prayers and Religious Observances in the Life-Cycle of the Jew.* Ktav 1977 $11.95. This abridgment of the Shulhan Arukh collects legal material relevant to present-day Orthodox practice, on such topics as prayer, dietary laws, and Torah study.

Birnbaum, Philip, trans. *Mishneh Torah: Maimonides' Code of Law and Ethics.* Hebrew Pub. 1974 $19.50 pap. $9.95. A readable translation of Maimonides' important code of Jewish law. This edition is greatly abridged.

Freehof, Solomon B. *The Responsa Literature and a Treasury of Responsa.* Jewish Pubns. 1963 o.p. Collection of the legal opinions written by Jewish authorities in response to queries from Jewish communities throughout the medieval and early modern world. Includes a brief introduction.

Ganzfried, Solomon. *Code of Jewish Law (Kitzur Shulhan Aruh).* 1864. Trans. by Hyam E. Goldin, Hebrew Pub. 1963 $17.50 pap. $11.95. Ganzfried's abridgment of the Shulhan Arukh soon gained widespread acceptance among Orthodox Jews. It remains the only version translated into English that contains all parts of the code.

Hurwitz, Simon. *The Responsa of Solomon Luria.* Bloch 2d ed. 1969 $10.00. The legal decisions by a sixteenth-century Talmudic authority in Poland. This anthology is in plain English but suffers from a lack of commentary and notation.

Jacobs, Louis. *A Tree of Life: Diversity, Flexibility and Creativity in Jewish Law.* Oxford 1984 $29.95. Argues that Jewish law grew organically during the medieval and modern periods in response to changing attitudes and needs. In the final chapter he proposes a "non-Fundamentalist" view of Jewish law.

Lampel, Zvi L., trans. *Maimonides: Introduction to the Talmud.* Judaica Pr. 1975 o.p. Translation of Maimonides' systematic commentary to the Talmud.

Twersky, Isadore. *Introduction to the Code of Maimonides (Mishneh Torah).* Yale Univ. Pr. 1980 $50.00 pap. $11.95. This impressive work of scholarship considers Maimonides' legal code from a variety of angles. Twersky analyzes the content and form of the *Mishneh Torah* and places it in the context of Jewish philosophic and legal history.

———. *Rabad of Posquieres: A Twelfth-Century Talmudist.* [*Semitic Ser.*] Harvard Univ. Pr. 1962 $22.50. Intellectual biography that places Abraham ben David (1125–98) into the context of the Jewish religious elite in southern France of the twelfth century. Focuses on his reaction to Maimonides' *Mishneh Torah,* with a short chapter on the emerging Cabala movement.

———. *Studies in Jewish Law and Philosophy.* Ktav 1982 $39.50. This collection of essays provides a good introduction to the scholarship of this authority on medieval Jewish law and philosophy, although some articles are quite technical and others are in Hebrew. The articles on the legal codes of Maimonides and Joseph Karo are excellent introductions to the topics.

Werblowsky, J. Z. *Joseph Karo: Lawyer and Mystic.* Oxford 1962 o.p. Study of Karo's diary, Maggid Mesharim, to show that the author of the standard code of Jewish law lived an ascetic and mystical life. Places Karo in the context of his contemporaries living in the Galilean city of Safed, the spiritual center of Jewish mysticism. This book sometimes assumes a knowledge of technical Hebrew terms.

BIBLICAL COMMENTARY

After the Rabbinic period, Jewish scholars continued to compile commentaries on the Hebrew Bible. These commentaries often took the form of line-by-line explanations of verses of Scripture. The medieval commentators frequently borrowed from, and elaborated on, the interpretations of the Bible found in Rabbinic Midrash. (See the main listings for Kimhi, Nahmanides, and Rashi in this chapter.)

Casper, Bernard. *Introduction to Jewish Bible Commentary*. Thomas Yoseloff 1960 o.p. An adequate introduction.

Jacobs, Louis. *Jewish Biblical Exegesis*. [*Chain of Tradition Ser.*] Behrman 1975 o.p. A good collection of primary sources, with clear explanations.

Saperstein, Marc. *Decoding the Rabbis: A Thirteenth-Century Commentary on the Aggadah*. [*Judaic Monographs*] Harvard Univ. Pr. 1980 text ed. $20.00. Reworking of a doctoral dissertation on Isaac ben Yedaiah, an author "ill-treated and forgotten." A readable and well-documented study of this biblical commentator and popularizer of philosophy to those who did not speak Arabic.

Smalley, Beryl. *The Study of the Bible in the Middle Ages*. Univ. of Notre Dame Pr. 1964 pap. $9.95. The best and most popular introduction to the mode of Jewish biblical commentary developed in northern and western Europe through 1300.

PHILOSOPHY

Medieval Jewish intellectuals learned about classical Greek philosophy, especially neo-Aristotelianism, from their Muslim counterparts. Jewish philosophers presented rational arguments proving the existence of God and the reasonableness of Jewish law. The controversies with the Karaites, who did not accept the authority of the oral Torah, provoked the so-called Rabbanites to vigorously defend the legitimacy of the Rabbinic tradition. In many ways, BARUCH SPINOZA's philosophy marks the transition from the medieval to the modern world. His ideas provoked a strong reaction during his day, but have since become commonplace. He questioned whether Moses actually wrote the Pentateuch and whether the Genesis story of creation is historically accurate. He argued that rationally derived natural law should take precedence over the received Torah. (See the main listings for Gersonides, Judah Ha-Levi, Maimonides, Nahmanides, and Saadia in this chapter and that for Spinoza in Chapter 5 in this volume.)

Abraham Ibn Daud. *The Exalted Faith*. Fairleigh Dickinson Univ. Pr. 1986 $75.00. This twelfth-century work by the first Jewish Aristotelian philosopher deals with scientific disciplines and pure philosophy.

Abrahams, Israel, ed. *Hebrew Ethical Wills*. Fwd. by Judah Goldin [*Lib. of Jewish Class.*] Jewish Pubns. 1976 pap. $10.95. In Jewish tradition, wills sometimes provided moral guidance to survivors rather than bequeathing property. Here is an anthology of such wills, especially from the medieval period.

Altmann, Alexander, and others, eds. *Three Jewish Philosophers*. Jewish Pubns. 1960 o.p. Introduction and selections of writings from Philo, Saadia Gaon, and Judah Ha-Levi.

Bleich, J. David. *With Perfect Faith: The Foundations of Jewish Belief*. Ktav 1983 $25.00 pap. $14.95. Collection of over 600 pages of writings by medieval Jewish philosophers, arranged according to Maimonides' 13 principles of faith.

Cooperman, Bernard, ed. *Jewish Thought in the Sixteenth Century*. Harvard Univ. Pr. 1983 text ed. $30.00 pap. $14.95. Collection of academic essays.

Glatzer, Nahum N., ed. *Faith and Knowledge: The Jew in the Medieval World.* Beacon Pr. 1963 o.p. Collection of sources by medieval religious authorities.

Husik, Isaac. *A History of Mediaeval Jewish Philosophy.* Jewish Pubns. 1948 o.p. The best introduction to medieval Jewish thought. Gives a synopsis of the thought of each major figure, placed in the context of medieval Arabic and classic Greek philosophy.

Jacob, Louis. *Jewish Ethics, Philosophy and Mysticism.* Behrman 1969 pap. $5.95. Short anthology of medieval Jewish thought, in three parts, according to the title.

——. *Theology in the Responsa.* Oxford 1975 $35.00. Analyzes the theological underpinnings of the legal opinions of rabbis from the medieval and modern periods. Arranged by century and by author.

Kane, Israel. *In Quest of the Truth: A Survey of Medieval Jewish Thought.* Vintage 1985 $8.95. A brief and uncritical introduction to some of the main thinkers and issues of medieval philosophy.

Lasker, Daniel J. *Jewish Philosophic Polemics against Christianity in the Middle Ages.* Ktav 1977 $25.00. Surveys the various modes of argumentation used to criticize Christianity.

Septimus, Bernard. *Hispano-Jewish Culture in Transition: The Career and Controversies of Raman.* Harvard Univ. Pr. 1982 text ed. $20.00. Study of the thought of Meir ha-Levi Abulafia (c.1165–1244) who lived in Toledo during the transition from Arab to Christian rule. Places him in the context of antirationalism and the controversies provoked by Maimonides' philosophy.

Sirat, Colette. *A History of Jewish Philosophy in the Middle Ages.* Cambridge Univ. Pr. 1985 $59.50

Twersky, Isadore, and Bernard Septimus, eds. *Jewish Thought in the Seventeenth Century.* Harvard Univ. Pr. 1986 text ed. $25.00 pap. $12.50. Eclectic collection of academic essays.

MYSTICISM

In addition to the development of legal codification, biblical commentary, and philosophy, the medieval period witnessed new strains of Jewish mysticism. Medieval Hasidism, a popular folk movement, stressed communal charity and personal asceticism. *The Zohar,* or *Book of Splendor,* compiled in the thirteenth century but written in the style of Rabbinic literature, led to the development of an esoteric mystical tradition called the Cabalah. New modes of biblical interpretation emerged that found deeper levels of meaning hidden in the sacred text. The Cabalists reflected on God's various attributes and emanations and saw their spirituality and ethics as bringing unity and redemption to a world marked by disunity and strife. (See Nahmanides' and Scholem's main listings in this chapter.)

Abelson, Joshua. *Jewish Mysticism: An Introduction to Kabbalah.* 1913. Hermon 1981 pap. $5.95. This classic work treats selected topics rather than attempting a comprehensive account of the topic.

Ben Zion, Raphael. *The Way of the Faithful: An Anthology of Jewish Mysticism.* 1945. Judaica Pr. 1981 o.p. Ben Zion claims his translations "transmit the spirit of the work, even at the occasional sacrifice of scientific precision."

Bension, Ariel. *The Zohar in Moslem and Christian Spain.* Intro. by Denison Ross, Hermon repr. 1974 o.p. Gives a synopsis of the *Zohar* and shows its relationship to Christian and Muslim mystics in medieval Spain.

Blumenthal, D. R. *Understanding Jewish Mysticism: A Source Reader.* [*Lib. of Jewish*

Learning] Ktav 2 vols. 1978–82 ea. $20.00 pap. ea. $9.95. Vol. 1, *The Mekabah Tradition and the Zoharic Tradition;* Vol. 2, *The Philosophic-Mystical Tradition and Hasidic Tradition.* The best introduction and overview of Jewish mysticism.

Bokser, Ben Zion. *The Jewish Mystical Tradition.* Pilgrim Pr. 1981 o.p. An anthology of mysticism through the ages with introductions to each major figure and text.

Dan, Joseph, and Ronald C. Kiener, eds. *The Early Kabbalah.* Pref. by Moshe Idel [*Class. of Western Spirituality*] Paulist Pr. 1986 $13.95 pap. $10.95. Readable translations of works by mystics from Safed.

Dan, Joseph, and Frank Talmage, eds. *Studies in Jewish Mysticism.* Ktav 1982 $25.00. Eclectic collection of academic papers, accessible to a lay audience.

Fine, Lawrence, trans. *Safed Spirituality, Rules of Mystical Piety and Elijah de Vidas' Beginning of Wisdom.* [*Class. of Western Spirituality*] Paulist Pr. 1984 $12.95 pap. $9.95. Excellent collection of teachings by six mystics from sixteenth-century Safed.

Green, Arthur. *Jewish Spirituality from the Bible through the Middle Ages.* Paulist Pr. 1985 o.p. Historical account of Jewish mysticism by various scholars. Views mysticism as part of the core of Judaism, not an appended curiosity.

Hyamson, Moses, trans. *Duties of the Heart by R. Bachya ibn Paquda.* 1925. Feldheim bilingual ed. 1968 o.p. Originally published in Arabic in the eleventh century, this mystical instruction manual bears the influence of medieval Sufi piety.

Jacobs, Louis, ed. *Jewish Mystical Testimonies.* Schocken 1977 pap. $8.95. Anthology of personal testimonies of mystical experiences from the biblical to the modern period, with an introduction, commentaries, and bibliography.

Matt, Daniel Chanah, ed. and trans. *Zohar: The Book of Enlightenment.* [*Class. of Western Spirituality*] Paulist Pr. 1982 $12.95 pap. $9.95. An excellent introduction that places the *Zohar* in the context of prior Jewish mysticism and traces its influence on later Judaism. The selection of passages (the 150 pages of translation represent only 2 percent of the massive original) highlights material that is particularly evocative and accessible to a modern audience. Notes are placed at the end to facilitate easy reading.

Meltzer, David, ed. *The Secret Garden: An Anthology on the Kabbalah.* Seabury 1976 o.p. A source book of Cabalistic texts.

Rosenberg, Roy A. *The Anatomy of God.* Ktav 1973 o.p. Translated selections of the *Zohar* not included in the Soncino Press edition translated by Simon and Levertoff (see below).

Safran, Alexandre. *The Kabbala: Law and Mysticism in the Jewish Tradition.* Feldheim 1975 o.p. A theological treatise that attempts to show that Jewish mysticism and legal observance derive from the same principles.

Sharot, Stephen. *Messianism, Mysticism, and Magic: A Sociological Analysis of Jewish Religious Movements.* [*Studies in Religion*] Univ. of North Carolina Pr. repr. of 1982 ed. 1987 pap. $12.95. Analysis of medieval and modern popular charismatic movements and their relationship to political and economic conditions.

Simon, Maurice, and Paul Levertoff, trans. *The Zohar.* Soncino Pr. 1934 $75.00 pap. $55.00. A complete translation, except for the section appearing in Rosenberg's translation.

Trachtenberg, Joshua. *Jewish Magic and Superstition.* Atheneum 1970 text ed. pap. $6.95. An extensively documented, yet readable, study of Jewish folk religion through 1600. The customs and beliefs exposed in this book often contrast markedly with "official Judaism" as portrayed by the religious elite.

Weiner, Herbert. *Nine and a Half Mystics: The Kabbala Today.* Macmillan 1986 pap. $8.95. A popular, personal account of a present-day Jewish mystical movement based on the Cabala.

Religious Movements

KARAISM

Karaism was a Judaism that denied the belief that at Sinai God had revealed the Torah in two media, oral and written. Karaites accepted the revealed status of the written Torah only. They therefore rejected the authority of the rabbis, who taught and applied the law of the Talmud and related writings. Karaite Judaism flourished in the Byzantine Empire, the Middle East, and in southern Russia and the Ukraine, producing its own literature of biblical exegesis and other religious writings. It was regarded as a heresy by the proponents of the Judaism of the dual Torah, which predominated.

Ankori, Zvi. *Karaites in Byzantium: The Formative Years, 970–1100. [Columbia Univ. Studies in the Social Sciences]* AMS Pr. repr. of 1959 ed. 1977 $28.50. A social and religious history of the Karaites. Follows the efforts of the group to adjust to the shift from Islamic to Orthodox Christian rule in Asia Minor.

Birnbaum, Philip. *Karaite Studies.* Hermon 1971 o.p. A collection of technical articles, including reproductions from the beginning of the century, that discuss both sides of the Karaite-Rabbinite controversy.

Isaac ben Abraham of Troki. *Faith Strengthened.* 1970. Trans. by Moses Mocatta, Hermon 1975 pap. $9.75. A polemic against Christianity and an attack on the New Testament by a Lithuanian Karaite who lived from 1533 to 1594.

Mann, Jacob. *Texts and Studies in Jewish History and Literature.* Ktav 2 vols. rev. ed. 1970 $99.50. Massive collection (some 1,600 pages) of Karaite literature from the Near East, Asia Minor, and Eastern Europe.

Nemoy, Leon, trans. *Karaite Anthology: Excerpts from the Early Literature. [Judaica Ser.]* Yale Univ. Pr. 1952 $45.00. This standard reference for Karaism presents translations of Arabic, Hebrew, and Aramaic writings, arranged by author. Includes a collection of Karaite liturgy.

SHABBETAIANISM

Between 1665 and 1666 a messiah, Sabbatai Zevi, made himself known through his prophet, Nathan of Gaza, and won the recognition of a sizable part of the Jewish world in both Islamic and Christian countries, with supporters from Egypt in the south to Poland in the north, from Turkey in the east to the Netherlands in the west. Sabbatai Zevi preached the doctrine that the Messiah would inaugurate an age in which the laws of the Torah no longer applied; therefore a mark of his messianic status was the violation of the laws of the Torah. The Judaism of the dual Torah had always maintained that the Messiah would keep and not violate the law, teaching the doctrine of the Messiah as a sage and rabbi. Sabbatai Zevi ultimately converted to Islam, and most of his followers returned to the Jewish community led by the sages of the day. (See also Stephen Sharot's sociological analysis under Mysticism, above.)

Scholem, Gershom. *Sabbatai Sevi: The Mystical Messiah.* Trans. by R. Zwi Werblowski *[Bollingen Ser.]* Princeton Univ. Pr. 1973 $67.50 pap. $22.50. This massive work gathers and analyzes the primary source material for the first time, explaining the cultural and religious environment in which this messianic movement caught fire.

HASIDISM

A movement of intense piety, Hasidism began in the person and teachings of a wonder-worker, Ba'al Shem Tov, Master of the Good Name, who died in 1760.

Hasidism taught that the Torah called for rejoicing in God and in creation, and furthermore that the Zaddik, or holy man, was an instrument of God's sanctification and salvation. The deeds and doings of the Zaddik, therefore, served as a medium of revelation, much as the Torah itself had served. Opposed by sages who saw in the dual Torah the media of revelation, Hasidism brought schism to the Jewish communities of Poland, the Ukraine, and White Russia. Three generations beyond the time of the Master of the Good Name, the Hasidim began to write down stories of the great Zaddikim, or holy men, and these stories served to express a yearning for sanctification in the here and now and for salvation in the coming of the Messiah. Hasidic communities continue to thrive in the United States and the State of Israel. (See the main listings of Ba'al Shem Tov, Buber, and Nahman in this chapter.)

Buber, Martin. *Hasidism and Modern Man.* Ed. and trans. by Maurice Friedman, Horizon Pr. 1972 pap. $5.95. Writings on the contemporary relevance of Hasidism by the man responsible for bringing its message to an audience outside eastern Europe.

———. *The Origin and Meaning of Hasidism.* Trans. by Maurice Friedman, Horizon Pr. 1972 pap. $5.95. A more analytic treatment of Hasidism, in which Buber traces the history of the movement and compares it with biblical prophecy, Spinoza, Freud, Shankara, Meister Eckhart, Gnosticism, Christianity, Zionism, and Zen Buddhism.

———. *Tales of the Hasidim.* Schocken 2 vols. 1961 pap. ea. $5.95–$6.95. A creative retelling of tales by and about various Hasidic masters.

———. *Ten Rungs: Hasidic Sayings.* Trans. by Olga Marx, Schocken 1962 pap. $3.95. Short collection of witty and inspirational sayings related to everyday life.

Dan, Joseph, ed. *The Teachings of Hasidism.* Behrman 1983 text ed. pap. $9.95. Anthology of writings by the first generation of Hasidic masters (1780–1811), arranged by topic. The selections seem disjointed because the editor does not clearly identify the author or the original literary context of each citation.

Dresner, Samuel H. *Zaddik: The Doctrine of the Zaddik According to the Writings of Rabbi Yaakov Yosef of Polnoy.* Pref. by Abraham H. Heschel, Schocken 1974 pap. $4.95. Theological discussion based on writings of Rabbi Yaakov Joseph of Polnoy. Discusses the role of the Zaddik as the charismatic link between God and the community of followers.

Green, Arthur, trans. *Upright Practices: The Light of the Eyes.* [*Class. of Western Spirituality*] Paulist Pr. 1982 $13.95 pap. $9.95. Translation of the works of Nahum of Chernobyl on spiritual depth and on the book of Genesis.

Green, Arthur, and Barry Holtz, eds. *Your Word Is Fire: The Hasidic Masters on Contemplative Prayer.* [*Spiritual Masters Ser.*] Paulist Pr. 1977 o.p. The stated purpose of this anthology of Hasidic prayer is "devotional rather than academic."

Harris, Lis. *Holy Days: The World of a Hasidic Family.* Macmillan 1986 pap. $7.95; Summit 1985 $18.95. A staff writer from the *New Yorker* magazine reports on her many visits to a Lubavitcher family. She explores the religious fervor, the role of women, and the history of the Lubavitcher Hasidic movement.

Heinemann, Benno. *The Maggid of Dubno and His Parables.* 1967. Feldheim rev. ed. 1978 $11.95. Anthology, with a brief biography of a Hasidic master who lived from 1741 to 1804 and was noted for imaginative interpretations of biblical verse in order to answer ethical and religious questions.

Jacobs, Louis. *Hasidic Prayer.* Oxford 1972 $17.95; Schocken 1978 pap. $4.95. Describes the unusual theory of prayer developed by Hasidic masters.

———. *Hasidic Thought.* Behrman 1976 o.p. Collects short pieces of writing from 35

Hasidic masters. Each selection is preceded by an introduction and followed by a thought-provoking commentary.

Langer, Jiri. *Nine Gates to the Chassidic Mysteries.* Ed. by Seymour Rossel, trans. by Stephen Jolly, intro. by Herbert Weiner [*Jewish Legacy Ser.*] Behrman 1976 text ed. pap. $4.95. Popular introduction to Hasidic thought.

Mahler, Raphael, trans. *Hasidism and the Jewish Enlightenment: Their Confrontation in Galicia and Poland in the First Half of the Nineteenth Century.* Jewish Pubns. 1985 $29.95. This study places Hasidism not only against the background of its more traditional opponents (the Mitnaggim) but also against the background of the secularists (the Maskilim).

Menahem Nahum of Chernobyl. *The Light of the Eyes: Homilies to Genesis.* Trans. by Arthur Green [*Class. of Western Spirituality*] Paulist Pr. 1982 o.p. Collection of homilies on the book of Genesis appearing in English for the first time.

Mintz, Jerome R. *Legends of the Hasidim: An Introduction to Hasidic Culture and Oral Tradition in the New World.* Univ. of Chicago Pr. 1968 $15.00 1974 pap. $14.95. Studies American Hasidism since the arrival of followers in New York during the 1940s and 1950s. Mintz collects almost 400 tales, many of which refer to the early years of Hasidism, and discusses the social function of storytelling in the contemporary Hasidic community.

Netanyahu, B. *Don Isaac Abravanel: Statesman and Philosopher.* Jewish Pubns. 1972 pap. $6.95. Study of "an encyclopedic scholar, a philosophic thinker, a noted exegete, and a brilliant writer." Analyzes his highly mystical and apocalyptic messianism.

Newman, Louis I. *The Hasidic Anthology.* Schocken 1975 o.p. Originally published in 1934, this anthology collects over 500 pages of short sayings on every imaginable topic.

Rabinowitsch, Wolf Zeev. *Lithuanian Hasidism.* Schocken 1971 o.p. Detailed historical study of the early Hasidic movement. Traces the development and demise of family dynasties.

Rotenberg, Mordecai. *Dialogue with Deviance: The Hasidic Ethic and the Theory of Social Contraction.* Inst. for the Study of Human Issues 1983 text ed. $27.50. Study in the tradition of Max Weber attempts to define the religious ethic of eighteenth-century Hasidism using sociological and psychological categories.

Wiesel, Elie. *Four Hasidic Masters and Their Struggle against Melancholy.* Fwd. by Theodore Hesburgh [*Ward-Phillips Lectures in Eng. Language and Lit. Ser.*] Univ. of Notre Dame Pr. 1978 $9.95 1979 text ed. pap. $4.95. Four moving lectures on four lesser-known Hasidic masters, by the famous novelist and recipient of the Nobel Prize for peace.

——. *Somewhere a Master: Further Tales of the Hasidic Masters.* Summit 1984 pap. $6.95. Biographies of nine Hasidic masters.

——. *Souls on Fire: Portraits and Legends of Hasidic Masters.* Summit 1982 $17.50 pap. $7.95. A popular introduction to the spirit of early Hasidism, written passionately and poetically.

MODERN JUDAISM

History of the Jews

The Jews' histories naturally followed diverse paths. Modern history began in the West with the secularization of politics in the late eighteenth and nineteenth centuries, moving from the westernmost fringes of the United States, France, Britain, and Holland eastward into Germany, Hungary, and beyond. Through the nineteenth century Jews acquired rights as citizens, but they also lost the right to govern their own affairs and to live in their own segregated world and by their own law. As Christianity lost its hold on the politics of the West, other political movements succeeded, with nationalism becoming one of the most powerful. Nationalism as a principle of politics brought with it the conception of the nation-state, in which all citizens conformed to a single law, and that made difficult the Jews' explanation of the ways in which they preserved a difference from others.

GENERAL

Goldscheider, Calvin, and Alan Zuckerman. *The Transformation of the Jews.* Univ. of Chicago Pr. 1986 $24.95 pap. $10.95. A comparative study of processes of modernization in Jewish communities throughout the world, showing that sociological factors, rather than ideology, were the primary motivations for change.

Grayzel, Solomon. *History of the Contemporary Jews from 1900 to the Present.* 1960. Atheneum 1969 text ed. pap. $4.95. A useful survey of the facts of the matter.

De Lange, Nicholas. *Atlas of the Jewish World.* Facts on File 1984 $35.00. This fact-filled coffee-table book surveys the history and culture of modern Jewry by country.

Mahler, Raphael. *A History of Modern Jewry.* Schocken 1971 o.p. An argumentative and engaging argument about class struggle in the modernization of Jewry. A socialist reading worth considering.

Mendes-Flohr, Paul R., and Jehuda Reinharz. *The Jew in the Modern World: A Documentary History.* Oxford 1980 $35.00 text ed. pap. $17.95. An anthology of important primary sources about Jews and Judaism written from many angles.

Meyer, Michael A. *The Origins of the Modern Jew: Jewish Identity and European Culture in Germany, 1749–1824.* Wayne State Univ. Pr. repr. of 1967 ed. 1972 pap. $7.95. An account of the modernization of Jewish thought and culture and the founding of Reform Judaism in Germany.

Sachar, Howard M. *The Course of Modern Jewish History.* Dell rev. & enl. ed. 1986 pap. $12.95. Engaging narrative, well written and easy to read, covering all the important topics in a highly competent way.

Sharot, Stephen. *Judaism: A Sociology.* Holmes & Meier 1976 text ed. $29.50. A comparative study of Judaism and Jewish life with special attention to how and why Jews did and did not become acculturated in the various environments in which they lived.

Steinberg, Milton. *The Making of the Modern Jew.* 1934. Univ. Pr. of Amer. 1987 pap. $14.50. The best analysis of the situation of Jews in modern culture, as penetrating now as when it was written more than 50 years ago.

EUROPE

While Jews in the West argued that one could be different in religion while sharing the nationalism of the country in which they lived (whether French or German or British or Italian), not everyone agreed. Some regarded Jews as alien, regardless of how long they had lived in their places of birth and residence. Doctrines of Jew-hatred, developing from secular sources and reinforced by long centuries in which Jews had been portrayed by Christianity as deicides, yielded a political movement known as anti-Semitism. Political parties took shape around Jew-hatred, teaching the doctrine that the solution to social problems lay in the segregation, expulsion, and ultimately the murder of the Jews. The history of the Jews in modern Europe is the story of the ultimate success of those political parties.

The largest Jewish population in the world in the nineteenth century was in the Russian Empire, which had acquired Poland and its ancient Jewish community, as well as Lithuania, White Russia, and the Ukraine. The Austro-Hungarian Empire and the German Empire also ruled over Jewish communities in eastern Europe. The history of the Jews in the nineteenth century in Europe is the story of the breakup of that massive population, its movement to great cities in Germany and the West, its processes of industrialization and modernization, and its migration to the far West—the United States and Canada in particular. The history of those who stayed in Poland and Russia came to an end, along with the histories of the Jews in all other continental European countries, in the murder of nearly six million Jews by the German government and its allies from 1933 to 1945.

Adler, Hans G. *The Jews in Germany from the Enlightenment to National Socialism.* Univ. of Notre Dame Pr. 1969 o.p. A history of the Jews in nineteenth- and twentieth-century Germany.

Albert, Phyllis Cohen. *The Modernization of French Jewry: Consistory and Community in the Nineteenth Century.* Univ. Pr. of New England 1977 $40.00. A sociological and demographic account of the institutions of French Jewry from Napoleon to the Dreyfus affair and how they adapted to modernization.

Avni, Haim. *Spain, the Jews and Franco.* Trans. by Emanuel Shimoni, Jewish Pubns. 1981 $19.95. Argues that Franco saved Jews' lives during the Nazi period.

Bakan, David. *Sigmund Freud and the Jewish Mystical Tradition.* Beacon Pr. 1975 o.p. Tries to link Freud's psychological theories to the Jewish mystical tradition, showing that Freud got important ideas from that tradition. A curiosity.

Baron, Salo W. *The Russian Jew under Tsars and Soviets.* Macmillan rev. ed. 1976 $14.95. An excellent survey of the history of the Jews in Russia from the end of the eighteenth century to our own time.

Bauer, Yehuda. *The Holocaust in Historical Perspective.* Univ. of Washington Pr. 1978 $18.00 pap. $8.95. A set of lectures on the historical lessons of the Holocaust by one of the pioneers in historical research in that subject.

Bermant, Chaim. *Troubled Eden: An Anatomy of British Jewry.* Basic Bks. 1970 o.p. A penetrating and acute social commentary on the Jews in Britain in the contemporary period.

Dawidowicz, Lucy S. *The Golden Tradition: Jewish Life and Thought in Eastern Europe.* Schocken 1984 pap. $11.95. An anthology of memoirs, letters, and other documents covering the cultural life of east European Jews from the nineteenth century; the best treatment of its subject.

———. *The War against the Jews, 1933–1945.* Bantam 1976 pap. $10.95; Free Pr. 1986 $22.95; Holt 1975 $15.00. One of the best histories of the mass murder of Jews in World War II. Argues for the centrality of anti-Semitism in Hitler's program.

———, ed. *A Holocaust Reader.* Behrman 1975 pap. $9.95. An anthology of primary sources on the subject, designed as a companion volume to the author's *The War against the Jews.*

Dobroszycki, Lucjan, and Barbara Kirshenblatt-Gimblett. *Image Before My Eyes: A Photographic History of Jewish Life in Poland, 1864–1939.* Schocken 1977 $29.95 1979 pap. $19.95. This collection of photographs—street scenes, family portraits, people at work—gives a vivid picture of Jewish life in Poland before it was destroyed by the Holocaust.

Flannery, Edward. *The Anguish of the Jews: Twenty-Three Centuries of Antisemitism.* Paulist Pr. rev. ed. repr. of 1964 ed. 1985 pap. $12.95. A history and analysis of anti-Semitism, showing the various sources of Jew-hatred over time.

Gay, Peter. *Freud, Jews and Other Germans: Masters and Victims in Modernist Culture.* Oxford 1978 $22.50 1979 pap. $9.95. An account of the development of Jewish culture in the context of the modernization of German society.

Gilbert, Martin. *The Holocaust: A History of the Jews of Europe during the Second World War.* Holt 1987 pap. $12.95; Hill & Wang 1979 pap. $6.95. A very human account, through the words of victims themselves, of what happened in Europe, joining historical fact to personal reminiscence.

————. *The Jews of Hope.* Penguin 1985 pap. $6.95. Documents the contemporary struggle of many Soviet Jews to maintain their ethnic identity and to emigrate. Includes illustrations and personal accounts along with a brief history of Jewish life in Russia over the centuries.

Gilboa, Yehoshua. *The Black Years of Soviet Jewry: 1939–1953.* Little, Brown 1971 o.p. Examines the devastating effect of Stalin's purges on the Jewish community.

Gilman, Sander L. *Jewish Self-Hatred: Anti-Semitism and the Hidden Language of the Jews.* Johns Hopkins Univ. Pr. 1986 text ed. $28.50. A sociological, psychological, and literary study of how a group responds to negative stereotypes. Analyzes the language of Jews from Karl Marx to Anne Frank. Highly recommended.

Glatstein, Jacob, and others. *Anthology of Holocaust Literature.* Atheneum repr. of 1968 ed. 1972 text ed. pap. $6.95. A useful anthology on the stated subject.

Gordon, Sarah. *Hitler, Germans, and the "Jewish Question."* Princeton Univ. Pr. 1984 $40.00 pap. $14.50. Detailed analysis of Hitler's conception of the Jews.

Greenberg, Louis. *Jews in Russia: The Struggle for Emancipation.* Ed. by Mark Wishnitzer, fwd. by Alfred Levin, AMS Pr. 2 vols. in 1 repr. of 1965 ed. 1982 $27.50; Schocken 2 vols. in 1 repr. of 1965 ed. 1976 pap. $11.95. This work remains a classic study of the movement for civil rights by Russian Jews in the second half of the nineteenth century.

Heller, Celia S. *On the Edge of Destruction: Jews of Poland Between the Two World Wars.* Columbia Univ. Pr. 1977 $34.00; Schocken repr. of 1977 ed. 1980 pap. $8.95. This scholarly account presents the Jews from World War I to the eve of World War II in Poland. Now superseded by Ezra Mendelsohn's *The Jews of East Central Europe.*

Hilberg, Raul. *The Destruction of the European Jews.* Holmes & Meier 3 vols. rev. ed. 1985 text ed. boxed set $159.50 pap. $14.95. The pioneering work on the subject, still the single best account of what happened. Candidly discusses how Jews were occasionally drawn into cooperating with the Nazis.

Hyman, Paula. *From Dreyfus to Vichy: The Remaking of French Jewry 1906–1939.* Columbia Univ. Pr. 1979 $28.00. A successful monograph on the social and religious history of French Jews in the early part of this century.

Kahn, Lothar. *Mirrors of the Jewish Mind: A Gallery of Portraits of European Jewish Writers of Our Time.* Thomas Yoseloff 1968 o.p. Excellent introduction to important European Jewish writers, introducing a variety of central European figures in particular.

Katz, Jacob. *Out of the Ghetto: The Social Background of Jewish Emancipation, 1770–1870.* Harvard Univ. Pr. 1973 $18.50; Schocken 1978 pap. $6.95. A history of the impact of the social and political changes that overtook the Jews in the nineteenth century, as the corporate community gave way to individual citizenship.

Klepfiscz, Heszel. *Culture of Compassion: The Spirit of Polish Jewry from Hasidism to the Holocaust.* Ktav 1983 $25.00. A collection of articles originally published in Yiddish that give a sympathetic account of the religious and cultural life of Polish Jewry.

Kochan, Lionel, ed. *The Jews in Soviet Russia since 1917.* Oxford 3d ed. 1978 pap. $9.95. This collaborative effort is objective and comprehensive, covering events through 1976. The best survey of the subject.

Kosler, Franz. *Napoleon and the Jews.* Schocken 1976 o.p. Readable account of Napoleon's efforts to liberate the Jews from the ghetto and to restore a modern form of ancient Jewish nationalism.

Malino, Francis, and Bernard Wasserstein, eds. *The Jews in Modern France.* Univ. Pr. of New England 1985 $32.50. A history of the Jews of France in the last two centuries.

Marcus, Jacob R. *The Rise and Destiny of the German Jew.* Ktav rev. ed. 1971 $15.00. A good history of the Jews in the nineteenth century, surveying their political progress and achievements on the eve of the advent of nazism and their destruction.

Marrus, Michael R. *The Politics of Assimilation: The French Jewish Community at the Time of the Dreyfus Affair.* Oxford repr. of 1971 ed. 1980 pap. $19.95. An analysis of the Jewish response to the anti-Semitism generated by the conviction of Dreyfus, a Jewish military officer falsely charged with treason.

Mendelsohn, Ezra. *The Jews of East Central Europe: Between the World Wars.* Indiana Univ. Pr. 1983 $27.50. The definitive treatment of the interbellum European Jewish community.

Parkes, James W. *The Emergence of the Jewish Problem, 1878–1939.* Greenwood repr. of 1946 ed. 1971 o.p. An excellent account of the rise of modern anti-Semitism as a political movement, especially in eastern Europe, and suggested solutions to the so-called Jewish problem, such as the Balfour Declaration.

Poliakov, Leon. *Harvest of Hate: The Nazi Program for the Destruction of the Jews of Europe.* Fwd. by R. Niebuhr, Greenwood repr. of 1954 ed. 1971 lib. bdg. $22.50; Holocaust Pubns. 1979 pap. $12.95; Schocken rev. ed. repr. of 1954 ed. 1979 pap. $5.95. Links anti-Semitic doctrine and thought to the Holocaust and spells out the story of the destruction of European Jewry.

Reinharz, Jehuda. *Fatherland or Promised Land: The Dilemma of the German Jew, 1893–1914.* Univ. of Michigan Pr. 1975 o.p. Analyzes the choices in politics and ideology that confronted German Jewry at the time of political emancipation.

Rozenblit, Marsha L. *The Jews of Vienna, 1867–1914: Assimilation and Identity.* [*Modern Jewish History Ser.*] State Univ. of New York Pr. 1984 $44.50 pap. $16.95. Utilizes demographic information to tell the story of the various means of social integration used by the Jews as they moved from small towns to the cosmopolitan world of Vienna at the turn of the century.

Schwarzfuchs, Simon. *Napoleon, the Jews and the Sanhedrin.* [*Littman Lib. of Jewish Civilization*] Fairleigh Dickinson Univ. Pr. 1979 o.p. Napoleon called a "sanhedrin" of rabbis and asked them whether the Jews were loyal citizens of France or belonged to some other country. This is the best study of that sanhedrin and the answers it gave to Napoleon.

Sichronovsky, Peter. *Strangers in Their Own Lands: Young Jews in Germany and Austria Today.* Basic Bks. 1986 $14.95. Discusses the attitudes and situation of the remnant of the Jewish community left in Germany and Austria after the Holocaust.

Spiegelman, Art. *Maus: A Survivor's Tale.* Pantheon 1986 pap. $8.95. The story of one man's experience in the Holocaust is told by his son, skillfully using the medium of the cartoon. The Jews are represented as mice, the Nazis as cats, and the Poles as pigs. Highly recommended for any audience.

Suhl, Yuri, ed. *They Fought Back: The Story of the Jewish Resistance in Nazi Europe.* 1967. Schocken 1975 $9.95. Tells the story of the Jewish underground during World War II.

Tal, Uriel. *Christians and Jews in Germany: Religion, Politics, and Ideology in the Second Reich, 1870–1914.* Trans. by Noah J. Jacobs, Cornell Univ. Pr. 1975 $35.00. Explains how the theological confrontation between Judaism and Christianity spilled over into politics. Shows the limits of German liberalism vis-à-vis the Jews.

Tec, Nechama. *When Light Pierced the Darkness: Christian Rescue of Jews in Nazi-Occupied Poland.* Oxford 1986 $19.95. Analyzes the psychological and ethical motivations of the "righteous gentiles" in Poland who acted to save Jews during the Holocaust.

Wasserstein, Bernard. *Britain and the Jews of Europe 1939–1945.* Oxford 1979 $25.00. Surveys the efforts of Britain to help the Jews save their lives during the period of the mass murders and shows that the matter enjoyed a very low priority.

Weinberg, David H. *A Community on Trial: The Jews of Paris in the 1930's.* Univ. of Chicago Pr. 1977 $22.00. An account of the political pressures of anti-Semitism on Paris Jews before World War II. Helps account for the extensive collaboration of the French in carrying out the mass murder of French Jewry.

Zipperstein, Steven J. *The Jews of Odessa: A Cultural History, 1794–1881.* Stanford Univ. Pr. 1986 $32.50. An account of a Jewish community in Russia during its period of modernization.

NORTH AMERICA

The Jews came to the United States in large numbers from the middle of the nineteenth century. They were part of a large wave of migration from central Europe, particularly Germany, and settled in the now-opening territories of the South and the Middle West. At the end of the nineteenth century a still larger wave of Jews migrated from eastern Europe, particularly White Russia, the Ukraine, Poland, Rumania, Hungary, and Lithuania. Numbering in the millions, those Jews settled in the cities in which their labor was needed, creating in the large metropolitan areas of the Northeast and Middle West vast communities. From the early twentieth century the children of immigrant Jews entered politics, professions, business, and various cultural ventures. They came to form an important component of American life.

Altshuler, David, ed. *The Jews of Washington, D.C.: A Communal Anthology.* Rossel Bks. 1986 $17.95. An illustrated anthology on the Jewish community in the nation's capital.

Belth, Nathan C. *A Promise to Keep: The American Encounter with Anti-Semitism.* Schocken 1981 pap. $7.95. Tells the history of anti-Semitism as a political and cultural force in America and the effort to combat it by the Anti-Defamation League of B'nai B'rith.

Cohen, Naomi W. *Encounter with Emancipation: The German Jews in the United States, 1830–1914.* Jewish Pubns. 1984 $25.95. A very readable social history describing the struggle of German-Jewish immigrants to make a life for themselves in the United States.

———. *Not Free to Desist: The American Jewish Committee 1906–1966.* Jewish Pubns. 1972 o.p. History of an important American Jewish political organization.

Cohen, Steven M. *American Modernity and Jewish Identity*. Methuen 1983 $24.00 pap. $9.95. An analysis of the cultural history of American Jews in the recent past and the formation of their identity.

Ehrman, Eliezer L., ed. *Readings in Modern Jewish History: From the American Revolution to the Present*. Ktav 1977 o.p. Anthology on American Jewish history.

Elazar, Daniel J. *Community and Polity: The Organizational Dynamics of American Jewry*. Jewish Pubns. 1976 pap. $9.95. Analyzes the organizational and institutional structure of American Jewry.

Feingold, Henry L. *Zion in America*. [*Amer. Immigrant Ser.*] Hippocrene Bks. rev. ed. 1981 pap. $10.95. Solid narrative history of U.S. Jews.

Forster, Arnold, and Benjamin Epstein. *The New Anti-Semitism*. McGraw-Hill 1974 o.p. Defines new forms of intellectual anti-Semitism in the United States.

Glazer, Nathan. *American Judaism*. Univ. of Chicago Pr. rev. ed. 1972 $12.50 pap. $7.50. A classic history of Judaism in America, with particular attention given to the social foundations of Judaic religious life and expression.

Goldscheider, Calvin. *Jewish Continuity and Change: Emerging Patterns in America*. [*Jewish Political and Social Studies*] Indiana Univ. Pr. 1986 $24.95. Brilliant analysis of the principles of communal coherence and the strength of the ethnic ties within Jewry; interprets change and shows continuity.

Goldstein, Sidney, and Calvin Goldscheider. *Jewish Americans: Three Generations in a Jewish Community*. Univ. Pr. of Amer. repr. of 1968 ed. 1985 text ed. pap. $13.50. Model demographic study of Jews' social, economic, and religious life and practice.

Handlin, Oscar. *Adventure in Freedom: Three Hundred Years of Jewish Life in America*. McGraw-Hill 1954 o.p. Interpretation of the history of the Jews in America within the setting of American life.

Herberg, Will. *Protestant, Catholic, Jew: An Essay in American Religious Sociology*. Univ. of Chicago Pr. repr. of 1955 ed. 1983 pap. $11.00. The original statement of the thesis that there is a civil religion or religious style affecting all religions in America. Shows how the three religions of democracy grow more and more like one another.

Hertzberg, Arthur. *Being Jewish in America: The Modern Experience*. Schocken 1980 pap. $7.95. A set of episodic essays and reflections by a controversial rabbi.

Higham, John. *Send These to Me: Jews and Other Immigrants in Urban America*. 1975. Johns Hopkins Univ. Pr. 1984 text ed. $22.50 pap. $8.95. An account of the experience of the Jews and other groups in American cities; among the best histories of the immigrant generations.

Himmelfarb, Milton. *The Jews of Modernity*. Basic Bks. 1973 o.p. A set of random thoughts by an acute observer.

Howe, Irving. *World of Our Fathers: The Journey of the East European Jews to America and the Life They Found and Made*. Harcourt 1976 $14.95; Pocket Bks. 1978 pap. $6.95; Simon & Schuster 1983 pap. $12.95. A much-acclaimed, illustrated account of the cultural life of the immigrant generations.

Janowsky, Oscar I., ed. *American Jew*. [*Essay Index Repr. Ser.*] Ayer repr. of 1942 ed. 1977 $18.00. Essays on the state and condition of American Jews.

Joselit, Jenna W. *Our Gang: Jewish Crime and the New York Jewish Community, 1900–1940*. Indiana Univ. Pr. 1983 $19.95 pap. $9.95. A well-documented study of crime as a means of upward mobility for Jewish immigrants in New York.

Karp, Abraham J. *Haven and Home: A History of the Jews in America*. Schocken 1985 $24.95 1986 pap. $9.95. An optimistic portrayal of American Jewish history from 1654 to the present, emphasizing the diversity of Jewish communities and experiences.

———, ed. *The Jewish Experience in America: Selected Studies from the Publications of the American Jewish Historical Society*. Ktav 5 vols. 1969 o.p. Anthology of American Jewish history.

Kessner, Thomas. *The Golden Door: Italian and Jewish Immigrant Mobility in New York City, 1880–1915*. Oxford 1977 text ed. $22.50 pap. $8.95. Readable demographic study of the impoverished Jewish and Italian immigrants in New York. Testifies to the openness of American society.

Learsi, Rufus. *The Jew in America: A History*. Ktav rev. ed. 1972 $11.95. One of the earliest histories of American Jews; still readable.

Libo, Kenneth, and Irving Howe. *We Lived There Too: A Documentary History of Pioneer Jews and the Westward Movement of America, 1630–1930*. St. Martin's 1984 $24.95 1985 pap. $13.95. A documentary history of the role of Jews in the western expansion of the British colonies and the United States. Many interesting illustrations and stories about little-known people.

Liebman, Charles S. F. *The Ambivalent American Jew*. Jewish Pubns. 1973 o.p. Penetrating sociological analysis of the consciousness and attitude of American Jews.

Marcus, Jacob R. *Early American Jewry*. Ktav 2 vols. 1953 o.p. Anthology of materials on the Jews in colonial times by the leading historian of the period.

———, ed. *Memoirs of American Jews: 1775–1865*. Ktav 1955 o.p. Anthology of memoirs; quite readable.

Moore, Deborah D. *At Home in America: Second Generation New York Jews*. Columbia Univ. Pr. 1981 $26.50 pap. $13.00. Major study of the children of the immigrants as they made their way in the life of New York City.

Morse, Arthur D. *While Six Million Died: A Chronicle of American Apathy*. Overlook Pr. repr. of 1966 ed. 1983 o.p. Describes the indifference of the Roosevelt administration to the murder of European Jews while the Holocaust was taking place.

Neusner, Jacob. *Israel in America: A Too-Comfortable Exile?* Beacon Pr. 1985 $14.95 1986 pap. $8.95. Relates the history of Judaism in America to the social experience of American Jews.

Oren, Dan A. *Joining the Club: A History of Jews and Yale*. Yale Univ. Pr. 1986 $29.95. Documents the long history of anti-Semitism at Yale University.

Perlmutter, Nathan, and Ruth Ann Perlmutter. *The Real Anti-Semitism in America*. Arbor House 1982 o.p. The national director of the Anti-Defamation League and his wife express less concern for the Ku Klux Klan and the neo-Nazis than for the anti-Semitism and anti-Zionism of intellectuals, diplomats, and other people in powerful positions.

Rieder, Jonathan. *Canarsie: The Jews and Italians of Brooklyn against Liberalism*. Harvard Univ. Pr. 1985 $22.50 1987 text ed. pap. $8.95. Analyzes the recent trend toward political conservatism among lower-middle-class Jews and Italians in Brooklyn.

Rischin, Moses. *The Promised City: New York's Jews, 1870–1914*. Harvard Univ. Pr. 1977 pap. $8.95. Best history of the Jews in New York City ever written.

Rochlin, Harriett. *Pioneer Jews: A New Life in the Far West*. Houghton Mifflin 1984 $17.95. Large-format book with photos on every page. Tells the story of Jewish participation in the development of the American frontier through 1912.

Rosenberg, Stuart E. *The Search for Jewish Identity in America*. Anchor 1965 o.p. Classic essays by a leading rabbi on the formation of Jewish identity.

Rothchild, Sylvia. *A Special Legacy: An Oral History of Soviet Jewish Emigres in the United States*. Simon & Schuster 1985 $17.95 1986 pap. $8.95. Recent interviews with refugees from the Soviet Union who have come to America.

Schoener, Allon. *The American Jewish Album: 1654 to the Present*. Rizzoli 1985 $45.00

pap. $25.00. Beautiful coffee-table book, with an interesting collection of photographs, essays, and first-person accounts.

Sidorsky, David, ed. *The Future of the Jewish Community in America*. Jewish Pubns. 1973 o.p. A collection of solid essays on the culture and society of U.S. Jewry.

Silberman, Charles E. *A Certain People: American Jews and Their Lives Today*. Summit 1985 $19.95 1986 pap. $9.95. Argues that Jews have found general acceptance and are no longer oppressed by anti-Semitism in America at this time.

Sklare, Marshall. *America's Jews*. Random 1971 pap. $9.00. A systematic account of American Jewry.

——, ed. *The Jews: Social Patterns of an American Group*. Greenwood repr. of 1955 ed. 1977 o.p. Classic essays on various aspects of the sociology of American Jewry.

——. *The Sociology of the American Jew*. Behrman 2 vols. 1976 o.p. An anthology of valuable essays.

——. *Understanding American Jewry*. Transaction Bks. 1982 text ed. $21.95. The great sociologist introduces the sociology of U.S. Jewry.

Sklare, Marshall, and Joseph Greenblum. *Jewish Identity on the Suburban Frontier: A Study of Group Survival in the Open Society*. Univ. of Chicago Pr. 2d ed. 1979 lib. bdg. $27.50 pap. $6.95. Studies the attitudes of Jews in suburbs, particularly the children and grandchildren of immigrants.

Sleeper, James A., and Alan L. Mintz, eds. *The New Jews*. Vintage 1971 o.p. An account of the nascent fourth generation of American Jews and their trend toward the political left in the 1960s.

Waxman, Chaim I. *American Jews in Transition*. Temple Univ. Pr. 1983 $24.95 pap. $9.95. Scholarly study of American Jewish sociology.

Woocher, Jonathan S. *Sacred Survival: The Civil Religion of American Jews*. [*Jewish Political and Social Studies*] Indiana Univ. Pr. 1986 $25.00. Argues that the most influential ideology of American Jews is the commitment to common social institutions—federations, volunteerism, fund-raising, and education.

Wyman, David S. *The Abandonment of the Jews*. Pantheon 1986 pap. $8.95. Wyman documents the failure of the American Jewish community and the American government to come to the aid of Jews under Nazi control.

STATE OF ISRAEL

The history of Jews in what was then Palestine became joined to the Zionist movement at the end of the nineteenth century. In 1897 the Zionist Organization was organized in Basel, and European and American Jews began to work for the creation of a Jewish state in Palestine. In 1917 the British assumed the government of Palestine and issued the Balfour Declaration. This statement supported the establishment of a Jewish "homeland" in Palestine and respected the rights of the present inhabitants. Between 1917 and 1947 hundreds of thousands of Jews settled in Palestine. But from 1933 to 1945, the Jews in Europe, although facing the threat of murder by the German government under the Nazi party, were officially prohibited from entering the country in sizable numbers. In the aftermath of World War II, many of the Jews who had survived wanted to go to Palestine, and in 1947 the United Nations voted to create a Jewish and an Arab state in Palestine. In 1948, the Jewish state declared independence and survived a war by its Arab neighbors. Today, over three million Jews reside in the State of Israel, along with over a million Arabs.

Begin, Menachem. *The Revolt*. Nash repr. 1977 $12.95. A memoir by the leader of a Jewish underground in the years leading up to Israel's independence. Describes his violent and courageous struggle against the British military and the mainstream Jewish organizations.

Black, Edwin. *The Transfer Agreement: The Untold Story of the Secret Pact between the Third Reich and Jewish Palestine.* Macmillan 1984 $19.95. A well-documented account of the secret deal in 1933 between the World Zionist Organization and Nazi Germany to allow 60,000 Jews to emigrate to Palestine in return for a complicated reimbursement scheme.

Collins, Larry, and Dominique Lapierre. *O Jerusalem.* Pocket Bks. 1980 pap. $3.95. The story of Israel's War of Independence is captured in this popular work of historical fiction. Portrays the war from a variety of angles—Jewish, Arab, and British.

Elon, Amos. *The Israelis: Founders and Sons.* Penguin 1983 pap. $7.95. A great writer recaptures the history of the State of Israel from its founding until the present, through the biographies of major figures.

Fein, Leonard J. *Israel: Politics and People.* Beacon Pr. 1967 o.p. A political scientist describes the politics of the new state.

Heilman, Samuel. *The Gate behind the Wall.* Summit 1985 $15.95. Vignettes of religious life in contemporary Jerusalem, by an Orthodox Jewish sociologist.

Liebman, Charles S., and Eliezer Don Yehiya. *Religion and Politics in Israel.* [*Jewish Political and Social Studies*] Indiana Univ. Pr. 1984 $17.50. The first systematic work on the relationship between state-supported Orthodox Judaism and the politics of the Jewish state.

Naamani, Israel T., David Rudavsky, and Abraham I. Katsch. *Israel: Its Politics and Philosophy.* Behrman 1977 o.p. A standard account of the Zionist ideology and political reality in the State of Israel.

Oz, Amos. *In the Land of Israel.* Trans. by Maurice Bartura Goldberg, Harcourt 1983 $12.95; Random 1984 pap. $5.95. A great novelist interviews Arabs and Jews in Israel and clearly records the diversity and increasing divergence of opinion. Compelling reading.

Sachar, Abram. *The Redemption of the Unwanted: From the Liberation of the Death Camps to the Founding of Israel.* St. Martin's 1983 $19.95 1985 pap. $9.95. The story of the survivors of the concentration camps and how they were brought to what was then Palestine and given new lives.

Sachar, Howard M. *A History of Israel: From the Rise of Zionism to Our Time.* Knopf 1979 $12.95. A great historian tells the story of Zionism and the State of Israel in a vivid and compelling narrative.

Said, Edward W. *The Question of Palestine.* Random 1980 pap. $4.95. An articulate analysis of the history and politics of the Arab-Israeli conflict from a Palestinian-Arab point of view.

Sanders, Ronald. *The High Walls of Jerusalem: A History of the Balfour Declaration and the Birth of the British Mandate for Palestine.* Holt 1983 $24.95. The best and most recent book on the Balfour Declaration.

Schenker, Hillel, ed. *After Lebanon: The Israeli-Palestinian Connection.* Pilgrim Pr. 1983 $18.95. During and after the Israeli invasion of Lebanon in 1982, Israeli Jews and Arabs, in the middle and left of the political spectrum, discuss the consequences of the war and the future prospects for peace.

Spiro, Melford E. *Kibbutz: Venture in Utopia.* Harvard Univ. Pr. 1975 pap. $7.95; Schocken rev. ed. 1963 o.p. Popular account of the collective communities and how they experimented in new forms of social life.

Sykes, Christopher. *Crossroads to Israel 1917–1948.* [*Midland Bks.*] Indiana Univ. Pr. repr. of 1965 ed. 1973 pap. $8.95. Excellent book on the period of the British Mandate.

Vital, David. *Zionism: The Formative Years*. Oxford 1982 $34.50. The best history of the beginnings of Zionism, both as ideology and as organization. Acutely detailed.

Weiner, Herbert. *The Wild Goats of Ein Gedi*. Atheneum 1970 o.p. The story of the mystical side of Judaism in general, with much attention to mystical Judaism in the State of Israel today.

OTHER COUNTRIES

Histories of Jews in other countries tend to conform to a fairly simple pattern. As the vast Jewish settlement in eastern Europe began to send forth emigrants from the mid-nineteenth century onward, small streams found their way to those parts of the world in which European settlement was getting under way. Communities took shape in Australia, South Africa, Canada, and Argentina. Secondary settlements of Jews from Muslim countries took root in a few places as well, particularly Brazil. From 1933 to 1945 small numbers of Jews were admitted to other Latin American countries as well.

De Felice, Renzo. *Jews in an Arab Land: Libya, 1835–1970*. Trans. by Judith Roumani, Univ. of Texas Pr. 1985 $27.50. The ups and downs of a Jewish community in North Africa.

Deshen, Shlomo, and Walter P. Zenner. *Jewish Societies in the Middle East: Community, Culture and Authority*. Univ. Pr. of Amer. 1982 lib. bdg. $30.50 text ed. pap. $14.25. Sociological and anthropological studies of Middle Eastern Jewish communities by various authors.

Elazar, Daniel J. *Jewish Communities in Frontier Societies: Argentina, Australia, and South Africa*. Holmes & Meier 1983 text ed. $44.50. Social studies of Jewish communities in former European colonies by a well-known political scientist.

Elkin, Judith L. *Jews of the Latin American Republics*. Univ. of North Carolina Pr. 1980 o.p. Account of the Jews in the Spanish- and Portuguese-speaking countries of the Western Hemisphere.

Haddad, Heskel M. *The Jews of Arab and Islamic Countries: History, Problems and Solutions*. Shengold 1984 $12.95. A good, brief historical, sociological, and demographic survey of Sephardic Jews from the medieval period to the present. Includes a study of the relations between Ashkenazi and Sephardic Jews in Israel today (that is, between Jews of Western and non-Western descent).

Kessler, David. *The Falashas: The Forgotten Jews of Ethiopia*. Schocken 1985 pap. $7.95. The story of the Jews of Ethiopia, descendants of Israelites who settled in pre-Christian times. They preserved their traditions for thousands of years and only recently returned to the Land of Israel to avoid famine and persecution.

Landau, Jacob M. *Jews in Nineteenth Century Egypt*. [*Studies in Near Eastern Civilization.*] New York Univ. Pr. 1969 o.p. A scholarly account of the inner life of the Jewish community in Egypt in the imperial period, with a large collection of documents.

Leslau, Wolf, trans. *Falasha Anthology*. [*Judaica Ser.*] Yale Univ. Pr. 1951 $26.00. This volume collects the ancient writings of the Falashas, some as old as the ninth century. With a 40-page introduction on Falasha history, literature, and religion.

Ozeri, Zion M. *Yemenite Jews: A Photographic Essay*. Schocken 1985 $19.95. Pictures of a colorful Jewish community, now settled in the State of Israel.

Pollak, Michael. *Mandarins, Jews and Missionaries: The Jewish Experience in the Chinese Empire*. Jewish Pubns. 1983 pap. $10.95. This study of the ancient Jewish community of China, which maintained a separate identity through the nineteenth century, portrays the experience of Jews in a non-Christian and non-Islamic environment.

Rejwan, Nissim. *The Jews of Iraq: 3000 Years of History and Culture.* Westview Pr. 1986 $30.00. Descended from the Jews who settled in Babylonia in 586 B.C., Jews in Iraq in recent times went through a turbulent history, until they collectively fled to the State of Israel in the 1950s.

Ross, Dan. *Acts of Faith: A Journey to the Fringes of Jewish Identity.* Fwd. by Raphael Patai, St. Martin's 1982 $15.95; Schocken 1984 pap. $8.95. Ross describes various groups on the boundary of the Jewish people—either geographically or theologically—including the Falashans of Ethiopia, the Chuetas of Majorca, the Bene Israel of India, the Samaritans, and the Karaites. Explores the perennial question of who is and is not a Jew.

Sachar, Howard M. *Diaspora: An Inquiry into the Contemporary Jewish World.* Harper 1985 $27.00 1986 pap. $10.95. Comprehensive treatment of the Jewish communities outside North America and the State of Israel since 1945.

Saron, Gustav, and Louis Hotz, eds. *The Jews in South Africa: A History.* Oxford 1955 o.p. A reliable history of the sizable Jewish community that settled in South Africa in the nineteenth century.

Strizower, Schifra. *The Bene Israel of Bombay: A Study of a Jewish Community.* [*Pavilion Social Anthropology Ser.*] Schocken 1971 o.p. A social-anthropological study of the small Jewish community in India.

Weisbrot, Robert. *The Jews of Argentina: From the Inquisition to Peron.* Jewish Pubns. 1979 $12.50. The history of the large Jewish community in Buenos Aires, and smaller communities in the pampas. Argentina contains the world's fifth largest Jewish community.

Wiznitzer, Arnold. *Jews in Colonial Brazil.* Columbia Univ. Pr. 1960 o.p. An account of the earliest Jewish settlements in the Western Hemisphere.

Jewish Thought

Jewish thought covers a variety of subjects. Some Jewish thought attends to political issues, inquiring what sort of social entity the Jews comprise. Some thought is of a religious character. It treats what it means to be a believing Jew under the conditions of contemporary culture and society. Some thought covers the histories of Jews, treating those histories as a single unitary and harmonious history and proposing to specify the "lessons" taught by that history. In these and other ways Jewish thought forms the intellectual component of the existence of the Jewish people. Nearly all Jewish thought took place in European settings; there is no important literature of thought deriving from Jews in the Muslim world.

GENERAL

Bergman, Samuel Hugo. *Faith and Reason: An Introduction to Modern Jewish Thought.* B'nai B'rith 1961 o.p. A brief and well-presented outline of how some important Jewish thinkers have reconciled the perceived conflict between faith and reason.

Berkovits, Eliezer. *Major Themes in Modern Philosophies of Judaism.* Ktav 1974 $25.00 pap. $11.95. An Orthodox rabbi's account of topics in modern Judaism.

Cohen, Arthur A. *The Natural and the Supernatural Jew: An Historical and Theological Introduction.* Behrman repr. of 1962 ed. 1979 text ed. pap. $6.95. An account of a number of modern systems of Judaic thought, together with the author's own reflections on some basic issues of religiosity.

Eisen, Arnold M. *The Chosen People in America: A Study in Jewish Religious Ideology.* [*Modern Jewish Experience*] Indiana Univ. Pr. 1983 $20.00. Traces the concept of chosenness in American Jewish intellectual history through 1980. Shows how the notion of ethnic distinctiveness conflicts with the desire for assimilation into American society.

Neusner, Jacob. *Understanding Jewish Theology: Classical Issues and Modern Perspective.* Ktav 1973 pap. $11.95. Anthology on the themes of God, Torah, and Israel and the people of God, in classical and modern Judaic thought.

Rawidowicz, Simon. *Studies in Jewish Thought.* Intro. by Benjamin Ravid, Jewish Pubns. 1975 o.p. Brilliant and original thinker on Jewish social philosophy and history presents his best ideas.

Rotenstreich, Nathan. *Jewish Philosophy in Modern Times: From Mendelssohn to Rosenzweig.* Holt 1968 o.p. The German Judaic tradition of thought presented by a master.

Sandmel, Samuel. *The Several Israels, and an Essay: Religion and Modern Man.* Ktav 1971 $10.00. Leading Reform Judaic theologian presents elegant essays on Judaic thought.

ENLIGHTENMENT

The French and German Enlightenment produced a heritage of skepticism and rationalism that affected some Jewish thinkers as well. They turned to the Jewish community with a program of intellectual reform, specifically proposing that Jews enter European culture, learn to read and speak European languages instead of their own Jewish language (Yiddish), and bring to their holy books and their religion the rationalist values of the age. Although not numerous, the Jewish disciples of Enlightenment exercised considerable influence. They began to write in Hebrew, producing secular as well as religious writings; they took an interest in science and politics; and they brought to the Jewish community some of those secularizing ideas that were reshaping European culture and politics.

Hadas, Moses, ed. *Solomon Maimon: An Autobiography.* Schocken 1967 o.p. A basic account of a critical figure in the eighteenth-century Enlightenment with a wealth of information about the contemporary cultural and social setting.

Hertzberg, Arthur. *The French Enlightenment and the Jews.* Columbia Univ. Pr. 1968 o.p. Argues that Voltaire was an anti-Semite and that the French Enlightenment was a source of Jew-hatred. Also an excellent history of eighteenth-century French Jewry on the eve of emancipation.

Jospe, Alfred, ed. *Jerusalem and Other Jewish Writings by Moses Mendelssohn.* Schocken 1969 o.p. The founder of modern Judaic thought and of Reform Judaism is here presented in a fine anthology.

SCIENCE OF JUDAISM (WISSENSCHAFT DES JUDENTUMS)

In the German universities of the early nineteenth century, a new approach to learning took shape, called *Wissenschaft*, translated into English as "science." *Wissenschaft* referred to learning that was systematic, critical, encompassing, and not merely a repetition of received information but a search for explanation and theory. The earliest Reformers in Judaism looked to scientific method, or *Wissenschaft*, as the correct means for the reformation of Judaism. This they wished to accomplish by a critical rereading of the sources of Judaism and a reconstruction of the history of the Jews along lines of science, rather than credibility or theology. *Wissenschaft des Judentums*, or science of Judaism, also took hold among Conservative Jews, and in the twentieth century in western Orthodoxy as well. At stake among all these groups was a factual and informed knowledge, based on criticism and philological learning, of the Jews' past. See also under Conservative Judaism (below).

Geiger, Abraham. *Judaism and Its History: In Two Parts.* Trans. by Charles Newburgh, Univ. Pr. of Amer. repr. of 1911 ed. 1985 text ed. pap. $17.50. A series of popular lectures on the nature of Jewish history given in 1865 in Frankfurt by an important figure in the development of Reform Judaism and Jewish historiography.

Graetz, Heinrich. *The Structure of Jewish History and Other Essays.* Ktav 1975 $20.00 pap. $14.95. Essays on Jewish history and historiography by one of the founders of the field. Schorsch's introduction is the best guide to the system of the founder of Jewish historiography in modern times.

Jospe, Alfred, ed. *Studies in Jewish Thought: An Anthology of German Jewish Scholarship.* Wayne State Univ. Pr. 1981 $32.50. An eclectic collection of writings by important figures in the *Wissenschaft des Judentums* movement on Rabbinic literature, mysticism, and medieval and modern theology.

EARLY TWENTIETH-CENTURY GERMAN-JEWISH THEOLOGY

Theology forms a subdivision of Jewish thought. It took up the task of setting forth and explaining the beliefs of Judaism as an ideal theoretical system. The theologies of Judaism in the nineteenth and early twentieth centuries were written mainly in German and followed the outlines and concerns of German Protestant theologians. This mode of reflection has been preserved to the present day, principally by Reform Judaic scholars, although in the twentieth century Conservative and Orthodox Judaic theologians have also undertaken the same systematic task of setting forth the principles of the faith and explaining and defending them. (See also the main listings for Baeck, Buber, Cohen, and Rosenzweig in this chapter.)

Mosse, George L. *German Jews beyond Judaism.* [*Modern Jewish Experience*] Indiana Univ. Pr. 1985 $20.00 pap. $7.95. Lectures about the intellectual optimism of the highly educated and cultured German Jews at the beginning of this century.

Oppenheim, Michael. *What Does Revelation Mean for the Modern Jew?* E Mellen 1985 lib. bdg. $39.95. Philosophic monograph on a concept that has been interpreted in new ways over the past 50 years.

POST-HOLOCAUST THEOLOGY

Beginning in the 1960s, Jewish thinkers began to come to terms with the theological dilemma of the Holocaust. Age-old questions of theodicy emerged with an acute sense of urgency. The responses have been varied and contradictory. On one side, Richard Rubenstein asked how Jews could remain faithful to a God who could allow such a tragedy to occur. On the other side, Emil Fackenheim responded that for Jews to give up faith after the Holocaust would give Hitler a posthumous victory. (See Fackenheim's and Rubenstein's main listings in this chapter.)

Berkovitz, Eliezer. *Faith after the Holocaust.* Ktav 1973 o.p. An Orthodox Judaic theologian affirms the received faith of Sinai and argues that the Holocaust is not unique, but rather an extension of typical Christian anti-Semitism.

Cohen, Arthur A. *The Tremendum: A Theological Interpretation of the Holocaust.* Crossroad NY 1981 o.p. Effort at original thought on the subject, marked by absence of clarity.

———, ed. *Arguments and Doctrines: A Reader of Jewish Thinking in the Aftermath of the Holocaust.* Jewish Pubns. 1970 o.p. An important anthology of contemporary theology on the problem of evil and other issues raised by the Holocaust.

Neusner, Jacob. *The Jewish War against the Jews: Reflections on Golah, Sholah, and Torah.* Ktav 1984 $12.95. Argues against the centrality of the Holocaust in the formation of contemporary Judaic consciousness.

Roskies, David G. *Against the Apocalypse: Responses to Catastrophe in Modern Jewish Culture.* Harvard Univ. Pr. 1986 pap. $9.95. Challenges the view that the Holocaust is without precedent or analogy in Jewish thought. Compares the Jewish response to the Holocaust with the way Jews have responded to over a century of European persecutions and pogroms.

CONTEMPORARY THEOLOGY

See also the main listings for Heschel, Rubenstein, Soloveitchik, and Waskow in this chapter.

Axelrad, Albert S. *Meditations of a Maverick Rabbi.* Rossel Bks. 1985 $8.95. Beloved Hillel rabbi at Brandeis University and left-wing activist states his religious convictions and his opinions on a wide range of topics.

Bamberger, Bernard J. *The Search for Jewish Theology.* Behrman 1978 pap. $4.95. The construction of a new system of Jewish theology by a Reform rabbi.

Berkovitz, Eliezer. *Not in Heaven: The Nature and Function of Halachah.* Ktav 1983 $12.00. Discusses the dynamic interaction of traditional Jewish law and the changing situation of Jewish life. Deals with contemporary issues that arise in a pluralistic, democratic environment, including conversion and the status of women.

Breslauer, S. Daniel. *A New Jewish Ethics.* E Mellen 1983 lib. bdg. $19.95. The construction of a pluralistic and ecumenical theology of ethics and interpersonal relations, inspired by the writings of Martin Buber.

Cohen, Arthur A. *The Myth of the Judeo-Christian Tradition.* Harper 1970 o.p. This iconoclastic study challenges the common assumption that Jews and Christians share a uniform tradition. The author argues for "the invigoration of prophetic radicalism, a dissent from the harmonious conservatism of inherited religion."

The Condition of Jewish Belief: A Symposium Compiled by the Editors of Commentary Magazine. Macmillan 1966 o.p. The answers of over 30 prominent rabbis to five burning questions of the day, such as "Is God dead?" and "Are the Jews the chosen people?" This collection documents the thinking of the mainstream rabbinical establishment in the 1960s.

Eisen, Arnold M. *The Chosen People in America: A Study in Jewish Religious Ideology.* [*Modern Jewish Experience Ser.*] Indiana Univ. Pr. 1983 $20.00. Traces the concept of chosenness in American Jewish intellectual history to 1980.

Hartman, David. *A Living Covenant: The Innovative Spirit in Traditional Judaism.* Free Pr. 1985 $21.60. Looks to Jewish tradition to establish a "covenantal religious anthropology capable of participating adequately in the challenges of modernity."

Herberg, Will. *Judaism and Modern Man.* Atheneum 1970 text ed. pap. $8.95. An analysis of how American Jews have responded and should respond to the challenges and opportunities of modern society.

Kaufman, William E. *Contemporary Jewish Philosophies.* Pref. by Jacob Neusner, Univ. Pr. of Amer. repr. of 1976 ed. 1986 text ed. pap. $12.25. A good survey of modern thinkers, carefully introduced, with the author's own proposals as well.

Neusner, Jacob. *Stranger at Home: "The Holocaust," Zionism, and American Judaism.* Univ. of Chicago Pr. 1981 $15.00 1985 pap. $8.95. On the relationship of American Jewry and the State of Israel.

Rosenthal, Gilbert S. *Four Paths to One God.* Bloch 1973 $8.95 pap. $5.95. A Conservative rabbi judges other peoples' Judaisms.

Schacter-Shalom, Zalman, and Donald Gropman. *The First Step: A Guide for the New Jewish Spirit.* Bantam 1983 o.p. A great Jewish spiritual leader proposes creative new models for Jewish practice.

Singer, Howard. *Bring Forth the Mighty Men: On Violence and the Jewish Character.* Funk & Wagnalls 1969 o.p. Reflections on the nature of "being Jewish" by a brilliant writer and social critic.

Wine, Sherwin T. *Judaism beyond God: A Radical Need to Be Jewish.* Prometheus Bks. 1986 pap. $13.95; Society for Humanistic Judaism 1985 pap. $13.95. Argues that Judaism and Jewish ritual can still be meaningful to Jews who do not believe in God. Humanistic Judaism emphasizes the intellectual and ethical dimensions of Jewish tradition.

Wolf, Arnold Jacob, ed. *Rediscovering Judaism: Reflections on a New Theology.* Quadrangle 1965 o.p. Reform rabbis reflecting on the renewal of Judaism.

Wyschogrod, Michael. *The Body of Faith: Judaism as Corporeal Election.* Seabury 1983 $24.95. A philosophic argument for the chosenness of Israel, the Jewish people, in a corporeal framework.

FEMINISM AND WOMEN'S STUDIES

One of the most lively issues facing Judaism today is the reevaluation of Jewish history, theology, and practice in light of changing attitudes and roles of women and men. Now that women have been ordained by the Reform, Conservative, and Reconstructionist movements, they are bringing new perspectives into a tradition that has been defined predominantly by men. Traditionalists claim that there is no reason for change. Conservatives believe that the tradition can adapt to accommodate new concerns. Radicals argue that Judaism must be transformed completely.

Aschkenasy, Nehama. *Eve's Journey: Feminine Images in Hebraic Literary Tradition.* Univ. of Pennsylvania Pr. 1986 text ed. $29.95 pap. $15.95. Traces the migration of female images through the Jewish tradition, concentrating on the Bible and recent literature. Gives special attention to two recurrent images—the "deadly seductress" and the "formidable giver of life."

Baum, Charlotte, and Sonya Michel. *The Jewish Woman in America.* Dial 1976 $8.95. Collection of essays on various aspects of the history of American Jewish women.

Biale, Rachel. *Women and Jewish Law: An Exploration of Women's Issues in Halakhic Sources.* Schocken 1984 $18.95. An attempt to reconcile contemporary concerns of women with the traditional sources of Jewish law.

Brayer, Menachem M. *Jewish Women in Rabbinic Literature.* Ktav 2 vols. 1986 text ed. ea. $20.00 pap. ea. $11.95. Vol. 1, *A Psychohistorical Perspective;* Vol. 2, *A Psychosocial Perspective.* An important compendium of sources from the Talmud to modern Orthodoxy. Examines woman's role in Judaism as wife, mother, educator, guide, martyr, and religious leader. Usually defends the traditional viewpoint against feminism.

Bristow, Edward J. *Prostitution and Prejudice: The Jewish Fight against White Slavery, 1870–1939.* Schocken 1983 $21.95. Bristow cites police reports, government studies, and newspaper accounts to explain the rapid growth in Jewish female prostitution in central and eastern Europe during the second half of the nineteenth century, and the response of the Jewish community as a whole.

Christ, Carol P., and Judith Plaskow. *Womanspirit Rising: A Feminist Reader in Religion*. Harper 1979 pap. $8.95. A collection of essays that place Jewish feminist thought in the context of general efforts to create new traditions of women's spirituality.

Greenberg, Blu. *On Women and Judaism: A View from Tradition*. Jewish Pubns. 1983 pap. $5.95. The best explanation of the Orthodox position on women's issues.

Henry, Sondra, and Emily Taitz. *Written Out of History: Our Jewish Foremothers*. Biblio NY 2d rev. ed. repr. of 1978 ed. 1983 $12.95 pap. $9.75; Bloch 1978 text ed. $12.50. This book gives attention to the women who have been pushed to the margins of Jewish history and forgotten, from the Bible to the present. Interesting reading but not reliable for scholarship.

Heschel, Susannah, ed. *On Being a Jewish Feminist*. Schocken 1983 $20.00 pap. $9.95. A collection of 24 feminist essays by men and women, many of which have been published previously, with a good introduction by the editor.

Kaplan, Marion. *The Jewish Feminist Movement in Germany: The Campaigns of the Judischer Frauenbund, 1904–1938*. [*Contributions in Women's Studies*] Greenwood 1979 lib. bdg. $29.95. An original and extensively documented study of Bertha Pappenheim (1859–1936) and the organization she established to promote woman suffrage and to fight prostitution and other social ills. Pappenheim is better known as Freud's "Anna O."

Koltun, Elizabeth, ed. *The Jewish Woman: New Perspectives*. Schocken 1976 pap. $7.95. A collection of essays on women, written from a variety of perspectives, that were originally published in a special issue of *Response* magazine in 1973.

Marcus, Jacob Rader. *The American Jewish Woman: A Documentary History*. Ktav 2 vols. 1981 vol. 1 $15.00 vol. 2 $35.00. The first volume is a comprehensive history of Jewish women in America, covering social, political, and religious topics. The second volume collects relevant documents, letters, memoirs, and essays.

Meiselman, Moshe. *Jewish Woman in Jewish Law*. [*Lib. of Jewish Law and Ethics*] Ktav 1978 $9.95. An antifeminist polemic that defends the traditional images and roles of woman.

Morton, Leah (pseud. Elizabeth G. Stern). *I Am a Woman and a Jew*. Intro. by Ellen Umanski [*Masterworks of Modern Jewish Writing*] Wiener repr. of 1926 ed. 1986 pap. $9.95. Autobiography from the first decade of this century by a Jew in a gentile world, a professional woman in a man's world of journalism and management. Having given up her Jewishness, she later developed a passionate pride in her tradition.

Ruether, Rosemary R. *Religion and Sexism: Images of Women in the Jewish and Christian Tradition*. Simon & Schuster 1974 pap. $10.95. An important collection of articles by various scholars on the view of women expressed by various documents of the Jewish and Christian traditions. Analyzes the Hebrew Bible, New Testament, Church Fathers, Talmud, Canon Law, the Reformation, and German Protestantism.

Schneider, Susan. *Jewish and Female: Choices and Changes in Our Lives Today*. Simon & Schuster 1984 $19.95. A guide for Jewish women full of practical information. Includes essays encouraging women to take on new roles.

Religious Movements

Each Judaism, each Judaic religious movement, has claimed that it continues the entire history of Judaism and represents the natural and logical next step from Sinai to the present day. Orthodoxy alleged that the sole legitimate and authentic Judaism, deriving from Sinai, was Orthodoxy today. Reform Judaism linked itself to reforming movements in the past and held that Reform Judaism today stands for the authentic and true Judaism, such as the prophets had set forth in their day. Conservative Judaism appealed to the processes of scholarship to identify in the past the necessary and essential Judaism that, in the present day, Conservative Judaism would embody. In these and in other ways each Judaism alleged that it formed the increment of the past and stood in a linear relationship to Sinai. This mode of legitimation in theological terms affirmed, in behalf of each Judaism, the authority of Sinai (for Orthodoxy) or of Sinai and of history (for Reform and Conservative Judaisms).

GENERAL

Blau, Joseph L. *Judaism in America: From Curiosity to Third Faith.* Univ. of Chicago Pr. 1976 $6.00 1978 pap. $4.95. A simple and clear introduction to the major movements of Judaism in America—Orthodox, Reform, Conservative, and the like.

———. *Modern Varieties of Judaism.* [*Lectures on the History of Religions*] Columbia Univ. Pr. 1966 $22.00 pap. $9.00. Good account of the modern Judaisms of the West.

Cohen, Elliot E., ed. *Commentary on the American Scene.* Knopf 1953 o.p. Selected essays from *Commentary* when the magazine concerned itself with Judaic rather than mainly political-conservative themes.

Cohen, Steven M. *American Modernity and Jewish Identity.* Methuen 1983 $24.00 pap. $9.95. Examines how various Judaic systems responded to modernity, including Reform and Conservative Judaism, as well as Jewish political liberalism and American Zionism.

Goodman, Saul L., ed. *The Faith of Secular Jews.* [*Lib. of Jewish Learning*] Ktav 1976 $25.00 pap. $11.95. Explains the position of Jews who are Jewish but not religious.

Isaacs, Harold R. *Idols of the Tribe: Group Identity and Political Change.* Harper 1977 o.p. Includes attention to American Jews in Israel as an example of how political change affects new definitions in religion.

Neusner, Jacob. *American Judaism: Adventure in Modernity.* Ktav 1972 pap. $9.95. Introduces the issues of history of religion to describe and interpret Judaism in America.

———. *The Death and Birth of Judaism: The Impact of Christianity, Secularism and the Holocaust on Jewish Faith.* Basic Bks. 1987 $21.95. Explains the modernization of Judaism in consequence of political change and interprets seven modern Judaisms against the background of contemporary history.

———, ed. *Understanding American Judaism: Toward the Description of Modern Religion.* Ktav 1975 2 vols. pap. ea. $11.95. Vol. 1, *Toward the Description of a Modern Religion: The Synagogue and the Rabbi;* Vol. 2, *The Sectors of American Judaism: Reform, Orthodoxy, Conservatism, and Reconstructionism.* Anthology of diverse writings about the three Judaisms of America, the rabbi, the synagogue, the community, and the consciousness of ordinary Jews.

Raphael, Marc Lee. *Profiles in American Judaism: The Reform, Conservative, Orthodox and Reconstructionist Traditions in Historical Perspective.* Harper 1984 $20.45. A clearly written survey of the history, ideology, and institutions of Reform, Conservative, Orthodox, and Reconstructionist Judaism.

Rudavsky, David. *Modern Jewish Religious Movements.* Fwd. by Abraham Katsch,

Behrman 3d ed. rev. repr. of 1967 ed. 1979 text ed. pap. $9.95. Account of the modernization of Judaism.

REFORM JUDAISM

Founded in early nineteenth-century Germany and enjoying enormous success in twentieth-century America, Reform Judaism took the position that change is legitimate and necessary, and that each generation had the task of finding a Judaism suitable to its circumstances. A means of preserving strong links and loyalties between a Judaism and the many Jews who wished to live a secular life and also a Judaic life, Reform Judaism solved the problem of making possible a Judaic life segregated from the politics and culture of the Western nations in which Jews lived. Reform Judaism maintained that certain aspects of Judaism, concerning ethics and morality, for example, took priority. To be a good Jew one did not have to keep dietary taboos but did have to practice justice and mercy and live an ethical life. Reform therefore proved the instrumentality for accommodating the desire of large numbers of Jews to live in a mixed society, not in a ghetto, and to live like their gentile neighbors but also in some ways different from them. See also under Science of Judaism (*Wissenschaft des Judentums*) above. (See Borowitz's main listing in this chapter.)

Blau, Joseph L., ed. *Reform Judaism: A Historical Perspective.* Central Conference of Amer. Rabbis 1973 o.p. Anthology of writings by Reform rabbis, spanning a period of 80 years.

Borowitz, Eugene B. *Reform Judaism Today.* 1973–77. Behrman 3 vols. 1983 text ed. pap. ea. $9.95. Vol. 1, *Reform in the Process of Change;* Vol. 2, *What We Believe;* Vol. 3, *How We Live.* Thought-provoking essays designed to facilitate discussion among Reform Jews.

Borowitz, Eugene B., and Joseph L. Blau, eds. *Reform Judaism, A Historical Perspective: Essays from the Yearbook of the Central Conference of American Rabbis.* Ktav 1973 o.p. Anthology of rabbis' writings.

Goldman, Edward A., ed. *Jews in a Free Society: Challenges and Opportunities.* Ktav 1978 $12.50. Eclectic collection of essays, celebrating the centennial of the Reform rabbinical school, on Jewish life in America and the purpose and potential of Reform Judaism.

Levy, Beryl Harold. *Reform Judaism in America: A Study in Religious Adaptation.* Bloch 1933 o.p. Early account of the history of Reform Judaism.

Marcus, Jacob R. *Israel Jacobson: The Founder of the Reform Movement in Judaism.* Ktav 1972 $12.50. Standard biography of an early Reformer.

Marcus, Jacob R., and Abraham J. Peck, eds. *The American Rabbinate: A Century of Continuity and Change, 1883–1983.* Ktav 1985 text ed. $20.00. Important picture of the character of the Reform rabbinate.

Martin, Bernard, ed. *Contemporary Reform Jewish Thought.* Quadrangle 1968 o.p. Account of important Reform theological positions by their authors.

Petuchowski, Jakob J. *Prayerbook Reform in Europe: The Liturgy of European Liberal and Reform Judaism.* UAHC 1969 $13.50. The story of how the prayer book became an arena for the reform of Judaism and how Reform Judaism reached the liturgy it presently follows.

Philipson, David. *Reform Movement in Judaism.* Ktav rev. ed. 1967 $20.00. The classic history of the nineteenth-century European phase of Reform Judaism, with presentation of primary source material.

Plaut, W. Gunther, ed. *The Growth of Reform Judaism: American and European Sources until 1948.* UAHC 1965 $10.00. Continuation of the following listing.

———. *The Rise of Reform Judaism: A Sourcebook of Its European Origins.* UAHC 1963 $10.00. The best anthology on the origin of Reform Judaism.

Umansky, Ellen M. *Lily Montagu and the Advancement of Liberal Judaism: From Vision to Vocation.* E Mellen 1984 $49.95. Biography of an important figure in early twentieth-century Liberal Judaism—the British equivalent of American Reform. Explores the world of English Jews, especially women, immersed in modern culture.

Weiner, Max. *Abraham Geiger and Liberal Judaism: The Challenge of the Nineteenth Century.* Jewish Pubns. 1962 o.p. The founder of Reform Judaic theology and scholarship in its Western and modern mode is here given his best biography and anthology in English.

ORTHODOX JUDAISM

In Germany and the United States, Orthodoxy took shape as a self-conscious Judaism in reaction to Reform Judaism. It maintained that change could not be declared in response to transient problems, and that Jews had to obey the Torah because God had revealed the Torah at Sinai. No knowledge and no science stood in judgment on the Torah, which was eternal, unchanging, and divine in origin and authority. Orthodoxy at the same time held that Jews could get a secular education and engage in life in close association with gentiles. Preserving the way of life and worldview of the received Judaism of the dual Torah, Orthodoxy recognized that Judaism would constitute a religion, rather than a completely encompassing politics and culture.

The Judaism of the dual Torah, with its definition of the Jews as a holy people living a holy life essentially separate from everyone else, may be called "traditional." That is because it was a received way of life that did not involve self-conscious affirmation, but simply an ongoing participation in patterns of life and thought that were received as unchanging and eternal. In this sense we should regard the Judaism of the dual Torah as it flourished in eastern Europe before World War II and as it flourishes in the State of Israel today, as well as in the United States and western Europe, as different from the Orthodoxy that came to expression in nineteenth-century Germany and twentieth-century America. This Judaism of the dual Torah held, and holds, that the Jews do not need to accommodate themselves to the requirements of Western civilization, should not waste time better devoted to study of the Torah by learning Western science and culture, and should form an essentially segregated and self-contained world, as (so it is maintained) the Jews did for all the centuries since Sinai. Dominating the world of yeshivas—centers for the full-time study of the Talmud and related sacred sciences—this kind of Judaism, although closely related to Orthodoxy, should be seen in its own terms, as an essentially separate Judaism, with its own social policy, its own types of institutions, its own politics and culture, distinct from that of the Westernized and modernized Orthodoxy. (See Hirsch's and Soloveitchik's main listings in this chapter.)

Bulka, Reuven P. *Dimensions of Orthodox Judaism.* Ktav 1983 o.p. Large collection of essays by various authors describing the ideology of modern Orthodoxy.

Friedman, Thomas. *Damaged Goods.* Permanent Pr. 1984 $17.95 1985 pap. $10.95. An informative and humorous account of second-generation Holocaust survivors in Brooklyn yeshivas (Orthodox religious schools) during the 1960s. Tells the story of an Orthodox dropout tempted and repulsed by secular society and the issues of the tumultuous 1960s.

Glenn, Menahem G. *Israel Salanter: The Story of a Religious-Ethical Current in Nine-*

teenth-Century Judaism. Bloch 1953 o.p. The first biography in English of a leading ethical thinker of nineteenth-century Orthodoxy.

Goldberg, Hillel. *Israel Salanter: Text, Structure, Idea.* Ktav 1982 $25.00. Biography of the founder of the Musar Movement (nineteenth-century movement that focused on the traditional and ethical component of Judaism). Salanter emerges as a creative thinker who was interested in understanding and altering the unconscious as well as in the study of the Talmud.

Heilman, Samuel C. *The Gate Behind the Wall.* Summit 1985 $15.95. An Orthodox Jew offers an insider's sociological study of Talmud study groups in Jerusalem. Succeeds as a personal account and as a sociological analysis.

———. *Synagogue Life: A Study in Symbolic Interaction.* Univ. of Chicago Pr. 1976 $12.95 pap. $9.95. Description of a close observer of an Orthodox synagogue and its everyday life.

Helmreich, William B. *The World of the Yeshiva: An Intimate Portrait of Orthodox Jewry.* Free Pr. 1982 $19.95; Yale Univ. Pr. 1986 pap. $14.95. Close observations of an Orthodox yeshiva on an everyday basis, together with a large-scale study of the entire movement.

Kurzweil, Zvi. *The Modern Impulse of Traditional Judaism.* Ktav 1985 $12.95. Outlines the position of centrist Orthodoxy in contradistinction to more extreme perspectives. Essays on tolerance, democracy, and the equality of women.

Liberles, Robert. *Religious Conflict in Social Context: The Resurgence of Orthodox Judaism in Frankfurt-Am-Main, 1838–1877. [Contributions to the Study of Religion Ser.]* Greenwood 1985 lib. bdg. $29.95. A sociological analysis of early Orthodoxy that demonstrates that the movement was not on the verge of collapse prior to Hirsch, as many people assume.

Liebman, Charles S. *Orthodoxy in American Jewish Life.* Amer. Jewish Comm. 1966 o.p. A sociological description of the religious and communal institutions of American Orthodoxy.

CONSERVATIVE JUDAISM

Conservative Judaism was born in Germany in the middle of the nineteenth century as a mediating movement between Reform Judaism and Orthodox Judaism. It shared the affirmation of Judaic religious observance of Orthodoxy but also the critical and scholarly policies of Reform Judaism. Conservative Judaism permitted change, like Reform, but change only in accord with the historically valid patterns by which the Judaism of the dual Torah had always produced change. In America, Conservative Judaism attained substantial success as a movement of the Judaic center. For the most part, it involved essentially observant and Orthodox rabbis preaching a middle-of-the-road Conservative Judaism to memberships made up of unobservant and therefore fundamentally Reform Jews. From 1920 to 1970 Conservative Judaism has been the most numerous of American Judaisms, but today is giving way to a strong trend toward Reform on the one side and a resurgent Orthodoxy on the other. See also under Science of Judaism (*Wissenschaft des Judentums*) above. (See Kaplan's main listing in this chapter.)

Davis, Moshe. *The Emergence of Conservative Judaism: The Historical School in 19th Century America.* 1963. Greenwood repr. of 1965 ed. 1977 o.p. Account of the beginnings of Conservative Judaism in America (1840–1902).

Siegel, Seymour, and Elliot Gertel. *God in the Teachings of Conservative Judaism.* Ktav 1985 $20.00. Anthology of theological writings by Conservative rabbis.

Sigal, Phillip. *The Emergence of Contemporary Judaism: The Foundation of Judaism from Biblical Origins to the Sixth Century A.D.* 1977. Pickwick 2 pts. 1980 text ed. pap. set $39.75. Conservative rabbi describes the beginnings of Conservative Judaism.

Sklare, Marshall. *Conservative Judaism: An American Religious Movement.* Univ. Pr. of Amer. repr. of 1977 ed. 1985 text ed. pap. $12.75. Sociological study of Conservative Judaism as the religion of the second generation of American Jews.

Steinberg, Milton. *A Partisan Guide to the Jewish Problem.* Univ. Pr. of Amer. repr. of 1945 ed. 1986 text ed. pap. $13.50. Leading thinker of Conservative Judaism lays out the Jewish problems as he sees them.

Waxman, Mordecai, ed. *Tradition and Change.* United Synagogue Bk. 1958 o.p. The best anthology of Conservative Judaism.

SOCIALISM

In eastern Europe during the second half of the nineteenth century, thousands of working-class Jews, together with members of the Jewish intelligentsia, turned to socialism as an answer to the continual persecution of the Jews. They considered anti-Semitism to be a consequence of socioeconomic injustice and advocated communist revolution. The Bund, the first Jewish socialist party, was established in Vilna, and quickly spread from Lithuania to Poland and the Ukraine. The early socialists advocated universal goals, but during the last decade of the century, a Jewish movement emerged, emphasizing the particular experience and culture of the Jews. Zionist socialism, incorporating the doctrine of territorialism, developed as an offshoot to Jewish socialism. When Russian-Jewish radicals arrived in the United States during the 1880s, Yiddish-language workers' parties, newspapers, and organizations flourished. Jews populated the sweatshops of the Lower East Side of Manhattan, producing a situation ripe for union organizing. Jewish activists organized the United Garment Workers of America (1891) and other important unions. Most of the unions had a socialist ideology, but one Jew, Samuel Gompers, who helped establish the American Federation of Labor in 1886, sought to keep his union apolitical.

Avineri, Shlomo. *Moses Hess: Prophet of Communism and Zionism.* [*Modern Jewish Masters Ser.*] New York Univ. Pr. 1987 $25.00 pap. $12.50. Examines the thought of Moses Hess (1812–75) and its relationship to Zionist socialism of the early twentieth century.

Buber, Martin. *Paths in Utopia.* Intro. by E. Fischoff, Beacon Pr. 1958 pap. $7.95. The idealist version of socialism laid out by the great social philosopher.

Deutscher, Isaac. *The Non-Jewish Jew and Other Essays.* Oxford 1968 o.p. Jewish socialist figure describes the position of secular Jews attracted to socialism.

Epstein, Melech. *Profiles of Eleven.* Intro. by Jacob Neusner, Univ. Pr. of Amer. repr. of 1965 ed. 1987 text ed. pap. $16.75. Biographies of 11 men who figured prominently in the Jewish socialist movement among the immigrant generation of 1880–1920.

Fishman, William J. *Jewish Radicals, 1875–1914: From Czarist Stetl to London Ghetto.* Pantheon repr. 1975 o.p. A detailed study of the various Jewish radical movements from 1870 until World War I.

Frankel, Jonathan. *Prophecy and Politics: Socialism, Nationalism, and the Russian Jews, 1862–1917.* Cambridge Univ. Pr. 1981 $72.50 1984 pap. $19.95. Classic account of the Jews and socialism in eastern Europe.

Goodman, Saul L., ed. *The Faith of Secular Jews.* [*Lib. of Jewish Learning*] Ktav 1976 $25.00 pap. $11.95. Secular, socialist Jews express their deepest convictions.

Green, Nancy L. *Pletzl of Paris: Jewish Immigrant Workers in the Belle Epoque.*

Holmes & Meier 1985 $39.55. Analysis of the Jewish immigrant labor movement in Paris during the Gay Nineties.

Johnpoll, Bernard K. *The Politics of Futility: The General Jewish Workers Bund of Poland, 1917–1943.* Cornell Univ. Pr. 1967 o.p. The story of the Jewish socialist movement in Poland.

Levin, Nora. *Jewish Socialist Movements, 1871–1917: While Messiah Tarried.* [*Littman Lib. of Jewish Civilization*] Oxford 1978 $32.00. Popular account of Jewish socialism that traces the history of the Bund in prerevolutionary Russia and the development of the American Jewish labor movement and socialist Zionism.

Liebman, Arthur. *The Jews and the Left.* [*Contemporary Religious Movements*] Wiley 1979 o.p. Political science study of the Jews in the left-wing movements of the twentieth century.

Mendelsohn, Ezra. *Class Struggle in the Pale.* Cambridge Univ. Pr. 1970 o.p. The founding, in competition with Zionism, of the Jewish socialist movement in Russia and Russian Poland.

Porter, Jack Nusan, and Peter Drier. *Jewish Radicalism: A Selected Anthology.* Grove 1973 o.p. An anthology of articles, manifestos, and poems from American Jewish radical newspapers and journals.

Portnoy, Samuel A., ed. and trans. *Vladimir Medem: The Life and Soul of a Legendary Jewish Socialist.* Ktav 1979 $25.00. The most important intellectual figure in the Jewish socialist movement.

Sorin, Gerald. *The Prophetic Minority: American Jewish Immigrant Radicals, 1880–1920.* [*Modern Jewish Experience*] Indiana Univ. Pr. 1985 $24.95. Engaging account of the Jewish labor activists and socialists, emphasizing ethnicity as a motivation for their ideology.

Tobias, Henry J. *Jewish Bund in Russia from Its Origins to 1905.* Stanford Univ. Pr. 1972 $30.00. The earliest years of the Jewish socialist movement.

Wistrich, Robert S. *Revolutionary Jews from Marx to Trotsky.* Fwd. by James Joll, Barnes & Noble 1976 o.p. Socialists who happened to be Jews, as distinct from Jewish socialists, described in biographical studies.

———. *Socialism and the Jews: The Dilemmas of Assimilation in Germany and Austria-Hungary.* [*Littman Lib. of Jewish Civilization*] Oxford 1982 $37.50. Analyzes the role the Jewish question played in the politics of the German and Austrian Social Democratic parties before 1914. Considers the issue of Jewish emancipation, the problem of political anti-Semitism, and the emergence of Jewish nationalism. Considers the evolution of German and Austrian Jewry from a new angle.

YIDDISHISM

Yiddishism was a language-oriented movement, allied with Jewish socialism, identifying the Yiddish language as the instrument by which the Jews would express their culture and collective consciousness. Since most of the Jews in eastern Europe and a great many in the United States spoke Yiddish, for a time the movement achieved considerable influence. It fostered the writing of fiction and serious nonfiction in Yiddish and the development of instruments of education and culture for the propagation of the language. The Jewish socialists made use of Yiddish as the means of reaching the Jewish masses and identified Yiddishism as the cultural dimension of their movement. (See also Volume 2, Chapter 17, Yiddish Literature.)

Epstein, Melech. *Profiles of Eleven.* Intro. by Jacob Neusner, Univ. Pr. of Amer. repr. of 1965 ed. 1987 text ed. pap. $16.75. Account of the earliest Yiddish-speaking socialists.

Howe, Irving, and Eliezer Greenberg, eds. *Voices from the Yiddish: Essays, Memoirs, Diaries*. Univ. of Michigan Pr. 1972 o.p. The best anthology of the Yiddishist movement.

ZIONISM

Zionism, founded in 1897, declared that the Jews are a people and required a state. The Zionist movement therefore identified the Jews as a political, not solely a religious, group, and maintained that the Jews' problem was a political one. They held that anti-Semitism was deeply embedded in Europe, and that the Jews had to evacuate Europe to save their own lives. Building a Jewish state in Palestine formed the principal goal of political Zionism, which achieved success in 1948. Zionist thought extended to political questions on the definition and program of the coming state, and also to cultural ones concerning the definition of the Jewish people and the description and meaning of the history of the Jewish people. Zionism formed one of the principal sources for the definition of Jewish thought and scholarship in the first half of the twentieth century.

Agus, Jacob. *Banner of Jerusalem: The Life, Times, and Thought of Abraham Isaac Kuk*. Bloch 1946 o.p. Biography of an Orthodox rabbi who also was a leading Zionist figure.

Ahad Ha'am. *Nationalism and the Jewish Ethic: Basic Writings of Ahad Ha'am*. Ed. by Hans Kohn, Schocken 1962 o.p. A good anthology of Asher Zvi Ginsberg, who took the name Ahad Ha'am (meaning "one of the people")—a leading Zionist theoretician of the early twentieth century, with strong interest in cultural issues.

Avineri, Shlomo. *The Making of Modern Zionism: Intellectual Origins of the Jewish State*. Basic Bks. 1981 $15.50 1984 pap. $7.95. History of Zionism by an important political figure and scholar.

Cohen, Naomi. *American Jews and the Zionist Idea*. Ktav 1975 pap. $9.95. Account of the development of Zionist ideology among American Jewry.

Dubnow, Simon. *Nationalism and History: Essays on Old and New Judaism*. Ed. by Koppel S. Pinson, Atheneum repr. of 1958 ed. 1970 o.p. Account of a Jewish nationalist who did not favor moving all the Jews to the Land of Israel but wished the Diaspora communities to survive.

Elon, Amos. *Herzl*. 1975. Schocken 1986 pap. $12.95. Stunning biography of the founder of modern Zionism, by far the best work ever done on the subject.

Halkin, Hillel. *Letters to an American Jewish Friend: A Zionist's Polemic*. Jewish Pubns. 1977 pap. $6.95. Polemic against Jews living in the Diaspora.

Halpern, Ben. *The American Jew: A Zionist Analysis*. Schocken repr. of 1956 ed. 1983 pap. $6.95. Powerful analysis of the weakness of the American Jewish commitment to Zionism.

———. *The Idea of the Jewish State*. [*Middle Eastern Studies*] Harvard Univ. Pr. rev. ed. 1969 $30.00. Profound analysis of the political foundations of Zionist thought.

Hertzberg, Arthur, ed. *Zionist Idea: A Historical Analysis and Reader*. Atheneum repr. of 1959 ed. 1969 text ed. pap. $7.95; Greenwood repr. of 1959 ed. 1971 $23.50. Classic anthology of writings about Zionism from the beginnings to the mid-1950s.

Herzl, Theodor. *The Jewish State*. Trans. by Harry Zohn, Herzl 1970 o.p. The influential book by the founder of political Zionism, Theodor Herzl (1860–1904). He argued that Jews will never be accepted into Western society, and that the only real solution to their economic and social problems would be the founding of a Jewish state in Palestine.

Kaplan, Mordecai. *A New Zionism.* Herzl 1955 o.p. New theory of Zionism, deriving from Ahad Ha'am's ideas on Jewish culture, making room for the notion of Jews living outside of the Land of Israel.

Laqueur, Walter. *A History of Zionism.* Schocken repr. of 1972 ed. 1976 pap. $12.95. The best history of Zionism, beginning to the present.

Lilker, Shalom. *Kibbutz Judaism: A New Tradition in the Making.* Associated Univ. Prs. 1982 $14.95; Norwood 1982 lib. bdg. $19.50. Argues that the life-style and ideology of the secular kibbutz represents a Jewish religion, even if the members do not actually consider themselves religious.

Mendelsohn, Ezra. *Zionism in Poland: The Formative Years, 1915–1926.* Yale Univ. Pr. 1982 text ed. $42.00. An excellent in-depth account of the rapid growth of Zionism in Poland.

Meyer, Isidore S., ed. *Early History of Zionism in America.* Amer. Jewish Hist. Soc. 1958 o.p. Monograph on the early history of Zionism.

Poppel, Stephen M. *Zionism in Germany, 1897–1933: The Shaping of a Jewish Identity.* Jewish Pubns. 1977 $7.95. Analytic study of the Zionist movement in Germany, its ideas and leadership, before Hitler.

Rabinowicz, Harry M. *Hasidism and the State of Israel.* [*Littman Lib. of Jewish Civilization*] Oxford 1982 $24.95. Tells the story of the twentieth-century, pro-Zionist Hasidic movement and its transplantation to the State of Israel after the Holocaust. Discusses the role of the Land of Israel in Hasidic ideology from its origins.

Rubenstein, Amnon. *The Zionist Dream Revisited: From Herzl to Gush Emunim and Back.* Schocken 1984 $14.95. The leader of an Israeli centrist party contrasts the old-line labor Zionism, dominant in the early twentieth century, with the contemporary right-wing hawks of the Gush-Emunim movement.

Urofsky, Melvin I. *American Zionism from Herzl to the Holocaust.* 1975. Doubleday 1976 o.p. Tells the story of the Zionist institutions and ideology among American Jews during the first half of this century.

RECONSTRUCTIONISM

In the twentieth century an offshoot of Conservative Judaism, Reconstructionism, established itself within a naturalist (rather than a supernatural) theology, and emphasized the idea of God as the power that makes for salvation. Reconstructionism laid great stress on Jewish peoplehood and emphasized the keeping of religious rites as an expression of loyalty to the people, rather than as obedience to God's will. Today Reconstructionist Judaism has its own seminary, the Reconstructionist Rabbinical College in Philadelphia, as well as an organization of rabbis and of synagogues. It is a fully articulated Judaism in America. (See also Kaplan's main listing in this chapter.)

Alpert, Rebecca T., and Jacob J. Staub. *Exploring Judaism: A Reconstructionist Approach.* Reconstructionist Pr. 1985 $11.95 pap. $5.95. A brief introduction to Kaplan's thought and the contemporary practice and institutions of the Reconstructionist movement.

Eisenstein, Ira. *Reconstructing Judaism: An Autobiography.* Reconstructionist Pr. 1986 $17.95. An autobiography by a key figure in the development of Reconstructionism as a movement.

Miller, Alan W. *God of Daniel S. in Search of the American Jew.* 1968. [*Brown Class. in Judaica Ser.*] Univ. Pr. of Amer. repr. of 1969 ed. 1986 text ed. pap. $13.25.

Review of all modern theologies of Judaism from the perspective of Reconstructionism. Powerful apologetic for Reconstructionism.

REVERSIONARY JUDAISM

Since World War II, and particularly in recent decades, a movement of reversion to Judaism has characterized large numbers of formerly secular Jews in both the State of Israel and America, as well as in Europe. This does not constitute a single Judaism, since it may be expressed by a higher standard of adherence to Judaic religious practices within Reform congregations, as much as a conversion by a secular Jew to Orthodoxy. The pattern is relative, therefore, and often involves moving one step toward a more traditional pattern, rather than a complete revolution in the believer's life and thought. Reversionary Judaism has, however, received its most effective institutional expression within Israeli Orthodoxy. Israeli yeshivas and communities of the pious have undertaken vigorous efforts to receive Jews of little or no background and to educate and train them into the Judaism of the dual Torah. In the United States, too, Orthodoxy has received and assimilated both less observant Orthodox and Reform and Conservative Jews, not to mention formerly quite secular ones, and has formed of these returnees large and vigorous communities of observant persons. (For works on contemporary Hasidism, see under Medieval Judaism: Hasidism in this chapter.)

Aviad, Janet. *Return to Judaism: Religious Renewal in Israel.* Univ. of Chicago Pr. 1983 lib. bdg. $20.00 pap. $8.95. Solid sociological study of the reversionists in the context of the institutions of Israeli Orthodoxy.

Levin, Michael Graubart. *Journey to Tradition: The Odyssey of a Born-Again Jew.* Ktav 1986 $14.95. The personal story of a young Jew who moved from a null position to Orthodoxy, but subsequently left Orthodoxy because, despite ample learning and strict observance, he could not find acceptance there.

BA'AL SHEM TOV. c.1700–1760

According to Hasidic tradition, Israel ben Eliezer Ba'al Shem Tov revealed himself as a healer and leader on his thirty-sixth birthday. His following expanded rapidly and soon encompassed a large part of eastern European Jewry. He employed Cabalistic categories and terminology, but emphasized personal experience and salvation over the redemption of the world. The Ba'al Shem Tov spoke of a God directly accessible to human beings through prayer and joyous celebration. Many legends developed during his lifetime and afterward about his miracles and charismatic personality. (See also under Medieval Judaism: Hasidism in this chapter.)

BOOKS ABOUT BA'AL SHEM TOV

Buber, Martin. *The Legend of the Baal-Shem.* Schocken repr. of 1955 ed. 1969 pap. $7.95. A theological introduction to Hasidism and a creative retelling of the legends concerning the charismatic founder of Hasidism.

Heschel, Abraham J. *The Circle of Baal Shem Tov: Studies in Hasidism.* Ed. by Samuel H. Dresner, Univ. of Chicago Pr. 1985 $24.95. Lucid and passionate essays on four figures from the inner circle of the founder of Hasidism: Pinchas of Korzec, Nahman of Kosov, Gershon Kutover, and Isaac of Drohobyez.

BAECK, LEO. 1873–1956

Leo Baeck was born in Lissa (now Leszno), Poland, to a family of distinguished rabbis. He studied at the Conservative Jewish Theological Seminary of Breslau and then at the Hochschule für die Wissenschaft des Judentums in Berlin. In 1905 he wrote *The Essence of Judaism* in response to Adolf von Harnack's *The Essence of Christianity*, and to the general mood of Christian chauvinism and anti-Semitism. Baeck was the most prominent Jewish leader in Germany when the Nazis came to power in 1933. He remained as the outspoken leader of the Berlin Jewish community until he was deported to the Theresienstadt concentration camp in 1943. After the war, he became the chair of the World Union of Progressive Judaism in London and occasionally taught at the Reform seminary in Cincinnati. (See also under Modern Judaism: Early Twentieth-Century German-Jewish Theology in this chapter.)

BOOKS BY BAECK

The Essence of Judaism. 1905. Schocken rev. ed. 1961 pap. $8.50. Apologetic work defending Judaism against criticism from insiders and outsiders. Explains Judaism as a coherent ethical system.

This People Israel. 1955. Holt 1964 o.p. Philosophy of Jewish peoplehood.

Judaism and Christianity: Essays. 1958. Trans. by Walter Kaufmann, Atheneum repr. of 1958 ed. 1970 o.p. Baeck agrees with Hermann Cohen that Judaism constitutes "ethical monotheism," and that this form of religion is superior to Christian "romanticism."

BOOKS ABOUT BAECK

Baker, Leonard. *Days of Sorrow and Pain: Leo Baeck and the Berlin Jews.* Oxford 1980 pap. $9.95. The best account of Leo Baeck's heroic and inspiring leadership of the Berlin Jewish community during the period of its demise at the hands of the Nazis.

Friedlander, Albert H. *Leo Baeck: Teacher of Theresienstadt.* Holt 1968 o.p. A good book on the leading German Judaic Reform theologian of the twentieth century.

BOROWITZ, EUGENE. 1924–

Borowitz is the most original and influential Reform Jewish thinker of today. A Reform rabbi and professor at Columbia and the Hebrew Union College in New York, he is the founder and editor of *Sh'ma: A Journal of Jewish Responsibility,* a lively publication that promotes open discussion of controversial topics from all Judaic perspectives. He rejects the notion that Judaism is based on a heteronomous tradition or Jewish law. Instead, he stresses the importance of autonomous choice and personal faith. Borowitz claims that a covenantal relationship to God forms the core of Reform Jewish theology and ethics. (See also under Modern Judaism: Reform Judaism in this chapter.)

BOOKS BY BOROWITZ

A New Jewish Theology in the Making. Westminster 1968 $6.50. The first articulation of Borowitz's theological system.

The Masks Jews Wear: Self-Deceptions of American Jewry. Simon & Schuster 1973

$8.95. Provocative and timely challenge to American Jews to come to terms with Jewish identity as an internal spiritual and ethical commitment.

Contemporary Christologies: A Jewish Response. Paulist Pr. 1980 pap. $7.95. For the first time, a Jewish theologian thoroughly examines and responds to contemporary Christian doctrines of Christ—Catholic, Protestant, liberal, neo-Orthodox, evangelical, and postmodern. Highly recommended.

Choices in Modern Jewish Thought: A Partisan Guide. Behrman 1983 text ed. $9.95. An analysis and subjective appraisal of the thought of the major Jewish philosophers of the twentieth century, from Hermann Cohen to Joseph Soloveitchik.

Liberal Judaism. UAHC 1984 pap. $8.95. Constructs a theological system, expressing Reform attitudes toward the Jewish people, God, the Bible, ethics, and Jewish life-style. Emphasizes a covenantal relationship with God and the importance of autonomous choice in Reform Judaism. Addressed to an intellectual audience.

BUBER, MARTIN. 1878–1965

Martin Buber was born in Vienna, the son of Solomon Buber, an important scholar of Midrashic and medieval literature. Martin Buber studied at the universities of Vienna, Leipzig, Zurich, and Berlin, under Wilhelm Dilthey and Georg Simmel. As a young student, he joined the Zionist movement, advocating the renewal of Jewish culture as opposed to Theodor Herzl's political Zionism. At age 26, he became interested in Hasidic thought and translated the tales of Nahman of Bratslav. Buber is responsible for bringing Hasidism to the attention of young German intellectuals who had previously scorned it as the product of ignorant eastern European Jewish peasants. Hasidism had a profound impact on Buber's thought. He credits it as the inspiration for his theories of spirituality, community, and dialogue. Buber also wrote about utopian socialism, education, Zionism, and respect for the Palestinian Arabs, and with Franz Rosenzweig, he translated the Bible. He was appointed to a professorship at the University of Frankfurt in 1925, but when the Nazis came to power he received an appointment at the Hebrew University of Jerusalem. (See also under Medieval Judaism: Hasidism, and Modern Judaism: Early Twentieth-Century German-Jewish Theology in this chapter.)

BOOKS BY BUBER

The Writings of Martin Buber. Ed. by Will Herberg, New Amer. Lib. 1974 o.p. Anthology presenting Buber's principal writings.

I and Thou. 1936. Trans. by S. G. Smith [*Hudson River Ed. Ser.*] Peter Smith 1986 $14.75; Scribner 1970 $20.00 pap. $6.95. The most important single work of the eminent philosopher of religion and Judaism. Develops a theory of interpersonal relations based on openness and respect, and claims that God exists in the genuine encounter of one person with another.

The Prophetic Faith. 1942. Peter Smith 1986 $15.75. Buber's interpretations of the religion of the prophets.

Between Man and Man. 1947. Trans. by Ronald Gregor Smith, Macmillan 1985 pap. $6.95; Peter Smith 1986 $15.25. An elaboration of the principles presented in *I and Thou,* with discussions of the theory of education and the thoughts of Kierkegaard, Kant, and others.

Two Types of Faith: The Interpretation of Judaism and Christianity. 1961. Macmillan

1986 pap. $7.95. Buber's open-minded encounter with Jesus, Paul, and the teachings of Christianity.

On Judaism. Ed. by Nahum Glatzer, Schocken 1972 pap. $7.50. A collection of important essays on the nature of Judaism.

BOOKS ABOUT BUBER

Berry, Donald L. *Mutuality: The Vision of Martin Buber.* State Univ. of New York Pr. 1985 $39.50 pap. $14.95. A short discussion of Buber's philosophy of dialogue.

Diamond, Malcolm L. *Martin Buber: Jewish Existentialist.* Gannon 1968 lib. bdg. $17.50. The single most accessible account of Buber's thought seen as a whole system.

Friedman, Maurice. *Martin Buber: The Life of Dialogue.* Univ. of Chicago Pr. 3d ed. rev. 1976 pap. $13.00. Important scholarly account of the relationship between Buber's life and thought.

COHEN, HERMANN. 1842–1918

The son of a cantor, Hermann Cohen studied at the Jewish Theological Seminary at Breslau, but gave up a rabbinical career to study philosophy. He devoted himself to the analysis of Platonic and Kantian idealism and became full professor at the University of Marburg at the young age of 34. His personal philosophy placed ethics at the center of human experience. Late in life, he left Marburg to teach at the Hochschule für die Wissenschaft des Judentums in Berlin. Whereas his early writings located the realm of ethics within autonomous human reason, his work in Berlin saw God as the foundation for any ethical system. (See also under Modern Judaism: Early Twentieth-Century German-Jewish Theology in this chapter.)

BOOKS BY COHEN

Religion of Reason out of the Sources of Judaism. 1919. Trans. by Simon Kaplan, intro. by Leo Strauss, Ungar 1971 o.p. First published posthumously, this classic text develops the doctrine of the uniqueness of God. Cohen holds that Judaism is rooted in reason and therefore can be logically derived and systematically explained.

Reason and Hope: Selections from the Jewish Writings of Hermann Cohen. Ed. and trans. by Eva Jospe, Norton 1971 o.p. Anthology of writings by the important German Jewish philosopher.

BOOKS ABOUT COHEN

Dietrich, Wendell S. *Cohen and Troeltsch: Ethical Monotheistic Religion and Theory of Culture.* Scholars Pr. GA 1986 text ed. $23.95 pap. $18.95. The best treatment of Hermann Cohen in English. This monograph traces the influences on Cohen's thought, compares him to Ernst Troeltsch, and discusses the contemporary relevance of their thought.

Kaplan, Mordecai. *The Purpose and Meaning of Jewish Existence.* Jewish Pubns. 1964 o.p. An epitome of and commentary on Hermann Cohen's *Religion of Reason out of the Sources of Judaism.*

Melber, Jehuda. *Hermann Cohen's Philosophy of Judaism.* Jonathan David 1968 o.p. Good introduction. Makes Cohen's difficult philosophy accessible. Shows the influences of classical Jewish sources and Kantian philosophy on his philosophic system.

FACKENHEIM, EMIL. 1916–

Fackenheim was born in Halle, Germany, and ordained at the Hochschule für die Wissenschaft des Judentums in Berlin in 1939. In 1940 he went to Canada and thus narrowly escaped the devastation of the Holocaust. Fackenheim became a professor at the University of Toronto, where he has made important contributions to the study of Hegel and German idealism. The 1960s saw a radical change in his philosophy, as he attempted to come to terms with the horror of the Holocaust. He argued that the murder of Jews by the Nazis was qualitatively unique, a "novum" in history. He could no longer think in terms of timeless and abstract philosophic systems, which do not account for the possibility of this radical evil. Fackenheim claims that Jews must not allow the Holocaust to weaken their faith, lest Hitler be given a posthumous victory. He sees the establishment of the State of Israel as a testimony to Jewish defiance in the face of Nazi oppression. Fackenheim has recently moved to Jerusalem, where he articulates a Zionist view that Jewish life can be authentically lived once in the State of Israel. (See also under Modern Judaism: Post-Holocaust Theology in this chapter.)

BOOKS BY FACKENHEIM

God's Presence in History: Jewish Affirmations and Philosophical Reflections. Harper 1972 pap. $5.95. The most important statement of the leading Holocaust theologian in Reform Judaism.

Encounters between Judaism and Modern Philosophy: A Preface to Future Jewish Thought. Schocken repr. of 1973 ed. 1980 pap. $7.95. Uses philosophic categories to refine Jewish thought in the aftermath of the Holocaust. Discusses the implications of Kant, Hegel, Sartre, and Heidegger on contemporary Judaism.

To Mend the World: Foundations of Future Jewish Thought. Schocken 1982 $22.50 pap. $12.95. A reformulation and explanation of Fackenheim's post-Holocaust and Zionist theology.

GERSONIDES (LEVI BEN GERSHON). 1288–1344

Levi ben Gershon or Gersonides wrote 16 major works on religious, philosophic, mathematical, and medical topics. He spent most of his life in the major papal cultural centers of southern France and maintained extensive relations with Christian intellectuals. Gersonides was a supreme rationalist in the tradition of Maimonides, although they disagreed on a number of key points. Gersonides held that humans may attain certain positive knowledge of God, and that humans possess a speculative intellect that permits the perception of truth and the attainment of immortality. (See also under Medieval Judaism: Philosophy in this chapter.)

BOOKS BY GERSONIDES

Providence in the Philosophy of Gersonides. 1973. Trans. by David J. Bleich, Feldheim 1982 $7.95. Translation of the fourth part of Gersonides' *The War of the Lord.* The most accessible portion of this work appearing in English.

The Creation of the World According to Gersonides. Trans. by Jacob J. Staub, Scholars Pr. GA 1982 pap. $20.00. Part 6 of *The War of the Lord,* in which Gersonides rejects Maimonides' contention that the creation of the world can be known philosophically.

HESCHEL, ABRAHAM JOSHUA. 1907–1972

Heschel received his doctorate at the Hochschule für die Wissenschaft des Judentums in Berlin but was deported to Poland by the Nazis in 1938. He went to London in 1940 and after the war accepted a professorship in ethics and mysticism at the Jewish Theological Seminary in New York. Heschel articulated a depth theology, arguing that the divine-human encounter takes place at a deeper level than is attainable by the rational mind. He reached out to skeptical Jews and tried to make Judaism accessible and meaningful in the modern world. Heschel stressed the interdependence of God and humanity. God recognizes and supports ethical human action, and people express their faith through their actions. Heschel lived according to his word, and played an active role in social change, including the civil rights movement. (See also under Modern Judaism: Orthodox Judaism in this chapter.)

BOOKS BY HESCHEL

The Earth Is the Lord's: The Inner World of the Jew in Eastern Europe. 1950. Farrar 1978 $8.95. pap. $5.95. Heschel believed that the world of eastern European Jewry from the seventeenth through the nineteenth centuries was a "Golden Age." He explains that these Jews sanctified time, rather than space, thereby making the Sabbath and the holy days the center of their spirituality.

God in Search of Man: A Philosophy of Judaism. 1955. Aronson repr. of 1955 ed. 1987 $30.00; Farrar 1976 pap. $10.95; Hippocrene Bks. repr. of 1955 ed. 1972 lib. bdg. $29.00. Heschel's most important work, a full-scale theology of Judaism, covering all aspects of the faith as Heschel reads them. The paramount statement of Judaic theology of the mid-twentieth century.

Between God and Man: An Interpretation of Judaism. 1959. Ed. by Fritz Rothschild, Free Pr. 1965 pap. $8.95. Anthology of 41 essays by Heschel. The best introduction to Heschel's philosophy of religion.

The Insecurity of Freedom: Essays on Human Existence. Schocken repr. of 1966 ed. 1985 pap. $7.95. A collection of Heschel's political, ethical, and religious writings, on religion in a free society, civil rights, Zionism, and many other topics.

Israel: An Echo of Eternity. Farrar 1969 o.p. Discusses the role of Jerusalem and the Land of Israel in Jewish theology, with a chapter on the contemporary Arab-Israeli conflict.

A Passion for Truth. 1973. Farrar 1986 pap. $9.95. Comparison of a Hasidic rabbi, the Kotzker, and Kierkegaard. Tour de force of enormous dimensions.

The Sabbath: Its Meaning for Modern Man. Farrar 1975 pap. $4.50. A profound and poetic book on the meaning of the Sabbath and the sacredness of time in Judaism. Highly recommended.

I Asked for Wonder: A Spiritual Anthology. Ed. by Samuel H. Dresner, Crossroad NY 1983 pap. $8.95. A short collection of brief selections of Heschel's writings, unfortunately presented out of context.

BOOKS ABOUT HESCHEL

Merkle, John C. *The Genesis of Faith: The Depth Psychology of Abraham Joshua Heschel.* Macmillan 1985 $19.95. Traces the influences on Heschel's thought, such as the spiritual sources of faith, the mystery of creation, and the literary sources of Judaism.

Sherwin, Byron L. *Abraham Joshua Heschel*. John Knox, 1978 o.p. Short (50-page) discussion of ten important themes that pervade Heschel's work and of the actual and potential influence of his writings on Judaism and Christianity.

HIRSCH, SAMSON (BEN) RAPHAEL. 1808–1888

The foremost leader of nineteenth-century German orthodoxy, Hirsch had a background in Talmud in addition to some study of Greek and Roman classics at the University of Bonn. He is best known for his passionate advocacy of Orthodoxy and his polemics against the new Reform movement. He opposed any notion of historical development of Jewish laws and customs. Hirsch's ideas and methods continue to shape the lives of many contemporary Jews. (See also under Modern Judaism: Orthodox Judaism in this chapter.)

BOOKS BY HIRSCH

The Collected Writings. Feldheim 3 vols. 1984 ea. $15.75

The Nineteen Letters of Ben Uziel on Judaism. Trans. by Bernard Drachman, Feldheim 1969 $4.95; Shalom $27.50. The classic writing of the founder of German Orthodox Judaism attacks the early Reform movement. Written in the form of imaginary letters between a young intellectual with religious doubts and a passionate young Orthodox rabbi.

Horeb: A Philosophy of Jewish Laws and Observances. Trans. by I. Grunfled, Bloch $19.95; Soncino Pr. 1962 $19.95. Hirsch presents a detailed account of Jewish observance, explaining the ideas and values behind each law. An important book, but not designed to be read from beginning to end.

BOOK ABOUT HIRSCH

Rosenbloom, Noah H. *Tradition in an Age of Reform: The Religious Philosophy of Samson Raphael Hirsch*. Jewish Pubns. 1976 o.p. Authoritative intellectual biography of the founder of German Orthodox Judaism.

JOSEPHUS, FLAVIUS. c.A.D.38–A.D.100?

Josephus claimed to personally embody many strains of first-century Judaism: His family lineage connected him to the Hasmonean rulers and the priestly caste, his education and religious quest gave him experience with the three major sects of first-century Judaism, and his military command and defeat landed him on both sides of the Jewish War against Rome (A.D. 66–73). His unusual life makes his autobiography, *The Life*, interesting reading. More importantly, his historical works, *The Jewish War* and *The Jewish Antiquities*, record information about Jewish life in Palestine during the first century. His accounts are frequently subjective and apologetic, but they represent the only extant sources on many significant details of this pivotal century. Even though he became a Roman citizen, Josephus remained a committed Jew. His *Against Apion* (not published separately) is a polemical defense of Judaism that attacks anti-Jewish arguments and asserts the ethical superiority of Judaism over Hellenism. (See also Volume 3.)

BOOKS BY JOSEPHUS

Flavius Josephus: Selections from His Works. Ed. by Abraham Hasserstein, Viking 1974 o.p. Readable translation from the full range of Josephus's works. Designed for the nonspecialist.

The Jewish War. Trans. by G. A. Williamson, ed. by E. Mary Smallwood [*Penguin Class. Ser.*] 1984 pap. $6.95. An alternative translation, not to be ignored. Includes a glossary, maps, and appendices.

Josephus. Harvard Univ. Pr. 9 vols. 1926–65 ea. $12.95. This is the standard translation of the War, History, and other works.

BOOKS ABOUT JOSEPHUS

Rajak, Tessa. *Josephus: The Historian and His Society.* Fortress 1984 $24.95. The best contemporary biography of Josephus, judicious, informed, lucid, and well argued. No other recent work meets its standard. Highly literate and readable.

Rhoads, David M. *Israel in Revolution, 6–74 C.E.: A Political History Based on the Writings of Josephus.* Fortress 1976 o.p. A good account, but superseded by Rajak.

Thackeray, Henry. *Josephus: The Man and the Historian.* Ktav 1968 $20.00. A brief and somewhat dated but well-written and interesting biography, by a great Josephus scholar.

Williamson, G. A. *The World of Josephus.* Little, Brown 1960 o.p. This readable biography places Josephus in historical context. A good way to learn about the political and cultural circumstances of the first century.

JUDAH HA-LEVI. c.1075–1141

Judah Ha-Levi, a Spanish-born poet, philosopher, and physician, left a large volume of writings. His major philosophic work, *The Kuzari*, takes the form of a dialogue with a pagan king of the Khazars who seeks spiritual direction. Judah Ha-Levi asserts the superiority of Rabbinic Judaism over Christianity and Islam. He claims that the God of Israel is known through the received tradition and not through philosophy, with its syllogisms and mathematical reasoning. (See also under Ancient Judaism: Jewish Literature in Greek in this chapter.)

BOOK BY JUDAH HA-LEVI

The Kuzari: An Argument for the Faith of Israel. 1964. Trans. by H. Hirschfeld, Schocken 1966 pap. $4.95. Originally published in 1905, this clearly written translation remains the standard English edition. Includes a new introduction by Henry Slonimsky.

KAPLAN, MORDECAI MENAHEM. 1881–1983

Kaplan emigrated to the United States from Lithuania at the age of eight. After graduating from Columbia University in 1902, he was ordained a conservative rabbi by the Jewish Theological Seminary of America, where he taught for the next 50 years. His attempts to adapt Judaism to the modern world—particularly to the American situation—led to the establishment of a new movement, Reconstructionism. He saw Judaism as representing, first and foremost, a religious civilization, and proposed a Jewish theology shaped by Jewish experience and Jewish ethics. (See also under Modern

Judaism: Conservative Judaism, and Modern Judaism: Reconstructionism in this chapter.)

BOOKS BY KAPLAN

Dynamic Judaism: The Essential Writings of Mordecai M. Kaplan. Ed. by Emanuel S. Goldsmith and Mel Scult, Schocken 1985 text ed. $22.00 pap. $12.95. Short pieces arranged by topic, with an introduction on Kaplan's life and his view of Judaism.

Judaism as a Civilization: Toward a Reconstruction of American-Jewish Life. 1934. Jewish Pubns. 1981 $25.00 pap. $12.95. Most important theological statement of Reconstructionism.

The Future of the American Jew. 1948. Reconstructionist Pr. 1981 pap. $13.95. Classic work of the founder of Reconstructionism on the nature of the American Jewish community.

BOOK ABOUT KAPLAN

Libowitz, Richard. *Mordecai M. Kaplan and the Development of Reconstructionism.* [*Studies in Amer. Religion.*] E Mellen 1984 $49.95. Monograph on Kaplan that analyzes each of his many writings and describes the various figures who influenced his thought.

KIMHI, DAVID. c.1160?–1235?

David Kimhi advocated exegesis based on literal readings of the Bible. He synthesized and continued the work of his father and brother on the philology and grammar of the Hebrew language. Kimhi's emphasis on the simple meanings of texts contrasted with the homelitic style prevalent at the time. In his commentaries on Chronicles, Genesis, the Prophetic books, and the Psalms, he referred to Rabbinic Midrash, but was careful to distinguish eisegetical embellishments from exegetical analysis. Kimhi also composed polemical writings against the Christian claim to be the true and only Israel. (See also under Medieval Judaism: Biblical Commentary in this chapter.)

BOOK ABOUT KIMHI

Talmage, Frank E. *David Kimhi: The Man and the Commentaries.* [*Judaic Monographs*] Harvard Univ. Pr. 1976 text ed. $16.50. A clear and accessible study.

MAIMONIDES (MOSES BEN MAIMON). 1135–1204

Maimonides (Moses ben Maimon) was born in Cordoba, Spain, but spent his most productive years in Cairo, where he served as a royal physician. The Arabic cultural environment brought him into contact with classical Greek philosophy. Maimonides fused neo-Aristotelian philosophy with the Jewish legal tradition into a systemic whole. His main philosophic work, *The Guide for the Perplexed*, is an apologetic appeal to rationalists troubled by the corporeality of God in the biblical accounts. He proposes a philosophic interpretation of the Bible that emphasizes abstract and spiritual meaning over literal interpretation. Maimonides formulated the 13 principles of faith that represent the irreducible core of Judaism. (For his legal writings, specifically the codification of Jewish law in the Mishna see Medieval Judaism: Legal Codification and Commentary, and Medieval Judaism: Philosophy in this chapter.)

BOOKS BY MAIMONIDES

The Book of Knowledge. Trans. by Moses Hyamson, Feldheim 1981 $13.95. Translation of the first book of the Mishnah Torah, which is devoted to ethical issues, unlike the rest of the document.

The Guide for the Perplexed. Ed. and trans. by S. Pines, Univ. of Chicago Pr. 1963 $20.00

Treatise on Resurrection. Trans. by Fred Rosner, Ktav 1982 o.p. Annotated translation of a treatise, attributed to Maimonides, on the problem of God's unity, the messianic age, resurrection, and the world to come. (See Goldfield below.)

Ethical Writings of Maimonides. Ed. and trans. by Raymond L. Weiss and Charles E. Butterworth, Dover 1983 pap. $4.50; Peter Smith 1984 $14.25. Anthology of seven passages on various ethical and philosophic topics.

BOOKS ABOUT MAIMONIDES

Dienstag, Jacob I., ed. *Eschatology in Maimonidean Thought: Messianism, Resurrection and the World to Come.* Ktav 1983 $59.90. Philosophic essays on medieval views of the Messiah, immortality, and resurrection, with selections from Maimonides and an extensively annotated bibliography.

Goldfield, Lea Naomi. *An Inquiry into the Authenticity of Moses Maimonides' Treatise on Resurrection.* Ktav 1985 text ed. $19.95. Convincingly argues that the "Treatise on Resurrection" has been falsely attributed to Maimonides.

Goodman, Lenn E., ed. and trans. *Readings in the Philosophy of Moses Maimonides.* Gee Tee Bee 1978 text ed. $10.00. Good one-volume anthology by a brilliant scholar of medieval Jewish and Arab philosophy.

Hartman, David. *Maimonides: Torah and Philosophic Quest.* Jewish Pubns. 1976 o.p. Effort to reconstruct Maimonides' philosophic system so as to integrate his philosophic writing, namely, *The Guide to the Perplexed,* and his legal writings.

Heschel, Abraham Joshua. *Maimonides.* Trans. by Joachim Neugroschel, Farrar 1982 $15.00 pap. $7.25. Originally published in German in 1935, this is an engaging intellectual biography that brings to life Maimonides' faith and the pressing questions of his age. (See also Heschel's main listing in this chapter.)

Rosner, Fred. *Sex Ethics in the Writings of Moses Maimonides.* Bloch 1974 $7.95. Description of Maimonides' legal rulings and philosophic writings on sexuality and sex roles.

Twersky, Isadore. *A Maimonides Reader.* Behrman 1972 pap. $9.95. An anthology of Maimonides' philosophic and legal writings, with a strong introduction by Twersky.

NAHMAN OF BRATSLAV. 1772–1811

The great-grandson of the Ba'al Shem Tov, Nahman of Bratslav attracted attention from an early age. He continually provoked the ire of important anti-Hasidic and Hasidic figures and advocated a theory of "controversy" as a test of faith. He tells of the incredible obstacles he endured on a journey to Palestine as evidence of his being the Messiah. Much of what we know about Nahman comes from Nathan, his disciple and scribe. Nathan helped to establish the Bratslaver Hasidic movement that continues to flourish today in Jerusalem. Nathan records 13 tales, whose meaning is so powerful yet obscure that many authors have embellished them to make them accessible. (See also under Medieval Judaism: Hasidism in this chapter.)

BOOK BY NAHMAN OF BRATSLAV

The Tales of Rabbi Nahman of Bratslav. Trans. by Arnold Band [*Classics of Western Spirituality*] Paulist Pr. 1980 o.p. The only direct translation, without embellishment, of the strange and powerful stories of Nahman of Bratslav. Includes a short but excellent introduction that places Nahman into the context of Hasidic storytelling.

BOOKS ABOUT NAHMAN OF BRATSLAV

Buber, Martin. *Tales of Rabbi Nachman.* Trans. by Maurice Friedman, Horizon Pr. 1972 $5.95. Buber wrote in 1956, "My re-creation of the tales of Rabbi Nachman first appeared in print fifty years ago. I have not translated these tales, but retold them with full freedom, yet out of his spirit as it is present to me."

Green, Arthur. *Tormented Master: A Life of Rabbi Nahman of Bratslav.* Schocken 1981 pap. $11.95; Univ. of Alabama Pr. 1979 $30.00. One of the few academic treatments of the Hasidic movement. Green uses psychoanalytic categories to explain the unusual life and writings of this self-proclaimed "suffering Messiah." Highly recommended.

Kaplan, Aryeh. *Until the Mashiach: Rabbi Nachman's Biography, An Annotated Chronology.* Breslov Research Institute 1985 consult publisher for information. A detailed but uncritical study of the life of Nachman, by a leader in the contemporary Bratslav movement.

Schwartz, Howard. *The Captive Soul of the Messiah: New Tales about Reb Nachman.* Schocken 1983 $17.95. Another creative retelling of the life of Nachman—this time by a contemporary Jewish poet.

Steinsaltz, Adin. *Beggars and Prayers: Adin Steinsaltz Retells the Tales of Rabbi Nahman of Bratslav.* Trans. by Yehuda Hanegbi, Basic Bks. 1980 $11.50 1985 pap. $6.95. Here is yet another adaptation of six of Nahman's stories.

NAHMANIDES (MOSES BEN NAHMAN, also RAMBAM). 1194–c.1270

Moses ben Nahman, also known as the Rambam, was an important Spanish philosopher, mystic, biblical exegete, and poet. His commentaries on the Hebrew Bible were written late in life, in the Land of Israel, after he was expelled from Spain because of his frequent anti-Christian polemics. He focused on the deeper meanings of biblical passages as opposed to the surface meanings of words. He frequently cited Rabbinic and medieval commentaries, but took an independent stance sometimes critical of these works. Nahmanides' many comments on the Talmud and on Cabala, when taken as a whole, reflect an original mind that had considerable influence on the development of Jewish thought in Spain. (See also under Medieval Judaism: Biblical Commentary, Medieval Judaism: Mysticism, and Medieval Judaism: Philosophy in this chapter.)

BOOK BY NAHMANIDES

Ramban (Nahmanides) Commentary on the Torah. Trans. by Charles B. Chavel, Shilo 5 vols. 1971– $84.75. Collection of Nahmanides' commentaries to the Pentateuch, from Genesis to Numbers.

BOOKS ABOUT NAHMANIDES

Chavel, Charles B. *Ramban: His Life and His Teachings.* 1960. Feldheim 1963 pap. $5.95. A general introduction to the life, thought, and writings of Nahmanides, with extensive translations of his biblical commentaries.

Twersky, Isadore, ed. *Rabbi Moses Nahmanides: Explorations in His Religious and Literary Virtuosity.* Harvard Univ. Pr. 1983 text ed. pap. $9.50. Collection of essays, often quite technical, on Nahmanides' philosophy, mysticism, and biblical commentary.

PHILO JUDAEUS. c.20 B.C.–C.A.D. 50

Philo was born to a prominent family in the large and prosperous Jewish community of Alexandria, Egypt, and received an education in classical Greek philosophy. He interpreted Jewish tradition from the point of view of contemporary Hellenistic culture, by employing an original, allegorical method to synthesize biblical theology with Greek philosophy. His etymologies of biblical terms are philologically dubious, but highly imaginative. Philo represents the first Jewish thinker known to us who articulated a systematic theology. His philosophic writings had an enormous influence on the early Christian church and on medieval philosophy in general. (See also under Ancient Judaism: Jewish Literature in Greek in this chapter.)

BOOK BY PHILO

Philo. Ed. and trans. by F. H. Colson, Harvard Univ. Pr. 5 vols. 1929–62 ea. $12.95. The accepted translation.

BOOKS ABOUT PHILO

Berchman, Robert M. *From Philo to Origen: Middle Platonism in Transition.* [*Brown Judaic Studies.*] Scholars Pr. GA 1985 $29.95. An original thesis on the links between Philo and Origen, the Church Father.

Goodenough, Erwin R. *By Light, Light: The Mystic Gospel of Hellenistic Judaism.* Yale Univ. Pr. 1935 o.p. Links the thought and system of Philo to the Hellenistic philosophy of the time and place, interpreting Philo's thought as a system of a profoundly mystical character within the Platonic thought-world.

———. *An Introduction to Philo Judaeus.* Allenson 1962 text ed. $11.00. The best introduction to the subject.

———. *The Politics of Philo Judaeus: Practice and Theory.* Elliots Bks. 1938 $75.00. An original and important account of the political system of Philo and of the Jews of Alexandria, the most important Diaspora community in their day.

Mendelson, Alan. *Secular Education in Philo of Alexandria.* Ktav 1982 $20.00. Assesses Philo's appropriation of Hellenistic culture "alien" to his Jewish background. Overstates the distinction between Judaism and Hellenism.

Sandmel, Samuel. *Philo of Alexandria: An Introduction.* Oxford 1979 pap. $9.95. A useful introduction to the subject, not up to the masterful standard of Goodenough, but not to be forgotten.

Winston, David, and John Dillon. *Two Treatises of Philo of Alexandria: A Commentary on De Gigantibus and Quod Deus Sit Immutabilis.* Scholars Pr. GA 1983 pap. $15.00. A fresh translation and commentary on two important tractates.

Wolfson, Harry A. *Philo: Foundations of Religious Philosophy in Judaism, Christianity and Islam.* Harvard Univ. Pr. 2 vols. rev. ed. 1962 $55.00. Links the thought and system of Philo to the Judaic philosophy of a later time and different place, interpreting Philo's thought as a system of a profoundly rational, philosophical character within the Judaic-Rabbinic thought-world.

RASHI (SOLOMON BEN ISAAC). 1040–1105

Rashi (from the acronym for his full name, Rabbi Solomon ben Isaac) of Troyes, France, wrote the most famous medieval commentaries to the Hebrew Bible. His commentaries are written in a simple, lucid, and uniform style. He provides a synthesis of Rabbinic interpretation, altering and abridging Midrashic citations, as well as adding his own insightful comments. Rashi utilized the so-called peshat method of exegesis, which interpreted the Bible in terms of the world of ancient Israel. In this way, he explained complex and ambiguous passages by adducing details from the biblical world and by analyzing the Hebrew language. Rashi has also produced the most influential commentary to the Babylonian Talmud—no edition of this Talmud has been printed without it. (See also under Medieval Judaism: Biblical Commentary in this chapter.)

BOOKS ABOUT RASHI

Halperin, Herman. *Rashi and the Christian Scholars*. Univ. of Pittsburgh Pr. 1963 o.p. Compares the writings of Rashi and Nichlaus de Lyra to show the relationship between Jewish and Christian biblical exegesis during the medieval period.

Liber, Maurice. *Rashi: His Life and Works*. Trans. by Adele Szold, Hermon repr. of 1906 ed. 1971 o.p. This in-depth study remains the best introduction to Rashi's thought.

Shereshevsky, Esra. *Rashi: The Man and His World*. Hermon 1982 $17.50. Comprehensive biography that places Rashi's work in the context of the Jewish world in which he lived. Chapters on "the world through Rashi's eyes" gather remarks from his biblical and Talmudic commentaries in order to reconstruct details about daily life in the medieval world.

ROSENZWEIG, FRANZ. 1886–1929

Rosenzweig was born in 1886 to intellectual and assimilated parents. He studied philosophy, history, and classics. While he was at university, many of his friends and relatives converted to Christianity. He came close to converting, until a visit to an Orthodox synagogue on the eve of Yom Kippur inspired him to "return" to Judaism. His doctoral thesis *Hegel and the State* was published in 1920, and he then began to devote his energies to the construction of a Jewish philosophic system. The result, *The Star of Redemption* (1921), has become a classic, combining German idealism, existentialism, and Jewish tradition into a complex and enduring system. In 1921, a progressive paralysis set in and although he soon lost his mobility and power of speech, he continued his intellectual activities for seven years. Rosenzweig's wife deciphered his signals and, among other activities, he began a new translation of the Hebrew Bible (with Martin Buber, who finished it in the 1950s), utilizing a style of German that attempted to retain the spirit of the original Hebrew. (See also under Modern Judaism: Early Twentieth-Century German-Jewish Theology in this chapter.)

BOOKS BY ROSENZWEIG

The Star of Redemption. 1921. Fwd. by Nahum N. Glatzer, Univ. of Notre Dame Pr. repr. of 1971 ed. 1985 text ed. $30.00 pap. $12.95. Assumes a great deal of knowledge about German philosophy.

Judaism Despite Christianity: The "Letters on Christianity and Judaism" Between Eugen Rosenstock-Huessy and Franz Rosenzweig. Univ. of Alabama Pr. 1969 $16.50. Classic exchange of letters between two German soldiers during World War I, a German Christian of Jewish descent and a German Jew.

BOOK ABOUT ROSENZWEIG

Glatzer, Nahum N. *Franz Rosenzweig: His Life and Thought.* Schocken 2d ed. 1962 pap. $8.95. An engaging biography and anthology of his writings by a former colleague.

RUBENSTEIN, RICHARD. 1924–

Rubenstein, a former congregational rabbi and Hillel director at Harvard and the University of Pittsburgh, offers a very different response to the Holocaust. He claims that the only honest response after Auschwitz is the rejection of God. In place of traditional theology, Rubenstein fashions a new interpretation of the role of Jewish religion based on Freudian psychology and existentialist philosophy. Rubenstein always writes with candor and compassion, and his works are sure to provoke and enlighten. Since 1971, he has been a professor of religion at Florida State University. (See also under Modern Judaism: Post-Holocaust Theology, and Modern Judaism: Contemporary Theology in this chapter.)

BOOKS BY RUBENSTEIN

After Auschwitz: Essays in Contemporary Judaism. Bobbs 1966 pap. $10.28. Argues that belief in God is not credible after the radical evil of the Holocaust.

The Religious Imagination: A Study in Psychoanalysis and Jewish Theology. Univ. Pr. of Amer. repr. of 1968 ed. 1985 text ed. pap. $12.50. A psychoanalytic interpretation of the Judaism of the Talmud.

Power Struggle. Univ. Pr. of Amer. repr. of 1974 ed. 1986 text ed. pap. $12.75. "The story I have to tell is how a deeply disturbed individual was moved by his disease to become a religious leader. I am that individual." A fascinating, candid view of Hebrew Union College, Jewish Theological Seminary, Harvard Divinity School, Paul Tillich, Harry Wolfson, Saul Lieberman, and much more.

SAADIA GAON (SAADIA BEN JOSEPH AL-FAYUMI). 882–942

Born in Egypt, Saadia ben Joseph al-Fayumi became the leader or "Gaon" of the Babylonian Jewish community. He issued virulent attacks against the powerful Karaite movement, which rejected the authority of Rabbinic Judaism. Saadia is reputed to be the first medieval philosopher to write monographs on topics of Jewish law and the first to write in Arabic. Saadia was also the first Jew to elaborate systematic and formal proofs of the existence of God. He took an interest in liturgy, grammar, and astrology. His theological and mystical writings on the shekinah (divine presence) and the Ruah ha-Kodesh (holy spirit) influenced medieval Hasidism and Cabala. (See also under Medieval Judaism: Philosophy in this chapter.)

BOOK BY SAADIA GAON

The Book of Beliefs and Opinions. Trans. by Samuel Rosenblatt, Yale Univ. Pr. 1948 o.p. The standard translation of Saadia's major philosophic work, with a brief introduction and extensive notation. Understandable to a reader with a minimal knowledge of philosophy.

BOOK ABOUT SAADIA GAON

Malter, Henry. *Saadia Gaon: His Life and Works.* 1920. Hermon 1969 o.p. This detailed biography examines Saadia's philosophic, liturgical, and philological writings.

SCHOLEM, GERSHOM. 1897–1982

Gershom Scholem's contribution to the understanding of Jewish mysticism is so dramatic that it warrants a separate introduction. As a young student of mathematics he became a Zionist, and his interest shifted to Jewish history. Scholem moved from Germany to become the librarian of the new University and National Library in Jerusalem in 1923, and served as a professor at Hebrew University from 1935 to 1965. Before him, Jewish historians in the nineteenth and early twentieth centuries scorned the ignored mystical dimension of Judaism as a relic of premodern superstition and ignorance. Scholem's erudition and deep insight gave Cabala a scholarly audience. His writings are often difficult to read, but they are indispensable for any thorough knowledge of the subject of Jewish mysticism. (See also under Medieval Judaism: Mysticism in this chapter.)

BOOKS BY SCHOLEM

Major Trends in Jewish Mysticism. 1941. Schocken 3d ed. 1961 pap. $8.95. The classic book on the topic, which integrates a great deal of material to show the development and continuity of Jewish mysticism over the last two millennia. Based on a series of lectures given in 1938.

(ed.). *Zohar—The Book of Splendor: Basic Readings from the Kabbalah.* Schocken 1963 pap. $3.95. A short anthology without adequate annotation or explanation.

On the Kabbalah and Its Symbolism. 1965. Schocken 1969 pap. $6.95. Collection of essays focused on the symbolism, ritual, and ideas of medieval Cabala.

The Messianic Idea in Judaism and Other Essays on Jewish Spirituality. Schocken 1972 pap. $8.95. Another important collection of essays on topics spanning the entire history of Judaism.

On Jews and Judaism in Crisis: Selected Essays. Ed. by Werner J. Dannhauser, Schocken 1978. $16.50 pap. $7.95. Episodic observations on twentieth-century German and Israeli Jewry; not his most important book.

Origins of the Kabbalah. Trans. by Allan Arkush, ed. by R. J. Zwi Weblowsky, Princeton Univ. Pr. 1987 $47.50. This in-depth study demonstrates that Cabala existed in southern France in the twelfth century, prior to the composition of the *Zohar* in Spain at the end of the thirteenth century.

BOOKS ABOUT SCHOLEM

Biale, David. *Gershom Scholem: Kabbalah and Counter-history.* Harvard Univ. Pr. 2d ed. 1982 text ed. pap. $7.95. A good introduction to Scholem's thought and scholarship that places him in the context of the historical Science of Judaism movement and developments in German-Jewish philosophy.

Schweid, Eliezer. *Judaism and Mysticism According to Gershom Scholem: A Critical Analysis and Programmatic Discussion.* Trans. by David A. Weiner, Scholars Pr. GA 1985 $22.95 pap. $16.95. A critical reappraisal of Scholem's understanding of Jewish philosophy and mysticism. Not for beginners.

SOLOVEITCHIK, JOSEPH. 1903–

Born to a family of important rabbis, Soloveitchik has become the most important twentieth-century philosopher of Orthodox Judaism. He resides in Boston, but serves as the head of the Theology Seminary of Yeshiva University in New York. Soloveitchik is well schooled in modern philosophy; his doctoral dissertation at the University of Berlin was on Hermann Cohen's epistemology. His knowledge of Jewish law is unsurpassed. He brings together existentialism, neo-Kantian rationalism, and Orthodox faith into a complex system of thought. (See also under Modern Judaism: Contemporary Theology, and Modern Judaism: Orthodox Judaism in this chapter.)

BOOKS BY SOLOVEITCHIK

The Halakhic Mind: An Essay on Jewish Tradition and Modern Thought. Free Pr. 1985 $16.95. Originally written in 1944, and now published for the first time, this monograph argues that Orthodox Judaism represents a valid metaphysical and epistemological system, but liberal (i.e., non-Orthodox) Judaism does not. Here Soloveitchik defies the usual label given to him of neo-Kantianism. Difficult reading.

Halakhic Man. 1944. Trans. by Lawrence Kaplan, Jewish Pubns. 1984 $12.95. Classic statement of Orthodox rationalism in an excellent translation with notes and observations. Here Soloveitchik presents his famous existentialist typology of humanity based on the two personalities of Adam in the book of Genesis.

SPINOZA, BARUCH (or BENEDICT). 1632–1677

[SEE Chapter 5, "Modern Philosophy," in this volume.]

WASKOW, ARTHUR. 1933–

Arthur Waskow describes his own personal development as the growth "from Jewish radical to radical Jew." In the 1960s he was active in the movements for civil rights and against the Vietnam War. Since 1969, he has been a leader in the so-called Jewish renewal movement, promoting Havurah religious fellowship and political activism. He has taught at Temple University and Swarthmore College, and is currently on the faculty of the Reconstructionist Rabbinical College. (See also under Modern Judaism: Contemporary Theology in this chapter.)

BOOKS BY WASKOW

The Bush Is Burning: Radical Judaism Faces the Pharaohs of the Modern Superstate. Macmillan 1971 $5.95 pap. $1.95. In the heat of the 1960s, Waskow addresses the religious upheaval of young American Jews and makes a case for Jewishly motivated political action.

Godwrestling. Schocken 1978 pap. $7.95. Argues that Jewish theology requires ethical activism.

These Holy Sparks: The Rebirth of the Jewish People. Harper 1983 o.p. Explains, in a clear and passionate way, how the Havurah fellowship movement can serve to reunite the scattered "sparks" of Judaism and contribute to the restoration of personal and global wholeness.

(and others). *Before There Was a Before.* Adama 1984 $8.95. A delightful retelling of the story of the seven days of creation (with a non-gender-specific God) with playful illustrations by Amnon Danziger.

CHAPTER 11

Early Christianity

Karlfried Froehlich and Gary H. Gilbert

Understanding is the reward of faith. Therefore seek not to understand that thou mayest believe, but believe that thou mayest understand.
—St. Augustine of Hippo

Christianity not only represents a complex and fascinating religious tradition, but is also one of the leading influences in Western civilization. Christianity is a diverse and rich religious tradition that cannot be summarized adequately in a couple of pages. The brief introduction to the individual sections below will provide the reader with some basic information on the history and thought of Christianity from its beginnings up to the eve of the Reformation. There were four areas that received continuous attention throughout ancient and medieval Christianity. One issue that was often debated—particularly in the early centuries—was Christology. Very soon after Jesus' death, or possibly even during his life, he was thought of as divine. What was not immediately clear was the nature of his divinity. Associated with this issue was the understanding of the Trinity, the relation between God the Father, Christ, and Holy Spirit. The second topic of importance is soteriology (the doctrine of salvation through Jesus Christ). During this period Christians debated the roles of autonomous human actions and the grace of God in the process of salvation. Ecclesiology (the study of church doctrine) was another major topic of this period; the Church argued over who should be its leaders and who should select those leaders and by what criteria. The final debate that can be traced through this period involved the relation between reason and revelation. The quote from Augustine that begins this chapter characterizes one prevalent attitude toward this issue during the ancient and medieval Church, but this view was by no means the only one. Some Christians discounted the necessity of the intellect in matters of faith; others viewed philosophical proof of theological issues as not only possible, but necessary.

Much of what occurs in later Christianity has its antecedents in the ancient and medieval Church. Christianity did change, and change dramatically, in the period beginning with the Reformation and after, but the changes that occurred were not molded out of an entirely new piece of clay, but were primarily reshaped from existing material. The events and developments of Christianity in the modern period need to be understood in light of the ideas, events, and personalities discussed in the literature below.

527

GENERAL REFERENCES

Reference Works

Attwater, Donald. *The Penguin Dictionary of Saints*. Ed. and rev. by Catherine R. John, Penguin rev. ed. 1984 pap. $7.95. "This book is a work of quick reference to the lives and legends of the more important and interesting people among the Christian saints."

Brauer, Jerald C., ed. *Westminster Dictionary of Church History*. Westminster 1971 $27.50. A brief, reliable, one-volume dictionary giving "an immediate, accurate, introductory definition and explanation concerning the major persons, events, facts, and movements in the history of Christianity."

Cross, F. L., and Elizabeth A. Livingstone. *The Oxford Dictionary of the Christian Church*. Oxford 1974 $60.00. The best one-volume encyclopedia in the field, particularly strong in the areas of doctrine, biography, and worship.

Davies, J. G., ed. *The New Westminster Dictionary of Liturgy and Worship*. Westminster 1986 $29.95. Good basic information and up-to-date bibliography on a large number of items in a restricted subject area. Illustrated.

Douglas, J. D., and Earle E. Cairns, eds. *The New International Dictionary of the Christian Church*. Zondervan rev. ed. 1978 $29.95. Quick orientation to the entire sweep of church history, especially strong on biography. "The aim has been to steer a middle path between academic textbook and popular introduction."

Harvey, Van A. *A Handbook of Theological Terms*. Macmillan 1964 pap. $4.95. An explanation of over 300 theological terms that illumine the history of doctrine and help to differentiate Roman Catholic, Protestant, and Eastern Orthodox viewpoints.

Kelly, J. N. *The Oxford Dictionary of Popes*. Oxford 1986 $24.95. A useful reference tool covering the biographies of all popes through John Paul II in concise articles that reflect painstaking scholarship and the needs of the general reader.

Livingstone, E. A., ed. *The Concise Oxford Dictionary of the Christian Church*. Oxford 1977 o.p. Excerpts from the larger volume (see Cross and Livingstone above); no bibliographies.

McClintock, John, and James Strong. *Cyclopedia of Biblical, Theological, and Ecclesiastical Literature*. 1867–87. Intro. by Wilbur M. Smith, Baker Bk. 12 vols. 1981 text ed. $395.00. Makes available again the most comprehensive Protestant encyclopedia in the field of Bible and church history to originate in the U.S. in the nineteenth century. The authors were conservative Protestant scholars.

Macdonald, W. J., and others, eds. *The New Catholic Encyclopedia*. Publishers Guild 17 vols. repr. of 1967 ed. 1981 $550.00. A comprehensive multivolume religious encyclopedia. It contains 17,000 articles "on subjects ranging from the Doctrine of Atonement and St. Paul to Comic Books and International Trade." Outlook and bibliographies reflect the ecumenism and the solid scholarship of the mid-1960s. Indispensable for beginner and expert alike.

O'Carroll, Michael. *Theotokos: A Theological Encyclopedia of the Blessed Virgin Mary*. M. Glazier 1982 pap. $19.95. With its entries written in a crisp, clear prose and supplied with the latest bibliography, this volume by the leading American Mariological scholar is quickly becoming a standard tool for readers interested in any aspect of Mariology (the study of the Virgin Mary).

Rahner, Karl, ed. *Encyclopedia of Theology: The Concise Sacramentum Mundi*. Crossroad NY rev. & abr. ed. 1975 $49.50. A one-volume condensation of a major international Catholic theological dictionary featuring general survey articles on broad subjects.

Richardson, Alan, and John Bowden, eds. *The Westminster Dictionary of Christian Theology*. Westminster 1983 $24.95. Revised edition of Alan Richardson, ed., *A Dictionary of Christian Theology* (Westminster 1969 o.p.).

Smith, William, and Samuel Cheetham, eds. *Dictionary of Christian Antiquities: Being a Continuation of the Dictionary of the Bible*. Kraus Repr. 2 vols. repr. of 1880 ed. 1968 $148.00. A standard reference tool of the late nineteenth century that remains useful because of its thoroughness. It aims to give "a complete account of the leading personages, the institutions, art, social life, writings, and controversies of the Christian Church from the time of the Apostles to the age of Charlemagne." Illustrated with line drawings.

Thurston, Herbert K., and Donald Attwater. *Butler's Lives of the Saints*. Christian Classics 4 vols. repr. of 1956 ed. 1981 o.p. The four handsome volumes contain descriptions of the lives of the saints in over 2,500 separate entries that are organized according to the calendar of their commemorations. The first modern "Butler" was published from 1928 to 1952.

Wakefield, Gordon S., ed. *The Westminster Dictionary of Christian Spirituality*. Westminster 1983 $20.95. A modern ecumenical dictionary on the spiritual life and prayer. The authors represent the Protestant, Catholic, and Eastern Orthodox traditions.

Walsh, Michael, ed. *Butler's Lives of the Saints*. Harper 1985 $20.45. A one-volume abbreviated version of the above Thurston and Attwater work.

Histories

Aland, Kurt. *From the Beginnings to the Threshold of the Reformation*. Trans. by James L. Schaaf, Vol. 1 in *A History of Christianity*. Fortress Pr. 1985 $24.95. An admirably organized narrative of the sweep of early church history, edited from the classroom lectures of a renowned German expert. The text is supplemented by 33 pages of useful "chronological tables."

Atiya, Aziz S. *History of Eastern Christianity*. Kraus Repr. 1980 lib. bdg. $52.00. A comprehensive critical survey of the history, ancient and modern, of the non-Greek churches of the Near East. Professor Atiya, himself a member of the Coptic Church, covers the Copts and Ethiopians, the Jacobites of Syria, the Nestorians, Armenians, Maronites, and the St. Thomas Christians of South India.

Bainton, Roland H. *To the Reformation*. Vol. 1 in *Christendom: A Short History of Christianity and Its Impact on Western Civilization*. Harper 1966 o.p. This masterful survey for the general reader, originally written for the *Horizon History of Christianity*, is both exceptionally readable and uncompromisingly scholarly. Its brief chapters narrate a clear, coherent story without getting lost in details. Carefully selected illustrations with full explanations enhance the value of the book.

Bouyer, Louis, Jean Leclercq, and others. *History of Christian Spirituality*. Winston Pr. 3 vols. 1982 pap. $37.50. Vol. 1, *The Spirituality of the New Testament and the Fathers*, by Louis Bouyer and others; Vol. 2, *The Spirituality of the Middle Ages*, by Jean Leclercq and others; Vol. 3, *Orthodox Spirituality, and Protestant and Anglican Spirituality*, by Louis Bouyer and others. The three volumes, first published between 1963 and 1969, provide a full overview of the major figures, movements, concerns, and life-styles connected with the Christian spiritual endeavor.

The Cambridge History of the Bible. Ed. by Peter R. Ackroyd and others, Cambridge Univ. Pr. 1963–70. 3 vols. ea. $57.50 set $155.00 pap. set $47.50. Vol. 1, *From the Beginnings to Jerome*; Vol. 2, *The West from the Fathers to the Reformation*; Vol.

3, *The West from the Reformation to the Present Day*. In the years since their first appearance, the volumes of *The Cambridge History of the Bible* have established themselves as the standard treatment of the subject in English. Produced by a team of recognized experts, the essays provide a complete picture of all aspects of Bible history: text, translations, interpretation, distribution, and manuscript illumination.

Copleston, Frederick C. *A History of Philosophy*. Paulist Pr. 3 vols. 1975 ea. $17.95. Vol. 1, *Greece and Rome;* Vol. 2, *Medieval Philosophy: Augustine to Scotus;* Vol. 3, *Ockham to Suarez*. The first three volumes of this standard work in the history of philosophy deal extensively with the early Christian contribution to philosophical thought.

Cunliffe-Jones, Hubert, and Benjamin Drewery, eds. *A History of Christian Doctrine*. Fortress Pr. 1980 $29.95. This recent one-volume history of Christian theology, designed to replace the 1896 textbook of the same name by George Park Fisher (Intl. Theological Lib.), takes an unusual approach. Each chapter is written by a leading specialist in vivid prose with a minimum of documentation. The result is a fascinating mosaic of precise information, analysis, and insight.

Danielou, Jean, and Henri-Irénéé Marrou. *Christian Centuries: Vol. 1, First Six Hundred Years*. Paulist Pr. 1969 $22.95. One of the best historical treatments, engagingly written and of impeccable scholarship.

Dowley, Tim. *Eerdmans' Handbook to the History of Christianity*. Eerdmans 1977 $29.95. A basic popular survey written mainly by evangelical Protestant scholars presenting church history as a lively story highlighted by quotations from primary sources, color photographs, maps, and diagrams.

Frankiel, Sandra S. *Christianity: A Way of Salvation*. Harper 1985 pap. $6.95. An engagingly written, very basic introduction to Christianity emphasizing the broad lines of historical development and the analysis of fundamental themes. A simple "glossary" explains the most basic terms.

González, Justo L. *The Early Church to the Dawn of the Reformation*. Vol. 1 in *The Story of Christianity*. Harper 1983 pap. $12.95. A new college and seminary textbook written by a Latin American historian teaching in the United States. "This crisp retelling of Christian history . . . is filled with insight. González excels in the brief character sketch" (M. Noll).

———. *A History of Christian Thought*. Abingdon 3 vols. 1975 rev. ed. $59.95. Vol. 1, *From the Beginnings to the Council of Chalcedon in A.D. 451;* Vol. 2, *From Augustine to the Eve of the Reformation;* Vol. 3, *From the Protestant Reformation to the Twentieth Century*. A concise, comprehensive account of the development of Christian thought.

Harnack, Adolf. *History of Dogma*. Trans. by Neil Buchanan, Peter Smith 7 vols. in 4 repr. of 1895–1900 ed. $72.00. A classic in its field, this work substantiates Harnack's famous thesis that the development of Christian dogma is a consequence of the "Hellenization" of the earliest Christianity.

Hefele, Karl J. *A History of the Councils of the Church from the Original Documents*. Ed. and trans. by William R. Clark, AMS Pr. 5 vols. repr. of 1896 ed. 1974 $172.50. Hefele's work is the old standard treatment. Unfortunately, the English translation follows the original German, not the revised and enlarged French version by Henri Leclercq and others (1907–52).

Jedin, Hubert, and John P. Dolan, eds. *History of the Church*. Trans. by Anselm Biggs and others, Crossroad NY 5 vols. 1980–81 ea. $59.50. Vol. 1, *From the Apostolic Community to Constantine;* Vol. 2, *The Imperial Church from Constantine to the Early Middle Ages;* Vol. 3, *The Church in the Age of Feudalism;* Vol. 4, *From the High Middle Ages to the Eve of the Reformation;* Vol. 5, *Reformation and Counter*

Reformation. The best modern multivolume treatment of the entire period, representing a broad scholarly consensus on the Continent. The authors stand in the Roman Catholic tradition, but their outlook is not narrowly confined. The English edition includes the rich bibliographies of the original German.

Latourette, Kenneth Scott. *A History of Christianity.* Harper 2 vols. 1975 ea. $13.95. Volume 1, *Beginnings to 1500,* is a standard textbook of church history, emphasizing the expansion of Christianity, the cultural setting, and fringe movements. Latourette, one of the great missionary historians of the previous generation, writes as a Protestant Christian but in a decidedly irenic spirit.

Littell, Franklin H. *The Macmillan Atlas History of Christianity.* Macmillan 1976 $24.95. A comprehensive survey of church history illustrated by good maps and drawings. One third of the volume deals with the early and medieval period.

Lohse, Bernhard. *A Short History of Christian Doctrine: From the First Century to the Present.* Trans. by Ernest F. Stoeffer, Fortress Pr. rev. ed. 1978 pap. $9.95. This well-written, authoritative account organizes the material by major doctrinal themes: canon and greed, the Trinity, Christology, sin and grace, word and sacrament, and so forth.

Manschreck, Clyde L. *A History of Christianity in the World: From Persecution to Uncertainty.* Prentice-Hall 2d ed. 1985 text ed. $29.33. A re-edition of a popular 1974 book, half of which deals with the early and medieval church. It was written for undergraduates by a Chicago professor of divinity.

Pelikan, Jaroslav. *The Christian Tradition: A History of the Development of Doctrine.* Univ. of Chicago Pr. 4 vols. 1971–85 ea. $25.00–$27.00. Vol. 1, *The Emergence of the Catholic Tradition (100–600);* Vol. 2, *The Spirit of Eastern Christendom (600–1700);* Vol. 3, *The Growth of Medieval Theology (600–1300);* Vol. 4, *Reformation of Church and Dogma (1300–1700).* When complete, the five-volume set will be a magisterial evaluation of Christian doctrine and tradition, comparable to Adolf Harnack's classic *History of Dogma* (see above). Based mainly on primary sources, conversant with up-to-date scholarship, relevant to the questions and concerns of contemporary readers, and written in a deeply ecumenical spirit by an eminent religious historian, these volumes represent the best of contemporary history writing.

The Penguin History of the Church. Ed. by Owen Chadwick, Penguin 3 vols. 1964–70. Vol. 1, *The Early Church,* by Henry Chadwick, 1968 pap. $5.95; Vol. 2, *Western Society and the Church in the Middle Ages,* by R. W. Southern, 1970 pap. $5.95; Vol. 3, *The Reformation,* by Owen Chadwick, 1964 pap. $4.95. All of the volumes in this series are superb achievements of historical analysis and appealing presentation for the general reader as well as the specialist.

Petry, Ray C., ed. *Readings in the History of the Early and Medieval Church.* Vol. 1 in *A History of Christianity.* Baker Bk. repr. of 1962 ed. 1981 pap. $23.95. A beautifully organized and written survey that combines long excerpts from primary texts and connecting narrative in a careful synthesis. A wealth of illustrations adds to the volume's usefulness.

Pluth, Alphonsus, and Carl Koch. *The Catholic Church: Our Mission in History.* St. Mary's Pr. 1985 text ed. pap. $11.00. An ecumenically responsible textbook for Catholic college students, clearly written and attractively illustrated.

Schaff, Philip. *History of the Christian Church.* Eerdmans 8 vols. repr. 1960 ea. $17.95 set $143.60. While outdated in some respects, Schaff's *History* remains the most extensive treatment of the history of the Christian Church written by an American scholar. The original edition appeared between 1880 and 1910.

Tillich, Paul. *A History of Christian Thought.* Simon & Schuster 1972 pap. $11.95. Edited from the great Protestant theologian's famous classroom lectures at

Union Theological Seminary in New York, this book traces the main lines of doctrinal development in generally accessible language.

Walker, Williston. *A History of the Christian Church.* Rev. by Robert T. Handy, Scribner 4th ed. 1985 $35.00. The fourth edition of the classic one-volume textbook, thoroughly revised and brought up to date, still preserves the virtues of the original version: precise information, clear organization, and readable style.

Williams, Rowan. *Christian Spirituality: A Theological History from the New Testament to Luther and St. John of the Cross.* John Knox 1980 $10.95 pap. $8.95. This is an excellent, informative introduction that emphasizes the connections between theology and the spiritual life. Good bibliographical suggestions.

Topical Studies

Aulen, Gustav. *Christus Victor.* Intro. by Jaroslav Pelikan, Macmillan 1969 pap. $5.95. This seminal study by an eminent Swedish theologian and churchman challenges the common understanding of atonement as objective satisfaction and proposes the patristic theology of "recapitulation" as the proper alternative.

Bailey, D. Sherwin. *Homosexuality and the Western Christian Tradition.* Shoe String repr. of 1955 ed. 1975 $22.50. Written in 1954 by an Anglican scholar as background for a comprehensive report on the issue by the Church of England, this reliable survey concentrates on biblical, historical, and legal aspects of the question.

Bainton, Roland H. *Christian Attitudes toward War and Peace: A Historical Survey and Critical Reevaluation.* Abingdon 1979 pap. $7.75. Compellingly written, this masterful essay traces Christian attitudes toward war and peace from the "just-war" theory through the modern peace movement. Bainton does not hide his pacifist sympathies.

Boswell, John. *Christianity, Social Tolerance, and Homosexuality: Gay People in Western Europe from the Beginning of the Christian Era to the Fourteenth Century.* Univ. of Chicago Pr. 1980 $35.00 pap. $12.95. Boswell's study has quickly become the most authoritative treatment of its subject available today. Appendix 2 presents a number of relevant texts and translations.

Brown, Harold O. *Heresies: The Image of Christ in the Mirror of Heresy and Orthodoxy from the Apostles to the Present.* Doubleday 1984 $17.95. A wide-ranging and knowledgeable account primarily of Trinitarian and Christological heresies, written by "an irenic evangelical scholar" (G. H. Williams).

Delehaye, Hippolyte. *The Legends of the Saints.* Folcroft 1907 $37.00. In this fascinating volume one of the founders of scientific hagiography explains the laws by which legends develop.

Graef, Hilda. *Mary: A History of Doctrine and Devotion.* Christian Classics 2 vols. repr. of 1965 ed. 1985 pap. $21.00. The best brief account in English of the historical development of Mariology written for a general readership. Volume 1 deals with the era of the early and medieval church.

Jones, Cheslyn, and Edward Yarnold, eds. *The Study of Liturgy.* Oxford 1978 $27.00 pap. $13.95. An excellent new standard work in this field, covering the early and medieval period thoroughly. The book was written by three well-known Oxford scholars to replace the old text by William K. L. Clarke and Charles Harris, *Liturgy and Worship* (Macmillan 1932), now out of print.

Klauser, Theodor. *A Short History of the Western Liturgy.* Trans. by John Halliburton, Oxford 2d ed. 1979 text ed. pap. $10.95. This substantial survey is probably the best introduction to all aspects of Western worship available in English today.

The concise text, written by one of the foremost German scholars, is followed by thorough bibliographical sections.

McGinley, Phyllis. *Saint Watching*. Crossroad NY 1982 pap. $6.95. "A warm, humorous, and affectionate book of prose about the saints she likes. . . . Here is an ecumenical book written for all people who like people" (*LJ*).

McGinn, Bernard, and John Meyendorff, eds. *Christian Spirituality from the Apostolic Fathers to the Twelfth Century*. Crossroad NY 1985 $49.50. This valuable collection of scholarly yet clearly written essays forms volume 16 of a new publication venture: *World Spirituality: An Encyclopedic History of the Religious Quest*. Part 1 discusses "Periods and Movements"; Part 2, "Themes and Values."

McGrath, Alister E. *Iustitia Dei: A History of the Doctrine of Justification*. Cambridge Univ. Pr. 1986 $39.50. The first full history of this important doctrine, this careful study is of considerable ecumenical significance.

Meyendorff, John. *Christ in Eastern Christian Thought (Le Christ dans la théologie Byzantine)*. St. Vladimir's 1975 pap. $10.95. A clearly written, lucid introduction to the theological answer given by the Eastern Orthodox Fathers to the question: Who was Jesus Christ? ". . . Meyendorff's book is intended for the serious student of theology" (*Kirkus*).

———. *The Orthodox Church: Its Past and Its Role in the World Today*. St. Vladimir's repr. of 1962 ed. 1981 pap. $8.95. Meyendorff, the leading Eastern Orthodox theologian in the United States, wrote this ecumenically oriented introduction to the tradition of the Eastern Church. Considerable attention is given to the Russian Church and modern Eastern Orthodox churches.

Niebuhr, H. Richard, and Daniel D. Williams. *The Ministry in Historical Perspective*. Harper repr. of 1956 ed. 1983 o.p. An important collection of essays discussing the historical development of the Christian priesthood and ministry. The chapters on the early and medieval church were written by John Knox, George H. Williams, and Roland Bainton.

Ruether, Rosemary R. *Religion and Sexism*. Simon & Schuster 1974 pap. $10.95. The 14 essays of this provocative book provide an excellent introduction to the issue of sexism in Christian history, challenging stereotypes and raising new questions.

Ruether, Rosemary R., and Eleanor McLaughlin. *Women of Spirit: Female Leadership in the Jewish and Christian Traditions*. Simon & Schuster 1979 pap. $10.95. Going beyond the mere documentation of the marginal role of women in the two traditions, the 13 essays of this volume want to contribute "both toward the recovery of important chapters of women's history and toward the charting of the paradigms of female leadership."

Spidlik, Tomas. *The Spirituality of the Christian East: A Systematic Handbook*. Trans. by Anthony P. Gythiel, Cistercian Pubns. 1986 $48.95 pap. $17.00. This rather ambitious, but competently composed, manual discusses in a systematic fashion all important topics connected with the theology of the spiritual life in the Christian East. It is one of the best sources of bibliography in the field.

Tavard, George H. *Woman in Christian Tradition*. Univ. of Notre Dame Pr. 1973 o.p. A theological treatment of the topic by a leading Catholic ecumenical scholar who is thoroughly familiar with the historical background.

Underhill, Evelyn. *The Mystics of the Church*. Attic Pr. repr. of 1925 ed. 1975 o.p. Underhill a foremost authority on mysticism, wrote this little masterpiece in 1925 as a concise introduction to the vast literature of Christian mysticism.

Walsh, Michael. *An Illustrated History of the Popes: St. Peter to John Paul II*. St. Martin's 1980 $19.95. An entertaining account of the historical papacy, written by an eminent Roman Catholic journalist and splendidly illustrated.

Warner, Marina. *Alone of All Her Sex: The Myth and the Cult of the Virgin Mary*.

Random 1983 pap. $10.95. A very readable, thoughtful exploration of the background, development, and function of Marian devotion drawing on history, mythology, psychology, and the visual arts.

White, R. E. *Christian Ethics: The Historical Development.* John Knox 1981 pap. $11.95. This extensive survey is meant "to bring the student reasonably equipped to the threshold of the current debate." Chapters 1–8 cover early Christianity up to Erasmus.

Source Collections

Ancient Christian Writers: The Works of the Fathers in Translation. Paulist Pr. 1946–   . 46 vols. to date ea. $11.95–$24.95. This well-established series, begun by Johannes Quasten and Joseph C. Plumpe under the auspices of the Catholic University of America in 1946, presents authoritative translations of a wide range of early Christian writings. At present, the editors are Johannes Quasten, Walter J. Burghardt, and Thomas C. Lawler.

The Ante-Nicene Fathers: Translations of the Writings of the Fathers down to A.D. 325. Ed. by Alexander Roberts and James Donaldson, Eerdmans 10 vols. repr. of 1884–97 ed. 1951 o.p. While not exhaustive, the volumes in this series present the older standard translations into English of the major works of the earliest church fathers. In the case of many of these works, no other English translation is available. The introductory material is often outdated, but the wealth of texts renders the series indispensable even today.

Barry, Colman J., ed. *Readings in Church History.* Christian Classics 3 vols. in 1 1985 pap. $50.00. A very useful documentary sourcebook that presents texts illustrating the various aspects of church history with special emphasis on thought and doctrine. Arranged in chronological order, the readings consist of substantial portions of a given work rather than brief excerpts. The editor is a well-known American Benedictine scholar, the abbot of St. John's Abbey, Collegeville, Minnesota.

Bettenson, Henry, ed. *Documents of the Christian Church.* Oxford 2d ed. 1970 pap. $8.95. The best brief anthology of important documents from the history of the church; more than half of the material comes from the early and medieval period.

———. *Early Christian Fathers: A Selection from the Writings of the Fathers from St. Clement of Rome to St. Athanasius.* Oxford repr. of 1956 ed. 1969 pap. $9.95. For each author, the excerpts are topically arranged, illustrating his thinking on a rich variety of doctrinal themes.

———. *The Later Christian Fathers: A Selection from the Writings of the Fathers from St. Cyril of Jerusalem to St. Leo the Great.* Oxford 1972 pap. $8.95. A continuation of the preceding volume, covering the period from the early fourth century to ca. 460 A.D. ". . . a work that constitutes a comprehensive one-volume collection of materials relating to the trinitarian and christological controversies" (*Christian Century*).

Cistercian Father Series. Ed. by Basil M. Pennington, Cistercian Pubns. 1970–   . 43 vols. to date ea. $7.95–$26.95 pap. ea. $3.25–$13.95. Begun in 1970, this rapidly expanding series offers excellent modern translations, many for the first time, of the works of medieval Cistercian writers, notably St. Bernard of Clairvaux, but also less-known figures.

Classics of Western Spirituality. Paulist Pr. 1974–   . 54 vols. to date ea. $12.95–$18.95 ea. pap. $9.95–$16.95. Originally planned as a total of 60 volumes, this series of original translations from the works of the Western spiritual and mystical tradition has turned out to be very successful and popular. The end, it seems, is not yet in sight. Among the figures of the early and medieval Christian Church we find Origen, Athanasius, Gregory of Nyssa, Augustine, John Cassian, John Climacus, Maximus Confessor, Gregory Palamas, Richard of St. Victor, Francis and Clare, Bonaventure, Meister Eckhart, John Tauler, and several women mystics: Hadewijch, Juliana of Norwich, Catherine of Genoa, Catherine of Siena. The series was begun in 1974.

The Fathers of the Church. Catholic Univ. of America Pr. 1947– . 76 vols. to date vols. 1–74 set $1,137.12 vol. 75 $19.95 vol. 76 $29.95. The series of new translations, founded by Ludwig Schopp in 1947 and originally published by its own corporation, continues to present reliable English translations of patristic literature. Of approximately 100 projected volumes, 76 have been published, following no particular order. The present editorial director is Professor Thomas P. Halton of the Classics Department at The Catholic University of America.

Leith, John H., ed. *Creeds of the Churches: A Reader in Christian Doctrine from the Bible to the Present*. John Knox 3d ed. 1982 pap. $11.95. The documents in this weighty little volume make for fascinating reading. The first 60 pages present major doctrinal affirmations from the New Testament to the Council of Florence (1438–65).

The Library of Christian Classics. Westminster Pr. 1950 to date 16 vols. ea. $8.95–$34.95. Most volumes of this essential series, which makes available translations of major Christian writings before 1600, are back in print in attractive paperback editions. Each volume is under the editorship of an acknowledged authority and contains superbly written introductions along with the texts. The bibliographies have not been updated in the reissues.

Neuner, J., and J. Dupuis, eds. *The Christian Faith in the Doctrinal Documents of the Catholic Church*. Alba House rev. ed. 1982 o.p. A classic compendium of authoritative documents from all periods of church history defining the official teaching of the Roman Catholic Church on major topics of Christian doctrine. "The documents are organized in chronological order around themes, so that the development of teaching . . . at various periods in the history of the Church becomes apparent."

Schaff, Philip. *The Creeds of Christendom*. Baker Bk. 3 vols. 1983 $75.00. Schaff's monumental *Creeds*, first published in 1877, remains the standard sourcebook of theological affirmations by major Christian churches all over the world. Volume 1 traces *The History of Creeds;* Volume 2 contains the *Greek and Latin Creeds*, with English translations.

A Select Library of the Nicene and Post-Nicene Fathers of the Christian Church. Ed. by Philip Schaff and others, Eerdmans 1956 28 vols. series 1 and 2 $18.95 per vol. The handsome set continues the *Ante-Nicene Fathers* in two series. Series 1 presents the works of St. Augustine (Vols. 1–8) and St. Chrysostom (Vols. 9–14) under the editorship of the great American church historian Philip Schaff; Series 2 includes in 14 volumes works by Eusebius, Athanasius, Basil the Great, Gregory of Nyssa, Ephrem the Syrian, Hilary, Jerome, Gregory the Great, and others. The second series was edited by Philip Schaff and Henry Wace.

Thompson, Bard, ed. *Liturgies of the Western Church*. Fortress Pr. repr. of 1962 ed. 1980 pap. $9.95. A very useful collection of orders of worship and similar materials from various traditions, especially the Protestant Reformation. The early centuries are represented by Justin Martyr, Hippolytus, and the text of the traditional Roman Mass.

THE EARLY CENTURIES (to c. A.D. 600)

The early centuries of Christianity were witness to the gradual Christianization of the Roman Empire. Beginning as a small sect within Judaism, Christianity quickly found converts among members of various classes of Greco-Roman society. At the end of its first 300 years it is estimated that 10 percent of the inhabitants of the empire were Christian. With Constantine's edict of toleration (313) and later Theodosius I's establishment of Christianity as the imperial religion (390), conversions to Christianity increased greatly. Missionaries converted people not only of Greek and Latin culture, but also "barbarians," such as the Germanic tribes. By the dawn of the Middle Ages, Christianity was the religion of the land that was once the Roman Empire.

The growth of Christianity, however, was not accomplished without difficulties. Christians faced not only external threats, philosophical condemnation, and sporadic instances of violence and persecution from their neighbors, but also internal division. Groups propounded differing, often contradictory, doctrines and beliefs, each group believing itself to have the correct understanding, to be "orthodox." Many of the more important issues, such as the Trinity and the nature of Christ, were settled at a series of councils, most important during this period being those of Nicea (325), Constantinople (381), and Chalcedon (451). By the end of this period two major centers of Christianity emerged: Rome, which as the church founded, according to tradition, by the Apostle Peter, became the center of the Roman Catholic Church; and Constantinople, the center for the Orthodox Church.

Special Histories

Ayer, Joseph C., ed. *A Source-Book of Ancient Church History from the Apostolic Age to the Close of the Conciliar Period.* AMS Pr. repr. of 1913 ed. 1979 $64.50. Ayer compiled this anthology as a companion to go with any good textbook. Chronologically arranged, it illustrates the main events, movements, and controversies to the ninth century. The connecting narrative gives a very brief factual account of church history.

Bainton, Roland H. *Early Christianity.* Krieger repr. of 1960 ed. 1984 text ed. pap. $7.50. In one small volume, Bainton combines one of the best brief accounts of early church history with an excellent selection of "Documents and Readings" in English translation.

Bruce, F. F. *The Spreading Flame: The Rise and Progress of Christianity from Its Beginnings to the Conversion of the English.* Eerdmans repr. of 1961 ed. 1980 pap. $14.95. Bruce, a leading evangelical New Testament scholar in Britain, emphasizes the time of the New Testament and the beginnings of Christianity in Britain.

Davies, John G. *The Early Christian Church.* [*Twin Brooks Ser.*] Baker Bk. repr. of 1965 ed. 1980 pap. $9.95; Greenwood repr. of 1965 ed. 1976 lib. bdg. $24.00. A chronologically organized account of the progress of Christianity as a religious movement, giving special attention to doctrine, worship, and Christian art and architecture. This fine book is intended for the general reader.

Frend, W. H. *The Rise of Christianity.* Fortress Pr. 1984 pap. $24.95. In this learned but lively book of more than 1,000 pages, the distinguished British church historian unfolds the story of Christianity's victory to A.D. 604. His model is Adolf Harnack's *Expansion of Christianity* (see below), which he wants to rewrite in the light of modern scholarship, including new archaeological and literary evidence. Furnished with notes, chronological charts, and a full bibliography, this is the most thorough treatment of the period available today.

Grant, Robert M. *Augustus to Constantine: The Thrust of the Christian Movement into the Roman World.* Harper 1970 o.p. An excellent survey by one of the foremost authorities in early Christian studies. The strength of Grant's presentation is its careful attention to the political and religious conditions of the Roman Empire and their impact on Christianity.

Harnack, Adolf. *The Expansion of Christianity in the First Three Centuries.* Ed. and trans. by James Moffatt [*Select Bibliographies Repr. Ser.*] Ayer 2 vols. repr. of 1904–05 ed. 1972 $64.00; ed. and trans. by James Moffatt, Irvington repr. of 1904 ed. $56.00. While largely superseded in details, Harnack's book is the classic study of the early spread of Christianity in the Roman Empire. The author tried to distinguish fact from fiction by a meticulous analysis of the sources.

Kidd, Beresford J. *A History of the Church to A.D. 461.* AMS Pr. 3 vols. repr. of 1922 ed. 1976 $82.50. At its time, this was the most detailed standard history of the first four centuries written by an English scholar. Kidd had an astonishing command of the sources and documented his account thoroughly in the notes and in a companion volume, *Documents Illustrative of the History of the Church to A.D. 461* (Macmillan 1920), which is not in print at the present time. The volumes are still valuable as reference tools because of their thoroughness.

Lebreton, Jules, and Jacques Zeiller. *The History of the Primitive Church.* Gordon Pr. 1949–52 $80.00. Vol. 1, *The Church in the New Testament: From the Death of St. John to the End of the Second Century;* Vol. 2, *The Church in the Third Century.* These are the first two volumes in the English translation of the famous French series *Histoire de l'Eglise*, edited by Fliche and Martin. The translation follows the French original rather closely.

Lietzmann, Hans. *A History of the Early Church.* Meridian Bks. 4 vols. in 2 1961 o.p. Vol. 1, *The Beginnings of the Christian Church;* Vol. 2, *The Founding of the Church Universal;* Vol. 3, *From Constantine to Julian;* Vol. 4, *The Era of the Church Fathers.* Lietzmann's volumes remain true classics in the field. Telling the story in a lively and readable style, they represent the harvest of decades of scholarly work on the major themes of early Christian history by the author and his generation.

Roberts, Peter. *In Search of Early Christian Unity.* Vantage 1985 $18.00. A somewhat uneven narrative account of church history through the seventh century written "for laymen by a layman." The author is a noted British MP and an ardent advocate of Christian unity.

Wand, J. W. C. *History of the Early Church from A.D. 500.* Methuen 4th ed. 1975 pap. $11.95. Written in 1934 by a well-known Anglican churchman and former bishop of London, this concise survey has remained a favorite textbook because of its reliable information and its balanced judgment. The new edition has some additional notes but has not been revised.

Christianity in the World of the Roman Empire

In the famous correspondence between the Emperor Trajan and PLINY THE YOUNGER (see Vol. 2), then Governor of Bithynia, Trajan informed Pliny that

Christians who refused to recant their allegiance by making the proper sacrifices and oaths should be punished, but they should not be sought out actively. This policy set the tone for the relations between Christians and the imperial government up to the middle of the third century. The sporadic acts of violence against Christians that did occur during this period were usually popular hostility and not imperial policy. In 250, Decius was the first emperor to sanction a general persecution of Christians. The persecution lasted intermittently for several years, after which came a period of 40 years of relative peace. In 303, the persecutions were resumed by Diocletian. Churches were destroyed, sacred books confiscated, clergy imprisoned and compelled to offer sacrifice. This official policy ended ten years later when Constantine, who in the previous year had, at least nominally, converted to Christianity and issued the "Edict of Milan" ending the persecution and officially recognizing the Christian churches. Finally, in 390 Theodosius I made Christianity the official imperial religion.

Barker, John W. *Justinian and the Later Roman Empire*. Univ. of Wisconsin Pr. 1966 text ed. pap. $10.95. Written for the general reader, this responsible account brings to life a crucial time of transition between antiquity and the Christian Middle Ages. The focus is not on biography but on the broader context of politics and religion in the empire.

Baynes, Norman H. *Constantine the Great and the Christian Church*. Gordon Pr. 1974 lib. bdg. $59.95; [*World History Ser.*] Haskell repr. of 1930 ed. 1972 lib. bdg. $75.00; [*Raleigh Lectures on History*] Longwood repr. of 1929 ed. 1977 $4.50. The classic statement of the view that the early sources depicting Constantine as a convinced Christian are trustworthy has been reissued with an important preface that traces the debate over Baynes's thesis in the past few decades.

Benko, Stephen. *Pagan Rome and the Early Christians*. Indiana Univ. Pr. 1985 $20.00 1986 pap. $7.95. This interesting study tries to show that pagan suspicions about early Christians were often not as unfounded as many people believe.

Browning, Robert. *The Emperor Julian*. Univ. of California Pr. 1976 pap. $4.95. The most recent full-length biography of the fourth century Roman Emperor whom Christians call "the Apostate." The study is particularly valuable because of the close attention paid to methods and results of modern social history.

Burckhardt, Jacob. *The Age of Constantine the Great*. Trans. by Moses Hadas, Univ. of California Pr. 1983 pap. $9.95. The English translation presents the classic interpretation of the Constantinian era as an age of disturbing transition by the greatest cultural historian of the nineteenth century.

Cochrane, Charles N. *Christianity and Classical Culture: A Study of Thought and Action from Augustus to Augustine*. Oxford repr. of 1944 ed. 1957 pap. $10.95; Peter Smith 1984 $18.00. Cochrane's book, first published in 1941, remains one of the most intriguing interpretations of the history of ideas both "pagan" and Christian and their interaction during the first four centuries of our era. The focus is on the shifting self-understanding of church and society.

Cunningham, Agnes. *The Early Church and the State*. [*Sources of Early Christian Thought Ser.*] Fortress Pr. 1982 pap. $7.95. A collection of fresh translations of key documents from the second to the end of the fourth century with a brief introduction.

Dodds, E. R. *Pagan and Christian in an Age of Anxiety: Some Aspects of Religious Experience from Marcus Aurelius to Constantine*. Norton repr. of 1965 ed. 1970 pap. $5.95. This is the famous but controversial study of the religious mood of the early Christian centuries that uses the Christian and pagan images of each other as illustrations of a common world of religious experience.

Doerries, Hermann. *Constantine and Religious Liberty.* Elliots Bks. 1960 $39.50. The Terry Lectures delivered at Yale in 1959 by the author of one of the best modern biographies of the Emperor Constantine, translated by Roland Bainton, the foremost church historian of his generation in the United States.

Fox, Robin L. *Pagans and Christians.* Knopf 1987 $35.00. This fascinating tome by a brilliant British historian links the story of early Christianity through the fourth century to the religious world of the Roman Empire at every point. Full of intriguing detail, yet eminently readable, it makes full use of recent advances in historical method and archaeology. The book represents accessible scholarship at its best.

Gager, John. *Kingdom and Community: The Social World of Early Christianity.* Prentice-Hall 1975 text ed. $14.95. The essays in this provocative volume attempt to understand early Christianity as one religious cult among others in the empire. They include "Religion and Society in the Early Roman Empire" and "The Success of Christianity."

Grant, Robert M. *Gods and the One God.* Westminster 1986 $16.95. This new book by an eminent historian of the early church skillfully introduces the reader to the religious conflict between Christians and their neighbors in the empire. Without a heavy technical apparatus, Grant discusses not only the mutual image of the two sides but also the influence of pagan religious concepts on distinctive Christian doctrines such as those of God, Christ, and the Holy Spirit.

Green, Michael. *Evangelism in the Early Church.* Eerdmans 1970 pap. $7.95. This study deals primarily with the methods, motives, and strategies of Christian evangelism as a proclamation of salvation and an invitation to conversion rather than the impact of the message on the Roman world.

Greenslade, Stanley L. *Church and State from Constantine to Theodosius.* Greenwood repr. of 1954 ed. 1981 lib. bdg. $19.50. Three lectures by the celebrated author of *Schism in the Early Church* given before a general audience and tracing the main development of Christianity as a state religion during the decisive century.

Hillgarth, Jocelyn N., ed. *Christianity and Paganism, 350–750: The Conversion of Western Europe.* Univ. of Pennsylvania Pr. rev. ed. 1986 lib. bdg. $25.00 pap. $10.95. This revision of *The Conversion of Europe, 350–750* (1969) presents an excellent anthology of relatively inaccessible sources that illustrate the slow penetration of Christianity into the changing society of Western Europe.

Hinson, E. Glenn. *The Evangelization of the Roman Empire: Identity and Adaptability.* Mercer Univ. Pr. 1981 $22.00. A good, broadly conceived study written by a church historian in the Free Church Tradition. The well-documented book starts from the assumption of the missionary nature of the church and tries to describe the contribution of theology and Christian life-styles to the missionary task.

Hoffman, R. Joseph, trans. *Celsus: On the True Doctrine.* Oxford 1987 $18.95 pap. $7.95. A brief study and new translation of the fragments of a famous anti-Christian treatise preserved in its rebuttal by the church father Origen.

Jaeger, Werner. *Early Christianity and Greek Paideia.* Harvard Univ. Pr. 1985 text ed. pap. $5.95; Oxford repr. of 1965 ed. 1969 pap. $4.95. The Carl Newell Jackson Lectures at Harvard for 1960 present an outstanding classicist's view of the reception of Greek learning into early Christianity. The book is adapted to the interests of a general audience.

Jones, A. H. *Constantine and the Conversion of Europe.* [*Medieval Academy Repr. for Teaching Ser.*] Univ. of Toronto Pr. repr. of 1948 ed. 1979 pap. $8.95. In this small but weighty volume, the leading authority on this period gives a clear, straightforward account of the Constantinian turn. Jones remains unconvinced by doubts about Constantine's serious Christian intentions.

Krautheimer, Richard. *Three Christian Capitals: Topography and Politics.* Univ. of California Pr. 1983 $35.00. These fascinating lectures give rich insights into the architectural features of Christian Rome, Milan, and Constantinople against the general background of fourth- and fifth-century politics. The book is beautifully illustrated.

McCullough, W. Stewart. *A Short History of Syriac Christianity to the Rise of Islam.* Scholars Pr. GA 1982 $21.95. The only general introduction in English to a field of study that finds great interest among church historians today.

McMullen, Ramsey. *Christianizing the Roman Empire, A.D. 100–400.* Yale Univ. Pr. 1984 $18.00. Drawing on his vast knowledge of the historical evidence, the author, professor of classical history at Yale, gives a clear account of the way the common people heard and assimilated the Christian message. His lucid text is supported by ample notes.

Mattingly, Harold. *Christianity in the Roman Empire.* Norton 1967 pap. $4.95. In six brief chapters, the author, an authority on ancient coins, gives a popular survey of church-state relations during the first three centuries. The appendix contains pertinent passages from primary sources, explanatory notes, and illustrations of imperial coins.

Ruether, Rosemary R. *Faith and Fratricide: The Theological Roots of Anti-Semitism.* Winston Pr. 1974 pap. $8.95. An important book whose author argues that the historical roots of modern anti-Semitism reach deep into classical history, including the New Testament and the church fathers.

Simon, Marcal. *Verus Israel.* Trans. by H. McKeating, Oxford 1985 $57.00. The English translation of the French original finally makes generally available one of the truly essential books on the subject.

Sordi, Marta. *The Christians and the Roman Empire.* Trans. by Annabel Bedini, Univ. of Oklahoma Pr. 1986 $22.50. A major study of the changing status of Christians in the Roman Empire, describing the persecutions and social conflicts as part of the religious rather than the political sphere. Translated from the Italian.

Wilken, Robert L. *The Christians as the Romans Saw Them.* Yale Univ. Pr. 1984 $22.50 pap. $8.95. This fresh look at early Christianity from the outside, written with a thorough knowledge of the sources yet unencumbered by technical discussions, opens up new and often surprising vistas that every reader will enjoy.

———. *John Chrysostom and the Jews: Rhetoric and Reality in the Late Fourth Century.* Univ. of California Pr. 1983 text ed. $32.50. A scholarly study of the social relations between Christians and the vigorous Jewish community of the city of Antioch, based on an analysis of eight sermons against the Jews by the church father Chrysostom.

Christian Doctrine and Heresies

During the early centuries of Christianity, numerous beliefs developed that attempted to answer questions fundamental to the religion. What is the nature of God and how is the relation among the members of the Trinity, the Father, the Son, and the Holy Spirit, understood? What is the relation between the earthly Jesus and the divine Christ? How are the sacraments, such as baptism and the Eucharist, to be understood and performed? What is Christian Scripture and how should it be interpreted? What is the human condition and do free will and grace affect that condition? There were several differing, sometimes contradictory, positions for each question. It took several centuries for the demarcation between "orthodox" doctrine and "heretical" belief to be clearly established. During this period, there were several important heretical groups, including Gnostics, who taught, among other things, that it was the true God, God the Father, who sent Jesus, and that salvation was given to an elect group through the knowledge (Greek "gnosis") of revealed truths. Other great controversies of the early centuries included Donatism, which divided the church over who had the authority to administer the sacraments; Arianism, which debated whether Christ is coeternal with the Father or created; and Pelagianism, which was concerned with whether human salvation could be affected by human free will and the role of God's grace.

Armstrong, D. M., ed. *The Cambridge History of Later Greek and Early Medieval Philosophy.* Cambridge Univ. Pr. 1967 $82.50. Despite its comprehensive scope, this massive handbook authored by a team of specialists contains a wealth of basic information and bibliography on Christian thought and thinkers to the early Middle Ages.

Bauer, Walter. *Orthodoxy and Heresy in Earliest Christianity.* Ed. by Robert A. Kraft and Gerhard Krodel, Fortress Pr. 1979 pap. $2.50. The main thesis of this seminal German work is that orthodox Christianity in many places was preceded by heretical forms of the faith so that the boundaries between orthodoxy and heresy must be seen as rather fluid in earliest times. The second German edition, from which the translation was prepared, contains two essays by Gerhard Strecker, including one on the controversy over Bauer's thesis. The American editors have made some modifications that help the reader greatly.

Burkitt, Francis C. *The Religion of the Manichees: Donnellan Lectures for 1924.* AMS Pr. repr. of 1925 ed. 1979 $29.00. Burkitt's masterful study, which is based on three Donnellan Lectures given at Dublin in 1924, ranks as the best general introduction to Manichaeism even though recent textual finds have changed the picture of the movement considerably. Burkitt addresses all major questions, such as sources, history, and teachings of this fascinating religion, remnants of which survived for many centuries.

Burns, J. Patout, ed. *Theological Anthropology.* [*Sources of Early Christian Thought Ser.*] Fortress Pr. 1981 pap. $7.95. A valuable sourcebook featuring new translations of patristic texts with an emphasis on the Pelagian controversy in which Saint Augustine was involved.

Chadwick, Henry. *Early Christian Thought and the Classical Tradition: Studies in Justin, Clement, and Origen.* Oxford 1984 text ed. pap. $11.50. Based on four lectures delivered in 1962, these delightful essays interpret the main themes of early Christian apologetics with great subtlety but in a language that is able to hold the attention of the general reader.

Danielou, Jean. *A History of Early Christian Doctrine before the Council of Nicea.* Trans. by John A. Baker, Westminster 3 vols. 1973–77 ea. $27.50. This massive trilogy, which was planned by the French cardinal for publication in English, presents a constructive synthesis of early Christian thought in terms of its Jewish, Hellenistic, and Latin components. As a scholar, Danielou was especially concerned with the distinctive phenomenon of Jewish Christianity and with the typological interpretation of Scripture.

Doresse, Jean. *The Secret Books of the Egyptian Gnostics.* AMS Pr. repr. of 1960 ed.

1979 $27.50; Inner Traditions Intl. 1986 pap. $14.95. One of the earliest and still most authoritative introductions to the ancient Gnostic writings discovered in Egypt after World War II, including the enigmatic Gospel of Thomas with 118 purported sayings of Jesus. The author, a French coptologist, was one of the first scholars to examine the spectacular find.

Frend, W. H. *The Donatist Church: A Movement of Protest in Roman North Africa*. Oxford 1985 $42.00. This is the detailed and scholarly standard history of the schismatic Donatist church of North Africa, now in a third printing with a new foreword.

———. *The Rise of the Monophysite Movement: Chapters in the History of the Church in the Fifth and Sixth Centuries*. Cambridge Univ. Pr. 1972 $74.50. In his characteristically lively style, the author explores the history of the most important group of Christological dissidents after the Council of Chalcedon (451) down to the Arab conquest. His narrative blends secular and ecclesiastical history with the history of doctrine and sheds new light on an understudied period that is of great ecumenical importance.

Grant, Robert M., ed. *Gnosticism: A Source Book of Heretical Writings from the Early Christian Period*. AMS Pr. repr. of 1961 ed. 1985 $32.50. Contains a standard collection of primary sources on Gnosticism in reliable English translations with brief introductory notes. It does not include the Nag Hammadi texts, which became available after its first publication.

Gregg, Robert C., and Dennis E. Groh. *Early Arianism: A View of Salvation*. Fortress Pr. 1981 $5.00. This controversial study, the first serious attempt at revising the image of the Arian heresy in decades, argues that Arius was less concerned with the question of God and the Trinity than with Christ as the model of a redeemed, mature humanity exemplified in the Christian Church.

Grillmeier, Aloys. *Christ in Christian Tradition*. Trans. by John Cawte, John Knox 1987 $34.95. This book in its present English form constitutes the most authoritative history of Christology in the ancient church. Written by a Roman Catholic scholar, it is precise in detail and is thoroughly documented.

Harnack, Adolf. *Marcion: The Gospel of the Alien God*. Trans. by John E. Steely and Lyle D. Bierma, Labyrinth Pr. 1987 $30.00. This important translation project makes available to English-speaking readers Harnack's monumental study of Marcion, the second-century heretic, which is based on the full range of early sources. The translators used the enlarged second edition of 1921. It is well known that Harnack had considerable sympathy with Marcion's "Pauline" Christianity.

Jonas, Hans. *Gnostic Religion: The Message of the Alien God and the Beginnings of Christianity*. Peter Smith 1963 2d ed. rev. $18.50. This weighty book by a well-known philosopher has become a classic in its field. Jonas not only describes the full range of Gnostic systems and writings, including Marcion, the so-called Hermetic literature, and Manichaeism, but attempts a comprehensive synthesis, interpreting Gnosis as a pervasive mind set present everywhere in the early centuries of the Christian era. The second edition contains a new chapter on the Nag Hammadi documents and an epilogue.

Kelly, J. N. *Early Christian Creeds*. Longman 3d ed. 1981 text ed. $16.95. This is the most recent edition of a widely used textbook that explains clearly and thoroughly the text, the history, and the meaning of all the important Christian creeds from the New Testament to the so-called Apostles' Creed, which, in its modern form, probably originated in early medieval France.

———. *Early Christian Doctrines*. Harper rev. ed. 1978 pap. $10.95. Kelly's masterly survey, organized by doctrinal themes within a chronologically ordered basic framework, remains undoubtedly the standard text in the field. The recent edition includes a new chapter on Mariology.

Lieu, Samuel N. *Manichaeism in the Later Roman Empire and Medieval China*. Longwood 1985 $54.00. This is a pioneering scholarly study of Manichaeism that not only discusses Mani and the beginnings of the movement, taking into account recent discoveries, but traces the religion's development in China, where Manichaeans existed until c.1600.

Norris, Richard A., Jr., ed. and trans. *The Christological Controversy*. [*Sources of Early Christian Thought Ser.*] Fortress Pr. 1980 pap. $7.95. A selection of essential primary texts in new translations, furnished with a concise introductory sketch.

Pagels, Elaine. *The Gnostic Gospels*. Random 1979 $14.95 1981 pap. $3.95. Drawing on the new Nag Hammadi writings, this provocative essay by a first-rate scholar makes a spirited plea for justice on behalf of Gnostic Christianity, which, she argues, was suppressed because it challenged the power structures of an authoritarian church.

Prestige, George L. *Fathers and Heretics*. [*Bampton Lectures*] Allenson 1940 o.p. In the famous Bampton Lectures of 1940, a great patristic scholar gives an engaging account of some important theological controversies of the third and fourth centuries. His sketches of the protagonists are little masterpieces: Bishop Callistus of Rome, Origen, Athnasius, Apollinaris, Nestorius, Cyril of Alexandria.

——. *A God in Patristic Thought*. Fortress Pr. 2d ed. 1952 o.p. An old classic (1936) by a master historian, this book traces the development of the doctrine of God and of the Trinity in a comprehensive fashion without becoming shallow.

Robinson, James M. *The Nag Hammadi Library in English*. Trans. by members of the Coptic Gnostic Library Project of the Institute for Antiquity and Christianity, Harper 1978 $23.03 pap. $11.95. Produced by a team of specialists, this is the first complete and authoritative English translation of the Gnostic books from the early Christian era that were found in a jar in Egypt shortly after World War II.

Rudolph, Kurt. *Gnosis: The Nature and History of Gnosticism*. Harper 1982 $28.45 pap. $14.95. This impressive book is probably the most comprehensive historical investigation to date of the entire Gnostic movement in the ancient world. It includes sections on Manichaeism and the Mandaeans. The translation is based on the second German edition (1980).

Rusch, William G., ed. *The Trinitarian Controversy*. [*Sources of Early Christian Thought Ser.*] Fortress Pr. 1980 pap. $7.95. An excellent selection of primary sources, mainly from the Arian controversy of the fourth century, which is also useful through its concise introduction to the persons and issues involved.

Russell, Jeffrey B. *Satan: The Early Christian Tradition*. Cornell Univ. Pr. 1981 $29.95 1987 pap. $10.95. A sequel to the same author's *The Devil* (Cornell Univ. Pr. 1977 $32.50), this carefully documented study discusses the theology and symbolism connected with evil from the second to the fifth century.

Turner, Henry E. *The Pattern of Christian Truth: A Study in the Relations between Orthodoxy and Heresy in the Early Church*. [*Bampton Lectures*] AMS Pr. repr. of 1954 ed. 1977 $47.50. In these Bampton Lectures the author wants to trace the pattern of doctrinal orthodoxy with particular reference to the three principal sources of theology—Scripture, tradition, and reason in answer to the thesis of Walter Bauer.

Von Campenhausen, Hans. *Virgin Birth in the Theology of the Ancient Church*. Allenson 1964 pap. $10.00. A careful critical investigation of the rise of early Christian Mariology from the New Testament to fathers and councils of the fourth and fifth centuries, written by a leading Protestant church historian.

Walker, Benjamin. *Gnosticism: Its History and Influence.* Borgo Pr. 1986 lib. bdg. $24.95. "A concise survey of gnostic thought from its pre-Christian origins to its modern manifestations," written for a wider public by a sympathizer.

Wallace-Hadrill, D. S. *Christian Antioch: A Study of Early Christian Thought in the East.* Cambridge Univ. Pr. 1982 $37.50. This is the first intensive study of the tradition of one of the great centers of Christian antiquity whose "school" helped in shaping Christian doctrine and controversy. Well-written and thoroughly documented, it gives a comprehensive answer to the question of what the label "Antiochian" meant in the early church.

Wand, John W. *The Four Great Heresies.* AMS Pr. repr. of 1955 ed. 1985 $29.00. In this slim volume, the former Bishop of London discusses clearly and succinctly the main tenets of the Arian, Apollinarian, Nestorian, and Eutychian heresies.

Wiles, Maurice F. *Making of Christian Doctrine.* Cambridge Univ. Pr. 1967 $32.50 pap. $11.95 o.p. This important study by the Regius Professor of Christian Doctrine at Oxford outlines convincingly the fundamental factors that contributed to the formulation of early Christian doctrine: Scripture, the experience of worship, and specific theological convictions concerning salvation.

Wiles, Maurice F., and M. Santer, eds. *Documents in Early Christian Thought.* Cambridge Univ. Pr. 1976 $42.50 pap. $12.95. A very helpful sourcebook featuring excerpts from the major church fathers on doctrinal topics such as God, Trinity, Christ, Holy Spirit, sin and grace, tradition and Scripture, church. Each section opens with a very brief historical introduction.

Wolfson, Harry A. *The Philosophy of the Church Fathers: Faith, Trinity, Incarnation.* Harvard Univ. Pr. 3d rev. ed. 1970 $32.50. Following the method of his classic study on Philo the Jew, the famous Harvard historian of philosophy develops the thesis that early Christian doctrines were the result of a recasting of Christian beliefs in the form of a Greek philosophy. A volume on other doctrines was planned but never written. The value of the book lies in its mastery of the sources and Wolfson's power of a synthetic vision.

Life in the Christian Church

In addition to the developments in doctrine, the church paid great attention to matters affecting the Christian life, including church structure, prayer, liturgy, and ethical issues such as Christian participation in military service and human sexuality. One important facet of this life was monasticism. From the deserts of Egypt and Syria, Christians both individually and in groups set themselves off from the rest of the world and pursued a life of perfection. Most of our knowledge of early Christian life comes from literary sources, but is greatly enhanced by the numerous remains from the ancient catacombs, churches, and various pieces of iconography.

Bradshaw, Paul F. *Daily Prayer in the Early Church: A Study of the Origins and Early Development of the Divine Office.* Oxford 1982 $26.00 pap. $9.95. This fine book gives an informative account of the practice of daily prayer, public and private, among early Christians, tracing its roots in Jewish practices. Much attention is devoted to the monastic development that led to the idea of specific hours being set aside for liturgical prayer.

Brown, Peter. *The Cult of the Saints: Its Rise and Function in Latin Christianity.* Univ.

of Chicago Pr. 1980 lib. bdg. $15.00 1982 pap. $7.95. In his own inimitable style, Brown tells the story of a major shift in Christian popular piety, throwing light on social and cultural conditions as much as on a phenomenon of religious devotion. The book grew out of a series of lectures delivered as the Haskell Lectures at the University of Chicago.

Cadoux, C. John. *The Early Christian Attitude to War: A Contribution to the History of Christian Ethics.* Gordon Pr. $69.96; Harper 1982 pap. $9.95. This old standard treatment of the subject covers the period before Constantine and argues the thesis that Jews and early Christians "closely identified their religion with peace" and therefore disapproved of war.

Chitty, Derwas J. *The Desert a City.* St. Vladimir's 1977 pap. $9.95. An important contribution to its field, this learned study traces the details of the earliest history of Christian monasticism in an imaginative synthesis of the literary and archaeological sources.

De Vogue, Adalbert. *The Rule of Saint Benedict: A Doctrinal and Spiritual Commentary.* Trans. by John B. Hasbrouck, Cistercian Pubns. 1983 pap. $25.95. The fruit of many years of careful study, this book by an acknowledged authority in the field of Benedictine studies contains a fascinating and eminently readable discussion of this foundational document of Western monasticism.

Dix, Dom G. *The Shape of the Liturgy.* Harper 1982 $24.50. A classic of long standing, this brilliant essay by a great Anglican monk and scholar had a considerable influence on the revival of liturgical studies since 1945. Touching on many aspects of liturgical life but concentrating on the Eucharist, the author stresses the Jewish roots of the central act of Christian worship.

Eno, Robert B. *Teaching Authority in the Early Church.* M. Glazier 1984 $15.95 pap. $9.95. A carefully selected and annotated volume of readings on a crucial question that covers such issues as the canon of Scripture, apostolic tradition, creeds, councils, and the authority of the Roman bishops through the fifth century.

Forell, George W. *History of Christian Ethics: From the New Testament to Augustine.* Augsburg 1979 $15.95. The first major effort at a synthesis of this kind in decades, this volume by a well-known Lutheran ethicist presents a very informative, balanced survey that takes into account historical advances and contemporary interests.

Giles, Edward, ed. *Documents Illustrating Papal Authority, A.D. 96–454.* Hyperion Pr. repr. of 1952 ed. 1979 $28.00. Today this inconspicuous volume is the standard collection in English of the primary texts that allow the reader to trace in great detail the development of the idea of papal primacy in the early church.

Gorman, Michael J. *Abortion and the Early Church: Christian, Jewish, and Pagan Attitudes in the Graeco-Roman World.* Inter-Varsity 1982 pap. $4.95; Paulist Pr. $4.95. Gorman has carefully collected and responsibly interpreted the scattered evidence that clearly points to a general rejection of abortion by early Christian as well as Jewish and Stoic writers in a permissive Roman society. He does not hide his own anti-abortion sympathies.

Grabar, Andre. *Christian Iconography: A Study of Its Origins.* Princeton Univ. Pr. 1980 $66.00 pap. $15.95. In this basic essay by one of the best-known interpreters of early Christian art the focus is on the way early Christian imagery was composed and used. The authoritative text is supplemented by more than 340 black-and-white illustrations.

Greer, Rowan A. *Broken Lights and Mended Lives: Theology and Common Life in the Early Church.* Pennsylvania State Univ. Pr. 1986 $19.50. Rather than trying to argue a thesis, the author pursues the *theme* of the impact of theology on the

Christian life in the early centuries. His book pleads for a sympathetic understanding of the fathers and the richness of their thought in our consideration of a common Christian spirituality.

Harnack, Adolf. *Militia Christi: The Christian Religion and the Military in the First Three Centuries (Militia Christi: Die Christliche Religion Und Der Soldatenstand In Den Ersten Drei Jahrhunderten).* Trans. by David M. Grace, Fortress Pr. 1981 $3.00. The first English edition of Harnack's brief but important essay in two parts ("The Christian as Soldier" and "The Christian Religion and the Military Profession") is enhanced by a short introduction tracing the impact of Harnack's book.

Helgeland, John, and others. *Christians and the Military: The Early Experience.* Fortress Pr. 1985 pap. $5.95. An excellent, straightforward analysis of the historical situation that combines extensive quotations from the sources with interpretation and a brief narrative framework. The authors conclude that "early Christian attitudes toward military service seem to be at least ambiguous."

Jungmann, Josef A. *The Early Liturgy to the Time of Gregory the Great.* Trans. by Francis A. Brunner [*Liturgical Studies Ser.*] Univ. of Notre Dame Pr. 1959 $12.95. In clear, nontechnical language, a master of the field sketches the entire development of Christian worship summing up his own research and that of other specialists.

———. *The Mass of the Roman Rite: Its Origins and Development.* Trans. by Francis A. Brunner, Christian Classics 2 vols. repr. of 1951 ed. 1986 pap. $39.95. The reprint makes available again the major modern in-depth analysis of the Roman Mass originally published between 1951 and 1955. The bulk of the work simply follows the outline of the traditional worship service and traces the history of each component through the centuries.

Kannengiesser, Charles, ed. *Early Christian Spirituality.* Trans. by Pamela Bright [*Sources of Early Christian Thought Ser.*] Fortress Pr. 1986 pap. $7.95. Ten representative texts from the Eastern and Western traditions are preceded by an introduction placing the selections in their historical context.

Kee, Howard C. *Miracle in the Early Christian World: A Study in Sociohistorical Method.* Yale Univ. Pr. 1983 $30.00 pap. $9.95. This study by an eminent New Testament scholar makes a serious attempt to read early Christian miracle stories in the framework of the general religious attitudes and practices in the Roman Empire.

Laeuchli, Samuel. *Power and Sexuality: The Emergence of Canon Law at the Synod of Elvira.* Temple Univ. Pr. 1972 $9.95. This engaging study tries to uncover the human drama behind the language of the laws passed by a fourth-century church synod. Many rulings concerned sexual misconduct.

Louth, Andrew. *The Origins of the Christian Mystical Tradition.* Oxford 1981 $29.95 pap. $9.95. The British author has written a thorough, very sympathetic introduction to early Christian mystical theology, weaving extensive quotations from primary sources into the interpretive narrative. Special attention is paid to the philosophical background (Plato and Philo) and to a comparison with St. John of the Cross.

McNamara, Jo Ann. *A New Song: Celibate Women in the First Three Christian Centuries.* Harrington Park repr. of 1983 ed. 1985 pap. $8.95; Haworth Pr. 1983 text ed. $29.95. This excellent study by a feminist historian tries to draw a more adequate picture of the role of communities of celibate women in early Christianity who "carved out a new niche for themselves in the social structure" and were the pioneers of a Christian freedom achieved by asceticism.

Mancinelli, Fabrizio. *Catacombs and Basilicas: The Early Christians in Rome.* Scala Bks. 1981 pap. $9.95. This book is particularly valuable for its superb pictures in full color, which give the reader a vivid impression of the most ancient monuments of Christian Rome. The text is brief but informative.

Musurillo, Herbert. *The Acts of the Christian Martyrs: Text and Translations.* Oxford 1972 $52.00. The best recent collection of the early reports on Christian martyrdom, usable both by the specialist and the general reader.

Phan, Peter C. *Social Thought.* M. Glazier 1983 $17.95 pap. $12.95. A good collection of excerpts from the fathers of the first five centuries, together with a brief general introduction.

Quasten, Johannes. *Music and Worship in Pagan and Christian Antiquity.* Trans. by Boniface Ramsey, Pastoral Pr. 1983 $10.95. Translated from the second German edition (1973), this fascinating, rich book is the only comprehensive treatment of the subject available.

Rader, Rosemary. *Breaking Boundaries: Male-Female Friendship in Early Christian Communities.* Paulist Pr. 1983 pap. $6.95. In this important study, a social historian of early Christianity investigates a major early Christian alternative to marriage in the relation between men and women. Rader finds a great deal of evidence for the phenomenon.

Shotwell, James T., and Louis R. Loomis, eds. *See of Peter.* Hippocrene Bks. 1965 lib. bdg. $49.00. An extensive collection of texts on Roman primacy from the New Testament to Pope Damasus (died 384). The volume was part of the Columbia University Records of Civilization series.

Snyder, Graydon F. *Ante Pacem: Archaeological Evidence of Church Life before Constantine.* Mercer Univ. Pr. 1985 $19.95. A scholarly but straightforward introduction to the archaeological remains of early Christianity giving accurate information, bibliography, and English translations of inscriptions. The book is carefully illustrated with black-and-white photographs, line drawings, and maps.

Stevenson, J. *The Catacombs: Rediscovered Monuments of Early Christianity.* [*Ancient People and Places Ser.*] Thames & Hudson 1978 $19.95. The best recent introduction to all aspects of the Christian catacombs in Rome and elsewhere. The book is beautifully laid out and profusely illustrated.

Swift, Louis J. *The Early Fathers on War and Military Service.* M. Glazier 1984 $15.95 pap. $9.95. This volume presents judiciously chosen brief excerpts from the Christian literature of the early centuries within the framework of a narrative that stresses the variety of viewpoints and the changes.

Veilleux, Armand, trans. *Pachomian Koinonia.* Cistercian Pubns. 2 vols. 1981–83 pap. ea. $10.00–$12.95. The first comprehensive collection of the sources from the circle of the founder of the communal religious life in fourth-century Egypt.

Von Campenhausen, Hans. *Ecclesiastical Authority and Spiritual Power in the Church of the First Three Centuries.* Trans. by J. A. Baker, Stanford Univ. Pr. 1969 $25.00. This penetrating analysis by an eminent church historian discusses the conflict over authority among early Christians: Who has authority and why? Which tradition is authoritative? The main focus is on the emergence of a variety of church offices in the first and second centuries.

Waddell, Helen. *The Desert Fathers.* Barnes & Noble repr. of 1936 ed. 1974 text ed. $9.25; Univ. of Michigan Pr. 1957 pap. $7.95. First published in 1936, this little book contains a classic selection from the wisdom of the early monks culled from the *Vitas patrum*, the standard Latin translation of the "Sayings of the Fathers."

Womer, Jan L. *Morality and Ethics in Early Christianity.* [*Sources of Early Christian*

Thought Ser.] Fortress Pr. 1987 pap. $7.95. A representative choice of texts from early Christian and patristic writings that are ably introduced by the editor-translator.

Church Fathers and Writers

Goodspeed, Edgar J. *A History of Early Christian Literature*. Ed. by Robert M. Grant [*Midway Repr. Ser.*] Univ. of Chicago Pr. rev. & enl. ed. 1966 pap. $13.00. The masterly survey from the beginning to A.D. 325, which one of the most distinguished American scholars authored in the 1930s, was revised by Robert M. Grant of Chicago.

Quasten, Johannes, ed. *Patrology*. Trans. by Placid Solari, Christian Classics 4 vols. 1983–86 set $85.00. Quasten's impressive volumes are the indispensable repertory of the fathers and of all early Christian literature. For each author, there is a brief biography, a detailed analysis of the literary legacy with a listing of English translations and bibliography, and an overview of the main teachings. Volume 4, published for the first time in English in 1986, deals with the Latin fathers on the fourth and fifth centuries.

Ramsey, Boniface. *Beginning to Read the Fathers*. Paulist Pr. 1985 pap. $9.95. Adapted from lectures given before the monks of Gethsemani Abbey in Kentucky, this helpful book skillfully introduces the reader into the thought world of the fathers. It is arranged by topics and includes suggestions for a "Patristic Reading Program."

Squire, Aelred, ed. *Fathers Talking: An Anthology*. Cistercian Pubns. 1986 $12.95 pap. $6.95. This slim volume offers a thoughtful selection of excerpts from Origen, Popes Leo I and Gregory I, Augustine, and Cyril of Jerusalem for meditative reading.

Von Campenhausen, Hans. *The Fathers of the Greek Church*. Pantheon 1959 o.p.

———. *The Fathers of the Latin Church*. Stanford Univ. Pr. 1964 $32.50. These two volumes by one of the best German church historians, classics in their field, contain excellent and lively biographies of the major church fathers from the second through the fifth centuries.

Wiles, Maurice. *The Christian Fathers*. Oxford repr. of 1966 ed. 1982 pap. $6.95. A topical introduction to the teaching of the fathers covering the image of God; the divinity of Christ; the Incarnation, sin, and salvation; sacraments; church; and ethics. Brief biographical notes at the end.

Young, Frances M. *From Nicea to Chalcedon: A Guide to the Literature and Its Background*. Fortress Pr. 1983 $22.95. This useful book analyzes the doctrinal developments of the crucial period from A.D. 325 to A.D. 451 by giving a thorough, reliable account of all the pertinent writings of the fathers and their critics.

AMBROSE, SAINT. 340?–397

Ambrose was Bishop of Milan during the last quarter of the fourth century. His work as bishop had a lasting influence on the relation between the church and secular authority. He was a counselor to several emperors and sought an alliance between the Roman state and Christianity, perceiving "the Emperor to be in the Church and not above it." The most significant demonstration of this belief was his demand for penance and excommunication of Roman Emperor Theodosius I for ordering a massacre of civilians in Thessalonica. Ambrose was well known for his preaching and defense of orthodoxy and is in part responsible for the conversion of Augustine. His writings include sermons and hymns and treatises on the sacraments, ethics, and ascetical subjects. He was a supporter of monasticism in northern Italy, and is ranked as one of the four doctors of the Latin Church.

BOOKS BY ST. AMBROSE

A Select Library of the Nicene and Post-Nicene Fathers. Ed. by Philip Schaff, Eerdmans 2d ser. repr. 1974 o.p. Volume 10 includes "Duties of the Clergy," "Holy Spirit," "Death of Satyrus," "Belief in the Resurrection," "Christian Faith," "Mysteries," "Repentance," "Virgins," "Widows," and selected letters. These documents, except the letters, comprise some of Ambrose's important dogmatic and ethical treatises and sermons.

Hexameron, Paradise, Cain and Abel. Trans. by John J. Savage [*Fathers of the Church Ser.*] Catholic Univ. Pr. 1961 $34.95. The "Hexameron" contains nine homilies divided into six books concerning the scriptural account of the six days of creation. "Paradise" and "Cain and Abel" are early homiletical works.

Seven Exegetical Works. Trans. by Michael P. McHugh [*Fathers of the Church Ser.*] Catholic Univ. Pr. 1972 $29.95. The exegetical works contained in this volume are "Isaac or the Soul," "Death as a Good," "Jacob and the Happy Life," "Joseph," "Patriarchs," "Flight from the World," "Prayer of Job and David."

Theological and Dogmatic Works. Trans. by Roy J. Deferrari [*Fathers of the Church Ser.*] Catholic Univ. Pr. 1963 $21.95. The first treatise, "Mysteries," represents addresses given to the newly baptized during Easter week. It treats the rites and meaning of the sacraments of baptism, confirmation, and Holy Eucharist. The second treatise, "Holy Spirit," is an attack on the Macedonians, a semi-Arian heresy. The third and fourth treatises, "Sacrament of the Incarnation of our Lord" and "Sacraments," address the issue of the sacraments especially as they were taught to the newly baptized Christians.

BOOK ABOUT ST. AMBROSE

Paredi, Angela. *Saint Ambrose: His Life and Times.* Univ. of Notre Dame Pr. 1964 o.p. This very readable book explores both the life of Ambrose and relevant Church history of the fourth and fifth centuries.

APOSTOLIC FATHERS

The name "Apostolic Fathers" was given in the seventeenth century to a group of Christian writers from the earliest times who may have been contemporary to the apostles and their immediate successors but whose writings were not accepted into the New Testament canon even though some early biblical manuscripts contain one or two of them along with other New Testament writings. Normally, the group comprises First Clement (Clement of Rome), Second Clement, the letters of Ignatius and Polycarp, the Martyrdom of Polycarp, the Didache or Teaching of the Apostles, the Epistle of Barnabas, the Letter to Diognetus, and the Shepherd of Hermas.

Barnard, L. W. *Studies in the Apostolic Fathers and Their Background.* Schocken 1966 o.p. Twelve essays on various works of the Apostolic Fathers, with major emphasis on the "Letter of Barnabas" and aspects of the development of early Christianity.

Goodspeed, Edgar J., trans. *The Apostolic Fathers: An American Translation.* Harper 1950 o.p. This volume contains "Doctrina," "Didache," the "Letter of Barnabas," "First Clement," "Second Clement," "Hermas," "Letters of Ignatius," "Letter of

Polycarp to the Philippians," "Martyrdom of Polycarp," "Apology of Quadratus," "Fragments of Papias," and "Diognetus." Each text is accompanied by a brief introduction.

Grant, Robert M., ed. *The Apostolic Fathers: A New Translation and Commentary.* Nelson 6 vols. 1964–68 o.p. Vol. 1, *An Introduction,* by Robert M. Grant; Vol. 2, *First and Second Clement,* by Robert M. Grant and Holt H. Graham; Vol. 3, *The Didache and Barnabas,* by Robert A. Kraft; Vol. 4, *Ignatius of Antioch,* by Robert M. Grant; Vol. 5, *Polycarp, Martyrdom of Polycarp, Fragments of Papias,* by William Schoedel; Vol. 6, *Hermas,* by Graydon F. Snyder. Each volume contains a substantial introduction to the relevant texts, translation, detailed commentary, and helpful bibliography.

Kleist, James A., trans. *The Epistles of St. Clement of Rome and St. Ignatius of Antioch.* Paulist Pr. 1946 $12.95. Contains "The Didache," "The Epistle of Barnabas," "The Epistle and Martyrdom of St. Polycarp," "The Fragments of Papias," "The Epistle to Diognetus."

Lake, Kirsopp. *The Apostolic Fathers.* [*Loeb Class. Lib.*] Harvard Univ. Pr. 2 vols. repr. of 1912–13 ed. ea. $12.95. These volumes contain Greek-English facing pages of the "Letter of Barnabas," "First Clement," "Second Clement," "Letters of Ignatius," "The Letter of Polycarp to the Philippians," "Didache," "Shepherd of Hermas," "Martyrdom of Polycarp," and "Epistle of Diognetus."

Lawson, John. *A Theological and Historical Introduction to the Apostolic Fathers.* Macmillan 1961 o.p. A primarily theological and spiritual introduction to these writings, with chapter-by-chapter brief commentaries on "First Clement," "Second Clement," "Didache," "Letters of Ignatius," "Martyrdom of Polycarp," "Letter of Barnabas," "Hermas," and "Diognetus."

Lightfoot, J. B., ed. *The Apostolic Fathers.* [*Twin Brooks Ser.*] Baker Bk. repr. of 1891 ed. 1984 pap. $17.95. Contains only the English translations from Lightfoot's major study (see below).

————. *The Apostolic Fathers, Clement, Ignatius, and Polycarp: Revised Texts with Introductions, Notes, Dissertations, and Translations.* Baker Bk. 2 pts. in 5 repr. of 1889–90 ed. 1981 $89.95. Lightfoot's famous volumes present the fullest scholarly discussion of the Apostolic Fathers in any language. The Baker reprint comes in handsomely bound volumes.

Schoedel, William. *Ignatius of Antioch: A Commentary on the Seven Letters of Ignatius.* Fortress Pr. 1985. $34.95. A scholarly commentary on the authentic writings of Ignatius.

Staniforth, Maxwell, trans. *Early Christian Writings: The Apostolic Fathers.* Intro. by Andrew Louth, Penguin 1987 $5.95. The text and brief introduction are given to "First Clement," "Letters of Ignatius," "Letter of Polycarp to the Philippians," "Martyrdom of Polycarp," "Diognetus," "Letter of Barnabas," and "Didache."

AUGUSTINE OF HIPPO, SAINT. 354–430

[SEE Chapter 3 in this volume.]

BASIL OF CAESAREA, SAINT. c. 330–379

Basil, also known as Basil the Great, is included as one of the Cappadocian Fathers, the leaders of philosophical Christian orthodoxy in the later fourth century. Basil was born in Cappadocia (in present day southeastern Turkey) and educated according to the best pagan and Christian culture of his day. He briefly pursued the monastic life in Syria and Egypt. Although he returned to his homeland, he remained influential in the monastic life of

Asia Minor. In 370 he succeeded Eusebius as Bishop of Caesarea, a post he held until his death. Basil was continuously involved in defending orthodoxy against many of the significant controversies of the fourth century. His most important work was as leader in the intellectual defense of Nicene Christianity. He was a champion of the term *homoiousios* ("like in substance to the Father"), and argued that it had the same implications as the Nicene *homoiousios* ("of one substance"). One of his most important treatises, "On the Holy Spirit," argued against the belief of those denying the divinity of the Holy Spirit.

BOOKS BY ST. BASIL OF CAESAREA

A Select Library of the Nicene and Post-Nicene Fathers. Ed. by Philip Schaff, Eerdmans 2d ser. repr. 1974 o.p. Volume 8 contains "On the Holy Spirit," the "Hexaemeron," and the letters.

Ascetical Works. Trans. by M. Monica Wagner [*Fathers of the Church Ser.*] Catholic Univ. Pr. 1950 $26.95. This volume contains 16 treatises addressed to ascetics, rules based on teaching of the Gospel directed at the laity, monastic problems, and various homilies on ascetical questions.

Exegetic Homilies. Trans. by Agnes C. Way. [*Fathers of the Church Ser.*] Catholic Univ. Pr. 1963 $19.95. Nine homilies on the "Hexaemeron" and 13 on various Psalms.

Letters. Trans. by Agnes C. Way [*Fathers of the Church Ser.*] Catholic Univ. Pr. 2 vols. 1951–55 o.p. The first volume contains letters 1–185, the second 186–368; trans. by Roy J. Deferrari and M. R. P. McGuire [*Loeb Class. Lib.*] Harvard Univ. Pr. 1926–34 4 vols. ea. $12.95. The complete letters are included with a Greek text. Volume 4 also includes the "Address to Young Men on How They Might Derive Benefit from Greek Culture."

BOOK ABOUT ST. BASIL OF CAESAREA

Murphy, M. Gertrude. *Saint Basil and Monasticism.* AMS Pr. repr. of 1930 ed. 1982 $14.75. Good, solid biography.

CASSIAN, SAINT JOHN. c.365–c.435

St. John Cassian, an important figure in the early history of monasticism, can be considered "one of the principal architects of the western monastic system." He joined a monastery at Bethlehem, but left soon after to study monasticism in Egypt. Eventually he found his way west, spending a short time in Rome and settling in Marseilles, where he founded two monasteries. He collected much of his knowledge on monastics and monasticism in his *Institutes* and *Conferences*. The former work was used by Benedict of Nursia in his famous monastic Rule. Cassian's theological importance and legacy comes in his disagreement with the Augustinian views of grace and predestination. He maintained that "the first steps towards the Christian life were ordinarily taken by the human will and that Grace supervened only later." His views, traditionally described as "Semi-Pelagianist," received widespread support in the monasteries in the West.

BOOK BY ST. JOHN CASSIAN

A Select Library of the Nicene and Post-Nicene Fathers. Ed. by Philip Schaff, Eerdmans 2d ser. repr. 1979 o.p. Volume 11 contains the "Institutes," "Conferences," and "Incarnation of the Lord."

BOOK ABOUT ST. JOHN CASSIAN

Chadwick, Owen. *John Cassian.* Cambridge Univ. Pr. 2d ed. 1968 $32.50. A very readable introduction to the life and thought of John Cassian.

CHRYSOSTOM, SAINT JOHN. c.354–407

John Chrysostom, whose life and career center around Antioch and Constantinople, is noted for his preaching, exegesis, and liturgical reforms. He was interested in monasticism and the life of the ascetic. For a period of some years he lived as a hermit. He was especially gifted in his powers of oratory (Chrysostom means "golden mouthed"). His skills were especially directed to the instruction and moral reformation of the people of Antioch. In terms of scriptural exegesis he spoke for a literal interpretation of the text against the allegorical school that was prominent in Alexandria. In 398 he became Patriarch of Constantinople. During his tenure he seriously angered the Patriarch of Alexandria and the empress, who eventually had Chrysostom removed from office in 403 and later exiled, first to Antioch and later to Pontus, where he died.

BOOKS BY ST. JOHN CHRYSOSTOM

A Select Library of the Nicene and Post-Nicene Fathers. Ed. by Philip Schaff, Eerdmans 2d ser. repr. 1979 o.p. Vol. 9, Letters, Homilies, "On Priesthood," "Instructions to Candidates for Baptism"; Vol. 10, Homilies on the Gospel of Matthew; Vol. 11, Homilies on Acts of the Apostles; Vol. 12, Homilies on First and Second Corinthians; Vol. 13, Homilies on Galatians and Ephesians; Vol. 14, Homilies on the Gospel of John and Hebrews.

Baptismal Instructions. Trans. by Paul Harkins, Newman 1963 o.p. A complete series of eight instructions on baptism.

Homilies on Genesis. Trans. by Robert C. Hill [*Fathers of the Church Ser.*] Catholic Univ. Pr. 1985 $29.95. The volume contains Homilies 1–17.

On Virginity: Against Remarriage. Trans. by Sally R. Shore, intro. by Elizabeth A. Clark, E Mellen 1984 $49.95. This volume, part of the Studies in Women and Religion series, contains two treatises important for Chrysostom's views on women, virginity, asceticism, and marriage. The introduction to the translations provides a helpful discussion of these views.

CYPRIAN OF CARTHAGE, SAINT. c.200?/210?–258

Cyprian was Bishop of Carthage during the middle of the third century, a time of persecution against the church and division within it. Cyprian converted to Christianity around 246 and soon became Bishop of Carthage. Within months of his assuming this position, the Christian community was faced with the Decian persecutions. Cyprian was forced to flee the city and lead the church from exile. He returned to Carthage two years later. During his absence many Christians had lapsed from their faith, and many more had secured "libelli pacis," certificates stating that they had sacrificed to the pagan idols in order to avoid imprisonment. Much of Cyprian's remaining career involved the issue of schismatic groups that grew out of the reintroduction of lapsed Christians into the church. Cyprian demanded the rebaptism of schismatics by properly consecrated clerics. If the bishop leading the community of believers was not holy, then the community itself ceased to be part of the church. For Cyprian, "there is no salvation outside the Church." These issues continued to be a burning problem for the church in North Africa, which led to the Donatist controversy of the fourth and fifth centuries. During the Valerian persecutions in 258 Cyprian was arrested and eventually martyred in Carthage. Cyprian's writings are known especially for their attention to church, the ministry, and the sacraments.

BOOKS BY ST. CYPRIAN OF CARTHAGE

Ante-Nicene Fathers. Ed. by Alexander Roberts and James Donaldson, rev. by A. C. Coxe, Eerdmans repr. 1978 o.p. Volume 5 contains Cyprian's letters and several treatises including "On the Unity of the Church," "On the Dress of Virgins," "On the Lord's Prayer," "An Address to Demetrianus," "On the Vanity of Idols," "On the Mortality," "On Works and Alms," "On the Advantage of Patience," "On Jealousy and Envy," "Exhortation to Martyrdom," and "Testimonies Against the Jews."

Treatises. Trans. by Elizabeth Keenan, Mary Hannah Mahoney, and George Edward Conway [*Fathers of the Church Ser.*] Catholic Univ. Pr. 1957 $29.95. Contains 13 treatises written by Cyprian, including "On the Unity of the Church" and "The Lapsed."

The Lapsed and Unity of the Church. Trans. by Maurice Bevenot, Eastern Orthodox Bks. pap. $2.95. These two important treatises of Cyprian deal with the aftereffects of the Decian persecutions.

The Lapsed. Trans. by Maurice Bevenot, Oxford 1971 o.p. The Latin text of this treatise is given with an English translation.

Letters. Trans. by Rose Bernard Donna [*Fathers of the Church Ser.*] Catholic Univ. Pr. 1964 $29.95. This volume contains letters 1–81.

BOOK ABOUT ST. CYPRIAN OF CARTHAGE

Hinchcliff, Peter. *Cyprian of Carthage and the Unity of the Christian Church.* Chapman 1974 o.p. A scholarly, yet nontechnical, biography of the third-century Bishop of Carthage. The work functions as a "useful guide to the course of Cyprian's career" (Gerald Bonner, *Journal of Ecclesiastical History*).

EUSEBIUS OF CAESAREA. c.260–c.340

Eusebius is best remembered for his important writings. His most celebrated, *Ecclesiastical History,* provides a history of Christianity, sometimes without critical judgment of the veracity of certain events, from the apostolic age down to the early fourth century. It is primarily this work that earned Eusebius the title of the "Father of Church History." His other writings, including *Preparation for the Gospel, Onomasticon, Commentaries on the Psalms,* and *Isaiah,* contain quotations from classical authors now lost, allegorical interpretations of biblical texts, and a valuable work on biblical topography. Theologically, Eusebius had a close association with the Origen-ist tradition; his teacher Pamphilus was a student of Origen, and had sympathy for the Arian cause, although he himself was not Arian. He held the position of Bishop of Caesarea beginning around 315 until his death c.340.

BOOKS BY EUSEBIUS OF CAESAREA

A Select Library of the Nicene and Post-Nicene Fathers. Ed. by Philip Schaff, Eerdmans 2d ser. repr. 1979 o.p. Volume 1 contains "Ecclesiastical History" and the "Life of Constantine."

Ecclesiastical History. Trans. by Roy J. Deferrari [*Fathers of the Church Ser.*] Catholic Univ. Pr. 1953 Bks. 1–5 $18.95 1955 Bks. 6–10 $17.95; trans. by Kirsopp Lake and J. E. L. Oulton [*Loeb Class. Lib.*] Harvard Univ. Pr. 2 vols. 1980 ea. $13.95. An important source, although not always historically accurate, for our knowledge of early church history. The Loeb Classical Library edition contains a Greek text.

BOOKS ABOUT EUSEBIUS OF CAESAREA

Barnes, Timothy D. *Constantine and Eusebius.* Harvard Univ. Pr. 1981 text ed. $37.50 1984 pap. $12.50. A scholarly study of "the history of the Constantinian age and the personalities of two of that period's most important figures" (Gerald Virna, *Anglican Theological Review*). An extensive bibliography accompanies the text.

Chesnut, Glenn F. *The First Christian Histories: Eusebius, Socrates, Sozomen, Theodoret, and Evagrius.* Mercer Univ. Pr. 2d ed. rev. 1986 $34.95. A learned study that examines "the historiography of the early eastern Christian historians" (E. Glen Hinson, *Church History*). The study focuses on how each of the authors dealt with the motifs of fate and fortune in Rome and the Roman emperors. Special attention is given to the writings of Eusebius.

Grant, Robert M. *Eusebius as Church Historian.* Oxford 1980 $36.00. A careful and detailed study of the influence of ecclesiastical-political realities on the writing of Eusebius's "Church History."

GREGORY THE GREAT (POPE GREGORY I). c.540–604

Gregory, who became pope in 590, oversaw great changes in the church. He was an able pastor and theologian, a promoter of monasticism, and, most significantly, a reformer of the Western Church who expanded the prestige and the authority of the papacy. Most of his activities were concerned with the practical shape of the Christian life. He made important changes in the liturgy; wrote an influential treatise, "Pastoral Rule," that set out directives for the pastoral life of a bishop; developed a doctrine of purgatory; wrote treatises, such as his *Morals on the Book of Job*, that contributed to monastic spirituality. He also promoted the conversion of the Arian Visogoths to Catholicism, initiated the conversion of the Anglo-Saxons in England, and reformed the administration and expenditure of the revenues of the landed estates that supported orphanages, schools, and hospitals. Notwithstanding the great influence Gregory had on the church as it entered into the Middle Ages, he is remembered for his humility. He rejected the suggestion of the Patriarch of Constantinople to style himself the "Universal Patriarch"; rather, he referred to himself as "the servant of the servants of God."

BOOKS BY GREGORY THE GREAT

A Select Library of the Nicene and Post-Nicene Fathers. Ed. by Philip Schaff, Eerdmans 2d ser. repr. 1979 o.p. Volume 12 contains the "Book of Pastoral Rule," in which, according to Schaff, Gregory "sets out the directives for the pastoral life of a bishop" and letters. Volume 13 contains the remainder of Gregory's letters.

Pastoral Care. Trans. by Henry Davies, Newman 1950 o.p. The translator states that the treatise "sets forth the awesome character and difficulties of the office of the priesthood," and shows "how to fulfill the duties that go with it as they should be fulfilled."

BOOKS ABOUT GREGORY THE GREAT

Evans, G. R. *The Thought of Gregory the Great.* Cambridge Univ. Pr. 1986 $39.50. A brief study of Gregory's thought, in particular (in the author's words) "his attempt to bring active and contemplative together and his theology."

Richards, Jeffrey. *Consul of God.* Methuen 1980 $27.95. A substantial scholarly biography of Gregory, concerned primarily with his influence on church organization and the development of the papacy.

JEROME, SAINT. c.347–419

Jerome was the greatest scholar of the ancient church. Most of his mature life was spent in study in various parts of the Eastern Mediterranean. In approximately 372, he set out for the East and stayed in Antioch for a short period, eventually settling as a hermit in the Syrian desert for four or five years. He then spent some time in Constantinople, and in 382 returned to Rome, where he became secretary to Pope Damasus. During his brief residence in Rome, he began his revision of the Bible into Latin translated from the original languages. The culmination of his work, which took over two decades, was the Vulgate. He returned to the East in 385 and eventually settled in Bethlehem, where he ruled a newly founded monastery and devoted the rest of his life to study and writing.

In addition to the Vulgate his writings include biblical commentaries and treatises concerning linguistic and topographical material written in order to help in the interpretation of Scripture.

BOOKS BY ST. JEROME

A Select Library of the Nicene and Post-Nicene Fathers. Ed. by Philip Schaff, Eerdmans 2d ser. repr. 1979 o.p. Volume 3 contains "Lives of Illustrious Men," short biographies of Christian writers from the apostles to himself. Volume 6 contains treatises and prefaces to his biblical commentaries and the letters.

Dogmatic and Polemical Works. Trans. by John Hritzu [*Fathers of the Church Ser.*] Catholic Univ. Pr. 1965 $21.95. The volume contains "On the Perpetual Virginity of the Blessed Virgin against Helvidius," "Apology against the Books of Rufinius," and "Dialogue against the Pelagians."

Homilies on Psalms. Trans. by Marie L. Ewald [*Fathers of the Church Ser.*] Catholic Univ. Pr. 1964 $23.95. Fifty-nine homilies on various Psalms.

Homilies on Psalms and Other Texts. Trans. by Marie L. Ewald [*Fathers of the Church Ser.*] Catholic Univ. Pr. 1966 $15.95. Fifteen homilies on the Psalms, 10 on the Gospel of Mark, and 12 more on various writings and topics.

Select Letters. Trans. by E. A. Wright [*Loeb Class. Lib.*] Harvard Univ. Pr. repr. of

1933 ed. 1980 $12.95. A selection of letters of various types and contents. A Latin text accompanies the translation.

BOOKS ABOUT ST. JEROME

Clark, Elizabeth A. *Jerome, Chrysostom and Friends: Essays and Translations*. E Mellen repr. of 1979 ed. 1983 $49.95. This volume contains two essays on the attitude toward male-female relationships in fourth-century Christianity. In addition, there are translations of relevant primary texts, including two concerning Chrysostom's friend and supporter, Olympias (the "Life of Olympias" and "Narration Concerning St. Olympias"), and Chrysostom's "Instruction and Reflections Directed against Those Men Cohabiting with Virgins" and "On the Necessity of Guarding Virginity."

Kelly, J. N. *Jerome: His Life, Writings and Controversies*. Christian Classics repr. of 1975 ed. 1980 o.p. A comprehensive and scholarly biography dealing with Jerome's personality and multifaceted career.

ORIGEN. 185?–254?

[SEE Chapter 3 in this volume.]

TERTULLIAN. c.160–c.230

Tertullian, a convert to Christianity, lived and wrote in the North African city of Carthage. Although he probably never held a clerical post, his influence on Christianity, especially in the West, was enormous. His writings include a long list of apologetic, theological, controversial, and ascetic works. He never shied away from discoursing against those he believed to be expounding against the "rule of faith." He is the first major Christian author to write in Latin. Tertullian's theological interests centered around his concern for the purity and holiness of the church. The importance of these issues eventually led Tertullian to join the Montanist sect, which emphasized the immediacy of the spirit, ecstatic prophecy, and a moral strictness.

BOOKS BY TERTULLIAN

Ante-Nicene Fathers. Ed. by A. Clevland Coxe. Eerdmans repr. 1978 o.p. Volume 3 contains apologetic treatises, including "On Idolatry" and "Apology"; antiheretical treatises, including "Against Marcion"; and ethical treatises, including "On Baptism," "Repentance," and "Patience." Volume 4 contains various treatises, including "Exhortation to Chastity."

Adversus Marcionem (Against Marcion). Trans. and ed. by Ernst Evans, Oxford 2 vols. 1972 o.p. A Latin text accompanies the translation.

Apology and Spectacles. Trans. by Gerald H. Renall [*Loeb Class. Lib.*] Harvard Univ. Pr. repr. of 1931 ed. 1977 o.p. A Latin text accompanies the translation of these two treatises.

Apologetical Works. Trans. by Rudolph Arbesmann, Emily Daly, and Edwin Quain [*Fathers of the Church Ser.*] Catholic Univ. Pr. 1950 $29.95. The volume contains "Apology," "Testimony of the Soul," "To Scapula," and "On the Soul."

Disciplinary, Moral, and Ascetical Works. Trans. by Rudolph Arbesmann, Emily Daly, and Edwin Quain [*Fathers of the Church Ser.*] Catholic Univ. Pr. 1959 $27.95. The volume contains "To Martyrs," "Spectacles," "Apparel of Women," "Prayer," "Patience," "Chaplet," "Flight in Time of Persecution."

Treatises on Penance. Trans. by William Le Saint, Newman 1959 o.p. The volume contains "On Patience" and "On Purity," the latter document being written during Tertullian's Montanist period.

Treatise against Hermogenes. Trans. by J. H. Waszink, Newman 1956 o.p. The introduction briefly explains Hermogenes' views on creation and matter, which Tertullian rejected.

Treatises on Marriage and Remarriage. Trans. by William Le Saint, Newman 1951 o.p. The volume contains "To His Wife," "Exhortation to Chastity," and "Monogamy." In these documents Tertullian speaks against remarriage and shows signs of sympathies with Montanist beliefs in purity.

BOOKS ABOUT TERTULLIAN

Barnes, Timothy D. *Tertullian: A Historical and Literary Study.* Oxford 1985 $45.00. A scholarly and detailed study of the life of Tertullian and the sources that provide much of the information about him. The work sets Tertullian in his pagan and Christian historical context. There are numerous appendixes on specific issues relating to Jerome, Tertullian, African Christianity, and Roman history.

Bray, Gerald L. *Holiness and the Will of God: Perspectives on the Theology of Tertullian.* John Knox 1980 $3.25. The author states that this book, directed at the informed general reader, attempts "to reflect seriously on Tertullian's theology," in particular how he conceived of sanctification and holiness and related issues including asceticism, the understanding of Scripture, and anthropology.

MEDIEVAL CHRISTIANITY

Special Histories

The study of Christianity in this period, roughly 600 to 1500, is practically inseparable from the study of the history and culture of Western civilization in general. Although church and state could often function as one, there was a recurring conflict between the two, especially over the question of what power lay rulers had in church affairs. The period saw the development of Christianity in several areas, especially ecclesiastical, spiritual, liturgical, theological, doctrinal, monastic, and architectural. This time also witnessed the growing division between the Eastern and Western churches and the Crusades, which initially were aimed at recapturing Jerusalem from the Muslims.

Despite the almost universal allegiance to the authority of the church, based on its interpretation of Scripture and ecclesiastical traditions, individuals and groups continually challenged the established doctrines and structures. Various attempts were made to reform the church. Some of these reformers, such as the Cathari in Western Europe and John Hus in Czechoslovakia, were thought to go beyond the bounds of reform and were deemed heretical. These attempts to reform the Church, attempts both within the established structure and outside of it, paved the way for the Protestant Reformation, which would permanently change the face of Christianity.

Bainton, Roland H. *The Medieval Church.* [*Anvil Ser.*] Krieger repr. of 1962 ed. 1979 pap. $7.50. The first half of this book provides a very brief introduction to the history and thought of the church in the medieval period. The second half includes primary documents that correspond to and illuminate the chapters in the first half.

Baldwin, Marshall W. *The Mediaeval Church*. Cornell Univ. Pr. 1953 pap. $4.95; fwd. by Edward W. Fox, Greenwood repr. of 1953 ed. 1982 lib. bdg. $22.50. A brief treatment of the church during the period from 800 to 1300, focusing on the mission of the church, understood to be the worship of God and the sanctification of souls.

Barraclough, Geoffrey. *The Crucible of Europe: The Ninth and Tenth Centuries in European History*. Univ. of California Pr. 1976 $36.50 pap. $8.95. A very readable study of the political history of the ninth and tenth centuries in Europe, with special attention to the Carolingian Empire.

Bolton, Brenda. *Medieval Reformation*. [*Foundations of Medieval History Ser.*] Holmes & Meier 1983 text ed. $22.50 pap. $14:75. A general introduction to the Renaissance of the twelfth century. Bolton provides an "account of the varied attempts which were made in the period to transform the life of the Church and the way the hierarchy responded to them."

Cannon, William R. *History of Christianity in the Middle Ages*. [*Twin Brooks Ser.*] Baker Bk. repr. of 1960 ed. 1983 pap. $9.95. Written in textbook style, this book provides a synthetic history depicting the development of Christianity, both its doctrinal and its institutional aspects, in both the East and the West, from 476 to 1453.

Deanesly, Margaret. *History of the Medieval Church, 590–1500*. Methuen 9th ed. 1969 pap. $12.50. A very well written short study of the church in this period with particular emphasis on the social and personal aspects of church history.

Hamilton, Bernard. *Religion in the Medieval West*. Arnold 1986 text ed. pap. $14.95. The book, directed to the interested general reader, focuses on the interaction between the church and lay society. The three sections explore the faith taught by the institutional church, the extent to which the laity understood and practiced this faith, and noninstitutional faiths that existed between the sixth and sixteenth centuries, including dissident Christian voices, popular religion including magic, and non-Christian religions.

Huizinga, Johan. *The Waning of the Middle Ages: A Study of the Forms of Life, Thought, and Art in France and the Netherlands in the XIVth and XVth Centuries*. St. Martin's repr. of 1924 ed. 1985 $25.00. A classic examination of the forms of life and thought in France and the Netherlands in the fourteenth and fifteenth centuries, a "crucial moment in history when the Middle Ages gave way to the great energy of Renaissance," according to the author.

Oakley, Francis. *The Western Church in the Later Middle Ages*. Cornell Univ. Pr. 1985 $32.50 text ed. pap. $9.95. An examination of the late medieval period that discusses various subjects, such as political history, the institutional church, liturgy, devotional practice, canon law, mysticism, and monasticism. Also included are biographies of several important figures of the period.

Russell, Jeffrey. *A History of Medieval Christianity*. Harlan Davidson 1968 pap. $8.95. A general history of ancient and medieval Christianity with particular attention on two forces for reform in the church, prophecy and order.

Southern, R. W. *The Making of the Middle Ages*. David & Charles 1987 pap. $13.95. An excellent treatment of "the influences that molded the history of Western Europe from the late tenth to the early thirteenth century."

Spitz, Lewis W. *Renaissance and Reformation*. Concordia 2 vols. 1980 pap. ea. $15.50. A very readable intellectual history of two crucial periods in history. The section on the Reformation pays particular attention to ecclesiastical developments of the era. The author often uses biographical sketches of the intellectual leaders of a region or movement, thereby "allowing the leading actors of the drama to speak for themselves." Extensive bibliographies with each chapter.

Wallace-Hadrill, John Michael. *The Frankish Church.* Oxford 1983 $59.95. The volume is a collection of essays on various subjects dealing with the Frankish Church, which, taken together, provide an excellent account of the church in the Merovingian and Carolingian periods. The work demonstrates "how the Frankish Church influenced and adapted to a cultural climate that itself was being shaped by a multitude of factors" (William T. Foley, *Church History*).

Eastern Churches and Crusades

The Orthodox Church began in the eastern part of the Roman Empire, spread to Russia and other parts of eastern Europe, and today consists of several churches independent in their administration, but sharing a common faith. Differences between the Western and Eastern churches can be traced back to an early period. During the Middle Ages the two churches grew increasingly estranged from one another until their disagreements finally erupted into an open and lasting schism. Two dates have been suggested as the beginning of the schism: 1054, when the Roman church excommunicated Michael Caerularius, Patriarch of Constantinople, and the patriarch excommunicated legates of the Roman church; and 1204, when crusading forces from the West sacked Constantinople. The causes of the schism, however, developed over centuries and therefore cannot be dated exactly. One particular difference between the two traditions is the veneration of icons in the Orthodox church. Icons, flat pictures with representations of Jesus, Mary, or the saints, are used in public and private worship, and are believed to exercise beneficient powers. During the eighth and ninth centuries, a factious, sometimes violent, debate was waged over whether the worship of icons should be permitted. The struggle, referred to as the iconoclastic controversy, failed, however, to dislodge their use in the East or in the West, for that matter.

Part of the history of the Eastern church and its relations with the West is the phenomenon of the Crusades. The first Crusade was preached by Pope Urban II in 1095 with the original objective of recovering the Holy Land from Islam. This was accomplished in 1099 but the Holy Land was lost back to the Moslems very soon. The causes of the Crusades were complex, including ideological, social, and economic factors. Later Crusades were also directed against non-Christians outside the Holy Land and against Christian heretics, such as the Albigensian Crusade of the thirteenth century aimed at a group of Cathari in southern France.

Atiya, Aziz S. *The Crusade: Historiography and Bibliography.* Greenwood 1976 lib. bdg. $22.50. A companion to the book *Crusade, Commerce and Culture* (Indiana Univ. Pr. 1962) by the same author. This volume provides extensive bibliographical information on the literature of the Crusades from both Christian and Muslim worlds.

Cowdrey, H. E. *Popes, Monks and Crusaders.* Hambledon 1983 $40.00. A collection of scholarly articles written over a period of 13 years, about half of which are on issues and events concerning the Crusades.

Dvornik, Francis. *Byzantium and the Roman Primacy.* Fordham Univ. Pr. rev. ed. 1979 pap. $7.50. A general study of the political history to the background of the division between Eastern and Western Christianity. The author argues that the Byzantine Church acknowledged the primacy of the pope while at the same time being interested in preserving its own autonomy. This attitude, however, began to change in the eleventh century and culminated in the complete schism coming as a result of the sack of Constantinople in 1204.

——. *Early Christian and Byzantine Political Philosophy: Origins and Background.* Dumbarton Oaks 2 vols. 1966 $50.00. A scholarly and thorough study of political philosophy over two millennia in the Ancient Near East, Ancient Greece, the Hellenistic world, the world of Judaism, the Roman Empire, and early Christian and Byzantine societies. Extensive bibliographies accompany each chapter. The work is important for an understanding of the relation between church and state in antiquity.

Erdman, Carl. *The Origin of the Idea of Crusade.* Trans. by Marshall W. Baldwin and Walter Goffart, Princeton Univ. Pr. 1977 $52.50. This volume, originally published in German in 1935, is an important and erudite investigation of the history of, as the author states, "what was in the minds of the men who planned and carried out the first crusade." Erdman argues that the Crusade was a culmination of a centuries-long development based on holy war and Christian knighthood. The true aim was the liberation of the entire Eastern Church by a holy war.

Geanakoplos, Deno J. *Byzantine Church, Society, and Civilization Seen through Contemporary Eyes.* Univ. of Chicago Pr. 1986 $32.50 pap. $18.95. A very useful sourcebook of texts arranged topically concerning Byzantine ecclesiastical, social, and political history. Also included are several helpful chronological lists and maps.

——. *Emperor Michael Palaeologus and the West, 1258–1282: A Study in Byzantine-Latin Relations.* Shoe String repr. of 1959 ed. 1973 $29.50. This scholarly volume, in the words of the author, "examines the relations between Eastern and Western Christendom during the reign of the thirteenth century Byzantine Emperor Michael VIII Palaeologus."

——. *The Interaction of the "Sibling" Byzantine and Western Cultures in the Middle Ages and Italian Renaissance (330–1600).* Yale Univ. Pr. 1976 $47.00. "This collection of essays is tied together by the common theme of Byzantine-Latin cultural relations" (Alice-Mary Talbot, *Journal of the Amer. Academy of Religion*). Most of the chapters are scholarly in the approach they take to their subject, but the prologue, which utilizes sociological analysis in the survey of Greek-Latin cultural relations, is especially helpful for the general reader.

Hopko, Thomas, ed. *Women and the Priesthood: Essays from the Orthodox Tradition.* St. Vladimir's 1983 pap. $7.95. The essays contained here provide a scriptural, historical, and theological context regarding women and the priesthood. The authors present various reasons against allowing women to become Orthodox priests.

Hussey, J. M. *The Orthodox Church in the Byzantine Empire.* [*History of the Christian Church Ser.*] Oxford 1986 $59.00. Although written for the nonspecialist, this book provides an informed discussion of the history of the Byzantine Church, both its internal events and its relations with the West, from the seventh century to 1453. A second section is devoted to ecclesiastical concerns of the Orthodox Church in Byzantium.

Lossky, Vladimir. *Orthodox Theology: An Introduction.* St. Vladimir's 1978 pap. $5.95. This volume includes an English translation of a series of related articles concerning various doctrinal issues important to the Orthodox Church, including the Trinity, creation, and Christology. Included are numerous quotations from Eastern authors, chiefly the Cappadocian Fathers, illustrating these beliefs.

Magoulias, Harry J. *Byzantine Christianity: Emperor, Church and the West*. Wayne State Univ. Pr. 1982 pap. $7.95. This slender volume contains a general survey of Christianity in the Byzantine Empire focusing on four topics: the relation between Christianity and the emperor, various fringe and heretical groups in the East, types of mysticism, and relations with the West.

Meyendorff, John. *Byzantine Theology: Historical Trends and Doctrinal Themes*. Fordham Univ. Pr. 2nd rev. ed. 1987 pap. $10.00. A very useful introduction to Byzantine religious thought. The first half of the book discusses Byzantine theology within its historical context from the fifth through the fifteenth centuries. The second half provides a systematic discussion of various doctrines important to the theology including creation, man, Jesus Christ, the Holy Spirit, God, and the Eucharist.

———. *Byzantium and the Rise of Russia*. Cambridge Univ. Pr. 1981 $82.50. A detailed and scholarly examination of the complex ecclesiastical and cultural relations between Byzantium and Russia in the twelfth through fourteenth centuries and the diplomatic activity of the fourteenth-century ecclesiastical leaders. The author also touches on the influence of Byzantine spirituality, liturgical order, and art on the Russian Church.

Nicol, D. M. *Church and Society in the Last Centuries of Byzantium*. [*Birkbeck Lectures*] Cambridge Univ. Pr. 1979 $32.50. These lectures provide the historical framework for the last two centuries of the Palaeologian period through an analysis of three situations that particularly marked the internal life of the empire: the Arsemite schism, Palamite controversies, and the question of union with Rome. The author attempts to show that despite the fall of the empire, the spirit of Byzantium was preserved by the Orthodox Church.

Ouspensky, Leonid, and Vladimir Lossky. *The Meaning of Icons*. Trans. by G. E. Palmar and E. Kadlovbousky, St. Vladimir's rev. ed. 1982 $35.00 pap. $25.00. A valuable theological and art historical study of the iconography in the Orthodox Church, with most attention devoted to Russian icons. The volume provides a "rich source for understanding the Orthodox Christian icon" (John Rexine, *Greek Orthodox Theological Rev.*).

Queller, Donald E. *The Fourth Crusade*. [*Middle Ages Ser.*] Univ. of Pennsylvania Pr. 1977 pap. $10.95. A valuable, detailed account of how the Fourth Crusaders came to conquer Constantinople. The author "traces the progress of the Crusade from its inception until the establishment of the Latin Empire of Constantinople" (Joseph O'Callaghan, *Theological Studies*). Also included is an extensive bibliography of primary and secondary sources related to the Fourth Crusade.

Riley-Smith, Jonathan S. C. *The First Crusade and the Idea of Crusading*. Univ. of Pennsylvania Pr. 1986 $32.95. The book focuses on religion, particularly monasticism, as the inspiration for crusading. Riley-Smith states that "Pope Urban II's appeal to lay knights in 1095–6 was the culmination of the movement of the Church towards lay people which had begun earlier in the eleventh century" to infuse secular life with monastic values. The author shows how the idea of crusading was transformed by the dreadful experiences of the army on the march and the euphoria that followed the capture of Jerusalem into a new association of ideas that found its way into the narrative accounts of eyewitnesses.

Runciman, Steven. *The Byzantine Theocracy*. Cambridge Univ. Pr. 1977 $32.50. This volume contains a series of lectures delivered in 1973 on the subject of church and state in Byzantium. The short, balanced treatment gives, states the author, "an account of the Byzantine Empire whose constitution was based on a clear religious conviction: that it was the earthly copy of the Kingdom of Heaven."

———. *The Eastern Schism*. AMS Pr. repr. of 1956 ed. 1983 $24.50. Discusses the historical background of the schism between the Western and Eastern churches, focusing on the impact the Crusades had on this division. Runciman argues that the Eastern schism was not fundamentally caused by differing opinions on the procession of the Holy Spirit or the bread of the sacrament. The final schism did not occur in 1054, but later, according to the author, "when papal ecclesiastical and theological demands were backed by the aggressive public opinion of the west insisting on subjugation of the East and when public opinion of the Orthodox East, remembering the Crusades and the Latin East, saw in papal supremacy a savage form of alien domination."

Schulz, Hans Joachim. *The Byzantine Liturgy*. Intro. by Robert Taft, Pueblo Pub. 1986 pap. $17.50. A discussion of specific authors and documents important for understanding Byzantine liturgy between the fourth and fifteenth centuries.

Ware, Timothy. *Orthodox Church*. Penguin 1963 pap. $5.95. A simple, balanced introduction to the Orthodox Church divided into two sections, the first providing a general history from the fourth century to the present. The second section, on faith and worship, discusses various topics, including God and humans, the sacraments, ecclesiology, and liturgy. The author has consciously designed the book to help promote better ecumenical relations between East and West.

Emperors, Popes, and Councils

The Middle Ages witnessed several important events that influenced the internal workings of the church and the relation between the church and secular authorities. In the investiture controversy the church and secular leaders battled over whether the secular leaders had the authority to appoint persons to religious posts. Lay investiture was prohibited in 1075 by Pope Gregory VII, although such practices continued to varying degrees in certain parts of western Europe. A severe test to the institution of the papacy came during the fourteenth century when for a time two, and later three, men claimed the title of pope. This Great Schism, as it is sometimes called, lasted until 1417, when the Council of Constance elected Martin V as sole pope. The schism of the papacy provided fuel to the conciliar theorists who believed the supreme authority in the church lies not with the pope, but with a general council. Although later papal decrees significantly curtailed the power of the councils, the conciliar movement can be viewed as an important influence leading to the Reformation.

Barraclough, Geoffrey. *The Medieval Papacy*. [*Lib. of World Civilization*] Norton 1979 text ed. pap. $7.95. A well-written introduction for the general reader in which the author describes the "various factors which historically helped to shape the development of the medieval papacy." The volume is rich with photographs of medieval art.

Brooke, Zachary N. *The English Church and the Papacy, from the Conquest to the Reign of John*. AMS Pr. repr. of 1931 ed. 1982 $42.00. This published version of lectures delivered between 1929 and 1931 examines the relation between the English church and the papacy in the eleventh and twelfth centuries, at a time when the English church was forced to accept the centralizing policy of the Roman church.

Cantor, Norman F. *Church, Kingship and Lay Investiture in England, 1089–1135.* Octagon 1969 $26.00. This scholarly volume investigates the history of church-state relations in England during the Gregorian reforms and investiture controversy. "It carefully weighs," writes Cantor, "the issues and analyzes the causes for the failure of the movement, which was decisive for the future history of the English Church." Special attention is given to the episcopal career of Archbishop Anselm.

Crowder, Christopher. *Unity, Heresy, and Reform, 1378–1460.* Limestone Pr. 1987 pap. $15.50. Crowder has collected 35 documents concerning the attempt to end the schism in the Roman Church. They are organized around the five councils responsible for dealing with the problem. Each document is prefixed with a short introduction placing the excerpt in its historical context.

Gill, Joseph. *The Council of Florence.* AMS Pr. repr. of 1959 ed. 1981 $37.50. A detailed study of the fifteenth-century council, which "dealt a death-blow to Conciliarism" and attempted to unite the separated churches of East and West.

Izbicki, Thomas M. *Protector of the Faith: Cardinal Johannes de Turrecremata and the Defense of the Institutional Church.* Catholic Univ. Pr. 1981 o.p. A scholarly volume focusing on the ecclesiology of Turrecremata, the Dominican cardinal who was a dominant papal apologist of the fifteenth century. Izbicki attempts to show that Turrecremata was not the papal extremist earlier scholars understood him to be.

Richards, Jeffrey. *The Popes and the Papacy in the Early Middle Ages, 476–752.* Methuen 1979 o.p. This book focuses on the political, administrative, and social aspects of early papal history, from the fall of the Roman Empire to the rise of the Frankish Empire. Richards points out: "This period saw a successful resistance to a succession of Eastern heresies; an increasing involvement in the social services; and, increasing involvement in politics, diplomacy, and war."

Swanson, R. N. *University, Academics, and the Great Schism.* Cambridge Univ. Pr. 1979 o.p. This book, a revision of Swanson's dissertation, examines the participation of universities in the post-1378 schism and the theories that were developed in academic circles to help heal the schism and restore a united papacy.

Thomson, J. A. *Popes and Princes 1417–1517: Politics and Polity in Late Medieval Church.* [*Early Modern Europe Today Ser.*] Allen & Unwin 1980 text ed. $14.95. Papal history between the Council of Constance and the Lutheran Reformation is treated in this volume. Thomson argues that "the various princes of Europe holding threat of another general council over the Popes, asserted their authority in their own national churches and reduced the relatively passive, politically reactive papacy to a mere principality itself."

Tierney, Brian. *The Crisis of Church and State, 1050–1300.* Prentice-Hall 1964 pap. $6.50. This volume contains selected extracts from various documents revealing ideas behind the conflict between the church and the secular authority. Tierney has prefaced a very helpful introduction providing the historical background of the documents.

Tillman, Helene. *Pope Innocent III.* Trans. by W. Sax, Elsevier 1980 $64.00. A scholarly biography of the thirteenth-century pope.

Ullmann, Walter. *A Short History of the Papacy in the Middle Ages.* Methuen 1974 pap. $16.95. Beginning in the waning days of the Roman Empire, this work shows how the papacy developed in the Middle Ages. Designed for the general informed reader, it is not a summary of individual biographies of the popes, but traces the development of the institution.

Christian Thought and Doctrine

Much of Christian thought during the Middle Ages was devoted to an inquiry into the relation between reason and revelation. Is it necessary, or even possible, for reason to prove the Christian truths that are known through faith or revelation? Two major events played a significant role in these debates. First was the rise of Scholasticism, the application of logical and dialectical principles to philosophical and theological problems. The culmination of this intellectual development was the theological syntheses ("summae"), the most famous being the *Summa Theologica* of Thomas Aquinas written during the second half of the thirteenth century. The second important influence on Christian thought was the translation of Aristotle's works into Latin and their dissemination in western Europe beginning in the twelfth century. These writings had a great impact on the thinkers of this period, most notably Aquinas. Not all the developments in Christian thought during the Middle Ages were based on rational thought. Several individuals and groups emphasized mystical elements within Christianity. Some of their views, such as those of Joachim of Fiore, were condemned by the ecclesiastical authorities.

Baldwin, John W. *The Scholastic Culture of the Middle Ages: 1000–1300.* [*Civilization and Society Ser.*] Heath 1971 pap. $8.95. This slender volume provides a very good textbook description of early Scholasticism. The work begins with an overview of medieval society in the eleventh through thirteenth centuries. "Against this background Baldwin traces the development of education and scholasticism, concentrating on the changing institutional structure of Medieval education" (William Courtenay, *Church History*).

Bynum, Caroline W. *Jesus as Mother: Studies in the Spirituality of the High Middle Ages.* Univ. of California Pr. 1982 text ed. pap. $9.95. The five studies in this book are concerned with the complex relations between the individual and the community, and women and clerical authority. In the author's own words, the work "examines key images and words which religious people of the twelfth and thirteenth centuries used to present their theories about the soul's journey to God and then situates these images and the words in the experience of the individuals or groups that produced them."

Cassirer, Ernst, and others, eds. *The Renaissance Philosophy of Man.* Univ. of Chicago Pr. 1956 pap. $10.95. According to the author, "the purpose of this volume is to acquaint the informed student with certain major thinkers of the early Italian Renaissance through translations of some of their more important works." The writers examined are Francesco Petrarca, Lorenzo Valla, Marsilio Ficino, Giovanni della Mirandola, Pietro Pomponazzi, and Juan Luis Vives. Also included is a general introduction to the thought of the period.

Chenu, M. D. *Nature, Man, and Society in the Twelfth Century: Essays on New Theological Perspectives in the Latin West.* Trans. by Lester Little, Univ. of Chicago Pr. 1979 pap. $7.95. Nine essays that together represent a "classic study in the medieval interrelationships of theology and history" (Ray Petry, *Church History*). Much attention is given to the varieties and types of Platonism found in the twelfth century.

Cohen, Jeremy. *The Friars and the Jews: The Evolution of Medieval Anti-Judaism.* Cornell Univ. Pr. 1984 pap. $10.95. This work "focuses on the friars' attack upon the Jews, the basic ideas and theological considerations that underlay their anti-Jewish activities and polemics" during the period between the fourth Lateran Council (1215) and the Black Death (1347–50). During these decades the friars "reshaped" the Western Church's "theology of the Jew," resulting in, among other things, expulsion of the Jews from much of western Europe.

Evans, G. Rosemary. *The Language and Logic of the Bible: The Earlier Middle Ages.* Cambridge Univ. Pr. 1985 $32.50. This book examines how the study of the Bible was transformed in the Middle Ages by the penetration of grammatical and dialectical studies.

———. *Old Arts and New Theology: The Beginnings of Theology as an Academic Discipline.* Oxford 1980 text ed. $34.95. An examination of the interaction between theology and the liberal arts and the development of theology into an academic discipline during the twelfth century, when the methods of investigation used in teaching the liberal arts began to be applied to theology.

Gilmore, Myron P. *The World of Humanism, 1453–1517.* [*Rise of Modern Europe Ser.*] Greenwood repr. of 1952 ed. 1983 lib. bdg. $45.00. This volume gives the general reader a survey of the social, economic, religious, scientific, and artistic developments, and the relation among them, at the end of the medieval period and the beginning of the Renaissance, a period that saw, among other things, the flowering of humanism.

Gilson, Étienne. *History of Christian Philosophy in the Middle Ages.* Random 1955 o.p. This textbook-like volume "provides the general reader with an introduction to the history of Christian philosophy from Justin Martyr in the second century up to Nicholas of Cusa in the fifteenth century whose work stands on the border line of a new historical period," according to the author. The text is organized chronologically around the important figures of early Christian philosophy and is accompanied by extensive notes.

———. *The Spirit of Medieval Philosophy.* Scribner 1936 o.p. This volume contains 20 lectures given from 1931 to 1932 that present a recognizable phenomenon of Christian philosophy. Gilson states that the "spirit of Medieval philosophy is the spirit of Christianity penetrating the Greek tradition, working within it, drawing out of it a certain view of the world specifically Christian."

Kantorowicz, Ernest H. *The King's Two Bodies: A Study of Medieval Political Theology.* Princeton Univ. Pr. 1981 $58.00 pap. $13.95. A scholarly study examining a religious strand within the political theory of later medieval England. The author shows how jurists in England worked out a political theory of "two bodies of the king" from the Christological doctrine of the two natures of Christ.

Kieckhefer, Richard. *Unquiet Souls: Fourteenth Century Saints and Their Religious Milieu.* Univ. of Chicago Pr. 1984 $24.95. This valuable contribution to the study of medieval saints analyzes the theological assumptions of the hagiography of fourteenth-century saints. The dominant motifs are found to be "patience, extraordinary identification with the Passion, extreme self-perception of oneself as a sinner," and inner spirituality as seen in experiences of rapture and revelation.

Knowles, David. *The Evolution of Medieval Thought.* Random 1964 pap. $4.76. Provides the general informed reader with a very good account of what the author calls "the rise and decline of a great and ambitious intellectual structure which the thirteenth century brought to a precariously stable apogee and which the fourteenth century saw disintegrate."

Kretzmann, Norman. *The Cambridge History of Later Medieval Philosophy: From the Rediscovery of Aristotle to the Disintegration of Scholasticism 1100–1600.* Cambridge Univ. Pr. 1982 $85.00. This scholarly and voluminous work contains the collaborative efforts of 41 scholars whose work provides up-to-date research on numerous areas of the history of medieval philosophy, including literature, logic, metaphysics and epistemology, natural philosophy, ethics, and political theory. The contributors aimed to show the continuity of intellectual concerns of medieval and contemporary philosophy.

Kristeller, Paul O. *Renaissance Thought: The Classic, Scholastic and Humanistic Strains.* Peter Smith $15.50. In these lectures, delivered in 1954, Kristeller attempts to demonstrate "the impact and influence of classical studies and of ancient sources upon the philosophical and general thought of the Renaissance period." Two additional essays in this edition provide further information on the medieval antecedents of Renaissance humanism and how Renaissance thinkers "transformed their admired classical course and incorporated them into their own novel modes of thought."

Lasker, Daniel J. *Jewish Philosophical Polemics against Christianity in the Middle Ages.* ADL $15.00. The published version of Lasker's dissertation, this book examines the rise of philosophical Jewish anti-Christian materials in the twelfth century, documents that were later a common feature of medieval Jewish literature. Lasker has focused on the philosophical refutation of four Christian doctrines, the Trinity, Incarnation, transubstantiation, and Virgin Birth.

Leff, Gordon. *Medieval Thought from Saint Augustine to Ockham.* Humanities Pr. repr. of 1958 ed. 1978 $15.50. A general introduction to the philosophical thinking of the Middle Ages.

Le Goff, Jacques. *The Birth of Purgatory.* Trans. by Arthur Goldhammer, Univ. of Chicago Pr. 1984 $25.00. This scholarly book, according to the author, "traces the formation of the idea of purgatory from its Judeo-Christian antiquity to its emergence in the second half of the twelfth century, when the idea of purgatory finally took hold in the West, and beyond into the next century . . . examines the psychological, social, economic, and intellectual setting that contributed significantly to the shaping of the doctrine of purgatory."

Oberman, Heiko A. *Forerunners of the Reformation: The Shape of Late Medieval Thought.* Trans. by Paul L. Nyhus, Fortress Pr. 1981 o.p. Designed for the nonspecialist, in Oberman's words, the book "introduces the reader to aspects of such major themes as conciliarism, curialism, mysticism, scholasticism, 'devotio moderna,' and the impact of Renaissance humanism." A general introduction provides an overview of the period, stressing the continuity of the fourteenth and fifteenth centuries with the Reformation period.

————. *The Harvest of Medieval Theology: Gabriel Biel and Late Medieval Nominalism.* Labyrinth Pr. repr. of 1963 ed. 1983 pap. $17.50. A complex and detailed work that examines nominalist thought, especially that of Gabriel Biel, a fifteenth-century Scholastic philosopher. The author argues against the position that "in Biel and other nominalists, the 13th century synthesis of faith and reason had decayed" (E. L. Mascall, *Church Quarterly Review*).

Ozment, Steven E. *The Age of Reform 1250–1550: An Intellectual and Religious History of Late Medieval and Reformation Europe.* Yale Univ. Pr. 1980 $45.00 pap. $13.95. A very good general account of the intellectual and religious history of the period. Ozment traces the roots of the Reformation in late medieval times.

Petry, Ray C. *Late Medieval Mysticism.* [*Lib. of Christian Class.*] Westminster 1980 pap. $12.95. Selections from the writings of persons important to the mystical thought of medieval Christianity, including three men associated with the abbey of St. Victor, Francis of Assisi, Bonaventure, Ramon Lull, Meister Eckhart, Richard Rolle, Henry Suso, Catherine of Siena, Jan van Ruysbroeck, the "German Theology," Nicholas of Cusa, and Catherine of Genoa. A brief introduction accompanies the texts of each author. A general introduction provides a historical background to mysticism up to the late Middle Ages.

Rogers, Elizabeth F. *Peter Lombard and the Sacramental System.* Richwood Pub. repr. of 1927 ed. 1976 lib. bdg. $19.50. Most of this book, which is the published version of the author's dissertation, is a translation of Peter Lombard's "Sentences," Book 4, Distinctiones 1–26. The author has prepared an introduction to the sacraments from the early church to the time of Peter Lombard.

Russell, Jeffrey B. *Lucifer: The Devil in the Middle Ages.* Cornell Univ. Pr. 1984 text ed. $26.95 1986 pap. $12.95. A study of the disparate views of the devil in the Middle Ages and the relation of the devil to evil as seen from theology, philosophy, literature, drama, homiletics, hagiography, folklore, and the visual arts.

Smalley, Beryl. *Study of the Bible in the Middle Ages.* Univ. of Notre Dame Pr. 1964 pap. $9.95. A general survey of biblical studies during the Middle Ages, with most attention paid to the studies in universities and monastic communities. Smalley describes the origins and development of medieval literal interpretation, especially in the twelfth and thirteenth centuries.

Szarmach, Paul E., ed. *An Introduction to the Medieval Mystics of Europe.* State Univ. of New York Pr. 1985 $44.50 pap. $14.95. Fourteen essays on various topics including Augustine, St. Bernard, Jewish mysticism, Aquinas as mystic, Juliana of Norwich, women mystics, Meister Eckhart, and Nicholas of Cusa. The corpus serves as an introduction to mysticism of the period for the informed reader.

Tavard, George H. *Holy Writ or Holy Church: The Crisis of the Protestant Reformation.* Greenwood repr. of 1959 ed. 1978 lib. bdg. $22.75. A brief study of patristic and early medieval treatments of the relation between the attitudes toward Scripture and tradition, and "a more detailed account of the positions taken by numerous writers from the fourteenth century through the Council of Trent . . . and through the Elizabethan period in England" (John Cobb, *Interpretation*). Between the extremes of emphasis on Scripture only, and the authority of the church, existed the traditional church position of reliance on church and Scripture.

Trinkaus, Charles. *The Scope of Renaissance Humanism.* Univ. of Michigan Pr. 1983 text ed. $28.50. As the author points out, this volume, containing essays written over a period of 40 years, centers on an "effort to evaluate the historical importance of Renaissance humanism both in the context of Italian and Northern Renaissance and in the larger perspective of its place in the history of Western Civilization."

Ward, Benedicta. *Miracles and the Medieval Mind: Theory, Record and Event 1000–1215.* State Mutual Bk. 1982 $69.00; [*Middle Ages Ser.*] Univ. of Pennsylvania Pr. 1982 pap. $13.95. This volume, a revision of the author's doctoral thesis, provides a helpful study of the view of miracles in the period between 1000 and 1215. Ward argues that the "role of the miraculous changed in the twelfth century under the joint pressures of theologians, philosophers and the evidence required in canonization proceedings."

Weinberg, Julius R. *A Short History of Medieval Philosophy.* Princeton Univ. Pr. 1964 pap. $9.95. A general introduction to the major figures and philosophical ideas of the period. It includes sections on Islamic and Jewish thought.

Christian Life and Culture

In western Europe, Christian life and culture was for most people synonymous with life and culture in general. The titles in this section discuss some of the more important and interesting aspects of this culture, including the making of pilgrimages; the veneration of relics; the rise of various heretical groups such as the Cathari, Waldensians, and Lollards; and the attempt by ecclesiastical authorities to control and eliminate such groups, often through the use of inquisitions, the practice of penance and indulgences, and the expansion of monastic and other religious orders, such as the Dominicans and Franciscans.

Atkinson, Clarissa W. *Mystic and Pilgrim: The "Book" and the World of Margery Kempe.* Cornell Univ. Pr. 1983 text ed. $29.50 pap. $9.95. This book begins with an epitome of the "Book" of Kempe and then traces the familial and social relations and those with the church and clergy of this fifteenth-century mystic. The author places Kempe in the tradition of women mystics in the later Middle Ages.

Baldwin, John W. *Masters, Princes, and Merchants: The Social Views and Reforms of Peter the Chanter and His Circle.* Princeton Univ. Pr. 2 vols. 1970 $63.00. In this solid study, rich in documentation, Baldwin provides an "analysis of the ideas of the circle of Peter the Chanter," a group of teachers in Paris whose central concern was individual righteousness.

Brooke, Rosalind, and Christopher Brooke. *Popular Religion in the Middle Ages.* Thames & Hudson 1985 pap. $10.95. This book provides a general appraisal of Christianity as understood and practiced by the laity. Since this group left few written documents, much of the evidence used in the analysis comes from such material evidence as relics, church buildings, and other religious objects.

Cohn, Norman. *Pursuit of the Millennium: Revolutionary Millenarians and Mystical Anarchists of the Middle Ages.* Oxford rev. ed. 1970 pap. $11.95. Traces the history of millennial sects of Europe, groups that believed, in Cohn's words, in a "miraculous event in which the world would be utterly transformed." The period covered is from the eleventh to the sixteenth centuries.

Davies, Horton, and Marie Helene Davies. *Holy Days and Holidays: The Medieval Pilgrimage to Compostela.* Bucknell Univ. Pr. 1982 $30.00. A scholarly but very readable description of the sacred and secular aspects of "the medieval pilgrimage to Compostela, the third most important pilgrimage site after Jerusalem and Rome" (Howard Happ, *Theology Today*).

Eckenstein, Lina. *Women under Monasticism: Chapters on Saint-Lore and Convent Life between A.D. 500 and A.D. 1500.* Russell repr. of 1896 ed. 1963 o.p. This book presents an inquiry into the cult of women saints and some accounts of the general position of women, primarily English and German, under monasticism in order to gain a better appreciation of the influence and activity of women connected with Christianity.

Ferrante, Joan M. *Woman as Image in Medieval Literature from the Twelfth Century to Dante.* Labyrinth Pr. repr. of 1975 ed. 1985 pap. $8.95. This study focuses on the symbolic treatment of women in the literature of the twelfth and thirteenth centuries, concluding with the writings of Dante. The author argues that a change took place from a positive presentation in the twelfth century to a much more negative portrayal in the thirteenth. Dante's writings, however, are unique in portraying women as complete human beings. This change reflects the alienation and fragmentation of the psyche occurring in society in general.

Fleming, John V. *An Introduction to the Franciscan Literature of the Middle Ages.* Franciscan Herald Pr. 1977 $10.95. A general discussion of the major literary works written by Franciscans during the thirteenth and fourteenth centuries.

Franzten, Allen J. *The Literature of Penance in Anglo-Saxon England.* Rutgers Univ. Pr. 1983 $27.50. Traces the development of penitential literature especially as found in Irish, English, and Frankish penitential handbooks.

Fry, Timothy, and Imogene Baker. *The Rule of St. Benedict in English.* Liturgical Pr. 1982 $2.25. The editors provide a very readable translation of this important monastic Rule along with a Latin text and notes. An extensive introduction to the text traces the origins of monasticism in the East and its establishment in the West. Several appendixes investigate particular topics pertaining to the text in more depth.

Geary, Patrick J. *Furta Sacra: Thefts of Relics in the Central Middle Ages.* Princeton Univ. Pr. 1978 $26.50. This is a study of accounts from the ninth to the twelfth centuries that told of and often condoned the theft of sacred relics.

Gies, Joseph, and Frances Gies. *Women in the Middle Ages.* Harper 1980 pap. $4.95. The first part of this book provides a general discussion of women in the Middle Ages. The second part examines particular women and types of women, including women in monastic and royal life and urban working women.

Hamilton, Bernard. *The Medieval Inquisition: Foundations of Medieval History.* Holmes & Meier 1981 text ed. $24.50 pap. $14.95. A general introduction to the actions undertaken by the inquisitions of the Middle Ages, which began in the thirteenth century.

Hardison, O. B., Jr. *Christian Rite and Christian Drama in the Middle Ages: Essays in the Origin and Early History of Modern Drama.* Greenwood repr. of 1965 ed. 1983 lib. bdg. $55.00. A detailed analysis examining the close connection between religious ritual and drama, the emergence of liturgical drama, and the origins of medieval drama.

Haskins, Charles H. *The Renaissance of the Twelfth Century.* Harvard Univ. Pr. 1971 pap. $7.95. A very readable general examination of the twelfth-century revival of the "Latin classics and their influence, the new jurisprudence and the more varied historiography, the new knowledge of the Greeks and Arabs and its effects upon Western science and philosophy, and the new institutions of learning," as stated by the author.

Hunt, Noreen, ed. *Cluniac Monasticism in the Central Middle Ages.* Shoe String 1971 o.p. A collection of ten valuable essays surveying the principal area of Cluniac scholarship, including Cluniac spirituality, the expansion and influence of Cluniac monasticism, and the role of the Cluniacs in the Crusades.

Knowles, David. *The Religious Orders in England.* Cambridge Univ. Pr. 3 vols. 1948–79 pap. ea. $19.95–$24.95. A thorough investigation of the organizational history of the religious orders from the thirteenth century until their dissolution in the sixteenth century.

Laistner, Max. *Thought and Letters in Western Europe, A.D. 500–900.* Cornell Univ. Pr. 2d ed. 1966 pap. $12.95. A general survey of the literature and the study of literature in western Europe from the fifth through the ninth centuries.

Lambert, Malcolm. *Medieval Heresy: Popular Movements from Bogomil to Hus.* Holmes & Meier 1977 $54.50. A general introduction to the popular heretical movements between the eighth and fifteenth centuries, movements with a substantial following among laypeople that deviated from papal teachings. Special attention is given to the Cathari, Waldensians, Lollards, and Hussites.

Lawrence, C. H. *Medieval Monasticism: Forms of Religious Life, Western Europe in the Middle Ages.* Longman 1984 text ed. pap. $12.95. A short but detailed and very readable survey of monasticism. The author traces the "growth of the monastic tradition as a whole in its social context from its origins in late antiquity down to the later Middle Ages."

Lea, Henry C. *History of Auricular Confession and Indulgences in the Latin Church.* Greenwood 3 vols. repr. of 1896 ed. 1968 lib. bdg. $67.25. A scholarly and detailed study of the origin and development of the practice of confession and indulgences.

Leclerq, Jean. *The Love of Learning and the Desire for God: A Study of Monastic*

Culture. Trans. by C. Mishrashi, Fordham Univ. Pr. 3d ed. 1985 pap. $10.00. These lectures explore the relation between learning and study and spirituality in monastic communities of the Middle Ages.

Leroy-Ladurie, Emmanuel. *Montaillou: The Promised Land of Error.* Trans. by Barbara Bray, Random 1979 pap. $6.95. A detailed study of Montaillou, a small French village that actively supported the Cathar heresy.

Leyser, Henrietta. *Hermits and the New Monasticism: A Study of Religious Communities in Western Europe, 1000–1150.* St. Martin's 1984 $25.00. This study surveys the phenomenon of hermitism or solitary monastic life and focuses on its eventual fusion with monasticism through the emergence of new communal forms of the hermitic life-style.

Little, Lester K. *Religious Poverty and the Profit Economy in Medieval Europe.* Cornell Univ. Pr. 1983 pap. $10.95. This informative survey traces the relationship between the church and the newly emergent profit economy of medieval Europe, especially in Italy and France, between 1000 and 1300.

McGinn, Bernard. *The Calabrian Abbot: Joachim of Fiore in the History of Thought.* Macmillan 1985 $24.95. This series of essays examines the background, thought, and later influence on medieval writers of the thought of Joachim of Fiore, an important apocalyptic figure of the Middle Ages. The work focuses on Joachim's understanding of Scripture and the doctrine of the Trinity.

——. *Visions of the End: Apocalyptic Traditions in the Middle Ages.* [*Records of Civilization Sources and Studies*] Columbia Univ. Pr. 1979 $38.00. A very helpful anthology of texts accompanied by substantial introductions placing each selection in its historical context. The texts provide a useful introduction to medieval apocalypticism.

McNeill, John T., and Helena M. Gamer. *Medieval Handbooks of Penance.* Hippocrene Bks. 1965 lib. bdg. $40.00. Most of this volume contains selections from numerous Irish, Welsh, Anglo-Saxon, and Frankish penitential documents and legal documents relating to penance. A solid introduction sets the documents in their historical and social contexts and provides a brief history of penance in the ancient Church and the use of penitentials.

Moore, R. I., ed. *The Birth of Popular Heresy.* [*Documents of Medieval History Ser.*] St. Martin's 1976 $25.00. A selection of texts, many previously untranslated, of the main sources relating to heresy in the eleventh and twelfth centuries, including popular dissent in the eleventh century, the emergence of anticlericalism in the twelfth century, the infiltration of Eastern dualism in the West, and the establishment and early organization of the Cathari.

Nichols, John A., and M. Thomas Shank, eds. *Medieval Religious Women I: Distant Echoes.* Cistercian Pubns. 1984 pap. $11.95. The first of three projected volumes on medieval religious women presents in a historical vein the variety of life-styles open to religious women from the fourth to the fifteenth centuries. The 14 essays address a wide variety of special subjects from "the lives of consecrated women in the fourth century" (JoAnn McNamara, medieval scholar) to St. Bernard of Clairvaux.

Payer, Pierre J. *Sex and the Penitentials: The Development of a Sexual Code 550–1150.* Univ. of Toronto Pr. 1984 $27.50. An examination of the church's attitude toward sexuality as found in medieval penitential literature. The author focuses on the sexual contents of the Welsh, Irish, Anglo-Saxon, and Frankish penitential texts, the transmission and reception of these texts, and how they were incorporated into later collections of ecclesiastical law up to the twelfth century.

Pennington, Basil. *The Last of the Fathers.* St. Bede's 1983 pap. $14.95. A discussion of the writings and thought of the major figures in this monastic community.

Primary attention is paid to Bernard of Clairvaux, William of St. Thierry, Guerrie of Igny, and St. Aelred of Rievaulx.

Peters, Edward, ed. *Monks, Bishops, and Pagans: Christian Culture in Gaul and Italy.* [*Middle Ages Ser.*] Univ. of Pennsylvania Pr. 1975 text ed. pap. $10.95. The volume contains pertinent sources in translation, including *The World of Gregory of Tours*, translated by W. C. McDermott.

Power, Eileen, and M. Poston. *Medieval Women.* Cambridge Univ. Pr. 1976 pap. $8.95. This collection of essays provides various portraits of medieval women, including mistresses of great households, heiresses, owners of businesses, scholars, and nuns.

Russell, Jeffrey B. *Dissent and Reform in the Early Middle Ages.* AMS Pr. repr. of 1965 ed. 1982 $36.00. A thorough examination of the dissenting and heretical groups that appeared in western Europe up to the thirteenth century. Russell argues that these groups were exaggerations of or reactions against reform movements of the Western Church.

———. *A History of Witchcraft: Sorcerers, Heretics and Pagans.* Peter Smith 1983 $16.75; Thames & Hudson 1982 pap. $10.95. "The author continues to argue that witchcraft during the witch-craze era (14th–17th centuries) derived from heretical groups and individuals rebelling against Christian authoritarianism. But, as Russell's subtitle indicates, he regards sorcerers practicing imitative magic (especially in primitive cultures) and pagans worshipping the Earth Goddess (especially modern wiccans) as an integral part of witchcraft. Russell's book strikes a nice balance between scholarship and readability" (*LJ*).

———. *Witchcraft in the Middle Ages.* Cornell Univ. Pr. 1984 $35.00 pap. $10.95. A scholarly "demonstration of how the political, social, economic, religious, and intellectual developments during the Middle Ages either fostered or militated against the growth of witchcraft" (Walter Bense, *Church History*). Russell focuses on the close relationship between witchcraft and heresy in this period.

Shannon, Albert C. *The Medieval Inquisition.* Augustinian College Pr. 1983 $15.00 pap. $10.00. This book, directed to those who appreciate the position of the church, traces the growth of the repression of heresy to its culmination in the Inquisition.

Tentler, T. *Sin and Confession on the Eve of the Reformation.* Princeton Univ. Pr. 1977 $44.00. The theology of penance implicit in the practical manuals for confessors is related to the practice of the sacrament. The author examines "the social functions of discipline and consolation served by the sacrament" (John Payne, *Church History*).

Thurston, Herbert. *The Holy Year of Jubilee: An Account of the History and Ceremonial of the Roman Jubilee.* AMS Pr. repr. of 1900 ed. 1980 $38.45. A comprehensive history of the practice and theory of the Jubilee Year, the practice of granting to those who make the pilgrimage to Rome during the proclaimed year a complete remission from punishment of their sins, from its beginning in 1300 to the end of the nineteenth century.

Tuchman, Barbara W. *A Distant Mirror: The Calamitous Fourteenth Century.* Ballantine 1980 pap. $8.95; Knopf 1978 $25.00. This work, written by a Pulitzer prize–winning author, is a very readable popular account of the fourteenth century, concentrating on French chivalry. The author has constructed her narrative around the figure of Euguerrand de Coucy VII, whom she describes as "the most skilled and experienced of all the knights of France." He serves as a paradigm for the fortune and fate of the nobility of the period. A splendid work of art and skillful writing.

Von Simpson, Otto G. *The Gothic Cathedral: Origins of Gothic Architecture and the*

Medieval Concept of Order. Princeton Univ. Pr. 1973 $29.95 pap. $9.95. The book examines what early Gothic architecture tells us about the religious thought of that period. Von Simpson deals at length with the Abbey of St. Denis and Chartres Cathedral.

Wakefield, Walter L. *Heresy, Crusade, and Inquisition in Southern France, 1100–1250.* Univ. of California Pr. 1974 $40.00. A solid account of the rise of the heretical groups—the Cathari and Waldensians—in southern France, the prosecution of the heresy, including the Albigensian Crusade fought in the thirteenth century, and the inquisition that stemmed from it.

Warren, Ann K. *Anchorites and Their Patrons in Medieval England.* Univ. of California Pr. 1985 $42.00. A full and detailed study of the anchorites, medieval English religious recluses, and the patrons who supported them from the twelfth through the sixteenth centuries.

Weinstein, Donald, and Rudolph Bell. *Saints and Society: The Two Worlds of Western Christendom, 1000 to 1700.* Univ. of Chicago Pr. 1986 $25.00 pap. $13.95. An investigation of the legends of the saints for what they tell us about medieval religious values, especially the life stages of childhood, adolescence, and adulthood, and notions of sanctity, for the period 1000 through 1700.

Wemple, Suzanne F. *Women in Frankish Society: Marriage and the Cloister, 500–900.* Univ. of Pennsylvania Pr. repr. of 1980 ed. 1985 text ed. pap. $18.95. The work focuses on the legal and economic position of women in Frankish religious and secular society during the early Middle Ages. Wemple shows how "Medieval women were far more visible, vocal, and powerful than their sisters in antiquity."

ALAN OF LILLE. d.1203

Alan of Lille was a poet, theologian, and preacher, who combined vast intellectual energy with a passion for poetry. He held an almost mystical view of learning and study, believing that rational powers, along with spiritual ones, should be employed in a search for God.

BOOK ABOUT ALAN OF LILLE

Evans, G. Rosemary. *Alan of Lille: The Frontiers of Theology in the Twelfth Century.* Cambridge Univ. Pr. 1983 $54.50. An examination of Alan's work in terms of his work as a theologian.

ANSELM OF CANTERBURY, SAINT. 1033?–1109

Anselm was Archbishop of Canterbury and one of the foremost thinkers among the earlier Scholastics. He broke with most earlier theologians by defending the faith with intellectual reasoning instead of employing arguments built on scripture and other written authorities. It is Anselm who first elaborated the ontological argument for the existence of God. (See also Chapter 3 in this volume.)

BOOK BY ST. ANSELM OF CANTERBURY

Why God Became Man? (Cur Deus Homo). Trans. by Jasper Hopkins and Herbert Richardson, E Mellen 1980 o.p. Anselm's famous argument for the necessity of the Incarnation.

BOOKS ABOUT ST. ANSELM OF CANTERBURY

Eadmer. *The Life of St. Anselm, Archbishop of Canterbury.* Ed. and trans. by R. W. Southern, Oxford 1972 $52.00

Evans, G. Rosemary. *Anselm and a New Generation.* Oxford 1980 $32.50. Evans examines the thinking on the questions Anselm faced as dealt with by his contemporaries and the generation that followed.

———. *Anselm and Talking about God.* Oxford 1978 $29.95. An examination of Anselm's thought about God and the process of thinking behind those thoughts. Evans not only investigates what Anselm said, but attempts to understand what Anselm himself thought he was saying.

Hopkins, Jasper. *A Companion to the Study of St. Anselm.* Univ. of Minnesota Pr. 1972 $13.95. A clear synthesis of Anselm's philosophical and theological thought. Hopkins first discusses Anselm's basic writings and the sources that influenced him, such as Aristotle, Boethius, and Augustine, and then examines various topics important in Anselm's thought.

———, ed. *Anselm of Canterbury.* Trans. by Herbert Richardson, E Mellen 4 vols. 1919 $149.95. These volumes contain the major works of Anselm. Vol. 1, "Monologion," "Proslogion," "Debate with Gaunilo," "A Meditation on Human Redemption"; Vol. 2, "Philosophical Fragments," "De Grammatico," "On Truth," "Freedom of Choice," "The Fall of the Devil," "The Harmony of the Foreknowledge, the Predestination, and the Grace of God with Free Choice"; Vol. 3, two letters concerning Roscelin, "The Incarnation of the Word," "Why God Became a Man," "The Virgin Conception and Original Sin," "The Procession of the Holy Spirit," and three letters on the sacraments. Volume 4 is entitled *Hermeneutical and Textual Problems in the Complete Treatises of St. Anselm* (E Mellen 1976 $49.95).

Southern, Richard W. *Saint Anselm and His Biographer.* Cambridge Univ. Pr. 1963. The book functions almost as a commentary on the *Life of St. Anselm* by his biographer, Eadmer (above). In the process Southern examines the relation between the originality of Anselm's thought and the traditions in which he was educated.

BERNARD OF CLAIRVAUX, SAINT. 1090?–1153

[SEE Chapter 3 in this volume.]

BONAVENTURE, SAINT. 1221–1274

[SEE Chapter 3 in this volume.]

DUNS SCOTUS, JOHN. c.1265–1308

[SEE Chapter 3 in this volume.]

ECKHART, (JOHANNES) MEISTER. c.1260–c.1328

Meister Eckhart was a German Dominican mystic, whose central concern was the relation of the soul to God. He regarded "the innermost essence of the soul as something uncreated, not only 'like' God in a creaturely resemblance, but truly 'one' with God" (Bernard McGinn, *Meister Eckhart*). Eckhart's thinking offended orthodox sensibilities as pantheistic and he was accused of heretical teachings.

BOOKS BY MEISTER ECKHART

Meister Eckhart: A Modern Translation. Trans. by Raymond B. Blakney, Harper 1941
   pap. $8.95
Meister Eckhart: The Essential Sermons, Commentaries, Treatises, and Defense. Ed. by
   Bernard McGinn, pref. by Huston Smith, Paulist Pr. 1981 $13.95 pap. $11.95

BOOK ABOUT MEISTER ECKHART

McGinn, Bernard, ed. *Meister Eckhart: Teacher and Preacher.* Pref. by Kenneth J.
   Northcott [*Class. of Western Spirituality Ser.*] Paulist Pr. 1986 $15.95 pap. $12.95.
   "Texts that illustrate the diversity of one of the most enigmatic and influential
   mystics of the Western Christian Traditions" (Publisher's catalog).

ERASMUS OF ROTTERDAM. 1466?–1536

[SEE Chapter 4 in this volume.]

FITZRALPH, RICHARD. c.1295–1360

Richard Fitzralph was Archbishop of Armagh in Ireland and an important figure in Anglo-Irish ecclesiastical history. Prior to becoming archbishop, he served as chancellor of Oxford and this brought him into contact
with the younger Wyclif. He promoted the interests of the secular clergy
against the friars, and argued that voluntary begging was against the teaching of Christ.

BOOK ABOUT FITZRALPH

Walsh, Katherine. *A Fourteenth Century Scholar and Primate: Richard Fitzralph in
   Oxford, Avignon, and Armagh.* Oxford 1981 $65.00. A thorough and balanced
   biographical study of the career of Fitzralph.

HUS, JOHN. c.1372–1415

John Hus was a Bohemian reformer and a well-known preacher in
Prague. His thinking was influenced by the Czech reform movement and the
writings of Wyclif. He taught that the true church consists only of the
predestined and that the "only law of the Church is the Bible, above all the
New Testament, and, like Wyclif, ruled out the extrabiblical traditions of
canon law but did not deny the teaching authority of the ancient fathers
and doctors." Hus was excommunicated in 1411 for his teachings, and in
1415 at the Council of Constance he was tried and convicted of heresy. He
suffered death at the stake. Popular in Bohemia during his life, Hus became
a national hero.

BOOKS ABOUT JOHN HUS

Spinka, Matthew. *John Hus: A Biography.* Greenwood repr. of 1968 ed. 1978 lib. bdg.
   $37.50. This book provides a scholarly portrait of Hus's life and its dramatic end
   at the Council of Constance in 1415.
———. *John Hus at the Council of Constance.* Columbia Univ. Pr. 1965 o.p. Primarily
   a translation of Peter of Mladonovice's eyewitness account of Hus's execution at
   Constance. A useful introduction concerning the conciliar movement, including
   some of Hus's letters and documents relating to the final years of his life.

JOACHIM OF FIORE. c.1132–1202

In a series of works known as *The Everlasting Gospel*, the mystic Joachim of Fiore put forth the view of a Trinitarian conception of history. The first period, that of the Father, is the age when humans lived under the Law until the end of the Old Testament dispensation. The second, that of the Son, is lived under grace and covers the New Testament dispensation. Joachim thought this period lasted for 42 generations of 30 years each. The final age, that of the Holy Spirit, was to be inaugurated in 1260 and would see "the rise of new religious orders destined to convert the whole world." Joachim's apocalyptic thinking was very influential among the Franciscan Spirituals.

BOOK ABOUT JOACHIM OF FIORE

West, Selno C., and Sandra Zimdars-Swartz. *Joachim of Fiore: A Study in Spiritual Perception and History.* Indiana Univ. Pr. 1983 $20.00. A good introduction to Joachim's thought, the book examines his use of patristic and medieval sources, his exegetical method, and his interpretation of the Incarnation and the relation between Christ and the Holy Spirit. A brief biographical sketch is included.

NICHOLAS OF CUSA. c.1401–1464

[SEE Chapter 4 in this volume.]

PATRICK, SAINT. c.390–460

St. Patrick, the "Apostle of Ireland," was born in Britain. At age 16 he was captured by Irish pirates and carried into slavery in Ireland, where he labored in bondage for several years. He eventually escaped and returned to Britain, where he trained for the Christian ministry. At some point Patrick was sent to Ireland, where he spent the rest of his life evangelizing, conciliating local chieftains, ordaining clergy, and organizing the common life of monks and nuns. The few facts known about Patrick were embellished by his biographers in the Middle Ages.

BOOK ABOUT ST. PATRICK

Hanson, R. *The Life and Writings of the Historical St. Patrick.* Winston Pr. 1983 $11.95. The volume, designed for the general reader, contains Patrick's "Letter to Coroticus" and "Confession" with accompanying commentaries to each. It opens with a general introduction to the life and thought of Patrick.

THOMAS AQUINAS, SAINT. 1225?–1274

[SEE Chapter 3 in this volume.]

WOMEN WRITERS

The visionary and poetic books of women religious writers of the Middle Ages have in many cases become spiritual and devotional classics.

BOOKS ABOUT WOMEN WRITERS

Collis, Louise. *Memoirs of a Medieval Woman.* Harper 1983 pap. $7.95. This book is based on the memoirs of Margery Kempe's *The Book.* It provides a biographical sketch of her life from the time of her wedding in 1393 up to her dictation of her memoirs.

Dronke, Peter. *Women Writers of the Middle Ages: A Critical Study of Texts from Perpetua (203) to Marguerite Porete (1310).* Cambridge Univ. Pr. 1984 $57.50 pap. $15.95. As the author states, this is a "presentation and interpretation of a substantial range of texts composed by women from the beginning of the third century to the end of the thirteenth century—to explore the ways women helped to shape the earliest Christian writing in a Western language, and observe their particular contributions to Western literature over a millennium." Dronke focuses on texts that illuminate women's awareness of themselves.

WYCLIF, JOHN. c.1330–1384

John Wyclif was an English philosopher, theologian, and reformer. Many of his beliefs varied from traditional Church teachings, and some views put him outside of the orthodox fold. He argued, for instance, that ecclesiastical authorities not in a state of grace could be deprived of their endowments by civil authority, and that there was no scriptural foundation for the religious orders. He also argued against the doctrine of transubstantiation, desiring rather to emphasize the moral and spiritual effects of the Eucharist, a position later condemned by the English church. Wyclif's greatest influence was, interestingly, not in England but in Bohemia, where John Hus preached Wyclif's theology.

BOOKS BY JOHN WYCLIF

The English Works of Wyclif. Ed. by F. D. Matthew, Kraus Repr. repr. of 1880 ed. $44.00

Select English Writings. Ed. by Herbert E. Winn, AMS Pr. repr. of 1929 ed. 1978 $18.50

On Universals: The Tractatus de universalibus. Ed. by Ivan Mueller, tr. by Anthony Kenny, Oxford 1985 $39.95 text ed. $72.00

An Apology for Lollard Doctrines Attributed to Wicliffe. Ed. by James H. Todd, AMS Pr. repr. of 1842 ed. 1983 $28.00

BOOKS ABOUT JOHN WYCLIF

Dahmus, Joseph H. *The Prosecution of John Wyclif.* Shoe String repr. of 1952 ed. 1970 $17.50. A study of Wyclif's career in general and his struggle with the church in particular.

Hall, Louis B. *The Perilous Vision of John Wyclif.* Nelson-Hall 1983 lib. bdg. $23.95. A popular account of the life and times of Wyclif.

Hudson, Anne, ed. *Selections from English Wycliffite Writings.* Cambridge Univ. Pr. 1981 pap. $18.95. A representative anthology of 27 passages with commentaries "of Lollard ideas and preoccupations and the different types of Lollard tracts, sermons, satire, and biblical translation."

Mudroch, Vaclav. *The Wyclif Tradition.* Ed. by Albert C. Reeves, Ohio Univ. Pr. 1979 $15.00. An analysis of the judgments and evaluations of Wyclif made in the sixteenth and seventeenth centuries.

Stacey, John. *John Wyclif and Reform.* AMS Pr. repr. of 1964 ed. 1979 $18.00. In the author's words, a readable "assessment of Wyclif's place as a forerunner of the reformers of the sixteenth century."

CHAPTER 12

Late Christianity

W. Fred Graham

There are moments in the history of humankind that seem to be pregnant with future possibilities—although not so much by virtue of the clear promises that they offer, as because the old ways have run their course and it is necessary to venture in new directions.
—JUSTO L. GONZALEZ, *A History of Christian Thought*

Even if the whole world goes to smash, God can make another world.
—MARTIN LUTHER, quoted in Ronald Bainton, *Erasmus of Christendom*

The history of Christianity from 1500 on can be seen as the story of the gradual relaxation of the religious impulse among the peoples of western Europe and North America. Or it can be understood as the era in which Christianity moved out of the backwaters of Europe into the newly discovered parts of the globe, growing from a parochial religion to its present status as the most populous faith on earth. Even its great rival, atheistic communism, can be read as either a highly successful enemy, destroyer of the faith in lands, especially in Russia, where Orthodox Christianity once reigned without rival; or as a weakening, parricidal faith—derivative of and dependent on its parent religion—that has brought a variant of Christianity into lands where the ordinary religious message had not penetrated well. In this reading, Marxism is bound to weaken and the true faith to increase, as, indeed, we find happening today in Russia and China.

Probably both readings are correct. Few will deny that in Europe and the Americas the religious permeation of society that obtained in the fifteenth century has declined. In western Europe, all art was once Christian art, all economics Christian economics. The great buildings and the great wars were cathedrals and crusades, while today the public square seems largely untouched by the dictates of prophet or priest. The common term for this desacralizing of society is secularization. But a long view of history also finds Christianity globally vibrant. Jesus' birthday and his resurrection are celebrated in every nation on earth, even in militantly atheist Albania and militantly Muslim Pakistan. If the splitting of the church in the West into Roman Catholic and Protestant served to hasten the secularizing of society, the resulting revivals of sectarian Christianity sparked missionary movement in heroic proportions. And where Protestant and Catholic have foundered, the stepchild, Pentecostalism, bids fair to root out pagan vestiges

577

within the endemic Christianity of South and Central America, and to cooperate with those same tendencies in tribal Africa, making that continent the largest Christian continent on earth.

Although the following pages could be arranged in a number of ways, the editor has followed a consciously historical outline, beginning with the Reformation—Protestant and Roman Catholic—and moving through the Enlightenment and the nineteenth century, and on to the present time. A number of movements—institutional and theological, as well as popular—are noted within each epoch, and they and their leaders serve as the gathering points for the bibliography that follows.

GENERAL REFERENCE WORKS

Gorman, G. E., and Lyn Gorman. *Theological and Religious Reference Materials.* [*Bibliographies & Indexes in Religious Studies.*] Vol. 1, *General Resources and Biblical Studies;* Vol. 2, *Systematic Theology and Church History.* Greenwood 1984–85 lib. bdg. $47.50–$49.95. According to the preface, Volume 3 will deal with practical theology and related subjects in the social sciences; Volume 4 will treat comparative and non-Christian religions.

Religious and Inspirational Books and Serials in Print, 1987. Bowker 1987 $89.00. A comprehensive listing of nearly 60,000 books (arranged by author, title, and subject) and 3,600 serials (by subject and title) of currently available American publications in religion, metaphysics, theology, ethics, and related subjects.

Religious Reading: The Annual Guide. McGrath 1975–86 pap. ea. $25.00. Each volume attempts to list all religious publications for the year from all American publishers. Entries arranged by subject area. Current and accurate.

Sheehy, Eugene P., and others, eds. *Guide to Reference Books.* Amer. Lib. Assn. 10th ed. 1986 text ed. $50.00. Devotes 50 pages to works on religion divided into subject categories with subdivisions.

Wilson, John F. *Research Guide to Religious Studies.* Ed. by Thomas P. Slavens [*Sources of Information in the Humanities Ser.*] Amer. Lib. Assn. 1982 lib. bdg. $22.50. Useful for finding direction in conducting preliminary searches.

DICTIONARIES, ENCYCLOPEDIAS, HANDBOOKS

The Church

Barrett, David, ed. *World Christian Encyclopedia: A Comparative Survey of Churches and Religions in the Modern World, A.D. 1900 to 2000.* Oxford 1982 text ed. $145.00. This is probably the only comprehensive survey of all branches of Christianity all over the earth. Special attention is given to church growth and to fringe groups. Indexes and many statistics.

Broderick, Robert C., ed. *The Catholic Encyclopedia.* Nelson rev. ed. 1987 pap. $18.95. A one-volume dictionary for the nonspecialist.

Cross, Frank L., and Elizabeth A. Livingstone, eds. *The Oxford Dictionary of the Christian Church.* Oxford 1974 $60.00. Standard work that includes Eastern Christianity and Vatican II changes in Catholicism. "The most representative general dictionary of the church" (*Theological and Religious Reference Materials*).

Douglas, James D., and others, eds. *The New International Dictionary of the Christian*

Church. Zondervan rev. ed. 1978 $29.95. Useful in the way the Cross volume (see above) is, covers much territory, Evangelical in outlook.

Eliade, Mircea, ed. *The Encyclopedia of Religion.* Macmillan 16 vols. 1986 $1,100.00. This series is intended to replace the Hastings *Encylopedia of Religion and Ethics* (see below). Influenced heavily by the history of religions approach of its editor, it includes work by many of the best scholars in nearly every field of religious study. An outstanding reference work.

Hardon, John A. *Modern Catholic Dictionary.* Doubleday 1980 $22.95. A modern up-to-date dictionary with Roman Catholic orientation.

Hastings, James, ed. *Encyclopedia of Religion and Ethics.* Scribner 13 vols. 1961 o.p. Found in many libraries, this is old but comprehensive and still very useful.

Livingstone, Elizabeth A., ed. *The Concise Oxford Dictionary of the Christian Church.* Oxford 1977 o.p. The abridged version of *The Oxford Dictionary of the Christian Church.* "Probably the most adequate single volume dictionary in its field" (*Theological and Religious Reference Materials*).

Loetscher, Lefferts A., and others, eds. *Twentieth Century Encyclopedia of Religious Knowledge: An Extension of the New Schaff-Herzog Encyclopedia of Religious Knowledge.* Baker Bks. 2 vols. 1955 o.p. Brings Schaff-Herzog into the middle of the present century, especially in church history.

Mead, Frank S., and Samuel S. Hill. *Handbook of Denominations in the United States.* Abingdon 8th ed. 1985 text ed. $10.95. Brief history, doctrines, government, and statistics of more than 200 American denominations. This brief compendium is handy for reference or for beginning study.

Melton, J. Gordon, and James V. Geisendorfer. *A Directory of Religious Bodies in the United States.* Garland 1977 lib. bdg. $40.00. Nearly 1,300 religious groups are listed and clustered into families, e.g., the Lutheran family, as well as under such headings as mail-order churches, neopaganism.

——. *The Encyclopedia of American Religions.* McGrath 2 vols. 1978 o.p. Compares more than 1,000 groups with Catholics, Baptists, and Lutherans.

——. *The Encyclopedia of American Religions, First Edition Supplement.* Gale 1985 text ed. pap. $75.00

New Catholic Encyclopedia. Ed. by William J. McDonald and others, Publishers Guild 17 vols. repr. of 1967 ed. 1981 set $550.00. Ecumenical in scope and nontechnical for the most part, good emphasis on biography. Volumes 16 and 17 are supplements.

The New Schaff-Herzog Encyclopedia of Religious Knowledge. Ed. by Samuel M. Jackson and others, Baker Bks. 13 vols. repr. of 1908–14 ed. 1949–50 o.p. Based on an original German publication, this is especially valuable for biography and for ancient and modern religions. Like Hastings in its broad coverage. See Loetscher (above) for supplement.

Piepkorn, Arthur C. *Profiles in Belief: The Religious Bodies of the United States and Canada.* Harper 4 vols. 1977–79 ea. $20.00–$30.00. Objective and comprehensive from a Lutheran-Ecumenical perspective. Invaluable tool.

Ethics and Theology

Cobb, John B. *Varieties of Protestantism.* Westminster 1960 o.p. Outline of nine basic Protestant theologies.

Ferm, Deane W. *Contemporary American Theologies: A Critical Survey.* Harper 1981 pap. $8.95. Brief and clear introductions to the main features of modern theologies in America, including Roman Catholic and conservative Protestant.

Fremantle, Anne, ed. *The Social Teachings of the Church*. New Amer. Lib. 1963 o.p. Texts and selections from the 13 major social encyclicals from Pope Leo XIII to John XXII. Subject index.

Gaynor, Frank. *Dictionary of Mysticism*. Citadel Pr. 1973 pap. $2.45. Alphabetically arranged definitions of 2,200 terms used in religious mysticism, psychical research, etc.

Gonzalez, Justo L. *History of Christian Thought*. Abingdon 3 vols. rev. ed. 1975 $56.00. Like his earlier volumes, an amazingly surefooted survey. Protestant but objective.

Häring, Bernard. *The Law of Christ*. Trans. by Edwin G. Kaiser, Paulist Pr. 3 vols. 1961–66 ea. $17.95. Recognized as a watershed in Roman Catholic moral theology. Annotated to make a handbook.

Harrison, Everett F., ed. *Baker's Dictionary of Theology*. Baker Bks. 1960 pap. $12.95. Acquaints readers with areas of disagreement in modern theology from conservative standpoint. Helpful bibliographies.

Harvey, Van A. *Handbook of Theological Terms*. Macmillan 1964 pap. $4.95. Useful in comparing the traditions since both Protestant and Catholic views are given on use of terms.

Henry, Carl F. H., ed. *Baker's Dictionary of Christian Ethics*. Baker Bks. 1978 o.p. Signed articles on ethical issues with brief bibliographies. Conservative Protestant.

Hordern, William E. *Layman's Guide to Protestant Theology*. Macmillan rev. ed. 1968 pap. $4.95. Clearly written account of theological movement from the Protestant reformers to the twentieth century, with particular attention to twentieth-century theologians, the major ones examined carefully.

Keeley, Robin, ed. *Eerdmans' Handbook to Christian Belief*. Eerdmans 1982 $24.95. Evangelical, clear, and careful.

Kliever, Lonnie D. *The Shattered Spectrum: A Survey of Contemporary Theology*. John Knox 1981 pap. $10.95. Picks up six prominent theological schools of thought since World War II and examines each carefully and in fairly easy style.

Macquarrie, John. *Principles of Christian Theology*. Macmillan 2d ed. 1977 text ed. pap. $17.95. A large book, presenting in ecumenical fashion current theological directions and issues.

———, ed. *Dictionary of Christian Ethics*. Westminster 1967 $18.95. A standard dictionary with no particular line of thought. Eighty contributors, brief bibliographies.

Placher, William C. *A History of Christian Theology: An Introduction*. Westminster 1983 pap. $16.95. Excellent one-volume survey of history of Christian thought, with last seven chapters covering Reformation to present.

Rahner, Karl, and Herbert Vorgrimler. *Concise Theological Dictionary*. State Mutual Bk. 1982 $59.00. Short articles on Roman Catholic theology, incorporating material generated by Vatican II. Excellent reference data.

Rahner, Karl, and others, eds. *Encyclopedia of Theology: The Concise Sacramentum Mundi*. Crossroad NY rev. & abr. ed. 1975 $49.50. The single-volume edition of the 6-volume work with some revision. Bibliographies.

———. *Sacramentum Mundi: An Encyclopedia of Theology*. Herder 6 vols. 1968–70 o.p. A widely popular book that has appeared in five other European languages. Based on the work of more than 600 Roman Catholic theologians, it attempts to present current developments and differences in all areas of theology.

Richardson, Alan, ed. *Dictionary of Christian Theology*. Westminster 1969 $13.95. Alphabetically arranged short articles for students. Good for beginners.

Church History

Barry, Colman J., ed. *Readings in Church History*. Christian Classics 3 vols. in 1 1985 pap. $50.00. Collection of primary materials illustrating important events, movements, thinkers. Volumes 2 and 3 cover the Reformation to the modern period.

The Book of Saints: A Dictionary of Persons Canonized or Beatified by the Catholic Church. Crowell 5th ed. 1966 o.p. This 740-page dictionary provides concise biographical data on some 2,200 saints. Sources of information are documented for further study.

Bowden, Henry W., and Edwin S. Gaustad, eds. *Dictionary of American Religious Biography*. Greenwood 1976 lib. bdg. $45.00. There are 425 biographical sketches of people who have helped shape America's religious traditions. Well annotated.

Brauer, Jerald C., ed. *Westminster Dictionary of Church History*. Westminster 1971 $27.50. An 887-page resource for definitions and explanations of facts, movements, events, and persons in church history.

Delaney, John J. *A Dictionary of Saints*. State Mutual Bk. 1982 $45.00. Up-to-date compendium of 5,000 saints.

———. *Pocket Dictionary of Saints*. Doubleday 1983 pap. $6.95

Dowley, Tim, ed. *Eerdmans' Handbook to the History of Christianity*. Eerdmans 1977 $24.95. Seventy scholars have contributed to this handy description of the history of Christianity, divided into seven chapters with numerous subdivisions where movements and persons are presented. Popular but good scholarship with many aids but no bibliography.

Eberhardt, Vernon C. *A Summary of Catholic History*. Herder 2 vols. 1961–62 o.p. The second volume begins with 1453 and carries the story to modern times. Indexes, appendixes, and bibliography. Fills gap for Roman Catholic surveys between one-volume summaries and Jedin's massive work (see below).

Jedin, Hubert, and John Patrick Dolan, gen. eds. *The History of the Church*. Crossroad NY 10 vols. 1980 set $495.00. Translation of Jedin's *Handbuch der Kirchengeschichte*, this is a solid history from a Catholic viewpoint, but seeks objectivity and veracity. Bibliography and index for each volume.

Latourette, Kenneth S. *A History of Christianity*. Harper 2 vols. 1975 ea. $13.95. Dean of American church historians summarizes his life's work in these volumes. Accurate and ecumenical.

Littell, Franklin H. *The Macmillan Atlas History of Christianity*. Illus. by E. Hausman, Macmillan 1976 $24.95. Excellent set of 197 maps and commentary focusing on intellectual, ethical, and expansionist aspects of Christianity from beginning to present.

Manschreck, Clyde L. *A History of Christianity in the World: From Persecution to Uncertainty*. Prentice-Hall 2d ed. 1985 text ed. $25.95. Bibliography. Moderate Protestant view of history of church.

Moyer, Elgin, and Earle Cairns. *Wycliffe Biographical Dictionary of the Church*. Moody 1982 $19.95. Formerly entitled *Who Was Who in Church History*, this volume includes brief biographical sketches of 2,000 religious leaders, Christian and non-Christian. Protestant in emphasis.

Neill, Stephen C., and others. *Concise Dictionary of the Christian World Mission*. Abingdon 1971 o.p. Covers all aspects of missions from ecumenical perspective. Brief articles by 200 specialists treat the spread of Christianity in various lands, topics relating to missionary work, and provide biographies of leaders. Islamic and Buddhist missions also lightly described. An "indispensable reference work in its field" (*Theological and Religious Reference Materials*).

Walker, Williston. *A History of the Christian Church*. Rev. by Robert T. Handy, Scribner 4th ed. 1985 $35.00. First published in 1918, its steady and fair coverage are continued in Handy's revision. Index and maps.

THE REFORMATION OF THE SIXTEENTH CENTURY: 1500–1560

Alternately characterized as "that infamous sundering of the Body of Christ" and "the rediscovery of the pure bride of Christ," the Reformation was not limited to the Protestant movements, but was also a reformation in church practice and morality by the Roman Catholic church, and a fixing of her theology in a form that lasted until the Second Vatican Council (1962–1965). At one time the Protestant reformers were vilified by Roman Catholic historians, but the works of Joseph Lortz in Germany, John Todd and Philip Hughes in England, and Robert McNally in the United States have concurred in recent decades in acknowledging good cause for the Protestant zeal, while still lamenting the end of unified Western Christianity. The Orthodox churches of the East escaped the divisiveness that has since characterized Christianity in the West. The principal reformers are listed separately at the end of this section.

Background: Before the Reformation

Cohn, Norman. *The Pursuit of the Millennium*. Oxford rev. ed. 1970 pap. $11.95. The left wing, or "stepchildren," of the Middle Ages comes to the surface—sometimes violently—after Luther. See also listings under The Radical Reformation, for Leonard Verduin and George Williams.

Gilson, Étienne. *History of Christian Philosophy in the Middle Ages*. Christian Class. 1955 o.p. In about 830 pages, all anyone wants to know about the subject. Some of Luther's rejection of philosophy, the "devil's whore," can be seen here.

Hudson, Anne, ed. *Selections from English Wycliffite Writings*. Cambridge Univ. Pr. 1981 pap. $18.95. Addresses the problem of whether the English Reformation existed already as a primarily underground movement when Henry VIII rejected papal ecclesiastical control over England in order to get his divorce.

Kaminsky, Howard. *A History of the Hussite Revolution*. Univ. of California Pr. 1967 o.p. In 580 pages of highly regarded scholarship John Hus and his followers, the Unitas Fratrum, are brought to light.

Knowles, David. *The English Mystical Tradition*. Harper 1961 o.p. Small, but broad in scholarship and even wisdom. By the dean of English students of monasticism.

Lambert, Malcolm. *Medieval Heresy: Popular Movements from Bogomil to Hus*. Holmes & Meier 1977 $54.50. Good clear account of various medieval movements, such as Albigensian, Waldensian, Hussite, and others.

Lerner, Robert E. *The Heresy of the Free Spirit in the Later Middle Ages*. Univ. of California Pr. 1972 $40.00. Brief, but careful, study of a wider sort of heresy than the title suggests. A short bibliography.

McFarlane, Kenneth B. *John Wycliffe and the Beginnings of English Nonconformity*. Verry 1952 $6.00. Small, fine study that has held its own with later studies of Wycliffe and his followers.

Oakley, Francis. *The Western Church in the Later Middle Ages*. Cornell Univ. Pr. 1985 $32.50 text ed. pap. $9.95. Good survey by top scholar.

Oberman, Heiko. *Forerunners of the Reformation: The Shape of Late Medieval Thought*. Trans. by Paul Nyhus, Fortress Pr. 1981 pap. $12.95. Selections from religious reformers before Luther.

———. *The Harvest of Medieval Theology: Gabriel Biel and Late Medieval Nominalism*. Labyrinth Pr. repr. of 1963 ed. 1983 pap. $17.50. Although focused on the nominalist theologian Gabriel Biel, this is a good survey of late medieval theology and philosophy.

Ozment, Steven E. *The Age of Reform 1250–1550: An Intellectual and Religious History of Late Medieval and Early Reformation Europe*. Yale Univ. Pr. 1980 $45.00 pap. $13.95. Defies usual periodization in order to put the Reformation into a medieval perspective and to show that Luther stood in a line of reformers.

———, ed. *The Reformation in Medieval Perspective*. New Viewpoints 1971 $12.50. pap. $3.45. Concentrates on the pre-Luther period, but shows continuities and radical breaks with the reforming tradition.

Spinka, Matthew. *John Hus: A Biography*. Greenwood repr. of 1968 ed. 1978 lib. bdg. $37.50. Brief and enjoyable.

———, ed. *Advocates of Reform: From Wyclif to Erasmus*. Westminster 1953 o.p. Selections from major works of pre-Reformation critics of church and society, Wycliffe, Hus, and others. Useful.

General Studies of the Reformation

Chadwick, Owen. *The Reformation*. [*History of the Church Ser*.] Penguin 1964 pap. $5.95. Balanced study by one of the leaders in British history. Indexes and bibliographies.

Dickens, A. G. *Reformation and Society in Sixteenth-Century Europe*. Harcourt 1966 text ed. pap. $11.95. Good on preconditions for reform; has glossary of theological terms and a reading list in English.

Eisenstein, Elizabeth. *The Printing Press as an Agent of Change*. Cambridge Univ. Pr. 2 vols. in 1 1980 pap. $23.95. Omits political considerations, studied in her later volume (below).

———. *The Printing Revolution in Early Modern Europe*. Cambridge Univ. Pr. 1984 $37.50 pap. $9.95. Fascinating examination of uses of printing as religious and political propaganda.

Elton, G. R. *Reformation Europe, 1517–1559*. Harper 1968 o.p. An unbiased book that sets the Reformation in its broader context very clearly.

Gerrish, Brian. *Reformers in Profile*. Fortress Pr. 1967 o.p. This is a handy introduction to several prereformers, Erasmus, and major reform leaders, such as Luther, Zwingli, Calvin, Cranmer, Simons, and (for Catholicism) Loyola. Each profile painted by an expert.

Green, Robert W., ed. *Protestantism and Capitalism and Social Science: The Weber Thesis Controversy*. [*Problems in Amer. Civilization Ser*.] Heath 2d ed. 1973 text ed. pap. $5.50. Presents in handy fashion arguments for and against the thesis that Protestantism was responsible for the rise of capitalism. Good notes and suggestions for further reading.

Grimm, Harold J. *The Reformation Era: 1500–1650*. Macmillan 2d ed. 1973 text ed. $34.00. Excellent treatment, supplemented by 65 pages of bibliography.

Harbison, E. Harris. *The Age of Reformation*. Greenwood repr. of 1955 ed. 1982 lib. bdg. $22.50. At 133 pages, the briefest study listed. Fruit of life's work by a dean of American historians. Index and suggestions for further reading.

Hillerbrand, Hans J., ed. *The Protestant Reformation*. Harper 1968 pap. $6.95. Lively account making good use of pamphlet literature, as well as major works on all sides. Good bibliography.

———. *The Reformation: A Narrative History Related by Contemporary Observers and Participants*. Baker Bks. 1978 pap. $11.95. Quotations and illustrations before and during the Reformation, with brief commentary. Gives sharp flavor absent in objective accounts.

Hughes, Philip. *A Popular History of the Reformation*. Hanover House 1957 o.p. Although this work by a Catholic historian has the *nihil obstat* and the *imprimatur*, it is not anti-Protestant. Index, but no bibliography.

Lortz, Joseph. *The Reformation in Germany*. Trans. by Ronald Walls, Herder 1968 o.p. Lortz was the first Catholic historian to present Luther in a favorable light. Originally published in 1939, this work focuses on Germany.

Moeller, Bernd. *Imperial Cities and the Reformation*. Ed. by H. C. Erik Midelfort and Mark U. Edwards, Jr., Labyrinth Pr. repr. of 1972 ed. 1982 text ed. pap. $5.95. Three essays that appeared separately in German. Studies problems in research for the era, the role of the German humanists, and of imperial cities. Excellent footnotes but no bibliography.

Mosse, George L. *The Reformation*. Peter Smith 3d ed. 1963 o.p. Viewpoint of author, well known for studies of nazism and Jewry, makes this a unique study.

Ozment, Steven E. *The Reformation in the Cities: The Appeal of Protestantism to Sixteenth-Century Germany and Switzerland*. Yale Univ. Pr. 1975 $28.50 pap. $8.95. Broader than Moeller's work, it looks at humanists as well as city councils. Necessary study, with smooth narrative flow and 70 pages of notes.

———, ed. *Reformation Europe: A Guide to Research*. Center for Reformation Research 1982 $18.50 pap. $13.50. Essays by experts in different facets of Reformation history, this is a must for the serious student or researcher. Each essay is bibliographic.

Spitz, Lewis W. *The Protestant Reformation 1517–1559*. [*The Rise of Modern Europe Ser.*] Harper 1984 $22.45 1986 pap. $8.95. Recent and by a noted historian, it contains the latest research. The 45-page bibliography is up-to-date and that alone makes this a necessary work.

Todd, John M. *Reformation*. Doubleday 1971 o.p. Balanced study by a Catholic biographer of Luther, with bibliography and index.

The Radical Reformation: Anabaptists, Spiritualists, and Evangelical Rationalists

It is difficult to lump all the left-wing reformers under one name. George Williams uses the three headings employed above, and perhaps that is the best that can be done to cover the fantastic array of religious nonconformists of the sixteenth century. The major reformers—Luther, Zwingli, Calvin, leaders of the English Reformation—all concurred with Roman Catholics in believing that church and state, religion and society, should be one. Indeed, it seemed to all of them "*frénétique et fantastique*" to think that a society could hold together if not bound by the ties of a common religion.

Not so these folk. Although they disagreed among themselves, all of them wanted a clear separation of state and church, the former belonging to

Satan and the latter to Christ. They all wanted to restore the primitive church, the small band of true believers whose light shone in a dark world. Some are denoted Anabaptists to show that their detractors identified them primarily by their insistence on believers' baptism, which, in practice, meant the rebaptism of folk already baptized as infants. Others are called Spiritualists, for they held the activity of the Holy Spirit within the believer to be even more important than the Bible. In the next century the Quakers (Society of Friends) institutionalized that position in the form we recognize today. The Evangelical Rationalists were Evangelical because, like Luther, they held to justification by faith alone, but their rationalism led them to deny doctrines that had to be accepted on faith, like the deity of Christ and the Trinity. Their existence in Poland lasted scarcely two generations, but they have cast a long shadow down the history of Christianity.

Armour, Rollin S. *Anabaptist Baptism.* Herald Pr. 1966 $16.95. Studies views of baptism on part of Anabaptist leaders and, surprise, they differ in many respects. Drew critical reviews when published.

Bak, Janos, ed. *The German Peasant War of 1525.* Biblio Dist. 1976 $26.00. Thomas Müntzer was a religious radical before he was led by divine inspiration into heading the folk rebellion in middle Germany. This book has a very good bibliography for further study. Contains essays that set forth various conflicting opinions on Müntzer and on the war itself.

Bender, Harold S. *Anabaptists and Religious Liberty in the Sixteenth Century.* Ed. by Charles S. Anderson, Fortress Pr. 1970 o.p. Tiny book by the dean of Reformation Anabaptist studies in which he shows their consistent desire to separate church and state.

Clasen, Claus-Peter. *Anabaptism: A Social History, 1525–1618.* Cornell Univ. Pr. 1972 o.p. Clearly written and with a large bibliography. The author believes one can quantitatively assess Anabaptist social history.

———. *The Anabaptist in South and Central Germany, Switzerland, and Austria.* Mennonite Historical Society 1978 o.p. Has been called the "major research achievement of twentieth-century Anabaptist studies." It omits the radicals of northern Germany and the Netherlands.

Davis, Kenneth R. *Anabaptism and Asceticism: A Study in Intellectual Origins.* Herald Pr. 1974 $15.95. Argues that there are spiritual and intellectual ties between medieval monks and the Anabaptists. Good intellectual history.

Durnbaugh, Donald F. *Believer's Church: The History and Character of Radical Protestantism.* Herald Pr. repr. of 1968 ed. 1985 pap. $12.95. Brings the stress of radical Protestants on church-state separation and pacifism into this century. Excellent study.

Friedmann, Robert. *The Theology of Anabaptism.* Herald Pr. 1973 $12.95. That Anabaptists were not primarily theologically minded is apparent from this 175-page book (with bibliography), which is adequate for the subject.

Goetz, Hans J. *Profiles of Radical Reformers.* Herald Pr. 1982 pap. $9.95. A handy brief work that includes profiles of all the important radical leaders: Müntzer, Karlstadt, Hus, Hutter, Denck, and 15 more.

Gross, Leonard. *The Golden Years of the Hutterites.* Herald Pr. 1980 $17.95. Primarily a study of second generation Anabaptists in southern and eastern Europe, just before their savage persecution by the Austrian Empire.

Klaassen, Walter. *Anabaptism in Outline: Selected Primary Sources.* Herald Pr. 1981 pap. $12.95. Writings from major leaders, as well as confessional statements and debate materials.

Littell, Franklin H. *The Anabaptist View of the Church*. Starr King 1958 o.p. Nearly a classic, this centers on the restoration of the primitive church from its Constantinian "Fall," and the pacifism of the Anabaptists.

Ozment, Steven E. *Mysticism and Dissent: Religious Ideology and Social Protest in the Sixteenth Century*. Yale Univ. Pr. 1973 $33.00. Traces mystical belief from pre-Reformation German thought through left wingers of the Reformation, like Müntzer and others, and shows the link between them and social protest, e.g., the Peasants' War.

Packull, Werner O. *Mysticism and the Early South German-Austrian Anabaptist Movement, 1525–1531*. Herald Pr. 1977 $19.95. Too obviously a doctoral dissertation, but still a readable way to see the origins of southern radicals.

Rupp, Gordon. *Patterns of Reformation*. Fortress Pr. 1969 o.p. Rupp, dean of English Reformation historians, is always enjoyable. This is described as an "entertaining study of two wayward radicals, Müntzer and Carlstadt" (Lewis Spitz).

Ruth, John L. *Conrad Grebel: Son of Zurich*. Herald Pr. 1975 $9.95. Admiring but not critical. Harold S. Bender (see above) also has done some work on this leader of the Swiss Brethren whom Zwingli persecuted in and near Zurich.

Scribner, Bob, and Gerhard Benecke. *The German Peasants' War 1525: New Viewpoints*. Allen & Unwin 1979 text ed. pap. $11.95. Described as "the most effective introduction to the subject."

Stayer, James M. *Anabaptists and the Sword*. Coronado Pr. 2d rev. ed. 1976 $15.00. Stayer argues that the one unifying idea was not theological, but political, namely, their attitude toward government authority (the sword).

Stayer, James M., and Werner O. Packull, eds. *The Anabaptists and Thomas Müntzer*. Kendall-Hunt 1980 text ed. pap. $11.95. Usually the leader of the Peasants' Revolt is regarded as a Spiritualist, a man who thought he had a direct pipeline to God. Here is an anthology and a good introduction.

Verduin, Leonard. *The Stepchildren of the Reformation*. Eerdmans 1964 o.p. By a Calvinist who sees the radicals as existing long before the Reformation, but only coming into the open with Luther.

Wilbur, Earl M. *A History of Unitarianism*. Harvard Univ. Pr. 2 vols. 1947–52 o.p. Vol. 1, *A History of Unitarianism, Socinianism and Its Antecedents;* Vol. 2, *In Transylvania, England, and America*. This is the most cited work, but appears to do more with later Unitarianism than the serious scholar of the Reformation might want. Has a brief biography of Socinus.

Williams, George H. *Radical Reformation*. Westminster 1962 $24.95. More than 900 pages, this was the first major study by a person who had no denominational ax to grind. Has a good section on what he calls the Evangelical Rationalists, including information on Socinus and his uncle Laelius Socinus, who promulgated Unitarian ideas in Italy. Because of its size, it is almost a catalog, although it reads well enough. The bibliography is in the footnotes.

Williams, George H., and Angel M. Mergal, eds. *Spiritual and Anabaptist Writers*. [*Lib. of Christian Class.*] Westminster 1977 pap. $11.95. The radicals were prolific writers but this is about the only good-sized English translation of some major writings. The second part of this edition is on Evangelical Catholicism, especially the Spaniard humanist writer Juan Valdes.

Zuck, Lowell H., ed. *Christianity and Revolution: Radical Christian Testimonies, 1520–1650*. [*Documents in Free Church History Ser.*] Temple Univ. Pr. 1975 $29.95 pap. $12.95. Excerpts from various radicals, especially reflecting their relationship with their enemies. Long end notes serve as bibliography.

The English Reformation: From Henry VIII to the Elizabethan Settlement

It has been said recently that English historians still do not know what their Reformation was like. Was it essentially a political matter? G. R. Elton presents that view, concentrating on the consolidation of religious and political power under Henry VIII, whose religious contribution was to reject papal claims in the land and to burn overzealous Protestants. Or was it basically a religious fermentation that destroyed the old church, for which Henry's policies happened to allow some grudging measure of freedom? Certainly the resulting Church of England was more like the Roman Catholic church than the churches of Luther, the Reformed or the left wing, at least in deliberately retaining the governing role of bishops. Indeed, it was the episcopal rule that drew the ire of Puritans after the Elizabethan Settlement, and provided most of the fireworks for the later history of church reform in England.

Beginning students should be aware that Henry VIII not only rejected the pope's control of the English church, but he closed the monasteries, thus putting an enormous amount of land and money in royal hands. These lands were often given or sold cheaply to local nobles, thus strengthening the power of the king. A fuller Reformation came in under the rule of his young son, Edward VI, and through the genius of Thomas Cranmer, archbishop of Canterbury (chief church official in the land), who guided this essentially Reformed movement and wrote the justly renowned *Book of Common Prayer*, the order for worship in England. A brief return to Roman Catholicism took place under Henry's daughter Mary, whom the Protestants dubbed "Bloody" for her killing of Protestants, including Cranmer. But Protestantism of the Anglican variety returned for good under his next daughter, Elizabeth I, whose presence in the womb of Anne Boleyn had made Henry more earnestly seek the divorce that first moved him to break with the pope.

Baker, Derek, ed. *Reform and Reformation: England and the Continent 1500–1750.* Blackwell 1980 $45.00. Helpful articles on various aspects of the Reformation in England. Not a first book to read; compare with Dickens (see below) and Powicke (see below).

Baker, J. Wayne. *Heinrich Bullinger and the Covenant: The Other Reformed Tradition.* Ohio Univ. Pr. 1980 $24.95. Zwingli's son-in-law was very influential in England through his sermons.

Bromiley, G. W. *Thomas Cranmer.* Attic Pr. repr. of 1956 ed. o.p. Definitive but brief, only about 100 pages. By a recognized scholar.

Capp, Bernard. *English Almanacs, 1500–1800: Astrology and the Popular Press.* Cornell Univ. Pr. 1979 $55.00. A much more important form of popular literature than today and therefore offering insights into popular religious beliefs at the time of the Reformation.

Christianson, Paul K. *Reformers and Babylon: Apocalyptic Visions in England from the Reformation to the Outbreak of the Civil War.* Univ. of Toronto Pr. 1978 o.p. Many of the English thought that Christ was about to begin his 1,000-year rule with England as its center. This view became common in nineteenth-century America and is reflected in theologies as diverse as the Millerites, the Oneida Community, and the Mormons.

Clebsch, William A. *England's Earliest Protestants, 1520–1535.* Greenwood repr. of

1964 ed. 1980 lib. bdg. $22.50. The best single volume on the pioneers of reform in England, with attention to Barnes, Firth, Tyndale, as well as to the reforming aspirations of Thomas More.

Cranmer, Thomas. *The Work of Thomas Cranmer.* Ed. by G. E. Duffield, Fortress Pr. 1965 o.p. Omits *The Book of Common Prayer,* which was largely Cranmer's work, but his other writings are here and are commented on expertly.

Cross, Claire. *Church and People, 1450–1600.* Humanities 1976 o.p. There is a good bibliography attached to this work, which argues what the title says, that the Reformation was the defeat of churchly powers by the laity.

Dickens, Arthur G. *The English Reformation.* Schocken 1968 pap. $8.95. Dickens is always good, and many regard this as the best single book on the English Reformation, showing it in all its delightful confusion.

Duffield, G. E. *The Work of William Tyndale.* Fortress Pr. 1965 o.p. Tyndale lost his life because he translated the Bible into English and had it smuggled into Henry VIII's England. Basic work.

Elton, G. R. *England under the Tudors.* Methuen 2d ed. 1974 pap. $19.95. Elton is dean of English scholars of the Reformation and always good. Makes perhaps more of politics and less of religion than Dickens.

———. *Reform and Reformation: England 1509–1558.* Harvard Univ. Pr. 1979 $27.50 pap. $8.95. Draws together 25 years of research.

Erickson, Carolly. *Bloody Mary.* St. Martin's 1985 pap. $9.95. Like Antonia Fraser and Barbara Tuchman, Erickson writes large but nontechnical books for the general public. For poor Mary Tudor, see also the entries for Prescott, Richardson, and Ridley.

———. *Mistress Anne: The Exceptional Life of Anne Boleyn.* Summit 1984 $17.95 1984 pap. $10.95. Good nontechnical account of the second wife of Henry VIII, who lost her head over him, but produced the girl, Elizabeth, who would knit the nation together.

Finucane, Ronald C. *Miracles and Pilgrims: Popular Beliefs in Medieval England.* Rowman 1977 o.p. Plates, bibliography, and a useful look at popular religion as the Reformation approaches.

Firth, Katherine R. *The Apocalyptic Tradition in Reformation Britain 1530–1645.* Oxford 1979 $45.00. Although a revised Ph.D. dissertation, this work reads well and gives insight into the wild side of the Reformation. (See also Christianson above.)

Heal, Felicity, and Rosemary O'Day. *Church and Society in England: Henry VIII to James I.* Shoe String 1977 $23.50. Helpful articles on a plethora of topics about both church and society in a revolutionary age.

Hughes, Philip E. *Theology of the English Reformers.* Baker Bks. rev. ed. 1980 o.p. Good study by one who agrees with Reformist theology.

Hunt, Ernest W. *Dean Colet and His Theology.* [*Church Historical Society Ser.*] Allenson 1956 o.p. This is a small study of Erasmus's friend, whose reforming views were realized more violently than he would have wanted.

Jordan, Wilbur K. *Edward VI: The Threshold of Power.* Allen & Unwin 1970 o.p.

———. *Edward VI: The Young King.* Allen & Unwin 1968 o.p. Together these two volumes tell most readers everything they want to know about the boy king in whose name Protestantism was fully established through the politics of his governors and the religious genius of Thomas Cranmer.

Kendall, R. T. *Calvin and English Calvinism to 1649.* Oxford 1979 o.p. Small but useful study of those who were later called Puritans and the problems predestination gave them as pastors.

More, Sir Thomas. (See Chapter 4 in this volume.)

Parker, Thomas H. L. *English Reformers*. Westminster 1966 o.p. Vignettes of Tyndale, Ridley, Latimer, Cranmer, and others. Good place for a beginner to start, for Parker is trustworthy.

Powicke, Maurice R. *The Reformation in England*. Oxford 1941 o.p. Old and very brief, therefore oversimplifies the scene, but in a way that the student is not misled very much. Read Powicke, then Dickens (above), and then smaller studies of individuals.

Prescott, Hilda F. *Mary Tudor*. Macmillan rev. ed. 1962 $6.00. Good-sized, rather popular study of the much-maligned queen that goes a good way toward exonerating her for the burning of nearly 300 heretics in the six years of her reign. (See also the entries for Erickson, Richardson, and Ridley.)

Reynolds, Ernest E. *Thomas More and Erasmus*. Fordham Univ. Pr. 1966 $25.00. Correspondence between the two humanist scholars with their somewhat different responses to the Reformation.

Richardson, Walter C. *Mary Tudor, the White Queen*. Univ. of Washington Pr. 1969 o.p. Praised as a good account of her life, her marriage to Philip of Spain, the tragedy of her reign.

Ridley, Jasper. *The Life and Times of Mary Tudor*. Weidenfeld & Nicolson 1973 o.p. Although by a good scholar, this is an easy-to-read coffee-table book about Mary and her times.

——. *Thomas Cranmer*. Darby Bks. repr. of 1962 ed. 1983 lib. bdg. $65.00. This is the basic biography that Ridley excels in. Easy to read, but based on thorough scholarship.

Rupp, Ernest G. *Six Makers of English Religion, 1500–1700*. [*Essay Index Repr. Ser.*] Ayer repr. of 1957 ed. $16.75. Discusses Tyndale, Cranmer, and John Foxe, author of the *Book of Martyrs*, as well as Milton, Bunyan, and Isaac Watts, the hymnwriter.

——. *Studies in the Making of the English Protestant Tradition*. Cambridge Univ. Pr. 1947 o.p. The first part fits this period in a solid way.

Scarisbrick, J. J. *Henry VIII*. Univ. of California Pr. 1968 pap. $8.95. Best modern biography, but a bit daunting at 560 pages.

Thomas, Keith. *Religion and the Decline of Magic*. Scribner 1986 pap. $17.95. Surveys English folk religion during this period. A long book, but so well organized that it makes it easy to study particular aspects of religion or magic, e.g., astrology, witchcraft.

Wilson, Derek. *A Tudor Tapestry: Men, Women, and Society in Reformation England*. Univ. of Pittsburgh Pr. 1972 $28.95. A book that looks at the Reformation the way ordinary English men and women must have experienced it. Although important people are in the tapestry, William and Anne Ayscough, knight and wife, are picked out in detail.

The Catholic Reformation: From 1500 through the Council of Trent

The Catholic Reformation or the Counter-Reformation? In the sense that the Roman Catholic church had the resources within itself to purge the institution of the corruptions of simony, nepotism, and a host of feudal ills, it was certainly a Catholic Reformation. But in the sense that the strongest stirrings for change came from men like Luther and others, who were either excommunicated by or rejected the Roman communion and founded churches outside that jurisdiction, it was necessarily a Counter-Reformation. Even the Council of Trent, which met intermittently from 1545 until 1563, can be seen either as the summarizing and clarifying of the church's long traditional theology and practice, or as a way to state theology in opposition to the Protestants.

The great leaders were not popes and bishops, but were people like Ignatius of Loyola, founder of the Society of Jesus (Jesuits), or Saint Teresa of Avila, who combined obedience with a radical spirituality centered on the Passion of Christ. It was the Jesuits especially who raised the theologians and built the schools to produce an educated ministry, the strongest challenge the scholarly Protestants threw at the Church of Rome. Jesuits tutored the bishops in theology at the Council of Trent. Jesuits saved a remnant for the church in England and encouraged kings and emperors to remain true to the faith in many lands. Jesuits stormed the rapidly opening East for the gospel, almost as fast as Portuguese and Spanish conquistadors searched for its wealth. Companions to the early explorers were Jesuit missionaries, men like Hennepin and Marquette, whose names are known even to schoolchildren in America. The listings also include books about Peter Canisius, Francis Xavier, and, in the "Later Developments" section that follows, Cardinal Bellarmine.

Brodrick, James. *St. Francis Xavier, 1506–1552.* Wicklow Pr. 1952 o.p. Good-sized tome on a man who took the gospel to India, China, and Japan; a great explorer and observer, as well as missionary.

———. *St. Peter Canisius.* Loyola Univ. Pr. 1962 $19.95. More than 800 pages is a bit much, but Canisius is often regarded as the one who saved half of Germany from the Lutherans. Brodrick is always inclined to "see no evil" in his heroes.

Christian, William A., Jr. *Local Religion in Sixteenth-Century Spain.* Princeton Univ. Pr. 1981 $28.00. The sort of solid story we need for more lands. Some modern scholars believe that the masses of rural folk were largely un-Christianized during the Middle Ages. This was not true of Spain, Christian shows.

Delumeau, Jean. *Catholicism between Luther and Voltaire: A New View of the Counter-Reformation.* Trans. by Jeremy Moiser, Westminster 1977 $21.50. Although mostly on France, this is not as "narrow" as most French studies. His is the thesis that most people were not Christianized in the Middle Ages; he argues that the Reformation and Catholic Reformation accomplished the conversion of the masses of Europeans to Christianity. Useful also for the period after the Council of Trent.

Dickens, A. G. *The Counter Reformation.* Norton 1979 pap. $7.95. Solid book and not too big by a noted Reformation historian.

Douglas, Richard M. *Jacopo Sadoleto, 1477–1547: Humanist and Reformer.* Harvard Univ. Pr. 1959 o.p. Sadoleto and Calvin had a published correspondence over the validity of the Reformation.

Evennet, H. O. *The Spirit of the Counter Reformation.* Univ. of Notre Dame Pr. 1970 pap. $4.95. A positive evaluation of the Catholic Reformation, especially of the Council of Trent, which many historians, both Catholic and Protestant, have understood as a narrowing and hardening of the church's theology and practice.

Gleason, Elizabeth G. *Reform Thought in Sixteenth Century Italy.* Ed. by James A. Massey [*Amer. Academy of Religion Texts & Translations Ser.*] Scholars Pr. GA 1981 text ed. pap. $10.95. In regrettable typescript format, Gleason has translated and edited reforming documents from Italy—some by those who will break with Rome (Ochino) and others by men who will lead reform (G. Carafa, who became Pope Paul IV). Handy sourcebook with clear introductions.

Iggers, Georg G. *New Trends in European Historiography.* Wesleyan Univ. Pr. rev. ed. 1984 pap. $12.95. Obviously for those who want to know how history is written, with the chapter on changes in writing about the Catholic Reformation very clearly set forth.

Janelle, Pierre. *The Catholic Reformation*. Bruce 1949 o.p. Rather a classic telling of the story, with special emphasis on the Catholic humanist as key to the success of the Catholic Reformation. Reads very well.

Jedin, Hubert. *A History of the Council of Trent*. Nelson 5 vols. 1957–63 o.p. This is the standard history that all scholars have used as point of departure. Jedin, who died in 1980, was dean of Catholic historians in Europe. See his listing (above) under Dictionaries, Encyclopedias, Handbooks: Church History.

McNally, Robert E. *The Unreformed Church*. Sheed & Ward 1965 o.p. McNally, a Jesuit, argues that the late medieval church was unreformed in worship, in its view and use of Scripture, in its administration, and in its spirituality. Thus, he argues that the Reformation was inevitable. Small and easy to follow.

Olin, J. C. *The Catholic Reformation: Savonarola to Ignatius Loyola*. Christian Classics 1969 o.p. A collection of reforming epistles, speeches, confessions, rules for new orders, and the like, all introduced within the context of the Reformation. Not the first book one would consult, but very useful for seeing firsthand what people thought needed reforming.

O'Malley, John W. *Praise and Blame in Renaissance Rome: Rhetoric, Doctrine, and Reform in the Sacred Orators of the Papal Court, 1450–1521*. Duke Univ. Pr. 1979 $25.00. Links Reformation and Renaissance and shows how difficult the role of a reformer was in cosmopolitan Italy.

Schenk, Wilhelm. *Reginald Pole: Cardinal of England*. Longmans 1950 o.p. Long the standard biography of Mary Tudor's chief churchman, a humanist, and a reformer in his own right.

Schroeder, H. J., trans. *Canons and Decrees of the Council of Trent*. TAN Bks. repr. of 1941 ed. 1978 pap. $8.00. The older printing had Latin on one side and English on the other; a recent printing eliminated the Latin. No commentary, but simply the decision of the bishops as finally promulgated.

Wright, A. D. *Counter Reformation: Catholic Europe and the Non-Christian World*. St. Martin's 1982 $25.00. The book ranges widely over a number of subjects, from science to witchcraft, and explores the problems that Catholic theologians had with the doctrine of predestination.

CALVIN, JOHN. 1509–1564

Born Jean Cauvin in Noyon, Picardy, France, Calvin was only a boy when Luther first raised his challenge concerning Indulgences. He was enrolled at age 14 at the University of Paris, where he received preliminary training in theology and became an elegant Latinist. However, following the dictates of his father, he left Paris at age 19 and went to study law, first at Orléans, then at Bourges, in both of which centers the ideas of Luther were already creating a stir.

On his father's death, Calvin returned to Paris, began to study Greek, the language of the New Testament, and decided to devote his life to scholarship. In 1532 he published a commentary on Seneca's *De Clementia*, but the following year, after experiencing a "sudden conversion," he was forced to flee Paris for his religious views. The next year was given to the study of

Hebrew in Basel, and to writing the first version of his famous *Institutes of the Christian Religion*, which he gave to the printer in 1535.

The rest of his life—except for a forced exile of three years—he spent in Geneva, where he became chief pastor, without ever being ordained. When he died, the city was solidly on his side, having almost become what one critic called a "theocracy." By then the fourth and much-revised edition of his *Institutes* had been published in Latin and French, commentaries had appeared on almost the whole Bible, treatises had been written on the Lord's Supper, on the Anabaptists, and on secret Protestants under persecution in France. Thousands of refugees had come to Geneva, and the city— energized by religious fervor—had found room and work for them. Though Calvin was sometimes bitter in his denunciation of those who disagreed with him, intolerant of other points of view, absolutely sure he was right on the matter of predestination, he was nonetheless one of the great expounders of the faith. From his work the Reformed tradition had its genesis, and from his genius continues to refresh itself.

BOOKS BY CALVIN

Calvin's Commentaries. Baker Bk. 22 vols. repr. 1979 $495.00. For the Old Testament only nineteenth-century translations of the commentaries are available in English.

Calvin's New Testament Commentaries. Ed. by David W. Torrance and Thomas F. Torrance, Eerdmans 12 vols. 1960 set $131.40. Unlike the case with Luther, there is no English compendium of all of Calvin's works, thus the multiple listings.

Calvin: Institutes of the Christian Religion. Trans. by Ford Lewis Battles, ed. by John T. McNeill [*Lib. of Christian Class.*] Westminster 2 vols. 1960 $34.95. Calvin's major theological work.

Calvin: Theological Treatises. Ed. by J. K. S. Reid [*Lib. of Christian Class.*] Westminster 1978 pap. $8.95. Most shorter writings, translated with notes, including church ordinances, catechisms, church visitation orders, his reply to Cardinal Sadoleto, and more.

Tracts and Treatises of the Reformed Faith. Ed. and trans. by Thomas F. Torrance and Henry Beveridge, Eerdmans 3 vols. 1958 o.p. A larger selection than Reid's work (see below).

BOOKS ABOUT CALVIN

Armstrong, Brian G. *Calvinism and the Amyraut Heresy: Protestant Scholasticism and Humanism in Seventeenth-Century France.* Univ. of Wisconsin Pr. 1969 $30.00. Very early the tensions in predestinarian theology began to surface, as did questions of how the new Protestantism should be expressed theologically.

Balke, Willem. *Calvin and the Anabaptist Radicals.* Trans. by William J. Heynen, Eerdmans 1982 o.p. Examination of Calvin's polemics against religious left wingers. Somewhat biased toward Calvin.

Cochrane, Arthur C. *Reformed Confessions of the Sixteenth Century.* Westminster 1966 o.p. Confessions from Switzerland, Germany, France, and Belgium, influenced by Zwingli and Calvin.

Douglass, Jane D. *Women, Freedom, and Calvin.* Westminster 1985 pap. $11.95. Only serious study of Calvin's "feminist" position by a major historian.

Dowey, Edward A. *The Knowledge of God in Calvin's Theology.* Columbia Univ. Pr. 1952 o.p. Classic work on how God is known in Calvin's thought.

Duffield, Gervase, ed. *John Calvin.* Eerdmans 1966 o.p. Articles by major Calvin scholars on various aspects of his thought and activity.

Graham, W. Fred. *The Constructive Revolutionary: John Calvin and His Socio-Economic Impact.* Michigan State Univ. Pr. repr. 1987 $9.95. After a brief history of Calvin in Geneva, this work summarizes Calvin's social and economic thought and assesses its influence. Also examines Weber's thesis on Calvinism and capitalism.

Höpfl, Harro. *The Christian Polity of John Calvin.* Cambridge Univ. Pr. 1985 pap. $14.95. Best work on Calvin's understanding of church and state.

Innes, William C. *Social Concern in Calvin's Geneva.* Pickwick 1983 pap. $22.50. Less Calvin and more Geneva than Graham (above).

Leith, John H. *Introduction to the Reformed Tradition: A Way of Being in the Christian Community.* John Knox rev. ed. 1981 pap. $10.95. Complements McNeill (below) with more on theological development, liturgy, and impact on culture.

McDonnell, Kilian. *John Calvin, the Church and the Eucharist.* Princeton Univ. Pr. 1967 o.p. Roman Catholic priest sympathetically examines doctrines of the church and of Christ's presence in Holy Communion.

McKim, Donald K. *Readings in Calvin's Theology.* Baker Bk. 1984 pap. $15.95. Includes helpful excerpts from McNeill (below), Battles (above), who translated *Institutes,* and many more.

McNeill, J. T. *The History and Character of Calvinism.* Oxford 1967 pap. $12.95. This is the single best overview of Calvinism's later history, including Huguenots, Presbyterians, and others in the Reformed churches.

Monter, E. William. *Calvin's Geneva.* Krieger repr. of 1967 ed. 1975 o.p. Good for relations between church and state, Calvin and city government in Geneva.

Muller, Richard A. *Christ and the Decree: Christology and Predestination in Reformed Theology from Calvin to Perkins.* Labyrinth Pr. 1986 lib. bdg. $30.00. Best place to examine predestination in Calvin and his followers.

Parker, T. H. *John Calvin: A Biography.* Westminster 1976 $10.95. By all accounts the best and most up-to-date biography.

Partee, Charles, ed. *Calvin and Classical Philosophy.* Heinman 1977 $30.00. Examines Calvin's uses of the ancients and argues that Calvin is not a philosopher, but a pure theologian.

Reid, W. S., ed. *John Calvin: His Influence in the Western World.* [*Contemporary Evangelical Perspectives Ser.*] Zondervan 1982 o.p. Articles on Calvinistic influence on various Western nations. No other work does this with any system.

Richard, Lucien J. *The Spirituality of John Calvin.* John Knox 1974 o.p. By a Roman Catholic, a careful study of Calvin's piety or Christian "life-style."

Selinger, Suzanne. *Calvin against Himself: An Inquiry in Intellectual History.* Shoe String 1984 $29.50. A psychological study of Calvin by an art historian that is raising controversy. Carefully considers other scholarship and relates Calvin to Luther.

Wendel, François. *Calvin: Origins and Development of His Religious Thought.* Trans. by Philip Mairet, Labyrinth Pr. 1986 pap. $14.95. Classic study and one of the first works to read on Calvin, along with Parker's biography (see above).

Wolterstorff, Nicholas. *Until Justice and Peace Embrace.* Eerdmans 1983 $13.95. Although a philosophy of economics in the modern world, this gives an excellent account of Calvin's social thought and its economic consequences.

IGNATIUS OF LOYOLA, SAINT. 1491–1556

Inigo Lopez de Loyola was born into a wealthy Basque family in northern Spain. Small, but quick of mind and body, he won appointment as a page to a wealthy confidant and treasurer to King Ferdinand. Filling his mind with chivalrous and amorous adventures from popular books, he was fired with a militant ardor that was later to transfer readily from secular to religious activities. As a young man he was cited several times for acts of violence. When the French invaded Navarre in 1521 and attacked Pamplona, Loyola counseled defense to the death, and during the subsequent bombardment one of his legs was broken and the other injured by a cannonball. The small garrison surrendered; Loyola's life changed abruptly.

Recovering from his wounds and the operations undergone to lengthen his broken leg, Ignatius (as he now began to call himself) turned to reading stories of the saints and of Christ. He quickly developed an aversion to worldly ideals and resolved to serve and imitate Christ alone. He lived in a cave in Manresa for 11 months in total poverty and there finished the first edition of his *Spiritual Exercises*. Though they were not finished to his satisfaction until 1541, he soon began to use them to help retreat leaders and penitents to structure their days of devotion.

After a brief visit to Jerusalem, he returned to Spain where he continually fell afoul of the Inquisition. To escape its restrictions, he traveled to the University of Paris, took a master's degree in philosophy, and gathered a company of nine companions who, in 1540, were canonically confirmed by Pope Pius III as the Society of Jesus. The next year he was elected superior-general for life. Loyola's amazing abilities as spiritual director, organizer, and money raiser are revealed in his massive correspondence and in the instant success of his new order. By the time of his death, the society numbered nearly 1,000 members. Already they were leaders in the Catholic Reformation, missionaries wherever Spanish and Portuguese ships sailed, and faculty for the many seminaries the church set up to counter the Protestant insistence on an educated ministry. Ignatius was canonized in 1622.

BOOKS BY ST. IGNATIUS

The Autobiography of St. Ignatius Loyola, with Related Documents. Trans. by Joseph F. O'Callaghan, Peter Smith 1974 $16.00. His own account, well edited and translated.

Spiritual Exercises. Trans. by Lewis Delmage, Daughters of St. Paul 1978 $4.00 pap. $2.25; trans. by Louis J. Puhl, Loyola Univ. Pr. 1968 o.p. Many translations of and commentaries on this spiritual classic have been published over the years; these are fairly recent and readable.

BOOKS ABOUT ST. IGNATIUS

Brodrick, James. *The Origin of the Jesuits*. Greenwood repr. of 1940 ed. 1971 lib. bdg. $22.50. Good introduction for beginning students, since the author curbs himself to about 275 pages of material on Loyola and his small band of proto-Jesuits.

——. *St. Ignatius Loyola: The Pilgrim Years, 1491–1538*. Farrar 1956 o.p. Solid and adulatory, as befits one Jesuit writing about the founder of the Society of Jesus.

Rahner, Karl, and Paul Imhof. *Ignatius of Loyola.* Collins 1979 $14.95. An interpretive essay with splendid old engravings and color photographs. This is the coffee-table Ignatius, if one can characterize anything with an essay by Rahner so simply.

LUTHER, MARTIN. 1483–1546

At age 22, the young Luther, destined for a career in law, was so terrified during an electrical storm that he vowed to become a monk. Two years later he was ordained a priest, but this did not quiet the storms raging in his soul. Despite incessant prayer, fasting, self-flagellation, and a journey to Rome for his Augustinian order, the fear of hell clung to him, causing bitter depressions that he called *Anfechtungen* (onslaughts). His superior, John Staupitz, pushed him into studying for a doctorate in theology, a degree he earned at Wittenberg a year after going there to teach in 1511.

At Wittenberg, a university founded in 1502 by the prince elector of Saxony, Frederick the Wise, he worked through the letters of Paul, finally understanding—in what he afterward called his "tower experience"—that being right with God (justification) is a matter of faith or trust in the death of Christ for one's sins, not a matter of performing enough meritorious works to induce God to be merciful. However, no sooner had he begun to experience the release and joy of sins forgiven than he felt compelled to fight the traffic in Indulgences in Germany. Indulgences, paper writs promising release from purgatory, which were being hawked across the river from Wittenberg and attracting people from the city, seemed to Luther to promise salvation upon the payment of money. In protest, he posted his Ninety-five Theses (whether by nailing or mailing is not clear), which soon led to trouble with Rome. It was by the sale of Indulgences that the archbishop of Mainz was recouping the vast sums he had paid the pope to secure a second princedom within the church. When the popularity of Luther's attack led to decreased sales, the church was forced to take notice, and a series of debates over church authority ensued that further radicalized the priest-professor. In 1520, Luther was excommunicated by the pope, and he began seriously that same year to urge reformation of church and society in three treatises: *An Address to the German Nobility; The Babylonian Captivity* (in which he argued that there are but two sacraments); and *The Freedom of the Christian Man.*

Outlawed by the Emperor Charles V after his appearance at the imperial Diet of Worms ("Here I stand, I can do no other"), he was given protection by Frederick and spent his remaining years translating the Bible from the original languages into German (completed in 1534), reforming the church in those parts of Germany where the rulers were favorable, preaching, engaging in doctrinal debate, and teaching his beloved students at the University of Wittenberg. In 1525 he married a former nun, Katherina von Bora, and they raised six children.

Luther is credited—or blamed—for the origin of Protestantism and praised for his translation of the Bible and for setting in his home life the ideal for the Lutheran pastor's family. He died while visiting churches, and his work was carried forward by his young friend and scholar Philip Melanchthon. Perhaps the most noteworthy item in modern scholarship about Luther is the high praise he now receives from many Roman Catholic scholars, who admire his courage and his theology, while deploring the split he created in Western Christendom.

BOOKS BY LUTHER

Works. Concordia and Fortress Pr. 55 vols. 1955– various prices. The German edition of Luther's writings now stands at 110 volumes and the count is still rising. The English translation gives students a chance to read much of Luther, although there are still gaps in the offerings. For a helpful guide to the translation, there is a cross-reference and index by Heinrich J. Vogel.

Three Treatises. Trans. by C. M. Jacobs and others, Fortress Pr. rev. ed. 1970 pap. $4.50. Luther's three treatises of 1520 drew widespread support for him in Germany; his excommunication followed.

BOOKS ABOUT LUTHER

Althaus, Paul. *The Theology of Martin Luther.* Trans. by Robert C. Schultz, Fortress Pr. 1966 $16.95. By the dean of German Luther scholars. Very sympathetic.

Atkinson, James. *Martin Luther and the Birth of Protestantism.* John Knox repr. of 1968 ed. 1981 pap. $5.25. Deals with both his life and theology in readable style.

Bainton, Roland H. *Here I Stand: A Life of Martin Luther.* 1950. New Amer. Lib. pap. 1977 $3.95; Peter Smith $13.75. Superb and popular study with many illustrations; has gone through many printings and still fascinates.

Boehmer, Heinrich. *Martin Luther: Road to Reform.* Trans. by John W. Doberstein and Theodore G. Tappert, Meridian 1957 o.p. Shows the young Luther and his development toward the role of reformer.

Dickens, A. G. *Martin Luther and the Reformation.* Harper 1969 o.p. Useful for beginning students. Contains 184 pages with illustrations but no bibliography.

Edwards, Mark U. *Luther's Last Battles: Politics and Polemics, 1531–1546.* Humanities text ed. 1983 $28.50. By 1530, when he was 47, Luther had been excommunicated, married (at age 41), and the Augsburg Confession had been adopted. Biographers have tended to overlook his last 15 years. Edwards deals with his anger and frustration, relationship with Jews, his hopes, fears, and his death.

Edwards, Mark U., and George Tavard. *Luther: A Reformer for the Churches—An Ecumenical Study Guide.* Fortress Pr. 1983 pap. $5.50; Paulist Pr. 1983 pap. $4.95. Only 96 pages with a bibliography, the dual publication indicates its use in Protestant and Catholic study groups. Both authors are distinguished scholars in the Reformation period.

Erikson, Erik H. *Young Man Luther.* Norton 1962 pap. $5.95. Neo-Freudian interpretation of Luther's conversion experience; on this study John Osborne based his play *Luther.*

Gerrish, Brian A. *Grace and Reason: A Study in the Theology of Luther.* [*Midway Repr. Ser.*] Univ. of Chicago Pr. 1979 text ed. pap. $11.00. Although a doctoral dissertation-turned-book, it is clear and useful in the controversy over Luther's use of philosophy.

Harran, Marilyn J. *Luther on Conversion: The Early Years.* Cornell Univ. Pr. 1983 $29.95. Analyzes Luther's thoughts on conversion with a final word on his own. Read this with Erikson (see above).

Hendrix, Scott H. *Luther and the Papacy: Stages in a Reformation Conflict.* Fortress

Pr. 1981 $15.95. Definitive work on Luther's gradual disenchantment with the papacy and his final dismissal of the pope as Antichrist.

Manns, Peter. *Martin Luther: An Illustrated Biography.* Intro. by Jaroslav Pelikan, Crossroad NY 1983 $14.95. The only coffee-table Luther.

Olin, John C., and others, eds. *Luther, Erasmus and the Reformation: A Catholic-Protestant Reappraisal.* Greenwood repr. of 1969 ed. 1982 lib. bdg. $22.50. Has articles by some of the best-known scholars on the two Reformation figures, and on the aftermath of their polemics concerning the freedom or bondage of the human will. One needs to know something of the thought of each to appreciate this volume.

Olivier, Daniel. *Luther's Faith: The Cause of the Gospel in the Church.* Concordia 1982 pap. $13.95. Outstanding Roman Catholic interpretation of Luther's theology published by the most conservative Lutheran publisher.

Prenter, Reginald. *Spiritus Creator.* Muhlenberg Pr. 1953 o.p. Classic study of the Holy Spirit as corollary to Luther's insistence on the centrality of the Bible.

Rupp, Gordon. *Luther's Progress to the Diet of Worms.* Harper 1964 o.p. By the dean of Luther scholars, very useful for Luther's earlier thought and work.

Rupp, Gordon, and Philip S. Watson, eds. *Luther and Erasmus: Free Will and Salvation.* Westminster 1978 pap. $8.95. Luther insisted that the human will is not free, and Erasmus publicly disagreed. This confirmed Erasmus in his determination not to follow Luther's revolt. Both their treatises on the freedom and bondage of the will are edited and translated in this useful volume.

Schwiebert, Ernest G. *Luther and His Times: The Reformation from a New Perspective.* Concordia 1950 $23.95. In 900 pages, the most exhaustive study of Luther and his environment, including Wittenberg, its ruler, and its university. Very pro-Luther.

Steinmetz, David C. *Luther and Staupitz: An Essay in the Intellectual Origins of the Protestant Reformation.* Duke Univ. Pr. 1980 $18.50. Where did Luther get his theology? From his Augustinian superior, or must we look elsewhere? A necessary study in the origins of Luther's thought.

Tappert, Theodore G., ed. and trans. *The Book of Concord: The Confessions of the Evangelical Lutheran Church.* Fortress Pr. 1959 $14.95. This book amounts to the confessional digest of Lutheran theology. It contains some of Luther's own works, such as his *Small Catechism*, the Augsburg Confession (1530), and the Formula of Concord (1580), which capped Lutheran theology a generation after Luther.

Todd, John. *Luther: A Life.* Crossroad NY 1982 $17.50. Up-to-date appreciation of Luther from Roman Catholic viewpoint.

MENNO SIMONS. 1496?–1561

Little is known of Menno's early life, except that he was of peasant stock, went to monastic schools, and that he was ordained a Praemonstratensian Order priest in 1524 and served several parishes in his native Friesland. His religious struggles began while he was relatively young, according to his own accounts, and centered on the sacraments. That he had difficulty affirming the real presence of Christ in the bread and wine of the Mass does not necessarily mean that the influence of Luther had reached his North Sea region, for antisacramentarian views had long permeated the Low Countries. He also rejected the validity of infant baptism, but this seems to have come after he began serious study of the Bible.

By 1528 he had become known as an Evangelical preacher, and by 1536 he found it prudent to go into hiding. The next year he became the leader of some scattered Anabaptist groups, and at about the same time he married. No doubt many of his followers were people who had been confused over the Anabaptist takeover of the city of Münster, the institution of polygamy and religious terror there, and the destruction of the conspiracy by combined Lutheran and Catholic forces in 1535.

Although one can fruitfully study Menno's thought by examining his views on the sacraments, or pacifism, or even on the "heavenly flesh" of Jesus (a view found in some of the church fathers), it is really his doctrine of the church that anchors his thought and that of the Mennonites, followers who took his name to define themselves. Luther and Calvin worked for a pure church, but Menno insisted on one. Since the church is the pure bride of Christ, it must be pure; thus, excommunication and the ban (exclusion from the church and shunning of those excluded) became marks of the true church. Unfortunately, such rigor produces division, and, to combat it, Menno's writings took on a harshness that had not been there in the beginning. Harried, persecuted, a price on his head, he finally settled in Holstein and continued to guide Anabaptist thought and practice by his pen until his death.

BOOK BY MENNO SIMONS

The Complete Writings of Menno Simons. Ed. by John C. Wenger, trans. by Leonard Verduin, Mennonite Pub. 1983 $24.95. Includes a brief biography by Harold S. Bender. This is the basic source for anyone who does not read Dutch.

BOOKS ABOUT MENNO SIMONS

Krahn, Cornelius. *Dutch Anabaptism.* Herald Pr. 1981 o.p. Devotes considerable attention to Menno Simons, as well as examining proto-Anabaptism in the Netherlands.

Littell, Franklin H. *A Tribute to Menno Simons: A Discussion of the Theology of Menno Simons, and Its Significance for Today.* Herald Pr. 1971 o.p. Highly adulatory and by a non-Anabaptist.

ZWINGLI, HULDRYCH (also HULDREICH). 1484–1531

Although of peasant stock, Zwingli's family was well off, and he received a first-rate education, culminating with a master's degree at the University of Basel in 1506. In that year he became parish priest in Glarus, where his pastoral duties led him to question the sending of Swiss youth as mercenary soldiers to Italy. Despite his doubts, he served as chaplain to the Glarus contingent of the pope's armies in 1513 and 1515 and earned a papal pension for his good work. Because he was in the good graces of Rome, his earliest movements for reform were not opposed by the church.

He pursued his interests in classical studies and music, corresponded with the famous humanist ERASMUS, and by 1516—a year before Luther wrote his Ninety-five Theses against the traffic in Indulgences—had probably reached what came to be Protestant convictions about the role of Scripture and justification by faith. After serving for two years as pastor in Einsiedeln, he was called to the office of people's priest at the Great Minster in Zurich, although some objected to his passion for music, and others to his passion for a young girl he was said to have seduced (and probably had). In 1520, his reforming views having become stronger, he persuaded the city council to back him in a move requiring scriptural support for all the affairs of the church. Since the Bible does not explicitly require celibacy for church leaders, Zwingli was free to marry, which he did in 1524.

As it became clearer that Zwingli, like Luther, was breaking with Rome, opposition to him began to harden. On the one hand, some former supporters now wanted more radical reformation: they wished to sever connections between church and state and insisted on believers' baptism. After many debates, a number of such opponents were arrested and one even put to death, ironically, by drowning. On the other hand were those Swiss cantons that wanted to remain Roman Catholic. Their opposition led to military conflict, and Zwingli, once more acting as chaplain, was killed during an intercantonal battle at Kappel in 1531. He was succeeded as pastor by his son-in-law Heinrich Bullinger, whose writings probably had a much greater influence on the subsequent progress of the Reformation, especially on its Reformed side.

In 1529, two years before his death, Zwingli had met at Marburg with Luther and other reformers in an attempt to mend their differences. Only the question of the Eucharist proved beyond agreement. Luther insisted that the risen Jesus gives his flesh to those who receive Communion, taking the words "This is my body" with a literalism that Zwingli, ever the rational humanist, could not accept. The break was unmendable.

BOOK BY ZWINGLI

Selected Writings of Huldrych Zwingli. [*Pittsburgh Theological Monographs: New Ser.*] Pickwick 2 vols. 1984 ea. $19.95. Vol. 1, *The Defense of the Reformed Faith*, trans. by E. J. Furcha; Vol. 2, *In Search of True Religion: Reformation, Pastoral, and Eucharistic Writings*, trans. by H. Wayne Pipkin.

BOOKS ABOUT ZWINGLI

Baker, J. Wayne. *Heinrich Bullinger and the Covenant: The Other Reformed Tradition.* Ohio Univ. Pr. 1980 $24.95. About the only recent work on Zwingli's son-in-law, head pastor of the church in Zurich after Zwingli died, who had a great influence not only in Switzerland, but in the Rhineland and England through his published sermons.

Bromiley, G. W., ed. *Zwingli and Bullinger.* [*Lib. of Christian Class.*] Westminster 1979 pap. $8.95. Lengthy excerpts from the writings of the two churchmen. The student can always depend on Library of Christian Classics for solid translation, editing, and commentary.

Courvoisier, Jacques. *Zwingli: A Reformed Theologian.* John Knox 1963 o.p. Accurate, but very brief, and therefore for the beginning student.

Farner, Oskar. *Zwingli the Reformer: His Life and Work.* Shoe String 1968 o.p. About 100 pages, very readable and, like Courvoisier, accurate.

Potter, G. R. *Zwingli.* Cambridge Univ. Pr. 1984 pap. $18.95. Most recent biography, up-to-date, very careful and readable. Probably best single work. Maps and bibliography. Not to be confused with the author's *Ulrich Zwingli* (1977), which is a bibliography on the Swiss reformer, published in London by the Historical Association.

Rilliet, Jean. *Zwingli: Third Man of the Reformation*. Trans. by Harold Knight, Westminster 1964 o.p. A standard work that reads easily. More popular than Potter, less so than Courvoisier or Farner (see their entries above).

Stephens, W. P. *The Theology of Huldrych Zwingli*. Oxford 1985 $52.00. The only full discussion of his theology in English, although Potter's biography also contains a good discussion of Zwingli's thought.

THE REFORMATION IN ITS LATER DEVELOPMENTS: 1560–1648

One of the frustrations of historians is dividing history into periods. It is necessary to do so, if only to teach courses that end when the semester ends, and to write books with beginnings and endings. One way to periodize the Reformation Era is to take a date of about 1560 and say that from 1517, when Luther posted his Ninety-five Theses (whether he nailed them or mailed them, we can at least say that he "posted" them), until about 1560 the Reformation was in its formative stage. So from then to 1648, when the Treaty of Westphalia ended the Thirty Years' War in Germany and pretty much set the present Catholic-Protestant boundaries, comes the Later Period, or the Consolidation, or (in Lewis Spitz's term) its Second Surge.

A number of deaths and settlements makes 1560 an attractive date to distinguish the fresh movements for reform from its Consolidation in both Catholic and Protestant circles. In 1564 the reforming Catholic Council of Trent finished its work of internal reform, but most of the reforming had yet to be done. Luther died in 1546, the year after the council began; and Calvin died in 1564, the year before it ended. In England the Elizabethan Settlement was ratified by Parliament in 1559, and that same year John Knox came to Scotland and introduced the Reformation there, that great "spider that sat down beside her" (Mary Queen of Scots).

But this periodization does not fit in every region. France became embroiled in its terrible Wars of Religion soon after 1560, and peace did not come conclusively until the Protestant Henry of Navarre, later Henry IV of France and converted to Catholicism, granted his former fellow Protestants partial freedom in his Edict of Nantes in 1598. In Ireland one can hardly say that the Reformation was over in 1648, for it was not until 1690 that Catholic James II, deposed as King of England the year before, was defeated by his Protestant son-in-law, William III, at the Boyne. It was that victory that sealed Ireland in its present mold, with Ulster largely a Protestant enclave in a Catholic island.

Our treatment will be much more cursory here, although the Puritan rebellion in England will be well annotated. A few last sections will conclude the Reformation Era, including one on Art and the Reformation.

Post-Luther Lutheranism in Germany and Scandinavia

Theologically Lutherans had to formulate Luther's somewhat sprawling theology into something approaching a system. Most historians of theology think issues such as Christ's presence in Holy Communion were pretty well solidified by 1580, when the Formula of Concord became the norm for Lutheran theology. In terms of expansion, the various Scandinavian countries all became predominantly Lutheran by the end of the century. This was fortunate, for it was only the intervention by Sweden's King Gustavus Adolphus in the Thirty Years' War (1618–48) that saved Protestantism in Germany from being destroyed or exiled by the Hapsburg Empire. The Treaty of Westphalia (1648) is always used by German historians to mark the end of the Reformation Era, since it required the various principalities of Germany to take on the religion of the local ruler, so that even today Germany is Lutheran or Catholic or (in a few places) Reformed on the basis of that treaty.

The Thirty Years' War is standard work for secular histories, so no books for that conflict will be listed below. Instead, consult the chapter on World History in Volume 3.

Bergendoff, Conrad J. *Olavus Petri and the Ecclesiastical Transformation in Sweden (1521–1552): A Study in the Swedish Reformation.* AMS Pr. repr. of 1928 ed. 1985 $32.50. It is difficult to find good work in English on the Reformation in Sweden and Finland. (See Michael Roberts below.)

Dunkley, Ernest H. *The Reformation in Denmark.* [*Church Historical Society Ser.*] Allenson 1948 o.p. A brief study that is clear and concise. The brief bibliography—almost every work written in Danish—shows how hard it is to find sustained studies of the Reformation in Denmark.

Elert, Werner. *The Structure of Lutheranism: The Theology and Philosophy of Life of Lutheranism, 16th and 17th Centuries.* Trans. by Walter A. Hansen, Concordia 1974 pap. $13.95. Discusses the arguments before and after the Formula of Concord (1580), which united German Lutheranism in one line of thought.

Jungkuntz, Theodore R. *Formulators of the Formula of Concord.* Concordia 1977 pap. $8.50. A study of those like Brenz, who forged Lutheran Orthodoxy after Luther.

Klug, Eugene F. *From Luther to Chemnitz on Scripture and the Word.* Eerdmans 1971 o.p. Lutheranism grew much more conservative in its understanding of Scripture after Luther, who had a tendency to dismiss Scriptures that "preached not Christ."

Larsen, Karen. *A History of Norway.* Princeton Univ. Pr. 1948 $60.00. A large work, but only two chapters on the Reformation in Norway. Unfortunately, writers in English are only interested in Vikings, and the rest of Norwegian history is a blank.

Lohff, Wenzel, and Lewis Spitz, eds. *Discord, Dialogue, and Concord: Studies in the Lutheran Reformation's Formula of Concord.* Fortress Pr. 1977 o.p. Excellent study of the formation of Lutheran Orthodoxy after Luther. Melanchthon's role is given particular attention in several of the articles.

Manschreck, Clyde L. *Melanchthon: The Quiet Reformer.* Greenwood repr. of 1958 ed. 1975 lib. bdg. $27.25. A classic study of Luther's friend and colleague that is careful and trustworthy. In 350 pages, both his life and doctrine are examined.

Midelfort, H. C. Erik. *Witch Hunting in Southwest Germany, 1562–1684: The Social and Intellectual Foundations.* Stanford Univ. Pr. 1972 $26.50. Sometimes historians forget that religion is more than worship and doctrine. It is also fear, superstition, alienation, and death. This book, with its big bibliography on witchcraft during the period, is highly regarded by those who research this field.

Moeller, Bernd. *Imperial Cities and the Reformation: Three Essays.* Ed. and trans. by H. C. Erik Midelfort and Mark U. Edwards, Jr., Labyrinth Pr. repr. of 1972 ed. 1982 text ed. pap. $5.95. The cities that hosted officials of the Hapsburg Empire tended to go Protestant. Why? An early study that has been supplemented somewhat by later ones of individual cities.

Pauck, Wilhelm. *The Heritage of the Reformation.* Free Pr. 1961 o.p. Good summary of the positive and negative effects of the Reformation Era.

Preus, Robert D. *The Theology of Post-Reformation Lutheranism.* Concordia 1972 $16.95. Comprehensive on Lutheran thought and struggle from the late sixteenth to the early eighteenth century, by an author sympathetic to the dogmatics of Lutheran Orthodoxy. Excellent coverage for Lutheran argument and post-Luther personalities.

Roberts, Michael. *The Early Vasas: A History of Sweden, 1523–1611.* Cambridge Univ. Pr. 1968 o.p. A new edition is planned soon of this good, comprehensive study of both religion and politics as Sweden became Protestant.

———. *Gustavus Adolphus: A History of Sweden, 1611–1632.* Longmans 3 vols. 1953–58 o.p. A follow-up to the preceding entry. If only we had comparable studies of the Reformation period in the rest of Scandinavia! Not having those we are left with Dunkley (see above) on Denmark or general histories like Larsen's for Norway (see above). Roberts also handles the Reformation in Finland, which was under the control of Sweden at the time.

Scharlemann, R. P. *Thomas Aquinas and John Gerhard.* Yale Univ. Pr. 1964 o.p. Gerhard (1582–1637) was the greatest theologian of post-Lutheran Orthodoxy. Aquinas is examined as well in order to see just how scholastic later Lutheran theology became, since Aquinas was the dean of the medieval schoolmen.

Strauss, Gerald. *Luther's House of Learning: Indoctrination of the Young in the German Reformation.* Johns Hopkins Univ. Pr. 1979 o.p. When it appeared, arguing that Luther's Reformation penetrated into the faith of the people very, very slowly, this book caused quite a stir. It is a seminal work, and his thesis, like Delumeau's, needs challenging to see whether it is true.

Waddams, Herbert M. *The Swedish Church.* Greenwood repr. of 1946 ed. 1981 lib. bdg. $22.50. Shows how little work in English has been done on Sweden after Roberts's (see above) monumental labors. Helps put the Reformation in perspective by looking at later church history.

Reformed Struggle after Calvin

The struggles in the Reformed branch were of two kinds: fighting political and religious enemies without, and fighting antipredestinarians within, especially the Arminians in the Netherlands and England. (The struggle between Calvinism—usually in its Puritan form—and Arminianism in England will be dealt with in the next section.) The second struggle was for the very life of Protestantism in France, the Low Countries, the Palatine region of present-day Germany, Hungary, Poland, Rumania, and England. In each place Calvinism was identified as a subversion of the social order, and political and military efforts were made to destroy it. General works such as that of W. Stanford Reid, or McNeill's *The History and Character of*

Calvinism, or Menno Prestwich's *International Calvinism* will need to be consulted for some of these areas. Indeed, for places like Hungary or Rumania, the person who reads English only must be content with the sketchy chapters to be found in general histories of the epoch.

Armstrong, Brian G. *Calvinism and the Amyraut Heresy: Protestant Scholasticism and Humanism in Seventeenth-Century France.* Univ. of Wisconsin Pr. 1969 $30.00. Armstrong argues that under Theodore Beza's leadership, Reformed theology became scholastic, hair-splitting, defending points like predestination, and missing the evangelical core of Calvin's own thought.

Baird, Henry M. *History of the Rise of the Huguenots of France.* AMS Pr. 2 vols. repr. of 1879 ed. 1970 set $90.00 ea. $45.00. A classic, with much information, but dated because of its partisanship.

Bangs, Carl. *Arminius: A Study in the Dutch Reformation.* Ed. by Joseph D. Allison, Zondervan rev. ed. 1985 pap. $10.95. A solid study of the man and the theology that split Calvinism in twain over the issue of predestination and election.

Bray, John. *Theodore Beza's Doctrine of Predestination.* Humanities 1975 o.p. Balanced and judicious study of the doctrine that came to be regarded as both norm and fighting center of Reformed theology.

Davis, Natalie Z. *Society and Culture in Early Modern France: Eight Essays by Natalie Zemon Davis.* Stanford Univ. Pr. 1975 $27.50 pap. $10.95. Eight separate essays, all useful, by one who knows French archives like no other American scholar.

Geyl, Pieter. *The Revolt of the Netherlands 1555–1609.* Barnes & Noble repr. of 1958 ed. 1980 text ed. $26.50 pap. $9.95. The revolt was against Spanish rule, and therefore Calvinism slowly came to be identified with Dutch patriotism. But it was a slow process, and at least half of the Netherlands has remained Roman Catholic to this day. Here is the real (and true) story of cutting dikes to keep enemy troops at bay, as well as less dramatic episodes in Dutch history. Geyl, a noted European scholar, has also written a two-volume work that picks up Dutch history after 1609, *The Netherlands in the 17th Century.*

Gray, Janet G. *The French Huguenots: Anatomy of Courage.* Fwd. by Gordon H. Clark, Baker Bk. 1981 pap. $8.95. The author's sympathies are with the Huguenots, but she tells the story ably. Her graphic account of the Saint Bartholomew's Day Massacre shows why it has always colored Protestant views of Catholic intolerance. See Sutherland for another account.

Kingdon, Robert M. *Myths about St. Bartholomew's Day Massacres, 1572–1576.* Harvard Univ. Pr. 1988 $30.00. The carefully planned killings of Huguenot nobles gathered in Paris for a royal wedding was followed by sporadic massacres throughout France. This study includes accounts of the massacres, both Protestant and Catholic reactions to the massacres, and treatises on politics and religion arising from the atrocities.

Mattingly, Garrett. *The Armada.* Houghton Mifflin 1962 pap. $9.95. A great story, linking the execution of Mary Queen of Scots with the determination of the Spanish king Philip II to do a "Bay of Pigs" on England. Court intrigue in France, the killing of the Protestant nobility on St. Bartholomew's Day—a thundering history written by an outstanding scholar.

Parker, Geoffrey. *The Dutch Revolt.* Cornell Univ. Pr. 1977 $35.00. A good account.

Prestwich, Menno, ed. *International Calvinism.* Oxford 1985 $49.95. Excellent study of various aspects of later Calvinism. Three chapters follow Huguenots in their diaspora after the revocation of the Edict of Nantes (1685); there is a chapter on Scotland, one on Hungary, and other excellent material.

Raitt, Jill. *The Eucharistic Theology of Theodore Beza: Development of the Reformed*

Doctrine. Scholars Pr. GA 1972 pap. $9.95. In the sixteenth century people thought the real differences among the reformers were their views on Christ's presence (or absence) in Holy Communion. This issue divided Luther and Zwingli, as well as later Lutherans and Calvinists. Raitt explores Beza in a brief work (90 pages) with some comparisons to other major thinkers.

Reid, W. Stanford, ed. *John Calvin: His Influence in the Western World.* [*Contemporary Evangelical Perspectives Ser.*] Zondervan 1982 o.p. Articles on Calvinistic influence on various Western nations. Probably covers more nations than any other study, but (except in the chapter on Hungary) assumes that predestination is the hallmark of Reformed theology.

Rothrock, George A. *The Huguenots: A Biography of a Minority.* Nelson-Hall 1979 $21.95. This 200-page work is good for beginning study, with some plates and bibliography. Compare with Gray and Sutherland.

Salmon, J. H. *Society in Crisis: France in the Sixteenth Century.* St. Martin's 1975 o.p. Much good material in this compilation.

Sutherland, N. M. *The Huguenot Struggle for Recognition.* Yale Univ. Pr. 1980 text ed. $40.00. Very scholarly tome in which the author argues that, with Protestantism existing as an aggressive enclave within the body of the nation, it was difficult for France to remain united.

Zoff, O. *The Huguenots.* Trans. by E. B. Ashton and Jo Mayo, Allen & Unwin 1943 o.p. Stimulating work by a friendly Catholic writer who obviously likes the Huguenots.

The Radical Reformation after the Death of Menno Simons, 1561

Historians have not paid much attention to the Anabaptists and others after their early struggles in Switzerland and northern Germany. And much of what has been written is found in denominational histories, some of which will be listed in the appropriate section under Christian Religion in America. Several books that may be helpful are listed here.

Bittinger, Emmert F. *Heritage and Promise: Perspectives on the Church of the Brethren.* Brethren rev. ed. 1983 pap. $6.95. Basic historical survey, with attention to doctrinal controversies and life-style changes.

Durnbaugh, Donald F. *The Believers' Church.* Herald Pr. repr. of 1968 ed. 1985 pap. $12.95. Contains historical sketches of a number of leaders and groups, such as Brethren, Mennonites, Hutterites, and others, and connects them with American churches today.

Durnbaugh, Donald F., and others, eds. *Church of the Brethren Past and Present.* Brethren 1971 pap. $6.95. Various aspects of history, church government, worship, and social concerns for the nonspecialist.

Estep, William R. *The Anabaptist Story.* Eerdmans 1975 pap. $7.95. Basic and accurate on most forms of the left wing of the Reformation and its modern descendants.

The Reformation in Great Britain:
From the Elizabethan Settlement to 1700

No sooner had Elizabeth settled on a uniform policy for religion, when she was disturbed by radicals of two sorts. On one side were the Catholic *récusants* (refusers), who refused to sign the oath acknowledging that she was governor of the church in England; on the other were militant Calvinists, the Puritans, who objected to ceremonialism in worship and to the bishops she appointed to rule the church. These disaffections led in two directions: Catholics were implicated in plots to replace her with Mary Stuart, Queen of Scots, who had fled to England in the 1560s when her marital scandals turned the Scots against her. Elizabeth eventually felt forced to execute her cousin Mary (1587). The radical Protestants, on the other hand, grew in numbers until, two rulers later, they rebelled against Charles I and, led by Oliver Cromwell, established a decade of quasi-religious rule in the land. The rise, triumph, and fall of puritanism has occasioned as vast a body of literature as has Luther's revolt, but only a little of it can be listed below.

Between Elizabeth and the unfortunate Charles—whose head Cromwell removed—was the rule of James VI of Scotland, son of poor Mary, who in 1603 became James I of England. He united the two realms, had a Bible translation named for him, and began the Plantation of Ulster, which led to British control over Ireland until 1921.

ENGLAND

Arnott, Anne. *Valiant for Truth: The Story of John Bunyan.* Fwd. by Blanche Stuart, Eerdmans 1986 pap. $5.95. Compare with Greaves (below). A popular biography of the author of *Pilgrim's Progress,* sympathetic and challenging.

Barbour, Hugh. *The Quakers in Puritan England.* Friends United Pr. repr. of 1964 ed. 1985 pap. $14.95. Solid study that includes George Fox and also the environment against which his movement demands to be studied.

Collinson, Patrick. *The Elizabethan Puritan Movement.* [*Lib. Repr. Ser.*] Methuen 1982 $60.00. Five hundred pages are about all most people want to know about the English Puritans. Here is a straightforward account by a dependable historian.

Foxe, John. *Foxe's Book of Martyrs.* Ed. by W. Grinton Berry, Baker Bk. 1978 pap. $7.95. This book labeled Mary Tudor as "Bloody Mary" for her killing of Protestants and is the first Protestant martyrology, to be followed by many more.

Fraser, Antonia. *Cromwell: The Lord Protector.* D. I. Fine repr. of 1973 ed. 1986 pap. $11.95. In more than 700 pages, this popular historian has included about all that is known of the doughty Puritan soldier and regicide.

———. *King Charles I.* Weidenfeld & Nicolson 1978 o.p. A book on the king Cromwell beheaded.

———. *Royal Charles: Charles II and the Restoration.* Dell 1986 pap. $9.95; Knopf 1979 $19.95. On Charles's son, who came to the throne when Richard Cromwell, inheritor of the Commonwealth on his father's death, proved inadequate to the task.

Greaves, Richard L. *John Bunyan.* Eerdmans 1969 o.p. A good biography of the greatest of the Puritan writers, the tinker-author of *Pilgrim's Progress.*

———. *Society and Religion in Elizabethan England.* Univ. of Minnesota Pr. 1981 o.p. In more than 900 pages the inexhaustible Greaves gives the reader all she or he ever wanted to know about religion, including Puritans and Catholics, in the time of Elizabeth.

Greaves, Richard L., and R. Zaller, eds. *Biographical Dictionary of British Radicals in the Seventeenth Century.* Humanities 1984 text ed. $90.00. Just what the beginning scholar needs to locate all of the English left-wing Puritans and other disturbing people.

Haller, William. *The Rise of Puritanism.* Univ. of Pennsylvania Pr. repr. of 1938 ed.

1972 pap. $14.95. Moderate-sized book by a recognized historian, whose reputation for this solid work remains firm despite later studies.

Hill, Christopher. *Change and Continuity in Seventeenth-Century England.* Harvard Univ. Pr. 1975 $20.00. Hill tends to let his socialism interpret his historiography, but he can be relied on for the facts. As with Collinson (see above), he has a number of books on the sixteenth and seventeenth centuries.

———. *God's Englishman: Oliver Cromwell and the English Revolution.* Harper 1972 pap. $7.95. In about half as many pages as Fraser, Hill discloses Cromwell, leader of a socioreligious revolution. Although Hill's socialism is apparent in a few places, this is pretty straightforward and well written, as befits work by a real scholar in the period.

Hooker, Richard. *Of the Laws of Ecclesiastical Polity.* Ed. by P. G. Stanwood, Harvard Univ. Pr. 1980 text ed. $65.00. Hooker's "laws" have always been regarded by Anglicans as the "middle way" between the extremes of Roman Catholicism and Calvinism.

Jones, Rufus M. *George Fox: Seeker and Friend.* Allen & Unwin 1930 o.p. The best of the old biographies.

Kingdon, Robert M. ed. *"The Execution of Justice in England," by William Cecil, and "A True, Sincere, and Modest Defense of English Catholics," by William Allen.* Cornell Univ. Pr. 1965 o.p. Cecil, premier adviser to Elizabeth I, argues the legitimacy of prosecuting Catholic missionaries to England. Allen, director of the Catholic seminary in Douai, France, where English priests were trained for that mission, argues that it was right for Mary Tudor to kill heretics because heresy was illegal, but not right for Elizabeth since the heresy laws had been expunged from the books. A marvelous study of intolerance from the original documents, expertly edited.

Meyer, Arnold Oskar. *England and the Catholic Church under Queen Elizabeth.* Trans. by J. R. McKee, Routledge & Kegan 1967 o.p. This reprint of an older edition is still regarded as remarkably accurate and dispassionate, as John Bossy says in his introduction to this edition.

Morgan, John. *Godly Learning: Puritan Attitudes towards Reason, Learning, and Education, 1560–1640.* Cambridge Univ. Pr. 1986 $49.50. Americans inherit a Puritan view of education, and this is a very useful book in getting at the heart of Puritan concepts; includes education of the ministers, the "godly household," the role of the teacher, and more.

Noble, Wilfred Vernon. *The Man in Leather Breeches: The Life and Times of George Fox.* Philos. Lib. 1953 o.p. "This popular biography will be enjoyed by readers who like a well-told tale, with plenty of adventure and pathos" (*New Statesman & Nation*).

O'Day, Rosemary. *The English Clergy: The Emergence and Consolidation of a Profession, 1558–1642.* Humanities 1979 o.p. Excellent study of a sometimes privileged and sometimes embattled elite.

Paul, Robert. *The Lord Protector.* Eerdmans 1964 o.p. Of the three books listed on Cromwell himself, this is the only one by an author who sympathizes with his basic commitments; despite that, it is the harshest in its judgment. A very good book.

Seaver, Paul S. *The Puritan Lectureships: The Politics of Religious Dissent, 1560–1662.* Stanford Univ. Pr. 1970 $30.00. Huge bibliography is attached to an important study of the way merchants and others got around laws against Puritan preachers by hiring them to present lectures.

Stannard, David E. *The Puritan Way of Death: A Study in Religion, Culture, and Social*

Change. Oxford 1977 $19.95 pap. $8.95. The kind of study that gets the reader deep into the mind of a culture.

Stone, Lawrence. *The Family, Sex and Marriage: England 1500–1800*. Harper 1977 $30.00 abr. ed. 1980 pap. $8.95. The rise of the modern family is charted—exhaustively. Stone's interdisciplinary work is well known in several fields.

Wallace, Dewey D., Jr. *Puritans and Predestination: Grace in English Protestant Theology, 1525–1695*. [*Studies in Religion*] Univ. of North Carolina Pr. 1982 $29.95. All the theological issues between Puritan and Anglican, Calvinist and Archbishop Laud's style of Arminianism are dealt with carefully in this excellent work.

Walzer, Michael. *The Revolution of the Saints: A Study in the Origins of Radical Politics*. Harvard Univ. Pr. 1982 text ed. pap. $7.95. A seminal work that argues that the Puritan revolt was the public expression of the Western world's conviction that the political realm belongs to people, not to inheritors of privilege. Here is the key to the various ways in which Puritanism broke with the past, and to the rise of capitalism and of modern science, both of which also arose in the Puritan milieu.

Watkins, Owen. *The Puritan Experience*. Schocken 1972 o.p. The Puritans are explored through their diaries.

Wildes, Harry E. *Voice of the Lord: A Biography of George Fox*. Univ. of Pennsylvania Pr. 1964 o.p. The most recent biography, based on contemporary scholarship.

SCOTLAND

The brief list that follows contains works that cover the whole of the Scottish Reformation. Since Cowan, Donaldson, Makey, and Wormald are active historians, one can find in their notes and bibliographies direction for further research.

Cowan, Ian B. *The Scottish Covenanters, 1660–1688*. Verry 1976 o.p. These are the folk whose rejection of Charles I's prayer book sparked a war between Scotland and England, a war that the Puritans in Parliament took advantage of to mount an army against the king, led by Oliver Cromwell.

———. *The Scottish Reformation: Church and Society in Sixteenth-Century Scotland*. St. Martin's 1982 $25.00. By one of the two deans (Donaldson is the other) of Scottish historians.

———, ed. *The Enigma of Mary Stuart*. St. Martin's 1971 o.p. Was she a saint, martyred by cruel Scottish Presbyterians through the agency of her cruel cousin Elizabeth of England? Or was she "our fair devil Queen," as one contemporary Protestant writer called her? Here are all the materials that relate to the decisive points in her reign, where scandal and tragedy conspired to cost her both her son and the throne, and eventually her life. Allows the reader to decide.

Donaldson, Gordon. *All the Queen's Men: Power and Politics in Mary Stewart's Scotland*. St. Martin's 1983 $21.95. Scotland's emeritus church historian gives us an overview of Scotland's nobility at the time of Mary, and the wonder is that she could function at all amid so much duplicity; a truly *katzenjammer* story.

———. *Mary Queen of Scots*. Verry 1974 o.p. Two hundred pages and therefore to be preferred to Fraser's (see below) longer story for those in a hurry. Donaldson repeats some of the documentation of Cowan.

———. *Scotland: The Shaping of a Nation*. David & Charles 1975 o.p. Donaldson is always clear and sometimes argumentative, particularly when he claims that Knox wanted a church run by bishops.

Fraser, Antonia. *Mary Queen of Scots*. Delacorte abr. ed. 1978 $17.95; Dell 1984 pap. $5.95. Fraser's work is always popular and balanced, though the reader gets more Mary and somewhat less social scenery than in the scholarly works about people like Mary, her son James I, and Cromwell.

Henderson, G. D. *Religious Life in Seventeenth-Century Scotland*. Cambridge Univ. Pr. 1937 o.p. Old but good, as he turns from royalty and nobility and General Assembly of the Kirk, to the way the faith was practiced in those turbulent times.

Knox, John. *John Knox's History of the Reformation in Scotland*. Ed. by Ralph S. Walker, State Mutual Bk. 1985 $20.00. This book, which has had several earlier editions, is the place to go for understanding Knox's prophetic self-image as an "Elijah" sent to destroy the religion of "Baal" (Romanism) in Scotland.

McGregor, Geddes. *The Thundering Scot: A Portrait of John Knox*. Westminster 1957 o.p. The briefest of the biographies, written by a man who has distinguished himself in writing theology.

Makey, Walter H. *The Church of the Covenant 1637–1651: Revolution and Social Change in Scotland*. Humanities 1979 text ed. $31.75. Provides a larger look at the Covenanters than Cowan's work, with the aim of examining those who scratched their names in blood as part of a thoroughgoing social revolution.

Reid, W. Stanford. *Trumpeter of God: A Biography of John Knox*. Baker Bk. repr. of 1974 ed. 1982 pap. $8.95. This is the most positive toward the Scottish reformer and is based on a thorough study of the basic sources. Clearly written.

Ridley, Jasper. *John Knox*. Oxford 1968 o.p. This, the most detailed of the books on Knox listed here, is written by the biographer of many of the great names in the Reformation period in Great Britain.

Wormald, Jenny. *Court, Kirk, and Community: Scotland, 1470–1625*. [*New History of Scotland Ser*.] E. Arnold 1981 text ed. pap. $14.95. Highly praised look at three levels of Scottish society during the turbulent years of religious and social revolution.

The Catholic Reformation after the Council of Trent

Probably the best place to begin is with some of the general histories of Christianity or of Christian thought that are gathered at the beginning of the sections on Christian history and again under General Reference Works and Dictionaries, Encyclopedias, Handbooks: Church History in this chapter. Gonzalez, *History of Christian Thought* (Volume 3, Chapters 8 and 14), is highly recommended (see under Dictionaries, Encyclopedias, Handbooks: Ethics and Theology in this chapter). The studies listed below tend either to be regional or to deal with such individuals as Saint Teresa of Avila or Saint John of the Cross.

Bossy, John. *The English Catholic Community, 1570–1850*. Oxford 1976 $39.95 pap. $5.95. Although covering a greater span than our U.S. period, a valuable study especially because it compares Catholic and Protestant groups that were legislated against in Great Britain.

Brodrick, James. *Robert Bellarmine, Saint and Scholar*. Newman Pr. 1961 o.p. This is a rewriting of an earlier two-volume work. Bellarmine, theologian and political thinker, has sometimes been credited with providing part of the theoretical basis for the development of democratic thought.

Copleston, Frederick. *Mediaeval Philosophy: Ockham to Suarez*. Vol. 3, pt. 2 in *The History of Philosophy*. Doubleday 1953 pap. $5.50. Contains a clear account of the thought of the Jesuit Suarez, whose theology most clearly guided the church both at Trent and afterward.

Corish, Patrick J., and Elma Collins, eds. *The Catholic Community in the Seventeenth and Eighteenth Centuries*. Longwood 1981 $9.95 pap. $6.95. Relatively small (155 pages), this book examines the Irish during the Protestant Ascendancy, which began about 1700. A beginner's book and useful for that.

Dunn, Richard S. *The Age of Religious Wars, 1559–1689*. Norton 2d ed. 1979 text ed. pap. $7.95. One means of pushing back Protestantism was the use of force, of which the Thirty Years' War is the best or worst example. Dunn looks at the whole age through the spectacles of warfare.

Garstein, Oskar. *Rome and the Counter-Reformation in Scandinavia*. Universitet 1980 $40.00. Massive scholarship in a neglected area.

John of the Cross, Saint. *The Complete Works of Saint John of the Cross*. Trans. by E. Allison Peers. Newman Pr. 1946 o.p. The writings of Saint John of the Cross and of his friend Teresa of Avila (or Teresa of God) established a "norm for spirituality" for Catholics that has power today. His *Ascent to Mt. Carmel* and *The Dark Night of the Soul* are classics.

Knox, Ronald A. *Enthusiasm: A Chapter in the History of Religion with Special Reference to the Seventeenth and Eighteenth Centuries*. Christian Classics 1983 pap. $14.95. Although even Knox seemed to acquiesce in the common judgment that this is a "bad book," it is nonetheless entertaining in its discussion of two French Catholic movements, Jansenism and Quietism.

O'Connell, Marvin R. *The Counter Reformation: 1559–1610*. Ed. by William L. Langer [*Rise of Modern Europe Ser.*] Harper 1974 o.p. Described as the best work on the Catholic Reformation after the Council of Trent.

Parker, Geoffrey. *Europe in Crisis, 1589–1648*. Cornell Univ. Pr. 1980 pap. $7.95. This small study covers all phases of the Hapsburg emperors' nearly successful attempts to eliminate Protestantism in Germany by military force. Very complete bibliography.

———. *Philip II*. Little, Brown 1978 o.p. Compact study of the Spanish king who managed to bankrupt the richest nation in Europe by his efforts to overcome Protestants by intrigue and by his failed Armada.

———, ed. *The Thirty Years War*. Methuen 1985 $32.95. Articles by various well-known scholars about the last of the great religious wars in which probably one in every three Germans died.

Sedgwick, Alexander. *Jansenism in Seventeenth-Century France: Voices from the Wilderness*. Univ. of Virginia Pr. 1977 $17.95. Jansenism, sometimes called Catholic Calvinism, was a strong force in France and Ireland, and the Jesuits bent every effort to destroy it at Port Royal and in the schools. But as one of its adherents, the philosopher and mathematician Pascal, demonstrated, it was a theology with a heart.

Teresa of Avila, Saint. *The Conquest of the Perfect Love*. Amer. Class. College Pr. 2 vols. 1986 $189.75. Contains a number of her writings, including *The Way of Perfection* and the autobiography, both justly regarded as classics of spiritual devotion. See also her friend Saint John of the Cross (above).

———. *The Interior Castle, or The Mansions*. Amer. Class. College Pr. 2 vols. 1984 set $197.85. Written late in her life to describe the soul's progress through seven mansions to the inmost chamber where it is united with God.

Art and the Reformation

A few works on this subject seem appropriate here. Some of the Protestant groups had a strong Hebrew flavor in their rejection of the graphic and plastic arts in worship and devotion. Here Lutheranism and, in general, Anglicanism demurred. All the churches, Protestant and Catholic, thought highly of music and developed it in various ways, the Protestants especially developing large bodies of congregational hymnody and, in Germany, the chorale.

Andersson, Christiane. *From a Mighty Fortress: Prints, Drawings, and Books in the Age of Luther, 1483–1546*. Pref. by Frederick Cummings, Detroit Institute of Arts 1983 pap. $10.00. This is a 400-page catalog of a large exhibition, with an index that should be useful to art historians interested in the Reformation Era in Germany.

Christensen, Carl C. *Art and the Reformation in Germany*. Ohio Univ. Pr. 1981 $18.95. This book examines both theory and practice among the German reformers, radicals as well as Luther. About as close to a comprehensive book as we have, at least for Germany.

Crew, P. Mack. *Calvinist Preaching and Iconoclasm in the Netherlands, 1544–1569*. Cambridge Univ. Pr. 1978 $37.50. This is not only a good study of image-breaking and the role (or nonrole) of the Calvinist preachers in that, but also of the essentially conservative nature of the early Calvinists in the Low Countries.

Eire, Carlos M. *War against the Idols: The Reformation of Worship from Erasmus to Calvin*. Cambridge Univ. Pr. 1986 $37.50. After a good look at Luther and his response to iconoclasm, the story switches to Geneva and Calvin, where idolatry is seen as the Calvinist "shibboleth." Recent and thorough.

Garside, Charles, Jr. *The Origins of Calvin's Theology of Music, 1536–1553*. [*Transactions Ser.*] Amer. Philosophical Society 1979 o.p. This tiny study distinguishes Luther and Calvin on music.

———. *Zwingli and the Arts*. Da Capo repr. of 1966 ed. 1981 lib. bdg. $25.00. Of all the major reformers Zwingli was the most thoroughly indoctrinated into humanism. Why does he have the reputation of being the one most averse to painting, sculpture, and music? An excellent study.

Harbison, Craig. *The Last Judgment in Sixteenth-Century Northern Europe: A Study of the Relation between Art and the Reformation*. Garland 1976 lib. bdg. $55.00. A dissertation that won an award that included its publication, and critics say it is a commanding study.

Lang, Paul H., ed. *Music in Western Civilization*. Norton 1940 $34.95. Has an excellent discussion of Luther's contribution.

Liemohn, E. *The Chorale*. Muhlenberg Pr. 1953 o.p. Many think the German chorale, especially as developed by J. S. Bach, is the epitome of liturgical music. Here is the classic study of a classic form.

Nettl, Paul. *Luther and Music*. Trans. by Ralph Wood, Russell repr. of 1948 ed. 1967 o.p. Just what the title says. Straightforward study by one who knows the era well.

Panofsky, Erwin. *The Life and Art of Albrecht Dürer*. Princeton Univ. Pr. 1955 $50.00. pap. $20.95. Dürer was already famous when he became a Lutheran and at one point was even hired by Henry VIII. A well-known art historian examines his work and the theological background, including some study of other reformers and their attitudes toward art in religious observance.

Phillips, John R. *The Reformation of Images: Destruction of Art in England, 1535–1669*. Univ. of California Pr. 1974 $34.50. This study moves the reader right through the English Reformation, from Henry VIII through the English Civil War and the temporary victory of the Puritans.

THE AGE OF REASON: CHRISTIANITY
IN THE EIGHTEENTH CENTURY

The eighteenth century is usually dated from the publication of NEWTON's (see also Vol. 5) *Principia Mathematica* in 1689 and ends with the revolutions near the end of the century, especially the French in 1789. It is marked economically as the age of colonial expansion and of the Industrial Revolution. In religion, especially Protestantism, there was a tearing asunder of the Christian soul: on the one hand were felt the strong demands of rational religion, allegiance to a God who made nature's laws and let them be, a religious spirit that found the Bible incredibly crude, primitive, and superstitious; on the other hand were those who centered on the indwelling Spirit of God—the German and Reformed Pietists on the Continent, and the Methodists and Quakers in Great Britain. Catholicism experienced a weakened papacy, so servile to the rulers of the "Catholic bastions" (Daniel-Rops) that Jesuits, attempting to bring a measure of humanity to slaves and people oppressed by colonialism, were suppressed in 1764. This was also the period of John Wesley, whose revivals began Methodism and in whose own experimental spirituality and love for the new sciences of experimentation the sundered soul was reknit.

Aaron, Richard I. *John Locke.* Oxford 3d ed. 1971 $42.00. If historians of the political process look to Locke as the champion of constitutionalism, those in religious history see him as a major force for "natural" or deistic religion, as contrasted with "revealed" or biblical religion.

Chadwick, Owen. *The Popes and European Revolution.* Oxford 1981 $84.00. The first six chapters are an excellent overview of the work of the popes during this period. Chapter 1, "The Religion of the People," is a marvelous look at popular religion in Catholic countries.

Cragg, Gerald R., ed. *The Cambridge Platonists.* Univ. Pr. of Amer. repr. of 1968 ed. 1985 text ed. pap. $17.75. Contains excerpts from the philosopher-theologians whose reasonable faith undoubtedly influenced Newton.

———. *The Church and the Age of Reason.* [*History of the Church Ser.*] Penguin 1961 pap. $4.95. Probably the surest guide to this period, with all the major figures discussed, whether Catholic or Protestant, philosopher or church leader.

———. *From Puritanism to the Age of Reason.* Cambridge Univ. Pr. 1966 o.p. Spans the brief period from the end of Cromwell's Puritan theocracy to this age of skepticism.

———. *Reason and Authority in the Eighteenth Century.* Cambridge Univ. Pr. 1964 o.p. Thoroughly explores the "battle for the Bible" conflict between natural and revealed faith.

Daniel-Rops, Henri. *The Church in the Eighteenth Century.* Vol. 7 in *The History of the Church of Christ.* Trans. by John Warrington, Dutton 1964 o.p. A Roman Catholic viewpoint is interesting for the light it casts on the struggles of Protestantism. The author also surveys the "feeble papacy" and the demise of the Jesuits in the middle of the century.

Frei, Hans W. *The Eclipse of Biblical Narrative: A Study in Eighteenth- and Nineteenth-Century Hermeneutics.* Yale Univ. Pr. 1974 pap. $10.95. "Discusses with unusual sensitivity changes in the way people read the Bible" (Placher).

Gay, Peter. *The Enlightenment: An Interpretation.* Norton 2 vols. Vol. 1, *The Rise of*

Modern Paganism; Vol. 2, *The Science of Freedom* 1977 pap. $11.95; Simon & Schuster rev. ed. 1985 pap. $15.95. Volume 1 focuses on religion and the philosophic issues that contributed to the rise of skepticism, deism, and the like.

Henry, S. C. *George Whitefield: Wayfaring Witness.* Abingdon 1957 o.p. Whitefield, John Wesley's Calvinistic friend, evangelized in England and the colonies and even won the praise of the worldly Ben Franklin.

Hume, David. *A Treatise of Human Nature.* Ed. by T. H. Green and H. Hodge Grose, Darby 2 vols. repr. of 1898 ed. 1981 lib. bdg. $200.00; ed. by L. A. Selby-Bigge and P. H. Nidditch, Oxford 1978 text ed. pap. $10.95; ed. by Ernest G. Mossner, Penguin 1986 pap. $6.95. This tough-minded Scot woke Kant from his "dogmatic slumbers." His understanding of how knowledge is gained undermined both religion and science.

Kant, Immanuel. *Critique of Practical Reason.* Trans. by Lewis W. Beck, Bobbs 1956 pap. $7.20. He argued that there are tenets that must be regarded as true because they are basic to the moral life, such as that God exists, that God rewards and punishes in the afterlife, that the self is free to do right and wrong. On this slender philosophy is Kant's Natural Religion hung.

———. *Religion within the Limits of Reason Alone.* Trans. by Theodore Greene and Hoyt H. Hudson, Harper 1960 pap. $7.95. He equated grace, so important to Luther, not with knowledge of the way of salvation, or with trusting Christ, but with the soul's becoming worthy of God's favor. Here salvation is turned into a free act of the person, thus reversing Luther's stress on God's initiative.

Lessing, Gotthold. *Lessing's Theological Writings: Selections in Translation.* Trans. by Henry Chadwick, Stanford Univ. Pr. repr. ed. 1957 pap. $3.25. His optimistic and rational Christianity was influential on educated Protestants everywhere.

Locke, John. *An Essay Concerning Human Understanding.* Ed. by A. O. Woozley, New Amer. Lib. 1974 pap. $8.95; ed. by Peter H. Nidditch, Oxford repr. of 1975 ed. 1979 text ed. pap. $12.95. He argued that the mind begins as a clear slate, a *tabula rasa,* with no inborn ideas; so moral and religious belief must not be argued on the basis of such ideas, but on the basis of experience, from which come reality and truth.

———. *The Reasonableness of Christianity and a Discourse of Miracles.* Ed. by I. T. Ramsey, Stanford Univ. Pr. 1958 pap. $6.95. Locke's predeist rationalism was prelude to American constitutionalism and to draining the supernatural out of religious thought. The result will be a simple and rational Christianity, one available outside the Scripture, and an end to mystical and theological speculation, in a word, deism.

Nichols, James H. *History of Christianity, 1650–1950: Secularization of the West.* Wiley 1956 o.p. Very surefooted guide through this period. His subtitle indicates the direction of society in matters religious.

Orr, James. *English Deism: Its Roots and Its Fruits.* Eerdmans 1934 o.p. Old but comprehensive and succinct.

Schweitzer, Albert. *J. S. Bach.* Trans. by Ernest Newman, Paganiniana Pubns. 2 vols. 1980 set $19.50. Here is a great soul, *le grand docteur,* writing about Luther's music, soul, Bach.

Weinlick, J. R. *Count Zinzendorf.* Abingdon 1956 o.p. A German noble and churchman, Zinzendorf rescued persecuted Moravians from Bohemia at his estate, Herrnhut, and then brought a colony to Pennsylvania that became part of the Pennsylvania Dutch.

Wirt, Sherwood E., ed. *Spiritual Disciplines: Devotional Writings from the Great Christian Leaders of the Seventeenth Century.* Good News 1983 pap. $7.95. One way to overcome a common assumption that all the leaders were deists except the

Wesleys is to read this little volume of extracts from the writings of so many genuine saints, Catholic and Protestant.

WESLEY, JOHN. 1703–1791

Wesley's life, begun in a poor parish at Epworth in Lincolnshire, spanned the century of the Enlightenment, during which human happiness, based on the new sciences, was confidently predicted. It was also the century of the Industrial Revolution, whose factories swallowed up the new cities' teeming masses, imprisoning them in lives that were brutish and short. His father, Samuel, was a pastor so hated that his parishioners once set their home ablaze; his mother, Susanna, was a practical saint who bore 19 children in 21 years, of whom only nine survived infancy. At age 11, John was sent away to school in London and was soon at Oxford, of which all his memories were pleasant. He left Oxford briefly to be his father's assistant, but in 1729 returned to lecture on Greek and philosophy. There he and his younger brother Charles founded an informal club, which was dubbed by its detractors the Holy Club, and its members derided, because of their dutiful religious observances, as Methodists.

After their father's death, the two Wesleys went to Georgia, to the colony of imprisoned debtors settled by James Oglethorpe. On the voyage they were impressed by the simple faith of some German Moravians who exhibited no fear when their ship was tossed by storms that sent terror to the hearts of the two pious brothers. Things worked out badly in Georgia— there is some mystery about a failed romance there—and the brothers returned to England where John underwent his dark night of the soul. In 1738 that ended when, as he recorded in his journal, "I felt my heart strangely warmed."

The rest of his life John spent in spreading the gospel of the wondrous grace of God throughout Great Britain, including Scotland and Ireland. He rode thousands of miles, organized religious societies in every major center, insisted on loyalty to the Church of England (he was, after all, a priest), wrote copiously, and with Charles published hymnbooks for the societies. There was in John Wesley none of the ignorant ranting of the evangelical preachers. He was an Oxford man, faithful to the church. It was only with the greatest reluctance that he ordained men to preach in the colonies. Above all, he was an organizer of talent and power. Wherever the population was growing and people uprooted from the countryside and thrust into the cities needed a warmhearted message and a practical ministry to help debtors, miners, and the out-of-work, there his ministry made a profound impression. His own failed marriage, his refusal to take the side of the colonies in their just grievances against England, the refusal of the Anglican church to accept his societies as part of its churches—none of these failures dims the brilliance of "this man sent from God, whose name was John."

BOOKS BY WESLEY

The Works of John Wesley. Ed. by Albert Outler, Oxford 1964 o.p. Outler, a scholar who usually works with the ancient fathers of the church, here edited Wesley's works expertly for the person who wants Wesley's life and thought in his own words. Outler is also the author of a biography of Wesley.

The Journal of John Wesley. Ed. by Percy L. Parker, Moody 1974 o.p. The reader can find all four volumes of Wesley's journals, which were published during his lifetime, even as he wrote them. But this condensation will suffice for most.

BOOKS ABOUT WESLEY

Cannon, William R. *The Theology of John Wesley with Special Reference to the Doctrine of Justification.* Univ. Pr. of Amer. repr. of 1974 ed. 1984 text ed. pap. $12.75. Not new, but a competent and moderate-sized work. Schmidt's work (below) is more detailed and in the Germanic style, although also readable.

Green, Vivian H. *The Young Mr. Wesley.* St. Martin's 1965 o.p. A detailed account of Wesley's years as a student at Oxford.

Harmon, Rebecca Lamar. *Susanna, Mother of the Wesleys.* Abingdon rev. ed. 1968 pap. $7.50. One of several available popular studies of John and Charles Wesley's mother. No one seems to write about their father.

Heitzenrater, Richard P. *The Elusive Mr. Wesley: John Wesley His Own Biographer.* Abingdon 2 vols. 1984 pap. ea. $9.75. Allows Wesley to tell in his own words the story of his life, with minimal input from the author.

Lindstrom, Harold. *Wesley and Sanctification: A Study in the Doctrine of Salvation.* Fwd. by Timothy L. Smith, Zondervan repr. of 1946 ed. 1984 pap. $8.95. Wesley theologically is best known for his doctrine of "entire sanctification" or "Christian perfection," although Methodists differ over the centrality of this doctrine. This study focuses on a doctrine that has helped split American Methodists into Wesleyan and plain Methodists.

Pudney, John. *John Wesley and His World.* Scribner 1978 o.p. With 125 illustrations, this is the coffee-table Wesley that all Methodist homes should display.

Schmidt, M. *John Wesley: A Theological Biography.* Abingdon 2 vols. 1962–73 o.p. The definitive theological study of Wesley.

THE AGE OF REVOLUTION: CHRISTIANITY IN THE NINETEENTH CENTURY

If we follow the custom of historians by beginning the century with the French Revolution (1789), and if we think of the enormous changes that people experienced during the 1800s, with all authority seemingly demolished and human thought and expectations turned upside down, we shall capture the spirit of the age in a nutshell: revolution. And it took all forms. In France the royal couple was beheaded; in England DARWIN (see Vol. 5) traced the less than divine descent of man. MARX (see also Vol. 3) set the stage for international communism. Missionaries, Catholic and Protestant, left the relative safety of Europe and America and took the gospel almost literally everywhere. Popes wrote defensive works and great social encyclicals, and in 1870 were declared infallible, under certain conditions. In the bibliography that follows, we shall ignore the so-called warfare between science and religion, for there is a special section on that. The expansion of Western Christianity through missionary labors also has a separate section. And American Christianity we shall handle in the next section as one piece.

There were a number of thinkers of great renown—men like HEGEL and Schleiermacher among the Protestants, and Loisy and Pope Leo XIII for Catholicism—as well as figures of special interest, such as John Henry Newman, England's most celebrated convert to Catholicism, for all of whom references will be found below.

Altholz, Josef L. *Churches in the Nineteenth Century.* Bobbs 1967 o.p. For the beginner, this modest book offers a good starting point. It has the advantage of covering in a brief survey all the churches, including the Eastern Orthodox, and all the movements.

Barry, Colman J., ed. *Readings in Church History.* Christian Classics 3 vols. in 1 1985 pap. $50.00. Almost everything is covered here in succinct summaries, with each section loaded with major statements or excerpts from major writers. For example, the declaration by Pope Pius IX on the Immaculate Conception of the Virgin Mary is here, as well as his condemnation of modernism. Both Protestant and Catholic high points are covered.

Chadwick, Owen. *The Popes and European Revolution.* Oxford 1981 $84.00. Chapters 7 and 8 give a fine survey of this period.

———, ed. *The Mind of the Oxford Movement.* Stanford Univ. Pr. 1961 $18.50. This High Church or medievalist movement among Anglicans produced great scholarship, as well as a few notable converts to Rome. (See also the various listings for Cardinal Newman in this chapter.)

Collier, Richard. *The General Next to God: The Story of William Booth and the Salvation Army.* Dutton 1965 o.p. A good size and style for this readable study.

Feuerbach, Ludwig. *The Essence of Christianity.* 1854. Fwd. by Richard Niebuhr, Harper 1957 pap. $6.95; Peter Smith 1958 $18.25. The essence, oddly enough, is atheism. The introductory essay of Karl Barth makes this special: the great modern theologian of God's transcendence and the theologian of God's absence under one cover.

Gargan, E. T. *Leo XIII and the Modern World.* Sheed & Ward 1961 o.p. Leo was the author of powerful modern social encyclicals and the condemner of modernism within the church. Short pieces illustrative of his work with helpful introductions by the editor.

Gerrish, B. A. *The Old Protestantism and the New: Essays on the Reformation Heritage.* Univ. of Chicago Pr. 1983 lib. bdg. $38.00. After essays on Erasmus and the reformers, Gerrish turns to the rise of science and the theologies that respond, those of Friedrich Schleiermacher and of Ernst Troeltsch.

Hales, E. E. *The Catholic Church in the Modern World.* Doubleday 1958 o.p. A sure guide from the French Revolution through the pontificate of Pius XII, John XXIII's predecessor. Especially good on relations between church and state. Handles both the Continent and the States.

Harnack, Adolph. *What Is Christianity?* Intro. by Rudolf Bultmann, Fortress Pr. 1986 pap. $12.95; Peter Smith 1958 $17.50. Greatest nineteenth-century church historian, Harnack followed Hegel in patterning his work on the early church, finding that Catholic Orthodoxy was a synthesis of Petrine and Jamesian legalism or Jewish Christianity and its opposite, Pauline and Johannine Hellenism. Marvelously formative for the liberal mind, especially in Germany and America.

Latourette, Kenneth S. *Christianity in a Revolutionary Age.* Greenwood 5 vols. repr. of 1958 ed. 1973 lib. bdg. set $160.50. Every pastor bought this massive and authoritative work, placed it in his study, and never looked at it again. By the man who was dean of American church historians for the first half-century.

Nietzsche, Friedrich. *The Portable Nietzsche*. Ed. by Walter Kaufmann [*Viking Portable Lib.*] Penguin 1977 pap. $7.95. The German atheist had a profound influence on theologies much more orthodox.

Petry, M. D. *Alfred Loisy: His Religious Significance*. Cambridge Univ. Pr. 1944 o.p. Loisy was perhaps the greatest of the modernist thinkers condemned by the pope just as the period ended (1907).

Phillips, Charles S. *The Church in France, 1848–1907*. Russell repr. of 1936 ed. 1967 o.p. The Catholic church in France between the revolutions of the bourgeoisie and the proletariat.

Ranchetti, Michele. *The Catholic Modernists: A Study of the Religious Reform Movements, 1864–1907*. Trans. by Isabel Quigly, Oxford 1969 o.p. Scholars regard this as a fair and definitive study of Catholic modernism.

Reardon, Bernard M. *Religious Thought in the Nineteenth Century*. Cambridge Univ. Pr. 1966 $49.50. pap. $16.95. Complements Smart (see below), by using the words of the great thinkers of the century. Very useful once the student has some of the names straight and perhaps a slight grasp of intellectual movement through the period.

———, ed. *Roman Catholic Modernism*. Stanford Univ. Pr. 1970 $20.00. Glance at the works by Ranchetti and Vidler and the reader can see that by about 1970 the winds of change from Vatican II were causing folk to ask if there were precedents for change in the monolithic thought that had characterized Romanism.

Redeker, Martin, ed. *Schleiermacher: Life and Thought*. Trans. by John Wallhausser, Fortress Pr. 1973 o.p. An excellent way to get into the Father of Liberal Theology is through this translation of his own *apologia*, edited and introduced ably here. Excerpts from Schleiermacher appear in *Religious Thought* by Reardon (above); the volume listed by Smart (below) has a good chapter on him and an excellent bibliography.

Smart, Ninian, and others, eds. *Nineteenth Century Religious Thought in the West*. Cambridge Univ. Pr. 3 vols. 1985 ea. $49.50. All the thinkers of the century are given chapters of about 40 pages, from Kant to Troeltsch, including nontheologians like Marx. Also contains introductions to schools. A bibliography concludes each chapter. This is a first-class source.

Stearns, Peter N. *Priest and Revolutionary*. Harper 1967 o.p. This is a sympathetic study of Lamennais, priest turned revolutionary thinker, and one of the odd ones of Catholic modernism.

Steele, Harold. *I Was a Stranger: The Faith of William Booth, Founder of the Salvation Army*. Exposition Pr. 1954 o.p. A short work of only 175 pages.

Vidler, Alexander R. *The Modernist Movement in the Roman Church*. Gordon Pr. 1976 $69.95. Vidler's 1930s study of Catholic modernism won awards when it was published and it has stood the test of time. The later edition adds material relating modernism to the changes that the Second Vatican Council brought about in the Catholic church.

———. *A Variety of Catholic Modernists*. Cambridge Univ. Pr. 1970 o.p. Earlier work than Ranchetti's, but also good.

Welch, Claude. *Protestant Thought in the Nineteenth Century*. Yale Univ. Pr. 2 vols. repr. ed. 1986 ea. $25.00. The bibliography contains everything useful, and the commentary is excellent. Scholars assign this to students for its clarity.

KIERKEGAARD, SØREN. 1813–1855

[SEE Chapter 5 in this volume.]

NEWMAN, JOHN HENRY, CARDINAL. 1801–1890

Born in London, Newman had an evangelical experience in 1816, the same year he enrolled at Trinity College, Oxford. In 1822, he was elected a fellow of Oriel College and slowly began to be drawn toward the High Church tradition, partly because of a personal bereavement and partly because of friendships with Hurrell Froude, John Keble, and Edward Pusey. Ordained an Anglican priest in 1825, he was vicar of the university church of Saint Mary the Virgin, where he gained fame as a preacher. In 1833, with the publication of the first *Tract for the Times*, Newman launched the Oxford movement, a High Church movement within Anglicanism that emphasized Catholic elements in the Church of England and within the early church. During this period he argued for the traditional *via media*, which held that the Anglican church was the only true representative of the unbroken tradition of the church fathers, both Rome and the Protestants falling to either side.

However, through further research into the early church he came finally to believe that his own church was schismatic; he resigned from his parish and his university fellowship and, in 1845, converted to Roman Catholicism. After study in Rome, he founded an oratory (a Catholic religious society of diocesan priests) in Birmingham. It was later moved to nearby Edgbaston, where he remained for the rest of his life, except for nearly a decade of teaching at the Catholic University of Dublin.

Controversy was Newman's great delight. He argued for development of doctrine against Catholic theologians, a viewpoint now commonplace. He defended Rome against Protestant attack in work after work. His editorship of the *Rambler*, which published lay opinion, earned him the animosity of his bishop. And he refused to attend the First Vatican Council, at which papal infallibility was declared, because he thought its definition was unripe and misplaced for the time. But he weathered all these controversies, earned the respect of his opponents, Protestant and Roman Catholic, and was awarded the cardinal's hat in 1879. Among his works, his *Apologia Pro Vita Sua* (1864) and *The Idea of a University* (1873) are regarded as classics in religion and intellectual education.

BOOKS BY NEWMAN

Apologia Pro Vita Sua. 1864. Ed. by A. D. Culler, Houghton Mifflin 1956 pap. $6.50; ed. by David De Laura, Norton 1968 text ed. pap. $11.95. His autobiographical defense of his movement into Orthodoxy and then into Roman Catholicism.

The Idea of a University. 1873. Ed. by Martin J. Svaglic, Univ. of Notre Dame Pr. 1982 text ed. pap. $9.95. Newman's most famous work on education.

Letters of John Henry Newman: A Selection. Ed. by Derek Stanford and Muriel Spark, Newman Pr. 1957 o.p. "An admirable introduction to John Henry the man" (*New Statesman*).

A Packet of Letters: A Selection from the Correspondence of John Henry Newman. Ed. by Joyce Suggs, Oxford 1983 $19.95. The scholar will know, and the beginning student not care, about the 31-volume Birmingham Oratory edition of *The Letters and Diaries of John Henry Newman*, with various dates and published by several houses.

BOOKS ABOUT NEWMAN

Bouyer, Louis. *Newman: His Life and Spirituality*. Kennedy 1958 o.p. The life of an English convert written by a French convert. Excellent handling of some of the tender spots in Newman's human relationships.

Chadwick, Owen. *Newman*. [*Past Masters Ser.*] Oxford 1983 $12.95 pap. $3.95. For the student who wants great scholarship cutting itself down to an 80-page book. Chadwick is always good.

Dawson, Christopher H. *The Spirit of the Oxford Movement*. AMS Pr. repr. of 1934 ed. 1976 $16.50. A Catholic intellectual of the twentieth century examines Newman's greatest contribution to Anglican religious thought in the nineteenth, the Oxford movement.

Harrold, Charles F. *John Henry Newman: An Expository and Critical Study of His Mind, Thought and Art*. Shoe String repr. of 1945 ed. 1966 o.p. Sympathetic approach by a non-Catholic, with special attention to his conversion and to his literary efforts.

Weatherby, Harold L. *Cardinal Newman in His Age: His Place in English Theology and Literature*. Vanderbilt Univ. Pr. 1973 $16.50. Good study of Newman's place in theology and literature.

CHRISTIANITY IN THE TWENTIETH CENTURY: 1914 TO THE PRESENT

One way to describe Christianity in our century is to say that in the global arena Christian adherents have grown by exponential leaps, whereas in its homeland of Europe its members have shrunk, its energies have faltered. Already peoples who have been evangelized only a generation or two are talking of sending missionaries to Europe, where in Protestant and Catholic nations alike the faith seems to speak strongly to neither the intelligentsia nor to the common people. In America the strength of Christian practice, and maybe even theology, seems to have passed from the old denominations and is now in the hands of more evangelical groups.

Theologically, something of the same picture holds, though not so clearly. Theology has always been the forte of the Germans, and from Karl Barth's massive protest against liberalism's optimism after World War I, until the 1970s, one could still talk of theology being made in Germany, processed in England, and sold in America. But with the controversy over the short-lived Death of God theologies in the mid-1960s and the advent of new liberation theologies in former colonial regions, Christian theology too has taken on a non-European complexion.

In the lists that follow the reader will find a General Religion and Theology section, followed by Liberation Theologies, the latter divided into Latin American, Black, and Women's. Also, some major figures in twentieth-century religious life will receive separate biographical and bibliographic listings.

These will be followed by a few books on Eastern Orthodoxy and on issues in science and religion.

General Religion and Theology

The books below were chosen to illustrate the thought or career of some major figures who do not receive separate biographical treatment, and to give surveys of various kinds, either in theology or ethics.

Barrett, David, ed. *World Christian Encyclopedia: A Comparative Survey of Churches and Religions in the Modern World, A.D. 1900 to 2000.* Oxford 1982 text ed. $145.00. The only comprehensive survey of all branches of Christendom everywhere; special attention to church growth; statistics abound.

Blazynski, George. *John Paul II: A Man from Krakow.* Weidenfeld & Nicolson 1979 o.p. As soon as Karol Wojtyla became the first non-Italian pope since the sixteenth century, a flood of books came out, most by Polish authors. This one is compact and reads well.

Bloesch, Donald. *The Future of Evangelical Theology.* Doubleday 1983 o.p. The author is one of the major voices in modern Evangelicalism and a mainline churchman. He has written many books, but this one allows him to summarize, reflect, and plead for Evangelical unity.

Bultmann, Rudolf. *Kerygma and Myth.* Ed. by Hans Bartsch, trans. by Reginald H. Fuller, Harper 1961 o.p. Bultmann, apostle of demythologizing the gospels, is criticized and responds to his critics.

———. *The New Testament and Mythology, and Other Basic Writings.* Ed. and trans. by Schubert M. Ogden, Fortress Pr. 1984 $12.95. Bultmann died in 1976, and here a disciple has collected materials that are accessible to the ordinary reader.

Cobb, John B., Jr., and David R. Griffin. *Process Theology: An Introductory Exposition.* Westminster 1976 pap. $8.95. Process theology, with its developing deity and its Whiteheadian language, deserves a good introduction, and Cobb is its major theologian anywhere.

Cox, Harvey. *Religion in the Secular City: Toward a Postmodern Theology.* Simon & Schuster 1985 pap. $7.95. Want to know where theology is headed? Read the latest Coxist pronouncement.

Curran, Charles. *Critical Concerns in Moral Theology.* Univ. of Notre Dame Pr. 1984 text ed. $16.95. Although it is the general tenor of his approach to ethics that cost Curran his teaching position at Catholic University, probably the sharpest disagreements are found in this book, with matters sexual heading the list.

———. *Directions in Catholic Social Ethics.* Univ. of Notre Dame Pr. 1985 text ed. pap. $8.95. Various articles by the Catholic church's most controversial ethicist on population control, peace and war, health care, and more.

Doig, Desmond. *Mother Teresa: Her Work and Her People.* Illus. by Rahgu Rai, Harper 1980 pap. $11.95. Small text with many pictures, some of them in color. There are no scholarly studies of the saintly missionary.

Dowley, Tim, ed. *Eerdmans' Handbook to the History of Christianity.* Eerdmans 1977 $24.95. Seventy scholars have contributed to this, and the twentieth century is handled very adroitly.

Ferm, Deane W. *Contemporary American Theologians: A Critical Survey.* Harper 1981 pap. $8.95. Brief and clear introductions to the main features of modern theologies in America, including Catholic and conservative Protestant.

Flannery, Austin, ed. *Vatican Council II: The Conciliar and Post Conciliar Documents.*

Franciscan Herald vol. 1 1976 pap. $7.95; Liturgical Pr. vol. 2 1983 pap. $9.95. Few events have so changed the face of modern Catholicism as Vatican II (1962–65). These volumes contain the 16 constitutions and decrees of Vatican II with many subsequent clarifying and implementing documents. The best compilation.

Gilkey, Langdon. *Naming the Whirlwind: The Renewal of God-Language*. Bobbs 1969 o.p. The author is probably the dean of all American theologians, Protestant and Catholic, and this is probably his major work. It is not easy reading.

Hebblethwaite, Peter. *The Year of Three Popes*. Collins 1979 $8.95. Gives the reader an idea of the uproar in Rome when Pope Paul VI died and was followed by John Paul I, who lived in office but 30 days (yes, you can find books that say he was murdered), and was succeeded by the present John Paul II. The author is a sure guide.

Hebblethwaite, Peter, and Ludwig Kaufmann. *John Paul II: A Pictorial Biography*. McGraw-Hill 1979 o.p. Here is the coffee-table Pope John Paul II. Lots of colored photos and a good text.

Henry, Carl F. *God, Revelation and Authority: God Who Speaks and Shows*. Word Bks. 6 vols. 1976–79 vols. 1–2 ea. $22.95 vols. 3–6 ea. $24.95. Henry and Bloesch are Evangelicalism's major theologians. Bloesch (see above) is relatively easy to read, while Henry requires deep ploughing.

Hordern, William E. *A Layman's Guide to Protestant Theology*. Macmillan rev. ed. 1968 pap. $4.95. A clearly written account of theological movements from the Protestant reformers to the twentieth century, with particular attention to twentieth-century theologians, the major ones examined carefully. A good book.

Keeley, Robin, ed. *Christianity in Today's World: An Eerdmans Handbook*. Eerdmans 1985 $29.95. Like other Eerdmans' handbooks; many scholars looking at the astonishing variety of Christians in Africa, Asia, and Latin America. A major reference work.

Kliever, Lonnie D. *The Shattered Spectrum: A Survey of Contemporary Theology*. John Knox 1981 pap. $10.95. Picks up six prominent theological schools of thought since World War II and examines each carefully in fairly easy style. Popular.

Lamb, Matthew L. *Creativity and Method: Studies in Honor of Rev. Bernard Lonergan, S.J.* Marquette Univ. Pr. 1981 $29.95 pap. $19.95. Lonergan is the epitome of Catholic theology, but nearly impossible to get hold of. Here his disciples explain him to each other and to the reader.

McBrien, Richard P. *Catholicism*. Winston Pr. 2 vols. 1980 set $45.00. Want to know where the church is today? A very modern theologian with a strong commitment to the historic faith tells you where.

———. *Catholicism Study Edition*. Winston Pr. 1981 pap. $24.50

McCormick, Richard A., and Paul Ramsey, eds. *Doing Evil to Achieve Good: Moral Choice in Conflict Situations*. Univ. Pr. of Amer. repr. of 1978 ed. 1985 text ed. pap. $11.75. This book was chosen because it also introduces the reader to the major Protestant ethicists. The reader is guided to other works by both editors.

Macquarrie, John. *Twentieth Century Religious Thought: The Frontiers of Philosophy and Theology*. Scribner 1983 text ed. pap. $19.95. A handbook with summaries of about 150 theologians and philosophers that make it a handy reference tool for beginner and practitioner alike.

Muggeridge, Malcolm. *Something Beautiful for God: Mother Teresa of Calcutta*. Harper 1971 $18.45 pap. $6.95; Walker repr. of 1971 ed. 1985 pap. $8.95. Brief, full of photos and conversations with Muggeridge, who was the first one to "discover" her for the West.

Neill, Stephen C., and others, eds. *Concise Dictionary of the Christian World Mission*.

Abingdon 1971 o.p. International and ecumenical in scope, this excellent source covers all facets of missions. Brief articles by more than 200 specialists treat the missionary work and provide biographies of missionary leaders. An "indispensable reference work in its field" (Gorman).

Ogletree, Thomas W. *The Death of God Controversy*. Abingdon 1966 o.p. Although the movement came and went in two years, it had a lasting effect. Here three of its major proponents argue their case; the editor has a good introduction.

Rahner, Karl. *The Christian Commitment: Essays in Pastoral Theology*. Trans. by Cecily Hastings, Sheed & Ward 1963 o.p. Rahner at his pastoral best, when his theology sounds less Germanic than usual.

———. *Foundations of Christian Faith: An Introduction to the Idea of Christianity*. Crossroad NY 1982 pap. $16.95. Usually regarded as the best brief exposition of his theology. The longer statement is in the 20 volumes of *Theological Investigations*.

———. *Karl Rahner in Dialogue*. Crossroad NY 1986 $18.95. Reviewers say the essential Rahner is here, including comments on Hans Küng's conflict with the church and modifications on his church of the future.

———. *A Rahner Reader*. Ed. by Gerald McCool, Crossroad NY 1975 pap. $10.95. Excerpts and shorter materials; about 375 pages.

Robinson, John A. *Honest to God*. Westminster 1963 pap. $7.95. A thoroughly bad book that had an enormous impact. Brief and to the point.

Rouse, Ruth, and Stephen C. Neill, eds. *A History of the Ecumenical Movement, 1517–1948*. Westminster 2 vols. rev. ed. 1970 o.p. The necessary book to read on the ecumenical movement, formation of the World Council of Churches, Vatican relations.

Schillebeeckx, Edward. *God and Man*. Trans. by Edward Fitzgerald and Peter Tomlinson, Sheed & Ward, 1969 o.p. Although not the Dutch Catholic theologian's latest book, it indicates some of the reasons he got in trouble with the Vatican.

Spink, Kathryn. *The Miracle of Love: Mother Teresa of Calcutta, Her Missionaries of Charity, and Her Coworkers*. Harper 1982 $15.00. Twice as long as Muggeridge's work (see above), with many color photos and what almost amounts to a biography.

Tracy, David. *Analogical Imagination*. Crossroad NY 1981 o.p. He wrestles with the pluralism in thought-worlds today, showing the importance of the "classical writings" in each tradition (e.g., Bible, Augustine, etc., for Christianity; Qu'ran for Islam), and argues their abiding importance rather than the official interpreters of the faith. Difficult reading.

———. *Blessed Rage for Order: The New Pluralism in Theology*. Harper 1979 pap. $9.95. Young Roman Catholic theologian lays out the philosophic grounds on which theology can be built in an age that is not religiously literate.

Verhey, Allen. *The Great Reversal: Ethics and the New Testament*. Eerdmans 1984 pap. $13.95. Paul Ramsay, Stanley Hauerwas, James Gustafson, and his student, Allen Verhey, are probably Protestantism's major ethicists. This is refreshing work, easy to read and thoughtful for any level of student.

Weger, Karl-Heinz. *Karl Rahner: An Introduction to His Theology*. Crossroad NY 1980 $10.95. Best English-language summary, with some attention to his life.

Williams, George H. *The Mind of John Paul II: Origins of His Thought and Action*. Harper 1981 $26.95. This book is unusual because it was written by a Protestant Reformation scholar, who came to know Cardinal Wojtyla before anyone had an idea he would become pope. Solid and perhaps for the scholar only.

Wojtyla, Karol. *Love and Responsibility*. Trans. by H. T. Willetts, Farrar 1981 o.p.

The present pope begins his study of human love with "the sexual urge" and goes on with a thorough scholar's analysis of sex, love, chastity, and marriage, with a section on birth control.

Liberation Theologies

Liberation theology, arising in the 1970s, appears to have a few major themes. First, it is theology "from below," that is, from the standpoint of oppressed people, not from college and seminary professors who are attacking or defending established literary positions. Next, it readily admits its debt to the Marxist "scientific" analysis of the ills of capitalism and colonialism. (See Novak's work below for criticism.) Finally, it differs according to the place of its origin: Latin American liberationists and middle-class American women liberationists do not always see the same issues as important. The books listed are generally recent ones that will not only state a case, but will also lead the reader back through earlier works in a rapidly changing field.

LATIN AMERICAN LIBERATION THEOLOGY

Alves, Rubem. *What Is Religion?* Trans. by Don Vinzant, Orbis Bks. 1984 pap. $4.95. Most of the liberationists are Roman Catholic, but Alves and José Miguez Bonino are noted Protestant authors.

Berryman, Philip. *The Religious Roots of Rebellion: Christians in Central American Revolutions.* Orbis Bks. 1984 pap. $19.95. Tells the story of recent revolutionary activity from a Christian perspective and in great detail.

Brockman, James R. *The Word Remains: A Life of Oscar Romero.* Orbis Bks. 1982 $12.95. "This is not a complete biography of El Salvador's martyred archbishop but rather the story of the last few years of Romero's life and work . . . highly recommended, both as a biography and as an insightful account of the situation in Central America" (*LJ*). See also listing below for Erdozain.

Dussel, Enrique. *A History of the Church in Latin America: Colonialism to Liberation.* Eerdmans 1981 $21.95. Best one-volume treatment of the subject of colonialism and the church, including recent revolutions (e.g., El Salvador, Nicaragua).

Erdozain, Placido. *Archbishop Romero: Martyr of Salvador.* Orbis Bks. 1981 pap. $4.95. Oscar Romero, shot to death at the altar, is examined and eulogized as a fighter for liberation, albeit a peaceful one (his writings are listed below).

Freire, Paulo. *Pedagogy of the Oppressed.* Trans. by Myra B. Raymos, Continuum 1970 pap. $9.95. A basic book, like Gutierrez's, which remains a sort of liberationist classic, although that term had hardly been coined when he wrote it.

Gutierrez, Gustavo. *A Theology of Liberation.* Ed. and trans. by Sister Caridad Inda and John Eagleson, Sr., fwd. by Robert McAfee Brown, Orbis Bks. 1973 o.p. This is the basic theology of the movement, for the author is careful to dialogue at length with European theology. The foreword is by an American theologian whose recent writings have tended to be of this genre, and who is always worth reading.

Hall, Mary. *The Impossible Dream: The Spirituality of Dom Helder Camara.* Orbis Bks. repr. of 1979 ed. 1980 pap. $2.48. This Brazilian leader is one of the patron saints of the oppressed in Latin America, a scrappy, yet irenic battler for the poor, the Indians, and all who lack freedom.

Lernoux, Penny. *Cry of the People: The Struggle for Human Rights in Latin America—The Catholic Church in Conflict with U.S. Policy.* Penguin 1982 pap. $7.95. Particularly readable because the author is a journalist who can write the story without neglecting the research.

Novak, Michael. *Freedom with Justice: Catholic Social Thought and Liberal Institutions.* Harper 1984 $17.45. A spirited and learned attack on all leftward leaning within his church, by an articulate spokesman for the so-called New Right.

Romero, Oscar. *The Church Is All of You.* Ed. and trans. by James R. Brockman, Winston Pr. 1984 pap. $6.95. Collection of writings by the Salvadoran liberationist churchman whose biography by Brockman is listed above.

———. *Voice of the Voiceless: The Four Pastoral Letters and Other Statements.* Trans. by Michael J. Walsh, Orbis Bks. 1985 pap. $9.95. In addition to the pastoral letters to the faithful of El Salvador, he writes to the American Protestants of the National Council of Churches, and even to President Carter. Always the concern is that outsiders understand the violence in his land, violence that martyred the peaceful bishop.

BLACK LIBERATION THEOLOGIES

Cone, James H. *A Black Theology of Liberation.* Orbis Bks. 2d ed. 1986 pap. $9.95. Like Gutierrez's for Latin American liberation theology, Cone's work is the one that most seriously tries to put this theology into the larger context, which means relating it to the Barthians, Niebuhrians, and others. This is the most mature statement of this theology.

Frazier, E. Franklin, and C. Eric Lincoln. *The Negro Church in America.* Schocken 1973 pap. $4.95. Actually, this is two small books in one: the first by the noted black historian, who died in 1959; the second by a notable black theologian and historian, who follows with an analysis written after Montgomery, *Brown* vs. *Board of Education,* and the assassination of Martin Luther King, Jr.

Nelsen, Hart M., ed. *The Black Church in America.* Basic Bks. 1971 text ed. $10.75. Articles and book chapters old and more recent, including material from about every major writer, including all the ones listed in this bibliography.

Roberts, James D. *Black Theology Today: Liberation and Contextualization.* [*Toronto Studies in Theology*] E Mellen 1984 $49.95. Articles written at different times, edited together into a good analysis of movements in black theology, with some ties to Latin American theology.

Washington, Joseph R., Jr. *Black and White Power Subreption.* Beacon Pr. 1969 o.p. One of the earlier books on black theology and black power. "Subreption," in canon and Scottish law, is "the obtaining of a dispensation from ecclesiastical authority or a gift from the sovereign by concealing the truth."

———. *Black Sects and Cults.* Univ. Pr. of Amer. repr. of 1973 ed. 1984 text ed. pap. $10.50. A major theologian looks at the side of black Christianity which is most visible when viewed from the street, but which gets very little attention in print. Their intention, he argues, is to be power communities.

Wilmore, Gayraud S., and James H. Cone, eds. *Black Theology: A Documentary History, 1966–1979.* Orbis Bks. 1979 pap. $14.95. Wilmore's introductions are very informative, as are Cone's. This 600-page collection of documents ranges all the way from the National Committee on Black Churchmen, to a paper on black Catholic theology, to black theology and black women. Good collection, chosen for breadth and related well to central issues.

WOMEN'S LIBERATION THEOLOGIES

Bainton, Roland H. *Women of the Reformation in France and England.* Beacon 1975 o.p. If Bainton did it, it is good Reformation history.

Carson, Anne, ed. *Feminist Spirituality and the Feminine Divine: An Annotated Bibliog-*

raphy. [*Feminist Ser.*] Crossing Pr. 1986 lib. bdg. $39.95. Probably the best catalog of materials in the field with an annotation toward the "goddess" ideal in feminist religious matters.

Daly, Mary. *Beyond God the Father: Toward a Philosophy of Women's Liberation.* Beacon 2d rev. ed. 1985 $18.95 pap. $8.95. Although the author has done later work (this was originally published in 1973), nothing exploded on the scene like this bitter, careful analysis and attack on patriarchy in Christian thought and practice.

Greaves, Richard L., ed. *Triumph over Silence: Women in Protestant History.* [*Contributions to the Study of Religion Ser.*] Greenwood 1985 lib. bdg. $35.00. This 300-page work summarizes the struggles of women to be heard or to lead. By a careful historian.

McHaffie, Barbara J. *Her Story: Women in Christian Tradition.* Fortress Pr. 1986 pap. $9.95. Amazingly able survey of women in the early church, medieval, Reformation, and Puritan attitudes, and the struggle by women in these epochs. The later history covered well, also. Gives good bibliography in a good number of areas. A one-volume treasure.

Mollenkott, Virginia R. *Women, Men, and the Bible.* Abingdon 1977 pap. $8.95. The author is a literary scholar and an Evangelical, and thus is able to throw light from several directions on the women's struggle.

Ruether, Rosemary R., and Rosemary S. Keller. *Women and Religion in America.* Harper 3 vols. 1982–86 pap. vol. 1 $10.95 vol. 2 $24.45 vol. 3 $26.45. Since the third volume ends just as the second wave of feminism was beginning in America (women's suffrage constituted the first), it appears that the series is to continue, although this is not stated in any of the excellent introductions to a myriad of studies of women in America, Protestant and Catholic, liberal and Evangelical, social movers and church reformers. Most of the articles are accompanied by documents, so this constitutes a most thoroughgoing analysis, justifying the claim that men have written American history as a story for men, and now it must be redone with the other half of the population included in order to see what really happened.

Scanzoni, Letha, and Virginia R. Mollenkott. *Is the Homosexual My Neighbor? Another Christian View.* Harper 1980 pap. $8.95. Here Mollenkott is teamed with another Evangelical, a sociologist, and their convictions on the rights of the homosexual have helped split the Evangelical community in this regard, and thus in the whole area of women in the church.

BARTH, KARL. 1886–1968

Up every morning to the strains of Mozart, to bed each night after an evening of beer and cigars with his students—it is hard to credit that the Basel theologian is probably the most prolific writer Christendom has ever produced. His gigantic *Church Dogmatics* runs well over 12,000 pages in English translation, yet there is also a great body of occasional writing, tossed off in his spare time, it would seem. Indeed, Barth would be worthy of mention if only for his first published work, a commentary on "The Epistle to the Romans."

In 1918, when he published this study, Barth was a young pastor in his native Switzerland. The guns of World War I could still be heard, their angry shells destroying, perhaps forever, the liberal optimism of Continental theology. Where was the progress young Barth had learned about from Harnack in Berlin? Where was human rationality, dispelling the noisome holes of ignorance and superstition, when the great leaders of Christendom descended to the barbarity of trench warfare? Turning to St. Paul's greatest epistle, as AUGUSTINE and Luther had before him, Barth clutched it, he said, like a man clutching at a rope when he is falling, only to discover that the rope is attached to the church bell and he has just awakened the city from its slumbers.

He secured a post at the University of Bonn, but Hitler objected to his work with the Confessing Church (see Bonhoeffer), and he was forced to return to his own country, there to produce all his great tomes. Turning theologians from their rational optimism, Barth has driven them to consider again the power of the Word of God: that acted, spoken, inscripturated, incarnated Word was always his chief theme. Against it, all human pride and pretension, all schemes for Utopian societies, all theologies based on anything other than the Bible and Christ have proven transient. His objectors reply that his God is too far away (like KIERKEGAARD he spoke of the "infinite qualitative distinction" between God and man), that he ignores scientific advances, that he cares little for dialogue with other religions. But they never complain of lack of erudition or ecumenical concern. To some he is the greatest theologian the church has produced. He died as he had hoped, with his *Dogmatics* still unfinished.

BOOKS BY BARTH

The Epistle to the Romans. 1919. Trans. by Edwyn C. Hoskyns, Oxford repr. of 1933 ed. 1968 pap. $12.95. Neo-orthodox theology began with this volume, just as the Protestant Reformation began with Luther's studies on Romans.

Church Dogmatics: The Doctrine of God. 1936–69. Trans. by Geoffrey W. Bromiley and others, Attic Pr. 5 vols. 1956–77 o.p. This is a portion of Barth's major work, occupying his whole life, even as he churned out volume after volume of occasional writings.

The Humanity of God. 1956. Trans. by John N. Thomas, John Knox 1960 pap. $5.95. The elderly Barth pokes some fun at the earlier Barth. A helpful corrective to some of the *Church Dogmatics*.

BOOKS ABOUT BARTH

Bromiley, Geoffrey W. *An Introduction to the Theology of Karl Barth*. Eerdmans 1979 pap. $8.95. Who better to interpret Barth than his faithful translator, a theologian in his own right?

Busch, Eberhard. *Karl Barth: His Life from Letters and Autobiographical Texts*. Trans. by John Bowden, Fortress Pr. 1979 o.p. In his declining years Barth chose Busch for this work, and he has performed it well. Some 500 pages with a number of indexes.

Casalis, George. *Portrait of Karl Barth*. Doubleday 1963 o.p. A brief life.

BONHOEFFER, DIETRICH. 1906–1945

Born in Breslau, Germany, now part of Poland, Dietrich and his twin sister, Sabine, were raised in a home where the intellect was encouraged. His father was a physician and professor of psychiatry at the University of

Berlin. Scholars like the famous church historian Adolph von Harnack, Ernst Troeltsch, theologian and sociohistorian, and MAX WEBER (see Vol. 3), a founder of modern sociology, were guests of his parents. A precocious student, he early decided on the church and theology as his life's work, evidencing a degree of independence of thought that was at odds with the reverence in which his fellow students held their professors. He was a product of liberal studies, but was much influenced by Karl Barth's recovery of Orthodoxy, an influence evident all through his writings.

His doctoral dissertation, *Sanctorum Communio: A Dogmatic Investigation of the Sociology of the Church*, was published in 1930, by which time he was teaching theology at the University of Berlin. Then followed a year's study in the United States (he liked the social concern of American students, but not their disdain of theology) and leadership of the World Alliance of Churches, where his flair for languages and his genial disposition won him many friends. These American and British friends tried unsuccessfully to dissuade him from returning to Germany after the rise of Hitler in 1932. But he went back and, joining the so-called Confessing Church of those who resisted "Germanizing" the church, he conducted an illegal seminary in Finkenwalde. Out of this experience came his *Life Together*, and out of his struggles to encourage Christians to resist the Nazis came his study of the Sermon on the Mount, *The Cost of Discipleship* (tr. 1948).

Although he escaped military duty by joining the intelligence service, he was eventually arrested and imprisoned by the gestapo and was linked to the attempt on Hitler's life, as were his brother Klaus and friends of the family who occupied high posts in the military. His *Letters and Papers from Prison* (tr. 1953), his testimony of faith, gave the American Death of God movement the term "religionless Christianity." Together with a few others, he was killed at Flössenburg prison, where the prison doctor wrote of him: "I have hardly ever seen a man die so entirely submissive to the will of God." Although some interpreters of his work concentrate on his undeveloped idea of religionless Christianity, he is probably best understood as a radical theologian of the Word of God.

BOOKS BY BONHOEFFER

The Cost of Discipleship. Macmillan 1963 pap. $4.95; Peter Smith 1983 $13.50. His major work on the Sermon on the Mount.
Letters and Papers from Prison. Macmillan enl. ed. 1972 pap. $6.95. Here are his thoughts from the concentration camp on religionless Christianity.
Life Together. Harper 1976 pap. $6.95. Only 120 pages, but it allows the new reader to see the radical commitment that Hitler caused Christians to make.

BOOK ABOUT BONHOEFFER

Bethge, Eberhard. *Dietrich Bonhoeffer*. Harper 1977 pap. $19.95. This is the definitive biography of the scholar, martyr, and friend, by one who knew Bonhoeffer well and has edited most of his works.

JOHN XXIII, POPE. 1881–1963

Born Angelo Giuseppe Roncalli, the son of peasants who rented land as sharecroppers, he early demonstrated intellectual abilities that saw him through seminary studies in Bergamo, near his home, and on to his ordination in 1904. For a number of years he worked with Catholic women's and youth organizations under the bishop of Bergamo. In World War I he served as a medical sergeant and as chaplain, and after the war was active in the Society for the Propagation of the Faith, with its headquarters in Rome. In 1925, he was appointed to the first of several diplomatic missions, first among the Catholic minority in Bulgaria, then in Turkey, where he set the precedent of introducing Turkish into the Mass, and in Greece, where during World War II military operations destroyed any opportunity he might have had to work with the Orthodox majority and confronted him, as well, with hatred of Italians, fueled by the Italian army's occupation of the country.

As the war began to heat up on French soil, he was appointed papal nuncio to France and arrived in Paris at the very end of 1944. There, for almost a decade, he worked with first the Germans and then the French government to heal the wounds of warfare, to keep the church intact through rapid changes of government, to keep Catholic schools alive, and to deal with the French bishops who saw the increasing secularization of the nation and the failing religious allegiance of the people as signs pointing to the need for radical new measures to propagate the faith. Nevertheless, it is true that the worker-priest movement, which he watched at first with approval, received its deathblow during his pontificate.

After serving as patriarch of Venice and being made cardinal (1953), he was elected by the College of Cardinals in 1958 to succeed Pius XII. The major accomplishment of his pontificate was the calling of the Second Vatican Council, whose arguments and decrees seemed revolutionary in their time (1962–65), and whose ripples continue to move the barque of Rome to this day. Thirty-nine non-Catholic observers attended with his blessing, special provision being made for translation from Latin documents and speeches, and it is perhaps not surprising that one of the first conciliar decrees was to allow the vernacular to replace Latin in the liturgy. He died of a gastric ulcer on June 3, 1963.

BOOKS BY POPE JOHN

Journal of a Soul. Trans. by Dorothy White, Doubleday repr. of 1965 ed. 1980 pap. $7.95. His diary is necessary reading for those who want to understand the saintly revolutionary.

The Teachings of Pope John XXIII. Ed. by Michael Cinigo, trans. by Arthur A. Coppotelli, Grosset 1967 o.p. All the essential encyclicals, letters, occasional teaching.

BOOKS ABOUT POPE JOHN

Bolton, R. *Living Peter: A Biographical Study of Pope John XXIII.* Allen & Unwin 1961 o.p. An unusual study for it follows the pope in his earlier career and shows his relationships to Orthodoxy and to the Anglican Church.

Hebblethwaite, Peter. *Pope John XXIII: Shepherd of the Modern World.* Doubleday

1985 $19.95. This is the largest and most recent of the many studies of the great pope, and the author is a skilled interpreter of things Roman to English-speaking audiences. Has a good bibliography.

KÜNG, HANS. 1928–

Küng is Swiss and was born in a middle-class family. He studied in Rome for seven years, obtaining his licentiate in philosophy and theology from the Gregorian University there, and then receiving his doctorate in theology from the Catholic Institute in Paris. Since 1960 he has been a professor at Tübingen University, where he taught dogmatic and ecumenical theology until his permission to teach Catholic theology was removed as a consequence of statements judged to be contrary to official doctrine. Since 1980 he has taught at the University of Chicago and the University of Michigan, and occasionally in Europe as well.

His difficulties with the church began with the publication *The Church* and became very hot with the publication of *Infallible? An Inquiry*. More recently, his *On Being Christian* has raised the question of whether his theology is not simply rational Protestant theology of the turn of the century. Official inquiries were held, statements were exchanged between Küng and the Conference of German Bishops, and the Rome-based Congregation for the Doctrine of the Faith, but no agreement was to be had. Küng continues to declare himself a loyal member of the Roman Catholic church and seems unlikely to leave its priesthood or to be excommunicated.

BOOKS BY KÜNG

The Church. Doubleday 1976 pap. $6.95

The Christian Challenge. Trans. by Edward Quinn, Doubleday 1979 o.p. Since Küng is given to writing long books, it is good to have a shortened version of *On Being Christian*, one of his major theological works.

Does God Exist? An Answer for Today. Random 1981 pap. $10.95. More than 800 pages of Küngiana, in which the reader can see how mightily the theologian wrestles with major nonreligious spokespersons.

Eternal Life: Life after Death as a Medical, Philosophical, and Theological Problem. Trans. by Edward Quinn, Doubleday 1984 $15.95 1985 pap. $9.95. More temperate in space at 270 pages.

Infallible? An Inquiry. Doubleday 1983 pap. $10.95. It was this book that brought Küng into conflict with Rome, since he argues that Paul VI's encyclical against birth control, which was meant to be infallible teaching, has since been rejected by the church.

Küng in Conflict. Ed. and trans. by Leonard Swidler, Doubleday 1981 o.p. Here in more than 600 pages is the story of Küng's conflict with Rome. Well told and well documented.

LEWIS, C(LIVE) S(TAPLES) (pseud. of Clive Hamilton). 1898–1963

C. S. (Jack) Lewis was born in Belfast, Northern Ireland, to a middle-class Protestant family. His father was a lawyer, his mother the daughter of an Anglican clergyman. Flora Hamilton Lewis died when Jack was nine, but not before she had taught him the rudiments of Greek and Latin. He and his brother Warren had their early schooling at public (private) schools in England, but Jack persuaded his father to allow him to be privately educated by William Kirkpatrick who, while preparing him rigorously in logic and languages, told Lewis's father that he had no talents except those of a scholar.

His schooling at Oxford was interrupted by military duty in World War I. Lewis served in the trenches and was wounded, as he says, by an English shell that fell short. Mustered out, he returned to Oxford and plunged into his studies, receiving "firsts" in Greats (classics and philosophy) and in English. He was then offered a fellowship in English at Magdalen College and thereafter crowded his writing into a busy schedule of lecturing and tutoring students who were facing exams.

Lewis became a believing Christian and re-entered the Anglican Church in 1931. Among those who helped him through atheism to theism and finally to classical Christian doctrine were the author and fellow-scholar J. R. R. TOLKIEN (see Vol. 1), author of *The Hobbit* and *The Lord of the Rings,* and Owen Barfield, lawyer, theosophist, scholar, and author of many influential books. Not long after his conversion Lewis's defenses of the faith began to appear: *Pilgrim's Regress* (1933) and *The Problem of Pain* (1940) were followed by the work that established his reputation as a shrewd observer of human nature, *The Screwtape Letters* (1942). Largely on the basis of that and other apologetical works, *Time* magazine placed him on its cover with the legend: "Oxford's C. S. Lewis, His Heresy: Christianity."

In 1954 Lewis was appointed professor of medieval and renaissance literature at Cambridge, a post he held until his death. In 1956 he married an American, Joy Davidman, who died of cancer in 1961. Lewis himself was stricken with a series of illnesses and died on November 22, 1963, the same day as Aldous Huxley, and also the day John F. Kennedy was assassinated. (See also Volume 1.)

BOOKS BY LEWIS

The Chronicles of Narnia. Macmillan 7 vols. 1983 set $79.95. 1986 pap. set $39.95. These popular children's stories were originally published separately, each with its own title. They begin with *The Lion, the Witch and the Wardrobe* and end with *The Last Battle.*

The Screwtape Letters. 1942. Collins 1979 $9.95; Macmillan rev. ed. 1982 pap. $1.95. Published in many editions, these are letters from Uncle Wormwood, very low in the Lowerarchy of Hell, to his nephew Screwtape on how to tempt an Englishman.

BOOKS ABOUT LEWIS

Carpenter, Humphrey. *The Inklings.* Ballantine 1981 pap. $3.50. The beautiful thing about this work is that it includes J. R. R. Tolkien and Charles Williams and their friends, while concentrating on Lewis. Carpenter did a good (although authorized) biography of Tolkien, and this is just as good.

Gibb, Jocelyn. *Light on C. S. Lewis.* Macmillan 1965 o.p. Although this is a series of essays on Lewis by people who knew him or have critiqued his work, the best thing here is the complete bibliography of Lewisiana.

Green, Roger L., and Walter Hooper. *C. S. Lewis: A Biography.* Harcourt 1976 pap.

$7.95. To date this is the definitive biography; in about 300 pages the authors catch the Lewis most people knew. Hooper is the official curator of Lewis's papers.

TILLICH, PAUL JOHANNES. 1886–1965

Paul Johannes Tillich was born into a German Lutheran pastor's family in that part of Germany that is now Poland. He attended several universities, earning the doctorate in philosophy in 1910, then taught at several more from 1919 to 1933. Removed from his professorate at Frankfurt by the Nazi government, he emigrated to the United States, with the encouragement of Reinhold Niebuhr, and taught at Union Theological Seminary in New York (1933–55), Harvard (1955–62), and the University of Chicago (1962–65). The fullest biography, including some fairly lurid material of a psychosexual nature, can be found in the appreciative work by Wilhelm Pauck and Marion Pauck.

The student who wants to encounter Tillich at his most succinct might turn to *The Courage to Be* (1952) or *The Theology of Paul Tillich* (1982). He is sometimes classified as Neo-orthodox, but that label does not fit him as well as it does Karl Barth who had small regard for Tillich's "theology of correlation," where responding to the world's questions is seen as the proper way of practicing theology. For Barth the starting place was never the world, but always God's Word.

BOOKS BY TILLICH

The Shaking of the Foundations. Scribner 1948 pap. $7.95. Should be read with *The New Being*, for *Shaking* has a good deal of the prophetic "no," while *The New Being* is more positive.

Systematic Theology: Life and the Spirit, History and the Kingdom of God. 1951–63. Univ. of Chicago Pr. 3 vols. in 1 1967 $49.95 1976 pap. $11.00. Here is Tillich's summary of the method and material of his work. The first-time reader should begin with one of the books listed above.

The Courage to Be. Yale Univ. Pr. 1952 pap. $6.95. As suggested in the biographical narrative this is perhaps the best place to begin reading Tillich.

The New Being. Scribner 1955 pap. $5.95. Some of his shorter essays and sermons. The power of the prophetic preacher is clear and urgent.

The Theology of Paul Tillich. Ed. by Charles W. Kegley, Pilgrim Pr. rev. ed. 1982 pap. $10.95. Includes 15 short critiques of his theology by noted writers (not all of them theologians), and his own 20-page reply. This edition lists all of Tillich's voluminous writings, great and obscure.

BOOKS ABOUT TILLICH

Pauck, Wilhelm, and Marion Pauck. *Paul Tillich: His Life and Thought.* Harper 1976 $15.00. Very good study that shows Tillich in all his intellectual glory and with all his moral warts. Has an excellent bibliography.

Tavard, George H. *Paul Tillich and the Christian Message.* Scribner 1962 o.p. A major American Catholic theologian assesses the positive and negative consequences of Tillich's Christology. Acute and fair.

CHRISTIAN RELIGION IN AMERICA

An Englishwoman who visited the United States in the 1830s wrote: "The almost universal profession in America of the adoption of Christianity . . . compels the inquiry . . . what sort of Christianity it is that is professed, and how it is come by. There is no evading the conviction that it is to a vast extent a monstrous superstition that is thus embraced by the tyrant, the profligate, the wordling, the bigot, the coward, and the slave; a superstition which offers little molestation to their vices, little rectification to their errors; a superstition which is but the spurious offspring of . . . divine Christianity" (Harriet Martineau, *Society in America*).

Certainly, of all the aspects of religious life that fascinated the European visitor in the last century, the separation of state and church, with its corollary, the voluntary church, was the one that interested them most. All European lands had an established church. In some, no other church could exist, but in all of them the nonestablished bodies were scorned or feared, and regarded as aberrations. To be properly Spanish was to be Catholic; the name for Rumanians is the same as adherents to the Rumanian Orthodox church; all important Englishmen were Anglicans, even if—as CHURCHILL (see Vol. 3) said later—it meant to be like a flying buttress, supporting the church from the outside.

In the bibliographies that follow, no attempt has been made to be exhaustive. However, the reader who needs information on persons, periods, movements, or schools of thought will find plentiful guidance, either in the bibliographies or the general works listed below. Almost no facet of religious America has gone unresearched, and the diligent student can find what is wanted with a little perseverance.

Bibliographies

Ahlstrom, S. E. *A Religious History of the American People.* Yale Univ. Pr. 1972 $50.00 pap. $18.95. For the beginning student this is a handy guide to the whole history of religion in America. In addition, the bibliographies are superb and include material for a great number of Christian denominations, as well as for groups that have made a conscious split with historic Christianity: Shakers, Christian Scientists, Swedenborgians, Steinerists, Mormons, Jehovah's Witnesses, Baha'is, Spiritualists, and Seventh-Day Adventists. The writing is lively enough and the interpretation very fair. Justly regarded as the preeminent work in its field.

Burr, Nelson R., ed. *Critical Bibliography of Religion in America.* Princeton Univ. Pr. 2 vols. 1961 o.p. Burr's bibliography, as it is always called, constitutes Volumes 3 and 4 of *Religion in American Life,* edited by James W. Smith and A. Leland Jamison, which is listed under General Studies (below). Burr's is the basic bibliography, providing in its table of contents a helpful organization of vast amounts of material.

————. *Religion in American Life.* [*Goldentree Bibliographies in American History Ser.*] Harlan Davidson 1971 $15.95. A condensation of and supplement to the preceding entry.

General Studies

Ellis, John Tracy. *American Catholicism*. Ed. by Daniel J. Boorstin, Univ. of Chicago Pr. 2d ed. 1969 pap. $10.00. Ellis invented the field and is still its master.

———. *Documents of American Catholic History*. Regnery 2 vols. 1967–68 o.p. Volume 1 covers the churches, including the Spanish colonies, to 1866; Volume 2 covers from then until the 1960s. Good introduction to Roman Catholicism in America.

Ellis, John Tracy, and Robert Trisco. *A Guide to American Catholic History*. ABC-Clio 2d rev. ed. 1982 lib. bdg. $29.85. An early work, but still useful. Shows the church before Vatican II had any influence on the church or on the historian.

Gaustad, Edwin S. *Historical Atlas of Religion in America*. Harper rev. ed. 1976 o.p. Maps, charts, tables, and text provide an excellent guide to the expansion and development of religious institutions in America. Non-Christian religions are covered. Numerous indexes.

———. *Religious History of America*. Harper 1974 pap. $10.95. Although superseded in size and coverage by Ahlstrom, this smaller account is more accessible and fair in every respect.

———, ed. *A Documentary History of Religion in America since 1865*. Eerdmans 1983 pap. $19.95. Skillfully edited primary sources that are placed together to tell the story.

Greeley, Andrew M. *The Catholic Experience: An Interpretation of American Catholicism*. Doubleday 1967 o.p. People forget that Greeley, tarred by the brush of his recent flashy novels, has always been and is a trenchant, insightful, and faithful exponent of the faith. This is a very good book.

Hudson, Winthrop. *Religion in America: An Historical Account of the Development of American Religious Life*. Macmillan 4th ed. 1987 text ed. $20.00. About as brief, at 400 pages, as a good work on religion in America can be. Its recent republication in a new edition allows the author to tie a few things together that others leave in the 1960s or 1970s. Written by one of the deans of religious studies in the United States.

Mead, Frank S., and Samuel S. Hill. *Handbook of Denominations in the United States*. Abingdon 8th ed. 1985 text ed. $10.95. Brief history, doctrinal views, polity, and statistics on more than 200 American denominations. Each is the soul of brevity.

Melton, James G. *The Encyclopedia of American Religions*. McGrath 2 vols. 1978 o.p. Surveys about 1,200 distinct religious groups, comparing practices and beliefs with Roman Catholic, Lutheran, and Baptist practice and belief.

Melton, James G., and James V. Geisendorfer. *A Directory of Religious Bodies in the United States*. Garland 1977 lib. bdg. $40.00. Nearly 1,300 religious groups, some not in Mead (see above), are listed. In addition to standard groups, e.g., the Baptist family, are such headings as mail-order churches and neopaganism.

Noll, Mark A., and others, eds. *Eerdmans' Handbook to Christianity in America*. Eerdmans 1983 $24.95. This is the coffee-table version of the subject. A test of several areas, e.g., women's causes, liberalism, and modernism, finds the work judicious, fair, and succinctly written. Many illustrations. Another good work by Eerdmans.

Piepkorn, Arthur C. *Profiles in Belief: The Religious Bodies of the United States and Canada*. Harper 4 vols. 1977–79 $20.00–$30.00. An invaluable reference tool for the reader who wants to dive in more deeply than the handbooks above allow. Objectivity guaranteed.

Smith, H. Shelton, and others, eds. *American Christianity: An Historical Interpreta-*

tion with Representative Documents. Scribner 2 vols. 1960 ea. $45.00. Fine collection of sources and documents with 1607–1820 covered in the first volume. Each chapter has numerous notes and bibliography. A standard source.

Smith, James W., and A. Leland Jamison, eds. *Religion in American Life.* Princeton Univ. Pr. 4 vols. 1961 o.p. Volumes 1 and 2 are interepretive essays. For Volumes 3 and 4, see above under Bibliographies for Burr, *Critical Bibliography of Religion in America.*

Vollmar, Edward R. *The Catholic Church in America: An Historical Bibliography.* Scarecrow Pr. 1963 o.p. Full bibliography until its publication date; after that the reader must rely on Ahlstrom's briefer bibliography.

The Yearbook of American and Canadian Churches. Ed. by Constant H. Jacquet, Jr., Abingdon 1985 pap. $15.95. This annual is a handy guide to everything about churches: their names, seminaries, church-related schools, religious periodicals, and statistics for membership and finances. It lists all ecumenical bodies as well.

French and Spanish Colonies

Most readers forget that the Spanish and French beat the English, Swedish, and Dutch to what is now the continental United States by about a century.

Kennedy, John H. *Jesuit and Savage in New France.* Yale Univ. Pr. 1950 o.p. Good account of brave people who, for the most part, failed because of the white pressure on the native American.

Picon-Salas, Mariano. *A Cultural History of Spanish America from Conquest to Independence.* Univ. of California Pr. 1966 o.p. Covers a great deal of material in a reasonable amount of space.

Other Useful Books

What follows is the editor's choice for the 20-odd most helpful interpretations of the religious experience in America.

Bellah, Robert N. *Habits of the Heart: Individualism and Commitment in American Life.* Harper 1986 pap. $7.95. A follow-up and extension of the earlier work, listed below.

Bellah, Robert N., and Philip E. Hammond. *Varieties of Civil Religion.* Harper 1982 pap. $7.95. Develops the famous construct of Bellah, a sociologist of religion, on the unacknowledged civil religion, which is part of, yet transcends, any particular faith or denomination.

Bratt, James D. *Dutch Calvinism in Modern America: A History of a Conservative Subculture.* Eerdmans 1984 pap. $13.95. Someone has called the Dutch the Jews of Christian America, and their emergence from the ethnic cocoon is interesting, as well as promising for religion in America.

Greeley, Andrew M. *The American Catholic: A Social Portrait.* Basic Bks. 1977 pap. $9.95. Like Hadden, Greeley is a sociologist (and lately a somewhat prurient novelist). Here he develops his understanding of the communal Catholic, one who is estranged from the institutional church, but is staunchly Catholic nonetheless.

Hadden, Jeffrey K. *Gathering Storm in the Churches.* Doubleday 1969 o.p. In what begins as a study of the race issue, Hadden concludes that clergy and laity are split over the meaning of the church, over the Christian message, and over the issue of authority. This led to his later *Why Conservative Churches Are Growing.*

Herberg, Will. *Protestant, Catholic, Jew: An Essay in American Religious Sociology.* Univ. of Chicago Pr. repr. of 1955 ed. 1983 pap. $11.00. Seminal work on self-understanding in America by a scholar who invented his own credentials.

Hill, Samuel S., Jr. *Southern Churches in Crisis.* Holt 1967 o.p. First major historical study of the southern churches entering the modern era.

Hochfield, George, ed. *Selected Writings of the New England Transcendentalists.* New Amer. Lib. 1966 o.p. Hutchison (below) will tell more accurately what transcendentalism has meant to American liberal theology, but here are the basic writings of folk like Emerson and Thoreau, with enough annotation to set the stage.

Hutchison, William R., ed. *American Protestant Thought in the Liberal Era.* Univ. Pr. of Amer. repr. of 1968 ed. 1985 text ed. pap. $10.75. The liberal mind in America existed prior to the Social Gospel, which is its finest flowering. Here is the whole scene.

McLoughlin, William G. *Modern Revivalism: Charles Grandison Finney to Billy Graham.* Ronald Pr. 1959 o.p. The author is *the* historian of that old American institution, the revival. See also his biographies of Billy Sunday and Billy Graham (below).

Marsden, George M. *Fundamentalism and American Culture: The Shaping of Twentieth-Century Evangelicalism, 1870–1925.* Oxford 1980 pap. $8.95. Written by a staunch conservative, it is the best book in the field. Notes and bibliography are unexcelled. (See also Sandeen and Sweet below.)

Marty, Martin E. *Modern American Religion: The Irony of It All, 1893–1919.* Univ. of Chicago Pr. 1986 $24.95. This is the first of four volumes that are projected to run to the close of the century. This one begins with the World Parliament of Religions and ends with the close of World War I.

————. *A Nation of Behavers.* Univ. of Chicago Pr. 1980 pap. $9.00. The leading interpreter of religion in America, professor and editor, Marty here presents six new maps (as he calls them) of religious allegiance in America: mainline and Evangelical churches, fundamentalism, pentecostal-charismatic religion, the new religions, ethnic religions, and civil religion. Expertly done and easy to grasp.

Mead, Sidney E. *The Lively Experiment: The Shaping of Christianity in America.* Harper 1963 pap. $6.95. In this and the following entry, Mead develops his view of the Religion of the Republic, which transcends particular faiths. A variant on civil religion pursued acutely. For the reader who already knows some of the facts.

————. *The Nation with the Soul of a Church.* Mercer Univ. Pr. 1985 $9.75. He states as his theme that "there is an unresolved tension between the theology that legitimates the constitutional structure of the Republic and the theology taught in most denominations in America." Interesting for even beginning students of American history.

Meyer, Donald. *The Positive Thinkers: Religion as Pop Psychology from Mary Baker Eddy to Oral Roberts.* Pantheon 1980 $15.95. Good background and analysis of this perennial version of faith, represented today by an increasing number of television preachers.

Miller, Perry. *The New England Mind: From Colony to Province.* Harvard Univ. Pr. 1983 text ed. pap. $8.95. Miller practically discovered the Puritans and their enduring importance for understanding religion in America.

Moore, Joan W. *Mexican Americans.* Prentice-Hall 2d ed. 1976 text ed. pap. $15.95. Not an adequate study of religion among Mexican Americans, but the best we can do for now. This is the largest Catholic ethnic minority in America, solidly Catholic, but (they say) not adequately ministered to by the church.

Niebuhr, H. Richard. *The Kingdom of God in America.* Harper 1937 o.p. Seminal work in which he traces the movement from the seventeenth-century's passion for God through the passion to change the social order for God. All studies of religion in America assume the work of Niebuhr.

O'Dea, Thomas F. *The Catholic Crisis.* Beacon 1968 o.p. This sociologist of religion finds that American Catholics approve of the changes brought about by Vatican II, but are estranged by them as well.

Powell, Milton B. *The Voluntary Church: American Religious Life Seen through the Eyes of Its European Visitors.* Macmillan 1967 $5.95. One can only really see the radical newness of American denominationalism by seeing it through the eyes of wondering Europeans. Many of their predictions have come true.

Sandeen, Ernest R. *The Roots of Fundamentalism.* Univ. of Chicago Pr. 1970 o.p. Along with Marsden's, one of the best studies of the conservative Protestant tradition.

Smith, Timothy. *Revivalism and Social Reform: American Protestantism on the Eve of the Civil War.* Johns Hopkins 1980 text ed. pap. $8.95. At one time American Evangelicals had a passion to change society, of which the abolition of slavery was a chief part. Why? And when did they lose it? Smith's is the definitive work. For a later interpretation see Marsden (above).

Sweet, Leonard I., ed. *The Evangelical Tradition in America.* Mercer Univ. Pr. 1984 $25.95. The editor's 85-page introduction "makes the volume well worth the price for any student of the subject."

Wilson, John F. *Public Religion in American Culture.* Temple Univ. Pr. 1979 lib. bdg. $24.95. 1981 pap. $9.95. James Madison's notion of public religion, not Jefferson's hasty "wall of separation," has really characterized the core of civil religion in America. A wise study of the way religion operates in America even when it appears to be hidden in the churches.

Wilson, John F., and John M. Mulder, eds. *Religion in American History: Interpretive Essays.* Prentice-Hall 1978 text ed. pap. $21.95. Twenty-seven essays that have had an impact on the reinterpretation of America's religious past. A rich source for the reader who already knows something about religious history in America.

Popular Religious Personalities in America

It seems appropriate here to single out for attention a few of the significant figures in American religious life whose careers, though interesting and important, have not received the fuller treatment accorded in the biographical sections. Of the ones included here, only Jonathan Edwards was a theologian. Indeed, except for the brothers Niebuhr, Reinhold and H. Richard, theology has not been America's forte. These three were chosen because in their day they have represented to a great many Americans what American Christianity was all about.

JONATHAN EDWARDS. 1703–1758

Colonial New England pastor and theologian, he has been called "the last Calvinist" and is widely regarded by scholars as one of the most creative minds ever grown on American soil. The literature is immense. The following are all solid studies, chosen because they explore different facets of his life and work.

Aldridge, Alfred Owen. *Jonathan Edwards.* [*Great American Thinkers Ser.*] Twayne 1966 o.p. Short and readable. A brief introduction in which the author manages to capture the flavor of the man and his work. For the beginning reader on Edwards.

Cherry, Conrad. *The Theology of Jonathan Edwards*. Doubleday 1966 o.p. Cherry calls Edwards's life an "American tragedy," because Edwards told his congregation in Northampton, Massachusetts, what the Puritan faith was at a time when they no longer wanted it. See also the listing for Patricia Tracy (below).

Davidson, Edward H. *Jonathan Edwards: The Narrative of a Puritan Mind*. Harvard Univ. Pr. 1968 o.p. In about 140 pages, the author tells the story of the development of Edwards's thought by relating it to his biography. Not an unusual approach, but in this case very effective.

De Lattre, Roland. *Beauty and Sensibility in the Thought of Jonathan Edwards*. Yale Univ. Pr. 1968 o.p. The new reader should read Aldridge (above) or Winslow (below) before tackling this book.

Holbrook, Clyde A. *The Ethics of Jonathan Edwards: Morality and Aesthetics*. Univ. of Michigan Pr. 1973 o.p. Edwards never separated beauty or morality from each other, or from God, giver of both. Holbrook digs deeply here, carrying on a debate with the other best book on the subject, Roland De Lattre's (see above).

Levin, David, ed. *Jonathan Edwards: A Profile*. Hill & Wang 1969 o.p. A curious book in a way, yet useful in that Levin allows Edwards to speak for himself, from diary extracts, and then prints some excellent articles by other writers, including some in this list.

Miller, Perry. *Jonathan Edwards*. [*Amer. Men of Letters Ser.*] Greenwood repr. of 1949 ed. 1973 lib. bdg. $25.00; intro. by Donald Weber, Univ. of Massachusetts Pr. repr. of 1949 ed. 1981 text ed. pap. $11.95. Miller rediscovered the "New England mind," and he calls this the biography of the life of a mind. Solid.

Tracy, Patricia. *Jonathan Edwards, Pastor: Religion and Society in Eighteenth-Century Northampton*. [*Amer. Century Ser.*] Hill & Wang 1980 $14.95 pap. $5.95. Here is the Northampton story told expertly. A slice of social history, full of real people.

Winslow, Ola E. *Jonathan Edwards, 1703–1758: A Biography*. Macmillan 1940 o.p. Though not devoid of theology, this is nonetheless a popular telling, and the book the general reader might begin with.

DOROTHY DAY. 1897–1980

Day, Dorothy. *By Little and By Little: The Selected Writings of Dorothy Day*. Ed. by Robert Ellsberg, Knopf 1983 o.p. A good selection of works by the editor of *The Catholic Worker*, American Catholicism's most famous communist.

———. *From Union Square to Rome*. Ayer repr. of 1938 ed. 1978 $17.00. A brief story of her conversion from atheistic Marxism to Catholic communism.

———. *The Long Loneliness: An Autobiography*. Intro. by Daniel Berrigan, Harper 1981 pap. $7.95. Her autobiography, although written a bit early in her life.

Ellis, Marc H. *Peter Maurin: Prophet in the Twentieth Century*. Paulist Pr. 1981 pap. $9.95. This Saint Francis in modern times was Day's right hand in their House of Hospitality. Her words on his death must be read.

Klejment, Anne, and Alice Klejment. *Dorothy Day and the Catholic Worker: Bibliography and Index*. Garland 1985 lib. bdg. $52.00. Simply a listing of all her editorials and articles, cross-indexed. For the specialist.

Miller, William D. *Dorothy Day: A Biography*. Harper 1984 pap. $10.95. Justly praised biography of the saint of the New York slums.

———. *A Harsh and Dreadful Love*. Doubleday 1974 o.p. The story of the Catholic Worker movement, of which Day and Peter Maurin were the spark and the drive. At 500 pages, it is still easy reading.

WILLIAM FRANKLIN (BILLY) GRAHAM. 1918–

America's foremost evangelist since the 1950s and still going strong in the 1980s.

Ashman, Chuck. *The Gospel According to Billy.* Intro. by Rod McKuen, Lyle Stuart 1977 $8.95. This is a journalistic look at the Graham message and the techniques used by Graham's evangelistic team. The author does not like Graham, nor what he terms the Jeu Bu$ine$$. A bit of a hit-and-run.

Bishop, Mary. *Billy Graham: America's Evangelist.* Putnam 1978 o.p. This is the coffee-table Graham, with lots of pictures and just enough text to tell the story.

Frady, Marshall. *Billy Graham: A Parable of American Righteousness.* Little, Brown 1979 o.p. This is the biggest book on Graham, more than 500 pages, and while Frady is a journalist, it is a fairer and more able analysis than Ashman's (see above). Frady doesn't like many things Graham says, but he likes and respects the man.

McLoughlin, William G. *Billy Graham: Revivalist in a Secular Age.* Ronald Pr. 1960 o.p. As a historian of revivalism, McLoughlin is uniquely qualified to understand Graham's place within that tradition. Those who like Graham will be disturbed by some of the author's judgments, which were made of necessity before Graham became somewhat of a statesman, more responsible in his dictates, especially after his entanglement in the Nixon affair.

Pollock, John. *To All Nations: The Billy Graham Story.* Harper 1985 $15.45. This is an authorized biography, a follow-up of an earlier volume by the same author. Such biographies are biased in favor of the subject, of course, but Pollock appears to keep his balance pretty well.

KING, MARTIN LUTHER, JR. 1929–1968 (NOBEL PEACE PRIZE 1964)

Son and grandson of Baptist preachers, King was born into a middle-class black family in Atlanta, Georgia. At Morehouse College his early concerns for social justice for blacks were deepened by reading THOREAU's (see Vol. 1) essay "Civil Disobedience." He enrolled in Crozer Theological Seminary and there became acquainted with the Social Gospel movement and the works of its chief spokesman, Walter Rauschenbusch. Mahatma Gandhi's practice of nonviolent resistance (*ahimsa*) became for him later a tactic for transforming love into social change.

After seminary, he postponed his ministry vocation by first earning a doctorate at Boston University School of Theology. There he discovered the works of Reinhold Niebuhr and was especially struck by Niebuhr's insistence that the powerless must somehow gain power if they are to achieve what is theirs by right. In the Montgomery bus boycott it was by economic clout that the blacks broke down the walls separating the races, for without black riders, the city's transportation system nearly collapsed.

The bus boycott took place in 1954, the year King and his bride, Coretta Scott, went to Montgomery, where he had been called to serve as pastor of the Dexter Avenue Baptist Church. Following the boycott he founded the Southern Christian Leadership Conference (SCLC) to coordinate civil rights organizations. Working through black churches, demonstrations were held all over the South, and attention was drawn, through television and newspaper reports, to the nonviolent demonstrations by blacks that were being put down violently by white police and state troopers. The federal government was finally forced to intervene and pass legislation protecting the right of blacks to vote and desegregating public accommodations. For his nonviolent activism, King received the Nobel Peace Prize in 1964.

While organizing a "poor people's campaign" to persuade Congress to take action against poverty, King accepted an invitation to visit Memphis, Tennessee, where sanitation workers were on strike. There, on April 4, 1968, he was gunned down while standing on the balcony of his hotel. Though today King is the only religious leader, save Jesus, who has an "official day" in most states, and his nonviolent strategy to win racial equality was the major cause for rewriting the laws of the nation, not everyone admired him, as the reader can see from the short bibliography below.

BOOK BY KING

A Testament of Hope: The Essential Writings of Martin Luther King, Jr. Ed. by James M. Washington, Harper 1986 $22.00. This really does have most of the essential writings: King's *Strength to Love* and *Stride toward Freedom* appear to be intact in this recent collection.

BOOKS ABOUT KING

Bennett, Lerone, Jr. *What Manner of Man: A Biography of Martin Luther King, Jr., 1929–1968.* Johnson Chi. 1969 $12.95. This is the coffee-table King. There is also a nonillustrated paperback, same author, title, publisher and date, but with more text.

Garrow, David J. *The FBI and Martin Luther King, Jr.* Norton 1981 $15.95; Penguin 1983 pap. $5.95. A trifle garish for serious scholarship, but seems to verify the conviction of King's followers that J. Edgar Hoover hated King more than he hated the Mafia.

King, Coretta S. *My Life with Martin Luther King, Jr.* Avon 1970 o.p. Published very hastily after King's assassination, this nevertheless catches the intimate King. Critics say it glosses over his weaknesses.

Lewis, David L. *King: A Biography.* [*Blacks in the New World Ser.*] Univ. of Illinois Pr. 2d ed. 1978 $32.50 pap. $9.95. Very good, but written in the heat of the controversies immediately following his death. The reader might want to check Oates (below) for a more reflective account as well.

Lokos, Lionel. *House Divided: The Life and Legacy of Martin Luther King.* Arlington House 1969 o.p. The death of King made him a martyr just as Lokos was researching and writing the great exposé of the communist fellow-traveler M. L. King, Jr. The author did not like King—the man, his tactics, his impact on the laws of the nation.

Oates, Stephen B. *Let the Trumpet Sound: The Life of Martin Luther King, Jr.* Harper 1982 $24.45; New Amer. Lib. 1985 pap. $4.95. This book is big at 500 pages, but reads well. In addition, the biographer is a sound scholar and biographer.

MERTON, THOMAS. 1915–1968

Born in France, Merton was the son of an American woman, an artist and poet, and her New Zealander husband, a painter. He lost both parents before he had finished high school, and his younger brother was killed in World War II. Something of the ephemeral character of human endeavor marked all his works, deepening the pathos of his writings and drawing him close to Eastern, especially Buddhist, forms of monasticism.

After an initial education in the United States, France, and England, he completed his undergraduate degree at Columbia University. His parents, nominally Friends, had given him little religious guidance, and in 1938 he converted to Roman Catholicism. The following year he received a master's degree from Columbia, and, in 1941, he entered Gethsemani Abbey in Kentucky, where he remained until a short time before his death.

His working life was spent as a Trappist monk. At Gethsemani he wrote his famous autobiography, *The Seven Storey Mountain* (1948); there he labored and prayed through the days and years of a constant regimen that began with daily prayer at 2:00 A.M. As his contemplative life developed, he still maintained contact with the outside world, his many books and articles increasing steadily as the years went by. Reading them, it is hard to think of him as only a "guilty bystander," to use the title of one of his many collections of essays. He was vehement in his opposition to the Vietnam War, to the nuclear arms race, to racial oppression.

Having received permission to leave his monastery, he went on a journey to confer with mystics of the Hindu and Buddhist traditions; he was accidentally electrocuted in a hotel in Bangkok, Thailand, on December 10, 1968.

BOOKS BY MERTON

The Asian Journal of Thomas Merton. Ed. by Naomi B. Stone and others, New Directions 1973 pap. $8.95. In these 445 pages, some of them introductions and commentary, the reader catches a glimpse of a lively mind wrestling with Eastern spirituality, comparing it with the great Benedictine tradition.

Conjectures of a Guilty Bystander. Doubleday 1966 pap. $5.95. Racism, the heroism of Martin Luther King and his nonviolent activists, growing concern over Vietnam. No bystander was Merton.

Geography of Holiness: The Photography of Thomas Merton. Ed. by Deba Prasad Patnaik, Pilgrim Pr. 1980 o.p. One hundred pages of pictures, most taken by Merton.

The Literary Essays of Thomas Merton. Ed. by Patrick Hart, New Directions 1981 $39.95 pap. $14.95. Fine essays introduced by a careful friend and critic of Merton.

Mystics and Zen Masters. Farrar 1986 pap. $8.95. In this 300-page work Merton tells the reader what he expected to find when he went to Asia. A good companion to what he actually found, as recorded in *The Asian Journal.*

The Secular Journal of Thomas Merton. Farrar 1959 pap. $3.95; Peter Smith 1983 $12.00. Provides background for his biography, *The Seven Storey Mountain.*

The Seven Storey Mountain. Harcourt 1948 $15.95; Hippocrene Bks. repr. ed. 1978 lib. bdg. $32.00; Walker repr. ed. 1985 pap. $19.95. His most-read classic. Many of the extreme positions he took not too long after entering the Trappists he modified later.

A Thomas Merton Reader. Ed. by Thomas P. McDonnell, Doubleday 1974 pap. $6.50. More than 500 pages, containing much of his important writing that is not included elsewhere in this listing.

BOOKS ABOUT MERTON

Furlong, Monica. *Merton: A Biography*. Harper 1985 pap. $8.95. The author is a well-known writer on theological matters, and her judgments seem accurate. She does not discount the bitterness Merton felt toward authority at the monastery, or the spiritual struggles he went through, but she accentuates his turn outward when this "desert" (as he called it) had been traversed. A good book.

Rice, Edward. *The Man in the Sycamore Tree: The Good Life and Hard Times of Thomas Merton*. Harcourt 1985 pap. $6.95. Rice, an old and enduring friend of Merton's, believes that Merton's life would have been more joyful and positive had he not spent most of it in a monastery.

Wilkes, Paul, ed. *Merton: By Those Who Knew Him Best*. Harper 1984 $13.95. Like *C. S. Lewis at the Breakfast Table*, this is an appreciation and personal glimpse collection.

NIEBUHR, REINHOLD. 1892–1971

WALTER LIPPMANN (see Vol. 3) once called Niebuhr the greatest mind America had produced since Jonathan Edwards. It was fitting, then, that Niebuhr died at home in Stockbridge, Massachusetts, in the town where Edwards had been pastor, and that his funeral was held in the church where Edwards had preached. He was born in Wright City, Missouri, and his father was a German immigrant who served those German-speaking churches that preserved both the Lutheran and Reformed (Calvinist) traditions and piety. After seminary in St. Louis, he studied for two years at Yale, and the master's degree he received there was the highest degree he earned. Rather than work for a doctorate, he became a pastor in Detroit, where in his 13 years of service a tiny congregation grew to one of 800 members. Part of his diary from those years was published in 1929 as *Leaves from the Notebook of a Tamed Cynic*.

During that time he began to attract attention through articles on social issues; as he said, he "cut [his] eyeteeth fighting [Henry] Ford." But the socialism to which he was attracted soon seemed naive to him: human problems could not be solved just by appealing to the good in people, or by promulgating programs for change. Power, economic clout, was needed to change the systems set up by sinful groups, a position expressed in his 1932 book, *Moral Man and Immoral Society*. Tough and brash, it exposed the shallow optimism of liberal thought and was in its way as revolutionary as Karl Barth's commentary on Romans a decade earlier was for German theology. By this time Niebuhr was teaching at Union Theological Seminary in New York, where he spent the rest of his career. His wife, Ursula, became head of the religion department at Barnard College; his brother H. Richard, who became nearly as famous as Reinhold, taught at Yale.

Reinhold Niebuhr's theology always took second place to ethics. He ran for office as a socialist, rescued Paul Tillich from Germany, became a strong supporter of Israel, gave up pacifism, and was often too orthodox for the liberals, too liberal for the orthodox. His *The Nature and Destiny of Man* is one of the few seminal theological books written by an American. In it he reiterates a theme that led some to place him in the Barthian camp of Neo-orthodoxy: the radical sinfulness of the human creature. But he was never as interested in Christ as God's unique response to human sin as others in the Augustine-Luther-Calvin-Barth continuum, and the label probably fits him less than it does Barth or Bonhoeffer. The human condition as illumined by the Christian tradition—that was always the arena in which he worked.

BOOKS BY NIEBUHR

The Essential Reinhold Niebuhr: Selected Essays and Addresses. Ed. by Robert M. Brown, Yale Univ. Pr. 1986 $19.95. Includes bibliography of his work and works about him. Edited by a colleague and a theologian nearly as celebrated as his subject, so the introduction is valuable too.

Leaves from the Notebook of a Tamed Cynic. Da Capo repr. of 1929 ed. 1976 lib. bdg. $25.00; Harper 1980 pap. $5.95. Written as Niebuhr left a 13-year pastorate in Detroit to become America's most celebrated home-grown theologian. Brief and very enjoyable.

Moral Man and Immoral Society: A Study in Ethics and Politics. 1932. Scribner 1960 pap. $9.95. This is an amazingly acute evisceration of philosophies of progress and reason, and almost a blueprint of later struggles for equality among minority people.

The Nature and Destiny of Man. 1941–43. Scribner 2 vols. 1949 o.p. His major theological work.

BOOKS ABOUT NIEBUHR

Fox, Richard W. *Reinhold Niebuhr: A Biography.* Pantheon 1986 $19.95. We are fortunate to have this full-blown study of the man, his life and thought, in readable form. It contains judicious evaluations of earlier works and a very good bibliography.

Patterson, Bob E. *Reinhold Niebuhr.* Word Bks. 1977 $8.95. The quickest way into Niebuhr's mind and thought.

ORTHODOXY: EASTERN CHRISTIANITY MOVES WEST

From the very beginning of Christian history all the major Christian centers—save Rome—were in the eastern Mediterranean region, places like Jerusalem, Ephesus, Alexandria, and Constantinople. Throughout the centuries several barriers arose to what had at one time been easy communication between the churches of the East and those within the orbit of Rome. Language changed, as the Western churches turned to Latin, where their ancestors in faith had used the common Greek of trade around the Mediterranean basin. The Eastern churches tended to stick with the languages of the people—Greek for the Greek-speaking, Arabic, Coptic, Armenian, and a dozen more. Politically, power centered in Constantinople, modern Istanbul, Turkey, and the Eastern churches may have lost some spiritual power vis-à-vis the state in the Caesaro-papism that developed there. And ecclesiastically Rome's bishop began to demand acknowledgment that his jurisdiction was a universal one, a claim the Eastern churches found aggrandizing, not rooted in the histories they have ever been fond of. Indeed, a slogan of the Eastern churches toward Rome is that "St. Peter had primacy of honor, but not of jurisdiction."

One can find several dates to mark the final sundering of relations between Eastern churches and the one Western church, but 1054 is the date usually accepted. Among various language groups liturgies developed and within regions systems of hierarchy were established—where they had not been established almost from the beginning, as, for example in Greece. Moscow received its own patriarch, second in the Eastern churches only to the patriarch of Constantinople. The Crusades sometimes ravaged the Eastern churches more than they did Turkish-dominated Islam; indeed, the cruelties of the Crusaders' empire in the Holy Land were responsible for the church there losing thousands of converts to Islam, for Suleiman was a more compassionate ruler over Christians than were the barbarian Christians from the West.

In our era the major event was a nonevent: the Eastern churches experienced no Protestant Reformation. No Martin Luther arose to challenge the hierarchy; no Reformed tradition produced Puritans intent on painting over the icons on the screen before the altar. Perhaps because of this, a fairly unbroken tradition stretches back as far as the historical eye can see, losing itself somewhere in the dimness surrounding the church of the first or second century.

The books below are generally regarded as accurate introductions to Orthodoxy.

Attwater, Donald. *The Christian Churches of the East.* Bruce 2 vols. rev. ed. 1961 o.p. Volume 1 covers churches in communion with Rome (Melkite, Maronite, etc.), with a chapter on monasticism in the East. Volume 2 surveys the Orthodox churches, the Nestorians and Monophysites. "A sound reference work and a key starting place for inquiries" (*Theological and Religious Reference Materials*).

Ellis, Jane. *The Russian Orthodox Church: A Contemporary History.* Indiana Univ. Pr. 1986 $39.95. This work sticks to the Russian scene from the mid-1960s, so its more than 500-page length allows for considerable depth and interpretation.

Fortescue, Adrian. *The Orthodox Eastern Church.* B. Franklin 1969 $25.50. "Frequently reprinted, this work covers the history, theology, liturgical structure of the Orthodox Church before and after the Great Schism to modern times" (Gorman).

Fouyas, Methodius. *Orthodoxy, Roman Catholicism and Anglicanism.* Oxford 1972 o.p. Describes the beliefs and practices of the three churches and examines the prospects for their reunion.

Lossky, Vladimir. *Orthodox Theology: An Introduction.* St. Vladimir's 1978 pap. $5.95. This is a textbook and reads somewhat like one, but provides fundamental concepts in Orthodox theology.

Maloney, George A. *A History of Orthodox Theology since 1453.* Nordland 1976 $39.50. This nearly 400-page book examines developments since the fall of Constantinople to the Turks in five of the Orthodox traditions: Russian, Greek, Serbian, Bulgarian, and Rumanian. Sound analysis and condensation of major trends, with good bibliographies.

Meyendorff, John. *Byzantine Theology: Historical Trends and Doctrinal Themes.* Fordham Univ. Pr. 2d rev. ed. 1983 pap. $9.00. Excellent study by one of Orthodoxy's best historians of theology.

———. *The Orthodox Church: Its Past and Its Role in the World Today.* St. Vladimir's 1981 pap. $8.95. A useful introduction, but Ware (below) is probably better for the new reader in this field.

Schmemann, Alexander. *Russian Theology, 1920–1965: A Bibliographic Survey.*

Union Theological Seminary (Virginia) 1969 o.p. Excellent introduction to Orthodox theology since 1920, and not confined to Russian.

Ware, Timothy. *Orthodox Church.* Penguin 1963 pap. $4.95. Highly regarded because, as a convert, he knows the stumbling blocks to Western appreciation of the ornate and "Byzantine" character of Orthodoxy. There is a good bibliography as well.

ISSUES IN SCIENCE AND RELIGION

The rise of science created a new paradigm (see Barbour below) for the understanding of the cosmos and humans within it. Three separate crises have rocked Christianity as its paradigm—an odd mixture of biblical religion with Aristotelian science, with the Ptolemaic earth-centered cosmology as backdrop—has been shattered. The first of these was the displacement of earth as the center of the universe; the second was the reduction of life and especially human life to that of the animal, as Darwinism explained a trial-and-error development where God had no place; the last has been the effort of modern biology to explain life by a genetic process of complex chemistry with a vigorous reductionism, which is now denied in modern physics, but affirmed on the biological level. The small list below addresses these various questions, all of them within a Christian framework, all written by respected scientists or theologians.

Barbour, Ian G. *Issues in Science and Religion.* Harper 1971 pap. $8.95. Barbour, like Peacocke (below), is both scientist and theologian. This book covers clearly and well almost any subject in the science-religion field up until its publication. It is, however, a little overwritten.

———. *Myths, Models, Paradigms.* Harper 1976 text ed. pap. $6.95. A very helpful study of the languages of science and religion, a key problem in interpreting each to the other.

Bowker, John. *The Religious Imagination and the Sense of God.* Oxford 1978 text ed. $32.50. Bowker is a leader among a large group of scholars at Oxford who comprise a think tank on issues relating faith to the modern world. Here he reexamines some of the themes William James dealt with at the turn of the century, writing cogently and clearly.

———. *The Sense of God: Sociological, Anthropological, and Psychological Approaches to the Origin of the Sense of God.* Oxford 1973 o.p. Shows that the sense of God's existence and presence are known even in the behavioral scientific analysis and practice. Read this book first, since it begins his Wilde Lectures on science and religion, followed by *The Religious Imagination.*

Gilkey, Langdon B. *Creationism on Trial: Evolution and God at Little Rock.* Harper 1985 pap. $12.95. Enjoyable account by a theologian who was called to testify at the creationist textbook trial in Arkansas. He tells a good story and gives lessons in the methods of studying both science and religion, finding that some theologians do not know what science is, nor do some scientists!

———. *Religion and the Scientific Future.* Mercer Univ. Pr. repr. of 1970 ed. 1982 text ed. $13.95. Best study of the possible downfalls of both areas of life and study if care is not given. Warning: not as readable as *Creationism on Trial.*

Moore, J. R. *The Post-Darwinian Controversies.* Cambridge Univ. Pr. 1979 $57.50 pap. $24.95. An interesting study, explaining that the author of the first fundamentalist tract on evolution actually believed that evolution was true, but Darwin was wrong. Solid study by a theological conservative.

Peacocke, A. R. *Creation and the World of Science: The Bampton Lecturers.* Oxford 1979 $22.50; Univ. of Notre Dame Pr. repr. of 1979 ed. 1985 text ed. pap. $9.95. Like Barbour (above), Peacocke is a practicing scientist and a theologian. This is the single best defense of Christianity as intellectually respectable in an age of science. It needs a bibliography, but the footnotes will lead the careful reader to other good studies.

Polinghorne, John. *One World: The Interaction of Science and Theology.* Princeton Univ. Pr. 1987 $17.50 pap. $7.95. Peacocke's physicist colleague at Cambridge decided to become an Anglican clergyman as science led him to theology. This is a much easier telling of the science-religion relationship than is Peacocke's, shorter and clearer for the general reader, but not as satisfying to the initiated. Laced with good insights.

Russell, Colin A. *Cross-Currents: Interactions between Science and Faith.* Eerdmans 1985 pap. $10.95. The single best volume on the science-religion issues before Darwin by a scientist who knows his way around religious language.

Teilhard de Chardin, Pierre. *The Phenomenon of Man.* Trans. by Bernard Wall, intro. by Julian Huxley, Harper 1975 pap. $7.95. The author, a Jesuit, spent his life as a paleontologist. His search for the divine in the midst of evolutionary change is exciting for those who can read his partially invented language.

Trinklein, F. E., ed. *The God of Science.* Eerdmans 1971 o.p. Various statements by scientists that demonstrate the capacity for belief by experts in physics, biology, and chemistry.

CHAPTER 13

The Bible and Related Literature

Prepared by Staff Editors

> Of course the Bible is not a book. Because it is all bound together a literature covering seven or eight centuries is mistaken for a single volume. This is Christianity's fault. The only book the Bible resembles is an anthology.
> —ISRAEL ZANGWILL

The Bible was written over a period of some 1,400 years (1300 B.C.–A.D. 100). Very few of its many contributing authors have been identified, and there are no known original manuscripts, only copies of copies and translations. Scholars used Hebrew manuscripts of the Old Testament dating from the ninth to eleventh centuries A.D. and the earliest complete New Testament manuscripts dating from the fourth century A.D. The oldest Gospel text in scholars' possession is a papyrus fragment from John 18:31–33, written in Greek, probably early in the second century, which describes the arraignment of Jesus before Pontius Pilate. Present-day versions of the Bible were, with a few exceptions noted, based on these manuscripts.

The very first thing a prospective student of the Bible must realize is that its contents, the vast sacred literatures of Jews and Christians, were not originally written in English. For that matter, they were not written in languages that are still spoken today as the sacred authors spoke them. The classical Hebrew of the Old Testament books belonged to the centuries before the Babylonian exile, in the sixth century B.C., and did not survive the 60-year exile as a common people's language. Its place among the Hebrew repatriates of Palestine was taken by Aramaic, the related Semitic tongue of the region of their exile and the language of a few late portions of the Jewish Scripture. This language, in its turn, barely survived the extinction of Jewish civilization in the Holy Land following the Arab conquests. Finally, the Greek of the New Testament period, which was the common coinage of a triumphant world culture, declined with that culture and echoes only intermittently in the spoken Greek of today.

A "language bridge" has had to be built, therefore, between this trilingual biblical heritage, on the one side, and modern readers, with their myriad of modern languages, on the other side, and of course no such bridge could ever be constructed without sustained and concerted efforts at interpreting the authors' statements as they wrote them. Any bibliography of biblical study has to begin, therefore, with the sources of the original texts, even if a majority of readers cannot aspire to the level of specialization that would

645

make the original texts accessible. A realization that what we read on any page of the Bible has a whole history of translation behind it, and that all translation is ruled by the very words and intentions of the original author, makes an indispensable first step in understanding this hallowed literature.

The translation activity that produced our English bibles was not merely a process of word substitutions. After all, to render any writer's speech accurately in a language other than that of the writing is to recapture all the special turns of expression, all the nuances and shadings, indeed all the plays of irony, hyperbole, and other types of inferential expression, that were given in the original. Knowledge of all these expressive features of some "dead language" of antiquity comes mainly from the way its writings were translated in periods and regions closer to them. This means that besides the original writings themselves, called "texts" in our arrangement, a biblical translator has to maintain close consultation of the classic translations, called "versions" here, which became the models and monitors of modern-language versions. Only the most important of the classical versions, the Greek and the Aramaic of the Old Testament and the Latin of both Testaments, can receive passing notice in a general-purpose bibliography such as this one.

The Greek of the New Testament is not the Attic dialect of the classical writers but the new language of "Hellenism," the Greek world culture, whose migrations and urban "melting pots" poured a molten mix of foreign-language habits, particularly Semitic ones from the East, into the exquisite vessel of the Hellenic tongue. A suggestive but risky comparison is the effect of the American "melting pot" on the English language, which U.S. domination of world affairs has promoted as the international medium of commerce and diplomacy. The New Testament documents part of the process of blending a "common" (koine) Greek out of its polyglot tributaries by the frequent quotation and imitation of the translated Hebrew Scriptures in New Testament writings. The Greek versions of the Old Testament antedated the Christian Scriptures, some by as much as 250 years, and deeply influenced the argument and diction of their authors. What we read in the original New Testament text, therefore, is not just a Greek language flattened and homogenized by uncultivated speakers, but a new stage of an incomparably rich and expressive tongue, expanded and reornamented by the idioms of just such widely quoted "foreigners" as the Hebrew sages.

REFERENCE WORKS

In the lists that follow, the principal "critical editions" of the original texts of both Testaments are given first; then the most authoritative access tools, grammars, and dictionaries, which assist any reading of the original, and finally bibliographies. Critical editions are those that list variant manuscript readings for uncertain passages in an accompanying annotation footnoted to the text.

Critical Editions of Original Texts

The Hebrew text of the Old Testament emerged in increasingly standardized form during the earliest age of rabbinical scholarship, the second to the fifth centuries A.D., and received a near miraculous standardization during the sixth to eighth centuries A.D. through the work of scholars called the Masoretes, who copied with rigid discipline, painstakingly evaluated the manuscripts on hand, and introduced vowel signs to a language previously written with consonants only. New manuscripts of some Hebrew Scriptures were found among the famous Dead Sea Scrolls from Qumran, beginning in 1947, and though these go back hundreds of years before the Masoretes, their readings evaluated so far roundly endorse the accuracy and fidelity of the Masoretic text.

Aland, Kurt, ed. *Synopsis of the Four Gospels.* Amer. Bible Society 1983 $5.95. Because of the literary relationships of the Gospel texts, especially the frequent formal parallels found among the three Synoptics (Matthew, Mark, Luke), an indispensable tool of Gospel study is the edition of their texts in parallel columns. This edition features Greek and English columns on facing pages for the convenience of students who cannot use the Greek by itself.

Aland, Kurt, and others, eds. *The Greek New Testament.* Amer. Bible Society 3d ed. 1983 $8.50. This is the same basic text as that of Nestle and Aland (below), but its advantage is its more attractive format, which includes captions for English-speaking readers and a simplified critical notation. Helpful formats of this edition available from the Bible Society include one with facing pages containing the Revised Standard English Version (see below under Texts and Versions of the Bible, English Versions) and one attaching a concise Greek-English dictionary at the back of the volume.

The Holy Scriptures of the Old Testament: Hebrew and English. Amer. Bible Society 1961 $16.00. Here is a useful edition of the Hebrew text, without critical notes, alongside columns containing the venerable King James Version (see below under Texts and Versions of the Bible, English Versions). Neither the Hebrew nor, *a fortiori*, the seventeenth-century English can be considered up to date, but a beginner with Hebrew is assisted by the immediate visibility of a translation for each verse.

Nestle, E., and Kurt Aland. *Novum Testamentum Graece.* Amer. Bible Society 26th ed. 1979 $8.00. This latest critical edition of the Greek New Testament is the work of an international committee of foremost textual scholars and represents the most authoritative text and most complete presentation of variant readings. An extensive introduction gives invaluable information concerning the manuscripts used to reconstruct the text and the procedures of their evaluation.

Rudolf, W., and H. P. Rüger, eds. *Biblia Hebraica Stuttgartensia.* Amer. Bible Society 2d ed. 1984 $19.00. A greatly improved critical edition of the Masoretic bible, meaning one that lists divergent manuscript readings for each unstable passage in footnotes to the sacred text established by the editors. This edition represents the latest stage in the critical evaluation of this century's extensive manuscript discoveries.

Principal Access Tools

Bauer, W., F. W. Gingrich, and F. W. Danker. *A Greek-English Lexicon of the New Testament and Other Early Christian Literatures.* Trans. by William F. Arndt,

Univ. of Chicago Pr. 2d ed. rev. & enl. 1979 lib. bdg. $45.00. This English adaptation of the fourth edition of the celebrated German work, widely recognized as the finest New Testament dictionary, includes material from the fifth edition and enrichments by the English-language editor.

Blass, F., and A. Debrunner. *A Greek Grammar of the New Testament and Other Early Christian Literature.* Trans. by Robert W. Funk, Univ. of Chicago Pr. 1961 $30.00. This German work in English translation is first among New Testament Greek grammars, of which there are many, in varying degrees of depth, for the student to choose from.

Funk, Robert W. *A Beginning-Intermediate Grammar of Hellenistic Greek.* Scholars Pr. GA 3 vols. 2d ed. rev. 1973 text ed. pap. $19.50. Includes appendixes, paradigms, and an index. A separate workbook is also available. This expository grammar, which explains the morphology and grammar of the common tongue as it emerged from the classical, makes an especially wise investment for the student in early stages of mastering biblical Greek.

Gesenius, William. *Hebrew-Chaldee Lexicon to the Old Testament.* Trans. by S. P. Tregelles, Eerdmans 1949 $12.95. This hoary nineteenth-century product has been revised here and there in this century and remains the most convenient unabridged Hebrew-Aramaic dictionary, with surveys of usage accompanying each definition. The more comprehensive and up-to-date lexicon by L. Koehler and W. Baumgartner, *Lexicon in Veteris Testamenti Libros* (distributed by the same publishing house), is an unwieldy German-English amalgamation that will discourage all but the specialist.

Gesenius, William, and E. Kautzsch. *Gesenius' Hebrew Grammar.* Trans. by A. E. Cowley, Oxford 2d ed. 1910 $29.95. Though some of its treatments are out of date, this exhaustively documented and illustrated grammar is still the best reference tool available in English. It is just that, however: a specialist's reference work, not a beginner's helpmate.

Greenlee, J. Harold. *A Concise Exegetical Grammar of New Testament Greek.* Eerdmans 5th ed. rev. 1987 pap. $5.95. This is a thorough revision of a popular, "user-friendly" instrument recommended for students in early stages of New Testament textual study.

Holladay, William L. *A Concise Hebrew and Aramaic Lexicon of the Old Testament.* Eerdmans 1971 $27.95. This condensed version of the foremost Hebrew-Aramaic lexicon (by L. Koehler and W. Baumgartner; see Gesenius annotation above) is well suited for students beginning their study of the two Old Testament languages.

Johns, Alger F. *A Short Grammar of Biblical Aramaic.* Andrews Univ. Pr. rev. ed. repr. of 1963 ed. 1972 text ed. pap. $7.95. A short beginner's tool, presupposing knowledge of biblical Hebrew.

Liddell, H. G., and R. Scott. *A Greek-English Lexicon.* Oxford 1966 $89.00. This immense lexicon, devoted mainly to classical Greek but including word usages from the Old and New Testaments, is the kind of major purchase only the aspiring specialist will make. A supplement was published by E. A. Barber and others by Clarendon in 1968 and a dated (1871) abridgment of earlier editions of the lexicon (reprinted by Clarendon in 1979) might prove more practical for the student of modest aspirations.

Weingreen, Jacob. *A Practical Grammar for Classical Hebrew.* Oxford 2d ed. 1959 $15.95. This is the most popular beginner's grammar, offering only the most basic information together with exercises, tables of forms, and a short vocabulary.

Zerwick, Max. *A Grammatical Analysis of Greek New Testament.* Loyola Univ. Pr. 1974 pap. $16.00. This valuable companion for the beginner identifies Greek forms and finely shaded word meanings verse by verse throughout the New

Testament, first the Gospels and Acts (Vol. 1) and then the letters and the Apocalypse (Vol. 2). Cross-references for grammar are to Zerwick's *Biblical Greek Illustrated by Examples,* translated by J. Smith and published by the Biblical Institute of Loyola University in 1963.

Bibliographies

Included in this category are several bibliographies that appear continuously and therefore could also be classified as serials. Listed here are only those items considered most helpful for the person striking out in Scripture study. In addition, the reader should consult articles in such periodicals as *The Bible Today, The Biblical Archaeologist, Biblical Research, Biblical Theology Bulletin, Catholic Biblical Quarterly, Interpretation: A Journal of Bible and Theology, Journal of Biblical Literature,* and *Semeia: An Experimental Journal for Biblical Criticism.*

Aune, David E. *Jesus and the Synoptic Gospels: A Bibliographic Study Guide.* Ed. by Mark L. Branson, Inter-Varsity 1981 pap. $2.95. Includes an introduction that lists basic reference works, literary criticism, tradition criticism, historical criticism, and theological study of the Gospels. Entries are annotated, guidance is very sound. Similar study guides are promised from the same auspices in Pauline literature, intertestamental Judaism, Pentateuchal studies, and second-century Christianity.

Childs, Brevard S. *Old Testament Books for Pastor and Teacher.* Westminster 1977 pap. $4.95. For the Protestant pastor/teacher; includes Old Testament text and translations, commentaries extensively evaluated, introductions to the Old Testament, history, theology. It is a helpful guide to a very large field.

Danker, Frederick W. *Multipurpose Tools for Bible Study.* Concordia rev. ed. 1970 pap. $12.50. This is an extensive and valuable listing of the main resources needed for serious study of both Testaments, together with explanations of their use and relationship to the interpretive enterprise as a whole.

Fitzmyer, Joseph A. *An Introductory Bibliography for the Study of Scripture.* Loyola Univ. Pr. rev. ed. 1981 o.p. One of the very finest bibliographies of its kind. The 555 entries, extensively and incisively annotated, embrace bibliographies, periodicals, texts and versions, introductions, lexica, grammars, concordances, dictionaries, commentaries, archaeology, history, theology, apocryphal and other contemporary writings, and religious milieu of the Bible. We are fortunate that the compiler undertook this laborious revision of the earlier bibliography (1961) he had published jointly with the late G. S. Glanzman.

Hurd, John C., Jr., ed. *Bibliography of New Testament Bibliographies.* Allenson 1966 text ed. pap. $8.50. As the title indicates, this directs the student quickly to the bibliographies available on individual books, sections, and topics pertaining to New Testament study. It is a remarkable resource, though it is no longer current.

New Testament Abstracts. Weston School of Theology triannual 1956 to date $24.00 per year. Published three times a year by the Weston School of Theology, this very important service abstracts the most important articles and book reviews that have appeared in Catholic, Protestant, and Jewish periodicals on topics and texts in the New Testament, offering short précis in English of materials published in all major European languages as well as English. Contents of each issue are broken down by topics and by New Testament books, whose internal order is followed in the listings. It is an indispensable tool for any research in the area.

Nober, Petrus, and J. Swetnam. *Elenchus Bibliographicus Biblicus.* Loyola Univ. Pr. 1972 o.p. This enormous undertaking lags behind the current year because of its immensity and the irreplaceable labors of its late founder. Biblical studies, both books and articles, are listed in the thousands, from many countries and languages, under both topical and biblical headings (Latin), embracing biblical exegesis and all its associated disciplines.

Old Testament Abstracts. Catholic Bibl. Assn. triannual 1978 to date $14.00 yearly subscription. Modeled after *New Testament Abstracts* (see above) and offering a parallel if necessarily more limited service, this trimestrial publication is under the auspices of the Catholic Biblical Association of America. Its purview extends to the most important publications in Old Testament and related disciplines, which it extracts competently and clearly. It, too, offers a service not duplicated elsewhere, at least in English.

TEXTS AND VERSIONS OF THE BIBLE

Ancient Versions

The oldest translations, or "versions," of the Hebrew Bible were products of both the Jewish Diaspora, following the Babylonian exile (587–539 B.C.), and the great institution that linked far-flung Jewish communities with their tradition, the Synagogue. The Greek translation was undertaken in Alexandria, Egypt, in the third century B.C. and bears a name, the "Septuagint," that echoes the legend of its accomplishment by a symbolic "70" translators. The Aramaic paraphrases grew out of the practice of the Palestinian synagogues and are called "targums" (translations). Out of reverence for the original Hebrew, the Aramaic paraphrases were never written down until the fifth century A.D., but there was undoubtedly a fixed oral tradition of Aramaic renderings of the Hebrew by the time of Jesus.

Brenton, L. L. *The Septuagint Version of the Old Testament and Apocrypha.* Amer. Bible Society 1976 o.p. A convenient edition with facing English columns, but both Greek and English are dated and flawed.

Friedlander, Albert H., ed. *The Five Scrolls.* Central Conf. of Amer. Rabbis 1984 $12.00. This "volume contains five selections, one for each of the 'five scrolls' of the Hebrew Bible—Song of Songs, Ruth, Lamentations, Goheleth (Ecclesiastes), and Esther. For each of the five the book presents a new translation, along with a brief introduction and a short liturgy to precede the ritual reading of the scroll itself in Reform temples. [This bilingual edition presents Hebrew and English texts on facing pages]" (*Choice*).

Jellicoe, Sidney. *The Septuagint and Modern Study.* Eisenbrauns repr. of 1968 ed. 1978 $12.50. A survey of this century's Septuagint research, covering its origins and transmission, then questions of its text and language.

McNamara, Martin, and others, eds. *The Aramaic Bible.* M. Glazier 19 vols. projected in set 1987– . ea. $27.95–$49.00. A professional translation of the targums with critical annotations and a lengthy introduction to each volume. Relationships between the English and the Aramaic original, plus variant readings and emendations, are offered in the notes. Five of the 19 volumes are now available (Jonathan of the Former Prophets, Isaiah, Ezekiel, Jeremiah, and Genesis).

Rahlfs, A., ed. *Septuaginta*. Amer. Bible Society repr. of 1935 ed. 1979 $16.00. The Greek text is the editor's reconstruction from major manuscripts, but its critical foundation and textual apparatus are inadequate. While we wait the completion of the following edition, this one remains the most convenient and popular.

Sperber, A. *The Bible in Aramaic Based on Old Manuscripts and Printed Texts*. Amer. Bible Society 4 vols. 1959–73 o.p. A critical edition of various targums, concluding with a study of the relationship of the targum to the Hebrew Bible (Vol. 4B). The edition is the best available to date.

Weber, R., ed. *Biblia sacra iuxta vulgatam versionem*. Amer. Bible Society 2 vols. 1969 $35.00 2 vols. in 1 $22.00. A manual edition of the Vulgate Latin version of the St. Jerome (fourth century) based on the major critical editions. This Latin text can also be obtained in facing-page editions with the Greek of Nestle and Aland (see above under Critical Editions of Original Texts).

English Versions

From the introduction of Christianity into Britain until the late fourteenth century, translation of the Bible into English was fragmentary and sporadic, being held back by the Western church's wariness of lay use of Scripture and the "profane" vernacular dialects (as against the officially sanctioned Latin Vulgate). The Oxford scholar John Wyclif (c.1330–84) (see Chapter 11 in this volume), precursor of the Reformation in England, supervised the first complete English translation (1382–84), and this began a tradition of English renderings, including those of William Tyndale (1525–31) and Miles Coverdale (1535), that produced the authorized Bibles of the Church of England under Henry VIII (1539), Elizabeth I (1568), and, most enduring, the "authorized version" commissioned by James of Scotland in 1611. Even at this stage, however, study of the Hebrew and Greek originals was still in its infancy, and the more adequate foundation of the English Bible in them would have to await much later revisions, the Revised Version of 1881 to 1885 and the celebrated Revised Standard Version (see below) of 1946 to 1952. As for the routed Roman Catholics of England, their scholars in exile produced a New Testament at Rheims in 1582, then the Old Testament at Douay (1609–1610), but both were slavishly dependent on the Latin Vulgate and desperately needed the considerable revision given them under Bishop Richard Challoner (1749–1763). English bibles for Catholics could not be fully based on the original texts until the pontificate of Pius XII, in the middle of the twentieth century, and the very recent New American Bible (see below) is among the first fruits of that revolution.

Bruce, F. F. *History of the Bible in English*. Oxford 3d ed. 1978 pap. $8.95. Its title suggests the very large and fascinating subject matter that is attempted here. The work effectively attunes its reader to the complexity and the marvelous consistency of the tradition of English renderings.

The Complete Bible: An American Translation. Univ. of Chicago Pr. rev. ed. 1939 o.p. This American effort, better known as the "Chicago Bible," was spearheaded by E. J. Goodspeed's initiative to bring the New Testament out from under the shroud of archaic "biblical" English. This bible is one of the first to accomplish the shift to attractive modern idiom.

The Geneva Bible: A Facsimile of the Fifteen-Sixty Edition. Intro. by Lloyd E. Barry,

Univ. of Wisconsin Pr. 1969 $95.00. "[This Bible] was a landmark in the history of the English Scriptures and language, second in influence in England, Scotland and America only to the Authorized Version of 1611.... While not the official Bible, [this] became, nevertheless, the Bible of the people. It was printed in roman type rather than in black letter, circulated in handy quarto rather than in the large unwieldy folio volumes that had been common. Divided into verses to help the memory and containing indices of names and subject material, it went through 120 editions before the King James Version was printed in 1611. One thing which must have made this book so influential was that the rather accurate and felicitous translation of the word-as-printed rescued the Bible from the vagaries of the word-as-tradition.... What also gave to the Geneva Bible its influence were the explanatory introductions to each book of the Bible and the marginal notes" (*N.Y. Times Book Review*).

The Holy Bible: King James Version. Amer. Bible Society 1974 pap. $7.95; NAL 1974 pap. $7.95. This monument of English literature is the "authorized version" of 1611, which continues in diligent use among more conservative, "evangelical" Christians who abhor any modernizing of the biblical language. The King James Version has fed "Bible English" into the language over generations, with the result that many of its phrases became epigrammatic in their period form and clash with any attempt to render the thought in a more functional vernacular for today. Although it was, of course, a towering literary achievement and is justly celebrated for the depth of its interpretative insight by seventeenth-century standards, the King James Version speaks an English that is often opaque to even cultivated readers today, and the translators' access to the texts was obviously obstructed by the primitive philology and historical science practiced in their era. This honored version remains in widespread use, but many users seem to relish its hieratic spell while failing to comprehend what it says. The New King James Version (Nelson 1982) presents the old text with stylistic revisions aimed at narrowing the gap between the King James Version and modern English usage. It does not, however, surmount the critical weaknesses nor the basic idiomatic barriers of its ancestor.

The Holy Bible: New International Version, Containing the Old Testament and New Testament. Zondervan 1978 o.p. This is a very conservative, but very respectable, translation into modern English by an interdenominational team of Protestant scholars of "evangelical" persuasion. A measure of their conservatism is the absence of the deuterocanonical (apocryphal) books of the Old Testament, which most modern versions include out of a concern for context and understanding, not denominational loyalty.

The Holy Bible: Revised Standard Version. Dell 1974 pap. $8.95. This celebrated revision of the King James Version according to the requirements of modern speech and scholarship followed earlier revisions of 1885 (British) and 1901 (American) and represented an international Protestant enterprise. The ongoing revision process now involves Roman Catholic and Jewish scholars as well. An "ecumenical edition," called *The Common Bible* (Collins 1973), presents the Apocrypha, that is, the Septuagint's additions to the Hebrew Bible, which were traditionally included in Catholic bibles, still in a separate section but between the two Testaments. An edition is even offered to the Greek Orthodox that includes Psalm 151 and 3 Maccabees, which belong to their scriptural canon. The Revised Standard Version is the English bible of choice for students because of its fidelity to the original texts, the consistency of its vocabulary, and the unique felicity of expression that it inherits from its ancestor, the King James Version. In its review, *Choice* said: "As a literary event the Common Bible offers little that is new but as an ecclesiastical and cultural event it is a step forward in ecumenical cooperation."

The Jerusalem Bible. Ed. by Alexander Jones, Doubleday 1978 $19.95. "[This Bible] is meant for the ordinary reader; the volume is also meant to be admired as well as consulted. . . . It may surprise people who are familiar with Dali's 'Last Supper' and his 'Crucifixion' to find that the new illustrations . . . are quite abstract; and some of them are all the more powerful. . . . No doubt the presence of these paintings has greatly increased the cost of the volume . . . but the cost would have to be high in any event. The pages are large (8 × 11½") and not only is the binding magnificent but the new large text with verse numbers at the left where they belong, is readable, beautiful, and, of course, expensive. The paper, barring cataclysm, is supposed to be durable enough to last for 1500 years. . . . This is a family book, with the traditional charts for inscribing all sorts of family data. All in all, an admirable piece of work" (*Best Sellers*).

Kubo, Sakae, and Walter Specht. *So Many Versions?* Zondervan rev. & enl. ed. 1983 pap. $9.95. An incisive critical review of 15 English versions produced in this century.

May, H. G., and Bruce M. Metzger. *The New Oxford Annotated Bible with the Apocrypha.* Oxford 1977 $27.95. One of the the best of the annotated editions, presenting the Revised Standard Version with introductions to each biblical book and footnoted explanations of points in the text. It enjoys broad interconfessional endorsement and is a truly first-class study bible.

The New American Bible: Translated from the Original Languages with Critical Use of All the Ancient Sources; with Textual Notes on Old Testament Readings. St. Anthony Guild 2 vols. in 1 consult publisher for information. The product of members of the Catholic Biblical Association of America, this fresh translation replaces earlier Catholic translations bound to the Latin Vulgate and the old Douay-Rheims version from the Counter-Reformation. The Old Testament is generally superior, the New Testament weakened by its disorderly production under the call of the Second Vatican Council for new vernacular readings. A needed revision is now complete and should bring this bible to first-class status in both critical and stylistic aspects.

The New English Bible with the Apocrypha. Oxford 1970 $19.95 pap. $15.95. This is one of the most pleasing of the innovating modern translations of the Bible into English. It was planned under British Protestant auspices and has the benefit of the latest stages of biblical and textual scholarship.

The New Jerusalem Bible. Ed. by A. Jones, Doubleday rev. ed. 1985 $24.95. This highly attractive and successful Roman Catholic annotated version was based on a critically acclaimed French vernacular translation, and its recent revision was undertaken to correct serious deficiencies in both the English biblical text and the rendering of the excellent annotations.

The Prophets—Nevi'im. Jewish Pubns. 1978 $9.00. A new translation of the Holy Scriptures according to the Masoretic text, second section. "The translation is conservative in rendering the Hebrew text; however the translators have been informed in their work by the Dead Sea Scrolls, the Septuagint, Targum, Peshitta, the Vulgate, and modern translations and commentaries. A conscious attempt has been made to avoid obsolete words and phrases. . . . The end result is a translation [which] . . . is readable and accurate without being slavishly literal. . . . [Included] is a table of Scripture readings for Sabbaths, festivals, and special days with references to both the Torah and the Prophets. . . . [This is] a valuable modern English translation of Hebrew Holy Scriptures" (*Choice*).

Sandmel, Samuel, and others, eds. *Oxford Study Edition: The New English Bible with the Apocrypha*. Oxford 1976 $27.95 pap. $19.95. With the excellent modern English rendering go annotations from Jewish, Catholic, and Protestant scholars, making this a perfect companion resource to *The New English Bible with the Apocrypha* (see above).

Throckmorton, B. H. *Gospel Parallels: A Synopsis of the First Three Gospels*. Nelson 4th ed. 1979 $9.95. This all-English (Revised Standard Version) edition of the Huck-Lietzmann gospel synopsis offers a less complicated and cheaper alternative to the Aland *Synopsis of the Four Gospels* (see above under Critical Editions of Original Texts) that is also available in wholly English format and includes John's Gospel, whereas Throckmorton restricts John to pertinent footnote citation.

The Torah: The Five Books of Moses. Jewish Pubns. 2d ed. 1967 $9.95. A new translation of the Holy Scriptures according to the Masoretic text, first section. A "New Jewish Version," this endeavor represents a fresh translation by American Jewish scholars, adhering closely to the received Hebrew text but adding notes on textual problems and variant readings.

Weigle, L. A. *The New Testament Octapla: Eight English Versions of the New Testament in the Tyndale–King James Tradition*. Nelson 1962 o.p. The interested student can compare eight older English versions, including the King James Version and the Revised Standard Version, which represent milestones in the history of the English Bible.

The Writings. Jewish Pubns. 1982 $10.95. The new translations convey in modern language the directness, simplicity, and sublime piety of the Hebrew Bible.

Chronology of Principal Versions

1382. WYCLIF BIBLE

John Wyclif (or Wycliffe, Wiclif, Wickliffe) (c.1330–84) initiated the first complete translation of the Bible from the Vulgate into English in order to reach the people directly. He himself translated the Gospels and probably the rest of the New Testament and part of the Old Testament. He entrusted the editing to John Purvey, who completed the translation (c.1388).

1525–1566. TYNDALE BIBLE

The first printed English Bible was William Tyndale's New Testament. His translation of the Pentateuch was issued in 1530 with revisions of both in 1534 to 1535. Tyndale began his translation of the New Testament from Greek into the vernacular and, finding publication impossible in England, left for Hamburg (1525); he completed at Worms the printing of 3,000 New Testaments in small octavo, which were smuggled into England and there suppressed by bishops (only five or six copies are now extant). Constantly harassed, he was finally imprisoned, strangled, and burned at the stake, in spite of intercession by Thomas Cromwell.

1535–1537. COVERDALE BIBLE

Miles Coverdale was a former colleague of Tyndale who completed the work left unfinished by Tyndale's death in prison. It was produced in Germany in 1535.

1537. MATTHEW'S BIBLE

With the royal approval of Henry VIII in 1537, a new translation appeared. Supposedly the work of Thomas Matthew, it is more likely that it was the work of John Rodgers, another colleague of Tyndale. To avoid the embarrassment of official sponsorship of work most decidedly that of the executed Tyndale and of Coverdale, a fictitious translator's name may have been used.

1539. THE GREAT BIBLE

Authorized by Henry VIII in 1538, this was a revision of the text of Matthew's Bible. Every parish was ordered to have a copy of this bible in its church with half the cost to be borne by the parishioners. It was known as the Great Bible because of its massive size. The Psalms in the Protestant Episcopal Prayer Book through the revision of 1928 followed this translation. A long preface by Archbishop Cranmer in the second edition of 1540 has caused it to be sometimes known as the Cranmer Bible.

1560–1644. THE GENEVA BIBLE

The first bible in Roman type, it became therefore very popular. It was also the first English Bible to use marginal notes and verse divisions. It is often known as the "Breeches" Bible because of the rendering of Genesis 3:7: "They sewed figge-tree leaves together, and made themselves breeches." It was published by English exiles in Geneva and brought to America by the Pilgrims. An edition of this version was the first bible printed at the Cambridge University Press in 1591; its publication broke the monopoly in bible production in England, held up to that time by the king's printer in London. It was the favored Bible in England for half a century because of its excellent translation, though its Calvinist slant was a source of irritation to King James I.

1568–1606. THE BISHOP'S BIBLE

A revision of the Great Bible; each book bears the initials of the bishop who translated it. The 1602 edition was made the basis of the King James Version.

1582–1610. DOUAY VERSION

This was a translation published at the English College in the town of Douai in northern France. Modern editions differ somewhat from the original, but the Bible used by Roman Catholics at the present day is, on the whole, the Douay translation. The new Confraternity Version (see below) is intended to replace the Douay Version in the United States. The Roman Catholic Bible differs from the Protestant Bible not only in rendering but also in the order of the books, the titles of the books, and the number of the books. The books of the Apocrypha are accepted as canonical and appear in the Roman Catholic Bible scattered among the various books of the Old and New Testaments. The peculiarity of the Douay Version, also known as the Douay-Rheims Bible, by which it is distinguished from Protestant versions, is the fact that it was translated from a Latin manuscript. The earliest manuscripts of the Old Testament are in Hebrew, and of the New Testament in Greek. When Rome conquered the world, and Latin became the speech of the people, there was need of a translation of the Bible into Latin, into the vulgar language—the language of the *vulgus*, the crowd. The Douay Version is a translation of the Latin translation called the Vulgate. The Vulgate (c.383–405) was the work of Saint Jerome (Eusebius Hieronymus, c.340–420), one of the four doctors of the church, who spent most of his life in a monastery in Bethlehem, writing a large number of ecclesiastical works.

1611. KING JAMES VERSION

The King James Version is known as the Authorized Version, although, as a matter of fact, it was never authorized by the king. It was, however, initiated by him as the result of a Puritan complaint that the Coverdale Authorized Version, revised as the Bishops' Bible (1568), was not accurate. He appointed a group of scholars to undertake the task of fresh translation. Later editions had printed on their title pages, "Appointed to be read in the churches," which probably gave rise to the legend of authorization. The King James Version was made between 1607 and 1611, during the lifetime of Shakespeare—the Golden Age of English literature. It was translated by 54 scholars and is the most famous English Bible. The late Dwight Macdonald (1906–1982) (like many who value the Bible as literature) regretted the fact that those who, with justice, set out to *correct* this translation usually went too far and bowdlerized great passages. For many the King James, with all its imperfections, can never be surpassed for poetry, religious feeling, and majesty and loveliness of utterance. In *Against the American Grain* (1952), in his essay on the Revised Standard Version called "Updating the Bible," Macdonald writes: "The King James Version is probably the greatest translation ever made. It is certainly 'The Noblest Monument of English Prose,' as the late John Livingston Lowes called his essay on the subject. 'Its phraseology,' he wrote, 'has become part and parcel of our common tongue.... Its rhythms and cadences, its turns of speech, its familiar imagery, its very words are woven into the texture of our literature.... The English of the Bible ... is characterized not merely by a homely vigor and pithiness of phrase but also by a singular nobility of diction and by a rhythmic quality which is, I think, unrivalled in its beauty.' ... The speed with which it was accomplished was possible only because it was not so much a new translation as a synthesis of earlier efforts, the final form given to a continuous process of creation, the climax to the great century of English Bible translation." The *New King James Version* was published in 1982.

1661–1663. The Algonquian Bible

The first Bible printed in America was not the King James Version but a translation by John Eliot for the Algonquian Indians called the Up-Biblum God.

1881–1885. The English Revised Version

The Revised Version of the King James was begun in 1870 at the Convocation of Canterbury by two committees, British and American, the latter advisory only. The New Testament was issued in 1881, the Old Testament in 1885, and the Apocrypha in 1895, by the Oxford and Cambridge University Presses. In 1901 the surviving members of the American Committee published through Thomas Nelson Publishing Co., then of New York, the American Revised Version embodying the readings they had previously suggested and other improvements. The revisions had been undertaken for two reasons:

1. The discovery of fresh Bible manuscripts spurred revision. When the King James Version of the Bible was made, there had not yet been discovered three early manuscripts of the Bible: the Vatican manuscript, fourth century (in the Vatican library, Rome); the Sinaitic manuscript, fourth century (discovered on Mt. Sinai, and long in Leningrad, purchased in 1934 by the Trustees of the British Museum for £100,000 from the Soviet government, the highest price ever paid for a manuscript or printed book); the Alexandrian manuscript, fifth century (in the British Museum). The discovery of these three manuscripts gave to translators a Bible text older and more accurate than any they had had before, and so much new light was thrown on obscure passages in the Scriptures that a fresh translation was not only warranted but demanded.

2. The second reason for revision was the archaic character of the language of the King James Version; so many words in the King James Version are obsolete, or have lost their original meaning, that modern readers no longer understand them in their

intended sense. For instance, David prays the Lord to enlarge his feet. In the Revised Version, the word *enlarge* is changed to *set free*. This original meaning of the word survives today in the phrase *at large,* meaning "free."

The translators of the Revised Version did not put the Bible into modern English—other translators have done that—but they did revise archaic words that are misleading in sense in the present day, and they corrected many mistranslations. An updated edition of the American Standard Version was published as *The New American Standard Bible* in 1971.

1917. THE JEWISH VERSION

Published by the Jewish Publication Society of America, *The Holy Scriptures According to the Masoretic Text* was produced in "Bible English." An earlier translation, made by Isaac Leeser in 1853, in Philadelphia, was a single-handed effort and was never widely read by Jews. Up to this time, the English Bible used by those professing Judaism has been either the King James Version or the Revised. Orthodox Jews have preferred the King James Version because it does not use the name Jehovah, the ineffable name that never occurs in the Jewish version. The Hebrew Bible (Old Testament only) is not called the Holy Bible, but the Holy Scriptures. Actually, in fact, the word *Bible* does not occur in the Bible itself. It came from the Latin *biblia*, from the Greek *biblia*, plural of *biblion*, the diminutive of *biblos*, "book"—"little book."

The paragraphing of the Jewish version follows that of the Revised Version. Verse divisions, uniform with those of the King James Version, are indicated in small type. The correspondence is in some cases approximate rather than identical, because the Jews divide the Old Testament into 24 books, while the Protestants divide it into 39 books. The order of the Hebrew Bible is also slightly different from the order of the Protestant. The Hebrew Bible ends with an incomplete sentence, the twenty-third verse of 2 Chronicles, "let him go up." In the Protestant Bible the Book of Ezra follows after 2 Chronicles and completes the sentence, "let him go up to Jerusalem which is in Judah."

The Revised Translation of the Holy Scriptures for Jews was undertaken in 1955 by the Jewish Publication Society. It is a complete revision of the 1917 version and embodies all the latest findings of modern biblical scholarship for all people, together with a modern text that is free from all archaism of language and therefore is more understandable to Jewish laymen. The first volume of *A New Translation of the Holy Scriptures According to the Masoretic Text* is the *Torah*, which appeared in 1963; in 1978 the second volume, *The Prophets*, was published; and in 1982 *The Writings* appeared.

1945–1949. THE KNOX VERSION

This Roman Catholic version was translated into modern English by Monsignor Ronald Knox in England and is officially approved by the Roman Catholic Church.

1946–1952. THE REVISED STANDARD VERSION

The authorized revision of the American Standard Version. Important manuscripts and fragments became available that were not known in 1611 or even in 1901 when the American Standard Version appeared. An old Syrian version of the Gospels, probably of the second century, was found in a monastery on Mount Sinai; in 1933, a fragment of Tatian's Harmony of the Four Gospels was discovered at Dura on the Euphrates; and most important of all was the discovery of fragments of 12 manuscripts, now known as the Chester Beatty manuscripts, 3 of them from the New Testament, which may date as early as the first half of the third century. In addition to the biblical documents, a great number of Greek papyri and papyrus fragments were unearthed in Egypt. These writings were contemporary with the New Testament and, together with inscriptions, furnished new meaning to Greek words and phrases as they were used in the years when the New Testament was written.

In 1928, a committee of 15 scholars was appointed by the International Council of Religious Education, with which the educational boards of 44 of the major Protestant denominations of the United States and Canada are associated, and to which the copyright of the American Standard Version had been transferred. Lack of funds delayed the work, which was finally begun in 1937. The committee was divided into two sections, one for the Old Testament and one for the New. Dean Luther A. Weigle of the Yale Divinity School served as chairman of the whole committee, and the executive secretary, from 1937 until his death in 1944, was the beloved scholar James Moffatt. The New Testament appeared in 1946, the Old Testament in 1952, and the Apocrypha in 1957.

The publication of the Revised Standard Version of the Holy Bible in September 1952 aroused great public interest and a new sales record was set: 1,600,000 copies in the first six weeks after publication. There is also a Catholic edition of the Revised Standard Version; however, it is no longer in general use.

1961–1970. THE NEW ENGLISH BIBLE (SOMETIMES CALLED THE OXFORD BIBLE)

An entirely new translation from the original Greek into current English, this version was prepared under the direction of all leading Protestant churches in the British Isles. The New Testament appeared first in 1961 and was published in its second edition in 1970. A new translation of the Old Testament and the Apocrypha was published in 1970. Scholars of different denominations and from a number of British universities took part in the work. They made a faithful rendering of the best available Greek texts and made use of the most recent biblical scholarship. The new translation was directed by the Joint Committee of the Churches, which consisted of representatives of the Church of England, the Church of Scotland, the Methodist Church, the Congregational Union, the Baptist Union, the Presbyterian Church of England, the Churches in Wales, the Churches in Ireland, the Society of Friends, the British and Foreign Bible Society, and the National Bible Society of Scotland. "In assessing the evidence, the translators have taken into account (a) ancient manuscripts of the New Testament in Greek, (b) manuscripts of early translations into other languages, and (c) quotations from the New Testament by early Christian writers. . . . In particular, our knowledge of the kind of Greek used by most of the New Testament writers has been greatly enriched since 1881 by the discovery of many thousands of papyrus documents in popular or nonliterary Greek of about the same period as the New Testament. . . . Taken as a whole, our version claims to be a translation, free, it may be, rather than literal, but a faithful translation nevertheless, so far as we could compass it. . . . But always the overriding aims were accuracy and clarity. . . . The translators are as conscious as anyone can be of the limitations and imperfections of their work. No one who has not tried it can know how impossible an art translation is. . . . Yet we may hope that we have been able to convey to our readers something at least of what the New Testament has said to us during these years of work, and trust that under the providence of Almighty God this translation may open the truth of the scriptures to many who have been hindered in their approach to it by barriers of language" (Introduction).

There was simultaneous publication worldwide jointly by Cambridge University Press and Oxford University Press.

1966. THE JERUSALEM BIBLE

Originally a modern translation in French prepared by Dominican scholars in Jerusalem (1956), La Bible de Jerusalem became The Jerusalem Bible when it was translated into English in 1966. A new edition titled *The New Jerusalem Bible* was published in 1985.

1970. CONFRATERNITY VERSION

Generally known as the Confraternity Edition, the Confraternity Version is a new translation, the first made from the original Hebrew and Greek languages for Roman Catholics, and intended to replace the Douay Version for public reading in the United States. The Confraternity revision of the New Testament translation was made in 1941.

The new translation of the Old Testament, made in accordance with directives of the late Pope Pius XII in his encyclical letter of September 30, 1943, was sponsored by the Bishops' Committee of the Confraternity of Christian Doctrine. These translations made their first appearance in 1952, with the work completed in 1970 and published as *The New American Bible.* The *New York Times Book Review* said: "It was a stroke of genius to give a new name to the awkwardly designated 'Confraternity Version of the Bible' and call it, in its final definitive edition, 'The New American Bible.' . . . The English of the new version is simple and natural and exhibits none of the painful Latinity of the Douay version. While they were putting the Bible into standard modern English, the translators were also able to take advantage of the remarkable achievements of recent Catholic, Protestant and Jewish scholarship."

Textual Criticism

By way of introduction, it should be observed that the original texts of the Bible came down through handwritten (manuscript) copying, long before the invention of the printing press. The variations of reading, both deliberate and accidental, that transmission by hand inevitably entailed create the need for a complex discipline for restoring the author's original text. The highly refined norms of this discipline, and the typical procedures of its application to disputed passages, are the subject of works listed below. The student should bear in mind, however, that textual criticism cannot achieve conclusive results operating by itself, apart from the other methods of interpreting the sacred writers' thoughts. All component disciplines of biblical interpretation must be in communication and cooperation with one another since determining what an author *wrote* and determining what was *meant* are complementary and interacting pursuits.

Aland, Kurt, and Barbara Aland. *The Text of the New Testament.* Trans. by Erroll F. Rhodes, Eerdmans 1987 $29.95. An introduction to the critical editions of the New Testament, and to the theory and practice of modern textual criticism, by the most authoritative practitioners of the discipline. This is an excellent primer for anyone starting out in this forbidding area.

Cambridge History of the Bible. Cambridge Univ. Pr. 3 vols. 1987 pap. $47.50. A vast survey of the phases and vicissitudes of the Bible's transmission.

Metzger, Bruce M. *The Early Versions of the New Testament.* Oxford 1977 $24.95. Indispensable witnesses to the scriptural text, the ancient translations, Eastern and Western, including the ancestor languages of those currently spoken, are introduced and evaluated as mediators of the Greek text of the New Testament.

————. *Text of the New Testament: Its Transmission, Corruption, and Restoration.* Oxford 2d ed. 1968 $13.95. This is a work of fully comparable stature to that of the Alands (see above), though less up to date, by one of the foremost practitioners of New Testament textual criticism. It is especially intended to appeal to students whom this daunting discipline would normally tend to discourage.

————, ed. *A Textual Commentary on the Greek New Testament.* Amer. Bible Society 1975 $5.45. This volume is intended to be used with Aland, *The Greek New Testament* (see above under Reference Works, Critical Editions of Original Texts), and offers a brief documentation and explanation of the editors' decisions on major variant readings. It is a unique reference tool for study of the New Testament text.

Wurthwein, Ernst. *The Text of the Old Testament (Text Des Alten Testaments).* Trans. by Erroll F. Rhodes, Eerdmans 1980 text ed. $16.95. An indispensable workbook for the study of the Hebrew text, this classic introduces both the many witnesses to the text and the steps in the procedure for restoring it in the presence of conflicting variant readings.

HISTORICAL BACKGROUND OF THE BIBLE

Histories of Judaism and Early Christianity

Recognition that the writings of the Bible came from specific locations in the distant human past and were essentially conditioned by their time and place has been the intellectual foundation of modern biblical studies. Three periods should be studied as indispensable background for the sacred books: the history of Israel from the period of the Patriarchs (c.1750 B.C.) through the Babylonian exile (587–539 B.C.), the history of the intertestamental period from after the exile through the time of Christ, and the history of the New Testament period. These are, at any rate, the broad and very unequal periods to which most historical-background titles are devoted.

HISTORY OF ISRAEL

Albright, William Foxwell. *From the Stone Age to Christianity: Monotheism and the Historical Process.* Johns Hopkins Univ. Pr. 2d ed. 1957 o.p. This is still a classic, though it is highly systematic and too conservative by present standards. Albright is a towering figure in the disciplines of biblical language and archaeology.

Bright, John. *A History of Israel.* Westminster 3d ed. 1981 $18.95. Although this presentation is still within the conservative principles of the Albright school, it fully deserves the high praise it has drawn from reviewers and teachers who have used it.

Edwards, I. E., and N. G. Hammond, eds. *The Cambridge Ancient History.* Cambridge Univ. Pr. 4 pts. 1981 pap. ea. $34.50–$39.50. Of the third edition, only 3 of the 12 volumes of the older edition (1925–39) are available, which brings coverage to the Assyrian Empire (to 600 B.C.). Wide coverage of the world of the Old and New Testaments will be found by the student wishing to know their larger historical context.

Hayes, John H., and J. Maxwell Miller, eds. *Israelite and Judaean History.* [*Old Testament Lib.*] Westminster 1977 $27.50. This collection of 11 major essays, surveying discussion of periods through the Roman era, offers a wide-ranging critical assessment of the contributions of major schools of thought. A table of Israelite and Judaean kings and a section of period maps enhance its considerable value.

Noth, Martin. *A History of Israel: Biblical History.* Harper 2d ed. 1960 $16.95; Westminster 3d ed. 1981 $18.95. This is another classic, representing the critical temper opposite that of Albright (above) and Bright (above) and differing from them most markedly in its account of Israel's early history.

INTERTESTAMENTAL PERIOD

Foerster, Werner. *From the Exile to Christ: A Historical Introduction to Palestinian Judaism.* Trans. by G. E. Harris, Fortress Pr. 1964 pap. $10.95. This account is as competent and comprehensive as it can be given the large holes in the source material. The main source is the Jewish historian Flavius Josephus (see titles by Thackeray listed below under Apocryphal and Other Writings Related to the Bible).

Hengel, Martin. *Judaism and Hellenism: Studies in Their Encounter in Palestine during the Early Hellenistic Period.* Trans. by John Bowden, Fortress Pr. 2 vols. 1981 o.p. The first volume is text, the second notes, already indicating the rich fund of information on the intertestamental period that is offered by this work. It is indispensable to students of that period, and students of the New Testament as well.

Koester, Helmut. *History, Culture, and Religion of the Hellenistic Age.* Vol. 1 in *Introduction to the New Testament.* De Gruyter 1982 $32.95 1987 text ed. pap. $16.95. A survey of the age that began with the conquests of Alexander the Great, equipped with maps, photos, and a glossary, dedicated to setting the proximate historical context for New Testament study.

NEW TESTAMENT PERIOD

Bultmann, Rudolf. *Primitive Christianity: In Its Contemporary Setting.* Trans. by Reginald H. Fuller, Fortress Pr. repr. of 1956 ed. 1980 pap. $8.95. A true classic, surpassed in some respects, but demonstrating with its crisp compression and breadth of primary-source coverage the gigantic stature of its author.

Conzelmann, Hans. *History of Primitive Christianity (Geschichte Des Unchristentums).* Trans. by John E. Steely, Abingdon 1973 pap. $8.95. A brief survey of the period following Jesus' death up to C.A.D. 100, given with a sharply profiled criticism and perhaps some hypercriticism.

Lohse, Edward. *The New Testament Environment.* Trans. by John E. Steely, Abingdon 1976 pap. $10.95. Divided into Jewish and Hellenistic Roman "environments," this work sketches both contemporary political history and currents in religion and culture. It is a convenient reference work for even the casual student and is an excellent choice for beginners.

Schürer, Emil. *A History of the Jewish People in the Age of Jesus Christ (175 B.C.–135 A.D.): A New English Version.* Ed. by Matthew Black and Martin Goodman, Fortress Pr. 3 vols. in 4 bks. 1973–86 ea. $34.95–$44.95. This nineteenth-century classic is given a new adaptation, with new information and up-to-date bibliographies, to maintain its stature as an irreplaceable authority on the subject. A one-volume condensation of the earlier edition of Schürer's great work is available from Schocken (1961).

Biblical Archaeology

Although archaeology is among the younger sciences, scarcely yet 150 years old, it is one of the principal contributors to the modern revolution in biblical interpretation. The investigation of ancient sites and of the literatures found at them, or near them, has given us exciting new terms of comparison for what we read in the Bible. For example, the excavations of the ancient Babylonian civilization at Mari, and the discovery of written tablets at places like Amarna on the Nile and Ras Shamra in coastal Syria, shed startling light on many features of lore and language previously considered unique to the Old Testament. Spectacular sites in Israel itself, including Hazor and Tel Dan in the North, Caesarea on the coast, Capharnaum on the lakeshore, Megiddo on the central plain, Jericho and Qumran near the Dead Sea, and the sector of the temple-mount in Jerusalem, have illumined the whole course of the region's history, from the distant beginnings of civilization down through the successive conquests of the Arabs, the Crusaders, and the Turks. The following titles are selected from among the most authoritative in this breathlessly expanding field.

Albright, William F. *The Archaeology of Palestine.* Peter Smith rev. ed. 1976 $11.25. A survey of archaeological techniques and sites, with a final section devoted to a picture of people and customs in Palestine in the periods brought to light by the excavations.

Avi-Yonah, Michael, ed. *Encyclopaedia of Archaeological Excavations in the Holy Land.* Prentice-Hall 4 vols. 1975 ea. $25.00. A comprehensive survey of 155 sites and topics drawn from the contributions of 68 scholars, many of whom led the excavations on which they report.

Finegan, Jack. *Archaeology of the New Testament: The Life of Jesus and the Beginning of the Early Church.* Princeton Univ. Pr. 1970 $60.00 pap. $10.50. One of the better discussions of sites and symbols connected with Christian beginnings, culling the best information and presenting it in highly readable prose.

Kenyon, Kathleen M. *Archaeology in the Holy Land.* Nelson 1985 pap. $12.95; Norton 4th ed. 1979 $10.95. A discussion by one of the trailblazing archaeologists of her science's illumination of Palestinian history from the earliest periods through the post-exile.

Murphy-O'Connor, Jerome. *The Holy Land: An Archaeological Guide from Earliest Times to 1700.* Oxford pap. 1986 $9.95. More a studious tourist's guide than a primer in archaeological science, this small volume is nevertheless a wonderful companion for Holy Land visits, elegantly written and lightly seasoned with the author's native humor and long experience on the scene.

Biblical Geography

To any historical investigation, geography is one of the principal coordinates, together with chronology. An appreciation of the location and natural circumstances of biblical sites adds appreciably, sometimes substantively, to the understanding of biblical texts. The features of the land the Israelite invaders coveted as they approached from the east, the stark contrasts between the fertile and barren regions different tribes obtained, the bucolic hills of Galilee, the stunning beauty of the Jordan Valley, and what it so clearly meant to "go *up* to Jerusalem," are only a few among the many points where biblical geography impinges on the biblical text.

Aharoni, Yohanan. *The Land of the Bible: A Historical Geography.* Trans. by A. F. Rainey, Westminster rev. & enl. ed. 1980 $19.95. A first-class expository work, giving first the setting and historic features of the Holy Land, then its historical development from the Canaanite period through the early post-exile.

Aharoni, Yohanan, and Michael Avi-Yonah. *The Macmillan Bible Atlas.* Macmillan rev. ed. 1977 $25.95. An excellent joint effort of two premier archaeologists with map specialists features 264 maps, pertaining to every period of biblical history, each accompanied by full and effective explanation.

Grollenberg, Luc H. *The Penguin Shorter Atlas of the Bible.* Trans. by Mary F. Hedlund, Penguin 1978 pap. $7.95. This is perhaps the foremost atlas, annotating more than 400 maps, charts, and pictures with more information than one will find in other publications of this genre.

May, Herbert G., and G. H. Hunt, eds. *Oxford Bible Atlas.* Oxford 3d ed. 1985 $18.95 pap. $10.95. A small and succinct atlas, with 26 maps, accompanied by explanations of biblical history from the Patriarchs through the travels of Paul.

Vogel, E. K., ed. *Bibliography of Holy Land Sites.* Vol. 42 in *Hebrew Union College Annual.* Ktav 1971 $65.00. A valuable listing according to biblical sites, arranged alphabetically.

Apocryphal and Other Writings Related to the Bible

The Apocrypha is the name given to 14 books written between 200 B.C. and A.D. 100, the period between the Old and the New Testament, or "intertestamental period." The word *apocrypha* comes from a Greek word meaning "hidden," or "spurious." The Roman Catholic Church accepts the books of the Apocrypha as of like inspiration with the other books of the Bible; the Protestant Church considers them of lesser inspiration, and excludes them from the accepted canon.

The interpreter cannot study the bible in isolation from its environment, as we have seen, and this applies above all to its literary "environment," constituted by contemporary writings of Jewish or Christian authors never received into the biblical canon, and also by literary products of other cultures closely adjoining and illuminating the biblical. Only collections and discussions considered of first interest to students of biblical exegesis are included here.

Barnstone, Willis, ed. *The Other Bible.* Harper 1984 $24.45 pap. $14.95. This is a wide-ranging collection of esoteric passages from the Pseudepigrapha, the Dead Sea Scrolls, the early Kabbalah, the Nag Hammadi Gnostic literature, and so forth, with brief introductions acquainting the neophyte with the kinds of Jewish and Christian literature that never gained mainstream recognition so as to become official, "sacred" literature. Here is a good beginning for someone wholly unfamiliar with the vast fringes of the Judeo-Christian Scripture.

Barrett, Charles K., ed. *New Testament Background: Selected Documents.* Harper pap. $6.95. A wide selection of documents—Roman, Hellenistic, and Jewish—including interesting specimens of the Greek papyrus manuscripts is presented in excerpts keyed to the interpretation of the New Testament.

Beyerlin, Walter, ed. *Near Eastern Religious Texts Relating to the Old Testament.* Trans. by John Bowden [*Old Testament Lib.*] Westminster 1978 $22.00. Texts from five cultures that touched Ancient Israel—Egyptian, Mesopotamian, Hittite, Ugaritic, and North Semitic—are arranged under subheadings to assist their comparison with the Bible.

Cartlidge, David R., and David L. Dungan. *Documents for the Study of the Gospels.* Fortress Pr. 1980 $16.95 pap. $10.95. An assortment of selections from Christian apocrypha and popular religious texts of Judaism and Hellenism, given lively translations and introductions, and organized for the illumination of familiar features of the Christian Gospels.

Charlesworth, James H., ed. *The Old Testament Pseudepigrapha.* Doubleday 2 vols. 1983–85 ea. $40.00. Vol. 1, *Apocalyptic Literature and Testaments*; Vol. 2, *Expansions of the Old Testament and Legends, Wisdom and Philosophical Literature, Prayers, Psalms and Odes, Fragments of Lost Judaeo-Hellenistic Works.* Fresh translations, by an international team of scholars, of a vast literature produced by Jews and Christians between 200 B.C. and A.D. 200, inevitably attributed to ideal figures of the Old Testament and claiming to contain God's revelation. The 52 writings are accompanied by detailed introduction and footnoted commentary. They do not include the so-called Apocrypha, which were part of the Greek Bible's (Septuagint's) Old Testament and have been considered "biblical" in the Roman Catholic tradition.

———. *The Pseudepigrapha and Modern Research with a Supplement.* Scholars Pr. GA 1981 pap. $12.95. A brief but useful introduction to each document in the field is followed by discussion of scholarly views of its background and message. This is a valuable companion to the preceding entry.

Colson, F. H., and G. H. Whitaker. *Philo with an English Translation.* [*Loeb Class. Lib.*] Harvard Univ. Pr. 10 vols. 1929–62 ea. $12.95. This is the Loeb collection of the writings, Greek original with facing English, of Philo Judaeus, the great Hellenistic-Jewish expositor of the Scriptures who was a contemporary of St. Paul. Philo is an irreplaceable source for an otherwise underdocumented sector of Judaism in the New Testament period.

Cross, Frank M. *The Ancient Library of Qumran and Modern Biblical Studies.* [*Haskell Lectures Ser.*] Greenwood repr. of 1958 ed. 1976 lib. bdg. $22.50. A highly informative introduction, including an account of the discoveries and their investigation, by a major participant in the process.

Danby, Herbert, trans. *The Mishnah.* Oxford 1933 $45.00. This is a full translation of the earliest body of rabbinical literature, collected around A.D. 200 and representing schools that grew up after the fall of Jerusalem in A.D. 70. Its preservation of some Pharisaic traditions from earlier periods accounts for its use, sometimes problematic, by New Testament scholars.

Dupont-Sommer, A. *The Essene Writings from Qumran.* Trans. by G. Vermes, Peter Smith 1973 $13.50. Fitzmyer (see below) considers this the best translation of the Qumran scrolls in English, supplying the original column and line numbers for easy location of passages under discussion.

Fitzmyer, Joseph A. *The Dead Sea Scrolls: Major Publications and Tools for Study.* Scholars Pr. GA 1975 pap. $10.50. An excellent, classified bibliography furnishes guided access to the famous discoveries of Khirbet Qumran, near the Dead Sea, beginning in 1947, comprising a Jewish sectarian literature spanning the period from c.200 B.C. to A.D. 70.

Foerster, W. *Gnosis: A Selection of Gnostic Texts.* Trans. by R. M. Wilson, Oxford 2 vols. 1972–74 o.p. Vol. 1, *Patristic Evidence*; Vol. 2, *Coptic and Mandean Sources.* This is an important collection of Christian (and post-Christian) testimonies to the mysterious phenomenon of Gnosticism, a late-Hellenistic religious movement, probably of pre-Christian origin, whose influence on the Christian sources remains among the liveliest debates of biblical studies.

Gaster, Theodor H. *The Dead Sea Scriptures.* Doubleday 2d ed. 1976 pap. $7.95. A popular translation of most of the scrolls with introductions and a useful analytical index.

Grant, Robert M., ed. *The Apostolic Fathers: A Translation and Commentary.* Nelson 6 vols. 1964–68 o.p. Authoritative expositions of the honored writings that followed directly upon the New Testament books in the esteem and usage of the early church, and also coincided in time with the later New Testament books. The first volume of the six contains a comprehensive introduction to this literature by the author. The importance of these writings for the historical context of the New Testament, particularly its later books, cannot be overstated and, in fact, is all too often understated.

Hennecke, Edgar. *New Testament Apocrypha.* Westminster 2 vols. 1963–66 vol. 1 $20.95 vol. 2 $32.50. This is the most authoritative presentation of the numerous "gospels" and apostles' "acts," "instructions," and so on, which proliferated in early Christianity without gaining entrance to the official Christian Scripture. Introductions and bibliographies are unsurpassed, but the texts are all in translation.

James, Montague R., trans. *Apocryphal New Testament.* Oxford 1924 $34.50. A convenient, one-volume collection, now more than 60 years old and lacking more recent discoveries and scholarly perspective.

Jonas, Hans. *The Gnostic Religion: The Message of the Alien God and the Beginnings of Christianity.* Beacon 1958 pap. $10.95; Peter Smith 1958 2d ed. rev. $18.00. A fascinating introduction that helps, among other things, to promote a clearer understanding of the declining Hellenistic culture in which Christianity, among other religious movements from the East, achieved its rapid expansion.

Kee, Howard Clark. *The Origins of Christianity: Sources and Documents.* Prentice-Hall 1973 $14.95. Excerpts from contemporary documents illustrate political and religious history, religious and philosophical currents, and literary conventions pertinent to Christian beginnings.

Pfeiffer, Robert H. *History of New Testament Times.* Greenwood repr. of 1949 ed. 1972 lib. bdg. $23.00. Though it is outdated, this work covers the Apocrypha, which are now printed in most English bibles, more extensively than any other.

Pritchard, James B., ed. *The Ancient Near East in Pictures Relating to the Old Testament.* Princeton Univ. Pr. 2d ed. 1969 $126.75. More than 750 pictures, with explanatory text, illustrate various aspects of Ancient Near Eastern life and religion. This source should be used as a companion to the following entry, and an abridged combination of both can be found in J. B. Pritchard, *The Ancient Near East* (Princeton Univ. Pr. 2 vols. 1958–76 vol. 1 $28.50 vol. 2 $30.00).

———. *Ancient Near Eastern Texts Relating to the Old Testament.* Princeton Univ. Pr. 3d ed. 1969 $65.00. This is the collection of absolutely first importance for Old Testament study. It has grown through successive editions as the Near Eastern library itself has grown through successive discoveries.

Robinson, James M. *The Nag Hammadi Library.* Harper 1978 $23.03 pap. $11.95. This is the first translation of Coptic manuscripts discovered in Egypt in 1945, which document a mostly Gnosticized, often wildly heterodox, Christianity of the second and third centuries A.D. Forty-seven writings are included in the collection.

Sandmel, Samuel. *Philo of Alexandria: An Introduction.* Oxford 1979 pap. $9.95. A convenient and informative primer for the student beginning an acquaintance with this important Jewish voice.

Strack, H. L. *Introduction to the Talmud and Midrash*. Atheneum 1969 text ed. pap. $8.95. An elderly, but still useful, primer for the student seeking access to the vast rabbinic literature.

Thackeray, H. St. J. *Josephus: The Man and the Historian*. Ktav rev. ed. 1968 $20.00. This is an introduction by the historians' master translator.

Thackeray, H. St. J., and others. *Josephus with an English Translation*. [*Loeb Class. Lib.*] Harvard Univ. Pr. 10 vols. 1926–65 ea. $12.95. This collection for Josephus, the Palestinian-Jewish historian of his people, furnishes a good Greek text and facing English translation. In his two great works, the *Jewish Antiquities* and *Wars of the Jews*, Josephus offers a record of events in the period between the Testaments and the New Testament period, much of which cannot be found elsewhere. His sources are occasionally uncertain or dubious, and his apologetic intention usually controls his presentation; but if we did not have his works, we would be unable to reconstruct most of the Jewish history that frames the New Testament Scripture.

HISTORY, METHOD, AND MAINSTREAM SPECIMENS OF MODERN BIBLICAL STUDY

The field of biblical study is as vast and diverse as the Bible's human constituency, and so any survey of literature in this field has to depend at least partially on the bibliographer's own background and perspective for its principles of selection. We shall try to list only what is important and widely influential in anyone's judgment, though we shall have to depend on some personal assessments to determine what is currently "mainstream" in a field of study that is now more genuinely "ecumenical" than ever before in modern history.

Histories of Biblical Interpretation

To include this heading in the bibliography is to recognize that the way the Bible is interpreted depends very much on where in the history of human knowledge and culture the interpreter stands. After the patristic and medieval periods of church history, when biblical interpretation remained strictly subordinate to church tradition and tilted more and more in favor of figurative and moralistic senses of the sacred text, Martin Luther (see Chapter 12 in this volume) raised a clarion cry for the literal sense and the manifest intention of the written word, which was to become the first recourse in pursuit of Christian revelation. Luther's call germinated during the continental Renaissance and bore its fruits, sometimes bitter for the Protestant churches, in the historical and critical study of Scripture unleashed by the Enlightenment (roughly 1775 onward). When we speak of "biblical criticism" nowadays, we mean that trend of analytical interpretation, rooted in the Reformation, slowly modulated and warily embraced by the mainline churches (now including Roman Catholicism), which seeks to understand the biblical text through exacting research of the author's original intention, grounded in the full social and linguistic context of the writing. Although some very recent trends of interpretation point away from this historical sense again toward the inherent features and aesthetic impressions of the text, most scholars still see the need to forge a consensus among the multitudes who look to the Bible for norms of conscience, and they find the only viable authority of such a consensus in the charism of the original author.

Obviously the long history sketched here so lightly demonstrates again and again that the meanings found in the Bible depend on the questions put to it and the changing vantage points of the questioners. The following titles are the best for researching that complex and colorful history.

Cambridge History of the Bible. Cambridge Univ. Pr. 3 vols. 1987 pap. $47.50. See above under Texts and Versions of the Bible, Textual Criticism.

Clements, Ronald E. *One Hundred Years of Old Testament Interpretation.* Westminster 1976 pap. $7.95. Selecting major currents and figures in modern Old Testament criticism, this survey covers the Pentateuch and historical books, Prophets, Psalms, Wisdom, and Old Testament theology.

Epp, Eldon J., and George W. MacRae, eds. *The New Testament and Its Modern Interpreters.* Fortress Pr. 1987 text ed. $24.95. Essays providing an overview of major accomplishments in all areas of New Testament studies since the 1940s.

Grant, Robert M., and David Tracy. *A Short History of the Interpretation of the Bible.* Fortress Pr. 2d ed. rev. & enl. 1984 pap. $10.95. This is the best and most engaging short sketch of the long and tortuous story. The new edition adds three chapters by David Tracy under the promise of bringing the book "into its new port" of modern interpretive theory and agenda.

Hatch, Nathan O., and Mark A. Noll, eds. *The Bible in America: Essays in Cultural History.* Oxford Univ. Pr. 1982 $22.50 pap. $6.95. This is a collection of eight essays. "The book's primary focus is on the changing and increasingly diverse assumptions about the Bible's unity and authority which guided its Protestant interpreters in the years from the American Revolution to the 1930s. Essays by Nathan O. Hatch and Timothy P. Weber, for example, [seek to] illuminate the tensions created by the commitment of nineteenth-century Protestants both to the individual's freedom to interpret the Bible and to the proposition that an unbiased reader would inevitably uncover in its pages a single, eternal message" (*Journal of American Academic Religion*).

Johnson, Luke Timothy. *The Writings of the New Testament: An Interpretation.* Fortress Pr. 1986 $34.95 pap. $18.95. "A sustained interpretation of the origins and functions of the documents in the early church. Among the most significant interpretative chapters are those that survey the individual books, chapters on the claims of the first Christians, on resurrection faith, and on the memory of Jesus in the church.... Its usefulness is enhanced by indexes and especially informative annotated bibliographies following each chapter" (*Choice*).

Kraeling, E. G. *The Old Testament Since the Reformation.* Schocken 1969 o.p. First published in 1955, this is a history of theological attitudes toward the Old Testament in the Reformed churches from Luther to the present.

Kugel, James L., and Rowan A. Greer. *Early Biblical Interpretation.* [*Lib. of Early Christianity*] Westminster 1986 $16.95. This survey promises to fill an unfortunate gap in scholarly coverage of the history of biblical interpretation, the exegesis of Scripture by the Fathers of the church.

Kümmel, Werner G. *The New Testament: The History of the Investigations of Its Problems.* Trans. by S. MacLean Gilmour and Howard Clark Kee, Abingdon

1972 o.p. This is the most important and valuable survey for the New Testament, covering pace-setting continental scholarship from the Enlightenment through 1930, and offering salient passages from landmark works as well as introductions to them.

Neill, Stephen. *Interpretation of the New Testament, 1861–1961.* Oxford 1964 pap. $10.95. The reading here is much easier and more engaging than in Kümmel's work, which Neill counterbalances with his greater critical reserve and better account of British contributions.

Nickelsburg, George W., and Robert A. Kraft, eds. *Early Judaism and Its Modern Interpreters.* Fortress Pr. 1986 $24.95. A collection of essays covers Judaism as society, culture, and religion in the Greco-Roman context, treating recent scholarship and recent discoveries pertaining to its history and literature.

Rhymer, Joseph, ed. *The Bible in Order.* Doubleday 1976 o.p. All the writings that make up the Bible, arranged in their chronological order according to the dates at which they were written, or edited into the form in which we know them, seen against the history of the times as the Bible provides it. "Using the Jerusalem Bible version, Rhymer reorganizes the Scriptures into the time frame of their writing. Each book of Scripture is thus seen in its relation to the contemporary religious experiences which stimulated it. Generally, each section consists of an introduction, historical background drawn from various biblical sources, and the biblical text itself" (*LJ*).

Tucker, Gene M., and Douglas A. Knight. *The Hebrew Bible and Its Modern Interpreters.* Scholars Pr. GA 1985 $22.50 pap. $14.95. This essay collection for the Old Testament corresponds to the Epp and MacRae symposium on the New Testament listed above. Fifteen articles cover developments in the study of major segments of the Old Testament from around 1945 to the present.

Von Campenhausen, Hans. *The Formation of the Christian Bible.* Trans. by J. A. Baker, Fortress Pr. 1977 pap. $10.95. This is the fascinating story, told by a true expert, of the emergence of a Scripture comprised of "Old" and "New" Testaments as the outcome of a fierce struggle against Christian renunciation of the Hebrew Scriptures.

Methods and Principles of Biblical Exegesis

The student wishing to locate a mainstream of biblical study, in which a momentum of cooperative and progressive investigation of the sacred books has been built up in the twentieth century, might look to the following titles for guidance on accepted methods and principles of interpretation.

Guides to Biblical Scholarship. Ed. by D. O. Via, Jr., and G. M. Tucker, Fortress Pr. 1969 ea. pap. $4.50–$4.95. This is a series of small, attractive paperbacks offering explanations and paradigms of the component methodologies employed by modern biblical criticism. Listed here are titles considered most useful, arranged in the order a newcomer might wish to follow: *The Historical-Critical Method* (E. Krentz, 1975); *Form Criticism of the Old Testament* (G. Tucker, 1971); *Tradition History and the Old Testament* (W. E. Rast, 1972); *The Old Testament and the Archaeologist* (H. Darrell Lance, 1975); *The Old Testament and the Historian* (J. M. Miller, 1976); *Sociological Approaches to the Old Testament* (Robert R. Wilson, 1984); *What Is Form Criticism?* (E. V. McKnight, 1969); *What Is Redaction Criticism?* (N. Perrin, 1969); *Literary Criticism of the New Testament* (W. Beardslee, 1970); *Letters in Primitive Christianity* (W. G. Doty, 1973); *What Is Structural Exegesis?* (D. Patte, 1976); and *Canon and Community* (J. A. Sanders, 1984).

Kaiser, Otto, and Werner G. Kümmel. *Exegetical Method: A Student's Handbook.* Trans. by E. V. Goetchius and M. J. O'Connell, Seabury rev. ed. 1981 pap. $5.95. A convenient and readable guide to the historico-critical method of Old Testament (Kaiser) and New Testament (Kümmel) exegesis, detailing the steps an interpreter must follow in any comprehensive investigation of the meaning of a passage.

Kee, Howard C. *Christian Origins in Sociological Perspective: Methods and Resources.* Westminster 1980 $9.95. This work introduces the recent trend of applying the social sciences to the reconstruction of a more adequate social context for interpreting the New Testament writings.

Koch, Klaus. *Growth of the Biblical Tradition.* Scribner 1968 lib. bdg. $24.50. This is an excellent introduction to the twentieth century's dominant methodology of scriptural exegesis, divided between exposition of the method and selected examples of its application. It is a "must" for any serious student of the field.

Lohfink, Gerhard. *The Bible, Now I Get It: A Form Criticism Handbook.* Doubleday 1979 pap. $7.95. This is a truly delightful primer in the concept and application of form criticism, adorned with clever cartoons that tell much of the story by themselves. It is a "natural" for neophytes who would like to be won over to the discipline.

McKnight, Edgar V. *Meaning in Texts: The Historical Shaping of a Narrative Hermeneutics.* Fortress Pr. 1978 o.p. The author surveys recent attempts to harness the philosophy of linguistics in a new methodology of biblical interpretation. This is a pleasant introduction to a daunting enterprise.

Marshall, I. Howard, ed. *New Testament Interpretation: Essays on Principles and Methods.* Eerdmans 1978 o.p. Eighteen essays by scholars of decidedly conservative, evangelical allegiance offer, nevertheless, a fair and informative survey of the discipline: its history, critical methods, objectives, and contemporary relevance.

Soulen, Richard N. *Handbook of Biblical Criticism.* John Knox 1981 pap. $11.95. This is a very useful handbook of technical terms and tools for biblical study, highly recommended as a standby for beginners in the field. Since the abbreviations routinely used in reference to biblical manuscripts and reference works, as well as the specialist's names for the Bible's parts and formats, are often daunting to the newcomer, this kind of glossary, with concise explanations given each entry, could prove a valued friend. A list of major representative works in the field is also included.

Stuhlmacher, Peter. *Historical Criticism and Theological Interpretation of Scripture: Towards a Hermeneutics of Consent.* Trans. with an intro. by Roy A. Harrisville, Fortress Pr. 1977 o.p. An important essay by a foremost New Testament exegete signaling new trends in the agenda of Scripture scholarship in Germany. The writer stands in the tradition of Bultmann and Käsemann (see below under Selected Masterworks on Biblical Topics and Authors, New Testament), but is taking a new and independent direction in assessing the responsibility of criticism to the Bible's roots in history and in the life of the church.

Westermann, Claus. *Essays on Old Testament Hermeneutics.* Trans. by J. L. Mays, John Knox 1979 o.p. Contributions by prominent Christian scholars explore different aspects of the quest for meaning in Old Testament texts, mainly in pursuit of the Old Testament's message and authority for the Christian believer.

Introductions to the Two Testaments

The genre of biblical "introduction" involves a special kind of book, which is usually arranged in the order of the biblical books and systematically unfolds the historical background, authorship, and salient literary features of each, at least so far as these are matters of current consensus or working hypothesis. The student consults these books for the underpinnings of interpretation, rather than for interpretation itself. They give information to start with, but also assumptions in need of further testing, in any new work of exegesis on a given sacred book.

Alter, Robert, and Frank Kermode, eds. *The Literary Guide to the Bible.* Harvard Univ. Pr. 1987 $29.95. "The authors utilize the full range of critical tools to analyze structure, thematic patterns, narrative techniques, poetic form, and symbolic systems of the books of both Old and New Testaments. Few previous works have treated literary study of the Bible in such a comprehensive way" (*Booklist*).

Anderson, Bernhard W. *Understanding the Old Testament.* Prentice-Hall 4th ed. 1986 $28.95. A mainstay of Old Testament courses for more than 30 years, this thorough and balanced introduction is adorned with attractive maps, charts, and illustrations, and remains one of the best manuals for nonspecialized instruction.

Anderson, G. W. *Tradition and Interpretation.* Oxford 1979 $34.50. Thirteen essays offer a detailed "state of the question" in the major segments of Old Testament study, quite useful for those who wish to delve deeper into the business of scientific exegesis. Though not strictly an "introduction," it will serve as a handy adjunct thereto for the serious student.

The Bible Reader: An Interfaith Interpretation. Prepared by Walter M. Abbott and others. Bruce 1976 $7.95 pap. $3.95. "The task the four editors—each of a different religious tradition—set themselves in preparing this book was to select and set into perspective those passages from the Bible that have shaped and influenced Western civilization in what is commonly called our Judeo-Christian heritage. . . . [Each selection] is introduced by a short discussion of its influence on and use in art, literature and music. The biblical texts themselves are taken from various translations: Protestant, Catholic and Jewish. And the notes that follow each selection explain how the passage is understood by various religions and often . . . the role it plays in the worship and traditions of each group" (*America*).

Bornkamm, Günther. *The New Testament: A Guide to Its Writings.* Trans. by Ilse Fuller, Fortress Pr. 1973 pap. $4.95. Very brief and quintessential, done by a master, this is a true beginner's book, placing the books in the setting of the infant Christian churches and their development.

Davies, W. D. *Invitation to the New Testament.* Doubleday 1969 o.p. Another introduction for the general reader, substantially larger and more broadly informative than the preceding entry.

Eissfeldt, Otto. *The Old Testament: An Introduction.* Harper 1965 $14.95. This is the classic introduction, still unsurpassed in its scope and depth, and especially valuable for the attention it gives to the prehistory of the books in oral tradition and literary sources.

Fohrer, Georg. *Introduction to the Old Testament.* Trans. by D. E. Green, Abingdon 1968 o.p. The scope and technical detail of this introduction nearly match those of the preceding entry. The two are indispensable tools of the professional student.

Gottcent, John H. *The Bible: A Literary Study.* G. K. Hall 1986 $17.95 pap. $6.95. "The aim is to guide readers through some close readings of biblical texts, infer patterns or general ideas of human experience therefrom, and use these patterns to help clarify contemporary experience and observation. After introductory comments on the history of the Bible, its cultural significance, and literary study of the Bible, Gottcent offers individual analyses of 12 texts chosen from the Hebrew Bible and four from the Christian New Testament" (*Choice*).

Koester, Helmut. *History and Literature of Early Christianity.* Vol. 2 in *Introduction to the New Testament.* De Gruyter 1982 $32.95 1987 pap. $16.95. This volume, whose companion is listed above under Histories of Judaism and Early Christianity, Intertestamental Period, places the New Testament books within a broadly reconstructed history of the early churches and a literary context enlarged by the Nag Hammadi papyrus discoveries.

Kümmel, Werner G. *Introduction to the New Testament.* Trans. by Howard C. Kee, Abingdon rev. ed. 1975 $16.95. This is the best New Testament introduction in terms of scope and authority, accredited by its author's unrivaled acquaintance with the literature and his judicious, moderate stance on issues of dispute.

Lohse, Edward. *The Formation of the New Testament.* Trans. by Eugene M. Boring, Abingdon 1981 pap. $9.95. A convenient, readable treatment of the development of the writings, beginning with the oral traditions that preceded them, done by a popular and authoritative scholar.

Perrin, Norman, and Dennis C. Duling. *The New Testament: An Introduction.* Harcourt 2d ed. 1982 text ed. pap. $15.95. The author was among the most influential American biblical scholars, and his approach here illustrates the legacy of literary criticism and comparative religion that he left in his works on the New Testament.

Rosenberg, Joel. *King and Kin: Political Allegory in the Hebrew Bible.* Indiana Univ. Pr. 1986 $29.50 pap. $10.95. "Focusing on the Garden story, the Abraham cycle, and the Davidic history, Rosenberg contributes a detailed study of the complexity and richness of allegory as a fundamental form of the art of biblical narrative. . . . Rosenberg's study affirms the impressive intertextual affinities and thematic integrity of the Bible's complex composition as seen through its use and development of allegory. . . . Excellently annotated" (*Choice*).

Schmidt, Werner H. *Old Testament Introduction.* Trans. by M. J. O'Connell, Crossroad NY 1984 $27.50. "The book gives insight after insight into the meaning of individual passages and even whole collections of texts. . . . Because it omits lengthy recitations of the history of scholarship, it treats quite fully those topics it covers. Because it is always abreast of current scholarship, the book will be too technical occasionally for the beginning Old Testament student; in general, though, it should be comprehensible to any educated readers who will devote their whole attention to it. The most serious shortcoming is the almost total attention to German authors and concomitant omission of American scholars" (*Choice*).

Bible Dictionaries and Concordances

A concordance is an alphabetical index of principal words in partial contexts, showing the places where the words occur in their full contexts, and is sometimes limited to common words, exclusive of proper names. There are concordances to the works of SHAKESPEARE (see Vol. 2), WORDSWORTH (see Vol. 1), TENNYSON (see Vol. 1), and others, but the Bible concordance is the most frequent. One Bible concordance differs from another in completeness, the number of words included; in the version of the Bible concorded; and in the inclusion or exclusion of the books of the Apocrypha.

A Bible dictionary contains short descriptive articles about people, places, things, and customs mentioned in the Bible. It explains the meaning of such terms as *phylactery, prophet, ark, Nazarite, Apocalypse,* and so on. A Bible dictionary differs from a concordance in that it lists many words and phrases that do not occur in the Bible itself, such as *Bible, Sabbatical Year, Ten Commandments, Lord's Prayer.* A dictionary defines; a concordance locates words.

Both tools belong to the indispensable equipment of biblical interpretation, and both develop into extensive, scientific enterprises the ancient marginal notations on biblical manuscripts that offered word statistics, keyword meanings, and interpretive cross-references.

Aland, Kurt. *Vollständige Konkordanz zum griechischen Neuen Testament.* De Gruyter 2 vols. 1975–78 $73.50. This is the "state of the art" in biblical concordances of the original text, giving all the Greek words, down to conjunctions and particles, with their contexts in alphabetical listing (Volume 1), then offering statistical and analytical surveys of word usage by each New Testament author (Volume 2). A standard reference for New Testament scholars.

Andersen, Francis I., and A. Dean Forbes. *Eight Minor Prophets: A Linguistic Concordance.* Biblical Res. Assocs. 1976 pap. $25.00

———. *A Linguistic Concordance of Ruth and Jonah: Hebrew Vocabulary and Idiom.* Biblical Res. Assocs. 1976 pap. $15.00. "This book on Ruth and Jonah is a linguistic concordance in beautifully computer generated pointed Hebrew text. [The authors] use the analytic and large scale data processing power of the computer to abstract (or wrench entire, as it were) the skeleton of Hebrew grammar from the very body of the text. Their research is at the 'atomic' level of the Hebrew language (as might be expected from two former physicists who are now very competent linguists and Bible scholars) and certainly shows up the deficiencies of earlier grammatical studies" (*Journal of Biblical Literature*).

Barr, James. *Semantics of Biblical Language.* Oxford 1961 $30.00. This, of course, is not a biblical dictionary, but a well-founded warning about their use. It stresses the need to determine word meanings from an attentive study of context rather than abstract etymologies and contoured histories of usage.

Botterweck, G. Johannes, and Helmer Ringgren, eds. *Theological Dictionary of the Old Testament.* Trans. by J. T. Willis and D. E. Green, Eerdmans 5 vols. 1977–86 ea. $25.00–$27.50. This invaluable reference work on the Hebrew vocabulary of the Old Testament reached its fifth volume in 1986 and the divine name "Yahweh," still less than halfway through the Hebrew alphabet. It is a specialist's tool, but richly rewarding to all who labor to gain access to it.

Brown, Colin, ed. *New International Dictionary of New Testament Theology.* Zondervan 3 vols. 1975–78 $100.00. This dictionary groups words according to related ideas and concentrates on their theological significance, true to its concern to provide a pastoral resource for preachers and catechists.

Buttrick, George A., and Keith R. Crim, eds. *The Interpreter's Dictionary of the Bible.* Abingdon 5 vols. 1976 $112.00. The subtitle is "An illustrated encyclopedia identifying and explaining all proper names and significant terms and subjects in the Holy Scriptures, including the Apocrypha, with attention to archaeological discoveries and researches into the life and faith of ancient times." A "must" for English-speaking students.

Hammond, N. G., and H. H. Scullard, eds. *Oxford Classical Dictionary.* Oxford 2d ed. 1970 $49.95. Handy in its one-volume, concise format, this is an authoritative reference book for the Greco-Roman antiquity, thus important background for part of the Bible.

Hatch, Edwin, and Henry A. Redpath. *A Concordance to the Septuagint and Other*

Greek Versions of the Old Testament (*including the Apocryphal Books*). Baker Bks. 3 vols. in 2 repr. of 1906 ed. 1983 $75.00. As the only concordance to the Greek Old Testament, this is an extremely valuable tool, though its authority is limited by the fact that it was based on only four major biblical manuscripts and has not the benefit of up-to-date textual criticism.

Katz, Eliezer. *A Classified Concordance.* 4 vols. Bloch 1964–70 ea. $30.00–$40.00. Vol. 1, *The Torah;* Vol. 2, *The Early Prophets;* Vol. 3, *The Later Prophets;* Vol. 4, *The Writings.*

Kittel, Gerhard, ed. *Theological Dictionary of the New Testament.* Trans. by Gerhard Friedrich, Eerdmans 10 vols. $299.50. This monumental resource, of which Volume 10 is a massive index, follows the Greek alphabet with the most significant vocabulary of the New Testament, grouped by root word. With its weaknesses, especially in Volumes 1 to 4 (see James Barr above), it is still an awesome achievement and an irreplaceable tool for the exegete. An abridged, one-volume condensation (1,392 pages), concentrating on the theological meaning of each word, is also available.

Mandelkern, Solomon. *Heichal Hakodesh Concordance to the Old Testament.* Shalom $95.00

————. *Veteris Testamenti concordantiae Hebraicae atque Chaldaicae.* Schocken 9th ed. 1971 o.p. Numerous corrections and additions have accrued to this work since it first appeared 90 years ago, but it is still the best concordance to the Hebrew and Aramaic text of the Old Testament, divided by word forms within the section devoted to each word, and thus invaluable to the student of the original languages.

Miller, Madeleine S., and J. Lane Miller, eds. *Harper's Bible Dictionary.* Harper 8th ed. 1973 $18.95. A very comprehensive revision of this handy reference volume greatly enhances its authority and currency.

Morrison, Clinton. *An Analytical Concordance to the Revised Standard Version of the New Testament.* Westminster 1979 $19.95. This is a compromise concordance for students unable to investigate the Greek vocabulary. Besides listing English words in alphabetical order with their occurrences, it also groups them according to the original Greek words they translate, and an index lists transliterated Greek words alphabetically to show how many ways each is translated in the Revised Standard Version. Other English-language concordances will lack these access keys to the original languages. See, for example, *Nelson's Complete Concordance of the Revised Standard Version Bible* (Nelson 2d ed. rev. 1972 $29.95) and *Nelson's Complete New American Bible Concordance* (Nelson 1977 o.p.).

Moulton, W. F., and A. S. Geden, eds. *A Concordance to the Greek Testament.* Fortress Pr. 1978 $54.95. This was the most popular concordance of the Greek New Testament before the publication of the Aland (see above) concordance, which has wholly surpassed it in textual foundation and completeness.

The New Westminster Dictionary of the Bible. Ed. by Henry Snyder Gehman, Westminster 1970 $22.95. "Like its earlier edition, this is an excellent work destined to become the study companion of all students of the Bible. . . . The new volume includes more than 5000 entries . . . including biblical books, persons, places, and themes" (*ADRIS Newsletter*).

Schmoller, A. *Concordance to the Greek New Testament.* United Bible 1983 pap. $11.00. Although it does not pretend total coverage of every Greek word in the New Testament, this handy instrument is worth mentioning because of its convenient format accompanying Aland, *Greek New Testament* (see above under Reference Works, Critical Editions of Original Texts).

Wigoder, Geoffrey, and others, eds. *The Illustrated Dictionary and Concordance of the Bible*. Macmillan 1986 text ed. $100.00. "This lavishly-illustrated dictonary/concordance, printed on high-quality paper, is comprehensive and authoritative as well as aesthetically pleasing. It provides identification and biblical sources for 'every name and place mentioned in the Old and New Testaments'—over 3500 Biblical names are identified. Also included are entries for religious concepts, rituals and feasts, tribes and dynasties. The photographs (1500 in full color) certainly are the book's most striking feature; all are of superior quality and as instructive as they are beautiful" (*School Library Journal*).

Wigram, George V. *The Englishman's Hebrew and Chaldee Concordance of the Old Testament: Numerically Coded to Strong's Exhaustive Concordance*. Zondervan 1983 $40.45. "George V. Wigram, whose name appears on the title page and cover of the volume, is the compiler of the original edition of 1843. The concordance itself follows the alphabetic order of the Hebrew and Aramaic words, under which are the concordance entries of Strong. There are Hebrew-English and English-Hebrew indexes, as well as appendixes of Hebrew and Aramaic proper names and a table of chapters and verses cited. Of course the Authorized Version is used for the English passages" (*Amer. Ref. Bks. Annual*).

Commentaries

The most comprehensive guide to biblical interpretation is the verse-by-verse commentary, in which the author assembles all the philological, historical, and contextual data on each passage to support his or her understanding of its meaning. Scholarly commentaries usually furnish an introduction to the book at the beginning, with discussions similar to those found in the Introductions listed above, after which specific explanations follow the order of the biblical text by chapter and verse. The entries will follow this order: (1) one-volume commentaries on the whole Bible; (2) prominent commentary series, in which single volumes on individual books might be sought; (3) a few particularly excellent commentaries on popular books on the Bible that appear outside of series.

ONE-VOLUME COMMENTARIES

Black, Matthew, and H. H. Rowley. *Peake's Commentary on the Bible*. Nelson 1962 $39.95. A cooperative effort by the best British and American biblical scholars, this reference volume gives a reliable introduction and explanation for all the sacred books (not including the Old Testament Apocrypha), together with some excellent introductory articles on biblical topics, a section of maps, and a fine index. The necessarily constricted format of a one-volume commentary will limit the inquirer's satisfaction and, at best, whet the appetite for further investigation. (This applies to the following entry as well.)

Brown, Raymond E., ed. *The Jerome Biblical Commentary*. Prentice-Hall 1969 $59.95. This effort of U.S. Roman Catholic scholars parallels *Peake's Commentary* but adds more extensive topical articles and commentary on the Apocrypha. The quality of the contributions varies, of course, but the one-volume package is immensely valuable and hard to duplicate.

Laymon, Charles M., ed. *The Interpreter's One-Volume Commentary on the Bible*. Abingdon 1971 $24.95. "It is slanted not so much to the specialist or to the theological student as to the layman, the Sunday school teacher, and the busy parish minister. It has a profusion of pictorial illustrations, some forty-eight general articles on a wider range of topics than is normally covered, including some on the use of the Bible in preaching and in teaching children and adults, and sixteen useful color maps. The commentaries follow the (Protestant) order of the biblical books and, except where indicated, are based on the RSV. Each commentary and article concludes with a brief bibliography. The Apocrypha is included" (*Theology Today*).

Neil, William. *Harper's Bible Commentary.* Harper 1975 pap. $7.95. "It contains no technical word studies, no sketchy comments on individual verses for which commentaries of the same scope are famous (or infamous!), no detached essays on special themes. Instead, the results of historical, critical, and linguistic studies are introduced unobtrusively (sometimes so subtly as to go unnoticed), as the author describes the whole sweep of each book" (*Interpretation*).

MULTIVOLUME COMMENTARIES

These commentaries are multivolume series. In some cases, the series are still ongoing; in others only some of the titles are still in print. Within a series, the price of each volume may not be the same. Because of these differences, the reader should consult the publisher or *Books in Print* for information concerning availability and prices of particular titles.

Anchor Bible. Doubleday 15 vols. 1964–   . ea. $10.00–$16.00. This important series now counts nearly 30 volumes on Old Testament books, 15 on New Testament, and 3 or 4 on Apocrypha. The quality ranges all the way from excellent to poor, so one should look up the reviews on the volume to be consulted. Contributors are mostly American and include Jews, Protestants, and Roman Catholics.

Augsburg Commentary on the New Testament. Augsburg 1980–88 10 vols. pap. ea. $8.95–$19.95. This series, about half complete (mostly in the epistles, but now including Acts and John), consists of succinct commentaries, with minimum technical and bibliographic detail, based on the English Revised Standard text and geared to laypeople, students, and pastors. Contributors are top-level scholars in the field, making the product surely one of the better ones at this level.

Augsburg Commentary on the Old Testament. Augsburg 1984–88 7 vols. $19.95–$36.95. This is at the same level and quality as its New Testament counterpart (above) but is as yet less than one quarter underway.

Cambridge Bible Commentary. Ed. by Peter R. Ackroyd [*New Testament Ser.*] Cambridge Univ. Pr. 1963 17 vols. ea. pap. $6.95–$12.95. Small volumes, succinct and geared for the general reader, now include all of the New Testament and much of the Old. The base text is the New English Bible with the Apocrypha (see above under Texts and Versions of the Bible, English Versions).

Harper's New Testament Commentaries. Ed. by H. Chadwick and others, Harper. The purpose here is basic understanding, not in-depth criticism, for the reader who does not know Greek. Contributors include British and American Protestant scholars, and both content and style can be highly recommended.

Hermeneia: A Critical and Historical Commentary on the Bible. Ed. by F. M. Cross and Helmut Koester, Fortress Pr. 19 vols. 1971–   . $17.95–$39.95. Still in relatively early stages (9 New Testament, 6 Old Testament, 1 Apostolic Father), this series promises the most up-to-date and technically sophisticated level of commentary available to the English-speaking reader. A large, visually attractive format separates the rich technical and bibliographic annotation from the main expository line and quotations from the original texts or in foreign languages are parenthetically translated. Entries thus far are mostly translated and updated works by foremost German Protestant scholars.

The Interpreter's Bible. Ed. by George A. Buttrick, Abingdon 12 vols. 1957 ea. $22.95 set $260.00. This series covers both Testaments and includes extensive introductions and background essays as well as exegetical and homiletic commentary. King James and English Revised Standard texts are printed in parallel columns accompanying the textual comment. The series is dated and uneven, but much of its informational content remains useful.

The New Century Bible Commentary. Ed. by Ronald E. Clements and Matthew Black, Eerdmans 30 vols. 1981– . ea. pap. $5.95–$18.95. This, too, is a nontechnical series on both Testaments, featuring brief introductions and interspersed commentary with lead phrases from the English Revised Standard version. Contributors are high caliber, mostly British, mostly Protestant.

The New International Commentary on the New Testament. Ed. by F. F. Bruce, Eerdmans 15 vols. 1964– . $12.95–$24.95. This series and the one following are twins, both featuring moderately technical commentary for serious students, and both hewing to a strongly conservative Protestant-evangelical platform of "the Scriptures as the infallible Word of God." The New Testament series is currently outpacing the Old Testament.

The New International Commentary on the Old Testament. Ed. by E. J. Young, Eerdmans 8 vols. 1976– . $14.95–$29.95

The New International Greek Testament Commentary. Ed. by W. W. Gasque and H. H. Marshall, Eerdmans 3 vols. 1979– . $15.95–$35.00. Still in very early stages, this series is based on the latest Greek text (Nestle and Aland), and means to provide scholarly, detailed comment for serious, professional students of the original writings. The series will undoubtedly share the conservative tilt of the two preceding entries but should be, on the whole, more critically responsive and more uniformly rewarding.

New Testament Message: A Biblical Theological Commentary. Ed. by W. Harrington and D. Senior, M. Glazier 22 vols. 1980–82 ea. pap. $5.95–$12.95. A series for the general reader by Roman Catholic scholars that uses the Revised Standard Version and explains the argument of larger sections rather than commenting verse by verse. Entries are uneven, but some are quite good and worth the newcomer's while.

Old Testament Library. Ed. by Peter R. Ackroyd and others, Westminster 1962– . $4.00–$27.50. This series includes both commentaries and topical treatises and now boasts 19 distinguished commentaries on Old Testament books, many being translated German works, and all at a high scholarly level without exceeding the grasp of the nonspecialist.

Old Testament Message. M. Glazier 23 vols. 1981 text ed. $235.00 pap. $165.00. This companion project to the *New Testament Message* (above), following the same procedure under the same auspices, is now underway with volumes on the Pentateuch.

Pelican New Testament Commentaries. Penguin 1963– . pap. $2.50–$3.25. A series of small, compact paperback volumes for beginners and outsiders to biblical study, this project brought out the four Gospels early on, and now the remaining New Testament books are on a slower schedule. The English text is the Revised Standard Version, the critical standard rather rudimentary.

Proclamation Commentaries: The New Testament Witnesses for Preaching. Ed. by Gerhard Krodel, Fortress Pr. 1978–81 $2.95–$8.50. This collection of slender volumes is a counterpart of the *New Testament Message* (above) under Protestant auspices and at mostly higher quality. The series includes sectional introductions (Synoptics, Paul) as well as individual verses in keeping with their slender format. The subtitle explains the intention and argument of the series.

Proclamation Commentaries: The Old Testament Witnesses for Preaching. Fortress Pr.
1978–81 $2.95–$8.50. Much the same can be said of the Old Testament companion series, which is newer and only shortly underway.

IMPORTANT COMMENTARIES OUTSIDE OF SERIES

Ebeling, Gerhard. *Truth of the Gospel: An Exposition of Galatians.* Fortress Pr. 1985
$19.95. A master expositor gives a wide audience his best in this work on Paul's
sharpest controversial response to his critics. Greek words in the exposition are
both transliterated and translated for the nonspecialist.

Fox, Everett. *In the Beginning: A New English Rendition of the Book of Genesis.*
Schocken 1983 $14.95. "Fox achieves his goal remarkably well without as much
impairment of English rhetorical style as might have been expected. The commentary is brief, but adequate.... The results of this exercise in rhetorical
criticism are as brilliant as they are unexpected, with fresh and thrilling insights for the English reader" (*LJ*).

———. *Now These Are the Names: A New English Rendition of the Book of Exodus.*
Schocken 1986 $16.95. "This translation of the Book of Exodus with commentary
and notes is the second volume of its kind by Everett Fox of Clark University. Like
its predecessor [see above], this translation embodies the translation principles of
the German translation of Martin Buber and Franz Rosenzweig.... The author's
more explicit attention to the growing scholarly interest in the literary dimensions
of the text, and the acknowledged usefulness of this scholarship for his own translation and commentary, make this on the whole a more useful volume than his
translation of Genesis. A list of suggestions for further reading (all but two in
English) enhances the usefulness of the work for both the interested layperson and
the scholar" (*Choice*).

Gordis, Robert. *The Book of Job: Commentary, New Translation and Special Studies.*
[*Moreshet Ser.*] Ktav 1977 $45.00. A lifetime of work on one of the Bible's peren-
nial fascinations comes to fruition in this magisterial commentary.

Haenchen, Ernst. *The Acts of the Apostles: A Commentary.* Westminster 1971 $29.95.
This work has reigned for nearly 30 years as the Acts commentary to which all
others must respond. Expository line and technical notes are separated, but not
always successfully.

Käsemann, Ernst. *Commentary on Romans.* Trans. by Geoffrey W. Bromiley, Eerdmans 1978 $25.95. An unfortunate mingling of exposition and bibliographic anno-
tation daunts the reader of this massive work on Paul's monumental letter. The
nonspecialist will need daring to approach this one, but will be richly rewarded.

Kraus, Hans-Joachim. *Psalms 1–59.* Augsburg 1987 $36.95. The translation of this
premier commentary on the psalms is an event of first importance for the
English-speaking world, for the work is unrivaled even at 30 years from its
original German edition. The commentary combines detailed critical information with nourishing exposition of the meaning and consequence of the psalm
texts.

North, Christopher R. *The Second Isaiah Introduction, Translation and Commentary
to Chapters 15–55.* Oxford 1964 $25.00. Here is perhaps the leading English-
language work on one of the most fascinating and influential voices in all the
Bible (Chapters 40 to 55 of the book of Isaiah).

Oesterley, W. O. E. *The Psalms: Translated with Text-Critical and Exegetical Notes.*
Macmillan 1962 o.p. This is a venerable work in the noble tradition of the
"workbook" commentary, which informs and stimulates the student's own interpretive labors rather than preempting them.

Schnackenburg, Rudolf. *The Gospel According to St. John*. Crossroad NY 2 vols. 1980 ea. $39.50. This is the last word in scientific and theologically nutritious commentary, unquestionably the finest on the Gospel of John in any language. The topical excursus sections repay the steep price of the set by themselves.

Schweizer, Eduard. *The Good News According to Luke*. Trans. by David E. Green, John Knox 1984 $23.95. This and the following two entries form a fine trio of Synoptic Gospel commentaries that combines this author's solid scholarship with a generous outreach to the general reader and the result is a model of informative and stimulating commentary.

———. *The Good News According to Mark*. Trans. by Donald Madvig, John Knox 1970 $18.95

———. *The Good News According to Matthew*. Trans. by David E. Green, John Knox 1975 $19.95

Westermann, Claus. *Genesis: A Commentary*. Trans. by John J. Scullion, Augsburg 3 vols. 1985–86 text ed. ea. $21.95–$34.95. Monumental in both size and stature, this outstanding commentary rewards the specialist with its dense detail, and the hungry spirit with its steadfast theological stewardship. Its translation for English-speaking readers is a taxing but welcome public service, which well deserves first mention here among the outstanding commentaries published outside of series.

Selected Masterworks on Biblical Topics and Authors

The principal authors and literary categories of the Bible all have their pathfinding works in modern biblical research. The titles in this section have been chosen either because they have won pathfinder status in their area or because they uniquely capture the spirit and fruits of current study in the area. The fact that so many of the works are translated from the German is testimony to the leadership of German scholars in this field, but also to the fact that ongoing work often responds to, and moderates, the lead taken by the Germans.

OLD TESTAMENT

Alter, Robert. *The Art of Biblical Poetry*. Basic Bks. 1985 $17.95. The author's "investigation of biblical poetry first [attempts to] explain the basic convention of semantic parallelism, with particular attention to its dynamics, its thrust toward narrative development and its power of intensification. Then in the hope of illustrating what a difference poetry makes in the Bible, he extends and refines these generalizations about the system of biblical verse in individual studies on Job, Psalms, the Prophets, Proverbs and the Song of Solomon" (*America*).

The Book of Isaiah. Jewish Pubns. 1978 $12.50. "A committee of eminent scholars prepared the text, using the latest Biblical research to render the Hebrew into contemporary English. . . . [The] 36 magnificent full-page pen-and-ink drawings by Chaim Gross . . . [make] visible the prophet's concern for peace and justice and making the book a contribution to both art and theology" (*LJ*).

Charlesworth, James H., ed. *The Odes of Solomon*. Scholars Pr. GA 1977 pap. $8.95. "[There is] a very brief but informative introduction and a full bibliography. Dr. Charlesworth's aim is thus to present the textual evidence with the minimum of interpretative comment. It is possible, though, to infer from scattered remarks in the notes that he inclines to the view that the original language of the Odes was Syriac. In the preface he clearly states his opinion that they are 'the earliest Christian hymn-book and therefore one of the most important early Christian documents' " (*TLS*).

Collins, Maureen P., ed. *Song of Love: Selections from the Song of Songs*. Association Pr. 1971 $4.95. "This small but sensitively edited volume is a thoughtful and provocative reminder that the Song of Songs is, if anything, first of all a celebration of human love. 'As a lily among brambles, so is my love among maidens' may not be the modern swain's way of describing his loved one; but when the words are accompanied by a picture of a beautiful wife in a laundromat they take on new meaning. . . . The beautiful husband and wife in the photographs breathe new life into the Old Testament words, which in turn, deepen our understanding of the spirit of man expressing itself in the manifold aspects of human wedded love" (*America*).

Crenshaw, James L. *Studies in Ancient Israelite Wisdom*. Ktav 1974 $59.50. A most distinguished and enthralling addition to the author's masterful survey of *Old Testament Wisdom* (John Knox 1981 $16.95 pap. $12.95) traditions and Wisdom books. No finer guide to this biblical stratum exists.

Gunkel, Hermann. *The Legends of Genesis: The Biblical Saga and History*. Intro. by William Albright, Schocken 1984 pap. $5.50. The translation of the introduction to his Genesis commentary by one of the pioneers of Old Testament form criticism offers a classification of scriptural story-types that remains in service among today's scholars.

———. *The Psalms: A Form-Critical Introduction*. Ed. by John Reumann, trans. by Thomas M. Horner, Fortress Pr. 1967 pap. $2.50. Once again this scholar stands at the threshold of Old Testament understanding with his classic diagnosis of psalm types and their life settings in Israelite and Jewish society.

Hanson, Paul D. *The Dawn of Apocalyptic: The Historical and Sociological Roots of Jewish Apocalyptic Eschatology*. Fortress Pr. rev. ed. 1979 $16.95 pap. $12.95. Here, from the most widely quoted author on the movement, is a rewarding study of the outlook and literature that form a major link between the two Testaments.

Koch, Klaus. *The Prophets*. Trans. by Margaret Kohl, Fortress Pr. 2 vols. 1982–84 pap. ea. $10.95. Vol. 1, *The Assyrian Period;* Vol. 2, *The Babylonian and Persian Periods*. This is an excellent introduction to the thought of the individual prophets of the Bible by one of the leading scholars of their literature and periods.

Kraus, Hans-Joachim. *Theology of the Psalms*. Trans. by Keith Crim, Augsburg 1986 $24.95. A concise statement of the faith content and religious significance of the Old Testament's songbook, most of which derived from the liturgical rites of the temple at Jerusalem. The nourishing exposition and theological insight here are typical of this leading commentator on the Book of Psalms (see his commentary above under Important Commentaries Outside of Series).

Mitchell, Stephen. *Into the Whirlwind: A Translation of the Book of Job*. Doubleday 1979 o.p. "Mitchell has produced a translation sometimes literal, usually quite free, but always conscious of the poetic meter and reflective of the spirit and intent of the original. He has not hesitated to omit, transpose, and improvise in order to turn the Hebrew (the most difficult in the Old Testament) into a rhythmic, strong-minded, contemporary English" (*Choice*).

Mowinckel, Sigmund. *The Psalms in Israel's Worship*. Trans. by D. R. apThomas, Abingdon 1962 o.p. The Norwegian scholar's towering achievement in psalm study corrected and complemented Gunkel's (see above). Moreover, his expository talent and his translator's charism make this the best handbook for psalm study currently in the marketplace.

Noth, Martin, and Bernhard W. Anderson. *A History of Pentateuchal Traditions.* Scholars Pr. GA 1981 $22.00. This landmark tradition-criticism of the Pentateuch endeavors to trace the history of principal themes from their spoken origins (oral tradition) to the written form they took at the point of the books' composition.

Russell, D. S. *The Method and Message of Jewish Apocalyptic.* [*Old Testament Lib.*] Westminster 1964 $19.95. Among his several writings on this topic, the author's larger treatise, well written and documented, will prove most rewarding for the serious inquirer.

Von Rad, Gerhard. *The Message of the Prophets.* Trans. by D. M. G. Stalker, Harper rev. ed. 1967 pap. $10.95. This is an extract from the author's celebrated *Old Testament Theology* (see below under Biblical Theologies), revised by him for nontheologians and additionally revised by the translator. No better survey of the subject could be found by a reader from any walk of life.

———. *The Problem of the Hexateuch and Other Essays.* Trans. by E. Trueman Dicken, Fortress Pr. 1966 pap. $17.50. Not only the title essay, but others here as well acquaint the reader with the critical principles and historical thesis of a scholar who, perhaps more than any other, has forged the contemporary consensus on basic matters of Pentateuch criticism.

Westermann, Claus. *Basic Forms of Prophetic Speech.* Trans. by H. C. White, Westminster 1967 o.p. An indispensable key to understanding the prophets is furnished here by a premier Old Testament scholar. The key is the set speech forms in which the prophets expressed themselves—now familiar trademarks of their books.

———. *Praise and Lament in the Psalms.* Trans. by Keith Crim and Richard Soulen, John Knox rev. & enl. repr. of 1965 ed. 1981 $12.95 pap. $9.95. An important and influential contribution to the same field travels in a different direction from Mowinckel (see above) with Gunkel's (see above) heritage. Organization and style are, however, less attractive here.

Wilson, Robert R. *Prophecy and Society in Ancient Israel.* Fortress Pr. 1980 pap. $11.95. Already widely influential is this recent treatise that corrects the lingering romantic portrait of the prophets as isolated free spirits, warring against their society from outside its institutions.

New Testament

Barclay, William. *The New Testament: A New Translation; Vol. 1, The Gospels and the Acts of the Apostles.* Collins 1968 $4.95. The professor of divinity and biblical criticism at Glasgow University "indicates that he was guided by two aims: to make an intelligible translation and to provide one which did not need a commentary. A brief introduction is given to each book; the final chapter is devoted to the subject of translating the New Testament and provides the stance from which Mr. Barclay translated" (*LJ*).

Beker, J. Christian. *Paul the Apostle: The Triumph of God in Life and Thought.* Fortress Pr. 1980 $22.95 pap. $14.95. Already celebrated as the most important book on Paul in recent years, this wordy treatise systematically applies the character of Paul's letters to the search for a coherent center of his thought. A briefer, related essay, more popular in format, is Beker's *Paul's Apocalyptic Gospel* (Fortress Pr. 1982 pap. $7.95).

Bornkamm, Günther. *Jesus of Nazareth.* Trans. by I. MacLuskey and F. MacLuskey, Harper 1960 o.p. It is a classic by now and conclusive evidence of the rich fruits borne, even amidst bitter controversy, by the Bultmann school of gospel criticism (see below). In very readable translation, it should be near the top of the list for every serious newcomer.

———. *Paul.* Trans. by D. M. Stalker, Harper ed. 1971 $15.95. With both biographical and theological sketches, the distinguished exegete gives us an unsurpassed handbook for Pauline study. It is written for the general reader, of whom it will be demanding.

Bornkamm, Günther, and others. *Tradition and Interpretation in Matthew.* Westminster 1963 $13.95. These are the foundational essays in the contemporary redaction (editorial) criticism of the Gospel of Matthew. They might be consulted after Stanton's symposium (see below).

Brown, Raymond E. *The Churches the Apostles Left Behind.* Paulist Pr. 1984 pap. $4.95. This is a short, well-written survey of the "subapostolic period," covering the books written in apostles' names after their deaths (Pastoral epistles, Colossians/Ephesians, I Peter, and so on) and the early church concerns reflected in this enterprise.

Bultmann, Rudolf. *The History of the Synoptic Tradition.* Trans. by John Marsh, Basil Blackwell 2d ed. repr. of 1968 ed. 1972 $39.95; Harper 1963 pap. $9.50. A dense reference book, and not for the fainthearted, this is a foundational treatise in modern Gospel criticism and an indispensable compass point for any continuing research in the field. A more digestable, popular skimming of its contents is given in the Harper Torchbook, *Form Criticism,* by Bultmann and K. Kundsin (edited by F. C. Grant, 1962).

———. *Jesus and the Word.* [*Hudson River Ed. Ser.*] Scribner $20.00. Bultmann reaps the historical and theological harvest of his Gospel criticism in this popular and widely read essay. Its skepticism about the Gospels' historical content was excessive and has been duly moderated by his students, Bornkamm (above) and Käsemann (below).

Conzelmann, Hans. *The Theology of St. Luke.* Trans. by G. Buswell, Fortress Pr. 1982 pap. $9.95. This was the first stroke in the most recent trend of compositional study of Luke-Acts. It is not easy to read and might be consulted along with the Keck and Martyn collection (below).

Dibelius, Martin. *From Tradition to Gospel.* Trans. by Bertram L. Wooff, Attic Pr. 1971 $27.50. This pioneering work of form criticism, complementing Bultmann's (above) is more concise and readable, though less comprehensive and conclusive, than the latter's treatise.

Käsemann, Ernst. *Essays on New Testament Themes.* Fortress Pr. 1982 o.p. This collection, by a foremost Bultmann student, includes a trend-setting essay on the historical Jesus that moderated his master's skepticism on the subject.

———. *Perspectives on Paul.* Fortress Pr. repr. of 1971 ed. 1982 o.p. Seminal essays by one of the most stimulating Pauline interpreters of our day make engrossing and demanding fare for the very serious student of Paul.

———. *The Testament of Jesus: A Study of the Gospel of John in the Light of Chapter 17.* Fortress Pr. 1978 pap. $3.95. Provocative, even radical, this is nevertheless a landmark treatise to which everyone feels obliged to respond. It might be read with Bornkamm's fine essay in John Ashton, ed., *The Interpretation of John* (Fortress Pr. 1986 pap. $7.95).

Keck, Leander E., and J. Louis Martyn, eds. *Studies in Luke-Acts.* Fortress Pr. 1980 pap. $8.95. Widely quoted, watershed essays are included in this collection of studies on both larger issues and individual passages.

Marxsen, Willi. *Mark the Evangelist*. Trans. by Roy A. Harrisville, Abingdon 1977 o.p. These essays inaugurated the compositional criticism of the Gospel of Mark, currently a crowded field of exegetical output.

Sanders, E. P. *Paul and Palestinian Judaism: A Comparison of Patterns of Religion*. Fortress Pr. 1977 $32.95 pap. $19.95. A controversial but widely admired and richly documented treatment of the understanding of the Mosaic Law presumed in Paul's writing that happens to include, as perhaps its most valuable feature, a survey of views on Paul's central concept of divine "righteousness" by M. T. Brauch.

Schweitzer, Albert. *Paul and His Interpreters: A Critical History*. Trans. by W. Montgomery, Schocken 1964 o.p. As he did for Jesus (below), Schweitzer here announces for Paul a liberation from nineteenth-century liberal theology in favor of the native Jewish apocalyptic thinking that nourished the Apostle.

———. *The Quest of the Historical Jesus*. Trans. by W. Montgomery, Macmillan 1961 o.p. This classic belongs to world literature, not just to theology. It chronicles the many failures and the unsuspected successes of the nineteenth century's "gold rush" in pursuit of the real Jesus. It is a "must" for every serious inquirer in this field.

Schweizer, Eduard. *Church Order in the New Testament*. Trans. by Frank Clarke [*Student Christian Movement Pr. Ser.*] Oxford 1961 pap. $9.95. A widely quoted survey of the New Testament books for the community organization they reflect brings out, with clarity and consistency, a pivotal criterion for discerning the later, postapostolic writings.

Smith, D. Moody. *Johannine Christianity: Essays on Its Setting, Sources, and Theology*. Univ. of South Carolina Pr. 1985 $17.95. A distinguished career in the research of John's Gospel (and letters) is epitomized in these fine essays, whose moderation in assessing and employing current trends recommends them to the serious Johannine student.

Stanton, Graham, ed. *The Interpretation of Matthew*. [*Issues in Religion and Theology Ser.*] Fortress Pr. 1983 pap. $7.95. Several landmark essays in Matthean criticism complement Bornkamm, *Tradition and Interpretation in Matthew* (above).

Stuhlmacher, Peter. *Reconciliation, Law and Righteousness: Essays in Biblical Theology*. Trans. by Everett R. Kalin, Fortress Pr. 1986 $24.95. Included are very important essays on Paul's thought by one of his best and most influential present-day interpreters.

Taylor, Vincent. *The Formation of the Gospel Tradition*. St. Martin's 1968 o.p. A highly respected British voice reacts to the early work of the form critics in Germany. It is warmly recommended for a conservative slant on that momentous movement.

Telford, William R., ed. *The Interpretation of Mark*. [*Issues in Religion and Theology Ser.*] Fortress Pr. 1985 pap. $7.95. Eight influential essays illustrate the current state of the Marcan question and complement (and correct) those of Marxsen (above).

Tuckett, Christopher, ed. *The Messianic Secret*. [*Issues in Religion and Theology Ser.*] Fortress Pr. 1983 pap. $7.95. Important essays attack the crucial issue raised in Wrede (below) and should be read with it.

Weiss, Johannes. *Jesus' Proclamation of the Kingdom of God*. Trans. by David L. Holland, Scholars Pr. GA 1985 pap. $9.75. Here, with introduction, is the monumental treatise of 1892 that changed a whole generation's view of Jesus' basic message and set the stage for all approaches to it in this century. (See current discussions of the matter in Bruce Chilton, ed., *The Kingdom of God in the Teaching of Jesus* [Fortress Pr. 1984 pap. $7.95], to complement that of Weiss.)

Wrede, William. *The Messianic Secret.* Trans. by J. C. Greig, Attic Pr. 1971 o.p. This turn-of-the-century work, together with that of Weiss (above), shattered the idealistic Jesus portraits of the preceding generation and prescribed a radically new approach to the Gospel's documentation of Jesus' life.

Biblical Theologies

This genre, usually in the form of a "Theology of the Old Testament" or a "Theology of the New Testament," attempts to organize the vast contents of either Testament in a systematic fashion, either according to guiding ideas or as illustration and orchestration of a historical process. Whether one chooses a concept or a view of history as the guiding principle, the project is very risky, and modern research has tended to discourage it by revealing the complexity and diversity of the biblical testimonies. As a result, biblical theologies are at least a threatened, if not an endangered, species in our day. Here are only the monumental survivors.

Bultmann, Rudolf. *The Theology of the New Testament.* [*Contemporary Theology Ser.*] Scribner 1970 text ed. pap. $15.95. Even though one can now see its defects and critical prejudices quite clearly, this is an irreplaceable treasure, especially for its treatment of early traditions, Paul, and John. There can be no New Testament literacy without reading and digestion of the work, which like that of Von Rad (below) is predicated on the diversity of the constituent voices.

Conzelmann, Hans. *An Outline of the Theology of the New Testament.* Trans. by John Bowden, Harper 1969 o.p. The title reflects the more modest ambition one now entertains for the biblical theology. The work is in the Bultmann tradition but a step forward from the master in terms of scholarly currency and flexibility. It is a rich reference work for all serious students of the New Testament.

Eichrodt, Walther. *Theology of the Old Testament.* Trans. by J. Baker [*Old Testament Lib.*] Westminster 2 vols. 1967 ea. $22.95. This work is a modern classic inasmuch as it applies historical methodology to the organization of Old Testament thought, yet it attempts to unify it around the theme of "covenant."

Jeremias, Joachim. *New Testament Theology.* Trans. by J. Bowden, Scribner 1971 $30.00. The highly respected author never got beyond this first volume of his theology, but everyone can benefit from its erudition, and many will appreciate its more conservative stance on the recovery of Jesus' authentic words.

Kümmel, Werner G. *The Theology of the New Testament According to Its Major Witnesses: Jesus-Paul-John.* Trans. by John E. Steely, Abingdon 1973 $17.95. Less likely to achieve "classic" status, this is nevertheless a useful coverage of the chosen "witnesses," though its exclusion of other New Testament voices clearly shows where it understands the heart of the Gospel to be found.

Von Rad, Gerhard. *Old Testament Theology.* Trans. by D. M. G. Stalker, Harper 2 vols. 1962–65 ea. $16.95–$17.95. Here, in our opinion, is the finest of the genre, a "must" for all students of the Old Testament, even casual ones. It attempts no unifying thematic but lets each tradition speak for itself and the polyphony of the Hebrew Scripture to ring forth gloriously.

CHAPTER 14

Minority Religions and Contemporary Religious Movements

Robert S. Ellwood

It is the customary fate of new truths to begin as heresies and to end as superstitions.

—THOMAS HENRY HUXLEY

There is only one religion, though there are a hundred versions of it.

—GEORGE BERNARD SHAW

Religious America has long presented two spectacles to the world, and to itself. In one, it is a "Christian nation," established by devoutly believing Founding Fathers and patriots, endowed with a sacred mission, and generally righteous in its dealings. In this picture, valid pluralism at the most embraces the conventional "three faiths" to which the great majority of Americans adhere: Catholicism, Protestantism, and Judaism. However much it may involve a mythologizing of the American past, this view is undoubtedly reinforced today by the fact that the rate of church attendance in America, mostly, of course, in "mainline" churches and synagogues, is among the highest in the world, and according to public opinion polls an extraordinarily high percentage of Americans claim that they are believers and that religion is important to them.

But we must not forget the other image of religious America, also remarked on by the world and, gladly or grudgingly, admitted by most Americans as well. That is the America of riotous religious diversity, hosting virtually every spiritual option in the world, spawning new sects and cults profligately. This perspective too has its truth. Owing both to immigration and domestic creativity, nearly every major American city boasts not only its traditional American places of worship but also its Buddhist temples, Hindu centers, Muslim mosques, and sanctuaries of a congeries of exceptional faiths old and new, whether Spiritualist churches with their deep nineteenth-century roots and/or products of the spiritual exuberance of the 1960s "counterculture" ranging from ashrams to Zen.

This chapter deals with a part of the diverse spectrum. The bibliography

684

will be of religious movements in the United States (though a few important works on European background will be cited) outside conventional Judaism and Christianity, and not primarily ethnic in character (i.e., it will not include Japanese-American Buddhist churches, ethnic Muslims, predominantly black and Native American groups). It will include studies of groups from nineteenth- and twentieth-century America in the esoteric, communal, or Eastern traditions that have drawn followers from several sectors of American society, and have had a certain impact on American life generally. The limiting definition of groups covered is "bent" in a few instances to include Christian and ethnic groups such as Jehovah's Witnesses and the "Black Muslims," about which there is widespread interest and a significant literature. Listings on individual movements will essentially consist of a very limited number of basic texts of the group itself, together with current works of independent scholarship on it.

NINETEENTH-CENTURY MOVEMENTS

The young American republic was a fertile field both for Christianity in its various forms and for unconventional spiritual movements. Broadly speaking, these movements had roots in a European philosophical tradition that can be traced back to ancient Neoplatonism and even before, and flourished in the Renaissance, but with the rise of modern science had been in recession as a dominant worldview. This Western Neoplatonism and its progeny emphasized the unity of the cosmos, the priority of mind and spirit to matter, the concept of "correspondences" (i.e., relationships between different planes of reality, as between signs of the Zodiac and human personality), and the "Great Chain of Being" idea that ranks of angelic or spiritual beings greater and lesser than humans lie between the lowest levels of creation and God. It was easy to move from theoretical acceptance of this outlook to belief in concrete manifestations of it such as spirits and magic. Though adherence to objective manifestations of the older worldview, such as the earth-centered Ptolemaic astronomy, dwindled to virtually nothing in the seventeenth and eighteenth centuries, not a few people continued to affirm the spiritual significance of such ideas as correspondences and the Great Chain of Being. Increasingly, though, they found themselves marginal to mainstream science and religion alike.

By the early nineteenth century, however, something of the spiritual side of the old worldview was being revived under the powerful impetus of several new movements that gave it a contemporary face and sociological grounding. These include Swedenborgianism and Mesmerism (discussed later), and Freemasonry with its image of lodges in which one can be initiated into ancient and secret wisdom. In the background was the vogue for Romanticism, with its exaltation of feeling and inner experience as ways of knowing, and its idealization of the past, and for philosophical Idealism not far removed from Neoplatonism. In America, on one level the new mix produced the Transcendentalism of EMERSON (see Vol. 1) and THOREAU (see

Vol. 1). On another, vivid movements such as Spiritualism, which has been called "Swedenborgianism Americanized," and later Theosophy, Christian Science, and "New Thought" emerged.

The young American nation was also fascinated by social and even sexual experimentation. It was dotted with utopian communities, often based on unconventional religious doctrines, testing new forms of social organization and sexual arrangements from celibacy to polygamy. We will present such groups as the Oneida community, the Shakers, and the Latter-Day Saints (Mormons). Some groups that were considered radical in the nineteenth century have now become well established and conventional while others have disappeared. All, however, help demonstrate that religious diversity and experimentation in the United States is no new thing.

General Works

Albanese, Catherine L. *Corresponding Motion: Transcendental Religion and the New America.* Temple Univ. Pr. 1977 $29.95. A useful book on Transcendentalism for the student of religious movements, since it emphasizes its religious character and themes.

Bridges, Hal. *American Mysticism: From William James to Zen.* CSA Pr. 1977 pap. $3.95. A useful and readable introduction to the world of American mystical experience and its relation to intellectual currents.

Cross, Whitney R. *The Burned-Over District: The Social and Intellectual History of Enthusiastic Religion in Western New York, 1800–1850.* Cornell Univ. Pr. 1982 pap. $9.95; Hippocrene Bks. repr. of 1950 ed. 1981 lib. bdg. $31.50. A classic study of the matrix out of which Spiritualism, Mormonism, and their movements of the nineteenth century emerged.

Ellwood, Robert S. *Alternative Altars: Unconventional and Eastern Spirituality in America.* [*Chicago History of Amer. Religion Ser.*] Univ. of Chicago Pr. 1979 lib. bdg. $12.95 pap. $5.50. A theoretical and historical study focusing on the concept of an ongoing pattern of "emergent religion" in American life and on Spiritualism, Theosophy, and Zen as major examples.

Foster, Lawrence. *Religion and Sexuality: The Shakers, the Mormons, and the Oneida Community.* Univ. of Illinois Pr. 1984 pap. $9.95. An excellent study of the three movements in the nineteenth century, emphasizing their highly contrasting sexual arrangements, but putting them in the larger context of ideology, religious experience, and cultural environment.

Jackson, Carl T. *The Oriental Religions and American Thought: Nineteenth-Century Explorations.* Greenwood 1981 lib. bdg. $27.50. An exceptionally fine piece of scholarship that emphasizes the impact of Hinduism and Buddhism on American writers, and provides invaluable background for understanding the popularity of Eastern-based groups and movements in the spiritual life of this country.

Judah, J. Stillson. *The History and Philosophy of the Metaphysical Movements in America.* Westminster 1967 o.p. A comprehensive treatment of Spiritualism, Theosophy, Christian Science, and the "New Thought" groups in the broader context of American culture. Judah emphasizes the healing aspects of these movements and the ways in which they are varied expressions of a single "metaphysical" theme.

Kerr, Howard, and Charles L. Crow, eds. *The Occult in America: New Historical Perspectives.* Univ. of Illinois Pr. 1983 $22.95. A collection of historical essays by various authorities, covering such topics as Spiritualism, Theosophy, Christian Science, and "Women in Occult America."

Leventhal, Herbert. *In the Shadow of the Enlightenment: Occultism and Renaissance Science in Eighteenth-Century America.* New York Univ. Pr. 1976 o.p. Provides invaluable background for the nineteenth century. Here one can see how European occultism and the Renaissance worldview took root in America to offer substance for later movements.

Melton, J. Gordon, ed. *Encyclopedia of American Religions.* Gale 2d ed. 1986 $175.00; McGrath 2 vols. 1978 $135.00. Very comprehensive reference work, especially in the area of new and unconventional groups. An essential resource for the study of minority religions.

Webb, James. *The Occult Underground.* Open Court 1974 $18.95. A discussion of nineteenth-century Theosophy, Christian Science, secret societies, and so on, in Europe and America. Webb interprets these movements as fearful reactions against modern reason and science; the reader should keep this perspective, which not all authorities would share, in mind. But the book is highly readable and based on extensive research.

CHRISTIAN SCIENCE

The Church of Christ, Scientist, was founded by Mary Baker Eddy (1821–1910), a New England woman who believed that she had been healed in a remarkable manner in 1866; she later referred to that event as her discovery of Christian Science. She published the first edition of her major book, *Science and Health with Key to the Scriptures,* in 1875. The Church was incorporated in Boston in 1879. Healing through treatments that inculcate belief in the ultimate unreality of evil and disease has always been important to Christian Science. Basic doctrine presents God as the sole true reality, the "divine Principle of all that really is," and sin and sickness, like matter, as objects of erroneous belief. The Christian Science Church has no clergy, but "practitioners" exercise leadership roles, especially in healing treatments. Worship is simple and centers around readings from the Bible and *Science and Health.*

BOOKS ABOUT CHRISTIAN SCIENCE

Braden, Charles S. *Christian Science Today: Power, Policy, Practice.* SMU Pr. 1958 $19.95. An important study, though now somewhat dated.

Eddy, Mary B. *Science and Health with Key to the Scriptures.* 1875. First Church $25.00 pap. $10.50. The basic text.

———. *Manual of the Mother Church.* 1908. First Church standard ed. $7.00. More than merely a book of operating procedures, the *Manual* offers important insights into ideas and their application.

———. *Prose Works.* 1925. First Church standard ed. $22.00. Essential works, apart from *Science and Health,* by the discoverer of Christian Science.

Gottschalk, Stephen. *The Emergence of Christian Science in American Religious Life.* Univ. of California Pr. 1974 $20.95 pap. $4.95. The most comprehensive treatment of Christian Science history and teaching in the nineteenth century.

Peel, Robert. *Christian Science: Its Encounter with American Culture.* Doubleday

1965 o.p. A basic work on the rise of Christian Science and its meaning in American life.

———. *Mary Baker Eddy.* Holt 3 vols. 1971–77 o.p. Vol. 1, *The Years of Discovery;* Vol. 2, *The Years of Trial,* Vol. 3, *The Years of Authority.* By far the best and most comprehensive biography of the discoverer of Christian Science.

COMMUNAL GROUPS

The Shakers were far from the only communal group with a religious basis in nineteenth-century America. Others include the Oneida community, a long-prosperous settlement in upstate New York celebrated for its practice of "complex marriage"; Fountain Grove in California, founded by the intriguing mystic and former Spiritualist and Swedenborgian Thomas Lake Harris; and Amana in Iowa, which (like Oneida) eventually moved from sect to successful corporation.

Among the most interesting is the succession of spiritual communes in New Harmony, Indiana. Founded in 1814 by George Rapp, a German, as a celibate, pietistic settlement, it was sold in 1825 to Robert Owen, the celebrated British industrialist and philanthropist, who established a cooperative community along his own utopian lines. The experiment cost him most of his fortune, however, and Owen returned to England in 1828, where he later became a Spiritualist. One of his sons who remained in America, Robert Dale Owen, pursued an interesting and varied life of romance, politics, communalism, and Spiritualism.

Books about Communal Groups

Barthel, Diane L. *Amana: From Pietist Sect to American Community.* Univ. of Nebraska Pr. 1984 $19.95. The most extensive study of this important community.

Bestor, Arthur. *Backwoods Utopias: The Sectarian Origins and the Owenite Phase of Communitarian Socialism in America: 1663–1829.* Univ. of Pennsylvania Pr. 2d ed. 1970 $31.50 pap. $12.95. A solid study of American communalism in its colonial and British sectarian roots.

Cole, George D. *Life of Robert Owen.* Biblio Dist. 1965 o.p. A standard life.

Dare, Philip N. *American Communes to 1860: An Annotated Bibliography.* Garland 1986 $34.00. A valuable bibliographical resource, with brief summary of each group's history.

Demaria, Richard. *Communal Love at Oneida: A Perfectionist Vision of Authority, Property and Sexual Order.* [*Texts and Studies in Religion*] E Mellen 2d ed. 1983 $49.95. A valuable study of Oneida's exceptional theology of love and its sexual practice.

Harrison, John F., ed. *Utopianism and Education: Robert Owen and the Owenites.* [*Class. in Education Ser.*] Teachers College Pr. 1969 text ed. pap. $6.00. Interpretation of the work of this great social visionary and founder of the New Harmony Owenite community.

Hinds, William A. *American Communities.* Citadel Pr. repr. 1973 pap. $2.45; [*Amer. Utopian Adventure Ser.*] Porcupine Pr. 3d ed. repr. of 1908 ed. 1975 lib. bdg. $39.50; Peter Smith 1971 $12.00. A classic account of such celebrated nineteenth-century American utopias as Economy, Zoar, Bethel, Aurora, Icaria, the Shakers, and Oneida, based largely on personal observation.

Hine, Robert V. *California's Utopian Colonies.* Univ. of California Pr. 1983 text ed.

$24.00 pap. $6.95. An account of Fountain Grove, the Theosophical community at Point Loma, and other early California spiritual and utopian communities.

Kring, Hilda A. *The Harmonists: A Folk-Cultural Approach*. Scarecrow Pr. 1973 $17.50. The best modern study of the Rappites, properly called the Harmony community, a Protestant celibate movement that lasted in several locations, including New Harmony, Indiana, from 1805 to 1905.

Leopold, Richard W. *Robert Dale Owen*. Hippocrene Bks. repr. of 1940 ed. 1969 lib. bdg. $31.50. A substantial biography of Robert Owen's distinguished son, who continued his Communalist and Spiritualist work.

Lockwood, George B. *The New Harmony Communities*. AMS Pr. repr. of 1902 ed. 1975 $34.50. Still the most comprehensive history of these planned communities, giving extensive attention to the Rappites and the work of Robert Owens.

Mandelker, Ira L. *Religion, Society, and Utopia in Nineteenth-Century America*. Univ. of Massachusetts Pr. 1984 lib. bdg. $22.00. A sociological study of utopian communities and their relation to the outside world, focusing on the Oneida community as an example.

Nordhoff, Charles. *Communistic Societies of the United States: From Personal Visit and Observation*. Intro. by Mark Holloway, Dover repr. of 1875 ed. pap. $6.95. Classic firsthand account of Amana, Harmony, Zoar, the Shakers, and Oneida, among others, with emphasis on the religious creed of each.

Parker, Robert A. *A Yankee Saint: John Humphrey Noyes and the Oneida Community*. [*Amer. Utopian Adventure Ser.*] Porcupine Pr. repr. of 1935 ed. 1973 lib. bdg. $27.50; Shoe String repr. of 1935 ed. 1973 $29.50. A standard biography of the controversial perfectionist of the Oneida community.

Thomas, Robert D. *The Man Who Would Be Perfect: John Humphrey Noyes and the Utopian Impulse*. Univ. of Pennsylvania Pr. 1977 $18.50. A life of the unforgettable visionary who founded the Oneida community.

Whitworth, John McKelvie. *God's Blueprints: A Sociological Study of Three Utopian Sects*. Routledge & Kegan 1975 o.p. An excellent study of the Shakers, the Oneida community, and the modern Bruderhof.

THE LATTER-DAY SAINTS (MORMONS)

The Church of Jesus Christ of Latter-Day Saints, or the Mormon Church as it is popularly called, has been the most successful of distinctive new religious movements originating in the United States. The recipient of the revelation that inaugurated Mormonism was Joseph Smith (1805–1844), who in 1822 was told in a vision by the angel Moroni where to find certain buried tablets. These were retrieved, translated, and published (in 1830) by Smith as the *Book of Mormon*, which Mormons regard as a major supplement to the biblical scriptures. It described sacred events, including an appearance of Jesus Christ, in early America. With the help of these revelations Smith called on the faithful to abandon apostate churches and restore pure religion.

Many vicissitudes followed, including violent mob action against Mormons and Smith's murder, leading up to the settlement of Utah by Mormons under Brigham Young (1801–1877) beginning in 1847. By this time the controversial practice of polygamy (ceased in 1890) had commenced.

Mormon theology accepts some conventional Christian doctrines, such as belief in God, the work of Christ, and free will, but includes such distinctive ideas as the concept of God as finite, of a material body, and of God having attained His position through growth. Several LDS churches exist; the largest, headquartered in Salt Lake City, is highly organized and well known for its effective missionary work.

BOOKS ABOUT THE LATTER-DAY SAINTS

Alexander, Thomas G. *Mormonism in Transition: The Latterday Saints and Their Church, 1890–1930.* Univ. of Illinois Pr. 1986 $19.95. An important historical work on the development of the LDS church.

Arrington, Leonard J., and Davis Bitton. *The Mormon Experience: A History of the Latter-Day Saints.* Knopf 1979 $17.50; Random 1980 pap. $5.95. A very full, rich historical account of Mormonism; a good first book to read on the subject. Both authors are members of the LDS church, but have written as scholars as well as believers.

Brodie, Fawn M. *No Man Knows My History: The Life of Joseph Smith.* Knopf o.p. An important though controversial investigation of Smith.

Bushman, Richard L. *Joseph Smith and the Beginnings of Mormonism.* Univ. of Illinois Pr. 1984 $17.95. A comprehensive, well-written summary of early Mormonism, based on the acceptance of Mormon documents at face value. A good introduction to the LDS perspective on their origins.

Flake, Chad J., ed. *A Mormon Bibliography, 1830–1930: Books, Pamphlets, Periodicals, and Broadsides Relating to the First Century of Mormonism.* Univ. of Utah Pr. 1978 $80.00. A basic resource for students of Mormonism.

Hill, Donna. *Joseph Smith: The First Mormon.* Signature Bks. rev. ed. repr. of 1977 ed. 1983 pap. $5.95. A sympathetic portrayal.

Leone, Mark P. *Roots of Modern Mormonism.* Harvard Univ. Pr. 1979 $17.50. A new look at the development of Mormonism, emphasizing economic factors and the presence of diversity as well as conformity in the Mormon world.

O'Dea, Thomas F. *Mormons.* Univ. of Chicago Pr. 1964 pap. $10.00. Still the best overall introduction by a sociologist of religion.

Shields, Steven L. *The Latter Day Saints Churches: An Annotated Bibliography.* Garland 1986 $67.00. Covers material from 1931–1986 on the LDS, the Reorganized Church of Latter-Day Saints, and smaller groups in the Mormon tradition.

Shipps, Jan. *Mormonism: The Story of a New Religious Tradition.* Univ. of Illinois Pr. 1985 $14.50. A new, compact, brilliant, and insightful study of the religion by a non-Mormon, emphasizing its originality as a new religion.

Smith, Joseph, Jr. *Book of Mormon, 1830.* [*Heritage Repr. Ser.*] Herald Hse. 1970 $12.00 1973 pap. $4.00. The book translated from the Golden Plates by Joseph Smith.

————. *Doctrine and Covenants of the Church of Jesus Christ of Latter-Day Saints: Containing the Revelations Given to Joseph Smith, Jun, the Prophet, for the Building Up of the Kingdom of God in the Last Days.* Ed. by Orson Pratt, Greenwood repr. of 1880 ed. 1971 lib. bdg. $29.75. A fundamental Mormon scriptural text. Inexpensive editions, often bound with a companion work, *The Pearl of Great Price*, are widely available through the LDS church.

MESMERISM

The Viennese-educated physician Franz Anton Mesmer (1734–1815), whose practice in Paris during the 1780s aroused great controversy, is considered the modern father of Mesmerism or hypnotism. His experiments indirectly contributed greatly to the development of psychotherapy and psychosomatic medicine. He also substantially influenced nineteenth-century Spiritualism and occultism.

Mesmer believed that healing can be affected by "animal magnetism," a universal force that can be transmitted from one person to another by stroking gestures. These operations could easily put patients into a hypnotic trance in which suggestibility was high and material from the unconscious could rise to the surface. Mesmer himself came to believe that animal magnetism could awaken latent powers of extrasensory perception, healing, and wisdom.

In the 1830s and 1840s, Mesmerism became a vogue in America, with Mesmerist experimentation, medical healings, and stage performances popular. When Mesmerist trance was combined with Swedenborgian cosmology to produce the trance mediumship of discarnate spirits, the result was Spiritualism.

Though several biographies of Mesmer exist, current literature on Mesmerism in America is unfortunately slight.

BOOKS ABOUT MESMERISM

Buranelli, Vincent. *Wizard from Vienna: Franz Anton Mesmer.* Putnam 1975 o.p. A good, readable biography of Mesmer.

Fuller, Robert C. *Mesmerism and the American Cure of Souls.* Univ. of Pennsylvania Pr. 1982 $23.00. Despite an occasionally arch tone, the best book on the subject.

Tatar, Maria M. *Spellbound: Studies on Mesmerism and Literature.* Princeton Univ. Pr. 1978 $34.00. Affords important insights into the cultural significance of Mesmerism in both Europe and America.

NEW THOUGHT

The New Thought movement is centered in ideas, similar to those of Christian Science, that God is all, mind is basic, good thoughts create good realities, and evil and sickness are the result of false beliefs. A major source of this teaching is Phineas Quimby (1802–1866) of Maine, a one-time student of Mesmerism. He was mentor of Mary Baker Eddy, discoverer of Christian Science, as well as of other early New Thought teachers, such as Warren Felt Evans and Julius Dresser. The principal differences between New Thought and Christian Science are organizational rather than doctrinal. While the Christian Science Church is a highly structured institution, New Thought has been a diverse movement of individuals, independent churches, and often loosely organized denominations. Among the New Thought groups are Unity, the Church of Divine Science, and the Church of Religious Science. Ideas of the New Thought type, sometimes spoken of as "positive thinking," have also been widely popularized by prominent clergymen of "mainline" churches, such as Norman Vincent Peale and Robert Schuller.

BOOKS ABOUT NEW THOUGHT

Braden, Charles S. *Spirits in Rebellion: The Rise and Development of New Thought.* SMU Pr. 1963 pap. $15.95. The best scholarly study of this movement.

Dresser, Horatio W., ed. *The Quimby Manuscripts*. 1921. Citadel Pr. 2d ed. 1984 pap. $9.95. Edited material by and about the principal founder of New Thought.

Fox, Emmet. *The Emmet Fox Treasury*. Harper repr. 1979 pap. $15.95. Basic works of one of the most articulate and readable of New Thought teachers; a good introductory sample.

ROSICRUCIANISM

The term *Rosicrucian* (from the Latin for the tradition's symbol: the rose and the cross) alludes to a body of esoteric wisdom and an ancient order that allegedly possesses it. The wisdom is essentially based on the worldview of Neoplatonism and the Renaissance, already mentioned, including the mentalism, the separate destiny of the soul from the body, astrology, the symbolic meaning of alchemy, and correspondences. The name and the concept of a secret order first appeared in Germany in the famous tract *Fama Fraternitatis*, published in 1614, when the older worldview was already coming under the onslaughts of modern science. Its account of a certain Christian Rosenkreuz and his quest for secret wisdom, as well as the idea of an ancient Rosicrucian order, are regarded as allegorical by most scholars.

The name, however, stuck. It is now used loosely for a body of occult learning in the Renaissance style, of the type cited above, and more concretely for certain modern groups that have adopted the label. A Rosicrucian society was established in Pennsylvania in 1694, and both in America and elsewhere numerous groups called themselves by that designation in the eighteenth and nineteenth centuries. At least five such orders are extant in America today, the oldest being the Fraternitas Rosae Crucis founded in 1868; the best known is undoubtedly the international Ancient Mystical Order Rosae Crucis, headquartered in San Jose, California, which advertises widely. Little independent literature on modern Rosicrucianism exists.

BOOKS ABOUT ROSICRUCIANISM

McIntosh, Christopher. *The Rosy Cross Unveiled: The History, Mythology and Rituals of an Occult Order*. State Mutual Bk. 1980 $30.00. A readable introduction to the entire tradition.

Melton, J. Gordon, ed. *Encyclopedia of American Religions*. Gale 2d ed. 1986 $175.00; McGrath 2 vols. 1978 $135.00. In the "General Reference Works" section in Volume 2, the reader will find a summary of the history of Rosicrucianism and the major American groups.

THE SHAKERS

The United Society of Believers in Christ's Second Appearing, commonly called Shakers, was a significant feature of nineteenth-century American spiritual life. Clustered in celibate rural communes from Maine to Kentucky, the Shakers combined an outward life of hard work and plain living with an inner world of sacred dance and strange visions. Their numerous practical inventions, simple well-made furniture, and lively songs are now parts of American lore.

The founder was Ann Lee (1736–1784), called Mother Ann. Raised in the slums of Manchester, England, she experienced a religious transformation through an ecstatic group known as the "Shaking Quakers" and came with a few fellow believers to America in 1774. Two years later the first community was established near Albany, New York. At its peak, around 1830, Shakerism had some 19 communal houses of several hundred souls each. Today, less than a dozen still practice the Shaker way of life.

Shaker belief centered on the dual nature of God, male and female principles being equally present in the divine. As the male aspect had appeared in Jesus Christ, so had the female in Mother Ann. Thus the "Second Appearing" had already come. The Society was called to live the life of the new age of perfection following that event, when men and women were absolutely equal and the lower passions transcended, and human beings could pursue lives of free cooperation together. To this ideal the quiet empire of Shaker communities testified.

Shaker worship was elaborate, combining precision marches and dances with spontaneous gifts of tongues and song. In 1837 a great Spiritualistic movement swept through the Shaker world, with many reports of visits by past worthies from biblical figures to Mother Ann. Despite emotional excess, these manifestations led to the fine Shaker art that endeavors to capture glimpses of another world on paper.

The literature, both primary and secondary, on the Shakers is extensive and growing. Below are a few books that may serve as starting points.

BOOKS ABOUT THE SHAKERS

Andrews, Edward D. *The Gift to Be Simple: Songs, Dances, and Rituals of the American Shakers*. Dover 1940 pap. $3.95; Peter Smith $12.75. Valuable insights into Shaker forms of expression.

————. *People Called Shakers: A Search for the Perfect Society*. Dover 1953 pap. $5.50; Peter Smith new & enl. ed. $15.50. A standard introduction by an eminent student of Shakerism.

Evans, Frederick W. *Autobiography of a Shaker and Revelation of the Apocalypse*. AMS Pr. repr. of 1888 ed. 1986 $19.50; [*American Utopian Adventure Ser.*] Porcupine Pr. lib. bdg. $25.00. Classic autobiography and statement of a leading nineteenth-century Shaker and social radical.

Melcher, Marguerite F. *The Shaker Adventure*. Shaker Mus. 1980 pap. $8.95. A good popular introduction.

Procter-Smith, Marjorie. *Women in Shaker Community and Worship: A Feminist Analysis of the Uses of Religious Symbolism*. [*Studies in Women and Religion*] E Mellen 1985 lib. bdg. $49.95. A well-researched feminist insight into the unique faith and society of the Shakers.

Richmond, Mary L., ed. *Shaker Literature: A Bibliography*. Univ. Pr. of New England 1976 text ed. $60.00. An exhaustive resource for primary and secondary materials on the Shakers.

Sasson, Sarah D. *The Shaker Spiritual Narrative*. Univ. of Tennessee Pr. 1983 text ed. $19.95. A fascinating look at the inner world of Shaker experience, with its visions and spiritual journeys, through the intimate journals of members of the community.

Whitson, Robley E., ed. *The Shakers: Two Centuries of Spiritual Reflection*. [*Classics of Western Spirituality Ser.*] Paulist Pr. 1983 $13.95 pap. $9.95. An excellent, well-introduced collection of writings by Shakers.

SPIRITUALISM

The formal beginning of the Spiritualist movement is generally attributed to the famous "Rochester rappings," tapped messages in code first heard at home in upstate New York in 1848 by two young girls of humble background, Margaret and Kate Fox. But, as we have seen, the way had been abundantly prepared. Not only were Swedenborgianism and Mesmerism at hand, but just the year before Andrew Jackson Davis (1826–1910), the chief philosopher of nineteenth-century American Spiritualism, had published his major work, now out of print, *The Principles of Nature: Her Divine Revelation and a Voice to Mankind* (1847). A practicing Mesmerist, Davis had delivered the manuscript of some 800 pages out of trance, it being recorded by scribes. Philosophically, much of it is little more than Swedenborg paraphrased, but it adds to Swedenborg's metaphysics an exuberant optimism, characteristic of America at this juncture, full of faith in progress and ever-brighter democratic futures without end.

For a decade or so after 1848, when sensational newspaper articles about the Fox sisters' encounter had provoked a thousand imitative attempts at contacting the Other Side, Spiritualism was an enthusiasm. Trance mediumship, seances, listening for rappings, and even "physical phenomena" such as the manifestation of spirit trumpets and levitation were widely reported. Spiritualism was vigorously attacked and defended, but it was talked about. Its ideology was Swedenborgian and Mesmerist, often joined to Davis's progressivist social idealism. After the Civil War, despite occasional revivals, Spiritualism maintained a much quieter existence, but persists to this day. Its direct and indirect influence on later movements, such as Theosophy and New Thought, as well as on the rise of scientific psychical research, is significant. The literature about Spiritualism is still sometimes either highly sympathetic or antagonistic, reflecting the strong feelings this colorful American movement has always evoked.

BOOKS ABOUT SPIRITUALISM

Bragdon, Ruth. *The Spiritualists: The Passion for the Occult in the Nineteenth and Twentieth Centuries.* Prometheus Bks. 1984 pap. $11.95. A general history written from a highly skeptical viewpoint.

Doyle, Arthur Conan. *The History of Spiritualism.* [*Perspectives in Psychical Research Ser.*] Ayer repr. of 1926 ed. 1975 $22.00. A classic history by the creator of Sherlock Holmes; Doyle was himself a Spiritualist believer and writes sympathetically.

Fornell, Earl W. *The Unhappy Medium: Spiritualism and the Life of Margaret Fox.* Univ. of Texas Pr. 1964 o.p. Though unfortunately very limited in its treatment of the religious and cultural background of Spiritualism, and less than profound in its understanding of the troubled spirit who was one of its inciters, this is an interesting biographical introduction to her.

Goldfarb, Russell M., and Clare R. Goldfarb. *Spiritualism and Nineteenth-Century Letters.* Fairleigh Dickinson Univ. Pr. 1978 $20.00. A summary of nineteenth-century Spiritualism and references to it in British and American literature.

Kerr, Howard. *Mediums, and Spirit-Rappers, and Roaring Radicals.* Univ. of Illinois Pr. 1972 o.p. A study, much more comprehensive than the Goldfarb work, of Spiritualism in nineteenth-century American literature and social movements.

Moore, R. Laurence. *In Search of White Crows: Spiritualism, Parapsychology, and*

American Culture. Oxford 1977 $22.50. A rich, well-documented investigation of Spiritualism and the scientific studies of psychic phenomena that it inspired. Though accused of excessive skepticism by parapsychological critics, Moore attempts to be evenhanded and shows appreciation for the cultural meaning of the subject in American life.

Nelson, G. K. *Spiritualism and Society.* Schocken 1969 o.p. A study of Spiritualism from a sociological perspective. Though emphasizing the movement in Britain, its insights are of value to students of it everywhere.

SWEDENBORGIANISM

Emanuel Swedenborg (1688–1772), the Swedish scientist and mystic, had a profound impact on nineteenth-century unconventional spiritual movements. Of brilliant intellect, Swedenborg began his career in science and engineering. In midlife, however, after the onset of a remarkable series of visions, he turned to religion. His experiences include spiritual journeys to the realms of departed spirits, which he saw as educative rather than dedicated to reward and punishment. Applying his extraordinary mind to the philosophical and theological understanding of what he had seen, Swedenborg revived not only the Neoplatonist doctrine of the separate destiny of the soul from the body in an eternity of growth and glory but also the concept of correspondences. He held that appearances in our time and space are but reflections of realities and events in the spiritual world.

A small but influential church, the Church of the New Jerusalem, commonly called the "New Church," was founded in England based on the teachings of the Swedish sage, and established in America as early as 1792. It has kept the ideas of Swedenborg alive to play a role on the larger stage of American intellectual life. Their influence can be seen in movements like Transcendentalism, Spiritualism, Theosophy, and New Thought; indeed, the 1840s, seminal for that collection of interwoven causes, has been called the decade of the "Swedenborgian wave."

Swedenborgianism affected common people in the New World as well as intellectuals. John Chapman ("Johnny Appleseed," 1774–1845) was a convinced apostle of that cause and spread tracts popularizing it as well as apples on the upper frontier. With Swedenborg's vivid portrayals of the life of the departed in mind, it is little wonder that Spiritualism's advocacy of conversation with them was soon to come.

BOOKS ABOUT SWEDENBORGIANISM

Block, Marguerite. *The New Church in the New World.* Swedenborg 1984 $12.95. The best treatment of Swedenborgianism in America to date.

Meyers, Mary A. *A New World Jerusalem: The Swedenborgian Experience in Community Construction.* [*Contributions in Amer. Studies*] Greenwood 1983 lib. bdg. $29.95. A study of Bryn Athyn, Pennsylvania, the center of the general Church of the New Jerusalem, the smaller of the two Swedenborgian churches in America; focuses on the community's response to physical and ideological incursions from without.

Swedenborg, Emanuel. *True Christian Religion.* Swedenborg 2 vols. ea. $10.00 set $19.00 pap. ea. $6.50 set $11.00. Perhaps the most lucid and comprehensive of Swedenborg's numerous theological writings.

Toksvig, Signe. *Emanuel Swedenborg, Scientist and Mystic.* [*Biography Index Repr. Ser.*] Ayer repr. of 1948 ed. 1972 $25.00. A standard biography of Swedenborg.

THEOSOPHY

The Theosophical Society was founded in 1875 in New York by the author of the basic Theosophical literature, Helena Petrovna Blavatsky (1831–1891); Henry Steel Olcott (1832–1907), its first president; and others. The major works of Blavatsky, *Isis Unveiled* (1877) and *The Secret Doctrine* (1888), postulate an ancient, primordial wisdom underlying all religions preserved through the ages in esoteric circles, whose tenets can now be presented as an alternative to modern dogmatic religion and materialistic science. They include the eternal interaction of consciousness and matter to shape the manifested universe, the existence of advanced souls (called Masters or Mahatmas) as teachers of mankind, and the evolution of the world and of individuals ("pilgrims") through many cycles of existence. After the publication of *Isis Unveiled*, Blavatsky and Olcott went to India, where the movement became influential and certain Eastern ideas, such as karma and reincarnation, came to be more central to its ideology. In turn Theosophy, despite a tumultuous history, has played an important role in popularizing Eastern religion and philosophy in the West. Its own distinctive teaching, however, is founded as much on the Western Neoplatonist and occultist tradition as on Oriental lore, though it sees a fundamental unity between the two.

BOOKS ABOUT THEOSOPHY

Blavatsky, Helena P. *Isis Unveiled: A Master-Key to the Mysteries of Ancient and Modern Science and Theology.* 1877. Theosophy repr. of 1877 ed. 1931 $17.00; Theos. Univ. Pr. repr. of 1877 ed. 1976 $20.00 pap. $14.00. Blavatsky's first major work.
———. *The Secret Doctrine: The Synthesis of Science, Religion, and Philosophy.* 1888. Theosophy repr. of 1888 ed. 1925 $18.50; ed. by Boris De Zirkoff, Theos. Pub. House 7th ed. 1980 $45.00. The most important Theosophical text.
Campbell, Bruce F. *Ancient Wisdom Revived: A History of the Theosophical Movement.* Univ. of California Pr. 1980 $18.95. The fullest independent scholarly history.
Olcott, Henry S. *Old Diary Leaves, First Series: America 1874–78.* Theos. Pub. House 6 vols. 1973 $7.50 ea. Fascinating though highly personal account of Blavatsky and the early American life of the Theosophical Society by its first president. The volumes carry Olcott's recollections of Blavatsky and Theosophy up to 1898.

TWENTIETH-CENTURY MOVEMENTS

Most of the new religious movements cited above that appeared in nineteenth-century America have continued into the late twentieth century, albeit less in the public eye. But certain new stages in unconventional spiritual life have also been reached.

Oriental religion packaged in specific denominational forms for occidentals first made its appearance at the very end of the nineteenth century in the wake of the celebrated World's Parliament of Religions, held in Chicago in 1893 in conjunction with the Columbian Exposition. There, for the first time, swamis, Zen masters, and other Eastern religious spokesmen well prepared for the task addressed, and often very favorably impressed, Western audiences in the West. Some, such as Swami Vivekananda of Vedanta and the Zen teacher Soyen Shaku, were soon instrumental in founding centers of their tradition in America for Western students. These increased in numbers and influence throughout the first half of the twentieth century.

Many other Eastern teachers came as well. Indeed, a dominant feature of such movements, beginning perhaps in the decade following World War I, has been a great emphasis on the role of charismatic individuals—swamis, gurus, masters—rather than of more abstract teachings. The same could be said of new movements more in the Western tradition too, such as "I Am" or Scientology.

After World War II, this strand of American spirituality deepened through the popular philosophical writings of such eclectics as ALDOUS HUXLEY (see Vol. 1) and Alan Watts, and explored new life-styles in the "Beatnik" Zen associated with writers like JACK KEROUAC (see Vol. 1) and GARY SNYDER (see Vol. 1). The next great phase, however, was the much-discussed "counterculture" of the 1960s, when enthusiasm for the East, the occult, and spiritual adventure seemed to go hand-in-hand with emerging "youth culture." Many new unconventional religious groups appeared, some growing phenomenally in that decade and the early 1970s. Much controversy was engendered. By the late 1970s and the 1980s, most of the 1960s-generation new religions had become more institutionally stabilized and enjoyed only modest rates of growth. Some continued, though, to exhibit a salient feature of the groups of the 1960s, a desire to embrace not only new ideas and the leadership of a charismatic individual but also a total life-style, expressed in dress, diet, career values, and perhaps communalism. As we have seen, these characteristics are by no means novel in America, having rich nineteenth-century precedents, yet in the 1960s they were often displayed with a flamboyance and a special emphasis on youth that made them highly visible, to the excitement of some and the acute discomfort of others.

General Reference Works: Directories, Encyclopedias, and Bibliographies

This section includes works covering several different twentieth-century groups that are organized for reference use—directories, encyclopedias, and general bibliographic works.

Choquette, Diane, comp. *New Religious Movements in the United States and Canada: A Critical Assessment and Annotated Bibliography.* [*Bibliographies and Indexes in Religious Studies Ser.*] Greenwood 1985 lib. bdg. $39.95. A basic research tool.

Khalsa, D. K. *The New Consciousness Sourcebook.* Borgo Pr. 1985 $19.95. Listing of new and unconventional groups alphabetically and geographically, with self-description. Also gives assorted "health" and "new age" type stores, restaurants, services, publications. Incomplete but useful.

Melton, J. Gordon. *Biographical Dictionary of American Cult and Sect Leaders*. [*Lib. of Social Sciences*] Garland 1986 lib. bdg. $39.95. Fundamental information on 267 individuals important in minority religions.

———. *The Encyclopedic Handbook of Cults in America*. [*Lib. of Social Sciences*] Garland 1986 lib. bdg. $24.95. Essential information on some 500 American religious groups. A "cult" is defined nonpejoratively as a "first-generation religion." A major reference tool.

Melton, J. Gordon, and James V. Geisendorfer. *A Directory of Religious Bodies in the United States*. [*Reference Library of the Humanities*] Garland 1977 lib. bdg. $40.00. Supplements Melton's *Encyclopedia of American Religions*, with addresses. Inevitably quickly becomes out-of-date for some groups but a valuable resource. Periodic revisions planned.

General Descriptive and Historical Works

This section presents books covering several or all twentieth-century new religious movements in historical or descriptive narrative form.

Barker, Eileen, ed. *New Religious Movements: A Perspective for Understanding Society*. [*Studies in Religion and Society*] E Mellen 1982 $69.95. Useful collection of essays.

———. *Of Gods and Men: New Religious Movements in the West*. Mercer Univ. Pr. 1984 $26.50. Collection of essays by leading scholars on new movements in both Europe and America.

Braden, Charles S. *These Also Believe*. Macmillan 1949 o.p. Still a valuable resource on older groups, such as Theosophy, I Am, New Thought, Father Divine, and others.

Bromley, David, and Anson Shupe. *Strange Gods: The Great American Cult Scare*. Beacon Pr. 1982 $21.95 pap. $8.95. A book for the general reader that summarizes major groups while seeking to dispel popular misconceptions about "cults." Critical of the "anticult" stance.

Ellwood, Robert S., Jr. *The Eagle and the Rising Sun: Americans and the New Religions of Japan*. Westminster 1974 $7.95. Description of Tenrikyo, Nichiren Shoshu, and other Japanese "new religions" in America, with emphasis on occidental converts to them.

———. *Religious and Spiritual Groups in Modern America*. Prentice-Hall 1973 pap. $21.95. A survey of unconventional and Eastern American groups. Second edition coauthored by Harry Partin (Prentice-Hall 1988 text ed. pap. $17.00).

———, ed. *Eastern Spirituality in America: Selected Readings*. Paulist Pr. 1987 $16.95. Text by leading proponents of Vedanta, Zen, and other Eastern teachings in America, with historical introduction.

Fracchia, Charles A. *Living Together Alone: The New American Monasticism*. Harper 1979 o.p. Reports on new forms of monasticism, including Hindu and Buddhist communities in America for occidentals.

Glock, Charles, and Robert N. Bellah, eds. *The New Religious Consciousness*. ADL $29.50 pap. $6.95; Univ. of California Pr. 1976 $36.50 pap. $11.95. Valuable collection of readable papers based on field research on a number of groups, well introduced by the editors, both prominent sociologists of religion.

Needleman, Jacob. *New Religions*. Crossroad NY 1984 pap. $10.95. A very readable introduction based on the 1960s experience.

Needleman, Jacob, and George Baker, eds. *Understanding the New Religions*. Harper 1978 $17.50 pap. $8.95. Scholarly papers from a variety of perspectives.

Pavlos, Andrew J. *The Cult Experience*. [*Contributions to the Study of Religion*] Greenwood 1982 lib. bdg. $29.95. An introduction to the subject. Often helpful, though sometimes overgeneralized and based on secondhand material.

Richardson, James T., ed. *Conversion Careers: In and Out of the New Religions.* Sage 1978 o.p. Good sociological and psychological case studies on a variety of groups.

Shupe, Anson D., Jr. *Six Perspectives on New Religions: A Case Study Approach.* [*Studies in Religion & Society*] E Mellen 1981 $49.95. Approaches to new religions, including criminological, philosophical, anthropological, psychological, sociological, and historical. Reading lists and discussion questions.

Tipton, Steven M. *Getting Saved from the Sixties: Moral Meaning in Conversion and Cultural Change.* Univ. of California Pr. 1982 lib. bdg. $21.95 pap. $8.95. An excellent, readable sociological study centering on three movements: EST, a Zen Center, and a youth-oriented fundamentalist Christian center. The premise is that, in the 1970s, groups like these channeled and tamed the spiritual energies of the 1960s.

Tiryakian, Edward A., ed. *On the Margin of the Visible: Sociology, the Esoteric, and the Occult.* Krieger 1974 o.p. Good collection of scholarly essays.

Ungerleider, J. Thomas. *The New Religions: Insights into the Cult Phenomenon.* Merck, Sharp & Dohme 1979 o.p. Balanced report based on psychological investigations.

Veysey, Laurence. *The Communal Experience: Anarchist and Mystical Communities in Twentieth Century America.* Univ. of Chicago Pr. 1978 pap. $7.95. Highly competent research on several groups, including a Vedanta ashram and Gurdjieff community.

Webb, James. *The Occult Establishment.* Open Court 1976 $19.95 pap. $9.95; State Mutual Bk. 1976 $35.00. Study of the occult in twentieth-century political and social life in Europe and America. Interesting material, though the author's hypotheses may not be convincing to all.

Wuthnow, Robert. *Experimentation in American Religion: The New Mysticisms and Their Implications for the Churches.* Univ. of California Pr. 1978 $31.00. Scholarly sociologial study based on the San Francisco Bay Area, illuminates underlying spiritual trends that help interpret the meaning of new religious movements.

Zaretsky, Irving I., and Mark P. Leone, eds. *Religious Movements in Contemporary America.* Princeton Univ. Pr. 1974 $71.00 pap. $18.50. Excellent essays on a variety of groups.

General Works on Controversial Issues

Understandably, new religious movements have brought controversy, and this has been expressed in full-length books as well as articles. Indeed, an "anticult" set of groups and publications has arisen that some observers perceive as a movement in its own right. Arguments have swirled around charges that intensive religious groups, often labeled "cults," "brainwash" initiates to make them psychologically unable to leave, and countercharges that such rhetoric is exaggerated and inflammatory, disregarding the rights of individuals to make their own religious choices. The practice of "deprogramming," the intentional removal and deconversion of adherents of "cults," has likewise spawned vehement debate between proponents and those who see it as no better than kidnapping and gross violation of religious freedom. Behind these debates lie far-reaching issues concerning the psychology of religious movements, their legal status, and their relation to the larger society. This section will not deal with philosophical and theological responses to new religions, but to controversies regarding their psychological and legal position vis-à-vis the lives of individuals.

Melton, J. Gordon, and Robert L. Moore. *The Cult Experience: Responding to the New Religious Pluralism.* Pilgrim NY 1982 pap. $8.95. A balanced overview for the general reader.

Richardson, Herbert W., ed. *New Religions and Mental Health: Understanding the Issues.* [*Symposium Ser.*] E Mellen 1980 $39.95; Rose Sharon Pr. 1980 pap. $11.95. Essays by 15 writers, generally opposed to "deprogramming" and "brainwashing" explanations.

Robbins, Thomas. *Civil Liberties, "Brainwashing" and "Cults": A Select Annotated Bibliography.* Graduate Theological Union of Berkeley 1981 o.p. A useful guide to the complex of interrelated issues suggested in the title.

Robbins, Thomas, and Dick Anthony, eds. *In Gods We Trust: New Patterns of Religious Pluralism in America.* Transaction Bks. 1980 text ed. pap. $12.95. Useful collection of scholarly essays.

Rudin, A. James, and Marcia R. Rudin. *Prison or Paradise?: The New Religious Cults.* Fortress Pr. 1980 $4.95. A strongly "anticult" discussion; combines genuine concern with some questionable information and assumptions.

Saliba, John A. *Psychiatry and the Cults: An Annotated Bibliography.* Garland 1986 $60.00. Highly recommended.

Shepherd, William C. *To Secure the Blessings of Liberty: American Constitutional Law and the New Religious Movements.* Crossroad NY 1985 $12.95 pap. $8.95. A thorough discussion of the legal issues, based on the premise that "the law knows no heresy."

Shupe, Anson D., Jr., and others. *The Anti-Cult Movement in America: A Bibliographic History.* Garland 1984 $22.00. An important introduction to the nature and literature of the opposition the new religions have evoked.

——. *The New Vigilantes: Deprogrammers, Anti-cultists and the New Religions.* Sage 1980 o.p. A study of the anticult movement.

Theological and Philosophical Responses to the New Religions

A vast amount of writing has attempted to assess the new religious movements, above all of the 1960s generation, and the overall worldview many of them imply, from philosophical or theological perspectives. Some of the assessments have been basically sympathetic, perceiving the movements as harbingers of important cultural and spiritual change, or signifying the opening up of new and positive kinds of experience. Others have seen disturbing signs of narcissism or even totalitarianism in them. Still other critics have challenged these new religious movements from the standpoint of different beliefs, especially those of conservative Christianity. Only a sampling of this literature is presented here, emphasizing those works of general rather than highly partisan or denominational character.

Cox, Harvey. *Turning East: The Promise and Peril of the New Orientalism.* Simon & Schuster 1977 $9.95 1979 pap. $7.95. A sensitive, sometimes critical, interpretation by a liberal Christian theologian.

Enroth, Ronald. *A Guide to Cults and New Religions.* Inter-Varsity 1983 pap. $5.95.

Descriptions together with evangelical Christian responses by a sociologist of religion.

Johnston, William. *The Inner Eye of Love: Mysticism and Religion.* Harper 1978 pap. $6.65. Written by a distinguished Jesuit theologian interested in dialogue between the mystical traditions of all religions; offers deep-level understanding of the contemporary quest that has produced new religious movements of Eastern or mystical orientation.

Martin, Walter. *The New Cults.* Vision House 1980 pap. $8.95. The perspective of a balanced, well-informed evangelical writer.

Needleman, Jacob. *Consciousness and Tradition.* Crossroad NY 1982 o.p. An analysis of modern spiritual malaise, with attention to the importance of traditional wisdom conveyed through several contemporary movements; recommended as a response by a sympathetic philosopher.

Newport, John. *Christ and the New Consciousness.* Broadman 1978 o.p. A good conservative Christian response; presents the evangelical Christian critique without resorting to inflammatory rhetoric.

Modern Theosophical Groups

The Theosophical movement has continued to be a vital force in the alternative spirituality of the twentieth century. Three major Theosophical societies have existed throughout the century, one of them until 1942 was centered in an important utopian community in Point Loma, San Diego. The largest, the Theosophical Society headquartered in Adyar, Madras, India, experienced severe vicissitudes until the 1930s under the brilliant but controversial leadership of Annie Besant and C. W. Leadbeater, who professed psychic powers and whose further refinements of the doctrines of the Masters produced a "second generation" of Theosophical literature. Above all, Besant and Leadbeater sponsored the career of J. Krishnamurti (1895–1986), first hailed as a Theosophical "World Teacher," who later broke with all organized groups to establish a major independent career as a spiritual teacher.

Other movements that sprang out of a Theosophical background in the twentieth century can only be named: the Anthroposophy of the remarkable philosopher and visionary Rudolf Steiner, the teachings and meditation groups of Alice Bailey, the I Am activity, modern Gnostic churches, the Liberal Catholic Church. The following list contains biographies and other works on persons and institutions connected with twentieth-century Theosophy or such related groups as these. For general books on Theosophical teaching and history see the bibliography under Nineteenth-Century Movements, General Works.

Bailey, Alice A. *Unfinished Autobiography.* Lucis 1970 $19.00 pap. $10.00. The life of the founder from her own perspective.

Easton, Stewart C. *Rudolf Steiner: Herald of a New Epoch.* Anthroposophic 1980 pap. $10.95. A study of the founder of Anthroposophy.

Greenwalt, Emmett A. *The Point Loma Community in California, 1897–1942: A Theosophical Experiment.* AMS Pr. repr. of 1955 ed. 1979 $26.00. Ample historical and sociological account.

Lutyens, Mary. *Krishnamurti: The Years of Awakening.* Avon 1983 $5.95; Farrar 1983

$15.00. The first volume of the most important study of Krishnamurti by one of his disciples.

———. *Krishnamurti: The Years of Fulfillment.* Avon 1984 pap. $4.95; Farrar 1983 $15.50. A valuable biography of the mature Krishnamurti.

McDermott, Robert A., ed. *The Essential Rudolf Steiner.* Harper 1983 pap. $10.95. Basic writings of the founder of Anthroposophy.

Nethercot, Arthur H. *First Five Lives of Annie Besant.* Univ. of Chicago Pr. 1960 o.p. The first volume of the major biography of Besant.

———. *Last Four Lives of Annie Besant.* Univ. of Chicago Pr. 1963 o.p. A continuation of the title above.

Pruter, Karl, and J. Gordon Melton. *The Old Catholic Sourcebook.* Garland 1983 $39.00. Brief descriptions and full bibliographies on churches in the modern Gnostic and Liberal Catholic traditions, among others.

Sheehan, Edmund W. *Teaching and Worship of the Liberal Catholic Church.* Ed. by William H. Pitkin, St. Alban Pr. 1978 pap. $2.25. A standard summary issued by the church.

Steiner, Rudolf. *Anthroposophy: An Introduction.* Trans. by V. Compton Burnett, Anthroposophic 1983 pap. $7.00. A good first book to read among the many works by the founder of Anthroposophy.

AMERICAN ZEN AND OTHER BUDDHISM

Buddhism in the United States has two traditions, ethnic and occidental. The former is represented by the temples and churches of Japanese-Americans, Thai-Americans, and others from largely Buddhist countries. Our concern will be with the latter, Buddhist centers serving Americans of occidental background who have found Buddhism through a personal spiritual quest. Most occidental Buddhists have been attracted to one of three forms of the religion: Zen, Nichiren Shoshu, and Tibetan (Vajrayana) Buddhism. Zen is known for its quiet seated meditations, its emphasis on simplicity and immediacy of life, and its rich cultural expressions. Nichiren Shoshu, also from Japan, has prospered since midcentury both in Japan and abroad through the vigorous efforts of its lay missionary arm, Soka Gakkai; it is a modern Buddhism that stresses chanting and dynamic living. Tibetan Buddhism, complex, colorful, and psychologically profound, has drawn a highly dedicated following. A growing interest in the southern or Theravada school of Buddhism, especially its meditation method called *vipassana*, can also be discerned.

Thus far books on American Buddhism are largely limited to general accounts and personal narratives. As background, a vast literature exists on Buddhism in general, and especially on Zen and Tibetan religion. Much material can also be found on the "Beat" Zen of the American 1950s from biographical and literary perspectives.

BOOKS ABOUT AMERICAN ZEN

Ames, Van Meter. *Zen and American Thought.* Greenwood repr. of 1962 ed. 1978 lib. bdg. $26.50. A classic study of parallels between Zen and American thought.

Dator, James Allen. *Soka Gakkai: Builders of the Third Civilization—American and*

Japanese Members. Univ. of Washington Pr. 1969 o.p. Dated, but a fundamental study of this movement.

Earhart, H. Byron. *The New Religions of Japan: An Annotated List of Books Published in English.* Univ. of Michigan Pr. Center for Japanese Studies 2d ed. 1983 o.p. A basic resource for Nichiren Shoshu and other Japanese "new religions" in America and their Japanese background.

Fields, Rick. *How the Swans Came to the Lake: A Narrative History of Buddhism in America.* Shambhala 1986 pap. $14.95. A full and interesting history with illustrations of American Buddhism of all schools.

Kapleau, Philip. *The Three Pillars of Zen: Teaching, Practice, Enlightenment.* Doubleday 1980 pap. $9.95. A standard text on the theory and practice of Zen for Westerners, with lectures by Zen Masters and valuable narratives of Zen experiences by both Eastern and Western students.

Kerouac, Jack. *Dharma Bums.* Buccaneer Bks. 1976 lib. bdg. $16.95; New Amer. Lib. 1959 pap. $2.95; Penguin 1971 pap. $6.95. A very influential novel of the 1950s "Beat" Zen epoch.

Layman, Emma M. *Buddhism in America.* Nelson-Hall 1976 pap. $13.95. A basic history.

Prebish, Charles. *American Buddhism.* Duxbury Pr. 1979 o.p. A good overview, emphasizing Buddhist movements appealing to occidentals.

Watts, Alan W. *Way of Zen.* Random 1974 pap. $4.95. An important introduction of Zen to the West by a noted interpreter of it in the tradition of D. T. Suzuki.

ASTROLOGY

Astrology represents a movement or sphere of influence in the twentieth-century world rather than a particular group, though a few small astrological churches and institutions have arisen. Its main influence is on the millions who read astrological books, periodicals, or newspaper columns, or the smaller but still large numbers who have professional horoscopes cast, or do their own. Many explanations have been offered for this continuing interest in the ancient art, both by believers and nonbelievers. But serious independent studies of astrology as a social phenomenon are few. In addition to the works listed below, general histories of occultism and related topics will contain information on astrological history and practice.

BOOKS ABOUT ASTROLOGY

Adams, Evangeline. *Astrology for Everyone.* Dodd repr. of 1931 ed. 1981 pap. $5.95. Reprint of a classic work by a founder of modern American astrology.

Omarr, Sydney. *My World of Astrology.* Wilshire 1965 $7.00. Anecdotal autobiography and philosophy of one of America's leading astrologers.

BAHA'I

The Baha'i faith originated in Persia (Iran) in the mid-nineteenth century through the ministry of Baha Ullah (1817–1892), believed by his followers to be the major prophet of our age, proclaiming a new universal religion. Having roots in Islam, Baha'i believes also in a succession of prophets, including the founders of the great religions. It differs from Islam in believing that Muhammad was not the last prophet, but that the list has continued past Muhammad to include its founder. Baha'i is monotheistic and affirms immortality, but the emphasis tends to be ethical and social; the new age inaugurated by the prophet Baha'u'llah will be one in which humanity must realize its unity, overcoming the prejudice, inequality, and war that set it against itself, and to these ends Bahaists dedicate themselves. Worship is simple but the sense of community among Bahaists is strong. The faith first came to America around 1892, and has become well established, as may be seen by its headquarters in the United States, the beautiful Baha'i temple on the shores of Lake Michigan in Wilmette, Illinois.

BOOKS ABOUT BAHA'I

Baha'u'llah. *Gleanings for the Writings of Baha'u'llah.* Baha'i 1976 $17.95 pap. $12.95. A basic introduction to the founder of Baha'i and his writings.

Bjorling, Joel. *The Baha'i Faith: An Historical Bibliography.* [*Reference Lib. of Social Science*] Garland 1985 lib. bdg. $35.00. A necessary resource for the student of Baha'i.

Cole, Juan R., and Moojan Momen, eds. *From Iran East and West.* Vol. 2 in *Studies in Babi and Baha'i History.* Kalimat 1984 $19.95. Example of modern historical scholarship within the Baha'i movement.

Esslemont, J. E. *Baha'u'llah and the New Era: An Introduction to the Baha'i Faith.* Baha'i 5th rev. ed. 1980 pap. $4.50. A very readable first book of the faith.

Hatcher, William, and James D. Martin. *The Baha'i Faith: The Emerging Global Religion.* Harper 1985 $14.45. A sympathetic scholarly study; a good introduction to the faith for students.

Lee, Anthony A., ed. *Circle of Unity: Baha'i Approaches to Current Social Issues.* Kalimat 1984 pap. $9.95. A good entree to modern Baha'i thought.

THE BLACK MUSLIMS

The "Black Muslims," originally called the Nation of Islam and later the World Community of Islam in the West and finally American Muslim Mission, began as a movement expressing alienation and nationalism among American blacks. Although the founder was W. D. Fard, the most effective organizer was Elijah Muhammad (Elijah Poole, 1897–1975), who shaped it into a militant, separatist community of black converts to an Islam with distinctive features centering in the special divine destiny of the black race. After the death of Elijah Muhammad, leadership was assumed by his son Wallace Muhammad, who has led the movement to admit whites and adopt a more normative Islamic faith and practice. Despite a strict moral and dietary code, the Black Muslims have enjoyed considerable success. Among the best-known converts was Malcolm Little, better known as Malcolm X, assassinated in 1965.

BOOKS ABOUT THE BLACK MUSLIMS

Hall, Raymond L. *Black Separatism in the United States.* Univ. Pr. of New England 1978 text ed. $30.00. Background together with accounts of the movement.

Lincoln, C. Eric. *The Black Muslims in America.* Greenwood repr. of 1973 ed. 1982 lib. bdg. $29.75. A classic, basic account, though dated now in some particulars.

Lomax, Louis E. *When the Word Is Given: A Report on Elijah Muhammad, Malcolm X, and the Black Muslim World.* Greenwood repr. of 1964 ed. 1979 lib. bdg. $22.50. A major study.

Malcolm X. *Autobiography of Malcolm X.* Ballantine 1977 pap. $2.75. A much-read and discussed book by a prominent Black Muslim.

Marsh, Clifton E. *From Black Muslims to Muslims: The Transition from Separatism to Islam, 1930–1980.* Scarecrow Pr. 1984 $16.50. Historical narrative of a major development, toward normative Islam, in the movement's growth.

Pinkney, A. *Red, Black and Green.* Cambridge Univ. Pr. 1976 $39.50 pap. $7.95. The black nationalist background and the Black Muslims.

GURDJIEFF, G. I. 1872?–1949

Georges I. Gurdjieff was a modern magus who began public work in Russia on the eve of the revolution and later headed a celebrated center in France. Though controversial, his work attracted dedicated disciples, some of them prominent persons. We are asleep, Gurdjieff taught, and need the shock of awakening; to this end he sponsored experiences of dance, exercise, hard labor, and sometimes surprise or acute frustration. The Gurdjieff work continues through several organizations. The literature on Gurdjieff and his activity is relatively extensive, for he attracted followers well able to express themselves in words, and so unforgettable was his power and personality that not a few of them felt compelled to narrate the experience. The following is only a sampling of the books, mostly by former students, about this enigmatic spiritual teacher.

BOOKS BY GURDJIEFF

Beelzebub's Tales to His Grandson. Dutton 1973 $40.00 pap. $29.95. A massive work outlining his teachings through the medium of colorful parables and accounts of human folly.

Meetings with Remarkable Men. Trans. by Alfred R. Orage, Dutton repr. of 1963 ed. 1969 pap. $6.95. One of Gurdjieff's principal works; describes his alleged encounters with Eastern spiritual teachers, mostly Sufi.

BOOKS ABOUT GURDJIEFF

Anderson, Margaret. *The Unknowable Gurdjieff.* Weiser repr. of 1962 ed. 1969 pap. $7.50. An interesting memoir.

De Hartmann, Thomas, and Olga De Hartmann. *Our Life with Mr. Gurdjieff.* Cooper Square Pr. 1964 $17.50; Harper rev. ed. 1983 pap. $7.95. Readable account by a couple who shared Gurdjieff's adventurous escape from revolutionary Russia and his work in the West.

Gurdjieff Foundation of California, and J. Walter Driscoll. *Gurdjieff: An Annotated Bibliography.* [*Lib. of Social Sciences*] Garland 1984 $50.00. A basic resource.

Ouspensky, P. D. *Fourth Way.* Random 1971 pap. $7.95. Work on the path to enlightenment by Gurdjieff's major philosophical disciple.

———. *In Search of the Miraculous: Fragments of an Unknown Teaching.* Harcourt 1965 pap. $6.95. A large-scale treatise by a philosopher and sometime associate of Gurdjieff deeply influenced by his ideas.

Peters, Fritz. *Boyhood with Gurdjieff.* Capra Pr. 1980 o.p. Compelling narrative of a childhood influence by the mysterious master.

Walker, Kenneth. *Gurdjieff: A Study of His Teaching.* Allen & Unwin 1980 pap. $5.95. A good introduction to the intellectual side of Gurdjieff's teaching.
Webb, James. *The Harmonious Circle: The Lives and Work of G. I. Gurdjieff, P. D. Ouspensky, and Their Followers.* Putnam 1980 o.p. One of the few studies of this movement by an outsider. Well researched and documented.
Wilson, Colin. *The War Against Sleep: The Philosophy of Gurdjieff.* Borgo Pr. 1986 lib. bdg. $19.95; Newcastle Publishing rev. ed. 1986 pap. $7.95; Weiser 1980 pap. $6.95. A brief summary of Gurdjieff by a well-known writer.

THE HARE KRISHNA MOVEMENT

Among the most colorful and controversial of the new religious movements is the Hare Krishna, properly the International Society for Krishna Consciousness. It was founded by Swami Bhaktivedanta (1896–1977), who came to the United States in 1965 to promote the practice of bhakti, or devotional Hinduism. The movement's object of worship is Krishna, regarded as the "Supreme Personality of Godhead." The movement's ecstatic devotionalism, and insistence on strictly traditional "Vedic" dress, diet, and way of life, as well as its widespread scale of literature, have attracted much attention. Its ornate and opulent temples have become showplaces in a number of cities and rural areas. At the same time, the communalism and interesting life-histories of many occidental adherents have made the movement the subject of several good sociological studies.

BOOKS ABOUT HARE KRISHNA

Bhaktivedanta, Swami A. C. *Krsna Consciousness: The Matchless Gift.* Bhaktivedanta 1974 pap. $1.95. A good introduction by the founder.
Burr, Angela. *I Am Not My Body: A Study of the International Hare Krishna Sect.* Advent 1984 text ed. $35.00. A good sociological study, using attitudes toward the body as a touchstone of interpretation. Based on the movement in Britain, but generally applicable.
Daner, Francine J. *The American Children of Krsna: Case Studies in Cultural Anthropology.* Holt 1976 text ed. pap. $9.95. Good early sociological study.
Gelberg, Steven, ed. *Hare Krishna Hare Krishna: Five Distinguished Scholars in Religions Discuss the Krishna Movement in the West.* [*Press Eastern Philosophy and Lit. Ser.*] Grove 1983 pap. $7.95. Transcriptions of interviews with five nonmember but basically sympathetic theologians and Indologists on the Krishna movement.
Judah, J. Stillson. *Hare Krishna and the Counterculture.* [*Contemporary Religious Movements Ser.*] Wiley 1974 o.p. The first major study of the movement and still valuable.
Rochford, E. Burke. *Hare Krishna in America.* Rutgers Univ. Pr. 1985 $25.00 pap. $11.00. A readable and valuable participant-observer sociological study.
Shinn, Larry D. *The Dark Lord.* Westminster 1987 $16.95. An important study of Krishnaism in both India and America, based in part on extensive interviews with adherents.

JEHOVAH'S WITNESSES

The Jehovah's Witnesses are a controversial Christian denomination noted for its biblical literalism, conspicuous streetcorner and door-to-door evangelism, and expectations for the imminent return of Christ and Judgment. From time to time the movement has encountered difficulties over such issues as refusal to salute the flag or accept blood transfusions, and internal defections because of unfulfilled prophecies and its authoritarian character, but losses have been made good by new recruits.

The organizer of Jehovah's Witnesses, though that name was not adopted until 1931, was Charles Taze Russell (1852–1916), who founded its well-known magazine *The Watchtower* in 1879, and preached and wrote widely on his ideas of Bible interpretation. Only gradually did a denomination emerge among the various groups and informal followings that appeared in the wake of Russell's labors. Now, however, the movement is highly organized from the top down, and members are expected to give primary loyalty to it, living in expectation of the coming Kingdom of God and taking no part in politics or other unnecessary activities of the present world.

BOOKS ABOUT JEHOVAH'S WITNESSES

Beckford, James A. *The Trumpet of Prophecy: A Sociological Study of Jehovah's Witnesses.* Halsted Pr. 1975 o.p. A classic sociological account.

Bergman, Jerry. *Jehovah's Witnesses and Kindred Groups: An Historical Compendium and Bibliography.* [*Social Science Ser.*] Garland 1985 lib. bdg. $53.00. An important scholarly tool.

Botting, Heather, and Gary Botting. *The Orwellian World of Jehovah's Witnesses.* Univ. of Toronto Pr. 1984 $25.00 pap. $9.95. A social study.

Harrison, Barbara G. *Visions of Glory: A History and a Memory of Jehovah's Witnesses.* Simon & Schuster 1978 o.p. A sensitive account, both scholarly and personal, by a former member.

Penton, M. James. *Apocalypse Delayed: The Story of Jehovah's Witnesses.* Univ. of Toronto Pr. 1985 $24.95. The major work on the subject by an academic scholar; comprehensive and reliable.

Russell, Charles Taze. *Studies in the Scriptures.* Watchtower Bible & Tract Society 1886–1904 6 vols. o.p. Representative works by the principal founder of Jehovah's Witnesses.

Sterling, Chandler. *The Witnesses: One God, One Victory.* Regnery-Gateway 1975 o.p. A good general introduction.

White, Timothy. *A People for His Name: A History of Jehovah's Witnesses and an Evaluation.* Vantage 1967 o.p. A thorough historical study.

THE "JESUS MOVEMENT"

A much-discussed American religious phenomenon in the early 1970s was the "Jesus Movement," a trend toward evangelical Christianity among young people, particularly many who had been involved in the drugs, mysticism, and protest of the 1960s. The movement took many forms, from highly intensive communal groups like the Children of God to normative evangelical churches and collegiate organizations. Despite the alienation of the extremist "Jesus" groups, observers tended to see the movement as a way of coming to terms with the personal chaos often engendered by the 1960s experience, and of reintegrating into the mainstream of American life. As the 1970s drew to a close, the movement had subsided as a distinct social phenomenon but, without doubt, was reflected in the fresh vigor apparent in evangelical Christianity.

BOOKS ABOUT THE "JESUS MOVEMENT"

Drakeford, John W. *Children of Doom*. Broadman 1972 o.p. Readable study of a Children of God commune.

Ellwood, Robert S. *One Way: The Jesus Movement and Its Meaning*. Prentice-Hall 1973 o.p. An account with interpretation of the movement's place in American culture.

Enroth, Ronald M. *The Story of the Jesus People: A Factual Survey*. Attic Pr. 1972 pap. $5.95. An interesting and important overview, with descriptions of various groups and centers; readable.

Mills, Watson E. *Charismatic Religion in Modern Research: A Bibliography*. Ed. by David M. Scholer, Mercer Univ. Pr. 1985 text ed. $14.50. A research bibliography including works on the "Jesus Movement."

Pritchett, W. Douglas. *The Children of God/Family of Love: An Annotated Bibliography*. Garland 1984 lib. bdg. $33.00. A basic resource on one of the most talked-about "Jesus Movement" groups.

Richardson, James T., and others. *Organized Miracles: A Study of a Contemporary, Youth, Communal, Fundamentalist Organization*. Transaction Bks. 1979 $19.95. A careful, fascinating sociological account of a "Jesus Movement" commune.

NEOPAGANISM, WITCHCRAFT, AND MAGIC

Among the most interesting, and possibly significant, developments in alternative religion since the mid-twentieth century has been a marked rise in the number of groups practicing paganism, witchcraft, and ceremonial magic. Though related, these three phenomena are not identical. Pagans, or neopagans, are concerned with reviving polytheistic religions of the pre-Christian past, such as those of the ancient Celts, Greeks, Egyptians, or Norsemen, or with creating fresh religions in their spirit. Modern witchcraft, or Wicca as its followers often call it, shares neopaganism's pluralistic and harmony-with-nature mood, but has certain ritual traditions of its own together with a special emphasis on a supreme God and Goddess. The role of the Goddess in Wicca has particularly attracted persons interested in feminist spirituality. Followers of modern witchcraft in Europe and America insist it should not be confused, as it sometimes is, with Satanism. Workers of ritual or ceremonial magic do eleborate evocations of deities in rites that owe much to medieval Cabalism and Renaissance occultism.

Reliable literature on these fascinating groups by independent scholars is sparse. Few works can be found on neopaganism and witchcraft, but the best current sources of information are the periodicals of the movement itself. On ceremonial magic in America there is virtually nothing of book-length, although a number of studies exist of its English precursors, the famous turn-of-the-century Order of the Golden Dawn and the career of the celebrated Aleister Crowley.

BOOKS ABOUT NEOPAGANISM, WITCHCRAFT, AND MAGIC

Adler, Margot. *Drawing Down the Moon: Witches, Druids, Goddess-Worshippers and Other Pagans in America Today*. Beacon 1981 pap. $10.95 1986 rev. and enl. ed. pap. $14.95. By far the best book on the subject.

Farrar, Janet, and Stewart Farrar. *The Witches' Way: Principles, Rituals and Beliefs of*

Modern Witchcraft. Phoenix WA repr. of 1984 ed. 1986 $23.95. A very complete summary of attitudes and practice in modern witchcraft.

Holzer, Hans. *Pagans and Witches.* Woodhill 1979 pap. $1.95. Popular in tone, but one of the few books in the area.

Melton, J. Gordon. *Encyclopedia of American Religions.* Gale 2d ed. 1986 $175.00; McGrath 2 vols. 1978 $135.00. The fullest summary of magic, witchcraft, and neopagan groups in America.

————. *Magic, Witchcraft and Paganism in America: A Bibliography.* [*Philosophy and Religion Ser.*] Garland 1982 lib. bdg. $44.00. A fundamental resource, offering not only basic bibliography, but a valuable historical perspective in the introductory material.

Scott, Gini G. *The Magicians: A Study of the Use of Power in a Black Magic Group.* Irvington 1984 text ed. $22.50 1982 pap. $10.95. A rare and very interesting study, based on participant observation.

Starhawk. *Dreaming the Dark: Magic, Sex, and Politics.* Beacon Pr. 1982 $15.95 pap. $9.95. Statement by a leading figure in contemporary witchcraft.

————. *The Spiral Dance: Rebirth of the Ancient Religion of the Goddess.* Harper 1979 pap. $10.95. The basic ritual and rationale of modern witchcraft and goddess-worship.

THE PEOPLE'S TEMPLE

The People's Temple first came to dramatic world attention on November 18, 1978, when 912 members of the movement died in a mass suicide, or in a few cases were killed, in Jonestown, its settlement in the jungles of the small South American nation of Guyana. The People's Temple had been founded by the Rev. Jim Jones, who started as a fairly conservative white "mainline" Protestant minister, but later, as he worked with inner-city, largely black congregations in Indianapolis and then San Francisco, became increasingly radical in politics and apocalyptic in religion. His social work was highly respected, but at the same time disturbing rumors surfaced concerning the personal loyalty he demanded and the regimentation of his flock. After an exposé article in the magazine *New West*, he took his followers August 1977 to the Guyana location where he intended to establish an agricultural commune and sit out the nuclear holocaust he was expecting. By this time he allegedly combined his vision with extreme ego-inflation, identifying himself with God and Christ. The mass suicide followed new attempts by the outside world, in the person of a U.S. congressman and journalists, to contact his isolated sanctuary.

Most literature on the People's Temple centers on the enigmatic personality of Jim Jones and on trying to understand the shocking and tragic event of November 18, 1978.

BOOKS ABOUT THE PEOPLE'S TEMPLE

Levi, Ken, ed. *Violence and Religious Commitment: Implications of Jim Jones's People's Temple Movement.* Pennsylvania State Univ. Pr. 1982 $24.50. Interpretations of the group and the suicides by a number of scholars.

Naipaul, Shiva. *Journey to Nowhere: A New World Tragedy.* Penguin 1982 pap. $5.95. An overview of the tragedy and its meaning.

Reiterman, Tim, and John Jacobs. *Raven: The Untold Story of the Reverend Jim Jones and His People.* Dutton 1982 $17.95. The best full biography of Jim Jones.

Reston, James, Jr. *Our Father Who Art in Hell: The Life and Death of Jim Jones.* Times Bks. 1981 o.p. A basic account of Jones and Jonestown by a prominent journalist; makes much use of tapes Jones made of his talks.

Rose, Stephen. *Jesus and Jim Jones.* Pilgrim NY 1979 $8.95 pap. $6.95. A discussion of ethical and religious issues raised by the People's Temple events.

Weightman, Judith M. *Making Sense of the Jonestown Suicides: A Sociological History of Peoples Temple.* [*Studies in Religion and Society*] E Mellen 1984 $49.95. The most important scholarly study.

Wooden, Kenneth, ed. *The Children of Jonestown.* McGraw-Hill 1980 pap. $5.95. An account of Jones's custody and treatment of children at Jonestown.

Yee, Min S., and Thomas Layton. *In My Father's House: The Story of the Layton Family and the Reverend Jim Jones.* Berkley Pub. 1982 o.p. The movement through the eyes of one involved family.

SATANISM

Satanism must be clearly distinguished from such practices as neopaganism and witchcraft since it is not concerned to revive pre-Christian or non-Christian worship, but rather to honor precisely that entity that for the Judeo-Christian tradition supremely epitomizes evil and antagonism to God. It thus has overtones of ultimate rebellion. Satanists can, however, be divided into two groups: those persons, often sociopathic, for whom Satan is truly evil and will reward those who serve him by doing evil; and those for whom Satanism is actually a benign religion, inculcating no more than the indulgence of "natural" drives that the other God would have us repress. The best-known example of the latter is the Church of Satan in San Francisco.

Although there has been much sensationalistic writing about Satanism, little reliable scholarship exists on the subject in America. Journalistic sources may also be pursued, though they must be used with caution.

BOOKS ABOUT SATANISM

La Vey, Anton S. *Satanic Bible.* Avon 1969 pap. $3.95. Basic text of the famous Church of Satan in San Francisco.

———. *The Satanic Rituals.* Avon 1972 pap. $3.75. Rites of the Church of Satan.

Lyons, Arthur. *The Second Coming: Satanism in America.* Dodd 1970 o.p. Now dated, but the only independent book on the subject. Journalistic in style.

Rhodes, H. T. *The Satanic Mass.* Citadel Pr. 1974 $7.95 1975 pap. $3.95. A classic study of the European background of modern Satanism.

SCIENTOLOGY

Few modern movements have generated the success or controversy of Scientology. It was founded by the science fiction writer L. Ron Hubbard (1911–1986), who began his psychospiritual work in the early 1950s with the teaching called Dianetics; Scientology was established in 1952 and grew rapidly as a part of the 1960s scene. The basic teaching is a highly dualistic view of the soul, or "thetan," as separate from the body but trapped in it, and in the matter-energy-space-time universe. Scientological "processing" involves ways to "go clear"—delete the "engrams" implanted in the mind by previous negative events, often in past lives—and then to become an "operating thetan." A "clear" is said to be "at cause" of his or her life, totally free. Controversy has surrounded the fees charged for "processing" and alleged tactics used by Scientologists against critics and in their ongoing battles with governments regarding tax status and other issues.

Despite the size and importance of Scientology, there are few independent studies of it, though a vast amount of in-house publications and journalistic literature remains to be mined.

BOOKS ABOUT SCIENTOLOGY

Hubbard, L. Ron. *Scientology: The Fundamentals of Thought.* Church of Scientology of New York 1983 $20.00. One of L. Ron Hubbard's voluminous publications; a good basic introduction to the philosophy of Scientology.

Wallis, Roy. *The Road to Total Freedom.* Columbia Univ. Pr. 1977 $27.50. The preeminent independent account.

UFO RELIGIONS

Since the modern series of reported sightings began in 1947, UFOs (Unidentified Flying Objects; also called flying saucers) have attracted religious as well as scientific and popular attention. Within a few years, certain individuals, often called contactees, claimed communication from beings aboard the mysterious objects. Sometimes it took the form of visits from them, and even rides on UFOs to distant planets for the contactee; at other times it was only mediumistic communication reminiscent of Spiritualism. In those contacts of religious significance, inevitably the space beings were portrayed as morally and spiritually vastly superior to humans, and bearers of important messages to humanity conveyed by the contactee. We were urged to reform, to put aside war, and to join a galaxy full of advanced and happy worlds. Out of these communications emerged a set of small but interesting religious groups. Literature on them is spotty, but the following diverse sources should serve to introduce the reader to the world of UFO religions.

BOOKS ABOUT UFO RELIGIONS

Adamski, George. *Inside the Spaceships: UFO Experiences of George Adamski 1952–1955.* GAF Intl. repr. of 1955 ed. pap. $9.95. One of the classic "contactee" accounts; Adamski was the first and most influential person to claim communication and a religious message from UFO beings.

Curran, Douglas. *In Advance of the Landing.* Abbeville Pr. 1986 pap. $16.95. Readable and informative survey of UFO beliefs; well illustrated.

Festinger, Leon. *When Prophecy Fails: A Social and Psychological Study of a Modern Group That Predicted the Destruction of the World.* Harper 1964 pap. $6.95. A much-discussed sociological study based on participant observation of a UFO group; interesting not only for the account of the group and its response to the failure of its prophecy but also for the issues of sociological ethics and methods it raises.

Jacobs, David M. *The UFO Controversy in America.* Indiana Univ. Pr. 1975 $17.50. A good, readable but scholarly history; contains a chapter on contactees and religious groups.

Jung, C. G. *Flying Saucers: A Modern Myth of Things Seen in the Sky.* Princeton Univ. Pr. 1978 $6.95 A much-cited book by a world-renowned analytic psychologist on the archetypal or symbolic meaning of UFOs and the reasons why they easily become religiously significant.

Rasmussen, Richard M. *The UFO Literature: A Comprehensive Annotated Bibliography of Works of English.* McFarland & Co. 1985 lib. bdg. $29.95. A valuable resource for the whole field.

Story, Ronald D., ed. *The Encyclopedia of UFOs.* Doubleday 1980 $29.95. A fascinating volume covering all aspects of the subject; includes articles on UFO religion and major religious figures.

UNIFICATION CHURCH

Officially, the Holy Spirit Association for the Unification of World Christianity, the Unification Church was founded in Korea in 1954 by the Rev. Sun Myung Moon. Rev. Moon declared that Jesus had appeared to him in 1936 and asked him to take on the task of establishing the Kingdom of God on Earth by reordering human society in accordance with hierarchical, puritanical principles. These are presented in the faith's basic text, *Divine Principle*, which also shows elaborate parallels between history before and since the time of Jesus suggesting that the world is ready for a new messianic figure, a role which many "Moonies," as Unificationists are popularly called, see fulfilled in Moon.

The Unification Church has received much criticism for authoritarianism, allegedly deceptive recruiting practices, and avoidance of paying taxes on businesses operated by the church and on Rev. Moon's personal income. As a result of his conviction on a charge of tax evasion, Rev. Moon spent 13 months in jail between 1984 and 1985. Since coming to the United States in 1959 the movement has steadily endeavored to enhance its intellectual credentials by improving the education of leaders and sponsoring scholarly conferences. The literature on the Unification Church reflects such highly varied perceptions of its nature and role in American, and world, society.

BOOKS ABOUT THE UNIFICATION CHURCH

Barker, Eileen. *The Making of a Moonie: Choice or Brainwashing?* Basil Blackwell 1984 $19.95 1986 pap. $9.95. A very highly regarded sociological study.

Bromley, David G., and Anson D. Shupe, Jr. *Moonies in America: Cult, Church, and Crusade.* [*Sage Lib. of Social Research*] 1979 $29.00 pap. $12.50. A thorough sociological study.

Fichter, Joseph H. *The Holy Family of Father Moon.* Leaven Pr. 1985 pap. $7.95. By a prominent Catholic sociologist.

Horowitz, Irving L., ed. *Science, Sin and Scholarship: The Politics of Reverend Moon and the Unification Church.* MIT 1978 $16.50 pap. $7.95. Selected papers, often critical, on the Unification Church and its politics.

Lofland, John. *Doomsday Cult: A Study of Conversion, Proselytization, and Maintenance of Faith.* Irvington enl. ed. 1981 $29.00 text ed. pap. $12.95. A classic early study of the Unification Church.

Mickler, Michael L. *The Unification Church in America: Sects and Cults in America.*

[*Bibliographical Guides Ser.*] Garland 1986 lib. bdg. $19.00. An invaluable resource.

VEDANTA

Among the oldest of Eastern movements in America are those sponsored by the Ramakrishna Mission, frequently called the Vedanta Societies. Its origins go back to the life and teaching of Ramakrishna (1834–1886), a saintly modern Hindu mystic who emphasized the unity of all religions as paths to God-realization. Swami Vivekananda (1863–1902), a disciple of his, attended the World Parliament of Religions in Chicago in 1893, where he made a lasting impression; in 1897 he established Vedanta Societies in several American cities to offer philosophical Hinduism and certain devotional practices to Westerners. The spiritual leadership of these societies is in the hands of swamis who are monks of the Ramakrishna Order, originally established among students of Ramakrishna. The teaching, which is basically in the advaita (nondualist) Vedanta tradition, emphasizes the oneness of all things as manifestations of the Brahman or God, and the presence of the divine within each individual as the true Self. The Vedanta Societies have not grown dramatically, but, by presenting an intellectually sophisticated version of Eastern lore, have attracted a complement of writers and thinkers, and have had a significant role in the spread of Eastern ideas in the West.

BOOKS ABOUT VEDANTA

Damrell, Joseph D. *Seeking Spiritual Meaning: The World of Vedanta.* [*Sociological Observations Ser.*] Sage 1977 o.p. An excellent sociological document.

French, Harold W. *The Swan's Wide Waters: Ramakrishna and Western Culture.* Associated Faculty Pr. 1974 $17.95. A useful historical account.

Isherwood, Christopher. *My Guru and His Disciple.* Farrar 1980 $12.95; Penguin 1981 pap. $4.95. A beautifully written and quite frank account of Swami Prabhavananda of the Vedanta Society of Southern California by one of his most prominent disciples, the distinguished novelist and playwright Christopher Isherwood.

———, ed. *Vedanta for the Western World: A Symposium on Vedanta.* Vedanta Pr. 1945 pap. $7.95. Interpretation of Vedanta by literate adherents addressing European and American seekers.

OTHER GROUPS OF EASTERN BACKGROUND

A number of groups of Eastern derivation, Hindu and others, have flourished in America. (Buddhist groups have already been considered.) Most have not received sustained outside study, but are significant parts of the spiritual scene. These include yoga groups, of which one of the best known is the Self-Realization Fellowship, founded by Paramahansa Yogananda (1893–1952). An important modern spiritual teacher was Meher Baba (1894–1969), noted for a long period of smiling silence, whose doctrine combined ideas from Hinduism and Sufism or mystical Islam. Many people both in India and the West consider Satya Sai Baba (1926–   ), a Hindu teacher celebrated for his reputed miracles, an avatar or appearance of God in the world. Transcendental Meditation, a simple technique offered by the Maharishi Mahesh Yogi (1911?–   ), sensationalized in the 1960s through its temporary endorsement by the Beatles and other stellar entertainment figures, became a major vogue in the 1970s, and still maintains a significant following. A smaller but likewise interesting group is Eckankar, founded by Paul Twitchell (1910?–1971), presenting techniques of "soul travel" and divine realization. The Divine Light Mission, of the then "teenage guru" Maharaj Ji (1958–), had a meteoric rise and fall in the early 1970s and still exists. An even more sensational growth and decline was the fate of the Rajneesh movement, celebrated for its wealth and its Oregon commune until the expulsion of the founder, Rajneesh (1931–), from the United States in 1985.

BOOKS ABOUT OTHER GROUPS OF EASTERN BACKGROUND

Baba, Meher. *The Everything and the Nothing.* Meher Baba Info. 1963 pap. $3.45; Sheriar Pr. repr. of 1963 ed. 1976 $4.95 pap. $2.95. The fundamental spiritual philosophy of Meher Baba.

Bharti, Ma Satya. *Death Comes Dancing: Celebrating Life with Bhagwan Shree Rajneesh.* Routledge & Kegan 1981 pap. $9.95. An account of life with Rajneesh.

Downton, James V., Jr. *Sacred Journeys: Conversion and Commitment to Divine Light Mission.* Columbia Univ. Pr. 1979 $25.00. A sociological study of the Divine Light Mission.

Lane, David C. *The Making of a Spiritual Movement: The Untold Story of Paul Twitchell and Eckankar.* [*Understanding Cults and Spiritual Movements Ser.*] Del Mar Pr. 1983 pap. $9.95. An illuminating outside study of Eckankar and its founder.

Mahesh Yogi, Maharishi. *Transcendental Meditation.* New Amer. Lib. 1973 pap. $4.95. A basic presentation by the founder of Transcendental Meditation.

Sandweiss, Samuel H. *Sai Baba: The Holy Man and the Psychiatrist.* Birth Day 1975 $8.25 pap. $4.25. A good introduction to the world of Sai Baba by a Western convert.

Twitchell, Paul. *The Tiger's Fang.* IWP Pub. 1979 $5.95. An introduction to basic concepts of Eckankar by its founder.

Yogananada, Paramahansa. *Autobiography of a Yogi.* Self-Realization Fellowship 12th ed. rev. 1983 $10.95 pap. $2.95. The influential autobiography of the founder of the Self-Realization Fellowship.

Name Index

In addition to authors, this index includes the names of persons mentioned in connection with titles of books written, whether they appear in introductory essays, general bibliographies at the beginnings of chapters, discussions under main headings, or "Books About" sections. Persons mentioned in passing—to indicate friendships, relationships, and so on—are generally not indexed. Editors are not indexed unless there is no specific author given; such books include anthologies, bibliographies, yearbooks, and the like. Translators, writers of introductions, forewords, afterwords, etc., are not indexed except for those instances where the translator seems as closely attached to a title as the real author, e.g., FitzGerald's translation of the *Rubáiyát of Omar Khayyám*. Main name headings appear in boldface as do the page numbers on which the main entries appear.

Aaron, Richard I., 154, 611
Abbott, Nabia, 441
Abel, Reuben, 9
Abelard, Peter, 85
Abelson, Joshua, 481
Abelson, Raziel, 9
Aberle, David F., 373
Aboulafia, Mitchell, 279
Abraham Ibn Daud, 479, 480
Abrahams, Israel, 474, 480
Ackrill, J. L., 44
Adams, Charles J., 323, 377, 388, 396, 415
Adams, Evangeline, 703
Adams, Marilyn McCord, 101
Adams, Robert, 343
Adams, Robert M., 151
Adamski, George, 711
Adelmann, F. J., 20
Adickes, Erich, 175
Adkins, Arthur W., 32
Adler, Elkan N., 477
Adler, Hans G., 487
Adler, Margot, 708
Adler, Morris, 471
Adler, Mortimer J., 44, 224
Adorno, T(heodor) W., 226
Aelred of Reivaulx, 80

Affifi, Abul E., 436
Afnan, Soheil M., 434
Agnon, S. Y., 451
Agrippa of Nettesheim, Henry Cornelius, 111
Agus, Jacob, 508
Ahad Ha'am, 508
Aharoni, Yohanan, 663
Ahern, Emily M., 386
Ahlstrom, S. E., 631
Ahmad, Aziz, 417
Aiken, Henry D., 136
Ajami, Fouad, 417
Akhavi, Shahrough, 417
Alan of Lille, 572
Aland, Barbara, 659
Aland, Kurt, 529, 647, 659, 672
Albanese, Catherine L., 686
Albert, Phyllis Cohen, 487
Albert the Great, 86
Albright, William F., 350, 660, 662
Aldridge, Alfred Owen, 635
Alegria, Ricardo E., 372
Aletrino, L., 417
Alexander, Ian W., 18
Alexander, Peter, 154

Alexander, Robert L., 349
Alexander, Samuel, 154
Alexander, Thomas G., 690
Alford, C. Fred, 275
Ali, Syed A., 441
Aliotta, Antonio, 227
Allan, D. F., 44
Allard, Jean-Louis, 278
Allen, Don C., 103
Allen, E. L., 232
Allen, George, 411
Allen, H. J., 47
Allen, Henry E., 418
Allen, Michael J. B., 119
Allen, Percy S., 117
Allen, R. E., 34, 59
Allison, Henry E., 160, 175
Alon, Gedalyahu, 456
Alpern, Henry, 6
Alpers, Antony, 367
Alpert, Rebecca T., 509
Alston, William P., 10
Alter, Robert, 670, 678
Althaus, Paul, 596
Altholz, Josef L., 615
Althusser, Louis, 188
Altmann, Alexander, 166, 480
Altshuler, David, 490

715

Title Index

Titles of all books discussed in *The Reader's Adviser* are indexed here, except broad generic titles such as "Complete Works," "Selections," "Poems," "Correspondence." Also omitted is any title listed with a main-entry author that includes that author's name, e.g., *Collected Prose of T. S. Eliot*, and titles under "Books About," e.g., *Eliot's Early Years* by Lyndall Gordon. The only exception to this is Shakespeare (Volume 2), where all works by and about him are indexed. To locate all titles by and about a main-entry author, the user should refer to the Name Index for the author's primary listing (given in boldface). Whenever the name of a main-entry author is part of a title indexed here, the page reference is to a section other than the primary listing. In general, subtitles are omitted. When two or more identical titles by different authors appear, the last name of each author is given in parentheses following the title.

The ABC of Relativity, 294
The Abandonment of the Jews, 493
Aboriginal Women, Sacred and Profane, 368
Abortion and the Early Church, 545
About Philosophy, 16
About Wordsworth and Whitehead, 315
Abraham Geiger and Liberal Judaism, 504
Abstract of a Treatise of Human Nature, 169
The Abyss of Despair, 475
Activation of Energy, 309
Activity of Philosophy, 16
Acts of Faith, 496
The Acts of the Apostles, 677
The Acts of the Christian Martyrs, 547
Adages, 117
Adam, the Baby, and the Man from Mars, 244
Addresses to the German Nation, 167

Adieux, 301
The Advancement of Learning, 141
Adventure in Freedom, 491
Adventures of Ideas, 314
Adventures of the Dialectic, 281
Adversity's Noblemen, 110
Adversus Marcionem (Against Marcion), 556
Advocates of Reform, 583
The Aesthetic Dimension, 275
Aesthetic Theory, 227
Aesthetics: Lectures on Fine Art, 187
African Islam, 419
African Philosophy: A Historico-Hermeneutical Investigation of the Conditions of Its Possibility, 17
African Philosophy: An Introduction, 17
African Philosophy: Myth and Reality, 17
African Philosophy: Myth or Reality, 17
African Religions, 368

African Traditional Religion, 369, 422
After Auschwitz, 523
After Lebanon, 494
Against Epistemology, 227
Against the Academicians, 89
Against the Apocalypse, 499
Against the Musicians (adversus Musicos), 41
The Age of Adventure, 109
Age of Analysis, 224
The Age of Constantine the Great, 538
An Age of Crisis, 166
The Age of Criticism, 106
The Age of Ideology, 136
Age of Reason, 137
The Age of Reform 1250–1550, 566, 583
The Age of Reformation, 583
The Age of Religious Wars, 1559–1689, 609
The Ages of the World, 208
The Aims of Education, 314
Aishah, 441
Akhenaton: The Heretic King, 345

743

Subject Index

This index provides detailed, multiple-approach access to the subject content of the volume, employing the subject headings as entry terms. Arrangement is alphabetical. Collective terms for authors are included, e.g., *Philosophers*, *Writers*, but the reader is reminded to use the Name Index to locate individual writers.